Edward Garbett, Samuel Martin

The family prayer book

Morning and evening prayers for every day in the year

Edward Garbett, Samuel Martin

The family prayer book
Morning and evening prayers for every day in the year

ISBN/EAN: 9783337281823

Printed in Europe, USA, Canada, Australia, Japan

Cover: Foto ©Lupo / pixelio.de

More available books at **www.hansebooks.com**

THE

FAMILY
PRAYER BOOK;

OR,

Morning and Evening Prayers for Every Day in the Year.

WITH

PRAYERS AND THANKSGIVINGS FOR SPECIAL OCCASIONS.

EDITED BY

THE REV. EDWARD GARBETT, M.A.,

INCUMBENT OF CHRIST CHURCH, SURBITON, AND LATE BOYLE LECTURER;

AND

THE REV. SAMUEL MARTIN,

MINISTER OF WESTMINSTER CHAPEL, AND CHAIRMAN OF THE CONGREGATIONAL UNION FOR 1862-3.

LONDON:
CASSELL, PETTER, AND GALPIN.

1864.

INTRODUCTION.

IT would be superfluous to expatiate to those, into whose hands this publication is likely to fall, on the obligations of Prayer, since a personal experience can alone suggest the want which this Volume is intended to supply. Like all other things of Divine institution, prayer is commended by benefits as varied as the aspects in which it can be regarded. It is a duty, for Christ has commanded it; a privilege, for we speak to God himself; an instinct of self-interest, for how else shall our wants be supplied? a necessity, for the full heart must find some mode of utterance; a happiness, for in prayer the Christian enjoys that immediate intercourse with his Heavenly Father, through Christ Jesus, which will constitute hereafter the very bliss and glory of heaven.

Nor is Family Prayer commended by reasons less cogent or varied than private supplication. It is a formal witness to the Unseen, an act of solemn allegiance to Him in whom we live, and move, and have our being. It is the expression of those religious interests and sympathies which the members of a family have in common, neither so general as those of the congregation, nor so closely personal as those of the individual. It is the means of mutual intercession, and the channel through which larger supplies of the Holy Spirit may be sought, sealed as it is with Christ's especial promise to united prayer. It is the truest bond of family affection, the spring of mutual sympathy, an instrument in the education of character, and the foretaste of a heavenly and an enduring relationship.

But the recognition of the duty is more easy than its satisfactory performance. There are some persons so richly endowed with fervency of spirit, tenderness of feeling, and freedom of utterance, that their extemporaneous outpourings of devotion constitute the best mode of family worship which can be suggested. But such gifts are not common, and it cannot be expected that all fathers of families should feel themselves competent to discharge such an office, either with comfort to themselves or with edification to others. To maintain its continuous performance without running either into eccentricity on the one side, or into monotony on the other, requires greater endowments than men can ordinarily be supposed to possess; and no warmth of feeling or fluency of language are in themselves sufficient.

An exact doctrinal knowledge must underlie all enlightened devotion. The free language of the heart is, we admit, very different from the definitions of theology, and must be measured by a widely different standard. Nevertheless, they are intimately related, and mutually react upon each other. The creed of the intellect necessarily guides the affections of the heart. Yet the process is often reversed, and an unscriptural mode of feeling leads little by little into an unscriptural mode of thinking. The relation between the head and the heart is so close, that no permanent discrepancy can exist between them. Not only the subjects of prayer, but its whole tone and character, are affected by the doctrinal creed. How differently, for instance, must the man feel and express himself before God, who believes in the total depravity of human nature and the sovereignty of Divine grace, from the man who believes with the Rationalist in human perfectibility, or with the Romanist in the *opus operatum* of the sacraments. Hence, a solid knowledge of Divine truth, and that devout familiarity with Scripture which saturates, as it were, the very heart with its tone and spirit, are the first requisites for the conduct of family devotion.

But when the substance of prayer has thus been secured, it still remains to regulate its expression. In private prayer this element scarcely enters into consideration, because here the relation is immediate between the soul itself and the God with whom it speaks. But when prayer becomes the common act of a number, the case is different. Some one must become the mouthpiece of all the rest, and the devotion of the whole circle can only be real, free, and unrestrained, in proportion as the thoughts and feelings of all are reflected in the language of the speaker. Hence the language should be simple, natural, unaffected. There should be no effort at ornament to distract, no coarseness of speech to offend. Conventionalisms, familiar to one man, but strange to another, should be avoided. Nothing, in short, should divert attention from the object and purpose of prayer to its outward form and vehicle. Affectionate, without familiarity; earnest, without effort; simple, without affectation, the language of prayer should be the outward reflection of prayer itself, by a process as natural as that which moulds the leaves of the bud after the shape of the blossom it encloses.

But when the matter and manner of prayer are both adjusted, it is still necessary to arrange the topics in such order as shall best quicken interest and promote edification. The recurrence of the same unalterable wants in every family circle makes it the more important to vary, as much as possible, the aspects under which they may be presented. In no way can this be accomplished with so much propriety, as by following the inexhaustible stores of Holy Scripture. What so natural, as that the portion of God's Word read should give its character to the prayer that follows, suggesting its salient topics, and colouring, with its own divine hues of promise or of warning, its confessions and its thanksgivings, its ascriptions and its supplications?

On these principles the present Volume of Prayers for Family Use has been compiled. It will be found to be pervaded everywhere with the distinctive principles of evangelical truth, and to breathe throughout an entire harmony of thought and sentiment. The high reputation of its Contributors, and the care with which the whole has been revised, encourage the hope that nothing will be found in it contrary to sound doctrine. The number of writers who have rendered their valuable assistance has tended to secure variety of style, and to prevent poverty of thought and individual peculiarities of expression. The portions of Scripture have been carefully selected from the authorised version, with a view to elucidate Scripture by Scripture, and to combine in one consistent course of instructive reading the various books of the Old and New Testaments. The connecting thought which has been present in the mind of the Editors may not in all cases be equally transparent; but it is believed that the heart of the worshipper may be conscious of a harmony of teaching, where the head may fail to analyse the exact connection out of which it has sprung.

That the object aimed at in this volume has been carried out imperfectly and with some defects, is most readily admitted. Diversities of judgment in the details of such a work must necessarily be expected. It is probable that the editors themselves, when they quietly revise their own work, may become conscious of faults which they would be the first to acknowledge and deplore. If the design is even partially realised, they must be thankful for this measure of success; and conscious of the sense of responsibility before God, in which their work was undertaken, must leave the rest to the forgiving mercies of their Master, and the indulgent judgment of their Christian brethren.

They humbly commend the Volume to the blessing of Him who hears and answers prayer through that gracious Saviour by whom alone we have access unto the Father. May He be pleased to assist with his Holy Spirit all those who use these prayers as the utterances of their family worship! Without His help, all forms whatever will be useless: with it, the forms supplied in this Volume may become instinct with spiritual blessing, and every home, where prayer is offered, be as the house of God and as the gate of heaven.

LIST OF CONTRIBUTORS.

The Right Rev. the LORD BISHOP OF MAURITIUS.
The Right Rev. the LORD BISHOP OF MELBOURNE.
The Right Rev. the LORD BISHOP OF SYDNEY.
The Very Rev. the DEAN OF DROMORE.
The Very Rev. the DEAN OF GLOUCESTER.
The Very Rev. the DEAN OF WATERFORD.
The Ven. the ARCHDEACON OF DERBY, M.A., Canon of Lichfield, and Vicar of Chesterfield.
The Ven. the ARCHDEACON OF SURREY, M.A., Canon of Winchester, and Vicar of Farnham.
Rev. W. ACWORTH, M.A., Vicar of Plumstead.
Rev. B. ADDISON, M.A., Incumbent of St. John's, Newcastle-on-Tyne.
Rev. T. ALEXANDER, M.A., Chelsea.
Rev. C. R. ALFORD, M.A., Principal of the Metropolitan Training College.
Rev. H. ALLON, Islington.
Rev. J. ANGUS, D.D., President of Regent's Park College.
Rev. R. ASHTON, Secretary of the Congregational Union, London.
Rev. C. T. ASTLEY, M.A., Vicar of Margate.
Rev. E. AURIOL, M.A., Rector of St. Dunstan's, West.
Rev. T. W. AVELING, Kingsland.
Rev. R. BALGARNIE, Scarborough.
Rev. J. BATEMAN, M.A., Vicar of North Cray, Kent.
Rev. J. BEAZLEY, Blackheath.
Rev. C. D. BELL, M.A., Incumbent of Ambleside.
Rev. S. B. BERGNE, Secretary of British and Foreign Bible Society.
Rev. R. W. BETTS, Peckham.
Rev. W. BEVAN, Canonbury.
Rev. J. BIGWOOD, Brompton.
Rev. C. W. BINGHAM, M.A., Rector of Melcombe Horsey, Dorchester.
Rev. C. M. BIRRELL, Liverpool.
Rev. D. BLOW, Regent's Park.
Rev. J. BOLTON, M.A. (the late), Incumbent of St. Paul's, Kilburn.

Rev. R. BRINDLEY, Bath.
Rev. H. F. BROCK, M.A., Incumbent of Christ Church, Doncaster
Rev. W. BROCK, Jun., Hampstead.
Rev. T. BROMLEY, M.A., Incumbent of St. Mary's, Leamington.
Rev. J. W. BROOKS, M.A., Vicar of St. Mary's, Nottingham, and Prebendary of Lincoln.
Rev. J. MORTON BROWN, D.D., Cheltenham.
Rev. Dr. BUCHANAN, Glasgow.
Rev. W. M. BUCKE, M.A., Chaplain to the Magdalen Asylum, London.
Rev. C. BULLOCK, Rector of St. Nicholas, Worcester.
Rev. W. M. BUNTING, M.A., Highgate.
Rev. J. BURDER, M.A., Clifton.
Rev. J. BURNS, D.D., Paddington.
Rev. A. B. BURTON, M.A., Rector of Holy Trinity, Southampton.
Rev. W. BURTON, Frome.
Rev. A. BUZACOTT, B.A., Romford.
Rev. L. H. BYRNES, B.A., Kingston.
Rev. Dr. CAIRNS, Berwick.
Rev. G. CALTHROP, M.A., Incumbent of Trinity Church, Cheltenham.
Rev. Canon CAMIDGE, M.A., Vicar of Wakefield.
Rev. J. R. CAMPBELL, D.D., Bradford.
Rev. E. G. CECIL, Portsmouth.
Rev. F. S. C. CHALMERS, M.A., Rector of Beckenham.
Rev. J. CHALMERS, M.A., Tottenham.
Rev. Canon CHAMPNEYS, M.A., Vicar of St. Pancras.
Rev. J. M. CHARLTON, M.A., Western College, Plymouth.
Rev. C. F. CHASE, M.A., Rector of St. Ann's, Blackfriars.
Rev. C. F. CHILDE, M.A., Rector of Holbrook, Suffolk.
Rev. Professor CHRISTMAS, M.A., Lecturer of St. Peter's, Cornhill.
Rev. H. CHRISTOPHERSON, New College Chapel, St. John's Wood.

LIST OF CONTRIBUTORS.

Rev. B. S. CLARKE, M.A., Incumbent of Southport.
Rev. T. J. CLARKE, M.A., Incumbent of St. Paul's, Southport.
Rev. E. CLAY, B.A., Incumbent of St. Margaret's, Brighton.
Rev. C. CLAYTON, M.A., Fellow and Tutor of Caius College, Cambridge, and Examining Chaplain to the Bishop of Ripon.
Rev. W. COCKIN, M.A., Rector of St. George's, Birmingham, and Examining Chaplain to the Bishop of Durham.
Rev. J. COLBOURNE, M.A., Incumbent of St. Matthias, Bethnal Green.
Rev. E. R. CONDER, M.A., Leeds.
Rev. G. W. CONDER, Leeds.
Rev. W. COOKE, D.D., London.
Rev. J. CORBIN, Hornsey.
Rev. A. G. CORNWALL, M.A., Chaplain in Ordinary to the Queen, and Rector of Beverstone, Gloucestershire.
Rev. H. O. CROFTS, D.D., Leeds.
Rev. J. H. CROWDER, M.A., Minister of the Octagon Chapel, Bath.
Rev. S. CRUMP, Kentish Town.
Rev. F. CRUSE, M.A., Incumbent of St. Jude's, Southwark.
Rev. T. CURME, M.A., Vicar of Sandford, Oxon.
Rev. T. H. DAVIES, M.A., Incumbent of Christ's Church, Ramsgate.
Rev. U. DAVIES, M.A., Incumbent of St. Matthew's, Islington.
Rev. C. H. DAVIS, M.A., Chaplain to the Stroud Union.
Rev. J. DAVIS, Secretary to Evangelical Alliance.
Rev. E. DAVYS, M.A., Vicar of Peterborough.
Rev. G. DESPARD, M.A., Incumbent of St. Paul's, Kilburn.
Rev. J. W. K. DISNEY, M.A., Vicar of St. Saviour's, Retford.
Rev. G. T. DRIFFIELD, M.A., Rector of Bow.
Rev. T. D. K. DRUMMOND, M.A., Incumbent of St. Thomas's, Edinburgh.
Rev. J. EADIE, D.D., Glasgow.
Rev. Canon EDEN, M.A., Vicar of Wymondham, Norfolk.
Rev. J. EDMOND, D.D., Highbury.
Rev. C. W. EDMONSTONE, M.A., Incumbent of St. John's, Upper Holloway.
Rev. C. EVANS, M.A., Rector of St. Clement's, Worcester.
Rev. W. FAIRBROTHER, Highgate.

Rev. J. FERGUSON, D.D., St. John's Wood.
Rev. G. W. FISHBOURNE, Stratford.
Rev. J. B. FIGGIS, B.A., Brighton.
Rev. G. FISK, LL.B., Vicar of Great Malvern, and Prebendary of Lichfield.
Rev. J. FLEMING, Kentish Town.
Rev. W. FLEMING, M.A., Incumbent of Christ Church, Hornsey.
Rev. B. FIELD, Northampton Square, London.
Rev. J. FLETCHER, Christchurch, Hants.
Rev. G. T. FOX, M.A., Rector of St. Nicholas's, Durham.
Rev. J. B. FRENCH, Richmond.
Rev. H. J. GAMBLE, Upper Clapton.
Rev. S. GARRATT, M.A., Incumbent of Trinity Church, St. Giles-in-the-Fields.
Rev. S. GEDGE, M.A., Vicar of All Saints, Northampton.
Rev. Canon GIRDLESTONE, M.A., Vicar of Halberton, Devon.
Rev. R. GLOVER, M.A., Incumbent of Christ Church, Dover.
Rev. E. GODSON, M.A., Curate of Shepton Mallett.
Rev. C. J. GOODHART, M.A., Minister of Park Chapel, Chelsea.
Rev. J. GRAHAM, Craven Chapel.
Rev. J. H. GRAY, M.A., Incumbent of St. Barnabas, Isle of Man.
Rev. R. W. GREAVES, M.A., Rector of Tooting.
Rev. T. GREEN, M.A., Principal of Church Missionary Institution, Islington.
Rev. R. GUNNERY, M.A., Incumbent of St. Mary's, Hornsey Rise.
Rev. J. GUTHRIE, M.A., Albany Chapel, Regent's Park.
Rev. J. S. HALL, Falcon Square Chapel, London.
Rev. J. HAMBLETON, M.A., Minister of the Chapel of Ease, Islington.
Rev. A. HAMPSON, Stoke Newington.
Rev. Canon HASTINGS, M.A., Rector of Martley, Worcestershire.
Rev. A. M. HENDERSON, Pentonville.
Rev. C. HEBERT, M.A., Vicar of Lowestoft.
Rev. J. HILL, Ventnor.
Rev. J. H. HINTON, M.A., Devonshire Square Chapel, London.
Rev. J. HOBY, D.D., Hackney.
Rev. B. S. HOLLIS, Islington.
Rev. H. C. HOWARD, Curate of St. Matthew's, Islington.
Rev. C. R. HOWELL, Finchley.
Rev. J. M'CONNELL HUSSEY, M.A., Incumbent of Christ Church, North Brixton.

LIST OF CONTRIBUTORS.

Rev. H. D. INGRAM, Paddington.
Rev. J. JAMIESON, D.D., Glasgow.
Rev. J. S. JENKINSON, M.A., Vicar of Battersea.
Rev. A. JENOUR, Incumbent of Blackpool.
Rev. J. KEELING, M.A., Incumbent of St. Paul's, Lisson Grove.
Rev. D. KELLY, M.A., Incumbent of Trinity Church, Gough Square, Fleet Street.
Rev. W. KENDALL, M.A., Association Secretary, Church Pastoral-Aid Society.
Rev. J. KENNEDY, M.A., Stepney.
Rev. W. H. KILLICK, M.A., Rector of St. Clement Danes, Strand.
Rev. J. S. KNAPP, Incumbent of St. John's, Portsea.
Rev. W. LANDELS, Regent's Park.
Rev. W. LAYCOCK, M.A., Incumbent of St. Anne's, Halifax.
Rev. G. LEA, M.A., Incumbent of Christ Church, Birmingham, and Prebendary of Lichfield.
Rev. W. LEASK, D.D., Ware.
Rev. J. LEECHMAN, M.A., LL.D., Hammersmith.
Rev. J. LEES, M.A., Incumbent of St. Mark's, Tollington Park.
Rev. J. LEIFCHILD, M.A., Regent's Park.
Rev. T. LESSEY, Arundel Square, Islington.
Rev. J. W. LESTER, D.D., Incumbent of St. Luke's, Lower Norwood.
Rev. W. G. LEWIS, Westbourne Grove, Bayswater.
Rev. Sir C. R. LIGHTON, Bart., M.A., Vicar of Ellastone, Staffordshire.
Rev. E. LILLINGSTON, M.A., Incumbent of St. George's, Edgbaston, Birmingham.
Rev. R. LONG, M.A., Association Secretary, Church Missionary Society.
Rev. J. LOUTIT, Plymouth.
Rev. S. M'ALL, Hackney College.
Rev. W. M'ALL, M.A., Incumbent of St. Mary's, St. George's East.
Rev. D. M'ANALY, Incumbent of Penge.
Rev. J. MACFARLANE, D.D., Clapham.
Rev. H. M. M'GILL, D.D., Glasgow.
Rev. R. MAGUIRE, M.A., Incumbent of Clerkenwell.
Rev. E. MANNERING, Bishopsgate Chapel.
Rev. G. MANSFIELD, M.A., Vicar of Finchingfield, Essex.
Rev. S. MARCH, Erith.
Rev. Canon MARSH, D.D., Rector of Beddington, Surrey.
Rev. C. D. MARSTON, M.A., Rector of St. Mary's, Bryanston Square.
Rev. R. H. MARTEN, B.A., Lee.
Rev. J. H. MILLARD, B.A., Maze Pond Chapel.

Rev. Canon MILLER, D.D., Rector of St. Martin's, Birmingham.
Rev. W. A. MOCATTA, M.A., Association Secretary, Church Missionary Society.
Rev. C. F. S. MONEY, M.A., Incumbent of St. John's, Deptford.
Rev. J. MOORHOUSE, M.A., Incumbent of St. John's, Fitzroy Square.
Rev. J. V. MUMMERY, F.R.A.S., Secretary of Book Society, and to Congregational Board, London.
Rev. W. M. MUNGEAM, B.A., Incumbent of St. Peter's, Southwark.
Rev. T. NOLAN, B.D., Incumbent of St. Peter's, Regent Square, St. Pancras.
Rev. G. OSBORNE, D.D., Secretary, Wesleyan Missionary Society.
Rev. J. PATTESON, M.A., Rector of Christ Church, Spitalfields.
Rev. J. S. PEARSALL, Eccleston Chapel, Pimlico.
Rev. J. PEDDIE, D.D., Edinburgh.
Rev. G. PERRY, M.A., Minister of Fitzroy Chapel, St. Pancras.
Rev. B. PHILPOT, M.A., Vicar of Lydney, Gloucestershire.
Rev. D. PITCAIRN, Torquay.
Rev. A. PRICE, B.A., Minister of the Lock Chapel.
Rev. E. T. PRUST, Northampton.
Rev. W. M. PUNSHON, M.A., Islington.
Rev. A. RALEIGH, Canonbury.
Rev. J. RANDERSON, Lincoln.
Rev. T. R. REDWAR, M.A., Incumbent of St. Thomas's, Chancery Lane.
Rev. W. REED, London.
Rev. H. R. REYNOLDS, B.A., Cheshunt College.
Rev. R. W. REYNOLDS, M.A., Incumbent of St. Stephen's, Spitalfields.
Rev. J. RICHARDSON, M.A., Vicar of St. Mary's, Bury St. Edmunds.
Rev. J. W. RICHARDSON, Rosendale, Dulwich.
Rev. A. ROBERTS, M.A., Rector of Woodrising.
Rev. R. ROBERTS, Huddersfield.
Rev. W. ROBERTS, B.A., Notting Hill.
Rev. W. ROBERTS, Halifax.
Rev. W. ROBERTSON, M.A., Hamilton.
Rev. D. ROBINSON, M.A., Curate of Henbury, Bristol.
Rev. Canon SALE, M.A., Vicar of Sheffield.
Rev. F. G. SANDERS, B.A., Curate of Southport.
Rev. J. SCOTT, M.A., Incumbent of St. Mary's, Hull.
Rev. F. SCOTT, M.A., Rector of Wappenham.
Rev. T. H. SHARPE, M.A., Vicar of Codicote, Herts.
Rev. G. SMITH, Trinity Chapel, Poplar.

LIST OF CONTRIBUTORS.

Rev. GERVASE SMITH, Islington.
Rev. A. W. SNAPE, M.A., Incumbent of St. Mary Magdalene, Southwark.
Rev. J. SPENCE, D.D., Poultry Chapel.
Rev. J. STACEY, Sheffield.
Rev. W. M. STATHAM, Brompton.
Rev. E. STEANE, D.D., Camberwell.
Rev. H. STEBBING, D.D., Rector of St. Mary's Somerset, Thames Street.
Rev. J. R. STOCK, M.A., Rector of Allhallows, Thames Street.
Rev. J. STRATTEN, Paddington.
Rev. A. B. SUTER, B.A., Incumbent of All Saints, Stepney.
Rev. G. TAIT, M.A., Rector of St. Matthew's, Bath.
Rev. A. C. THOMAS, Cross Street, Islington.
Rev. P. THOMSON, Grosvenor Street Chapel, Manchester.
Rev. W. L. THORNTON, M.A., Editor to Wesleyan Conference.
Rev. A. W. THOROLD, M.A., Rector of St. Giles-in-the-Fields.
Rev. S. A. TIPPLE, Upper Norwood.
Rev. J. H. TITCOMB, M.A., Incumbent of St. Stephen's, South Lambeth.
Rev. F. TRESTRAIL, Secretary, Baptist Missionary Society.
Rev. J. W. TWEDDLE, Westminster.

Rev. L. TUGWELL, M.A., Incumbent of St. Andrew's, Lambeth.
Rev. H. VACHELL, M.A., Rector of St. John's, Horseydown.
Rev. M. H. VINE, M.A., Rector of St. Mary-le-Bow, Cheapside.
Rev. J. VINEY, Highgate.
Rev. S. WADDY, D.D., Chelsea.
Rev. E. WAITE, M.A., Leatherhead.
Rev. S. A. WALKER, M.A., Rector of St. Mary-le-Port, Bristol.
Rev. H. WALSH, M.A., Rector of Bishopston, Wilts.
Rev. W. WELLS, M.A., Vicar of Carbrooke, Norfolk.
Rev. F. A. WEST, Governor of New Kingswood School, Bath.
Rev. C. WHITE, M.A., Incumbent of Haslington, Cheshire.
Rev. J. B. WHITING, M.A., Rector of Broomfield, Essex.
Rev. W. WILKINSON, M.A., Incumbent of St. Mary's, Sheffield.
Rev. D. F. WILSON, M.A., Vicar of Mitcham, Surrey.
Rev. J. G. WILSON, M.A., Assistant Editor to Wesleyan Conference.
Rev. S. A. WINDLE, Chaplain of Mariners' Church, Kingstown.
Rev. W. WINDLE, M.A., Rector of St. Stephen's, Walbrook.
Rev. J. WRIGHT, M.A., London.

THE
FAMILY PRAYER-BOOK;

OR,

Morning and Evening Prayers for Every Day in the Year.

| MORNING.] | FIRST WEEK.—LORD'S DAY. | [EVENING. |

READ IN HOLY SCRIPTURE GENESIS I.

ALMIGHTY and Everlasting God, Creator of heaven and earth, accept our thanksgiving for all thy mercies, for Thou art the Lord our God. We especially praise Thee, O God, for the protection wherewith Thou hast kept us during the past night, and for the renewed mercies of another day. Thou hast stretched thy shield over this household, and beneath thy care we have dwelt in safety. Continue thy care over us throughout the day, and enable us to please Thee in all our thoughts, and words, and works. Bestow upon us such health and strength that we may be ready, both in body and soul, to do thy will; and give us all such things as Thou seest to be good for us.

Thou who didst command the light to shine out of darkness, shed the light of thy truth into our souls. Thou knowest, O Lord, what the day will bring forth, and neither our weaknesses nor our temptations are hidden from Thee. Fulfil towards us thy promises, and grant us such grace that we may walk in thy faith and fear all the day long, for Thou art round about our path, and spiest out all our ways.

We beseech Thee, also, for all those who are near and dear to us. We commend to thy fatherly goodness all thine afflicted people. And as Thou hast made of one blood all nations of men, teach us so to love one another that we may rejoice with those who do rejoice, and weep with those who weep. Be in the midst of this family, to guide us in our devotions before Thee and in our intercourse with each other. Endow all thy ministers with grace and wisdom, and all thy congregations with the hearing ear and the understanding heart. Shed thy blessing, O God, on thy Church and people. Grant that thy Word may be widely preached throughout the world, and so prosper it with thy Spirit that many sinners may be gathered unto Thee. Hear us, we beseech Thee, for the sake of thy Son Jesus Christ our Lord. Amen.

READ IN HOLY SCRIPTURE ST. JOHN I. 1—18.

OUR Father which art in heaven, we assemble ourselves as a family at the end of the first Sabbath in this New Year, to confess our sins, to thank Thee for thy goodness to us, and to seek thy blessing upon this closing day's engagements. Blessed be God who daily loadeth us with benefits, and who hath richly blessed us this day. By thy grace we have not forsaken the assembling of ourselves together, as the manner of some is, but we have loved the habitation of thy house. Sanctify to our spiritual profit the public reading of the Scriptures, the preaching of the Gospel of thy grace, and all the ordinances of thy Church. Suffer us not to be forgetful hearers, but make us doers of thy Word. May the sweet savour of Church worship abide with us, and by means of all the religious privileges which we enjoy, whether public, private, or domestic, may we bring forth much fruit. In every place, as in many things, we all offend. We have sinned in thy house this day, and have come short of thy glory. We would be humbled by the thought that even in the place where prayer is wont to be made, and even in acts of worship, we grieve Thee and break thy laws. Father in heaven, forgive us, we beseech Thee, and may we now and always feel that the blood of Jesus Christ our Saviour cleanseth us from all sin.

One thing, O merciful Father, we specially ask of Thee, that during this New Year our knowledge of the Saviour may greatly increase. May we know Him as the Word made flesh, and as the only-begotten Son of the Father, and may our experience be that He is full of grace and truth. Grant, we pray Thee, that in every period of life we may be qualified to say, "I know whom I have believed, and am persuaded that He is able to keep that which I have committed unto Him against that day." And now bless us with thy protection during the night, that we may lay ourselves down in sleep and safety, secure from evil, and quiet from fear of evil, through Jesus Christ our Saviour. Amen.

[1]

[Morning.]   FIRST WEEK.—MONDAY.   [Evening.

READ IN HOLY SCRIPTURE PSALM CIV.

READ IN HOLY SCRIPTURE HEBREWS I.

O LORD our God, Merciful and Almighty Father! our hearts would respond to the psalm of praise which we have just been reading, and with our souls and all that is within us we would now bless *Thee*. For sleep and safety during the night; for life, and health, and strength this morning; for food and raiment, and a dwelling-place; and for all that supplies the needs of the body, we thank *Thee*. For all Thou art unto us as our Father; for the gift of thy Son our Saviour—for the sending of the Holy Ghost, our Regenerator and Comforter; and for the sacred volume which gives us the knowledge of thyself and of Jesus Christ whom Thou hast sent, we bless *Thee*. We receive from Thee every day mercies more than we can number, and blessings more precious than we can describe; and we are sensible of obligations which these words of worship do not express. Accept, therefore, O merciful Father, not merely the praises of our lips, but the unuttered gratitude of our hearts.

And we beseech Thee to hear us, O Lord God, when we ask that thy mercy may follow us throughout this day—may it attend us in all our labours, and in all our recreations; in all our trials, and in all our temptations. Often move us to think of Thee, and may our meditation of Thee be sweet; may we be glad in the Lord. Open our eyes to see the manifold works, and thy riches, of which this earth is full. Especially enable us to inquire into and to meditate upon the exceeding riches of thy grace, and the unsearchable riches of Christ, so that we may sing unto the Lord as long as we live, yea, sing praises to our God while we have any being.

We acknowledge ourselves to be defiled with the exceeding sinfulness of sin, and to be unworthy to receive any gift from Thee. Grant, therefore, that with the spirit of praise there may be ever united in our hearts the spirit of true humility; and that whenever we speak of Thee, it may always be with a penitent and believing heart.

We especially confess to Thee that we have often been unmindful of thy love to us, and that we have shown our unthankfulness by restraining praise, by coldness and indifference of heart, and by disobedience to thy commandments. Mercifully forgive us. We resolve, by the help of thy grace, to show forth thy praise, not with our lips only, but also with our lives, by giving up ourselves to thy service, and walking before Thee in holiness and righteousness all our days.

Accept, Father of all mercies, this our morning sacrifice of worship, for our Lord Jesus Christ's sake. Amen.

GRACIOUS art Thou, O God, and blessed is thy name: for Thou dost give us life, and health, and all things. Thou art our God, and we will praise Thee; Thou art our God, and we will exalt Thee.

We give Thee humble and hearty thanks, O merciful Lord, for thy guardian care over us in our goings out and in our comings in. For all our mercies, personal, social, and domestic; for food, and raiment, and shelter; for the preservation of life and health; for every pleasure we have enjoyed, and every mutual affection which has gladdened our homes, we glorify thy goodness, O our God.

We acknowledge, O holy and heart-searching Judge, that we have not deserved any of thy mercies: for we, like sheep, have gone astray. It is of thy mercy only that we are not consumed.

O God, the Father of our Lord Jesus Christ, who didst give thine only-begotten Son to make known unto us thy will, and to bear the penalty of our transgressions, mercifully pardon and accept us. O God the Son, who didst humble thyself to the death upon the cross, that Thou mightest purge away our sins, and art now ascended into heaven, cleanse us in thy most precious blood. O God the Holy Ghost, who didst guide the minds of prophets and apostles to write thy Word, open our minds to understand thy will, and prepare our hearts to do it. Blot out as a thick cloud our transgressions, and as a cloud our sins.

Teach us, O Lord, so to number our days that we may apply our hearts unto wisdom. Awaken and ever increase in us an earnest anxiety about the things belonging to our peace, that we may live as strangers and pilgrims who seek another country, even a heavenly. Let us not love the world, nor the things of the world, more than we love Thee. Be Thou alone our strength in life, our hope in death, and our exceeding great reward for evermore.

Send down, we beseech Thee, thy Holy Spirit, to cleanse from our hearts any evil thoughts which may have been suggested to us during the day, either from within or from without. Accept, through Jesus Christ thy Son, whatever sincere love and obedient service thine own grace hath enabled us to render unto Thee, and be not extreme to mark the negligences and ignorances with which they have been accompanied.

To thy protection we commit ourselves and all whom we love. Keep us in peace through the hours of the darkness: and if it be thy pleasure, raise us to see another day; if not, take away the fear of death and receive us into thy kingdom, through Jesus Christ our Lord. Amen.

[Morning.]   FIRST WEEK.—TUESDAY.   [Evening.

READ IN HOLY SCRIPTURE GENESIS II.

O GOD our Father, enable us to feel in this our prayer, that Thou art very near to us, and that we are very near to Thee; that thine ear is hearkening to our prayer, and thy hand outstretched to bless us. With all our hearts we thank Thee for the protection and rest of the night and the mercies of the day. Thou hast renewed to us the bounties of thy providence and the riches of thy grace. O Lord, we desire to see thy love in all these things. Help us to use them as for Thee, and to remember, day by day, that of all these talents we must give account at the Great Day.

Forgive us, O God, all our forgetfulness of Thee, and of thy mercy to us—all our disobedience of thy commands. Awaken in us every day a deeper sense of our own emptiness, and reveal to us more clearly the fulness and sufficiency of Jesus. Through Him alone we hope for peace and blessing.

And now, O God, when another day is before us, with its temptations, and opportunities, and duties, we look upward to Thee for preserving and sustaining care. The life which Thou didst inbreathe at the first we commit to thy precious keeping. Leave us not to ourselves, for if Thou withdraw thy care we fall and perish. Thou knowest, O God, the craft of the great enemy, and what ignorant and feeble creatures we are; Thou knowest the power of the world's temptations, and how unable we are in our own strength to meet and overcome them. Lord, help us. Preserve us from falling. Uphold us in the narrow way, that our footsteps slip not. Set a watch over our lips, that we offend not in word. Make our conscience so tender and sensitive, that we may shrink at the approach of evil, and touch not the forbidden thing. Remind us constantly of thy presence, and hide thy word in our hearts, that we may not sin against Thee. We know, O Lord, that whatever Thou deniest us is denied in mercy, and whatever Thou commandest is commanded in mercy. Kindle in our hearts such love to Thee, that thy commandments may never be grievous. It is Thou who hast placed us where we are, and given us our work to do. We desire in our station and calling to please Thee in all things. If Thou seest us wandering from the ways of godliness, speak to our hearts by thy Holy Spirit, and turn our feet again into thy paths.

Lord, we pray not for ourselves alone, but for all whom we love. Sanctify to us and to them the earthly relationships by which thy providence has knit us together. Let not one of us be found wanting in the day when Thou makest up thy jewels; but make us thine, and keep us thine for evermore. Hear us, O God. We ask Thee for all, and thank Thee for all, in the name of Jesus Christ, thy dear Son, our Saviour. Amen.

READ IN HOLY SCRIPTURE ISAIAH XL. 1–11.

O GOD, whose providence ordereth all things in heaven and earth, glory be to thy great Name for the mercies of this day. If we have had strength for the daily task; if we have been protected in the midst of dangers; if home comforts have been ours; if we have had peace in the midst of much to trouble us, and a secret sense of thy love hath sweetened our toil, it is all of thy favour. If we have been steadfast in the face of temptation, not unto us, O Lord, but unto thy Name be all the praise. For these, and all thy gifts, we adore thee, O thou Fountain of grace and Father of mercies. We did not deserve thy goodness, but Thou hast had mercy, and even now waitest to be gracious. Oh, add to all thy gifts the gift of a thankful heart, that we may be stirred up to see what we can render to Thee for all thy benefits.

We come to Thee, O God, just as we are: sinful, do Thou forgive us: guilty, do Thou cleanse us: unholy, do Thou sanctify us: ignorant, do Thou teach us: in a world of sorrow, do Thou comfort us: uncertain of life, for all flesh is as grass, do Thou establish our faith in thy Word, which standeth fast for ever; and give us the hope of a blessed immortality. Oh, that the glad tidings of thy Gospel may melt our hearts anew, and make them contrite and believing. Level whatever hinders the perfect work of thy Spirit within us. Break down all pride and conceit of our own goodness. Cast out all selfrighteousness. Humble us, O God, by thy teaching and discipline. Make us meekly submissive to all thy will. In all things prepare us for the coming of Jesus in the power and glory of the Father, to judge the living and the dead. Oh, that in that day we may be found of Him in peace, without spot or stain.

Lord Jesus, Thou art the good Shepherd of the sheep. Thou stoopest to the youngest and weakest of thy flock, bearing them in thine arms, and carrying them in thy bosom. Regard with special favour the children of this household. Convince them of their own sinfulness, and unfold to them the meaning of thy Cross and Passion. Have pity on the unconverted among us. Spare them, O God, and by thy Spirit root out their hardness of heart and unbelief. Forbid it, Lord, in thy mercy, that even one of us should neglect thy great salvation.

Take us now under thy protection. Pour out thy choicest blessings on all whom we love. Strengthen the hands of thy ministers. Magnify thy grace in the conversion of souls. Make known thy glory far and wide, that all the world may see it; and hasten thy kingdom. We ask all through Jesus Christ our Lord. Amen.

[Morning.] **FIRST WEEK.—WEDNESDAY.** [Evening.

READ IN HOLY SCRIPTURE HEBREWS IV. 1—11.

GLORIOUS art Thou, O God, and adored for ever and ever be thy name. Thy ways are not as our ways, nor thy thoughts as our thoughts. As we now recall thy goodness, deepen in us, O Lord, a feeling of thankfulness and praise. We confess with shame and sorrow we have not loved Thee and lived for Thee as we ought. We have received thy gifts, and too often have forgotten the Giver. Convince us of our sin, and cleanse us from its stain.

Lord, thou hast given us the promise of rest and peace in Jesus. Increase our faith, lest through unbelief we come short of it and perish. Give us peace of conscience now by the assurance of forgiveness from all sin, and of our adoption into thy family. Amid all the buffetings of temptation, and the anxieties and cares of life, enable us to stay our souls on Thee, and thus to be kept in perfect peace. Give us rest with thyself hereafter, in that better land where neither sin nor temptation can beset us. Forbid it, Lord, in thy mercy, that we should fail of a place in thy kingdom. We fear, not because we doubt thy truth or despair of thy love: we fear for ourselves. We fear lest at any time our hearts should become hard and insensible through the deceitfulness of sin or the engrossments and pleasures of the world. Thou knowest how weak is our faith, and how inconstant our best and holiest resolutions. Give us, O Lord God, constancy of purpose, and the grace of unfailing perseverance, that we may hold fast our confidence even to the end. Show us the exceeding sinfulness of unbelief, and preserve us from ever dishonouring Thee and imperilling our own souls by doubting thy truth. Especially, O Lord, keep us mindful that this earth is not our rest. Teach us to look forward with an earnest and lively hope to the coming of the Lord, and our own entrance into the rest which remaineth for his people.

We pray for all with whom Thou hast united us in the ties of relationship and affection. We pray for all men: for the ungodly at home, and the heathen abroad. Enlighten them by thy truth: bring them humble and penitent to the feet of Jesus. Take the veil from the eyes of the Jew: reveal to him Christ his Redeemer and King. We pray for the Church of Christ, that every member thereof may truly and godly serve Thee. We pray for all in authority: overrule all that they do for the enlargement of the Redeemer's kingdom, and the increase of godliness in the land.

Lord, accept Thou our unworthy services. Receive us for Jesus' sake. To him, our exalted Saviour, with Thee, O Father, and Thee, Holy Ghost, be honour and praise for evermore. Amen.

READ IN HOLY SCRIPTURE ST. LUKE I. 1—25.

O GOD, at the close of another day we fall low at thy mercy-seat. May we not only bend the knee before Thee but also the heart. And may we come with boldness to thy throne, by that new and living way, even by our Saviour Jesus Christ. We acknowledge, Holy Father, our transgressions and sins. If we say that we have no sin, we deceive ourselves, and the truth is not in us; but if we confess our sins, Thou art faithful and just to forgive us our sins, and to cleanse us from all unrighteousness.

We have sinned this day in thought, word, and deed. We have done things which we should not have done, and we have left undone many things which we ought to have done; but there is forgiveness with Thee, that Thou mayest be feared, and the blood of Jesus Christ thy Son cleanseth from all sin. May that blood be sprinkled on our souls, and our sins, which are many, be all forgiven and for ever blotted out.

We thank Thee for thy gracious dealings towards us throughout this day. We thank Thee for food and raiment, for health and strength, for home, and peace, and happiness. May these thy mercies long be continued to us, and do Thou thyself never leave and never forsake us.

Graciously grant, Heavenly Father, that as each day passes away we may be found nearer unto heaven, walking, as Zacharias and Elizabeth, in all the commandments and ordinances of the Lord, blameless. Give us more and more of the Spirit of Christ. Impress thine own image more deeply on our souls. Subdue in us all evil passions which hinder our growth in godliness and true holiness. Help us to cast away our besetting sins. Deepen our love to Thee, and confirm and strengthen our faith. And thus, living in thy fear, and doing thy will, may we be ready, whenever our summons may come, to enter into the joy of our Lord.

And now we commit ourselves to thy care and keeping this night. Watch Thou beside our beds, and grant that we may awake in the morning filled with thy Spirit, to do Thee better service than we have done this day. We beseech Thee to bless all for whom we ought to pray. Those near and dear to us, may they be very near and dear to Thee. Those in any sorrow, trial, need, or necessity do Thou remember, and be unto them a very present God in their season of affliction.

Hear us, Holy Father, in these our petitions. Pour down upon us the abundance of thy mercy; forgiving us those things whereof our conscience is afraid, and giving us those good things which we are not worthy to ask, but for the sake and through the merits of Jesus Christ our Lord. Amen.

[Morning.]   FIRST WEEK.—THURSDAY.   [Evening.]

READ IN HOLY SCRIPTURE GENESIS III.

O GOD! Thou art the Creator of all things: with Thee is the fountain of life. Thou didst make man at first in thine own image, and after thy likeness, to reflect thy glory in righteousness and true holiness. But, alas! how soon and how totally did he fall away from Thee! We humble ourselves before Thee as members of a fallen race. We with our fathers have sinned: we have done wickedly. Unto the Lord our God belongeth righteousness, but unto us shame and confusion of face, as at this day. We have not trusted Thee: we have not obeyed thy Word. The tempter has tempted us, and led us far astray. We have been drawn by the love of the world. We have sought the pleasures of sense. We have forgotten thy holy law. We have often put out the hand to forbidden things. We too have fallen by our iniquity. O Lord, convince us deeply of our sin, and work in us, by thy Holy Spirit, true repentance, which needeth not to be repented of, and a sincere faith in our Lord Jesus Christ.

We adore thy manifold wisdom and the riches of thy grace in the promise which softened the fall of our first parents in Eden, and which, in its last fulfilment, will repeal the curse over all the earth. We thank thee for Him who came in the fulness of time, made of a woman, made under the law, to redeem them that were under the law, that we might receive the adoption of sons. We thank Thee that he has finished the work given him to do. May we behold him coming to us now, travelling in the greatness of his strength, speaking in righteousness, and mighty to save. Teach us to admire his spotless life. Lift us up that we may behold his greatness and his beauty. Above all, bring us in penitent and humble trust to his cross, and help us to rely with unwavering confidence on that atoning sacrifice which he offered for us. Thus receiving Christ, and him crucified, as our salvation, may we walk in newness of life. Teach us to know the power of his resurrection. Give us the fellowship of his sufferings, and conform us increasingly unto his death. O Lord, graciously bend our will to thine: constrain our affections, and lift them up to spiritual things: cleanse our consciences from dead works: take all our nature into thy holy keeping, and let us be living sacrifices unto Thee.

Preserve us this day: guide all our steps: shield us from all evil: assist us in every duty. May all the days of our earthly pilgrimage, under thy gracious guidance, be leading us on to the heavenly rest; and may we all meet at length in our Father's house above. We ask all in the name of our only Lord and Saviour, Jesus Christ. Amen.

READ IN HOLY SCRIPTURE ST. LUKE I. 26–38.

O ALMIGHTY and Everlasting God, who hast caused all Holy Scripture to be written for our learning, give us grace to receive with meekness and faith the portion which we have now heard. We thank Thee for that inestimable love which led Thee to give thy Son—thine only Son—to take our nature upon him, and to be made flesh without spot of sin, that we might be free from all sin. We thank Thee, O Lord, for that example of faith which Thou hast given us in the mother of our Lord, whose spirit rejoiced in God her Saviour. We pray Thee to give us all the same precious faith; enable us to receive the message of thy Word with the same readiness of mind. Teach us to submit to thy will concerning us, with the same loving humility. Strengthen us to leave the difficulties which we know, and those also which we do not know, to that never-failing providence which ordereth all things both in heaven and earth. Enable us to commit ourselves and our characters calmly into thy hands, anxious only to be right with Thee, and having no doubt that *Thou* wilt make our righteousness as clear as the light.

Oh, may the Holy Ghost—the Lord and Giver of life—form Christ within our hearts. May it please Thee to reveal thy Son in us, that he may dwell in our hearts by faith. Set up within us thy kingdom, which is righteousness, peace, and joy in the Holy Ghost. Oh, that Thou wouldest bring every thought within us, every temper, every motive, every disposition, into obedience to the law of Christ. May the Spirit of Truth rule and direct our minds, and may we watch continually and keep the door of our lips. May no corrupt communication—no words that are not true, or profitable, or kind—ever come forth from our lips, which are not our own, but Christ's; and may we speak only that which is good to the use of edifying, which may minister grace to the hearers.

O Lord Jesus, Thou thyself hast assured us that whosoever shall do the will of thy Father which is in heaven, the same is thy brother, and sister, and mother. We bless Thee that we may all thus be thy kinsmen according to the Spirit—the children of God by faith in Thee—whom Thou, tho root and offspring of David, art not ashamed to call thy brethren. Oh, give us grace to live as becometh this our high and holy calling; and as Thou, Lord, art holy, so may we strive and pray to be holy in all manner of conversation. We beseech Thee to prepare us now to dwell with Thee hereafter, that when Thou comest in thy kingdom, O Lord, thou son of David, we may, with all thy holy angels and all thy redeemed saints, be admitted to behold thy glory.

O God, grant this for thy dear Son's sake. Amen.

[5]

[Morning.] **FIRST WEEK.—FRIDAY.** [Evening.]

READ IN HOLY SCRIPTURE ROMANS I. 18—25.

O LORD, our God! our Creator, our Preserver, our Redeemer, our Judge! We are unworthy to take thy holy Name upon our lips, to enter into thy presence, and to supplicate thy favour. We are guilty sinners: unholy and unclean. We acknowledge our iniquity: we confess our vileness. O God, have mercy upon us!

Thy wrath, O God, is revealed from heaven against all ungodliness and unrighteousness of men. Thy just sentence is—"The soul that sinneth, it shall die." *We are* "worthy of death." Lord! we read thy power, thy wisdom, thy goodness, in the glorious works of thy Almighty hand: we discern them in our own bodies, so fearfully and wonderfully made: we see them in the returning day, in the revolving seasons, in the fruits of the earth, and in the wonders of the great deep. But, alas! too often have we forgotten Thee, our Maker and Preserver, in whom we live, and move, and have our being: too often, while we have professed with the lip to serve Thee, have we in our lives denied Thee, and "held the truth in unrighteousness." We confess with shame and confusion of face that too often, since we have known Thee, have we "glorified Thee not as God, neither have we been thankful:" we have "worshipped and served the creature," idolising the very comforts and blessings Thou hast given us, rather than thyself, our Creator, "who art blessed for ever." Blessed God! Thou hast further revealed thyself to us in thy Holy Word as the God and Father of our Lord Jesus Christ: we have heard thy gracious message, but how coldly have we received the message! how little have we been affected by the manifestation of thine infinite love towards us thy sinful creatures! Great, indeed, is our guilt in forgetting Thee our Almighty Creator and gracious Preserver! Oh, how much greater our sin in forgetting thy redeeming love in the Lord Jesus Christ! "Have mercy upon us, O God, according to thy lovingkindness: according unto the multitude of thy tender mercies, blot out our transgressions." Oh, may the precious blood of Jesus cleanse us from all sin! Shed abroad in our hearts the love of Jesus, by thy Holy Spirit!

Help us this day to live under the abiding influence of thy goodness, grace, and love. May the love of Christ constrain us to live not to ourselves, but to Thee our God. Teach us, by happy experience, that thy service is perfect freedom. May it be the resolve of our hearts, as well as the profession of our lips—"O Lord our God, other lords beside Thee have had dominion over us; but by Thee only will we make mention of thy Name." Amen.

READ IN HOLY SCRIPTURE ST. MATTHEW I. 18—25.

O GOD, who art always more ready to hear than we to pray, be gracious unto us, we beseech Thee, and accept us for Christ's sake.

We thank Thee, O Lord, for the multiplied mercies of this day. In the midst of its dangers Thou hast kept us safely. O our God, we are monuments of thy forbearance and love. Our hearts have been cold and dead, when they should have kindled with grateful love: our feet have been sluggish to duty, when they should have run in the way of thy commandments; in all things, O God, we have come short of thy glory. Could we but see ourselves as Thou seest us, we should be ashamed to lift up our eyes unto Thee. Guilty as we are, and unrighteous — stained with the defilement of many transgressions—we cast ourselves on thy mercy. Lord, whither can we turn for pardon and peace but to Thee? For Jesus Christ's sake, O God, let not our sins be remembered. We recall, with adoring hearts, the name of thy dear Son, and take comfort. It tells of thy mercy and grace to a guilty world. Thou didst give thy Son Jesus Christ to save his people from their sins: to reveal unto us all thy love: to proclaim to us thy grace, and restore in us the righteousness we have lost. Graciously give us the assurance of our acceptance in him. If any of us are unconverted, do Thou convert them. By the attraction of thy love, draw us all near to thyself: subduing our rebellious wills, melting the hard heart to a true repentance, and quickening within it the faith which looks unto Jesus, and in him finds joy and peace.

And, O Lord Jesus, deliver us from the power of sin. Take away all that opposes Thee and hinders the full accomplishment of thy purposes of mercy towards us. Let the thought of thy love stir up in us a jealous watchfulness against the unholy thoughts and tempers that mar thy work in our hearts and lives. Lord, we desire to be like Thee; to have the mind that was in Thee; to be walking in thy footsteps; and to have the constant sense of thy love.

O God our Father, take us and all that are dear to us into thy care and keeping. Spread around us during the night the shield of thy protecting power. Give us all sweet and refreshing sleep, and turn away evil from our dwelling.

Carry the Gospel to those who know it not, or, knowing it, have turned away from its heavenly message. Go forth, O God, in the power of thy truth, and gather into the fold the estranged and the wandering. Thy kingdom come: thy will be done in earth as it is in heaven. Lord God, hear us in these our prayers and thanksgivings, for Jesus' sake. Amen.

[MORNING.]   FIRST WEEK.—SATURDAY.   [EVENING.

READ IN HOLY SCRIPTURE GENESIS IV.   READ IN HOLY SCRIPTURE ST. LUKE I. 39—56.

ALMIGHTY and most gracious Lord God, who invitest us to come to Thee as our reconciled Father in Jesus Christ, give unto us, we beseech Thee, thy Holy Spirit as the Spirit of adoption, that we may draw near to Thee unfeignedly in his all-prevailing name. We confess that we are unworthy to come into thy presence, for we are guilty, sinful, and unprofitable creatures. We have nothing which we can offer to commend us to thy favour; but we beseech Thee to give to each of us a true and living faith in the Lamb of God, which taketh away the sins of the world. We bless Thee that his blood speaketh better things than the blood of Abel. May it plead effectually for us before thy throne of grace. May it be sprinkled on our consciences, and purge our souls from dead works to serve Thee, the living God.

Make us mindful this day of our solemn obligations to Thee in all our undertakings and doings, and give us grace that we may be kept unspotted from the world. Preserve us from evil. Direct the thoughts of our minds and the affections of our hearts, that they may be in accordance with thy holy Word and will. We thank Thee for thy great goodness in having preserved us in safety to the closing day of another week. Enter not into judgment with thy servants for anything Thou hast seen amiss in us during the time that is past, and grant that we may so spend this day that it may be a suitable preparation for the sacred season of the approaching Sabbath. Keep far from us, as a Christian family, everything that may tend to stir up evil passions, wrath, strife, envy, or jealousy, and may we live together in holy love and peace, as it becomes brethren of the same household.

Bless our Sovereign and the members of the Royal Family. Direct the counsels of our rulers for the furtherance of peace and godliness, and the extension of thy kingdom amongst us. Spiritually bless thy ministers this day in preparing for the responsible duties of the morrow. Guide them to the contemplation of such subjects as may most tend to the edification and spiritual benefit of their people. Comfort those who mourn. Look upon any who are suffering for conscience' sake, or who are testifying for the Gospel of thy dear Son in the midst of opposition or danger. Restrain the ungodly, and make the very wrath of man to praise Thee. O God, we beseech Thee to grant that we may be found amongst thy true people, and that with all thy redeemed ones we may have our everlasting portion in thy glorious kingdom, for Jesus Christ's sake. Amen.

O LORD God, the high, the holy, the gracious God, in tenderness and compassion look upon us, as in the name of Jesus we humbly kneel at thy footstool. Be present in our midst, and reveal thyself unto us as Thou dost not unto the world.

Raise our hearts in praise for the mercies of this day, and let thine ear be open to our prayer. Thou causest thy sun to rise on the evil and the good, and sendest rain on the just and the unjust. Thy mercy reacheth unto the heavens, and thy faithfulness to all generations. We, too, have experienced thy love. Thou hast done for us great things, and holy is thy name. Even when we were yet without strength, Christ died for us. Our day of grace has been prolonged, while others have been called to their great account. Thou hast satisfied us out of thy goodness, and enriched us with blessings that have been withheld from others. Thine everlasting arms have upheld us, and the mightiness of thy protection has been round about us. Our table has been spread by thy hand. The raiment that clothes us and the dwelling that shelters us are of thy giving. The faith which enables us to grasp thy promises, and the repentance which bows us now at thy feet in sorrow for sin, and the grace of thy Holy Spirit which guides and keeps us in the narrow way, are of thy giving. We magnify Thee, O Lord, for this and all thy mercy. Oh, that our hearts may now rejoice in God our Saviour. Help us, heavenly Father, to consecrate ourselves, body, soul, and spirit, more lovingly and obediently than ever to thy service.

Have mercy upon us, O our God, for the sins of this day. If thou wert extreme to mark what is done amiss, who could stand before Thee? But there is mercy with Thee, and the blood of Jesus Christ cleanseth us from all sin. Wash us, Lord, in the fountain once opened for sin and uncleanness. Shed upon our souls the peace which springs from the assurance that our sins are forgiven, and that thy providence is making all things work for good to us so long as we love Thee. Deepen in us a spirit of true humility. Increase our faith, and enable us to look up undoubtingly for the fulfilment of thy Word. Help us to deny ourselves and bear meekly the cross of Christ. Give us a righteous abhorrence of all evil, that we may indeed be the sons and daughters of the Lord God Almighty. Let the light of thy love shine on our path, and grant us the sure hope of eternal life in thy dear Son. In his name we commend ourselves, and all who are dear to us, to thy care. Oh, watch over us and bless us, and answer our prayers for his sake. Amen.

[Morning.] **SECOND WEEK.—LORD'S DAY.** [Evening.

READ IN HOLY SCRIPTURE I. JOHN III. 11—24.

READ IN HOLY SCRIPTURE ST. LUKE I. 57—80.

O HEAVENLY Father, who hast in thy gracious providence kept us in safety through the watches of the night, accept our sacrifice of prayer and thanksgiving.

We pray, Holy Father, that thy protecting goodness may be around us this day. Be with us in whatever we may think or do. Wherever we go, do Thou go; wherever we abide, do Thou abide. Ever be with us, to guide, to help, and to bless us.

And may we remember that this is thy day, and keep it holy unto Thee. Banish all worldly cares, all wandering thoughts. Fix our hearts upon things above. And when we go up to thy house of prayer, may we worship Thee in spirit and in truth.

Bless, O Heavenly Father, especially thy minister whom thou hast set over us. Grant that the influences of the Holy Spirit may be abundantly poured out upon him this day! May he hold up the Cross in all simplicity, plainness, and affection. May thy Word fall as into good ground, and bring forth fruit—some thirty, some sixty, and some a hundred-fold.

Lord Jesus, be in the midst of all assemblies of thy people to-day. Let thy Word have free course and be glorified. May sinners be saved; the unconverted changed; the dead in trespasses and sins quickened; the sleeper aroused; the mourning penitents comforted; the broken in heart healed; the waverers decided; the backsliders humbled; and the righteous built up in their most holy faith. Bless the Word of thy grace to them all.

And bless, O Lord, all near and dear to us. Bless our parents, friends, and relatives. Bless the poor, the destitute, the dying, the outcast, the afflicted, and him that hath no helper.

And now, O Lord God, we again ask for ourselves. May we love one another as thou hast given us commandment. Help us to bear with each other's failings or infirmities. Increase in us a spirit of kindness, so that we may love in deed as in word. May we ever feel for those who possess not the many mercies of our own lot. If our brother hath need, may we never shut up the bowels of compassion from him. O Lord, thy Son did die for us guilty sinners: may we ever be ready to deny ourselves for the sake of those in necessity around us. Fill our souls with love, both to Thee and to our fellow-creatures. Subdue in us all hatred, all ill-will; root out of our hearts all bitterness. Enable us to be kind one to another, to be forgiving if we have any cause of offence, and ever to remember Him who graciously forgave us.

These, and all other mercies, we ask, Holy Father, in the name and through the mediation of our Lord and Saviour Jesus Christ. Amen.

O LORD God of our fathers! we desire to bow humbly at thy footstool. We approach Thee in the name of our Lord Jesus Christ. We make mention of his righteousness. Draw near unto each of us, O Lord: make us feel thy presence: and give us that holy reverence and solemn awe which is the due of the Creator from his creatures, of the Father in heaven from the children on earth. And do Thou, O Holy Spirit, breathe on our souls and inspire our speech, that our communion may be with the Father, and with the Son, and with the Holy Ghost: one God.

We bless Thee, O our Father, for sparing us to see another day of the Son of Man. May the public services of thy House be blessed to our souls. May the Word preached be profitable to us, being mixed with faith: and may our Sabbath day's sins be blotted out, and not remembered against us. Thou hast seen and knowest all that we have said, and done, and been this day. We confess our sins before Thee: we confess the sins of thought, the sins of feeling, the sins of desire, the sins of imagination, the secret sins, and those which may have been open. We confess each and all of the sins of omission and of commission of which each of us has been guilty this day. Give each of us grace, O Lord, we earnestly beseech Thee, for Christ's sake, to make hearty and humble confession of our individual sins before Thee ere we retire to rest, and to seek pardon through the merits of the precious blood of Jesus. We join in supplicating this mercy on each and all of us now. O Lord, our God, for thine own name's sake, and for the Lord Jesus Christ's sake, pardon our iniquity, because it is great. And grant, O Lord, that we, being delivered from the hand of our enemies, may serve Thee without fear, in holiness and righteousness before Thee all the days of our life. Save us, O God, from the hand of our enemies, and from all them that hate us. Keep us ever from the strife of tongues.

Take us into thy very special care this evening. Spread the sheltering shadow of thy wings over our household. Keep us and ours, and all near and dear to us, during the darkness. Waken us to life and health in the morning. Give us grace to begin the labour of the week in thy fear and favour, and may our Sabbath devotions sweeten the performance of all our duties through the coming week.

O Lord our God, bless our Sovereign and our dear native land, and all for whom we ought to pray; and may the beauty of the Lord our God be upon us and ours for ever and ever: for the Lord Jesus Christ's sake. Amen.

[MORNING.] SECOND WEEK.—MONDAY. [EVENING.

READ IN HOLY SCRIPTURE PSALM XXXIX.

ALMIGHTY and eternal God, since it is appointed unto all men once to die, so teach us to number our days that we may apply our hearts unto wisdom. Raise us by thy Spirit from the death of sin unto the life of righteousness. Renew us in thine own image. Let not self-pleasing nor man-pleasing be our aim; but in singleness and purity of heart may we please Thee. Oh, that we may live soberly, righteously, and godly this day. Oh, that our life may be hid with Christ in God; that neither the cares of the family or of business, neither the duties of our calling nor the pleasures of the world, may make us earthly-minded or earthly-hearted, but that we may walk in the Spirit, as those whose citizenship is in heaven. Help us by thy grace so to watch, and pray, and wait, that when death comes to us we may have nothing to do but to die. Take us, when we die, to thyself. Give us now the earnest of thine indwelling Spirit, to assure us that, in the day of the Lord, mortality shall be swallowed up of life. We would find in Jesus, who died and rose again for us, our rest and comfort, and the ark of our salvation. We rejoice in the glorious hope that our portion shall be with the children of the resurrection, who can die no more. Strengthen us, O our God, that we may fear no evil in the prospect of death. Thou givest grace to live, Thou wilt give grace to die.

We commend ourselves to thy fatherly care this day. Prepare us for every duty, every care, and every temptation. Teach us to use the world as not abusing it. We would enjoy thy gifts thankfully, cheerfully, and moderately.

Above all, give us pardon and peace, that we may walk before Thee and with Thee in faith and holiness. We have many who are dear to our hearts; some near, some afar off. Visit them with thy mercy, preserve them from harm, guide them safely amid all the dangers of their earthly pilgrimage, and grant that in thy goodness they and we may meet at last in thy kingdom. May this household live in love to-day. Let no angry temper, no unruly tongue, no sinful lust mar our peace and unity. Give us a spirit of forbearance and meekness. May our love to Thee bind us more closely in love to one another. Have mercy upon all men. Bless thy Church's work in this and in every land. Quicken her missionary zeal. Multiply her missionaries a thousand fold, and cheer their hearts in the midst of trial and opposition. Stablish and bless thy true churches already formed amid the darkness of other lands. Hasten the coming of thy kingdom, and let the whole earth be filled with thy glory. We ask it for Jesus Christ's sake. Amen.

READ IN HOLY SCRIPTURE ST. LUKE II. 8–20.

O GOD the Holy Ghost! wake up our sluggish hearts to praise, by the glad tidings which this Scripture brings. We would dwell with grateful adoration on the marvel of grace and love of which it tells. The Word was made flesh! Thou, the Creator, hast clothed thyself with the humanity of thy erring creatures. This is, indeed, thy crowning mercy to our rebellious and guilty world. Lord, never suffer the familiar truth to become a common thing to us, neither kindling emotion nor exciting thankfulness. But for this we had been lost for ever and ever! Enable us to see in the birth of Jesus Christ the fulfilment of thine everlasting counsels. Through long years of waiting, thy Word cheered the hearts of thy people; and when the fulness of time was come, thy dear Son, the brightness of his Father's glory, and the express image of his person, was made flesh and dwelt among us, and men beheld his glory, the glory as of the only begotten of the Father, full of grace and truth.

O God, how can we praise Thee enough for this thy goodness! Forgive us the indifference with which we often hear of thy redeeming love. Pardon the coldness of our hearts, our deadness to spiritual things, and the weakness of our faith. In mercy take away the veil from our eyes, and unfold to us all the meaning and significance of that scene in Bethlehem on which we have looked. May we learn from it thy tenderness and compassion towards us: may we see in it the Divine provision for our deep need. Lord, increase our faith, that we may embrace with all our hearts the message of mercy which thy incarnation brings us from Thee. Blessed indeed are our eyes, which see what kings and prophets longed to see, but saw not. O Jesus, Thou art born unto us a Saviour. Save us from the guilt of sin, by washing us in thine atoning blood. Save us from the love of sin, by kindling within us the love of God. Save us from the power of sin, by the indwelling energies of thy sanctifying Spirit. Oh, may this thy name be ever precious to us, comforting our hearts when sad, inspiring us with courage when fainting, and constraining us, by the mercies it recalls, to deny ourselves, and in all things conform ourselves to thine image.

Impress, Lord, on our hearts the high responsibility which these Gospel privileges entail. Oh, suffer none of us to neglect thy great salvation. Visit with thy grace all who are dear to us. Send forth far and wide thine everlasting Gospel. Let us see the day dawn in which glory shall be to God in the highest, peace in all the earth, and good will among all men. Hasten it, Lord, in thine own good time, for Jesus' sake. Amen.

[9]

[Morning.] **SECOND WEEK.—TUESDAY.** [Evening.

READ IN HOLY SCRIPTURE GENESIS VI.

O GOD, pour down upon us the spirit of praise and prayer, lost we draw nigh to Thee with our lips, while our hearts are far from Thee, and thus add to our other many transgressions the sin of insincerity and untruthfulness towards Thee. Truly Thou dealest with us not after our sins, and rewardest us not after our iniquities. Time and memory would fail us to recount thy mercies. Oh, help us to proclaim our thankfulness, not only now, in the uplifted song of praise, but through all the day, in the hearty obedience of the life.

And while Thou acceptest our praise, turn not away, O God, from our prayer. We plead His name and righteousness who hath promised that whatsoever we shall ask in prayer, believing, we shall receive. Lord, we believe; help Thou our unbelief. All the number of our sins are known to Thee: the sins of thoughtlessness and levity, the sins against light and knowledge, sins against the warnings of conscience and the strivings of thy Spirit. Thou hast measured all their greatness and enormity. And yet, O Lord, thy power to save transcends them all. Who is a God like unto Thee, that pardoneth iniquity, and passeth by transgression? We have fallen from righteousness, and the imaginations of our hearts are evil continually. We turn away in faith from ourselves to Jesus, and his atoning sacrifice, and take comfort. O Lord, with Thee is plenteous redemption; cleanse us, we beseech Thee, from all unrighteousness.

O gracious Spirit, the Spirit of holiness and love, dwell Thou within us this day, that we may be kept in the faith and fear of God. We pray that we may not grieve Thee by neglecting thy promptings to what is good, or by wilfully despising thy warnings against sin. We would walk with God through all the day; do Thou, O God, walk with us, and by precious tokens of thy presence make us conscious that Thou art near. In dependence on thy strength we enter on the day's duties, and earnestly plead that Thou wouldest enable us to do them as in thy sight, with singleness of eye and purity of motive. Shield us in the midst of temptation. Guide us through all perplexities. Whenever our will clashes with thine, may we in all things prefer thy will to our own, and be ready to deny ourselves daily, and bear whatever cross thou layest upon us.

Mercifully regard the children of this family. By nature dead in trespasses and sins, and the children of wrath, make them, by thy life-giving Spirit, children of grace. In thy hands we leave ourselves, and all who seek an interest in our prayers. Seal them thine and keep them thine for ever, in Jesus Christ our Lord. Amen.

READ IN HOLY SCRIPTURE ISAIAH IX. 1—7.

LORD Jesus, we bend with adoring hearts before the mystery of thy incarnation. Thou, the Mighty God, the Everlasting Father, the Prince of Peace, didst lay aside the robes of thy Eternal Majesty, and humble thyself to our nature, sharing our weakness, and bearing our sins. Oh, enlarge our hearts with a knowledge of thy self-sacrificing love, and enable us to realise to ourselves thy grace and all-sufficiency. Thou art wonderful in thy being: one with us, bone of our bone, and flesh of our flesh, and yet God over all, blessed for ever! Wonderful art Thou in thy cross and passion, in thy death and resurrection, and in the overflowing compassion which moved Thee to live, and suffer, and die for us men and our salvation. Lord, when we think of all Thou hast done for us this and every day, and all that Thou art doing, and all Thou hast promised to do, we feel that thy love passeth knowledge. We can but wonder and adore. Oh, reveal to us more and more of thyself, that we may grow in grace and in the knowledge of Thee, our Lord and Saviour, Jesus Christ. Thou art able to save to the uttermost all that come to God by Thee. Lord Jesus, save us. Save us from the condemnation which our sins deserve. Cleanse us from the guilt of all sins which Thou hast seen in us during the day now past—sins of ingratitude and coldness of heart towards thyself —sins of the heart, sins of the lips, sins of the life. O Lord, they are all known to Thee. Blot them from thy remembrance, and let them be seen no more.

In Thee, O Saviour, are hid all the treasures of wisdom and knowledge. Thou art the Counsellor. None teacheth like Thee. Oh, leave us not in ignorance of all we should know, and all we should do. Let us hear thy voice in the Holy Book, and in the daily dealings of thy providence. Teach us by thy Spirit, and impress deeply thy divine lessons on our hearts. Keep us in safety amid the dangers of daily life. Call us back when we wander. Uphold us when we slip. Restore us when we fall. Guide us, Lord, by thy counsel here, train and teach us in thy way, and afterwards, in thine own good time, take us to glory.

We ask, O Lord, the same blessings for others. Bestow them on all who are dear to us, and especially on all among us and around us who are yet in the darkness of spiritual death. Shed the bright beams of thy grace and glory in their hearts. Extend thy sway through all the earth. Hasten the day when Jew and Gentile shall bow the knee at thy footstool. Keep us safely this night, and if it please Thee, raise us again, refreshed and strengthened, for the duties of another day. Grant it, O Lord, for thy great name's sake. Amen.

[Morning.] SECOND WEEK.—WEDNESDAY. [Evening.

READ IN HOLY SCRIPTURE GENESIS VII.

READ IN HOLY SCRIPTURE ST. LUKE II. 25—40.

ETERNAL God, our gracious Father and ever-living Friend, grant that the words of our lips and the meditation of our hearts may now be acceptable in thy sight, O Lord, our strength and our Redeemer.

We want, O Lord, a deeper conviction of our sinfulness and danger through sin. Teach us how hateful sin is in the light of thy countenance. Impress on our hearts the testimony Thou hast given against it in the destruction of the old world. By thy Holy Spirit reveal to us the disease of our hearts, and make us sensible of our helplessness to save ourselves. O God the Holy Ghost, purge our darkened sight, that we may see Divine things plainly, and discern especially the excellence and glory of thy dear Son, our only ark of safety and deliverance when the tempest of thy wrath bursts on the world. Bestow a stronger faith, that we may grasp more firmly the exceeding great and precious promises of thy Word. We pray for a brighter hope, that we may bear about with us the earnest and pledge of the heavenly inheritance. We desire a warmer love, that our hearts may glow with grateful affection, and constrain us in all things cheerfully to do thy will. Oh, for that joy and peace in believing which are the privilege of thy saints! Oh, for that experience of the Divine life which will testify that we have indeed taken refuge in Christ, and found deliverance from condemnation and death through his precious blood-shedding. Lord, these are all thy gifts—bestow them on us, we pray Thee, and by thy Spirit work them within us. Wisdom and strength are thine, O Lord: withhold them not. Clothe us with the spotless robe of Christ's righteousness, and mould us into his image and likeness. By thy grace bring every thought and disposition into subjection at thy footstool, that thy will may be our will, and thy Word in all things our law. Above all things, preserve us, O God, from unbelief of thy coming judgments, and suffer us not to walk in the old way which wicked men have trodden. Oh, that none of us may turn aside from the open door of mercy, and perish eternally in the day of thy wrath!

We acknowledge with heartfelt praise the mercies of the night now past. Evermore make us mindful of thy goodness. Go with us now to the varied duties of the day: leave us not to ourselves or to the devices of our great enemy. Preserve us and all whom we love in the midst of surrounding evil and the temptations of besetting sins. Be this our desire: so to let our light shine before men that they, seeing our good works, may glorify Thee, our God and Father in heaven. Lord, hear us and mightily help us, for Jesus Christ's sake. Amen.

LORD God Almighty! another of our days has now passed away, never to return again; and Thou hast seen and known all that has been amiss in our thoughts, and words, and ways. Lord, what can we say, and wherewith can we present ourselves before Thee? We are sinful, helpless creatures: but we lift our eyes to Jesus who died for us, and is now exalted to the right hand of God, a Prince and Saviour, to give repentance and remission of sins. For his sake, blot from the book of thy remembrance whatever stands recorded against us, and let it not witness to our condemnation in the great day.

Thanks and praise are due to Thee, O God our Father, for the mercies of the day. Enable us to take account of thy goodness, and to treasure in our hearts the constant remembrance of thy gracious dealings with us from day to day. Our blessings might have been curses, and our joys sorrows, but for thy lovingkindness and compassion. Accept the offering of our unfeigned thankfulness, not only for these daily gifts of thy providence, but also for the more precious gifts of thy grace. Grant, we beseech Thee, that our hearts may rejoice in these blessings. Let the light of thy love ever shine upon our path, cheering us with the abundance of its consolations, and kindling within us a spirit of hearty obedience to all thy will.

We know not, O God, what the night may bring forth. We place our life and strength in thy care and beneath thy protection. Give us all to sleep in quietness, and speak to our hearts, as we lie down, words of comfort and of peace. We long, O God, for the clearer and brighter experiences of thy grace. We desire to grow in holiness as we grow in years. Grant that through thy teaching and blessing we may become wiser and better every day. We know not what is thy will concerning us, whether to live or to die. If it please Thee, spare us till we have made our calling and election sure. And, oh! grant that when our race of life is run, and the last of our days on earth shall have dawned, we may face death without a fear, and be enabled to say with Simeon, "Lord, now lettest Thou thy servant depart in peace, according to thy word, for mine eyes have seen thy salvation."

Help us, O Lord, in all our necessities. Thou knowest what will be good for us. Give us, we beseech Thee, a quiet and humble spirit, and in mercy bend our own will into perfect conformity to thine. We ask these blessings, and all things else that Thou seest good for us, and for those dear to us, in the name of thy dear Son, our Saviour, Jesus Christ. Amen.

[Morning.] SECOND WEEK.—THURSDAY. [Evening.

READ IN HOLY SCRIPTURE ST. MATTHEW XXIV. 36—51.

READ IN HOLY SCRIPTURE ST. MATTHEW II.

O THOU holy Lord God, humble our minds, we beseech Thee, under a just apprehension of thy glorious majesty and of thy coming judgments. Suffer us neither to be unmindful how in ancient time Thou broughtest swift destruction upon an ungodly world, nor that Thou art reserving the world which now is for the judgment of the last day. We adore thy great goodness in giving us those forewarnings of its approach which we have now read in the words of our blessed Saviour. Oh, help us to be watchful; and since we know not when the time shall be, enable us to live as faithful servants, who wait for their Master's coming.

But who may abide the day of thy coming, and who shall stand when Thou appearest? O Lord God, we humble ourselves before Thee as we remember our manifold sins. We have lived too much in the indulgence of our carnal affections; we have found our pleasure too much in the gratification of our senses; too eagerly have we pursued the world. Oh, let thy Holy Spirit withdraw our hearts from all that would still more debase and pollute our nature, and direct them into the love of God and the patient waiting for Jesus Christ.

And grant, O most merciful Father, for his sake, the forgiveness of all our sins, which we thus humbly confess before Thee. O Lamb of God, hast not Thou borne our sins in thine own body on the tree? We plead thy sufferings and atoning death. Our sole trust is in thy precious blood and righteousness. Grant that being now justified by faith, we may spend the rest of our life in loving obedience to thy holy will.

Accept, we beseech Thee, heavenly Father, our thanksgiving for all thy lovingkindness towards us. Thine eye hath watched over us through the darkness of the night, and thy hand hath raised us up to meet the new duties of another day. Strengthen us for all the requirements of active life, or for the patient endurance of thy holy will. Bestow upon us, in thy fatherly bounty, the gifts of thy providence, and fill our hearts with compassion for the destitute. We commend one another to thy protection and love, and to Thee we also commend all who are dear to us. Do thou, O God, remember them for good. Be gracious to all who especially need thy help. Sanctify all tribulations and sorrows; succour the distressed; comfort the broken-hearted; preserve the young from the follies and dangers of youth, and sustain the aged and dying with the blessed hope of eternal life. All these gifts we humbly ask in the ever adorable name of our Lord Jesus Christ, to whom, with the Father and the Holy Spirit, one God, be glory everlasting. Amen.

O HOLY God! help us to draw near to Thee with lowly reverence and godly fear. We glorify Thee as the King eternal, immortal, invisible, who hast revealed thyself to us in the person of thy Son. We rejoice that the Word was made flesh, and dwelt among us, partaking of our sorrows, and acquainted with our griefs. We adore the providence that turned from him the wrath of Herod, and preserved a life so precious to the world. May our rulers desire, in all honesty, to know and worship him, and worthily magnify his holy name. We bless Thee that we have thy Word, as the star that leads us to the Saviour. May it shine in every dark place!

Help us now, O God, like the wise men of old, to approach unto Jesus, and to offer to him the homage of our hearts as our King, and worship him as God over all. May he control all our thoughts and affections, that we may always live to his glory. May the corruptions of our nature be entirely subdued, our tempers be sanctified, and our dispositions be brought into harmony with the mind of Christ. May our thoughts be pure, and our words truthful and loving. May we hate sin with a perfect hatred, as that which thou abhorrest, which brings misery and ruin to men. Pardon all our transgressions, for the sake of thy dear Son, whose atoning blood we plead as the ground of our hope of forgiveness. Let it be our delight to do the will of our Father who is in heaven. To this end may we grow in the knowledge of thy Word and will; and, with deeper convictions of obligation and duty, more heartily serve and love Thee.

Make this home a scene of domestic peace and happiness, where the law of kindness and forbearance shall reign, and where selfishness shall be unknown. Abide with us at all seasons and under all circumstances. Sanctify the sorrows of life to all who are called to bear them; especially overrule for good the bereavements that so often desolate our dwellings. May parents who, like Rachel, mourn over the death of their children, be comforted by the assurance that of such is the kingdom of heaven. May all who are spared to us live before Thee as thy children; and when the hour of our departure comes, receive us, O God, to thyself; and grant that we and all dear to us may for ever be with thee Lord.

Graciously watch over us during the night on which we have entered. Suffer no evil to befall us, no plague to come nigh our dwelling. May the morning find us prepared for the duties of the new day. Grant us these blessings, and all others that we need, but have forgotten to ask, for the sake of thy dear Son Jesus Christ, our only Mediator and Advocate. Amen.

[Morning.] SECOND WEEK.—FRIDAY. [Evening.

READ IN HOLY SCRIPTURE GENESIS VIII.

LORD God Almighty, our Creator, Preserver, and Father, all power is thine. Thou canst create and Thou canst destroy; Thou canst kill and make alive; Thou canst raise the dead, and preserve alive in the midst of death. Who would not fear Thee, Lord of all power and might? We would ever speak to Thee with reverence and godly fear, but at the same time with the confidence which thy faithfulness and goodness invite.

We have deserved destruction on account of our sins, but Thou hast not rewarded us according to our iniquities. Blessed be God, who daily loadeth us with benefits, even the God of our salvation. For the redemption which is in Christ Jesus our Lord, glory be to the Father, and to the Son, and to the Holy Ghost.

Remember not against us, O Lord, the sins of our youth, or any of our iniquities; but remember us with the favour Thou bearest unto thy people. Remember us all, the youngest and the oldest, the weakest and the strongest. Remember us all, to save us with an everlasting salvation, and to do us good all the days of our lives. And wilt Thou help us, O Father of our spirits, to remember Thee? As we begin and end each day, may we remember Thee. As we commence and finish our daily work, may we remember Thee. In the midst of our kindred, friends, and neighbours, may we remember Thee. In all times of sorrow and of joy, in all seasons of trial and of temptation, may we remember Thee. In all places and in all scenes, help us to remember Thee. May we remember Thee with love and with joy, with hope and with child-like confidence. May we remember Thee to obey Thee, to give Thee thanks continually, to cast all our cares upon Thee, to serve and to glorify Thee, and to present to Thee our bodies living sacrifices, holy and acceptable, which is our reasonable service.

We also pray that we may be assisted at all times to remember Thee, not merely by thy Word and by thy Holy Spirit's ministrations, but also by beholding the works of thy hands. As we see the seasons change from seedtime to harvest, from summer to winter; as we see day follow night, and night succeed to day; may we remember Thee, and think of Thee as ever faithful to thy promises, and mindful of thy covenant. We ask yet further, that as Noah, and his sons, and his wife, and his sons' wives with him, were saved from the flood, so in like manner we may be saved as a family from thy wrath; and may we assemble around thy throne in heaven a family unbroken—a family entirely saved. This great mercy, and all the blessings which we need, we ask in our gracious Saviour's name. Amen.

READ IN HOLY SCRIPTURE EPHESIANS III.

O GOD, the Father of our Lord Jesus Christ, of whom the whole family in heaven and earth is named, in mercy regard us who now as a family are gathered at thy footstool. Glory be to thy Name for this gracious Word to which we have now listened. What motives it supplies for praise! What encouragement it gives for prayer! To us in these Gospel days is made known the mystery long kept secret, that even for us Gentiles, as well as for thine ancient people, there have been stored up the unsearchable riches of Divine grace and power. Oh, that we may be made partakers of thy mercy, and that even in us and in our salvation the angels and archangels in heavenly places may see the manifold wisdom of God.

Lord, we come boldly to thy throne of grace. Thou hast not spared thine own dear Son, but delivered him up for us all, and Thou art able, through him, to do exceeding abundantly above all that we ask or think. We plead these assurances of thy Holy Book: we remind Thee how Thou hast exalted Jesus to thy right hand in glory to intercede for us. For his sake, O God, grant us thy peace: for his sake enrich us with spiritual blessing.

How great have been thy mercies to us this day! Thou hast fed and clothed us: we have gone in and out to our daily task, and Thou hast spread around us the shield of thy power and protection. Thou redeemest our lives from destruction, and crownest us with the gifts of thy lovingkindness. Bless the Lord, O our souls, and all that is within us bless his holy Name. Thou knowest our frame, and rememberest that we are dust. Thou dost not always chide, nor keep thine anger for ever. Oh, suffer us never to forget Thee, O thou Father of mercies! or to be unthankful recipients of thy bounty.

Especially we pray, O God, that according to the riches of thy glory we may be strengthened by thy Spirit in the inner man. O Jesus, come and dwell in our hearts, that being rooted and grounded in love, we may share with all thy saints in the knowledge and experience of thy love, and be filled with all the fulness of God. Guide us, we beseech Thee, to a deeper acquaintance with thy Truth. We are weak: do Thou uphold us. We are ignorant: do Thou teach us. We know not what may befall us as a family, or singly and alone. We commit ourselves to thy keeping, O Thou who never sleepest. Keep our souls clear of every sinful thought, and raise us, if it be thy will, to the duties of the coming day. We ask all for Christ's sake, to whom, with Thee and the Holy Ghost, be glory in the Church, throughout all ages, world without end. Amen.

[Morning.] SECOND WEEK.—SATURDAY. [Evening.

READ IN HOLY SCRIPTURE GENESIS IX. 1–19.

READ IN HOLY SCRIPTURE ST. LUKE II. 41–52.

O THOU that hearest prayer, and hast declared that whoso offereth praise honoureth Thee, we raise our eyes and our hearts to thy throne. Thine is the kingdom for ever and ever, and Thou rulest over all. We praise Thee, O God: we acknowledge Thee to be the Lord. All the earth doth worship Thee, the Father everlasting. To Thee all angels cry aloud, the heavens and all the powers therein. To Thee cherubim and seraphim continually cry, Holy, Holy, Holy Lord God of Hosts. Heaven and earth are full of the majesty of thy glory. How great our privilege, Lord, that we can speak to Thee, and Thou wilt not disdain our offering: that we can spread at thy footstool, in the name of Jesus, the confession of our sins, and wants, and weaknesses, and Thou wilt not send us empty away! Day by day thou renewest the tokens of thy mercy and love. Despite our countless sins, Thou never weariest of blessing us. Oh, that we may never weary of praising Thee.

Fulfil to us, we beseech Thee, this day, thy promise in Jesus Christ. Heaven and earth shall pass away, but thy word shall not pass away. Enable us, in the midst of all fears and dangers, to see the bow of mercy in the cloud, and to take courage. If afflictions come upon us, may we have grace to receive them as of thy sending, and to bear them without a murmur, remembering that whom the Lord loveth he chasteneth, and that it is through much tribulation we must enter into rest. Under all circumstances confirm our faith in thy Gospel. Let no doubting or unbelief cloud our spiritual sight. Open more fully to us the meaning of thy Word, and enable us to use it as the lamp of our feet and the light of our path. O God, let nothing separate us from the love of Christ. If Thou be for us, who can be against us? If Thou justify us, who can condemn? If Christ has cleansed us in his blood, and pleads our cause in his all-prevailing intercession, who can lay anything to our charge? O Almighty Saviour, endue us with thy strength, and we shall be more than conquerors in every conflict.

Lord, look in thy love on all whom we love. Such of them as are still wanderers from thy fold, in the broad way of sin and death, seek out and bring in. Oh, may they live before Thee! Be gracious to the young among us: win their hearts to thyself: preserve them from the temptations peculiar to youth, and under thy training and discipline may they grow in grace as they grow in years, and learn even now that the ways of wisdom are ways of pleasantness, and all her paths are peace. Lord, grant this, and all other petitions, through Jesus Christ our Lord. Amen.

AGAIN, O God, we are called to thank Thee for thy great mercy towards us. Thou hast ordered our steps through the day, and now in thankfulness and peace we will lay ourselves down to rest, confiding in thy care, who alone makest us to dwell in safety. Forgive, Lord, all that thou hast seen amiss in us. Put it away from before Thee, and cancel the guilt of it for ever. Create in us a clean heart, and renew in us a right spirit. So unfold to us the riches of thy saving grace, that we may live not for ourselves, but for Thee; and let our light so shine before men, that they may see our good works, and glorify our Father which is in heaven.

Lord Jesus, Thou wast made in all things like unto us, sin only excepted. As the child, the boy, and the man, Thou hast had experience of our life, and hast set us an example that we may walk in thy steps. Thou wast very God, and yet —oh, inscrutable mystery!—Thou didst grow in wisdom and in favour with God and man. Impart, we beseech Thee, to us the very mind that was in Thee. By thy Holy Spirit, impress on us thy likeness and image. Thou didst choose a lowly state, when angels would have done thy bidding, and all the riches of heaven and earth were at thy command. Make us contented with such things as we have, and enable us to do our duty in whatever station it may please Thee to place us. Thou didst bear the burden of human labour, and thereby hast made it honourable. Be with us in all our work from day to day, and teach us that how lowly soever our place, we may glorify Thee in it by singleness of eye and purity of motive. Thou didst do and suffer in all things the Father's will. Enable us by thy Spirit to crush every rising passion, and subdue every rebellious temper. Teach the young among us from thy example to be obedient to their parents, to bear meekly the restraints of home, and thus to prove themselves thy faithful servants and disciples, sharing thy cross, and in all things following Thee.

Shelter us, O God, to-night beneath thy protecting wing. We look forward with thankfulness to the rest and peace of the Lord's day. Oh, prepare us to enjoy the sacred season, and to profit by its services. Prepare also thy ministers for their holy work. Kindle in their hearts a burning zeal for thy glory and a fervent love for souls. Teach them thy truth, that out of their own experience they may teach others. Put a word in their tongues, O God, that shall be useful to all, that the hard heart may be softened, the mourning be comforted, and all thy people edified. Hear us, O Lord, and help and save, for the sake of Jesus, our adorable Lord and Redeemer. Amen.

[MORNING.] THIRD WEEK.—LORD'S DAY. [EVENING.

READ IN HOLY SCRIPTURE 2 PETER III.

LORD of the Sabbath, in thy mercy listen to our prayer. Thou art the long-suffering God, or we had not now been kneeling together in peace at thy footstool. Often have we grieved thy Spirit by the wilfulness and waywardness of our hearts: still Thou sparest us, not because our transgressions are of small account with Thee, nor because thine arm is not strong to punish and destroy, but because thy mercies are great, and thy compassions fail not. Thou art not willing that we should perish. For thy name's sake, O God, and in pity to our souls, let not thy forbearance towards us fail of its purpose. Give us thy Holy Spirit to arouse and quicken us. Such of us as have never yet repented of their multiplied transgressions against Thee, convince of their sin : show them the fearful peril of trifling with grace and opportunity. In such of us as have already sorrowed for sin after a godly sort, do Thou deepen the sense of sin. Lord, take these hearts of ours, unholy, impure, stained as they are, and make them clean in the fountain once opened for sin. Renew and sanctify us by thy grace, that we may be transformed ever more and more into the image and likeness of thy dear Son.

We thank Thee, heavenly Father, for the mercies of the past night. This is the day which the Lord hath made : oh, that we may rejoice and be glad in it! Forgive, O God, past neglect, and let it not cause Thee now to withhold thy blessing. Be Thou with us all the day, and work in us to will and to do of thy good pleasure. As we kneel in prayer, teach us our emptiness, that we may yearn to be filled out of thy fulness. Feed us with the bread of life which came down from heaven. Give us of the living waters which flow from the throne of God and the Lamb. As we lift up our voices in praise, oh! kindle within us a heavenly fervour by the recollection of thy goodness and mercy. Let not thy Gospel witness against us to our condemnation, but make it the savour of life unto life—a message of love and peace welcome to our souls, for which we shall glorify Thee at the close of the day.

Pour down thy Spirit abundantly on all who shall meet in thy house of prayer; prepare them to receive thy Word. Lead many this day to the cross. Let thy Word have free course and be glorified. Touch the hearts of thy ministers with fire from heaven, and make them wise to win souls to Christ. Make bare thine arm among the nations. Awaken in thy Church an earnest longing for His coming who shall make all things new; and grant that when He cometh we may all be found of Him in peace, without spot, and blameless. Grant it, O Lord, for his sake. Amen.

READ IN HOLY SCRIPTURE ST. LUKE III. 1–22.

ALMIGHTY God! who art merciful and gracious, slow to anger, abundant in goodness and truth; who willest not the death of a sinner, but rather that he should turn from his evil way and live; grant unto us that godly sorrow which worketh repentance unto life, that by faith in thy Son we may obtain redemption through his blood, and the forgiveness of our sins, according to the riches of thy grace; and, receiving the adoption of children, may become heirs according to the hope of eternal life.

O God! who searchest the hearts and triest the reins of the children of men, search us and try us, and see what way of wickedness there is in us, and lead us in the way everlasting. Preserve us from resting in any outward privilege or ordinance, and fix our faith on Him who is the only fountain of mercy, grace, and peace. Renew us in the spirit of our minds, that we may bring forth fruits meet for repentance, and worthily magnify thy name.

Eternal God! the Father of our Lord Jesus Christ, who at his baptism didst declare him, by a voice from the excellent glory, to be thy beloved Son, we give Thee thanks for thine unspeakable gift. Sprinkle our hearts with his most precious blood; justify us freely through the redemption that is in him. Baptise us with the Holy Ghost, and make us meet for the inheritance of the saints in light. Oh, that in the great day of separation, when Jesus shall sift the wheat from the chaff, the precious from the vile, we may all of us be garnered safely in thy kingdom!

Father of all our mercies! accept our humble thanksgiving for the blessings of this day. May it please Thee to remember us as a family, with all who are dear unto us by the ties of nature and affection. Let the continued dew of thy blessing be on them and on us. Bless to our souls all the ordinances of thy house. Forgive the sins of our holy services. Apply thy Word with power to our hearts, and the hearts of all who have heard it. Look in mercy on the unconverted among us. Reveal to them the terrors of the Lord, and awaken them to flee from the wrath to come while the day of grace lasts.

Show us thy marvellous lovingkindness, O Thou that savest by thy right hand those that put their trust in Thee. Keep us as the apple of thine eye, and hide us under the shadow of thy wings; so will we lie down, and none shall make us afraid. Give thine angels charge over us, to keep us in all our ways. Satisfy us early with thy goodness, and make us joyful in Thee. All this we beg in the name and through the mediation of our only Saviour Jesus Christ. Amen.

[15]

[Morning.] THIRD WEEK.—MONDAY. [Evening.

READ IN HOLY SCRIPTURE GENESIS XI. 1—9.

ALMIGHTY Lord God, the Maker of all things, who from thy throne beholdest all the dwellers upon earth, be pleased most graciously to look upon us at this time.

We acknowledge that we have sinned and done amiss, and have need to bow at thy footstool in great lowliness of spirit. Thy dealings with us and all thy creatures have been most kind and tender — worthy of our greatest confidence and love.

Thou hast wisely counselled, admonished, and corrected us. Thy judgments, from time to time, have been abroad in the earth; yet we have too often been unmindful of them, and not learnt to do thy righteous will.

But we beseech Thee to enter not into judgment with us, thine unworthy servants. Spare us, good Lord, and pardon our manifold offences, for thy dear Son's sake.

And as we, through thy gracious providence, have been permitted to enter upon the duties of another day, we would seek thy guidance, protection, and blessing. May we this day be delivered from the great snare of putting our trust in any earthly good, power, or creature, and from seeking our happiness in the world apart from Thee.

Be pleased also to instruct us in the nature of thy will, the character of thy laws, and the way of peace and safety, so that we may be kept under the protection of thy fatherly love, and have a perpetual fear and love of thy holy name and Word.

In our prayers we would bear before Thee the wants of the world in which we live. It has gone astray from thy testimonies; the strife of tongues prevails; confusion and every evil work are seen in the dwellings of many; and the way of peace is not sought or loved. We therefore beseech Thee, in compassion to our fallen world, to increase and make more pure and efficient the agencies employed for its conversion.

Send forth thy Holy Spirit upon all flesh. Make thy ways known; thy saving health among all nations. Oh, let the people soon learn to be of one heart and tongue, and united to praise Thee. Then shall the earth bring forth her increase, and God, even our own God, shall give us his blessing.

As members of a Christian family we would implore thy favour and blessing upon us. Pour into each of our hearts that most excellent gift of charity, the bond of peace and of all virtues. Keep us from all things hurtful, and bestow upon us all such gifts as will be profitable for us both in time and eternity: and grant that, when we have served Thee upon earth, we may glorify Thee in heaven, through Jesus Christ our Lord. Amen.

READ IN HOLY SCRIPTURE ST. LUKE IV. 1—13.

MOST holy Lord God, we draw near to Thee in the name of Jesus Christ, to praise Thee for the favours and deliverances of the day which has passed. May our evening's sacrifice of praise and thanksgiving be acceptable in thy sight, O Lord, our strength and our Redeemer.

We desire to acknowledge our dependence upon Thee, and that we are under thy rule and governance. Thou knowest all that we have done, endured, suffered, or purposed in our minds to do this day. Thou hast understood our thoughts afar off, and there has not been a word in our tongue but Thou, O Lord, hast known it altogether.

Whatever, therefore, has been wrong in our conduct or spirit, or wherein we have failed to do thy will, to be watchful, and to resist temptation, be pleased, through thy manifold and great mercies in Christ Jesus, to pardon and forgive. Thou, O Lord, knowest that we are placed in so many and great dangers that, by reason of our frailty, we cannot always stand upright. But we are encouraged, in our approaches to thy Majesty, by remembering that when we offend against thy holy law, if we confess our sins, Thou art willing, for thy Son's sake, to forgive us our sins, and to cleanse us from all unrighteousness.

That we may hereafter faithfully serve Thee, impress upon our minds the truths of thy holy Word. Grant that with meek hearts and due reverence we may receive the truths of that portion of it we have now read. May we never forget that we are constantly exposed to the evil devices of Satan and the corruptions of our own deceitful hearts.

If in thy dispensations towards us we should ever be so tempted and tried as to be brought into great straits and difficulties, may we remember the example of our Saviour, who, though tempted as we are, was yet without sin. May we never make it our only or chief care to obtain the bread which perisheth, but may we be taught by thy Word to do and suffer thy will.

Deliver us from the great sin of unbelief. May no hasty desire, no feeling of presumption, ever lead us rashly to engage in anything, but may we in all our ways seek thy direction, and humbly trust in Thee.

Save us also from the baneful influence of the world. Grant that its seductive power may never subdue our spirits to its service; but preserve us, we beseech Thee, ever ready, both in private, at the family altar, and in thy house, to worship Thee, the one living and true God.

Hear these our prayers, protect us through the night, refresh us with quiet rest; and to Thee will we ascribe the praise, for Christ's sake. Amen.

[MORNING.]   THIRD WEEK.—TUESDAY.   [EVENING.

READ IN HOLY SCRIPTURE GENESIS XII.

O GOD, our Creator and Preserver, Thou proclaimest to us day by day thy goodness and truth. The streams of thy bounty never fail. In the light and in the darkness thine eye is ever upon us. Thou art at our right hand and our left, sustaining us by thy power, and enriching us with thy mercy. O God, we feel that we owe all our temporal blessings, as well as our spiritual, to thy love in Christ Jesus. Life, and health, and strength, and all that Thou bestowest, are ours, because He redeemed us. For thy gifts alike in creation, in providence, and in grace, we offer at thy footstool our tribute of fervent praise.

The stains of sin mar and defile all that we do. We can but cry, Unclean, unclean. Oh, let our cry enter into thine ears, and bring down from above thy forgiveness and pardon. Constantly do we need thy strength. We are impotent of ourselves to stand against temptation, unless Thou uphold us, that our footsteps slip not. God, Thou knowest our weakness and shortcomings, pour down upon us the abundance of thy grace. Bear with the weakness of our faith, and supply all our need according to thy riches in glory by Jesus Christ our Lord.

We know not, O God, what this day will bring forth for us. All its circumstances are known to Thee, its trials and temptations, its perplexities and its dangers. It is our comfort to know that nothing happens but as Thou seest fit, and that all the issues of life and death are in thy hand. Prevent us, O Lord, in all our doings with thy most gracious favour, and assist us with thy continual help, that in all our works begun, continued, and ended in dependence on Thee, we may glorify thy holy name, and finally, by thy mercy, obtain everlasting life. Wean us, O God, from the love of the world and worldly things. Enable us to hold all things as from Thee, and to be ready at all times cheerfully to sacrifice even what is dearest to us at thy bidding, and to follow Thee whithersoever thou leadest us. Oh, that we may count all things but loss compared with Christ our Redeemer and Lord; that the savour of Christian piety may abound in our life and conversation. May we have grace to avoid all evil, and even the appearance of evil, lest we bring dishonour on the holy name of Jesus, or cause the enemies of the Lord to blaspheme.

Graciously grant us thy protection during the day. Spread around us all the shield of thy power, and turn aside whatever evil may threaten our bodies or souls. Make known the glory of the Saviour to those who know Him not, that in Him Jew and Gentile may be blessed. Hear us, O God, for thy dear Son's sake. Amen.

READ IN HOLY SCRIPTURE HEBREWS II.

FATHER of all mercies, beneath whose sheltering providence we have this day been preserved, look down upon us, we beseech Thee, in these our evening prayers. To whom else can we come for protection through the dark shadows of the night? To whom can we bring our cares for relief, or our sins for pardon, but to Thee, O Heavenly Father, who hast promised to supply all the wants of thy children for the sake of Jesus Christ our Mediator? In his blessed name, therefore, we now draw near thy throne, and ask for the gifts of thy covenant grace. Blot out all our transgressions. Sanctify us by thy Holy Spirit. Let thy Word dwell richly in our hearts. Thou hast honoured us above angels by granting us the revelation of thine eternal love in Christ Jesus. Yet how little have we prized the excellency of this knowledge! How often do we forget thy promises, and neglect thy precepts! O Lord, lay not these sins to our charge. Remember that we are but dust. Accept us for Jesus' sake.

O blessed Jesus, we turn to Thee in this our conscious weakness, and thank Thee for that divine compassion which has not left us comfortless. We glorify the riches of thy love which led Thee to become partaker of our own flesh and blood. Precious to us now is all thy power of sympathy with our sorrows, and of help in our temptations! Blessed, for ever blessed be thy name, that we can live by faith on the assurance of thy glorified manhood, and see Thee on Jehovah's throne as the great Captain of our salvation, not being ashamed even to call us brethren! Lord, into thy faithful hand we commend ourselves day by day. Wilt Thou not keep us, and bring us among many sons to glory! Thou art our only Shepherd. Thou art the Lord our Righteousness. Oh, for a deeper sense of thy love, and a larger measure of the indwelling of the Holy Ghost! Oh, for that faith and patience which will enable us to inherit the promises! We desire to follow Thee in all faithfulness, and whenever we stray from the right path, to hear thy voice behind us saying, "This is the way, walk ye in it."

Gracious God, give us these blessings, we beseech Thee. And if any now among us be still strangers to Thee, add to thy gift of mercy, and this very evening bestow upon them the spirit of repentance and faith. Quicken us all, that we may be more wholly and constantly thine. Bless our children, friends, and country. Bless thy Church, with its ministers at home, and its missionaries abroad, and its members everywhere. And all we ask, O God, is for Christ's sake, to whom with Thee, O Father, and Thee, O Eternal Spirit, be honour and glory, world without end. Amen.

[17]

[MORNING.] **THIRD WEEK.—WEDNESDAY.** [EVENING.]

READ IN HOLY SCRIPTURE 1 PETER II. 11—25.

READ IN HOLY SCRIPTURE ST. JOHN I. 19—34.

FATHER of mercies and God of all grace, we bless and praise Thee for all the kindness Thou hast shown unto us in the commencement of another day. Thou hast preserved us during the watches of the night, and by thine hand our eyes have been opened to see the morning light. Blessed be thy holy name for refreshing sleep, for convenient food and raiment, for health and strength, and for all thy mercies which Thou givest us so richly to enjoy. Teach us to take all the comforts of life from thy hand, and in their use to be truly thankful unto Thee, O Lord; and when Thou sendest sorrow or trouble of any kind, help us to believe that Thou doest all things well, and to say, "Thy will be done."

We beseech Thee, good Lord, to refresh and strengthen our souls with that portion of thy sacred Word which we have read. Make us true pilgrims, such as feel that this world is not their rest, and teach us daily to walk as in thy sight. Keep us, holy Father, from fleshly lusts, which war against the soul. In all the business of life let integrity and uprightness preserve us. Make us peaceable subjects, good neighbours, faithful servants, loving relatives, and true followers of thy dear Son Jesus Christ. In thought, and speech, and conduct may we be made like unto Him, who did no sin, neither was guile found in his mouth. If our patience shall be tried this day by unkindness or injustice, preserve us, O God of peace, from anger and resentment, so that our fellow-men may take knowledge of us that we have been with Jesus, and have learnt of Him. Guide our rulers with heavenly wisdom; prosper our country, and let peace and plenty enrich our native land. Have mercy upon all who are suffering affliction, and help them who have no earthly helper. We confess before Thee, O Lord, our manifold sins and transgressions. Pardon us for the sake of Him who his own self bare our sins in his own body on the tree. Bestow upon each one of us now bowing down at thy footstool that faith in Jesus which purifieth the heart and worketh by love. Grant unto us that true repentance which leadeth unto life, and is not to be repented of. Redeem us from all iniquity, receive us graciously, and love us freely. Let the fruits of holiness abound in our lives, so that we may adorn the doctrine of God our Saviour in all things; and when we shall depart from this life, may we sleep in Jesus, and rise to dwell for ever amid the joys which are at thy right hand. These our humble prayers and praises we present in the name of our Lord Jesus Christ, to whom with Thee, O Father, and the Holy Spirit, be all praise and glory for ever. Amen.

O GOD, the Father of our Lord Jesus Christ, for his sake baptize us also with the Holy Ghost, that we may now draw nigh unto Thee in the spirit of adoption, crying, Abba, Father. But, Father, we have sinned against heaven, and in thy sight, and are not worthy to be called thy children. We own with shame that we have turned every one to his own way: Thou alone knowest how often we have sinned in thought, word, and deed against Thee. Yet, merciful Father, thy Word, which tells us of our sins, tells us also of thy readiness to show mercy, and directs us to behold the Lamb of God which taketh away the sin of the world. Thou hast so loved the world, as to give thine only begotten and well-beloved Son to die, the just for the unjust, that He might bring us to Thee. For his dear sake, O Father, forgive us our sins, and receive us graciously.

O Lamb of God, that takest away the sins of the world, take away our sins; grant us thy peace; sprinkle our consciences with thy blood; plead for us as our Advocate with the Father. May thy spotless righteousness be reckoned for our righteousness, that being justified by faith in Thee, we may have peace with God. Be Thou still, and always be to us, the Lamb of God, which takest away sin; take away from us all love of sin. Heavenly Father, for Jesus Christ's sake, give us daily thy Holy Spirit, to constrain us to follow Him as our pattern while trusting in Him as the propitiation for our sins. Forgiven much, may we love much; loving Thee, may we try to please Thee in all things; may we, and our poor, imperfect services be daily accepted in the Beloved; and thus may we be preparing while on earth to dwell with Thee for ever in heaven.

O Lord, the whole world lieth in wickedness before Thee; may we feel as we ought for our fellow-sinners. Send forth, we pray Thee, faithful men to point sinners to that Lamb of God, that they also may look to Him and live. May many see One standing among them whom they know not, and discover with delight that, by the application of this one sacrifice once made, He still taketh away the sin of the world. Send the Holy Ghost, and give success to all the endeavours of thy servants to make straight the way of the Lord, and prepare men for his glorious coming. May they all, like John the Baptist, have lowly views of themselves, and exalted views of the Lord Jesus.

Hear us, Heavenly Father, in these our prayers for his name's sake. Accept our praises for all thy many mercies, and especially for thine unspeakable gift of that all precious Lamb of God, thy Son our Saviour. To Him, with Thee and the Holy Ghost, be glory, now and ever. Amen.

[Morning.] THIRD WEEK.—THURSDAY. [Evening.

READ IN HOLY SCRIPTURE GENESIS XIII.

GREAT and gracious God, we desire that, like thy servant of whom we have now been reading, we may have an altar in every place where we dwell. We know that we cannot live without Thee, and we would never forget to acknowledge Thee, the Author of all our mercies, and the God of our salvation. On this family altar we would now lay our offering of praise and prayer. Condescend to accept it through the Great High Priest of our profession; and let the fire of God, though unseen, fall upon it, enlightening and purifying all our souls. Send into our hearts the Spirit of thy Son, crying, Abba, Father. May He renew us in the spirit of our minds. May He deliver us from the power of sin and Satan, and enlarge our hearts that we may run the way of thy commandments. Help us, O Lord, against ourselves, that we, through the Spirit, may mortify the deeds of the body. Make us, like faithful Abraham, meek and peaceable. May we be willing to yield even to our inferiors whatever we may with a good conscience, rather than live in strife and contention. God forbid that we should cause the way of truth to be evil spoken of, or that those who are enemies to thy cause and Thee should be encouraged by our conduct to continue in sin. Rather may they see in us the fruit of the Spirit, which is love, joy, peace, long-suffering, gentleness, goodness.

Pardon, O Lord, we pray Thee, all our past sin and folly. Too often have we not only failed to show forth these graces, but have done the works of the flesh and the will of the devil. But we betake ourselves to Thee. We return unto the Lord, from whom we have fallen by our iniquity. Have mercy upon us according to thy lovingkindness. Accept us in thy Son. Wash us in the fountain which Thou hast opened for sin and uncleanness, and make us clean.

For the mercies of the past night, and for all the good gifts of thy providence bestowed upon us, we humbly thank Thee. We pray that thy guidance and protection may be granted to us throughout this day. Be about our path, as Thou hast been about our lying down. Bless and keep all whom we love. May the love of Jesus consecrate our mutual affection, and knit us together in everlasting bonds. Oh! that none of us may remain unreconciled to Thee, or uncleansed and unforgiven. Especially, O Lord, look in mercy upon the young members of this family. Speak to their hearts by thy gracious Spirit, that they may give the morning of their lives to Thee, and have their names even now written in the Book of Life. We ask it all for the Lord's sake. Amen.

READ IN HOLY SCRIPTURE ST. JOHN I. 35—51.

O MOST good and merciful Lord God, Father of our Lord and Saviour Jesus Christ, behold us met together this night before the throne of thy grace. Give ear unto our prayers, and attend unto the voice of our humble petitions. We thank Thee for the mercies of the day past, and for all the opportunities Thou hast given us of showing our love to Thee. We confess that we have not made such use of them as we might have done, had our souls been more steadily bent upon running the way of thy commandments. While we mourn over our sins and shortcomings, we pray Thee, O God, to direct our eyes unto Jesus Christ, the Lamb of God, who taketh away the sins of the world. May we lay our guilt and offences upon Him, believing that his blood cleanseth us from all sins, and that by his stripes our souls shall be healed.

Give us grace, we beseech Thee, rightly to follow the Lord Jesus. Make us his true disciples, and give us such hearty love to Him, and such readiness and power to obey his commandments, that He may never be ashamed of us, but own us as his now, and at the last, when he makes up his jewels.

We pray not for ourselves only, but for all whom we know, especially for our relatives, friends, and neighbours, and those with whom we live or work. Grant to them, as well as to us, the saving knowledge of Jesus. May they, with us, be brought to Christ, and encouraged to forsake all ungodliness, and follow Him without delay. Give success to all ministers, missionaries, and teachers, whose occupation is specially to lead others to Christ. Prosper them in their work, and may many by their means be led to know their Lord and Saviour.

And now, O God, who art ever present, and who seest us even when we are alone, we beseech Thee to watch over us this night; we commend ourselves to thy kind care. Keep us when we have no power to keep ourselves, during the silent hours of darkness. Preserve us from danger, but above all deliver us from evil. Restore our souls by thy Holy Spirit, make us to love thy Word and thy service, and as each day passes over us, grant that it may find us further advanced in the paths of righteousness, and better prepared for living with Thee in heaven, after having served our generation according to thy blessed will. These petitions we humbly present unto Thee, O God, through Him whom Thou hearest always, Jesus Christ, thy Son, our Saviour, to whom, with Thee and the Holy Spirit, one eternal God, we would give all praise, and honour, and glory, now and for ever. Amen.

[Morning.] **THIRD WEEK.—FRIDAY.** [Evening.

READ IN HOLY SCRIPTURE ST. LUKE XII. 13–31.

OUR Father and our God, we again bow at thy footstool, and offer Thee our morning worship. Every day Thou dost renew thy mercies to us, and every day would we renew our praise to Thee. For the protection and repose of the past night, and for the health and comforts we enjoy this morning, we devoutly thank Thee. Oh, may a sense of thy constant goodness to us lead us to cherish constant gratitude and love to Thee, and prompt us to a life of cheerful obedience and willing service.

We thank Thee, O thou fountain of light, for all the teaching of thy Holy Word. We especially praise Thee that Thou hast, in these latter days, spoken to us by thy Son. Help us to listen to his words, and to profit by them. Help us to take heed and beware of covetousness. Impress upon our minds a sense of the supreme value of that which is spiritual and heavenly; and save us, oh, save us, we beseech Thee, from that delay or neglect that would leave us unprepared for our final summons. So do Thou enrich us by thy grace, and help us to lay up treasure in heaven, that when our souls are required of us, we may be enabled, with calm and humble confidence, to resign them into the hands of Him who hath redeemed them with his blood.

So long as it is thy will that we should remain on earth, do Thou help us to confide in thy Fatherly goodness and care. May we not dishonour Thee by distrusting Thee. If we have burdens to bear, help us to cast them upon the Lord. If the future should appear dark to us, help us to believe that light will arise in the darkness. When we cannot see our way, may we be willing that Thou shouldest lead us. May the changes of earth lead us to rejoice in thine unchangeableness; and may the failures of earthly supplies send us to that fountain which can never fail. We thank Thee, O our Father, that Thou hast promised that our bread shall be given us, and our water shall be sure. We thank Thee that in our past history no good thing has been withheld from us. May the experience of the past strengthen our confidence for the future. May we take no anxious thought for the morrow, but leave that trustfully with Thee. And do Thou, O God of providence and grace, make our hearts strong and glad in the belief that, as Thou dost clothe the lilies and feed the ravens, Thou wilt never forget nor forsake us.

Defend us, O Lord, from all the dangers of this day. Guide us in every difficulty. Aid us in every duty. Keep us from temptation, and every hurtful snare. Help us to walk in thy fear all the day long, and finally bring us to thine eternal kingdom, for Jesus Christ's sake. Amen.

READ IN HOLY SCRIPTURE PSALM LXXII.

O THOU by whom kings do reign and princes decree justice, we gratefully acknowledge thy goodness in guiding us through the busy hours of the past day, and bringing us to its close in peace and security. For all thy gracious dealings with us, we render to Thee our unfeigned thanks. We have had food and raiment, health and happiness, peace of conscience, and whatever else Thou seest good for us. All these blessings thy hand has provided and thy bounty bestowed, and to Thee we give the praise.

Amongst all the temporal blessings which we have received at thy hands, not the least is that of good governance under a rightful sovereign. May she long reign over us in peace and confidence, and may all the royal family be the recipients of thy choicest blessings. For all our governors and judges, also, for all our legislators and public officers we pray, that they may so adjudge the causes and claims of the people, that injustice and oppression may be removed, and that thy servants may lead a peaceable and quiet life, in all godliness and honesty.

But, O thou Father of our Lord Jesus Christ, prepare us to receive thy Son as our universal King. We earnestly pray that his dominion may extend from sea to sea, and from the river to the end of the earth. Let the people that dwell in the wilderness bow before Him, and those who inhabit the uttermost parts of the earth do homage unto Him. Let kings fall down before Thee, and all people do Him service.

O thou blessed Saviour of our souls, who didst redeem us at the cost of thine own precious blood, to Thee we turn with holy joy and humble adoration. May thy glorious person be had in reverence, and thine earthly temples held in honour. There let prayer and intercessions be made continually to Thee; there let men offer the sacrifices of praise and thanksgiving. O thou King of saints, who perpetually sittest at the right hand of thy Father, receive the supplications which are presented in thy prevailing name, and grant great success to the Gospel which proclaims Thee and honours the Father.

Blessed be the Lord God, the God of Israel, who only doeth, and can do these wondrous things for us. He is our King, and He saves us; He alone delivers us from our enemies; He alone spares his people and pardons their iniquities. Pardon our offences, for they are many; pardon them for Jesus Christ's sake, for He is our atoning Lamb, which taketh away the sin of the world. Then shall our hearts be filled with thy praise, as the whole earth shall one day be filled with his glory. Amen and Amen.

[Morning.] THIRD WEEK.—SATURDAY. [Evening.

READ IN HOLY SCRIPTURE GENESIS XIV.

ALMIGHTY God, our Heavenly Father, give us access to Thee this morning, through Jesus Christ our Saviour, and enlarge, day by day, our desires after spiritual blessings.

We thank Thee, O Lord, for the rest and protection we have enjoyed during the past night. Suffer us not to forget all the benefits we receive at thy hands, but give us that due sense of all thy mercies, that our hearts may be unfeignedly thankful. Let our gratitude for spiritual blessings be seen in our holy and consistent lives. Help us to adorn the doctrine of God our Saviour in all things; make it the rule of our lives. In all the concerns of daily life enable us to be consistent with our Christian profession. Help us in difficult circumstances to do justly, to love mercy, and to walk humbly with God. In our dealings with those who know not Thee, keep us doubly watchful; let us not go beyond nor defraud them in any matter. May we have grace to walk in wisdom towards them that are without. Teach us to value the acquaintance and prayers of those who serve Thee, and ever to show them the respect which thy Word enjoins.

Help us now to enter upon our daily duties in a Christian spirit; prepare us by thy grace for all the events of the day. Amidst the busy occupation of the day suffer us not to forget the worth of our souls. Let us not be deceived by the vanities of the world. Thy providence calls upon us to be in the world; oh, let us not be of it! Teach us the secret of true religion. Unite us to Christ Jesus. Help us to realise our dependence upon Him all day long. May He be the ground of all our hopes, the object of our love, and the pattern of our lives. Watch over us until the day shall close; prepare us to expect temptation; give us the victory over it; preserve our bodies in health and safety; and sanctify all that befalls us. Increase our desires for the good of others. Open our bowels of compassion for all the sinful and guilty around us. O Lord, bless all our relatives, friends, and acquaintances. Have pity upon the multitudes who have no pity upon themselves; open their eyes to see their danger, and lead them to flee for safety to Thee. Finally, O Lord, revive thy work in the world. Lay this desire upon all thy faithful people. Put it into the hearts of all Christians to pray this prayer. Let prayer ascend up from thy true Church on earth without ceasing. O Lord, give thy dear Son the heathen for his inheritance, and the uttermost parts of the earth for his possession.

Hear these our supplications, O Heavenly Father, and graciously answer us, for the sake of our Lord and Saviour Jesus Christ. Amen.

READ IN HOLY SCRIPTURE ST. JOHN 11.

ALMIGHTY God, our Heavenly Father, help us now to worship Thee in spirit and in truth. We come to Thee in our Saviour's name; we plead his merits; we rest on his gracious promise that what we ask faithfully we shall obtain effectually, to the relief of our necessities, and to the setting forth of thy glory. Incline our hearts to come to Thee in faith and prayer for every needful good.

We thank thee, O merciful Father, for all the comforts and enjoyments of this life, and for the many temporal blessings with which we are surrounded. While we thankfully use these good gifts, may we not abuse them, but may our hearts be ever lifted up in grateful love to Thee, our bountiful and never-failing benefactor.

We praise thy holy name for giving thine only Son to be unto us both a sacrifice for sin and an example of godly life. Give us grace that we may daily endeavour ourselves to follow the blessed steps of his most holy life. Help us to walk even as He walked. Like Him, may we go about doing good. May it be our meat and drink to do our Father's will. May our days on earth, like his, be spent in works of holy, active loving-kindness. Make it ever our happiness to promote the happiness of others, and as our blessed Lord deigned to show his sympathy in his people's joys, and to sanctify by his presence their lawful pleasures, so may we learn to rejoice with them that do rejoice, and thus to adorn the doctrine of God our Saviour in all things. We bless Thee, O Lord, for thy Holy Word, which is able to make us wise unto salvation, through faith which is in Christ Jesus. Help us, we beseech Thee, so to read its sacred pages as daily to draw from it some useful lesson of life. Oh, give us an increasing love and reverence for that blessed Book. May it show us the greatness of our need; may it reveal Christ Jesus to us in all the fulness of his love, in all the freeness of his salvation. Thou, O Lord, art the inexhaustible fountain of life; may thy Holy Spirit bring each one of us to Him who alone is able and willing to give us of the water of life freely. Thou hast said, "Open thy mouth wide, and I will fill it." We come to Thee, O Lord, trusting in this thy word, and earnestly beseech Thee now to grant us thy grace and heavenly benediction, that we may live in the constant obedience of thy will.

O Lord, we pray not only for ourselves, but for those we love. Grant to them all the fulness of the blessing of the Gospel of Christ. Take them and us under thy merciful protection this night. May no evil befall us. Grant us refreshing rest, and raise us up in the morning to serve Thee with all our hearts, for Jesus Christ our Saviour's sake. Amen.

[MORNING.]   FOURTH WEEK.—LORD'S DAY.   [EVENING.

READ IN HOLY SCRIPTURE HEBREWS VII. 11—28.

READ IN HOLY SCRIPTURE PSALM XLV.

ALMIGHTY GOD, the Father of our Lord Jesus Christ, who hast appointed the Sabbath for man, a day of rest for the exhausted body, and of refreshment to the weary spirit; we would approach Thee first in the simplicity of this family service, before assembling together in the midst of thy worshipping people. Give us grace so to improve our earthly Sabbaths, that at the last an entrance may abundantly be ministered to each of us into thine everlasting Sabbath, the rest that remaineth to the people of God.

We bless Thee for thy mercy to each of us through the night, and that we are all in safety before Thee this morning. Cause us to be in the Spirit on this Lord's day, that we may worship Thee in spirit and in truth. Meet us in the sanctuary, and bless the company of our fellow-worshippers as well as ourselves. Bless also all thy ministers. Make thy word from their lips to be with power to every heart amongst us; let it come to us as a message from Thee; let the inward grace accompany and quicken each outward ordinance to-day, so shall we realise thy presence, and feel that God is with us of a truth.

O Father, we would remember all that are near and dear to us. We would ask thy mercy and grace upon them also. We pray for our Queen and country; for thy Church militant here on earth, at home and abroad; for thy faithful missionaries to the Jew and the heathen. May thy Word have free course and be glorified. Let not the enemy of souls have advantage over us. Let him not take away the word from our hearts, but help us all to believe and to be saved.

O Lord Jesus Christ, Thou only Mediator between God and man, who art the same yesterday, and to-day, and for ever, the only Son of the Father, consecrated for evermore the Great High Priest, who art holy, harmless, undefiled, and separate from sinners, God over all, blessed for evermore, whose blood cleanseth from all sin, who art able to save to the uttermost all that come to God by Thee, our Hope, our All, who canst be touched with a feeling of our infirmities, have compassion on us, we beseech thee, and upon all who are out of the way. For thy name's sake, pardon our iniquity, for it is great.

O eternal Spirit, proceeding from the Father and the Son, do Thou help our infirmities, and make intercession for us. Do Thou lead us into all truth, and sanctify us with its power.

O merciful God, may Christ in us, the hope of glory, be an anchor of the soul, sure and stedfast, to be realised in its fulness, in the day of the Lord Jesus. Lord, hasten it in thy time. Lord Jesus, come quickly. Amen.

O THOU, who art the King of kings and the Lord of lords; Thou art good, though men are evil. Thou hast given thine only begotten Son to die for our sins, and thy Holy Spirit to quicken us to newness of life. We thank thee if we have been made partakers of this grace. Help us to love Thee with all the love of our hearts; and to serve Thee with all the service of our lives. We thank Thee for the kingdom of Christ upon earth; that this sick and sorrowful world is thus healed and blessed by Him; and that all nations are to be blessed in Him and to call Him blessed.

We thank Thee for the righteousness of his rule, and for the beauty of his holiness. May we imitate his perfect example; be like Him in all piety towards God, and in all virtue towards men: thus may we be holy members of his kingdom, and help its coming upon earth.

We thank Thee that Thou hast made thy Son our Saviour head over all things to his Church. We bless Thee that of his fulness we may all receive, and grace for grace. God of all grace, may the Church live as the true Bride of thy beloved Son, adorned with the garments of salvation and the beauty of holiness, manifesting to the world that loving yet reverent attachment which is a meet response to his surpassing love. Do Thou graciously perfect it, and remove from its members every inconsistency. Help us to seek thy glory. Take out of our hearts all worldly-mindedness, and all spiritual selfishness. Bless all the members of this family. Let our children be a seed to serve Thee; make them simple concerning evil, and wise to that which is good. May they be children of the Father's house, and the Church be their home from their earliest years. In spiritual goodness and beauty may they grow up in it saints from their childhood; and when our hands shall fail, may they bear the ark of the Lord, and uplift the standard of the cross more nobly and zealously than we have done.

Holy Father, we thank Thee for the manifold mercies of this thy day; for thy protection from its evils, and for thy gifts of its goodness; for the ordinances of thy house, and the preaching of thy Word. Forgive our poor returns; our forgetfulness, ingratitude, and sin.

Mercifully protect us during the night, and give us sleep that may refresh us and strengthen us to serve Thee on the morrow.

Bless all our relatives and friends, and have mercy upon all men, for the sake of Him whose name we bear, and we will render to Thee, the Father of an infinite Majesty, and to thine honourable, true, and only Son, and to the Holy Ghost the Comforter, everlasting praises. Amen.

[Morning.] FOURTH WEEK.—MONDAY. [Evening.

READ IN HOLY SCRIPTURE GENESIS XV.

ALMIGHTY and everlasting God, who didst make thyself known in ancient times to thy faithful servant Abraham, be pleased to reveal thyself unto us. As obedient children we desire to walk in the steps of his faith, and as heirs of the promise, to look for thy blessing in Jesus Christ our Lord. Come to us as Thou hast promised, and take up thine abode with us. Graciously shed abroad the love of God in our hearts by thy Holy Spirit, that we may love Thee better, and ever be disposed to keep thy commandments. Most unworthy are we to receive such tokens of thy love and mercy. Our sins have deserved thy wrath and condemnation, but Thou hast taught us that Christ is the propitiation for our sins. For His sake impute not iniquity to us, but account us righteous in thy sight.

O most gracious God, send the Spirit of adoption into our hearts, crying, Abba, Father. Cause us to know that we are indeed thy children through faith in Christ Jesus, the seed of Abraham, and heirs according to the promise. Oh, may we ever walk worthy of our high vocation. Save us from falling into any kind of sin; keep us by thy power through faith unto salvation. Thou art our shield and exceeding great reward. Protect us, O God, from all evil, and preserve us in thy fear and love all our lives long. May we stedfastly walk with Thee all the days of our life, ever looking for that blessed hope and the glorious appearing of God our Saviour, who gave himself up for us, and redeemed us from all iniquity.

Pour out upon us the spirit of grace and supplication, that we may never cease to pray, and thus receive thy promised blessing. Help our infirmities, blessed Lord, by thy Holy Spirit, and let us not faint in coming to thy throne of grace. Let no wandering thoughts intrude; let nothing defile our souls and hinder our prayers this day. Do Thou fill us with thy Spirit. Bring every thought and imagination into obedience to thy blessed will, and grant that we may have sweet communion with the Father and the Son.

O gracious God, bless us and our family, our relations and friends, with thy richest blessings in Christ Jesus. May all receive out of his fulness grace for grace.

Let thy way be known on earth, thy saving health among all nations; may all the families in the earth be blessed in Christ according to thy promise. May He be the light of the Gentiles and the glory of thy people Israel.

Receive these our supplications which we present unto Thee this day, not trusting in our own righteousness, but in thy manifold and great mercies, through Jesus Christ, our only Mediator. Amen.

READ IN HOLY SCRIPTURE ST. JOHN III. 1–21.

O LORD God, our Father, which art in heaven, it is good for us to draw near unto Thee. We call upon Thee, O Lord, of thy great mercy to fill our hearts with the wonderful words we have read from thy holy Gospel. Send down thy Holy Spirit, that we may understand what we read. If by thy grace we have been born again, may the Holy Ghost work in us to will and to do of thy good pleasure. May He be our Teacher, our Guide, and our Comforter, and bring all things to our remembrance, whatsoever Christ Jesus hath said unto us. O thou great Searcher of all hearts, if there be one among us this night who is not yet born again, one who has not believed in the Son of God, hear our prayer, that before he lays himself down to sleep he may have a new heart created within him. Take away the stony heart out of his flesh, and renew a right spirit within him, for thy mercy's sake, O Lord.

Almighty God, we humbly beseech Thee to accept our thanks for the great goodness Thou hast shown to all of us throughout this day. We bless Thee for all the good things which the Lord our God hath given us. Thou crownest our life with loving-kindness and tender mercies. What manner of persons ought we to be! But, Lord, we confess with shame that we have sinned against Thee, and are not worthy this night that Thou shouldest come under our roof. Lord, have mercy upon us! Christ, have mercy upon us! Let the blood of the cross be found upon us, now, and in the hour of death, and at the day of judgment.

Hear us, O heavenly Father, we implore Thee, when we pray for all our absent relatives and friends. The Lord bless them and keep them. Make them thy sons and thy daughters. May they all be born again. May they all believe in Jesus Christ, whom Thou hast sent. May our whole family be numbered with thy saints in glory everlasting. Be merciful, O God, we humbly beseech Thee, to our neighbours, to our country, and to all who rule over us. More especially we pray for our Sovereign, and for all the members of the royal household. Let great grace be upon them all.

And now, O Lord, we commend ourselves to thy care during this night. Thou never slumberest, never sleepest. May we lay ourselves down in peace and sleep, for Thou, Lord, only makest us to dwell in safety. So teach us to number our days that we may apply our hearts unto wisdom. O Lord, hear us; O Lord, forgive; and supply all our need, for Jesus Christ's sake, to whom, with Thee and the Holy Ghost, be all honour and glory, world without end. Amen.

[MORNING.]   FOURTH WEEK.—TUESDAY.   [EVENING.

READ IN HOLY SCRIPTURE PSALM CXXXIX. 1—12.

ALMIGHTY and everlasting God, once more, through thy kind and gracious providence, we are gathered, a united family, at thy footstool. Thou hast given us sleep and rest; Thou hast renewed our strength. We have awakened with fresh energy for the duties of the coming day.

We thank Thee for these great and ever-recurring blessings; Thou art, indeed, ever mindful of us. During the hours of darkness Thou hast watched over us. Whilst lying in unconscious sleep thine eye has never closed. Trouble has come to many during the past night, yet Thou in thy goodness hast kept and guarded us. Through thy loving-kindness we are enabled to offer up our praise and thanksgiving.

We thank Thee for thy Word read. May we ever feel conscious that thine eye is upon us; may we never lose sight of thy all-pervading presence. Whatever our occupation may be this day, whatever the duties which we may be called upon to fulfil, may we remember Thou God seest us. And as Thou didst open up a fountain in the desert to Hagar of old, so open, O Lord God, the fountain of thy grace, that in our constant weaknesses and necessities we may be comforted and strengthened by thy help.

We know not, O Lord, what may befall us this day; we know not what temptations may assault us; we know not what dangers may beset our path: Thou knowest all, O God! Help us graciously by thy mighty power; if we are tempted, help us to resist and overcome; and if dangers arise, send us a speedy deliverance: direct our every footstep, and lead us and bless us in all things. And not only, O Lord God, do Thou protect and guide us, but do Thou graciously help us to manifest in our conduct a Christian character. In all our doings may we act with sobriety and uprightness, as those who have one day to give an account of things done in the body, whether they be good or bad.

But, O Lord God, we cannot maintain this holy life unless Thou thyself pourest out upon us thy Holy Spirit. Of ourselves we can do nothing; our good resolutions we cannot carry into effect; we are weak and utterly impotent without thy gracious favour. Help us, O Lord God! help us, and Thou shalt have the praise and the glory.

And now we go forth in thy strength; leave us not, forsake us not, but be with us throughout every hour and every moment of the day.

These and all other mercies, together with the forgiveness of our sins, we humbly ask in and through the name of Jesus Christ, our blessed Lord and Saviour, to whom, with Thee and the Holy Spirit, be glory and praise now and ever. Amen.

READ IN HOLY SCRIPTURE HEBREWS VII. 25—VIII.

ALMIGHTY God, the God and Father of our Lord Jesus Christ, and *our* God and Father in and through Jesus Christ, we draw near to the throne of thy grace in his name. Thou, O God, art rich in mercy. Thou desirest not the death of the sinner, but that he should turn from his way and live; and therefore Thou didst give thine only begotten Son, that whosoever believeth on him should not perish, but have eternal life.

O God, for his sake we pray Thee to pardon all our sins; to justify us freely by faith in Him; to give us peace with Thee, through Him who is our peace. We beseech Thee to adopt us into thy family; to make us thy children; to give us a good hope through grace; yea, for his sake to receive us graciously and love us freely.

We acknowledge before Thee our ignorance. Of ourselves we understand not heavenly things. O Lord, open Thou our eyes, that we may behold wondrous things out of thy law. Send upon us thy Holy Spirit, that Christ may be revealed in us, that the things of Christ may be shown unto us, that our faith and love may be strengthened, that we may be filled with joy and peace in believing, and abound in hope through the power of the Holy Ghost.

We bless Thee for our great High Priest and Intercessor at thy right hand, the Advocate whose pleading always prevails with Thee. We bless Thee that He is touched with the feeling of our infirmities, and was in all points tempted like as we are, yet without sin. May we be enabled through Him to come boldly unto the throne of grace, that we may obtain mercy, and find grace to help in time of need. We bless and glorify thy name that He ever liveth, and is able to save them to the uttermost that come unto Thee by Him. O Lord Jesus, our High Priest, save us, or we perish.

Nor for ourselves only would we plead, but also for all men, that like blessings may be bestowed on them. Thou art our Father, and we are all thy offspring. Oh, let the time speedily come, when both Jews and Gentiles shall be brought to enjoy the fulness of the blessings of the Gospel of Christ; when thy kingdom shall come, and thy will be done on earth as it is in heaven. O God, pour out abundantly of thy Spirit, that thy Word may mightily prevail, and be glorified. Let the day dawn when they shall not teach every man his neighbour, and every man his brother, saying, Know the Lord, but when all shall know Thee, from the least to the greatest.

We ask all in the name of our Lord Jesus Christ, to whom, with the Father and the Holy Spirit, we ascribe everlasting glory. Amen.

[Morning.] **FOURTH WEEK.—WEDNESDAY.** [Evening.

READ IN HOLY SCRIPTURE EPH. IV. 17–32.

O GOD, most mighty and most merciful, behold us, thy creatures, thy children, as we draw near thy throne. We adore Thee as our Creator and Upholder: Thine eye has again watched over us, and thine arm protected us. We praise Thee for the rest of the night, and the new mercies of the morning. We reverence Thee as our King and Lord; we acknowledge that thy government is supreme, thy commandments righteous and true. We approach Thee as our Father, to whom we have been reconciled in Jesus Christ, and made nigh by his precious blood. Thou hast pitied us; Thou didst remember us in our low estate, and bear long and patiently with our sin. And now Thou lovest us; every day we believe Thou art bending down to help and heal our weakness, to forgive us our sins, and to cleanse us from all unrighteousness. We say together, "Bless the Lord, O our souls, and forget not all his benefits!"

Teach us, then, O our Father, to live this day as thy forgiven children. Forbid that we should be hasty and uncharitable with others, when Thou art so forbearing and long-suffering to us. Help us always to remember that it is only by thy great love that we are saved; that Thou hast saved us in order to make us like thyself. May the thought of thy purity, therefore, make us pure; the recollection of thy truthfulness keep us from being false in lip or in life; may thy mercy make us merciful. In the company of others this day, oh! may we be indeed thy followers, as dear children. Keep Thou the door of our lips, of our hearts. Enable us to adorn the doctrine of our Saviour in all things. In our intercourse together at home, may we be careful to speak and act the truth; to avoid all offence; to be patient if we are provoked; to forgive freely if we are injured. And in our own hearts give us thy Holy Spirit; make them thy dwelling-place, that so we may have friendship with Thee, and be in the fear of the Lord all the day long. Oh, that this day, each of us, from the youngest to the oldest, may do some good in the great world where we live!

Take care of us to-day, O God. Keep us from disease, we pray, from accident, from strife, and, above all, from sin. Draw the hearts of the children before Thee to Jesus, that they may be his now in the days of their youth, and his for ever and ever. Give us wisdom and strength for every duty; sanctify to us every pleasure; uphold us under every burden; and may the evening, when it comes, find us at thy footstool, with a new song upon our lips!

We present our praise and our prayer in the name of Jesus Christ our Saviour. Amen.

READ IN HOLY SCRIPTURE ST. JOHN III. 22–36.

O LORD God Almighty, we this evening bow ourselves before thy footstool, in the name of Jesus Christ our Saviour and Mediator. We are unworthy to come into thy presence, by reason of our heinous sins; but Thou encouragest lost sinners to seek mercy and salvation, and willest not that we should perish. Grant us, O Lord, the true baptism: the baptism of thy Holy Spirit. Send into our hearts the Holy Ghost, to convince us more and more of our deep sinfulness, and to reveal to our souls the exceeding preciousness of Christ. May the same Holy Spirit conform us to the Saviour's likeness, making us willing to humble ourselves, that he may be exalted. Clothe our souls with true humility; and grant that we may exhibit in our conduct the meekness and gentleness of Him who said, "Take my yoke upon you, for I am meek and lowly in heart."

Grant, also, we beseech Thee, that we, like thy servant John the Baptist, may serve Thee with all our hearts, and be ready, through evil report and good report, to bear testimony to thy love to us in Christ Jesus. Teach us to rejoice greatly in the advance of the Redeemer's kingdom, and in the salvation of souls. Incline us willingly and thankfully to receive the revelation which Thou hast made to mankind by thy dear Son; and to know that "thy Word is truth." O Father, Thou lovest thy Son; and Thou hast given all things into his hand. Out of the fulness of grace that is treasured up for us in Christ, bestow upon us, we pray Thee, all that Thou seest to be needful for us. Above all, give us a saving faith. Grant that we may so believe in the death and merits of Christ, that we may become inheritors of everlasting life. Oh, grant that no one of us, now kneeling before thy face, may reject our only hope of salvation, by neglecting Christ. Take out from every one of us the evil heart of unbelief, for Thou hast solemnly warned us that "he that believeth not the Son shall not see life, but the wrath of God abideth on him." We deserve thy wrath; but, O Lord, enable us to believe that the Lord Jesus endured thy wrath on our behalf, and to rejoice that he was wounded for our transgressions, and that with his stripes we are healed.

Graciously look upon the children of this family. Oh, that they may be filled with the Holy Ghost, even from their earliest years, and ever serve Thee in faithfulness and love. Preserve and keep us through the night, and if it be thy will renew to us morning mercies, for the sake of Jesus Christ our only Lord and Saviour, to whom, with Thee, O Father, and Thee, O Holy Ghost, we would ascribe all honour and glory, world without end. Amen.

[25]

[MORNING.] FOURTH WEEK.—THURSDAY. [EVENING.

READ IN HOLY SCRIPTURE GENESIS XVII.

O LORD God, by whose gracious help alone we can render an acceptable service of prayer and praise, pour down upon us thy promised Spirit. Incline our wills to engage heartily in this our morning worship: kindle within us a spirit of thankfulness; increase our faith, enlarge our desires after heavenly things, and enable us to worship Thee now and at all times in sincerity and truth. We are sinful and unworthy, but Jesus is our advocate with the Father. We plead his merits. Lord, according to thy gracious word, accept us, pardon us, and bless us for his sake.

Glory be to thy name for the mercies of the night. Oh, how great is thy goodness to us, O Lord, from day to day. Morning by morning and evening by evening Thou preservest us and keepest us. Continue, we beseech Thee, thy gracious guardianship and care over us through all the day. In the midst of its duties, and temptations, and difficulties, be Thou ever near us, and succour us according to our need, that in nothing we may fail of our duty to God or man. We thank Thee for the spiritual privileges which Thou hast bestowed upon thy believing people in making them thy children by adoption and grace. We pray Thee for the continual indwelling of the Holy Ghost, that our souls may be cleansed and sanctified; that we may be Christians not in name only, but in deed and in truth, living in the Spirit, and walking worthily of our high calling. O God, by thy grace mortify and subdue in us every sinful temper and every unholy desire. Mightily strengthen us from above, that with all Christian courage we may cast away from us all that is hateful and displeasing to Thee. Oh, help us to strive after higher things—to aim at a loftier standard of Christian character, and thus to go on unto perfection. Seal us by the Spirit, and grant that we may live as the children of God and heirs of the promises wherewith Thou hast blessed us in thy dear Son.

Lord, look down in thy love on the whole Church of Christ. Endue all the professing members thereof with thy grace, that they may be more and more conformed to the image of thy dear Son, and enjoy more abundantly the precious gifts which Thou bestowest through him. Oh, make them and us more unworldly in spirit. Awaken in them and us a deeper interest in the spread of the Redeemer's kingdom. Stir up the desire of all hearts for the ingathering into thy fold of Jew and Gentile, and the fulfilment of the sure promise that in Christ all nations shall be blessed. O God, let these our prayers and thanksgivings enter into thine ears, and bring forth an answer of peace, for Jesus Christ's sake. Amen.

READ IN HOLY SCRIPTURE 1 JOHN V.

LORD God, Thou hearest and answerest prayer, and biddest us cast our care upon Thee, for Thou carest for us. For the sake of thy dear Son, and in fulfilment of thy gracious promises, hear, and answer, and bless us. Manifold as are our wants, Thou canst supply them; open to us now the treasures of thy love, and bestow all that Thou seest us to need, whether of life and strength for the body, or of grace and peace for the soul. We ask it, O God, believing in thy promises to which we have now listened, and remembering all the love with which Thou hast loved us, and the mercy which Thou hast shown to us in Jesus Christ our Lord.

We praise Thee, O God, for the record which thou hast given us of thy Son, that in him we have life, the life that is spiritual and eternal. We pray that we may have Christ for our own, and that, having him, and believing in him as our Saviour and our God, his life may be our life, and that, because he liveth, we may live also. O Lord, we believe; help thou our unbelief. We believe that Jesus is the Son of God, that he came to seek and to save that which was lost, that he lived, and suffered, and died for us, and that he is ascended up far above all heavens, and at thy right hand in glory pleadeth our cause. Lord, let us have the sure witness in our own hearts, testifying to our acceptance in Christ, and that we have been born of God. Give us true peace of conscience, that, if we are thine, no fear of condemnation may haunt and disturb us. Give us such faith in thy dear Son that we may know that we have eternal life. And, oh! grant that the evidence of these blessings may be seen in our hearts and constant obedience to thy commandments. Bring our hearts into such perfect unison with thy will, and fill us with such a sense of thy love, that thy commandments may never seem grievous, but the law of perfect happiness and peace. Grant also, O God, that in the power of a true faith, we may resist all the temptations of the world, and come off more than conquerors through Him who hath loved us. Lord, let us not be condemned with the world. Raise us above it in thought, and motive, and inclination, that neither the lust of the flesh, nor the lust of the eye, nor the pride of life may draw us away from Thee.

Lord, be with us through the hours of darkness, and give to us, as Thou dost give to thy beloved, sleep. Spread around us, and all whom we love, the shield of thine unslumbering care. Let neither wicked man nor wicked spirit come near to harm us. We lay ourselves down to sleep, trusting to thy protection. Keep us now and ever as thine own children, for the sake of Jesus Christ, Amen.

[Morning.]   FOURTH WEEK.—FRIDAY.   [Evening.

READ IN HOLY SCRIPTURE ROMANS IV.

O ALMIGHTY and merciful God, who givest liberally and upbraidest not, bestow upon us, we pray Thee, all the things that accompany salvation. Impute not against us our many sins, known and unknown; and graciously enable us to enjoy day by day the comforting sense of thy forgiveness. Unworthy and guilty in ourselves, we plead the saving righteousness of thy dear Son. Cover us with it, O God, that our sins may be hidden from thy sight, and that we may be found without fault before thy throne. Create in us the clean heart, and renew us, from day to day, in knowledge and true holiness. Fill our hearts with all joy and peace in believing, that we may abound in hope through the power of the Holy Ghost. Work in us to will and to do of thy good pleasure whatsoever is well-pleasing in thy sight. Grateful for the blessings of the past night, we desire to consecrate ourselves afresh this morning to thy service. Oh, help us to live not to ourselves, but to Him who died for our sins, and rose again for our justification, and now ever liveth to make intercession for us.

Especially, O God, we pray for a strong faith, that in all things we may give glory to Thee by our unwavering confidence in thy word and in thy love. We trust, O Lord, not in ourselves or our principles, but only in thy promises. Confirm our faith, that we stagger not in unbelief. Thy counsels of old are faithfulness and truth. What Thou hast promised Thou art able to perform. In thy hands we place ourselves, body, soul, and spirit. Work in us thy holy will, conform us to the image and likeness of thy dear Son, and grant that we may be numbered with thy saints in glory everlasting.

Extend the same favours, O Lord, to our relations, neighbours, and friends. Endue them with thy Holy Spirit; enrich them with thy heavenly grace. Let thy Gospel be preached to all nations, and unite Jews and Gentiles in one fold under the good Shepherd, Jesus Christ our Lord. Prosper all societies formed to promote thy glory and the peace and happiness of mankind. Succour the tempted, give patience to the afflicted, comfort the persecuted, and give peace to the dying. Grant that the rising generation may remember Thee, and walk in thy ways. May all thy ministers diligently feed thy sheep, and especially the lambs of thy flock. Bless thy Church, and enable all who love the Lord Jesus Christ in sincerity to abound in love and humility towards one another, that Christ's people may be one, and that the world may know that Thou hast sent him. Hear us, O God; grant us thy presence and protection through the day, and do for us above all that we can ask or think, for Jesus Christ's sake. Amen.

READ IN HOLY SCRIPTURE ST. JOHN IV. 1—42.

GRACIOUS Father and God, heaven is thy throne and earth thy footstool, and Thou inhabitest eternity. Blessed be thy name, that Thou wilt also dwell in the humble and contrite heart. Come, Lord, and abide with us and in us. Let us now feel thy presence among us, and, oh! enable us by thy grace to worship Thee in spirit and in truth.

Thou hast preserved and upheld us this day in such health and strength as is good for us. Out of thine own fulness Thou hast supplied our wants, and with the bounties of thy providence hast nourished and clothed us. Wake up our hearts to thankfulness and praise; teach us how undeserving we are, and teach us how much we owe to Thee. Grievous, and great, and many have been our sins and shortcomings in thy sight. Weighed in thy balances we are found wanting; Lord, pity us. Blessed Saviour, who didst visit and teach the guilty and impure when on earth, and draw them to thyself by the power of the Spirit, have mercy upon us. Show us our sinfulness, and reveal thy power and willingness to save. Let nothing keep us from Thee, or hide from us thy glory. Thou, O God, art the Fountain of living waters; we desire to drink daily at the streams of thy love, and to receive thy Holy Spirit in such abundant measure that it may be in us as a well of water springing up to everlasting life. Give us truer conceptions of our own emptiness and of thy fulness. Grant us an ever-deepening experience of the riches of thy grace and love in Christ Jesus, that the signs of the new life may abound in us more and more, and men take knowledge of us that we have been with Jesus. O Lord, so transform us into his likeness, and give us the mind that was in him, that we may tread in his footsteps, and make it our meat and drink to do thy will.

Look in mercy, O Lord, we beseech Thee, on the world at large. Give grace to thy Church, that it may scatter far and near the incorruptible seed of the truth, and look up earnestly and believingly for thy blessing and the promised harvest, in which sower and reaper shall rejoice together. O God, let it not be in vain that thy Gospel is preached from day to day, to the healthy and the sick, to the living and the dying. Let it not be in vain that the precious tidings of the Saviour's love have come to us, and those that are dear to us. If as yet we have been deaf to thy voice, open our ears now, we pray Thee, and soften and subdue us to a true repentance. To thy kind care we commit ourselves for the night, and all whom we love. Watch us, preserve us, and above all, save us eternally. We ask all for thy dear Son's sake. Amen.

[27]

[MORNING.] **FOURTH WEEK.—SATURDAY.** [EVENING.]

READ IN HOLY SCRIPTURE GENESIS XVIII. 1–15.

GRACIOUS Lord God, as Thou didst appear unto thy servant Abraham of old, so appear unto us this morning. Be in our midst as we humbly kneel at thy mercy-seat. May we feel that Thou art present. Banish from our minds all that may distract or disturb them. Let our thoughts be fixed upon Thee; and thus, through thy Holy Spirit, may we offer unto Thee an undivided sacrifice of heart and soul.

We thank Thee, gracious Lord, for all the mercies of the past night. Whilst we have slumbered, Thou hast been wakeful and watchful: whilst we have been lying in helpless sleep, exposed to many dangers, thine eye has never closed.

We desire to give our first thoughts to Thee. We desire that the thanksgiving of love should first arise to Thee. We desire to begin the day with God. Before going into the world, before entering upon our several duties, before mixing with those around, we would, as one united family, bow the knee, and come into thy presence.

We know, O Lord, that we cannot keep in our Christian course this day without Thee. We know that temptations cannot be resisted, that difficulties cannot be overcome without thy help. We shall want wisdom to guide us, and strength to aid us; and to whom, O Lord, can we go but unto Thee?

We come asking humbly but earnestly for these mercies. We may be much tried this day, we may be much tempted, we may have to face many and great daugers; we know not what may happen: but we know that if Thou art with us, on our right hand and on our left, we are safe. Be with us, O Lord God, and grant that we may realise thy presence.

And should we be tempted to doubt because of any seeming difficulty, may we remember that nothing is too hard for Thee; that though some things are impossible with men, all things are possible with Thee. May we call to mind thy wonders of old. Thou didst work for thy people great deliverances. May we feel that it will be the same in thy dealings with us. May we cling with unwavering belief to thy power, and to the covenant of thy love with all thy children.

We pray for the forgiveness of our sins. We pray for our besetting sins to be rooted out. We pray to become holy.

We pray also for all estates of men in their several vocations and ministry. We pray for thy Church, that it may be kept in the right way. We pray for the coming of Christ in power and great glory. Even so, come, Lord Jesus. Hear us and answer us, O God, for the sake of our only Mediator, Jesus Christ. Amen.

READ IN HOLY SCRIPTURE ST. JOHN IV. 43–54.

O LORD, our Heavenly Father, in approaching Thee at this time, we desire humbly to acknowledge our unworthiness, and to confess our sin: yet we bless Thee that Thou hast made us welcome through Jesus Christ thine only Son. Thou hast mercifully preserved us during another day, and we bow before Thee in thankfulness for all thy goodness to us. We lament, O Lord, that not a day passes over us which is not marked by imperfections and shortcomings. We have sinned against Thee this day; but we rejoice that we have an advocate with Thee the Father, even Jesus Christ the righteous, whose blood can wash away all our sin. We thank Thee, O God, for the record which Thou hast given us of all that Jesus did, and taught, and suffered during his sojourn among men; and we pray that by the teaching of thy Spirit every part of his earthly history may be full of holy instruction and influence to us. May we yield to him the homage, love, and worship which are his due. May none of us be like those in his own country who refused to honour him; but may we all submit to his authority, to be ruled by his love, and saved by his grace. To whom can we go, as creatures morally diseased, but to Him who is the Physician of souls? To whom, O Lord, can we look, as creatures by nature spiritually dead, but to Him who came to give life to perishing men? Help us, therefore, to bring our emptiness to his fulness, and our souls, guilty and polluted as they are, to his atoning sacrifice and healing grace, that we may live anew in him. And grant, O Lord, we beseech Thee, that our faith may be simple and strong: that in believing we may rest on the Saviour's word, and through faith rise to liberty, and joy, and hope. Thus may we all accept thy mercy in Christ, realise thy presence, and seek day by day to live to thy glory, so as to find the blessedness of those who are at peace with Thee, and who rejoice in thy salvation.

We pray, O Lord, for all whom we love, that every needful blessing may descend on them, and that they may know the power and preciousness of thy Divine love. We pray for our country, and for the progress of thy Gospel in our own and in every land. May the time soon come when the Saviour's name be everywhere adored, and his Gospel everywhere triumphant.

Now we commit ourselves to thy gracious care. May we rest in safety under thy shadow; and may every day witness our growing devotedness to Thee, and our advancing meetness for thy glory. Hear us, O Lord; forgive and save; and to Thee shall be the praise, through Jesus, our strength and our Redeemer. Amen.

[Morning.]   FIFTH WEEK.—LORD'S DAY.   [Evening.]

READ IN HOLY SCRIPTURE GENESIS XVIII. 16–33.   READ IN HOLY SCRIPTURE ISAIAH LXI.

O LORD, our Heavenly Father, help us to come to Thee this morning with deep humility, sincerity, and faith. Thy Word has reminded us that sin is very grievous in thy sight. We confess before Thee, O Lord, that we are sinners. We remember with shame that our sins have been committed against the clearest light and knowledge. Thou hast sent thy beloved Son to die, a sacrifice for our sins, and thy good Spirit to cleanse us and to guide us in thy way; and yet, O Lord, we have lived in rebellion against Thee. We know, therefore, that our sins must be peculiarly offensive in thy sight. As Thou hast graciously taught us this, we humbly beseech Thee to make us to feel it deeply in our hearts. Humble us, O our Father, at the thought that we should have so often and so grievously offended Thee. Give us grace that with penitent hearts we may truly repent and turn to the Lord.

O holy and righteous Saviour, our Creator, Redeemer, and Judge, we humbly entreat the forgiveness of all our sins. Without thy mercy, Lord, we know it will be more tolerable for Sodom and Gomorrah in the day of judgment than for us. We implore, in the name of Jesus Christ, who died on the cross for us, the assurance of thy forgiving love. Throughout this day help us in thy strength to resist and overcome every temptation, and henceforth to live only to Thee.

We ask the assistance of thy Holy Spirit, that we may follow the example of thy servant Abraham, who commanded his children and his household after him to keep thy way. Make our house, O Lord, thy house; and so rule our hearts that we may ever be helpers together with Thee in promoting each other's holiness, happiness, and usefulness here upon earth, and hereafter may we all reign together with Thee in glory everlasting.

Upon all our dear relatives and friends we beseech Thee to bestow thy rich blessing. May those who love Thee rejoice continually in thy favour. And, O Lord, grant thy mercy especially to those who are yet in sin. Spare them, we beseech Thee, and, by thy Holy Spirit, change and sanctify their hearts, that they also may be all thine for ever.

We ask thy blessing on this, thy day, upon all the preachers of the Gospel throughout the world, and especially upon thy servant our beloved pastor. Prosper him and them, O Lord, in all their efforts for the extension of thy kingdom.

Accept our thanksgiving for thy protection through the night, and for the blessings we this morning enjoy. Be with us to guide and bless us throughout this day, for the sake of thy Son Jesus Christ our Lord. Amen.

O GOD, our heavenly Father, visit us this evening with the power of the Holy Ghost, and let thy Spirit descend and abide upon us. Thou hast given us many blessings, for time and for eternity; and this day we have been permitted to enjoy the means of grace in the services of thy sanctuary. We now draw nigh to Thee, in faith and humble confidence that Thou wilt hear our prayer, and bestow upon us a Sabbath evening's blessing ere we retire to rest. Let the good tidings of the Gospel of thy dear Son bind up the broken heart, and proclaim liberty to the captive soul. Let the acceptable year of the Lord come upon us with power, and find us willing to receive the Saviour, and to be accepted of him. Grant that the good news of salvation read and preached from thy Holy Word to-day may comfort all that mourn; and that the seed planted in our hearts may be as the good seed in the good ground, bringing forth fruit to thy praise and glory.

Thou knowest us, O God, better than we know ourselves. Teach us how low and how deep we have fallen, and what evil sin hath wrought within us. We sit in dust and ashes, and confess our sins before Thee. Let the unction of thy good Spirit, the oil of joy and gladness, refresh our souls, and clothe us with the garment of praise. We long for the time, O Lord, when Thou shalt make us to become fruit-bearing trees of righteousness, which thine own right hand hath planted. We pray Thee to make us the true Israel of God, restored to thy favour—prodigals returned, and reinstated in our Father's house, and for our shame receiving double at the good hand of the Lord, in an everlasting covenant, which shall not be cut off.

Oh, give to us this evening a fresh view of Jesus. Reveal thy Son in our hearts. Open the eyes of our understanding, that we may see by faith and realise thy presence here, and claim thy promises, which are yea and amen in Christ Jesus.

We beseech Thee also, O Lord, to impart to us heavenly peace, and the joys of thy salvation. Clothe us with the robe of righteousness—the spotless righteousness of thy dear Son; and thus arrayed, we shall be adorned as the spiritual bride of the Heavenly Bridegroom. Help us, O God of our salvation, to wait and look for the Bridegroom's coming.

We pray for domestic blessings, for thy Divine protection through the night, and such rest and peace as Thou seest good for us. Shelter us, Lord, beneath thy wings; and if it please Thee, raise us in safety to see the coming day. We ask all through the name and intercession of thy Son, our Saviour Jesus Christ. Amen.

[Morning.] **FIFTH WEEK.—MONDAY.** [Evening.

READ IN HOLY SCRIPTURE 1 TIMOTHY II.

GREAT and merciful God, we worship at thy footstool. New mercies received at thy hand call for new thanksgiving and praise. We bless Thee that once more we behold the morning light. Let thy favour rest upon us, unworthy though we be. Increase our knowledge of Christ, and bestow upon us more largely the graces of the Holy Spirit. Help us to raise our thoughts to heaven and heavenly things. Unite us more closely to Thee and to each other; and so united may we remain to the end of life—one in the fear of God, in the love of Christ, and in the hope of glory. Give to us, merciful Father, all the temporal good that we require. We thank Thee for the bounties of thy hand in times past. We thank Thee for health in the measure in which it has been granted to us, and for that gracious help we have received whenever, in trouble or difficulty, we have looked to Thee. So bless us, we beseech Thee, in the future, and let thy goodness and mercy follow us all the days of our life.

And now, Lord, as Abraham, thy servant, was allowed to intercede with Thee, do we desire to offer, so far as our weakness will permit, prayers, intercessions, and giving of thanks for all men. Cause godliness and honesty to prevail and to increase more and more amongst us. Dispose the hearts of those who are in authority to exercise their high office as under thine all-seeing eye, and in view of that account which all must render to Thee at last. May they hear, as Thou, O Lord, hearest, the cry of the oppressed; and, being both "a terror to evil-doers" and a "praise to them that do well," may they be the ministers of God unto their subjects for good. Grant, Lord, unto such rulers as truly confide in Thee support under every trial. Guide them in every time of perplexity, overrule all their plans and proceedings for good, and give unto them at length a crown of life.

And, O Lord, hear us when we offer "prayers for all men." Succour Thou the needy. Comfort those that are cast down. Save such as be contrite. Thou only knowest the *hearts* and the *wants* of the children of men; cause them, we beseech Thee, to trust in the shadow of thy wings. Specially do we pray that men everywhere may this day be enlightened by thy Spirit, and come to the knowledge of the truth. Reveal thy Son unto them, that through his infinite merits they may find pardon and peace.

These prayers for ourselves and others we offer, O Lord, through Christ, our only Saviour and Intercessor, who liveth and reigneth with Thee and with the Holy Spirit, one God blessed for evermore. Amen.

READ IN HOLY SCRIPTURE ST. LUKE IV. 14–31.

ALMIGHTY God, the Father of our Lord Jesus Christ, we thank Thee that we have heard of the wonderful grace and compassion of Him who came into the world to save sinners. We bless Thee that the land in which we live is filled with the fame of Him, and that the story of his great love is being told in these last days far and near. Oh, forgive us, merciful Father, that we have not glorified Him as we ought. We confess with sorrow our negligence and the hardness of our hearts, and humbly pray Thee for grace, that from henceforth our wandering eyes may be kept fastened on Him by whom Thou dost speak to us, and in whom are hid all the treasures of God. May our spiritual poverty be relieved out of his unsearchable riches; may He pour upon our spirits, when troubled and sad, the oil of joy. May his Divine power set us free from the sore bondage of sin, and in his light may we see light. Lord, increase our faith, and suffer not the clouds of doubt and unbelief to darken our hearts or dim the brightness of our confidence in thy promises. With unbounded trust we would look up to Thee, and in all things lean upon thy love and truth.

O God, our Father, in the name of Christ we cast ourselves upon thy loving care, beseeching Thee to bless us, according to our several necessities, with such things as Thou seest good for us. So reveal Thyself to us, and grant us such a sweet sense of thy presence, that while all is darkening around us we may have sunshine and joy within. Do Thou comfort our bodies with rest to-night. May we lie down in peace, and sleep, while Thou, O Lord, makest us dwell in safety.

We entreat Thee to remember with thy favour all our kindred, and those among whom we live; help us to do them good, and to seek their salvation, like the blessed Jesus, who did not forget Nazareth, where he had been brought up. May none whom we know and love reject Him as the Nazarenes did, but may his gracious words dwell in them richly in all wisdom. Let thy special grace be given to the little ones of this household. Lead them by thy Spirit to love what is good, and fulfil in them all thy purposes of mercy. O Lord, let the blessing promised to those who are not offended in Him rest upon us and all our dear ones; and so teach us to sit at his feet and learn of Him, that we may have grace rightly to discharge the duties, patiently to bear the troubles, and successfully to resist the temptations of life, and that, being made wise unto salvation, we may be brought at last to thy eternal glory. Hear and answer us, O Lord, for the alone sake of thy well beloved Son Jesus Christ, to whom, with thyself and the Holy Spirit, be everlasting praise. Amen.

[MORNING.] FIFTH WEEK.—TUESDAY. [EVENING.

READ IN HOLY SCRIPTURE GENESIS XIX. 1–30. READ IN HOLY SCRIPTURE ST. MATTHEW IV. 12–25.

ALMIGHTY and everlasting God, who dost govern all things, and in whom we live and move and have our being, accept our humble thanks for the mercies vouchsafed to us through another night. Grant that we may come to the throne of grace confessing our sins with contrite hearts, and pleading with earnest faith the merits of Jesus Christ. Thou who didst warn thy servant Lot to escape from the city of Sodom, lest he should be consumed with the wicked, hast also warned us to flee from the wrath to come, and lay hold on the hope set before us in the Gospel. Yet, O Lord, we have erred and strayed from thy ways like lost sheep. Altogether weak, unworthy, and full of sin, we have resisted the strivings of the Holy Spirit, and not hearkened to thy voice when Thou hast said, "Arise, and depart from your evil ways." Have mercy upon us, O God; deal not with us according to our sins, but for Christ's sake blot out all our transgressions. And if by thy grace we are resolved henceforth to live in Christ, and to walk not after the flesh, but after the Spirit, may we not look back with desire upon the pleasures of sin, but may we exercise ourselves to have a conscience void of offence toward God and man. When dangers threaten us, and temptations press heavily upon us, be Thou our refuge and strength. Lift upon us the light of thy countenance, and cause us to rejoice in thy salvation. Keep us back from all presumptuous sins—from sins of irreverence and self-sufficiency, of deliberate purpose, and of unsettled habit. Give unto us the spirit of watchfulness and prayer; deliver us from the sin which doth easily beset us, and from the sin to which we think we are not prone; make us to understand the purity of thy law and the deceitfulness of our own hearts, and cleanse Thou us from secret faults.

In tender compassion regard thy servants; cause thy face to shine upon us, and lead us in the way everlasting. Have mercy, O Lord, upon all who are oppressed by calamity, affliction, or bereavement, giving them the consolations of thy Gospel, and grace to say, "Thy will be done." Bless our Queen and all the members of the royal family; give prosperity to thy Church, and peace to all nations. Unite thy people in the fellowship of Jesus Christ, and in pity for the lost sheep of the house of Israel. Be gracious to all our friends, loving them as Thou hast loved us, with an everlasting love. Preserve us this day from all evil, and grant that we may be followers of Thee as dear children; that throughout life we may be faithful, loving, and without guile; and to Thee we shall ascribe all praise and glory, through Jesus Christ our Lord. Amen.

PRECIOUS to us, O Lord Jesus, is this record of thy character and labours. We hail Thee as the Day-spring from on high, which was to visit the world. Thou art the life and the light of men. We bless Thee that in the fulness of time Thou didst appear to the lost sheep of the house of Israel, as the predicted Sun of Righteousness; but we also praise Thee that in Galilee of the Gentiles, the people which sat in darkness saw great light, and to them which sat in the region and shadow of death light sprang up. We thank Thee that thy light has not been confined to Galilee, but that it has reached us. Let none of us close our eyes to this light. May it shine into our hearts.

But while we glory in Thee, O Lord Christ, for what thou art, we praise Thee for what thou hast done. As the great Teacher of man, Thou didst preach repentance and the kingdom of heaven when Thou wast on earth; and still Thou dost speak to us by thy Word, thy Spirit, and the preachers of thy Gospel. May none of us be disobedient to thy invitations and commands. We rejoice that Thou art able to save to the uttermost our souls and our bodies. Heal us, O Lord, for we have sinned against Thee.

As a family we come this evening to thy feet, O Jesus, remembering that our times are in thy hand. The temporal blessings we enjoy are more highly valued by us as thy gifts. The care and bounty of another day have laid us under deeper obligation to Thee. How many began this day who have not been permitted to see its close! How many have passed through suffering and trial, from which we have been preserved! But in the light of thy goodness our sins appear in their enormity. What neglect of Thee and opposition to thy will! What selfishness, earthliness, and unbelief! Have mercy upon us. Sprinkle us with thy precious blood. Sanctify us by thy Holy Spirit. Let thy goodness lead us to repentance. Make us more watchful, prayerful, earnest, and devoted.

Bless our relatives and friends. Regard with special favour the children of this family. Incline their hearts to do thy will, and teach them the preciousness of a Saviour's love. Comfort the sorrowful. Have mercy upon prayerless families, and hasten the time when incense and a pure offering shall ascend to Thee from all.

Watch over us during the night. Give rest and comfort. Let thine angels encamp around us, and when the fulness of the time shall come, exalt us to the blessedness and glory of heaven. And to the Father, the Son, and the Holy Spirit, shall be praise for evermore. Amen.

[Morning.]   FIFTH WEEK.—WEDNESDAY.   [Evening.]

READ IN HOLY SCRIPTURE ST. LUKE XVII. 11—32.

O GRACIOUS God, give to us the Spirit of grace and supplication. Enable us to worship Thee in spirit and in truth. Blessed Lord, draw nigh to us, and then we shall draw nigh to Thee. We are, indeed, by nature afar off from Thee. Our sins separate us from Thee. They rise up like a high mountain between Thee and us. Oh, that we may come to Thee through that new and living way which Jesus has consecrated for us through the rent veil of his flesh. In Him receive us graciously, and love us freely. In Him bless us with all spiritual and all temporal blessings this day. We thank Thee that thou hast preserved us to see the light of another day. We bless Thee that thou didst spread thy guardian wing over us during the past night. And now, Lord, renew thy mercies to us this morning. We need thy special care to sustain us under all the trials and temptations of life. We have no strength or sufficiency of our own. We confess our proneness to wander from Thee, and to yield to the snares and temptations which encompass us on every side. Keep Thou our feet, and then, and then only, shall we be safe. Hold Thou us up, O Lord. Guide us in the duties of this day. Enable us to set the Lord always before us. May we not forget that life is short, and that the Lord Jesus is at hand.

Make us to feel that this world is not our home. May the eye of our faith be steadily fixed upon the kingdom of heaven. May we seek first, in all things, and under all circumstances, the kingdom of God and thy righteousness. May we go forth to the duties of this day in the strength of our Lord, conscious at all times of thy presence and blessing. O our Lord, may not the world absorb our thoughts. Living *in* the world, may we be not *of* the world. May our treasure be in heaven, and our hearts be there also. May we receive grace to be willing to sacrifice health, reputation, yea, life itself, rather than lose thy favour. Be Thou our portion, and the lot of our inheritance for ever.

And now, O Lord, we beseech Thee to bless us all with thy Holy Spirit. Make all our relations and friends thy children. Take them under thy guardian care this day. Make them thine, and keep them thine for ever. Bless our beloved Sovereign, and bless our favoured country. Give wisdom to our senators, and enable them to rule in the fear of the Lord. Send forth thy light and thy truth into all lands. Hasten thine own coming, O Lord Jesus; and when Thou shalt appear, may we be found waiting for Thee.

Lord God, hear these our prayers, and grant these our requests, for the sake of Jesus Christ our Lord and Saviour. Amen.

READ IN HOLY SCRIPTURE ST. MATTHEW V. 1—16.

OUR Father, which art in heaven, we desire to glorify thy name. We are not worthy of the least of all thy mercies, and yet we are bidden by Thee to come and ask for the greatest of them all. We fall at thy feet, and ask Thee to make us citizens of thy heavenly kingdom. We have been selfish, and proud, and worldly, but we pray Thee to give us that Holy Spirit which can consume our lusts, and humble our pride, and enable us, from the depths of our spirits, to cry unto Thee, Abba, Father. We dare not disbelieve thy promise; and though often broken-hearted and crushed by our sins, we take Thee at thy word, and lay hold of thy strength, and desire nothing so much as to be at peace with Thee. We have an infinite need. May we hunger and thirst after thy righteousness. May we crave a peace that passes all understanding, and yearn after a joy that is unspeakable. We cry unto Thee to give us a perfect love, that can cast out all fear. We humble ourselves before Thee; Thou alone canst exalt us. We mourn; Thou alone canst comfort us. We are dark; Thou art able to shed such light upon us that we shall become children of the light and of the day, and be ourselves as lights in the world.

O God, Thou hast comforted us to-night by the gracious words of our Lord. He has blessed our hunger and thirst, our sense of helplessness, our consciousness of disease, our fears and our groanings. May we receive his righteousness, and be complete in Him. May his precious, atoning blood, cleanse us from all unrighteousness. May the purity of heart which He gives, the single eye which He bestows, see Thee, O living God. We wish to see Thee in Him, to see Thee in the dark mysteries of thy providence, in the wondrous things of thy law, and in the workings of our own hearts. We beseech Thee show us thy glory. Let us see Thee so clearly that this vision of thy face shall be an earnest of our purchased possession, a foretaste of heaven itself.

Another day is before Thee, and Thou seest all its sins, and neglect, and follies. Pardon and strengthen us. May to-morrow be a better, and happier, and holier day; and as the days pass by, may we have more of hope, and faith, and charity; more of Christ, and more of heaven in them. Watch over us, and all whom we love, to-night. Have mercy upon our sinful world. May all men acquaint themselves with Thee, and be at peace. O Christ, be our advocate with our Father and with thy Father to-night. And as we ask what we will, that it may be done unto us, may the Father be glorified in the Son: to whom, with the Holy Ghost, be all glory for ever. Amen.

[Morning.] FIFTH WEEK.—THURSDAY. [Evening.

READ IN HOLY SCRIPTURE 2 PETER II. 1—9.

O GOD! in whose hand are all our times, and who knowest how to deliver the godly out of temptations, save by thy name and judge us by thy strength. Let thy tender mercies come unto us, that we may live; and let thy merciful kindness be for our comfort, according to thy word. Thou, O Lord, art our confidence, and we beseech Thee to keep our foot from being taken; so will we walk in our way safely, and not be afraid of sudden fear, neither of the destruction of the wicked when it cometh. Deliver us, O Lord, from our enemies; we flee unto Thee to hide us. Mercifully send thine angel before us, to keep us in all our ways; and as Thou didst save thy servant Lot from the hand of unjust and cruel men, let it please Thee to preserve us in the hour of temptation, delivering our souls from death, our eyes from tears, and our feet from falling.

Almighty God, who requirest truth in the inward parts, create in us a clean heart, that we, escaping the corruption that is in the world through lust, may do those things which are well pleasing unto Thee, so that finally we may obtain the salvation that is in Christ Jesus, with eternal glory.

Father of all our mercies, we give thanks unto Thee for thy great goodness which Thou hast laid up for those that fear Thee, which Thou hast wrought for them that trust in Thee before the sons of men. Accept our morning sacrifice of praise for thy watchful care over us during the sleep and the silence of night—for renewed life, and health, and reason, and all the blessings of this life. Above all, we bless Thee for thine inestimable love in the redemption of the world by our Lord Jesus Christ, for the means of grace, and for the hope of glory. And we beseech Thee give us that due sense of all thy mercies, that our hearts may be unfeignedly thankful, and often we may show forth thy praise not only with our lips, but in our lives, by giving up ourselves to thy service, and by walking before Thee in righteousness and holiness all our days. Mercifully keep us this day from evil, and prosper us in the work of our hands. Bless us, O our Father, as a family, with all who are dear unto us. Hear us for the good estate of thy whole Church and for the salvation of all men. Let thy Word run and be glorified. Bring many hearts this day to thy dear Son in repentance and faith. Bless our country and our Queen, with all in authority over us. Comfort all who are in sorrow, and heal the broken in heart; and this we beg through Jesus Christ, our only Mediator and Saviour.

The grace of our Lord Jesus Christ, the love of God, and the communion of the Holy Ghost be with us all. Amen.

READ IN HOLY SCRIPTURE ST. MATTHEW V. 17—48.

O ALMIGHTY and gracious God, whose we are and whom we serve, we draw nigh to Thee this evening as a family, to adore and praise Thee. Very near and very gracious hast Thou been to us. Strength to labour, food to eat, a home to receive us, are the least of all thy gifts. Thou hast given us to have fellowship with Thyself and thy dear Son, and we know that the blood of Jesus Christ cleanseth from all sin. How else can we draw near to Thee in this our evening prayer? Breakers of thy law, condemned by it and by conscience, "our sin ever before us," what can we do? We can make no atonement, nor offer a ransom for our forfeited souls. But what we cannot do Thou hast done. "Christ has redeemed us from the curse of the law, being made a curse for us."

Delivered from the curse—a redeemed family, enable us to serve Thee in all holy obedience. Constrained by the love of Christ, never let us think little of sin, never let us live unto ourselves. Put thy law into our inward parts, and write it in our hearts; and be our God, and let us be thy people.

We thank Thee for thy law, which is holy, just, and good. Make it, in thy Spirit's hands, our guide, and our rule. Search us by it, show us ourselves, reprove us, humble us. Convince us of all sin. We ask Thee to spare no evil in us; we would be nearer and more like to Thee. O Jesus! let thy words ever abide in us: "Be ye perfect, even as your Father in heaven is perfect."

How much we owe Thee, O our God, for thy law; and to Thee, O our Saviour, that Thou hast taught us how broad, and spiritual, and searching it is. We do stand condemned by it for an impure look, an evil thought, and a hasty word. Keep us, O our God; keep our hearts, our lips, our ways; let us not offend Thee. Enable us to do what Thou hast commanded, and to cease to do what Thou hast forbidden. Teach us to love our enemies; to return good for evil; to remember others as Thou hast remembered us, that we may be the children of our Father which is in heaven.

O God, we confess this evening how much we have done that we ought not to have done. We pray Thee to forgive us. Remember what we are—poor sinners, so ready to fall, and quite unable to arise without Thee. Withhold not from us thy rich blessing, but grant us to lie down at peace with Thee, happy in thy forgiving love, confident in thy care, and looking forward with growing desire to the appearing of our God and Saviour.

Bless our dear relations and friends. Visit with thy salvation each heart and home around us; send thy Gospel to the heathen, and gather in thy ancient people, for Christ's sake. Amen.

[33]

[Morning.] **FIFTH WEEK.—FRIDAY.** [Evening.

READ IN HOLY SCRIPTURE GENESIS XXI. 1–21.

MOST gracious God, on coming into thy presence, we acknowledge Thee as the God of truth and power, and believe that what Thou hast promised Thou art able and willing to perform. Look favourably upon us and bless us, for the sake of Him in whom all thy promises are faithfulness and truth.

We entreat Thee to accept our humble offering of praise for having again permitted us to experience thy goodness during another night. It is of thy mercies we are not consumed.

We read in thy Word that Thou didst make unto thy servants of old, the patriarchs, many rich promises. These Thou didst graciously fulfil, in their protection and guidance, and in accomplishing thy Divine purposes concerning them. We praise Thee for these examples, written for our learning, and pray to be encouraged and instructed by them. May we rejoice that there are given to us also exceeding great and precious promises, so that by them we may be made partakers of the Divine nature. Grant that, having these, it may be our endeavour this day to cleanse ourselves from all sinfulness of the flesh and spirit. Bring us, we beseech Thee, O Father of all our mercies, more fully into the enjoyment of thy promises made to us in Christ Jesus our Lord. Renew and sanctify our hearts by thy Holy Spirit. Help us prayerfully to seek circumcision of the heart and the spirit: that we may worship Thee in the spirit, and rejoice in Christ Jesus, having no confidence in the flesh. Enable us faithfully to perform the duties in which we shall engage this day. As members of a Christian family, may we love each other fervently, and avoid everything in word and deed which would offend Thee and destroy that harmony which should exist among us. Grant that we may strive to carry into all our engagements the spirit of truth, peace, unity, and concord. Oh, forbid that we should be careless and unconcerned about these things. To this end impress our minds with the solemn truth that Thou God seest us; that wherever we are, whether at home or abroad, we cannot be where Thou art not.

O Lord, we now commit ourselves to thy care. Point out the way of safety in all that we have to do, and help us to walk therein. Oh, that we may listen this day in all things to the promptings and warnings of the Holy Spirit, and not grieve him by our wilfulness and disobedience. Thou knowest our weaknesses and wants, how many and constant they are. Oh, supply all our need out of thy abundance, and bring us safely to thy kingdom of glory, through Jesus Christ our Lord, in whose name we ask every blessing. Amen.

READ IN HOLY SCRIPTURE ROMANS XII.

O THOU fountain of all goodness! we thank Thee for thy watchful care over us this day, for the supplies of thy kind providence, and for the strength which has enabled us to discharge the duties of life. Follow, we pray Thee, with thy blessing all the lawful occupations of the day, and give success to all our endeavours to do good to others, and to get good to ourselves.

May our sins and imperfections, our mistakes and neglects, be all forgiven, for our Saviour's sake. Oh, sprinkle us afresh with his precious blood. Wash us, and keep us clean, that we may be enabled to perfect holiness in the fear of the Lord.

Do thou help us, O Lord, to gain wisdom from the experience of the past. May we not go needlessly into scenes and circumstances that have proved dangerous to us. May we never trifle with temptation. May we never think lightly of sin. In every hour of peril, O gracious Deliverer, be Thou at our right hand, and bring us off more than conquerors through Him who loved us.

May the lessons now read from thy Word be written upon our memories and our hearts. Save us from a spirit of resentment; help us to return good for evil, and to follow the example of Him who prayed even for his murderers. Save us from vain and lofty thoughts about ourselves, and help us to learn of Him who was meek and lowly in heart. Save us from slothfulness, from dishonesty, and from the spirit that engenders strife. O thou Giver of all grace, qualify us, we beseech Thee, for every office we have to fill and every duty we have to perform. May we serve the Lord even in our daily business; and may our common occupations be sanctified by godly motives prompting them, and by the religious spirit in which they are undertaken.

We acknowledge, O Thou who art our Creator and Redeemer, that by many ties we are thine. And now we desire, constrained by thy multiplied mercies toward us, to present ourselves a living sacrifice unto God. Graciously accept us in and through thy beloved Son. And may we be so filled with thy Holy Spirit, that henceforth we may continually live under the recollection that we are not our own, but thine.

We pray Thee to bless our relations and friends, our neighbours and our fellow-Christians. May they all share in thy fatherly protection, and be all partakers of thy heavenly grace. Do Thou guard our habitation during the night, and fit us all, if it please Thee, by refreshing sleep, for the duties and enjoyments of the coming day. Hear these our prayers, and breathe on us thy evening blessing, for Christ's sake. Amen.

[34]

[MORNING.] **FIFTH WEEK.—SATURDAY.** [EVENING.]

READ IN HOLY SCRIPTURE GALATIANS IV.

READ IN HOLY SCRIPTURE ST. MATTHEW VI. 1-18.

O LORD, our Lord, we thank Thee for the tender mercy and watchful care that have preserved our lives to the beginning of another day, and for the great and many blessings of every kind by which we are surrounded; but we more especially thank Thee that through the atonement of thy dear Son we may come unto Thee this morning as children to a loving Father; not as servants, but as sons, even as the sons and daughters of the Lord God Almighty. May we more thoroughly enjoy and more highly value the manner of love that has been bestowed upon us that we should be called thy children, and may we be helped to look forward with joyful expectation to that blessed time when we shall be with Thee, our Father, in the house of many mansions. We ask Thee to help us to-day to walk worthy of this high vocation whereunto we are called, and to assist us to show in our conduct, and by our words and spirit, whose we are and whom we serve. May our light so shine before men that they, seeing our good works, may glorify our Father in heaven. Give us grace and wisdom this day rightly to fulfil the duties devolving on us in our varied stations and relationships. Teach us, O God, our Father, in all things, to see Thee, and to do everything as to the Lord and not as unto men; not with eye-service, as men-pleasers, but as the children of God, doing the will of God from the heart. We pray Thee that Thou wouldst so send forth thy light and thy truth that all people may come to know Thee and to serve Thee as their Father. Gather out thy children from the uttermost parts of the earth; and may those who are now living far from Thee, without God and without hope in the world, be drawn by the teachings of thy blessed Spirit unto Jesus Christ, and through him call Thee Father.

May thy kingdom, O Lord, come into every land, and may Thy will be done on earth as it is in heaven. We would pray for all our kindred and friends, specially for those in affliction, whether of mind, body, or estate. It is our joy to know that although some whom we love may be far off from us, they cannot be far from Thee; thine eye is on them as it is on us, and Thou knowest all their needs. Lord, bless them, we pray Thee, with needful grace, and in thine own good time give them a happy issue out of all their afflictions.

To Thee we commit ourselves for this day. Defend us from the dangers which may beset us in body or soul. Constrain us, by the love of Christ, to do thy will and to please Thee in all things. Grant us these mercies and all else that is good for us according to thy gracious promises, for Jesus Christ's sake. Amen.

O LORD, the great and mighty God; the high and lofty One, that inhabiteth eternity, whose name is holy, in bowing at thy feet we remember that Thou hast said, "To this man will I look, even to him that is poor and of a contrite spirit, and trembleth at my word." Thou resistest the proud, but givest grace to the humble. We feel it to be condescension in Thee to permit us to approach Thee, and therefore would put far from us the thought that we can lay Thee under obligation by our prayers and services. Our goodness cannot reach to Thee. Save us from pride and self-complacency in our services. Give us a deep conviction of our weakness, imperfection, and sin, and convince us that not for our righteousness' sake, but for thy great mercy, in Christ Jesus, we are accepted by Thee. Deliver us, O Lord, from all hypocrisy; let us not draw nigh to Thee with the mouth and honour Thee with the lip, while the heart is far from Thee. Save us from doing our works that they may be seen of men, and grant that our charity and devotion may be acceptable in thy sight, who seest in secret and rewardest openly. Suffer us not to be deceived by a formal and external religion, which rests in prayers and gifts, and keeps back the soul from God. Thou searchest the hearts and triest the reins of men; therefore may we not offer to Thee heartless service. Purify us from all unworthy motive in thy service, and let us not regard iniquity in our hearts, lest Thou shouldst not hear us. Pour upon us the spirit of true worship; Thou who didst teach thy disciples how to pray, teach us to pray. While every evening on which we gather around our family altar we have cause for thankfulness and praise, specially so is it this evening. A week's mercies present themselves for acknowledgment.

Day has followed day, and thy goodness has been new every morning and fresh every evening. As a family, our bread has been given and our water has been sure. Death has not come up into our dwelling, and affliction has not been laid upon our loins. Bless the Lord, O our souls. But, alas! our sins stand out before us in the light of thy goodness; enter not into judgment with us. We look to the cross. For Christ's sake, O Lord, blot out our sins of omission and of commission.

And now the Sabbath draws on. Give us a preparation blessing; preserve us from all evil this night; give us, as thy beloved, sleep. Let us awake refreshed and fitted for the service of the Lord. To Thee we commit ourselves and all dear to us, and we pray that the whole earth may be visited with thy salvation. Now to the Father, the Son, and the Holy Ghost, be glory everlasting. Amen.

[35]

[Morning.]　　　SIXTH WEEK.—LORD'S DAY.　　　[Evening.]

READ IN HOLY SCRIPTURE GENESIS XXII. 1–19.　　READ IN HOLY SCRIPTURE ST. MATTHEW VI. 19–34.

WE bless Thee, most gracious God, that Thou hast been pleased to set apart one day in seven for thy own worship and the welfare of the human race. We thank Thee for the peace and the rest brought unto us by the Sabbath morning, and we humbly ask of Thee grace to help us, that we may serve Thee with reverence and with godly fear. Make this day a season of spiritual instruction and heavenly joy unto our souls. Wherever thy holy Word shall be proclaimed, and the way of salvation through Jesus Christ made known to-day, there, O Lord, bestow thy blessing. Hear the prayers and accept the praises of all saints, and grant unto all faithful preachers and teachers of thy truth grace from on high, so that poor sinners may come to the knowledge of our Lord and Saviour, and those who have believed in him may grow in grace and holiness.

Bless all our dear relations, friends, and neighbours, and in thy great mercy grant that our beloved children may know and serve Thee, and walk in thy ways all the days of their life.

Heavenly Father, we entreat Thee to apply to our hearts the lessons we have now heard from the ancient Scriptures. Make us the children of faithful Abraham, so that like him we may believe thy promises, obey thy commands, and patiently wait thy holy will. We adore Thee that Thou didst so love the world as to give thy only begotten Son a sacrifice for sin. Help us, good Lord, truly to believe in Jesus, and to rest assured that Thou wilt provide for all our wants, and conduct us in safety to thy heavenly kingdom. What can we render unto Thee in return for thy great love to us? A broken and contrite heart, O God, Thou wilt not despise. Feeling that we have nothing, and are nothing of ourselves, we cast ourselves at thy feet, and pray that we may love Thee more and serve Thee better than we have done before.

Fulfil, we beseech Thee, thy ancient promise that all nations of the earth shall be blessed in Christ. Smile upon all efforts to bring the heathen unto him, and let all sorrow, and ignorance, and sin be banished before the brightness of his glorious coming.

And now that we are about to go unto thy house, we praise Thee that we need no burnt offering, but we ask that the holy fire of love may glow in our hearts, that we may be free from all the cares and business of the world. Deliver us, O Lord, from all wandering thoughts and temptations of Satan, and grant unto us the pardon of all our sins, for the sake of our Lord Jesus Christ, to whom, with Thee, O Father, and the Holy Spirit, we will render all praise and glory, both now and for evermore. Amen.

ADORED be thy name, O God, for the many and undeserved blessings of this day. We thank Thee for its rest from toil. We thank Thee for its priceless privileges; we thank Thee for the ordinances of thy house, for the opportunities of prayer and of the hearing of thy Word; for whatever communion we have had with Thee, and for every assurance of thy grace which has fallen on our ears and our hearts. We feel, as we look back on the services of the day, how unworthy they have been of thy regard. We have not worshipped Thee as we ought; our desires have been contracted, our faith has been weak, our praises languid.

Oh, how little have we felt the guiltiness of the sins we have confessed; with what coldness of heart have we sought thy pardon! We confess, O God, the sin of our confessions, and pray Thee to pardon this and all those other sins which thy searching eye has detected in us. Let not this Sabbath-day be remembered to our shame and condemnation in thy judgment.

Gracious Spirit, it is thine to guide us into all truth, and to apply the Word of God with power to the heart. Arouse our consciences, we pray Thee, to feel that what we have heard and read this day is the message of the living God to us. Fix its lessons on our hearts, that we may remember them not only now as we look up from our knees to the throne of God, but to-morrow and every day, when we go forth to discharge the duties and face the temptations of busy life. Let not the Word sown this day fall to the ground. Deepen every impression which has been made in our own hearts or the hearts of others. Confirm and strengthen every resolution. O God, let thy truth be mighty, through Divine grace to subdue the strongholds of sin and the world to the love of Thee and of thy dear Son. May his praises be sung anew this night by many converted souls.

Lord, we are comforted by the assurance of thy fatherly care, as it is proclaimed to us by the grass of the field and the fowls of the air. Oh, let us never distrust Thee or doubt thy goodness. We will confide in Thee more and more. Lord, we believe; help our unbelief. Enable us to seek first and above all things thy glory and the fulfilment of thy work in our hearts, and to commit all our anxieties and cares to Thee. Preserve us, O God, from over-carefulness; and enable us so to pass through things temporal that we finally lose not the things which are eternal. We ask these things for ourselves and all who are dear to us, and we commend them and ourselves this night to thy holy keeping, in the name of our Lord and Saviour Jesus Christ. Amen.

[Morning.] SIXTH WEEK.—MONDAY. [Evening.

READ IN HOLY SCRIPTURE HEBREWS XI. 1—19.

O GOD, our Father, which art in heaven, look down upon us from thy dwelling-place; behold us gathered in the name of Jesus, thy dear Son, and for his sake grant the petitions that we desire of Thee.

Thou, O God, art good and gracious; Thou art a rewarder of them that diligently seek Thee; and though we see Thee not, yet we believe Thou art not far from any one of us, but especially near us now, when we draw nigh unto Thee.

Help us to come before Thee with true humility of heart, not trusting in our own righteousness, but in thy great mercy and pardoning love through Jesus Christ. Accept us in him. Look upon the sacrifice which he made for us; for he is the Lamb of God, who, by the sacrifice of himself once made, taketh away the sin of the world.

Grant us grace that we may henceforth serve Thee in newness of life; and may it be our daily endeavour so to live as to please Thee. Enable us, by the help of thy Holy Spirit, to walk before Thee in all holiness, uprightness, and godliness; and when our time to die shall come, may we rest in peace, and in certain hope of a resurrection to eternal life, through the merits of Jesus.

O Thou who art the God of all the families of the earth, be thou our God, our Guide through life. Keep us as we journey on to that heaven which we desire for our home. May we never seek our rest here; but by pressing forward and raising our thoughts and desires above earthly things, look for a better country, that is, an heavenly.

We pray Thee, O Lord, to increase the number of true believers. May thy Word have free course in our land. May thy Sabbaths be better observed. May the houses of prayer be filled with true worshippers. Bless all who preach thy Word; clothe them with righteousness; and may many, by their warning, be led to flee from the wrath to come, and to take refuge in Jesus, that they may be saved in the day of account.

And now, O Lord, we beseech Thee to accept our thanks for the mercies of the past, and for the renewal of them this morning; and we ask for thy special assistance to help us in every time of need that may occur to us this day. Thou knowest what is before us, and how great is our ignorance and weakness: if it be temptation, show us the way to escape, that we may be able to bear it; if it be trial, give us patience, and, in thine own good time and way, a happy end to the trouble. May thy good promises be ever before our minds, and grant that they may be fulfilled to us, for the sake of Jesus Christ, our Saviour. Amen.

READ IN HOLY SCRIPTURE PSALM CIII.

O THOU gracious and eternal Jehovah, who art the strength of all who trust thee, the light of all who see thee, and the life of all who love thee: Thou art most worthy of the praises of heaven and earth. Help us, a little band, whose hearts have been touched by thy love, to draw near unto Thee, that we may join the great company who do continually show forth thy praise. Glory be to thy holy name for all the blessings Thou hast conferred upon us during the day that is now drawing to a close. We thank Thee for all the comforts we have enjoyed, and for all the evils from which we have been spared; and we desire to be deeply grateful for the privileges enjoyed by us during the Sabbath which is past. May the good seed of the kingdom which has been sown in our hearts bring forth fruit in our lives, and in the lives of all who have been our fellow-worshippers. Teach us to hide thy Word in our hearts, so that we may not sin against Thee. And we pray Thee, good Lord, to comfort those who by sickness, or infirmity, or any lawful impediment, were deprived of the means of grace, and supply them, by thy good Spirit, with holy thoughts and heavenly desires.

Thou kind and merciful Father, we praise Thee for all thy bounties. Never let us forget thy love to us, for it is wonderful. We are of yesterday, and know nothing. Thou art the same yesterday, to-day, and for ever. Yet Thou dost not despise or forget us. We are guilty of sins without number. Thou art of purer eyes than to behold iniquity; yet Thou hast not dealt with us after our sins, nor rewarded us according to our iniquities. We die, but thine undying mercy endureth throughout all generations. Let the people praise Thee, O God; yea, let all the people praise Thee. Cause us to feel the uncertainty of our lives, and to be continually prepared for death; and grant that our children after us may sing of thy righteousness, and be a seed to serve Thee, and a generation to call Thee blessed.

May thy kind and watchful providence protect all beneath this roof during the night upon which we have entered; bless us with refreshing sleep; preserve us from danger, and let us rise in the morning, to pursue the duties of daily life in a spirit of humble faith and holy diligence, anxious in all things to do that which will please Thee. Forgive, most merciful God, all that has been amiss in us this day. In many things we all offend; but we bless Thee that the blood of Jesus Christ cleanseth us from all sin. Through him we ascribe unto Thee, Lord God Almighty, the kingdom, and the power, and the glory, world without end. Amen.

[Morning.] SIXTH WEEK.—TUESDAY. [Evening.

READ IN HOLY SCRIPTURE ST. JOHN VIII. 30—59.

O GOD of Abraham, Isaac, and Jacob, who keepest covenant with thy people for ever, help us, with the return of another day, to make suitable acknowledgments to Thee for the mercies of the past night. We bless Thee that through the hours of darkness Thou wast our protector from all evil. Now, while the light is shining around us, defend us from every danger, seen and unseen. Hold Thou us up, and we shall be safe.

We this morning renew our vows of obedience and service. Help us to keep them. We would again exercise our dependence upon Thee, and be childlike in our reliance. Give us a confiding heart, that trusts Thee where it cannot trace Thee; and an obedient heart, ready to do thy will without a murmur, and without a doubt. Make us ready thus to submit and deny ourselves, by the remembrance of thy wonderful love to us, in that Thou didst not withhold thy Son, thine only Son, from us. We rejoice that the day of Christ, which Abraham saw afar off with sacred joy, has dawned upon the earth; and that He who dwelt in the bosom of the Father has come into the world to save sinners, even the chief, having laid down his life as a ransom for many. May we, and all men, have that faith in thy blessed Son which shall lead to the saving of the soul. We would look with holy awe upon the Lamb of God who taketh away the sin of the world; and, while we mourn over the transgressions which rendered necessary so costly a sacrifice, we admire and adore the love that so freely gave him up for us all.

Under the influence of grateful feelings, may we faithfully discharge the duties of this day: be diligent in business, fervent in spirit, serving the Lord. As Thou hast formed us for thy praise, may we glorify Thee in our body and in our spirit, which are thine. May we recommend religion to all around us, by the evenness of our temper, the gentleness of our spirit, the truthfulness of our words, and the uprightness of our actions. If, during the day, temptation should assail us, and our easily besetting sins should seek to lead us astray, O God, forsake us not. And if, through the weakness of our faith and the deceitfulness of our hearts, we should sin against Thee, cast us not away from thy presence, and take not thy Holy Spirit from us.

Bless the whole world. Where ignorance exists, there send thy light and thy truth. Where sorrow dwells, send consolation. Where affliction and poverty are found, let thy goodness minister to the wants of them that are exercised thereby, and let the trials of earth prepare us for the blessedness of heaven. Grant all these mercies, O God, our loving Father, for Jesus' sake. Amen.

READ IN HOLY SCRIPTURE ST. MATTHEW VII.

O GOD, our heavenly Father, encouraged by the gracious promises of thy holy Word, we come to Thee. Thou art the fountain of all life and the source of all blessing. Thou art the Creator and the upholder of heaven and earth, and all things, visible and invisible. As children return to their home, seeking the blessing and protection of their parents, so we this night come to Thee as our heavenly Father. Reveal thyself to us, O Father, that we may see Thee. Stretch out thy hand to us, that we may lay hold upon Thee. Make us to feel thy love, that our hearts may grow warm with love to Thee. May thy presence and blessing make us so glad here in our earthly home, that we may anticipate with holy desire the time when we shall behold thy face, and dwell for ever with Thee in our heavenly home.

With a father's love, O Lord, thou hast watched over us every moment of this day. Thou hast gone before us, shedding thy blessing on our path. Though we have not seen Thee, thou hast been walking at our side, to strengthen, guide, and protect us. How good, how kind, how loving thou art, O Lord! We have not deserved this favour from Thee. Whilst Thou, O Father, hast been caring for us, we have been slighting Thee; whilst Thou hast blessed us, we have sinned against Thee. With shame and sorrow, O Lord, we confess our sins; and for the sake of Jesus Christ we beseech Thee to have mercy upon us, and pardon all our offences. Without thy forgiveness, O Lord, we cannot sleep this night in peace. Blot out our transgressions, and assure us of thy forgiving love.

We ask thy gracious assistance, O God, that we may henceforth live in obedience to thy law. Let thy Holy Spirit guide us, that we may enter in at the strait gate, and walk in the narrow way that leads to eternal life. We are prone to do evil; Holy Spirit, sanctify our desires, our thoughts and motives, that we may learn to do well. Dispose our hearts to love that which is holy, and help us to bring forth the fruits of holiness in our lives, to the praise and glory of God.

The shadows of evening close around us, and soon the darkness of death will cover us; then, O Lord, our state will be fixed for the judgment of the great day. We tremble, O Lord, at the thought that thou mightest then say to some of us, "Depart, ye cursed; I never knew you." Oh, that we may build upon the sure Foundation, that we may be saved in that day.

We pray for all our relations and friends, that Thou wilt mercifully grant them thy grace, and bring them to thy heavenly kingdom, through Jesus Christ our Lord. Amen.

[Morning.]   SIXTH WEEK.—WEDNESDAY.   [Evening.]

READ IN HOLY SCRIPTURE GENESIS XXIII.

READ IN HOLY SCRIPTURE ST. LUKE V. 1—16.

O OUR God, the God of all the families of the earth, regard us in thy mercy, and accept our prayer. We ought indeed to praise Thee and to trust in Thee. Day by day Thou hast blessed us; we have wanted no good thing; and better than all, Thou hast given to us thy dear Son. We thank Thee for him, thine inestimable gift. We thank Thee for thy Book which tells of the Saviour, and of how he lived, and suffered, and died for us. O God, awaken in us ever more and more a spirit of praise and thankfulness. Make us so to feel thy goodness, that it may be our desire and our joy to consecrate the life, and strength, and talents which Thou hast given to thy service.

O God, we confess, at thy footstool, our many misdoings, the coldness and deadness of our hearts under the experience of thy loving mercy, the weakness of our faith in thy promises, our frequent disobedience to thy commandments in thought, and word, and deed. Pardon us for these things, we pray Thee. Look upon thy dear Son, and for his sake refuse not our prayer.

Graciously be with us in all the varying circumstances of this day, and by thy Holy Spirit teach us more perfectly the knowledge of thy Word and will. Impress on our hearts the solemn lessons of the chapter we have now read. Grant that whenever Thou sendest to us the afflictive dispensations of thy providence, we may bow ourselves submissively beneath thy chastening hand. Grant that we may see in the death of others the evidence of our own mortality, and give all diligence to make our calling and election sure, that when Thou demandest an account of our stewardship, we may render it up with joy, and not with grief.

Enable us, in all our dealings with others, to be examples of Christian courtesy and unselfishness, of humility and meekness, showing the very mind of Christ, and striving in all things to be like him, and to tread in his footsteps, who did no sin, nor was deceit found in his mouth. Thou knowest, O God, how, through our sins and wickedness, we are sore let and hindered in running the race that is set before us; do Thou, in thy bountiful grace and mercy, help and deliver us, that this day we may be kept from all that would displease Thee.

Look, in thy compassion, upon all who are dear to us. May our relations and friends know both Thee and thy dear Son, and have all peace and joy in believing. Comfort them if they are in sorrow. Sustain and help them in every hour of need. Make all things work together for their spiritual and eternal welfare, and bring them and us in safety to thine everlasting kingdom, for the sake of Jesus Christ our Lord and Saviour. Amen.

L ORD Jesus, our blessed Saviour, we rejoice to know that Thou art the same yesterday, to-day, and for ever; that as in the days of thy life on earth Thou wert ever touched with pity for the infirmities of those who sought thy help, so now that Thou art ascended up on high, Thou ever livest to make intercession for us. Still may we come to Thee, assured that Thou wilt not turn away our prayer nor thy mercy from us. We ask Thee, O Lord, this night, to cleanse us from the leprosy of sin. We acknowledge that we are sinners before Thee, that we have no hope but in thy mercy, through Christ Jesus. We rejoice to know that we may come unto Thee, that Thou art a God pardoning iniquity, transgression, and sin, and that Thou hast sent thy Spirit into the world that our hearts may be drawn to the Saviour, and be cleansed from the defilement of all iniquity. We pray thee, O Lord, to make us holy, even as Thou art holy; to strengthen us with all might by thy Spirit in the inner man, that Christ may dwell in our hearts by faith; and to grant that every day we may grow more and more like Him who came to set us an example that we should walk in his steps.

We thank Thee for all the mercies that have attended us through the past day. Goodness and mercy have followed us all the days of our lives, and with grateful hearts we offer the sacrifice of praise and thanksgiving. Have mercy upon all our fellow-creatures who are destitute of the blessings that we enjoy; relieve the necessities of the poor; succour and comfort the sick and dying; break the yoke of the slave, and let the oppressed go free. Above all, we pray that the knowledge of Jesus may be spread throughout the earth, so that sin and misery may be known no more. May every effort made to extend this knowledge be blessed of Thee. Give success to the labours of all missionaries at home and abroad; encourage them in their work by thy gracious presence and evident blessing; give them the great joy of seeing the degraded and ignorant among whom they labour become enlightened and holy followers of the Lamb of God. Especially have mercy on the thousands in our own country who shut their eyes against the light of the Gospel, and choose darkness rather than light, because their deeds are evil. Save them, we pray Thee, and make our beloved country a holy and happy nation, serving Thee. Now, O Lord, we commit ourselves to thy care and protection for the night. It is our joy to know that while we are sleeping Thou art watching over us; that thy watchful eyes are ever open toward us. Hear our prayers and bless us now and for ever, for Jesus Christ's sake. Amen.

[MORNING.]   SIXTH WEEK.—THURSDAY.   [EVENING.

READ IN HOLY SCRIPTURE GALATIANS III. 13–29.   READ IN HOLY SCRIPTURE ST. LUKE V. 17–39.

O GOD, blessed be thy name that the great promise of a Saviour, which was given in Paradise, was revealed more fully through succeeding ages and generations; and that the law, in its commandments and ordinances, was constituted a schoolmaster to bring men to Christ.

How glorious is thy grace in Jesus the Redeemer! Not by works of righteousness which we have done, but according to thy mercy in Christ, we are saved. God forbid that we should seek to establish our own righteousness, but may we cordially submit to the righteousness of faith. Let the blessing of Abraham rest upon us through Jesus, and may those precious truths of thy Word which we have read this morning often come with power to our hearts.

We committed ourselves to thy protection and blessing on the past evening, and thou didst give thine angels charge over us. Under the shadow of thy wings we have rested securely. We laid us down and slept, and awaked, for the Lord sustained us. Now that a new day dawns upon us, with gratitude we implore Thee to shine into our hearts, and give us the light of the knowledge of thy glory in the face of Jesus Christ. We know not what is before us. Each day brings its duties and temptations, and lays us under fresh obligations.

Help us to commit ourselves to our several works and ways in thy fear. May we carry about with us a sense of thy presence everywhere and in all things, and be diligent in business, fervent in spirit, serving the Lord. Preserve us from the numerous temptations and enemies that may surround us, and help us to keep our hearts with all diligence, remembering that out of them proceed the issues of life.

Open thine hand, and graciously supply us with all necessary good. Let us, as a family, be prospered, in going out and coming in. May we seek to do good, as well as to get good, to-day. Bless our relatives and friends. May those who are unconverted be subdued to the obedience of faith. Let thy comforts delight the souls of all thy people.

Pour out thy Spirit upon the world, and let thy salvation fill the earth. Send forth more labourers to the great work of winning souls to Christ and edifying thy Church. Oh endue them with thy good Spirit. Make them wise themselves, that with wisdom they may teach others. Lord, grant them a large measure of thy presence, and great success in their work. Accept this our morning sacrifice, O Lord, and let the lifting up of our hands be as incense, through Jesus Christ our Lord. Amen.

GRACIOUS Lord God, Father of our Saviour Jesus Christ, be pleased to accept our united praise for the favours bestowed upon us during the day now about to close. Now that we are again assembled in thy presence to worship Thee, may our hearts be so impressed with a deep sense of thy fatherly goodness, that our souls may be devoutly raised in this our evening service. Truly we can say, Thou hast been mindful of us in all the dangers and duties through which we have been brought.

Yet in making these our grateful acknowledgments, we have abundant cause to come in deep humility before Thee, at the remembrance of our sins. How often we have offended against thy Divine Majesty this day, Thou only knowest. We cannot dissemble, nor hide any fault or misconduct from Thee. Give us, therefore, at this time, the spirit of true repentance; pardon our sins, negligences, and ignorances.

We are encouraged in our petitions by thine own Word. Thou biddest us to come in faith unto the throne of thy grace to seek mercy. It is Thou alone who forgivest our sins, healest our diseases, deliverest our souls from destruction, and crownest us with loving-kindness and tender mercies. Be pleased, we beseech Thee, O Father of mercy, for thy Son's sake, to pardon our offences and cleanse us from all unrighteousness.

That we may more faithfully serve Thee for the future, endue us with grace to amend our lives according to thy holy will. Let thine eternal Spirit so dwell in our souls and bodies, that whether we sleep or wake, live or die, we may be thine.

Impress our minds with a high sense of thy majesty, power, and glory. Help us all to see that thy works proclaim the greatness of thy name and the wondrous character of thy nature. Whenever we think or speak of Thee, whenever we offer praise and prayer, may it be with the recollection that Thou art the Lord God Almighty, glorious in holiness, fearful in praises, doing wonders. Keep also before our eyes thy Son Jesus Christ. Help us to study and adore his character, and so to follow his footsteps as becometh the disciples of a pure and holy Master.

Give thy blessing to our Sovereign, to the rulers of our land, and to the ministers and members of thy holy Church. Save the sick and all in any adversity.

To thy fatherly care we commend our family, relations, friends, and neighbours. The Lord bless us and keep us, and make his face to shine upon us, both now and evermore, for Christ's sake. Amen.

[40]

MORNING.] SIXTH WEEK.—FRIDAY. [EVENING.

READ IN HOLY SCRIPTURE GENESIS XXIV. 1—31.

MERCIFUL God and Father, fulfil now thy gracious promise, as in the name of thy dear Son we come into thy presence, and make known at thy footstool all our care. It is of thy goodness we have been kept safely through the night, and that in the renewed experience of morning mercies we are permitted to unite at thy footstool in thanksgiving and praise. Lord, let not thy daily blessings fall on cold and thankless hearts. How have we failed to realise the exceeding abundance of thy Divine compassions; how contracted is our knowledge of the precious and priceless gift of thy dear Son. Forgive us, we pray Thee, this and all our other sins. Speak peace to our souls, and make known to us our forgiveness, by shedding upon our hearts the sweet sense of thy reconciling love and pardoning grace.

In thy name and in thy fear we desire to go forth to the duties of this day. We look up to Thee for protection and guidance. Go Thou with us wherever we go; be Thou with us wherever we are. Stand Thou between us and all dangers. Turn aside the shafts of evil which may be launched against us by the malice of Satan, or the unkindness of our fellow-men. All our circumstances, in their minutest details, are known to Thee, and spread before thine all-seeing eye. Thou knowest our peculiar trials, whether at home or in the engagements of our daily calling. Thou knowest all that is in our hearts, the weak points of our character, the side on which we are most exposed to temptation, and the sins which most easily beset us. Lord, in thy mercy, and for the sake of Jesus Christ thy dear Son, strengthen our faith. Awaken us to greater watchfulness. Help us in every hour of our need and temptation. Give us tenderness of conscience. If we are proud, humble us, and inspire in us the meekness and gentleness of Christ. If we are forgetting Thee in the eager pursuit of worldly things, show to us that one thing is needful. If we are under the power of any sin, arouse us to struggle against it, and by thine Almighty Spirit break the bonds that hold us captive. Deliver us, O Lord God, and save us for thy great name's sake.

Hear us, we pray Thee, for all whom we love; we would send them a blessing by thy hand. Thou knowest what is best for them; watch over them all for good.

We pray that thy favour may be with us in all that we put our hands to this day. Prosper Thou our daily work, and enable us in all things to do that which is just and right before Thee and towards all men. Hear us, gracious God, and answer us; help us, keep us, and bless us, for Jesus Christ's sake. Amen.

READ IN HOLY SCRIPTURE ISAIAH LVIII.

WE humbly pray Thee, O God, to help us in this our evening service. Give us thy Holy Spirit to enkindle our affections, guide our thoughts, direct us to the petitions we ought to ask, and to teach us how to pray. We would ask only such things as are pleasing in thy sight. Thou knowest what is good for each one of us kneeling before Thee; but we do not, for we are ignorant even of all our needs. We therefore earnestly pray the Holy One to rule and direct our hearts whilst we call upon Thee.

We feel that we have omitted many things this day which it was our bounden duty to have done. We feel, too, that many things have been done which are not in accordance with thy Divine law. We bewail these our offences. We find them a grievous burden; but do Thou remove it; take it far off; roll it from our hearts. May each one of us feel in our own conscience that our transgressions are forgiven freely and fully, through the all prevailing atonement of thy dear Son.

And what mercies have we enjoyed! Our family circle still unbroken; health and strength still our portion; food and raiment still bestowed; guided and guarded still by thy fatherly love and goodness; and all kneeling here to thank Thee for thy continued lovingkindness, and to adore the hand that scatters upon our pathway so many and great bounties.

Evermore give us grateful hearts. Evermore, O Lord, incline us to praise and adore Thee, thou giver of all good things. Evermore grant us to feel that He who hath led us on hitherto will load us on in safety to the home of the blessed, which is above. We praise Thee, we laud Thee, we magnify Thee, we give thanks to Thee, thou good, and gracious, and loving Benefactor and Father.

And now that we are about to retire to our rest, keep us still under thy protection. We are helpless, exposed to many and great dangers, but we look to Thee; Thou that keepest Israel never slumberest. Thine eye is ever watchful. In safety keep us, and grant that our night's rest may, by thy mighty power, restore and fit us for the duties of the coming day.

Bless our relatives and friends; the poor and the destitute; the sick and dying: every man in his vocation and ministry; and forget not our native land. Remember our Queen and her family; our senators, our judges, and our magistrates; remember our pastors and teachers; and have mercy upon the heathen who know Thee not. Send unto them thy light and truth. Hasten the coming of thy Son. Hear us, we humbly beseech Thee, for the sake of our blessed Saviour Jesus Christ. Amen.

[41]

No. 6.

[MORNING.]   SIXTH WEEK.—SATURDAY.   [EVENING.

READ IN HOLY SCRIPTURE GENESIS XXIV. 32—67.   READ IN HOLY SCRIPTURE ST. JOHN V. 1—23.

WE would turn, O Lord God, our earliest thoughts to Thee. In thy providence Thou hast spared us during the hours of the past night, Thou hast kept watch beside our beds, Thou hast renewed our strength, and hast awakened us to find all our family circle blessed by Thee. We kneel now before Thee, and utter forth our united thanksgiving. O Lord God, we need thy help and protection throughout this day. We cannot go right, we cannot do right, we cannot even think right, without Thee. Be with us, then, O God, in all we think and do. Be with us in our goings out and in our comings in; and help us so to act that when we come to lie down at night our conscience may be free from sins against thy Divine law.

We feel, Lord, our own utter weakness. We feel that unless we have the constant indwelling of thy Spirit we cannot please Thee. There is much pride remaining within our breasts, much irritability of disposition, much impatience if trial comes upon us, much readiness of judging others, so that we are prone of ourselves to go astray. O Lord God, our faith is so weak, our love so lukewarm, our interest in Divine things so little, that unless thy Spirit strengthen, and enkindle, and keep alive our faith and love, we cannot but err and stray.

Keep us, then, O Lord God, keep our hearts aright; keep our very thoughts; keep our unruly tongue, keep us in all things; and grant that this day we may breathe the spirit of Jesus, and follow, in all our dealings with our fellow-men, the footsteps of our Divine Master. We would live to thy honour and glory.

If tempted, may we, by thy power, resist and overcome; but if it be thy will, lead us not into temptation. Give success to the work of our hands. May we be blessed in our business and pursuits. Thou knowest the needs of each and all, grant us help and blessing in accordance with these needs. Apportion strength according to our necessities. Bless our children; may they learn thus early to love and to serve Thee. May they be thy children. May their young hearts be touched by thy truth, and may they give themselves up to the Lord. Bless those that govern among us. May we remember that we have a Master in heaven. Bless us all with the spirit of love, of truth, and of a sound mind.

And now we commit all those for whom we ought to pray to thy blessing and keeping. Bless them according to their several necessities; give them in this world knowledge of thy truth, in the world to come life everlasting.

These and all other mercies we ask in the name and for the sake of Jesus Christ our Lord. Amen.

ALMIGHTY and merciful God, enable us to draw nigh to Thee at this time with one accord, in full assurance of faith, by thy dear Son Jesus Christ, the Lord our righteousness, who died the just for the unjust, that He might bring us unto Thee. We are not fit to come into thy holy presence, but thy dear Son has promised that whatsoever we ask in his name we shall receive.

O God, we thank Thee for thy fatherly care during the past day; for food and raiment, health and strength; for a peaceful home; and for the mutual help and comfort we have one of another. But still more do we bless Thee for the word of thy salvation; for all the means of grace we enjoy here, and the hope of glory in the world to come. We are unworthy of the least of all thy mercies. Oh, may thy goodness lead us to repentance. By thy blessed Spirit convince each of us this night of our sins, especially of the sins and shortcomings of the past day. May we be ashamed of our many iniquities, and feel that we are indeed miserable sinners, and have no power to help ourselves. O God, we thank Thee that Thou hast revealed to us a pool of Bethesda, a fountain opened for sin and uncleanness. Give us grace, each one, to step in, knowing and feeling the plague of our own hearts. Let the power of the Lord be now present to heal us. Wash us and make us white in the blood of the Lamb. May Christ himself draw near, and apply his precious merits and impart his virtues to each of us, that we may feel in ourselves that we are healed of our plague. O God, help us to walk as thy redeemed, and to adorn the doctrine of God our Saviour in all things. May our whole conversation be such as becomes the Gospel. Implant the same mind in us as was in the Lord Jesus; the same meekness, gentleness, and purity; the same heart for Thee and love to all men.

Bless us, O our God, and make us a blessing, separately, and also as a Christian household. Grant that the Son of peace may ever abide beneath this roof, that there be no secret or open wickedness here, and nothing in any member of this family which shall cause Thee to withdraw thy presence from us. Take us under thy gracious care this night. Preserve us from all accidents, sickness, and sad tidings, and from all that might grieve or vex us. Grant us that sleep which Thou seest good and needful for us. May our last thought be of Thee, and may we awake to find we are still with Thee. Bless all our dear friends with every temporal and spiritual mercy in Christ Jesus. Be Thou their God, and do for them and for us above all that we ask or think, now and ever, for the sake of Jesus Christ, our Lord and Saviour. Amen.

[Morning.]   SEVENTH WEEK.—LORD'S DAY.   [Evening.

READ IN HOLY SCRIPTURE PROVERBS III.

O GOD of Hosts, hear our prayer. Meet us in our worship. May we all be in the Spirit of the Lord on the Lord's day. Be merciful unto us, O God, through the merits of thy dear Son, our Saviour Jesus Christ. He died for our sins, but was raised again for our justification. We plead his righteousness alone. Give to thy servants, we humbly beseech Thee, fellowship with his sufferings, and let us know the power of his resurrection. May we be risen with Christ. May we seek, this day, those things which are above, where Christ sitteth on the right hand of God.

We present to Thee, O Lord, our offering of praise for the mercies of the past week. Thou hast defended and comforted us every night. Thou hast been always doing us good. If we are permitted to go up to thy holy temple, and to worship with thy people, of thy great goodness, go Thou with us. Let us worship God, who is a Spirit, in spirit and in truth. May we hear thy holy Word in all humility, and understand it, and believe it, and obey it from the heart. Assist thy servant who shall speak to us in thy name. May he speak as a good minister of Jesus Christ, and this day know nothing amongst men save Jesus Christ and him crucified. If, in thy providence, any amongst us be deprived of the services of the sanctuary, do thou, nevertheless, visit us with the joys of thy salvation, and open to us the Scriptures, and draw near to us in our private worship, and let our home be to us as the house of God.

We pray, O merciful Father, for all faithful pastors, and for all who confess Christ and acknowledge him to be the Lord. May they all this day receive help out of Zion, and be satisfied with the goodness of thy house, even of thy holy temple. May thy people everywhere keep the unity of the Spirit in the bond of peace. Hear us, O God, for all mankind, especially for those who, being aliens from the commonwealth of Israel and strangers to the covenant of promise, shall hear this day of Christ in our own land or on foreign shores. Send down upon them thy Holy Spirit. Take away the stony heart from every sinner, and give him a heart of flesh. O Lord, let thy word have free course, and be glorified. Let the people praise Thee, O God, yea, let all the people praise Thee. Soon let all lands keep their Sabbaths, and let the reign of righteousness spread over all the earth.

And now, may He who brought again from the dead our Lord Jesus, that Great Shepherd of the sheep, through the blood of the everlasting covenant, make us perfect in every good work, to do his will, working in us that which is well-pleasing in his sight, through Jesus Christ, to whom be glory for ever. Amen.

READ IN HOLY SCRIPTURE ST. JOHN V. 24—47.

O THOU, from whom cometh every good and perfect gift, we praise Thee for the blessings of this thy day, for the privilege of Christian worship, and for the Gospel of thy grace, the good news which have come to us concerning thy Son Jesus Christ, the Saviour of the world. We believe in Thee, O Saviour, as the Anointed One of God, to whom give all the prophets witness. Thou art the Way, the Truth, and the Life; the Bread that came down from heaven; the living Water, of which if a man drink he shall never thirst. Oh, draw us near unto Thee, we implore Thee. Let thy life be imparted to us; let thy love quicken and animate us. Speak words of power and of mercy to our darkened souls; open our understandings; turn our affections toward thyself; create in us clean hearts, and renew right spirits within us. If we be already among thy faithful ones, keep us always from sinking back into the sloth of unbelief; stimulate us to higher aims, fill us with purer motives; may it be our daily endeavour to grow in knowledge and in grace. If we be arising from the dead, aroused to a sense of sin and weakness, guide us to thy cross, O Lord Jesus; teach us how thy death was our life, how by thy stripes we are healed. If any of us be utterly dead in trespasses and sins, merciful Saviour, arouse them, we implore Thee; speak the word of authority, as of old in the streets of Nain, and by the cave of Bethany, and awaken them out of sleep. Oh, that we might all lie down this night reconciled through Thee to the Father, clothed in thy righteousness, sanctified by thy Spirit; that whether we live or die, wake or sleep, we might be the Lord's; and thus, when Thou comest in the glory of thy Father, to execute judgment, grant to us that we may be among the blessed company who come forth at thy call unto the resurrection of life.

And now, most merciful Father, we commend each other to thy keeping during the darkness of the night. Protect, we pray Thee, our persons, our property, our home. Though we be but a little group in thy great family, remember us; give thine angels charge over us; and Thyself, O thou Keeper of Israel, who never slumberest, be as a wall of fire about our dwellings. Be pleased, in like manner, to care for all our absent ones. Extend thy guidance to the perplexed, thy consolation to the sorrowful, thy charity to the homeless and destitute. Bless thy word to all who have heard it this day. Make it instrumental, even now, to the awaking of the careless, the comforting of the afflicted, and to the edification of all. Blot out, we implore Thee, all our transgressions; and receive us graciously, for the sake of Jesus Christ our Saviour. Amen.

[Morning.] SEVENTH WEEK.—MONDAY. [Evening.

READ IN HOLY SCRIPTURE HEBREWS XII. 14—28.

READ IN HOLY SCRIPTURE ST. MATTHEW XII. 1—21.

ALMIGHTY and everlasting God, we draw near to thy throne with deep reverence, adoring thy glorious perfections, confessing our sins, and supplicating thy gracious regard and unmerited mercy. Blessed be thy name that, through the blood which speaketh better things than the blood of Abel, we can come near to thy footstool. Give us grace to hear thy voice as thou speakest in thy Word and by thy Spirit, and ever to serve Thee with reverence and godly fear.

O our God, we thank thee for the gift of thy Son. May his life be our righteousness, his death our atonement and salvation; and his mighty intercession at thy right hand our constant and abiding security and help in every time of trouble. We thank Thee, O Lord, for the means of grace and the blessed privileges of the glorious Gospel of thy Son. Glory be to thy gracious name, we are permitted to draw near to Thee! Lord, give us simple, full, and strong faith in Christ for the salvation of our souls. Oh, forgive us all that has been wrong in the past; and grant us such spiritual strength for all future duties and difficulties, that in everything we may glorify thy holy name.

Thou, O Lord, art acquainted with all our affairs. Direct us in thine own way; show us the path of duty; and, for the sake of our blessed Redeemer, pour down upon us thy special blessing, and give us in rich abundance the help of thy Holy Spirit.

We acknowledge our sins, and are deeply grieved on account of our many transgressions; in thought, word, and deed, we have offended against Thee. We have broken thy laws, and have not profited by the many opportunities which have been graciously laid in our path. We have not been as grateful as we ought to be for thy mercies daily bestowed upon us. Forgive us, O Lord, for all these things. Take not thy Holy Spirit from us. Let us not fail of thy grace; nor for anything which this world can offer, barter our hope of eternal glory. Continue thy loving-kindness and thy gracious mercies towards us. Help us personally to honour thy great name. Let no bitterness or strife be found among us, but make us a family serving Thee and loving one another; willing to be guided by thy Word in all things that may happen to us.

We commend to Thee, O Lord, ourselves and all whom we love; our country and our gracious Queen; make all our great men good men; give them grace and courage to perform the duties of their high stations as in thy sight. Bless all thy ministers in their work; give them the signs of thy presence in converted and believing hearers. We pray for all in the name of Jesus Christ our Lord. Amen.

O ALMIGHTY God, unto whom all hearts be open and all desires known, cleanse the thoughts of our hearts by the inspiration of thy Holy Spirit; enable us to realise at this time thy presence in the midst of us, and to worship Thee in spirit and in truth.

We praise thee, O Lord, for the unnumbered mercies which have prevented and followed us; for all the blessings of this life; for the continuance to us of our faculties and powers of mind and body; but more especially for what we have individually experienced of thy loving-kindness, faithfulness, and power. Oh, may we show forth thy praise not only with our lips, but in our lives.

We come before thee, O Lord, as those who in some measure feel their sins and their sinfulness. In us dwelleth no good thing. Although we may have been preserved from many of those outward sins into which others have fallen, yet we would remember that the seed of every evil is within us, and that the principle of corruption constantly works in us, defiling our thoughts, corrupting our motives, drawing down our affections, and causing us sometimes even to doubt what Thou hast said. We must still come before Thee in the deepest humiliation, saying, Unclean, unclean.

Yet, O Lord, give us to know that while in ourselves we are sinners, in Christ we are saved; and enable us to rise to the enjoyment of those blessings wherewith Thou hast blessed thy people in Christ Jesus. We pray Thee to order all things for us as Thou seest best, and grant that as our day is so our strength may be.

And now, O Lord, we beseech Thee to bless those near and dear to us. We rejoice to feel that their state and circumstances are known unto Thee. If it be thy will, cause the light of thy truth to shine into the hearts of those yet in darkness. Turn Thou them, and they shall be turned; call Thou them, and they shall call upon Thee.

And do Thou, who wilt not break the bruised reed nor quench the smoking flax, carry on thy work wherever it is begun. Do Thou support the weak, protect the tempted, lift up them that are cast down, strengthen the feeble knees, and give joy for mourning, the garment of praise for the spirit of heaviness. Bless thy beloved people, by whatever outward name they may be called. Send many faithful labourers into thy harvest. Take us under thy care during the hours of darkness; and if it please Thee to spare us to another day, may we rise with thankful hearts to engage in every work to which Thou shalt see fit to call us. All this, and whatever else is good in thy sight, we ask in the name and for the sake of our Lord Jesus Christ. Amen.

[MORNING.] SEVENTH WEEK.—TUESDAY. [EVENING.

READ IN HOLY SCRIPTURE GENESIS XXVI. 1—26.

ALMIGHTY and most merciful Father, help us this morning to praise Thee for thy benefits, and may all that is within us bless thy holy name. We thank Thee for thy preserving care during the night. We laid us down and slept; we awaked, for Thou sustainedst us. Heavenly Father, we look to Thee for aid and succour during the day on which we have entered. We know not what may be its sorrows and its joys, its trials and temptations. But Thou knowest them all. Hide us under the shadow of thy wing. Make perfect thy strength in our weakness. Sprinkle, we beseech Thee, our hearts and consciences, and may the life we now live in the flesh be a life of faith in Jesus, who loved us, and gave himself for us.

O God, thou hast been the guide of thy people in every age; thou didst lead thy servants Abraham, Isaac, and Jacob, of old. In all their wanderings Thou wast with them, and didst never leave nor forsake them. Say to us as Thou didst to Isaac, "I will be with thee, and bless thee;" and enable us by thy grace to obey thy voice. Help us to walk in wisdom towards them that are without, and when temptation assails us, make therewith a way to escape, that we may be able to bear it. Grant us such a measure of blessing in our worldly callings as Thou seest good for us, but may we never, O Lord, whilst enjoying thy gifts, prove unmindful of the Giver.

May we endeavour, as much as in us lieth, to live peaceably with all men, never returning railing for railing, but contrariwise, blessing. Let not our dwelling become a place of contention, nor a place of hatred, but may it ever be to us a Bethel, the house of God and the gate of heaven. Grant that brotherly love may continue, and that all the graces of the Spirit may live, grow, and abound in us.

Bless all our relatives and friends. Look graciously on our beloved Sovereign, and all the members of the royal family. Continue thy favour to our country. Regard with thy pity and favour all orders and degrees of men. May the rich be poor in spirit, and the poor rich in faith. Comfort the sons and daughters of affliction; support them under their trials, and grant them a happy issue out of all their sufferings. Prosper all efforts for the promotion of thy Gospel both at home and abroad. Hasten the time when Jew and Gentile shall be one fold under one Shepherd, Jesus Christ.

Hear us, we pray Thee; pardon us; bless us; and do for us far more than, through our weakness and ignorance, we have been able to ask, for the sake of thy dear Son, Jesus Christ our Lord. Amen.

READ IN HOLY SCRIPTURE ISAIAH XLII.

O DIVINE Father, God of all the families of Israel, who hast created the heavens and stretched them out, who givest breath and spirit to them that walk upon the earth, we, the creatures of thy hand, come to bless Thee, and to call Thee Father in thy Son Jesus. In ourselves there is no good thing, but he is thine elect, in whom thy soul delighteth. Accept us in him. Of ourselves we know not how to pray as we ought, but give us, as Thou hast promised, thy Holy Spirit, that we may give glory unto Thee, and declare thy praise.

Lord, most holy and most merciful, impute not unto us our sins this day. We confess them now, each of us, to Thee. We would not hide them, nor excuse them, but bring them out, and lay them on Jesus. Oh, wash us, and make us clean. Deliver us not only from the punishment which our sins have merited, but from the power which they have over us, and, oh I ever keep us from presumptuous sins. Make our consciences tender; make thy law great and honourable in our sight. Make us to run the way of thy commandments with a perfect heart.

For Thou art a most tender Father, and the bruised reed Thou wilt not break, and the smoking flax Thou wilt not quench. We desire to bless Thee for thy love, while we humble ourselves in the dust for our exceeding unworthiness. We thank Thee for daily bread, for our happy home, for human kindness, for the precious love of friends, for opportunities of helping our brethren; but most of all, we bless Thee for the Son of thy love, and for the gift of thy Spirit, for the rivers of pleasure in thy house, and for the hope laid up for us in heaven. Grant, O Lord, that having this hope we may purify ourselves, even as Christ is pure.

And now we ask Thee to give us yet more out of thy fulness, and to continue to us thy mercy. If tribulation come upon us, enable us to suffer patiently. If prosperity shine upon us, teach us that every good gift cometh of Thee. Bless the children of this family with thine abundant grace. Give to all near and dear to us what we have asked for ourselves. Spare useful lives. Make peace where there is now war. Give bread where there is now hunger. In our own land, and in our own neighbourhood, strengthen thy ministers to preach thy Word. Set judgment in the earth, and make the isles wait for thy law. When we sleep, let thine everlasting arms be round about us; when we wake, meet us with sweet thoughts of Thee. Living or dying, let us be the Lord's; and when life is over, call us to sit down together at the marriage supper of the Lamb; for Jesus Christ's sake, to whom, with the Father and the Holy Spirit, be all praise and glory, now and ever. Amen.

[MORNING.] SEVENTH WEEK.—WEDNESDAY. [EVENING.

READ IN HOLY SCRIPTURE GENESIS XXVII. 1—29.

READ IN HOLY SCRIPTURE ST. LUKE VI. 12—38.

O THOU most gracious God, who hast been in all ages the confidence of thy people, we bless Thee that Thou dost still hear and answer prayer. We earnestly desire that the same Holy Spirit who taught men in ancient days to call upon thy name, may now instruct us, so that with reverence, with gratitude, with faith, and with all humility, we may bow at thy footstool. We thank Thee that Thou hast once again restored the day, and quickened all our powers of body and of mind. Thou hast given us refreshing sleep and safety during the hours of darkness, and we believe that the same power and mercy which have raised us up this morning will one day animate our dust, and raise us from the sleep of death. Let all the gifts of thy wise and holy providence fill our souls with thankfulness to Thee.

We come unto Thee, heavenly Father, in the name of Christ our Elder Brother. We would be clothed with his righteousness, and we plead in his name for the bestowal of that blessing which maketh rich, and addeth no sorrow to it. Make us to know our interest in those boundless blessings which proceed to men through Jesus Christ, who was the hope of the patriarchs, and who has been so distinctly made known to us in the Gospel of thy grace. Preserve us, O Lord, from all deceit and untruthfulness. Suffer not strife or division at any time to destroy our peace, or sever us from those dear to us by the ties of nature or of friendship. Teach us to wait for the fulfilment of thy promises, for Thou hast said, "I am the Lord; they shall not be ashamed that wait for me." Never let us do evil that good may come. May we choose affliction rather than sin, and walk in the truth all our days.

And now bestow upon each one of us before Thee a blessing, that shall abide with us throughout this day. Make our labour light by the assurance of thy love. Guide us continually by thy counsel, and keep our hearts in thy fear. Help us to live soberly, righteously, and godly, and bring us together again at the close of the day in peace and comfort, to praise thy holy name. Grant, Lord, that our children may be obedient, loving, upright, and honest; and put Thou thy fear into their hearts, that it may preserve them from evil. Bless all with whom we have to do this day. Teach them and us continually to render to one another that which is neighbourly in thy sight; and grant that all men may see in us the fruits of true religion, to the praise of thy holy name. Make our country and our beloved Queen the objects of thy constant care and kindness, and let all the earth rejoice in the knowledge of Thee, our God. We ask it through our ever adorable Redeemer and Saviour, Jesus Christ. Amen.

ALMIGHTY God, glorious in thy holiness, rich in thy mercies towards us in Christ Jesus, look down upon us, as once more we are gathered together at thy footstool. Pardon, oh! pardon, for Jesus' sake, the sins and follies of this day. We are too ready to lay up treasure upon earth. We shrink from the daily cross. We are apt to call the rich and great happy. We covet that which Thou hast in mercy kept back from us. We are quick to resent evil, and slow to forgive others. Oh, send the Spirit of thy Son into our hearts, that we may become like him. Give us of the true riches. Make us willing to suffer with Jesus, that we may hereafter reign with him. Grant us a large, a liberal, and a loving heart. Teach us to love our enemies. Supply all our need, according to thy most gracious promise, "I will never leave thee nor forsake thee." Watch over us this night, and refresh us for the duty and service of the morrow.

Bless, O Lord, each one of us with the grace we need at this time. Lead us to the fulness of grace which is treasured up in Christ Jesus. Bless also our dear relations and friends with all real good. Seal the younger ones among us with the seal of thy covenant love. Gather into thy fold those who are still wandering from Thee. Strengthen the weak and timid. Keep thine own people very near to Thee, abiding in Jesus. Bless also our sovereign the Queen, and all the royal family, and make us as a nation to fear Thee and work righteousness.

O Thou great Head of the Church, who in the days of thy flesh didst send forth thine apostles to prepare thy way, raise up a succession of faithful pastors, who shall fully preach thy Word, and be ensamples to the flock. Defend thy Church from all false teachers. Send thy Holy Spirit to accompany the ministry of thy Word with power, that sinners may be converted, and thy people grow up in Christ. And, O thou Lord of the harvest, send forth labourers among the heathen, and to the house of Israel, and greatly bless them. Hasten, O Lord, thy coming and thy kingdom, to the glory of thy great name.

With these our prayers accept, O Lord, our humble and hearty praises for all thy mercies towards us. We bless Thee for food and raiment, for friends and benefactors; above all, for the Gospel of thy grace, for thy written Word, thy holy Sabbaths, and for the hope of glory. All praise and honour be unto Thee, O Father, Son, and Holy Ghost, one Jehovah, for thy boundless love! Help us to praise Thee better here, and may we worship Thee perfectly in thine own kingdom hereafter, through Jesus Christ our Lord. Amen.

[Morning.]   SEVENTH WEEK.—THURSDAY.   [Evening.

READ IN HOLY SCRIPTURE GENESIS XXVII. 30—46.

READ IN HOLY SCRIPTURE ST. LUKE VI. 39—49.

O GOD, who makest the outgoings of the morning to rejoice, it is a good thing to give thanks unto Thee, O Lord, to show forth thy loving-kindness in the morning and thy faithfulness every night. Praise is comely for the righteous, and gladness for the upright in heart. We adore Thee for again restoring us to the activities of life. Thou hast been about our bed, and hast given us rest and sleep. Refreshed by the rest of the night, we come forth to the duties of another day; but while we enjoy light, and life, and all the temporal bounties of thy hand, we remember that man lives not by bread alone, but by every word that proceeds out of the mouth of God. We adore Thee for this provision of thy grace.

Bless to us that portion of thy Word now read. May its solemnity and importance deeply impress us. God forbid that we should lightly estimate the privileges with which Thou hast favoured us, lest at last we should have to exclaim in bitterness, "The harvest is past, the summer is ended, and we are not saved." May we firmly believe that whatsoever a man sows that shall he also reap; that he who sows to the flesh shall of the flesh reap corruption, and they that sow the wind shall reap the whirlwind. Deliver us from the profanity of Esau, who, by sinful appetite, involved himself in sorrow and bitterness. Help us to keep under our bodies, and bring them into subjection. May the Holy Spirit make us his temples, that holiness to the Lord may be written upon our bodies and our souls. Regulate, we beseech Thee, the thoughts of our hearts, and direct the actions of our lives. Teach us in all things to walk in the footsteps of thy dear Son. 'Oh, give us the grace which shall enable us so to improve the events and duties of life, as that each day may witness our victory over sin, and the cultivation of whatever is pure, lovely, just, and good. Suffer us not to give occasion to the enemy to blaspheme, or, like Jacob, to be the means of prompting others to anger and malice, but rather may we be blameless and harmless, the sons of God, without rebuke, in the midst of a crooked and perverse generation, and thus maintain a conscience void of offence both towards God and man. For this, may we set a watch over the door of our lips, that we may not sin. Hold Thou us up and we shall be safe.

Comfort us with thy love, and strengthen us for all duty with thy grace. Let us and all our friends be written among the living in the new Jerusalem. God be merciful to us, and bless us, and cause his face to shine upon us, that thy way may be known upon earth, and thy saving health among all nations, for Christ's sake, to whom, with the Father and the Spirit, be everlasting praise. Amen.

O LORD, our God, bless, we pray Thee, thy Word to our souls, and enable us to follow its teachings. Grant that it may be our constant aim to *do* as well as know thy will. Put thy laws in our minds, and write them in our hearts, that we may be thy people, and that thou mayest be our God.

Make us, we beseech Thee, pure and holy; create within us clean hearts, and renew right spirits within us. Sanctify our affections and desires, that it may be our joy to obey thy commandments and glorify thy name, and make us fruitful in all good works, to the glory of thy name. May our conduct ever prove that we are indeed the disciples of Christ. Give us grace to walk in his footsteps, and to look to him as our example, as well as our Saviour. May the same mind that was in Jesus be in us. May we cultivate his temper and disposition, and beholding, as in a glass, the glory of the Lord, be changed into the same image, from glory to glory, even as by the Spirit of the Lord.

Guide us, O God, we pray Thee, by thy Holy Spirit, into all truth. Forbid that we should be blind followers of the blind. Give unto us both light and sight. Open our eyes, that we may behold wondrous things out of thy law, and enable us to walk in the light, as children of light. Reveal unto us, we earnestly entreat Thee, the glory of the Saviour's character and work. Give unto us firm faith in the efficacy of his sacrifice, and the completeness of his atonement. Make us to realise the power of his blood to wash away all sin, to cleanse the soul from all pollution, and to render us perfectly acceptable to Thee. Forgive, we pray Thee, for his sake, all the sins that we have this day committed. Speak to us words of pardon and peace. Cause us to know that our sins are forgiven, and thus inspire us with full confidence in thy fatherly goodness, and child-like, loving trust in thy protection and care.

Accept our hearty thanks for all the mercies of this day—for health, food, and raiment; for the pleasures of friendship, for family endearments, for all the good we enjoy. Make each individual member of this household the object of thy love, and the partaker of thy grace, and bless all the inhabitants of the earth with the joys of thy salvation.

Watch over us during the hours of darkness; preserve us from all harm; refresh us with the sleep Thou givest to thy beloved, and raise us up on the morrow invigorated and refreshed for its duties. Guide us by thy counsel, and afterwards receive us to glory, for the sake of thy dear Son; and unto God the Father, God the Son, and God the Holy Spirit, as unto one God, we will render everlasting praise. Amen.

[Morning.]   SEVENTH WEEK.—FRIDAY.   [Evening.

READ IN HOLY SCRIPTURE PSALM XXXVI.

O GOD our Father, most gracious and compassionate, we thank Thee that the light of another day has dawned on us, and that we are permitted again to approach Thee in social worship, in the name of thy dear Son Jesus Christ. Be with us, we beseech Thee, and let thy Holy Spirit help our infirmities while we call upon Thee. We thank Thee for the portion of thy Holy Word which has just been read; and we pray that the savour of it may be in our hearts continually. May the fear of God be ever before our eyes, that we wander not into the ways of the transgressors, who delight in the works of iniquity, who devise mischief on their beds, and abhor not that which is evil. Lord, Thou knowest how often and how grievously we have sinned against Thee. We have trodden in dangerous ways, and Thou only hast known the greatness of our peril; but, blessed be thy holy name, thy mercy is in the heavens, and thy faithfulness reacheth unto the clouds. Thou, Lord, art the God who delightest in showing mercy and forgiveness. Oh, visit us with thy forgiving mercy, so shall we put our trust under the shadow of thy wings, and be abundantly satisfied with the river of thy pleasures. Lord, make us to know Thee in Christ Jesus as the Fountain of Life, and in thy light grant that we may see light. Continue to us thy loving-kindness, and give us a full experience of thy righteousness, even the righteousness of our God, which is by faith of Jesus Christ unto all and upon all who believe. We look for a free justification by thy grace in Christ Jesus, whom Thou hast set forth to be a propitiation, through faith in his blood, for the remission of sins that are past, that Thou mightest be just, and the justifier of those who believe in Jesus our Lord.

O our Father, when the workers of iniquity are falling around us, do Thou uphold us in righteousness; and when the foot of pride and the power of this world's wickedness are striving against us, interpose mightily for our deliverance. Help us ever to cast our care upon Thee, assured that Thou carest for us. Make us to delight in holiness; and to that end, we pray Thee, till us with thy Spirit. Increase our faith, and every other Christian grace, and incline and enable us to promote thy glory in all we think, and say, and do. Bless us as a family, according to our several states and circumstances, and extend a like blessing to our dear relatives and friends, even the blessing which maketh rich, and with which no sorrow is added. We ask these, and all other needful things, in the name and for the sake of Jesus Christ thy Son, our Lord. Amen.

READ IN HOLY SCRIPTURE 1 CORINTHIANS III.

O GOD, thy mercies are renewed every evening, and great is thy faithfulness. Sensible of thy goodness, we would not forget that much will be required from those to whom much is given. We have been solemnly reminded in thy Word of the responsibilities and obligations which attach to our Christian privileges. We are humbled by the remembrance of these responsibilities. We are constrained to confess how prone we are to allow sinful preferences and prejudices to hinder spiritual profit from the ministry of thy Word. Pardon, O Lord, this sinful disposition, and deliver us from it. May we ever look to Thee for the blessing without which there can be no increase, although Paul may plant and Apollos water. O Lord, Thou hast taught us that all things are ours, if we be Christ's; give us, we pray Thee, experience of the good things prepared for them that love Thee. Teach us not to glory in men, but humbly to rest on Thee alone.

And now, O our God, we supplicate for our souls the renewal of spiritual gifts. We are poor and needy: graciously supply all our need out of thy riches in glory by Christ Jesus. Make us increasingly partakers of the justifying and sanctifying riches of Christ, which are unsearchable. Apply afresh the blood of sprinkling to our consciences, and by thy Holy Spirit write thy law in our hearts, and work in us both to will and to do those things that are pleasing in thy sight.

Extend to others the Christian privileges which we enjoy. Pour out thy Spirit upon all flesh. Pull down the strongholds of sin and Satan in idolatrous lands. Bring home the outcast Jew. Break the oppressor's yoke, and scatter the people who delight in war. Strengthen thy ministering servants at home and abroad for their work. Increase their number, and cause them in every place to "triumph in Christ." Greatly prosper the labours of our own pastor. Bless him for our sake, that we may receive the greater benefit from his ministrations. May he both save himself and those who hear him. Look graciously upon our kindred and our friends. May their souls prosper and be in health. Sanctify every providence, whether of prosperity or adversity, to their spiritual good.

Finally, we pray Thee to preserve and protect this household during the hours of the night. Let no harm befall, and no terror disturb us. With thankful, penitent, and believing hearts, may we lie down in peace and take our rest; and with the morning sun may we arise to consecrate ourselves more devotedly to thy service, through Jesus Christ our Lord, to whom be honour and glory for ever. Amen.

[48]

[Morning.] **SEVENTH WEEK.—SATURDAY.** [Evening.]

READ IN HOLY SCRIPTURE GENESIS XXVIII. | READ IN HOLY SCRIPTURE ST. LUKE VII. 1—23.

HEAVENLY Father, for thy dear Son's sake, accept this our family tribute of prayer and praise. Thou art gracious and longsuffering, bearing patiently with our infirmities; even when we have sinned against thee, Thou art willing to receive us, if we come to Thee in godly sorrow, trusting not to our own righteousness, but to the atoning sacrifice of thy dear Son. Thou art the same yesterday, to-day, and for ever. All thy dealings with us are in tenderness and compassion. If Thou chastenest us for our disobedience, and by sharp trial makest our sin to find us out, it is that Thou mayest bring us back to thyself, as Thou didst Jacob thy servant, and give us peace and the assurance of thy blessing. Even when brought low by the conviction of our misdoings, Thou art near, to teach us that the gates of mercy are not closed, and that though we have dishonoured Thee by our sinful thoughts, and sinful words, and sinful acts, the way is yet open by which our supplications may ascend to Thee, and thy blessings come down upon us.

We praise Thee, O God, for the mercies of the night, and that Thou hast raised us in safety this morning. We desire to show our thankfulness by a heartier and more constant obedience to thy will. Give us, we entreat Thee, such a view of thy love to us, as shown in all our mercies, spiritual and temporal, as may constrain us to live, not for ourselves, but for Thee. In thy goodness and love be not far from us, but watch over us through all this day. Preserve us amid its dangers. Great is our need, but great also is thy sufficiency. Even our lawful calling may be a snare unto us, much more the temptations of the great enemy, and the secret promptings of our own evil hearts. O God, unable to keep ourselves, prone as we are to fall, we implore thy help and protection. In thy keeping we shall be safe: in thy strength we shall be strong. Kindle in our hearts such a zeal for godliness and truth, that we may abhor all that is fraudulent and deceitful, and set our faces like a flint against all solicitations to evil, come whence they may. And grant, O Lord, that ours may be a life much cheered by communion with Thee. We never can be where Thou canst not see us, or where Thou art not near us. May we more and more cherish the assurance of thy love, and, in the trustfulness of an undoubting faith, cast all our care upon Thee.

Hear us, merciful Father, in all we ask. Keep from harm this day all whom we love, and bless them with thy love. Lead them to the feet of Jesus who know Him not. Succour the tempted and tried. Lord, help and save, according to thy mercy in Jesus Christ our Lord. Amen.

O GOD, our Father, we come into thy presence this evening as thy children, claiming the privilege we have of drawing near to Thee in the Son of thy love. Jesus Christ is our brother; we are one with Him. And, as Thou dost not refuse to hear Him, Thou wilt not refuse to hear us.

Sprinkle our consciences afresh with the precious blood of Christ. We have sinned to-day, often and greatly; but now we bring our sins and spread them before Thee. O our Father, we thank Thee that He has made reconciliation for the sins of thy people, and that Thou wilt forgive, and dost forgive. We are grieved that we so grieve Thee. We rejoice that Thou dost blot out our iniquities and rememberest our sins no more.

Heavenly Father, we are beset with many enemies. In our own strength we cannot resist them; but we trust in our High Priest, who has himself suffered, being tempted. We know that He sympathises with us in our worst temptations. O Jesus, succour us; give us the victory. We cannot fight except Thou fight for us; we cannot conquer except Thou conquer for us. We can do nothing; and yet, through Thee and in Thee, we can do all things.

O our Father, look in mercy on those who are near and dear to us. Bless them, wherever they are. If they are not thine already, make them thy sons and daughters by faith in Christ Jesus. If they are thine, fill them with all the riches of thy grace.

Pour forth thy Spirit. May the Holy Ghost work mightily in all hearts, in miracles of grace and gifts, according to his own will, gathering multitudes to Christ from every nation, and people, and kindred, and tongue, and giving to each believer fresh power, fresh light, fresh joy, and fresh love.

Our God and Father, bless, we beseech Thee, thy suffering people in every part of the world. Enable those in sorrow to cast their sorrows on the loving heart of Jesus. Be with those who, in every land, are preaching the everlasting Gospel, and grant them great success. May all thy people glorify thy name, and shine as lights in the world.

Bless our Queen and our country. May thy name be honoured in our councils, and be a wall of fire around us. Watch over us this night. Let none be satisfied to sleep unsaved. We thank Thee that, whether asleep or awake, living or dying, in Jesus we are safe. Keep us under the shadow of thy wings, and fill our hearts with joy and peace in believing.

We ask all in the name of Jesus, thy dear Son, to whom, with Thee, O Father, and the Holy Ghost, be glory, praise, and power, henceforth and for evermore. Amen.

[Morning.]   EIGHTH WEEK.—LORD'S DAY.   [Evening.

READ IN HOLY SCRIPTURE PSALM XXXVII.

READ IN HOLY SCRIPTURE ST. MATTHEW XI. 1—19.

ALMIGHTY and all-seeing God, restored by thy mercy to see another Sabbath day, we would solemnly devote it to thy service, and spend it in rest and spiritual occupation, so as thereby to refresh both our hearts and bodies.

O Lord, in Thee do we trust. We are weak: do Thou strengthen us; dark: do Thou shine upon us; short-sighted: do Thou enlighten us. Help us to trust Thee when we cannot trace thy hand, assured that Thou doest all well, and that all things work together for good to those who love Thee.

Overrule our waywardness when we wander; teach us to act as ever in thy sight, not fearing what man can do unto us. O Thou that orderest all things according to the counsel of thy will, help us to commit our way unto Thee in perfect confidence, assured that Thou wilt bring to pass that which concerneth us. May it be the desire of our hearts to serve Thee, comforted by the assurance that so long as we hold fast by the Lord, none of our steps shall slide. Whatever be the lot of the wicked, the thoughtless, and the profane, may it never be ours. Keep us from becoming envious at the prosperity of others, especially of the ungodly, and suffer no prospect of gain ever to make us think lightly of sin.

Grant that many heavenly messages may pass up and down this day between our souls and Thee. May we take our part faithfully in public and private prayer, asking for our own need, and for that of our neighbours, and for Christ's Church throughout the world. Especially would we remember the aged, the young, and the afflicted. Build us up in our most holy faith; help us all to say, "I know in whom I have believed," and may we have a good hope of eternal salvation through Christ Jesus. May we keep before our eyes the doom of the transgressors, who shall be destroyed at the last, and be enabled in all cases to cast in our lot with the righteous, assured that it shall be well with them that fear the Lord. Grant us such a view of thy goodness in the sanctuary this day that we may learn our blessedness as children of God; and if any of us have any doubts as to our being born again, may we seek thy Holy Spirit to create us anew in Christ, that old things may pass away, and all things become new.

Bless our dear relations and friends; enable us to join them in spirit at thy footstool. Help all who this day shall instruct the young. Assist, Lord, thy ministering servants; enlighten their minds, inspire their tongues, prepare the hearts of the hearers, that thy Word may have free course and be glorified amongst us, and bring forth fruit to last for ever. These and all other mercies we ask in the name of Jesus our Lord. Amen.

GRACIOUS and glorious Lord God, Thou hast been very merciful to us this day, and we thank Thee for thy goodness. We praise Thee, O God the Father, who hast created us; and Thee, O God the Son, who hast redeemed us; and Thee, O God the Holy Ghost, who abidest with us and sanctifiest us. Strengthen our faith, we beseech Thee, in all thy love and truth. Let it not be shaken by the sorrows or temptations of life, nor allow us to be discouraged even though clouds and darkness hang at times around our path. If Thou seest trial good for us, enable us to receive it with meekness and submission, as of thy sending. Subdue in us at all times a spirit of repining or impatience. We are but weak and frail in ourselves, but in thy strength we may meet the secret promptings of doubt, and the open assaults of evil, and come off more than conquerors.

Bless to our hearts, O God, all the services in which we have been engaged this Lord's day. Forgive the sins and selfishnesses which have stained them, and let them be accepted for the sake of Him in whose name we have performed them. As each Sabbath comes round, may it be the means of increasing our knowledge of Divine things. Make so clear to us what Thou hast revealed, that we may not be offended at Christ or his truth, but ever adore Him as our Emmanuel, God with us, our great atoning Sacrifice, the Lamb of God which taketh away the sin of the world, our great High Priest, who can be touched with the feeling of our infirmities, our exalted King, who shall come again in the glory of his Father, and render to all according to their works. Fix what we have heard this day deeply in our hearts. Thou speakest to us in the bright tokens of blessing and in the sharpness of trial. Thou hast sent a message to us in the warnings of thy law and the invitations of thy Gospel. However Thou speakest to us, prompt us by thy Spirit at all times to say, "Speak, Lord, thy servant heareth." We ask this, O God, not alone for ourselves, but for others [for the children of this family,] for those who are bound to us by the ties of kindred and affection, for all who are yet in bondage to sin and Satan, for all who are suffering in mind, body, or estate. O God, heal the sick, quicken the dead in trespasses and sins, open the ears of those who are deaf to thy voice, and turn the feet of many into the way of thy commandments. Glorify thy name by a great increase, day by day, to the number of thy believing people.

Casting ourselves on thy care and protection for the night, we beseech Thee, O Lord, to grant us thy peace, for thy dear Son's sake. Amen.

[50]

[Morning.]   EIGHTH WEEK.—MONDAY.   [Evening.

READ IN HOLY SCRIPTURE HOSEA XIV.

READ IN HOLY SCRIPTURE ST. MATTHEW XI. 20—30.

GREAT and most merciful Father, we thank Thee for thy precious promises of mercy to penitent and backsliding souls. Lord, we repent of our sins. Oh! make our repentance deep and sincere, a repentance that needeth not to be repented of. We thank Thee for the gracious promise of thy Word. Convince, cleanse, and comfort the hearts of all sincere believers in Jesus Christ our Lord, and speak peace to all who forsake their sins and return to Thee. God of light, reveal to our souls the value of thy Spirit, that we may thirst for his truth and grace. God of love, reveal to us the power and willingness of our glorified Redeemer to send down this most excellent gift of thy Spirit into our hearts. May his grace drop on us as the rain, and distil on us as the dew, and make our heart as a watered garden bringing forth ripe fruits unto Thee. May the influences of thy blessed Spirit mingle with all our meditations and prayers. May his holy fire touch our hearts and lips with praise. May his quickening power animate us to all holy zeal and vigour in duty, and make us as the salt of the earth to our generation, so that our speech may be always with grace. Let his purifying energy penetrate to the inmost springs of thought, feeling, and action within us. May his grace so feed our lamp, that it may burn steadily in life, and through the valley and shadow of death.

O God, shed thy love abroad in our hearts by the Holy Spirit given unto us; and while we love Thee as our Father, may we love our fellow-men as the objects of thy love, and our fellow-Christians as thy children and our brethren in Christ. Prepare us by thy Spirit for all the dispensations of thy providence. May we bring forth the fruits of the Spirit in due degree and proportion. May we be taught of God to be moderate in prosperity, to be submissive in suffering, to be meek under opposition, to be gentle toward all men, and rightly to discharge every duty connected with our calling and walk. We thank Thee for past helps; and we trust Thee, Thou good and faithful God, for all future good, and for all grace to help us in every time of need. Bless thy Church with Pentecostal baptisms of thy Spirit. Revive, O Father, thy work in the midst of us. Let Divine power attend thy preached Gospel; and let the world be more deeply and widely convinced of its sin and its need of the great salvation of thy Son. We would realise our dependence on thy grace; keep us sensitively watchful lest we grieve the Holy Spirit of God, by which we trust we are sealed to the day of redemption. O God, grant it all, for Christ's sake. Amen.

O God, the Creator of all things, regard us, we entreat Thee, in this our prayer. How countless are thy blessings; how constant is thy care; how unwearied thy patience; how surpassing all knowledge is thy love! Lord, when we think of what we are, and in how many things, great and small, we have sinned against Thee, we can but adore thy mercy which spares us, and for the sake of Jesus forgives our guilt.

We come in thy name, O Lord Jesus, for Thou hast bidden us. We confess the sins which burden our consciences, and of which Thou hast this day seen us to be guilty. The evil thought, the impulse of unsanctified desire, the impatient temper, the idle word, the envious eye, the selfish purpose, the disobedient and rebellious will. Thou, Lord, hast seen it, and marked it, as we thus grieved thy Spirit, and turned a deaf ear to thy commands. Gracious Saviour, wash us in thy atoning blood, and give rest and peace to our anxious souls. And oh! enable us to learn meekly at thy feet all the lessons which thou wouldst teach us. Subdue the pride of our hearts, and all conceit of our own goodness and knowledge, that we may be as babes before Thee, and like little children hearken obediently to every message which thy Word brings to us. Lay thy yoke upon us, and give us such a sweet and abiding experience of thy love, as shall make it easy and light.

Gracious God, awaken in us a deep conviction of the greatness of our privileges, and remind us continually that to whom much is given of him will much be required. Thou hast indeed been good and merciful to us beyond multitudes of our fellow-creatures. Other nations are sitting in darkness and in the shadow of death, while we have the light of thy Gospel shining brightly among us. To others thy Word is a sealed book, but we can read it, none making us afraid. Lord, preserve us, we entreat Thee, from blindness of heart and contempt of thy Word. Enable us so to receive it, and to believe in it that not against us may the heathen rise up in judgment, and witness against our unbelief and our sin. Save us, O God, from so great a condemnation.

[Take under thy special teaching the younger members of this family. May they be thy disciples indeed. Let thy work in them be begun early, and graciously draw their hearts to Thyself, before they have been hardened by sinful habits and blunted by contact with the world.] Spread around us during the night the shield of thy care; and if it please Thee, raise us to see the morning light, and to serve Thee faithfully in the duties of another day, for thy dear Son's sake. Amen.

[51]

[Morning.] **EIGHTH WEEK.—TUESDAY.** [Evening.

READ IN HOLY SCRIPTURE GENESIS XXIX. 1—20.

O THOU who art the God of all the families of Israel, we bless Thee for the mercies of the darkness and of the daylight. Thou hast refreshed us with sleep, and awakened us again to active life. Supply all our needs, in food, and clothing, and various comforts; but, above all, grant us a sense of thy love and favour.

Oh, let our communion with Thyself be real and spiritual. Inspire in us that conscious fellowship with Thee, our God and Father, which shall enable us, at home and abroad, to go about all duties with cheerfulness. We do not know what a day may bring forth, but would own and trust Thee in all the relations, offices, and business of life. Guide us with thy wisdom, protect us with thy power, replenish us with thy grace, and uphold our feeble footsteps lest they slide.

We lay before Thee all that concerns us, and in all implore thy blessing. Whether we pursue the ordinary tenor of our way, or may be surprised into new and unlooked-for circumstances, may we feel equally assured of thy care, and depend upon thine overruling hand. As we commit our ways to Thee, so may we defer to thine unerring wisdom and unfailing goodness. Teach us, O Lord, a quiet submissiveness to thy will; and when we may be bewildered with doubt, or encompassed with darkness, help us cheerfully to consider that our pilgrimage is to a brighter world. May we look upon all that happens here in its relation to invisible and everlasting things. Deliver us from all distrust and suspicion. In patience may we possess our souls. Enable us to come boldly to thy throne, seeing we may with confidence look for mercy, and shall assuredly receive grace from the fulness of Christ. By looking to Jesus, may we be preserved from being weary and faint. Help us to rejoice in thy promises, and to plead them in our prayers. Let each soul present feel a deep concern to secure by faith a personal interest in all the blessings of thine everlasting covenant.

We bring our kindred and friends before Thee, and implore for them like blessings as for ourselves. Especially comfort and heal the sick. Succour the oppressed, and provide for the poor and destitute. Dispose all, according as they receive from Thee, to give to the needy. Above all blessings, be pleased to visit all men with the blessings of thy salvation. Pity the nations of mankind, and scatter the clouds of ignorance and error. Deliver the heathen from cruel idolatry. May the simple truths of the Gospel of Christ be cordially believed, and thy kingdom and glory be established for ever and ever. Hear and answer us for Jesus Christ's sake. Amen.

READ IN HOLY SCRIPTURE ST. LUKE VII. 36—50.

"IT is a good thing to give thanks unto the Lord, and to sing praises unto thy name, O Most High: to show forth thy loving-kindness in the morning, and thy faithfulness every night." Accept, O Lord, our united thanks for the mercies of this day. Thou hast preserved our going out and our coming in. Thou hast given us "bread to eat, and raiment to put on," and to these Thou hast added numberless other comforts. Many, O Lord, are thy wonderful works which Thou hast done, and thy thoughts which are to usward: they cannot be reckoned up in order unto Thee; if we should declare and speak of them, they are more than can be numbered. "Blessed be the Lord who daily loadeth us with his benefits, even the God of our salvation." "Give us that due sense of all thy mercies, that our hearts may be unfeignedly grateful."

We bless Thee for the Holy Scriptures, and ask Thee to give us the aid of thy Spirit, that we may be guided into all truth. We are encouraged by thy Word now read to ask Thee to dwell among us. We know we are not worthy that Thou shouldst come under our roof, but Thou art not a respecter of persons. Oh, make our hearts thy home. "Abide with us; for it is toward evening, and the day is far spent;" then "our tabernacle shall be in peace."

We confess with shame, O Lord, that we have ill requited thy favours. How little have we loved Thee in return for all thy love to us! Instead of daily remembering how much we owe Thee, we are prone to forget thy benefits. Oh, teach us the sinfulness of ingratitude, and of all our other sins, that we may confess and forsake them. We plead thy abundant mercy in Christ Jesus, "in whom we have redemption through his blood, the forgiveness of sins, according to the riches of his grace." Let each one of us hear thy voice saying to-night, "Thy sins are forgiven thee;" "thy faith hath saved thee;" and, having had much forgiven, may we love much.

Be with us during the night. May we lie down in peace with our fellow-creatures and with Thyself; may no plague come nigh our dwelling; may we have sleep and be refreshed; and when we awake, cause us to hear thy loving-kindness in the morning, and with all diligence to give ourselves to the work which in thy providence thou hast placed in our hands.

We present these petitions and thanksgivings, O Father, "in the name of our Lord Jesus Christ," to whom "blessing, and glory, and wisdom, and thanksgiving, and honour, and power, and might, be ascribed for ever and ever." Amen.

[Morning.]   EIGHTH WEEK.—WEDNESDAY.   [Evening.

READ IN HOLY SCRIPTURE GENESIS XXXI. 25—55.

MERCIFUL Father, who hast brought us in safety to this day, accept, we beseech Thee, our grateful thanks for thy protecting goodness. Awaken our hearts to lively gratitude for thy favours; forgive all our transgressions, and fill us with thy Spirit of love and life, that we may faithfully serve Thee.

Preserve us, gracious God, this day, from all the power of evil men whom we may be called to meet in the business and intercourse of life. Let them not be suffered to do us injury, nor to lead us away from Thee; and suffer us not in any measure to forget Thee, our protector and friend. We are weak and sinful creatures, and ever need thy support and guidance. Oh, preserve us from the expression or indulgence of any unholy temper or passion. When wrongfully accused, may we answer with meekness, and may our conduct be such, that with well-doing, we may put to silence the ignorance of foolish men. May we be faithful in all our relations with our fellow-men, and above all, ever faithful to Thee, feeling the greatness of thy claims upon us, and remembering continually thy redeeming love in the gift of thy beloved Son Jesus Christ our Lord.

O thou Father of all the families of the whole earth, bless our family. May we who are at its head live for Thee. May our example, in word, in temper, and in all our conduct, be influential for good. [May our children grow up in thy fear and love to be the servants of God, a blessing to their parents, and a benefit to their generation. May their hearts be truly affected by thy grace, that they may love that Saviour who has first loved them.] Help us, O God, ever to remember our accountability to Thee for the discharge of all our duties to each other, and may we in the spirit of our household and in its peace and harmony, "adorn the doctrine of God our Saviour in all things." May none of us permit any vain idol to pollute and injure our own souls and the souls of others, and bring upon us thy dread anger; but may we ever live as seeing Him who is invisible.

We would intercede with Thee, O God, on behalf of those who are endeared to us by ties of kindred or friendship; may they be thy friends. Bless all who are afflicted, and sanctify thy corrections to their spiritual profit, and so keep us that when we come to the close of this day we may have reasons for fresh gratitude in the abundant blessings of thy grace, through Jesus Christ our Lord, to whom, with the Father and the Holy Spirit, one God, we ascribe all power, and dominion, and praise, now, and for evermore. Amen.

READ IN HOLY SCRIPTURE ST. MATTHEW X. 1—23.

FATHER of mercies, we thank Thee that the season of rest has once more arrived, and that after the toils of the day it is our happiness to take thy holy name upon our lips, and to lift up our hearts in thy worship. Pardon all the sin that Thou hast seen in us this day; let us not retire to sleep with unforgiven guilt upon the conscience, but, looking unto Jesus, may we have peace with Thee, peace within, and peace with all beside. Glory be to Thee, O Lord, for all the mercies bestowed upon us hitherto. How precious are thy thoughts unto us, O God! how great is the sum of them! If we should count them, they are more in number than the sand; when we awake we are still with Thee.

Under the shadow of thy Almighty wings may we, and all we love, repose in safety through this night. Behold, O God, those who lie upon beds of pain, and comfort them. Hear the cry of the troubled, and of him that hath no helper. Let thy merciful care preserve those who are sailing on the broad ocean. Do Thou, gracious Saviour, who once hadst not where to lay thy head, befriend the friendless, shelter the outcast, and let all men know the riches of thy compassion and thy saving love.

Blessed for ever be thy holy name, O Lord, that Thou didst come into our world to save sinners, and that now on the throne of thy glory Thou dost still choose the poor of this world, and make them rich in faith and heirs of the kingdom. May we be thy loyal subjects, loving friends, and faithful disciples, and by thy grace enable us to bring our fellow sinners unto Thee. We thank Thee that the days of persecution are past in our land, and that we can call upon thy name, none daring to make us afraid. Keep us by thy mighty power from the corruption that is in the world; let us never grow cold toward Thee; never neglect thy Word or thy worship; but may we become more fervent in prayer, wax stronger in the faith, grow in every grace, and, enduring to the end, see Thee in thy heavenly kingdom, and serve Thee with everlasting joy and gladness. Bless those in less favoured lands who are persecuted for righteousness sake; strengthen them to endure as seeing Him who is invisible, and hasten the time when superstition and sin shall cease to afflict our race.

Bestow, O Lord, upon all our relations, friends, and neighbours the mercies which Thou seest they require. Comfort those of them who are aged; protect the young, and grant that all of them may, with us, when days and nights shall be no more, meet at thy right hand. And to Father, Son, and Holy Ghost we will ascribe all blessings and praise for ever. Amen.

[MORNING.]   EIGHTH WEEK.—THURSDAY.   [EVENING.

READ IN HOLY SCRIPTURE PSALM XXV.

OUR heavenly Father, by whose care we have been preserved through another night, accept our morning sacrifice of praise and thanksgiving. Thou art the God of salvation, and they who wait on Thee shall not be put to shame. Thou redeemest Israel out of all his troubles. In the midst of affliction and pain, thy people trust in Thee, and are upheld and comforted. Encompassed with enemies, they find Thee to be a wall of fire around them, their defence and glory. And we, encouraged by the experience of all ages, turn our eyes and hearts to Thee now, and ask that Thou wilt be our shield, our portion, and our joy. Show us thy ways, O Lord; teach us thy paths. We are very ignorant: do Thou enlighten us. We are very guilty: do Thou forgive us. We are very weak: do Thou strengthen us. We are very sinful: do Thou sanctify us. To whom shall we go but unto Thee? All thy ways are mercy and truth. The meek wilt Thou guide in judgment. The secret of thy presence and love is with them that fear Thee, and thy mercy endureth for ever.

We know not, O Lord, what this day may bring forth. But our times are in thy hands, and we desire to cast ourselves on thy care. Whatsoever duties devolve upon us, do Thou enable us to discharge them in thy fear, doing everything as unto the Lord. Should trouble come, do Thou enable us to bear it, and to submit to thy righteous will. Should temptation assail us, do Thou pluck our feet out of the net. May the thought that Thou seest us, be a stimulus to duty, a comfort under affliction, and a motive to flee from sin. And when the shades of evening return, may it be our privilege to record with grateful hearts that Thou hast not left nor forsaken us.

Bless, we pray Thee, all the families that call upon thy name; may there be light in their dwellings. May thy Church grow in knowledge, in purity, and in spiritual power. Have mercy on all mankind. Hasten the time, O Lord, when thy glory shall cover the earth, and there shall be nothing to hurt or to destroy in all thy holy mountain. Make us daily more and more thankful to Thee for our liberties and our Christian privileges: for our Bibles, our Sabbaths, and our sanctuaries. And grant that, nurtured as we are in thy knowledge, and fenced around by thy good providence, we may walk in the paths of righteousness, adorn the Gospel of God our Saviour, and grow in meetness for that holy state which sin shall never defile and sorrow never darken. Cleanse us, O Father, from all iniquity, and fill us with thy love.

We ask these blessings in the name and for the sake of Jesus Christ our Lord. Amen.

READ IN HOLY SCRIPTURE ST. MATTHEW X. 24—42.

TO whom, Lord Jesus, shall we go? Thou hast the words of eternal life. Through Thee alone can we draw nigh to the Father, by the help of the Holy Spirit. On Thee alone we depend, from day to day, from hour to hour, for grace, mercy, and peace: on Thee, who bore our sins in thine own body on the tree, and who ever livest to make intercession for us.

Grant that the lessons from thine own lips which we have now heard may be graven on our memory and heart. Make us willing to tread in thy steps, to go forth unto Thee without the camp, bearing thy reproach, and humbly looking for thine appearing in our behalf. Implant in us a filial fear of the Almighty, that we may fear none beside. Awaken us to a lively apprehension of thy providence in our minutest affairs. Give us grace to confess Thee before men, to deny ourselves, and willingly to give up all for thy glory; in thy saints to trace and to love thine image, and so to bear one another's burdens as to fulfil thy blessed law.

O glorious God! we wonder at thy condescension in permitting us thus to plead with Thee. If Thou, Lord, shouldest mark iniquities, O Lord, who shall stand? But thy love is greater than our guilt and misery. At thy own bidding we come to find refuge beneath the shadow of thy wings, until every calamity of life and of death shall be overpast. Have mercy, have mercy upon us. Pardon all that we have done amiss. Renew to each believing soul the assurance of thine accepting love. Help us to hate sin, to overcome the world, and to resist Satan. Apply thy truth, to warn, instruct, and stimulate us. May we prove its sanctifying virtue, and, by its exceeding great and precious promises, be partakers of the Divine nature. May we know how frail we are, and feel that eternity is nigh. May we live ready for our swiftly approaching change; and oh, remember us when Thou comest in thy kingdom.

Those great mercies we ask for ourselves, and for all whom we love. We commend to Thee our Queen, our country, and all classes around us, with the Jew and the Gentile, the bond and the free, in every land. Hasten thy reign of grace, and let all the people praise Thee.

Now, Shepherd of Israel, we rest in thy care. We are safe and happy while Thou art our Guardian. May our last thoughts and our first thoughts be, every day, thoughts of Thee. May we rise, if it please Thee to spare us a little longer, to serve Thee in the duties of a new day. And when the night of our sojourn on earth is gone, may we wake up to be for ever in thine own light. Even so, Lord Jesus. Amen.

[MORNING.] **EIGHTH WEEK.—FRIDAY.** [EVENING.

READ IN HOLY SCRIPTURE GENESIS XXXII. | READ IN HOLY SCRIPTURE REVELATION VII. 9-17

O THOU who didst make Thyself known to thine ancient people as the God of Abraham, the God of Isaac, and the God of Jacob, look with compassion upon us who desire to be numbered among the spiritual Israel, and are now assembled to offer unto Thee the sacrifice of prayer and praise. Like thy servant Jacob, we entreat Thee to grant us thy blessing. We are exposed to many perils, and we have no power to resist them; all our sufficiency is in Thee. To whom can we flee for succour but unto Thee, O Lord, who for our sins art justly displeased? We acknowledge that we are not worthy of the least of all thy mercies and of all the truth which thou hast shown unto thy servants; but enable us to enjoy the fulfilment of thy gracious promises given to the disciples of thy Son. Give us power, we pray Thee, to serve Thee with a willing mind, that we may enjoy the light of thy countenance and the assurance of thy protecting care. Bestow upon us wisdom to conduct ourselves aright, and ability to fulfil discreetly the duties that may this day devolve upon us. Set a guard, O God, over our lips, that we speak not unadvisedly; and do Thou bestow upon us the ornament of a meek and quiet spirit. Be with us in our going out and our coming in, and prosper the work of our hands. Give us grace to remember that, though unseen, Thou art about our path, and spiest out all our ways. May we daily remember that without Thee no man is strong, and no man is holy; may we look to the Wise for wisdom, and to the Strong for strength, and by thy Holy Spirit attain to that purity which is acceptable in thy sight.

We desire to dedicate ourselves anew to thy service; we acknowledge thy right to reign over us, and that thy service is perfect freedom. May our hearts become the throne of Christ, and our bodies the temples of the Holy Ghost. With these our supplications, we present unto Thee our thanksgivings for mercies temporal and spiritual. Our worldly comforts we owe to thy providence, our religious privileges we owe to thy grace. All we have and all we hope for are gifts from thy hand, for which we bless and praise thy holy name.

Remember, we beseech Thee, all for whom it is our duty to pray; especially all who are distressed in mind, body, or estate. Comfort and relieve them according to their several necessities, giving them patience under their sufferings, and a happy issue out of all their afflictions. These prayers for ourselves and others we offer unto thy Divine Majesty, through the intercession of thy Son Jesus Christ our Lord, to whom, with Thee and the Holy Ghost, be ascribed all honour and glory henceforth and for ever. Amen.

O LORD God, Lamb of God, Son of the Father, that takest away the sins of the world, receive our praises and our prayers. With joy we behold the Lamb that was slain now standing in the midst of the throne. We rejoice in thy glorious rest; we rejoice in thy government and care. As a family, blessed in Thee, we unite to call Thee blessed. For the mercies of this day we adore and laud thy name. All mercies flow to sinful man through thy sympathy and through thy merits. Thy death redeemed our forfeited life; thy bloody sweat earned for us the bread we eat; and to thy poverty and sorrows, as the Son of Man, we owe all the solaces of our lot. Teach us to give thanks always for all things to God, even the Father, by Thee; and oh, that the sense of thy dear-bought benefits may rivet thy claims on our hearts!

But exceeding great is thy love, O Lord Christ, unto such as have heartily embraced Thee as their Master and only Saviour. Their life in Thee is eternal, their consolation everlasting. Thou hast washed them from their sins in thy blood, and hast taught them to follow thy footsteps. Thou hast given them rest in thy salvation, and liberty in thy service, and triumph in a good hope through grace. Blessed Jesus, receive us into their number. By thy cross and passion, deliver us from the bondage of guilt and sin, and pour down into our hearts the Spirit of adoption, whereby we cry, Abba, Father. May we love Thee for thy love; and may we love not only thy salvation, but thy yoke, thy law, thy holy ways, and the very track of thy toiling, bleeding footsteps in this wilderness. And while striving to follow Thee, by the teaching of the Holy Ghost, may we be strengthened unto all patience with joyfulness, by the promises which Thou hast given us. How many are thy toil-worn, tempted, downcast servants. May the murmur of the "living fountains," and the chant of victory in the upper "temple" oftentimes fall upon their ear. How many are "the prisoners of the Lord," in dungeons or on beds of languishing. May "the heavens be opened" through thy Word; and may they "see visions of God" their Redeemer, and of the white-robed, happy multitude before his throne. So do Thou comfort their hearts, and brighten the tears, which God shall soon wipe away.

And now, Lord, vouchsafe to us and ours, ere we sleep, the assurance that we are thine; and when we awake, if on earth, may it be to do or suffer thy will; if in eternity, may it be to meet thy merciful welcome. But, whether on earth or in heaven, we will magnify thy grace, ascribing to God and the Lamb alone salvation for ever and ever. Amen.

[55]

[Morning.] **EIGHTH WEEK.—SATURDAY.** [Evening.

READ IN HOLY SCRIPTURE GENESIS XXXIII.   READ IN HOLY SCRIPTURE ST. MATT. XII. 22—37.

ALMIGHTY and merciful God, pour upon us the spirit of grace and supplication. We thank Thee for all thy goodness and mercy towards us during the past night. We laid down, and slept; we awaked, for the Lord sustained us. May our spared lives be evermore consecrated to thy happy service.

We ask thy blessing, O Lord, on the portion of thy Holy Word which has just been read. May the lessons it teaches be deeply impressed on our hearts, and be ever noted out in our lives. We see Thee there as the Protector of all that put their trust in Thee. May the gracious answer which Jacob received to his prayer encourage us to pray always, and never to faint. In all our ways may we acknowledge Thee, and do thou direct our paths. We know not, O Lord, to what dangers we may be exposed as we pass through this troublesome world. We are encompassed by enemies on every side. Our own evil hearts, and the temptations of the world, are ever leading us out of the only path of peace and safety. How often, alas! do our own sins bring us into difficulties, and cause our hearts to fail. Oh, help us to pour out our souls before Thee in earnest, persevering prayer, that so we may meet all our trials with calmness, confidence, and comfort, assured that in thine own good time we shall experience the mercy and faithfulness of our God. O thou whose never-failing providence ordereth all things in heaven and earth, who alone canst order the unruly wills and affections of sinful men, graciously hear us, that those evils which the craft and subtilty of the Devil or man worketh against us be brought to nought, and by the providence of thy goodness they may be dispersed. Thou, Lord, canst make even our enemies to be at peace with us.

Oh, shed forth, we beseech Thee, the spirit of love throughout this world of strife. May we ever be kindly affectioned one to another with brotherly love, in honour preferring one another. May all who see us take knowledge of us that we have been with Jesus, and have learned of Him who was holy, harmless, undefiled, and separate from sinners. In our intercourse with all men, and specially with those who are near and dear to us, help us to walk worthy of the Lord unto all pleasing, and make us fruitful in every good word and work. Thus may we be living epistles, known and read of all men.

Be with us this day. May thy Spirit guide, protect, and bless us. Assist us in all the duties of the station of life in which thou hast been pleased to place us; and if it be thy will, prosper all our plans with thy blessing. Grant this for Jesus Christ our Saviour's sake. Amen.

ALMIGHTY Father, we bless thy holy name for the mercies of this day. In Thee we live, and move, and have our being. Enable us to feel that we are not our own, and give us grace that we may not live as our own, but that we may live unto Thee. Forgive all that thou hast seen amiss in us this day. Enter not into judgment with thy servants, O Lord, for in thy sight shall no man living be justified. Wash away all our sins in the blood of thy dear Son.

Bless the words we have now read. May they be imprinted upon our minds, and sink deep into our hearts. Remove our spiritual blindness, and enable us to see Jesus in all his loveliness, and to behold wondrous things out of thy law. Take away our deadness of heart, and help us to praise thy name, and bear witness of Christ before all men. Help us to set a watch upon the door of our lips. May no idle words proceed out of our mouth, but sound and holy speech that may edify. We would remember that by our words we shall be justified, and by our words we shall be condemned, and that for every idle word we must give account in the great day. Whatsoever we have spoken amiss this day do thou graciously pardon; and whatever we have spoken that is profitable do thou graciously bless. Take from us all lukewarmness in our religion. May we remember that all who are not with Christ are against him. Keep thy servants from presumptuous sins, and let them not get dominion over us. May we never resist the strivings of thy Spirit, nor sin against the Holy Ghost. Graciously fill us with that Spirit, and make the fruits of holiness abound in us. O thou who art stronger than our strongest enemy, keep us ever stedfast in the way everlasting. May we as a household be bound together in love, and never be divided against each other. May we be united in the bonds of the Gospel, and love each other in the love of Christ Jesus. May our influence upon each other be always for good. May we bear each other's burdens, and strengthen each other's faith. If any before Thee know Thee not, and love not the Lord Jesus, oh! may thy Spirit quicken them, that we may none of us be separated from each other and from Thee in the day of Christ. O thou who searchest the hearts of all men, make us pure within, that we may be righteous in all our deeds. May we glorify our Father in heaven by bringing forth much fruit.

Go with us to our rest. May we lie down in thy love, and rise up in thy fear. O thou that neither slumberest nor sleepest, watch over us. Help us to serve Thee on the morrow better than we have served Thee to-day. Hear us, and answer us, for Jesus Christ's sake. Amen.

[Morning.] NINTH WEEK.—LORD'S DAY [Evening.

READ IN HOLY SCRIPTURE PSALM XCII.

O LORD most high! it is a good thing to give thanks unto thy name: to show forth thy loving-kindness in the morning, and thy faithfulness every night. Oh, how great is thy goodness which Thou hast laid up for them that fear Thee, which Thou hast wrought for them that trust in Thee before the sons of men.

And now we come to Thee through that blessed Saviour whose day this is. On it He rose; on it He showed himself alive, again and again, after He had suffered; on it He ascended; on it He poured out his Spirit; on it He specially visits his servants, and blesses their meetings and their work. For all this day brings to our memory, accept our thanksgiving: the finished work of Jesus Christ; his glorious sacrifice, and his resurrection and ascension, the pledge and type of our own. For all this day brings to our hope, accept our thanksgiving: rest when toils are over; things eye hath not seen, nor ear heard; a home where sin, and change, and death can never come. Let the cross, and the glory that followed it, fill our thoughts and hearts to-day. Say to each of us anew, "I am thy salvation."

Go with those of us who hope to worship in the great congregation. May we feel how awful is the place of religious assembly, and yet how blessed. Let our thoughts be fixed on Thee. While beholding thy glory, may we be changed into the same image. Beneath the light of thy truth and of thy favour, give us higher aims, and a more joyous, heavenly temper, and greater fruitfulness; that so we may flourish like the palm-tree, and grow like the cedars in Lebanon. Strengthen us thus, with all might, by thy Spirit, in the inner man. Stay with any of us who are prevented by thy providence from attending in thy house. Teach us to sanctify Thee in our hearts. Visit us with the favour Thou bearest to thy children. Help us to say, "This is the day the Lord hath made; we will rejoice and be glad in it." And if there be any dear to us, and yet far from Thee, graciously remember them. Our hearts' desire is, that they may be saved. Whatever else Thou givest or withholdest, oh, guide them in judgment, and teach them thy way.

Bless all who to-day shall be working or speaking for Thee. Clothe thy ministers with salvation. Wherever and by whomsoever the words of life are spoken, let them accomplish what Thou pleasest: let them prosper in the thing whereto Thou hast sent them. Let thy light and thy truth visit all nations, that thy kingdom may come and thy will be done on earth even as it is in heaven. These blessings we ask through Jesus Christ, our Redeemer. Amen.

READ IN HOLY SCRIPTURE JONAH II., III.

ALMIGHTY and gracious God, let thine ear be open to our prayer, and receive, we beseech Thee, with thy favour, our sacrifice of thanksgiving. When we think of our unimproved opportunities, our misspent Sabbaths, and of the sins and shortcomings of even this our holy day, we are ashamed, and confess before Thee, in self-abasement and humiliation, our great and manifold offences. Have mercy upon us, O Lord; deal not with us after our sins, but spare us and forgive us. We have nothing to answer Thee, nor any righteousness of our own to plead. We lay our mouths in the dust, and in the name of Jesus we crave thy forgiveness and blessing. Thou didst turn away from repentant Nineveh the wrath which it deserved. Avert from us the wrath which our misdoings have deserved, and shed on our souls the sweet and comforting assurance of thy peace.

Heavenly Father, let thy blessing follow all the engagements and exercises of this day. Much of sinfulness and unbelief has mingled with our services. We are conscious how unworthy they are of thy regard. But we trust they have been fragrant with the atoning merits of Jesus, and have risen as a sweet savour before Thee. Lord Jesus, thou hast been set forth among us as the crucified Redeemer, dying and rising again; and in thy resurrection testifying to us, as Jonah to the Ninevites, of the power and truth of God. Grant us thy grace, that the Word which we have heard read and preached may abide in our hearts as a message from above. O God the Holy Ghost, lay it upon our consciences. Let not the enemy snatch it away. Let not the cares, or temptations, or pleasures of the coming week choke it, and make it unfruitful. Apply it with power to our souls, that it may renew us into the image of Christ, and so sanctify us and increase in us all heavenly virtues, that we may be ripened for glory, and look forward with joy to the never-ending Sabbath of the heavenly kingdom.

Oh, look in mercy, gracious Lord, on the world that lieth in wickedness. Have pity on the souls of those that know Thee not, and snatch them as brands from the burning. Wherever minister, missionary, or teacher has spoken a word for Thee this day—whether of warning or entreaty, whether of doctrine or exhortation—bless their efforts, and make their message a savour of life unto life. We long, O God, for the accomplishment of thy purposes. We pray Thee to hasten the time when Jesus shall see of the travail of his soul and be satisfied, and the earth shall be filled with thy glory. Hear us, we beseech Thee, and accept us in Jesus Christ, our Lord. Amen.

[MORNING.] NINTH WEEK.—MONDAY. [EVENING.

READ IN HOLY SCRIPTURE GENESIS XXXV. 1—15.

READ IN HOLY SCRIPTURE ST. MATTHEW XII. 38—50.

ALMIGHTY and most merciful Father, who showest to them that be in error the light of thy truth, to the intent that they may return into the way of righteousness, we desire to bless and praise thy holy name for the instruction and encouragement which we may derive from considering thy dealings with thy servants of old, and especially with the patriarch of whom we have been reading.

Grant, we humbly beseech Thee, that we may remember all the way which the Lord our God has led us through this earthly wilderness, may recall our sins to remembrance, and fulfil the vows which we made in the day of trouble. May we recall past instances of Divine interposition in our behalf, and of communion with Thee, O Father of our spirits. May we call to mind the promises which Thou hast made to us to support and cheer us on our way, and humble ourselves before Thee for all failures, and especially for the many vows and resolutions which we have neglected to keep.

We desire, O Lord, to come before Thee, as humble suppliants for the mercy revealed and promised in thy Word through Jesus Christ. We rest simply on Him by faith; and while deeply lamenting our sins, we ask for the grace and strength of thy promised Spirit, that we may go and sin no more. Cleanse the thoughts of our hearts by the inspiration of thy Holy Spirit, that we may perfectly love Thee, and worthily magnify thy holy name. For thy Son, our Lord Jesus Christ's sake, forgive us all that is past, and grant that we may ever hereafter serve and please Thee in newness of life. Increase and multiply upon us thy mercy, that Thou being our ruler and guide, we may so pass through things temporal, that we finally lose not the things eternal.

May we carefully watch over the souls of those who are dear to us. May we bid them also to arise, and, with us, to seek the Lord; and do Thou graciously prosper our efforts, and crown them with success. Diffuse, we beseech Thee, the knowledge of salvation at home and throughout the world, and accompany the preaching of thy Word with the out-pouring of thy Spirit, that sinners may be converted and live, and the name of the Lord Jesus be magnified.

Accept our praises and thanksgiving especially for thy protection during the past night, and for all thy mercies, temporal and spiritual; and do for us, and all whom we should remember in our prayers, exceeding abundantly above all that we can ask or think, through Jesus Christ our Lord, to whom, with Thee and the Holy Ghost, be all honour and glory, world without end. Amen.

LORD God Almighty! Thou hast in mercy brought us to the close of another day. We would thank Thee most heartily for thy gracious favour. Thou hast covered our heads, Thou hast strengthened us by thy mighty power, Thou hast guided our steps, Thou hast permitted us again to kneel at thy footstool to recount the mercies of the day, and to give Thee heartfelt thanks. What are we, that Thou shouldest thus take knowledge of us? What are we, that Thou so regardest us? We are poor, weak, sinful creatures; and yet, how ever-mindful of us Thou art! how careful to preserve us in health! how tender in forgiving our many shortcomings! Again and again, at this quiet evening hour, we thank thee, O blessed Lord and God.

We thank Thee, too, for thy holy Word. We thank Thee for the portion we have just read and heard. May it warn us; may it at the same time encourage us.

Thou hast given us great and precious privileges; but to whom much is given, much, we know, will be required. Thou hast committed to our charge ten talents, privileges without number. May we use them aright. May we not allow them to rise in judgment against us. May those who have had but few privileges not be witnesses in the last great day against us. The queen of the south came from the uttermost parts of the earth to hear the wisdom of Solomon. May she never rise in the judgment against us; for we this night have heard the words of a greater than Solomon—Solomon's King and Lord.

And grant, O gracious Lord God, that the unclean spirit may be cast out of all our hearts. May every unruly lust and passion be overcome, and may our souls be filled with the light, and truth, and love which come from Thee. And may we so live that the unclean spirit once cast out may never more return. Oh, may we dread to sin, after the warning our Saviour this evening has given. Keep us, gracious Lord, by thy almighty power.

But there is sweet encouragement in thy holy Word. Our Saviour speaks of his brother, and sister, and mother. May we be of his kindred. We would be his entirely and for ever. O God, adopt us, by thy Spirit, into thy family, and make us the loving members of our elder Brother.

And now protect us throughout this night. Keep us in safety, and by thy gracious providence bring us to the beginning of another day.

Bless us and all men; and all these mercies, with the forgiveness of our sins, we ask in the name of Jesus Christ our Saviour. Amen.

[Morning.]   NINTH WEEK.—TUESDAY.   [Evening.

READ IN HOLY SCRIPTURE GENESIS XXXVII.

O MOST merciful and gracious God! morning and evening will we praise Thee for thy great goodness. May thy Holy Spirit teach us to pray aright, that we may ask of Thee those blessings which are best adapted to our spiritual and eternal welfare. We thank Thee for the promises which Thou hast given us that whatsoever we ask in faith, through Jesus Christ, our Mediator, we shall receive. Lord, increase our faith, that we may rest with stronger confidence upon thy Word, knowing that He who spared not his own Son, but delivered Him up for us all, will also with Him freely give us all things.

May we be deeply impressed at this time with the thought that Thou God seest us. Wherever we are, and in whatever we are engaged, we can never elude the observation of thine eye. The darkness hideth not from Thee, but the night shineth as the day. Thou compassest our path, and art acquainted with all our acts, purposes, desires, and thoughts. Whenever, therefore, we are tempted to do evil, may we shrink from its commission, because the eye of a just, holy, and loving God is upon us. And may we be kept from evil, not merely by the dread of Divine detection, but because our souls loathe it as an injury to ourselves and a dishonour to Thee. For all past sin we desire heartily and humbly to repent. Whether sin has been open or secret, more immediately against God or our fellow-creatures, whether in thought, word, or deed, we bring it in sincere confession, O Lord, to Thee, and beseech Thee to take away the awful burden from our souls, through the atoning sacrifice of our Lord Jesus Christ; and may thy Spirit enable us to prove our repentance and faith, by denying ungodliness and worldly lust, and walking diligently in the path of thy commandments.

Sanctify to our minds the solemn and instructive lessons suggested by that portion of sacred history just read. May we see the wickedness of envying others upon whom thy providence seems to smile more than upon ourselves. May we be very grateful for what we possess, and feel that we are not worthy of the least of thy mercies. May we shut out of our hearts every unkind and cruel purpose or thought. Preserve us from deceit and falsehood. Hide from us lying lips, and let integrity and uprightness ever preserve us. Grant us simple and childlike trust in thy providence, so that when events appear adverse, we may hope for an issue which shall make us wiser, holier, and happier for the discipline through which we have passed. Be Thou our guide through life, and at length bring us all to thy kingdom in heaven, through Jesus Christ our Saviour. Amen.

READ IN HOLY SCRIPTURE ST. LUKE XII. 1—12.

WE draw near to thy footstool, O gracious God, with all reverence and humility of mind, in the name of Jesus Christ, our Saviour. We thank Thee for the manifold and precious mercies of another day. We bless Thee for our reason, our speech, the exercise of our senses, and the use of our limbs. We adore Thee for the air we breathe, the light which has shone upon us, the food by which our bodies have been nourished. May our hearts be filled with gratitude to our Divine and unwearied Benefactor.

We are conscious of sin, infirmity, and shortcoming this day, and we lament and deplore it before Thee. We read with joy in thy Scriptures that if we confess our sins, Thou art faithful and just to forgive us our sins, and to cleanse us from all unrighteousness. We beseech Thee, O God, to fulfil thy promise in the person and experience of each one of us this night. O blessed Lord, put thy fear into our hearts—that holy fear which will make us unwilling to offend against Thee, in thought, or word, or deed, and which will enable us to put away every other fear. Teach us by thy Holy Spirit to know the things we ought to do, and faithfully to fulfil the same. Make sin hateful to us because it is so hateful to Thee. Give us a holy courage and boldness, that wherever we go, and whatever we do, we may not be ashamed of confessing that we know and love the Saviour, and that when He comes to be our Judge, He may confess us before the angels of God. May we ever remember that the fear of man bringeth a snare.

We know, O Lord, that Thou art about our path and about our bed, and spiest out all our ways. The very hairs of our head are all numbered, and not a sparrow falls to the ground without thy will. We therefore commend ourselves in humble confidence to thy guardianship for the night. May we fall asleep in peace with Thee, O God, in peace with our own minds, and in perfect charity with all the world. May the precious blood of sprinkling minister rest to our consciences, repose and safety to our souls. Number us with thy saints in glory everlasting.

Protect us and all our dear friends, whether at home, in foreign lands, or on the sea, this night, from every danger. Prepare us for our last hour; and when that shall come, may our minds be serene and tranquil, and without fear. May our sleep remind us of the blessed sleep in Jesus, and our awakening be to us the emblem and pledge of the glorious morning of the resurrection of the just.

And now to the Father, the Son, and the Holy Ghost, be equal and ceaseless praises. Amen.

[59]

[Morning.] NINTH WEEK.—WEDNESDAY. [Evening.

READ IN HOLY SCRIPTURE GENESIS XXXIX.

O LORD, help us, we pray Thee, so to read thy Word as to find it at all times profitable for doctrine, for reproof, for correction, and for instruction in righteousness. Through thy tender mercy we are permitted to begin another day, and we ask Thee to help each of us through all its hours, and in all its duties. May we be conscious that Thou art with us, and that we have the blessing of the Lord, that maketh rich. Thou hast assured us that they who delight in thy Word shall be as trees planted by rivers of water, and that whatsoever they do shall prosper. Lord, may it be thus with us to-day. Keep us from sin; keep us from error, from mistakes, and from all evil and danger; whatever we do, help us to do it unto Thee, and do Thou make it to prosper. And we especially ask Thee to keep us this day from temptation; let it never be too strong for us, but may we always see a way of escape, that we may be able to bear it. We know that the devil goeth about like a roaring lion seeking whom he may devour; we know something of our own utter weakness and sinfulness, and of our natural tendency to yield to his temptations. Hold Thou us up, therefore, or we cannot be safe; keep us by thy mighty power; strengthen us with all might by thy Spirit in the inner man, that we may be able to resist the devil. Help us to use the shield of faith, wherewith we may be able to quench all the fiery darts of the wicked one; and may we ever be encouraged in the midst of all our conflicts and strivings against evil, by the sympathy of Jesus, who was tempted in all points like as we are, yet without sin. Let us not be discouraged by any trials, or difficulties, or persecutions that may happen unto us; in all things may we seek to approve ourselves unto Thee, having a conscience void of offence. Help us cheerfully to commit our way unto Thee, our Lord, counting it a small matter what may be the judgment of men concerning us.

We offer Thee our hearty thanks for the blessings of another night, and for the unnumbered mercies by which we are surrounded this morning. Thy love, O Lord, is new every day. Oh, help us anew every morning to give ourselves up as living sacrifices unto Thee. We pray for all who are dear to us; give them all Thou seest needful for them in this world, and in the world to come grant them life everlasting. We pray for the whole world. Send out thy light and thy truth to the uttermost parts of the earth, so that all people may know Thee, the living God, and Jesus Christ whom Thou hast sent. Hear these our prayers and praises, O Lord, for the sake of our beloved Saviour. Amen.

READ IN HOLY SCRIPTURE ST. LUKE XII. 13—34.

OUR heavenly Father, we approach thy mercy-seat in the name of our Lord and Saviour Jesus Christ. We acknowledge with grateful hearts thy manifold mercies, and desire to celebrate thy praise. We bless Thee for our continued existence, for the bounties of thy daily providence, for thy great forbearance and long-suffering towards us, and for all the benefits bestowed upon us. We acknowledge Thee as the Father of lights, and the source of every good and perfect gift, whose goodness fills the earth, and whose tender mercies are over all thy works. We more especially bless Thee for thy great and infinite mercy, in sending thine only-begotten Son to be the one sacrifice for sin, and we adore Thee that by his gracious mediation we can come near to Thee, and be sure that Thou wilt accept us.

We adore and magnify thy name that Thou hast given unto us the Holy Spirit, to be our Guide and Sanctifier, and to assist us with his gracious aid in all our exercises of praise and prayer. Grant unto us now such a sense of our dependence and helplessness, that we may draw near unto Thee with reverence, humility, and fear. May we not lean to our own understanding, or trust in any righteousness or merit of our own, but confess our sins and negligences before Thee, and obtain forgiveness through the righteousness and sacrifice of our Lord Jesus Christ. Grant unto us such a knowledge of thy character that we may love Thee supremely, and such an assurance of thy favour, that we may rejoice continually in thy name.

Deliver us, O Lord, from all sinful anxiety about the things of this life. Deliver us from all covetousness and earthly-mindedness. Amidst the troubles and sorrows of this life, may it be our blessedness, as thy redeemed people, to rejoice in the hope of possessing the kingdom of eternal glory.

The lives which thou dost so mercifully preserve and bountifully sustain may we dedicate afresh to Thee as our most reasonable service; and may our whole body, soul, and spirit be sanctified by thy Holy Spirit, and washed in the fountain opened for sin and uncleanness. Preserve us, O Lord, from peril during the night; and if it please Thee, grant unto us refreshing sleep and a quiet spirit, that so we may be better prepared for doing or suffering thy holy will.

We pray for all our kindred, and for the prosperity of thy kingdom; for the welfare of our nation, and the diffusion of thy Gospel to all the nations of the earth. Hear us, O Lord, in thy dwelling-place, and when Thou hearest forgive, and accept us through Jesus Christ our Lord. Amen.

[Morning.]   NINTH WEEK.—THURSDAY.   [Evening.

READ IN HOLY SCRIPTURE PSALM XXXV.

O THOU Almighty Protector, who during the darkness of the past night didst cover us with the shadow of thy wing, we awake to behold the light of this morning in peace and health, because Thou hast kept us. Now that Thou hast raised us from sleep, continue thy protection to us against all our enemies. May those who malign us and contrive evil against us find that Thou dost confound them and put them to shame. Keep not silence. Be not Thou far from us. Plead Thou our cause, O Lord, when we cannot plead our own, and make our righteousness clear as the noon-day. If we are truly thy servants, we know that the world will hate us, but let not men wrongfully rejoice over us, who hate us without a cause. Stir up Thyself, and help us in all our need, as Thou didst thy servant Joseph when Thou wast with him, and didst show him mercy, and didst give him favour in the sight of the keeper of the prison.

We remember also how Thou didst appear on behalf of thy servant David, whose song of distress and deliverance we have now been reading. May thy Word encourage us in the midst of all our temptations. With the saints of ancient days may we look directly to Thee for aid, and for the righteous vindication of our cause. Thou hast it in the power of thy providential purposes to clothe with shame and dishonour all who magnify themselves against us.

Then, O Lord, shall our souls be joyful in Thee; they shall rejoice in thy salvation. Let us never be ungrateful for thy delivering mercy. With all our strength may we join in thy praises, and say, "O Lord, who is like unto Thee in goodness, power, mercy, and justice? Who is like unto Thee, who in thy great goodness deliverest the poor who have nothing to repay: who in thy great power defendest the weak, that have no strength; and comfortest the afflicted, who are in sorrow?"

Let thy name be magnified, O thou mighty and merciful Deliverer, who hast pleasure in the prosperity of thy servants; and may thy right hand be extended in favour of all who in any land are oppressed by their enemies for righteousness' sake. Let thy Church be secured by the saving strength of thy right hand, and defended from the malice and evil devices of all her enemies; so, O gracious Father, shall our tongues perpetually speak of thy righteousness and of thy praise. Help us by thy grace to live a life of praise and obedience. Let us not this day turn from the way of thy commandments. May the daily experience of thy love constrain us to follow, in all things, thy perfect will. Hear us, O God, through Jesus Christ our Lord. Amen.

READ IN HOLY SCRIPTURE ST. LUKE XII. 35—48.

MOST Holy God, who hast appointed a day in which Thou wilt judge the world in righteousness by Jesus Christ our Lord, vouchsafe to us, in thy mercy, that we may be numbered, in that day, among thy saints and the inheritors of thy kingdom.

We confess, O Lord, that we are utterly unworthy, in any merit of our own, to stand before the Son of Man. We have sinned against heaven and before Thee. We come to Thee with penitent and contrite hearts. We beseech Thee, for the sake of Him who loved us and gave Himself for us, to forgive us our sins, and to cleanse us from all unrighteousness.

Of thine infinite goodness and mercy, O Lord, suffer us not, through any weakness or folly of our own, or any temptations of the devil or of the world, to neglect thy will, and to leave undone the work which Thou hast given us to do. Suffer us not, at any time, to say in our hearts, "My Lord delayeth his coming;" but make us watchful, patient, humble, diligent, as the followers of Jesus Christ. Grant that we may always have our loins girt and our lights burning, and be ourselves as those who wait for their Lord.

Enable us faithfully to do Thee service in the several stations which in thy good providence Thou hast assigned to us, and so let our light shine before men. At all times and in all places make us to remember Thee; and the life we now live in the flesh may we live by the faith of the Son of God, looking for that blessed hope and the glorious appearing of the great God and our Saviour. Increase and multiply upon us thy grace, that we may abound unto every good word and work. Dispose us to seek the furtherance of thy true religion among men. Endue us with fervency of spirit, with holy zeal, and with constancy and devotion in our Master's cause. And oh, that it may be given to us to know the full blessedness of those whom the Lord, when he comes, shall find so watching and working for him.

We thank Thee, O Lord our God, for all the blessings of the past day: that we have been preserved in health and safety, and that Thou hast provided for all our earthly necessities. Above all, we thank Thee for our spiritual privileges and hopes, for the gift of thy Son our Lord, and for the promise of life in him.

And now we commend ourselves to thy fatherly care and protection for the coming night. Let thy blessing rest on every member of this house and family, and on all our relatives and friends. Grant us peaceful and refreshing rest, and may we rise with renewed strength to serve and glorify Thee, through Jesus Christ our Lord. Amen.

[Morning.] NINTH WEEK.—FRIDAY. [Evening.

READ IN HOLY SCRIPTURE GENESIS XL.

O OUR God and Father, who leadest thy people in a way they know not, blessed be thy name for all thy goodness to us and ours this morning, and all our life through. Thou art ever good, in chastisement as in blessing, when Thou deniest as when thou givest. With what tenderness dost Thou reprove us. The darkness Thou makest light; our sorrow Thou turnest into joy; and to us, struggling and tempest-tossed, Thou givest back the sweet calm of peaceful trust. Humbled, repenting, we fall before Thee; we confess; we adore. Great art Thou, O God; wise, loving, and faithful. Teach us how to praise and how to trust.

Wonderful are thy providences, as when Thou didst suffer thy servant Joseph to linger in prison. Thou art still the same, and thy footsteps are in the deep waters. To-day Thou mayest call us to suffer; we may stumble beneath some heavy cross. Stand Thou by us; give us the needed grace; refresh us with thy strengthening presence; subdue sin within us; check the oft-rising murmur; loosen us from earth; bind us closer to Thee. Teach us to fear sin more than suffering; to value more than ease and self-comfort thy presence and grace.

Let not our sorrows and trials make us selfish or idle. May we look kindly on our brother who is sad, comforting him with the consolations with which Thou hast comforted us. May we speak of Thee, our God, and tell of all thy wondrous works to us and all thy people, and trust Thee even when thy judgments are most unsearchable. Enable us to lighten, by words and deeds of blessing, what we cannot remove; and to plead for our brother as for ourselves at thy throne of mercy. Grant us, O Lord, to love our neighbour as ourselves.

If our kindness meet with no grateful return, but they whom we have remembered in their sorrow should in prosperity forget us, let us not repine. Recall to our sorrowing hearts how often we have thus treated Thee and thy goodness; how we have taken thy gifts, and forgotten the Giver; and may we have eyes watchful for our own sin rather than for our brother's. May we do good with a more single motive, with less self-seeking. May we cease from man, and cleave to Thee; for Thou wilt never forget us, O our God.

Bless this our family each moment in each duty as we need. Unite us in growing love to Christ and to each other; and grant us, if such be thy will, to meet again before Thee this evening in health, thankful and happy, to praise Thee for new mercies, for preserving grace, and for a desire, daily strengthening, to be thine and thine only, for Jesus Christ's sake. Amen.

READ IN HOLY SCRIPTURE ST. LUKE XII. 49—59.

GOD of all mercy and truth; Thou in whom we live, and move, and have our being; by whom alone our lives have been sustained and our reason continued, and from whom we receive every good and perfect gift; we meekly beseech Thee for thy Holy Spirit, that at the close of another day we may approach the throne of thy heavenly grace, with lowly, penitent, and believing hearts, and in our evening worship find acceptance with Thee.

We once more draw near to Thee, O Lord our God, to adore thy great and matchless name, to magnify thy abounding mercy, and to acknowledge thy fatherly goodness and love. Through all the days of our lives, in all our wanderings, labours, and troubles, amid dangers both seen and unseen, Thou hast been our Protector, Guardian, and Friend. And as the darkness of another night has gathered around our dwelling, we come to confess before Thee our manifold sins and iniquities, to cast ourselves on thy redeeming love, to implore thy forgiveness, and to supplicate thy saving strength. We humbly beseech Thee, our Father and our God, for the sake of thy dear Son, not to enter into judgment with us because of our transgressions, but in the midst of deserved wrath to remember with undeserved mercy.

Thou didst send thy Son into the world, not to condemn the world, but that the world through Him might be saved. By thy Holy Spirit Thou hast separated and art now separating a people to Thyself; a peculiar people, zealous of good works. Here Thou art calling the prince, there the peasant; here the child of tender years, there the profligate and profane; here the master, there the servant; for Thou art no respecter of persons. Nor shall thy truth and Spirit cease to work, burning like fire among men, until all thy people are gathered in, and made holy, "without spot, or wrinkle, or any such thing." Grant, O God, that in that day we may be found of Christ in peace, and enter into the joy of our Lord.

Lord, hear our prayers, and save us and all dear to us, and number us among thy jewels. Bless, we beseech Thee, all that have rule over us, and give them wisdom and justice; all that preach thy Gospel, and make them wise to win souls. Save thy people, O God, and bless thine inheritance; make haste to help the needy, the afflicted, and the dying; and speedily accomplish the coming of thy kingdom. Beneath the shadow of thy protecting love, holy Father, we desire this night to rest; and when that time comes when we are to awake no more on earth, give us all to live with Thee in heaven, for Christ's sake; to whom, with the Father and the Holy Ghost, be everlasting praise. Amen.

[Morning.]   NINTH WEEK.—SATURDAY.   [Evening.

READ IN HOLY SCRIPTURE GENESIS XLI. 1—36.   READ IN HOLY SCRIPTURE ST. LUKE XIII. 1—9.

ALMIGHTY God, whose compassions fail not, look, we beseech Thee, in loving-kindness and tender mercy, upon us here gathered together before Thee. We approach Thee in the all-prevailing name of Jesus Christ. Thou that hearest and answerest prayer, hide not thy face from us; but for thy dear Son's sake hearken to our cry, accept and bless us.

We thank Thee, gracious God and Father, for rest and preservation during the past night. Thou hast protected us when we could not protect ourselves. Thou hast watched over us, and brought us in safety to see the light of this day.

We beseech Thee to fit us for the duties of the day. Give us that preparation of the heart which is from the Lord. Grant that in thought, in word, and in deed, we may glorify Thee continually, remembering that we have been redeemed with the precious blood of Christ, and are therefore not our own, but bought with a price. Oh, may thy good Spirit teach us what we ought to do, and also give us power faithfully and diligently to fulfil the same.

We desire, O our God, to acknowledge thy hand in all the events of our daily life; for thy Word hath showed us that famine and plenty, abundance and scarcity, sorrow and joy, are ordered by Thee, and are the ministers of thy will. Teach us to trust Thee at all times, with a perfect heart. If we abound in the good things of this life, enable us to trace our blessings to thy bountiful hand. And shouldest Thou call upon us to suffer privation or sorrow, may we still believe that Thou doest all things well for them that put their trust in Thee. Grant, gracious Father, that, by the teaching of thy Spirit, the Lord Jesus Christ may become increasingly precious to our souls. May we feed on Him in our hearts by faith with thanksgiving. And as we beseech Thee to strengthen us by thy Spirit for the duties of life, so we beseech Thee to arm us for its trials. It may be our lot to encounter wrong-doing, or neglect, or oppression. Hard words may be spoken against us to-day. Hard things may be done. Give us, we humbly pray Thee, the meekness and gentleness of Christ. Being reviled, may we not revile again. May we commit our cause unto Thee, knowing that Thou wilt bring forth our righteousness as the light, and our judgment as the noon-day. And now send us forth, O Lord, to our work with thy blessing resting upon us. Bless also our friends and relatives. Bless our Queen and country, and all others for whom we should pray. O God, our God, hear us and answer us in these our prayers, for Jesus Christ, our Saviour's sake. Amen.

O THOU Preserver of men, in Thee we live, and move, and have our being. Thou holdest our souls in life. It is thy air that we breathe; it is on thy bounty that we live; we are every day fed at thy table; and when thou takest away our breath we die. Nor do we know the moment or the day when our souls will be required of us.

In the name of Jesus, the one Mediator between Thee and men, we would give Thee hearty thanks for all thy care over us and ours this day. It has been a day of mercy. Thou redeemest our lives from destruction, and crownest us with loving-kindness and tender mercy. Bless the Lord, O our souls, and forget not all his benefits.

We would take shame to ourselves that we have so often abused thy long-suffering. How little fruit have we borne to thy praise! O Lord, we have been worse than cumberers of the ground; we have borne corrupt fruit. Adored be the exceeding riches of thy grace for thy forbearance. Let thy long-suffering be our salvation. Cut us not down, but spare us yet another year, for the sake of the Great Intercessor, who ever lives to make intercession for all who come to Thee by him. Let all our trials only tend to loosen our attachment to the world, to make our hearts soft, and let thy Spirit be to them as the dew on the mountains of Sion. Let our souls live, and they shall praise Thee. Hast not Thou said, "I will be as the dew unto Israel?" Fulfil thy word, and be as the dew unto us.

For thy name's sake forgive us the trespasses which we have committed this day, as we forgive all who have trespassed against us. Bless the work of our hands; and now hide us under the shadow of thy wings. Suffer no harm to befall us, nor any plague to come nigh our dwelling. If it please Thee, give rest to our weary bodies, and so renew our strength for the duties of the morrow. If it should be our lot to be wakeful, with our souls may we desire Thee in the night, and meditate in thy law.

O most merciful Father, prepare us for the night of death and the morning of the resurrection. At whatever moment and in whatever form death may visit us, may we be found clothed in the wedding garment of Christ's righteousness, with our loins girded and our lamps trimmed, ready to enter into thy presence, and to dwell with Thee for ever.

All these praises and petitions we humbly present before Thee, O Lord, in the precious name of Jesus, who died the just for the unjust, to bring us unto Thee. And to Him, to Thee, and to the Holy Spirit, one God, be ascribed all honour and glory, world without end. Amen.

[63]

[Morning.] **TENTH WEEK.—LORD'S DAY.** [Evening.]

READ IN HOLY SCRIPTURE GENESIS XLI. 37—57.

O LORD, our heavenly Father, we bless Thee that our lives have been spared through the darkness of night, and that we are permitted to behold the light of another Sabbath-day. We desire, O Lord, to begin this day with Thee, and to enjoy thy presence and blessing throughout its sacred hours. We come, therefore, to ask that Thou wouldst give us thy Holy Spirit, that He may govern our thoughts, our words, and our actions this day; so that in all things we may please Thee our God. Bless thy holy Word which we have read. May its lessons be impressed upon our hearts by thy Holy Spirit. We admire and adore Thee for thine infinite goodness to the children of men. Even in the midst of thy judgments, thy mercy, thy condescension, and thy love appear most brightly. O Thou who didst give unto thy servant Joseph thy own Spirit, and didst raise him out of his prison to be a prince in Egypt and a blessing to the nations in time of famine, we humbly beseech Thee to be our God; and grant that in all our trials and afflictions we may be upheld by Thee, and be fitted by them for usefulness in thy Church and in the world.

This morning, O Lord, we ask thy special blessing to fit us for the privileges and duties of this sacred day. Draw our minds from all things that are merely earthly, and fix them on those things that are heavenly and divine. Reveal to us the fulness of thy love in Christ Jesus, and assure our hearts of an interest in his salvation. Prepare our minds for the solemn exercises of Divine worship. May we go to thy house in a humble, teachable, and fervent spirit, desiring only to meet Thee our God. In praise and in prayer help us to worship Thee in spirit and in truth. May we hold communion with the Father and his Son Jesus Christ, and listen to thy Word with deep attention, and with a desire to learn some lesson which may be profitable to our souls.

Be with all thy servants who to-day shall proclaim thy truth. May they preach with the power of the Holy Ghost sent down from heaven, so that sinners may be pricked in their hearts, and cry, "What must we do to be saved?" and thy people be built up in their most holy faith. Fill all Sabbath-school teachers, O Lord, with a sense of the value of their scholars' souls, and with a deep desire for their salvation. Help them to impart that truth by which the children shall be made wise unto salvation. Upon all our friends we beseech Thee to pour out thy Spirit, and grant that we and they may meet at last with all the redeemed in glory everlasting. Have mercy upon us, and accept our prayers and praises, for Jesus Christ's sake. Amen.

READ IN HOLY SCRIPTURE ISAIAH V. 1—25.

GRACIOUS and merciful art Thou, O our God; constant and unfailing is thy care, and exhaustless thy Divine goodness and compassion. What could have been done for us which Thou hast not done? From the beginning even until now thy preserving goodness hath sustained and kept us, and thy hand hath supplied our wants. We belong to a fallen race; but even when we were sinners and without strength, Thou didst not spare thy dear Son, but deliveredst him up for us all. We have had thy holy Word to be a lamp unto our feet, and a light unto our path. Ministers have spoken to us, in Christ's stead, the message of reconciliation. The way of access to thy footstool is open to us. Through thy dear Son Thou hast provided for us all that infinite mercy can find, and all that fallen man can need.

O Lord, we acknowledge thy great and undeserved goodness. How poor a return we have made for it; what scanty fruit we have brought forth. Thou hast borne with us long and patiently, and it is of thy mercy that we are not consumed. The power which could have destroyed us has been extended to bless us. O God, we blush for our ingratitude and sin. We adore Thee for thy long-suffering patience and forbearance. Spare us, we beseech Thee. Pour upon our hearts the precious gift of thy Holy Spirit, that He may quicken us to new life. Bless to our souls the Word which has this day been sown among us, that it may arouse us from our sluggishness and indolence, and warn us back from the sinful ways in which our feet have trodden, and stimulate us to greater diligence in thy service, that we may be trees of righteousness, the planting of the Lord, that He may be glorified.

We pray not for ourselves alone, O Lord, but for others: for those who are bound up with us in the bonds of kindred and affection, for those who dwell around us and in the midst of whom our lot is cast, and for all sorts and conditions of men. Thou knowest the measure of their opportunity and privilege, and the measure of their fruitfulness. Spare, O God, the unfruitful, and awaken them to see their danger and their sin. Visit with thy grace the fruitful, that they may bring forth much fruit to thy glory, and the honour of thy Gospel. May every Sabbath-day see a great enlargement of the Redeemer's kingdom, and the conversion of many souls, both among Jews and Gentiles, among the heathen abroad and the ungodly at home.

Take us into thy keeping, O God, for the night, and bestow upon us now and ever every needful and saving blessing, through Jesus Christ our Lord. Amen.

[Morning.] **TENTH WEEK.—MONDAY.** [Evening.

READ IN HOLY SCRIPTURE PSALM LXVI.

O LORD our God, Thou art very great; who is like unto Thee? Thou art God alone. The day is thine, and the night is thine; Thou hast prepared the light and the sun. O God, Thou hast made us, and not we ourselves; we are thy people, and the sheep of thy pasture. In thy hand our breath is, and thine are all our ways.

Blessed for ever be Thou, O our Father; Thou hast not turned away our prayer, nor thy mercy from us. We have cried unto Thee in our troubles, and Thou hast heard and delivered us. The living, the living, they shall praise Thee, as we do this day.

Wisely and graciously hast Thou dealt with us in every time of sorrow. Thou broughtest us into the net; Thou laidst affliction upon our loins. Our fears were many, our unbelief great, our murmurings loud. We asked, "Has the Lord forgotten to be gracious, and will He shut up his loving-kindness in displeasure?" But all the while—now we see it, now we praise Thee for it—Thou wert proving us, wert trying us as silver is tried. We went through fire and water, but Thou broughtest us out into a wealthy place.

O God, who holdest our souls in life, and dost not suffer our feet to be moved; who hast often, by thy providence, turned our sorrow into joy, consecrate us, body and soul, to thy service. Teach each one of us to live, labour, suffer, trust, so that Thyself and thy grace may be daily magnified in us. Grant us to remember all the way Thou, O Lord our God, hast led us, to humble us and prove us, to know what was in our hearts, whether we would keep thy commandments or no. In prosperity, let us not forget the vows of adversity. May we pay that which our lips have uttered and our mouths have spoken when we were in trouble.

Keep us from feigned prayers, from insincere dealing with Thyself and ourselves. If we regard iniquity in our hearts, Thou wilt not hear us, for Thou searchest the hearts and triest the reins; all things are naked and open before Thee, with whom we have to do.

Grant thy blessing on our daily toil. Let thy presence gladden us all the day long. Keep the thought of evil afar off. Give strength and victory in temptation. May we grow in grace, watching against sin, fearing self, hiding thy Word in our hearts, doing good, blessing others, living and longing for the coming of our Lord and Master; and so day by day walking in the light, as Thou art in the light, may the blood of Jesus Christ cleanse us from all sin. Accept our praises, we beseech Thee; grant these our petitions for thy dear Son's sake. Amen.

READ IN HOLY SCRIPTURE ST. MATTHEW XIII. 1–23.

FAITHFUL and ever-blessed God, who art Most High for evermore, who fillest heaven and earth! there is no darkness where the workers of iniquity can hide themselves, nor are thy children ever concealed from thy view. The day and the night are both alike to Thee.

We adore the riches of thy goodness towards us since last we bent the knee before Thee. We went forth to our work, and Thou hast upheld us. Our bodily wants Thou hast supplied. Thy grace has been bestowed in proportion as we have prized and sought it. Thou hast made the outgoing of the morning and the evening to rejoice; and now we meet again to speak good of thy name. Let not our eyes be so blind as not to see, let not our hearts be so dull as not to feel, the loving-kindness of the Lord.

But to us, O Lord, belongeth shame and confusion of face. We have sinned, we have done wickedly; we have been unthankful, insincere, unholy. We come, therefore, through Him whom Thou hast exalted to be a Prince and a Saviour. We make mention of his righteousness, and of his only. Cleanse us from the defilement our souls have contracted. Speak peace to our consciences. Justified anew from all things, may we rejoice in hope of thy glory.

And now, our Father, how can we thank Thee enough for the clear teachings of thy Word? Prophets and righteous men desired to see those things we see, and have not seen them; and to hear those things we hear, and have not heard them. Blessed are our ears, for they hear; and our eyes, for they see. Let thy Word abide in us, and thy Spirit enable us to understand it. Let not our hearts prove so hard that it cannot touch or enter them, but let it be as good seed cast into good ground, yielding ready and abundant fruit. Teach us to count the cost as well as to know the blessedness of obedience. If tribulation comes or persecution, may consolations abound even as sufferings abound. Help us to be on our guard against the corrupting and deadening influence of worldly cares and of worldly wealth. If riches increase, teach us not to set our hearts upon them. Our cares, teach us to cast them upon Thee.

We commend to thy blessing our friends and all the members of this family. Be with them and us through the hours of the night. We are safe only when Thou art our Defender; rich only when Thou art our portion; happy only when Thou art our good. If it please Thee, may we rise on the morrow with new strength for new duty. When we awake, may we be still with Thee. We ask all through Jesus Christ our Lord. Amen.

[65]

[Morning.] TENTH WEEK.—TUESDAY. [Evening.

READ IN HOLY SCRIPTURE GENESIS XLII. 1—24.

O LORD God, our heavenly Father, who art glorious in thy majesty, and yet dost stoop down to the weakest and meanest of thy creatures; we adore thy grace and power, which have kept us through the night now past. Oh, enable us to regard every returning day as a fresh witness of thy goodness, and to see in all daily blessings, and especially in the message of thy Word, cords of love by which Thou wouldest draw us to Thyself. Accept our thanksgivings. To Thee, O God, be all the praise and glory. Thou hast loved us with an everlasting love. Forgive, we beseech Thee, the coldness and sinfulness of our hearts, that we have loved Thee so little in return. Cleanse us from the guilt of unthankfulness, and awaken us to a deeper gratitude, and a heartier and holier service. Lord, we desire to live this day under thy protection. Watch Thou over us for good. We know not what is before us, nor what may be the trials and temptations which we shall meet. Be Thou with us in all that we do; and by thy Holy Spirit show us what is right, and give us strength and courage to do it.

Especially we pray Thee to give us a tender conscience, that we may not sleep in the ways of sin, nor be deaf to the voice of thy Word, nor grieve thy Spirit by our wilfulness and disobedience. O God, preserve us from spiritual blindness, from hardness of heart, and from contempt of thy Word and commandment. If trouble befall us, open our eyes to see thy hand in it; and if it bring our sin to remembrance, give us grace to confess that we are verily guilty, and to seek earnestly for pardon and forgiveness. Oh, that past faults and failings may make us watchful against the approach of temptation, and keep us humbly dependent upon thy guidance and help, without which we shall surely fall. Grant us, O God, as a family, every domestic blessing. May the love of Jesus abide in all our hearts, that drawing nearer day by day to Him, we may be drawn nearer to each other. Oh, that all of us may be thy people, the children of God, loving Thee, and bringing forth the fruits of the Spirit. Are any of us yet wanderers from Thee, O God? by thy Holy Spirit convince us of sin, arouse us to repentance, subdue our pride, quicken us from spiritual death, reveal unto us thy dear Son in the tenderness of his love, and the power of his saving grace. Salvation belongeth unto Thee. Oh, let none of us be found unsaved in the day of Christ's appearing. Merciful God and Father, we implore all these blessings, and we praise Thee for all thy goodness, in the name of Jesus Christ. For his sake accept us and our offering of prayer and praise, and give us peace. Amen.

READ IN HOLY SCRIPTURE ST. MATTHEW XIII. 24—43.

AT the close of another day, O Lord, we meet together to offer Thee our praises for thy great goodness to us, and to supplicate thy continued protection during the night. Keep us under the shadow of thy wings; let no evil befall us, suffer no plague to come nigh our dwelling. Each day brings us nearer to the close of life; and we specially ask Thee to prepare us, by the blood of Jesus Christ and the transforming power of thy Holy Spirit, for that last great day when Thou wilt send forth thine angels to gather out of thy kingdom all that offend and all that have done iniquity. May every one of us be found then in Christ; not having our own righteousness, but the righteousness which is by the faith of our Saviour. Keep us all from self-deception; let us not be as tares among the wheat, exposed to the awful misery of discovering our real position by the revelations of the great day of thine appearing. We know from the lips of our blessed Saviour that in that day many will say, "Lord, Lord, have we not prophesied in thy name, and in thy name done many wonderful works?" and that He will reply, "I never knew you; depart from me, ye workers of iniquity." O Lord, our Father, again we ask Thee to save every one of us from this awful doom. Make us know ourselves. Search us, O Lord, and try our hearts, and show us if there is anything that is keeping us from a simple trust in thy beloved Son, our Saviour Jesus Christ, as the only hope of our salvation. Help us to give all diligence to make our calling and election sure; to have our loins girded and our lamps burning, as servants waiting for their Lord's coming; so that whenever He shall come and call for us, we may be ready. And we ask this not only for ourselves, but for all who are dear to us, and for all mankind. Cause there to be an increased preparation in the hearts of all people for the coming of the Son of Man. Prosper and bless all efforts for the spread of the Gospel, both at home and abroad, and help us as we have opportunity to hold forth the Word of life, and to be as lights of the world, so that men seeing our good works may glorify our Father which is in heaven. We ask thy pardon for all the sins we have committed during the past day; with shame and contrition we confess before Thee that we have sinned in thought, in word, and in deed. If we looked only at our sins, we should despair; but we turn with thankful hope to the precious blood of Jesus Christ, who came into the world to save sinners. For his sake have mercy upon us and forgive us all our sins, and accept our prayers; and to Father, Son, and Holy Ghost be glory and praise for ever. Amen.

[Morning.]   TENTH WEEK.—WEDNESDAY.   [Evening.]

READ IN HOLY SCRIPTURE GENESIS XLII. 25—38.

O LORD God, thy mercies never cease. Day after day and night after night thy mercy surrounds thy children. During the hours of darkness Thou guardest our beds, Thou givest sleep to our eyes, Thou renewest our wearied strength; and now, refreshed and invigorated, we kneel before Thee in praise and thanksgiving.

How wonderful, O Lord, art Thou in all thy works! How wonderful in thy dealings with us poor weak and sinful creatures! May we walk worthy of thy goodness and love.

We pray Thee, O Lord, to be our Guide and Protector this day. Keep us from all sin, and give us grace to hate it. Let us not whisper to our conscience that our transgression is so secret that none can ever know it, for thou knowest all things, O Lord, even the very innermost thoughts of our heart. Make us to feel that, sooner or later, our iniquities will find us out. Keep us, therefore, O Lord our God, ever in thy trust and love, that we sin not against Thee.

And, O Lord, it may be that some of us may be tried very much with things working, as we think, against us. We may be in deep affliction of soul, and it may be all unknown to those around us. Some trial from Thee may be bringing us down to the very dust. We may be in bitterness of spirit. O Lord, may we not for an instant think that Thou art against us. May we not imagine for one single moment that Thou hast either forgotten or forsaken us.

No, O Lord our God: a woman may forget her child; but Thou never forsakest those who trust in Thee, and who love Thee. To those among us who may be suffering under trial give sweet and holy comfort; and as Thou didst cause all to work together for good for thy servant Jacob, so cause all to work together for the same gracious purpose for all thine afflicted people. Amid their afflictions may they not forget Thee, but feel, with Job of old, "Though He slay me, yet will I trust in Him."

And now, O Lord, again we ask Thee to keep us this day from all sin and all danger. Guide us by thy wisdom. Help us by thy blessing. May we so walk, as thy children, and so conduct ourselves, that men may behold in us the epistles of Christ. We pray that we may be useful to those around us. May we live, not only for ourselves, but for others. May we seek their good, as well as our own; and, above all, may we seek the eternal welfare of all.

We go forth in thy name. We depend on thy help. We trust in thy love. May we triumph in thy salvation. Hear us and answer us, for thy dear Son's sake. Amen.

READ IN HOLY SCRIPTURE ST. MATTHEW XIII. 44—58.

O GOD, unto whom all hearts be open, all desires known, and from whom no secrets are hid, subdue our hearts by the remembrance of our own unworthiness as we kneel at thy footstool. Humbly and reverently we come into thy presence. Turn not thy face away in displeasure, but according to thy great mercy in Christ Jesus, give us a token for good, and let us not be ashamed of our hope in Thee.

Blessed be thy name, O Lord our God, for the many mercies of this day. We owe it to thy watchful and tender care that we have been kept in safety, and that our day of grace is prolonged. Forgive us, we pray Thee, our frequent sins, and let them not be remembered. Let us know in our daily experience the healing power of Christ Jesus' blood, and have the peace which passeth all understanding. Thou hast given us thy Gospel, and gathered us into the number of thy professing people. O God, grant that we may be thine, not by profession only, but in deed and in truth. Teach us that it will avail us nothing to serve Thee with the lips, unless our hearts and lives be given to Thee. Carry on in us thy work, and let its power be seen in the holiness of our conduct. Check and subdue in us every disposition to formalism and hypocrisy, that we may be what we profess to be, true disciples of thy dear Son; and that when the great day of final separation shall come, we may not be cast away. Preserve us from spiritual hardness and insensibility. May our hearts be tender, receiving readily the impressions of thy Word, yielding cheerfully to the promptings of the Holy Ghost, and resisting firmly all the temptations of pride and unbelief. Thou hast brought us near to Thyself in the privileges we enjoy. Thou hast revealed to us Jesus, thy dear Son, and hast made clearly known unto us the way of salvation. Having spared Him not, but delivered Him up for us all, with Him Thou wilt freely give us all things. Lord, give us such an increase of faith that we may be willing to count all things but loss for the excellency of the knowledge of Christ Jesus, if so be we may be found in Him, clothed with his righteousness, and sanctified by his Spirit.

Take us now, we pray Thee, under thy protection. Let thy blessing rest on all who are dear to us. Let none of them remain in unbelief. [Especially visit with thy grace the children of this family. May they remember their Creator in the days of their youth, and, under the guidance of thy Holy Spirit, give their hearts now to the Saviour.] We lay our prayers and thanksgivings at thy feet. Accept them, we beseech Thee, for Jesus Christ's sake. Amen.

[Morning.] **TENTH WEEK.—THURSDAY.** [Evening.

READ IN HOLY SCRIPTURE GENESIS XLIII. 1–14.

O GOD, holy and true, who workest all things after the counsel of thine own will, and who in thy wisdom and love dost bring light out of darkness, order out of confusion, and joy out of sorrow; we acknowledge with gratitude and praise that just and true are all thy ways, and that in thy hand all things work together for good to them that love Thee. Be pleased to confirm our faith in thy promises, that we, casting all our care upon Thee, may be careful about nothing; and that, walking in the light of thy countenance, we may be filled with that peace which passeth all understanding. Remember, O Lord, thy word unto thy servants, upon which Thou hast caused us to hope; and perfect in us all the good pleasure of thy goodness, and the work of faith with power. Hear us when we call, O God of our righteousness. Thou hast enlarged us when we were in distress. Have mercy upon us, and hear our prayers.

Father of mercies, who makest our cup to run over, and preventest us with the blessings of thy goodness; accept, we beseech Thee, the freewill offerings of our mouth, and let our prayer come before Thee as incense, and the lifting up of our hands be as the evening sacrifice. Thou hast preserved our souls in life, and hast filled our hearts with food and gladness. We would bless Thee, the Lord, at all times; may thy praise be continually in our mouth. Oh, continue thy lovingkindness unto them that know Thee, and thy righteousness to the upright in heart. We commit our way unto Thee, we trust also in Thee; for Thou wilt bring forth our righteousness as the light, and our judgment as the noonday. We wait for Thee; our soul doth wait, and in thy word do we hope. Be pleased, O Lord, to fulfil our petitions, and bless us with all spiritual blessings in heavenly places in Christ Jesus.

We give thanks unto Thee, O thou Preserver of men, that we are alive every one of us this morning; and we beseech Thee, according to thy manifold mercies, to preserve us, and let goodness and mercy follow us all the days of our life. Be Thou our God; and remember those who are dear to us with the favour which Thou bearest to thy people. Let Israel rejoice in Him that made him, let the children of Zion be joyful in their King; for Thou takest pleasure in thy saints, Thou wilt preserve all them that trust in Thee.

O Lord, go before us, we beseech Thee, to keep us this day in the right path; and bless us in all that we put our hand unto, that of thine may we give Thee; and so fill us with thy grace, that whatsoever we do, we may do all to thy glory, through Jesus Christ our only Saviour. Amen.

READ IN HOLY SCRIPTURE ISAIAH VI.

ETERNAL and ever-blessed Saviour, who didst reveal Thyself to thy servant Isaiah, make Thyself known unto us, we pray Thee, in this our assembling at thy footstool. Thou art God of God, Light of Light, very God of very God. Thy glory covereth the heavens, and the earth is full of thy praise. Holy and reverend is thy name, O Lord of Hosts. Lord, what are we, that we should be permitted to speak unto Thee, before whom even angels veil their faces! Our hearts are unclean, our lips are unclean, our hands are unclean; in thought, and word, and deed, we have transgressed against Thee. We are vile in thy sight, whose eyes are as a flame of fire, searching the heart and reading the life.

O Lord Jesus, as we know our misery through sin, so enable us to feel our need of thy cleansing blood; that experiencing in our hearts the blessedness of thy peace, we may be ready to run in the way of thy commandments. Gracious Saviour, impart to us these blessings. Blot out our sins, whatever they be. Kindle in our hearts a lively sense of thy mercy, that with a holy zeal we may be ready to every good word and work, and realise ever more and more that thy service is perfect freedom.

We praise thy name, O our God and Father, for the many mercies of the day. To thy gracious providence we owe all our good. Life, health, strength, domestic comforts, a blessing on our daily toil; above all, the Gospel of thy dear Son and the gift of thy Holy Spirit, are of Thee, and to Thee will we give the glory. We pray that we may not prove unprofitable servants, laying our talents idly by instead of employing them to thy glory. O Lord, when Thou seest us slothfully or selfishly misusing the gifts of time, money, and opportunity, remind us, by the powerful impressions of thy Spirit on our hearts, of the solemn account we must one day give. Especially grant that thy Word may never become to us the savour of death unto death. Oh, forbid it, Lord, that we should resist its power and shut our ears to its warnings; sinful and ungrateful as we have been, cast us not away from thy presence, and take not thy Holy Spirit from us.

Be very gracious unto all whom we love. May each and all of them be partakers of thy grace in Christ Jesus. [Make the children of this family thy children, and daily renew them by thy Holy Spirit.] Guard us and our dwelling from all evil this night, and let us sleep beneath thy protection.

Hearken to these our prayers, and supply all our need, according to thy riches in glory by Jesus Christ our Lord. Amen.

[Morning.]   TENTH WEEK.—FRIDAY.   [Evening.

READ IN HOLY SCRIPTURE GENESIS XLIII. 15–34.

READ IN HOLY SCRIPTURE ST. MATTHEW VIII. 18–34.

O LORD, Thou art our God; the Author of our being, and the Giver of every good and perfect gift. All the blessings we enjoy come to us from Thee, through Him who, though exalted on high, and crowned with glory and honour, is our Saviour, and Brother, and Friend.

We rejoice that for our sake Jesus Christ submitted to humiliation, poverty, and pain; loving us when we were at enmity with Him, and seeking our welfare while He suffered for our sins. We rejoice that, having suffered, He is now exalted above all principalities and powers, a Prince and a Saviour, to give repentance and remission of sins. Especially do we rejoice that, on his throne in glory, He retains the same love for us as when He hung upon the cross, that He does not forget those whose nature He wears, but still thinks of us, and intercedes for us; and, as He bore our sin and shame, gives us a share in the fruits of his exaltation.

We thank Thee for all the blessings Thou hast bestowed on us through Him. Thou hast fed us and clothed us; Thou hast protected us from danger, and preserved our lives. In sickness and sorrow Thou hast sustained us; and in health Thou hast supplied our wants. And, looking back over all the way by which Thou hast led us, we are constrained to say, "Blessed be the Lord God, the God of Israel, who doeth wondrous things; and blessed be his glorious name for ever, and let the whole earth be filled with his glory. Amen and Amen."

We acknowledge likewise thy spiritual mercies in Christ Jesus, for all the means of grace, and for the hope of glory. Make us partakers of thy Spirit, and heirs of the kingdom of thy dear Son, that we may be his in the day when He maketh up his jewels.

Accept, O Lord, of our thanksgivings for these manifold mercies, of which we are most unworthy; and enable us to use thy gifts for thy service. May every renewed favour increase our love to Thee and devotedness to thy service. And, receiving so much ourselves, may we ever be ready, in the exercise of a true brotherly feeling, and according to the ability which Thou hast given, to minister to the welfare of others. Help us especially, in a family, to be considerate of each other's feelings. May Christian love characterise all our intercourse here. And, when the vicissitudes of life are past, may we have a happy meeting around thy throne.

Receive our thanks for the mercies of the past night. Grant us protection, and help, and guidance, and grace throughout the day. Forgive us our sins, and accept us and our services, for the Redeemer's sake. Amen.

ALMIGHTY and ever-living God, the Protector of all who trust in Thee, help us to look up to Thee now and at all times, in love, and reverence, and godly fear. Fill our hearts with grateful praise for the continued mercies of this day. Thou art indeed good and gracious to us. May we ever be mindful that it is from Thee that all good things do come, and that even the evils of life are overruled by Thee, and work for good to them that love Thee. Forgive, we earnestly beseech Thee, all that we have done, or said, or thought amiss this day. Thou art faithful and just to forgive the sins of all who believe in thy dear Son. Lord, we believe; help Thou our unbelief.

Gracious Spirit, anoint our eyes, that we may see.. Leave us not to grope in spiritual darkness. Take of the things of Jesus, and show them unto us, that in Him we may have peace, and be indeed the children of our Father in heaven. Merciful Saviour, Thou knowest our frame, and canst compassionate our weakness. Stretch out at this time thy merciful hand, and raise us up from the depths into which our sin has plunged us. Save us, Lord! save us, or we perish. We pray Thee also to help and succour us in all the trials and temptations of our daily life. Leave us not to be overwhelmed by them, nor permit them to bring us under the dominion and power of sin. When we find our cross heavy, do Thou share the burden with us, and enable us to bear it with patience and holy courage. Remembering thy sufferings for us, O Lord Jesus, may we never repine, but meet with cheerfulness and faith whatever trials, for the Gospel's sake, Thou art pleased to send to us, and be willing to count all things but loss for the excellency of the knowledge of our Lord and Saviour.

Preserve us, O Lord, this night in peace and safety. We have no power of ourselves to help ourselves. Keep us, we pray Thee, outwardly in the body, and inwardly in the soul, and fit us for the duties of another day. Let thy favour rest upon our dear relations and friends. Oh, grant that both they and we, the old and the young, may hearken to the call of Jesus, and follow Him at all cost. Lord, suffer nothing to hinder us. We desire, O Lord, to be thine entirely; to be free with the liberty wherewith Christ makes his people free, and to enjoy the witness of thy Spirit that we are indeed thy children. Pity, we pray Thee, all them that are yet led captive of the devil at his will. Cast out from their hearts the spirit of disobedience. Open their ears to hear the glad tidings of deliverance, and bring them to a right mind. We ask all, O God, through Jesus Christ our Lord. Amen.

[Morning.]   TENTH WEEK.—SATURDAY.   [Evening.

READ IN HOLY SCRIPTURE 1 PETER IV. 7—19.   READ IN HOLY SCRIPTURE ST. MATTHEW IX. 1—15.

O GOD Almighty, who givest us good things without number, without money, and without price; we lift our hearts to Thee in thanksgiving and in praise. We laid ourselves down, we slept, we awaked; for thou, O Lord, didst sustain us. Yet we are not worthy of the least of all thy mercies, or to present any offering to Thee; but, sinners as we are, do Thou receive us for his sake who Himself became our Surety, and ever liveth to make intercession for us.

Lord God, be gracious to us this day, and help us, we beseech Thee, to spend it as in thy sight, and with eternity in view. May we use the world as not abusing it, being temperate in all things, and watching unto prayer. Oh, fill our hearts with fervent charity towards all men, and especially towards those with whom we shall associate, whether at home or elsewhere. May we be intent, not on spying out their faults, but on furthering their interests, lovingly ministering to their wants, and seeking their happiness according to our ability. O God, save us from selfishness, in all its forms. Root it out of our souls, and grant that in things temporal and spiritual we may ever remember that we have nothing which we did not receive, and that Thou wilt soon require of us an account of our stewardship. May all our conduct, in public and in private, be regulated by the principles of thy Word; and then we shall not be ashamed, but Thou wilt in all things be glorified, through Jesus Christ.

Be with us, heavenly Father, amidst the varied troubles of our daily life, that, taught and strengthened by thy good Spirit, we may rest thankfully in thy will, knowing that whom the Lord loveth He chasteneth. And should we be called to suffer for Christ's sake, may we arm ourselves with his mind. May we never be ashamed of his name, but rejoice in the privilege of being partakers of his sufferings; so that when his glory shall be revealed, we may be glad with exceeding joy. But forbid, we earnestly implore, that, through forgetfulness of Thee, we should at any time bring shame and sorrow to our own souls, and give occasion to thine enemies to blaspheme.

Pardon all our past sins. Draw us to Thyself by thy constraining love; and when the day is ended, may we feel that we have made some progress in the way to heaven and Thee. Shed every blessing on all whom we love, wherever they may be. Bless thy Church. Let the time to favour Zion, yea, the set time, come; that thy glory may be revealed, and all flesh see it together. O Lord, hear; O Lord, forgive, and save us evermore, for the alone merits of Jesus Christ, our Lord. Amen.

O LORD, our heavenly Father, we come before Thee at the close of another day—another day of labour and of toil, but a day in which thy kind hand has still been about us for good. But, O Lord, we would have we failed to walk with Thee! how have we failed of being, like our blessed Redeemer, always employed in doing thy will! As for us, we seem, at best, just to serve Thee for a little while, and then to forget Thee; but with Him it was, all the day long, unceasing service and unceasing love. Forgive the sins of our holy things, that they are so cold, and of our unholy things, that they are so frequent.

Lord, we would come to Thee through Him who died for our sins and rose again for our justification. For his sake receive and help us. Polluted and helpless as we are, we come to Thee, O our God, for cleansing and deliverance, that we may be pardoned, strengthened, and renewed. Heal us, we pray Thee, and purify us from all our iniquities. Who can forgive our sins but Thou alone? Lord, give us living faith, that in thy Son Jesus we may obtain the fulness of thy blessing. Lord, we are blind, but we believe that Thou canst give us sight. Open Thou our eyes, that we may behold the wondrous things of thy Word.

Nor would we pray unto Thee, O Lord, for ourselves alone. We would bring before Thee in prayer all those who are dear to us. [Our children,] our friends, our relatives, our household; may they all live before Thee. It may be that some of those dearest to us may at this moment be us dead before Thee. Lord, for his sake who purchased for us the gift of thy blessed Spirit, raise those who know Thee not from the death of sin unto the life of righteousness. May the Saviour speak by his Spirit to their hearts, "I say unto thee, Arise!"

Nor look upon our families alone; but upon our friends, our neighbourhood, our country. Lord, pour down thy blessing on this land of ours. Thou hast blessed thy work within our borders, and yet, O God, among us, as in thine own Israel, there are many wandering far from Thee, as sheep that have no shepherd. Lord, look upon thy Church, and have mercy upon the world. Increase the number of thy faithful shepherds; preserve from wandering the sheep already in thy fold. Collect thy dispersed flock, and according to our Saviour's promise, let there be one fold and one Shepherd. Gather the number of thine elect, and hasten thy kingdom. Hear us for his sake who alone is worthy, thy beloved Son, Jesus Christ, to whom, with Thee and the Holy Ghost, one God, be all glory, and praise, and honour, for ever and ever. Amen.

[70]

[Morning.] **ELEVENTH WEEK.—LORD'S DAY.** [Evening.]

READ IN HOLY SCRIPTURE GENESIS XLIV.

O GOD, we adore thy blessed name, and pray that our hearts may be kindled by the remembrance of thy glory. Before the mountains were brought forth, or ever Thou hadst formed the earth and the world, even from everlasting to everlasting, Thou art God. Thou art the Almighty God, who doest as Thou wilt in heaven above and in earth beneath. Thou art the holy God, who hatest and abhorrest sin. Thou art the faithful and true God, whose promises stand fast for ever and ever. Hear Thou from heaven, thy dwelling-place; and when Thou hearest have mercy and forgive, and do for us according to the riches of thy grace and love in Jesus Christ our Lord.

From our very hearts we thank Thee, heavenly Father, for all thy mercy to us, and especially for the day of rest, and the ordinances of the house of prayer. By thy Spirit so work in us to will and to do, that these blessings may not be in vain. We beseech Thee ever to deepen in us the conviction of our own unworthiness. When we confess our sins publicly before Thee this day, fill us with shame at the remembrance of them. Let thy grace work in our hearts, humbling us before the cross of thy Son, and preparing us to hear with joy the message of thy pardoning grace and reconciling love. Glory be to thy name that thy hand is not shortened that it cannot save, nor thine ear heavy that it cannot hear. Implant in our hearts the comforting sense of thy forgiveness, that being justified by faith, we may have peace with God through thy dear Son, and rejoice in hope of thy glory.

In the midst of all our trials and temptations, enable us to see that Thou art teaching us. If thy hand be laid upon us in chastisement, and Thou callest our sins to remembrance, as Thou didst the sins of Judah and his brethren, at the same time reveal to us thy mercy, that we may not be overwhelmed by the fear of thy wrath. Keep us ever humble and watchful against the sinfulness of our hearts, and the temptations of evil around us. Be Thou in all things our Shield and Strength, and let thy good Spirit guide and help us.

According to thy promise, be present with all who this day meet in thy name. Preserve us from all that would distract the mind, or cause us to forget that Thou art near. Give wisdom to thy ministers, and let none of their words fall to the ground. Have mercy on many who are now estranged from Thee. Draw them to thy house, and sow the seed of the Word in their hearts. Glorify thy dear Son, and let Him see this day of the travail of his soul. O God, in thy mercy answer us, and bless us for his sake. Amen.

READ IN HOLY SCRIPTURE ST. MATTHEW IX. 18–33.

GRACIOUS Father, we thank Thee for thy fatherly care, for the renewal of religious opportunities, and for all thy goodness towards us on this thy day. We bless Thee for health of body, for soundness of mind, and for our daily food and raiment. We thank Thee for the enjoyments of home, for all our domestic blessings and comforts. We praise Thee for thy holy Word which we have been privileged to read and hear, for the ordinances of thy house, and for the service of the family altar, with which we would conclude the engagements of this day. May we rejoice amidst bereaving providences that our kindred and friends are continued to us; and that while we are surrounded by disease and death, we are alive to praise Thee. Enable us gratefully to acknowledge all thy benefits, and not to forget those tokens of thy daily kindness. We confess our secret faults, and presumptuous offences. We approach Thee, O Lord, not as righteous persons needing no repentance, but as those who have often vexed thy good Spirit by our transgressions against Thee. We humbly pray that our sins may be blotted out as a cloud, and our iniquities as a thick cloud. Take away from our hearts the love of evil, and may we experience the cleansing of the atoning blood of Jesus. May thy rich grace be bountifully supplied to us, that we may have wisdom and ability both to know and do thy will.

Make us anxious to redeem the time, and to employ our life for the benefit of our fellow-men, and for the manifestation of thy glory. May our faith in the Lord Jesus be constantly increased; and as in the days of his flesh he gave sight to the blind, and raised the dead, so may we experience the operations of his Holy Spirit, in being spiritually enlightened, and raised from the death of sin to newness of life.

We mourn the sinfulness which we daily witness in the world. How many are perishing for lack of knowledge, and lie under the power and dominion of Satan. The harvest truly is plenteous, but the labourers are few. Raise up, O God, and send forth more labourers. Beat down by thy truth all superstition and error. Let the Gospel of the kingdom be preached with power and much assurance, so that many around us may be saved. Restore thine ancient Israel to favour. Prosper all missionary efforts both at home and abroad, that righteousness and peace may bless the world.

Mercifully bless our kindred and friends. Comfort the poor, the afflicted, and desolate. Thy kingdom come. Thy will be done in earth as it is in heaven. We ask all, O God, in the name and through the intercession of our Lord and Saviour Jesus Christ. Amen.

[Morning.] **ELEVENTH WEEK.—MONDAY.** [Evening.

READ IN HOLY SCRIPTURE GENESIS XLV.

ALMIGHTY God, the Holy One of Israel, Father of the whole family in heaven and earth, we present ourselves before Thee in worship and adoration. Our voice shalt Thou hear in the morning, and day by day will we direct our prayer unto Thee, and will look up. We thank Thee for peace and safety during the night, and for the refreshment and strength received in sleep; and now that our faculties are restored, and another day is before us, we pray for the forgiveness of past sins and follies, and ask that we may be kept from again being guilty of the offences against Thee which Thou hast graciously pardoned.

We are only safe as Thou keepest us. Great and many dangers beset our path. Our own hearts are prone to evil. Continually we see the good, but prefer the evil. The good that we would we do not, and the evil that we would not that we do. We are frail and feeble, without strength of our own to stand upright. Lord, look in thy mercy upon us, and preserve us from falling. Clothe us with the armour of God, that the shafts of temptation, and sin, and Satan may hurt us not. Remove the hindrances that prevent our spiritual progress. Suffer us not to be tempted beyond what we can bear. Let thy name be glorified in our godly walk and conversation, that we may not do harm to religion, nor bring dishonour on thy name by inconsistency and sin.

Grant, O Lord, that the lesson of thy Word now read may be fixed deeply in our hearts. May it show us how Thou makest all things work together for good to thy people, and how, though sorrow may endure for a night, joy cometh in the morning. May we learn from it the duty of forgiveness, and be ready at all times to do good to them that have injured us, and to pray for them that despitefully use us. O God, forgive us our trespasses, as we forgive them that trespass against us. Oh, let this our household be a God-fearing family, abounding in love to Thee and to one another. Let no fruits of bitterness spring up to trouble us. We desire that Jesus may dwell with us, shedding on all our hearts the bright beams of his precious presence, and drawing us all to Himself by the bands of everlasting love. Grant, Lord, that when the shades of evening shall come down upon the world again, we may be privileged to look back on a day which has been without wilful offence against God or man.

We present at thy footstool these our prayers and thanksgivings, trusting in the grace and mediation of our Lord and Saviour Jesus Christ, to whom, with the Father and the Holy Ghost, one eternal Jehovah, be unending praise. Amen.

READ IN HOLY SCRIPTURE ISAIAH LXII.

O HEAVENLY Father, our Almighty and gracious God, thy good hand has been upon us all the day through, and in thine exceeding mercy we are again gathered as a family at thy throne of grace. Oh, let not this our evening service of prayer and praise be cold and formal. Stir up our hearts to devotion, that we may have joy and gladness in thy presence, and feel that the brightness of thy love is shining upon us. Forgive all that we have done wrong this day. Cleanse our consciences in the atoning blood of thy Son, and increase our faith, that as thy children we may take hold of the promises to which we have listened, and cheerfully obey the precepts of thy Word.

O Lord, enlarge our hearts with zeal for thy glory, and a desire for the coming of thy kingdom. How feebly have we realised the encouragement which Thou hast given us in this chapter to plead with Thee for the success of the Gospel, and the accomplishment of thy gracious purposes to our lost and guilty world. Lord, let not this our unbelief and lukewarmness remain unforgiven. Arouse us from our apathy, and kindle within us from this hour a fervent zeal for the honour of thy name and the triumph of thy truth.

Awaken in thy Church a deeper anxiety for thy glory. Pour down the spirit of prayer and supplication on all thy believing people. Excite them to increased labours for Thee, and to more self-denying sacrifices for the advancement of the Gospel. Revive thy work in the midst of us. Let Christians feel more intensely the preciousness of Christ to themselves, and the obligation which lies upon them to make Him known to others. Call forth an increasing band of faithful ministers. Teach them by thy own Spirit, and endue them with Divine gifts. Give abundant grace to all who now preach thy truth. Reveal it with power to their own hearts, that they may proclaim it more clearly and powerfully to others. Be with our missionaries in other lands. Lift up their hands when they hang down, and strengthen their feebleness. Go forth, O Lord, in thy righteousness and truth, and level in the dust the strongholds of sin and Satan. To the ends of the earth let it be seen that Thou art God, and Thou alone; and that the word in thy mouth is truth. Take the veil from the eyes of the Jew. Stir up thy people to remove every stumbling-block from his path, and hasten the day when thy name shall be known upon earth, and thy saving health among all nations.

Grant, O God, that the words of our mouth and the meditation of our hearts may be acceptable in thy sight, through Jesus Christ our Strength and Redeemer. Amen.

[Morning.]   ELEVENTH WEEK.—TUESDAY.   [Evening.

READ IN HOLY SCRIPTURE PSALM XXX.

HOLY and ever-blessed God, the Father of our spirits, the framer of our bodies, the preserver of our lives; in approaching thy throne this morning, we come with humble boldness, making mention of the name and pleading alone the merits of the Lord Jesus Christ. We are sinners, and feel our need of a Saviour. Burdened by a sense of our own unworthiness, but remembering thine own gracious command, in all things to make known our requests unto Thee, we now bow our knees, and offer unto Thee the thanksgivings of grateful and adoring hearts.

O Lord, thou art good, and ever doing good; gracious art Thou in all thy ways. All of us in thy presence have again been the recipients of Divine protection and sparing mercy. Through the silent hours of the night Thou hast sustained us; and while many have been awake through suffering, we have slept and been refreshed. During the season in which darkness has overshadowed our dwelling, we have been free from dangers, both from within and from without; and now ere we enter on the duties and demands of another day, we implore the pardon of all our sins, and unwavering guidance in the way of holiness; that, as a family and household, we may be kept an unbroken circle in the fellowship and love of our God.

Holy Father, in thus approaching into thy presence, we desire to plead the great work of thine own well-beloved Son, who died on the cross, and ever liveth to make intercession for us. When our world was lying in sin, none in it righteous, no, not one, and when no eye pitied and no hand helped the perishing, blessed be thy gracious name, thine eye pitied, and thy hand wrought redemption. For this great salvation we would adore and bless Thee. But, Lord God, the world as yet is far from enjoying the glad tidings of great joy which are for all people. We therefore earnestly beseech Thee, O most blessed God, to send forth light and truth to the ends of the earth, to lead men out of darkness into marvellous light, to subdue their hearts to Thyself, to make an end of war, and so to take to Thyself thy great power and reign, that speedily the kingdoms of this world may become the kingdoms of thy dear Son.

Bless the poor, O God, and save the dying. Let the afflicted be sanctified, and the sorrowing be consoled. And may we all so remember our latter end, as to number our days and apply our hearts to wisdom; that in thine own kingdom at last, with the innumerable host of the redeemed, we may praise Thee for ever and ever, through Jesus Christ, our Lord. Amen.

READ IN HOLY SCRIPTURE ST. MATTHEW XIV. 1—14.

O ETERNAL God, in whom we live, and move, and have our being, we bless Thee for the protecting care which has been around us this day. Dispose our hearts, we pray Thee, to come into thy presence with holy thankfulness and devout adoration.

Thou knowest, Lord, how this whole world lieth in wickedness; whenever the overflowings of ungodliness make us afraid, grant that our trust and our confidence may be in Thee. We adore thy goodness that our lot is cast in this favoured land, where the course of things is so peaceably ordered by thy governance, that thy Church is able to serve Thee in godly quietness, and the families of our Israel may sit each under his own vine and under his own fig tree, none making us afraid.

But forasmuch as thy holy Word has taught us that they who reign with Christ must first suffer with Him, we pray Thee, gracious God, to prepare us to bear with meekness, patience, and constancy the afflictive dispensations of thy providence, in whatever form they may present themselves. Give us the self-denial and boldness, even unto death, of thy servant John the Baptist; nay, more, give us the spirit of thy dear Son Jesus, who endured the cross, despising the shame, and is set down at the right hand of the throne of God. In the hour of our sore temptations, in our conflicts with indwelling sin, in the mortification of self, in the fight of faith, and until the glad hour of final triumph, be Thou, O Lord, our strength and our defence. When our hearts are overwhelmed within us, lead us to the Rock that is higher than we. Thou, O blessed Jesus, art that Rock; Thou hast been our shelter and a strong tower from our enemies; keep us, we pray Thee, even unto the end. That we may walk more closely with Thee, and grieve not thy Holy Spirit, make us, O merciful God, very watchful against all occasions of sin, from without and from within. May we have grace to abstain from the very appearance of evil, and to be on our guard against all places, and all company, and all habits of worldly conformity, whereby we may be surprised into sin. Thus do Thou enable us to keep ourselves in the love of Thee, looking for the mercy of our Lord Jesus Christ unto eternal life.

Now, heavenly Father, we desire once again to commend ourselves to thy keeping for the coming night; may we lay us down in peace, assured that Thou, Lord, wilt make us dwell in safety; may we rise refreshed and strengthened to renew our work of faith and labour of love, until we rest with Thee in glory, through the only merits of our blessed Lord and Saviour Jesus Christ. Amen.

[MORNING.] **ELEVENTH WEEK.—WEDNESDAY.** [EVENING.

READ IN HOLY SCRIPTURE GENESIS XLVI. 1—7, 26—34.

READ IN HOLY SCRIPTURE ST. JOHN VI. 1—21.

WE devoutly acknowledge Thee, O Lord, as the supreme object of our adoration, reverence, and love. Bestow on us the precious gift of faith, that we may always trust in Thee. Each day and each hour may we hear thy voice speaking to our inmost souls. May we all do thy will cheerfully, as in the sight of the Lord. Even in those things which contradict our natural inclinations, may we learn to obey Thee. Throughout this day may we have the deep consciousness that Thou art with us, directing our steps, inspiring our thoughts, and regulating our purposes. Let everything we do, whether secular or sacred, be done as in thy holy presence and for thy glory. Preserve us from the snares which may beset our path. Destroy our selfishness, and teach us to love others even as ourselves. Give us a growing love of all holiness, and a growing hatred of all sin. In the midst of an evil world, give us thy Holy Spirit, that we may maintain a conscience void of offence toward God and toward men.

We adore Thee, O Lord, as the Fountain of all our blessings. Accept, we pray Thee, of our united thanksgivings for thy watchful care throughout the night, for the mercies of the morning, and for the manifold blessings which tend to make our existence here below holy and happy. May all thy gifts be employed for Thee, and be rendered back to Thee in holy and acceptable service. In every gift may we recognise the Giver. Grant, we beseech Thee, O Lord, that our life may in all things be well-pleasing to Thee. We devoutly thank Thee for the gift of thy well-beloved Son, Jesus Christ, as the Saviour of sinners. May we so believe in Him that we may reap all the benefits of his death and passion upon the cross, and at last be counted worthy to share in the joys of his heavenly kingdom.

We pray Thee, O Lord, to bless our country with peace, and with that measure of prosperity which shall be most conducive to the furtherance of thy purposes of mercy and love. Let the wickedness of the wicked come to an end. Establish the reign of righteousness and truth throughout the world. [Be gracious, we beseech Thee, to the children of our household. Bless them with the grace of thy Holy Spirit, that they may be restrained from all evil, and be renewed in thy likeness.] And now, Lord, we commend ourselves, as a family, to thy fatherly care and protection during another day. Be thou our Guard and Guide. In every perplexity be Thou our wisdom. In every sorrow be Thou our solace. In every perplexity be Thou our shield and strength. Hear us, gracious Lord, in these our supplications, for the sake of Jesus Christ our only Saviour. Amen.

O LORD God, Most High, unworthy of ourselves to come into thy holy presence, we plead the name of thy dear Son. On his atoning merits and righteousness we rest our hope of acceptance. In gracious fulfilment of thy promise, do Thou for us exceeding abundantly above all that we ask or think. Show us, O God, our sinfulness. By thy Holy Spirit convince us how undeserving we are of thy daily goodness. Root out of our minds all pride and conceit of our own goodness; give us a deep insight into our own hearts and our many transgressions, that we may see our great need. Whatever in us has grieved thy Holy Spirit and defiled our own souls, graciously pardon. For thy name's sake remember not, we beseech Thee, our offences, but spare us, good Lord.

We praise Thee, O God, for the bounties of thy providence. We bless Thee that the same Divine power and compassion which supplied the hungry crowds that followed Jesus has ministered to our daily necessities. Enable us to read in these thy mercies the greatness of thy love, and in all thy past goodness to see a pledge of future grace. Especially, we beseech Thee to feed us with the bread of life. Awaken in us the hungering and thirsting after righteousness which will impel us to come daily to Jesus, that we may be filled. Our wants are many, but thou canst supply them all— strength in our weakness, protection from all dangers, and guidance in all perplexity. Be with us, we pray Thee, in the darkness and in the light. Keep us back from presumptuous and wilful sins, and direct our steps in thy ways, that we slip not.

Graciously, O God, look on all whom we would remember at thy footstool. Whatever earthly blessing Thou seest right and good for them, bestow. Above all, grant that they may be numbered among thy saints. May the young love and fear thee in the days of their youth, and the old be ripened, under the teaching and training of thy Spirit, for a place in thy kingdom of glory. Send forth the light of thy truth even to the uttermost parts of the earth. Grant that wherever it comes it may shine in many hearts which have hitherto been in darkness and the shadow of death, and guide them into the way of peace. Pour out thy Spirit on all thy Church. Illuminate all thy ministers with true knowledge and understanding of thy word. Give wisdom to all in authority, and courage to do that which is right in thy sight. Strengthen weak believers. Comfort sorrowing and bereaved hearts. Raise the fallen, and finally break down and subdue the power of Satan.

Hear us, O God; watch over us during the night, and bless us with all needful rest and sleep, for Jesus Christ's sake. Amen.

[MORNING.]   ELEVENTH WEEK.—THURSDAY.   [EVENING.

READ IN HOLY SCRIPTURE GENESIS XLVII. 1—12.

READ IN HOLY SCRIPTURE ST. JOHN VI. 22—40.

HOLY Father! in the Saviour's precious name we again present ourselves at thy footstool, to acknowledge thy protection through another night, and to implore a continuance of thy care through the dangers of another day. We have laid us down and slept, and awaked; for Thou hast sustained us. Now be pleased to give thine angels charge concerning us, to keep us in all our ways. Lord, make us to know our end, and the measure of our days, what it is; that we may know how frail we are, and apply our hearts unto wisdom.

O Lord, be our days few or many, days of joy or sorrow, let them not be days of sin—days on which we shall have to reflect in life's decline, and in death, with remorse or repentance. Oh, pardon all our past mis-spent days, and let the time past of our life suffice us wherein we have wrought the will of the flesh. Henceforth we would live in thy fear and to thy glory: but our strength is weakness; therefore hold Thou us up, and we shall be safe.

Impress our hearts, by what we have been reading, that life is a pilgrimage to eternity; and help us throughout the journey to keep the end in view. May we, by thy grace, be seeking, as the holy patriarchs did, a better country, that is, a heavenly. Be Thou to us, as to them, a Sun and a Shield. Direct and defend us, all through the wilderness, to the rest which remaineth to the people of God, and let not any of us come short of that rest.

Mercifully assist us now in the faithful discharge of all the duties of the day. Provide for our necessities. Order all our goings. Lead us not into temptation, but deliver us from evil; and unto all endeared to us by the ties of nature or friendship impart the blessings which they severally need. Comfort all who are in sorrow, and especially do we pray Thee to be the support of the infirm and aged. Should we attain threescore or fourscore years, may our hoary heads be a crown of glory, being found in the way of righteousness.

We again supplicate thy mercy on behalf of our gracious Monarch and all the royal family: our several ministers of state, and magistrates. Of thy goodness provide for the poor. For Christ's sake, the Lamb of God that taketh away the sin of the world, restore every prodigal to his Father's house. Hasten the fulfilment of thy word, "All the ends of the world shall remember and turn unto the Lord."

We now commit ourselves into the arms of thy love. Remember us for good, for our Lord and Saviour's sake; to whom, with Thee and the Holy Ghost, be all honour and glory for ever. Amen.

O HEAVENLY and loving Father, we praise Thee for thy gracious promise that every one who sees the Son, and believes in Him, shall have everlasting life. Give us thy Holy Spirit, that, taking of the things that are Christ's, He may show them to us. Grant us to grow continually in the knowledge of Jesus, and of the power of his resurrection, till we come to find that even in going to the grave there is no real death to them that are in Christ Jesus. When we are called by Thee to leave this world, may we fall to sleep, in sweet hope that nothing of Christ's shall be lost, but our very bodies be raised up at the last day. Send us now, we beseech Thee, a token for good, and give us refreshing sleep. Or if our eyes are held waking, be Thou near us, and the very darkness shall be light in Thee.

O kind Father, thou hast preserved and provided for us during another day. We thank Thee for the earthly bread which we have eaten, and which has come from thy hand, as surely as if we had gathered it, like the manna which of old fell from the skies. We praise Thee for strength to do our daily work. Let thy blessing rest on our accomplished tasks. Forgive us our forgetfulness of the true bread which came down from heaven. Let us ever seek first the kingdom of God and his righteousness. Blessed be thy glorious name that the entrance into the kingdom is not by works which we have done, but by believing on Him whom Thou hast sent. Lord, we hope in Him, we come to Him, sure that He will receive us, and never, never cast us out.

We commend to Thee, O gracious Father, with sympathy and compassion, all poor and destitute ones this night. Guide wanderers to the shelter of homes thou shalt open for them. Give the hungry food from hands prepared for them. Incline our hearts always to relieve, as Thou enablest us, the wants of the needy. And, O bountiful Provider of heavenly bread for the life of the world, pity all famishing souls. Awaken thy Church to scatter her stores more freely. Call men everywhere to the feast prepared for all peoples. Oh, that the salvation of Israel were come out of Zion! Oh, that men of every tongue, and nation, and tribe were taught no more to labour for that which is not bread, but to hearken to thy call, and eat that which is good, given by Thee for the life of the soul.

Now, O Lord, we commit to thy care, for the night, all the members of this family, young and old; and all our dear friends, far and near. Keep them night and day, till Thou bring them home; and to Thee shall be glory for ever, through Jesus Christ our Lord. Amen.

[75]

[Morning.]   **ELEVENTH WEEK.—FRIDAY.**   [Evening.]

READ IN HOLY SCRIPTURE GENESIS XLVII. 13—31.

READ IN HOLY SCRIPTURE ST. JOHN VI. 41—71.

HOLY Father, Lord of heaven and earth, we thank Thee for all thy goodness and mercy to us; goodness undeserved, and mercy great beyond our utmost thought. Thou hast again kept us in safety during the hours of the night, Thou hast blessed us with sleep, and the morning has brought to us fresh proofs of thy loving-kindness. We praise thy holy name for health and strength, and for the good which Thou hast mercifully provided for the refreshment of our bodies. Thou, O Lord, preservest man and beast. We beseech Thee to behold all who are suffering the bitter pangs of hunger, and send them help out of thy vast store-house; for the silver and the gold are thine, and the cattle upon a thousand hills.

Merciful Lord God, we thank Thee that we are not driven from our native land by famine, like thine ancient servant Jacob and his sons; that our Lord and Saviour has provided better blessings for all who confide in Him than those which Joseph obtained for his father's house. Let us daily feel that man liveth not by bread alone, but by every word that proceedeth out of the mouth of God. Feed us this day with the bread of life. Strengthen us, sanctify us, comfort us by thy everlasting Word, that it may be our guard and our guide; and when the time shall come that we must die, may thy sacred promises cheer and sustain us in death, and assure us of an entrance into thy kingdom.

We pray that thy gracious providence may watch over us throughout all the labours of the day; especially keep us from sin, that we may not grieve Thee. When we are beset by temptation, be Thou our strength, and in all our ways uphold, direct, and teach us. We beseech Thee, O Lord, to protect those who are exposed to great peril of life in their daily labours. We pray Thee to provide for the relief of those who are unemployed. Comfort the afflicted, support the aged, bless the bereaved, and cheer the dying through the precious blood of Jesus Christ.

Father of mercies, we entreat Thee to bless our country. As thou hast exalted our nation by so many privileges, so also grant unto us grace to serve and honour Thee. Let the wickedness of the wicked come to an end, but establish thou the just. Bring men of all classes to know, and love, and serve Thee. Bless our beloved Queen and all the royal family. Enlighten our rulers with heavenly wisdom, prosper our commerce, and give us peace by all means.

And now we cheerfully and thankfully betake ourselves to our daily duties. Be not far from us, O our God. To Thee we dedicate ourselves and all our service, through our blessed Saviour Jesus Christ. Amen.

O LORD our God, in Thee we live, and move, and have our being. Our life in the flesh hangs upon thy care, and is sustained by thy goodness. We receive daily bread, because thy compassions fail not. We are closing another day in peace, because it has been crowned with loving-kindness and tender mercy.

But man liveth not by bread alone. Our fathers did eat manna in the wilderness, and are dead. Though enriched with the blessings of this life, we, too, must lie down to die, and we know not the day nor the hour when the Son of Man shall come. So teach us to number our days that we may apply our hearts unto wisdom. Thou hast made us for endless life. Thou hast rendered us capable of bearing thine image and tasting thy joy; of being lights of the world, and temples of the living God; but we have sinned against Thee, O Lord, and are not worthy to be called thy children. By nature we are alienated from Thee, and dead in trespasses and sins; but Thou hast had pity upon us, and proposed to us reconciliation, and shown to us the way of life.

Thanks be unto God for his unspeakable gift, that He spared not his own Son, but gave Him, the true bread from heaven, that all who believe in Him may have everlasting life.

We pray that we may be taught of Thee, and become wise unto salvation; and that it may please Thee to draw our reluctant hearts to Christ, in whom Thou hast given us remission of sins. Through his obedience unto death, may we not come into condemnation, but pass from death into life. Quickened by his Spirit, may we rise from the death of sin to the life of righteousness. May we live a life of faith upon Christ, and hunger and thirst after righteousness. May our fellowship be with Thee, O God, and with thy Son Jesus Christ; and so closely unite us with Him that we may learn by experience what it is to eat his flesh and drink his blood. Thus nourished unto eternal life, may we increase in knowledge, grow in grace, abound more and more in love, wax stronger and stronger, rejoice in the hope of the glory of God, and be changed into the same image from glory to glory, by the Spirit of the Lord; that though our bodies perish day by day, our souls may live, looking for and hasting unto the glorious appearing of our God and Saviour Christ.

Hear our prayers for our [children and] kindred, that they all may be alive unto Thee, through Jesus Christ; serve Thee in newness of life in this world, and in the world to come have life everlasting. We ask all in the name and for the sake of Jesus Christ, our adorable Lord and Saviour. Amen.

[Morning.]	ELEVENTH WEEK.—SATURDAY.	[Evening.

READ IN HOLY SCRIPTURE GENESIS XLVIII.

LORD, we bless Thee that in a world of change and death Thou art ever the same. Be merciful unto us, we pray Thee, and grant that we may be followers of them who through faith and patience inherit the promises. Help us to live, as they did, as pilgrims and strangers upon earth. Whether our lives be long or short, may they be lives of faith upon the Son of God; and whom we die, may we enter upon the rest that remaineth for thy people. We thank Thee that the Day Spring from on high hath visited us, and that things which righteous men of old saw only through a glass darkly stand open to our sight. Lord, accept the offering of grateful and contrite hearts. We plead the merits of Jesus for acceptance with Thee. We beseech Thee to sprinkle us afresh with the blood of atonement. May the guilt of sin be cancelled, and its power be destroyed within us. May we cease to do evil, and learn to do well, perfecting holiness in the fear of the Lord. To this end grant us the aid of thy Holy Spirit, that He may take of the things of Christ, and show them unto our souls; and thus may Christ not only be the object of our trust, but the example we imitate.

We render hearty thanks unto Thee, O God, for thy watchful care during another night. Oh, help us to begin every day as if we entered upon life anew. May the precious hours of this day be well spent; yea, so spent as if it were the last. To Thee we now consecrate our renewed health and strength. May the secular duties of life be to us religious duties, because we seek thy glory in them. Help us to order all our affairs with discretion, and to regulate our entire life by the principles of thy Word. May those with whom we have intercourse take knowledge of us that we have been with Jesus, and that we are on our way to dwell in his presence for ever. Preserve us this day from the temptations of the wicked one. Keep our feet that they do not stumble, our eyes that they behold not vanity, our tongues that they utter no guile, our hearts that they be not disquieted by untoward events, and that we lose not the light of thy countenance. Grant us as much prosperity as shall be for our good; and when Thou sendest adversity, may we receive it from the hand of our Father, and may it contribute both to the health of our souls and the glory of thy name.

[We pray Thee to bless the children of this family; bring them all in early life to Jesus, that we may be a holy family, journeying to our Father's house above.] Let thy mercy be bestowed on all whom we love. We ask all, and we praise Thee for all, in the name of Jesus Christ. Amen.

READ IN HOLY SCRIPTURE PSALM CXXX.

O GOD! the God of the spirits of all flesh; Thou hast no pleasure in the death of the wicked, and savest such as be of a contrite spirit; pardon, we beseech Thee, the iniquity of thy servants, according to the greatness of thy mercy; and bless us with all spiritual blessings in heavenly places in Christ Jesus; that we, being sanctified through thy truth, and preserved by thy mighty power, may receive the salvation that is in Christ Jesus, with eternal glory.

Most merciful Father! out of the depth of our sin and ruin do we cry unto Thee; pitifully behold us in our low and lost estate; for if Thou shouldest mark iniquity, we could not stand. With Thee there is forgiveness, that Thou mayest be feared. Have mercy upon us, O Lord, according to thy loving-kindness; according to thy tender mercies, blot out our transgressions; granting us true repentance, with faith in our Lord Jesus Christ, and the hope of eternal life. We wait on Thee; our soul doth wait, and in thy word do we hope. O God, be not far from us; O our God, make haste for our help.

Our Father in heaven! who hast given us this day our daily bread, and hast prevented us with the blessings of thy goodness; we would sacrifice unto Thee with the voice of thanksgiving, and pay unto Thee that which we have vowed. Let it please Thee so to rule in our hearts by thy grace, that we may hate every false way, and be kept from the path of the destroyer. Pitifully look upon us in our weakness, and help us to take heed to our ways, that we sin not against Thee; but keeping our tongue from evil and our lips from speaking guile, may we worthily magnify thy holy name, and adorn the doctrine of God our Saviour.

O God, hide us under the shadow of thy wings, and let thy tender mercies come unto us, that we may live. Let thy merciful kindness be for our comfort, according to thy word; bless our substance, and accept the work of our hands; let it be well with us, and with our children after us, that we may prolong our days upon the earth. O Lord, who art our confidence and our hope, let it please Thee to keep us during the night. When we lie down, let us not be afraid; and let our sleep be sweet. Do Thou for us, and for our kindred, above all we ask or think. Build up Jerusalem, and let the righteousness thereof go forth as brightness, and the salvation thereof as a lamp that burneth.

And now let these our words wherewith we have made supplication before Thee, be heard by Thee, the Lord our God; and in thy faithfulness answer us through Jesus Christ, our only exalted Redeemer. Amen.

[Morning.]   TWELFTH WEEK.—LORD'S DAY.   [Evening.

READ IN HOLY SCRIPTURE PSALM LXXI.   READ IN HOLY SCRIPTURE ST. MARK VII. 1—23.

GRACIOUS God, accept our praises for all thy mercy to us, and grant that in all the religious duties of this holy day thy Spirit may kindle in us a fervent desire towards Thee, and maintain in us a constant remembrance that we are not our own, but thine. Thou hast bought us with a price, not with silver and gold, but with the precious blood of thy dear Son. May we be entirely consecrated to thy service and glory!

Lord, how many are the motives which Thou hast given us for trusting in Thee! Through infant years and later days thine eye has watched over us, and thy hand ministered to our wants. Thou hast cast our lot where we have been privileged to hear the blessed tidings of redeeming mercy. All things that pertain to life and godliness Thou hast abundantly bestowed. O God, we desire that our mouth may be continually filled with thy praise, and that in the experience of thy goodness we may lean upon Thee more and more. Renew to us, day by day, the tokens of thy love. May all thy dealings with us tend to the increase of our faith; and fill us, we beseech Thee, with all joy and peace in believing, that we may abound in hope through the power of the Holy Ghost.

Deliver us out of every trouble; disappoint the craft of the great enemy, and let us not fall under his power. Especially, O God, preserve us this day from his devices, and from all those earthly and sinful thoughts which would hinder our services of prayer and praise in the sanctuary. Calm and solemnise our hearts as we draw near to thy footstool. May we realise at once the greatness of thy majesty and the tenderness of thy pity. Let not the Word we shall hear be snatched from our hearts, or be choked by other things, but cause it to take root and bring forth fruit abundantly in holy and religious lives.

We pray for all congregations that shall meet in thy name this day, far and near. Let the signs of thy presence be seen among them in the earnestness of ministers and people. Give wisdom to all who shall teach thy Word, in public or in private, in the school or the congregation. May they be guided into all truth themselves, and be thereby fitted to guide others. Pour out thy Spirit, which alone can make effectual to salvation the message they shall deliver. Anxiously we pray, O God, that thou wouldst turn the feet of many to thy house to-day who have hitherto neglected its ordinances. Draw them by thy grace, and let them not hear in vain.

Commending ourselves and all whom we love to thy watchful providence, we ask these and all needful mercies at thy hand, in the name of Jesus Christ, our exalted Redeemer and Saviour. Amen.

ONCE, more, O God, in the multitude of thy tender mercies, we are permitted to draw near to thy throne of grace. We have had many religious privileges to-day, but we fear we have not used them as we ought to have done. Forgive the sins of our worship; wash our very services in the blood of the Lamb, and keep us at all times from honouring Thee with our lips, while our hearts are far from Thee.

Bless to our hearts, O God, the word of the truth of the Gospel which our ears have heard to-day. Bless the portions of thy Holy Book to which we have listened, and oh, fasten upon our souls the solemn words of the Saviour which we have just read. Keep us from the defilement that cometh out of the heart. From all deadly sin, from envy, hatred, malice, and all uncharitableness, good Lord, deliver us.

Heavenly Father, and Saviour, and Comforter, it grieves us to think that our hearts are so dead, and our lips are so dumb, to speak thy praise. Yet, we beseech Thee, accept our humble tribute of thanksgiving, for Jesus' sake, and fit us for singing thy praises in a better way and in a brighter world.

We rejoice to think of Thee, eternal King, as the God who heareth and answereth prayer. May all the prayers to-day offered, according to thy will, return in blessings to many, many souls. Make thy Word preached this day to be the power of God unto the salvation of many who have heard it. Let thy Church now arise, and shake herself from the dust, and put on her beautiful garments; let all the ends of the world see the salvation of our God.

Bless the poor in their cottages; bless the sick upon their beds; bless the captives in their dungeon, especially those whom Satan hath bound; and, in blessing others, forget us not. Lord, we would see Jesus. Take the veil from our hearts, and let us behold the King in his beauty. Forgive us that we have grieved the blessed Comforter, and take not thy Holy Spirit from us. We desire to know more of Thee and thy love, which passeth knowledge, and to have a deeper experience of the work of thy grace in our hearts.

Gathered here as a family, we ask for family mercies. [Our children, ourselves, the dear ones at home, and the dear ones far away, bless them all, O Lord.] Make those who are already thine more like Thee, and oh, that all whom we love may live before Thee! And now for the hours of our nightly rest we cast ourselves on thy loving care. Guard us while we sleep, and when we awake may we be still with Thee. We ask all for the love of Jesus Christ our Lord. Amen.

[Morning.] **TWELFTH WEEK.—MONDAY.** [Evening.

READ IN HOLY SCRIPTURE GENESIS XLIX. 1—27.   READ IN HOLY SCRIPTURE ST. MARK VII. 24—37.

O GOD, Thou art our God, early will we seek Thee. Our voice shalt Thou hear in the morning; every day will we bless Thee, and praise thy name for ever. Preserved by thy care, O Thou who never slumberest, we again implore a Father's blessing from thy hands, and ask of Thee those things which are necessary as well for the body as the soul. We pray for guidance during this day. We are strangers here, seeking a better country; help us to live as those who know that this is not their rest. Let thy bountiful grace and mercy point out our way. Enable us to overcome difficulties, preserve us in the hour of temptation and weakness, and bring us safely to our journey's end.

O Thou compassionate and all-loving Father, who in Jesus Christ art willing to be our Father, who givest good gifts to thy children, behold us before Thee, waiting for those gifts which Thou alone canst bestow. Earnestly do we ask that Thou wouldst accept us through thy well-beloved Son, wouldst place us among thy children, and give us of their portion.

Bless us with strength of purpose and stability of mind. May we never look back, after putting our hands to the plough, but forgetting that which is behind, reach forward to the prize of our high calling in Christ Jesus. Teach us to value our privileges and rights as the sons of God, never to barter them for anything the world or the flesh may offer, but to endeavour to be blameless and harmless, as thy children in the midst of an evil world.

Bless us with calm and holy tempers, such as become the followers of the meek and loving Jesus; and give us resolution to put away from us all anger, wrath, and malice, forbearing one another, and forgiving one another, even as we hope to be forgiven of Thee, for Christ's sake.

Bless us with influence for good over our brethren, that we may seek their happiness, sorrowing with their sorrows, and rejoicing in their joy. If thou shouldst call us to rule, may we rule in the fear of the Lord; if to serve, help us to do it as serving the Lord Christ; that when He comes we may be approved in his sight, and give in our account with joy.

Bless our neighbours and friends with peace and prosperity in their homes, that all men may see that we are a people blessed and owned of Thee. Guide and direct our rulers, and all in authority. Clothe them with uprightness and truth, for the punishment of wickedness and vice, and the maintenance of thy true religion and virtue.

These mercies we seek from Thee, the mighty God, for the sake of thy Son our Saviour, Jesus Christ. Amen.

O LORD, we gratefully acknowledge that Thou hast done all things well. All our life long we have been the objects of thy care; and through all the way by which we have come, Thou hast watched over us. Thou hast shaped our course, and fixed the bounds of our habitation, and ordered aright that which concerns us. And now, O Lord, we give Thee thanks for thy providential guidance and guardianship, and for the unfailing bounty by which Thou hast supplied our wants. Grant, we entreat Thee, that the goodness and mercy which have been over us until now may follow us all the days of our life.

We are encouraged to trust Thee by the remembrance of thy past mercies. If sometimes thy ways have appeared dark and mysterious to our erring sight, the result has proved that all thy ways were right. Though Thou hast veiled thy face, Thou hast never withdrawn thy love; Thou hast shown us that when thou didst most clothe Thyself in clouds, it was only the better to fulfil thy wise design. Thou hast delayed to bestow, but Thou hast never denied us thy blessing; and the delay of which we have most complained has only been designed to try our faith, and to prepare us for the larger mercy. And whatever the way by which Thou hast brought us, Thou hast caused all things to work together for our good.

And now, O Lord, we come again to the fountain from which we have so often drawn. We cast ourselves again on the love which has never failed us. We deserve not the smallest of thy favours, nor the meanest place in thy house. We are not worthy to be called thy children, nor to be numbered among thy servants; for we have failed to honour Thee as a Father, and to serve Thee as a Master. But Thou, O Lord, art merciful; and though our wants are manifold as our sin is great, it is easy for Thee to supply them all. Even the crumbs of thy bounty are sufficient to enrich us; and Thou wilt not withhold these when Thou hast given us thy Son. Lord, for his sake do Thou supply our wants. Grant us a clearer sense of forgiveness and acceptance. Take away every feeling which interferes with our service. Let our ears be open to hear thy voice, our hearts and lips to show forth thy praise.

We commend to Thee our [children and] friends. Teach them day by day thy will. Deliver them from all evil, and preserve them safe unto thy kingdom and glory.

Accept of our thanksgivings for the mercies of the day. Have us and ours in thy holy keeping during the watches of the night. Guide us through life; and at death receive us to Thyself, for Christ's sake. Amen.

[MORNING.] **TWELFTH WEEK.—TUESDAY.** [EVENING.]

READ IN HOLY SCRIPTURE GENESIS L.

WE thank Thee, O Thou preserver of men, that this morning we are not found weeping over the dead body of any who compose our family circle, but that, having been favoured with sound and refreshing sleep, we now present ourselves at thy gracious footstool in the possession of health of body, vigour of mind, and earthly comfort. Whilst we render Thee our most grateful thanks for these undeserved mercies, we would pray for any into whose habitation death has entered, and who are now mourning over the loss they have sustained, Enable them to say, "The Lord gave, and the Lord hath taken away; blessed be the name of the Lord;" and grant them grace, that they sorrow not even as others which have no hope, for them also which sleep in Jesus will God bring with Him. Sanctify such solemn events for our good also, and for the good of all the living. O Lord God of the patriarchs, as Thou didst guide Jacob and Joseph, thy servants, through life, and didst sustain and comfort them in death, so guide us with thy counsel, and afterward receive us to glory.

We beseech Thee, O Lord, to give us this day a watchful spirit, that we may not say or do anything which shall be injurious to one another, or to any with whom we may associate. If we should act improperly, make us immediately sensible of our fault, and give us the grace of true humility to acknowledge and confess the same, seeking forgiveness from those we may offend; and if any should act towards us contrary to righteousness, may we be saved from indulging in a spirit of retaliation and enmity. As we hope for forgiveness from Thee for our manifold sins, so may we be ready to forgive others.

Incline us, O Lord! who art the Author of all goodness, to live the remainder of our lives according to thy glorious Gospel, which teacheth us that, denying ungodliness and worldly lusts, we should live soberly, righteously, and godly in this present world. Purify our hearts, by the power of the Holy Spirit, from the love of sin, especially the sin which doth so easily beset us; and fill us with such views of Thee, and experiences of thy favour, that we may love the Lord our God with all our heart, and with all our soul, and with all our mind. Enable us to discharge every duty aright, prayerfully trusting in thy wise, powerful, and beneficent providence. Grant, O Lord, that whatsoever our hand findeth to do this day, we may do it with our might, remembering that there is no work, nor device, nor knowledge, nor wisdom, in the grave, whither we must all, sooner or later, go. Hear us, O merciful Father, for the sake of Jesus Christ our Lord. Amen.

READ IN HOLY SCRIPTURE PSALM CXLVII.

O LORD, we praise Thee as our Creator; Thou madest us, and not we ourselves. We praise Thee as our Preserver; for in Thee we live, and move, and have our being. We praise Thee as our Redeemer; for in Thee we have redemption through Christ's blood, the forgiveness of sins, according to the riches of his grace. We praise Thee, O Jehovah, as his Father, who loved us from eternity; as the Son that died for us on the cross; as the Holy Ghost, that comforteth and sanctifieth us; and as the ever-blessed and undivided Trinity, to whom we would now ascribe glory, honour, praise, and power. Hear us, Lord, when we cry unto Thee.

We have sinned against Thee, and are not worthy to be called thy children. Father, forgive us; stretch forth thy hand and lift us up, and be our strength and our hope. Oh, create within us clean hearts, and renew within us right spirits. We cannot be happy till we become holy, and we can never be holy till thy Spirit take up his abode with us, and renew and sanctify us. Be pleased to reconcile us to Thyself.

Our Father which art in heaven, make us thankful for our numerous and undeserved mercies; above all, for Jesus, thine unspeakable gift. Help us to open our hearts when He knocks for admission. God forbid that we should shut Him out, and give entrance and entertainment to sin and Satan. Come, O Spirit of the Lord, open the gates of our affections, and let the King of Glory come in. We lament before Thee our weakness of faith, our feebleness of hope, and our deadness of affection. Our sins prevail against us, and are more in number than the hairs of our head; but we look to Thee for mercy. Kindle a holy love in our hearts, and cause all that is within us to bless thy holy name. Make thy will to be our will, and so we shall be filled with grace and peace. Feed us, O Lord, with the bread of life, of which, if we eat, we shall never die. Strengthened by this food, we will go on our way rejoicing, till it pleases Thee to take us to heaven, where we shall neither hunger nor thirst any more. Till then, O holy Saviour, hedge up our way, even though it be with thorns, that we go not aside from the path that leads to life everlasting. Help us continually to expect death and the judgment to come; help us, like the Apostle, to die daily; help us to resist the world, the devil, and the flesh; and when all thy purposes regarding us in this world have been accomplished, oh, receive our ransomed spirits into the kingdom of thy dear Son, that we may live and reign with Him for ever. We ask all for His name's sake. Amen.

[Morning.] **TWELFTH WEEK.—WEDNESDAY.** [Evening.

READ IN HOLY SCRIPTURE 2 CORINTHIANS V.

READ IN HOLY SCRIPTURE ST. MATTHEW XV. 29—39.

O GOD, our Father, suffer us to draw nigh to Thee this morning with our morning sacrifice of prayer and thanksgiving. Help us to live this day in thy faith, and fear, and love; and in our life and conduct enable us to walk by faith, and not by sight.

Teach us, O God, the solemnities of the future—the things that shall be, and that must be hereafter. Teach us that we are but dying creatures, living here for a season, and then to pass away. In thy Holy Book we have read this morning about this perishable body, and about this imperishable soul of ours. Oh, teach us to learn the lessons of thy Word, and to value its timely teachings. Teach us how frail are these bodies, and how uncertain is this life; that the body is but a movable tent, an earthly tabernacle, that must one day dissolve, that is even every day dissolving. Fix our affections on things above, and teach us not to rest the foundation of our hopes on the shifting sands of this passing world; but to push forward, and look upward, away from the crumbling clay to the building of God, the house not made with hands; away from that which is temporal and temporary to that which is eternal in the heavens.

Lord, give us spiritual foresight in time to provide for eternity. Teach us so to live that we may not fear to die; and may we so die that we may live for evermore! While we are at home in the body may we be clothed upon with Christ; and then, when we shall depart from the body, we shall not be cast out naked, but shall be clothed upon with immortality. Grant that whether present or absent, we may be accepted of Him; that, living or dying, we may be the Lord's.

Prepare us for judgment. Let us love Jesus as our Friend, our Redeemer, our Advocate, and we shall not fear Him as a Judge; for He that hath loved us, and bought us, and pardoned us, and accepted us in this the day of salvation, will not condemn us in the great day of his appearing. Let the love of Christ constrain us, and lead us no longer to live unto ourselves, but unto Him which died for us and rose again. Thus consecrate our days to thyself, O God, by thine anointing Spirit, and receive us as thy servants, and admit us into the adoption of thy Son.

We give Thee thanks, O God, for thy continued goodness. Thou hast sustained us while we slept, and hast kept us from the perils and dangers of the night season. We now commit ourselves to thy good keeping during this day, and humbly pray that Thou wouldst preserve us by thy providence, and at last receive us into thine everlasting kingdom, through Jesus Christ our Lord. Amen.

ALMIGHTY and most gracious God, who knowest our wants and hast compassion on our infirmities, we beseech Thee to assist us by thy grace whilst we offer up our evening prayer.

We come to Thee as weak and guilty creatures, and we entreat Thee to forgive the sins which we have this day committed against Thee by thought, word, and deed, and to strengthen us with might by thy Spirit, that we may successfully strive against our besetting evil passions, and run with patience the race that is set before us, looking unto Jesus, the author and finisher of our faith.

We thank Thee for thy goodness to us in supplying our wants. We are dependent on Thee, O Lord, for life and all that we need, and we desire to recognise thy hand in all our daily circumstances; and whilst we use with moderation and gratitude this world's enjoyments which thy bounty bestows upon us, we pray Thee to enrich our souls with those spiritual gifts whereby we may daily grow in grace, and become meet for the inheritance of the saints in light.

Incline our hearts to seek first the kingdom of God and his righteousness, and cheerfully to trust in Thee to prosper our efforts to provide things honest in the sight of all men; and if it should please Thee to visit us with disappointment or affliction, let thy grace accompany thy dispensations, so that we may humble ourselves under thy mighty hand, and bear with patience and resignation the trials which Thou seest to be needful for us. Let thy blessing accompany our daily study of thy Holy Word, and grant that what we read therein may be so carried to our hearts by thy Holy Spirit that it may guide, strengthen, and comfort us in all our ways, and make us wise unto salvation through faith that is in Christ Jesus.

We know that this world, with all its objects and enjoyments, passeth away. Incline us to seek more earnestly that eternal inheritance which Christ hath purchased for us; and may a lively faith in his merits enable us to live in this world with our affections set upon things above, so that, amidst all the changes and chances of this mortal life, our hearts may surely there be fixed where true joys are to be found.

To thy gracious care and protection we commend ourselves and all that belongs to us. Let thy gracious hand be over us to keep us from all evil. Refresh us with such sleep as is needful to fit us for the duties of another day. May we daily grow in grace, and in the knowledge and experience of thy Gospel; and whenever it shall please Thee to take us out of this world may we be received into thine everlasting kingdom, through our Lord and Saviour Jesus Christ. Amen.

[81]

[Morning.]   TWELFTH WEEK.—THURSDAY.   [Evening.

READ IN HOLY SCRIPTURE EXODUS I. 1—14.

O THOU that hearest prayer! quicken us, we beseech Thee, by thy Spirit, that we may worship Thee in spirit and in truth; and grant us access to Thee, by faith in Christ Jesus. Another day is before us. We know not what it may bring forth. Unexpected trials may sadden us, or unexpected mercies may cheer us. Feeling the uncertainty of the future, we seek renewed grace, and strength, and wisdom, to sustain, direct, and guide us under all the circumstances that may befall us. Prepare us for whatever Thou art preparing for us.

If temporal mercies are continued to us, if the enjoyment of family and social privileges be prolonged, if our household abide in safety this day, we beseech Thee to preserve us from the peril of prosperity, by adding to all thy other gifts the grace which alone can fill our hearts with a sense of dependent gratitude.

Or, should it seem good to Thee to visit us with affliction, we pray for a submissive, resigned, and patient spirit. We pray for the gift of faith, to enable us to trust Thee where we cannot trace Thee. We know thy people are often chosen in the furnace of affliction. We know that the rigour of Egyptian bondage went before the deliverance of Israel from the oppression of their cruel taskmasters. If, therefore, trial be before us, Lord, increase our faith! Grant that we may hear the rod and who hath appointed it; that we may see GOD in our affliction, and so see *good* in it.

And now, heavenly Father, committing all that is uncertain to thy gracious providence, we pray for present grace for present duty. Whether it be our province to rule or serve, to be active in the world or diligent in the home, shed abroad thy love in our hearts, by thy Holy Spirit, that our day's work may be a work of faith, our day's labour a labour of love. Let thy presence go forth with us. Suffer us not to forget Thee, and fall into sin; but in every temptation be Thou at our right hand, and make a way for our escape. May it be our aim to adorn the doctrine of God our Saviour in all things; and to this end grant that we may abide in Christ.

We supplicate thy blessing upon all near and dear to us. Bless them with all spiritual blessings in Christ Jesus. Be gracious to our land, and to our Sovereign. Regard all conditions of men. Succour the oppressed. Break the fetters of slavery in every land. Comfort the sorrowful and bereaved, and in Thine own time, and in thine own way, set up thy kingdom of righteousness, peace, and joy in the Holy Ghost, in the hearts of men, through Jesus Christ our Lord. Amen.

READ IN HOLY SCRIPTURE ST. MATTHEW XVI. 1—12.

O LORD our heavenly Father, who hast taught us in thy holy word to have our conversation in heaven, enable us while we live *in* the world to live *above* it, renouncing its lusts and vanities, and seeking Thee only, as our exceeding great reward. Deliver us from all trust in secular knowledge, and from a vain satisfaction in sense; and, above all, from a worldly mind in our spiritual things. Take from us the carnal heart, which looks for Thee only in the rich, and mighty, and wonderful things of the world; and give us the spiritual mind which can see Thee best in love, and meekness, and holiness. Give us a spiritual ear to catch the still small voice of the promised Comforter, that so the earnest of the spirit of Jesus may be our all-sufficient sign from heaven in the dangers and troubles of our daily life. Teach us to read the signs of the time, not only in the world around us, but in the word of thy truth, and in the course of thy providence; and while we mourn in ourselves and others the abounding of error and wickedness, enable us to stay our hearts upon the assurance of thy promise, that when the enemy cometh in like a flood, the Spirit of the Lord shall lift up a standard against him.

O Thou who feedest the young ravens that call upon Thee, and the cattle upon a thousand hills; who satisfiest the poor with bread, and spreadest thy bountiful table for all the multitudes of mankind; feed us, we beseech Thee, with that bread of heaven which giveth life unto the world. We thank Thee and praise thy holy name for all temporal blessings; but we beseech Thee to enable us to seek *first* the kingdom of God and his righteousness, that we may know the love of Christ which passeth knowledge, and be filled with all the fulness of God.

We feel and bewail the deceitfulness of our own heart, and that the leaven of sin lingers in it at its best estate. Cleanse us from our sin in its guilt and power. Take away our natural enmity to Thee. Wash us in the atoning blood of our Redeemer, and purge us throughly from our iniquities. Join us more closely to our risen Lord; quicken in us his life, and perfect in us his love, that henceforth we may not live to ourselves, but to Him that died for us and rose again. And when our hearts faint and fail through unbelief, remind us of the truth and mercy that have followed us all the days of our life; that, resting on thy love, and patiently awaiting thy time, we may trust Thee even in the thick darkness. These prayers and praises we offer to Thee, beseeching Thee, O Father, to bring us and all whom Thou hast taught us to remember at thy throne of grace, to that eternal feast of joy and love which Thou hast promised us in Jesus Christ our Lord. Amen.

[MORNING.]   TWELFTH WEEK.—FRIDAY.   [EVENING.

READ IN HOLY SCRIPTURE PSALM V.   READ IN HOLY SCRIPTURE ST. MATT. XVI. 13—23.

O LORD, without whom nothing is strong, nothing is holy, we would begin this day with Thee, and ask that we may have Thee with us through the day. Lord, cause thy face to shine upon us, and thereby make our faces to shine, and fill us with strength for all the duties and burdens of the day. We give Thee hearty thanks, O God, for the sleep which has refreshed and recruited us, after the labours of yesterday; for the sweet morning light which raises us again to our toil. Thou hast blessed us, and we are blessed; no pestilence walking in the darkness has smitten us, no evil thing has come nigh our dwelling; we laid ourselves down and slept; we awoke, for Thou didst sustain us. Accept, we beseech Thee, through thy Son Jesus Christ, our morning sacrifice of praise.

And now, O Lord, do thou go forth with us to our work; let not our hands lose their cunning, nor our minds their intelligence; make us diligent in business, and grant us comfort and success in all we undertake; prepare us for whatever thy fatherly goodness may have in store for us to day, whether of joy or sorrow, and help us both to suffer and to do thy will. O God, we are sadly prone to go astray from thy commandments, and many temptations will beset our path; but may the thought that Thou hatest all workers of iniquity restrain us. Moved with fear, may we shrink from vexing thy love and incurring thy displeasure. Do Thou keep our lips that they speak no falsehood, but may truth characterise and hallow all our communications. Do Thou lead us in thy righteousness, that we may not be beguiled, by the enemy of souls, into any sin. Let us not listen to his seductions, nor lend an ear to his promises, for there is no faithfulness in his mouth; but give us grace to trust only in Thee, and under the shadow of thy wing may we abide all the day long. Defend us, we beseech Thee, with the shield of thy power. Make our hearts glad with the sunshine of thy favour. Look in mercy on the world which lieth in wickedness. Day by day snatch many souls as brands from the burning. Arouse slumbering and lukewarm Christians. May thy Church serve Thee, and seek thy glory with a warmer zeal. Endue thy ministers with the wisdom which cometh from above, and encourage them by the manifest tokens of thy blessing.

These mercies we entreat, according to thy will and our several necessities, not only for ourselves, but for every one whom we love, and for all men, in the great name of our blessed Advocate and Saviour Jesus Christ, to whom, with Thyself and the Holy Spirit, be all honour and glory for ever. Amen.

BLESSED Lord Jesus, we adore Thee as the only begotten Son of God; the brightness of the Father's glory, and the express image of his person. Thou art the Christ, the Son of the living God; our only Saviour, our eternal Friend. We build all our hopes upon thy person, thy righteousness, and thy finished work. Ever may we be bound to Thee by ties of gratitude and love. Blessed is he who believeth in Thee. Blessed are we, that out of our sin and sorrow we may look unto Thee for salvation.

Bestow upon us, O God, such zeal for thy glory, and so much of the patience of thy kingdom, that we may gladly endure persecution and scorn for thy name's sake. Since Thou didst bear the cross for us, let us not refuse any cross of thine; only strengthen us in thy ways, and leave us not without the supports of thy sacred Spirit. Pardon us, O Lord, that we have done so little to spread abroad thy praise, and to bring our follow-men to the knowledge of thy grace. Arm us, we beseech Thee, with courage, and fill our hearts with so much love to Thee that we may make all around us know how great, how good, and how precious a Saviour Thou art.

May we ever, as Thou hast taught us, prize the soul beyond the body, eternity beyond time, and heaven beyond earth. Make us content to be poor in this world, if only we are rich in faith and heirs of the kingdom; and in that great day when Thou shalt judge the secrets of all men, grant unto us, through thy precious blood, to find acceptance with Thee and everlasting life.

We thank and bless our God for all the goodness and the truth which have been shown us this day. We praise Thee, Lord, for all the mercies bestowed on us, and for our preservation from the innumerable evils which have compassed us about. Pardon all Thou hast seen in us opposed to thy sacred will. Teach us to do thy will. We humbly and earnestly ask that forgiveness of sin which Thou hast mercifully promised to bestow upon all who seek it, through thy dear Son Jesus Christ. Keep us in safety through the night; bless our habitation and all whom it contains. Kindly grant us sweet sleep; preserve us from all disturbance and all danger, and in the morning grant us to rise refreshed and strengthened for our labour. Have mercy, O God, upon all our relations, friends, and neighbours; bestow upon them all needful good, both temporal and spiritual. Hear the prayers which any offer on our behalf, as well as our prayers for all the families that call upon thy name; for we approach Thee in the name of our Lord Jesus Christ, unto whom, with Thee, O Father, and the Holy Spirit, be praise and glory for ever. Amen.

[Morning.]   TWELFTH WEEK.—SATURDAY.   [Evening.

READ IN HOLY SCRIPTURE EXODUS II.

O LORD God Almighty, the Maker of all things in heaven and earth, the day is thine, the night also is thine; Thou createst the light and the sun. We thank Thee that thou hast raised us from sleep, and given us to see the light of another day. We are not worthy of these repeated acts of thy goodness; for we have sinned against Thee in thought, word, and deed. Thou mightest justly have left us in darkness, in the night of hopeless gloom and despair; but because Thou delightest in mercy we are still spared. Oh, let the day star shine upon our hearts, and chase away all the darkness of sin! We pray for pardon through Jesus Christ, who has died for our sins and risen again for our justification. Give us the witness of the Holy Spirit that we are thy children, adopted into thy family, and made heirs together of the hope of eternal life.

This day supply all our wants. Feed us with food convenient for us; let our bread be given us, and our water be sure. As thou didst graciously care for thy servant Moses, and even from infancy to hoary hairs didst protect him from all dangers, and deliver him in all temptations, so guard, guide, and defend us, we beseech Thee. Let the examples of thy special care for thy people in the days which are past lead us so to trust in Thee, that we may not be tempted to seek our wealth or profit by any means which would incur thy displeasure, and place us beyond the range of thy special providence and regard. May we always endure temptation and trial as seeing Thee, the Invisible!

Feed our souls, we pray Thee, with the bread of heaven. Let us earnestly labour for the bread which endureth unto everlasting life. Let our treasure and our heart be in heaven. Let us ever feel that the supply of our temporal wants is not all we need; and as the people of old by faith still looked to the land of promise, and longed for it as their final resting place, so, while thankful for temporal mercies, would we most earnestly pray for final admission into the rest which remaineth for the people of God. May we esteem even the reproach of Christ greater riches than all which the world can give, and in all things bear the cross patiently while we have respect unto the recompence of the reward. Let us ever feel that this is not our home, that the heavenly Canaan is our true country, and that we are constantly travelling to it. We pray to be more and more fitted for that rest by thy renewing and sanctifying Spirit. Watch over all the members of our family; restrain and sanctify them in all things by thy grace, and bring them and us finally to a heavenly home, for the sake of Jesus Christ our adorable Lord and Saviour. Amen.

READ IN HOLY SCRIPTURE EPHESIANS II. 13—22.

ALMIGHTY and everlasting God, we adore the greatness of thy love in preserving our lives, and bringing us nearly to the close of another week. Truly it is of thy mercy that we are not consumed. It is not of our own carefulness that we are permitted to bow before Thee in the possession of so much health and comfort. Many of our fellow-creatures during the week have had to pass through much and severe trial; many have been visited with great sickness and mortality; some with pestilence, famine, and sudden death. But Thou hast mercifully preserved us, and given us another opportunity of drawing near to the throne of thy grace, and seeking pardon through Christ our Redeemer.

We confess our need of coming penitently into thy presence. We have committed many offences, in thought, word, and deed, against thy Divine Majesty. Help us truly to repent, and to be heartily sorry for these our misdoings. Give us grace that, by faith in our Saviour Jesus Christ, we may seek and obtain forgiveness for all that is past, and strength whereby we may ever hereafter serve and please Thee in newness of life, to the honour and glory of thy name.

We beseech Thee, most merciful Father, upon this the eve of thy holy day, so to affect our minds that they may be withdrawn from all unnecessary care and worldly concern. Fix our thoughts upon the word of thy truth and upon Christ, who hath brought us, once strangers from the covenant of promise, nigh unto Thyself, and hath given us access by the Spirit to the throne of thy grace. Lead us also to magnify thy holy name for having made so great provision for thy Church upon earth. Enable us highly to value its privileges; make us, by thy saving and sanctifying power, fellow citizens with the saints, and obedient and affectionate members of thy family and household. Being thus blessed, may we seek, in dependence upon Thee, the prosperity of thy Church. Give to its pastors a large measure of thy grace and heavenly benediction, so that by their life and teaching they may set forth thy glory in the salvation of men.

Grant also that we and all thy people may be built upon the foundation of the apostles and prophets, Jesus Christ himself being the chief corner stone. May we be constantly seeking to become a holy and perfect temple, in which thy praises may be sung, thy pure truth taught, thy glory seen, and thy presence felt.

Now, O Lord, we commit ourselves [our families], and all for whom we should pray, to thy protection this night. We ask every blessing for the sake of our Saviour Jesus Christ. Amen.

[MORNING.] **THIRTEENTH WEEK.—LORD'S DAY.** [EVENING.

READ IN HOLY SCRIPTURE HEBREWS XI. 23—40.

O LORD God Almighty, no man hath seen Thee at any time; no man can see thy face and live. But verily God is in this place, though we cannot see Him. Wherever two or three are gathered together in thy name, there art Thou; for, "the only-begotten of the Father, He hath revealed Thee." And, lo; He is with us alway, even unto the end of the world.

We bless and magnify thy name that we have had fathers in thy Church, who now, by faith and patience, inherit the promises. They saw the Redeemer's day, and were glad. They waited for thy salvation, O Lord. We beseech Thee to grant unto us, by thy Holy Spirit, like precious faith, that we may trust to a Mediator whom we have not seen, as they also did before He came. Lord, we believe; help Thou our unbelief.

Thanks be unto thy mercy and goodness for another of the days of the Son of Man. We rest from our labours, as Thou, O Lord, didst rest, when thy work was done. We would be in the Spirit of the Lord on the Lord's day. Take us up to thy courts with thanksgiving, and to thy gates with praise. It is good for us to draw near unto God. Endue thy ministers with righteousness, and make thy chosen people joyful. Satisfy thy poor with bread. May thousands hear the joyful sound of thy Gospel, and be blessed. Let thy Word prosper, being mixed with faith in them that hear it. Our fathers wandered in deserts, and in caves of the earth; they resisted unto blood; they were persecuted, afflicted, tormented; but we, this day, sit every man under his own vine and under his own fig-tree, none daring to make afraid. What hath God wrought! God help us to walk this day according to our high calling of God in Christ Jesus.

And now we beseech Thee, O our Father, to accept our acknowledgments for the safe slumber of another night. The Shepherd of Israel, who never slumbers, never sleeps, has been with us. We laid ourselves down in peace, and slept, for Thou, Lord, only madest us to dwell in safety.

Let thy Word, which we are about to hear, sink deep in all our souls, and bear fruit unto everlasting life. Send thy blessing upon all thy churches. Heal the divisions of the body of Christ. Let great grace be upon Israel.

And now will we go, if Thou permit us, to the altar of God—to God, our exceeding joy. We will worship and bow down, and kneel before the Lord our Maker. Strengthen us, we beseech Thee, out of Zion. And, unto the Father, the Son, and the Holy Ghost, ever one God, be the kingdom, the power, and the glory, now and evermore. Amen.

READ IN HOLY SCRIPTURE ST. MATTHEW XVII. 1—13.

ALMIGHTY God, the Father of our Lord Jesus Christ, the Author and Giver of every good and perfect gift, send down thy Holy Spirit to teach us how to pray.

We approach Thee in the name of thy dear Son; we make mention of his righteousness only; and we adore Thee for the great love and tender mercy which Thou hast ever shown to us. O Lord, we are unworthy of that love; from our birth we have gone astray; our hearts are deceitful above all things, and desperately wicked; in us there dwelleth no good thing. Even to-day we have sinned grievously. O Lord, righteousness belongeth unto Thee, but unto us confusion of face. Pour out thy Holy Spirit upon us. Quicken our cold hearts; revive our drooping love; increase our faith. Give us such a sight, by faith, of Jesus, so reveal to us his preciousness, that we may be filled with a burning desire to be over with Him.

Lord Jesus, show us thy glory. We would see Thee. Oh, change us into thine image, from glory to glory, even as by the Holy Spirit. Make us more heavenly minded, more loving, more gentle, more holy. So conform us to Thyself, that our will may be swallowed up in thy will, and that we may be living epistles of Thee, known and read of all men.

Heavenly Father, glorify thy Son in us. Bring down every thought in our hearts into subjection to Him. Let our influence be exercised for Him. Make us, as a family and as individuals, to shine as lights in the world. In all our intercourse one with another, make us forbearing and kind, anxious each to promote the other's good, and willing always to give place one to the other.

Above all, O God, keep us living in the daily expectation of the glorious appearing of Christ. Let that day soon dawn when the knowledge of thy glory shall cover the earth even as the waters cover the seas. Bless thy Word wherever it has been spoken to-day. Make it effectual, through the Holy Ghost, to the conversion of sinners and the building up of believers. Be especially with our own minister; help him in his study of thy Word, and use him as an instrument in bringing many souls to Jesus.

And now, O Lord, take care of us to-night. Protect us, body and soul. Help us quietly and peacefully to rest on Christ; and give us such a good hope through grace, that we may be well assured that whether we wake or sleep, whether we die or live, we are thine. Hear us, heavenly Father, and do exceeding abundantly for us above all that we can either ask or think, for Jesus Christ's sake. Amen.

[Morning.] **THIRTEENTH WEEK.—MONDAY.** [Evening.

READ IN HOLY SCRIPTURE EXODUS III.

HOLY Lord God Almighty, who dost from thy throne behold all the dwellers upon earth, regard us favourably as now we worship Thee. May we ever remember, in our approaches to Thee, that the place where we stand is holy ground. It is infinite condescension in Thee to listen to our praises and prayers; for we are as yesterday, and know nothing, while Thou art the great "I Am," the ever-living God. Yet though Thou art the high and lofty one, encouraged by thy gracious invitation, we look up to Thee, and ask that thy blessing may rest upon us all this day. Help us conscientiously to fulfil its various engagements, that we may glorify Thee. Give us bodily strength for every duty. Control our minds and hearts, that we may think and feel aright. Thus may all our powers be consecrated to Thee; and we remember, when we have done this, that of thine own have we given Thee.

We adore Thee for the many tokens of thy love and care with which thy people have been favoured in the past. Thou hast preserved thy Church amid the dangers by which it has been assailed. Though the bush has been surrounded by fire, yet hast Thou not suffered it to be consumed. No weapon formed against thy servants has prospered.

We thank Thee, O God, that thy promises extend to every one of thy people, and that like as a father pitieth his children, so the Lord pitieth them that fear Him. Thou knowest their sorrows, and wilt not lay upon them more than they can bear. We bless Thee for the assurance of thy loving pity. May it be enjoyed by us even when the shadow of grief passes over our dwelling.

We thank thee that no obstacles prevent us from worshipping Thee; that in our sanctuaries and homes we can offer the sacrifice of thanksgiving, and call upon the name of the Lord. We bless Thee for the inestimable privileges we possess in this favoured land. Truly, the lines have fallen to us in pleasant places. May we understand our responsibilities; as much has been given to us, may we love much, and serve Thee heartily.

Yet, Lord, grant that, amid all our mercies and enjoyments, we may remember we have not yet come to our rest. Help us to live as pilgrims and sojourners, who have here no continuing city, anticipating one in heaven, where, in the everlasting sunshine of thy smile, our wanderings and our woes shall be forgotten; where we shall behold thy face in righteousness, and being made like unto Thee, shall enter into the joy of our Lord. Prepare us for that eternal home; and grant us all needful blessings, with the pardon of all our sins, for the sake of Jesus Christ, our atoning High Priest and Advocate. Amen.

READ IN HOLY SCRIPTURE 2 PETER I.

O HEAVENLY Father, we approach thy throne at the close of another day, in the name and through the merits of our great High Priest, now pleading for us above. Thou hast in condescension and love been speaking to us by thy Word; help us now, by the gracious aid of thy Holy Spirit, to speak to Thee in humble, heart-felt prayer.

We acknowledge before Thee, O Lord, the corruption of our nature—the sins of our heart, of our lips, and of our lives. Thanks to thy blessed name for the gift of thy Son. Through Him, O Lord, give us all things that pertain to life and godliness. In Him we put our trust. May thine exceeding great and precious promises be our comfort and stay; through them may we be partakers of the Divine nature, and escape the pollutions and perils of the wicked world in which we dwell.

We pray that our religion may be of the right kind. Give us the precious faith of thy chosen. May the only ground of our hope be the perfect righteousness of our God and Saviour Jesus Christ. Help us to add to this faith all the excellences that should adorn the Christian character. Forbid it, O Father, that we should be idle or unfruitful in our profession. Daily bestow upon us rich supplies from above, that we may give all diligence to make our calling and election sure. And at last, when we have finished our course below, grant us an abundant entrance into the everlasting kingdom of our Lord and Saviour.

Impress us, O our Father, with a deep conviction of our mortality. Thanks to thy name, we can look beyond death and the grave. When we trust in Jesus, and follow Him, and look for glory through his infinite mercy, we are not following cunningly devised fables. We thank Thee, O Lord, for the evidence that Jesus is the Christ. We think of Him as transfigured on the holy mount, when his face did shine as the sun, and his raiment was white and glistening. We praise Thee for the testimony of the eye witnesses of his majesty. Above all, we bless Thee for thy voice from the excellent glory, declaring Him to be thy beloved Son, in whom Thou art well pleased. Lord, help us to trust in Him; to rejoice in his glory, and to anticipate the time when He will change our vile body, and fashion it like to his glorious body. Till then, O Lord, enable us to hold fast thy faithful word, as a light shining in a dark place. May we buy the truth, and sell it not. May the holy words which holy men of God spake by the Holy Ghost be our solace and guide, till the shadows of time depart, and the glories of eternity burst upon us. Then may we live with Jesus, our exalted Saviour, in eternal day! Hear us, O Lord, for our Redeemer's sake. Amen.

[Morning.]   THIRTEENTH WEEK.—TUESDAY.   [Evening.

READ IN HOLY SCRIPTURE EXODUS IV. 1—23.

READ IN HOLY SCRIPTURE ST. MATTHEW XVII. 14—27.

O ETERNAL Lord God, most mighty and gracious Protector, we, thine unworthy servants, do humbly present ourselves before Thee in the name of thy Son Jesus Christ.

We desire to offer Thee our unfeigned thanks for having again permitted us to meet at the family altar, in the enjoyment of so many and great mercies. Put a new song into our mouths, even praise unto thy holy name.

We adore the wisdom and goodness of thy providence over the children of men. For though Thou art the high and lofty one, that dwellest in the heavens, yet Thou beholdest those that dwell upon earth. Thou openest thine hand and satisfiest the desire of every living thing. Thou upholdest all that fall, and raisest up those that are bowed down. Thou art nigh unto all that call upon Thee, and thine ear is open to their cry. We therefore beseech Thee, thou covenant-keeping God, to have respect unto thy people now as in days of old. Oh, defend and protect them from all that would hurt and oppress them. Do Thou be pleased, in thy goodness, to raise up holy and devoted men, mighty in the truth of thy Word and in the power of the Holy Ghost. Qualify them for thy service. Make them valiant for thine honour, and daily prepared to be the leaders of thy people through the wilderness of this world to the better inheritance of the saints in light.

We beseech Thee also to bless us as members of thy Church on earth. Teach us by thy Word and Spirit all the good purposes of thy blessed will, and the work Thou hast given us to perform. We confess and deplore our ignorance, and inability, in our own strength, to work for thy glory. Do Thou strengthen us, as Thou didst thy servants of old. Make us willing and prompt to act, to speak, and think for Thee. Leave us not to ourselves, but defend us from falling into any sin, error, or danger, and grant that all our doings may be ordered by thy counsel.

Whatever duties await us, give strength to discharge them. If we are called, in thy providence, to rule, may we do it in thy fear, knowing that our Master is in heaven; if to obey, may we do it in singleness of heart, as unto Christ. If to instruct, to admonish, or to reprove, may we not hesitate or forbear, seeking thy help. Do Thou speak to us; put thoughts into our hearts and words into our mouths, that with meekness we may so instruct and convince those that oppose, that they may have no evil thing to say against us and thy truth.

Be with us this day. Watch over our footsteps. Keep us from all danger and sin, and at the last receive us unto Thyself, through Jesus Christ our Lord. Amen.

O LORD, our heavenly Father, we, thy children, draw near to Thee at the close of another day, to thank Thee for thy mercies, and to worship at thy footstool. May thy Holy Spirit prepare our hearts for devotion, and may we be accepted through the atoning merits of the one great sacrifice, even of the Lamb of God, which taketh away sin.

We bless Thee for the favour shown us in the supply to us of temporal comforts. We humbly acknowledge that we have forfeited our common mercies by our sins, and have deserved thy just anger. It is of the Lord's mercies that we are not consumed. But we bless Thee, O God, with a deeper gratitude for our spiritual mercies; especially for thy blessed Word; for showing us the Saviour, full of compassion, ready to heal the sickness and to pity the infirmities of all who apply to Him for help, whether for body or soul. We mourn that we have come so seldom to Jesus, and so coldly pleaded for ourselves and for our friends. We have been a faithless and perverse generation, but we now confess and bewail our unbelief. O Lord, increase our faith, that, strong in the help of thy Holy Spirit, we may stand fast in every time of trial. We have been easily, because willingly discouraged, and have soon counted that to be impossible with God which was only impossible with men. Lord Jesus, forgive our unbelief, and let it no more have dominion over us; but may we expect thy grace to be sufficient for us, whenever we are called to any great trials, or to any difficult duties, because Thou hast appointed the trial and required the obedience. Teach us to copy thy example of fulfilling all righteousness; of uniting wisdom with fidelity; of regarding every ordinance of man for the Lord's sake; and with meekness of wisdom, putting to silence the ignorance of foolish men. May we learn to unite all obedience to human laws with the fear of God, and to sanctify our ordinary engagements by the Word of God and prayer.

Heavenly Father, we implore the forgiveness, through Christ, of all the known and unknown sins of this day, and especially of our want of trust in thy promise and grace. We now place ourselves and our families and friends in thy hands, Thou gracious, watchful Shepherd, to be defended this night from all perils and dangers. Shelter us beneath thy protection; and grant that in the morning we may each give himself, with renewed strength of purpose, as a living sacrifice to Thee. We ask all mercies and blessings in the only name of Jesus Christ, our Lord and Saviour, to whom with Thee, O Father, and Thee, O Holy Ghost, be eternal praise and glory. Amen.

[Morning.] **THIRTEENTH WEEK.—WEDNESDAY.** [Evening.

READ IN HOLY SCRIPTURE EXODUS V.

WITH holy awe, yet with filial confidence, we approach thy throne of grace, O heavenly Father; and, while humbling ourselves before Thee, under a deep consciousness of our own unworthiness, we yet draw near with boldness in the all-prevailing name of Jesus Christ. We rely on the assuring promise of thy Word, that whatsoever we ask in his name we shall receive. Much have we to ask, for much we need; much have we to confess, for greatly have we sinned. Grant to us at this time hearts to pray, and give us the spirit of praise. Pour out upon us the Holy Ghost, that He may teach us our necessities, and dictate our supplications.

We remember with gratitude that thine eye is ever upon us; that He who is our Protector and Friend neither slumbereth nor sleepeth, and that the humblest of thy people are precious in thy sight. Impress this cheering thought upon our minds, so that we may not despond amid difficulties, nor despair amid disappointments. May we recall to mind how Thou hast wrought deliverance for thy people in the days of old, and that Thou, the unchangeable God, canst deliver now. Reveal to us more and more the glorious victory of Christ, and enable us to be more than conquerors through Him that loved us. May we know Him as the Deliverer out of Zion, who gives liberty to the captive and freedom to the slave.

Grant, O mighty God, that Satan may be trodden down under our feet, and that the standard of the Lord may be lifted up against the flood of iniquity in our land. Raise up amongst us faithful witnesses for thy truth, who may speak in love, and earnestly contend for the faith once delivered to the saints. May they cry aloud and not spare, lifting up their voice like a trumpet. May their bold testimony be honoured of Thee in the conversion of many souls, and the discomfiture of those who oppose thy Word. May the record of thy love have free course and be glorified, the kingdom of Christ extended; and from north to south, from east to west, may earth echo with the sound, "Know the Lord." Reveal thine arm in the midst of the world, that wondering nations may cry, "See what God hath wrought!" Teach us so to experience thy sympathy and love that in all our nights of trial or days of joy we may draw near to Thee, assured that into a Father's ear we may pour the complaint of our sorrows, or the grateful tribute of our rejoicing hearts. Enrich us with all spiritual blessings, and so guide us through things temporal that we finally lose not the things eternal. Grant these our prayers for the sake of thy beloved Son Jesus Christ. Amen.

READ IN HOLY SCRIPTURE ST. MATTHEW XVIII. 1—20.

O LORD our God, infinite and eternal; Thou fillest heaven, and the heaven of heavens cannot contain Thee; yet Thou art pleased to dwell with them that are of an humble and contrite heart. We beseech Thee to cause us to feel that Thou art here present with us, who offer Thee thanksgiving for thy goodness towards us through the day past.

Unite our hearts. Teach us, by thy Holy Spirit, to agree together in prayer and in praise. Help us to believe in the Lord Jesus Christ, who ever liveth and reigneth at thy right hand, that, putting our trust in Him, we may ask and receive all needful grace, and that our joy may be full.

Search us, O God, and know our heart; prove us, and know our thoughts. See if there be any way of wickedness in us, and lead us in the way everlasting.

Grant that each one who now bows down before Thee may be humble and lowly as a little child, made a new creature in Christ Jesus. Make our consciences tender. Pardon our unbelief. Give us meekness and lowliness, even as our blessed Lord and Saviour was meek and lowly, and has left us an example that we should walk in his steps. Yet, Lord, we cannot follow Him unless Thou lead us; and therefore we implore Thee to stretch out thy mighty hand, and lead us, even the weakest member of this thy flock, in the paths of righteousness for thy name's sake. Pity our weakness. Forgive our wanderings. Restore our souls; and bring Thou every thought into captivity to the obedience of Christ.

Thou openest, and no man shutteth; Thou shuttest, and no man openeth; and that which thy inspired servants declare to be bound on earth is bound in heaven. Therefore, we pray Thee, enlighten our mind to understand thy written Word. Save us from condemnation; keep us in the perfect liberty of God's children. From all vain desires, from every besetting sin, from every hurtful pleasure, and from the love of the world, which is enmity against Thee, good Lord, deliver us.

Shepherd of souls, bring back them that have wandered from thy flock, and fill heaven with gladness for the dead that are alive again, and for the lost that are found. Destroy the enmity of sinners against thyself, and shed upon all who call themselves thy children the Spirit of thy Son who loved them, and gave Himself for them.

If we have any enemies, forgive them, and turn their hearts. If any man hath aught himself against any one of us, we pray Thee so to incline the heart of the offender that we, being reconciled one to another may be all forgiven, and meet at last at thy right hand, through Jesus Christ our adorable Redeemer. Amen.

[Morning.] THIRTEENTH WEEK.—THURSDAY. [Evening.

READ IN HOLY SCRIPTURE PSALM LXXXVIII.

O THOU from whom all blessings flow, and with whom is no variableness, nor shadow of turning, bow down thine ear, we beseech Thee, and listen to our morning prayer. It is of thy goodness that we have slept in peace and safety, and that we can again unite in praise and thanksgiving at thy footstool. Blessed be thy holy name for all thy mercy to us. May it lead us to a deeper repentance for sin, and cause us to be more and more ashamed of our past ingratitude towards Thee, and of our forgetfulness and disobedience to thy commandments.

We know not what a day may bring forth, or now, in a moment, we may be brought into grievous sorrow and temptation. Teach us, therefore, O God, to be humble, patient, and submissive, and to count all things but loss for the excellency of the knowledge of Christ Jesus our Lord. Enable us always to trace thy hand in all that concerns us, and to desire, above all things, that thy dealings with us may mould us more and more into the image and likeness of thy dear Son. Give us thy Holy Spirit this day. May thy Word be hid in our hearts, that we may not sin against Thee. By thy power uphold and defend us, and let not our feet wander from the ways of thy commandments. In ourselves we are frail and feeble, and our wills infirm of purpose; leave us not then, we pray Thee, but be with us, and watch over us in all our goings out and comings in. Cleanse us from every sin in the atoning blood of Jesus, and give to our hearts the peace which passeth all understanding.

Look in thy compassion on all who are in trouble and necessity. Grant them the tokens of thy presence, and fill them with the consolations of thy Spirit. As Thou hast commanded us to love our brethren, and to bear one another's burdens, so we beseech Thee to hear our prayers for all thy suffering people. To such as mourn under the heavy pressure of sin, do Thou give peace. Show them the sufficiency of the Saviour, and the merits of his perfect sacrifice. To such as weep under bereavement, do Thou make Thyself known as the Father of the fatherless and the God of the widow. To those who are distressed by worldly anxieties, give faith in thy promises, that they may cast their care on Thee, and hear thy voice speaking to them in trial.

May thy mercy continue to rest on our land. May our Queen be enabled to rule in thy fear, and may all in authority under her be endued with wisdom and grace to do what is just and right in thy sight. Bless all thy ministers in their work, and shed on all whom we would remember at thy throne the fulness of thy grace and love. Hear us, gracious Father, for Jesus Christ's sake. Amen.

READ IN HOLY SCRIPTURE 1 PETER V.

GRACIOUS and merciful God, our heavenly Father, in whom we live, and move, and have our being, brought by thy parental care to the close of another day, we would again draw near to thy throne of grace, and ere we retire to rest offer to Thee our evening sacrifice of prayer and praise.

We thank Thee for the mercies of this day, for our temporal supplies, for food and raiment, and all the present comforts we have been permitted to enjoy. May we never forget from whom all blessings come; but tracing up every mercy to Thee, the fountain of all good, may our souls, and all that is within us, praise and bless thy holy name.

Above all, we would thank Thee for thine unspeakable love in our redemption by thy dear Son. For his sake pardon whatever Thou hast seen of evil in us this day, and blot out all our sins by his atoning blood, that being justified by faith in him, we may have peace with Thee our God, and rejoice in the hope of thy glory.

And do Thou, who art the giver of all grace, and who hast, we humbly trust, made known to us thy truth, and called us to thy eternal kingdom, perfect thy work within us. Daily more and more strengthen us in our souls. Especially, we beseech Thee, by thy Spirit, to make us humble. Root out of our hearts all pride and self-conceit. Give us the very mind that was in Christ, that we may submit ourselves in all things to thy will, and by our meekness and humility adorn the Gospel of thy dear Son.

Deliver us from all error in doctrine, and from all evil in practice. Confirm and settle us in the true faith of the Gospel, that we may not be carried about by divers and strange doctrines; but keeping stedfast hold of Thee and thy Word to the end of our lives, may finally, when the chief Shepherd shall appear, receive a crown of glory that fadeth not away.

To thy love and mercy we commit ourselves for the night, casting all our care upon Thee, in the assured belief that Thou carest for us. Do Thou who never slumberest nor sleepest, with whom the darkness and the light are both alike, watch over us for good. With humble and thankful hearts we would retire to rest, and lie down under the shadow of thy wings. Grant us refreshing sleep, that we may be fitted to fulfil whatever duties and meet whatever trials Thou, in thy wisdom, mayest appoint for us.

May the Lord bless, preserve, and keep us; may He mercifully cause his face to shine upon us.

We ask all, O God, in thy dear Son's name, to whom, with Thee and the Holy Spirit, we would ascribe all glory and honour, majesty and dominion, for ever and ever. Amen.

[Morning.] THIRTEENTH WEEK.—FRIDAY. [Evening.

READ IN HOLY SCRIPTURE EXODUS VI. 1—13.

READ IN HOLY SCRIPTURE ST. MATTHEW XVIII. 21—35.

ALMIGHTY and self-existent God, who hast made Thyself known to us by thy name, Jehovah, assist us to worship Thee. Keep back thy servants from presumptuous sins; inspire us with confidence in thy mercy and faithfulness, and let our morning sacrifice be acceptable in thy sight.

We thankfully acknowledge thy goodness in preserving us from the dangers of the past night. We laid us down and slept, we awaked, for the Lord sustained us. We bless Thee for the supply of our bodily wants, for the light of thy holy Word, and above all, for the wondrous provision which Thou hast made for our present and everlasting salvation. Thou who didst hear the groaning and pity the wretchedness of thine ancient people, hast had compassion on us. In our utter misery thine eye pitied us, and thine arm brought salvation. We adore Thee, gracious Father, for the unspeakable gift of thy beloved Son, and for the assurance that with Him Thou wilt give us all things that pertain to life and godliness. Thou hast redeemed us without money, even with the precious blood of Christ; and as thy servant Moses was commissioned by Thee to proclaim thy merciful designs to his brethren, his kinsmen according to the flesh, so by thy grace the ministers of thy Word publish to us the good tidings of salvation. Give us, we pray Thee, to feel our need of redemption through Jesus; forbid that, in anguish of spirit, we should despair of thy mercy; but, with believing hearts, may we accept the pardon which Thou offerest unto us.

May we, O God, be delivered from the yoke of Satan, from the seductions of the world, from the depravity of our own hearts, and be introduced into that spiritual liberty which thy Son came to preach and to give to us. If He make us free, we shall be free indeed : may we experience his ability to save to the uttermost them that come to Thee through Him; and may we thus become thy people, and prove that Thou art to us a God. Help us, as thy redeemed servants, to do thy will, to resign ourselves to thy disposal, and thus to magnify thy grace.

Be present with us throughout this day : preserve us, if consistent with thy will, from accident, disease, and sudden death; give us victory over temptation; guide us in all our perplexity; help us to act in our worldly business as under thine inspection, and in all things may we serve the Lord Christ. Guide us with thy counsel, and ultimately bring us to that country which is better than the earthly Canaan, and in which we shall see Thee as Thou art, and be happy and safe in thy presence for ever. We ask it for Christ's sake. Amen.

O THOU adorable Father, whose goodness has preserved us throughout another day, whose wisdom has ordered our goings, and whose power has strengthened our feebleness; we give Thee hearty thanks for thy parental kindness which has supplied all our wants, watched over our faltering steps, and kept us and those dear to us safe from harm. We come to Thee to ask thy blessing at the close of the day. We would confess with true contrition our sins and offences in thy sight, and earnestly, through Jesus Christ, implore thy forgiveness. Have mercy upon us, O God, have mercy upon us, and blot out all our transgressions. We cannot say we will render Thee all thy due, for we have nothing to pay. We are poor, undone, helpless creatures, utterly ruined and lost; only thy mercy can raise us : only thy *free* forgiveness can save us. Our hearts are troubled and overwhelmed when we consider our sins; but we flee to Thee, through the all-sufficient sacrifice and mediation of Jesus Christ. Accept us in Him; and let us have the seal of thy forgiving love upon our hearts—the testimony of thy Spirit with ours that we are the children of God, restored to our Father's embrace, and comforted with his love.

And, O Lord, grant us, we beseech Thee, the spirit of thy children, loving, meek, and good. So renew our hearts by the Spirit of grace, that we may love our brethren around us. When they offend against us, help us to remember how often and grievously we have offended against Thee; and remembering thy goodness toward us, may we, from our heart, forgive them. Purge out from our souls all malice, and hatred, and revenge; and make us kind, loving, forbearing, and forgiving. May we never call forth thine anger by any manifestation of unholy anger against our fellows; but ever live in peace and harmony, following his blessed example who when He was reviled reviled not again; when He suffered, He threatened not, but committed Himself to Him that judgeth righteously. And if this day we have fallen into any uncharitableness or hastiness of temper, or angry words, we beseech Thee forgive us, and make us watchful over our spirits for the future, that we may not again offend Thee.

Bless, O God, all the members of this family. Let every heart be renewed by thy grace; let us live before Thee in holy love, seeking each other's good. Give us this night that rest which is needed to restore our strength for to-morrow's duties; and if we should know no to-morrow here, may we wake in that world where there is no night, to be for ever with the Lord. Grant these our humble petitions, O God, for the sake of Jesus Christ, our Lord and Saviour. Amen.

[Morning.] THIRTEENTH WEEK.—SATURDAY. [Evening.

READ IN HOLY SCRIPTURE EXODUS VII.

O GOD, Thou art our God, early will we seek Thee. Mercifully be Thou nigh unto us, that in seeking we may find Thee.

Thou, O Lord, art very great; Thou art clothed with honour and majesty, but Thou art also very good, and thine unsearchable greatness is softened to our view by thine unspeakable goodness. Both in the works of thy hands and in the ways of thy providence Thou hast made Thyself known to the sons of men, so that in their forgetfulness of Thee they have ever been without excuse. When they have hardened themselves against Thee, Thou hast not withdrawn thy compassions from them. Thou hast even come out of thy place, and shown signs and wonders in the midst of them, for Thou hast no pleasure in him that dieth, but wouldst have all men come to repentance and live.

We thank Thee, O God, that Thou hast in so many ways spoken unto us; in the heavens, which are ever telling of thy glory, and in the earth, which is ever full of thy riches. Thy providence, which daily loadeth us with benefits, is daily addressing us in accents of fatherly love. Even the things which aforetime were said unto others are now said unto us, upon whom the ends of the world are come. Chiefly do we bless Thee that Thou hast spoken unto us by thy Son, who is heir of all things. Save us, we pray Thee, from hardening our hearts, as did Pharaoh of old, against thy Word; lest, like him also, we perish at last through unbelief. Especially may we have grace to hear Him in whom Thou art ever well pleased, and whose words are spirit and life to all who receive them; for if they escaped not who refused him that spake on earth, much more shall not we escape, if we turn away from Him that speaketh from heaven.

Enable us, in full surrender of ourselves to thy guidance, to enter upon the duties of this day thankful for the love which has watched over us during the night, and quick to hear that still small voice of thy Spirit which is given to instruct us, and to teach us in the way that we should go. Preserve us, O Lord, from the deceitfulness of our own hearts, and from the corruption that is in the world through lust. Fortify us against the devices of Satan, and against the malice of those who whet their tongues like swords, and bend their bows to shoot their arrows, even bitter words. Give us the spirit that always watches and always prays. Though in the world, and engaged in worldly business, may we walk with God, and each day obtain a greater likeness to Him, until, in the end, we receive an abundant entrance into his everlasting kingdom, through our Lord and Saviour Jesus Christ. Amen.

READ IN HOLY SCRIPTURE 1 COR. XIII.

GREAT God of love, and grace, and truth, we adore, we praise, we glorify Thee. Thou art our Father in Christ, and Thou art our King. All thy laws are wise, all thy words are true, all thy ways are good, all thy works are great. We thank Thee for the privilege and ordinance of prayer. Help us now to worship Thee in spirit and in truth. Accept us in the Son of thy love. Answer us according to thy wisdom, and mercy, and faithfulness. Oh, our Father, we thank Thee for the grace given us by the Holy Ghost! If we have passed from death unto life, if we have laid aside the foolish things of sin and unbelief, it is because Thou hast taught us. Every good gift, and every perfect gift, has been from Thee. We thank Thee for all Thou hast wrought in us. Because Thou hast given, we ask Thee still to give such things as may be good. Keep us from pride of heart, even from every form of that pride which is so unseemly and offensive in thy presence. Lord, give us faith in thy dear Son, in his atoning blood, in his prevailing intercession, in his coming glory. Lord, give us a well-founded hope that our souls shall be saved in the day of his appearing. We ask for spirituality of mind and heart. We pray that Thou wouldst make us a consecrated people to thy praise.

Oh, our Father, teach us how truly to love Thee and to love all that bear thy image! Help us to be unselfish. Write thy new name upon our hearts —thy name of love. We thank Thee for the mercies of the day which is about to close. Father, help us to remember the heaven where there is no night. Teach us to look for the home in which we shall see face to face. Enable us, before sleep closes our eyes, to have a living look to Jesus. Teach us to know that our sins have been covered and cancelled through the blood of sprinkling. Give us the comfort of the Holy Ghost, the seal of our sonship, the witness of our acceptance in the Beloved. Shed thy light upon all our souls. Thou knowest what we are and what we need. Oh, suit thy gifts to our necessity! Bless us in body and in soul. Be with us in life and death.

[Look upon our children, and make them thy children also.]

Watch over our home, and make us to be of the household of faith and family of God. Sanctify, strengthen, guide, deliver us. We would be ever thine, altogether thine, all thine. Lord, have mercy upon us. Christ, have mercy upon us. Lord, have mercy upon us. So shall we love Thee, so shall we live for Thee, so shall we live with Thee for ever. Lord, hear our prayer, for Christ our Saviour's sake. Amen.

[Morning.] **FOURTEENTH WEEK.—LORD'S DAY.** [Evening.]

READ IN HOLY SCRIPTURE EXODUS VIII. 1—19.   READ IN HOLY SCRIPTURE ST. MARK IX. 33—50.

GRATEFUL to us, O Lord our God, is the light of any day which dawns upon us, as the token of thine unfailing kindness and ceaseless thoughtfulness towards us; but this day, the day of the Lord, is especially grateful to us. Thou hast made the Sabbath for man, and crowned it with privileges and blessings. May we be in the Spirit on the Lord's day. May it not be felt to be a burden by any of us, but may we hail it as the holy of the Lord honourable, and say in the gratitude of our hearts, "This is the day which the Lord hath made, we will rejoice and be glad in it." May we consecrate its hours to high and heavenly objects; not doing our own ways, nor finding our own pleasure, nor speaking our own words, but keeping it holy and honourable unto the Lord. May we this day eat of heavenly manna and drink of living water, and thus be nourished up to life eternal.

May this domestic service prepare us for the various exercises of the day. Let the Word of God now read shed its light upon all our minds, and exert a salutary influence upon all our hearts. Mighty art Thou, O Lord, to vindicate thine honour and to punish the sin of man. Thy power is over all thy works. Means and instrumentalities are ever available to Thee. Thou hast but to speak, and it is done. All creatures minister to thy will; but, alas, how deep and deadly is the enmity of the human heart. Plagues and judgments fail to reduce it to penitence and submission. Thy grace alone can melt the soul to contrition and to love. Deliver us by thy grace, O Lord, from unbelief and hardness of heart. Make us willing and obedient. Go with us to thy house, and let thy Word prove the power of God unto our salvation. Let thy ministers be clothed with salvation, that thy saints may shout aloud for joy. May we be solicitous, not only to obtain good, but to do good this day.

Bless all who shall be occupied in works of faith and labours of love. Let such as shall be engaged in imparting instruction to the young, in the family and in the Sunday school, be greatly blessed, and all who seek to spread thy truth be prospered with thy favour.

Oh send out thy light and thy truth throughout our land. Have mercy upon our fellow-countrymen who forsake thy sanctuaries, break thy Sabbaths, and run in the way of death. Enlighten their minds and change their hearts.

Bless distant nations. Render missionary efforts gloriously successful, and let the world be filled with thy salvation. May this Sabbath be to us a preparation for, and an earnest of, the Sabbath of heaven. Hear us, O Lord, for Jesus Christ's sake. Amen.

O LORD, our Lord, how excellent is thy name in all the earth. Thou art great, and greatly to be feared, for Thou doest wondrous things. Look from the throne of thy glory upon worms of the earth, who have now taken upon themselves to speak unto Thee. Help us to worship Thee in spirit and in truth. We have been surrounded this day with circumstances demanding our gratitude, and we praise Thee with joyful lips. The sound of the Gospel has saluted our ears, and Jesus Christ has been set forth before our eyes as crucified for our sins. Help us to improve our privileges, that we may be benefited by all we hear and learn. Impress upon our minds the solemn and delightful truths made known to us this day; and may we hide thy word in our hearts, that we sin not against Thee. Save us from the abuse of thy long-suffering and compassion, lest the things we have heard depart from us all the days of our life, and rise up to our condemnation in the judgment of the great day.

We thank Thee, O our God and Father, for the glad tidings of the Gospel as preached to guilty men. Thou hast sent forth the Word of salvation, proclaiming peace to them that are afar off and to them that are nigh. We bless Thee that it ever reached our shores, and by the power of thy Spirit turned our forefathers from the worship of idols to the service of the true God. We thank Thee that it is now going forth from this and from other lands to be proclaimed to all nations, and people, and tongues. What multitudes have hailed the messengers of mercy who have proclaimed it to-day! Dark minds have been enlightened, stubborn hearts have been subdued, and sorrowful spirits rendered glad by the proclamation of salvation, through the blood of the cross. Be pleased to follow with thy blessing the Word of life, wheresoever and by whomsoever it may be preached. Give an abundant increase to all who toil in thy vineyard. Never let thy servants labour in vain. May the pleasure of the Lord prosper in their hands, till all nations shall be blessed in Him, and all people call Him blessed.

Teach us to love and acknowledge all who are trying to do good in the name of Jesus. May we not willingly offend any of his followers, however lowly or feeble. Grant that we may always stand prepared by our words, and feelings, and actions, to do them good. May all our works be performed from love to Christ and with a view to his glory, so that we may not lose the reward He will graciously bestow. Grant that we may live peaceable and holy lives, and through thine infinite mercy be saved from future and eternal woe. We ask it for Christ's sake. Amen

[MORNING.] FOURTEENTH WEEK.—MONDAY. [EVENING.

READ IN HOLY SCRIPTURE EXODUS VIII. 20—32.　　READ IN HOLY SCRIPTURE ST. LUKE IX. 51—62.

O ALMIGHTY and everlasting God, at the opening of the day we come to pay our grateful homage to Thee. Thou art the God of all peoples upon the earth, but specially of those who believe and obey Thee. We acknowledge Thee to be *our* God, our Redeemer and Saviour.

We humbly beseech Thee of thy great mercy to write upon our hearts the lessons of thy holy Word we have now read. Fill us with a deep sense of thy love to thine own people, and of thy power to deliver and to defend them from all foes and all dangers. Impress us deeply with a sense of thy long-suffering and forbearance towards those who rebel against Thee, and of thy justice in punishing those who trifle with thy mercy. Deliver us, we beseech Thee, from the sins which brought upon Pharaoh and his people thy displeasure and thy wrath. Grant us the grace we need that we may be sincere in all our duties towards Thee and our fellow-men. May our repentance be deep and earnest, our faith be simple, and our love to Thee be true. Help us in the discharge of our duties towards thy people, that we may speak and act with prudence and with kindness, remembering, on all occasions, that they are thine, and that what is done to them is really done to Thee. Make us jealous for the honour, the happiness, and the usefulness of thy people. In our conduct towards the world, help us to be just and truthful. If we have enemies, detractors, or slanderers, oh, help us to bear with them! Give us grace to love them; and, by our meekness, humility, and consistency, may we commend ourselves to every man's conscience in thy sight; and so let our light shine before men, that they may glorify Thee, who alone worketh in us to will and to do.

For our relations and friends we ask that they all may live in thy faith, fear, and love, and ever enjoy thy guidance and favour. We pray for thy blessing upon the neighbourhood in which we live. May all who are around us be made partakers of thy salvation. We pray for our Queen and our country. We beseech Thee to pity and provide for the poor. Have mercy upon all who are afflicted and distressed. Carry the Gospel to our prisons, and deliver all who are in captivity to Satan. Oh, our Father, we pray that thy kingdom may come, and thy will be done on earth as it is in heaven! Accept, O Lord, our thanksgivings for thy watchful care over us through the night, for the health and comfort we now enjoy, and for the many mercies Thou hast given us. We implore thy guidance and help throughout this day. Keep us in the hour of temptation, and in all things help us to glorify Thee, for the sake of Jesus Christ our Lord and Saviour. Amen.

GRANT us, O Lord God, thy promised Spirit, that we may worship Thee in spirit and in truth. Help us to think of Thee as the fountain of all life, of all goodness, and of all joy. Grant unto us more deeply to feel what we owe to Thee for loading us with benefits, unworthy as we are.

We pray for grace, that our face may be more stedfastly set towards the Jerusalem above, while on our pilgrimage through this world. Make us willing to be strangers upon the earth. May we not feel at home here, knowing that Christ has prepared a place for his disciples in his Father's house. Yet help us, O Lord, to praise Thee, as we would now do, for all our home comforts here below. May we all learn of Jesus, not to mar, but always tenderly to promote the peace and wellbeing of all with whom we dwell, and to show piety at home. Make us deeply sensible of our many faults, in thought, and word, and act. We would make Christ's word a light and a lamp to our feet; and we pray that we may look at his pure and holy life while we listen to his voice. May we learn what He means by bidding us to follow Him; and oh forgive all the insincerity and the frailty of our sinful and infirm hearts. We need the cleansing of Christ's atoning blood, alike for our very professions and performances. O Lord, pardon us wherein we have lacked the spirit of meekness and goodness, or been unconcerned for thy glory.

We seek the renewal of peace, and hope, and joy, at his cross who there made atonement for our sins. Help us to put our trust beneath the shadow of thy wings, that we may rest securely, and sleep in peace. Whatever have been the events and circumstances of this day, we desire to acknowledge thy hand in all things, and pray that Thou wouldest make them, in thy wisdom and love, work together for good. Whatever anxieties arise, may we have faith to cast our cares upon Thee. Graciously take us under thy protection this night. Give us refreshing rest, and grant that when we awake we may feel that we are still with Thee.

Remember, O God, for good all whom we love. Enrich them, according to thy mercy, with the bounties of thy providence; but, above all, bestow upon them the riches of thy grace. If they are in sorrow, comfort them; if they are in perplexity, guide them; if weak, strengthen them. [May thy special favour rest on the young of our household. Draw their hearts to Thyself in the days of their youth, and teach them to remember Thee.] Pity the unconverted around us, and pour on their darkened souls the light of thy truth. We ask these and all other mercies in the name of Jesus Christ, thy dear Son, our Saviour. Amen.

[93]

[Morning.] FOURTEENTH WEEK.—TUESDAY. [Evening.

READ IN HOLY SCRIPTURE ISAIAH XI. 1—13.

READ IN HOLY SCRIPTURE HEBREWS X. 19—39.

HEAVENLY Father, we draw near to Thee with our hearty thanksgivings. To Thee we are indebted for the light of the morning, for life, for health, and for sound minds; above all, for Jesus Christ, the Light of the world. Each day we rise, we would call upon thy name, and make mention of thy faithfulness. Rested and refreshed with sleep, we would go to the duties and trials of a new day underneath the shadow of thy wings. Leaning upon our own understanding, we are sure to go astray; and trusting in our own strength, we are certain to fail. Oh, be pleased to direct our steps into the ways of thy precepts. Help us to set Thee the Lord constantly before us; and whilst Thou givest us our daily bread, give us also daily grace. When duty is to be done, may our hearts be inclined to it, and may our hands perform it diligently. When temptation approaches, put us on our guard, and open for us a door of escape. When opportunities of usefulness are presented, may we have the understanding to discern them, the heart to seize them, and the power to turn them to good account. Empty us of self, and fill us with the mind that was in Christ Jesus. Enable us to live for Thee; and when we again seek repose, may the blessing of our God descend upon us.

O God of the prophets, we would rejoice over their accomplished word. Hasten the time when the Gospel shall be preached among all nations, and when the rod out of the stem of Jesse shall wield its mighty power to the subjugation of all hateful passions, and to the rise and reign of pure and undefiled religion throughout the whole earth. May each of us, in our own experience, know the sanctifying influence of the cross of Jesus. Believing that in our corrupt human nature lie the seeds of all evil, we would come to that cross, and have them all destroyed there. We ourselves cannot root up such evils, but thy grace is sufficient for us. Create within us clean hearts; and may we be careful not to grieve thy Spirit, who seals us unto the day of redemption.

Father, we implore Thee for thy richest blessings. We ask not wealth, nor power, nor fame; but we ask the blessing that makes rich and adds no sorrow. Oh, give us not only the pardon of our sins, but the delightful conviction that they are all cast out of thy sight and out of thy remembrance. Thus may we have thy peace reigning within us, and taste even here the joys that are at thy right hand. Those our morning supplications we leave with Thee, and we now arise and go forth in humble faith that not only throughout this day, but even unto death, Thou wilt be our God and Guide. And all we ask is for Christ's sake. Amen.

MOST merciful God, we bless Thee that though utterly unworthy to approach Thee, we have boldness to come through Jesus Christ. We behold Him as our great High Priest within the veil, ever living to make intercession for us. We stand now before his cross, and from thence lift up our eyes to his throne. May our consciences be sprinkled afresh with atoning blood, that the sins of this day may be all forgiven, and we may lie down at peace with God. We give Thee thanks on behalf of those members of this family who have believed in Jesus. Help us to hold fast the profession of our faith without wavering. We would not be among those who draw back unto perdition, but of those who believe to the salvation of their souls. We lament before Thee that though we bear the name of Christ, we have so little of his image. We have followed Him, but, alas! at how great a distance! Blessed Jesus, wert Thou to regulate the bestowment of thy favour by our desert, long ere this we had been left to ourselves. We thank Thee for thy forbearance towards us. Make it a powerful motive to bring us nearer to Thyself. Our faith is weak: do Thou strengthen it. Our hope is dim: do Thou brighten it. Our love is cold: do Thou kindle it into a flame. Our souls cleave to the dust: quicken Thou us according to thy Word. Henceforth may we follow Thee fully, and may every closing day find us nearer to Thee, and fitter for the rest that remaineth for thy people.

Holy Spirit, sanctify to us all the events of this day. May afflictions wean us from the world. May disappointments loosen our affections from the things that are seen, and transfer them to the things that are eternal. Whatever prosperity Thou art pleased to send, may it not lift us up, but supply fresh materials for songs of praise. We beseech Thee to sanctify to us the reading of the Scriptures; may we ever find something precious therein which shall be as manna to our hungry souls. Help us to know our Lord's will, and to do it, or to bear it. Help us to study the life of Jesus, and in all things to walk in his footsteps, that at last we may be like Him, and see Him as He is.

We now commend ourselves to thy fatherly care. Suffer no enemy to molest our property, no disease to attack our persons, and permit not death to invade our home; but with sleep unbroken, and strength renewed, may we awake in the morning to serve our God. May we lie down as calmly to die as we lie down this night to sleep; so that falling asleep in Jesus, we may be satisfied with his likeness when we awake. We ask all in the name of Jesus Christ our Lord. Amen.

[94]

[MORNING.] FOURTEENTH WEEK.—WEDNESDAY. [EVENING.

READ IN HOLY SCRIPTURE EXODUS IX. 1–12. READ IN HOLY SCRIPTURE ST. LUKE X. 1–16.

HEARKEN unto the voice of our cry, our King and our God; for unto Thee will we pray. In the morning will we direct our prayer unto Thee, and will look up.

We thank Thee for the mercies of the past night, for Thou, Lord, only makest us dwell in safety. The day is thine, the night also is thine. Thou hast prepared the light and the sun. Many of our fellow-creatures during the night have passed into eternity, but we are alive and remain; and our prayer shall be to the God of our life. The living, the living he shall praise Thee, as we do this day.

Give us this day our daily bread. We desire not to eat the bread of idleness, but would be diligent in business, fervent in spirit, serving the Lord. May we ever seek an honest livelihood, and do Thou bless the work of our hands. Vouchsafe to keep us this day without sin. May we be in the fear of the Lord all the day long.

Bless this household. Let none of us, like Pharaoh, impiously exclaim, "Who is the Lord, that I should obey his voice?" May we exhort one another daily, lest any of us be hardened through the deceitfulness of sin. Shouldest Thou see fit to afflict us, let us not murmur, but submit to thy will.

Remember, O Lord, any that are suffering persecution for righteousness' sake. Let them not fear the wrath of any Pharaoh, but hold fast the profession of their faith without wavering. May they choose rather to suffer affliction with the people of God than to enjoy the pleasures of sin for a season, esteeming the reproach of Christ greater riches than the treasures in Egypt, having respect unto the recompense of the reward.

Give us grace for the special duties and trials of this day, and enable us to resist all temptations. May we live to thy praise, and walk worthy of our Christian vocation. May we be kind to all about us, and bear meekly with each other's infirmities, forgiving one another, as we trust God, for Christ's sake, has forgiven us. Let thine eye and thy hand be upon us all for good, and prosper us in all our plans and undertakings which are according to thy will.

Give wisdom to all our rulers. Preserve them from the fear of man, and enable them to act in all things as in thy sight, remembering the account they must one day give. Graciously pour out the Holy Spirit on thy Church, and daily increase the number of thy believing people.

Forgive, O Lord, all the imperfections of our supplications. Hear us for the Lord Jesus Christ's sake. Amen.

O GOD, our heavenly Father, we give Thee thanks for the privilege of drawing near to the throne of grace. During another day Thou hast supplied our need, and caused our comforts to abound. What shall we render unto Thee for all thy mercy and loving-kindness? Every day augments the sum of our obligations to love and serve Thee our God, and we bless Thee that, in infinite wisdom and goodness, Thou hast united our happiness with our duty. Thy ways are ways of pleasantness, and all thy paths are peace. May we love Thee with all our hearts, and daily grow in thy favour and image; and let us always make thy holy will our law, thy Word our guide, thine example our pattern, and thy glory the sole end of our being. How far, O Lord, have we hitherto fallen short of this! What ingratitude and folly, what neglect and waywardness, have marked our conduct. For the sake of thy dear Son, forgive us all iniquities, receive us graciously, and enrich us with all the graces of thy Holy Spirit. Especially, O Lord, reveal thy dear Son to us in all the glory of his Divine power, and in all the riches of his saving grace. May He dwell in our hearts by faith, and cause us to know the peace which springs from reconciliation with Thee, and the forgiveness of sins.

We commend all our loved ones to thy mercy. Make them all partakers of thy salvation; be Thou their portion, and the Guide of their life. We pray Thee also to bless our enemies; change their hearts, and make them thy friends. Remove far away from our own hearts all anger and malice, and help us to live in charity with all men. Remember, in thy compassion, all the sons and daughters of affliction, especially thine own children. Be with them in the furnace; and when Thou hast tried them, may they come forth like gold that is purified. Mercifully spare useful lives; and those who are drawing near the gates of death prepare for the eternal world. Fit us for death and judgment, that when Thou comest we may be ready to obey thy call, and enter into thy joy. Have compassion on all those who obey not thy Gospel and regard not the day of thy visitation. Oh turn Thou their hearts to Thyself, and let not the judgments of Chorazin and Bethsaida fall on them. And now, O Lord, we commit the keeping of both body and soul to thy care during this night. Almighty Keeper of Israel, give to thy beloved sleep, and may we rise in the morning with invigorated strength, to love and serve Thee our God in the duties of another day; and when days and nights with us are no more, may we be found in thy glorious kingdom, through Jesus Christ our Lord. Amen.

[Morning.]   FOURTEENTH WEEK.—THURSDAY.   [Evening.

READ IN HOLY SCRIPTURE EXODUS IX. 13–35.   READ IN HOLY SCRIPTURE JAMES I. 17–27.

WHO knoweth the power of thine anger, O God? who can stay thine hand, or say unto Thee, What doest Thou? Keep us, by thy grace, from hardening our hearts against Thee; and may we never, by our own sins, bring down thy judgment on ourselves or others. Hast Thou not, on account of sin, cursed the ground? Have mercy upon us, O God, miserable sinners. Bring not thy plagues upon our hearts. Make us not, by reason of our continued rebellion, examples of thy power and wrath. Give us to see what an evil and bitter thing sin is, and may we turn from its first approach as from the bite of a serpent or the sting of an adder. Oh that we may never be found amongst them who regard not thy Word; and keep us ever in mind that it is a fearful thing to fall into thy hands, O thou holy and righteous God! We bless Thee that Thou hast ever mingled mercy with judgment. Thou dost not smite without warning, nor threaten without showing a way of escape. Thou willest not the death of a sinner, but rather that all should turn to Thee and live. Give us true repentance. How often have we, like Pharaoh, when thy hand was upon us, confessed our sin, and vowed to serve Thee; but no sooner has the burden been removed than we have turned again to folly. Grant us thy Holy Spirit, that we may forsake sin as well as mourn for sin; and may the future of our lives be in strict obedience to thy commands. Thou hast, in the Son of thy love, provided a refuge from the storm and a covert from the tempest. May we fly to Him. Pardon us for his sake. Thou canst, through the atonement which He has made, be just, and yet the justifier of the ungodly. Accept us in the beloved; and when thy fierce anger burns in the judgments which are abroad, may we hide ourselves in Him till the indignation be overpast.

We bless Thee, O God, for raising up a prophet like unto Moses, and that Thou hast appointed Him to give deliverance to the captive and freedom to them that are bound. Unto Jesus may we hearken; and oh grant that by faith in Him we may be freed from spiritual bondage, from the passions of the flesh, the allurements of the world, the temptations of Satan, and be led to rejoice in the glorious liberty of the children of God. May we know the truth, and the truth make us free.

For the mercies of another day we thank Thee. Thou hast preserved us while we slept, and raised us in health and safety. Now, as we go forth to our duties, take us under thy protection, and make use of us for thy glory. We consecrate ourselves to Thee, body, soul, and spirit. Do for us exceeding abundantly above all we are able to ask or think, for Jesus Christ's sake. Amen.

O LORD God, at the close of another day, we lift up the voice of prayer. We call on Thee as the Father of our Lord Jesus Christ, and the Father of all them who truly believe in Him. We remember how He spake to his disciples of his Father and their Father, of his God and their God; and we ask, in his name, that we may know for ourselves the preciousness of this high relationship, and that in very deed we may be thy children, born again through the truth, and have faith to say "Abba, Father."

Forgive, we beseech Thee, all the sins of this day, and give us peace through Jesus Christ. We confess that in thy sight, O Thou holy God, we have deeply sinned and come short of thy glory; but looking up to Him who is the Lord our Righteousness, we earnestly pray for pardon, and ask that by thy Spirit we may be made every day more and more what we ought to be. Let thy Word be increasingly precious to us—be hidden in our hearts, and manifested in our lives. Lord, we would be not forgetful hearers, but doers of thy Word; witnessing to its power, and fulfilling its precepts. May our religion be pure and undefiled before Thee, our God and Father. Teach us, we beseech Thee, to bridle our tongues, to watch over our hearts, and to abound in all acts of Christian kindness and charity. Lord, enable us to keep ourselves unspotted from the world, that we may be preserved harmless amidst its temptations; and though living in it, yet have our hearts and our treasure in heaven.

O Lord, let none of us be self-deceived in regard to our state before Thee. Thou readest and searchest the very heart. If any of us be unconverted, show them their lost condition. Convince them of sin, reveal them to themselves; let them learn, under thy teaching, all their guiltiness, and in thy mercy bring them out of darkness into the light of thy love. Teach us that it is not enough to cry Lord, Lord; but that the heart must be changed, and the sins be blotted out, and the life be conformed to thy will. Oh, let not our religion be a vain one; but in heart and life may we be consecrated to Thee, loving Thee more, serving Thee better, and bringing forth the fruits of the Spirit in a ready obedience in all things to thy will.

We now go to rest for the night, commending each other, and all whom we love, to thy care. Lord, watch over us by thy gracious providence. If we live, may we awake to glorify Thee; if we die, may we sleep in Jesus. Hear us, we pray Thee, O our God, for his sake, to whom, with Thee and the Holy Ghost, our only God, be ascribed equal and undivided praise. Amen.

[Morning.]   FOURTEENTH WEEK.—FRIDAY.   [Evening.

READ IN HOLY SCRIPTURE PSALM LXVIII. 1—19.

O GOD of our salvation, our voice shalt Thou hear in the morning. We thank Thee for having watched over us through the night, for having refreshed us with sleep, and for bringing us in health and comfort to the beginning of another day. Defend us throughout its hours, and grant that we may not fall into any sin, neither run into any kind of danger. Thou art able to keep us from evil, and to comfort and support us in all the trials and duties of life. Thou hast been the refuge and helper of thy people in all generations. Thou didst guide thine ancient people in the wilderness, and encompass them with miraculous tokens of thy presence and care. Thou didst lead them to the goodly land promised to their fathers, refresh and confirm them in its possession, and provide of thy goodness for the poor. Guide us, we humbly pray Thee, through the pilgrimage of life, and give us day by day our daily bread. In mercy feed us with the bread of life. Cause us to drink of the living water that flows, for our refreshment and salvation, from Jesus Christ, the smitten Rock; and bring us to that better country which Thou hast promised to all them that love and serve Thee.

We thank Thee for the gracious revelation Thou hast made of thy character and will to the children of men, and we would rejoice in Thee as the all-sufficient God. A Father of the fatherless and a Judge of the widow art Thou. Thou openest the eyes of the blind. The outcast and forsaken are remembered by Thee. Thou hast sent thy dear Son, in our nature, to open the prison doors to them that are bound, and to set at liberty them that are bruised. Thou hast given the Word of salvation, and great is the company of them who preach it. Soon may the joyful tidings of repentance and remission of sins be preached in the name of Jesus among all nations. May those who are now afar off be made nigh. May those who are now degraded and dishonoured by the practice of sin be purified and forgiven, and be adorned by the beauty of holiness.

Thou wilt in very deed dwell with man upon the earth. We thank Thee that when Christ ascended on high he obtained gifts for men, even for the rebellious; and we bless Thee that the Divine Spirit has been shed abroad. May He take of the things of Christ and reveal them to us, so that Jesus may dwell in our hearts by faith, and our bodies may be temples of the living God. Daily would we bless Thee, as we are constantly loaded with benefits, and always would we rejoice in Thee as the God of our salvation. Be pleased to accept our worship, to pardon our sins, and to supply our various wants, for the sake of Jesus Christ. Amen.

READ IN HOLY SCRIPTURE ST JOHN VII. 1—13.

GREAT and glorious Lord God Almighty, who dwellest in light which no man can approach unto, whom no man hath seen, or can see; we come into thy presence in the name of thy well-beloved Son, who is the Mediator between Thyself and us. In no other name can we come, for there is none other name under heaven given amongst men whereby we must be saved. We adore Thee for Him as thine unspeakable gift, and for all the blessings that are promised and secured to us through his death. Because Thou hast not spared thine own Son, but delivered Him up for us all, Thou wilt with Him also freely give us all things. Grant us to feel our need of Him, and to find in Him all our salvation and all our desire. May we feel more and more our spiritual poverty, and more and more be made rich with his unsearchable riches. And as we thus receive of his fulness, oh, help us continually to show forth his praise. May his name be so dear to us that we shall delight to speak of Him. While our whole temper and conduct bear witness to our union with Him and our love to Him, may we be so add to our faith courage that we shall be bold to go without the camp bearing his reproach; not like those who, in the days of his flesh, did not speak openly of Him for fear of the Jews, but rather like those who, making mention of his righteousness, and of his only, rejoiced that they were counted worthy to suffer shame for his name's sake.

Accept, O Lord, of the praises we humbly bring to Thee for the mercy of this day. Thou hast given to us our daily bread, and with this all things that pertain to life and godliness. How precious are thy thoughts unto us, O God; how great is the sum of them! If we should count them, they are more in number than the sand. Continue these tokens of thy love, we pray Thee, as thy wisdom may see most fit; and ever enable us to say, "Because thy lovingkindness is better than life, my lips shall praise Thee. Thou art my portion, O Lord."

We implore the forgiveness of this day's offences through the intercession of our great High Priest, and commit the keeping of our souls to Thee for the night, as unto a faithful Creator. Be Thou, O Lord, our hiding place; preserve us from trouble, and compass us about with songs of deliverance. May no evil befal us, nor any plague come nigh our dwelling; but grant us, with the security of thy watchful presence, such a renewal of our strength, both of body and of mind, by the rest of this night, that we may be able to offer Thee on the coming day a more cheerful and acceptable service. We ask every mercy in the name of our Lord Jesus Christ. Amen.

[97]

No. 13.

[Morning.] **FOURTEENTH WEEK.—SATURDAY.** [Evening.

READ IN HOLY SCRIPTURE EXODUS X. 1—11.

READ IN HOLY SCRIPTURE ST. JOHN VII. 14—31.

ALMIGHTY and eternal God, Lord of heaven and earth, the world is full of thy glory. Help us to come near to Thee with reverence and godly fear, and to kneel at thy footstool, remembering that Thou art our Creator and our King. We ask for lowly hearts, such as become those who feel thy presence and thy majesty. We thank Thee that Thou hast revealed Thyself unto us not only as a God of glory, but as a God of grace, delighting in mercy, and pardoning iniquity, transgression, and sin. In Christ Jesus Thou art full of love towards us; and for his sake Thou wilt save and bless all who come unto Thee through Him. Thou givest us boldness of access into thy presence, that we may obtain mercy and find grace to help us in time of need. Behold us, Lord; we come to Thee, for Thou art our God. Look down, and let the light of thy countenance shine upon us.

We thank Thee that Thou makest Thyself known to us as a covenant-keeping God; faithful to thy gracious promises, providing for all the wants of thy people, defending them from their enemies, and working for their deliverance. Lord, we beseech Thee, provide for us; guard us this day from sin and danger; lead us not into temptation; or, if Thou permit us to be tempted, be near us to preserve our feet from falling. Let not the snares of the Evil One entrap us, nor the assaults of sin have power to subdue and overcome us. We would make the Lord our refuge, and abide for ever under the shadow of the Almighty.

Gracious God, look in mercy and love on the whole Church of Christ. Make thy people more and more a blessing to all around them. Especially be with thy ministers in their preparation for the labours of the coming Sabbath-day. May thy Spirit take of the things of Christ, and show them wondrous things out of thy Word. Give them clear views of thy truth. If they are in error, give them light and understanding. Endue them abundantly with thy grace; give them fervour of spirit, tender compassion for the weak and the perishing, and let the unction of thy grace be on all that they say and do. Increase the number of faithful labourers in thy vineyard. Raise up men to serve Thee in the ministry who shall be mighty in the Scriptures, and zealous for Christ. May all who have the training of future pastors receive wisdom and grace from above, that their labours may be blessed of Thee, and tend to the welfare of thy Church and the increase of the Redeemer's kingdom.

Be with us, and all who are dear to us, this day and for evermore. We ask every mercy for his sake who loved us and gave Himself for us, Jesus Christ thy dear Son, our Lord. Amen.

O GOD, the Creator and Governor of all things, again we bow before thy sacred Majesty. Though Thou art high, Thou hast respect unto the lowly. We approach Thee through the one Mediator, Christ Jesus: for his sake lift upon us the light of thy countenance, and give us peace.

We thank Thee for the manifold mercies which we have received from thy bountiful hand during the past week. Thou hast blessed our going out and our coming in; our lives have been precious in thy sight. Thou hast given us day by day our daily bread, Thou hast clothed us, and provided us with a comfortable habitation. Notwithstanding our forgetfulness of Thee, Thou hast mercifully remembered us. The consolations of thy Spirit have not been withdrawn from us; the adversary of our souls has not been permitted to devour us; and the trials by which we have been overtaken have been designed for our spiritual and eternal welfare. What shall we render unto the Lord for all his benefits towards us? May we take the cup of salvation, and call upon the name of the Lord. Fill our hearts with gratitude, and let all our powers be consecrated to thy service. We have not hitherto rendered unto Thee according to the benefits which Thou hast conferred. Oh, sprinkle our consciences with the blood of atonement, and enable us in the future to glorify Thee with our bodies and our spirits, which are thine.

We bless Thee for the appointment of the Sabbath-day. Prepare us for its holy exercises; and if we are permitted to enter upon them, may they be to us sources of spiritual comfort and edification. Let the Sabbath be to us not only a day of rest, but also a joy and a delight: and, like our Lord and Master, may we employ a portion of its sacred hours in works of love and mercy.

Graciously prepare thy servants who may be called to labour for Thee, for their respective duties, and make them instrumental in leading multitudes to Jesus. May many souls be quickened from the death of sin unto the life of righteousness. Let all the ends of the earth acknowledge Him to be the very Christ, and receive Him as their Saviour.

We now commend ourselves and all who are dear to us into thine hand. Preserve us during the night season, and may we rise in the morning with renewed strength and grateful hearts. Grant these our petitions for the sake of Jesus Christ our Lord, to whom, with Thee and the Holy Spirit, be all praise, and glory, and honour for ever. Amen.

[Morning.]   FIFTEENTH WEEK.—LORD'S DAY.   [Evening.

READ IN HOLY SCRIPTURE EXODUS X. 12—29.   READ IN HOLY SCRIPTURE ST. JOHN VII. 32—53.

O BLESSED God, Thou art indeed long-suffering and slow to anger. Thou hast not dealt with us after our sins, nor rewarded us according to our iniquities. We have often provoked thy displeasure, yet Thou hast made goodness and mercy to follow us all our days. When Thou hast smitten us, it has been to make us wise, and to bring us to hearken to thy voice of love. Lord, sanctify to us all past afflictions. Pardon our forgetfulness of those lessons, and grant that the lasting effect of thy discipline may be to keep us humble, watchful, and weaned in spirit from earth and earthly affections. Have compassion on all in affliction this morning. Be with thine own children in the furnace, and bring them forth purified. Keep the hearts of sinners from becoming hardened under thy dealings. May they humble themselves before Thee in their darkness and trouble, and come to Thee in Jesus with a true repentance. Oh, let none mock Thee with a false profession of sorrow for sin. Thou art a holy God, and requirest truth in the inward parts. Nor will thy word of threatening fall to the ground. When Thou visitest for sin, Thou workest fearful things in righteousness. Great, O Lord, and dread are thy resources for the punishment of transgression. Who can stand before Thee when Thou art angry? Our hearts may well tremble in awe of thy righteous judgments.

But Thou art calling us this morning to gratitude and joy. The darkness of the night has not brought us terror, and our eyes have been opened to see the morning. We hail it in thy name, for it is the morning that saw our Lord arise. Oh, make this day a blessed time of privilege and profit to our souls. In our closets, in our family, in the sanctuary, meet us, and bless us. Teach us to worship Thee, and give us this day our portion of bread from heaven. Bless our pastor in his sacred work. Bless all ministers of the Gospel and all Christian teachers this day, and make their labours effectual to win souls. Pour out thy Spirit as on the day of Pentecost of old, and let thousands of saved souls be added to the Church. We commend to Thee each member of this household as if by name. We commend to Thee all our kindred and friends. We pray Thee to bless the land we live in. Bless it with yearly harvests unblighted, and its people with grateful hearts. Bless our beloved Queen, and let her reign ever bring blessing to her subjects. Bless all lands. Let the people praise Thee, Lord; let all the people praise Thee. Let earth soon keep universal Sabbath, and ascribe to Thee, as we do now, dominion and glory, through Jesus Christ our Lord. Amen.

A LMIGHTY and most merciful Father, who in thy good providence hast brought us to the close of another day, we humbly thank Thee for thy loving-kindness, and for thy care over us, and would now commend ourselves and all that are near and dear to us to thy protection for the night.

We acknowledge, O Lord, that we are unworthy of thy least favours. In how many things have we sinned against Thee and done amiss this day! How many vain thoughts have lodged in our minds, how many idle words have escaped our lips, and how far have we fallen short in the actions of our life of that holiness which becomes thy people! But there is forgiveness with Thee, O our God, and plenteous redemption. Let the blood of Christ our Saviour cleanse us from all sin, and do Thou receive us, for his sake, into the arms of thy mercy now, and let us abide in thy love.

We bless thy holy name for all the spiritual privileges we enjoy. We thank Thee for the gift of thy Word, and for thy Holy Spirit which Thou hast sent to dwell with thy Church always, to quicken, sanctify, and comfort the souls of thy people. Grant unto us that we all who are here present may understand thy Word, and be filled with thy Spirit. Yet a little while, O Saviour, Thou art with us. Oh, give us grace that we may seek Thee day by day whilst Thou mayest be found. Make Thyself manifest to our hearts, that we may know Thee now by faith, and evermore increase in the love of Thee. Enable us to put away all doubt and misbelief, all sin and wickedness, all worldliness and vanity. And do Thou refresh us with thy heavenly consolations. Give us to drink more and more deeply of the streams of the fountain of life which is in Thee. Our soul thirsteth for Thee, O God our Saviour. Thou hast received of the Father gifts even for the rebellious. Therefore, send down upon us, in fulness of measure, thy Spirit, that we may rejoice in Thee, and be made meet for thine inheritance.

Keep us; O Lord our God, this night from all evil. Give us peaceful rest, and grant that we may rise in the morning fitted for the services and duties to which Thou mayest be pleased to call us. Bless all our relatives and friends. Do good to all who love us. Bless our Sovereign the Queen, and all in authority under her. Bless the ministers of thy Word and ordinances. Bless and keep all thy people; and have mercy on those who in ignorance or wilfulness are rejecting the Saviour. We ask all in Christ's most holy name, and to the Father, Son, and Holy Ghost, three Persons, one God, would ascribe all honour and praise, world without end. Amen.

[99]

[MORNING.] **FIFTEENTH WEEK.—MONDAY.** [EVENING.

READ IN HOLY SCRIPTURE ISAIAH LI. 9—16. READ IN HOLY SCRIPTURE ISAIAH LV.

ALMIGHTY and everlasting God, the Creator of heaven and earth, by whose never-failing providence all things are upheld and governed, look down in mercy, we humbly beseech Thee, upon us thy servants, who desire to begin this day by putting ourselves under thy guidance and protection. Thou, even Thou alone, art the God of all the families of the earth; to Thee alone belong glory, and honour, and power, for Thou madest all things, and for thy pleasure they are and were created.

Be with us, Lord, we beseech Thee, this day in our going out and coming in, and keep us in all our ways. Thou knowest our frame, and rememberest that we are dust. Strengthen us by thy Spirit in the inner man, that we, being strong in Thee and in the power of thy might, may lay aside every weight, and especially the sin that does most easily beset us, and run with patience the race that is set before us. Give us grace that we may faithfully and diligently fulfil all our appointed duties, and so have a conscience void of offence both towards Thee and towards men.

Thy hand is not shortened that it cannot save, nor thine ear heavy that it cannot hear. Oh, do Thou, who didst deliver thy people of old from hard bondage, and didst divide the waters of the sea, making a way for thy ransomed ones to pass over, deliver us from the guilt and bondage of sin, and make a way for us to escape from the sins and snares of the world, and from all the dangers and temptations to which we are exposed in this present life. Thou knowest, Lord, how weak and ignorant we are of ourselves; graciously strengthen, guide, and direct us, that we may walk in the way of thy precepts.

Amidst all our cares and distractions, enable us to feel conscious of thy presence, and to set Thee always before us. Thou art about our path, and observest all our ways. May we therefore strive to approve ourselves in all things to Thee, the heart-searching God. Suffer us not, gracious Lord, through fear of man, ever to be ashamed of thy name, but give us grace that we may boldly confess Thee before men, and be faithful witnesses for thy truth, both with our lips and in our lives.

Pour out thy heavenly grace abundantly on all who are dear to us [and especially on the younger members of this household]. May they all be numbered among thy saints, and be daily found at thy footstool praying for themselves as we now pray for them. Sow the seed of thy truth in all their hearts, that whatsoever from thy Word they may profitably learn they may indeed fulfil the same. Hear us, merciful Father, for the sake of our Lord and Saviour Jesus Christ. Amen.

ALMIGHTY God, we adore Thee as the author of our being, and bless Thee as the giver of every good and perfect gift. We thank Thee for thy gracious invitation to come to the waters of life, and to partake freely of all the blessings of thy grace. We have spent our money for that which is not bread, and our labour for that which satisfieth not; but now, through the grace of thy holy Spirit, we repent of our wickedness, and beseech Thee, O Lord, to give unto us the bread of life, that we may not perish, but live for ever.

We incline our ear, and come unto Thee, O Lord; and we implore Thee, of thy great goodness, to make an everlasting covenant with us, even the sure mercies of David. Thou hast given Him for a Witness to the people, a Leader in the way to heaven, and a Commander in all our conflicts with the powers of darkness. Oh, may the nations run unto Jesus for salvation; for it has pleased Thee that in Him should all fulness dwell, that men should be blessed in Him, that all nations should call Him blessed. Do Thou give unto us, O Lord, a new heart and a new spirit, that we may obey the Captain of our salvation, and may be also glorified with Him.

Through Jesus we now seek Thee, O Lord, and call upon Thee for salvation. Be found of us now, and evermore be near to save us to the uttermost. We have done wickedly in thy sight, and have deserved death for our sins. It is of thy mercy that we are not consumed. We would confess our sins, forsake our wicked ways and thoughts, and return unto Thee, our God, that Thou mayest have mercy upon us, and abundantly pardon our transgressions. We rejoice, O Lord, that thy thoughts to us-ward are thoughts of peace, and not of evil; that thy ways to penitent sinners are full of mercy. As the heaven is high above the earth, so great is thy mercy towards them that fear Thee.

Do Thou, O God, bless the preaching of thy most holy Word, that it may make the souls of men fruitful in every good word and work, even as the rain and snow make the earth bring forth and bud, that it may give seed to the sower, and bread to the eater. Grant thy ministers abundant success, that there may be joy in heaven over the repentance of sinners, and that thy Word may be fulfilled in the conversion of the world. O Lord, remember the Word upon which Thou hast caused us to hope, and grant that instead of error and ignorance may come up wisdom and knowledge, and instead of wickedness and misery may come up holiness and joy, for the benefit of men, and to the everlasting glory of thy great name. Hear us, O God, and bless us, for the sake of Jesus Christ, our Lord. Amen.

[Morning.] **FIFTEENTH WEEK.—TUESDAY.** [Evening.

READ IN HOLY SCRIPTURE EXODUS XI.

O LORD God, the Author and Giver of all good things, we again approach Thee in prayer and praise. Graciously assist us by thy Holy Spirit, that our morning sacrifice may be acceptable in thy sight. We thank Thee, O God of our life, for thy preserving care and for refreshing sleep; help us to devote ourselves and all that we have to Thee, which is our reasonable service; and may thy good providence watch over us during this day, protecting us in danger, guiding us in perplexity, and mercifully supplying all our need. We acknowledge ourselves, O Lord, to be unworthy of thy regard, and to be exposed to thy just displeasure, because we have sinned against Thee, violating thy righteous law, rejecting thy Gospel, and grieving thy Holy Spirit. Have mercy upon us, O God, giving us true repentance, a firm reliance on the atoning death of thy Son, and that full and free pardon offered in thy blessed Word. We pray also that the promised Comforter may dwell within us, and bear witness to our acceptance through Christ; and thoroughly sanctify our nature, so that we may perfectly love and worthily magnify thy holy name. Write thy precious Word in our heart. May our lives be so regulated by its precepts that we may please Thee in all things, and escape the judgments which Thou hast denounced against the ungodly. Look, gracious Father, in thy mercy, on those who are dear to us. Watch over them by thy providence. Teach and guide them by thy Holy Spirit, and grant that such of them as are unconverted may be turned from darkness to light, and delivered from the bondage of sin and Satan into the glorious liberty of the children of God. [We supplicate Thee also for the younger members of this family. To them also give thy grace, and draw them to Christ their Saviour.]

We pray also, O Lord, for thy Church throughout the world. Give peace and unity to thy people, fill thy ministers with wisdom and grace, clothe their word with power, and let all thine ordinances be seasons of refreshing from thy presence. We pray Thee to subvert all deadly errors, vanquish and overturn all opposition to thy truth, and let thy kingdom come with power and great glory. Hear us, O Lord, for our beloved country. Turn away ungodliness from our people, and bring them to the knowledge of thy salvation. Favour us with prosperity in our commerce and trade, direct our legislators into all truth, and give wisdom, equity, and mercy to our magistrates. Be gracious to our beloved Queen, and to all the Royal Family; and let thy compassion be extended to all mankind, through Jesus Christ our Lord. Amen.

READ IN HOLY SCRIPTURE ST. JOHN VIII. 12–30.

O THOU who art the Fountain of light and life, we draw near to Thee to offer up our evening worship, in the name of thy Son Jesus Christ. We acknowledge thy great goodness to us this day. Thou hast continued to us the use of our faculties and powers, and hast supplied us with all needful good.

We confess before Thee, O Lord, that we are altogether unworthy of the least of these thy favours. We have been unmindful of thy goodness and thy love. We have been ungrateful for thy mercies. We have neglected thy Word. We have transgressed thy commands. We mourn before Thee that to-day we have added to the number of our sins and to the amount of our guilt. Have mercy upon us, O Lord, we beseech Thee. Grant us penitence of heart, and by thy good Spirit lead us to sincere repentance. For the sake of Jesus Christ thy Son, blot out all our sins, and assure us of thy forgiving love.

O Thou who art the Light of the world, dispel from our minds all darkness of error and unbelief. Be in us the light of life. Grant that in all our relationships to each other and the world we may henceforth live as children of light. Help us, by conduct as well as conversation, to hold forth the Word of life. Through us do Thou graciously shine forth unto others, that they, seeing our good works, may glorify Thee our Father in heaven.

Most merciful Father, we beseech Thee to pour out thy blessing upon all who are dear to us. May our friends who love Thee continually enjoy thy favour. If any are in perplexity and sorrow, may thy wisdom and grace guide and comfort them. May those who are aged be sustained in their declining years by the consolations of thy love. May they enjoy such constant and intimate communion with Thee that they may ever feel themselves ready to enter into thy heavenly kingdom. May those who are young grow up into Jesus Christ, and adorn the doctrine of God our Saviour in all things. Of thine infinite mercy bring to thy Son Jesus Christ any whom we love who may be still living in sin and at enmity against Thee, and grant that all our relations and friends may be thy children, and heirs with us of eternal glory.

We pray for the extension of the Redeemer's kingdom. Let the nations which are now held in bondage by Satan be made free in Christ, and soon may the whole world see the salvation of God.

We now commit ourselves and each other unto thy care. Keep us from all danger through the night. Give us the rest we need, and grant, if it be thy will, that we may rise in the morning to serve Thee in newness of life, for the sake of Jesus Christ. Amen.

[Morning.] **FIFTEENTH WEEK.—WEDNESDAY.** [Evening.]

READ IN HOLY SCRIPTURE EXODUS XII. 1—20.

WE thank Thee, heavenly Father, that Christ our Passover has been slain for us; that Thou hast brought us out of the land of Egypt, and out of the house of bondage; that Thou hast released us from the thraldom of sin, delivered us from the power of Satan, and translated us into the kingdom of thy dear Son. We thank Thee that when we had no helper, when there was no eye to pity and none to deliver, thine eye took compassion on us, and thine arm wrought out salvation. We adore that love which condescended to our low estate, remembered us in our sin and misery, and snatched us as brands from the burning.

O God, we had no claim upon thy love; Thou mightest justly have left us to perish; we merited thine eternal wrath, but Thou hast not dealt with us according to our sins. Thou hast redeemed us with the precious blood of Christ, as of a lamb without blemish and without spot. Enable us ever to live under the influence of this love. Constrain us, by the mercies of Christ, to present our bodies a living sacrifice to Thee; and grant that, sprinkled with the blood of atonement, we may find mercy in that day when Thou shalt be revealed in flaming fire, taking vengeance on thine enemies.

Hasten the time, O Lord, we beseech Thee, when all our fellow-creatures in every part of the earth shall be made acquainted with Christ our Passover, and all the captives of Satan brought into the glorious liberty of the sons of God, so that the whole world may be filled with thy glory.

We desire to praise Thee, O Lord our God, for thy preserving care through another night. We laid ourselves down and slept, we awaked, for the Lord sustained us. We thank Thee for the measure of health and strength in which Thou hast raised us up. We gratefully recognise thy hand in all the mercies we enjoy. Thou hast spread our table for us, and supplied our returning wants. Give unto us thankful hearts, and enable us to consecrate all we have and are to thy service. Grant us thy presence throughout this day. Help us to keep a close watch over our steps, words, and thoughts, that we sin not in any way against Thee. Prepare us for the discharge of every duty; shield us from all harm; strengthen us in every temptation; and assist us to maintain a good conscience both toward God and man.

Bless every member of this family. May young and old be the partakers of thy grace, and in every relationship of life may we act as becometh the children of God.

Hear Thou, in heaven thy dwelling place, and when Thou hearest, forgive; and do for us exceeding abundantly above all we can ask or think, for the sake of thy dear Son. Amen.

READ IN HOLY SCRIPTURE ST. JOHN VIII. 31—45.

O THOU who art the light, and with whom is no darkness at all, we beseech Thee to enlighten our minds and help us to understand thy holy Word. We praise Thee for the words of grace and truth which dropped from the lips of thy well-beloved Son. May we delight to sit at his feet and learn of Him. May we be meek and lowly in heart, ready to receive whatever truth He is pleased to teach us, and ever willing to follow Him in all things.

Oh, make us his disciples indeed. May our actions proclaim more loudly than our words that we belong to Him; and may our whole lives be an exemplification of the doctrines and precepts of the Gospel. Deliver us, O Lord, from the slavery of sin, and from the bondage of our natural corruption. Let not the wicked one be allowed to lead us captive at his will. Give us grace to resist him whenever he may tempt us. May we never give the least encouragement to his suggestions, nor go unnecessarily into the way of temptation. O Jesus, who hast Thyself been tempted, succour us; succour us, we pray Thee, and plead for us, that our faith fail not.

We give Thee thanks, O most gracious God, that Thou dost permit us to call Thee our Father. Wilt Thou mercifully own us as thy sons and daughters, and give to us all the blessings of thine adopting love? May the truth as it is in Jesus make us free, that we may love Thee with all our hearts, and serve Thee with all our strength.

We desire to praise Thee, O Thou who fixest the bounds of our habitation, for our family mercies and for our national privileges. Ever would we thank Thee for the piety of our ancestors, and for all the influences that have affected for good our character and our life. Help us to profit by the instructions of the living and the dead; help us to follow their example so far as they followed Christ; but may we never trust to their piety or their prayers. Oh, save us, our God, we beseech Thee, save us from ever thinking that because we have had Abraham, or any one else, as our father, we are at liberty to do the works of the wicked one; but may we rather feel that our natural and family connections lay us under increased obligations to love, and obey, and serve Thee.

Accept our thanks for the multiplied mercies of this day. Pardon, we beseech Thee, our imperfections, neglects, and sins. Sprinkle our hearts afresh to-night with the blood of the everlasting covenant. Protect us through the hours of darkness, and refresh us by sleep for the duties of to-morrow. Grant us these and all needful blessings, for Christ's sake. Amen.

[Morning.]   FIFTEENTH WEEK.—THURSDAY.   [Evening.

READ IN HOLY SCRIPTURE EXODUS XII. 21—36.   READ IN HOLY SCRIPTURE ST. JOHN VIII. 46—59.

ALMIGHTY and most merciful God, great in holiness and terrible in power, who art the same yesterday, to-day, and for ever, the unchangeable God, we desire to draw near to Thee, pleading no other name and trusting to no other merit than the name and merit of Jesus Christ, thy Son, our Lord. We thank Thee, gracious God, that Thou hast been pleased to make known unto us the way of life. Give us grace, we beseech Thee, so to profit by the revelation of thy mind and will, that we may embrace and ever hold fast those truths which pertain to our well-doing in the life that now is, and to our prosperity in the life that is to follow. May we so reflect upon thy dealings with thine ancient people Israel, and the direful judgments denounced against the rejectors of thy commands, that we may be led in faith, in penitence, and in holy fear, to the Lamb of God who taketh away the sin of the world. As Christ our Passover was sacrificed for us, grant, by thy grace, that we may be made partakers of all the blessings which He died to secure. And as of ourselves we are not able to believe and to do those things which are pleasing in thy sight, we beseech Thee, strengthen us by power from on high for the right discharge of our duties to Thee and to our fellow-men; and grant, that we may be led so to embrace the offer of deliverance, by faith in Christ Jesus, that being rescued from all our spiritual enemies, we may be enabled to worship Thee with joyful hearts, and to serve Thee in newness of life.

As it is Thou, Lord, that liftest up or castest down, as it is thine to exalt or to abase, and as the silver and the gold are thine, and the hearts of all men are at thy control, teach us to know that our safety and our prosperity in things temporal are alike in thy hands. May we therefore look up to Thee for guidance in all our ways, and ever pray that Thou mayest direct our paths.

Now that we are about to enter on the duties of the day, be with us in our going out and our coming in, to prosper the work of our hands. Bestow upon us throughout the day a sense of thy presence; keep us in thy faith and fear; and when our duties on earth are finished, do Thou in mercy forgive us those things whereof our consciences are afraid, and give us those good things which of ourselves we are not worthy to ask, but which we venture to ask for ourselves, and for all for whom it is our duty to pray, through the intercession of Jesus Christ our Lord.

The Lord bless and keep us. The Lord make his face to shine upon us, and give us peace. The Lord be gracious unto us this day, henceforth, and for ever. Amen.

GIVE us, we beseech Thee, O Lord God, the spirit of prayer and praise, that this our evening worship may not be a vain and empty service, but be acceptable in thy sight, because fragrant with the merits of thy dear Son, who ever liveth to make intercession for us. We owe Thee, gracious Father, everlasting thankfulness. Our mercies this day have been many and great. Unspeakable, indeed, is thy loving patience and forbearance, for we are utterly unworthy of thy favour. We have gone astray, like lost sheep, from thy commandments, and in many things day by day have preferred our own will to thine, and the way of the world to thy precepts. Forgive us, O merciful God, all our sins—the sins of our secret thoughts, the sins of temper, the sins of the tongue, the sins of act, of which we may have been guilty this day. They are known to Thee; have compassion upon us, and blot them out for ever. O Lamb of God, that takest away the sins of the world, hear our prayer and grant us thy peace.

Gracious Father, we earnestly implore the gift of the Spirit, that He may dwell in our hearts, and incline us to think and to do such things as please Thee. Take from us all ignorance and hardness of heart, and enable us to receive with meekness thy Word, which is able to save our souls. We pray for the hearing ear and the understanding heart of thy children, and for the teaching of thy Spirit, who alone can guide us into all truth, and enable us to know the things which have been given to us by God. We pray for thy love to be shed abroad in our hearts, that we may live as in the light of thy countenance, and feel that thy commandments are not grievous. Deliver us from the bondage of sin, and self, and Satan, that, keeping Christ's sayings, we may be spared the second death, and have our life hid with Christ in God. May no unbelief be harboured in our hearts, nor love for what is sinful make us halt in the way of thy commandments, or turn a deaf ear to the warnings of thy holy book.

Mercifully be with us, O God, during the night. Do Thou comfort us and shelter us by thy protecting power. Spare us, if it be thy will, till the morning, and raise us up, strengthened in body and spirit, to serve Thee cheerfully in the duties of another day.

Let thy Divine favour and blessing rest on [the young of this household, and on] all whom we love. Endue them with thy grace, give them a heart-knowledge of thy Gospel, and cause them so to abound in the graces of the Spirit, that they may be seen to be the children of God, and faithful disciples of the Lord Jesus. In his name we ask these and all other mercies which we need. Amen.

[MORNING.] FIFTEENTH WEEK.—FRIDAY. [EVENING.

READ IN HOLY SCRIPTURE EXODUS XII. 37—51.

READ IN HOLY SCRIPTURE ST. JOHN IX. 1—23.

O LORD, teach us to pray. We bless Thee for our creation, preservation, and for all the blessings of this life; but above all, for our redemption, the redemption of our bodies and souls, by Christ Jesus our Lord. Oh, grant us thy grace to walk as thy redeemed ones. May we this day and ever remember that we are bought with a price, and that we are not our own. Set our souls free from every evil thing, and especially from that sin which doth so easily beset us. Baptise us afresh with the Holy Spirit, and enkindle within us a fervent love and holy zeal for thy name. May we have grace to be faithful to our high and holy calling. O Lord, hold Thou us up, and then we shall be safe. Receive us, O Lord, as Thou hast promised, and be a Father unto us for ever. Bless this whole family. Make it thy family. Be Thou our Father and our God. Make every heart thine own. Let not one of us be a stranger to Thee. May thy holy Word dwell richly in our hearts, and may we adorn it in our daily walk and conversation. May we live as pilgrims in the earth.

O Lord, strengthen us this day for all the duties, responsibilities, and trials of faith to which Thou shalt call us. May we not faint nor be weary in well-doing. Make us feel thy strength in our weakness. In the hour of difficulty and perplexity do Thou guide us. In the hour of temptation and danger do Thou deliver us. Leave us not a moment to ourselves. Safely guide us by thy counsel, and after our race is run receive us into glory.

O blessed Redeemer, may we experience the sanctifying efficacy of thy precious atonement this day. Sprinkle our consciences afresh with thy purifying blood. Give us thy peace, which the world can neither give nor take away.

We commend to thy guardian care, O Lord, our beloved Queen and our country. Oh, bless and sanctify to thy service all the Royal Family. Make this nation a holy people. Teach us to prize thy favour above all riches, and all honour, and all glory. Grant that we may be made a blessing in the earth. O Lord, we would also plead for those who plead for Thee. Bless the ministers of thy holy Word. Make them wise to win souls to Christ. Uphold them in all their laborious works for Thee. Especially bless our own minister. We pray that he may be filled with the Spirit, and that his ministrations may be continually blessed to us and to all his flock. And now, O our Lord, we commend ourselves and all who are dear unto us once more into thy hands; exceed our most fervent desires and petitions, for the sake of Jesus Christ, our blessed Lord and Redeemer. Amen.

O THOU who hearest prayer, we beseech Thee now to accept and help us. We cannot hold communion with Thee or realise thy presence without the help of the Holy Spirit. We desire now to plead with Thee this promise, "If ye then, being evil, know how to give good gifts unto your children, how much more shall your heavenly Father give the Holy Spirit to them that ask Him?" Gracious Father, give us now the Holy Spirit, to teach us and guide us into all truth. Oh, assist us to come to Thee as helpless children to a loving father. Send into our hearts the spirit of adoption, crying Abba, Father. It is because we are weak and sinful that we stand so much in need of thy help. Bow down thine ear and hear, for we are poor and needy.

Come, Holy Spirit, into our hearts, and speak to us of Jesus and his love. Come and help us to give up sin and to worship God. Come and make us wise, and holy, and happy. Come and make us like Christ. We are indeed sinful, but we know that Christ is a great Saviour. Be very gracious to us now. Help us to cast all our care upon God, and all our sins upon Jesus. Help us to feed upon thy holy Word. We thank Thee for all Thou hast done for us. Without Thee we cannot think a good thought, or pray aright. Bless us, then, we pray Thee, and bless to us that portion of Scripture we have just been reading, and which was written for our learning.

O Thou who art the light of the world, open our eyes, we beseech Thee. Enable us to see Thee, O Jesus, and to worship Thee as our Prophet, Priest, and King. Lighten our darkness, we beseech Thee, O Lord. Take away all blindness from our eyes, and all hardness from our hearts. In thy light may we see light. When evil thoughts and desires darken our minds, oh, do Thou graciously anoint us with thine own Spirit. May the Spirit of truth enlighten the eyes of our understanding. Blessed Saviour, Thou hadst compassion upon one who was born blind: have mercy now upon those who are blinded by sin. Thou dost often bring the blind by a way that they know not: guide us, we beseech Thee, in the way that leads to heaven. May thy Word be a lamp to our feet and a light to our path. Suffer us not to fall or wander from Thee. Be ever near to us. It is not night, blessed Saviour, if Thou art near.

Oh, may no earth-born cloud arise,
To hide Thee from thy servants' eyes.

Guard us sleeping; watch over us till the day dawns; and when we awake from the sleep of death, do Thou, who art the bright and morning Star, shine on us for ever and ever. Amen.

[Morning.]   FIFTEENTH WEEK.—SATURDAY.   [Evening.

READ IN HOLY SCRIPTURE PSALM LXVIII. 20—30.

O THOU gracious preserver of men, whose merciful providence has watched over us during the darkness and dangers of another night, receive our united thanksgivings for thy goodness. We bless Thee for the light of this morning, awaking us to so many mercies, of which we are utterly unworthy, and for the promise of all the blessings we may need this day. We know that our common mercies, too often received as if our due, and enjoyed without thought of their value or regard to the Giver, yet demand our heartfelt gratitude and praise. A sleepless night, with pain or weariness, would make us more highly value the rest we so commonly enjoy; and the loss of the mercies of our table and our home would make us more grateful for our comforts. O teach us to say from the heart, "Blessed be the Lord, who daily loadeth us with benefits, even the God of our salvation;" and let our bodies, thus fed and sustained, and the life thus lengthened and made comfortable by thy goodness, be a sacrifice to God, acceptable through Christ our Saviour.

We join in blessing Thee, O Lord, for the provision which Thou hast made for our souls, for that redemption we have in Christ, for that fountain of infinite merit at all times and to all men easy of access, for the blessings of personal forgiveness, and acceptance to thy favour, and for the gift of thy Holy Spirit, the source of infinite grace, the Author and Giver of life, and peace, and strength. We bless Thee that we are not cast out of thy presence, after all our ingratitude and disobedience; that through the intercession of thy Son we have the privilege to pray, and the promise of both mercy and grace. In thy Word and in thy sanctuary Thou hast made known Thyself to man; how Thou hast set thine heart upon him, and hast towards him thoughts of peace, and not of evil. We thank Thee that we are disposed by thy blessed Spirit to seek salvation by grace through faith, to trust in Christ alone, and to receive Him as our Prophet, Priest, and King. Oh, lead us into all truth, and teach us to do thy will. Help us to live by faith on the Son of God, who loved us, and gave Himself for us; and may his blessed love be continually in our hearts.

Grant these blessings, O heavenly Father, not only to this family, but to all our connections in life, that all grace, and peace, and every blessing, may be multiplied unto them also. Give thy ministers thine effectual help in preparing food for thy people. Bless our beloved Queen and our nation, and enlighten and save the world. Let these our prayers and praises come up with acceptance, through Jesus Christ, our Lord and Saviour. Amen.

READ IN HOLY SCRIPTURE ST. JOHN IX. 24—41.

ETERNAL God, the strength of all that trust in Thee, our hope and refuge in every time of need, hear us now that we call upon Thee, and in the name of thy beloved Son implore thy blessing. Most graciously hast Thou dealt with us. Another week's mercies have been added to the life-long loving-kindness which Thou hast shown towards us. Oh, add to all thy other bounties the gift of a thankful heart, and so inspire us by thy grace that we may perfectly love Thee, and worthily glorify thy name.

Thou, O Lord, searchest and triest our very hearts. Sins of which we are hardly conscious are seen by thine all-seeing eye. Secret thoughts and imaginations of evil which we have forgotten have been written in the book of thy remembrance Lord, could we but see ourselves as Thou seest us, we should blush and be ashamed to lift our eyes unto Thee. Merciful Father, cleanse us, we pray Thee, from all the guilt and defilement of these our transgressions. So put away our sin from before Thee that it may never more be seen. We plead the blood of Jesus Christ, and we earnestly desire that we may so see our sins in the light of his cross and passion, that we may abhor and forsake them, and strive every day to live more entirely according to thy will.

Reveal unto us, O God, the glory and sufficiency of Jesus Christ. Thou knowest how feeble is our comprehension of divine things; how little we have as yet understood of the glory of Jesus Christ, and of his wonderful suffering for all the sinner's need. Open our eyes, we pray Thee, that we may know and believe in Him as our adorable Emmanuel, Jesus our Saviour, Christ our King. Teach us all the meaning of his cross, and agony, and passion; raise our hearts to his throne, whither Thou hast exalted Him to give repentance and remission of sins. Give us such experience of his saving power and grace that we may have the witness in ourselves of forgiveness and acceptance, and be enabled to go on our way rejoicing.

Do Thou, Lord, take us into thy keeping for the night to which Thou hast brought us; and as the Sabbath-day dawns, grant us to be in a suitable spirit, thankful for renewed religious opportunities, and anxious to make them profitable for our growth in grace and in spiritual knowledge. Let thy favour rest on all whom we love. [Watch over the younger members of our family. Take them under thy special teaching, and by thy constraining love win them into thy fold. Let them hear the voice of Jesus the good Shepherd, and follow Him.] Prepare all thy ministers for the duties of the morrow, and make it a day of blessing unto us all, for Jesus Christ's sake. Amen.

[105]

[MORNING.] SIXTEENTH WEEK.—LORD'S DAY. [EVENING.

READ IN HOLY SCRIPTURE EXODUS XIII.

ALMIGHTY God, who didst deliver thy people from the land of Egypt, and from the house of bondage, and who dost now deliver from the bondage of sin them that repent and believe in Thee, accept the praises of thy servants whom Thou hast ransomed by the precious blood of Christ. Thou who didst command thy people to sanctify their first-born unto Thee, and who dost teach us that we are not our own, but are bought with a price, help us to give up to Thee that which most we love, and to consecrate to thy service all that we possess.

For the gifts of thy bounty in days past, for strength to serve Thee, for help in time of need, and for long-suffering towards us when our offences have provoked thy just displeasure, we humbly offer Thee, through Jesus, the sacrifice of praise. Casting off our burden of toil and care on this day of rest, we most humbly approach thy mercy-seat through the same Jesus, our great High Priest; and ask for grace to keep a solemn feast unto the Lord. This is the day which the Lord hath made; we will rejoice and be glad in it.

O God of mercy and of might, break Thou our bonds, and set us free. Let not sin have dominion over us, but bring us into the perfect liberty of the children of God. Let no unkindness towards any man hinder our prayers. Let not impenitence, nor pride, nor hardness of heart, nor unbelief prevent one soul from coming freely unto Thee, with whom there is forgiveness, that Thou mayest be feared. Grant us all grace, O King of Sion, that thy children may be joyful in Thee. Then we shall have power to cast away every idol, and live only to thy glory, freed from the things of guilt, and from the dread of hell.

And now, Father of Heaven, let thy good Spirit bear witness to us if we are indeed thy children, that we have been born from above, and can truly call Thee Father; then will we cast ourselves upon thy mercy for all that may befall us throughout this earthly pilgrimage. Thou so leadest the faithful through the wilderness, that neither the fiery serpent, nor the scorpion, nor the drought can hurt them. Thou feedest them with manna, and bringest water for them from the flinty rock. Send now the Angel of the Covenant, that He may go before us. Command the fiery pillar to give us light, and let us hear thy voice bidding us march onwards to the eternal country. Oh, give each member of our family to-day a foretaste of that rest. Save each one from the evil heart of unbelief in departing from the living God; and grant him faith, which only Thou canst give, that even now he may enter into the holiest by the blood of Jesus. Amen.

READ IN HOLY SCRIPTURE PSALM L.

O LORD God, searcher of the hearts, who knowest our necessity before we ask, and our ignorance in asking, give us now, we beseech Thee, thy help, that we may come into thy presence with reverence and godly fear. We are but dust and ashes before Thee; we have nothing we can call our own but our sins.

And yet, O most merciful and gracious God, we would remember that we have in heaven a great High Priest, who ever liveth to make intercession for us. Through Him we approach Thee as our Father. Give us, together with the spirit of holy reverence, the Spirit of adoption; and enable us to come boldly before Thee, that we may obtain mercy and find grace to help in time of need.

We thank Thee, O our Father, for the many mercies of another day, and that thine own holy day. We praise and bless thy name for all thy gifts to fallen man, for the appointment of a day of rest, for the revelation of Thyself in thy Word, for the ordinances of thy house, for the means of grace, as well as for all the temporal blessings which Thou dost so abundantly bestow upon us. Above all, we thank Thee for the unspeakable gift of thy dear Son, and for the salvation which has been again this day proclaimed to us through his atoning blood. Graciously forgive us the imperfection of our religious duties, and if, by wandering thought, or vain imagination, or by a trifling and cavilling spirit, we have offended against Thee this day, oh, wash us again in that fountain which Thou hast opened for the sin and uncleanness of thy believing people. And grant, gracious Father, that each succeeding Sabbath may incline our thoughts more to that rest which remaineth for the people of God.

We desire, O God, the felicity of thy chosen ones. Help us to desire it more. Thy blessing, we know, is upon thy people. It is Thou who makest them to prosper in their ways. Oh, help us to remember that from Thee alone is our fruit found; and may we be enabled, by the help of thy Holy Spirit, to exercise, under all circumstances, an unfailing reliance upon thy protecting, and quickening, and sustaining love. We would, also, greatly value thy written Word. May we find it a lamp unto our feet, and a light unto our path. Bless, O Lord, the public preaching of the Word this day. May thy Spirit clothe it with power. May sinners be converted, and thy people edified.

And now, gracious Father, we commend ourselves and all who belong us to thy guardian care. Graciously protect us and refresh us for the duties of the coming day, and may thy blessing abide upon us now and for ever, for Jesus Christ our Saviour's sake. Amen.

[MORNING.] SIXTEENTH WEEK.—MONDAY. [EVENING.

READ IN HOLY SCRIPTURE EXODUS XIV. 1—18.

READ IN HOLY SCRIPTURE ST. JOHN X. 1—18.

BLESSED and Almighty God, Thou knowest the way of the righteous. Thou didst lead thy people as a flock; with a mighty hand and a stretched out arm Thou didst deliver them, to get Thyself a glorious name, that men might trust in Thee for ever. Thou art still our Guide and our Deliverer. We look to Thee, where to go and where to rest. The pillar of cloud and of fire is before and around us still.

Another day of rest has come and gone. We enter again upon the labours of the week. We have heard thy Word : teach us to remember and keep it. Let us be not only hearers, but doers of the same. We have met thy people; visit us with the favour which Thou bearest to them. We have read of thy judgments; may we learn righteousness. We have been told of thy mercy; let not our hearts be hardened by it. And now, give us thy blessing and guidance, amid the duties and trials that are before us. If our work is arduous, may we remember Him through whom we can do all things. If our work is humble, teach us to ennoble it by the spirit in which it is done. Whether we eat or drink, whether we live or die, may we do all as unto the Lord. If our course is dark and uncertain, if our adversaries are many and powerful, be Thou our Light and our Salvation. Teach us to be still, and to know that Thou art God. Remember in love all that are dear to us. We thank Thee for them. Thou mightest have put them from us, and our acquaintance into darkness. If there are any of our kindred that are strangers to thy grace, hear us on their behalf. Our hearts' desire is that they may be saved. Teach us to win them to Christ. Let there be no division of our household in the great day.

We look beyond our own borders. We pray for lands where there is no light, and where the people perish. Have respect to thy covenant. Give the heathen to thy Son for his inheritance, and the uttermost parts of the earth for his possession. Awake, O arm of the Lord. Let Zion put on her strength, employ her resources—her might of faith, her power of prayer, her energy of love —for the salvation of men, and then let her trust in Thee. Gird thy sword upon thy thigh, O most mighty, and now give the kingdom to thy Son.

Hear us, our Father. Keep us, and continue thy loving-kindness to us. Go Thou forth with us into every engagement, sustaining and sanctifying us in them all. Thus may our whole spirit, and soul, and body be preserved blameless unto the coming of our Lord Jesus Christ. Accept our prayers and our thanksgivings through Him, thine own Son, our Redeemer, to whom with Thee and the Holy Ghost be everlasting praise. Amen.

ADORABLE Redeemer, the Apostle and High Priest of our profession, the very Door of salvation and of heaven, look graciously on us, who now desire to come to God by Thee.

Enable us, most blessed Jesus, to approach the throne of grace with a true heart, in entire dependence on the eternal Spirit, and pleading nothing but thy blood and righteousness.

We are indeed sinful, and have sinned more deeply than we know; yet here, prostrate at thy footstool, we are constrained to render thanks and praise to Thee, O God, the Father of our Lord Jesus Christ, who didst not spare thine own Son, but deliveredst Him up for us all, that He might be the Author of everlasting life to every one believing on his name. And Thee we glorify, Thou precious Saviour, who didst come with joy to do thy Father's will; so loving us, while we were yet thine enemies, as to become obedient unto death, even the death of the cross, that we might have life, and have it more abundantly. Thee, too, we bless and magnify, almighty Comforter, who in richest mercy dost open blind eyes to see the beauty of Christ; who dost reveal Him in the broken heart, turning all its grief to gladness; and who dost lead the souls of thy people to go in and out, and evermore find pasture.

O Father, Son, and Holy Ghost, one God, enrich us with the knowledge of Thyself; enfold us in the everlasting arms, write upon us thy new name, make us familiar with thy voice; and whithersoever Thou shalt go, oh, give us grace to follow. Another day has fled, to return no more. How richly have we proved thy faithfulness and love! We have lacked no good thing. Thou hast been our Shepherd, and we have not wanted. Blessed be God, who daily loadeth us with benefits, giving us not always what we would, but ever what is best. Mercifully forgive our sins. Of very many sins we have been conscious; but oh, how often do we grieve Thee, and not know it! For Christ's sake blot out all that is against us, and may we sleep this night in perfect peace, and with thy smile resting as a holy light upon our hearts. Suffer no evil to molest us; grant to us all the shelter of thy wings; and should wakeful moments come to us amid the silence and the darkness, oh, may we have communion with our God.

Be near to all we love. Visit with showers of blessing the universal Church, and let that happy day soon come when the fulness of thy mercy shall be made known, and there shall be one fold and one Shepherd. We ask all through the mediation of thy only Son, Jesus Christ our Lord. Amen.

[Morning.]   SIXTEENTH WEEK.—TUESDAY.   [Evening.

READ IN HOLY SCRIPTURE EXODUS XIV. 19—31.

READ IN HOLY SCRIPTURE PSALM XXIII.

ALMIGHTY God, our heavenly Father, we bless thy name for thy goodness to us during the past night, and in bringing us to the beginning of another day. May this day, and all days, be spent in thy service. May we work for Thee while it is day, because the night cometh when no man can work. May we redeem the time because the days are evil. In thought, word, and deed strengthen us to glorify thy name. Let us shine as lights in a dark world. May men take knowledge of us that we have been with Jesus. May we do nothing that is inconsistent with our holy profession, and never cause any to stumble by our worldliness or sinfulness.

Thou only knowest what lies before us. Thou only knowest what this day may bring forth. To Thee, therefore, we commend ourselves and all our affairs. Do Thou be our Guide. Let the pillar of thy presence go before us. May we ever hear a voice behind us, as we turn to the right hand or to the left, saying, "This is the way, walk ye in it." May the angel of thy presence abide with us this day and for ever. Do Thou Thyself encamp around us. May our very trials be overruled for good. May the deep waters of our afflictions open out a way for us to the good land. May our deepest sorrows be so sanctified by Thee as to be a wall of defence unto us on the right hand and on the left. Enable us to be victorious over every enemy, and to fight manfully under Christ's banner against sin, the world, and the devil; and may we at last receive the victor's welcome of "Well done," and enter into the joy of our Lord.

Grant that we, as a family, may grow in grace day by day. May we seek each other's good. May we be helpers to each other in every holy work. May we be a household in which Jesus delights to dwell. Teach us to regulate our actions according to thy Word. In ruling and serving may we remember that one is our Master, even Christ, and that all we are his servants. [May we, as parents and children, serve and glorify Thee. Make the young before Thee like unto the child Jesus. May they be subject unto their parents as He was. As they grow in stature may they grow in favour with God and man. May they ever be about their Father's business, even in their days of childhood and youth; and may they grow up to be blessings to all men, and living examples of the saving and sanctifying influence of the Gospel.] Let thy blessing rest upon all our relatives, and make them thine. Pour down thy Spirit upon the whole Church, and hasten the time when all shall know Thee, from the least to the greatest, because all shall be taught of God. We ask these blessings for Jesus Christ's sake. Amen.

GIVE ear, O Thou Shepherd of Israel; Thou that dwellest between the cherubims, appear unto us. We acknowledge that like lost sheep we have gone astray, we have turned every one to his own way. We are foolish and ignorant; and because our deeds are evil, we love darkness rather than light.

Restore now, we beseech Thee, our souls, and lead us in the path of righteousness for thy name's sake. Forgive the sins of this day; forgive our waywardness, our impatience, our morbid anxiety, our eagerness to obtain the bread that perisheth, our forgetfulness of that which endureth unto life eternal. Mercifully now replenish us with thy grace. Calm our hearts. Let us rest in the Lord, and wait patiently for Him. Make us, in quiet meditation on thy precepts, to lie down in green pastures. Lead us, by loving faith in thy promises, beside the still waters. Let sweet sleep refresh our weary bodies; let spiritual repose invigorate our souls.

O Thou who art the good Shepherd, Thou who hast given thy life for the sheep, make us to know thy voice. Keep us in thy fold. Let no man ever pluck us out of thy hand. Even though we walk through the valley of the shadow of death, tended by Thee, let us fear no evil; be Thou with us; let thy rod and thy staff comfort us.

Heavenly Father, encircle us, as a family, with thy love. Give thine angels charge concerning us. [Sanctify parental affection and care. Guard the young from all hurtful snares.] Let our household be a household of faith. May we all abide this night and for evermore under the shadow of the Almighty. Let no plague come nigh our dwelling. Take care of those who are dear to us. Comfort such as are in sorrow; cheer the dying; strengthen those who may have to pass the night in watching at their side. Be Thou the Father of all fatherless and motherless children. Let them not want, but supply all their need and the need of us all, according to the riches of thy glory by Christ Jesus.

Exalted Saviour, as the Shepherd of the sheep Thou hast been smitten for us. Gather together in one all thy scattered flock. Let there be one fold and one Shepherd. Help thy ministers to feed the flock of God. Gather the lambs with thy arm, and carry them in thy bosom. Reclaim those who are wandering; prepare all for thy promised coming; and grant that when, as the Chief Shepherd, Thou shalt appear, we may be acknowledged as thine, and abide with Thee for ever; and unto God the Father, Son, and Holy Ghost will we ascribe eternal praise. Amen.

[Morning.]　　　SIXTEENTH WEEK.—WEDNESDAY.　　　[Evening.

READ IN HOLY SCRIPTURE PSALM LXXVI.

ALMIGHTY and eternal Jehovah, we praise Thee that we can enter thy presence in the exercise of that perfect love which casteth out fear. We would at this time come as dear children to a loving Father, and thank Thee for preserving us through the perils and dangers of another night. Truly thy mercies are new every morning; great is the sum of them. Make us sensible of thy lovingkindness; give to us thankful hearts, and let us not forget thy benefits.

We have no power, no might of our own, to help ourselves. But our eyes are unto Thee. We would run to Thee as our sure refuge and rock of defence. We have heard with our ears, and our fathers have declared to us, the noble works that Thou didst in their days, and in the old time before them. As Thou wert pleased to work then, even so mercifully interpose in our behalf now. As thou didst preserve them, bless and keep us. Let no weapon forged against us prosper, and enable us to condemn every tongue raised against us in judgment.

Be pleased this day, and at all times, to give us an abiding sense of thy gracious and watchful providence. We trust that whatever may be the trials, the sorrows, the cares, and the disappointments which may beset us, Thou wilt be pleased to sanctify them to our eternal good. We would cast all our care on Thee, believing that Thou doest all things well. We come to Thee poor, empty, and needy. Give us all we need this day for this day's necessities. All good of every kind must come from Thee. Help us this day to walk consistently with our profession. May we have an abiding sense of thy presence. Enable us to live as those who love the Saviour. Let us do nothing which may grieve thy Holy Spirit, or cause thine enemies to blaspheme. Bless us in our avocations. May we do all things as unto Thee. Make us active in the discharge of every duty. Grant us opportunities for doing good, and bestow upon us the mind and spirit to make use of them.

And now, Lord, we commend ourselves to thy keeping, for we cannot keep ourselves. Hold Thou up our goings in thy paths, that our footsteps slip not. Look favourably on all who are dear to us [and especially bless with thy grace the children of our family. Draw their young hearts to Christ, and even from their childhood sanctify them to thy service]. Be with all thy ministers, and prosper them in their labours for Thee. Cause thy people to shine as lights in the world, that thy name may be glorified in them. We humbly beg every mercy in the name and for the sake of thy dear Son, our Saviour Jesus Christ. Amen.

READ IN HOLY SCRIPTURE ST. JOHN X. 19—42.

O GOD our Father, unto Thee, at the close of this day, we raise our hearts in praise and thanksgiving. Constant and unfailing is thy love, unwearied and exhaustless are thy divine compassions. Enable us now, we beseech Thee, to have blessed communion with Thee in this our family worship, and to enjoy in our souls the tokens of thy gracious presence. For all thy mercies to us, from the beginning until now, we thank Thee; for blessings bestowed, and evils, known or unknown, averted; for protection in the hour of danger, and strength in the time of temptation. If in any degree we have served Thee in the duties of our station this day, to Thee be all the praise. If we have been enabled to overcome evil, to thy grace and sustaining help we owe it, and to Thee be all the glory.

O Lord Jesus, we adore Thee for thy great love to sinners. Thou didst bear meekly and patiently the scornful reviling of men, and the unbelief and contradiction of the ungodly, and all for us and for our salvation. Enable us to see what suffering our sins have cost Thee, that we may hate them, and remember how hateful they are to Thee. Cleanse us, we beseech Thee, from all the guilt which our souls have contracted during the day, and by thy Spirit renew in us whatever graces have declined through the malice of the wicked one, the influence of the world, or the deceitfulness and infirmity of our own hearts. Mould us more and more into thine image and likeness. We believe, do Thou help our unbelief. Quicken and increase our love, and kindle our hopes by the bright anticipations of the glory which is yet to be revealed. We desire, O gracious Saviour, to tread in thy footsteps, and to live as in the constant presence of the things which are unseen and eternal. Speak to us day by day in thy Word, and by the impressions of thy Spirit on our hearts, and give us grace to know thy voice, and cheerfully and lovingly to follow Thee. If we are indeed thy sheep, oh, suffer us not to wander from thy fold. If thou seest us straying, turn us back; let us not find pleasure in any way of evil, but lead us into the way everlasting.

Thy providence, O Lord God, is over us and all that concerns us. We put ourselves, body, soul, and spirit, into thy hands. Do Thou what is good for us, and make all things tend to further thy work of grace in our hearts. Behold, in thy goodness, any of us who are strangers to Christ, and living without God in the world. Lord, in thy mercy, suffer them not to perish. Give them true repentance towards God, and faith in our Lord Jesus Christ. We ask all for his holy name's sake. Amen.

[Morning.]   SIXTEENTH WEEK.—THURSDAY.   [Evening.

READ IN HOLY SCRIPTURE EXODUS XV.   READ IN HOLY SCRIPTURE ST. LUKE X. 17—24.

O GOD, the strength of all them that put their trust in Thee, accept our united praises and thanksgivings for thy goodness towards us and all mankind. Many and great have been thy mercies. Our fathers have told us the noble works that Thou didst in their days, and in the old time before them. Thou wast their strength and their song, and didst become their salvation. Who is like unto Thee, O Lord, glorious in holiness, fearful in praises, doing wonders?

To us, also, Thou hast been a gracious and merciful God. Thou hast sent thy dear Son into the world to overcome the great enemy of our souls. Thou hast made a way for us through Him to everlasting life, and Thou hast given us the promise of thy Holy Spirit, to make us the children of God by faith in Christ Jesus, to soften our hearts, to sanctify our souls, to subdue our tempers, and to guide us in thy strength unto thy holy habitation. Oh, may we all be partakers of these blessings! Let none of us lose them by our negligence or unbelief. Increase our faith. Lead us to love Thee more and more, and grant that whatever is a hindrance to us may be put away. May we seek first thy kingdom and thy righteousness, and let thy right hand become powerful for us to overcome all our spiritual enemies.

O God, we are utterly unworthy to ask of Thee any blessing, but Thou hast encouraged us in thy Word to spread before Thee all our need.

Be with us during the day on which we now have entered. We know not what is before us. We may be expecting blessings, and may meet with disappointments; we may be expecting health, and may meet with sickness; we may be expecting joy, and may meet with sorrow. Be Thou round about us, to protect and deliver us; and should it please Thee that, instead of finding refreshment by the way, we should be called upon to taste of bitter things, let thy grace sanctify all our sorrows, and make it good for us to be afflicted. May we all come more frequently beneath the shadow of the cross, look up more trustfully on our suffering Redeemer. Help us to think of Him who was a Man of sorrows and acquainted with grief, that we faint not; and grant, O God, that the presence of Jesus may ever be with us in sorrow and in joy, that all things may work together for our good and thy glory.

O Lord, remember our dear relations and friends, and grant unto them the same blessings which we have asked for ourselves.

Bless likewise thy whole Church, and grant that souls may be increasingly added unto it. All this we ask through Jesus Christ our Lord. Amen.

O HEAVENLY Father, be pleased, for the sake of thy dear Son, to hear our prayers, and to accept our praises. We adore Thee that Thou hast endowed us with reason, and conscience, and with all those other faculties and powers which make us capable of knowing, and of loving and serving Thee. But we are sinners, and the natural man receiveth not the things of the Spirit of God, for they are foolishness unto him; neither can he know them, because they are spiritually discerned. Take away, we beseech Thee, the veil of blindness, and folly, and prejudice. May thy Holy Spirit direct, sanctify, and govern us in the ways of thy laws and in the works of thy commandments. O God, our fathers cried unto Thee, and were delivered; they trusted in Thee, and were not confounded; and never didst Thou say to any of the seed of Jacob, "Seek ye my face in vain." Bless us, we beseech Thee, with all spiritual blessings in Christ Jesus. May we be complete in Him. Dispose us to receive and rest on Him alone. May the life we live in the flesh be a life of faith in the Son of God, who loved us, and gave Himself for us. And being filled with all joy and peace in believing, may we be found fruitful in every good work, to the praise and glory of thy marvellous grace.

We thank Thee for the gift of our Sabbaths. Prophets and righteous men desired to see those things that we see, and did not see them; and to hear those things that we hear, and did not hear them. But blessed are our eyes, for they see; and our ears, for they hear. O thou God of salvation, we magnify thy mercy and grace for all the good done this day to the souls of men. Let the Gospel preached and heard be crowned with abundant blessing. And when, at length, thy ministering servants give in their account, may it be found that they have not laboured in vain, nor spent their strength for nought.

Fill the whole Church of God on earth with the spirit of truth, purity, and peace. Watch over thy flock wherever they are scattered; gather both Jews and Gentiles into thy fold, and hasten the time when there shall be but one flock and one Shepherd. Pour down thy blessing upon our Queen and our country. Pardon our national sins; continue to us thy favour; and make us a people fearing Thee, and working righteousness.

Take us, we beseech Thee, and all who are dear to us, under thy tender care this night. Shield us from danger; grant us quiet sleep; and, if it please Thee, spare us to enter on our duties tomorrow. May we do so in thy faith, fear, and love. Grant this, for the sake of Jesus Christ our Lord. Amen.

[110]

[MORNING.] SIXTEENTH WEEK.—FRIDAY. [EVENING.

READ IN HOLY SCRIPTURE PSALM LXXVII.

READ IN HOLY SCRIPTURE ST. LUKE X. 25—42.

O LORD God, our God and Father in Christ Jesus, protected by thine almighty power, we have been kept in peace and safety through the night. We would come before Thee this morning with thanksgiving for this and all thy mercies. Truly are they renewed to us every morning, daily dost Thou load us with thy benefits. From Thee cometh all our good—health, friends, food, raiment, every earthly comfort. But, above all, to thy grace and mercy do we owe it, that though we are full of infirmity, and tainted with sin, we are yet permitted continually to come to Thee for all we want. Thou hast promised to blot out our transgressions, and forgive us all our sins. Thou hast given thy Holy Spirit to renew and sanctify our sinful hearts. Cleanse us, O God, from all our guilt, and transform us into the likeness of thy dear Son.

O Lord God, our Saviour, make sin to be hateful to us; and give us to see more clearly and to feel more deeply thy loving-kindness towards us in that Thou keepest our souls in life, and givest us in Christ salvation from sin, and death, and hell.

Gracious Father, be with us through this day. Ignorant and helpless of ourselves, in Thee is all our strength and all our hope. We know not what it shall bring forth—trial and perplexity, joy or sorrow, health or sickness, continued life or unlooked-for death. Preserve us in the midst of temptation. Let not sin or Satan overcome us, or cause our feet to slip. Sustain our feeble steps. Prepare us, by thy grace, for every ordering of thy providence. Keep us from all murmuring and unbelieving thoughts. Let every sorrow speak to us from Thee, that we may know and correct whatever evil in us Thou art chastening with thy rebuke. And though thy way be trackless, as through the sea, and thy footsteps be not known, as those of one passing through deep waters, though thy purposes be hidden from us, yet grant that we may ever trust in Thee, for Thou changest not. Thou art girded with faithfulness, and ever puttest forth for good thine almighty power. O Lord God, Thou hast loved us freely. Thou hast given thy Son to die for us. Thou hast not refused us, in time past, the grace of the Holy Spirit, nor ever failed to do us good.

In all things thy goodness and mercy have followed us; we therefore, in humble confidence, commit ourselves and all dear to us to thy care this day. Such of us [all, young or old,] as are thine, enable to realize their high privileges; such as are yet estranged and ungodly, convert and bring into thy fold. O Lord, hear us; and when Thou hearest forgive, for Jesus Christ's sake. Amen.

O LORD our Righteousness, who only art worthy, permit us to call upon Thee this evening, and, after the mercies of another day, to give Thee thanks for all the goodness and mercy with which Thou hast been pleased to accompany our path. We would this evening confess ourselves before Thee as utterly unworthy of the least of all thy mercies. Forbid it, Lord, that we should boast ourselves in thy presence, or claim to ourselves any righteousness in thy sight. If we would inherit eternal life and become heirs of God, we must be born again, as his sons. Grant us this new birth, which will make us heirs of life; and so fill us with thy Holy Spirit, and sanctify our souls, that we may love Thee perfectly and follow Thee faithfully.

Take away from us all a spirit of self-righteousness. Oh, let us not strive to justify ourselves, but in lowliness of mind, and in self-abasement, may we find our righteousness in thy beloved Son, and know that in Him and through Him we receive the adoption of sons, the inheritance of heaven, and everlasting life.

Show unto us, O God, our state by reason of our sin; how sin hath sore smitten us, and Satan hath buffetted us, and stripped us, and wounded us, and left us half-dead, yea, utterly dead in trespasses and sins. Teach us the blessed lesson how Jesus, better than the Good Samaritan, came out of his way and out of his place to seek the wounded victims of Satan, and to take care of them, and heal them. O Thou good Friend of sinners, come and pour out into our wounded hearts the oil and wine of thy sweet mercy and Divine compassion. Lift us up from death in sin to the life of righteousness.

And enable us to imitate the example of thy Son, our living Saviour, by loving those that love us not, and by pouring the precious balm of kindness on the heads of those that hate us. Let all the world be "neighbours"—one with each other, one with Thee. Make wars to cease through all the earth; let love, and joy, and peace be multiplied; send forth the spirit of peace into all the world. Oh, that the nations of the earth may learn in Christian love to forget their national enmities, and join hand in hand in doing each other good. And to this end be pleased to grant to our own land the spirit of Christian love, and that she may send the messengers of Christ to all lands, to help the weak, and to strengthen the dying. Bless all missionary enterprises, and enable us all to choose that good part which shall not be taken from us. Let thy protecting care be about us during the night, preserve us from evil, and bless us in all things, for Jesus Christ's sake. Amen.

[111]

[Morning.] SIXTEENTH WEEK.—SATURDAY. [Evening.

READ IN HOLY SCRIPTURE EXODUS XVI. 1—10.

ALMIGHTY God and merciful Father, Thou hast said that Thou wilt be sanctified in them that come nigh Thee, and before all the people Thou wilt be glorified. We beseech Thee to put thy Spirit within us, that we may sanctify Thee in our hearts, and make Thee our fear and our dread, our confidence and our joy. And seeing that what we have read was written for our admonition upon whom the ends of the world are come, may we take heed to our spirits that we lust not after evil, as the people in the wilderness also lusted, and were destroyed of the destroyer.

How prone, O God, have we been to think of this world as our home, and not as a resting-place by the way! Or we have gloried in thy mercies as though we had not received them from Thee; and when Thou hast seen fit to remove them, we have repined as though Thou hadst taken away what was not thine own. In prosperity we have not been thankful, nor rendered according to the benefits received; nor have we been submissive in adversity. But spare us, good Lord, and let not thy wrath wax hot against us; correct us, but in thy mercy; rebuke us, but not in thine anger, lest Thou bring us to nothing.

Bread for the day Thou hast taught us to ask, and promised to bestow; having this, may we not murmur as though Thou hadst broken faith with us; but learn therewith to be content, and to labour chiefly, not for the meat that perisheth, but for that which endureth unto eternal life. Deliver us from an earthly mind, from a mind that would seek its happiness in the creature rather than the Creator, and from affections which cleave to things of time and sense as their supreme good. May thy Spirit maintain within us so decided a sway and predominance of heavenly and eternal things that it may be manifest to all that we are seeking a better country, that is, a heavenly one.

Under the hand of thy servant Moses Thou didst give the people manna, the type of the true; but Thou hast provided some better thing for us, even the true Bread which came down from heaven. We bless Thee for the gift of the Saviour, who has said, "I am the bread of life: he that cometh to me shall never hunger; and he that believeth on me shall never thirst." Give us, we beseech Thee, a spiritual desire, and evermore feed us with this bread through all the days of our pilgrimage, until Thou bring us to thy holy hill and thy heavenly sanctuary, to behold the glory of the Lord, and go no more out for ever. Be with us through all this day. Leave us not to ourselves, for we are weak, and unable to stand without Thee. Enrich us with the tokens of thy love, and preserve us from all evil, for Jesus Christ's sake. Amen.

READ IN HOLY SCRIPTURE PHILIPPIANS III.

ACCEPT our hearty thanksgivings, O gracious God and Father, for the mercies of the past day, and of the past week. Great indeed is thy goodness and long-suffering. May we be more and more grateful, and endeavour more diligently to show forth thy praise. Oh, that we may remember day by day that we are not our own; that all we are and all we have is thine, and that of thine own are we giving Thee even when we devote ourselves most fervently and obediently to thy service. Convince us, O Lord, of our sinfulness. We were born in sin, the children of wrath, and sin cleaves to our best and holiest services. We have no merit or goodness of our own. All our hope and trust are in thy dear Son. Oh, that we may be found in Him, our crucified and living Redeemer; and, clothed with his righteousness, be free from every spot and stain of sin. Grant that, having experience of thy saving grace, we may count all things but loss in comparison of the knowledge of Christ Jesus our Lord. Conform us, we beseech Thee, to his likeness. We desire, O God, to forget the things that are behind, and to press forward to higher attainments in godliness, to a larger acquaintance with thy Word, and a more abundant assurance of thy favour.

Forgive our past sloth and indolence. Let not our misuse of opportunities and privileges cause Thee to withhold from us grace and strength for the future. As citizens of a heavenly kingdom, may we live in the world beneath thy protecting care, and be kept from its evil while we look and wait for the coming of the Lord.

Take us, we pray Thee, and all who are dear to us, unto thy Divine care for the night. May our sleep be sweet and refreshing, so that we may rise strengthened in body and soul, and be ready to enter with thankfulness and joy on the duties of thy holy day. Prepare our hearts for them. Stir up in us deep and earnest desires for spiritual blessings; that, hungering and thirsting after righteousness, our souls may be filled out of thy fulness. O Lord, thou knowest how weak and ignorant we are, and how, through our own unbelief, we miss many mercies which Thou preparest for us. Increase our faith and enlarge our expectations, and let not the great enemy of our souls deprive us of our confidence in Thee, or make us ashamed of our hope in thy Word. Be with thy ministers in all their preparation for the Sabbath. Give them the anointing of the Holy One, that they may dispense thy Word with power.

Lord, hear us in thy mercy, and bless us, for the sake of thy Son Jesus Christ our Lord. Amen.

[Morning.] SEVENTEENTH WEEK.—LORD'S DAY. [Evening.

READ IN HOLY SCRIPTURE EXODUS XVI. 11—36.

READ IN HOLY SCRIPTURE ST. LUKE XI. 1—13.

ALMIGHTY God, who orderest all things in heaven and earth according to thy counsel, give us grace, we beseech Thee, reverently to acknowledge that Thou art just in all thy ways and holy in all thy works. Teach us to look up to Thee as our God and Father in Christ Jesus, who art able and willing, for his sake, to bestow upon us whatever is necessary as well for the body as the soul.

We are not worthy to come before Thee, much less to receive any favour at thy hands; for we have sinned against Thee. Instead of acknowledging Thee in all our ways, we have often walked in the light of our own eyes, and after the imagination of our own hearts. But we put our trust in the merits of thy Son, our Lord and Saviour, who gave Himself a sacrifice for sin, according to thy will. For his sake receive us graciously, and pardon whatever want of confidence we have shown towards Thee. Lead us henceforth, by the teaching of the Holy Spirit, to trust in Thee at all times. May we continually grow in thankfulness to Thee. Suffer us not in prosperity to forget Thee, or in adversity to think ourselves forgotten by Thee; but, confiding in thy providence and protection, grant that we may always do that which is righteous in thy sight.

Thou who of old didst command the clouds from above, and openedst the doors of heaven, and rainedst down manna upon thy people, continue to give us our daily bread. Feed us with food convenient for us. As man doth not live by bread alone, but by every word that proceedeth out of thy mouth, help us to hide thy word in our hearts, that we sin not against Thee. Blessed be thy name for returning Sabbaths. May this day be to us a season of rest, worship, and instruction. May we know, by the teaching of the Holy Spirit, what Jesus meant when He said, "I am the bread of life: he that cometh to me shall never hunger; and he that believeth on me shall never thirst." When we go up to the house of the Lord, cause thy blessed Gospel to come to us, not in word only, but in power and in the Holy Ghost, and in much assurance.

Be gracious to all who are detained, by sickness or other necessary cause, from the assemblies of thy people. Pity those who wilfully forsake thine ordinances, and bring them to repentance.

To thy care we commend ourselves and our friends. Bless our country, the Queen and all the Royal Family, and all conditions of men among us. Bless thy whole Church throughout all the world, and bring all mankind to the knowledge and obedience of thy Word. Hear these our humble supplications through Jesus Christ our Lord. Amen.

WE give Thee thanks, O God, that Thou hast given us such encouragement to approach Thee in prayer. We thank Thee for so many invitations, for such precious promises, and for so perfect a model to teach us how to pray; to all which Thou hast added the assurance of the ready ear of a Father, the powerful intercession of a great High Priest within the veil, and the gracious aid of thy own Spirit to help our infirmities. Oh, that now the Spirit may make intercession within us according to thy will.

Our iniquities might make us afraid to approach Thee, for they are many, and they are very heinous; but to whom can we go but to Thee? And Thou hast assured us that if we confess our sins, Thou art faithful and just to forgive us our sins, and to cleanse us from all unrighteousness. Our iniquities had separated between Thee and us; but, far as we had wandered, and deep as we had sunk, even then thine eye and thy heart were toward us for good, and in thy love and in thy pity Thou didst redeem us. Thou hast brought us nigh by the blood of Jesus, and given us access to Thee by one Spirit as unto a Father. Let that love which quickened us when we were dead in sin now raise us up together, and make us sit together in heavenly places in Christ Jesus; that as we have borne the image of the earthly, we may also bear the image of the heavenly, and show forth the praises of Him who hath called us out of darkness into his marvellous light.

We are naturally selfish, but Thou art boundlessly benevolent, delighting in mercy, and only waiting to see us fully conscious of our need, and taking the attitude and spirit of suppliants; and such is the overflowing kindness of thy heart, that Thou hast said, "Before they call I will answer, and while they are yet speaking I will hear."

Various have been the means employed this day to advance the kingdom of Christ among men; many have run to and fro that knowledge might be increased. Thy ministers have stood up and cried, "Behold the Lamb of God, which taketh away the sin of the world." Let it not be in vain. Prosper thy work abundantly in their hands. Glorify thy Son, and let the earth be filled with his praise. Let times of refreshing come from thy presence, and thy Church hear thy voice saying unto her, "Arise, shine, for thy light is come, and the glory of the Lord is risen upon thee." Let wars cease to the ends of the earth, and the kingdoms of the world become the kingdoms of the Lord and of his Anointed. Now blessed be the Lord God of Israel; and blessed be his glorious name for ever, and let the whole earth be filled with his glory. Amen and Amen.

[113]

[MORNING.] **SEVENTEENTH WEEK.—MONDAY.** [EVENING.

READ IN HOLY SCRIPTURE EXODUS XVII. | READ IN HOLY SCRIPTURE ST. LUKE XIII. 11—22.

GLORY be to Thee, O Lord, for all thy goodness to this family and household. Thou hast graciously heard and answered our prayers, and hast not withheld thy mercies from us. Thou hast kept us in quietness and peace, and hast renewed us in life and health this morning. We praise Thee, we bless Thee, we glorify Thee, O Lord God, heavenly King, God the Father Almighty.

Yet, O God, we confess that we do not love Thee as we ought. We mourn before Thee over the weakness of our faith and the coldness of our affections. To Thee we look for help. Thou hast promised to give thy Holy Spirit to them that ask Thee, and we beseech Thee to pour down his gracious influences upon us, that we may love Thee more and serve Thee better. Especially we beseech Thee to give us that due sense of all thy mercies that we may show forth thy praise, not only with our lips, but in our lives, by giving up ourselves to thy service, as a holy, lively, and reasonable sacrifice.

And now, O Lord, be with us during the day, and amid the labour and duties of the week upon which we have entered. Enable us to follow in all things the guidance of thy will. Make it our object not to please ourselves, but Thee; not to do our own will, but thine. Make us strong in faith and firm in hope, diligent in our daily callings, fervent in spirit before Thee, and kindly affectioned one towards another. Enable us to fight the good fight against sin, the world, and the devil; and to approve ourselves the faithful soldiers and servants of our Master. Enable us to stand in every time of temptation—sober and vigilant, and watching unto prayer. Strengthen our weakness, teach our ignorance, supply our wants; comfort us in sorrow, uphold us in every trial, and make us more than conquerors through Him that loved us.

Thou knowest, O Lord God, that we are not sufficient of ourselves to think anything as of ourselves, but our sufficiency is in Thee. Bestow upon us the spirit of grace and supplication, that earnestly asking help at thy hands, we may abundantly receive it. If Thou art with us, we are safe; if Thou leave us, we become like them that go down into the pit. Leave us not, neither forsake us, O God of our salvation. Bless us both in our bodies and our souls this day, and evermore.

Bestow upon our friends and relatives all the blessings we have asked for ourselves. Give thy special grace to all who are afflicted in mind, body, or estate. Bless all that shall be done in thy name during the week, either by ourselves or others; and hasten the coming of thy kingdom. We ask every blessing for the sake of Jesus Christ our Lord. Amen.

O GOD, by thy goodness and mercy we are brought to the close of another day; and ere we separate for the night, we would review the day as in thy presence. First of all we would glorify thy holy name for thy forbearance, grace, and love, whereby we have been spared, preserved, and all our wants supplied through the day. Alas, in contrast with thy goodness, we are reminded of our own several sins, negligences, and ignorances, that by thought, word, and deed, we have committed against thy Divine Majesty. O heavenly Father, in many things we offend Thee; and shouldest Thou be extreme to mark what is done amiss, who could stand? But there is forgiveness with Thee, that Thou mayest be feared. O God, we bless Thee for the gift of thy dear Son, in whom there is redemption through his blood, even the forgiveness of all sin. O holy and gracious Spirit, do Thou take of the things of Jesus, and show them to our souls. Give us grace to forsake our sins as well as to confess them, and to mourn over them with that godly sorrow that worketh repentance unto salvation not to be repented of. Grant that each of us may commune with our own hearts upon our beds this night, and be still, realising thy presence, offering the sacrifice of righteousness, and putting our trust in Thee.

O heavenly Father, Thou knowest the individual trials and temptations, the besetting sins, the infirmities and weaknesses, of each of us. Let mercy forgive us all that is past, and let grace be near to help us in every hour of coming need. O God, we come boldly to ask it, because our great and merciful High Priest Jesus, thy dear Son, ever liveth to make intercession for us.

O God, Thou wouldest not have us ignorant of the devices of the great enemy of our souls. We would watch and pray that we fall not into his snares. From the crafts and assaults of the devil, good Lord, deliver us. When the enemy cometh in as a flood, O Spirit of the Lord, lift Thou up a standard against him.

To thy fatherly goodness we commend ourselves now. Do Thou watch over us for good, that we may lay us down in peace and sleep; and if it be thy will, may we rise refreshed and strengthened for the duties of the coming day. The same merciful and protecting care we ask for all who are dear to us, near and far off.

Oh, give us thy peace all the days of our life, so that, when we have finished our course, we may lay us down in peace at last, and awake to be with Christ in the day of his coming and his glory. We ask all in the name of the same Jesus Christ thy Son, our Lord, to whom with Thee and the Holy Spirit, be glory everlasting. Amen.

[Morning.] SEVENTEENTH WEEK.—TUESDAY. [Evening.

READ IN HOLY SCRIPTURE 1 CORINTHIANS X. 1—15.   READ IN HOLY SCRIPTURE ST. LUKE XIII. 23—35.

ALMIGHTY God, heaven is thy throne, and the earth is thy footstool. All things above and below are the creatures of thy hand, and thy kingdom ruleth over all. Thou killest and makest alive, Thou puttest down and raisest up. Graciously accept our tribute of praise for watchful care and refreshing sleep by night, and for the renewed mercies of the morning. Lord, so work in us to will and do by thy good Spirit that we may cheerfully consecrate the strength which Thou givest us to thy praise.

We earnestly seek thy help and guidance through the day. Feeble and ignorant as we are, leave us not, O God, to ourselves, or to our own understandings. We live in a world of temptation. It meets us in our business and our pleasure; it besets us at home and abroad; and even our lawful calling may become a snare for our souls, and a hindrance to our salvation. Oh suffer us not, we beseech Thee, to be tempted beyond our strength. Give us a spiritual perception, that we may discern at all times the presence of evil, and be on our guard against it. Make a way for our escape in all our difficulties and perplexities. We commit our souls to thy keeping, and in thy faithfulness and love place all our trust. Be with us, O God, in every trial and conflict, and perfect thy strength in our weakness. Suffer us not to be lifted up with spiritual pride and self-confidence, but keep us humble, distrustful of ourselves, and looking only to Thee. We pray that we may never tempt Christ, or grieve thy Spirit by our unbelief and stubbornness of heart. Give us a tender conscience, that will shrink from sin with a holy abhorrence, and make us afraid to do, or say, or think anything which Thou hast forbidden.

Refresh us, O Lord, with the presence of thy indwelling Spirit. As waters flowed for the refreshment of Israel, so let the streams of life and peace which flow from the smitten Jesus comfort and gladden all our hearts. When tempted and tried, may we find courage in the remembrance that no trial befalls us but such as is common to man, and that the same afflictions are accomplished in our brethren in the world. Have mercy upon us, O God, and supply all our need: bestow upon us pardon for all sin and strength for all weakness, and let not our feet stumble in thy paths.

Let thy favour rest on all our relatives and friends; succour them in all their necessities, and give them the sweet experience of thy saving grace and love. We commend ourselves and them to thy Divine keeping. Protect, preserve, and bless us; bring us to the close of the day in health and peace, and at last receive us unto Thyself, for Jesus Christ's sake. Amen.

ALMIGHTY God, the Father of our Lord Jesus Christ, we come before Thee this night to thank Thee for thy goodness to us throughout the day. Whatever good we have received has come to us of thine undeserved mercy; whatever evil has happened to us, Thou, we know, wouldest have it become to us a means of good. Thou doest all things well. Grant that every promise of thy Word and every dispensation of thy providence may encourage our confidence in Thee, and bind our hearts more closely to thy service.

O Lord God, grant us grace this night, before sleep comes over us, to have communion with Thee. We know not but that before the morning light the Son of Man may come. Grant that we may not be among the unhappy ones, who shall seek in vain to enter into the kingdom; but number us among the blessed ones who having earnestly striven shall pass through the straight gate into thy presence with joy. O Lord, we lie down to rest in the darkness, looking to see again the light of day; grant that we may even so look through the gloom of the grave with a good hope to the light of everlasting day; and that, if spared to the morrow, we may rise from our beds to serve Thee better than in the day which is past. May every day see us growing in grace and in the knowledge of our Lord and Saviour; may our walk be more and more steady in holiness and in humility. May we feed continually by faith on Him who is the Bread of life, and be refreshed continually with the waters of grace from Him who is the everlasting Fountain.

May all our dear relatives and friends partake in full measure the blessings which we ask for ourselves; suffer none of them to receive thy grace in vain. [Especially regard with thy favour the children of our household; may they be indeed new creatures in Christ Jesus—the children of God, manifesting even from early years the fruits of the Spirit in all meekness and obedience]. Gather into thy kingdom increasing numbers of men from east, and west, and north, and south. But oh, grant that none of us who have already been called to know Thee, and have thy Word to instruct us, and thine ordinances to refresh us, may fail to find admittance, with the blessed company in heaven, to the marriage supper of the Lamb. On Him, O Lord God, is all our trust for the forgiveness of our sins and the renewal of our hearts. On Him would we fasten our affections. His steps would we follow. Oh, do Thou fill our hearts full with holy love. Help us to keep thy commandments; and make us meet for the inheritance of the saints in light, through Jesus Christ our Lord, to whom, with Thee and the Holy Ghost, be honour and praise. Amen.

[115]

[Morning.] SEVENTEENTH WEEK.—WEDNESDAY. [Evening.

READ IN HOLY SCRIPTURE EXODUS XIX.

READ IN HOLY SCRIPTURE ST. LUKE XIV. 1—24.

GRANT us grace now to approach Thee, O God, with filial reverence. Let thy voice this morning awaken our souls in songs of gladness and praise. Suffer not our hearts to be oppressed with the majesty of thy glory. Help us to listen, to obey, and to love.

We thank Thee for having spoken unto us by thy Son, and that He is not ashamed to call us brethren. Send forth the spirit of thy Son into our hearts, that we may have faith to call Thee Abba, Father. Blessed be thy name, that we can say, we are not come to the mount that might be touched, and that burned with fire, nor unto blackness, and darkness, and tempest; but unto Mount Zion, and the city of the living God, and to Jesus, the Mediator of the new covenant. Assist us, therefore, to give the more earnest heed to the things that we have heard, lest at any time we should let them slip. Suffer us not to refuse Him that speaketh, but so sanctify and cleanse us by the washing of regeneration and renewing of the Holy Spirit, that we may be enabled sincerely to resolve that all which the Lord hath spoken we will do.

O Lord, our God, we confess with shame that we have often broken thy commandments. In tenderness and strength Thou hast borne us as on eagles' wings, yet have we murmured and rebelled against Thee. Thou hast never been unfaithful to us, yet thy covenant have we not kept. As thy peculiar treasure hast Thou defended us; yet have we, like prodigal children, wasted thy substance. O Lord, have mercy upon us; rebuke us not in thy wrath, neither chasten us in thy hot displeasure. Help us, O God of our salvation, for the glory of thy name, and deliver us and purge away our sins, for thy name's sake. Thou art good, and doest good; teach us thy statutes.

O God, Thou who art the Holy Ghost, the Comforter, come, we beseech Thee, and abide with us this day. Subdue our pride. Restrain our lusts. Direct our thoughts. Purify our affections. Guard us from the beginnings of sin. Let not Satan get an advantage of us. Strengthen us for every duty. Make every care and every sorrow a blessing. Let our speech be always with grace. Teach us to do whatever is well-pleasing in thy sight, and so all the day long may the peace of God rule in our hearts.

Merciful Creator, prepare us to meet Thee in the hour of death—in the day of judgment, when the trumpet shall sound, and the dead shall be raised. Grant us then the victory through our Lord Jesus Christ. This we ask in his name, and unto Thee, O God, will we give glory and praise for ever. Amen.

ALMIGHTY God, Maker of all things in heaven and earth, we beseech Thee mercifully to hear us. Thou art the high and lofty one that inhabitest eternity, whose name is Holy, and we are sinful and impure, yet Thou hast bidden us to come boldly unto thy throne of grace. O God, we come conscious of our unworthiness, but trusting in thine own promise, through the merits of our great High Priest, whom Thou hast given to die for our sins and to rise again for our justification.

Bestow upon us, we beseech Thee, from day to day, a more lively sense of our countless obligations to Thee. We thank Thee for our creation; for Thou hast made us fearfully and wonderfully, and hast given us reason to understand thy will, and affections capable of loving Thee. Enlighten our understandings with the Holy Spirit to know thy will, and dispose our hearts to do it. We thank Thee for preservation—that Thou hast been pleased to keep all the members of this household safe from all evil. From our childhood unto this day Thou hast preserved us; Thou hast given us food, and clothing, and shelter, and all things we need. We thank Thee for redemption—for that inestimable love in which Thou didst give thy blessed Son to die for us. Especially we thank Thee for those members of this family to whose hearts Thou hast been pleased to reveal Him as the Saviour by whom they are redeemed, and the Master whom they obey; and on those amongst us who are yet strangers to Thee, we pray Thee by thy converting Spirit. We thank Thee for all the means of grace, and for the hope of glory. Enable us to set our affections on things above, and to look for and hasten unto the second coming and glorious appearing of our Lord and Master. Write upon our hearts the sense of all these thy mercies, that we may love Thee perfectly, and serve Thee devotedly all our days.

Conform our hearts, O blessed Lord God, after thine own image, that we may seek to be holy, even as Thou art holy. Make us to be the meek and lowly disciples of our meek and lowly Master. Abase us before Thee, that Thou mayest exalt us; Enable us to be humble in all our dealings with our fellow-men, that we may esteem others better than ourselves, in honour preferring one another. Help us to do good to all men for thy sake; to be kind and gentle, patient and forbearing, in all our dealings, that we may be the children of our Father who is in heaven; not rendering evil for evil, but blessing them that curse us, and praying for those that despitefully use us and persecute us. Fill us with thy Spirit here, and hereafter glorify us in thy kingdom, through the worthiness of thy Son Jesus Christ, our Lord. Amen.

[Morning.]   SEVENTEENTH WEEK.—THURSDAY.   [Evening.

READ IN HOLY SCRIPTURE HEBREWS XII. 18—29.

READ IN HOLY SCRIPTURE REVELATION XIX. 1–9.

O THOU ever-living God, who hast in all ages been the delight and the desire of those who know thy name; we kneel at thy footstool. Blessed be thy holy name for the way of approach to the throne of grace which Thou hast given us in thy dear Son Jesus Christ. We thank Thee for the spirituality, the simplicity, the sacred sweetness of Christian worship. Through the great High Priest of our profession we draw nigh. Unto Thee alone, Thou adorable Jehovah, do we render all our worship, and we hope for acceptance only through the blood of sprinkling. With reverence and with godly fear we would now come near unto Thee. How great is thy goodness, that Thou dost bow to our worship, and accept our feeble praise and imperfect prayer! Speak unto us, O Lord, by thy Word, and grant us wise, believing, and obedient hearts, that we may in all things live as subjects of that kingdom of grace which cannot be moved. We would be constrained by thy love to serve Thee truly; but, if need be, let thy terrors keep our rebellious hearts in awe of Thee.

Thou Father of mercies, who hast preserved us through the past night, we thank Thee for the safety and the sleep we have enjoyed, and we see thy kindness in the food provided for us this day. May every blessing we possess fill us with more love to Thee, and every trial we endure strengthen our trust in Thee. We go forth to the labours of this day depending on thy watchful providence. We desire to set the Lord ever before us; be Thou at our right hand, so that we may not be moved. Preserve us, if it please Thee, from all bodily injury; but, O our God, earnestly we pray Thee to defend and guard us from all sin. Give us grace to discharge all our duties to our fellow-men with integrity, uprightness, and charity. May some around us be made holier and happier by our conduct this day, and especially help us to make known to our fellow sinners the grace and the mercy of our Lord Jesus Christ. Give us courage and wisdom to reprove, and to warn, and to exhort; and may the tenderest love to our neighbour actuate us in all we think, or say, or do.

We pray for all in this house, and entreat Thee that [from the eldest to the youngest] all may be saved in the Lord with an everlasting salvation. Let thy merciful compassion be displayed to all the afflicted; sanctify bodily pain and worldly trouble, that they may lead men to Thyself. Comfort the aged, protect the young, bless all who are journeying by land or by water, show thy mercy to such as draw nigh unto death. These and all needful blessings, for others or ourselves, we supplicate through Jesus Christ, our adorable Redeemer and Saviour. Amen.

WE desire, O God our Father, to thank Thee for thy care and love towards us this day. Thou hast provided for our wants; Thou hast kept us and hast enriched us with all needful blessings.

We thank Thee especially for family mercies. We meet in peace; our home is the dwelling-place, we trust, of thy Spirit. Thou dost overshadow it. Ever abide Thou with us. Be Thou as a wall of fire round about us, and as our glory in the midst.

And yet, O Lord, We are unworthy of this blessedness, though we thus address Thee; we are among the evil and the unthankful. Thou mightest have led us forth with the workers of iniquity. We have no right to enter thus into thy presence; thy love in thy Son is our only plea. It is through his blood we have redemption, even the forgiveness of our sins, according to the riches of thy grace. Give us a deeper sense of his sufficiency and love.

We bless Thee, O God, that our ears have heard the Gospel, and that our eyes have seen some of the things Thou hast provided for them that love Thee. Millions have never heard and never seen; and millions who have heard and seen have rejected thy mercy, and have refused to listen to thy voice. Blessed are we if we are called to this feast; doubly blessed if we have obeyed the call. Help us to praise our God, with all his servants, with all that fear Him, both small and great.

And while we are thus thankful for present mercy, we lift our hopes and faith to things above. Victory and rest; freedom from sorrow, and change, and sin; things eye has not seen nor heart conceived—these are before us. We bless Thee for them, for the grace that is the earnest and pledge of them, for the revelation that in part discloses them. Teach us, while waiting for those things, and hastening to them, teach us to be holy in all our behaviour, and to live as pilgrims and strangers on the earth.

Hear our prayers for the afflicted and the persecuted. Sustain the hearts of all who obey and trust in Thee—in all lands and in every condition. Put down oppression and injustice, superstition and idolatry. Lord God Almighty, reign Thou from sea to sea, from the river to the ends of the earth.

Keep us to-night under thy care. Let thine eye be over us, thy hand around us. Spare us to enter to-morrow on new duties with renewed strength. Give like blessings to all we love, and let thy favours to us, and our friends, and our country, far exceed both our deserts and even our desires, for our Saviour's sake, to whom with Thee and the Holy Spirit, be all glory and praise, for ever and ever. Amen.

[117]

[Morning.] SEVENTEENTH WEEK.—FRIDAY. [Evening.

READ IN HOLY SCRIPTURE EXODUS XX. 1—21.

READ IN HOLY SCRIPTURE ST. LUKE XIV. 25—35.

ALMIGHTY and everlasting God, who didst reveal Thyself in old time by thy servant Moses, and who art the same yesterday, to-day, and for ever, enable us to approach Thee this morning with reverence and godly fear. Our eyes cannot see Thee, as when Thou wentest through the wilderness, when the earth shook, and the heavens dropped at thy presence; yet we know that Thou art here; for Thou art in every place, beholding the evil and the good. Our ears cannot hear Thee as when Thou didst come down upon Sinai with the sound of the trumpet and the voice of words; and yet we have listened to Thee in thy written Word, and we praise Thee for the gift of it. Prepare our hearts to feel thy power, and our lips to speak thy praise. Give us fervency of devotion, and simplicity of faith, in approaching to Thee. Teach us to ask for such things as shall please Thee; and where we are too weak and ignorant to speak unto Thee as we ought to do, let thy Holy Spirit make intercession for us, according to thy will.

Enable us, O God, to carry this constant remembrance of Thee into all our daily life, that thy presence may consecrate our home, may prosper us in all we do, and sanctify us in all that we enjoy. Whatever may befall us this day, give us grace to receive it as from Thee, that we may be both patient in suffering thy will and diligent in doing it. In the midst of our various occupations, let us all remember that Thou, O Lord, art about our path, and spiest out all our ways. Let not the recollection of Thee slip out of our hearts through our own carnal weaknesses, nor let it be forgotten amid the cares and pleasures of life. Fill us with such adoration of thy goodness, and such reverence of thy majesty, that thy fear may ever be before our eyes, that we sin not.

Write, we beseech Thee, thy law upon our hearts. Fix our souls upon Thee, that all this household may serve Thee, even Thee only. Thou art a Spirit, and we pray Thee to give us grace to worship Thee in spirit and in truth, to speak of Thee with godly reverence, and to dedicate unto Thee the firstfruits of our life. Teach us to love our neighbours as ourselves. Make us dutiful as children, obedient as subjects, submissive to those who are in authority, blameless in our conduct, just and true in all our dealings, kind in heart, temperate in pleasure, and diligent in business, that we may do our duty in that state of life into which it has pleased Thee to call us.

Pardon, O God, the ignorances and imperfections of our prayers, and do for us according to thine own riches in glory, through Jesus Christ our Lord. Amen.

O THOU that art the Father of mercies and the God of all comfort, at the close of another day we would approach Thee in the name of our adorable Redeemer. Help us to come with humility and with confidence. We humble ourselves before Thee as thy erring children. In many things we all offend. But we bless Thee that we can plead the merits of the dear Redeemer. Oh, give to us a sweet sense of pardon through the blood of Jesus Christ.

And while we praise Thee for pardoning mercy, we beseech Thee to carry on in us that work which we humbly believe Thou hast begun. May we be evidently among the number of thy people. Enable us to bear the cross, and to follow Jesus. May we, through good report and through evil report, ever witness a good confession. Give to us such a sense of the preciousness of Jesus that we may be willing to give up all to follow Him. May we ever have grace to say, "Whom have I in heaven but Thee, and there is none upon earth I desire beside Thee." Let us never be ashamed to acknowledge whose we are and whom we serve. We trust, O Lord, that through thy preventing grace we have put our hands to the Gospel plough. Suffer us not to look back at any time; but through thy help enable us to count all things but loss for the excellency of the knowledge of Jesus Christ our Lord.

We thank Thee for the mercies of another day. We bless Thee for our creation, preservation, and for all the blessings by which we have been surrounded. Thou hast fed us with food convenient for us. Thou hast watched over and protected us. If Thou hast preserved us from falling into gross sin, and from dishonouring the name we profess to love, to Thee, O Lord, would we ascribe all praise. We pray that the same blessings we ask for ourselves may also descend upon those who seek an interest in our prayers. Increase their faith, enlarge their hopes, inflame their zeal, and make them to be eager and earnest in the performance of thy will. Look down upon our unconverted friends and relatives, and bring them, we beseech Thee, to see and feel the preciousness of a Saviour's love. Enable them to realise their own deep needs, and to experience the presence and the fulness of thy great salvation.

And now, blessed Father, we commend ourselves to thy keeping. Shield us throughout the perils and dangers of another night. Let no harm come near our dwelling; let no ill dreams disturb our rest. Be Thou our Guardian, and bring us in safety to the beginning of another day. Hear us, we humbly beseech Thee, for the sake of Jesus Christ thy Son, our Saviour. Amen.

[Morning.]   SEVENTEENTH WEEK.—SATURDAY.   [Evening.]

READ IN HOLY SCRIPTURE JEREMIAH XXXI. 18—34.

O LORD our God and Father, we thank Thee that Thou changest not. Men fail, and generations pass away, but Thou art ever the same. For the sake of the Lord Jesus Christ, receive our prayer. Father, we pray Thee to give us a fuller sense of thy majesty, and a richer experience of thy mercy. We would not rush carelessly into thy holy presence; but keep us, so that we do not run foolishly from thy throne in fear. We plead that the blood of the atoning Sacrifice has been sprinkled before the mercy-seat. We praise Thee that thy love is shed abroad in our hearts, through the Holy Ghost which is given unto us.

We come with boldness, but with deep humility, before thy footstool. We desire to thank Thee, O God, for thy manifold gifts and grace. We are all here the living to praise Thee. We thank Thee for the good we have, and for the good we hope for in Christ Jesus our Lord. We thank Thee that the evil we have deserved has not come upon us, and that the blessings we have forfeited have not been withdrawn. We are monuments of thy mercy—illustrations of thy grace—examples of thy saving love and power. Oh, let thine eye of love be upon us as thy people. We are in a world which is full of temptation. Give us grace to be separate from the ungodly. Give us peace in the knowledge that we are a people formed for thy praise. We plead with Thee, through our ascended Saviour, and according to the teaching of the Holy Ghost which dwells within us, that we may know Thee and love Thee more. Father, reveal Thyself to us in thy dear Son. Take off the veil from our eyes, and make the light and comfort of thy truth and glory shine in upon our souls. Lord, enable us to understand the value of our soul, and the preciousness of the redeeming blood. Write thy law upon our hearts. Make us to love what Thou hast commanded, to hate what Thou hast forbidden, and to desire what Thou hast promised. Teach us to crucify the flesh, to overcome the world, and to set our affections on things above.

We are now going forth into the duties and dangers of our several worldly callings. O God, guide us and preserve us. May thy grace attend us. Use us, as Thou seest best, for the advancement of thy truth and kingdom in the world. Keep us, that we may bring no disgrace upon thy cause and people. Bless us, that wherever we are we may lift up our eyes unto Thee. From our youth, Thou hast been with us; to our death be Thou near us, for the sake of Jesus Christ our Saviour. Amen.

READ IN HOLY SCRIPTURE ST. LUKE XV. 1—10.

ALMIGHTY and everlasting God, thy property is ever to have mercy; we come to Thee, at the close of another week, humbly seeking that mercy. We have erred and strayed from thy ways like lost sheep. We have wandered from Thee each in his own way. Our sins of thought, word, and deed, are more than we can number. If Thou wert to enter into judgment with us, we could only be condemned in thy sight.

But, O God, we thank Thee that Thou hast mercy upon penitent sinners. Thou dost not desire our destruction, but our salvation. Thou art well pleased when sinners seek thy forgiving love. O God, this is not the manner of men. Although sinners like ourselves, they would look down upon us if they knew concerning us all that Thou knowest. Satan, too, tries to alarm us. But thy Word bids us lift up our hearts, and tells us that there is joy in heaven when sinners repent.

O God, grant unto us all real repentance. Make us truly contrite on account of sin, and deliver us from the paths of the destroyer. Let it be known in heaven, and felt in our hearts, that though we were lost, we have been found; and that though we were far off, we have been made nigh. But, alas, we are so prone to wander, that we shall go further and further from Thee unless we are kept in the keeping of thy grace. Keep us by thy mighty power, O blessed Jesus, and bring us safely to thy heavenly kingdom.

We humbly beseech Thee also to carry on the work of sanctification in our souls. Thine image, O God, has been marred and defaced by sin. Our affections have been misplaced, our understandings have been misdirected. Grant unto us thy Holy Spirit more and more. Change us into the image of Christ from glory to glory. Bless all the means of grace to the furtherance of thy work in us, and especially the ordinances of thy house on the approaching Sabbath. Let thy ministering servants be fed in their own souls, that they may be able to feed thy people. Help them to break the bread of life, and grant unto us all a portion at their hands.

We would lie down this night under thy protection, humbly beseeching Thee to cast all our sins into the depths of the sea; and if it be thy will, may we rise in the morning refreshed and strengthened to enjoy a sweet foretaste of the eternal Sabbath which remaineth for the people of God.

Bless all for whom we are bound to pray, and grant that they with us and we with them may finally be made partakers of thy glory.

Receive these our petitions, gracious God and Father, in the name and for the sake of Jesus Christ our Lord. Amen.

[Morning.] **EIGHTEENTH WEEK.—LORD'S DAY.** [Evening.

READ IN HOLY SCRIPTURE EXODUS XXIV.

O LORD, Thou glorious God, clothed with clouds as a robe of majesty, wherewith shall we approach thy throne, and worthily draw near thy footstool? Thou art the Lord Jehovah, the God of peace, the great and terrible God, dwelling in the light which no man can approach unto. Thou didst call thy servant Moses into thy presence; with him didst Thou speak; through him didst Thou command the offering of peace, the sprinkling of the blood, and the making of a covenant with thy people Israel.

But a greater than Moses is here; not thy servant, but thy Son, the Mediator of the better covenant; who, by the sacrifice of Himself, presented an offering unto God, and, by the blood of sprinkling, made atonement for the sins of men. O Lord God, we who stand afar off from thy glorious majesty are brought nigh by the blood of Jesus. Through Him we may come boldly to the throne of grace, and at Jehovah's footstool we find a mercy-seat. Introduced by Jesus, may we enter the cloud of thy glory, and with reverence and godly fear make known our wants to Thee.

After another six days' work and labour, we now would seek the rest of thy holy Sabbath, and in the secret of thy tabernacle would hold communion with Thee. We bless Thee for this day of rest. We would dedicate it to Thee, with all its sacred duties, with all its holy privileges, with all its blessed opportunities. We beseech Thee, Father, to reveal Thyself to us to-day, in the worship of thy house, in the reading of thy Word, and in the secret meditations of our hearts before Thee. Conduct us to thy house of prayer; solemnise our hearts in anticipation of the services of the sanctuary; and may this Sabbath be a spiritual festival to our souls. Let thy ministers be clothed in righteousness, and make thy chosen people joyful. Oh, teach the teachers this day, that they themselves, being taught of God, may teach transgressors thy ways, and that sinners may be converted unto Thee.

Be pleased to bless all the members of our family to-day, and be present with them whereover they may be. Let thy blessing abide on us, which Thou hast promised to the families that call upon thy name. Take away all our sins, Thou Lamb of God. Wash us in thy cleansing blood, O Thou gracious Saviour. Receive us graciously and love us freely, O Thou that art enthroned in the majesty of thy glory. Thou art our Redeemer; save us, O Christ. Thou art our Comforter; sanctify and bless us, O Holy Spirit. Thou art our Father; hear us now, O God, and ever help us, through the intercession of our only Saviour, Jesus Christ. Amen.

READ IN HOLY SCRIPTURE ROMANS X. 1—13.

O LORD God of the Sabbath, who dost hear in heaven, thy dwelling place, the prayers and praises of thy people upon earth, accept, for thy dear Son's sake, the tribute of our unworthy but most hearty and sincere thanksgivings. What are we that Thou shouldest be so mindful of us, and that Thou shouldest surround us with thy lovingkindness and tender mercy? We confess that this day we have not served Thee as we ought to have done. We have been too often cold in heart, formal in worship, and worldly in affection. If Thou hadst dealt with us according to our sins, Thou wouldest long since have cut us off in the midst of our transgressions. But there is mercy with Thee, and therefore will we fear Thee.

We pray Thee that this day may not close without leaving a blessing behind it, even grace and peace from Thee, our God. Enable us to retain in our hearts some message of thy truth, some lesson of thy loving wisdom, that during the ensuing week it may be a light unto our feet and a lantern unto our paths. Draw us, we beseech Thee, by thy constraining love, closer unto Thee, and to thy Son Jesus Christ that we may perfectly love Thee, and worthily magnify thy holy name.

We entreat Thee, O gracious Lord God, on behalf of all who have heard thy Word this day. As Thou didst exalt thy Son with great triumph unto thy kingdom in heaven, so draw the hearts of all men unto Him that they may find pardon and peace through his most precious blood. Grant that the Word preached this day may be to very many souls an incorruptible seed, springing up, through thy Spirit, unto everlasting life. Especially we would beseech Thee on behalf of those who are hearers of thy Word and not doers of it; who have a name to live, but yet are dead before Thee; who have either been indifferent to the salvation of their souls, or who, seeking to establish their own righteousness, have not submitted themselves to the righteousness that is of faith. Open Thou the blind eyes, that they may see wondrous things out of thy law.

We would likewise pray for those who have not heard thy Gospel. Oh, speak the word, that great may be the company of the preachers, who, both in our own and other lands, may preach the unsearchable riches of Christ. May very many sinners be translated from the power of darkness into the kingdom of thy dear Son.

Finally, Lord, we beseech Thee to accomplish the number of thine elect, and to hasten thy kingdom, that all may know Thee, even from the least unto the greatest. We ask all through the prevailing merits and intercession of thy dear Son Jesus Christ our Lord. Amen.

[Morning.] **EIGHTEENTH WEEK.—MONDAY.** [Evening.

READ IN HOLY SCRIPTURE HEBREWS IX. 1—12.   READ IN HOLY SCRIPTURE ST. LUKE XV. 11—32.

GRACIOUS Lord God, who art always more ready to hear than we to pray, and art able and willing to do for us more than we desire or deserve, pour down upon us the abundance of thy mercy. Forgive us all those things of which our consciences are now afraid, and give us those good things which we are not worthy to ask, but through the merits and mediation of thy Son, Jesus Christ, our Lord. We bless thy name, O God, for the light of thy Gospel. We thank Thee for the knowledge of redeeming mercy, and that we can come to thy footstool in the assurance that in Christ Thou hast reconciled the world to Thyself, and that whosoever cometh to Thee Thou wilt in no wise cast out. Draw us, O Lord, by thy Spirit. Bring us nearer and nearer to Thee by thy grace, and give us the comforting experience of thy forgiveness and thy love.

We praise Thee for the renewed mercies of the morning. Life, and health, and peace, are thine; and in such measure as Thou seest good, Thou distributest them. We pray that we may be more thankful for thy gifts, and may have the heart day by day to make them instrumental for thy glory. Especially we ask of Thee, O God, guidance and strength for this day's duty. May we be as in thy sight all the day long. Cheer us in the midst of discouragement and disappointment. Prosper the work of our hands, and let all our labour and toil be lightened by a sense of thy presence and of thy love. Let not temptation assail us; and if it does, let it not overcome us. As long as Thou seest fit for us to be in the world, keep us from the evil that is in it, that neither business nor pleasure may keep our hearts back from Thee, or so choke thy Word within us as to make it unfruitful. Deepen our love to Thee, that we may do all such things as please Thee. Increase in us true religion, and let its influence pervade our entire life, both at home and abroad. Nourish us with all goodness, and let it strengthen us with a holy courage to continue steadfast in the ways of thy commandments. May we be patient and meek in all our intercourse with others, and strive in all things to do unto them as we would they should do unto us. Keep us in safety to the end of our earthly career, and glorify us, with Thyself and thy dear Son, in the kingdom which is everlasting.

Shed thy choicest blessings on all whom we love. [Let the children before Thee be partakers of thy grace, and feel thy love shining brightly in their hearts. Do Thou train and teach them by thy Spirit. Make them thine now, and keep them thine for ever.] Hear us, O God, in these our prayers and thanksgivings, we pray Thee, for thy dear Son's sake. Amen.

O THOU infinite and everlasting God, we marvel at the long-suffering and loving-kindness which Thou hast extended to the sons of men. Thou art the Almighty, whose hand none can stay; the all-holy, who art of purer eyes than to behold iniquity; and yet Thou dost stoop from thy throne to bid us think of Thee as our Father. We have been again assured, from the lips of thy beloved Son, that, like as a father pitieth his children, so dost Thou pity all who return to Thee.

We acknowledge that we have wandered far from Thee. We have rejected thine authority, and despised thy mercy; we have forgotten our relationship to Thee, and lived like strangers and outcasts from thy family; we have even neglected the salvation which Thou hast sent us by the hands of Christ. Father, we have sinned against heaven and in thy sight, and are no more worthy to be called thy children.

But we would arise and come to Thee. O Lord Jesus, may thy grace cancel our guilt, and thy righteousness, like a robe, cover our uncleanness. We come again, O God, at the end of another day, confessing our sins, and imploring thy pardon; we come casting ourselves on thy fatherly compassion. Thou willest not the death of a sinner; Thou art in Christ reconciling the world unto Thyself; have mercy upon us, then, O God, according to thy loving-kindness; according to the multitude of thy tender mercies, blot out our transgressions. Give, also, the spirit of adoption, that we may cry, Abba, Father, and that we may know and believe the love which Thou hast to us. May we be in spirit, as well as in fact, the sons and daughters of the Lord Almighty.

And thus, O our Father, may we all lie down to rest as in the embrace of thine everlasting arms. We know not what a night may bring forth, or whether we shall see the light of another morning; but are we not safe in thy keeping, and may we, not lie down and sleep in peace under the shadow of thy wings? Doubtless Thou art our Father: let thy fatherly blessing rest upon all this household; let the youngest of us hear thy voice, and rejoice in thy mercy. Comprehend, we pray Thee, in thy care, all near and dear to any of us, in every place; bless the homeless and destitute, the orphan and widowed ones; look upon the prodigals and outcasts, and restore them; may the dead be brought to life, and the lost be found. Increase the number of faithful pastors, and pour out thy Spirit on all thy people. And with these our prayers, accept our unfeigned thanksgivings for thy perpetual mercies; and may the blessing of the Father, the Son, and the Holy Spirit rest upon us all, now and for ever. Amen.

[Morning.] **EIGHTEENTH WEEK.—TUESDAY.** [Evening.

READ IN HOLY SCRIPTURE HEBREWS IX. 13—28.

BLESSED art Thou, O Lord! Teach us thy statutes. Oh! grant us clearer apprehensions of heavenly things. Open Thou our eyes, that we may see wondrous things out of thy law. We are strangers in the earth; hide not thy commandments from us. We are sinners, and suppliants for mercy. Oh! help us, that we, turning from our iniquities, may now understand thy truth.

Great God! with Thee there is mercy; yea, there is forgiveness with Thee. Thou hast even engaged Thyself, by a gracious covenant, to grant pardon and eternal redemption to all who will take hold of its promises. We see Jesus bearing our sins, in mysterious sufferings on the cross, that He might put away sin from us. We see that without the shedding of his infinitely precious blood, there could be no remission, no peace to the guilty conscience, no access to thy holy presence, here or hereafter. O righteous Father! we tremble at thy word. We mingle awe with faith in coming to thy blood-besprinkled throne. But Thou hast done all things well. All that thy law required, thy love has provided and secured. Unto us a Son is given. For us He freely died, and ever lives to make intercession. And now, O Thou, mighty to save, we take hold of thy saving strength. By thy all-sufficient sacrifice, and by thy priesthood on thy throne, save us to the uttermost, who come unto God by Thee!

We thank Thee, O Father, for safety and rest during the night, and for the light of life and health this morning. Help us, we beseech Thee, to carry the influence of these heavenly things into all the scenes and duties of the day. May we set the Lord, our Redeemer, the Holy One of Israel, always before us. May thy hatred to sin stir us up to watch, and pray, and strive in thy Spirit's might against it. May the blessings of salvation, so free to us, because so dearly purchased for us by thy Son, inspire us with alacrity in his service, and prompt us, whatsoever we do, for our neighbours or for ourselves, to do it unto the Lord. May we adorn the profession of his Cross, by purity, humility, and meekness, by all goodness, and righteousness, and truth. May we ever fervently desire and invoke, as now we do, for all sorts and conditions of men, but especially for our kindred, friends, and countrymen, a saving knowledge of thy grace. And for ourselves and all whom we love and would remember before Thee we pray, O holy and merciful Saviour! that we all may be found of Thee, severally in death, and together in the last great day, in peace, without spot, and blameless, through the blood of the everlasting covenant. Amen.

READ IN HOLY SCRIPTURE ROMANS VIII. 1—15.

ETERNAL God, who art gracious unto all who come to Thee, enable us now to look up to Thee, in child-like confidence, as our Father in heaven. Oh! what love hast Thou shown unto us, that we should be called the children of God! Fill our hearts, we pray Thee, with a deep sense of thy goodness and mercy. Send the Spirit of thy dear Son into our hearts, that we may indeed love Thee, and trust Thee, and obey Thee as our Father.

We feel ashamed, O our Father, that in so many things we continually grieve and displease Thee. We owe it to thy merciful forbearance that we are not lying under condemnation, and that we can plead the blood of Jesus, thy dear Son, which cleanseth from all sin. Do Thou wash us, and we shall be clean. Do Thou forgive us in thy mercy, and then shall not our sins be remembered. And grant that we may have grace to see the loving hand of our heavenly Father in all the circumstances of our life, overruling outward events for good, and upholding and renewing our hearts by the guidance and strength of the Holy Ghost. We thank Thee, Lord, for all that Thou hast done for us. We cannot praise Thee enough for thy undeserved goodness. Help us to love Thee more, and to show our gratitude by a heartier consecration of ourselves and all that we are to thy service.

We desire, O God, to be growing in grace, and to experience more deeply and constantly the gracious work of thy Holy Spirit. We are often tempted to forget Thee. Leave us not, we pray Thee, to ourselves; but guide, and teach, and strengthen us day by day. May we, in thy strength, walk not after the flesh, but after the Spirit, and have a spiritual mind, which is life and peace. Mortify and subdue in us all that is displeasing to Thee—the sinful temper, the unruly desire, the hasty speech, the selfish spirit, and whatever else hinders the perfect work of thy Spirit within us—that we may live here in thy favour, and hereafter in thy presence and glory.

Look in mercy on all who are still unconverted. Show them their danger: open their eyes to see and make their hearts to feel how fearful a thing it is to fall into the hands of the living God. If any of them are yet without the Spirit of Christ, arouse them to flee from the wrath to come. Let none of us, O God, or any who are dear to us, receive in vain thy heavenly grace and message.

We commend ourselves to thy care. Be with us through the night. Shield us from evil, and give us refreshing rest and sleep. We ask all in the name of thy dear Son, Jesus Christ, our Lord. Amen.

[MORNING.] **EIGHTEENTH WEEK.—WEDNESDAY.** [EVENING.

READ IN HOLY SCRIPTURE EXODUS XXXI.

MOST glorious Lord God, our merciful and loving Father, in whom we live, and move, and have our being; in the multitude of thy tender mercies we once more approach Thee, from whom all good things proceed. And since Thou hast safely brought us to the beginning of this day, we beseech Thee to defend and direct us in the same; and as Thou hast blest us in our lying down and in our rising up, so protect and keep us in our going forth and in our coming home. It is in vain for us to labour, except thy blessing go with us; prosper us, therefore, we pray Thee, O Lord, in our several callings, and so guide us that all we take in hand may tend to thy glory, to the good of others, and to the comfort of our own souls. From Thee do come wisdom and understanding, and knowledge in all manner of workmanship. Strength and skill are thy gifts. Thou teachest the ploughman to open and break the clods of the ground. Thou hast created the smith to make and the waster to destroy. And because the Lord of life and glory did not disdain a lowly station, may we labour with cheerfulness, and study to be quiet and do our own business. Help us so to walk in thy fear, that in mirth we become not trifling, and in sorrow we sink not into despair. Instruct us by thy Word; soften us by thy grace; and humble us by thy corrections. May we see Thee, O God, in all things, and all things in the light of thy presence.

Suffer us not to be led away by the error of the wicked, but keep us, that no temptations may prevail to plunge us into intemperance, uncleanness, evil speaking, or aught that would defile our hearts, disturb our consciences, or destroy our peace.

In all the labours of life we would look forward to the Sabbath of rest; and we pray that when life and its labours shall close upon us, we may dwell with Thee, in the everlasting Sabbath of thy glorious presence. Till then, most merciful God, permit us not to neglect the means of grace, but bless this our family worship, and seasons of public worship, and make them all conduce to our personal holiness and to thy praise.

[Behold, Lord, our dear children, and put thy fear into their young hearts. Let thy good providence guard them and thy grace save them.] In mercy watch over all our friends, relations, and neighbours. Comfort and bless our beloved Sovereign, and grant that she and all her family may reign with thee in everlasting life. Prosper and preserve our country, and spread abroad the glory of thy holy name, and the kingdom of thy dear Son Jesus Christ throughout all the world. Now to the Father, Son, and Holy Spirit be all praise and glory for ever. Amen.

READ IN HOLY SCRIPTURE ST. LUKE XVI. 1—17.

O GOD, our Creator, Preserver, and continual Benefactor, we bless Thee at the close of another day, for all thy goodness and mercy towards us. Thou never weariest in doing us good. Our Lord, when He was upon earth, had not where to lay His head; but Thou hast made our lot far different. Thou hast given us food, raiment, and a habitation; and of the least of all thy mercies we are utterly unworthy. How much more unworthy must we be of the unutterable mercies of the covenant of thy grace!

O God, the Father of our Lord Jesus Christ, look not upon us, but look upon the face of thine Anointed. We come to Thee without a claim of our own, without one single recommendation in thy sight. But we come to Thee in the Name of thy dear Son. In Him and with his perfect sacrifice for sin Thou art always well pleased; and Thou art able to save to the uttermost them that come to Thee through Him. Oh, may thy good Spirit ever enable us so to come to Thee, that, being justified by faith, we may be at peace with Thee, because in Christ Thou art at peace with us; and may our peace in Jesus be like a river ever flowing forth from Him, as the smitten Rock in whom are all our fresh springs.

O eternal Spirit, the Author and Giver of all life in Jesus, bind our souls unto Jesus, in love and gratitude, for ever. Teach us to live not as our own, but as bought with a price; and may the life which we now live in the flesh be lived by the faith of the Son of God, who loved us, and gave Himself for us, the Just for the unjust, that He might bring us to Thee.

Make us, also, faithful in all our duties; faithful in that which is least as well as in that which is greatest; faithful in that which is another's as well as in that which is our own. We are but stewards, every one of us, of that which is thine. Thou art the one Proprietor and Owner of all. The earth is thine and all the fulness thereof. All things are of Thee, and for thy pleasure they are and were created.

Make us, therefore, to feel the great responsibility of our stewardship. May we be daily living and trading for our Lord and Master, and be ready to give in our account at a moment's notice, if so required. May we remember that One is our Master, and not try to serve God and Mammon. Give us a decided faith and a decided mind; and when we fail, and may be no longer stewards on earth, give us an abundant entrance into the everlasting habitations of the blest. We ask all for Jesus Christ's alone sake, to whom, with Thee and the Holy Ghost, be praise and glory for ever. Amen.

[MORNING.] EIGHTEENTH WEEK.—THURSDAY. [EVENING.

READ IN HOLY SCRIPTURE EXODUS XXXII. 1—14. | READ IN HOLY SCRIPTURE 2 CORINTHIANS VIII.

O GOD, the Protector of all that trust in Thee, without whom nothing is strong, nothing is holy, increase and multiply upon us thy mercy, that, Thou being our Ruler and Guide, we may so pass through things temporal, that we finally lose not the things eternal.

In our passage through the wilderness of this world, may thy Holy Spirit ever bring to our sight the truth of the written Word; and may that Word be constantly a lamp to our feet and a light to our path. And if human teaching speaks not according to the law and to the testimony, may we be assured that there is no light in it. Keep us mindful that nothing can supply the want of thy blessed presence, that no outward ordinances can of themselves effect that inward cleansing and that spiritual nourishment which Thou alone canst impart.

Give us grace, O Lord, to remember that, however free from the guilt of worshipping or bowing down to images of wood and stone, we are ever prone to spiritual idolatry; and may we resist every temptation to worship and serve the creature rather than the Creator, who is blessed for evermore. And to this end, we beseech Thee so to set before us the beauty and glory of our incarnate Redeemer, that we may be constrained by his love to say, Whom have we in heaven but Thee? and there is none upon earth that we desire besides Thee.

Alas! O Lord, we know but too well how grievously we have sinned against Thee in time past, by following the devices and desires of our own hearts, or the example and practice of those who know not Thee, rather than the plain directions of thy Word, and the leadings of thy Spirit. Well might thy wrath be hot against us; justly mightest Thou consume us. But spare us, we pray Thee, for thy name's sake, and hear the intercession of our great High Priest pleading for us at thy right hand.

Be with us, we beseech Thee, in all the duties of this day. Let thy Spirit abide with us, teaching us what we ought to do, and enabling us to do it as in thy sight and for thy glory. Shed thy blessings on all whom we love. Make them the temples of thy grace, and the devoted followers of the meek and lowly Jesus. Look upon the Church, enlarge its borders, and gather day by day into its fold many wandering souls. Give wisdom to all in authority, and guide their counsels. Sanctify and comfort the hearts of the sorrowing, and hasten the time when there shall be no more death, nor crying, nor sorrow, because the old things have passed away. Hear us, we pray Thee, for thy dear Son Jesus Christ's sake. Amen.

O THOU who art the God of all the families of the earth, and hast graciously promised to draw nigh unto those who approach Thee through thy dear Son, grant unto us some tokens of thy presence by filling our hearts with holy affections and heavenly desires. May none of us draw nigh unto Thee with our lips while our hearts are far from Thee; but may we all worship Thee in spirit and in truth. May we consider it our highest privilege to hold communion with Thee in prayer and supplication. Another day has now passed away, with all its mercies and its trials, its duties and its opportunities. Help us seriously to review its events, and to ask ourselves whether we have reason to hope that we are now fitter for heaven, as we are nearer to eternity. Oh, what cause have we to humble ourselves, and to pray, "Enter not into judgment with thy servants, O Lord." Blot out all our sins, for we have done what we ought not to have done, and we have left undone what we ought to have done. We thank Thee for thy forbearance and long-suffering; and pray that, for the time to come, should we be spared, we may be more diligent and faithful in serving Thee. May we be enabled, by a hearty surrender of body, soul, and spirit, to give ourselves to the Lord as a living sacrifice, holy, acceptable unto God, as a reasonable service. As we abound in the means of grace, may we also abound in faith and love, in knowledge, and in all diligence. Give us, we pray Thee, a deeper and truer knowledge of Divine things. Lord Jesus, manifest Thyself unto us as Thou dost not unto the world. May we know Thee in all the sufficiency of thy grace and the perfectness of thy atonement. Strengthen us against all temptation, and deliver us from the power of our great enemy. Show us the evil of sin, and kindle in our hearts a holy watchfulness and zeal against it. Give us the blessed experience of thy love, and constrain us thereby to deny ourselves and follow Christ.

Enlarge our hearts towards our fellow-creatures, and may we seek the salvation of all mankind. Pity heathen idolators, and take away the veil from the heart of the Jew. May we devise liberal things to the poor around us, and to the far distant heathen; and knowing the grace of our Lord Jesus Christ, may He spread abroad the knowledge of his salvation, that so his ways may be known upon earth, his saving health among all nations.

And now, O Shepherd of Israel, take us all into thy protection through the night. Refresh us with needful rest; and may we arise in the morning rejoicing in thy love. We ask all for Jesus Christ's sake. Amen.

[MORNING.] **EIGHTEENTH WEEK.—FRIDAY.** [EVENING.]

READ IN HOLY SCRIPTURE EXODUS XXXII. 15—35.   READ IN HOLY SCRIPTURE ST. LUKE XVI. 19—31

O LORD our God, we humbly and gratefully acknowledge Thee as the only true and living God. We mournfully confess the proneness of our hearts to depart from Thee. Other lords have had dominion over us. We have yielded up the empire of our souls to thy rivals, and thus dishonoured Thee. Graciously interpose on our behalf. For the sake of Jesus Christ thy Son, overthrow every usurper within us, and enthrone Thyself in our hearts. Destroy all idolatrous love for the creature, and cause our supreme affections evermore to go out after Thee.

Throughout this day be Thou our Guide and God. We are thine, O Lord, redeemed with precious blood: claim us fully. We are thy servants; may we serve Thee without weariness. We are thy children; may we love and honour Thee with constancy. In the midst of temptations be Thou round about us to shield us. Deprived of Thee, we are weaker than a bruised reed. On Thee, our Divine Helper, we therefore cast ourselves. Be gracious unto us and bless us. Fulfil in our experience the promises in which Thou hast caused us to hope. Let us realise a greater nearness to Thee this day than ever. And in order to this, may our trust in Thee be full, constant, and unwavering.

We adore Thee, O Lord, as the Father of all our mercies. We praise Thee for the instructions and admonitions of thy holy Word. By signal examples of thy sore displeasure on thine ancient people, Thou hast warned us against departing from Thee. May we take heed to the voice of thy judgments, and learn obedience. May we so obey thy voice, that we may be found among those who shall be counted worthy to live and reign with Thee for ever. We render Thee devout thanksgiving for the mercies and protection of another night, and for the bounties which thy hand has spread before us on the return of another morning. Let the gratitude we express be engraven on our hearts and developed in our lives.

We pray Thee, O Lord, to be very gracious to our relatives and friends absent from us. May they all truly know Thee, that they may truly love Thee. May thy Church universal be blessed, not only with peace, but also with prosperity. May thy people everywhere possess a holy ambition to adorn the doctrine of God their Saviour in all things, and to shed the light of a consistent piety on all around. May the coming of thy kingdom be thus hastened; and may the Saviour, whose right it is to reign, speedily claim for Himself the world He has redeemed. Hear us, O, Lord, in these our prayers, we most humbly beseech Thee, for the alone sake of Jesus Christ, our Strength and our Redeemer. Amen.

ALMIGHTY and most merciful Father, we humbly beseech Thee to bestow upon us the spirit of prayer, that we may draw near to Thee this evening with true hearts, in the full assurance of faith, and close this day in the enjoyment of thy favour and thy love.

We acknowledge, O Lord, the many mercies and blessings Thou hast granted to us this day. Thou, our heavenly Father, hast holden us in life, and continued to our use the faculties and capacities of our bodies and souls. We bless Thee, O Lord, for our reason, our sight, our hearing, our speech; and we thank Thee for the numberless supplies which have contributed to our enjoyment and happiness. We praise Thee for thy fatherly love and watchful care over us. Thou hast surrounded us every moment with the tokens of thy merciful goodness. To Thee, O God, we owe the homage of our hearts, and the best obedience of our lives.

Almighty God, we confess, and we deplore before Thee, that, in return for thy great and manifold mercies, we have often and grievously sinned against Thee. Pardon, we humbly beseech Thee, our thoughtlessness, our negligence, our ingratitude, our numerous and aggravated sins. We plead the merits of thy beloved Son Jesus Christ; for his sake graciously blot out all our transgressions, and help us henceforth to live to thy glory.

Impress upon our minds the solemn passage of thy holy Word we now have read. We ask of Thee the wisdom we need to use the things of this life, so that the recollection of them may not add to our misery hereafter. If in thy good providence our temporal lot be one of prosperity and success, oh, keep us from pride and vain glory, and especially keep us from despising the poor; oh, help us to remember the grace of our Lord Jesus Christ, who, though He was rich, yet for our sakes He became poor; and may his mind always be in us. If thou shouldest see fit to lead us through suffering, poverty, and want, oh, give us resignation to thy will, and grant that when the time of our departure from earth shall arrive, we may be carried by angels into Abraham's bosom.

Whilst we remain on earth, O Lord, we pray Thee to enable us to use all our talents according to thy will, remembering the account we must one day give. Awaken now, we beseech Thee, in all our minds, a deep concern for the salvation of our friends and relatives. Take away from us and from them all hardness of heart and contempt of thy Word; and, of thy infinite mercy, bring us all to Jesus Christ, that we may be happy in heaven for ever with Him.

Grant this, O God, for his sake. Amen.

[Morning.] **EIGHTEENTH WEEK.—SATURDAY.** [Evening.

READ IN HOLY SCRIPTURE EXODUS XXXIII.

O KING of kings, whose unveiled face no man can see and live, be gracious and merciful unto us, and make all thy goodness pass before us. Bring to our remembrance thy mercies, and the long train of thy kindness, and love, and forgivenesses. Melt our hard hearts with gratitude, and may we look on Him whom we have pierced, and mourn.

Spare us, good Lord, for we have sinned. We have done amiss and dealt wickedly. Like Israel, we have forgotten thy judgments and thy favours. Thy laws we have broken, and by our idols we have insulted Thee.

Blessed Saviour Jesus, intercede for us, as Moses pleaded for Israel. Thou art the true Mediator between God and man. Thou art indeed God; Thou sittest with thy Father on his throne, and at thy feet all angels cry aloud, "Holy, holy, holy, Lord God of hosts." But Thou art man, and wast made a servant for us. All praise and love be to Thee, Lord Jesus; for all our transgressions Thou hast made full satisfaction. In thy name we come to the throne of grace. Oh, plead for us, that we may be pardoned. Plead for us, that we may be blessed.

O God, the Holy Ghost, may thy presence go before us, and, like the pillar of the cloud, direct our way. If any of us have lived until now in ignorance or contempt of Thee, may they arise from sin, and commence a wiser and a happier life. May we all be holy, and unlike the world. Preserve us from open sin and from secret vice. Turn away our hearts, O Lord, from vanity, and enable us to improve our time, and daily to grow in grace. May we live but to please Thee, and, like Joshua, who loved to abide in thy tabernacle, may we ever find in Thee our solace and joy. Grant us grace to pursue our various employments this day as in thy sight, and to look up to Thee in every moment of need or temptation. Beat down Satan under our feet. May we hate and abhor all deceit and pride, all malice and strife. May we be unselfish and self-denying, and do our utmost to promote the happiness of every one on earth.

O Thou whose long-suffering is unspeakable, let thy power, thy glory, and the mightiness of thy kingdom be known unto men! Arise, O God, maintain thine own cause. Near and afar, let thy Word grow mightily, and prevail. We know not what a day may bring forth. Prepare us to meet thy righteous face; and, after this wilderness, admit us to the land that floweth with milk and honey, that we may see the felicity of thy chosen, and give thanks with thine inheritance, evermore, through Jesus Christ our Saviour, to whom be glory for ever. Amen.

READ IN HOLY SCRIPTURE JAMES V.

O LORD our God, who hast given us another day of mercy, and hast again patiently borne with our sins and infirmities, seal upon our souls thy forgiveness this night, and bless us all in Jesus Christ. The evils of our hearts are all known to Thee; and, oh, how much hast Thou seen amiss in us through this day! How little we have felt of love to Thee and to others; how much we have lived this day and hitherto to ourselves. Forgive any envy, malice, or uncharitableness which has prevailed in us; any impatience in our behaviour towards others, or any fretfulness under the dealings of thy loving hand. May we trust Thee in all thy providences, as very pitiful and of tender mercy; and in sickness and in health keep close to Thee in prayer, and ever have a heart to thank Thee for thine unceasing loving-kindness.

Pour out upon us continually the spirit of grace and of supplication; and grant to us and to thy whole Church more earnestness and perseverance in our intercessions on behalf of all men. Give us all to realise more the power of prayer, and to believe and plead with confidence all thy precious promises to thy praying people. Make our supplications, by thy blessed Spirit, to be effectual and fervent, and give us continually the answer of peace. We ask Thee for a more deep and earnest concern for the salvation of others. Oh, that the very weakest of us might be enabled so to walk as to save some soul from death; and grant that all our influence may be for good, and not for evil, towards any with whom we may have had intercourse this day. Set a watch before our mouth, and keep the door of our lips. Keep us from everything unworthy of that pure and holy name by which we are called. May we ever be found watching, with our loins girt and our lamps burning, as those that look for their Lord. May we never be weary in well-doing, knowing that in due season we shall reap if we faint not.

Keep our hearts steadfast in thy truth; and if we be reproached and persecuted for Christ's sake, may we patiently endure. Graciously comfort and support any that are suffering for his name. May they feel that they have in heaven an enduring inheritance, and may their testimony win others to the truth. Have pity upon those who are lovers of pleasure more than lovers of God. We commend ourselves and all dear to us to thy holy keeping this night, especially any of them who may be under thy chastening hand. May we and they rest in peace, through the blood of Jesus, and the comfort of the Holy Ghost. Bless us, O Lord, and accept these our prayers and praises, for Christ's sake, our adorable Redeemer and Saviour. Amen.

[MORNING.] **NINETEENTH WEEK.—LORD'S DAY.** [EVENING.]

READ IN HOLY SCRIPTURE ST. JOHN XIV. 1—14.

O THOU in whom we live, and move, and have our being, we bless Thee for having brought us, in thy providence, to the morning of another day of rest. We magnify Thee, our God and Father, for having raised from the dead thy Son Jesus, and exalted Him to thine own right hand; and for the everlasting rest which, through his atoning sacrifice, we trust to spend with Thee in heaven. Blessed be the God and Father of our Lord Jesus Christ, which, according to his abundant mercy, hath begotten us again unto a lively hope by the resurrection of Jesus Christ from the dead.

We come, under the shelter of his great name, seeking as a family thy blessing upon the means of grace to-day. Without Thee, we know they will be empty and barren. Oh, fill them with the power of thy Spirit! May we each have intercourse with Thee, the Father; manifest Thyself to us in the public worship of the sanctuary, and in our retirement at home; may the youngest of us find a way to Thee. And to this end teach us how to approach Thee through thy Son, the Mediator between God and man. May we see in Him the Way, the Truth, and the Life. O Saviour! thou who art evermore the same, guide our uncertain steps into the holy place. Show us the Father by revealing Thyself; and learning of Thee, may we find rest unto our souls. If any of our hearts are troubled and distracted with the cares and sorrows of life, speak to us words of peace and consolation; point us to the place prepared in thy Father's house for those that love Thee; remind us of thine own coming to receive us. Say to us, "Be not afraid; only believe." So in our own experience to-day may thy promise of sympathy be realised, and the Father be glorified in the Son!

We especially ask thy presence with us, O God, in the public worship in which we are about to engage. May we meet our fellow-worshippers in the fulness of the blessings of the Gospel of Christ. Grant that our praise and prayer may be the utterance of unfeigned wants; may we mingle faith with the reading of thy Word, and may our souls be prepared to receive thy Gospel gladly and thankfully. Be in all the congregations of thy saints; make the place of thy feet to be glorious. Clothe thy ministers with salvation, and let thy people shout aloud for joy; and may many lost sinners be brought this day out of darkness into thy marvellous light, and from the power of Satan into the kingdom of thy dear Son.

Accept our hearty thanksgiving for all the mercies of the night, and the health and comfort of the morning. May we love the place of thy worship, and delight to run in the way of thy commandments. We ask it for Jesus Christ's sake. Amen.

READ IN HOLY SCRIPTURE ST. LUKE XVII. 1—19.

O LORD, our heavenly Father, accept our united thanks for the privileges of this Sabbath-day. Grant us the aid of thy Holy Spirit, that we may offer unto Thee an acceptable sacrifice. Impress upon our minds the lessons which we have just read. May we learn not to be surprised at any trials we may meet with during our pilgrimage through this world of sin and temptation. If man in his wickedness should place stumblingblocks in our way, grant us grace still to persevere. We know that we are safe in thy protection; for Thou hast said, "Vengeance is mine, I will repay." To all thy people who are persecuted for righteousness' sake, grant the consolations of thy grace, and so overrule the conduct of their enemies, that the wrath of man may praise Thee. As Thou art gracious and merciful, and willest not the death of a sinner, we pray that all the persecutors of thy people may be brought to true repentance. Give to all thy saints the spirit of their Divine Master, that they may bless them that curse them, and pray for them who despitefully use and persecute them. Increase the faith of all thy servants, that they may be spiritual amidst worldliness, forgiving amongst enemies, and heavenly-minded whilst surrounded by the ungodly.

Enable us, O Lord, to understand and obey thy will at all times, and save us from all pride, that we may attach no merit to any of our duties. That we have any disposition or power to obey thy commandments, we owe to thy grace; whilst all our failings, which are many, belong to ourselves. Forgive the defects, infirmities, and sins which cleave to our most holy things. May we ever walk humbly with Thee, our God, counting it an honour to be thy servants, and leaving it to Thee to bless and reward us as Thou seest fit.

We thank Thee, O blessed Saviour, for the teaching of thy Word. In what Thou hast done, we see thy readiness to hear, and thine ability to answer prayer. As Thou didst restore the lepers to health, so heal our souls. Make us willing to obey thy commands, that we may obtain the fulfilment of thy promises. May we never pause in our obedience, seeking for reasons for the duties which Thou dost enjoin, but instantly fulfil them, that we may prove thy power to save. Forgive our past unthankfulness for the blessings we have received, and vouchsafe to us the spirit of gratitude, that we may glorify Thee on earth, and thus prepare to praise Thee for ever in heaven.

Defend us this night, O Lord, from all danger, and grant us refreshing sleep, for the sake of Jesus Christ our Lord, to whom, with Thee, O Father, and Thee, O Holy Ghost, be everlasting praise. Amen.

[Morning.]   NINETEENTH WEEK.—MONDAY.   [Evening.

READ IN HOLY SCRIPTURE EXODUS XXXIV. 1—14.

READ IN HOLY SCRIPTURE PSALM CXVI.

O LORD, thou art our God. Early will we seek Thee. The desire of our hearts is unto Thee, and to the remembrance of thy name. Whom have we in heaven but Thee? and there is none upon earth that we desire beside Thee. Having Thee, we have all. For Thou art Jehovah, merciful and gracious, long-suffering, and abundant in goodness and truth; keeping mercy for thousands, forgiving iniquity, transgression, and sin. Shine into our hearts, and cause us to see thy power, thy glory, and thy goodness, in the face of Jesus Christ, and may we be ready to count all things but loss for the excellency of the knowledge of Christ Jesus, our Lord.

But it is the Spirit that quickeneth: the flesh profiteth nothing. Without the Spirit, all is dead in us; but where Thou breathest, there is life. Evermore give us this breath of life. Heavenly Father, draw us by thy Spirit unto Jesus; reveal thy Son in us in all his fulness of love and all his preciousness, that we may give our hearts wholly unto Him, and know assuredly both his completeness in Thee and our own completeness in Him.

Hast not Thou appointed a ransom for the sinner? Out of Christ thou canst by no means clear the guilty; but in Christ Thou art faithful and just to forgive us our sins, and to cleanse us from all unrighteousness. Oh, wondrous love! that Thou shouldest not have spared Thine own Son, in order to spare a guilty people: that Thou shouldest have made Him to be sin for us who knew no sin, that we might be made the righteousness of God in Him! Oh, come, then, Spirit of truth and Spirit of life, come and take of the things of Christ and show them unto us; show us our deliverance from all wrath, all curse, all condemnation: show us our refuge in the cleft of the Rock that is higher than we; show us how, by his one offering, Christ hath perfected for ever them that are sanctified, that we may heartily rejoice in the strength of our salvation.

Write also thy law, we beseech Thee, on our hearts, even as thy hand did twice write it upon tables of stone. Teach us to adorn the doctrine of God our Saviour in all things. May our conversation this day be as becometh the Gospel of Christ, and may all that is in us bless his holy name.

Look, O Lord, with special favour upon our Queen and our country. Increase amongst us that righteousness by which a nation is exalted. Add daily to thy true Church such as shall be saved, and may streams of mercy and blessing go forth from us to the very ends of the earth. These and all our petitions we humbly offer in the name and through the mediation of thine own beloved Son, Jesus Christ, our Lord. Amen.

THOU, O God, art good, and Thou doest good continually. Thou hast done us good, and we desire to offer at thy footstool this evening our sacrifice of thanksgiving and praise. We thank Thee for the assurance that Thou wilt hear us in our own homes, as well as in the courts of the Lord's house. Through Jesus accept us, and give us thy Spirit, that the flame of devotion may burn brightly on thine altar.

With loving gratitude we acknowledge our entire dependence on Thyself. Another day has testified to thine unwearied love and watchful care. Thou hast taken us out and brought us in. Thine eye has guided, thine arm defended, thine hand sustained us. What are we, or what is our father's house, that Thou shouldest deal thus bountifully with us? We have deserved nothing but wrath; we have received nothing but mercy. What shall we render to the Lord for all his benefits toward us? We will take the cup of salvation, and call on thy holy name.

Like the Psalmist of whose experience we have been reading, we, too, have sometimes found trouble and sorrow. The gourd under whose shadow we have sat has withered; the brook of whose pleasant waters we drank has dried up; the idols of our hearts have been shattered, and darkness has gathered over us. The sorrows of death then compassed us, and the pains of hell then gat hold upon us. How innumerable, how aggravated, how inexcusable have appeared our sins! Oh, we thank Thee that then Thou didst help us: that Thou didst show Thyself a gracious God, long-suffering, and of tender mercy. May we ever go to Thee in all times of our guilt. Oh, give us faith in the Saviour, whose blood cleanseth from all sin; who is able to save to the very uttermost all who come to God by Him. May we look less to ourselves, and more to Him; and be enabled, whilst we look, to realise by faith our acceptance, and to say, "Return unto thy rest, O my soul, for the Lord hath dealt bountifully with thee."

Grant, too, we implore Thee, that our future lives may prove our gratitude. Whilst we live may we walk before Thee, unto all well-pleasing; and when the end of our course shall come, may we be numbered amongst thy saints in glory everlasting.

Take us under thy kind care and protection this night. Suffer no evil thoughts to disturb or defile us; keep us from the designs of ungodly men; shield us from devouring flames; may we lie down in peace, and rise again in health.

For our Saviour's sake we ask these and all other mercies; and to the Father, Son, and Spirit ascribe everlasting praise. Amen.

[Morning.]   NINETEENTH WEEK.—TUESDAY.   [Evening.]

READ IN HOLY SCRIPTURE EXODUS XXXIV. 21—35.

READ IN HOLY SCRIPTURE ST. LUKE XVII. 20—37.

ALMIGHTY and everlasting God, before whom angels veil their faces, how shall we, who have broken thy holy law, in thought, word, and in deed, now venture to draw nigh to Thee? We dare not approach thy throne had we not an all-prevailing Mediator, who ever liveth to make intercession for us. The thunders of Mount Sinai would make us afraid; but, thanks be unto God, we are brought within the bonds of a better covenant, and have access with boldness unto the throne of grace, through the blood and righteousness of Jesus Christ. Prepare our hearts now to draw nigh to Thee, as our reconciled God and Father. Give to us thy Holy Spirit, to be in us a Spirit of prayer and supplication, and vouchsafe an answer of peace.

May the moments thus spent in communion with Thee be seasons of refreshing from the presence of the Lord; so that when we enter upon the business of life, our countenances may shine with a holy brightness, and all around take knowledge of us that we have been with Jesus.

May our minds be thus fitted for the duties of the day, and the events which may betide us. May we carry our religion with us into the world, and so let our light shine before men, that others may glorify God on our behalf.

May thy holy precepts be written upon the fleshy tables of our hearts, so that we may delight in thy commandments, and find them ways of pleasantness and paths of peace.

We bless Thee for thy mercies to us in times past, for health of body and peace of mind, and for all other tokens of thy favour and loving-kindness. Be Thou our Guardian and Guide, even unto the end. Should trials or sickness come upon us, may we receive them as evidences of thy fatherly love, since Thou hast declared, "As many as I love, I rebuke and chasten;" and may they be sanctified to the good of our souls. And should the candle of the Lord still shine upon our dwelling, give us grateful hearts for unnumbered comforts. May the pillar and the cloud ever rest upon our tabernacle, and may we cheerfully follow the leadings of thy good providence.

Let thy favour rest on our country. Guide the deliberations of our rulers, and control all their plans and proceedings to the advancement of thy kingdom and the increase of godliness in the land. Have pity on the souls that know Thee not. Turn the feet of the wicked into the ways of righteousness, and bow the hearts of many this day in true repentance at the feet of thy dear Son. Bless all who are dear to us, and enrich us with the special tokens of thy love. We ask all in the name of our adorable Redeemer. Amen.

ALL thy works praise Thee, O God, and thy saints give thanks unto Thee. Adorable art Thou in thy glorious perfections: wonderful art Thou in thy works and ways; above all, in the great work of redeeming grace which Thou hast accomplished by thy dear Son. What are we that we should be the objects of thy tender love from hour to hour, and that even now, as we kneel in thy presence, Thou shouldest hear our prayer, and assure us of thy favour? Raise our hearts afresh in thankfulness and joy. Let us see more and more clearly what we owe to Thee; how great has been thy goodness towards us, and how rich and abundant is thy forgiveness, which saves from eternal condemnation all them who trust in Thee, through thy dear Son.

O God, we are sorry that, thus blessed, we have lived so unworthily and so sinfully. We repent us now before Thee of our many misdoings: of the coldness of our love to Thee, of our backwardness to do thy will, and of the occasions on which during the day now past we have been unmindful of our duty to Thee and of thy precepts. Accept our humble confessions, and through thy dear Son have mercy upon us, and grant us thy peace.

We pray Thee that Thou wouldest keep us in a spirit of watchfulness for the Saviour's second coming, that we may not sleep as do others, but look and long for the time when He shall come in the glory of his Father. May the thought of his searching judgment make us anxious to be sincere and without offence in this our day of trial; and stir up our hearts to a more constant diligence in every good word and work to which thy providence calls us. Keep us ever in mind, O Lord, that it will avail us nothing in that day to have enjoyed Christian privileges, unless we have believed in Jesus with all our hearts, and striven, amid the temptations of the world, to walk closely in his footsteps, and be prepared for his coming. If Thou hast converted us by thy Spirit, preserve us from backsliding. Let no mournful longings after the things we have forsaken damp the fervour of our love to Thee, or mar the entireness of our consecration to Thee.

Graciously pour out thy Spirit on all people. Wherever thy truth comes, let it be glorified. Wherever Christ is preached, let many hearts be bowed before Him. Guide into heavenly wisdom all thy ministers. Strengthen their hands, comfort their hearts, and show them more clearly all thy will. Accomplish the number of the elect, and hasten thy kingdom. We ask all these mercies, and we commend ourselves and all we love to thy gracious care, in the name of Jesus Christ our Lord and Saviour. Amen.

[Morning.] NINETEENTH WEEK.—WEDNESDAY. [Evening.

READ IN HOLY SCRIPTURE 2 CORINTHIANS III.

WE adore thy loving-kindness, O God, which has cared for us and protected us during the night. We praise Thee for the renewal to us of morning mercies. Give us at all times, we beseech Thee, a childlike confidence in thy love. We would look up to Thee as our Father in heaven, and would pray Thee ever to look down upon us as thy dear children, thy beloved in Christ Jesus. May we grieve with a godly sorrow over our many offences against Thee, and by thy Spirit's help be enabled to put away what is hateful in thy sight, and inconsistent with our high vocation. Blessed be thy name, O God, for thy forbearance. Thou knowest our frame, and what poor, weak, ignorant, and mistaken creatures we are. Have pity upon us, heavenly Father, and lift up the light of thy countenance upon us.

Let us preserve, we pray Thee, the constant remembrance of thy presence through all this day. Surrounded as we are by temptations, and with an evil heart within us, leave us not, we pray Thee, to ourselves. Watch Thou over us, and guard us against the devices of our great enemy. Let the prayer of the Saviour for his people be answered on our behalf. Keep us from evil. In all our conduct towards others, and in all the business of daily life, let it be seen that we have the fear of God before our eyes. Set a watch over our lips, that we offend not in word; and let our conversation be with grace. So deeply write thy law in our hearts, and let it so influence our lives, that we may be epistles of Christ, known and read of all men. Open our eyes, we beseech Thee, to see and to understand the glory of the Gospel. Let not Satan or sin blind us to the light of thy truth. Remove every veil of ignorance and prejudice, and enable us with open face to look upon Jesus, our exalted Redeemer and Saviour. Give us thy Holy Spirit, to be in us a Spirit of liberty, freeing us from the bondage of every besetting sin, and from the toils of the devil. We pray that we may not only be the true disciples of thy dear Son, but be changed more and more into his image and likeness, and walk even as He walked.

We commit ourselves, and all who are dear to us, to thy gracious keeping. May they enjoy an abundant measure of thy grace and blessing, and with us be daily prepared for an inheritance among thy sanctified and glorified people. We also pray for the enlarged outpouring of thy Holy Spirit on all who profess and call themselves Christians, that they may be more entirely consecrated to thy service, and seek more diligently thy glory, and promote more earnestly the extension of the Redeemer's kingdom. Grant us these our prayers, for Jesus Christ's sake. Amen.

READ IN HOLY SCRIPTURE ST. LUKE XVIII. 1-14.

O LORD God Almighty, Thou seest the hearts of the children of men, and of them that profess to pray unto Thee. We all now kneel before Thee, and in the eye of man there is no separation between us; but Thou discernest between the prayer of the proud and the sighing of a broken and contrite heart.

Lord, we are not worthy so much as to lift up our eyes unto Thee. Oh, convince us of our guilt! Take away our ignorance and self-esteem, and destroy all our false comforts. Give us godly sorrow for sin, and that with an aching heart we may pray as the publican prayed—"God be merciful to me a sinner."

Be merciful, O our God, and let thine anger cease from us. Be not displeased at us for ever. We have sinned against Thee this day, as in the days that went before it. Not only are our actions polluted by sin, but we ourselves are sinners. Our nature is unclean, and, like a corrupt tree, bringeth forth evil fruit. For thy Son our Lord Jesus Christ's sake, forgive us all that is past. We are miserable sinners; our hearts are evil; and if we have not fallen into the grossest wickedness, it is not of ourselves, but because thy goodness has restrained us. Nay, Thou knowest, O Lord, that thy loving mercies to us have been so great, and our privileges so many, that we may call ourselves the chief of sinners, for sin in us is exceedingly sinful.

Yet our trust is in thine abundant mercy, through Jesus Christ the righteous, who poured out his soul unto death for us, and bore the sins of many. Lord Jesus, bid us come to Thee. Do Thou wash us in thy most precious blood, that our sins may be mentioned against us no more. If the unjust judge listened to the widow's cry, O Thou, most faithful, most kind Father, hearken to our prayer, and grant us thy pardon this night. Without it we cannot rest. O Lord, deny us not the blessings we seek.

Protect us, gracious Father, during the hours of sleep; and if it please Thee to prolong our lives another day, renew our strength to serve Thee. Prepare us for the summons to quit these mortal scenes. In the dark moments of death be Thou our light; and in the day of judgment, good Lord, deliver us.

We beseech Thee with thy favour to behold our Queen and our country. Bless our neighbours as ourselves; and let our relatives and acquaintances find grace in thy sight. Have mercy upon this evil world. Come quickly, O Thou Son of Man! Put an end to sin and misery; and to Thyself, with the Father and the Holy Ghost, be all glory, now and evermore. Amen.

[Morning.] NINETEENTH WEEK.—THURSDAY. [Evening.

READ IN HOLY SCRIPTURE EXODUS XXXV. 30—XXXVI. 7.

READ IN HOLY SCRIPTURE ISAIAH LVII.

GRACIOUS and loving Father, in whom we live, and move, and have our being; by whose mercy we have awakened this morning from our sleep refreshed and strengthened, we bless Thee for this renewal of thy goodness. By Thee we have been sustained through the night, that we may be ready to fulfil the work given us to do. For these and all thy mercies, spiritual and temporal, we adore thy mercy. Grant our souls much of thy grace, and enable us to present our bodies this day a living sacrifice to Thee in all our service, and to consecrate all our ordinary employment to thy glory. From Thee alone cometh the power to fulfil even our worldly callings. Help each one of us ever to feel this entire dependence upon Thee in all the circumstances of our life. The wisdom and understanding which we need, even for our ordinary work, come only from thy Spirit. Grant, therefore, that we may be skilful in our various spheres of duty; not slothful in any business, but serving Thee. May we do nothing carelessly, but all as unto the Lord; nothing in our own sufficiency, but everything in dependence on Thee for its success and blessing. Sustain our minds in the strength needed for daily duty, and our bodies in the health sufficient for the fulfilment of our appointed service. May we ever labour as of the ability which Thou givest, and be preserved from indolence and slothfulness, as well as from pride and self-seeking. Above all, may we feel that we are bought with a price, and daily walk in the peace and power of thy salvation. May we thus count nothing our own; but, inasmuch as Thou hast given us all things in Christ, even wisdom and righteousness, sanctification and redemption, may we render all we have and are to Thee. Stir us up willingly to help the poor, as far as lieth in us, by personal service, and freely to give of that which Thou hast given us, as we have opportunity.

Make us all to walk this day as those whose bodies are the temples of the Holy Ghost. May we be clothed with the beauty of holiness; may our conversation be as it becometh godliness; may others take knowledge of us that we have been with Jesus. Grant us to feel more interest in the spiritual welfare of all around us, and make us ready in finding occasions of doing them good. May we carefully, through grace, check the corruptions of our evil nature; and may our temper at all times be such as to help forward unity and godly love in all forbearance and meekness. Bless all dear to us this day; preserve them and us, outwardly in our bodies by thy providence, and inwardly in our souls by thy grace. Hear our prayers and pardon all our offences, through Jesus Christ our only Saviour. Amen.

ALMIGHTY God, the High and Lofty One that inhabitest eternity; whose name is Holy; we give Thee humble and hearty thanks, that though Thou dwellest in the high and holy place, Thou dost dwell also with those who are of a contrite and humble spirit; to revive the spirit of the humble, and to revive the heart of the contrite ones. And we beseech Thee so to cleanse our hearts by the inspiration of thy Holy Spirit, that we, being delivered from this present evil world, and walking in newness of life, may have fellowship with Thee the Father, and with thy Son Jesus Christ.

O God, who searchest the heart, and triest the reins of the children of men; we have sinned and done evil in thy sight; we have erred and strayed from thy ways like lost sheep; we have followed too much the devices and desires of our own hearts; we have offended against thy holy laws; we have left undone those things which we ought to have done, and we have done those things which we ought not to have done; and there is no health in us. Have mercy upon us, O God, according to thy loving-kindness; according to the multitude of thy tender mercies, blot out our transgressions, and spare Thou them that confess their faults. Subdue the unholy passions of our souls, and save us from the corruption that is in the world through lust; deliver us from all evil; that we, cleansing ourselves from all filthiness of the flesh and spirit, and perfecting holiness in thy fear, may finally come to thine eternal kingdom, and be presented faultless through Jesus Christ our Lord.

Most merciful Father, spare thy people whom Thou hast redeemed, and suffer not the righteous to perish out of the land; neither be Thou wroth with thy servants, lest the spirit should fail before Thee, and the souls which Thou hast made. But Thou, O Lord, have mercy upon us, and grant that it may be well with us and with our children for ever. And as Thou hast promised to bless all that we set our hand unto, give us to eat of our bread to the full, and dwell in the land safely. Be merciful to our country and our kindred; be gracious to our Sovereign Lady the Queen and all the members of the Royal Family. Let our rulers be such as fear Thee; men of truth, and hating covetousness, that righteousness may be the stability of our times.

Into thy hands we now commit our spirits; grant that we may lie down, and none make us afraid. Give us the sleep of thy beloved; and when we awake, let us still be with Thee. Take also under thy care all whom we love, and let thy blessing rest upon them. All this we humbly beg for Jesus Christ's sake. Amen.

[MORNING.] NINETEENTH WEEK.—FRIDAY. [EVENING.

READ IN HOLY SCRIPTURE EXODUS XL. 1—16. READ IN HOLY SCRIPTURE ST. LUKE XVIII. 15—30.

O GOD, the Father of our Lord Jesus Christ, for thy mercy shown to us as a family, and as individuals, during the past night, we praise Thee. We bless Thee for preservation from numberless evils. We bless Thee for food, raiment, health, friends. Above all, we bless Thee for the gift of thy Son, to be unto us both a sacrifice for sin, and also an ensample of godly life; and for the promise of thy Holy Spirit to guide us into all truth.

We confess ourselves most unworthy of all this mercy and love. We are sinners, great sinners. Oh, be not extreme to mark what we have done amiss. Blot out as a cloud our transgressions, and as a thick cloud our sins. Pour out upon us this morning thy Holy Spirit. Raise up thy power, and come amongst us, and with great might succour us. Keep constantly before our minds to-day the remembrance of thy great love, and let it constrain us to avoid all sin, and to seek in word and work to glorify Thee. In all the manifold temptations to which we may be exposed to-day, be Thou with us, and strengthen us to resist and overcome them. In all the troubles that may befall us to-day, be Thou with us. Give us comfort, and a quiet mind. Enable us to see thy hand in all, and to believe that all is well. In all the difficulties in which we may be placed to-day, be Thou with us. Give us counsel and guidance; deliver us from impatience; help us to cast all our care upon Thee, and then quietly to wait for the way of escape which Thou wilt open to us.

And especially we pray Thee to make us useful to others to-day. By word and by example, help us to point them to Jesus. May we ourselves live, and speak, and act as those who have been separated to be thine own. May we ever show by our conduct that we have taken Christ for our Master and our Friend; that we are really resting upon Him as our wisdom, our righteousness, our sanctification, and our redemption; and that we have a good hope that hereafter we shall live and reign with Him.

Bless, O God, all our dear relatives and friends. Make them all thy children by adoption and grace.

Bless our beloved Queen, our rulers, and our country generally. Let peace and concord abound, and hasten that glad day when thy name shall be magnified throughout the whole world, and when the knowledge of thy glory shall cover the earth even as the waters cover the seas.

Pardon, O Lord, the imperfections of these our prayers, and do exceeding abundantly for us above all that we can either ask or think, for his sake in whose merits alone we trust, even Jesus Christ, thy dear Son, our Saviour. Amen.

WE thank Thee, O Lord, for the encouraging truth that the things impossible with men are possible with Thee. We adore Thee, O Christ, the Son of the living God, for having lived as man among men, and for having died for us men, and for our salvation. With the simplicity and confidence of children, may we receive thy kingdom into our hearts, accept thy rule, and cheerfully sacrifice ourselves and our all to thy will. May thy command be our law; thy will our rule. Take away sin from our hearts, that it may never separate us from Thee.

Help us, O Lord, ever rightly to appreciate the realities of eternity. Having the eye of faith fixed on things which are not seen, may we rise superior to the present world, and be ever ready to count all things but loss if we may gain Christ. Whenever the world would allure us from Thee, help us then, with a firmer hold and a stronger will, to cleave to Thee as our chief good, our joy, and our all.

O Lord our God, Thou art holy, but we are vile and sinful. With penitent hearts would we come to Thee, confessing our faithlessness. We mourn over our wilfulness, waywardness, and selfishness. Bestow upon us sincere sorrow for sin. Inspire us with that faith that will enable us to cast our burden of sin on Jesus Christ the Saviour. Notwithstanding our forgetfulness of Thee and our rebellion against Thee, reveal to us again thy mercy in Christ Jesus. O Thou Eternal Spirit, come now into our hearts, and bear thy witness to our acceptance with God. Chase away all darkness from our minds, and all doubt from our hearts, and fill us with thy glorious light. Be our Sanctifier, by sprinkling our consciences with the precious blood of atonement, that we may be the consecrated servants of Christ for ever.

And now, Lord, at the close of another day, we render Thee anew the homage of our hearts. Thou art worthy to be praised by all, but more especially by us, on whom Thou hast conferred so many benefits. We praise Thee that thy watchful eye has been upon us, and thy gracious hand underneath us, to protect and uphold us through the perils and duties of the day. Extend to us and ours the same loving care throughout the watches of the night, and may the morning find us with vigour renewed, and with a will more resolute than ever to love, and serve, and obey Thee, the God of our life. Let it please Thee, O Lord, to accept this our offering of praise, and to hear and answer our united supplications, for the alone sake of Jesus Christ, our only Mediator and Redeemer; and to the Father, Son, and Spirit be endless praise. Amen.

[Morning.] **NINETEENTH WEEK.—SATURDAY.** [Evening.]

READ IN HOLY SCRIPTURE EXODUS XL. 17—38.

GOD of our fathers, the God of Abraham, Isaac, and Jacob, the God and Father of our Lord Jesus Christ, bend thine ear to our morning prayer. Thou that sittest between the cherubim, shine forth. In the name of Jesus we would now enter within the vail, rejoicing to think that thy grace shines upon us from our Lord, the true mercy-seat. Give us faith to see the blood sprinkled upon that mercy-seat, and so to come boldly to the throne of grace. Lord Jesus, be thou our High Priest at God's right hand; bear our names upon thy breast-plate before Him, and grave them on the palms of thy pierced hands. And do Thou, blessed Comforter, teach us to pray.

We feel it to be a good thing to give thanks unto the Lord, and to sing praises unto thy holy name, O Most High. For making us so fearfully and wonderfully, with hands to work, and minds to think, and hearts to love, great Creator, we thank Thee. For opening thy hand, and satisfying the desire of every living thing, and for giving us day by day our daily bread, great Preserver, we thank Thee. For the light of the Gospel, for the gift of thy Son, for the grace of thy Spirit, Father of mercies, we thank Thee.

We praise Thee, O precious Redeemer, that when Thou tookest upon Thee to deliver man, Thou didst not abhor the Virgin's womb; and that when Thou hadst overcome the sharpness of death, Thou didst open the kingdom of heaven to all believers.

We praise Thee, Spirit of the living God, for striving with our hearts; for translating those of us who believe out of darkness into the kingdom of God's dear Son; for bearing with all our waywardness and with all our wickedness, and for still continuing to bring to our remembrance the words and works of our Saviour.

And now, holy Father, take us under thy care for the day. Let not the work of the world hinder us from working out our salvation with fear and trembling, but keep us always mindful that one thing is needful. If troubles and perplexities should come, help us to cast all our care upon Thee, and in our hours of pleasure be Thou our chief joy.

Temptations are very near, but do Thou, the good Shepherd, make us thy sheep, and keep and defend us from all the power of the enemy.

Grant that very often, in the midst of business or of pleasure, our hearts may ascend in prayer to Thee, though it be but for a moment;

"And help us this and every day
To live more nearly as we pray."

We ask it for Jesus' sake. Amen.

READ IN HOLY SCRIPTURE ST. MATTHEW XX. 1—16.

O MOST merciful God and Father, who art rich in mercy towards all who call upon Thee through thy dear Son, we beseech Thee, for his sake, to look upon us with favour, and to give us thy blessing. We can do nothing good of ourselves. We are utterly without strength. Sin taints and defiles all our actions. We desire, therefore, to humble ourselves beneath thy mighty hand, and to seek for pardon through the atoning blood of Christ. Oh, renew in us a right spirit, and teach us to walk in thy holy fear all the days of our life.

We bless Thee for having graciously preserved us during the past day, and for again permitting us to draw near to thy throne of grace. Give us prayerful hearts. Enlighten our eyes, that we may understand thy blessed Word. Help us to obey its precepts, and hide them in our memories, that we may not sin against Thee. Show us more perfectly that to be truly happy and useful upon earth, we must follow in the steps of Christ's most holy life, and seek to have the mind which was in Him. Set our affections on things above, that we may approve ourselves as his disciples, and be willing to take up our cross. Strengthen us, that we may never shrink from discharging our duty, whether towards God or towards man, and assist us to commend thy truth by the consistency of our lives and the purity of our speech. May our light so shine before men, that we may convince them that godliness is profitable for all things, and may persuade them to seek after the one thing needful.

Preserve us from a spirit of envy. May we always have grace to believe that Thou art good, and doest good. Keep us, O Lord, from an evil eye and proud heart, lest we convert thy mercies into occasions of discontent, and murmur against Thee. Give us that wisdom which cometh from above, and incline us to commit our way unto Thee with the confidence of thine adopted children. Confirm our faith in Christ, and make us ever thankful for that great love wherewith He loveth us. May no temptation from without, or indwelling frailty, separate us from Him, lest we become barren and unfruitful. Sanctify us by thy Holy Spirit, that we may daily grow in grace, and walk worthily of Thee, and do Thou keep us by thy power through faith unto salvation. Let thy fatherly hand ever be over us as a family, and over all whom we love. Guide us in our going out and coming in from this time forth and for evermore. Defend us this night under the shadow of thy wing, and grant us sweet repose, that we may be refreshed for the spiritual duties and engagements of the morrow, through Jesus Christ thy Son, our Saviour. Amen.

[MORNING.] **TWENTIETH WEEK.—LORD'S DAY.** [EVENING.]

READ IN HOLY SCRIPTURE HEBREWS V.

LORD God of Hosts! thanks to thy holy name that we see the light of another Sabbath. On this holy day of sweet and sacred rest Thou dost call us once more to special communion with our own hearts, with thy people, and with Thee. May we be in the Spirit on this Lord's day; and let this blessing be enjoyed by all thy people.

O Lord, we are unworthy to appear in thy presence and engage in thy service. Our nature is corrupt, our heart is depraved; our spirit, speech, and behaviour all testify against us. Alas! we are stamped and stained with proofs of our sinfulness. Wherewith shall we come before the Lord, and bow ourselves before the high God?

Our trust is in our great High Priest, who died the just for the unjust, that He might bring us to God. Eternal thanks for Him whom Thou hast appointed to this office on our behalf. We have not a high priest who cannot be touched with the feeling of our infirmity. He knows our frame, and grants us his sympathy and succour. Through Him we draw near with humble boldness to thy throne of grace. Our dependence is on his finished work—his prevailing intercession: We plead his name; we rely on his merits; we trust in his power and promise. We rejoice that He is the author of eternal salvation unto all them that obey Him. Behold, O God, our Shield, and look upon the face of thine Anointed. Grant that we and our services this day may be accepted through our great High Priest, Jesus Christ our Lord and Saviour.

O our Father, have compassion on us, for we are ignorant and compassed with infirmities. Give us pardon and peace through the blood of the Lamb, that we may worship Thee in sincerity and earnestness. May our sorrows, as well as our mercies, be sanctified to us; and, like thy beloved Son, may we learn obedience by the things which we suffer.

O Lord, we beseech Thee, bless abundantly the provisions of thy house on this thy day. May thy ministers have a double portion of thy Holy Spirit to aid them in their great work; and may we go to the sanctuary hungering and thirsting for thy grace. Alas! we have not prized our privileges, nor improved them as we ought. We have been dull of hearing; we need to have line upon line, and to be instructed again and again in the first principles of the oracles of God. This day meet with us, and bless us. As new-born babes, may we desire the sincere milk of the word. May we grow in faith and love, in meekness and spirituality, in activity and usefulness, and every gift and grace, till, through thine infinite mercy, we reach the measure of a perfect man in Christ Jesus our Lord. We ask every blessing for his sake. Amen.

READ IN HOLY SCRIPTURE ST. MATTHEW XX. 17–34.

O GOD, our Father, let thine eye be upon us in mercy, and thine ear be attentive to our prayer. We thank Thee that the way is open to thy footstool, and that through thy dear Son we may make known our requests unto Thee, and that Thou wilt receive our praise. Quicken in us by thy Spirit such a deep sense of thy love, that we may delight to draw near to Thee as thy children, and hold communion with our Father in heaven.

Especially, O God, may we have the grace to value thy Sabbaths, and highly to prize the opportunities which they bring to us. We confess that our frequent misuse of thy gifts might justly cause Thee to withhold them. Could we read the secrets of the heart as Thou hast read them, and recall all which Thou hast seen in us this day, of sin and irreverence, and forgetfulness, and formality, we should be ashamed of ourselves before Thee. How unmindful have we been of thy majesty! How little have we been conscious of thy presence. How cold have been our praises! How little have we felt of the sinfulness over which our lips have mourned, or of our need of the grace for which we have asked. Have compassion upon us, O our God; bear with our many infirmities, and forgive us all the sins of thy holy day. And, oh, renew us by thy Holy Spirit. Kindle within us more heavenly affections. Awaken in us purer and loftier desires. Give us, we beseech Thee, a spiritual mind, with its life and peace. And grant that as we think of our Redeemer's sufferings, and the life-long cross of trial which He bore, we may cheerfully bear our cross after Him; and if called to drink of the bitter cup of his people, may we not murmur, but count it all joy to be partakers of his sufferings. Correct all our blind and selfish desires, and enable us with humility and contentment to receive all thy gifts, and to use them as for Thee, the Giver.

Bless, O Lord, all the ministrations of thy Word, whether read or preached, this day, to ourselves or to others. We trust that it has been sown in many prepared hearts, and that, by the accompanying power of the Spirit, it may be glorified in the salvation and spiritual prosperity of many souls. Give, we beseech Thee, a double portion of blessing to all who have been prevented in thy providence from worshipping in the assembly of thy people, and enrich them with thy heavenly grace.

Let thy guardianship and care be on us for the night. May we and all who belong to us rest in peace beneath thy sheltering wing, and be raised in the morning strengthened to serve Thee in the duties of another day. Hear us, and answer us, for Jesus Christ's sake. Amen.

[134]

[Morning.]   TWENTIETH WEEK.—MONDAY.   [Evening.

READ IN HOLY SCRIPTURE LEVITICUS X.

READ IN HOLY SCRIPTURE 2 CORINTHIANS IV.

O GOD, who art of purer eyes than to behold iniquity, may we draw near to Thee by the new and living way which Thou hast consecrated for us.

While encouraged, by the promises of thy Word and the mediation of Christ, to come boldly unto the throne of grace, may we come with the boldness becoming a conviction of our guilt and a sense of our unworthiness, tempered by considerations of thine unsearchable greatness and perfect purity.

May our devotion be kindled with fire from the altar of our God, find a place in the golden censer of our great High Priest, and, presented with the prayers of all saints, be an offering of a sweet-smelling savour, acceptable to Thee through Jesus Christ.

It is of thy mercies that we are not consumed for having so often come before Thee in our worship with the strange fire of formality, self-righteousness, and a worldly mind. How, then, can we sufficiently adore thy long-suffering towards us, that a fire has not been kindled in thine anger, and come forth from thy presence, to consume us for our heinous sins against the authority of thy law and the mercy of thy Gospel?

We pray that our sins may be all forgiven for the sake of Christ, our paschal Lamb, who suffered the Just for the unjust. Purify and refine us by the Spirit of burning, the fire of thy Word, and the furnace of affliction.

Help us to learn wisdom from the conduct of thy servant Aaron, and enable us, like him, meekly to bow at all times to thy righteous judgments.

May we keep ourselves unspotted from the world dead in trespasses and sins. When corrected for our sins, may we be silent and submissive under the correction, and be quickened by it to serve Thee in newness of life. [Be gracious to our dear children, and convert them. Let not one of them live or die offering strange fire on thine altar; but let the beauty of the Lord our God be upon them, that, satisfied early with thy mercy, they may rejoice and be glad all their days.]

Help us this day to walk in the fear of God, and in the comforts of the Holy Ghost. Help us, in our intercourse with the world, to adorn the doctrine of God our Saviour in all things. Hold Thou us up, and we shall be safe; be our Arm every morning, and our Salvation in every time of trouble. Deliver us from every evil work, and preserve us unto thy heavenly kingdom. Let these our prayers, O Lord, be acceptable unto Thee, through Jesus Christ thy Son, our great High Priest, who ever liveth to make intercession for all who come unto Thee through Him. Amen.

HOLY and Divine Spirit, graciously quicken our minds, and abstract our thoughts from all worldly objects and cares, while we approach thy throne of grace to present our evening prayer.

We desire with gratitude to express our thanks for the mercies of the closing day. Thine hand hath led us, thy right hand hath holden us. We meet in peace and safety after the cares, and fatigues, and dangers of the day. We remember that our times are in thy hand, and to thy unwearying love we owe our comforts and mercies, and the special privileges that surround us at this time. Bring home to our hearts, gracious Father, the daily lessons taught us by thy providence, and sanctify to us the truths we have read from thy precious Word. We bless Thee for the holy ministry, and for all the gracious blessings which it has conferred upon the children of men. Oh, may all thy servants be inspired with the same Spirit as the apostle Paul, and preach the same Gospel, and find their joy and crown of rejoicing in the salvation of souls, and in the edifying of thy Church.

Pardon, we beseech Thee, O Lord, our manifold sins. Who knoweth how oft he offendeth against Thee? Cleanse Thou us from secret faults, and deliver us from every evil way; let no unholy temper, thought, or affection have dominion over us. We implore Thee to give us a clean heart, and put a right spirit within us, that we may walk by faith in Christ, and daily overcome evil with good.

O Lord, suffer not the business we are engaged in, or our home duties, or the pleasures of this world, to occupy our minds, to the exclusion of Thyself and of eternal things. Daily correct our tendency to worldly-mindedness, and increase our faith in the Gospel of thy Son our Saviour, that, strengthened by thy grace, we may seek first the kingdom of our God and of his righteousness. Sanctify to us the troubles and disappointments of life; may we have thy promises to cheer us, and thy peace dwelling in our minds.

Permit us to plead with Thee on behalf of our country. Shed thy choicest gifts on our beloved Sovereign, and on every member of the Royal Family. Give wisdom and uprightness to our senators, and bless the poor of our land; deliver them from want, and feed them with the bread of life. Forgive our national sins; promote affection and amity among all Christians; visit our churches with the showers of blessing, and increase their zeal for thy glory. Be our defence this night. Into the hands of our covenant God we commend our spirits, and all we ask is for Jesus' sake. Amen.

[135]

[Morning.] **TWENTIETH WEEK.—TUESDAY.** [Evening.

READ IN HOLY SCRIPTURE LEVITICUS XVI. 1—22.

READ IN HOLY SCRIPTURE ST. LUKE XIX. 1—10.

O LORD God, our heavenly Father, we rejoice in the renewed tokens of thy constant love. We would receive all thy mercies with thankfulness, acknowledging Thee as our Benefactor, and beseeching Thee for grace to show forth thy praise, not only with our lips, but in our lives.

Suffer not, we pray Thee, the daily recurrence of thy goodness to us to lessen the impressions of our obligation and responsibility to Thee. May we be humbled under a sense of our utter unworthiness to receive the least of all thy mercies. May we remember with adoring gratitude the mediation of thy beloved Son, our Redeemer, by whose meritorious obedience and atoning sacrifice we are brought nigh to Thee, to receive the blessings of thy providence, as well as the riches of thine heavenly kingdom.

Accompany, we pray Thee, with the illumination of thy Holy Spirit, the reading of thy holy Word. May we this morning have spiritual discernment of the Lord Jesus Christ, our Saviour, as the one High Priest of our profession. May we all look unto Him with a believing, contrite heart, and be saved. We acknowledge our manifold transgressions, the imperfection and evil which we bring with us to this service of praise and prayer. O our God, we are unable of ourselves to make atonement for sin; but we plead the one sacrifice of Christ, which taketh away sin. May our sins through Him be so forgiven as to be found no more for ever.

Grant unto us this day, O Lord, strength to fulfil our duties. Prosper Thou the work of our hands; sustain us in the hour of temptation, and suffer not the evil of the world to obtain the mastery over the affections of our heart, or the purposes of our mind. If called to endure affliction, grant us cheerful submission; and if called to witness the sorrows of others, help us to sympathise with and to alleviate them.

Exalted Saviour, walk with us this day, as our guide, our pattern, our counsellor, and our defence; and aid us to serve Thee. Should occasion offer, strengthen us to speak the word in season, that sin may be reproved, and the power of thy salvation may be revealed.

Remember with thy choicest favour the members of our family; convert and save the ungodly; strengthen the faith of those who believe. Bless our neighbourhood with increase of light, even the Gospel of Christ, who is the light of the world. Let his light shine more and more. Mercifully fulfil thy promises in our experience as a family. May thy favour be our portion; may thy blessing be our continual joy. Hear these our prayers, for Jesus Christ's sake. Amen.

O LORD God Almighty, the Author and Giver of every good and every perfect gift, we thank Thee for all the blessings of the past day. Thou hast supplied our wants by thy fatherly bounty and love. Thou hast restrained us by thy preventing grace, and we are now permitted to read thy holy Word, and to offer up our prayers to Thee for the forgiveness of all our sins.

We thank Thee that Thou art as willing to receive sinners now as Thou wast in the days of thy incarnation, when Thou didst bring salvation to the house of Zaccheus. Make us as anxious to see Thee, and as willing to receive Thee, as this penitent publican; and make us as willing to show the sincerity of our repentance by acts of benevolence and charity; and oh, let salvation come to this house. We rejoice to know that the Son of Man is come to seek and to save that which is lost. We are lost, by our wanderings, and unfaithfulness, and sin: do Thou save us. Give us faith in Jesus Christ, that we also may become sons of Abraham, who believed God, and it was counted to him for righteousness. Thus let us have peace with Thee, and lie down upon our beds with consciences void of offence before God and man. Preserve us from all the evils and dangers of the night. Give thine angels charge concerning us, that they may watch around our beds, as they have been about our path. Keep our house from fire, and the attacks of wicked men. Keep our bodies from disease and death, and refresh and strengthen us by sleep for the performance of the duties of the coming day.

Have mercy on the houseless wanderer, the destitute, and poor. Give support and shelter to the distressed. Be very gracious to the sick, who are tossing to and fro upon beds of languishing; comfort and sustain them in their suffering and weakness. Prepare the dying for death; cheer them in this last stage of their earthly journey; in the eveningtide let it be light about them. Mercifully defend and guide all who are far away upon the sea, pursuing their course over the dark, and trackless, and perhaps stormy waters. Be Thou their light and their help, and bring them in safety to the desired haven. Bless the members of our families, thy whole Church, and the world at large. Oh, hasten the time when the clouds and darkness of the night of sin shall be chased away by the rising of the Sun of Righteousness with healing in his wings; when the Day-dawn and Day-star from on high shall bring in the morning of a glorious day, and when all shall know Thee from the least unto the greatest. We humbly but confidently commit ourselves to thy care, and present ourselves and our prayers to Thee, in the name of Jesus Christ our Lord. Amen.

[Morning.] **TWENTIETH WEEK.—WEDNESDAY.** [Evening.

READ IN HOLY SCRIPTURE HEBREWS X. 1—22.

O LORD God, our God and Father in Jesus Christ, Thou art glorious in holiness, fearful in praises, doing wonders. Thou art of purer eyes than to behold iniquity; and yet Thou hast opened for sinful man a path of return to Thyself, by giving Jesus to be the new and living way. We bless Thee that we have boldness to enter into the Holiest, into thy sacred and awful presence, by his most precious blood.

We come, gracious Father, for cleansing: wash away, we pray Thee, every guilty stain in that Fountain opened for sin and uncleanness. Grant that our hearts may be sprinkled from an evil conscience, so that we may continually rejoice before Thee. We come to Thee for enlightenment: cause us to understand and to know that by one offering Jesus hath perfected for ever them that are sanctified. We come to Thee for grace to obey thy will in all things: may thy Holy Spirit put thy laws into our hearts, and write them in our minds. We come to Thee for steadfastness: make us bold to confess Christ before men. Keep us from ever being ashamed of Him and his words. Help us to endure even unto the end. And do Thou, by the continual supplies of thy grace, stablish, strengthen, settle us.

Grant, we pray Thee, that this day we may adorn in our lives the doctrine we profess. Help us, O our God and Father, to do the truth. Make us sincere, and without offence, and earnest in everything. Put away from us the way of lying. Cause us to hate every false way. May our deeds as well as our words be according to the truth; and help us, in all simplicity and godly sincerity, to follow the example of the Lord Jesus Christ.

Graciously bless us, O our God, in our daily work. May we do everything in the name of the Lord Jesus Christ, giving thanks to God and the Father by Him. And should temptation come, or perplexities embarrass us, oh, hold Thou up our goings in thy paths, that our footsteps slip not.

We desire, most merciful and gracious God, to remember before Thee all thine unspeakable goodness to us. Day by day Thou renewest thy mercies; Thou makest the outgoings of each morning and evening to rejoice. We thank Thee for food and raiment—for family comforts and blessings—for our many temporal mercies; but, above all, for the gift of Jesus Christ thy dear Son, and in Him for the means of grace and the hope of glory. May we show our thankfulness by lives devoted to thy service in the Gospel of thy Son.

Bless our dear relations and friends. Take them this day into thy holy care and keeping; and do for us and them more than we are able to ask or think, for Jesus Christ's sake. Amen.

READ IN HOLY SCRIPTURE ST. LUKE XIX. 11—27.

O ETERNAL God, the Creator and Preserver of all mankind, Giver of all spiritual grace, the Author of everlasting life, be pleased at this time to hear us from heaven thy dwelling-place; and when Thou hearest, forgive.

Thou, O Lord, knowest us altogether. Thou knowest each household, and its wants—each worshipper, and his desire—each bosom, and its sorrows—each heart, and its besetting sin; and Thou art able to supply all our need. Pour down upon us, we beseech Thee, the abundance of thy mercy, forgiving us those sins whereof our conscience is afraid, and giving us those good things which we are not worthy to ask but through the merit and mediation of Jesus Christ thy Son, our Lord.

We confess before Thee that we are unprofitable servants. Entrusted with precious talents, how often have we neglected to occupy them for Thee! What cause have we to lament many things done this day which we ought not to have done, and many things left undone which we ought to have done! Our faith has been wanting in simplicity and in sincerity, and therefore we have failed to glorify Thee in our bodies and in our spirits, which are thine. O Lord, we pray Thee, give us an increase of faith. Cause us to feel more deeply and constantly that we are not our own, that we have been bought with a price; and constrain us, by the love of Christ shed abroad in our hearts by the Holy Spirit, to walk in the way of thy commandments, and to adorn the doctrine of God our Saviour in all things. Suffer us not to be deceived, or to deceive ourselves, with false thoughts of Thee and thy service, as if Thou wert a hard Master; but grant that we may grow in grace and in the knowledge of our Lord and Saviour Jesus Christ.

We would remember before Thee all for whom we ought to pray. Give special grace to those who are called to occupy high places; preserve them from the perils of earthly greatness, and dispose them to walk humbly with their God. Visit with thy fatherly consolations all that are in danger, necessity, and tribulation. Sanctify trial and discipline to those who are exercised thereby. Bless us as a family. Let it ever be our united resolve, "As for us and our house, we will serve the Lord." Regard with thy favour the aged and the young, especially those among our own dear relatives. Grant that the aged may come to the grave in righteousness, as a shock of corn in its season, and that the young may grow up in godliness like the willows by the water-courses.

These our supplications and prayers, together with our thanksgivings for past unnumbered mercies, we humbly present in the name of Jesus Christ our Lord. Amen.

MORNING.] TWENTIETH WEEK.—THURSDAY. [EVENING.

READ IN HOLY SCRIPTURE LEVITICUS XXIII. 1—22.   READ IN HOLY SCRIPTURE PSALM CXIX. 73—88.

O LORD our God, we present ourselves before Thee this morning to ask thy blessing, and to acknowledge thy mercy. Thou hast dealt very graciously with us, and we beseech Thee now to give us thy Holy Spirit, and to enable us to pour forth our hearts before Thee in sincerity and truth. Grant, we beseech Thee, that we may live this day as those who are bought and cleansed with the precious blood of Christ. Six days we know we should work, always remembering whose servants we are, and that for every thought, and word, and act, we must give account to God. We know not what a day may bring forth, nor how a night may terminate; but we pray that both morning and evening, and all day long, our hearts may be sprinkled with the atoning blood of Christ, and that we may neither be injured by man nor by Satan.

To Thee we desire to present our bodies a living sacrifice, holy and acceptable through Christ. To Thee we would present the first-fruits of all our increase, and the first thoughts and desires of each day. We acknowledge that we are very sinful, and that the leaven of wickedness has been working within us; but we implore Thee to forgive us our sins, and to cleanse us from all unrighteousness. Strengthen, we beseech Thee, O Lord, the hands of all who are engaged in thy service, and grant that those who go forth weeping, bearing precious seed, may come again rejoicing, bringing their sheaves with them. We would especially pray for the peace of Jerusalem, and the ingathering of all her scattered tribes. Bless all societies whose object it is to send forth labourers into the harvest, and grant that the kingdom of Christ may soon be established.

Help us to feed more and more upon thy holy Word, receiving all Thou hast revealed with the simplicity and trustfulness of little children. May all who read thy Word be thereby strengthened and refreshed as by the bread of life. Enable us so to hide thy truth in our hearts, that we may not sin against Thee. Thou knowest, heavenly Father, the coming events of each day, its duties, temptations, and cares. Give us, we pray Thee, such a supply of thy grace, that we may walk according to thy will, and glorify thy name. Whilst remembering One, who though he was rich, yet for our sakes became poor, may we think with compassion upon the needy, and relieve their distress; and do Thou, whose blessing alone maketh rich, direct us with thy counsel now, and in the time of harvest gather us into thy heavenly garner, for Jesus Christ's sake, in whose name we ask, both for ourselves and all who are dear to us, these and all other mercies which Thou seest good for us. Amen.

WE worship and bow down, and kneel before Thee, O Lord, our Maker; for Thou art our God, and we are the people of thy pasture, and the sheep of thy hand. Thou art a great God, and of great compassion. We thank Thee for the many gifts of thy bounty during the hours of this day; but, above all, for thine unspeakable gift of our Lord Jesus Christ.

We acknowledge that we have gone astray like lost sheep. How often have we ungratefully forgotten Thee, and forsaken thy way! But we return unto the Shepherd and Bishop of our souls, who gave Himself for us to redeem us from all iniquity. Father, forgive us, for thy dear Son's sake.

Remembering all thy benefits, we dedicate our whole body, and soul, and spirit unto Thee, a living sacrifice. Give us understanding, that we may keep thy precepts. Sanctify us through thy truth. Strengthen us to serve Thee with perfect hearts and willing minds.

O Thou who hast been tempted in all points like as we are, yet without sin, be our Refuge and Shield in the hour of temptation. May we overcome evil with good. May we walk worthy of the holy name we bear, and show forth the praises of Him who hath called us out of darkness into his marvellous light. If we have to endure hatred and persecution, comfort us with the assurance that Thou wilt deliver the godly out of temptation. Leave us not, neither forsake us; but perfect thy will in our souls.

We pray for all who are near and dear to us. May those who know thy love be preserved blameless unto the end, and may our unconverted relatives be brought into the fellowship of thy dear Son.

Let thy kingdom come. Prosper the work of thy universal Church. Pour out thy Spirit upon all flesh. Bring the families of men into the blessing of faithful Abraham, that Jews and Gentiles may confess that Jesus is Lord, to the glory of God the Father.

O Lord, be Thou our keeper through the darkness of the night. Preserve us from all evil: preserve our bodies and our souls: preserve our going out and our coming in from this time forth, and even for evermore; and, at last, bring us to the mansions which are prepared in our Father's house, where there is no night.

O Thou that hearest prayer, accept our evening sacrifice; and when Thou hearest in heaven, thy dwelling-place, forgive, and answer, and do: granting unto us all spiritual blessings, and supplying all our need, according to thy riches in glory by Christ Jesus. Amen.

[188]

[Morning.] **TWENTIETH WEEK.—FRIDAY.** [Evening.

READ IN HOLY SCRIPTURE LEVITICUS XXIII. 23—44.   READ IN HOLY SCRIPTURE ST. JOHN XI. 1—29.

O HOLY, holy, holy, Lord God of hosts, in whose sight the heavens themselves are not clean, how shall we, miserable sinners of the earth, presume to approach thy footstool? We bless Thee that Thou hast provided a new and living way in Jesus Christ, our great High Priest, and that Thou hast invited us to draw near, through Him, with boldness to thy throne of grace. Help us to seek Thee this morning with godly reverence, and to worship Thee in spirit and in truth. Help us, O Holy Ghost, in all our infirmities, and enable us to pray with devout sincerity of heart.

We thank Thee, O heavenly Father, that Thou hast kept us through the past night in perfect safety, and raised us up refreshed with health and strength, and surrounded with new tokens of thy providence. Teach us ever to remember with grateful hearts that all these blessings flow directly from Thee. But, above all, we thank and praise Thee for our spiritual privileges, and especially that we have been permitted once more to read a portion of thy Holy Word. May we prize its sacred teaching; may we love to meditate upon its truths. Give us grace to honour thy Sabbaths, to attend with profit all thine ordinances, to devote to thy service the first-fruits of all our labour, and to dedicate ourselves, body, soul, and spirit, to thy service. Thou hast told us to-day how thy children of old did tabernacle in booths in the wilderness. Lord, these things remind us that here we have no abiding city, that we also are pilgrims and strangers upon earth. Give us such faith in Jesus, and such confidence in his finished work upon the cross, that when our earthly tabernacle of the flesh is dissolved, we may be able to look with bright assurance to that building of God, the house not made with hands, eternal in the heavens, prepared for them that love Thee.

And now, Lord, we go forth to the duties of another day. Hold Thou up our goings in thy paths, that our footsteps slip not. Make our bodies the temple of thy Holy Spirit to-day. Purify our minds; subdue our tempers; sanctify all our conversation. In our contact with the world, keep us amidst temptation. In all our dealing, may we do unto others as we would they should do unto us. Remove all eye-service. Make us diligent in business, fervent in spirit, serving Thee, O Lord, our God, so that whether we eat or drink, or whatsoever we do, we may try and do all to thy honour and glory.

Bless our Queen and country. Bless all the faithful ministers of thy Gospel. Bless especially our dear relatives and friends; and receive us all hereafter into thine own eternal kingdom, through Jesus Christ, our Lord and Saviour. Amen.

INFINITE and everlasting God, in whom we live, and move, and have our being, whose power sustains, whose wisdom guides, whose love enriches all that thy hands have made, accept our warmest thanks for the unnumbered mercies we have this day received at thy hand. Thy very thoughts unto us, O God, how precious are they! How great is the sum of them! If we should count them, they are more in number than the sand. And yet, alas! how few have been our thoughts of Thee, how poor our services, how faint our gratitude! We have forgotten Thee, whilst Thou hast been mindful of us. Our hearts condemn us. Lord, have mercy upon us, and help us to love Thee with all our hearts, and to show forth our love by a ready obedience to thy will.

Oh that we could live as seeing Him who is invisible! Oh that we might walk with God! then should we be safe from the tempting vanities of the world. How great is our danger! How needful that we should watch unto prayer! How grave and solemn our responsibility! Lord, who is sufficient for these things? Gird us with thy strength, O thou Most High! Hide us under the shadow of thy wings.

Let thy blessing rest upon us as a family. Make every member of our household a member of the body of Christ. Let the love which binds us together here be sanctified, so that we may be companions in the road to heaven. Let us not be separated at last. To this end may we be prepared to die, trusting only in the merits of our Lord Jesus Christ.

We worship Thee, O our Saviour. Thou art the Resurrection and the Life, and hast promised that whosoever liveth and believeth in Thee shall never die. Thou art God—God manifest in the flesh. As the Christ of God Thou hast spoken; and thy words we have now read. Thou hast acted; and the story of thy deeds we have listened to with wonder and delight. Thou canst now raise us from the death of sin, as Thou didst raise Lazarus from the grave.

Have we passed from death unto life? Then strengthen our life, and lead us on to spiritual maturity. Are we, or any who are dear to us, still dead in trespasses and sins? O Lord, listen to our earnest prayer, that now thy voice may be heard, saying, "Come forth and live!" This very night may we be delivered from the bonds which have bound us, and walk forth on the morrow in newness of life. Come and visit our slumbering souls, and let there be joy here and in heaven over the spiritual resurrection of those for whom we pray. Hear us, O Lord, for Jesus Christ's sake. Amen.

[139]

[Morning.]   TWENTIETH WEEK.—SATURDAY.   [Evening.]

READ IN HOLY SCRIPTURE ISAIAH I.

O THOU all-seeing and heart-searching God, regard, we beseech Thee, the supplications of thy servants who would now draw nigh to Thee in the name of thy Son, our only Saviour. We have now read of thy judgments against thy people because of their multiplied iniquities. O Lord, make this Scripture profitable to us for correction and instruction in righteousness.

With shame we must confess that we, individually and nationally, have sinned against Thee, and grievously offended thy Divine Majesty: we have been unmindful of thy love, have set at naught thy commandments, and preferred our own wills to thine. O Lord God, by thy Holy Spirit, make us heartily sorry for all our misdoings. O Lord, in the name of Jesus Christ we come to Thee for pardon and purification. Do Thou wash us, and we shall be clean. Wash us in the precious blood of Jesus, that we may become without spot or blemish in thy sight.

And, O Lord, help us against all the sinful tempers and habits which most beset us. Through thy grace may we be enabled to cease to do evil, and to learn to do well. May we use all our members as instruments of holiness unto Thee, and delight to run in the way of thy commandments.

Do Thou renew us in the spirit of our minds, and dispose us to love our neighbours as ourselves. May we bear one another's burdens, and be kind, tender-hearted, loving, and forgiving towards all men. O Lord God, for Jesus' sake help us thus to live; and make all things belonging to the flesh to die in us, and all things belonging to the Spirit to live and grow in us.

We pray, also, for the rising generation. God of love, grant that they may grow up to be a seed whom Thou shalt bless. Daily renew them by the Holy Spirit, and make them, as they increase in stature, to increase in wisdom and in favour with God and man. We pray for all connected with us, that they may be taught of Thee; and that true religion and piety may increase in our families and neighbourhoods.

O Lord, hear us for our country. Make us to be a people fearing Thee and working righteousness. Bless our Queen, and all the Royal Family. Do Thou counsel all their counsellors, and give them a right judgment in all things. Let thy wisdom guide our Parliament, and direct and prosper all their consultations to the advancement of thy glory, the good of thy Church, and the safety, honour, and welfare of our Sovereign and her dominions.

Heavenly Father, hear these our confessions, supplications, and intercessions for Jesus Christ's sake, our only Mediator and Advocate. Amen.

READ IN HOLY SCRIPTURE ST. JOHN XI. 30—46.

O FATHER of mercies and God of all comfort, the Author of our life and the Giver of all good things, we adore Thee for thy gracious dealings with us this day, and again look up to thy throne in the hope of continued mercy, for our deep need. We plead the name and righteousness of thy dear Son, and pray that through his mediation, whom Thou hearest always, our supplications and thanksgivings may be accepted, and that we may have an answer of peace.

It is our comfort to know, O God, that all things that concern us are in thy hand; that in our troubles and necessities Thou art near, even when we see Thee not, and that in all thy dispensations Thou hast a purpose of mercy towards us. May we in prosperity look up to Thee in grateful remembrance of thy love, and in adversity rely, without a doubt, on thy wisdom and grace. We recall, with thankfulness and praise, the tokens of Jesus' sympathy, and the assurance that He is touched with the feeling of our infirmities, and enters into our sorrows. We recall, with thankfulness and praise, the signs of his power, in that He could not only give sight to the blind and a tongue to the dumb, but even call from the grave them that were dead. Lord Jesus, reveal unto us more clearly thy tenderness and compassion, and cause us to experience the outgoings of thy power. Increase our faith. Have mercy on our unbelief, and enrich us abundantly with all spiritual blessings. Arouse our cold hearts to greater spiritual earnestness. Give us the faith which overcomes the world, and by the power of thy Spirit raise our affections to things above. Give us increased willingness in thy service, and a constant watchfulness against all sin; and so constrain us by a sense of thy love that we may find thy commandments pleasant, cheerfully bear every cross, and patiently submit in all things to thy all-wise and gracious will. Fill us with all joy and peace in believing, and cause us to abound in hope by the power of the Holy Ghost.

We pray, O God, for a great increase of true godliness in ourselves, in all whom we love, and in the world around us. May all thy people strive, in the station which Thou hast placed them, truly and godly to serve Thee, and to adorn the doctrine of our Saviour in all things. [Give to the children of this family thy Holy Spirit, and make them, by adoption and grace, even from their early years, thy children.] Take us all into thy protection, and preserve us, if it please Thee, to see the light and enjoy the blessings of another Lord's day. May it be a day of much grace and mercy to all thy people. Hear us and help us for thy dear Son's sake. Amen.

[Morning.] **TWENTY-FIRST WEEK.—LORD'S DAY.** [Evening.

READ IN HOLY SCRIPTURE LEVITICUS XXIV. 1—16.

READ IN HOLY SCRIPTURE JOHN XI. 47—57.

MOST gracious God, we bless Thee for another day of the Son of Man. May we be in the Spirit on the Lord's day. May we reverence it as the holy of the Lord, honourable, and call it a delight; and may we be glad when they say unto us, "Let us go into the house of the Lord."

O Lord, great reverence is due unto Thee in the meeting of thy saints, and holiness becometh thine house for ever. May we be sanctified to draw nigh unto Thee, and before thy people may we glorify thy great and blessed name. Oh, send out thy light and thy truth. Let them lead us: let them bring us to thy holy hill, and to thy tabernacles. Show unto us thy beauty and thy glory, and satisfy us with the goodness of thy house, even of thy holy temple.

O Thou that dwellest between the cherubim, shine forth. Our minds are blinded through the deceitfulness of sin. Our foolish hearts are darkened; but Thou art light, and in Thee there is no darkness at all. Oh, shine in our hearts, and give us the light of the knowledge of the glory of God in the grace of Jesus Christ. Do Thou anoint thy servants, who minister in thy house, with the gifts of the Spirit. May their lips keep knowledge, that we may hear the law of the Lord at their mouth. Enable us to take heed how we hear.

O Lord, we rejoice to believe that there is meat enough and to spare in our Father's house. Feed our souls this day with that Bread of Life which came down from heaven. May He who is that Living Bread be sweet unto our taste and precious to our souls. May we experience the truth of his own saying, "The words that I speak unto you, they are spirit, and they are life." May they be profitable unto us for doctrine and for reproof, for correction, and for instruction in righteousness.

O God, let us not be forgetful hearers of the Word, but doers also of the work. When we leave thy courts, let us not leave Divine things behind us. May we give men increasing cause to take knowledge of us that we have been with Jesus, and that we have learned of Him. May we sanctify the Lord God of Hosts in our hearts, and make Him everywhere our fear and our dread. Grant especially, O our heavenly Father, that the name of our dwelling may be, "The Lord is there."

As a family, may we live together in unity, and be all made, through grace, members of the household of faith, washed, and sanctified, and justified, in the name of the Lord Jesus, and by the Spirit of our God.

These things, O God, we humbly ask in the name and for the sake of thy blessed Son; and unto Thee be all the glory. Amen.

O GOD, the Father of our Lord Jesus Christ, permit us now to address Thee. We have publicly united in worshipping Thee this day, and now we would join in household worship. May the Spirit of light and truth promised to thy Church move us as a family to address Thee aright. First of all, we thank and bless Thee for the many mercies which we have this day enjoyed. As the heaven is high above the earth, so great is thy mercy towards us. We praise Thee for the gift of thy Sabbath, and for the events of which each Lord's day reminds us. We bless Thee that Thou didst not spare thine own Son, but didst freely deliver Him up for us all. We bless Thee that Christ died for the ungodly, and we thank Thee for the inestimable blessings that become ours by his death. We acknowledge to Thee that we need the blood of Christ to cleanse us from our sin; and that nothing but such a sacrifice can make our sins, which are as scarlet, white as snow. May we all know for ourselves the preciousness and the power of the blood of Christ.

And now hear us, most holy Father, when we entreat Thee to keep us from trampling under foot the Son of God, from doing despite to the Spirit of grace, and accounting the blood of the covenant, whereby we are sanctified, an unholy thing. May Christ be revealed to us in all the beauty of his person, and the glory of his work, and be increasingly precious to us all. May we live by his death, be healed by his stripes, and be in all respects saved by the redemption that is in his blood. Let not our so frequently hearing and reading of the Saviour make our hearts too familiar with thy words about Him, but may the frequency of the contact of our minds with these things deepen the impression of their importance and value. O Lord, grant that we may receive a full blessing from the religious engagements of this closing day.

But not for ourselves alone do we pray: we intercede for all the children of God; and we pray Thee to have mercy upon all men, that all may be saved, and come to the knowledge of the truth. Have mercy upon all who have heard the Gospel to-day, and who are in danger of neglecting it. Have mercy upon all who are aroused, and are in danger of sleeping again in the insensibility of sin. In innumerable cases let the Gospel, as preached to-day, be made manifest as the wisdom of God and the power of God. May thine own people receive much blessing. O Lord God, hear our prayers, receive our confessions, accept our thanksgivings, and in thy great mercy defend us from all the perils of the night, for Jesus Christ our Saviour's sake. Amen.

[Morning.] **TWENTY-FIRST WEEK.—MONDAY.** [Evening.

READ IN HOLY SCRIPTURE LEVITICUS XXV. 1—22.

READ IN HOLY SCRIPTURE PROVERBS I.

HOLY, holy, holy, Lord God of Hosts, before whom the seraphs veil their faces, and in whose sight the heavens are not clean, behold we have taken upon us to speak unto Thee, which are but dust and ashes. We acknowledge and bewail our manifold sins and iniquities, which we from time to time most grievously have committed, by thought, word, and deed, against thy Divine Majesty. Have mercy upon us, we beseech Thee. Pardon and deliver us from all our offences, and grant us all the assurance that we are accepted in thy beloved Son.

We thank Thee, O Lord, that Thou hast caused all holy Scriptures to be written for our learning. We bless Thee for the shadow of good things to come contained in the Law, and for the better things themselves revealed in the Gospel. By thy dear Son Thou hast caused the trumpet of jubilee to sound throughout the world. Thou hast anointed Him to preach the Gospel to the poor, to proclaim deliverance to the captives, to set at liberty them that are bruised, to preach the acceptable year of the Lord. Cause every one of us, we beseech Thee, to know the joyful sound. Deliver us from the bondage of sin, and introduce us into the glorious liberty of the Gospel. We plead likewise for all our dear relatives and friends. Behold now is the accepted time; behold now is the day of salvation. Oh, cause any of them who may still be the slaves of Satan to submit to the easy yoke of that gracious Saviour whose service is perfect freedom.

And not only do we ask Thee thus to bless our own immediate friends, but we beseech Thee also to have mercy upon all men. The whole world still lieth in wickedness. Thousands in our own land are still unconverted. Millions of the heathen are still bowing down to idols. Oh, let thy Gospel be preached throughout the whole earth, and cause them that are ready to perish to come unto Him who was lifted up upon the cross that He might draw all men unto Him.

And now, Lord, at the beginning of another day we dedicate ourselves anew to thy service. Preserve us in our going out and coming in. Guard us from vain thoughts. Set a watch before our mouths, and keep the door of our lips. Grant that we may fall into no sin, neither run into any kind of danger. Let us not be slothful in business; but whatsoever we do may we do it heartily, as unto the Lord, and not unto men. Enable us to be followers of Him who was holy, harmless, undefiled, and who went about doing good; and keep us unspotted from the world.

Now unto Him that is able to do exceeding abundantly above all that we ask or think, unto Him be glory in the Church by Christ Jesus throughout all ages, world without end. Amen.

WE adore Thee, O God, as the greatest and best of beings. Almighty power and perfect wisdom belong to Thee. All things, past, present, and to come, are perfectly known to Thee. Thou lovest righteousness and hatest wickedness. Thou art good and doest good.

We adore Thee as our Creator, giving Thee thanks for all those powers of thought and reason which Thou hast graciously bestowed upon us. Teach us by thy Spirit to use them aright, and enable us to know Thee and Jesus Christ whom Thou hast sent. Teach us to live as strangers and pilgrims, who seek another country, even a heavenly.

We thank Thee, O Lord, for the revelation of thy truth and the knowledge of thy will. Enlighten our consciences, that we may know that will; and strengthen our hearts, that we may do it. And whereas even our consciences are darkened and corrupted by sin, we thank Thee for thy holy Word, for the good Law, and for thy glorious Gospel. We thank Thee not only for the promises of thy Word, but also for its threatenings. Teach us to lay them to heart, that we may flee from the wrath to come, and may watch against everything that would displease Thee. Dispose us, O Lord, to keep far away from every path which leads to destruction.

Thou hast taught us if we lack wisdom and ask of Thee, Thou wilt liberally grant it, and upbraid us not; Lord, we ask for it, and beseech Thee to bestow it. May we not be numbered with those who mock at sin. Save us from the folly of those who, while troubled and careful about many things, neglect the one thing needful, and perish everlastingly. Stir up in us, we beseech Thee, a constant diligence to make our calling and election sure. Reveal to us more clearly the things that belong to our peace.

Many and grievous have been our sins during the day. We have not loved Thee as we ought. We have often forgotten thy precepts, and neglected to do what Thou hast commanded. Our hearts have been prone to evil when we should have followed that which was good. O God, forgive us all our sins, and put them away from before Thee for ever. May we lie down to rest at peace with Thee and with all men.

Graciously incline us so to act in future that we may count all things but loss which would stand in the way between us and Christ.

For the many blessings of the past day we adore and praise thy name. Make us more grateful for all thy mercies. We implore thy protection for the night. Let the shield of thy care be around us and all who belong to us. Bestow on them and us every needful blessing, for Jesus Christ's sake. Amen.

[Morning.] TWENTY-FIRST WEEK.—TUESDAY. [Evening.

READ IN HOLY SCRIPTURE LEVITICUS XXV. 35—55. READ IN HOLY SCRIPTURE ST. JOHN XII. 1—11.

O LORD, we worship and adore Thee, for Thou art our Maker, and we are the people of thy pasture, and the sheep of thy hand. We thank Thee for thy watchful care of us during the past night, and for the mercies of this new day. The day is thine, and the night also: Thou hast prepared the light and the sun. All our blessings come from Thee, and to Thee we desire to trace them, through whatever instrumentality they have been conveyed to us: Thou art the parent source, and there is not a blessing we enjoy which we can say has been deserved by us. We are miserable sinners. It is of the Lord's mercies we are not consumed, and because his compassions fail not. Thanks be to God for redemption in the blood of Christ, even the forgiveness of sins, according to the riches of his grace. Wash us in his precious blood. Sanctify us by thy Holy Spirit; and after guiding us safely through this vain world, bring us to the land of uprightness.

Impress on our minds the lessons taught us in that portion of thy holy Word which we have now read. Make us kind and gentle towards all men, and helpful especially to the poor, the afflicted, and the stranger. Enable us to consider ourselves stewards only of all that we possess, and let us be ready to distribute, willing to communicate, since with such sacrifices God is well pleased. Implant and cherish within us that love which is the fulfilling of the law. Endow us with the Spirit of Him who, though rich, became poor for our sakes, that we, through his poverty, might be rich. As we have opportunity, let us do good to all men, especially to them who are of the household of faith. We would remember them that are in bonds as bound with them, and them that suffer adversity as being ourselves also in the body.

We bless Thee that Christ came to proclaim liberty to the captive, and the opening of the prison doors to them that are bound. May the law of the Spirit of life in Christ Jesus make us free from the law of sin and death. Enable us more and more to walk at liberty, keeping thy precepts; and, O God, break every yoke, and let the oppressed go free. Deliver the nations from the bondage of ignorance, superstition, and sin. Remember in this respect thy Word unto thy servants upon which Thou hast caused us to hope. Have respect unto thy covenant; let the day of universal jubilee dawn, and gather all the redeemed sons of Adam to the enjoyment of their forfeited inheritance.

To thy care and blessing we commit ourselves throughout the day. Help us to order all our affairs with discretion. Keep us from evil, that it may not grieve us. We ask all through Christ. Amen.

HEAVENLY and merciful Lord God, be pleased to condescend and assist us in our offering of prayer and praise; and although we be unworthy, because of our offences, to offer unto Thee any sacrifice, yet we beseech Thee to accept this our bounden duty and service, not weighing our merits, but pardoning our iniquities, through Christ our Lord.

In presenting ourselves before Thee, we supplicate the help of thy Holy Spirit, that we may know the greatness of the love of thy Son, our Saviour, Jesus Christ. We rejoice to know that He was made in the likeness of man, and became obedient unto death, that He might be the resurrection and the life of all that believe in Him. Do Thou, O Lord, so dispose our hearts in return for thy redeeming love, that we may be unfeignedly thankful, and daily strive to show forth thy praise, not only with our lips, but in our lives. May we count no gift too costly, or service too humiliating, that we may be called to do for Thee, or for the least of thy saints; but may we present ourselves a living sacrifice, holy and acceptable unto God.

We acknowledge our constant need of seeking to be preserved from every false way. May we never wickedly assume a spirit of piety, or mere outward regard for thy truth. Save us from a feigned charity and concern for the poor, and from urging this as an excuse for withholding from Thee and thy cause that which Thou requirest at our hands.

Help us, O Lord, to behold the light of the knowledge of thy glory, as seen in the face of our Saviour, Jesus Christ. May his gracious presence be with us this night. Make us a household united in love—a family that Jesus will love to honour, and with which He condescends to abide.

We humble ourselves because of the sins of our fellow-creatures, and the many occasions on which the ungodly have taken counsel against thy great name and thy people to destroy them. O Thou Father of mercy, hasten the time when the wickedness of the wicked shall cease, and the just be established in the earth.

We would not be unmindful in our prayers of our Sovereign and the Royal Family. Grant that those in authority may be so directed in their counsels, that truth and justice, religion and piety, may be established among us. Have compassion upon all the afflicted. Comfort and relieve them according to their necessities, and give them a happy issue out of all their sufferings.

To thy protection we commit ourselves. Watch over us through the night; refresh us with invigorating sleep; and finally bring us to thy rest in glory, through Christ our Saviour. Amen.

[143]

[Morning.]   TWENTY-FIRST WEEK.—WEDNESDAY.   [Evening.]

READ IN HOLY SCRIPTURE LEVITICUS XXVI. 1–20.

O LORD our God, who reignest alone in the heavens above and on the earth beneath; who art a mighty and a jealous God, and wilt not give thy glory to another, cleanse our hearts from all idolatry of the flesh and of the spirit; crucify every affection, and cast down every imagination that would displace or dishonour Thee.

And that our love to Thee may increase and abound, stir us up to a more diligent and faithful employment of our many and precious privileges. Teach us to love thy Sabbath and reverence thy sanctuary. Fill our hearts with joy in thy service, that we may feel the Sabbath a delight, the holy of the Lord, honourable, rejoicing to honour Thee, and praise thy holy name. May this earthly rest be to us a lively memorial of thy creating and redeeming love, a pledge and foretaste of the rest without end. And, oh, our gracious Father, shed abroad the fulness of the Spirit on our fainting hearts, and enable us to rejoice in the fruition of thy blessed promise, "I will set my tabernacle among you, and I will walk among you; and I will be your God, and ye shall be my people."

We confess that we are unworthy of such privileges, because we too are a stiff-necked and gainsaying generation. But though we are thus evil, Thou hast encouraged us to come to Thee in the name and through the mediation of thy wellbeloved Son. In obedience to thy command, in reliance on thy promise, we now approach Thee by the new and living way which He has consecrated for us through his flesh. We come to Thee as blood-bought sinners, pleading our Saviour's merits, bold in his all-sufficient righteousness. In Him we pray Thee to come and dwell with us, and to make us thy sanctified temple; in Him we beseech Thee to walk with us through all the toil and trial of our earthly pilgrimage, to feed us with the bread of life, to guide us by the pillar of thy presence, and to bring us safely over the waves of Jordan to the promised Canaan of rest.

But while we specially pray for thine abiding presence and love, we seek also, for our journey, all needful temporal blessings. Thou hast commanded us to be anxious about nothing; and we therefore bring to Thee all our daily trials and cares. Thy wisdom knows what is best for us; thy love desires what is best; and we cry to Thee out of our ignorance and weakness, "Thy will be done."

Finally, we pray Thee, O Lord, to extend the same blessings we have sought for ourselves to all our fellow-creatures, and to make them, with us, members of thy household, and partakers of thine eternal inheritance, through Jesus Christ our Lord, to whom, with Thee and the Holy Ghost, be all praise and honour, now and for evermore. Amen.

READ IN HOLY SCRIPTURE ST. JOHN XII. 20–36.

O ALMIGHTY and most merciful Father, who hast glorified thy Son Jesus Christ, give us, for his sake, thy Holy Spirit, that we may draw near to thy throne of grace, trusting in Him who died for us and rose again.

We acknowledge that we are unworthy to come into thy presence; but Thou hast encouraged us to look to Thee as our Father and God in Christ, and to expect through Him, not only pardon of our sins, but all needful blessings. We do come to Thee, and beseech Thee to forgive us all our past sins, and to accept our thanksgivings, and to hear our prayers.

We heartily thank Thee for all the mercies of this day. All our blessings come from Thee; may we ever receive them as from thy hand, and try to show forth thy praise, not only with our lips, but in our lives.

Help us, O heavenly Father, to follow more closely the example of our Saviour Jesus Christ. May the great desire of our hearts be to glorify thy name and to walk according to thy holy will.

We rejoice, O our gracious God, that Thou hast glorified thy Son, that all power in heaven and in earth is in his hands, that He has triumphed over the prince of this world, and that He is head over all things for his Church. Grant that we may ever look to Him, and that, strong in his strength, we may overcome all our spiritual enemies. Look down in mercy, O merciful Father, upon all who are afar off from Thee, and bring them near by thy almighty grace. May they be drawn to Him who was lifted up upon the cross, and who is now at thy right hand in heaven; and may they be kept by the power of thy grace, through faith unto everlasting salvation.

O grant that those who have the light may walk in the light; rejoicing here in thy truth and love, may they rejoice hereafter in the light of thy glory.

Look down with thy favour and pity upon the dark places of the earth. Send forth thy messengers to tell of that loving Saviour who was lifted up that He might draw all men unto Him. May a rich and abundant blessing attend the labours of all who preach the unsearchable riches of Christ. Raise up faithful men for thy work. The harvest truly is plenteous, but the labourers are few. O Thou Lord of the harvest, send forth labourers into thy harvest.

We desire now to commend ourselves, and all who are dear to us, to thy loving care. Keep us in safety through the night, and raise us up in health for thy service to-morrow; and grant that when our days on earth are ended, we may enter into the rest that remaineth for the people of God, through Jesus Christ our Lord. Amen.

[Morning.] TWENTY-FIRST WEEK.—THURSDAY. [Evening.

READ IN HOLY SCRIPTURE LEVITICUS XXVI. 21—46.   READ IN HOLY SCRIPTURE ST. JOHN XII. 37—50.

HAVE mercy upon us, O God, according to thy loving-kindness; according unto the multitude of thy tender mercies, blot out our transgressions: for we have offended against thy holy laws, and misused thy benefits. Thou art a just God, who wilt by no means clear the guilty. But Thou art a Saviour, waiting to be gracious to all who truly repent. Oh, accept the sacrifice of broken and contrite hearts, and show Thyself faithful and just to forgive our sins, and to cleanse us from all unrighteousness. For the sake of thy dear Son, who offered himself a sacrifice for us, love us freely, and receive us graciously.

Thou hast promised to give thy Holy Spirit to them that ask Thee. Oh, that He may enable us to call Thee Father, and help us to bring forth fruits meet for repentance, in a devout and holy life. Teach us to do thy will; subdue every evil passion; deliver us from temptation; inspire us with pure thoughts; shed abroad in our hearts the love of Christ; draw our affections to heavenly things, that we may be happy in serving Thee with reverence and godly fear.

When Thou art pleased to send affliction upon us, we would meekly receive the chastening of the Lord, and humbly hope for a better life to come. Heal our sicknesses, relieve our distresses, and be a very present help to us in trouble. In bereavement, may we sorrow not as others who have no hope; and in death, may our blessed Lord, who ever liveth to make intercession for us, receive our spirits, and give us an inheritance among all them that are sanctified.

Bless our dear friends and kindred. Keep them in safety, give them the joy of thy salvation, and bring them with us to thy kingdom in glory.

O God of Israel, who didst make thy chosen people joyful when they kept thy statutes; who didst restore them to thy favour when they turned from their iniquities, bless our native land. We thank Thee for our Christian privileges, and for the prosperity and peace which Thou hast ordained for us. But we have been a sinful nation, O Lord. Forgive the ungodliness which abounds, and turn the wicked from their wickedness, that we may be a holy people, and extend to all lands the truth and power of thy glorious Gospel.

We praise Thee for the goodness which has crowned our lives, and for thy care over us while we have slept. And now, as we go forth to the varied duties of this day, we beseech Thee to guide us by thy counsel, and defend us from all sin.

May we all be thine, O gracious Father, through the redemption of thy dear Son, to whom, with Thee, and the Holy Ghost, be glory and blessing, ever world without end. Amen.

ALMIGHTY and Everlasting God, the Lord of life and of death, the Creator and Preserver of all mankind, we give Thee thanks that Thou hast mercifully brought us in safety and in peace to the close of another day. We know not through what dangers we have walked to-day, but Thou hast been our perpetual guard. We know not what snares have been laid for our feet by the enemy of souls; but Thou hast kept us from falling. We know not what arrows of death have been flying past us; but Thou hast kept us from harm. Incessant as our wants have been, Thou hast richly and abundantly supplied them. Thy gifts have been around us in measureless profusion and vastness, and we have lived in thy love. We would humbly rejoice now in thy favour to us, and praise Thee for thy goodness.

But how, O Lord, shall we praise Thee for thy forbearance, thy long-suffering, thy patience, thy gentleness, and thy tenderness towards us? We know we have done amiss; but we know not how evil our lives are in thy sight, and how imperfect has been our best obedience. Pardon us, O Lord, for the sake of Jesus, whose sacrifice we plead as our only ground of hope; and oh, help us to be more watchful for the future against those things in which we know that we have failed and sinned this day. Thou hast called us to imitate thy perfection. Send down the Comforter, who is the Holy Ghost, to take of the things of Christ, and show them unto us. Help us to set Thee always before us, and to make Jesus, thy dear Son, our rule and law of life. Preserve us from spiritual blindness and hardness of heart. Increase our faith in thy Word, and in Him whom it reveals, and grant that in and through Him we may surely attain unto life everlasting.

And now, O Lord our Father, we lie down to sleep, confident of thy protection. Until Thou willest it, we cannot sleep the sleep of death. We would not fear to die; but we pray that whenever Thou shalt call us to depart we may die as the friends of Jesus, and be ready, through thy grace, to give in our account to Thee with joy. Nor would we fear the approach of trouble and sorrow, for we know that all things are in thy hands. Thou makest all things to work together for good to them that love Thee: and we are sure of thy presence in our hour of need, and of all succour that we can want. We leave all with grateful confidence in thine hands.

If there be any of our friends in trouble this night, O Lord, comfort them. Be with all who sorrow or suffer; and so cause thy kingdom to spread in the world, that all men shall speedily rejoice in thy salvation. Hear us, O Lord, through Jesus Christ thy Son, our Saviour. Amen.

[Morning.] **TWENTY-FIRST WEEK.—FRIDAY.** [Evening.

READ IN HOLY SCRIPTURE NUMBERS III. 1—13.

READ IN HOLY SCRIPTURE ISAIAH LX.

GIVE ear, O Shepherd of Israel, to our morning prayer. We are thy people, and the sheep of thy pasture. We render Thee our hearty thanks for thy manifold mercies, and present our earnest request for thy continued care.

We come to Thee without fear, and yet without money and without price. We trust in the Son of thy love. His precious blood we plead. We are sinners looking to Jesus to be sanctified. Yet Thou art not repelled by our sinfulness. Blessed Saviour! our hope is fixed on Thee. Thou art a merciful and faithful High Priest. Lead us to the throne of grace. Acknowledge us as thy brethren; and, standing by thy side, may we receive a Father's smile for thy sake.

We believe in thine infinite power and love, O Thou Friend of sinners! Grant us the full assurance of this faith. Fill our hearts with peace and joy in believing. Let us be delivered from the thraldom of worldly fears, and from the delusion of worldly hope. May we seek no other good than Thee. May we fear no evil, since Thou art with us. Hast Thou not promised that nothing shall harm us if we are thine? Hast Thou not said, "I will never leave thee, nor forsake thee?" Thou hast given us thy Son; wilt Thou not with Him also freely give us all things? Let nothing separate us from the love of Christ.

Through another day's occupations may we honour Thee. Thou ordainest our lot; make us contented therewith. Teach us what to do, and what to shun. Lead us not into the path of danger. Guard us in the hour of temptation. May we ask and have thy blessing in every act, and word, and thought. May love actuate us in everything. Banish evil tempers from our hearts. Let not angry words be heard among us. May we show that we have been with Jesus, by the meek and gentle spirit we possess. And may we lead others to the Saviour by a kind and Christ-like character. May we be a holy and devout household, of which every member is a child of God by living faith. In each heart prepare thy banquet, and make thine abode. Lord, keep us, for we are weak, and can do nothing of ourselves.

Prosper, we pray Thee, the labour of our hands. Make us diligent in every appointed duty; exact in every allotted service. Impress us with a sense of our accountability to Thee. Nothing that we have is our own. All is thine, and we are thy stewards. Soon must we give an account of our stewardship. Make us faithful, O God, in that which is least, that we may at last have an abundant entrance into thy kingdom.

Grant this, O Lord, for Jesus Christ's sake. Amen.

ALMIGHTY God, who hast revealed thyself to us in Jesus Christ, through Him, the Son of thy love, we now approach Thee, bowing down in humblest adoration at thy footstool. Day by day Thou renewest thy mercies. Thou openest thy hand, and fillest us with good.

We thank Thee, O our God, that Thou hast preserved us amidst the temptations and dangers of the day. Forgive us, we pray Thee, the sins which this day we have committed; and enable us by thy grace, in the blessed experience of thy pardoning mercy, to live soberly, righteously, and godly in this present world, glorifying Thee in our bodies and our spirits, which are thine. We ask Thee, O gracious and bountiful God, to impart to us now a sustaining sense of thy favour. May we know Thee to be our God and Father in Jesus Christ. May the joy of the Lord be our strength. Give us, we pray Thee, that peace which passeth all understanding, and which the world can neither give nor take away.

And whilst we praise and bless Thee, O Father, for thy past lovingkindness, we would remember also thy goodness and grace manifested in the bestowment of the light of the Gospel. Thou hast been gracious unto our land. Thou hast given us, and continued among us, the knowledge of thy truth. Unlike other nations, who sit even now in darkness and the shadow of death, we enjoy all the blessings of Gospel teaching and Gospel privilege. Make us thankful for thy distinguishing mercy, and dispose our hearts to render ceaseless thanks unto Thee, our God, for all thy benefits towards us.

We rejoice, gracious God and Father, at all the comforting assurances of thy Holy Word. We pray Thee, great God, to hasten the coming of thy kingdom. Let the light break speedily through the thick darkness of a guilty world, and let the Sun of righteousness arise upon the nations with healing in his wings. Bless, we humbly beseech Thee, the labours of all those who labour for Thee. Strengthen the hands of thy missionary servants; and enable them, amid all their difficulties and discouragements, to believe that in due season they shall reap if they faint not. We bless Thee, gracious God, because thy Spirit hath so often clothed their word with power. We bless Thee because Thou hast already gathered out from among the Jew and Gentile a people to the glory of thy name. O Lord, put forth thy power. Make bare thy holy arm in the sight of a gainsaying world; and hasten the time when salvation, and strength, and the kingdom of our God, and the power of his Christ, shall have finally come. We ask all for Jesus Christ's sake. Amen.

[Morning.] **TWENTY-FIRST WEEK.—SATURDAY.** [Evening.]

READ IN HOLY SCRIPTURE NUMBERS IX. 1—5, 15—23.   READ IN HOLY SCRIPTURE ST. MATTHEW XXI. 1—17.

O LORD, our Father, from everlasting to everlasting Thou art God. By thy mercy we have come to the last day of another week. Swiftly indeed do our days pass away; "So teach us to number our days, that we may apply our hearts unto wisdom."

We confess that, like the people of whom we have been reading, we have often complained and displeased Thee. Forgive us all our sins, whether of ignorance, negligence, or wilfulness; and especially do we ask thy pardon for all our murmurings and complainings against thy providence, and against thy holy will. Enter not into judgment with us, we beseech Thee, O Lord, and hear us when we ask Thee graciously to bless us with a calm and thankful heart, free from all discontent and repinings. Cause us to feel that we are not worthy of the least of all thy mercies, and then show us what great things Thou hast done for us. In all times of our tribulation may we remember that Thou dost not afflict willingly, and may we see that Thou hast not dealt with us after our sins, nor rewarded us according to our iniquities. We bless Thee, Father of all mercies, for thy wondrous patience and forbearance, and for the manifold expressions of thy fatherly kindness. We beseech Thee to grant that thy goodness may incline us to be patient and gentle toward our fellow-men, bearing their burdens, as Thou hast taught us in thy Holy Word. We ask Thee, also, to show us the right use of all thy gifts, temporal and spiritual, so that we may profit by every blessing, and avoid the abuse of the least of thy mercies. When thou dost expose us to painful changes, may we not so think of the past as to be unmindful of present blessings; but help us to be of good courage, and graciously strengthen our hearts. So renew our strength day by day, that the yoke of our duty may be easy, and the burden of our responsibilities light.

Thou knowest the position which we severally occupy in this family. Thou hast appointed our duties and the various claims that are made upon us. Do not permit us, in any despondency of heart, to say, "I am not able to bear my burden;" but rather may we say, with thine apostle Paul, "I can do all things through Christ, who strengtheneth me." Even now make us strong through the grace that is in Christ Jesus, and may we be so consciously strengthened by thy mighty power, that this day may be unto us the brightest and best of the whole week. May our path, even to the end of our lives, be that of the shining light, shining brighter and brighter unto perfect day. We ask all in the name of our blessed Saviour Christ Jesus. Amen.

O LORD God, in whom we live and move and have our being, we would present to Thee our evening sacrifice of prayer and praise. Thou hast promised that when two or three are met together in thy name, Thou wilt be in the midst of them; vouchsafe, therefore, to look upon us around our family altar. May the incense of devout and heartfelt thanksgiving ascend before thy throne. Hear our supplications, gracious Lord, and give us an answer of peace.

We would review with gratitude the blessings of this day. Thy tender mercy hast sheltered us from every danger. Thy loving bounty has supplied us with food and raiment; and now by thy goodness we are permitted to assemble together in peace and safety. Bless the Lord, O our souls, and forget not all his benefits.

Of a truth, Lord, we are unworthy of the least of thy mercies. How often have we sinned against Thee this day. How often have we grieved thy Holy Spirit by thought, and word, and deed. How much have we left undone that we might have done. The good that we would, we do not; and the evil that we would not, that we do. Have mercy upon us, most merciful Father; pardon and forgive us all our sins; sprinkle our consciences to-night with the precious blood of our dear Redeemer, and help us by thy Holy Spirit for the future, that we may be able to love Thee more and serve Thee better.

O Lord Jesus Christ, thou King of kings and Lord of lords, keep us ever mindful of thy second coming. May we learn to look for the fulfilment of thy promise, "A little while, and ye shall see me." Grant that we as a family may be like the wise virgins, our lamps trimmed and our lights burning, looking for our Lord's return. Keep us holy. Keep us watchful, so that when the cry goes forth, "Behold, the Bridegroom cometh! Behold, thy King cometh unto thee!" we may be found ready to join that triumphant multitude which no man can number, ready to sing before thy throne, "Hosanna in the highest! Blessed is he that cometh in the name of the Lord!"

Gracious God, take us under thy care this night. We commend each other affectionately unto thy mercy. Watch over our dwelling. Shield us from all danger. Preserve us from all sin. Refresh us with rest, and raise us up on the morrow, invigorated and prepared once more to go forth on the duties of the day. Remember all those for whom we ought to pray. Give them every needful good in this life, and in the life to come eternal glory. And we ask it all in the name of Jesus Christ, our only Lord and Saviour, to whom be honour and glory for ever and ever. Amen.

[Morning.] **TWENTY-SECOND WEEK.—LORD'S DAY.** [Evening.]

READ IN HOLY SCRIPTURE NUMBERS X. 11—13, 29—36.

OUR Father which art in heaven, hallowed be thy name. We come gladly, gratefully, and humbly to thy throne on this Sabbath morning, and give Thee our heartiest thanks that Thou hast blessed the seventh day and hallowed it, and that we have awaked this morning to enjoy its rest and its sacred employments. How great is thy mercy to us, O Lord! Thou hast searched us and known us; Thou knowest our downsitting and uprising, and understandest our thoughts afar off. Thou compassest our path and our lying down, and art acquainted with all our ways. How much is there in us every hour to cause Thee displeasure, and to move thine holy anger against us. It is of the Lord's mercies that we are not consumed. We acknowledge with deep shame and contrition our great sinfulness, and thy perpetual and measureless mercy toward us. Thou hast not dealt with us after our sins, nor rewarded us according to our iniquities. As far as the east is from the west, so far hast Thou removed our transgressions from us. And now, O Lord, graciously prepare us for the great duties of thy holy day. We would be spiritual worshippers, bowing down before Thee with heart and soul, reverencing thy majesty and thy glory, and rendering unto Thee the homage of creatures and the allegiance of subjects. Fill our hearts with true devotion towards Thee. We would praise Thee for thy great love to us in the blessings of thy providence and in the gift of thy dear Son. We would once more confess our sins, and seek thy gracious forgiveness. Give us a contrite spirit, and show to us again that love of Christ which shall heal us, and strengthen us, and sanctify us. We would be learners in thy blessed book of truth. Open Thou our eyes to see, and our ears to hear, and cause our hearts to perceive. May our conscience be quick and tender within us, to apply to us the condemnations or the consolations of thy truth, and to bind us to those duties to which Thou dost this day call us.

And we humbly beseech Thee to help all thy ministers to-day. Pour out upon them abundantly thy Holy Spirit. Teach them what they shall say unto thy people, and bless their word to all who hear them. Especially we pray that if any of those whom we love are in special need of the consolations or convictions of thy Word, that Thou wilt mercifully direct the Word to them with power, that they may rejoice in this Sabbath day. And now, O Lord, our Father, return Thou unto the many thousands of Israel as they rest this day from life's journeyings and fightings. Glorify Thyself in the midst of them, and make thy chosen people joyful in Thee, for the sake of Jesus Christ our Lord. Amen.

READ IN HOLY SCRIPTURE PSALM VIII.

O LORD our God, glory be to Thee for thine exceeding great love towards us in the redemption of the world by our Lord Jesus Christ. What are we, that Thou shouldest have been so mindful of us? God of love, give us to believe in the Lord Jesus with all our heart; and may we in heart and mind thither ascend where He is gone before, and with Him continually dwell. We glorify Thee Thou hast given Him a name above every name, and hast exalted Him to be head over all things to the Church, which is his body. Lord, hasten the time when at his name every knee shall bow, and in all things He shall have the pre-eminence. And O Holy Ghost, help us to give Him the affection, and obedience, and honour we ought to do.

Great God of heaven and earth, we thank Thee for all the services and means of grace of this day. May none have worshipped Thee in vain; may every prayer have been heard, and thy Word everywhere been blessed. O Lord, we pray that thy presence may have been felt in every assembly of thy people this day; that the ignorant may have been taught, the mourners comforted, the weak strengthened, and every hungry soul filled with good things. We pray that the dead in sin may have been quickened, and many a lost sheep found this day. Grant, O Lord, there may be now joy in heaven because many have repented this day; and may all thy waiting people have grown in grace, and faith, and hope, and peace, and be strengthened to go on their way rejoicing.

O Lord, we entreat Thee that all ministers may have received much good and done much good this day. May thy Word read and preached have profited very many. May all missionaries, at home and abroad, have witnessed the power of the Gospel; and grant that no Sunday-school teacher may have taught or laboured in vain. We look to Thee for the advancement of thy kingdom in the world. Do Thou give the increase.

[We pray for all the young. Lord, pour thy Spirit upon our seed, and thy blessing on our offspring, as Thou hast promised. Out of the mouth of babes and sucklings do Thou ordain strength; and make our children to glorify Thee.]

Hear us, merciful Father, we beseech Thee. For Jesus Christ's sake pardon our offences, and all the iniquity of our holy things to-day, and accept every work of faith and labour of love.

Now take us, and all belonging to us, under thy protection this night. And when we lie down to sleep in death, may we awake in the morning of the resurrection, to give Thee perfect service and praise in thine eternal and glorious kingdom, through Jesus Christ our Lord. Amen.

[Morning.] **TWENTY-SECOND WEEK.—MONDAY.** [Evening.

READ IN HOLY SCRIPTURE NUMBERS XI. 1—15.   READ IN HOLY SCRIPTURE ST. MATTHEW XXI. 16–32.

O LORD, our preserver and benefactor, we thank Thee for thy continued care and kindness. We thank Thee for the safety and rest of the night, and for the blessings of the morning. All good comes from Thee. Thou givest us, day by day, our daily bread. Many of our fellow-creatures enjoy not our blessings. Not more than others we deserve, though Thou hast given us more. Be pleased, O Lord, with these favours, to impart to every one of us a grateful sense of thy goodness. Save us from that discontent, that ingratitude, and those lusts of the flesh which the people of Israel manifested at the time of which we have been reading. Whatever Thou seest fit either to deny us, or to take from us, help us, instead of murmuring, to say, with thy servant Job, "The Lord gave, and the Lord hath taken away; blessed be the name of the Lord." And suffer us not to regard any earthly blessing as our chief good. Help us to use the world as not abusing it, since the fashion of this world passeth away. May our treasure be in heaven, and may our hearts be there also. Enable us feelingly to say :—

"Thou bounteous giver of all good,
Thou art of all thy gifts Thyself the crown :
Without Thee we are poor, give what Thou wilt;
And with Thee rich, take what Thou wilt away."

While there be many that say, "Who will show us any good?" may our desire and prayer rather be, "Lord, lift Thou upon us the light of thy countenance."

While we thank Thee for food and raiment, and all the blessings of this life, we especially thank Thee for thine unspeakable gift, and for that heavenly teaching which enables us, in some measure, to discern its value. Thanks be to God for that bread of life, of which if any one eats he shall live for ever. Thanks be to God for that water of life, of which if a man drink he thirsts no more for sin and folly. Lord, now and evermore give us that bread of life and that water of life. May we have sincere faith in the Saviour, and understand what He meant when he spoke of eating his flesh and drinking his blood. May our participation of that spiritual food strengthen us both for doing and for suffering thy holy will. Thus help us to withstand and overcome all temptations, whether of the world, the flesh, or the devil. Enable us to do justly, to love mercy, and to walk humbly with our God ; and of thy great mercy forgive us all our sins.

We offer these our petitions and thanksgivings in his name, who having died for us, rose from the dead, and ascended on high, where He now lives as our High Priest and Intercessor, to whom be given all glory, now and ever. Amen.

O LORD, our God, at the close of another day we would lift up our souls unto Thee. Every day Thou art loading us with thy benefits, and giving us new cause to make mention of thy loving-kindness in the morning, and of thy faithfulness every night. Alas, that we are so unthankful and evil! Thou art ever mindful of us, but we are continually forgetting Thee: We cannot reckon up the sum of thy gracious thoughts towards us, and neither can we count the number of our sins. Oh, give us the grace of true repentance. Lead us anew this evening to the fountain opened for sin and for uncleanness; and as we have done iniquity in time past, may we do so no more.

Help us to lay to heart the solemn lesson of the barren fig tree. Oh, let us not also be cumberers of the ground, lest we, too, fall under thy righteous curse. Teach us to remember that herein is our heavenly Father glorified that we bear much fruit. Do Thou, O God, make us to abound in those works of righteousness which are, by Jesus Christ, to thy praise and glory. Without Thee we can do nothing. Make thy grace sufficient for us. Create in us a clean heart; renew in us a right spirit; and enable us to follow holiness, without which no man shall see the Lord.

We are unworthy of the least of thy mercies, but worthy is the Lamb that was slain. We bless Thee for the promise that whatsoever we shall ask in prayer in Christ's name, believing, we shall receive. Lord, we believe ; help Thou our unbelief. Supply all our need according to thy riches in glory by Jesus Christ. Having named his name, may we learn henceforth to depart from all iniquity. As He who hath called us is holy, may we also be holy in all manner of conversation; purifying ourselves as Christ is pure, and laying up treasure in heaven.

Oh, let us not think it enough to say unto Christ, "Lord, Lord;" neither let us trust in ourselves that we are righteous. In thy sight all our righteousnesses are as filthy rags. Thou, O God, lookest not on the outward appearance, but on the heart. May our hearts be sincere before Thee; and may Christ be made of God unto us wisdom, and righteousness, and sanctification, and redemption.

And now, O Lord, we would commit ourselves into thy hand for the night. When we lie down, may we take our rest in quiet ; and when we awake, may we be still with Thee. If Thou art pleased to spare us to see the light of another day, may the life thus preserved be spent in thy service, and devoted to thy glory. And now, O Lord, turn not away thy face from us, neither our prayers from Thee, for the sake of our Lord and Saviour Jesus Christ. Amen.

[149]

[Morning.] **TWENTY-SECOND WEEK.—TUESDAY.** [Evening.

READ IN HOLY SCRIPTURE NUMBERS XI. 16—33.

ALMIGHTY and Eternal Lord God, whose kingdom is everlasting and power infinite, have mercy upon us, and assist us, that we may worship Thee in an acceptable manner.

We acknowledge ourselves to be most unworthy; and pray that our souls may be deeply humbled under a sense of thy majesty and our sinfulness. Subdue within us all self-righteous feelings, and every desire contrary to the spirit of true worship. Create within us now, contrite, and believing hearts, that we may obtain of Thee, the God of all mercy, perfect remission and forgiveness of all our sins.

We confess that we can render no true and laudable service to Thee, nor engage in any undertaking to our profit and to thy honour, unless we are taught and strengthened by thy good Spirit. Do Thou, therefore, O God of all wisdom, graciously behold us now in thy presence. Instruct us in the duties of our calling. Show the way in which Thou wouldest have us go. Strengthen us to overcome every difficulty, hindrance, and temptation that may be in our path. Help us to guard against all carelessness of mind, looseness of thought, impropriety of speech, manner, and disposition.

We praise Thee for thy revealed will, and seek grace that we may profit by the lessons it is designed to teach, and be enabled to regulate our lives by its precepts and spirit. Grant that the misconduct of thy ancient people, their punishments, and every instance of thy forbearance and love towards them, may induce in our souls a holy caution and fear lest we resist thy rule. Deliver us from the love of unholy pleasures and pursuits, and from the innumerable dangers which surround us. Keep us from uniting at any time with the multitude in rebelling against thy authority, and in resisting those whom Thou hast in thy wisdom appointed to rule, guide, and instruct us. Grant that in dependence upon Thee, we may diligently cultivate a spirit of ready obedience and submission to thy rule. May we never restrain thy work in our souls, or in those of thy servants, but fervently pray that all may be richly endowed with heavenly gifts, and that thy spirit may abide upon them, qualifying them for every good word and work. That we may be preserved in thy fear this day, help us to live in dependence upon Thee. Leave us not to ourselves, but strengthen us from on high, and prosper all our ways.

We ask these favours, and every other which thou seest we need, not in our own name, or because of any merit in us, but in the name and for the sake of our only Lord and Saviour Jesus Christ. Amen.

READ IN HOLY SCRIPTURE ST. MATTHEW XXI. 33—46.

O GOD, the Father of our Lord Jesus Christ, the Father of mercies and the God of all comfort, we praise Thee, we bless Thee, we worship Thee, we glorify Thee, we give thanks to Thee, for the goodness and mercy which have followed us all the days of our lives, and especially for the manifold tokens of thy loving-kindness this day vouchsafed unto us. Above all things, we adore Thee for thine exceeding great love to our perishing souls. Thou hast not withholden thy Son, thine only Son, from us. Thou hast sent Him down from heaven into this world of sin to die for us, the just for the unjust, that by the one oblation of Himself once offered, He might open the kingdom of heaven to all believers. May we thankfully receive thine unspeakable gift. May we reverence thy Son. May we embrace, and ever hold fast, the blessed hope of everlasting life which Thou hast given us in Him; and at length be welcomed to our Father's house in heaven.

We thank Thee, O thou great husbandman, that Thou hast planted the vineyard of thy Church in this land, and that Thou waterest it continually with the dews of heaven, causing it to bring forth fruit and bud; but Thou hast taught us that, where much is given, there will much be required. Thou lookest that we shall bring forth fruit. We acknowledge, O Lord, that we are very barren and unfruitful. The vineyard of our souls we have not kept. Spare us, we beseech Thee, and cut us not down as cumberers of the ground, but cause thy Holy Spirit to breathe upon us, that we may bring forth the fruits of righteousness, love, joy, peace, long-suffering, gentleness, goodness, faith, meekness, and temperance. May these things be in us and abound, that we may be henceforth neither barren nor unfruitful in the knowledge of our Lord Jesus Christ.

O God of Abraham, of Isaac, and of Jacob, have compassion upon those into whose privileges we, sinners of the Gentiles, have now entered. The house of Israel was thine ancient vineyard. Thou plantedst it a noble vine; but through unbelief its branches have been broken off. Thou art able to graff them in again. Lord, be favourable unto Zion. Turn away ungodliness from Jacob, and cause all Israel to be saved.

And now, heavenly Father, before we lie down to rest, grant to each of us pardon and peace through the Son of thy love. Thou hast laid Him in Zion a precious corner-stone. Make Him precious to every member of this family. May we all come to Him, and be built up as lively stones, a spiritual house, an holy priesthood, to offer up spiritual sacrifices acceptable to Thee, through Jesus Christ our Saviour. Amen.

[Morning.]   TWENTY-SECOND WEEK.—WEDNESDAY.   [Evening.]

READ IN HOLY SCRIPTURE PSALM LXXVIII. 17—39.   READ IN HOLY SCRIPTURE PSALM II.

O MERCIFUL God, turn not away thy face from us because of our many sins, but, according to thy great goodness forgive, accept, and bless us. Thou art indeed gracious, and long-suffering and full of compassion. Thou puttest away thine anger even when we have grievously offended Thee, and sparest us even when we deserve thy wrath. Glory be to thy name for all thy mercies bestowed from day to day. Forbid it, Lord, that we should receive thy grace in vain, or that having heard the warnings of thy Holy Book, we should turn to them a deaf ear. Give us a true repentance for sin, and an earnest, but child-like faith in Jesus Christ, thy dear Son. Seal us with the Holy Spirit of promise, and abundantly enrich us with the experience of thy love.

We look up to Thee, O God, for guidance and protection, for wisdom and strength this day. In the prospect of its duties and cares, of temptations arising from our calling, and dangers of which we may be unaware, we desire to cast ourselves on thy mercy. Only as Thou keepest us shall we be safe; only as Thou shieldest us shall we be kept from evil and the Evil One. Leave us not, then, O God, nor forsake us. We are frail, and prone to sin. Thou knowest all our weaknesses. Hold up our goings in thy paths, that we slip not. We would go forth to our daily duty cheerfully, in the remembrance that Thou hast placed us where we are, and that even in the lowliest station, and among the humblest occupations, thy people have an opportunity of serving the Lord Christ. Enable us in all things to serve Thee. Whatsoever we do, in word or deed, may we do it as in thy sight, who seest in secret, and will reward us openly.

Preserve us, we beseech Thee, from unbelief and disobedience. Let not our times of blessing be times of forgetfulness. May thy goodness deepen in us a spirit of repentance, and thy love to us awaken our warmest love in return. Above all, we pray for the Holy Spirit, that He may guide us into all truth, show us our deep sinfulness, and reveal unto us the preciousness of thy dear Son.

Look graciously on all who belong to us, and bestow upon them thy choicest mercies. All their circumstances are known to Thee, their trials and temptations, their sorrows and perplexities. Help them according to their need, and prosper them in body and soul. [We implore thy grace and blessing for the children of our household. Oh, teach them by thy Spirit, and cause them daily to grow in grace, and in the knowledge of our Lord and Saviour Jesus Christ.] Hear us in these our prayers; and to Thee, O God, Father, Son, and Holy Spirit, ever one God, be honour and praise. Amen.

O GOD, Thou art King of kings, and Lord of lords. Thou art glorious in strength and fearful in praises, doing wonders. Thy counsel stands fast for ever, and the thoughts of thy heart to a thousand generations. We bless Thee for raising up thy Son Jesus Christ, and giving Him glory, that our faith and hope might be in Thee. We rejoice in the belief that He is at the right hand of power, and that He must reign until all his enemies have been made his footstool. It is in his name that we draw nigh unto Thee, and his righteousness that we plead as a reason why Thou shouldest be merciful unto us. O God, forbid that we should be found among the enemies of the Lord Christ, and be broken in pieces with his iron sceptre in the day of his wrath. We would submit to his government, and glory in his cross. We would take his yoke upon us, for it is easy, and his burden, for it is light, and, as his devoted, affectionate subjects, would receive, admire, love, and adore Him, putting our whole trust in Him for salvation, and walking in all his commandments and ordinances blameless, that when He who is our life shall appear, we also may appear with Him in glory.

We give Thee thanks for thy goodness to us throughout the past day, and throughout all our past lives. All thy paths drop fatness. Thou makest the outgoings of the morning and of the evening to rejoice. How precious is thy grace! Under the shadow of thy wings we put our trust. Bless to us all the events of thy providence, both prosperous and adverse; may they all work together for our good.

We commit ourselves to the watchful care of the Shepherd of Israel this night. May He who never slumbers nor sleeps keep us and ours. May He keep our souls. May He bless our going out and our coming in, from henceforth and for ever.

We ask of Thee pardon for the sins we have this day done. May we never lie down to rest with unrepented guilt upon our consciences. Teach us continually to repair to the blood of Jesus, and make fresh application to that fountain of atoning merit which cleanses from all sin. And as we are every day coming nearer to the eternal world, so may we every day advance from grace to grace and strength to strength, till we meet Thee in thy kingdom.

May thy blessing rest upon all who are dear to us, upon all who are united to us by friendship or religion. Yet we do not confine our good wishes to them; we pray for all mankind. May the promise to the great Intercessor be fulfilled, that when He shall ask of Thee, Thou wilt give Him the nations for his inheritance. To Him, with the Father and the Spirit, be glory for ever. Amen.

[MORNING.] TWENTY-SECOND WEEK.—THURSDAY. [EVENING.

READ IN HOLY SCRIPTURE NUMBERS XIII. 1, 2, 17—33. | READ IN HOLY SCRIPTURE ST. MATTHEW XXII. 1—22.

O MERCIFUL God, the Father of our Lord Jesus, for his sake look in thy mercy upon us, who at the beginning of another day draw near to Thee. We thank Thee for the blessings of the night past, for the health and strength which Thou hast continued to us, and for all the gifts of thy love which we enjoy this day.

O Lord, forgive all our sins, and enable us to serve Thee more faithfully for the time to come. We desire, O our Father, to walk with Thee this day, trusting in thy help, realising thy presence, and doing thy will. Keep us, we beseech Thee, from all sinful words and works; may our affections be set on things above; may we, in all our ways, acknowledge Thee, and our paths be directed by Thee in all things.

Thou seest us to be set in the midst of many dangers. Oh, be Thou our help in every time of need. May we ever look to Thee, and go forward without fear, knowing that, although our enemies are many and mighty, Thou who art on our side art stronger than all. May thy promises ever cheer our hearts, and may the hope of the inheritance which Thou hast given us in Christ Jesus animate us, amidst all our dangers and temptations, to press forward on our heavenly way. Keep us from unbelieving fears: while we have no confidence in ourselves, may we have full confidence in Thee, and may we feel assured that Thou wilt make us more than conquerors through Christ our Saviour.

Grant us now the grace of thy Holy Spirit, that we may rejoice in Him who loved us and gave Himself for us. May the spiritual comforts which we enjoy be to us a foretaste of the still greater blessing to which we look forward hereafter; so that we may each day more earnestly desire the possession of that good land which Thou hast promised to us. Look, O gracious Father, on all who are near and dear to us, keep them in thy ways. May they all be one with us in Christ. May his Spirit fill their hearts, and may they ever obey thy holy commandments, and walk in thy fear and love. Keep them from the evils of this sinful world, and renew to them day by day thy grace, that they may be followers of those who, through faith and patience, have inherited the promises.

We beseech Thee, O our God, for thy whole Church militant here in earth; may all who profess and call themselves Christians be led into the way of truth, and hold the faith in the unity of the Spirit, in the bond of peace, and in righteousness of life. Keep thy people from evil; and when the enemy comes in like a flood, do Thou raise up a standard against him. Hear us, O merciful Father, for Christ's sake. Amen.

O LORD God, the Almighty and Holy God, bow down thine ear and hear us. Open thine eye of pity upon us, and regard us favourably, for Jesus Christ's sake. We praise thy name for the mercies of the day now past. We owe it to thy forbearance that we have been spared, and to thy love, which passeth knowledge, that our wants have been so graciously supplied. Above all, we thank Thee for the rich and complete provision which Thou hast made for all our spiritual needs. Thou hast provided in thy dear Son sufficiency of grace and peace for all, and Thou hast declared that whosoever will may partake freely of thy grace. Lord, forbid it that we should turn aside from thy proffered mercy, or slight and refuse the pardon and peace which Christ hath obtained for us. Oh, come and dwell in our hearts by faith. We believe; oh, help our unbelief. Clothe us with the righteousness of Christ, that every stain of guilt may be covered and put away from before Thee. Being justified by faith, may we have peace with God, through Christ our Lord.

Carry on in our hearts, we pray Thee, the good work of thy grace and love. We desire to have a clearer evidence that we are indeed clothed in the garments of salvation, and that our names are written in the Lamb's Book of Life. Prepare us for the glory and purity of thine everlasting kingdom by the sanctifying work of the Holy Spirit on our hearts and tempers, that we may purify ourselves even as Thou art pure; and being ripened in all Christian graces, may have an entrance ministered unto us abundantly into the kingdom of our Lord and Saviour. We want more love to Thee: do Thou kindle our cold and careless hearts to praise and thankfulness. We want more of thy Spirit: may He reveal his presence more clearly within us, and draw us nearer and closer to Thee. We want to have more of the mind which was in Christ: Lord, implant it within us. Enable us to see the excellency of his life in all things, and to strive daily to tread in his footsteps.

Mercifully look on all who are united to us by ties of friendship or kindred. May they be dear to Thee in and through thy dear Son. Speak to them, O God, and bring thy Word with power to their souls. Convert the unconverted among them, and establish the converted in the faith and love of Jesus. Guard us through the night from dangers, known and unknown; from the temptations of spiritual enemies, and the designs of evil men. We cast ourselves entirely on thy omnipotent care. Give us refreshing sleep, and raise us in safety, prepared to engage with cheerful obedience in the duties of another day. Grant it all, for Jesus Christ's sake. Amen.

[152]

[Morning.]   TWENTY-SECOND WEEK.—FRIDAY.   [Evening.

READ IN HOLY SCRIPTURE NUMBERS XIV. 1–25.   READ IN HOLY SCRIPTURE REVELATION VI.

ALMIGHTY God, who hast been the Leader and Guide of thy people in all generations, we bow at thy sacred footstool this morning to thank Thee for all the way through which Thou hast hitherto conducted us; to humble ourselves before Thee in confession of our manifold transgressions; and anew to commit ourselves to thy wise and merciful guidance for what yet remains to us of our earthly pilgrimage.

Thou hast never been unmindful of us. The eye of thy mercy hath been ever upon us. Thy hand hath holpen us when we were weary. Thou hast fed us with food convenient for us, and our water has been sure to us. Our enemies Thou hast discomfited before us; and Thou hast led us by ways that we had not known, and paths that we had not trod; so that we are still on the road to that land of rest and plenty of which Thou hast spoken unto us. But how does it become us to humble ourselves before Thee at the remembrance of our constant unworthiness of the very least of thy mercies, of our multiplied acts of rebellion against Thee, and of our foolish as well as wicked departures from thy ways! We would confess also how we, like thy people of old, have sinned against Thee. Have mercy upon us, O God, and forgive us our great sins. Give us, we beseech Thee, a stronger faith in Thee, a more firm reliance on the truth of thy Word, a more entire submission to all thy will concerning us. Suffer us not to forget the multitude of thy mercies towards us, and enable us to bear meekly whatever trials thy providence may see fit to allot to us, that so patience may have in us its perfect work, and we, through faith and patience, may in due time inherit the promises.

At the commencement of a new day, we would desire especially to commit ourselves to thy guardian care and wise guidance for the duties and engagements of the day. Help us to live this day by faith in thy dear Son, realising his propitiatory work as the only ground of our acceptance with Thee, and confiding in his High-priestly intercession as the source of strength, light, wisdom, and happiness to us. Endow us, we beseech Thee, with the life-giving and comforting influences of thy Holy Spirit. Preserve us this day from evil associations, unhallowed tendencies, worldly lusts, and the snares of the devil. May we do some good and useful work this day for thy glory, and the welfare of our fellow-men. And do Thou bring us safely and peaceably to the close of the day, keeping our eyes from tears, our feet from falling, and our souls from death. Bless all those for whom we ought to pray. We ask it for the sake of Jesus Christ our Lord. Amen.

O LORD, our only Hope and Refuge, to Thee would we come in humble confidence, and to Thee would we ever cling. We adore thy ineffable condescension in revealing Thyself to us, and we bless Thee for thine infinite love, and for Christ, thine unspeakable gift. We would humbly and fully confess our sinfulness, and cast ourselves on thy great mercy. Oh, teach us to know ourselves. O Father, pity us, and save us. We have no help but in Thee. Bestow upon us, we earnestly implore Thee, the rich blessings of thy salvation. Raise us above the world, and lift us nearer to Thyself. Grant us thy favour, for it is life; and conform us to Christ's image, for it is perfection. Lord, strengthen us by thy good Spirit, for we are weak without Thee. Let the Divine life be more and more developed within us. Oh, let our hearts ever contemplate this pure and perfect Pattern, and may we be changed into the same image.

We pray that our souls may repose confidence in Thee amidst all changes. We desire never to be alarmed, but to rejoice that Christ is universal Governor; that the Lamb opens the sealed book of thy providence, and presides over all its dispensations. We rejoice that the pleasure of the Lord prospers in his hand. We rejoice that his martyrs were animated by courage, and that their blood glorified and ennobled his cause; and we pray that all his enemies may take warning. Oh, that his reign of truth, and peace, and love may be everywhere! The Lord hasten this happy period in his own time. May none of us find ourselves the enemies of Christ, without faith in Him, or love to Him. May we seek shelter in his love now, and be washed in the blood of the Lamb. God in his great mercy forbid that any of us should be found out of Him, and crying in our panic to the mountains and hills to fall upon us. Let the day of his wrath to an ungodly and rebellious world be the day of his highest and tenderest manifestation to us. May we all find mercy of Him in that day, and be accepted by Him; and may it be our eternal destiny to be with Him, to adore, and serve, and enjoy Him for ever and ever.

Accept, O our God, of our thanks for all this day's mercies, and forgive all the sins committed during its hours. Watch over us during the night, and keep us ever under the shadow of thy wings. Holy Father, guard us and ours. Our heart's desire and prayer for all our kindred is, that they may be saved. Lord, encircle us with thy fatherly arms. Our humble prayers we lay before Thee, and plead with Thee to accept them for Christ's sake; to whom, with the Father and the Holy Ghost, be all glory, now and ever. Amen.

[MORNING.] **TWENTY-SECOND WEEK.—SATURDAY.** [EVENING.

READ IN HOLY SCRIPTURE HEBREWS III.   READ IN HOLY SCRIPTURE ST. MATTHEW XXII. 23—46.

O LORD, who art merciful to us in our penitence, and patient towards us in our sin, let thy great love constrain us, let thy long-suffering subdue our hearts. We mourn our waywardness and wilfulness towards Thee. By the provisions of thy grace, and by the appeals which Thou hast addressed to us, Thou hast made our sin to be exceeding sinful. Thou hast sent thy Son, but we have not reverenced Him. Thou hast delivered Him to die for us, but we have not crucified the sins which crucified Him. Thou hast set before us his perfect life, faithful in all things, and delighting to do thy will; but we have not walked in his steps. Him Thou hast exalted to thy right hand, crowned with glory and honour, the head of all principality and power; and for this we praise Thee. Mercifully help us to consider the Apostle and High Priest of our profession, and to hold fast the rejoicing of our hope firm unto the end. Dispose our hearts to obey as He obeyed, to be faithful as He was faithful, to endure as He endured, so that we may be partakers of his heavenly honour and joy.

O merciful God, save us, we beseech Thee, from that hardness of heart which disregards his voice, which disbelieves his threatenings, and which is ever growing harder still through its own unbelief. Oh, may we hear what the Holy Ghost saith, and, while it is called to-day, accept thy proffered mercy; lest, like thine ancient people, we weary out thy patience, and be excluded from thy rest. It is thine to soften hard hearts. Help us to unbare ours to the influences of the Saviour's cross, to the approaches and strivings of the Holy Spirit. Keep us from the evil heart of unbelief, and from the way that leads from the living God. Let those solemn words of Holy Scripture, of signal warning and Divine entreaty, make us very humble before Thee, and fill us with sacred fear, lest we, too, because of our unbelief, should not enter into thy rest. From hardness of heart, and contempt of thy Word and commandment, good Lord, deliver us.

Let the impressions and purposes of this our morning worship abide with us through the day, and shed a hallowing influence on all we do. May we strive to be as holy as we pray to be. Keep us from bodily evils, and, above all things, from sin. And when the evening shall come, may it be to us a preparation for the Sabbath; and by quiet thoughts and communings with Thee, may we anticipate its rest and the joy of thy house. We ask these and all needful mercies for ourselves, our friends, and for all mankind, in the name of Jesus Christ our Lord; to whom, with Thyself and the Holy Spirit, be everlasting praise. Amen.

ALMIGHTY and everlasting God, whose years are throughout all generations, we humbly thank Thee that Thou hast called us unto eternal life through Christ our Lord. From Thee we had fallen into sin, darkness, and death; but the Son of Man hath come to seek and to save that which was lost. Eternal thanks to Thee, O Father, that by dying He destroyed death and him that had the power of death, being delivered for our offences and raised again for our justification. Give us, O Lord, to know Him and the power of his resurrection, and the fellowship of his sufferings, being made conformable unto his death. May a living faith in Him ever sustain us amidst the sufferings of this present time; and when the sorrows of death compass us about, may we each be able to say, "I know that my Redeemer liveth!" Comfort us concerning the departed that sleep in Him; and may we rejoice in his blessed words, that "the God of Abraham, of Isaac, and of Jacob is not the God of the dead, but of the living."

Be pleased, O merciful Father, to bring all nations out of the shadow of spiritual death. May the heathen find eternal life in the knowledge of Thee, the only true God, and of Jesus Christ whom Thou hast sent. May the Mahometan be directed to a better paradise. May the Jew welcome Him who is David's Son and David's Lord. May those among whom this Gospel has long been published bring forth the fruit thereof; so that the great love wherewith Thou hast loved them may constrain them everywhere to love Thee, the Lord their God, with all their strength, and to love one another with a pure heart fervently. Keep all who name the name of Christ from a false profession; and may no leaven of the Sadducees tempt them to doubt or despise the life and immortality which He hath brought to light.

While we thank Thee, O Lord, for spiritual gifts and privileges, we would also gratefully remember our temporal mercies. Through the labours, cares, and dangers of another week Thou hast safely brought us. We bless Thee for our domestic ties, and we pray that we may by thy grace so live together here as to be prepared for those higher relationships which Christ our Saviour shall form in that heavenly world, where all shall be as the angels of God. We confess our individual and family sins and shortcomings, and seek to lie down this night with the sweet sense of thy pardoning love shed abroad in our hearts. Prepare us for the rest and worship of the Sabbath; and when all our work below is ended, may we sleep in Jesus, and awake amidst the Sabbath of thy eternal love. We ask all for the sake of Jesus Christ our Lord. Amen.

[MORNING.] **TWENTY-THIRD WEEK.—LORD'S DAY.** [EVENING.

READ IN HOLY SCRIPTURE NUMBERS XIV. 26—45.

READ IN HOLY SCRIPTURE PSALM CX.

O LORD God, our voice shalt Thou hear in the morning, early will we direct our prayer unto Thee, and will look up. We are spared, and in health, because Thou defendest us. We laid us down and slept, we awaked, for the Lord sustained us; and it is Thou only who makest us to dwell in safety.

We desire to trust under the shadow of thy wings. Hold Thou us up always, and we shall be safe. Let our faith in Thee be strengthened. Let thy love be shed abroad in our hearts.

We adore Thee as the God of providence. Thou leddest thy people like a flock, by the hand of Moses and Aaron. Help us to remember that to us Thou hast given richer blessings: the atonement of thy Son, a greater High Priest; the guidance of thy Spirit, and a Leader who cannot err. May we prize our privileges, and improve them. Do not let us fall into the sins of thine ancient people. Save us from murmuring, as some of them murmured; and from tempting Christ, as some of them also tempted; and let us be filled with holy fear, lest, a promise being given us of entering into that rest, any of us should seem to come short of it.

We bless Thee for the Sabbath, and for the sanctuary. May our hearts be in tune for their services and enjoyments. May we wait upon Thee in thy house. Let us carry prepared hearts to the hearing of thy Word; and let it be a word in season to us. Let all ordinances lead us to Christ. Let his mind be formed within us by thy Spirit. Let his comforts rule our hearts. Let us be truly his followers; and may we be made strong by the service of the temple for the constant service of life.

Let thy ministers be anointed from on high with all boldness; may they preach thy truth. Send thy Spirit forth according to thy word, and this day may thy people be quickened into a higher life, and may many sinners be converted unto Thee. Look upon the ungodly around us, and upon the families who have not called on thy name. Bless every effort which is made to save them. Thou willest not that they should perish. Oh, let thy Spirit convince them of sin, and direct them to the Saviour of sinners.

Now, O heavenly Father, we humble ourselves in thy presence. We are sinners, and we would not hide our sin. We are unworthy to approach Thee, or to join in thy praises. Our hearts cleave to their evil ways, and start aside like a deceitful bow; in us, that is, in our flesh, there dwelleth no good thing. But Thou art plenteous in mercy unto all that call upon Thee. Pardon us, O Lord, and help us to serve Thee acceptably, for the Redeemer's sake. Amen.

ALMIGHTY God, from whom no secrets are hidden, we come into thy presence on the evening of the day which Thou hast hallowed, and which Thou hast set apart for thine own service. We bless Thee that we have been allowed to tread the courts of thy house, and to pay our vows unto the Lord in the presence of all his people. We bless Thee for the Word of thy grace, for the Gospel of our salvation, for the promised Spirit, and for the hope of heaven.

We trust that we have not wilfully sinned against Thee this day. But who knoweth his errors? In thy sight our best doings are folly, and our holiest thoughts unclean. Our temple services and all our sacrifices are marred by our sins. We thank Thee for the blood of sprinkling, and we pray that Thou wouldest apply it to us afresh. Let our persons, our families, our services, all be accepted through its power. We would not be satisfied unless our hearts are wholly given to Thee. Cleanse the thoughts of our hearts, and keep back thy servants also from presumptuous sins.

Let the words which we have heard this day be blessed to us. Let us be doers of the Word, not hearers only. Let our love prompt us to obedience, and let our obedience illustrate our faith. Save us from the self-righteousness which trusts in its own doings. Hide thy Word in our hearts, that we may not sin against Thee, and that we may have joy and peace in believing.

We pray for the success of thy Word which has been this day declared in thy house. Let it be quick and powerful; as a hammer, may it break the rock in pieces; as a fire, may it burn up the dross of sin. Let sinners be converted everywhere, and let thy people be filled with greater faith and zeal.

We thank Thee for the portion of thy Word which we have just read. If it please Thee, fulfil the promise in our sight. Let us see thy kingdom come, Christ ruling in the midst of his enemies, thy people made willing in the day of thy power. Especially we bless Thee for our great High Priest. We rely upon his sacrifice once offered. We plead his merits, which Thou canst not turn away. We humbly rejoice that we have an Advocate with the Father, Jesus Christ the righteous; and we ask, for his sake, the forgiveness of our sins, and inheritance at last in the kingdom of thy glory.

We commend ourselves this night to thy holy keeping. Watchman of Israel, guard us in our slumbers. Let us rise to serve Thee. Help us to live to thy praise; and at length may we see Thee as Thou art, through Jesus Christ our Lord. Amen.

[Morning.] **TWENTY-THIRD WEEK.—MONDAY.** [Evening.

READ IN HOLY SCRIPTURE PSALM XC.

READ IN HOLY SCRIPTURE ST. MATTHEW XXIII. 1–22.

BEHOLD us, O Lord, assembled before Thee to express our united thanksgivings for the mercies of the past night, and to commit ourselves, both as individuals and as a family, to the care of thy providence, and to the guidance of thy grace during the day. We know not to what trials we may be subjected, ere the sun go down; but thy people in all generations have felt themselves, under the protection of thy watchful and gracious providence, infinitely more secure than within the strongest and most solid dwelling-place; and we, animated by their recorded experience, pray that Thou wouldest give us also to know the blessedness of those whose refuge is the everlasting God, and around whom are extended the Almighty arms that formed the earth and the world.

We feel, O Lord, that we are not only dependent, but frail and short-lived creatures. Thou hast shown us in thy Word that all flesh is as grass; and not a week, scarce a day, passes over our heads, but we are reminded, by many impressive and solemn occurrences, that man, who is born of a woman, has but a short time to live. We know that by one man sin entered into the world, and death by sin. In the cutting off of our days, and in the pining sickness whereby Thou dost make an end of us, we see the continued infliction of the sentence denounced against sin, according to which Thou turnest man to destruction, and sayest, Return, ye children of men. Oh, grant that we may so far know the power of thine anger, that our minds may be duly affected with a profound awe of thy justice and holiness; that we may be led, by repentance and faith in the Saviour, to seek thy favour as the fountain of purest joys; and that, from a consideration of the shortness and miseries of this life, as well as of the certainty of death, we may earnestly devote ourselves to the study and practice of that true wisdom which consists in piety and the fear of the Lord. We have constant need, O gracious Father, that Thou shouldest so teach us to number our days; for we spend our years as a tale that is told, and are prone to live as if we were to live here always.

Under a deep sense of our sinfulness, we plead thy mercy in Christ. Oh, give us the delightful consciousness of thy returning favour, and supply us with the promised influences of thy Spirit; that in the renovation of our nature, manifested by the conversion of our hearts and the progressive holiness of our conduct, the beauty of the Lord our God may be reflected upon us; and becoming henceforth steadfast as well as zealous of good works, we may hope that our persons and services will be accepted through Christ. Amen.

BLESSED and exalted Saviour, we look up to Thee at the close of another day, and ask for thy blessing. Thou art in heaven, we on the earth. Thou dwellest in light, we are surrounded by darkness. Having finished the work given Thee to do, Thou hast taken thy seat at the right hand of power, and there Thou art directing all things according to thy will. We rejoice in Thee as our Prophet, Priest, and King. Sinners of the earth, we delight to remember that thy blood once shed on Calvary cleanseth from all sin. May that precious blood be sprinkled upon our consciences to-night, that being justified by faith, we may have peace with God.

Impress on our minds and hearts the precepts Thou hast just addressed to us in thy Word. Preserve us, O God, from the leaven of hypocrisy, that we may not have a name to live while we are dead. Cleanse, we beseech Thee, the thoughts of our hearts. Create in us clean hearts, renew right spirits within us. Preserve us from pride; help us to feel we are thy servants, not our own masters. May we be clothed with humility, and humble ourselves as little children, that we may be exalted by thy grace. Make us willing to sit at thy feet, and to learn of Thee to be meek and lowly in heart, that we may find rest unto our souls.

We seek pardon for the sins of the day. In many things we all offend. We have erred and strayed from thy ways like lost sheep, and there is no health in us. We have this day too much deserved thy rebuke as fools and blind. We see not as we ought our true interest, nor thy glory. The world too much absorbs our thoughts, and obscures the vision of eternal things. Lord Jesus, make us more spiritually-minded, which is life and peace. Thou wast always holy in thought, word, and deed. Though mingling with all classes of men, and ever active, Thou didst always that which pleased the Father. Thy meat and thy drink was to do his will. Make us, we pray Thee, more like Thyself. May we bear thy image, and reflect more perfectly thy character to the world.

Mercifully take us, O God, beneath thy care this night. Thou never slumberest nor sleepest, and when on earth didst often spend whole nights in prayer. While our weariness requires repose, let thy tender love be over us, thy watchful care protect us. Bless all dear to us, and all thy people everywhere, and prepare us for the world where we hope to see Thee as Thou art, and to be like Thee for ever. From our hearts we thank Thee for all Thou hast done for us, especially for the gifts of thy dear Son and the promise of the Spirit, and with our united spirits would render to Thee all honour and praise for ever and ever. Amen.

[MORNING.]   TWENTY-THIRD WEEK.—TUESDAY.   [EVENING.

READ IN HOLY SCRIPTURE NUMBERS XVI. 1–22.   READ IN HOLY SCRIPTURE ST. MATTHEW XXIII. 23–39

O THOU that dwellest between the cherubim, be pleased to shine forth on us; and as we now seek, by the blood of Jesus, to enter into that which is within the veil, give us access unto Thee, and do Thou speak unto us peace.

We have been guided by Thee, O God, very tenderly in all our way on earth. We have drank of the upper and the nether springs in Thee. And Thou hast added this to the numberless other blessings of our state, that Thou hast not spared thine own Son, but hast given Him up unto death for us all. Yet how often have we forgotten Thee, the God that madest us; how often have we lightly esteemed Thee, the Rock of our salvation ; how often, by the restless discontent and gainsaying of our hearts, have we grieved thy Spirit and provoked thy anger, so that it would be a righteous doom were we even now to die in our sins.

Oh, have mercy on us, for thy Son's sake, and for his righteousness' sake. Look upon us as we bow before his cross, as we there repent us of our sins, as we call upon Thee in sincerity and truth; and let the darkness of thine anger pass away, O our God, and receive us again graciously, and love us freely.

And this day, and all our days, may thy Spirit be shed within our hearts, in his baptism of power. May He subdue the rebelliousness of our mind and will. So may He work in us, that we may put on Christ, and be clothed evermore with the garment of his humility, his obedience, his trust. And with this, the very mind of Jesus, wrought in us, in all the ways of thy appointment, may we then be found no more striving against, but yielding ourselves the willing subjects of thy grace. In our health and weakness, in our labour and rest, in our privilege and privation, may we seek not our own will, but thine; may we walk before Thee as dear children; may we set our eyes continually on Him whom Thou hast ordained our High Priest in the heavens; and may He, as all our salvation and all our desire, be daily magnified in our body, whether it be by life or by death.

Guide us, then, and bless us, O God, throughout this day. Save our feet from falling, and our souls from death, and our eyes from tears. May those, also, whom we love have their portion in the love of Jesus. And may the kingdom of his grace everywhere advance, till the kingdom of his glory come, and all men shall call Him blessed, and the earth be filled with his praise.

Now unto Him that loved us, and washed us from our sins in his blood, and hath made us kings and priests unto God and his Father, to Him be glory and dominion for ever and ever. Amen.

IN the multitude of thy mercies, O Lord our God, we present ourselves at the throne of thy grace to-night. Thou hast been our guide and our guard through another day. Thou hast delivered us from dangers both seen and unseen. Many have been our wants, but Thou hast supplied them all. Make us truly grateful, and grant us thy Holy Spirit, to enable us to devote those lives to thy service which Thou dost so constantly make thy care. With deep humility and self-abasement, we acknowledge our unworthiness and our sins. We have done much that we ought not to have done, and have left much of our duty undone. We rejoice to know that thou delightest in mercy, and that with Thee there is plenteous redemption. Be merciful to us, for the sake of Jesus Christ; and pardon our iniquity, for it is great.

Thou didst of old speak unto thy people by thy servants the prophets, but Thou hast spoken unto us by thy Son, the Lord Jesus. May the lessons of instruction we have now derived from his words make a lasting impression on our hearts, and exert a practical influence on our conduct. Suffer us not to resemble the scribes and Pharisees, against whom such woes were denounced. Forbid it that we should be as whited sepulchres, which may indeed appear beautiful without, while within they are full of all uncleanness. May we hate and avoid hypocrisy and deceit. May we be among the pure in heart who shall see God. While we attend to the lesser matters of thy law, may we not omit the weightier matters of judgment, mercy, and faith. Permit us never to be blind guides, going astray from thy paths ourselves, and leading others astray too; but may thy Spirit lead us into all truth, and make us useful to those with whom we associate.

May we always be found watching and waiting for that time when it shall be said, "Blessed is He that cometh in the name of the Lord." Make us willing to suffer affliction and persecution for Him who suffered, the just for the unjust, that He might bring us to God. Grant that as a family we may all be not only the objects of thy protecting care, but partakers of thy saving grace. May those who are related to us, by the ties of nature and affection, be taken into relationship with Thyself.

By the tears Thou didst shed over Jerusalem, and by thy death on the cross to put away the sin of the world, we beseech Thee to pour out thy Holy Spirit upon all flesh.

And now, like as a hen gathereth her chickens under her wings, so do Thou graciously cover us with thine own Almighty power and love, that we may both lay ourselves down to sleep and awake in peace, for thy great name's sake. Amen.

MORNING.] TWENTY-THIRD WEEK.—WEDNESDAY. [EVENING.

READ IN HOLY SCRIPTURE NUMBERS XVI. 23—50.   READ IN HOLY SCRIPTURE JOEL II. 12—32.

O LORD our God, Thou art very great; Thou art clothed with honour and majesty. Clouds and darkness are round about Thee; righteousness and judgment are the habitation of thy throne. Help us to draw near unto Thee with reverence and godly fear, and to worship Thee in spirit and in truth.

Enter not into judgment with us, O Lord; for in thy sight shall no flesh living be justified. We bless Thee that Thou desirest not the death of a sinner, but rather that he should turn from his trespasses and live. Help us with our whole hearts to cease from sin, and to turn to Thee. May we be warned and instructed by the history of thy judgments. May we remember that if they escaped not who refused Him that spake on earth, much more shall not we escape if we turn away from Him that speaketh from heaven. Make us deeply sensible of the evil, guilt, and misery of sin; and strengthen our faith to lay hold on thy pardoning mercy, through thy beloved Son. Being justified by faith, may we have peace with God.

Accept our thanksgivings, heavenly Father, for thy great and constant bounty towards us. It is of thy mercies that we are not consumed, because thy compassions fail not. They are new every morning: great is thy faithfulness. We bless Thee for the safety and refreshment of the night, for the cheerful light of day, for the supply of our ever-returning wants, for the use of reason and all our powers, for the comfort of our earthly home, and for all the duties as well as the enjoyments of life. Help us to consecrate to Thee all we have and enjoy, to see thy hand in all thy gifts, to lean on thy strength in all our duties, to commit all our ways to Thee, and to set our best and strongest affections on things above, not on things on the earth.

Go with us, we beseech Thee, through the scenes and duties of this day. If it be thy will, keep our eyes from tears, and our feet from falling. But when sorrow, disappointment, or suffering, or difficult tasks and perplexing cares are appointed us, keep us near to Thee, stay our hearts on Thyself, uphold us by thy free Spirit, and let the strength of Christ be perfected in our weakness.

Bless each member of this household. [May our dear children live before Thee.] Mercifully remember all our beloved kindred and friends. Number them among thy children. Bless all Christian families, and the members of thy Church throughout the world. Bless our country, our Sovereign, and all our rulers; and grant to all nations freedom, truth, righteousness, and peace.

Mercifully hear our prayers, heavenly Father, for the sake of thy beloved Son. Amen.

O GOD, the Father of mercies, and God of all consolation, from Thee cometh every good and perfect gift. Thou openest thy hand, and suppliest the wants of every living thing. We are the witnesses of thy bounty and preserving care, in having commenced the various engagements of the day, in having had health and strength of body and of mind vouchsafed for their performance, in having tasted of thy goodness during its passing hours, and in now being gathered around this family altar, with one mouth and with one heart to present our oblation and sacrifice of praise, which we offer, and which we humbly pray may be accepted, through our only Advocate and Mediator, the Lord Jesus Christ.

Pity us, O Lord, and pardon all errors of judgment, all the infirmities of the flesh, the want of seasonable recollection, and the foolish prejudices into which we may have been betrayed; and through the blood of the Lamb who taketh away the sin of the world, pardon and absolve every one before Thee from all iniquity, transgression, and sin. O Christ, save us both now and evermore! Renew in us right spirits. Restore unto us the joys of thy salvation, and uphold us with thy free Spirit; then shall we teach transgressors thy ways, and sinners shall be converted unto Thee. Henceforth may we serve Thee acceptably in holiness and in righteousness all our days.

May the Gospel run, and the name of Jesus, Messiah, the Lord and Saviour, be glorified in all lands. May all nations be blessed in Him, and all peoples, kindreds, and languages call Him blessed. Greatly increase the success which has been already vouchsafed, and hasten the times of salvation for which Thou hast caused all thy servants in successive ages to look.

Finally, we commend to thy gracious protection thy servant, our Sovereign, the Royal Family, and all who are in authority. Grant to us, and to all the subjects of this realm, to live honest and peaceable lives, and to dwell in charity with all men.

We are now about to separate and retire to rest. May our sleep be sweet, because Thou, Lord, sustainest us. But if through pain of body or any other cause, we lie awake any portion of the night, may our meditations be profitable. May we commune with the Father of our spirits, the Fountain of all consolation. Preserve us from all dangers. Give us to rise refreshed with sleep, and then, as now, gratefully to record thy tender mercies; thus spending our short and uncertain life in the assured hope of resting with Thyself and with all thy saints in glory everlasting, through Jesus Christ, our only Lord and Saviour; to whom be all honour and glory. Amen.

[MORNING.] TWENTY-THIRD WEEK.—THURSDAY. [EVENING.

READ IN HOLY SCRIPTURE ST. JUDE.

READ IN HOLY SCRIPTURE ST. MARK XII. 35—44.

WITH the beginning of a new day, O Lord, we come to Thee as a family, in humble dependence on the Holy Spirit, to offer our praise and prayer. We desire ever to praise Thee for all Thou art in Thyself and for all Thou art to us. We praise Thee as the King of Kings, and Lord of Lords. We praise Thee as the Almighty Creator, the constant Preserver, the bountiful Benefactor, the gracious Redeemer, and the sovereign Judge of all mankind. It is in Thee we live, and move, and have our being; and from Thee alone we receive every good and perfect gift. Help us to remember that Thou wilt give us through Jesus Christ all blessings, both temporal and spiritual, if we seek them in his name; and in their enjoyment may we recognise thy love, and magnify thy name. Thou dost draw the curtains of darkness around thy children at night, so that they may rest after the toils of the day. We render to Thee our heartfelt thanksgivings for the peaceful and refreshing sleep Thou hast afforded us during another night. We know not what may be before us to-day. Do Thou preserve us from all accident, from all sickness, and especially from all sin. May we not deny Thee in thought, word, or deed; but, like Enoch, may our walk be close with our God. May the pillar of fire and of cloud which accompanied thy people of old, as they travelled through the wilderness, ever accompany us. Suffer us not to resemble clouds without water, or trees whose fruit withereth; but may we know that we are sanctified by God the Father, and may we be as trees of righteousness, the planting of the Lord, that Thou mayest be glorified.

Write on our hearts the lessons of instruction which we have read in thy Word, and graciously help us to build ourselves up in our most holy faith, praying without ceasing in the Holy Ghost. May mercy, and peace, and love be multiplied to us. May we keep ourselves in the knowledge and love of God, and be continually looking for the mercy of our Lord Jesus Christ unto eternal life, knowing that He cometh with ten thousands of his saints to the judgment of the great day. Make us diligent in the discharge of all the duties connected with our salvation. Enable us earnestly to contend for the faith which was once delivered unto the saints. Keep us from evil in all our necessary contact with those who acknowledge not thy dominion. Suffer us not to be overcome by evil, but may we overcome evil with good. Now unto Him that is able to keep us from falling, and to present us faultless before the presence of his glory with exceeding joy, to the only wise God, our Saviour, be glory and majesty, dominion and power, both now and ever. Amen.

WE praise and adore thy name, O God, for the mercies of this day. Strength for duty, and the supply of food and raiment, came from Thee. We acknowledge thy hand in all our blessings, and, above all, in the gift of thy dear Son. May the remembrance of his cross and passion awaken us to earnest thankfulness, and may the assurance of his resurrection, and ascension, and intercession, encourage in us a holy trust and confidence. Unworthy in ourselves, we plead his worthiness and merits. For his sake do us good, we beseech Thee, now that we kneel before thy throne, and send us not away unblessed or unforgiven. In many things we continually offend Thee and transgress thy holy law. Lord, be gracious unto us, and visit us not for our sins, but pardon us in thy mercy, and gladden our hearts by thy forgiveness. May we not rest without the assurance of thy mercy.

O God, preserve us, we beseech Thee, from the sin of hypocrisy. Implant in our hearts the undoubting conviction of thine omniscience, that we may shrink from attempting to deceive ourselves, or the world around us, or Thee. Thou discernest the thoughts and intents of the heart; and there is not a word on our lips but Thou, O Lord, knowest it altogether. We tremble when we think how Thou searchest us, and weighest all our motives in the balance of truth and righteousness, and we fly for refuge to Jesus, the Lamb of God, which taketh away the sin of the world. We pray for thy Holy Spirit. May He dwell in us, and cause our religion to be a religion of the heart, and not of mere outward show and profession. Oh, give us grace in all things to serve Thee in spirit and in truth, remembering that not he that commendeth himself is approved, but whom the Lord commendeth.

Implant also within us a spirit of self-denial and cheerful liberality. May we have in constant remembrance the great things which Thou hast done for us, and cheerfully do all we can for others. All we are and all we have is thine, and for our use of all things Thou wilt require an account at the great day. Graciously enable us, in the grateful sense of thy mercy, to honour Thee with our substance; and of what we have received at thy hand, be it much or little, may we conscientiously set apart a portion for Thee, and for the advancement of thy kingdom, and the comfort of our poor neighbours.

We pray for thy protection. Let it be above us and all who belong to us during the night, and preserve us from all dangers. Hear us, O God, and grant us an answer of peace, for Jesus Christ's sake. Amen.

[159]

[Morning.] **TWENTY-THIRD WEEK.—FRIDAY.** [Evening.

READ IN HOLY SCRIPTURE NUMBERS XX. 1—13. READ IN HOLY SCRIPTURE ST. MATTHEW XXIV. 1—14.

ALMIGHTY and most holy Lord God, by whose power the world is upheld; in whom we live, and move, and have our being; we praise and worship Thee as the Ruler of the world, and the Creator of all that is therein. All thy creatures speak of thy goodness and wisdom, though we confess that often we have loved and served the creature more than the Creator, and have neglected to see Thee in thy works and to hear Thee speak in thy Word.

Open our eyes every day to see Thee and the traces of thy working in this wonderful world, and to perceive that Thou art Lord of all. May the light of thy sun now risen on the earth remind us to greet with joy the rising upon our sinful world of the Sun of Righteousness with healing in his wings; and as the shadows of night are fled, so put to flight our sinful fears and doubts.

We acknowledge that it is in thy hand to kill and to make alive, to wound and to heal, and we would ever trust thy goodness. When we cannot fathom the depths of thy designs, may we never in haste condemn thy merciful purposes because we cannot clearly comprehend them all; and if Thou seemest to forsake us, may we cleave to Thee closer, till thy presence is restored to us.

O God, how often have we murmured against thy providence, and said in our hearts, "It is in vain to serve the Lord, and what profit have we in walking humbly before the Most High?" Our faith has been weak, and in the hour of need we have sat down in despair, when we ought to have prayed more earnestly to Thee, and taken comfort in thine exceeding great and precious promises.

Take away from us, we implore Thee, this spirit of murmuring and discontent. Teach us in whatsoever state we are, therewith to be content. While we use thy help for all our real necessities, let us be heartily satisfied with thy blessed will, even though it be different from ours.

Supply, we pray Thee, from thy fulness in Christ Jesus, all the wants of our souls. Refresh them, while wandering through the wilderness of this world, with the water of life; and may Christ ever be felt at hand in all our journey, to sustain our burdened souls, and strengthen us in the hour of weakness.

Deliver us from haste, and carelessness; from harshness of thought, and rashness of judgment; and if we are vexed with the ungodliness of the world, keep us from too speedily passing judgment on them, for Thou art the righteous Judge, strong and patient.

These mercies we ask in Christ's name, to whom, as also to Thee, O God the Father, and to Thee, O God the Holy Spirit, we ascribe all praise and power. Amen.

O GOD, in the review of another day's mercies, we exalt and praise thy name. Great indeed is thy goodness, great the riches of the forbearance, and thy long-suffering. We have provoked Thee by our sins, but Thou hast not turned away thy face from us. We have misused thy gifts of life, and health, and opportunity; yet still Thou continuest them. Oh, grant that thy gracious dealings with us may lead us to a deeper sense of sin; that in the light of thy mercy we may learn the grievousness of our disobedience, and be humbled at thy footstool. For thy Son our Lord Jesus Christ's sake, forgive us all our misdoings; all sinful thoughts, all sinful words and works: put Thou them out of thy remembrance, and let them not rise up again to our condemnation. Speak to us words of comfort and peace, and shed upon our souls the blessed assurance of thy reconciliation and forgiveness.

We pray Thee, O God, to give us a clearer insight into thy holy Word, that we may not be led astray by false teachers, and through the weakness and ignorance of our own hearts. Enable us to receive with meekness the Word which is able to save our souls, and to wait patiently till the revelation of the great day, for the clearing up of what is now dark and mysterious. Especially keep us watchful for the Lord's coming, that we may prepare to receive Him with joy when He shall come to be admired of his saints, and to be glorified in all that believe. Increase our desires for the enlargement of the Redeemer's kingdom, and stir up our hearts with an earnest zeal for his glory, that we may do all that in us lies to spread abroad in our own homes and in the world the glad tidings of his Gospel. Lord, write it on our own hearts. Enable us to experience, through thy grace, the comfort of its promises and the guidance of its precepts. Let its blessed effects be seen in our growth in grace, and in the knowledge of our Lord and Saviour Jesus Christ, that others may be drawn to Him, and believe in his name.

We beseech Thee to bless whatever has been done this day for thy glory. Make thy Gospel the saviour of life unto life to many souls. Look upon thy Church; heal its divisions, reconcile its contentions. Bring all thy people nearer to Christ; then will they be brought nearer to each other. Bring Jew and Gentile into thy fold, and hasten the time when thy Gospel shall have been preached as a witness to all nations, and the kingdom of Christ shall come.

Spread around our household this night the protection of thine almighty arm. We lie down to sleep, trusting in thy care and lovingkindness; keep us, bless us, and supply our need, according to thy riches in glory, by Jesus Christ our Lord. Amen.

[Morning.] **TWENTY-THIRD WEEK.—SATURDAY.** [Evening.

READ IN HOLY SCRIPTURE PSALM LXXXI.

O LORD, we adore Thee as the God who in times past didst speak unto the fathers by the prophets, but hast in those last days spoken unto us by thy Son. For all the deliverances granted to thine ancient people we humbly thank Thee; and we praise thy name that in Christ Thou hast saved us from a worse bondage than that of Egypt, having broken the yoke of our burden, and the rod of our oppressor. Give us grace continually to sing aloud unto God our strength; and being redeemed out of the hand of our enemies, may we serve Thee without fear, in holiness and righteousness before Thee all the days of our life.

Thou, Lord, in the days of old didst bless the families of thy people, feeding them with food convenient for them, and giving them water out of the rock. Thou, in thy manifold mercies, didst not forsake them in the wilderness; and when they called in trouble, Thou didst deliver them. We humbly beseech Thee to bless us as a family with bread from heaven, and to feed us with the heritage of Jacob our father. May every one of us be satisfied abundantly with the provisions of thy house; and may we hunger and thirst after righteousness, that we may be filled. Suffer none of us ever to err from thy ways, or harden our hearts from thy fear, lest Thou shouldest be turned to be our enemy, and fight against us. We confess and deplore the strength of evil and the weakness of our good resolutions. Assist us, O God of our salvation, with thine almighty grace, that we may evermore hearken unto Thee, and walk in thy ways.

O merciful God, be favourable also to our beloved country. Thou hast highly exalted us, like Israel of old, placing amongst us thy testimony and thy law, and answering us in the secret place of thunder. Forbid that there should be among us any strange god, or that we should listen to any voice but thine. Deliver us as a people from all unbelief and pride, from all hardness of heart and contempt of thy holy Word and commandment. Let the wickedness of the wicked come to an end, and let the righteous be established. Remove from the midst of us everything that offendeth and worketh iniquity; and let not our lukewarmness and coldness of heart grieve thy Holy Spirit. Teach us wherein we have fallen, to remember and do our first works, lest our candlestick should be removed out of its place. O our God, we are verily guilty; but thy compassions fail not; and we implore Thee to renew us to repentance, that thy covenant may be still with us. We ask all through Jesus Christ, our Saviour and Redeemer, to whom, with Thee and the Holy Ghost, be glory for ever and ever. Amen.

READ IN HOLY SCRIPTURE ST. MATTHEW XXIV. 15–35.

GRACIOUS and merciful God, our refuge and strength, a present help in every time of need, give us thy blessing, we beseech Thee, before we lay ourselves down to rest. We acknowledge the fatherly care with which Thou hast watched over and preserved us during the week, and the love which hath supplied all our wants. We thank Thee for giving us access to thy presence, and for the promise which assures us of acceptance through thy dear Son, who ever liveth to make intercession for us. We confess our sinfulness before Thee. By nature corrupt, we are continually transgressing thy commandments and contracting fresh guilt. Thou knowest our unworthiness, and settest our secret sins in the light of thy countenance. Have mercy upon us, O God, and put away our offences from before Thee. Forgive us for thy name's sake, and let us now find favour in thy sight.

O Lord Jesus, fit and prepare us for thy second coming. By thy Holy Spirit implant in our hearts a holy fear of sin; and so reveal unto us things unseen and eternal; that we may not be led astray by those which are seen and temporal. Fill our hearts with a lively expectation of thy glory, and sustain us under all trials and temptations by the sure hope of eternal life. Thy promises fail not; enable us to lean on them with all the confidence of loving hearts, knowing that heaven and earth must pass away rather than they should fail. Fulfil thy work of grace within us, transforming us more entirely into thy Divine likeness, and cheering our souls by the experience of thy peace and joy. May it be all our desire day by day to live for Thee, and in the discharge of every duty may we strive to please Thee.

We look forward, O God, with grateful hearts to the rest and privileges of thy holy day. As the Sabbaths come round and ever bring us nearer to eternity, oh, make us more earnest and diligent in the use of our opportunities, remembering that the night cometh in which none can work. In the prospect of the prayer and praise of the morrow, do Thou convince us of our sin, that we may long for spiritual blessings as the hart panteth for the water-brooks; and awaken in us a deep sense of all thy goodness, that we may bring to Thee the tribute of unfeigned thankfulness.

Take us all into thy gracious keeping for the night. Let nothing prevent or disturb our rest. Oh, that, waking or sleeping, we may be thine. We implore thy protection and blessing for all whom we love. In all their necessities do Thou help them. Hear us, heavenly Father, and do for us according to the riches of thy grace and love in Jesus Christ thy Son our Lord. Amen.

MORNING.] TWENTY-FOURTH WEEK.—LORD'S DAY. [EVENING

READ IN HOLY SCRIPTURE NUMBERS XX. 14–29. | READ IN HOLY SCRIPTURE ST. MATTHEW XXIV. 36–51.

O LORD our God, Thou art God alone, the high and holy One, robed in majesty. Thou hast made all things, and Thou preservest all things. All thy works praise Thee. Thy power is unbounded, thy wisdom is infinite, and thy tender mercies are over all thy works. Thou art light, and Thou art also love. Thy throne of glory is also a throne of grace. Feeling that we are so unlike Thee, may we now draw near with contrite hearts. We have sinned, and what shall we say to Thee? Lord, forgive us. Enter not into judgment with us. Save us, we implore Thee, for thy Son's sake. Send down upon us this day thy Holy Spirit. May the ascended Lord shed Him forth as at the time of Pentecost.

May this holy day be a day of revival in all thy churches. Oh, grant that thy people assembling for thy worship may be accepted by Thee. May the spirit of grace and supplication be largely given to them. Enable them to realise their position as a holy priesthood, and to lay on thine altar those spiritual sacrifices with which, for Christ's sake, Thou art well pleased. Abundantly bless us in thy house this day. Let our praises rise with acceptance, and let our prayers be answered beyond our expectations. May thy Word spoken to us be heard and accepted as thine in docility and faith, and may it nourish and sustain our souls. Oh, may thy Spirit bring it home to our hearts with power, so that we may live by it, and may always feel its power and consolation. Cause us to rejoice in the ordinances of thy house, and ever to implore a blessing upon them. May the rain from heaven fill the pools, so that the pilgrims may drink and be refreshed.

O Lord, glorify Thyself this day in saving many souls, and in reviving thine own people. We bless Thee for the assurance that, while thy servants on earth are not suffered to continue, by reason of death, Christ, the Minister of the true tabernacle, still lives, and lives for ever. As we have been reading in thy Word that Aaron died, and his robes were put on Eleazar, his son, so we find in thy Church a succession of pastors. But we rejoice that our great High Priest lives, and ever pleads for his people: reigns over them, and fills them with blessing. May the privileges which we enjoy soon be possessed by the whole world. Oh, raise our souls this day above the world. May we leave it behind and beneath us; and as we enter this house, may we feel thy gracious presence. May great grace be upon us, and may every Sabbath spent here be preparing us for the rest remaining to thy people. Lord, hear us, and do Thou for us above all that we can ask or think, for Jesus Christ's sake. Amen.

ALMIGHTY and merciful Father, the only wise God, to whom all events and all hearts are known, and from whom no secret is hid, we humbly thank Thee that although Thou hast hidden from us those secret things which belong unto Thee, and the times and seasons which Thou hast kept in thine own power, Thou hast plainly revealed unto us all things needful to life and godliness. Keep us, we beseech Thee, from presumptuous curiosity in regard to what Thou hast concealed, and from neglect, ignorance, or unbelief in regard to what Thou hast revealed. And in that day wherein Thou wilt bring every work into judgment, with every secret thing, whether it be good or whether it be evil, may we be delivered from condemnation, through the sacrifice and merit of thy dear Son, and be found in Him, not having our own righteousness, but that which is through the faith of Christ. Grant us our portion amongst those blessed servants whom their Lord, when He cometh, shall find ready. When Christ, who is our life, shall appear, then may we also appear with Him in glory.

We thank Thee, merciful Father, for the manifold and precious blessings of this day. We praise Thee for thy holy Word, for the worship and fellowship of thy Church, for the ministry of truth, and for all the means of grace. Pardon, we beseech Thee, our poor and imperfect improvement of all thy gifts, the sin which stains our best duties, and all that has been wrong or wanting in us to-day.

Have mercy on all to whom this day has been no Sabbath. Send thy light and truth to the nations which are yet in darkness. Strengthen and cheer our missionary brethren, and greatly prosper their work. Restore the lost sheep of the house of Israel. Bring to an end every false religion, all war, slavery, and injustice, and whatsoever hinders thy Gospel. Bless every faithful effort to spread thy Truth. Let many, heretofore careless and ungodly, be led, by what they have heard to-day, to seek thy mercy, and to believe thy Word. Pour thy Spirit, O Lord, on all flesh, and fill the earth with thy glory.

Graciously watch over us, and all dear to us, through this night. Refresh us, if it please Thee, with quiet rest, and fit us for all the duties and unknown scenes of a new week. Bless each member of our family, and all our kindred and friends. And when our days on earth are ended, may we be ready to follow those who have happily entered before us into thy presence, and to keep overlasting Sabbath with thy Church above, through Him who is gone to prepare a place for us, that where He is we may be also. Amen.

[MORNING.] **TWENTY-FOURTH WEEK.—MONDAY.** [EVENING.

READ IN HOLY SCRIPTURE NUMBERS XXI. 1—20.   READ IN HOLY SCRIPTURE ST. MATTHEW XXV. 1—13.

MOST merciful and gracious God, on the morning of a new day we come to Thee to acknowledge the blessings of another night, and to offer once more the tribute of grateful praise: "It is of the Lord's mercies we are not consumed, because his compassions fail not; they are new every morning; great is thy faithfulness."

We implore thy protection as we enter upon the day. Like Israel in the wilderness, we have many enemies; sin, Satan, the world, our own evil hearts, are ever opposing us in our journey to the heavenly Canaan, and we need to watch and pray always.

Mercifully defend us this day from all evil. By thine overshadowing providence keep us from bodily danger. By the power of thy Spirit guard us against our spiritual foes. We are strong only in thy strength. If Thou dost leave us, we fall. Hold Thou us up, and then we shall be safe; and may we ever take to ourselves the whole armour of God.

Preserve us, we beseech Thee, from a backsliding spirit. Thou knowest how prone we are to wander from Thee. Lord, keep us near thy side. May we seek our highest happiness in Thee and thy service.

We desire unfeignedly to bless Thee for Jesus Christ. As Moses lifted up the serpent in the wilderness, so the Son of Man has been lifted up, that whosoever believeth in Him might not perish, but have everlasting life. May we all look to Him. We have been wounded by sin, and are in danger of death. Oh, help us to look to Christ and live. We thank Thee that the way of salvation is so simple, that whosoever will may believe and be saved. Lord, help us to depend upon Jesus not for salvation alone, but for everything. This day will not pass without its cares, anxieties, perplexities, and temptations; in the midst of all these may we lean on the arm of our Saviour. We thank Thee for his fulness—that He is made unto us wisdom and righteousness, sanctification and redemption. Let the life we live in the flesh be a life of faith upon the Son of God.

Bless, we pray Thee, all for whom we should intercede; not only each member of this family, but all dear friends and relations, our country, the Church, and the world. May we try to live that the world may be better for our life. Give us grace to be active, useful, consistent, and holy. As the salt of the earth, may we not lose our savour, but exert such an influence to-day as through eternity shall prove a blessing to many.

Our Father, hear these our morning supplications. Let them come up before Thee as incense; and according to thy mercy, answer and accept us for Jesus Christ's sake. Amen.

O LORD God, in whom we live, and move, and have our being, through thy kind and watchful providence we have arrived at the close of another day. We thank Thee for the mercies of the day. Thou hast given us our daily bread, Thou hast sustained us in the enjoyment of health and strength, Thou hast permitted us to pursue our ordinary avocations in peace, Thou hast mercifully preserved us amidst many dangers unseen by us, Thou hast not suffered the enemy to gain an advantage over us; in various ways hast Thou made thy goodness to pass before us; and now Thou art causing the shadows of the night to gather around us, that we may seek needful repose and be refreshed from the toils of the day. Give us, O Lord, a blessing ere we separate for the night. May the sins of the day be forgiven, and our souls washed from every stain of guilt in that fountain which Thou hast opened for sin and for uncleanness. May we not seek repose with the burden of evil upon us; but delivered wholly from all guilt, and from all uncleanness of the flesh and of the spirit, may we lay us down at peace with Thee, at peace within ourselves and at peace with all men.

As each day draws to its close, help us, O Lord, to number our days, that we may apply our hearts unto wisdom; and so to live, that when summoned to enter our Master's presence, we may do it with joy, and not with grief. May it be our constant desire and aim to be ready for the coming of our Lord, that when the voice is heard saying, "Go ye out to meet Him!" we may have nothing to do but joyfully to obey the call. Whilst we are careful to preserve our lamps clean and bright, oh, may we never forget that this will profit us nothing unless we have oil in them, wherewith they may be caused to give light. Mercifully save us from having this to seek when the Bridegroom comes. Preserve us, we beseech Thee, from the folly of trusting to our fellow-creatures to help us to that of which no creature can have more than he himself absolutely needs. Help us ever to come unto Thee with our empty vessels, that Thou mayest fill them with the golden oil of thy grace. Keep us ever simply and earnestly confiding in Christ as our alone and all-sufficient Saviour. Endow us with the gifts of the Holy Ghost, that strengthened with all might in the inner man, we may stand fast in the day of trial, may walk worthy of the Lord unto all well-pleasing, may finish our course with joy, and may at last enter into the joy of our Lord. Hear us, O Father, and help us according to our need, since all that we ask is in the name and through the merit of our only Lord and Saviour Jesus Christ. Amen.

[Morning.]   TWENTY-FOURTH WEEK.—TUESDAY.   [Evening.

READ IN HOLY SCRIPTURE ST. JOHN III. 14—27.

READ IN HOLY SCRIPTURES 1 THESSALONIANS IV.

BLESSED Lord God, we, thine unworthy servants, enter into thy presence with thanksgiving for manifold mercies; for giving and sustaining life to this moment, and especially for thy protection and favour during the past night. May our prolonged lives, and the renewed health and strength which we are about to engage; may we bear with patience the trials and share the joys incident to our lot. May we so habitually remember thy name, and so cherish the spirit of prayer at all times and in all places, that through the prevailing intercessions of our Lord Jesus Christ, and the light, and strength, and succour of the Holy Spirit, we may be in the fear of the Lord all the day long. Graciously have regard to our individual circumstances and necessities, to the relations which we sustain to each other, to the temptations peculiar to our station and work. Implant in us those principles and habits which are essential to our character as the disciples of the meek and lowly Jesus, that we may, by thy grace, be in due time fitted for the fellowship of the redeemed in heaven.

We unitedly thank Thee for the love wherewith Thou hast loved us, in having given thy only begotten Son to suffer, the Just instead of the unjust, to bring us to Thyself; that—like as Moses lifted up the serpent in the wilderness—whosoever believeth in Him should not perish, but have everlasting life. We bless Thee that these glad tidings of great joy designed for all people, this Gospel of the grace of God, has been brought to us, and that we can now read in our native tongue the record of everlasting mercy in Christ Jesus. May thy Holy Spirit promised to us and to our children render the word and teaching of the Gospel effectual to our salvation.

Bless our land. Be the shield and protector of thy servant our Sovereign, and all the members of the Royal Family. Give wisdom to our counsellors, and sustain the magistrates in the execution of their offices. Give us grace to lead quiet and peaceable lives, in all godliness and honesty. Feed the hungry, clothe the naked. Be the husband of all widows, and the father of all fatherless and orphan children, and the refuge of the destitute. Comfort all who mourn. Lead the outcast, the wanderer, and the hard-hearted sinner to Christ. Strengthen thy people in all godliness, and finally bring us, and those to whom we are related by the ties of this transitory life, with the whole Church, to the rest of thine everlasting kingdom, through Jesus Christ our Lord. Amen.

ALMIGHTY and most gracious Father, we thank Thee for the clear and full revelation of thy will contained in thy holy Word. As it is our great privilege to live in a land where we have the free use of the Scriptures, may we ever bear in mind that to whom much has been given, of them much will be required. Having this infallible guide to direct us, may it be our fervent desire and daily aim to walk so as to please Thee. May we make it the object of our holy ambition to abound more and more in the attainments of Christian faith and holiness. Thy will concerning us is our sanctification. Oh, may we be fellow-workers with Thee in this holy and gracious purpose. Having given our hearts to Thee in the Gospel covenant, may we aspire after the complete renewal of our nature unto holiness; maintaining a vigilant control over our whole nature, and endeavouring to bring every thought and feeling, every passion and desire, into captivity to the obedience of Christ. As Thou hast called us into thy Church to be trained to holy habits in heart and conduct, may we be taught and enabled to walk worthy of our Christian vocation. As we know the commands which were given us by the Lord Jesus, may we remember that to neglect or break them is to despise God. May we, therefore, be careful that the Word of Christ may dwell in us richly in all wisdom and spiritual understanding, that through its sanctifying power we may, in all the circumstances and relations of life, faithfully do the good, and perfect, and acceptable will of God.

We thank Thee, most gracious Father, not only for the counsel which the Gospel affords us for the performance of duty, but also for the rich and unspeakably precious consolations it has opened up to us beyond death and the grave. We rejoice to know that when friends near and dear to us die, and what in them is mortal is laid in the grave, we are not left to sorrow as those who have no hope; for life and immortality have been clearly and fully brought to light by the Gospel. Enable us to remember the words of the Lord Jesus, how He said, "I am the Resurrection, and the Life; he that believeth in me, though he were dead, yet shall he live." May the faith and hope that we cherish in these glorious prospects reconcile our minds to thy providence, however painful and trying it may sometimes be, and may we look forward with delightful anticipation to the second coming of Christ, when those who sleep in Him shall be raised to glory, and death-divided friends shall meet to part no more.

Pardon the sins and shortcomings of this day, and take us under thy protecting care during the night, for Christ's sake. Amen.

[161]

[Morning.] **TWENTY-FOURTH WEEK.—WEDNESDAY.** [Evening.]

READ IN HOLY SCRIPTURE NUMBERS XXII. 1—19.   READ IN HOLY SCRIPTURE ST. MATTHEW XXV. 14—30.

LORD God Omnipotent, by whose mighty arm thy people were rescued from the bondage of Egypt, and were guided and guarded through the wilderness, Thou art the same yesterday, to-day, and for ever. Thou art as merciful as Thou art powerful, and art ever willing to deliver the fettered sinner from the bondage of corruption into the glorious liberty of the children of God. Deliver us, O Lord, we beseech Thee, from the guilt which we have contracted by our transgressions, and from that dreadful curse which has fallen upon us from the law which we have broken. What shall we render unto Thee, O Thou God of grace, for the unspeakable gift of thy beloved Son, who has redeemed us from the curse of the law by being made a curse for us; for now we can come boldly to the throne of grace, to ask for help in every time of need. We can plead the redeeming power of his sufferings and death, and the invitations and promises by which we are authorised to hope for pardon and eternal life. Oh, may the Spirit of glory and grace take of the things that are Christ's, and show them to us so clearly and so impressively, that we shall fully yield our souls to his care, and ever cherish the persuasion that He is able to keep what we have committed to Him until that day.

Deliver us, O Lord, from the love of the world. Remove far from us vanity and lies. Give us neither poverty nor riches. Feed us with food convenient for us, lest we be full and deny Thee, and say, "Who is the Lord?" or lest we be poor, and steal, and take the name of our God in vain. Give us, O Lord, a supreme love to Thee, as our Father in heaven, and cordial love to all thy children, for thine own sake, and for the truth's sake that is in them. Never may temptation, however powerful, induce us to curse any whom Thou hast blessed, or to put a stumbling-block or occasion of offence in the way of a fellow Christian. Give us, O Lord, the same mind which was in Christ, thy Son. Constrain us to receive Him as our example, as well as our Redeemer; and, while we cling to his cross, may we also humbly bow beneath his sceptre.

Thus may we all be distinguished by faith and holiness. As a family may we be united together, not only by natural relationship, but by a bond of faith and love to Christ Jesus; and having thus been one family on earth, may we be, throughout all eternity, united in heaven.

Now unto Him that is able to keep us from falling, and to present us faultless before the presence of his glory with exceeding joy, to the only wise God our Saviour, be glory and majesty, dominion and power, both now and ever. Amen.

O GOD, from whom cometh down every good and every perfect gift, the Father of lights, with whom is no variableness, and no shadow of turning, we, the creatures of thy bounty, and the children of thy grace, bow before Thee in reverence and godly fear. What are we, or what is our father's house, that we should have received of Thee so great mercies? Thine is the air we breathe; thine the food we eat; thine the raiment wherewith we are clothed; thine the life and health, and all the blessings of our earthly state. Above all, in the gift of thy love, Jesus Christ, thine are the things set before us by Thy Gospel which belong to our eternal peace.

We mourn that, so richly endowed of Thee, we have been unprofitable servants; that, in the midst of mercy so abounding and so varied, we have nourished cold and thankless hearts; that we have lost many golden opportunities, this day and every day; and that, in our unloving, indolent, and selfish lives, we have so mis-spent our time, that, if Thou wert now strict to call us to account, we must perish from thy presence.

Oh, spare us, good Lord, in the multitude of thy loving-kindnesses. Spare us, by the blood of thine own Son. Through Him redeem us from our past iniquity and folly, and be not angry with us for ever. And, with new opportunity, give us, we beseech Thee, now grace, whereby we may serve Thee acceptably, and with godly fear. May thy Spirit work within us, till there be deepened in our heart a sense of the awfulness of sin; till we shall be able to reckon up, and correctly to estimate, the talents Thou hast bestowed on us; and till each one shall feel, truly and lastingly, that for all these things God will bring us into judgment. Oh, help us to redeem the time. Strengthen our weak purposes. Set our hearts on high aims. So change and renew us inwardly, that we shall labour not for the meat that perisheth, but for that which endureth unto life eternal. May we, denying ourselves and taking up our cross daily, be followers of Him who went about continually doing good. And when, at thy second coming, we render Thee thine own at last, may it, through thy grace, be with holy usury; and, in our death and in judgment, may we hear thy voice saying, "Well done, good and faithful servant."

Now, under the shadows and silence of the night, do Thou give us rest in Thee, O God. And, oh, may the time speed on when the kingdom of our Lord shall everywhere be spread; when the throne of God and of the Lamb shall be in the midst; and his servants shall serve Him; and his name shall be in their foreheads. We ask it all, O heavenly Father, for Jesus Christ's sake. Amen.

[Morning.]   TWENTY-FOURTH WEEK.—THURSDAY.   [Evening.]

READ IN HOLY SCRIPTURE NUMBERS XXII. 20—35.

O ALMIGHTY God, heaven and earth are full of thy glory. Glory be to Thee, O Lord Most High. Thou dwellest in the light that no man can approach unto, and sittest above the water-floods as King for evermore. Thy throne is established of old, and from everlasting to everlasting Thou art God. Thou hast established the earth, and it abideth. Power and majesty are thine, and all things serve Thee. Holiness and truth are thine; Thou canst not look on iniquity, and all sin is an abomination in thy sight. Fill us, we beseech Thee, with a deep sense of thy greatness and purity, that we may bow at thy footstool with a lowly reverence. We feel, O Lord, that we have no righteousness of our own to plead before Thee. In thy sight we are stained with sin; and through our many transgressions we lie exposed to the curse of the law. Blessed be thy name that Thou hast not cast us out; and that even when we were yet sinners, and without strength, Christ died for us, and redeemed us from the curse of the law, being made a curse for us. Through Him, O Lord, we desire to stand before Thee. Being justified by faith, we desire to be at peace with Thee, and to rejoice in hope of thy glory. Seal to our hearts thy gracious promises, and let the light of thy reconciling love shine on us as we press on in the narrow way of life.

We thank Thee, O merciful Father, for the abundant gifts of thy providence, and especially for thy sheltering care and protection during the hours of darkness, and the renewal to us of this morning's mercies. May we consecrate to thy service the life Thou hast given, and use as in thy sight all the bounties which we have received from thy hand. O God, incline us to live not for ourselves, but to Thee, and to remember that Thou hast sent us into the world not to please ourselves or to have our own way, but to fulfil thy will. We are entering on the day's duties, and many are the dangers and temptations which beset our path. Preserve us, we beseech Thee, in the midst of them all, and let them not be the means of bringing us into sin. May we keep our hearts with all diligence, because out of them are the issues of life; and set a watch over the door of our lips, that we offend not with our tongues. Be with us in all our engagements and duties. Let nothing tempt us in them to disobey thy law or set lightly by thy will. If Thou seest us wandering, or Satan drawing us into any path of evil, mercifully prevent us, and turn us back into the ways of righteousness.

Hear us, O our God, and grant us all those blessings which Thou seest best for us, for Jesus Christ's sake. Amen.

READ IN HOLY SCRIPTURE 1 THESSALONIANS V.

O GOD, eternal, immortal, invisible, and everywhere present, who from the throne of thy glory beholdest all the dwellers on the earth, how can we present ourselves to Thee except through Jesus Christ, the way, the truth, and the life? Thou lovest the light, and all that is perfect and truthful. We therefore pray Thee that we may not be of the night, nor of darkness. Enable us to walk as children of the light. May our deeds be all wrought in and through Thee, as unto the Lord, and not unto men.

Another day taken from the sum of our lives reminds us how near is eternity, and the hour of the second coming of our Lord and Saviour. Forasmuch as we know not when He will come, make and keep us ever ready; may we be in readiness to obey the call to meet the Bridegroom, and have our loins girt, our feet shod, and our lamps trimmed, that that day may not overtake us as a thief. May we be Christ's now, and confess Him in the present sinful world, and so be confessed of Him before Thee and the holy angels.

We would remember before Thee in sorrow the sins and negligences of the past day. We have fought the good fight but weakly; and when putting on our armour, have boasted as he that putteth it off. May we henceforth trust ourselves less, and Thee more. Gird us for the battle against sin, the world, and the devil; strengthen our souls; grant us to overcome the wicked one, and make us more than conquerors through Him that loved us.

We bless Thee for all helps and assistance which Thou hast provided for us, for all who minister to us in holy things, and are over us in the Lord, and admonish us; we would account them as thy messengers to us for good, and pray Thee to bless their example and their counsels, and to reward them for their faithfulness to thy flock.

We pray that the many mercies we enjoy from thy hands may stir us up to do and feel more for others; rejoicing with them that rejoice, and weeping with them that weep. Take, therefore, from us all sharpness and bitterness of temper; and may the Holy Spirit teach us thy ways, and dispose our hearts to walk in them.

Help us to live in holiness and righteousness of life before Thee. As each day passes, may we be made more meet for the great change, and learn how, by earnest, humble faith and trust in Jesus and his atoning blood, we may lay down in peace and take our rest, for Thou makest us to dwell in safety. Bless all our friends and relatives with the abundant tokens of thy favour.

With our thanks for the mercies of this day, we offer up these our humble prayers, through Christ our Lord. Amen.

[Morning.] TWENTY-FOURTH WEEK.—FRIDAY. [Evening.

READ IN HOLY SCRIPTURE NUMBERS XXII. 36—XXIII. 12.   READ IN HOLY SCRIPTURE ST. MATTHEW XXV. 31—46.

LORD God Almighty, who dwellest in the high and holy place, whose name is Holy, in humility and reverence we kneel at thy footstool. We are unworthy to take thy name on our lips, or to come into thy presence, for we are guilty and undone, and of ourselves deserve thy wrath and condemnation. We thank Thee that Thou canst be gracious unto us, and that in thy dear Son we may come before thy Majesty and be sure of an answer of peace. According to thy promise do Thou supply our need, and enlarge our hearts with the experience of thy forgiving grace. We have dishonoured Thee by our many sins. We take shame to ourselves that we have been so forgetful of thy commandments, and that those around have seen in us so little of the mind of Christ. Have mercy upon us, and blot out our sins. Wash us in the fountain once opened for sin, and deliver us from the fear of thy displeasure.

Go with us, we pray Thee, to all the duties of this day. Assist us by thy Spirit that we may do what is just and right before Thee, and act towards all with whom we have to do as we would that they should act to us. When temptations beset us, be Thou near to help us. When Satan would ensnare us in his toils, do Thou deliver us. When our hearts are turning aside from the right way, speak to us, O Lord; and by the vivid impressions of thy Spirit on our hearts, cause us to hold on steadfastly in the footsteps of our Lord and Master, and, if need be, to bear the cross patiently after Him. Our wills and affections are unruly and subtle; enemies are ever on the watch to work our ruin. Lord, keep us vigilant, that we may not be drawn into any kind of sin, but that in the thoughts of our hearts, in the words of our lips, and all the actions of our life, we may honour Thee and show forth the power of thy grace and love.

Look down in tenderest pity, O God, on the world which lieth in wickedness. Turn the hearts of many this day from darkness to light, and bring them in repentance and faith to thy dear Son. Let all thy ministers see the signs of thy presence, and do Thou make them wise to win souls. Strengthen their hands, encourage their faith, and prosper abundantly their labours. Kindle in the hearts of thy believing people an earnest desire for the Saviour's coming, and make the diligent to be found of Him in peace, as servants who look for the Lord.

And now, commending ourselves and all who are dear to us to thy grace and protection, we ask all these mercies in the name of Jesus Christ, our Lord and Saviour; to whom and unto Thee and the Holy Ghost, one eternal and glorious God, be undivided and everlasting praise. Amen.

O LORD open Thou our lips, and our mouths shall show forth thy praise. Draw our hearts to Thyself, that we may magnify thy name and lay at thy feet a sincere and fervent offering. We have proved thy grace and mercy through another day, and now, before we lay ourselves down to rest, we acknowledge with thankfulness thy long-suffering and compassion, who dealest not with us after our sins, nor rewardest us after our iniquities. Have mercy upon us for the sins and shortcomings of the day, and grant us the assurance of thy forgiveness. We are frail and ignorant. Continually are we falling into sin, and yielding, against the warning of conscience, to what Thou hast forbidden. It is only of thine infinite mercy that we are spared. Oh, make us more jealous over ourselves, and more watchful against the encroachments of sin and the world, lest thy Spirit be quenched within us, and the light of his love and guidance be withdrawn.

We take comfort, O adorable Saviour, in the prospect of thy coming glory, when Thou shalt come in the majesty of the Father, with the holy angels, and when before Thee every knee shall bow. Help us to prepare to meet Thee on thy judgment throne, and give such diligence to make our calling and election sure by a cheerful obedience to thy will, that we may be found acceptable in thy sight, and receive that blessing which Thou wilt then pronounce to all who love and fear Thee, saying, "Come, ye blessed children of my Father, receive the kingdom prepared for you from the beginning of the world." Suffer us not, we pray Thee, to deceive ourselves, but may we seek day by day a greater conformity to thine image, and therefore the surer evidence of our being thy true disciples. Oh, create in us an earnest longing for eternal life with Thee in glory, when we shall see Thee face to face, and be delivered from the temptations which now beset our paths.

O God, impress deeply on the hearts of those who love Thee not, and reject thy great salvation, the awful truth of the coming judgment. Convince them of their unfitness to appear in the presence of Christ on that day. Arouse them to self-examination. Awaken them from their spiritual sleep, and stir them up to call upon Thee. Pour out thy Spirit on all thy believing people, and make them zealous of good works, full of loving-kindness and compassion to others, that thus they may reflect in the station of life in which Thou hast placed them, the gentleness and mercy of the Lord Jesus. Be Thou our protector for the night, and shed on our hearts and the hearts of all we love the sweet assurance of thy favour, for thy dear Son's sake. Amen.

[Morning.] **TWENTY-FOURTH WEEK.—SATURDAY.** [Evening.

READ IN HOLY SCRIPTURE NUMBERS XXIII. 13—30.

O GOD of our life, we call upon Thee at the beginning of another day; hear us, we beseech Thee, for the sake of thy dear Son, and enrich us with the continuance of thy goodness. Oh, may our hearts overflow with love to Thee as we count thy multiplied mercies, and think of all which Thou hast so graciously done for us. What forbearance towards our many infirmities and sins! What tenderness and compassion towards our many failings! What turning aside of threatening evils! What overruling of outward things for good! And now, O Lord, Thou hast added to all past countless blessings the rest and protection of another night, and the spiritual opportunities and temporal mercies of another morning. Oh, forgive the coldness of our hearts, that we so little feel thy goodness and so often forget Thee, even when enjoying thy gifts.

Leave us not, O God, to ourselves this day. It is our comfort to know that Thou changest not, that Thou art not a man that Thou shouldest lie, or the son of man that Thou shouldest repent. Give us strong faith that we may lean upon thy promises, and through mercy find in them strength and courage for all the varying circumstances of life. Preserve us this day from sin. Suffer us not, O God, to touch the accursed thing. In heart, and in speech, and in act may we honour Thee, and shrink from all that would grieve thy Spirit, or lay on our souls an increased burden of sin. May we be kept free from the entanglements which Satan spreads for the feet of thy saints, and set our affections more and more on the things which are above, where Christ sitteth at thy right hand in glory.

We pray that all whom we would remember at thy footstool may enjoy the experience of thy saving grace, that they and we may be one in Christ Jesus, children of God, and heirs of the kingdom. Bring such of us as are yet unconverted under the transforming power of thy Word and Spirit. Suffer them not to perish in their sin and unbelief. [Guide the hearts of the children who are dear to us to Jesus day by day, and tenderly influence them to do such things as please Thee. Make them thine, set thy seal on them, cause them to hear the voice of the good Shepherd, and to follow Him.] Be with all thy ministers in their preparation for the labours of the coming Sabbath. Enlighten them with Divine teaching, and show them more clearly the wonderful things of thy Word. Prosper all the labours of teachers and missionaries, and cause many to rejoice anew in the saving knowledge of thy dear Son.

Graciously fulfil these our petitions for his sake. Amen.

READ IN HOLY SCRIPTURE REVELATION XIV.

O GOD of all the families of the earth, our Father and our Saviour, we rejoice in that revelation of thine eternal power and Godhead which appears in all thy works; for the heavens declare thy glory, and the firmament showeth forth thy handywork. But we more abundantly rejoice in those Holy Scriptures which are addressed to us as sinners, and show how we may obtain pardon and salvation; for Thou hast laid upon Christ the iniquities of us all, and hast assured us that if we come unto Thee through Him, Thou wilt in no wise cast us out.

Lord, we believe in thy mercy and love in Christ Jesus; help Thou our unbelief; and enable us with full confidence to commit the keeping of our souls to his hands. Deliver us, O Lord, from going down to the pit by that ransom which Thou hast found for us. Let none of us who read thy Word, and now kneel before thee in prayer, neglect thy great salvation. May we fear lest, having a promise of entering into his rest, any of us should seem to come short of it. Remember us, O Lord, with the favour which Thou bearest to thy people. Cleanse us from all the defilements of flesh and spirit. Let no guile be found in our mouth. Help us to follow the Lamb whithersoever He goeth. Write thy name on our hearts and on our foreheads, that we may be recognised as thy children, the heirs of God and joint heirs with Christ; and at last may we be found without fault before the throne of God and the Lamb. May the great Shepherd of the sheep walk with us through the valley of the shadow of death, and bring us into the brightness of the glory that shines beyond. But all the days of our appointed time would we wait till our change comes; and while we are strangers and pilgrims here, we would live not unto ourselves, but unto Thee, and for the furtherance of thy Gospel in the world.

We thank Thee for the opportunities of usefulness we enjoy; and we pray that all institutions around us, which exist for the temporal and spiritual welfare of the world, may abundantly prosper by thy blessing. Call forth abundant labourers into thy vineyard, who may speedily convey the everlasting Gospel to all the dwellers upon earth. To-morrow is the rest of the holy Sabbath of the Lord. Give us refreshing sleep this night, O Lord, that we may be prepared for the privileges of thy holy day; and may all its sacred services be used by thy Holy Spirit to prepare us for the enjoyment of the rest that remaineth for the people of God.

And now may the grace of our Lord Jesus Christ, and the love of God, and the fellowship of the Holy Spirit, be with us all evermore. Amen.

[MORNING.] **TWENTY-FIFTH WEEK.—LORD'S DAY.** [EVENING.

READ IN HOLY SCRIPTURE MICAH VI.

GRACIOUS and merciful God, blessed be thy name, through Christ Jesus, for the care Thou hast taken of us during the night, for the comforts of the morning, and especially for the privileges of the day of rest. Oh, bless us, we beseech Thee, all the day long. Put away all our sin. Bestow on us a Sabbath spirit. Give us at once a serious and a cheerful mind. Help us in our secret places to draw near to Thee with a fervent heart, and in the assemblies of thy saints to worship Thee in spirit and in truth.

Precious are the truths which thy ministering servants will be declaring aloud this day. Oh, may the glad tidings of redemption through a crucified Redeemer be glad tidings indeed to ourselves. May we more deeply than ever feel our need of Jesus, as sinners guilty and undone; more solemnly than ever surrender our helpless souls into his hands; and more joyfully than ever realise our interest in his salvation. Let thy good Spirit fix thy Word in our memories, and write it in our hearts, that it may be a light to our steps, and a lamp to our path.

And bless thy Word to others, we entreat Thee, as well as to ourselves. Gird thy ministers with strength for their arduous toil, and grant them a sweet consciousness of thy help under a sense of their many weaknesses. Give to thy congregations the hearing ear and the understanding heart, that they may not only hear, but understand and obey. Make thy presence felt in the midst of thy waiting people, and make the place of thy feet glorious. While Jesus is lifted up, as Moses lifted up the serpent in the wilderness, may He draw all men unto Him. Edify thy saints, and bring sinners to the knowledge of Thyself. Comfort the mourners in Zion, and give them the oil of joy for the spirit of heaviness.

Compassionate those whom afflictive dispensations withhold from public ordinances. We pray for such as are laid on beds of languishing, that Thou wilt make all their bed in their sickness, and place underneath them the everlasting arms; and make Thou the sick chamber none other than the house of God and the gate of heaven.

Oh, spread thy Gospel throughout this and every land. Pity the multitudes by whom it is neglected, and who, in the midst of privileges, hasten so madly to perdition. Pity the wide-spread pagan lands which lie in the region and shadow of death. Hast Thou not given thy Son for them? Hast Thou not given them unto thy Son? Wherefore dost Thou delay the manifestation of thy power? Oh, pluck thine hand from thy bosom, and graciously accomplish the things whereof Thou hast spoken. Hear us, O Lord, for Jesus' sake. Amen.

READ IN HOLY SCRIPTURE REVELATION XX.

ETERNAL God, the First and the Last, we adore Thee that what eye had not seen, nor ear heard, neither entered into the heart of man to conceive, Thou hast been pleased to reveal to us by thy Spirit, through thine Apostles, that our faith should stand not in the wisdom of men, but in the power of God. And we humbly beseech Thee so to enlighten our minds in the knowledge of thy Son, Christ Jesus, that we may hold fast the profession of our faith steadfast unto the end. Being filled with all joy and peace in believing, may we abound in hope through the power of the Holy Ghost, and grow in grace and the knowledge of our Lord and Saviour Jesus Christ.

O God, who hast given unto us the rest of the Sabbath-day, and hast made us joyful in the house of prayer, let thine ear hearken unto the prayer which thy servants have prayed unto Thee this day. Accept our service of song and thanksgiving, and so help us by thy grace, that we, having heard thy Word, may, in an honest and good heart, keep it, and bring forth fruit; that through patience and comfort of the Scriptures we may have hope. Grant that being quickened together with thy Son, and raised up together, and made to sit together in heavenly places, we may know Him, and the power of his resurrection, and the fellowship of his sufferings; that we may attain unto the resurrection of the dead, and finally appear with Him in glory.

Be pleased, O Lord, to hasten the latter day glory by the more speedy advent of millennial light, and life, and love; when Satan shall be bound, the throne of iniquity be overthrown, the rod of the oppressor be broken, the captive be set free, and the kingdom of thy Son, which is righteousness, and peace, and joy in the Holy Ghost, be universally established. Accomplish the number of thine elect, and gather thy redeemed into one. Grant that our names may be written in the book of life, so that we may not be hurt by the second death; but having washed our robes and made them white in the blood of the Lamb, may we serve Thee day and night as priests in thy temple; and having come off more than conquerors, reign with our Lord in his kingdom for ever.

On our family, our kindred, and our country; on the one holy catholic Church, and on thy servants in the ministry of the Gospel; on all seminaries of learning; on all evangelical and missionary labours; on Jew and Gentile, bond and free, let it please Thee, O God, to command thy blessing; and unto Thee, O Father, with thy Son Jesus Christ, and the Eternal Spirit, be glory, world without end. Amen.

[Morning.] **TWENTY-FIFTH WEEK.—MONDAY.** [Evening.

READ IN HOLY SCRIPTURE NUMBERS XXIV.

READ IN HOLY SCRIPTURE ST. JOHN XIII. 1—19.

O THOU good and gracious God, who makest a hedge about thy people, and turnest aside the evil designs of their enemies, we owe Thee all: this life that Thou hast continued to us, with all its mercies, hopes, and opportunities of usefulness, this our unbroken and happy family, our safety during the night past, our health for the day on which we are now entering, and above all for this our most happy privilege of daily united prayer and praise.

It is good to draw nigh unto Thee. Teach us how to make the best use of these sacred moments. Open our hearts to receive the lessons of thy Word. Quicken our desires after Thee and the knowledge of thy ways. May the fruits of the Spirit abound in us more and more. If we be thine, enrich us yet more with thy grace, and enable us to serve Thee with a single eye, and a heart all thy own. If we be strangers to Thee, make Thyself known to us in all the riches of thy love in Christ.

Grant to us, as we go out and as we come in, thy most rich and satisfying blessing. Give to each of us whatever we need to-day for time and eternity. We have duties to discharge to Thee and our fellow-men—make us faithful in the doing of them: temptations to meet—grant us the victory over them: difficulties through which to pass— teach us to be patient, persevering, and hopeful: sorrows to bear—make them a gracious discipline and a most fruitful chastisement. Strengthen, sustain, and comfort us, O our Father, with all spiritual blessings in heavenly places in Christ Jesus.

Let us as a family be more united, more loving to-day. Let us bear and forbear, anxious to please, fearing to offend, thinking one for another, and finding our pleasure in each other's pleasure. [Grant to the parents to rule with wisdom, tenderness, firmness, and for God; to the children to obey affectionately and promptly, and as unto the Lord.]

Happy, O our God, are all they who put their trust in Thee, and dwell beneath the shadow of thy wings. How goodly are thy tents, O Jacob, and thy tabernacles, O Israel! blessed is he that blesseth thee, and cursed is he that curseth thee. So bless us as thy heritage, O our God, so acknowledge us as thy own peculiar people.

Hasten the coming of the Lord Jesus; remove all that hinders and opposes it. Spread from land to land, from heart to heart, the knowledge of his grace. Make ready a people prepared for Him. Pour out richly on Jew and Gentile thy converting, sanctifying Spirit. Pardon, accept, and bless us, for Jesus Christ's sake. Amen.

O ALMIGHTY God, at the close of another day we draw nigh to Thee in prayer. We bless Thee that we are permitted to come before Thee to confess our sins, to speak thy praise, and to implore thy forgiving mercy. Help us to approach Thee with a penitent, contrite, and devout heart.

We thank Thee, O Lord, that Thou hast given to us thy blessed Son, to be to us not only a sacrifice for sin, but also an example of godly life. Enable us most thankfully to receive that his inestimable benefit, and also daily to endeavour to follow the blessed steps of his most holy life.

We acknowledge, O Lord, that we have this day fallen far short of his perfect pattern, by evil thoughts and rash words, by indolence and negligence, by covetousness and worldly desires, by selfishness and pride. We have sinned against Thee, and provoked thy displeasure; but we pray Thee, O Lord, be merciful to us; wash us in the blood of the Lamb that was slain to take away the sins of the world. Take away all iniquity, receive us graciously, forgive us freely.

Holy Father, we thank Thee for receiving us into thy family in Christ. May his example be in our hearts, to follow it and to live by it. Let this mind be in us which was in Christ Jesus our Lord.

Give us, we pray Thee, a more simple faith on Christ, a more entire reliance on his redeeming grace. Enable us to walk more acceptably before Thee. Let thy Holy Spirit ever sanctify and teach us. Grant that as we have been baptised into the death of Christ, so by the continual mortifying of our corrupt affections, we may die with Him unto sin, and rise with Him unto newness of life.

And now, O Father, we commit ourselves to thy gracious care for another night; keep us from all things that may hurt us; above all, keep us from sin. Let our last thoughts before we sleep be of Thee, and raise us up again to see the light of another day.

We commend into thy hands all our beloved relations and neighbours: make them partakers of thy grace, and number them among thy children. Have pity on the afflicted, the fatherless, and widows: comfort and succour them in all their sorrows. We pray for our Sovereign and all the Royal Family, for the ministers and dispensers of thy holy Word and sacraments, particularly for him who is over us in the Lord. Endue them with wisdom, and make them zealous to serve Thee. Grant, O Lord, these our imperfect petitions, for thy dear Son Jesus Christ's sake, to whom, with Thee and the Holy Spirit, be everlasting praise. Amen.

[MORNING.] TWENTY-FIFTH WEEK.—TUESDAY. [EVENING.

READ IN HOLY SCRIPTURE 2 PETER II. 9—22.

READ IN HOLY SCRIPTURE ST. JOHN XIII. 20—38.

O LORD, Thou art a terrible God, and thy Word is as a sharp sword. Thou art a consuming fire, and wilt not spare the guilty. Permit us this morning to approach Thee with reverence and with godly fear; knowing that God is not mocked, and that whatsoever a man soweth that shall he also reap. Thy Word, so full of promise, and comfort, and consolation, is also a word of admonition, and a message of warning. Enable us to read both its promises and its threatenings with profit to our souls. We feel that we too often presume upon the long-suffering of God. Oh, teach us to deny ungodliness and worldly lusts, and to live righteously, soberly, and godly in this present evil world. Deliver us from temptation. We know that if we be thine Thou wilt deliver us, and wilt always make a way of escape for us. May we guard our lips, our tongues, our hearts, so that they offend not. Grant us that, by thy grace assisting us, we may not walk after the flesh, but after the Spirit. May we submit ourselves with all lowliness and humbleness of mind to those that are placed by Thee in authority over us—our Sovereign, our government, our parents, our teachers; and, above all, may we be in continual subjection to the leading and guidance of thy Holy Spirit, and may thy Word and doctrine be our rule of faith and conduct.

Keep us ever in the right way; let us not stray from the paths of uprightness and peace. May we love the way of righteousness, and walk therein. Give us grace to live this day to thy glory, lovingly engaged in thy service, walking in the way of thy commandments. Grant that this day we may fall into no sin, neither run into any kind of danger. May our souls be kept in perfect peace, our minds being stayed on Thee. We feel, O God, how prone we are to wander and stray from Thee. Keep us, we beseech Thee, steadfast in thy commandments. Let not Satan lead us captive, but in every time of temptation enable us to resist and overcome him.

O Lord, we beseech Thee to save us from the pollutions of the world, through the knowledge of the Lord and Saviour Jesus Christ. Forbid that we should be ever again entangled and overcome by the craft and subtlety of the devil. Increase and multiply thy mercy and grace upon us, and give us peace.

We pray for all who are dear to us. O God, bestow upon them all such blessings, spiritual and temporal, as Thou seest them to need. We pray for all who are labouring in the vineyard of thy Church. Guide and watch over and prosper them. These mercies we humbly ask in the name of Jesus Christ, thy dear Son, our Lord. Amen.

HOLY and merciful God, who hast spoken to us in these last days by thy Son Jesus Christ, we adore Thee that Thou didst send Him into the world to suffer for us in the flesh, and hast now glorified Him at thy right hand.

Enable us to be true disciples of Christ, and keep us from the deceitfulness of our own hearts, that we may not be guilty of saying, "Lord, Lord," with our lips, while we deny or betray our Master by our life.

Deliver us, we beseech Thee, from covetousness and every worldly lust; and let us not lean on our own strength in our purpose or endeavour to serve Thee. May the vanity and pride of our nature be destroyed and cast out; so that we shall walk humbly with our God. May thy strength be made manifest in preserving and sanctifying us.

We confess our heinous offences against Thee, and cry for mercy in the name of our Divine Mediator. May we be corrected and strengthened, so that we shall not any more wander from Thee, the Shepherd and Bishop of our souls. Form in us the spirit of children, that we may receive into our hearts the rule of Christ, and with grateful confidence cry unto Thee, "Abba, Father." Enable us to hold fast Jesus Christ, the beginning of our confidence, firm unto the end. Strong in the Lord and in the power of his might, may we withstand all temptation, and in every conflict come off more than conquerors.

We thank and praise Thee for thy bountiful goodness to us this day. By thy grace alone have we been preserved from evils into which we must have fallen. Thou hast given strength to our hand, and encouragement to our spirits. We bring our united thank-offering to thine altar. Cleanse from our souls the defilements of this day. Let the blood of sprinkling be upon us, and spread over and around us the shield of thy power, that the angel of destruction may not come near our dwelling.

All whom we love we commend to thy gracious keeping. May we have refreshing repose under the shadow of thy protection. If it please Thee to surprise us this night with any trouble, do Thou stay and strengthen our spirits, and give us perfect peace. Give us an early and happy waking on the morrow. May our first thoughts when we wake be of Thee, and our first desires and purposes be toward the keeping of thy commandments.

Teach us while we live to live to Thee, that when we die we may die to Thee. O our Father in heaven, to Thee we offer our evening prayer, and look for a gracious answer, in the name of our Divine and ever-blessed Redeemer, Jesus Christ. Amen.

[171]

[Morning.] TWENTY-FIFTH WEEK.—WEDNESDAY. [Evening.

READ IN HOLY SCRIPTURE NUMBERS XXVII. 12—23. | READ IN HOLY SCRIPTURE ST. MATTHEW XXVI. 17—35.

O LORD, the God of the spirits of all flesh, teach us to worship Thee in spirit and in truth. Thou art great, and greatly to be feared, and to be had in reverence of all them that are about Thee. Thou art holy, and of purer eyes than to behold iniquity. Thou art good, and the earth is full of thy goodness. Thou art merciful, and thy mercy endureth for ever.

We bless and praise Thee, O our God, that Thou hast kindly kept us through another night. We thank Thee for our safety, and for sleep, and for all the blessings brought to us with the morning light. Let our hearts be deeply affected by the riches of thy goodness, and may all thy gifts constrain us to love Thee more, and to serve Thee better than we have hitherto done.

We have been reminded by thy holy Word that there is no man that sinneth not. If thy faithful servant Moses by one transgression incurred thy displeasure, how much more have we, by repeated, countless acts of rebellion, deserved thine indignation! Enter not into judgment with thy servants, for in thy sight shall no man living be justified. We adore Thee, O Lord, that Thou hast cast our lot in this merciful day of Gospel grace, and we pray that renewed, sanctified, and preserved by the good Spirit of our God, we may be permitted not only to see, but to enter into that kingdom of glory which Thou hast prepared for all them that love Thee. Make us followers of Jesus; at his word may we go out and come in. To Him may we carry all our wants, cares, trials and sorrows, as they rise, and may we find relief by telling Him all that is in our hearts. We desire to set the Lord always before us. We would spend this day in thy fear. Let not any iniquity have dominion over us. Strengthen us, O God, in the hour of temptation; keep us every moment, that we may not stray from Thee.

If it please Thee, preserve unto us health and strength; make us diligent, contented, patient; establish Thou the work of our hands, yea, the work of our hands establish Thou it. Glorify Thyself in us, and by us. Let all our actions be influenced by love to Thee and love to our fellowmen; so that by honourable, upright, and useful lives we may bring a good report upon thy ways.

Pour down thy richest blessings on all who are near and dear to us, and unite them with us to Thee and to each other, in the everlasting bonds of faith and love to Jesus Christ. Make thy great and holy name to be praised throughout all the earth. Prosper thy Church universal, that by the spread of thy truth the ends of the earth may see the salvation of our God. Pardon, accept, and bless us for Jesus' sake. Amen.

HEAVENLY Father, we come to thy throne of grace this evening in the name of Him of whom the whole family in heaven and earth is named. We desire to approach Thee in the spirit of adopted children, whose privilege it is to say, "Abba, Father," and to give thanks for all the goodness and mercy which have followed us all the days of our life. We thank Thee for our experience of thy loving-kindness this day. Thou hast held us up, and we are safe; and Thou hast clothed and fed us, and given or withheld as Thou sawest best for our highest interest. O for grace to have no will of our own in anything, but to leave all to the will of our Father who is in heaven!

And now we pray, that as the blood of the paschal lamb was the sign of safety to the Hebrews, who used it according to Divine appointment, so the blood of Christ, our Passover, who was slain for us, may be sprinkled upon our consciences, to purge us from dead works, and to deliver us for ever from the wrath to come. Impress us deeply with the exceeding sinfulness of sin, of which there is no remission without shedding of blood; and with the great love wherewith Thou hast loved the world in giving thine only-begotten Son to die, that whosoever believeth in Him may not perish, but have everlasting life. May we yield ourselves entirely to Him, and believe on Him to the saving of our souls. Preserve us from the danger of being content with a mere profession of faith in the Saviour, lest in the hour of temptation we fall into sin and deny Him.

We desire to be placed continually under the care of the good Shepherd who was smitten for us. May He be to us the Shepherd and Bishop of our souls, who has sought and found us, and restored us to himself. Keep us in thy blessed fold, O Thou adorable Lord of the Church which Thou hast purchased with thy blood, and lead us by the still waters and the green pastures. Let us never stray from Thee. Let not the enemy and the destroyer have any power over us; but hold Thou us up, and we shall be safe; keep us, and no evil thing shall come near us. We beseech Thee to pardon all that Thou hast seen in our hearts and lives this day, inconsistent with a profession of the Christian name. Forgive worldly thoughts and feelings, hasty tempers, angry words, and corrupt passions; and bring every thought, we beseech Thee, in willing subjection to the authority of Christ. Preserve us in perfect safety and peace through the night, if it be thy holy will. Let our dwelling and persons be protected from every danger, and do more for us than we can ask, for Christ's sake. Amen.

[Morning.] **TWENTY-FIFTH WEEK.—THURSDAY.** [Evening.]

READ IN HOLY SCRIPTURE NUMBERS XXXII. 1–32.

ALMIGHTY God, we draw near to thy footstool in the name and through the intercession of thy dear Son. Another season of rest has been granted to us; we bless Thee for the mercy, and pray that we may be deeply thankful for all thy goodness to us. Make us to know the value of time and opportunity, and grant that every day which Thou addest to our life may be a day's progress in grace and in ripeness for the kingdom. Whatever of trial this day may bring to us, sanctify it to our souls. Let us not yield to the temptations of Satan, nor be overcome by the sin that is in our hearts. Grant to us that wisdom which is profitable to direct, and that grace which shall keep us from all evil. We have received unnumbered mercies at thy hand. Oh, let us never depart from thy love. Remember us, Lord, with the favour which Thou bearest unto thy people.

Bless to each of us the portion of thy Word now read. Cause its lessons to abide with us through the day. Oh, give us faith and strength to follow Thee entirely. Amid the snares which surround us, enable us to cleave unto Thee with full purpose of heart. We confess with sorrow how much the present world has engrossed our thoughts; how much we have forgotten that this earth is not our rest; and that, like Reuben and Gad, we have been too content to have our portion on this side Jordan. Convince us, we beseech Thee, of the danger of living at ease. Keep us from ever discouraging the hearts of thy children by holding back in the Christian warfare, or by magnifying the difficulties of the way. May we never, by self-indulgence, or the compromise of principle, put a stumbling-block in our brother's way.

And now, heavenly Father, that we are about to enter on the engagements of the day, do Thou mercifully go with us, and leave us not. Many are the temptations which continually beset us, and our own hearts are frail and ignorant. Almighty God, do Thou strengthen us. Gracious Spirit, do Thou teach us; show us the true and the right way, and give us a sound judgment in all things. Let thy choicest blessings rest on all whom we would remember at thy footstool. [Draw the hearts of the children before Thee to their Saviour, and train them up by the discipline of thy grace and providence in the ways of godliness and peace.] Give to all who shall receive any message from thy Word this day the listening ear and the understanding heart. Keep thy Church watchful for the Lord's coming, and enable us, whenever He cometh, to be found of Him in peace. Grant us these mercies, O God, for Jesus' sake. Amen.

READ IN HOLY SCRIPTURE GALATIANS VI.

O LORD, who hast taught us that all our doings without charity are nothing worth, and that by this shall all men know that we are thy disciples, if we have love one to another, send thy Holy Spirit, we pray Thee, and pour into our hearts that most excellent gift of charity, the very bond of peace and of all virtues, without which whosoever liveth is counted dead before Thee. We pray, O Lord, that thy Holy Spirit may keep us from all self-exalting thoughts, and make us gentle toward all our brethren. May we ever be ready to bear one another's burdens, by sympathy, counsel, or relief; and so fulfil the law of love. Keep us from all self-deception; and if in anything we are better than others, help us to remember who it is that has made us to differ.

Inspire us, we pray Thee, with an affectionate reverence for those who are over us in the Lord, and admonish us; and keep us mindful of the obligations we are under to them for those spiritual benefits which they have been the instruments of imparting to us. May we endeavour to strengthen their hands in all things, that they may give themselves to the work of the ministry, feeding and providing for the Lord's family, and seeking for Christ's sheep which are scattered in the midst of this naughty world.

Deliver us from all desire of making a fair show in the flesh, and courting acceptance by outward appearance. Remembering that the offence of the cross can never cease, may we not shrink from the persecution which will ever follow it, but strive to be conformed to the example of Him who for our sake endured the cross and despised the shame. May we seek that union with Him which consists neither in circumcision nor in uncircumcision, but in a new creation; and enable us to manifest the reality of this union by the deadness of our affections to worldly things, and by the earnestness with which we follow our heavenly calling.

Pardon, we pray Thee, O heavenly Father, our innumerable transgressions of thy holy law, and the grievous inconsistency of our lives with our profession. Pardon the iniquity of our holy things, the sins that cleave to our best duties, and wash them away in the blood that cleanseth from all sin.

Finally, accept our heartfelt thanks for all thy mercies in providence and grace. Graciously watch over us during the night, and preserve us and all who are dear to us from harm. If it please Thee, give us refreshing sleep, and raise us in the morning strengthened for thy service in the duties of the day.

Hear us, we pray Thee, for Jesus Christ's sake, our most blessed Lord and Saviour. Amen.

[Morning.] **TWENTY-FIFTH WEEK.—FRIDAY.** [Evening.

READ IN HOLY SCRIPTURE NUMBERS XXXV. 9—29. | READ IN HOLY SCRIPTURE ST. JOHN XIV. 1—14.

O RIGHTEOUS Father, and merciful Judge, we have sinned against Thee. We are verily guilty in thy sight, and thy displeasure is as the avenger of blood to our terrified consciences. Be merciful unto us, O God, be merciful unto us, for our soul trusteth in Thee; yea, in the shadow of thy wings will we make our refuge.

We thank Thee for having revealed to us that refuge in thy dear Son. Help us now and always by thy gracious Spirit to believe in Him, that we may never die. When we tremble at the thought of vengeance, send forth the Holy Ghost the Comforter into our hearts, and lead us to Jesus, the Mediator of the new covenant, and to the blood of sprinkling, that speaketh better things than that of Abel. We would flee from the wrath to come. We would escape unto Him for our life. Suffer us not wilfully or carelessly to neglect his great salvation, but give us grace to feel that Thou hast in thy mercy made Him our surety, that, as the heirs of promise, we might have a strong consolation who have fled for refuge to lay hold upon the hope set before us.

O Thou Almighty, unchangeable God, be a refuge for us this day. Accept our thanks for the protection and rest of the past night. And now, during the day, keep us from forsaking the shelter of thy grace. Go with us where we go; dwell with us where we dwell. Deliver us from all evil and mischief; from all blindness of heart; from pride, vain-glory, and hypocrisy; from envy, hatred, malice, and all uncharitableness. Mercifully defend us especially from our adversary the devil, a murderer from the beginning, and who walketh about as a roaring lion, seeking whom he may devour. Whatsoever we may have to do, at home or abroad, in the family or in our business, keep us, O Father, from making lies our refuge. Preserve us from vainly attempting to hide ourselves under falsehood; but let thy mercy and thy truth preserve us, according as we hope in Thee.

Bless, we beseech Thee, O God, our family, our relatives and friends, our country, and all the nations of the earth. Let brotherly love continue. Let all oppression, and murder, and cruelty, and war cease. Be Thou everywhere, in all lands, a strength to the poor, a strength to the needy in his distress, a refuge from the storm, a shadow from the heat, when the blast of the terrible ones is felt. Oh, let the nations be glad and sing for joy. Let the people praise Thee, O God; let all the people praise Thee.

This and every blessing we ask through Jesus Christ, our Lord and Saviour; unto whom, with Thyself, O Father, and the Eternal Spirit, be glory for ever. Amen.

O GOD, the Author and Giver of all good things, we now approach Thee with the voice of thanksgiving for the many mercies we have received at thy hand, and for the long-suffering goodness whereby we have been led in thy providence all this day long. We have merited nothing but continued chastisements through our manifold transgressions; but Thou hast not dealt with us according to our deserts. How many have been the provocations wherewith we have provoked Thee to anger this day: in temper, thought, desire, word, and action we have transgressed. Have mercy upon us. We plead for forgiveness through the alone death and merits of thy dear Son, and we thank Thee that, guilty and unworthy of any favour as we are, we can approach Thee with confidence through Him, and obtain mercy and ever find grace to help in time of need. May we ever bear in mind that there is an all-prevailing Advocate with Thee, who has made atonement for sin.

Make us diligent in every effort to advance our own souls' welfare and the spiritual good of others. Animate us with a full persuasion of thy grace being sufficient for us. Impress upon us the shortness as well as uncertainty of this present life, and the nearness of that period when our eternal destiny will be for ever fixed. Cheer us with the assurance that for all true disciples of the Lord Jesus there are mansions of bliss prepared, where troubles will for ever cease, and the presence of holiness and happiness never leave us. We are encouraged to pray for all men, that the light of thy truth may shine so effectually, that many may be partakers of its rich promises, and be occupants of the many mansions in thy house above.

Our own country and nation demand our special intercessory supplications. Oh, that Thou wouldest so bless it with the dew of Divine truth, that the barren parts might blossom and bear fruit, and rejoice as the garden of the Lord; and that from us might go forth an increased number to preach the Gospel in all lands.

Bless us now before Thee, and all our relations and friends. Such temporal things grant to us as Thou seest to be best for us; and in spiritual things supply all our need, according to thy riches in glory by Christ Jesus. We would remember before Thee all thy people. Enable them to fulfil their high calling as lights of the world.

We now commit ourselves to thy Divine keeping. These prayers and supplications we offer unto thy Divine Majesty, looking for acceptance and a gracious answer through the merits of thy Son Jesus, to whom, with Thee and the Holy Spirit, be glory for ever. Amen.

[174]

[Morning.]   TWENTY-FIFTH WEEK.—SATURDAY.   [Evening.

READ IN HOLY SCRIPTURE PSALM XXVII.

O LORD, who art the light and the salvation of thy people, we give Thee thanks that Thou hast raised us up this morning after the hours of sleep, and brought us together to pay our vows unto the Lord. We thank Thee for all the blessings of this life, for health and strength, for food and raiment, for relatives and friends, for home with all its comforts, and for the civil and social privileges which in our favoured country we are permitted to enjoy. Give us thankful hearts. Bless the Lord, O our souls, and forget not all his benefits. We beseech Thee, O Lord, to bless us all this day. From the temptations of the world, the flesh, and the devil, defend us, good Lord. In every temptation make a way for our escape, that we may be able to bear it. Hold Thou us up, and we shall be safe. Thou who art the strength of our life, strengthen us this day, to discharge every duty and to bear every trial. Should the storm of trouble be permitted to sweep across our path, may we hide ourselves in the pavilion of the Almighty. Should the enemies of our souls be permitted to assail us, may we retreat beneath the shadow of thy wings. Amid all earthly perplexities be Thou our guide. Teach us thy way, O Lord, and lead us in a plain path, because of our enemies. As earthly supports give way, may we find in Thee our trust; and as earthly friends fail, may we prove thy friendship only the more unfailing. When father and mother forsake us, when lover and friend are taken from us, and our acquaintance go into darkness, be Thou our comfort and our stay. By our experience of thy faithfulness in the past, may we be encouraged to trust Thee for all the future. Thou hast been our help; therefore leave us not, neither forsake us, O God of our salvation. When circumstances arise that are calculated to discourage our faith, may we wait upon the Lord, and be of good courage, that He may strengthen our hearts.

We beseech Thee, most merciful Father, to bless all the members of this family. Be gracious to all our relatives and friends. Smile upon our native land. Bless our gracious Sovereign and all the Royal Family. Give wisdom to our rulers, and a good understanding to all who are in authority over us. Remember the poor, and make them rich in spiritual blessings. Pour out the Spirit upon thy Church. Hasten the coming of the latter day glory. Then shall the earth yield her increase, and God, even our own God, shall bless us. God shall bless us, and all the ends of the earth shall fear Him. Accept, O Lord, our thanksgiving for all thy mercies, and grant these our prayers, through Jesus Christ our Redeemer; to whom be everlasting praise. Amen.

READ IN HOLY SCRIPTURE ST. JOHN XIV. 15—31.

O GOD, the high and holy One, we confess with shame that we have often grieved thy Holy Spirit by our sinful affections, our excessive attachment to earthly things, and our daily forgetfulness of Thee. This day, as it hastens to its close, bears witness against us. We implore thy forgiveness through the blood of Christ, and pray that before we sleep we may enjoy the sense of reconciliation with Thee by his death. Henceforth enable us to walk in the Spirit, that we may not fulfil the lusts of the flesh. Fill our souls with his enlightening and sanctifying presence, and guide us in all thy ways by His constant teaching. By thy Holy Spirit live in us and be our life, work in us and be our strength, shine in us and be our light, make our souls thy temple and our hearts thy throne. May the beauty of holiness be spread over our whole conduct. May we daily feel that we are truly the sons of God, because we are led by the Spirit of God.

We earnestly desire, O our Father, to be in constant communion with Thee, and to enjoy the privilege of that manifestation of our Saviour which He gives not to the ungodly world. Enable us, therefore, to prove our love to Thee by keeping thy commandments, that Thou mayest come unto us, according to thy promise, and make thine abode with us. Thou art the true dwelling-place of our souls, the strong habitation whereunto we would continually resort. Draw away our affections from all created good, by shedding abroad thy love in our hearts, and becoming the object and the end of our whole lives.

Amid all that is trying and depressing in this world, may we over share in that peace which our Lord hath left us, the present inheritance of his Church. Save us from inordinate anxieties, and gloomy forebodings of the future, which we desire to leave in thy gracious and sovereign hands; and may that peace which passeth all understanding continually keep our hearts and minds, through Christ Jesus.

Let this peace rest upon our spirits as we retire this evening to rest. We unfeignedly thank Thee for all the numberless mercies of the past day, and humbly supplicate the mercies of the night. Grant us that sleep which Thou dost give to thy beloved. Spread over us the wings of thy protecting providence; and in the morning may we be still with Thee, and arise as from the dead to a new life of holy and active service. In such service may all our future days be passed, until He who is gone to Thee the Father shall come again to receive us to Himself. We ask all this in his name, to whom, with Thyself and the Holy Spirit, be ascribed all honour and glory for evermore. Amen.

[Morning] TWENTY-SIXTH WEEK.—LORD'S DAY. [Evening.

READ IN HOLY SCRIPTURE DEUTERONOMY IV. 1—22.

READ IN HOLY SCRIPTURE ST. JOHN XV. 1—13.

WE praise Thee, O Lord, for the privileges of our favoured country, of which the return of thy holy day reminds us. Surely Thou hast not so dealt with any people. May we in this age worthily use, and maintain, and transmit to those who come after us the precious heritage of spiritual advantages which Thou hast graciously bestowed upon us. Thou art not calling us in these times to struggle amid persecutions and sufferings for the attainment and preservation of freedom to worship Thee. Under the shelter of a benign reign, we go forth this morning to join the multitude that keep holy day, no man forbidding us. The Lord bless and prosper the beloved Sovereign, for whose rule this land in all its borders gives Thee thanks; and fill with peace and joy the palace-homes of our country. Give to the Royal Family a happy Sabbath. Give to this household, and to every domestic circle where thy name is feared, a day of spiritual delight and profit; and grant, O Lord, that soon this sacred weekly rest may be rejoiced in by every family, high and humble, throughout the realm. Instruct this privileged nation so to know and follow thy statutes, that all the world may see us to be, through thy Word given to us, a wise and understanding people, and be drawn to serve the same gracious God.

Go forth to-day, O blessed and mighty Spirit of the Lord, with all those whose high office it is to set before assembled congregations thy glorious Gospel. Bless thy servant on whose ministrations we wait. Make him wise to win souls this day. Guide all those who go up to worship in the courts of thy house. What praise shall we render to Thee, O living and true God; because we do not gather ourselves together to bow down to graven images, or lift our eyes in worship to the hosts of heaven! What gratitude, also, should be ours, that we come not to Mount Sinai, with its blackness and tempest, but to Mount Zion; nor to altars on which animal oblations burn, but to scenes where praise and prayer, with contrite hearts, are the only sacrifices. May we joyfully offer them this day, in the name of Him by whose one offering all that believe are for ever sanctified.

Have mercy, O Lord, on the blinded worshippers of idols. Gather the scattered descendants of thine ancient people to the faith of the Messiah already come. Let the whole world speedily know Thee, the only true God, and Jesus Christ, whom Thou hast sent. Let thy kingdom be greatly advanced this very day. Let thy saints rejoice in Thee, and let there be joy in the presence of thine angels over many sinners won to repentance and salvation. Hear us in these our requests, and forgive and accept us, for Jesus Christ's sake. Amen.

O THOU great and glorious Jehovah, before whom angels veil their faces, while with unceasing praise they exalt thy name; pour out upon us the spirit of grace and supplication, that we may praise and adore Thee for the riches of thy redeeming love. May the Sabbath now closing prove to each of us a foretaste of the rest which remaineth for the people of God. Grant, O Lord, that many who rose this morning ignorant of the way of life, may have been born again of incorruptible seed, by the Word of God. Increase the number of thy spiritual watchmen, and add daily to thy Church such as shall be saved.

Forgive, O Lord, the sins of this day. Pardon the iniquity of our holy things, and graciously accept our imperfect services. If Thou, O Searcher of hearts, seest any of us still unchanged, and living only for this present world, let thy Spirit now prevail to open their eyes and lead them to Jesus, that we may be a household fearing Thee and working righteousness.

Blessed Jesus, Thou hast shown thy love to us in leaving the glory which Thou hadst with the Father before the world was, becoming a man of sorrows, and laying down thy life for us. Cause us to magnify the riches of thy grace by our lips and in our lives. We have been outwardly engrafted into Thee by baptism. Thou knowest whether by inward and spiritual regeneration we have been renewed into Thine image. Thou purgest the living branches, that they may bring forth more fruit. Oh, give us grace to profit by the precious discipline. Train us in self-denying godliness here, and make us meet for the enjoyment of thy presence hereafter. In the bright hope of the heavenly crown, make us cheerful bearers of the earthly cross. Remove all spiritual ignorance from our minds, and satisfy our hearts with true peace. Thy Word alone can make us clean. Grant that it may richly abide in us, so that we may walk in its holy precepts, hold fast its saving truths, and rejoice in its precious promises. Cause us to dwell together in brotherly love. Gracious Saviour, abide in us, that we may abide in Thee, and at length be glorified with Thee in thy coming kingdom.

Take us all, we pray Thee, O Father, into thy Divine protection for the night. If Thou blessest us, we shall be safe from all harm, whether it threaten the body or the soul. May the refreshment of the day of rest, with its spiritual privileges, and its seasons of communion with Thee, fit us to enter cheerfully on the fulfilment of thy will in the duties of the week. Thus living to thy praise now, we may look forward to thy glory hereafter. Grant it all for Christ's sake. Amen.

[Morning.] **TWENTY-SIXTH WEEK.—MONDAY.** [Evening.]

READ IN HOLY SCRIPTURE DEUTERONOMY IV. 23—40.

ALMIGHTY God, who dwellest in the light which is unapproachable; whom no one hath seen or can see; whose glory may not be given to another, nor thy praise to graven images; and who hast commanded us not to make to ourselves any likeness of anything in heaven above or in the earth, neither bow down to them nor serve them, for Thou art a jealous God: search us and try us, and see what way of wickedness there is in us, and lead us in the way everlasting. Be pleased so to fill our hearts with thy grace that we may abstain from those fleshly lusts which war against the soul, and walk before Thee in righteousness and holiness all our days.

O God, who art merciful and gracious, we acknowledge that we have erred and strayed from thy ways like lost sheep. We have sinned; we have done wickedly. But deal not with us after our sins, nor reward us according to our iniquity. Out of the depths we cry unto Thee. Oh, send forth thy mercy and truth. Let thy loving-kindness prevent us, for in Thee do we put our trust. Forsake us not, neither forget thy covenant, for we seek Thee with all our heart and with all our soul. Thou art rich in mercy to all that call upon Thee. Save us from our sins; grant us redemption through the blood of Christ; and so sanctify us in body, soul, and spirit by the Holy Ghost given unto us, that we may evermore keep thy statutes and thy commandments which Thou hast commanded us, that it may go well with us and with our children after us, that we may all have an inheritance among them that are sanctified, and finally be numbered with thy saints in glory everlasting.

O God, the day is thine; the night also is thine. We laid ourselves down, and have slept, for Thou hast sustained us. Thou hast prepared the light and the sun. Cause us to hear thy loving-kindness in the morning, for in Thee do we trust. Cause us to know the way wherein we should walk, for we lift up our soul unto Thee. Let thy hand, which is good, be upon us as a family, and bless us with thy favour, which is life. [Grant that our offspring may receive the adoption of children.] Be gracious to our kindred and our country, and guide the counsels of all in authority. Teach us to be subject unto the higher powers. Spare thy people, whom Thou hast purchased for a possession unto Thyself, and let all the ends of the earth see thy salvation.

O God, be not far from us. Make haste for our help; so shall our lips greatly rejoice, and our soul, which Thou hast redeemed. Perfect thy work in us, and preserve us to thine eternal kingdom, through Jesus Christ our Saviour. Amen.

READ IN HOLY SCRIPTURE ROMANS VI.

O MOST gracious Father, who art light, and in whom is no darkness at all; who hast called us with a holy calling unto fellowship with Thyself and thy Son Jesus Christ: we beseech Thee that this thy loving purpose of grace may daily be more and more fulfilled in us. Oh, how good hast Thou been to us, if this evening we are more humble, more truly conscious what sinners we are, more simply and gratefully dependent on Thee, thinking more of thy great grace and love which has borne with us another day, and, above all, blessing Thee for that blood which cleanseth from all sin.

In many things have we all offended this day. Very much that is evil Thou hast seen in us, in our thoughts, and words, and acts. Which of us ought not to be ashamed? We are not worthy so much as to lift up our eyes unto Thee, or to call Thee Father. Yet to whom can we go but unto Thee? And, oh, we ask Thee to receive us, to forgive us, to humble and bless us. Wash us throughly from our iniquity, and cleanse us from our sin. Create in us a clean heart, O God, and renew a right spirit within us.

Great are the riches of thy grace in Christ Jesus. But while we praise Thee, let us not presume; because thy grace abounds, let us not continue in sin. O Lord, Thou knowest the deceitfulness of our hearts, and how we wrong Thee, to-day by distrust, to-morrow by sinful presumption.

Grant us to remember that Thou hast given thy Son to be both a sacrifice for sin and an ensample of godly living. As He died for sin, enable us to die daily unto sin. As He was raised from the dead by the glory of the Father, so also may we walk in newness of life, yielding ourselves unto God, as those who are alive from the dead.

O our Father, suffering, shame, and death, these belong to us, for we have sinned, and these are the wages of sin; yet we ask Thee for life, love, thy grace here, thy glory hereafter. Gratefully do we thank Thee that thy gift is eternal life, through Jesus Christ.

Now, gracious God, add this also to thy other blessings, that we may lie down in peace with Thee, with each other, with all men, to-night. Grant these our wearied bodies, if it be thy will, unbroken, refreshing slumber. Keep us safely from sin, from danger, from disease, and all evil. We give ourselves up, Thee, with thy hands, body, soul, and spirit. Bless us and all our friends, and relatives, and neighbours; and do Thou for us and them according to thy tender mercies, and thy knowledge of our manifold weaknesses and wants, for thy Son Jesus Christ's sake; to whom, with Thee and the Holy Ghost, be all honour and glory. Amen.

[Morning.]   TWENTY SIXTH WEEK.—TUESDAY.   [Evening.

READ IN HOLY SCRIPTURE PSALM CXLVI.

O MOST merciful Lord, we thank Thee for the words of praise that Thou hast put into our mouths this morning. May these words of our lips be the expression of our inward gratitude to Thee. Fill our hearts with gladness as we meditate on Thine unspeakable love to us. Truly Thou hast been very gracious to us. Our mercies have been unspeakable. From the day of our birth until this hour, goodness and mercy have followed us. Bless the Lord, O our souls; and all that is within us, bless his holy name. Bless the Lord, O our souls; and forget not all his benefits. While we live will we praise Thee. We will bless Thee while we have any being.

May we know the unutterable happiness of having Thee for our God, through the precious atonement of thy dear Son. O God of Jacob, do Thou ever be our help; O God and Father of our Lord Jesus Christ, save us, and bless us, and sanctify us, and make us meet for glory. Whom have we in heaven but Thee? and there is none on earth that we desire in comparison with Thee. Suffer us not to put our trust in man, or to lean upon an arm of flesh. May we never seek our happiness from earth's pleasures, or our honour from earth's great ones. We would be happy only in thy love, and seek only the honour that cometh from above.

O Thou that openest the eyes of the blind, open our eyes. Enable us to see Thee as Thou art, and admire Thee as we ought. Give us this day all that we need. Feed us with the bread of life. Give us Thyself, blessed Jesus. Fulfil thy gracious promise, and grant that, feeding on Thee, we may live for ever.

O Lord, we are often bowed down with sorrows; do Thou ever raise us up again, and make us glad with the joy of thy countenance. We labour and are heavy laden with our manifold sins; do Thou take away our load, and give us rest in Jesus. Here we have no continuing city. This world is not our home. Give us the spirit of pilgrims, that we may live as strangers upon the earth; and fix our affections on things above. O Thou that relievest the fatherless and the widow, relieve us in all our sorrows, whensoever they oppress us. May we cry unto Thee in every time of trouble, and not cry in vain. O Thou who lovest the righteous, love us. May thy Spirit dwell richly within us. Reign in our hearts this day and for evermore. Establish thy kingdom in our hearts. Keep us this day from all dangers. Shield us from temptation. Protect us from all sin. Help us to serve and glorify Thee in all that we do; and to thy name shall be the praise for evermore. We ask all for the sake of Jesus Christ our Lord. Amen.

READ IN HOLY SCRIPTURE ST. JOHN XV. 13—27.

O HEAVENLY Father, accept through Jesus our evening offering of prayer and praise. Many have been thy thoughts of love towards us. How great is the sum of them! How safely we have gone out and come in, and how kindly have all our wants been provided for! But herein most especially hast Thou shown thy love towards us, that Thou hast sent thy Son to lay down his life for us, not as friends, but as enemies. Oh, thanks, new thanks, perpetual thanks, be to Thee for this unspeakable gift.

Once, indeed, we were enemies to Thee by wicked works; but now, through the blood of Jesus reconciled, Thou callest us friends. Accept graciously at our hands whatever we have done for thy sake and in thy strength this day; and in thy mercy forgive whatsoever thy holy eyes have seen amiss in us. Of many shortcomings and iniquities we ourselves are conscious; but how many more must have been manifest in thy sight! Blot out our iniquity as a cloud, and as a thick cloud our sins. Receive us graciously, and love us freely. Help us, O Lord, to take gratefully at thy hands whatever good Thou sendest, and to bear submissively every trial. Shall not all thy will be love? Like as a father pitieth his children, so Thou pitiest them that fear Thee; for Thou knowest our frame, and rememberest that we are dust. Be our refuge in every sorrow, our strength when heart and flesh faileth; and when Thou callest us to walk through the valley of the shadow of death, let thy presence cheer our path, and thy hand sustain our steps.

And now, heavenly Father, we commit ourselves to thy care through the night on which we are entering. While darkness covers us, and dangers are round about, let thine ever open eye be upon us, and thine almighty power be our guard. If it please Thee, give us sleep; or if our eyes be held waking, in the multitude of our thoughts within us let thy comforts delight our souls. If we see another morning, rejoice us with the light of thy countenance, and take our renewed life again under thy guidance and care; or if our eyes open no more on earth, receive us to thy fatherly arms, and to that happier world where there is no night, no weariness, and no sorrow.

Blessed be thy name, O God of our mercy, for the sweet hopes with which we are permitted to close this day. And now, having by prayer and supplication with thanksgiving made known our requests unto God, may the peace of God, which passeth all understanding, keep our hearts and minds, through Christ Jesus; to whom, with Thee, Holy Father, and the Blessed Spirit, be equal and everlasting praise. Amen.

[Morning.] **TWENTY-SIXTH WEEK.—WEDNESDAY.** [Evening.

READ IN HOLY SCRIPTURE DEUTERONOMY V. 1—21.

READ IN HOLY SCRIPTURE ST. JOHN XVI. 1--15.

HOLY, holy, holy, Lord God Almighty, who by thy great power and wisdom hast created all things, and dost uphold them by the word of thy power, we acknowledge Thee as the only cause of our preservation during the past night, as well as the Giver of our present existence. And now we go forth to the duties appointed to us in our several stations with prayer that we may never forget our obligations to Thee, to love Thee and to serve Thee. Help us to pray, that we may ask such things as Thou art ready to grant, and may find ourselves strengthened and cheered by this our service for the various employments of the day. May a present sense be given us, that as Thou hast been about our bed, so Thou wilt be about our path, spying out all our ways. May we therefore walk uprightly before Thee, for Thou requirest truth in the inner man. May our desire be to acquit ourselves always as thy servants, in all things doing thy will from the heart; not by constraint rendering Thee only the form of obedience, but constrained by love to Thee, for thy great love bestowed on us in the gift of thine own dear Son.

By thy Holy Spirit put thy laws into our minds, and write them in our hearts; then shall we have respect unto all thy commandments, and serve Thee with a willing mind. Let others seek what they will, and find their portion in what they can; give us grace to cleave to thy testimonies, and to find our meat and drink in doing thy will. Thy commandments are not grievous to such as know thy name; yea, in keeping of them there is great reward. Grant us, therefore, to seek thy precepts as our rule always; then shall we walk at liberty, not looking to be accepted by Thee on account of our obedience, but desirous to show ourselves thy dear children, by being followers of Thee in all holy conversation and godliness.

Thou knowest all the events that shall befall us this day, the persons with whom we shall have intercourse, the difficulties and dangers that may beset our path. Thou also knowest our weakness, and our proneness to err from thy commandments; prevent us, therefore, we beseech Thee with thy grace and goodness, keep us from all evil, and guide us in the paths of righteousness for thy name's sake.

We would remember before Thee our gracious Sovereign and all the Royal Family. May they be blessed and a blessing to our nation. Look down on our neighbourhood; let peace and godliness prevail among us. Make all our dear relations and friends partakers of thy best blessing. Hear us, and answer us graciously, for Jesus Christ's sake. Amen.

O BLESSED Spirit, Holy Comforter, whom the Father hath sent unto his people; we humbly call upon Thee at thy throne of grace this evening, and implore thy help and blessing in our present approach to Thee. Thou art the Teacher of thy Church and people. Oh, teach us, and first of all teach us how to pray. Thou art the Author of all prayer, the Giver of all peace, the Dispenser of all good gifts; be Thou the Hearer and the Answerer of our prayer this evening.

O Lord Jesus Christ, Thou hast ascended up on high, and to thy Church on earth Thou hast been pleased to send the Comforter, thy Holy Spirit. Send this comforting Spirit into our hearts to-night, we pray Thee. In all time of danger and persecution may we feel his presence near, and be supported by his strength.

O God and Father, send to us thy Holy Spirit to direct, govern, and sanctify both our hearts and bodies. 'Tis thine to send the Spirit to whomsoever Thou wilt; and Thou hast promised that Thou wilt give thy Holy Spirit to them that ask it. We now ask, O Lord, for Jesus Christ's sake, give unto us thy Holy Spirit! It is the Spirit who quickeneth; who is the Teacher of the Church, the Comforter of the afflicted, and the Reprover of the world. Seal thy people with this earnest of their inheritance, that Christ may be glorified in us, whether by life or by death. Guide us into all truth, and make us temples of the living God, consecrated, body, soul, and spirit, to thy service.

O Thou Triune Jehovah, Father, Son, and Holy Spirit, we bless Thee for all the choice gifts Thou hast been pleased to pour upon us. Lead us into all truth; fill us with all grace; bedew us with the unction of the Holy One; let us ever be partakers of that life-giving Spirit by which the soul liveth unto God, and abideth for ever. May that Spirit rule in our hearts and consciences, and sanctify and keep us holy unto the day of thine appearing.

We pray for an abundant outpouring of thy Spirit on all who profess and call themselves Christians. Go forth in the might of thy power and grace, O God the Holy Ghost. Convince the world of sin, because it believes not in Christ. Show to the unconverted their own unrighteousness, and reveal unto their hearts Christ, the Lord our Righteousness. Arouse them by the predictions of judgment, and bring them trembling and penitent to the feet of Jesus. Let the tokens of thy presence be seen in the Church of Christ, in the hearts and lives both of ministers and people. Guide the ignorant and erring into the way of truth, and prepare all men for the coming of the Lord. We ask all for Jesus Christ's sake. Amen.

[MORNING.]   TWENTY-SIXTH WEEK.—THURSDAY.   [EVENING.

READ IN HOLY SCRIPTURE DEUTERONOMY V. 22—33.   READ IN HOLY SCRIPTURE ST. JOHN XVI. 16—33.

GLORIOUS and holy Lord God Almighty, we, thy unworthy servants, draw nigh to Thee at the beginning of another day. We bless Thee for taking care of us during the night past, and for refreshing us with comfortable sleep. We beseech Thee to send us thy blessing through the day on which we have entered. Be with us in our going out and coming in. Dispose us to lift up our hearts to Thee whilst we are engaged in the works of our calling, and enable us to do all as in thy sight and to thy glory. We bless Thee, O Lord, for Jesus, the Mediator of the new covenant; that we are permitted to draw nigh to thy throne in his name, that we may obtain mercy, and find grace to help in time of need. We thank Thee that Thou speakest to us not from the mount that burned with fire, but from Mount Sion, through thy own beloved Son. We bless Thee, O Lord, that Thou invitest us to come to Thee, and that Thou vouchsafest to us thy covenant of peace. Oh, let thy blessed Spirit help our infirmities. Take away from us the spirit of bondage; give to us the spirit of faith and of fear, of love and a sound mind.

We have professed ourselves, O Lord, to be thy people; we have acknowledged aforetime, and we now acknowledge before Thee, our obligations to love and serve Thee; but we have too often broken our vows, we have turned aside out of thy ways. We humble ourselves before Thee, O God, because of our manifold transgressions and great sins. Thou mightest justly cast us away from thy presence, and refuse any more to be entreated of by us; but, O Lord, we beseech Thee, deal not with us according to our sins, recompense us not according as our iniquities deserve. Have respect for Him who knew no sin, but was made sin for us. Pardon, we pray Thee, all our sins, and let them no more have dominion over us. Enable us this day to love and to serve Thee. Write thy laws in our hearts. Strengthen us for all the duties of our holy calling. Make thy law precious to us, and enable us to keep it unto the end. Thou knowest, Lord, the secrets of our hearts. Shut not thy merciful ears to our prayers.

Bless all who are near and dear to us; our kindred, friends, and relations. We pray for our Sovereign and for those in authority. Guide them in all their deliberations, and overrule all that they do for the welfare of thy Church and the increase of godliness and truth in the land. Graciously prosper all the labours of thy ministers, and increase daily the number of thy believing and obedient people. We ask all in the name and for the sake of thy dear Son Jesus Christ, to whom be honour and glory for ever. Amen.

WE thank Thee, gracious Saviour, for the precious words of comfort Thou didst speak to thy disciples before Thou didst leave them and go to thy Father. Bestow upon us now that faith which will hear thy voice, and enrich our hearts with the peace and joy which Thou hast promised to them that believe. We confess that we have but poor and feeble views of the Father's love, and that too often we restrain prayer before God. Now that Thou art exalted above all principality and power, fulfil thy word unto us, upon which Thou hast caused us to hope. All hearts are open before Thee, and all desires are known unto Thee. Give us enlarged hearts, that we may expect great things from God; stir us up to ask and receive, that our joy may be full. Lead us into a growing experience of the love that passeth knowledge, that we may be cheerful in tribulation, steadfast in hope, fervent in spirit; and, like our great Leader, may also overcome the world. Continue, in thy mercy, to bestow upon us all that is needful for body, soul, and spirit; and when Thou shalt come a second time without sin unto salvation, let us be found amongst the subjects of thy redeeming grace.

Graciously grant us thy presence and protection through this night; cause us to feel that we are not alone, but that thine eye is upon us and thy heart toward us. Be pleased, O Lord, to give us safe and sweet sleep, and let no evil or fear of evil disturb the watches of the night. We thank Thee for the tender care which has been about our path during another day. We ascribe it to thy loving-kindness, that we have escaped calamity, disease, and death; and we call upon our souls and all that is within us to bless thy holy name. Forgive all that has been opposed to thy holy will in our thoughts, or words, or actions; and cleaving to the promise of thy forgiving love, let us close our eyes without a misgiving or a fear. And when the brief day of life shall come to its end, may we as calmly and as gladly sleep in death as we hope to rest this night upon our bed. [O Lord, in thy mercy bless our dear children, and give us grace to train them in thy fear. May our example, our instructions, and our prayers lead them into the good way, that they may walk before Thee all their days on earth, and dwell with Thee hereafter in heaven.] Have mercy upon all who are lying on beds of languishing. Preserve those who are journeying on the mighty waters, and hear our prayers that all men may trust in thy faithful providence and know thy saving grace. Hear us, O our God, for the sake of Jesus Christ, thy Son, our Lord. Amen.

[180]

[Morning.] TWENTY-SIXTH WEEK.—FRIDAY. [Evening.

READ IN HOLY SCRIPTURE DEUTERONOMY VI.

O LORD God of our fathers, we confess to Thee our great and manifold transgressions. We have turned from the way of thy holy commandments. We have followed the devices of our own foolish and proud hearts. We beseech Thee to have mercy upon us, and to turn our hearts to the obedience of thy holy laws.

Open our understanding to receive knowledge, and guide our erring and stumbling feet in the paths of wisdom. Fill us with reverence and love to Thee, our Father in heaven. Draw us into a childlike, confiding trust in our Divine and adorable Saviour. Enable us to have fellowship in our daily life with the ever-blessed Spirit.

We adore and bless Thee for thy great goodness in giving us thy Word. We rejoice before Thee that we have been taught to understand and receive thy mercy, made known to us in the teachings and life, in the atoning sorrows and death, of our blessed Lord and Saviour Jesus Christ. We desire daily to learn of Him. By thy grace and help we would hide these treasures of wisdom and knowledge in our hearts, that we may not sin against Thee.

We thankfully accept of thy good gift of life this morning. Thou hast watched over our sleep, and hast waked us into life, and we earnestly desire to live this day so as to please Thee. We go forth at thy bidding to our daily work. Make us strong and diligent in the doing of it. May thy law be written in our hearts, so that we shall this day avoid all that is evil, and follow that which is good. Let not cares harass us, or temptations ensnare us. Keep us from all sinful anger, and from every temper that does not breathe devotedness to Thee, our God, and charity to our neighbour. May we be able, in seeking our own good, to desire and devise benefit and happiness for all whom it may be in our power to befriend. Holy Saviour, who hast left us an example of holy human life, enable us by thy Spirit to follow thy steps.

Be pleased, O Lord, to dwell in our house. Make thy face to shine upon our native land. Bless our beloved Sovereign and the members of the Royal Family. May justice be administered in this realm with impartiality and truth.

Comfort every mourner. Deal graciously with the sick and troubled, and brighten by thy favour and love the dark path of the dying. Let thy Word have free course and be glorified in the conversion of many souls to Christ. Regard, we pray Thee, all our relations and friends. Pour down upon them all spiritual and temporal blessing. Accept our praises, and hear and answer our prayers, for the sake of Jesus Christ, thy Son and our Saviour. Amen.

READ IN HOLY SCRIPTURE ST. JOHN XVII.

ALMIGHTY God, the Father of our Lord Jesus Christ, through whom we have access to thy throne, give ear to us, while again we bow before Thee. We rejoice that we have such an Advocate with Thee as Jesus Christ the Righteous, who is the propitiation for our sins. On his intercession we rely for the acceptance of our evening sacrifice.

We praise Thee that through the day we have been under thy Divine protection; and that every want has been supplied with a bountiful hand. Pardon us if there has been any abuse of our mercies, or any failure in the recognition of their source. Bless us still, O our Father, and help us ever to cherish towards Thee filial love and gratitude.

We rejoice in the contemplation of the glorious work of thy Son, who for our salvation came down from heaven, and dwelt among us; hallowing our earth by his footsteps, and by his holy life and wondrous death obtaining eternal redemption for us. We exult in the assurance that He glorified Thee by the manifestation of thy name, and finished the work that Thou gavest Him to do; and that now He has returned to the glory which He had with Thee before the world was. Evermore may we depend upon the continuance of his love, on his pitiful remembrance of us, and on his powerful pleadings on our behalf, who are still in the world, struggling with the foes that beset our path, and looking to Him for succour in the hour of need. May we, while here, be kept from the evil around us, and thy truth work so mightily in our hearts, that under its influence we may shine as lights in the world.

Bind thy people together in the bonds of a holy friendship. With one Lord, one faith, one baptism, one God and Father of all, may they keep the unity of the Spirit in the bond of peace; be more united in effort and aim; and by love serving one another and Thee, constrain the world to believe that Thou hast sent thy Son. May it be their glory to make known the truth, that God was in Christ, reconciling the world to Himself. In this reconciliation may we all share, and when Christ, who is our life, shall appear, may we also appear with Him in glory. Daily may we be prepared for the better world, and when absent from the body may we indeed be present with the Lord.

Guard us from all evil amid the darkness of the night. Refresh our weary minds with quiet sleep; and with the new day and new duties, may there be given to us new strength and wisdom, that we may glorify Thee in our bodies and spirits, which are thine. Grant all, with the pardon of every sin, for Jesus' sake. Amen.

[MORNING.] TWENTY-SIXTH WEEK.—SATURDAY. [EVENING.

READ IN HOLY SCRIPTURE DEUTERONOMY VII. 1—16.

READ IN HOLY SCRIPTURE ISAIAH XLIX. 1—17.

O LORD God, who hast graciously made Thyself known to us in Christ Jesus, we adore Thee for Him as thine unspeakable gift to the world, and pray that for his sake we may obtain grace to help us in every time of need. We thank Thee for peaceful rest during the past night, for the light of this morning, and for all the blessings with which we are favoured. Every good and perfect gift cometh down from Thee, the Father of Lights, with whom is no variableness, neither shadow of turning; and whilst we live, and move, and have our being in Thee, help us to acknowledge Thee in all our ways, and do Thou direct our steps.

We know not what is before us this day; but, O God, we would commit ourselves to Thee, praying that our steps may not slide, and that we may not offend Thee with our tongue. Let us profit by the lesson we have read in thy holy Word at this time. May we remember that those who call upon thy holy name are to be separate from the world. Keep us from its vanity, and folly, and idolatry. May we not covet the things thou hast forbidden, lest they be a snare to our souls. Help us to remember that this is not our rest; but that our blessed Lord has gone to prepare a place for us, and that an inheritance that fadeth not away is reserved in heaven for all who are kept by the power of God through faith unto salvation. Bring us, in thine own good time, O Lord, when we shall have gone through our earthly pilgrimage, into that good land of promise, which is better than any earthly Canaan; and while we confess ourselves unworthy of lot or part in the inheritance of the saints in light, we rejoice Thou hast freely set thy love upon us, and hast redeemed us, not with corruptible things, as silver and gold, but with the precious blood of Christ, as of a lamb without blemish and without spot. Not by works of righteousness which we have done, but according to thy mercy Thou hast saved us, through the redemption that is in Him. Without money and without price Thou hast opened the fountain of life, and graciously called us to come and drink; and if we have been at all enabled to do this, the glory and the praise be thine!

We pray for the guidance and sanctifying influences of the Holy Spirit; for we know that those who are saved by grace will follow holiness. May we adorn the doctrine of God our Saviour in all things, and give evidence that we have passed from death unto life. Be mercifully pleased to give us this day everything we need, as well for the body as the soul, for we bless Thee Thou carest for both. Graciously hear and answer us, O God, for we ask all in the name of our Lord and Saviour Jesus Christ. Amen.

GREAT and gracious God, we are constrained to thank and praise Thee for the inestimable treasure of thy holy Word, so full of wondrous things, so suited to all our needs, and rich in glorious promises. It is through thy grace, and the instruction of thy Spirit, that we are able to delight ourselves in any measure in those heavenly truths Thou hast discovered to us; and very earnestly we crave increased enlightenment, purer hearts, stronger faith, a more sincere desire to know thy mind, so that thy Word may dwell within us richly, bringing forth much fruit through its effectual working.

Truly, Lord, thy dear Son, our Saviour Jesus Christ, by whom we come to Thee, is the first and last of all that Thou hast spoken to us; and to his voice we listen when our ears have been unstopped, and Thou hast taught us its sweet tones. Fain would we sit continually at his feet, receiving into the deepest places of our souls the words of life that come forth from his lips. May the wide world receive them, too; all the people, near and afar, and in the islands of the seas.

Lord Jesus, we desire to behold Thee; we would strive to know Thee in all thy grace and power, and to ponder with ever-deepening interest that better covenant of which Thou art the Mediator.

For our sakes Thou didst assume the form of a servant, and in suffering and sorrow didst complete the work of redeeming us. Praise and honour be unto Thee. Thou art Lord of all. Thou art given for a light to the Gentiles, and to be the glory of thy people Israel. Thou hast not toiled in vain, nor spent thy strength for nought; but thy right is with the Lord, and thy reward with thy God. Oh, may the contemplation of thy triumph feed our souls with strength and patience. How greatly dost Thou comfort us! Save us from ever being distrustful of thy love. How can we be? It is like no other love; purer, tenderer, stronger, incapable of change, and overlasting. We are graven upon the palms of thy hands, and thou wilt lead us by the living waters, where the sun smites not by day, neither the moon by night, and the days of our mourning shall be ended. By another day we and thy whole Church are nearer to that perfect bliss. Through every hour a deep, broad stream of blessing has followed us. Lord, accept our thanks, and mercifully blot out all our sins. Oh, forgive us, and make clean our hearts within us! Be with us through this night, Eternal God, to whom the darkness and the light are both alike. Ourselves, our dear ones, all we know and love, we cast upon thy goodness and thy truth, through Jesus Christ our Lord; to whom, with Thee and the Holy Ghost, be everlasting praises. Amen.

[MORNING.] TWENTY-SEVENTH WEEK.—LORD'S DAY. [EVENING.

READ IN HOLY SCRIPTURE DEUTERONOMY VIII.   READ IN HOLY SCRIPTURE ST. MATTHEW XXVI. 36–56.

O ETERNAL God, who hatest nothing that Thou hast made, we laud and magnify thy glorious name for thy long-suffering goodness. Every benefit which we enjoy is thy gift; all our spiritual blessings flow from Thee. It is through thy great love in sending thine only-begotten Son to bear our sins and open the kingdom of heaven to all believers, that we can approach Thee with confidence, and make known our requests before thy throne. Grant us, therefore, thankful hearts for all thy mercies. Enlighten our eyes, that we may see the numberless tokens of thy care which surround our path. Preserve us from grieving thy Holy Spirit by mistrusting thy loving-kindness, and assist us with thy grace, that we may acknowledge Thee in all our ways, and do those things which are pleasing in thy sight.

We bless Thee that Thou hast consecrated this day to thy service, and commanded us to keep it holy. May it always be honourable in our estimation. Teach us to observe it in a right spirit, that we may worship Thee with pure hearts fervently. Enable us to lay aside the cares and distractions of the past week when waiting on Thee in thy house, that we may be very attentive to hear thy Word, and thereby gain strength for glorifying Thee in our bodies and our spirits, which are thine. Let not our holy things become occasions of transgression, lest Satan get an advantage over us. Sanctify us, O Lord, that we may be instruments of usefulness to others, and make it evident that we are doers of the Word, and not hearers only.

Be with all thy ministering servants this day throughout the world, that they may deliver thy message with persuasive power. Thou alone canst give the increase, and bring nigh to Thee those who are afar off. Have compassion, therefore, upon the heathen, and those who are out of the way, that they may be turned from darkness to light. Fetch them home, blessed Lord, to thy flock, that they may experience joy and peace in believing.

Keep us, throughout the week, from evil thoughts and hardness of heart. While diligently discharging our daily duties, assist us to labour chiefly after that meat which endureth unto everlasting life. Increase our love for holy things, that we may never be ashamed of Thee. Nourish us with all goodness, that, being rich in faith, we may plentifully bring forth the fruits of the Spirit. Be with all our dear relations and friends, and grant that they may prosper both in body and soul. Watch over our country, and endow our rulers with judgment and firmness, that they may govern us with wisdom. Grant this for the sake of Jesus Christ. Amen.

MOST merciful God, who causest the outgoings of the morning and the evening to rejoice, we thank Thee for this holy day, for all its happy privileges; that we have taken sweet counsel, and gone to the house of God in company, beheld the beauty of the Lord, and inquired in his temple. May we value, above all earthly pleasures, the joy of serving and worshipping Thee. We ask thy blessing on all the holy occupations of the day. Accept our private supplications that we have presented at thy throne, and help us never to neglect the duty of secret prayer. Bless the public services of thy house upon which we have attended. May the words which we have heard with our outward ears sink deep into our hearts, and prove precious seed that shall bring forth much fruit. As our Sabbaths multiply, may our piety increase, and our graces grow. May the Saviour become increasingly precious, and the prospect of heaven more bright; and when the earthly Sabbath ceases, may we spend the eternal Sabbath with Thee, in thy presence, where there is fulness of joy, and at thy right hand, where there are pleasures for evermore.

We beseech Thee, O Lord, to bless this day, not only to ourselves, but to all who have observed its ordinances, or have been occupied in the vineyard of the great Master. Bless the preaching of thy holy Gospel everywhere. Gather many souls this day to Thyself. Prosper every sincere endeavour to do good. And may those who have spent this day in the sick chamber, or, like Jesus, in some Gethsemane of sorrow, receive the blessing of Him whose presence is not confined to temples made with hands, but who has promised to dwell in the humble and the contrite heart.

We thank Thee, above all thine other gifts, for the gift of a Redeemer to save our lost souls, Wash away our sins in his atoning blood. When we taste the joys of thy salvation, may we never forget the bitterness of the Saviour's sorrow, and often think of Him who in Gethsemane and on Calvary bore our sins and carried our sorrows. May we look to the Lord Jesus not only as our sacrifice, but also as our example. Teach us those lessons of humility, and patience, and meekness, and obedience, which Gethsemane should teach all Christ's disciples.

Prepare us for another week of activity. Defend us, good Lord, from all evil. Give us strength for every duty and trial. Deliver us in the hour of temptation. Help us to fight the good fight of faith, and to come off victorious at last, through the grace of our Lord Jesus Christ, to whom and to Thyself, O Father, and to the Holy Ghost the Comforter, be everlasting praises. Amen.

[MORNING.]   TWENTY-SEVENTH WEEK.—MONDAY.   [EVENING.]

READ IN HOLY SCRIPTURE DEUTERONOMY X.   READ IN HOLY SCRIPTURE ST. MATTHEW XXVI. 57—75.

O LORD, who art God of gods and Lord of lords, a great God and a mighty, we learn with thankfulness that Thou dost execute the judgment of the fatherless and the widow, and lovest even the stranger. Thou art also our praise; for Thou hast wrought more glorious things for us through our Lord Jesus Christ.

When we read of thy just requirements, we are humbled to the dust under a sense of our guilt and sinfulness. It is meet and right that we should walk in all thy ways, love Thee and serve Thee, our God, with all our heart and soul. But, O our Father, how grievously have we fallen short of all this! How often have we wickedly departed from thy ways; and instead of supremely loving Thee, lavished the affections of our immortal being upon perishing, and even upon sinful things. We unfeignedly confess that we have broken thy covenant, and forfeited every claim to thy regard, and are in ourselves helplessly exposed to thy righteous displeasure.

But we call to remembrance what Thou hast done for us through One greater than Moses. We desire to contemplate Thee as Thou art now revealed: not in a fiery law, but in the Gospel of thy Son, in whom we have redemption through his blood, the forgiveness of sins, according to the riches of thy grace. We flee from ourselves and our iniquities, to find a refuge in Him alone. We lay hold with the hand of our faith on the one atoning oblation, which he offered on our behalf; and we pray to be freely forgiven and accepted for his sake.

Write thy laws in our hearts, and impress the image of thy Son on our whole life. Uproot every evil principle which lurks within us; make our souls the temples of thy light and love, and take all our powers into thy service.

Uphold our goings this day; guide us in all that may be perplexing; aid us in the discharge of duty; defend us in all dangers and temptations; in all time of our weakness be over nigh with thy gracious succour, and save us from ever becoming to others an occasion of breaking the commandments of our God. Whatever Thou dost give or withhold of earthly good, may we ever feel that Thou alone art our inheritance. Accept the humble oblations of love which we may lay upon thine altar, and lead us onward day by day to that heavenly Canaan which Thou hast sworn to give to thy people for an everlasting possession.

We ask all this, and present our grateful acknowledgments of thy goodness, in the name of our Lord and Saviour, Jesus Christ; to whom, with Thyself and the Holy Spirit, be all the praise. Amen.

O SON of God, who for us didst become a man of sorrows and acquainted with grief; who wast despised and rejected of men, and now Thou art exalted to the right hand of God, strengthen us, we beseech Thee, with thy Spirit, and give us fellowship with thy sufferings, and prepare us for the triumphs of thy coming.

Believing in thy tender sympathy with us, we confess to Thee our weakness. Thou knowest what is in man. Pity our frailty; pardon our sin. We, too, have thought and spoken that which is false about Thee. We have denied Thee even in the presence of thy enemies. We are not worthy to be called by thy name. Oh, mercifully look upon us in thy compassion. Bring thy words to our remembrance, and thus, by thy loving Spirit, humble our vain-glorious hearts in true repentance. Rebuke us not in thy hot displeasure, but chasten us only in thy loving-kindness, that as Thou didst suffer for us in the flesh, we may be armed likewise with the same mind.

We thank Thee, O Lord, for having redeemed us from the curse of the law, by being made a curse for us. We pray Thee this night so to reveal Thyself to our hearts, that we may be filled with thy love. Whatever we have said or done against Thee this day, forgive. Whatever has been well-pleasing in thy sight, graciously own and prosper. In peaceful dependence upon Thee, permit us now to take our rest. When again we go forth into the temptations of the world, pray for us, O merciful Intercessor, that our faith fail not. Heal our backslidings. Recover us from our wanderings, and let not Satan, by the suddenness of his attack, gain any advantage over us. Hold Thou us up, and we shall be safe; and we will have respect unto thy statutes continually.

Holy Father, send forth, we entreat Thee, the Spirit of thy Son into the hearts of all mankind. Strengthen the Church in every land. Give the patience of Jesus to those who are being despitefully used and persecuted. Bring to nought the hatred and malice of all false witness against Him, who alone is the faithful and true Witness. Teach the kings and judges of the earth to submit themselves to the Lord's Anointed. Thy kingdom come; thy will be done on earth, as it is in heaven.

Have mercy, O Lord, upon the nation which Thou didst call by thy name. Let their sin in rejecting Messiah be forgiven. Take away their hardness of heart and unbelief. Hasten the time when there shall be one fold and one Shepherd. And now, for the sake of Jesus Christ, may the blessing of God Almighty, the Father, the Son, and the Holy Ghost, be amongst us and remain with us always. Amen.

[MORNING.] **TWENTY-SEVENTH WEEK.—TUESDAY.** [EVENING.

READ IN HOLY SCRIPTURE DEUTERONOMY XI. 1—17.

O LORD our God, we thank Thee for the rest and peace of the past night, for the light of a new day, and for all the domestic and temporal blessings of our lot. May our souls and all that is within us be stirred up to bless thy holy name. We have heard with our ears, and our fathers have told us what Thou didst in their day; and our own experience of thy goodness calls upon us to give thanks. Graciously enable us to love the Lord our God with all our mind and strength; then shall we indeed walk in the ways of thy commandments, and find our Saviour's yoke easy, and his burden light. May this law of love under which He has graciously placed us be ever pleasant to our hearts; and whilst we are in the wilderness, like thy people Israel of old, may we be supported and defended as they were. Enable us to take heed to ourselves, that our hearts be not deceived by the love of the world, or by its cares or troubles, or anything that may turn us aside from following our most blessed Redeemer.

Keep us mindful of our entire dependence upon Thee, and of our utter unworthiness of any mercy. We would never forget that by grace we are saved, through faith in Christ Jesus, whom Thou hast set forth a propitiation for our sins, that Thou mightest be just whilst justifying the ungodly; nor would we forget that if any man be in Christ he is a new creature. Cause us, therefore, whilst deeply humbled on account of our manifold transgressions, to bring forth the fruits of righteousness, which are to thy glory through Him. Give us the Holy Spirit to sanctify and comfort us, and to show us the things freely given us in Christ Jesus. Then shall we walk as children of light, and our feet shall be kept in the narrow path that leadeth unto life eternal. O Lord, we beseech Thee let us experience this most precious privilege, to be led of thy Holy Spirit. Then shall our faith not stand in the wisdom of men, but in the power of God; and we shall be able to say with thy servant the Apostle, "I know whom I have believed, and am persuaded that He is able to keep that which I have committed unto Him against that day."

O our Father, preserve our going out and our coming in this day. Prosper us in our lawful calling as far as it shall be for thy glory and the prosperity of our souls. Bless us in our basket and store, and enable us gratefully to receive what Thou art pleased to bestow upon us, and to avoid murmuring if Thou shalt see it right to withhold some things that we may desire. These, and every other needed blessing, we beg in the name and for the sake of our Lord Jesus Christ, to whom, with Thee and the Holy Spirit, be glory and praise for ever. Amen.

READ IN HOLY SCRIPTURE PSALM LI.

O ALL-MERCIFUL Father, we come this night with all our sins, negligences, and ignorances into thy compassionate presence. Have mercy upon us, O God, according to thy loving-kindness: according to the multitude of thy tender mercies blot out our transgressions. Wash us throughly from our iniquities, and cleanse us from our sins. We acknowledge our transgressions, and our sin is ever before us. The remembrance of them is grievous, the burden is intolerable. Look now upon the blood of thine everlasting covenant, and in mercy think upon thy penitent servants. Hide thy face from our sins, and blot out all our iniquities. Create in us new hearts, O God, and renew a right spirit within us. Cast us not away from thy presence, and take not thy Holy Spirit from us. Restore unto us the joy of thy salvation, and uphold us with thy free Spirit.

We spread out this night all our shortcomings before Thee. We would not dissemble one fault. Thou hast said, "Though your sins be as scarlet, they shall be as white as snow; though they be red like crimson, they shall be as wool." Fulfil now, O Lord, thy promise to us in Christ. We plead his atoning blood, that blood which cleanseth from all sin. We desire to avail ourselves of his one all-sufficient sacrifice. Apply his healing blood to our souls. Surely He was wounded for our transgressions; He was bruised for our iniquities. The chastisement of our peace was upon Him, and with his stripes we are healed. Help us to realise to-night the perfected work of justification. Accept us graciously for his sake. May we lie down in perfect peace, knowing that our repented transgressions are perfectly forgiven. Thy promises stand sure. We believe that Christ has loved us with an everlasting love, and that his sacrifice is a full and sufficient oblation for the sins of the whole world.

Into thine hands, O gracious Father, we commend ourselves and all that we love this night. Watch over us whilst we sleep. Give refreshment to our wearied bodies. Renew our spirits within us; and if it be thy holy will, enable us to go forth to our duties on the morrow with a good courage, thanking Thee for past mercies, encouraged by the remembrance of thine abiding faithfulness, persuaded that we are accepted in the Beloved, and that all things shall assuredly work together for our good. While we live may we glorify Thee in our bodies and our spirits, which are thine. Forgive, O Lord, the infirmity of these our petitions; and those things which for our unworthiness we dare not, and for our blindness we cannot ask, vouchsafe to give us for the all-sufficient worthiness of Jesus Christ, thine own dear Son. Amen.

[MORNING.] **TWENTY-SEVENTH WEEK.—WEDNESDAY.** [EVENING.

READ IN HOLY SCRIPTURE DEUTERONOMY XI. 18—32.　　READ IN HOLY SCRIPTURE ST. MATTHEW XXVII. 1—25.

O LORD, our heavenly Father, incline our hearts to keep thy laws. According to thy promise, put thy laws into our hearts, and write them in our minds; for we deeply feel our proneness to forget them, and to disobey them even when remembered. We acknowledge with shame how far we have been from rendering Thee our entire obedience, and we heartily thank Thee that Jesus Christ has borne the curse for us; that He who knew no sin was made sin for us, that we might be made the righteousness of God in Him. Thus redeemed, may we this day and every day live a life of faith on the Son of God. Help us especially, according to the directions we have just been reading, to study with increasing diligence thy holy Word. May it be in our thoughts when we sit in the house and when we walk by the way, when we lie down and when we rise up; and may we strive earnestly to be the means of making it known to others. As far as we have opportunity, help us to spread the knowledge of thy will; and specially we ask Thee to bless all societies which have for their object the circulation of the Holy Scriptures. May all obstacles to their diffusion be taken away, so that the Word of the Lord may have free course and be glorified. We thank Thee for our own privileges; that thy Word is so easy of access; that we may all read and study it, none daring to make us afraid; but we also remember the responsibility which this possession of Divine revelation brings upon us, knowing that unto whomsoever much is given, of him much will be required.

We offer Thee our thanksgivings for the mercies of the past night, and for the great blessings by which we are surrounded this morning. We thank Thee for refreshing sleep, for the renewed supply of all our wants, for loving friends, and for all the innumerable blessings which Thou hast bestowed upon us. Truly the lines are fallen to us in pleasant places, and we have a goodly heritage: help us to show our gratitude by living to thy service and glory. Every hour of this day help us to glorify Thee. Help us to watch and pray, lest we enter into temptation; to set a guard over our lips, lest we sin with our tongue; and especially to keep our hearts with all diligence. We ask Thee to help us to do all things as unto Thee, and to seek first the kingdom of God and his righteousness. Under all circumstances and in all places, may we remember that we are not our own; that we have been redeemed with no less a price than the precious blood of Christ; and may we earnestly strive to walk worthy of Him who hath called us to his kingdom and glory. Strengthen us by thy Holy Spirit, and to thy name shall be all the praise. We ask all in the name of Jesus Christ. Amen.

O THOU most high God, the Father of our Lord Jesus Christ, enable us, at the close of this day, to draw near to thy throne. We praise Thee for having invited us to come near. Thou dost rejoice to hearken to the cry of thy children, and art more desirous to bless them than they are to obtain thy blessing.

When we consider the dangers through which we have safely passed this day, we feel constrained to thank Thee. We might have been smitten by sickness; we might have fallen by fatal accident; we might have been overwhelmed by evil tidings; above all, we might have been overcome by temptations to forget Thee, to grieve Thee, and to cast off thine authority. What has preserved us from these calamities and crimes but thine own merciful providence and supporting grace? To Thee be all the praise.

How shall we duly praise Thee for the unspeakable love of thy dear Son, who was willing, for our sakes, to submit to the sorrows of which we have now read? It was for us He endured this contradiction of sinners, this contempt of the proud, this treachery of familiar friends; and afterwards the agonies of the garden, and the shame and suffering of the cross. Oh, preserve us from insensibility to such compassion. Help us to keep ever before our view what He became, and what He has now obtained for all them that believe in Him, so that looking unto Jesus, our love may abound yet more and more. We beseech Thee, O Lord, to grant us, as a family, the favour of thy continual presence. Dispose our hearts to love and serve one another for thy sake. Keep us from all uncharitable thoughts and unkind actions, and incline us to be patient, tender-hearted, and forgiving one towards another. [We especially commend to Thee those of our number who are absent from home, those who are exposed to the temptations of the world, and those who are of tender years, imploring Thee to grant them thy fatherly protection and saving grace.]

Make known, O Lord, the blessed Gospel which we possess to all mankind. Let all classes in our land be reached by the voice of those who faithfully proclaim it. From the throne to the cottage, in the dwelling of the rich and in the cell of the prisoner, may its glad tidings be heard and embraced. Gather thy people speedily from all nations, and hasten the day when the name of Jesus shall be everywhere as ointment poured forth.

Forgive the infirmities which accompany this approach to thy footstool; mercifully accept our grateful praises; and evermore keep our feet from falling, seeing that we ask all for the sake of Jesus Christ, our Redeemer and Lord. Amen.

[MORNING.]   TWENTY-SEVENTH WEEK.—THURSDAY.   [EVENING.

READ IN HOLY SCRIPTURE DEUTERONOMY XIII.

READ IN HOLY SCRIPTURE ST. JOHN XVIII. 28—40.

O LORD God of heaven and of earth, Thou art a great King above all gods. We confess with shame and confusion of face our multiplied sins against Thee, and the sins of our fathers. Spare us, O Lord God, and forgive us for Christ's sake. Turn not thy face away in displeasure, but have compassion upon us and accept our offering of prayer and praise. We beseech Thee, O Lord, to give us thy gracious Spirit, that we tempt not Christ, as some of thine ancient people tempted, and were slain in the wilderness. Vouchsafe to keep us this day from the sin of idolatry. Let us use this world as not abusing it. Let our chief treasure be in heaven, and our hearts be there also. And while diligent in business, preserve us from covetousness, which is idolatry.

We praise Thee and magnify Thee, O Lord God of our life, for another night's rest; for sleep and safety in the dark watches. Hitherto the Lord hath helped us. And now that Thou hast raised us up again to renewed life, let the dayspring of thy favour visit us from on high. May the Lord God be our sun and shield. Direct, we beseech Thee, the path of our feet. Lead us not into temptation, and deliver us from evil. O Lord, we entreat Thee lay upon us this day no burden which we are unable to bear; no burden of sorrow, no burden of temptation: with every trial do Thou make a way for our escape, that we may be able to bear it. We can do all things through Christ, who strengtheneth us. Hear us, we pray Thee, on behalf of all our kindred and all our acquaintance. Bring all our dear relations into thy family, and let Jesus, thy well-beloved Son, be the elder brother to all that are in our household. Let no kinsman of ours be found to be wanting when Thou, in the day of judgment, numberest up thy people.

We commend to Thee, Almighty Ruler of the nations, our beloved country. Give peace in our time. Send us now prosperity. O God, bless our Sovereign and all the Royal Family. Give grace to judges and magistrates to execute justice and to maintain truth.

We pray for all who suffer affliction, in mind, body, or estate; comfort and relieve them according to their several necessities; and may the trials of thy creatures, though at present not joyous, but grievous, work at last for good to them that are exercised thereby. And now we will go through this day in the strength of the Lord, and will make mention of his righteousness, even of his only.

Glory be unto the Father, and to the Son, and to the Holy Ghost: as it was in the beginning, is now, and ever shall be, world without end. Amen.

MOST blessed Lord, we adore Thee for thy matchless condescension and boundless love in enduring what Thou didst for us at the hands of sinful men. We are amazed that Thou shouldest suffer Thyself to be arraigned at the bar of an earthly judge, when the world will one day have to stand before thine own. While we rejoice at thine exaltation at the Father's right hand, we would always remember the humiliation to which Thou didst submit; thine agony and bloody sweat, thy cross and passion, thy sorrows, known and unknown. Our sins were laid upon Thee, and by thy stripes we are healed. Blot them out in thy precious blood. May we be assured by the inward witness of thy Spirit that no condemnation awaits us, and that our sins will be remembered no more. And while we rejoice in our freedom from the curse of sin, release us from its power. Grant that we may walk as children of the light, looking for the day of thy appearing.

Gracious Saviour, we rejoice that while no worldly kingdom was thine when treading our earth, all things are under thy control; that Thou sittest in the tranquillity of thine almightiness, overruling all the events of time. We beseech Thee to work mightily through the instrumentality of thine own truth, and to prosper all the efforts that are made in every department of Christian activity for the ingathering of thy redeemed. Let thy name be known upon earth, thy saving health among the nations. Encouraged by thine own Word, we look for a kingdom yet to come, and we pray for its establishment. Take unto Thyself thy great power, and let Jew and Gentile, bond and free, be gathered into thy redeemed fold. Put down all opposition to thy truth, and let the authority of thy Word be recognised, and its blessed influence felt in every part of the world.

We commend unto Thee the interests of our own land. Let thy choicest favours surround our Sovereign. Bless each member of the Royal Family. Have respect to the Government of the country, and give our rulers in each department the wisdom that is from above. Give peace and prosperity in our time, and may our posterity live to call Thee blessed.

Accept, O Lord, our united and hearty thanks for the mercies of this day. Let thy merciful pardon absolve us from all the sins we have committed. Give us that peace which Thou alone canst give. Abide with us through the silent hours of night. Refresh us with quiet rest and sleep. Shelter us beneath thy protecting wing, and if it be thy will, raise us in safety to see the morning light. Grant these our petitions for Christ's sake. Amen.

[MORNING.] **TWENTY-SEVENTH WEEK.—FRIDAY.** [EVENING.]

READ IN HOLY SCRIPTURE 2 JOHN.

BLESSED Lord, we adore Thee, the Fountain of Life, the Father of mercies, and God of all comfort. Thou art worshipped by the hosts of heaven; these are constantly employed in ascribing honour and glory to thy holy name. How shall we, who are but dust and ashes, approach Thee? We take encouragement at the remembrance of thy gracious character revealed in thy Word. Oh, that grace, mercy, and peace from Thee, our heavenly Father, may rest upon us. It is of thy goodness that we have been sustained and kept through another night. To Thee, therefore, we direct our prayer and praise. Be pleased to hear us out of thy holy hill, and further us with thy help and blessing, that through all the duties of this day we may truly serve Thee. Blessed be thy name for making known to us thy righteous judgments, and the mercy promised to us in Christ. We praise Thee for this token of thy love, and for sending thy Son in the flesh to make atonement for our sins. May we daily seek to understand and abide in the doctrine of Christ, to treasure it up in our hearts, and to bring forth its fruit in our lives. Preserve us, O Lord, from neglecting to obey thy commandments. As we have heard and been taught thy truth, so may we always walk in it, and confess our faith in Christ, and Him crucified. Help us carefully to look to ourselves, to examine our hearts, whether we be in the faith.

We specially pray for our souls to be deeply impressed with love to the Gospel of Christ, that our affections and sympathies may be with those who fear Thee and walk in thy ways. Deliver us from all false doctrine, heresy, and schism, and make us examples in spirit, faith, and charity. May we have no fellowship with those who are destitute of the truth, lest we be partakers of their evil deeds, and fail to show ourselves the true disciples of Christ.

Now that we are about to go forth into the world, to be exposed to its temptations and trials, let thy presence go with us. Enable us to overcome evil dispositions, and shun every false way. Strengthen us by thy Spirit, both in body and mind, faithfully to perform our duty, and to exhibit in our dealings a regard for integrity and truth, for peace and love. Grant that all we do may be begun, continued, and ended agreeably to thy will. May no evil or danger overtake us this day, but defend us by thy gracious and ready help. Hear these our supplications; pardon our sins. Grant that what we have asked according to thy will may be obtained, to the relief of our necessity and the setting forth of thy glory, through Christ our Lord. Amen.

READ IN HOLY SCRIPTURE ST. LUKE XXIII. 1—23.

O GRACIOUS God, the Father of mercies, and the Fountain of life and peace, look down from heaven, thy dwelling-place, and open thine ear to our prayers and thanksgivings. We adore thy goodness in stooping to the sinful and unworthy; and we pray Thee, for the sake of thy dear Son, who by his sufferings and death atoned for our sins, to have mercy upon us, and do for us according to our need.

We thank Thee for the blessings of this day. Thou hast shielded us from harm, and continued to us the supply of our bodily necessities in such measure as Thou seest good. Oh, enable us to trace all our blessings to thy hand, and to feel every day that the food which we eat, and the raiment which covers us, are of thy giving; and that all the kindnesses of others, and the friendships which sweeten them, spring out of thy tender love towards us. Above all, we praise thy name for the unspeakable mercies of thy redeeming grace. Lord, how undeserving we are of all that Jesus hath done for us. Show us the grievousness of our sins by the sufferings which He endured. Cause us to be ashamed of the transgressions which brought upon Him such shame. As we contemplate Him enduring the contradiction of sinners for us, kindle in us a heartier repentance, and a livelier faith, that we may obtain forgiveness, and through thy grace strive to sin no more. Cleanse us from the guilt of this day's sins. Whatever we have done wrong in thy sight, either towards Thee or those with whom we have had to do, pardon the offence, and blot it out for ever. We desire to lie down to sleep at peace with Thee and with all mankind.

We beseech Thee, O God, to carry on in us, day by day, the work of thy grace. Reveal Thyself more manifestly to us as our God and Father in Christ Jesus. Increase our knowledge of Divine things. Let thy Spirit take of the things of Christ and show them unto us. Preserve us from being led astray by false doctrine and false teachers, and keep us, we pray Thee, from the evil which is in the world. Lord, we desire to be thine, to have thy love shed abroad in our hearts, to know by experience the peace which passeth all understanding, and to rejoice in the hope of thy glory.

We commit ourselves and all whom we love to thy gracious protection for the night. Minister to all their necessities, as we pray Thee to minister to our own. Suffer none of them, young or old, to despise thy grace, or abide in unbelief and disobedience, but grant that they and we may be found in Christ, in the great day, in peace. We ask all for his name's sake. Amen.

[Morning.] TWENTY-SEVENTH WEEK.—SATURDAY. [Evening.

READ IN HOLY SCRIPTURE DEUTERONOMY XVIII. | READ IN HOLY SCRIPTURE ST. MATTHEW XXVII. 26—54.

O LORD and heavenly Father, we thy humble servants present unto Thee our morning sacrifice of praise and thanksgiving. Through the silent watches of the night thine eye has been over us, thine arm has sustained us, and it is Thou alone who hast permitted us to meet once more in peace and safety. Sanctify, we pray Thee, this day's duties and employments. As we go forth to our intercourse with the world, may we never forget that thy vows are upon us. May we be at all times what Thou wouldest have us to be—a peculiar people unto Thyself. May the time past suffice us to have wrought the will of Satan; henceforth we would live only unto Thee. Let thy fear be the ruling principle of our conduct, and in all we say and do may we seek thy honour and glory. Send down the Holy Spirit into our hearts, and enable us to keep ourselves unspotted from the evil that lieth around. Thou hast bidden us be perfect, even as Thou art perfect. Oh, beget in each one of us a likeness to Thee, our Father, and conform us more and more to thy holy mind and will. We thank Thee for having raised up in the person of thy Son the Great Prophet whom Thou didst promise. Enable us to take heed unto his voice, as He speaks to us in thy name. Recognising his Divine authority, may we know Him as the Way, the Truth, and the Life, without whom no man can draw near unto Thee.

We pray especially at this time for those whom Thou hast set apart to minister unto us in the Word and doctrine. Make them men of faith and prayer, determined to know nothing else save Jesus Christ and Him crucified. Be Thou their strength and portion, and may their reward be great in heaven. Assist them in their preparation for the coming Sabbath-day. Enable them rightly to divide the Word of truth. Give them the unction of the Holy One, that they may know all things, and so be preserved from error. Strengthen all those who have gone forth to proclaim in heathen lands the unsearchable riches of Christ. Under all their trials may they find Thee a very present help; and amid all their discouragements may they be sustained by the comfort of thy heavenly grace.

Bless our country and the Sovereign Thou hast set over us. Give our senators wisdom, and grant that in all their decisions they may be influenced from above. Overrule every passing event to the promotion of thy glory, and hasten the time when all shall know Thee from the least to the greatest; when the Redeemer shall take unto Himself his kingdom, and reign supreme over all the earth. And now, Lord, go with us this day where we go; dwell with us where we dwell; be our God and our guide even unto death. Amen.

O LORD Jesu Christ, who for our sakes was contented to be betrayed and given up into the hands of wicked men, we beseech Thee graciously to behold this family, to hear our prayers, and to vouchsafe a blessing. We would close this week with Thee; standing by thy cross, meditating on thy love, and recalling all that Thou hast done for us men, and for our salvation.

Thou didst leave the brightness of the Father's glory, and become incarnate upon earth. As an infant of days Thou wast carried down to Egypt, and as a man of sorrows Thou wast driven into the wilderness. Thou didst weep at the grave of Lazarus, and sit wearily on Jacob's well. Thou didst endure the contradiction of sinners and the desertion of disciples. Thy sweat was as it were great drops of blood in the garden of Gethsemane, and Thou didst bear the cross to the mount called Calvary. They scourged and crucified Thee: they pierced thy hands and feet, and mocked thy dying cry: and when thy sacred body was laid in the tomb, they sealed the stone and set the watch. In all these thy sufferings we see, as in a glass, the reflection of our sins. They are many and they are great. We were born in sin and shapen in iniquity. We mourn over the hardness of our hearts, the perversity of our wills, the wandering of our affections, our distrust, our unbelief, our forgetfulness of thy Word and commandments. If Thou, Lord, shouldest be extreme to mark what is done amiss, we could not abide it. But there is forgiveness with Thee. The blood which Thou hast shed speaketh better things than that of Abel. Grant, Lord, unto thy servants pardon and peace, that we may be cleansed from all our sins, and serve Thee with a quiet mind. Bestow all needful grace. Without Thee we can do nothing. Make thy strength perfect in weakness; that so, when we have done thy will, we may inherit thy promises, and be made partakers of thy heavenly treasure.

With these our prayers and supplications we would mingle unfeigned thanksgivings. Goodness and mercy have followed us. Thou hast redeemed our life from destruction, and crowned us with loving-kindness and tender mercy; and now Thou hast brought us safely through another week. At its close accept our evening sacrifice of praise, and ere we retire to rest, bless us, O our Father. Preserve us through the silent watches of the night. May our meditation of Thee be sweet; and for us may life be Christ, and to die gain.

Hear us, we beseech Thee, for the sake of thy Son Jesus Christ, who ever liveth, with the Father and the Holy Ghost, one God, world without end. Amen.

[MORNING.] TWENTY-EIGHTH WEEK.—LORD'S DAY. [EVENING.

READ IN HOLY SCRIPTURE EZEKIEL XIII. 1—16.

READ IN HOLY SCRIPTURE PSALM XXII.

MOST merciful and gracious God, the God and Father of our Lord Jesus Christ, we bless and praise thy holy name that Thou dost permit the most unworthy to come to thy throne of grace, when they come in the name of thy dear Son. Every day testifies to the truth, that in many things we offend all. But there is forgiveness with Thee. Being reconciled through the death of thy Son, we come to Thee crying, "Abba, Father." Accept our humble thanks for the care which Thou dost take of us night after night, and for the returning light of each successive day; but more especially do we thank Thee this morning for the best day of all the seven, the Sabbath-day. We thank Thee for the public ordinances of Divine worship instituted for the instruction and comfort of our souls. Grant that this day may not be a day of weariness to us, but a day of refreshing from the presence of the Lord. May we be in the Spirit on this the Lord's day, and worship Thee in spirit and in truth. If permitted to join the assemblies of thy saints, help us to pray in faith, persuaded that whatever good thing we ask in thy Son's name, Thou wilt do it. Enable us to open our mouths wide, that Thou mayest fill them. May we receive with meekness the engrafted Word which is able to save our souls. Let the dew of thy Holy Spirit descend on our souls, and water the good seed of the Kingdom.

Look with favour, we beseech Thee, on the ministers of thy Word, and enable them rightly to divide the Word of truth. Enable them to feed thy flock with the pure milk of the Word, and to preach, not themselves, but Christ Jesus the Lord. Prevent them from prophesying out of their own hearts, and crying "peace" when there is no peace. Whether men will hear, or whether they will forbear, cause thy servants to preach the Word, and to declare the whole counsel of God.

Bless all Sunday-schools, and make them nurseries in which shall grow many plants that will in due time be transplanted to the paradise above. Look in mercy on those who may be this day prevented from attending thine house of prayer, and help them to rejoice that,

"Where'er they seek Thee, Thou art found."

From the careless and indifferent take away all hardness of heart and contempt of thy Word and commandment. Have mercy, we beseech Thee, on all men, and hasten the time when all shall know Thee, from the least to the greatest, and when the earth shall be filled with the knowledge of the glory of the Lord, as the waters cover the sea. We ask all in the name of Jesus Christ our Lord. Amen.

HOLY Saviour, who upon the cross didst cry in an agony of soul, "My God, my God, why hast Thou forsaken me?" we thank Thee that Thou hast not forsaken us, but in thine infinite love hast died to save us. We would remember thy sufferings, and all the cruel revilings which Thou didst endure for us, when by the hands of wicked men Thou wast crucified and slain. They compassed Thee about; they gaped upon Thee; they pierced thy hands and thy feet; they parted thy garments, and cast lots upon thy vesture. Yet we praise Thee, holy Saviour, that in all this they fulfilled thy purpose of grace, to redeem us to God by thy blood. And now we thank Thee that, although Thou hast ascended on high, and sittest at the right hand of God, Thou art not ashamed to call us brethren; for Thou dost not despise the affliction of the afflicted, neither dost Thou hide thy face from them. Have mercy, O Lord, upon all who are troubled and distressed, and comfort or deliver them. Help us to come to Thee in all our afflictions. Our fathers trusted in Thee; yea, they cried unto Thee, and Thou didst deliver them. Deliver us also in all time of our sorrow. Be not far from us when trouble is near; and in the hour of deepest affliction, may we never feel that Thou hast forsaken us.

O Thou that inhabitest the praises of Israel, our praise also has been of Thee in the congregation to-day. We thank Thee that it has been our privilege to hear the joyful sound of the Gospel. We beseech Thee to bless to us all the services and religious engagements of the day. May the Word of Christ, which we have heard, dwell in us richly in all wisdom; and may a Sabbath blessing rest upon all our hearts to-night. With a humble and contrite spirit, O Lord, we remember the sins of this day. Forgive all that has been displeasing to Thee. Cleanse us from all sin, through the precious blood of Christ, and may we lie down in peace with grateful hearts. May it please Thee to give us the sweet refreshment of sleep. Defend us and our dwelling from all evil. Bless all our family circle, with all our dear relations and friends. Bless all faithful ministers of the Gospel, especially our own. Prosper all their labours. May the Word which they have preached to-day prove a savour of life to the hearers, that many may seek Thee, and be satisfied, and live for ever. Thine, O Lord, is the kingdom. Hasten thy glorious reign. Pour out thy holy Spirit upon all people, and may all the ends of the world remember and turn unto Thee, and all the nations worship before Thee. Hear us, O Lord, in these our prayers and praises, for Jesus Christ's sake. Amen.

[Morning.] TWENTY-EIGHTH WEEK.—MONDAY. [Evening.

READ IN HOLY SCRIPTURE PROVERBS XI.

READ IN HOLY SCRIPTURE ST. LUKE XXIII. 27—43.

ALMIGHTY and most merciful God, we most earnestly beseech Thee to grant unto us thy Holy Spirit, that we may now draw nigh to Thee with true and penitent hearts, and with a deep sense of our great wants.

We thank Thee for thy Holy Word. We bless Thee that we have been reminded this morning how Thou hast set before us in the journey of life a blessing and a curse: a curse, both for time and for eternity, if we despise thy favour and love, and a blessing free, increasing, and enduring for ever if we truly love and serve Thee. Every day teaches us that the way of transgressors is hard; that though hand join in hand, the wicked shall not go unpunished; while each day doth also assure us that the Lord loveth the righteous, and his ear is open unto their cry.

We entreat Thee to instruct us in the way of life. Oh, suffer us not to pass this day in thoughtlessness and sin. Let not the false wisdom of this evil world influence and rule our hearts. Grant unto us, we beseech Thee, heavenly wisdom, that we may humbly and eagerly seek to tread in the footsteps of our divine Redeemer. May we regard this world, with all its duties and its dangers, its joys and its sorrows, as He regarded it. Enable us to be faithful imitators of the holy Jesus, and let thy Spirit conform us in thought, and work, and word, to his good, and holy, and perfect will. Help us so that our hearts may ever be constrained by his love. We pray Thee to convince us of our sin, and of our need of his cleansing blood. We pray Thee to write deeply upon our memories the truth that through Him alone we gain all the blessings we require.

Lamb of God, that taketh away the sins of the world, take away our guilt; take away the love of sin, for only thus shall we be able to understand and be prepared to enter upon the holy life of faith in the Son of God who loved us and gave Himself for us.

We thank Thee, O God, that Thou hast watched over us during this past night. We thank Thee for this new day. May we begin it in thy fear and in thy love. May thy fear restrain us from sin, and keep us from yielding to temptation. May the love of Thee—the love shed abroad in our hearts by the Holy Ghost which is given us— constrain us to be diligent in business, fervent in spirit, serving the Lord. Give us a right understanding in all things, that we may ever do such things as please Thee. We beseech Thee to defend us from every kind of evil. Protect our bodies from disease, and save our souls from sin, and in all our words and actions enable us to glorify Thee this day, through Jesus Christ our Lord. Amen.

O MOST glorious and gracious Lord God, who dwellest in heaven, but beholdest all things below, look down, we beseech Thee, upon us. Turn not thy face from us by reason of our many sins, but have pity and help us. All our hope is in Thee; thy promises in Christ Jesus are faithfulness and truth. Hearken to our prayer, and, according to thy mercy, forgive us all our sins of thought, and speech, and act committed this day. We confess that we are guilty in thy sight, and undeserving of thy favour; but Thou canst be just, and yet justify those that believe in Jesus. Oh, accept us, for thy name's sake, and through the blood of the Covenant grant us the blessed assurance of thy pardon. Let us not lie down to sleep with unforgiven sin upon the conscience.

Blessed be thy great name for thine exceeding goodness during the past day. We owe life, and health, and all other blessings to Thee. Stir up our hearts to thanksgiving. Show us our own undeserving, that we may the better understand all the greatness of thy love. Take us for the night into thy keeping. Guard and defend us against all the evil which may threaten us. Give us refreshing sleep, and when we wake may we feel that we are still with Thee.

We desire, O Lord God, that as each day passes by, it may find us growing in grace, and in the knowledge of our Lord and Saviour Jesus Christ. Especially teach us more clearly all the meaning of his cross and passion. Enable us to realise the sufficiency of his death as the atonement for the world's sin, and to know that through his stripes we may be healed. We would copy the example of his uncomplaining meekness and patience. We desire to see our sins in his great sufferings, and to read in them the token of thy righteous anger against our transgressions. As we think how Thou didst not spare thy own dear Son, but delivered Him up for us all, and recall what He endured to save us, oh, excite our hearts with a burning zeal against the sins which caused Him thus to suffer. Imprint on our hearts the image of Christ crucified. By his cross stir up our minds to love Thee more, and serve Thee better.

We pray, O God, that the glad tidings of thy great love in Christ Jesus may be carried even to the uttermost parts of the earth, and bring light, and comfort, and peace to many hearts now in darkness and the shadow of death. Hasten the time when He shall see of the travail of his soul and be satisfied, and when all people shall be blessed in Him; and grant that in the day of his appearing not one of us may be found wanting. We ask all for his sake, to whom with Thee and the Holy Ghost be honour and praise. Amen.

[MORNING.]   TWENTY-EIGHTH WEEK.—TUESDAY.   [EVENING.

READ IN HOLY SCRIPTURE DEUTERONOMY XXVI.

READ IN HOLY SCRIPTURE ISAIAH LIII.

O GOD, praise waiteth for Thee. We deem it a privilege as well as a duty to offer at thy feet the sacrifice of thanksgiving, and with joyful lips to speak of thy loving-kindness. A new day, succeeding the safety and the refreshing rest of another night, adds to all thy past and pressing claims upon us, and lays us under deeper obligations to Thee. Again would we call upon our souls and upon one another to bless the Lord, and not to forget any of his benefits.

May the reading of Holy Scripture be sanctified to the enlightenment of our consciences and the guidance of our life. Help us prayerfully to observe thy hand in providence and in grace. Thy mercies are more in number than the sand, and we feel it to be good so to gaze upon their vastness and richness as to be touched, and melted, and moved by the contemplation. And grant, O Lord, that we may not be satisfied with mere feeling in reference to thy goodness, but may have such a due sense of all thy mercies that we may show forth thy praise, not only with our lips, but in our lives. Preserve us from the sin of covetousness. Awaken in us a spirit of self-denial. Enable us at all times with holy zeal to honour the Lord with our substance and with the first-fruits of our increase.

With a generous liberality may we sustain thy cause; asking with simplicity and deep solicitude, "Lord, what wilt Thou have me to do?" Upon us grant that the blessing of the widow and the fatherless, and him that was ready to perish, may rest; and in our giving and our doing, let all be done as to the Lord, for Christ's sake. But while, O Lord, we seek blessings for ourselves this day as a family, in the form of guidance, protection, and all needful grace, may we look beyond our domestic circle, and take up the patriotic prayer we have now read. Look down from thy holy habitation, from heaven, and bless thy people Israel, and the land which Thou hast given us. Bless our Sovereign, and the government of the nation. Hear us, O Lord, for all those who are ignorant and out of the way. Have mercy upon those who are in sorrow, and need thy special help. Minister to bruised and broken hearts.

And now, O Lord, we go forth to the duties of the day, looking to thy grace to render us active, earnest, holy, and useful. Help us each to commit himself to duty, not with eye-service, as men-pleasers, but as unto the Lord; and if we be spared to the evening, may it be to unite with glad hearts in glorifying the name of the Father, and the Son, and the Holy Ghost. Hear us, O Lord, and answer us, for Jesus Christ's sake. Amen.

ALMIGHTY God, we bless Thee for the gift of thy dear Son, and for the revelation which Thou hast given us in thy Word. Enlighten our minds, that we may behold his beauty; and reveal thine arm in our salvation, that we may enjoy his love. May He no longer appear to us as a root out of a dry ground, but become all our salvation and all our desire.

We confess that we too long despised and rejected Him: we hid our faces from Him, and esteemed Him not; but now we love Him, because we feel that He hath borne our griefs and carried our sorrows. Oh, grant that our fellow-creatures who still reject Christ may soon be convinced of their folly and wickedness, and turn unto Him with weeping and supplication, that they also may be saved.

Grant unto us, O Lord, a deeper sense of his amazing suffering for our sins. Take away all our unbelief and hardness of heart, that we may more clearly see, and more deeply feel, that Jesus was wounded for our transgressions, and was bruised for our iniquities; that the chastisement of our peace was upon Him; and that with his stripes we are healed.

We confess, O Lord, that all we, like sheep, have gone astray; we have turned every one to his own way; but Thou, in mercy to us, hast laid on Him the iniquity of us all. May we never forget his meekness and patience under suffering; his imprisonment, death, and burial for our sins; but over draw near to Thee through the all-perfect Mediator. For his sake forgive us our sins, restore us to thy favour and image, and impart to us that grace which will enable us to live to thy glory. It has pleased Thee, O Lord, to bruise Him; to put Him to grief; and to make his soul an offering for sin; that He might become the captain of our salvation, and bring many souls to glory. Grant, we beseech Thee, that his seed may become as the sand on the sea shore, and as the stars of the sky for multitude. Cause thy pleasure to prosper in his hand; may He see of the travail of his soul, and be satisfied. Oh, let the knowledge of Jesus Christ spread far and wide, until the ends of the earth see the salvation of our God. We pray that millions may be justified by his blood, and be saved by his life, for He has borne their iniquities; that He may take the spoil, and deliver our race from the destroyer. Hear Thou his intercessions for the transgressors; and grant that men, redeemed by his blood, may soon be regenerated by his Spirit to the praise of thy glorious grace. Watch over us during the night, be with us during the remainder of our lives, and bless us according to thy mercy, for Jesus' sake. Amen.

[Morning.] **TWENTY-EIGHTH WEEK.—WEDNESDAY.** [Evening.

READ IN HOLY SCRIPTURE PSALM CXII.

O FATHER Almighty, we draw near to thy footstool through the name of Jesus. Shed abroad the love of Christ in every heart, and touch our lips with a living coal from the altar before the mercy-seat. We bless Thee, we praise Thee, we magnify Thee. Thy mercies are fresh every morning, and thy loving-kindness is like the great deep. For all temporal mercies we give Thee thanks; for our food and raiment, for our health and strength, for our reason and freedom from pain. But above all we bless Thee for the gift of thine own dear Son. Without Him we can do nothing, for He is our only hope and stay, both for time and for eternity. Oh, grant us this day richly to enjoy those precious gifts which He has secured even for the rebellious ones, with his own blood upon the cross. May we always remember his dying love and feel his quickening power. May we go in his strength all the day long. Grant us to know the blessedness of the man that feareth the Lord, that delighteth greatly in his commandments. When we go forth to our appointed work, guide us, and teach us in the way wherein we should walk. We are foolish, and blind, and ignorant, and Thou only knowest what things shall befall us in the days that yet remain: but our eyes are unto Thee, O Lord. We wait for thy salvation. Hold Thou us up, and we shall be safe. In perplexity be Thou our guide; in darkness be Thou our light; in temptation be Thou our strength and stay. Power belongeth unto Thee; it is not in man that walketh to direct his steps. Help us then this day to guide our affairs with discretion. May we walk in love as thine own dear children; doing everything to thine honour, and with a single eye to thy glory. Enable us to keep our hearts with all diligence, denying ourselves, and taking up our cross and following Christ.

O blessed Saviour, look down upon the sheep of thy hand and the lambs of thy flock. Bless every member of this family, and make us altogether thine own. Fetch home the wanderers, comfort the penitent, establish the weak; and when we meet together this night, put into each of our mouths a song of thanksgiving for the mercies of the day. May we be enabled to look back upon a day spent in thy service, and to adore thy protecting faithfulness and preserving love; thus may we pass through the wilderness of this world, having our conversation in heaven, from whence also we look for the Saviour, who shall present us without spot, or wrinkle, or any such thing, before the throne of his Father's glory. Hear us, we beseech Thee, for we ask in faith, believing in thy promises, and again pleading the name of our only Mediator and Advocate, Jesus Christ. Amen.

READ IN HOLY SCRIPTURE ST. JOHN XIX. 25—42.

EVER blessed and most gracious God, help us at this time to offer the evening sacrifice of praise and thanksgiving for the manifold mercies of thy kind providence, and for the help of thy grace during the day that is now drawing to an end. Thou hast not forsaken us, and we would not forget Thee. Thou hast given us our daily bread, and we humbly trust thy blessing has been upon it; and now may the gratitude of our hearts be offered to Thee, and not the mere homage of the lips only.

We pray Thee deeply to impress us with the wonderful truths we have just read. Our Saviour suffered thus for us, and forbid, O Lord, that we should be mere formalists whilst approaching Thee in his name. He bore our sins in his own body on the tree, that we being dead unto sin, might live unto holiness, and bring forth fruit unto God. We glorify Thee for that blessed truth, "It is finished!" With believing hearts we would therefore draw near, and receive the free gift of everlasting life, offered us through the atoning sacrifice of Him who took our place, and redeemed us with his precious blood. Herein is love; not that we loved God, but that He loved us, and sent his Son to be the propitiation for our sins. We pray that this love may constrain us, that it may bind us to Christ, to his service, to his cause. Enable us to count all things but loss for his sake, and make it the desire of our hearts to be found in Him, not having our own righteousness, but his. Let us not be ashamed of the cross. Let us love, trust, follow, and adore Him who so freely loved us, and bore the shame and the sorrow that He might bring us to God. We thank Thee for giving us complete evidence of this great salvation. He that saw these wonders bare record, and his record is true; and it is written that we might believe. Lord, we believe the glad tidings, and pray that we may have the witness within; even thy Spirit witnessing with our spirits, that we are born of God.

Give to every one beneath this roof, and to all who are dear to us, the Spirit of Christ; for if any man have not the Spirit of Christ, he is none of his. If in any degree Thou hast enabled us this day to walk as the followers of the Lamb, we ascribe it wholly to thy grace, and give Thee all the praise. Perfect that which concerneth us, and leave us not until all the purposes of redeeming love are accomplished in our souls; so shall we, when life's last day on earth shall come, be received into heaven, and be for ever with the Lord. We pray Thee to forgive the sins of this day, and to keep us in safety, in peace, and in health this night, for the sake of our adorable Saviour, Jesus Christ. Amen.

[Morning.] TWENTY-EIGHTH WEEK.—THURSDAY. [Evening.

READ IN HOLY SCRIPTURE DEUT. XXVIII. 1—20.

O LORD, Creator of heaven and earth, and fountain of all happiness, we approach Thee this morning with the voice of thanksgiving. Thou hast granted to us peaceful rest, and hast greeted us with new blessings. The night is thine; the day also is thine, and thine are the powers of body and mind with which we are about to enter on our various duties.

We would meet the unknown events of this day with humble trust in thy mercy. We are indeed weak and irresolute, and easily overcome by evil, but we have ever found Thee ready to succour us in danger, and to give us deliverance from our enemies. We would put away from us all undue anxiety regarding the things of this life. Thou hast hitherto blessed us, and given to us all that is truly needful for our comfort and usefulness. We have seen thy goodness both in withholding and in granting to us these temporal gifts. Enable us, from the experience of thy past mercies, to draw the assurance of future good.

We praise Thee for the gift of thy Holy Word, for those histories of thine ancient people, for the precepts and promises of thy grace, and for the glad tidings of a Saviour. We feel our need of more humility, contrition, and love, in order to receive its lessons into our hearts, and to carry them out into our actions. We desire to thirst for thy testimonies, as the traveller thirsteth for living water, and as the hungry man for his daily bread; for it is by this that our souls live, and are made strong for thy service. Breathe upon us, most gracious Spirit, that we may be thus fed and sanctified.

We praise Thee that Thou hast in our days raised up so many faithful men for the translation and dispersion of thy Word among the nations. Greatly increase their number, and give to them fidelity and courage for their arduous and blessed enterprise, until all the people that sit in darkness shall see thy great light.

We commend to Thee our own country, our Sovereign, our legislators, our magistrates, with all sorts and conditions of men. Be especially gracious to the sick in body and in mind, and to all who shall this day encounter pain or peril, helping them to lean on Thee, who art a present help in trouble.

Be gracious to ourselves as a family. Keep us united to Thee and to each other. May we fear to offend and delight to serve Thee. Watch Thou over our spirits, that we speak not hastily with our lips, nor cherish an unkind thought towards any man. Thou art our King, our Deliverer, and our Saviour; and unto Thee, through Jesus Christ our Lord, we render eternal praises. Amen.

READ IN HOLY SCRIPTURE ST. JOHN XX. 1—18.

OUR Father which art in heaven, we would end this day as we began it, by seeking thy blessing.

We thank Thee for lives redeemed from destruction, for freedom from severe and overwhelming trials, for the preservation of all our bodily powers, for the supply of all our animal wants; and especially we thank Thee for the spiritual blessings which Thou hast granted to us so abundantly. We thank Thee for thine unspeakable gift, and for thy Holy Word, which reveals thy dear Son to us, not only as having died for our sins, but as having risen again for our justification, and as now and for ever living to make intercession for us. We thank Thee, that having thus risen from the dead, Christ has become the firstfruits of them that slept. May our hearts be filled with holy confidence in Him, the resurrection and the life, and may every one of us believe on Him, so that we may never die. May we know Christ Jesus the Lord, and the power of his resurrection, so that our whole natures may be conformed to his likeness. Help us to die unto sin, to rise again unto righteousness, and to have our affections so set on things which are above that we may constantly be stimulated and cheered by the blessed hope that when He who is our life shall appear, we shall also appear with Him in glory. Oh, grant that this blessed hope may deliver us from the bondage of sin, and from the absorbing influence of the things that are seen, so that the cares of this world may not choke the good seed, and make it unfruitful. O Lord our God, make us more spiritually alive, that we may be more entirely devoted to thy service: glorifying Thee by bringing forth much fruit. We ask thy pardon that in so many instances this day we have fallen short of doing thy will, that we have turned to our own way, and have yielded to temptation. Blessed be thy name that we have been taught that the blood of Jesus Christ cleanseth from all sin; and that if we confess our sins, Thou wilt be faithful and just to forgive us our sins, and cleanse us from all unrighteousness. Lord, grant that the knowledge of the blessed truth that there is forgiveness for every sin through the blood of Jesus may be more extensively known, not only among the heathen, the blasphemers, and the profane, but by those who are seeking by their own good works to atone for their guilt. Help all who feel sin to be a heavy burden to come to Jesus and find rest to their souls. We ask Thee, O Lord, to preserve us from all evil during this night; may our sleep be quiet and refreshing to us, and may it fit us for the duties of another day.

We ask all these mercies in the name of our blessed Saviour Jesus Christ. Amen.

[Morning.]   TWENTY-EIGHTH WEEK.—FRIDAY.   [Evening.

READ IN HOLY SCRIPTURE DEUT. XXVIII. 45—68.   READ IN HOLY SCRIPTURE ST. LUKE XXIV. 13—35.

ETERNAL God, we stand in awe of thy judgments, and remember with trembling thy hatred of iniquity. We have seen the manifestation of that hatred in the history of peoples and individuals. We have ourselves felt the misery of banishment from Thee on account of sin. Born in sin and shapen in iniquity, we have known what it is to live without God. But we adore Thee that Thou hast not left us in the darkness of our fallen state. We have been raised by Thee to the enjoyment of the privileges of sonship. Thou hast given us an interest in Him who died, the Just for the unjust, and we praise Thee that we have the blessed assurance that we are not orphans in a homeless world, but children living upon thy fatherhood, and looking for an inheritance beyond the grave. O Lord, we are thine; Thou hast redeemed us, and hast sent unto us the necessity of reconciliation, and given us the promise of thy gracious Spirit. May we be increasingly thankful for these inestimable mercies. Help us to keep our eyes steadily and steadfastly fixed upon Him who clothed Himself in our humanity, and by his one offering on the cross perfected us for ever. Let no cloud arise to obscure our vision, or dim our perception of his unutterable glory. In the blood that atones may we daily wash away our stains, and in the righteousness of Jesus may we now and for ever be justified.

We are journeying on in the pilgrimage of life, and daily grappling with the difficulties, trials, and temptations of the way. We are frequently weary, worn, and sad. Our strength is perfect weakness. Let us be supported by thine Almighty power. When temptations beset us, help us to resist them; when difficulties gather around us, let us be strengthened to overcome them; and when trials befall us, sanctify them to our good and thy glory. Grant unto us a spirit of submission to thy righteous will. Forbid, O Lord, that we should ever seek help from an arm of flesh rather than from Thee, the living God. Help us ever to realise thy presence. May we never be cast down with any darkening thought of thy distance from us, but may we be joyfully conscious that Thou art a God near and not afar off.

We would bear on our hearts before Thee all that we love, our kindred and friends. Let the joys of thy salvation be granted to each one. Have them, with us, this day in thy holy keeping. Throw around us thy sheltering arm. Let us fall into no sin, neither run into any kind of danger, and cause all things to work together for our good. We ask every blessing in the name of Jesus Christ our Lord, to whom, with Thee and the Holy Spirit, be everlasting praise. Amen.

O GOD, Father of mercies, and God of all grace, we thank Thee that Thou didst so love the world as to send thy well-beloved Son, that through Him we might have everlasting life. We thank Thee for the decease which He accomplished at Jerusalem, because He was wounded for our transgressions, and bruised for our iniquities. We thank Thee, moreover, O Lord, that Christ is risen from the dead, and become the firstfruits of them that slept. Because He lives, we shall live also. We bless Thee, O Lord our Saviour, for thy communion with thy disciples as they journeyed, and were sad by the way: Thou didst reveal Thyself to them, and comfort them; we beseech Thee, do the same now to us, thine unworthy servants. Abide even with us, for it is toward evening, and the day is far spent. Manifest Thyself to us as Thou dost not unto the world, and then truly, O Lord, at eventide it shall be light.

Almighty God, we ask thy gracious pardon for all that Thou hast seen amiss in every one of us this day. With Thee is plenteous forgiveness; let the blood of Jesus Christ thy Son cleanse us from all sin. And now remember us according to the greatness of thy mercy, and protect us from all perils and dangers of this night. Thou art the Shepherd of Israel, never slumbering, never sleeping: watch over us in our slumbers; let no evil come nigh our dwelling; let us rest under the shadow of thy wing. Hear us, O Lord, for all homeless and friendless wanderers, strangers in great cities, who have not where to lay their heads. Do Thou, O God, provide of thy goodness for the poor. Incline the hearts of thy people to show pity to the needy and sorrowing; to feed the hungry, and to clothe the naked; and to be merciful as their Father who is in heaven is merciful.

Look down this night upon all our absent friends and connections. Thou art not far from every one of them; grant to each of them, for Christ's sake, in this world knowledge of thy truth, and in the world to come life everlasting.

O Lord, Thou hast exhorted us by thine Apostle to offer prayers and supplications for kings and for all that are in authority, that we may live quiet and peaceable lives in all godliness and honesty. Bless our Monarch with every good gift. May the princes of the royal house live before Thee. Let thy kingdom come, O God, and thy will be done on earth as it is done in heaven. Give us day by day our daily bread. And lead us not into temptation, but deliver us from evil. For thine is the kingdom, and the power, and the glory, for ever and ever. Hear us, and have mercy upon us, for Jesus Christ's sake. Amen.

[Morning.] TWENTY-EIGHTH WEEK.—SATURDAY. [Evening.

READ IN HOLY SCRIPTURE MALACHI I.

READ IN HOLY SCRIPTURE ST. LUKE XXIV. 36–49.

O LORD God, our Father in heaven, graciously enable us to worship Thee in spirit and in truth. Preserve us from the sin of drawing near with our lips, while our hearts are far from Thee. Thou art ever more ready to hear than we to pray. For thy dear Son's sake, hear us now, and give us an answer of peace.

Glory be to thy great name for the mercies of the past night, and of the returning day. Continue, we beseech Thee, thy gracious favour and protection. Now that we are entering again on the duties of the station in which Thou hast placed us, endue us with thy heavenly grace, and grant us such increase of wisdom and strength, that we may walk circumspectly before all men, and say and do nothing this day that would dishonour thy name. Let a blessed conviction of thy reconciling mercy abide in our hearts, and the love of Christ constrain us in all things cheerfully and diligently to do such things as please Thee. O God, Thou knowest the weakness of our sinful nature, and our proneness to turn aside from Thee. Hold up our goings in thy paths, that our footsteps slip not. Cheer us continually with the bright tokens of thy love. Enable us to resist all temptations from within or without, and in thy strength to deny ourselves and follow Christ. Oh, enable us to give Thee our hearts' best and truest service, remembering that Thou art a great King, the God and Father of all, blessed for evermore.

Pour out thy Holy Spirit on the whole Church. Increase the faith and love of thy believing people, and make them zealous for thy glory. Cause them to shine as lights in the world, and to hold forth the Word of life. Enlarge the number of faithful ministers, and multiply abundantly the agencies for spreading abroad the knowledge of Jesus Christ and Him crucified. Guide all who are in error, and who have turned from the simplicity of the Gospel to the wisdom of man, back again to the truth as it is in Jesus. Look in thy compassion on the dark places of the earth, and for the sake of thy dear Son hasten the time when they shall be enlightened with the light of thy Gospel. Lord, we long for the fulfilment of the promise, that, from the rising of the sun to the going down of the same, thy name shall be great; when from the lips of Jews and Gentiles shall rise the anthems of everlasting praise to thy glory.

Regard with thy favour all who are dear to us. Overshadow them this day with the wings of thy love, and preserve them from evil. [By thy Spirit touch the hearts of the children of our family, and make them thine, now and for ever.] Accept our praise for all thy goodness, and answer our prayers for Jesus Christ's sake. Amen.

EVERLASTING Lord God, Thou art worthy of the highest worship of all thy creatures. Enable us to present such an offering as shall come up before Thee as incense, and let the lifting up of our hands be as the evening sacrifice.

Great is thy goodness in preserving our lives, and permitting us again to enter into thy presence. We would call upon our souls and all within us to unite in blessing thy holy name. Truly Thou art merciful beyond our hopes, and bountiful beyond our wants. Dispose us, therefore, to come before Thee with grateful hearts, and to seek thy favour through the merits of our Redeemer, Jesus Christ. We confess with shame that we have offended against thy holy laws, and followed too much the devices and desires of our own evil hearts. Do Thou give us to feel that godly sorrow which worketh repentance, and grace to follow thy blessed will in all our ways. All glory be to Thee for the gift of thy Son, who suffered, died, and rose again from the dead, that repentance and remission of sins might be preached in his name. We beseech Thee, for his sake, to have mercy upon us. Pardon our sins, and as when on earth Thou didst speak peace to thy disciples and returning penitents, so now speak to us. Calm our fears, and fill our hearts with joy and peace through believing.

We give thanks to Thee for the glad tidings of salvation, and for making plain the way to heaven. Be pleased to open our understanding, that we may know all things written in the law and the prophets, in the psalms and the gospels, concerning Jesus. Impress them upon our hearts, that we may be constrained to testify of them to others, and be thy true and faithful witnesses, conforming our lives to thy will, and the example of our Saviour Christ. Send, we beseech Thee, the Holy Ghost, the Comforter, to guide us into all truth, that we may have a right judgment in all things, and rejoice in his light and comfort. Endue us with power from on high faithfully to discharge the duties of our calling, and by patient continuance in well-doing, to glorify Thee. Accept our prayers on behalf of thy holy Church, that every member of it, in his vocation and ministry, may truly serve Thee. Look in compassion upon the heathen. Make known to all nations the Gospel of Jesus, and the remission of sins in his name. Visit, we pray Thee, every member of our family, and all for whom we should pray, with thy grace and heavenly benediction. Let thine eternal Spirit so dwell in us, that at the last we may be exalted unto the same place whither our Saviour Christ is gone before, who reigneth with Thee and the Holy Ghost, one God, world without end. Amen.

[Morning.]   TWENTY-NINTH WEEK.—LORD'S DAY.   [Evening.]

READ IN HOLY SCRIPTURE DEUTERONOMY XXXI. 1–13.   READ IN HOLY SCRIPTURE ST. JOHN XX. 19–31.

BLESSED Lord, who hast preserved us through the dark and silent hours of the night, and brought us in health and safety to see the light of another day, accept our morning sacrifice of praise and thanksgiving. We are journeying towards the place of which the Lord hath said that he would give it us, and we would acknowledge thy goodness in time past, and trust Thee for the time to come. Thou hast borne with our manners, led us in the right way, fed us with food convenient for us, and refreshed us with living water from the Rock: and now that thy pillar of a cloud is stayed upon the tabernacle, we would abide in our tents, and welcome the day of rest. O Thou who art the Lord of the Sabbath day, make this a day of rest to our souls. May no worldly thoughts intrude, no anxious cares disturb, no sore temptations harass us; but may we be kept in peace, and have fellowship with the Father, and with his Son Jesus Christ.

Meet us in thine house of prayer, O Lord. Revive thy work in the midst of the days. Rebuild the decayed places in the temple. Rekindle the flame of love upon the altar. Pour out a spirit of prayer and supplication. May we be upon our watch to hear what the Lord shall say unto us, and what we shall answer when we are reproved. Our hearts are hard; Lord, soften them by thy grace, and then mould them into thine image.

We mourn over broken Sabbaths, wasted opportunities, wandering thoughts, idle words, unprofitable services in time past. Lord, let this be to us a good day, a day of grace, a day of growth. May love be quickened, and every good purpose confirmed in us.

We pray not only for ourselves, but for the whole body of the faithful. May the whole Church receive a blessing this day. May she break out on the right hand and on the left. Lengthen her cords and strengthen her stakes. Let all her ministering servants be taught of God, and have a word put into their mouths that no adversary shall be able to gainsay or resist. Let sinners be converted, and saints be edified and built up in their holy faith. Shine, Lord, into the dark places of the earth. May the heathen world cease from that which cannot profit, and cast their idols to the moles and to the bats. May they take the Saviour's easy yoke upon them, and learn of Him who is meek and lowly in heart, and thus find rest unto their souls.

All these our prayers we humbly offer in the name of Him whom Thou hearest always, and who is our Advocate with the Father, Jesus Christ the righteous. Amen.

O LORD Jesus Christ, who hast manifested Thyself this day in the assemblies of thy people, we pray Thee, at its close, to visit us at our family altar. The shadows of evening have gathered around us, and once more we are about to retire to rest. As Thou didst appear at this time to thy disciples of old, so be present now in the midst of us, and breathe upon our souls the blessing of peace. We thank Thee for all the mercies of another Sabbath; for all the privileges and means of grace which Thou hast afforded us. We thank Thee for the joyful sound of thy Gospel, and that thou hast thereby made known to us, unworthy though we be, the way of pardon and life. Follow the labours of thy ministering servants with the enriching grace of thy Holy Spirit. Bring home thy Word with power to the hearts of all who have heard it. May angel messengers even now be carrying away from earth to heaven the glad tidings of salvation accepted. Comfort all who are sorrowing for sin; point them to the open fountain of thine own most precious blood; and to all who are turning the eye of faith upon a risen Saviour, say, as Thou art ever wont, "Be of good cheer; thy sins are forgiven."

Forbid it, Lord, that any should reject the offers of mercy which Thou hast so freely made; take away all pride and prejudice, all carelessness and indifference. Cause thine own people to take heed, lest even in them there be found an evil heart of unbelief. Give to each of us more simple faith. We would trust Thee not only in what is bright, but also in all that may seem dark. Cause our confidence to be strong at all times and in all circumstances. Deal tenderly with us, as Thou didst deal with thine erring disciple Thomas. Behold us, we pray Thee, with the same pity and compassion. Correct us whenever we go astray. Strengthen us wherever we are weak. Show Thyself in all things our sympathising High Priest. Though we have not seen Thee, Lord, yet may we love Thee, and grant that by faith we may be able to rejoice with joy unspeakable and full of glory.

Thou art acquainted with all our wants, and we place ourselves entirely in thy hands. As Thou hast knit us together in the ties of earthly relationship, so may we all be one in Thee. Let some savour of this holy day attend us throughout the week. Let its hallowing influence be seen in all our thoughts, and words, and works; and when our life of toil and service is ended here, may we enter into that rest which remaineth for the people of God. Hear us in these our prayers, and to Thee, with the Father and the Holy Ghost, will we give the glory, now and for ever. Amen.

[Morning.] TWENTY-NINTH WEEK.—MONDAY. [Evening.

READ IN HOLY SCRIPTURE DEUT. XXXI. 14—30.

WE present ourselves before Thee, most holy God, on this the morning of a new day. Although we see no pillar of cloud, and hear no sound of thy voice, may we feel that Thou art very near to us; and may our souls be filled with reverence and humility in thy sacred presence. We adore Thee that we are found bowing at thy throne of grace, surrounded by so many mercies which we have not deserved. We confess that we, like thy people of old, have wrought many evils before Thee, and have greatly provoked Thee. Yet we beseech Thee, O Lord, have mercy upon us, and forgive us. We know and confess that thy law is a witness against us that we have sinned and rebelled against Thee. But we fly, O Lord, from the law to the cross. Thy holy law convicts and condemns us; but we thank Thee that Christ redeems us from the condemnation of the law, and justifies us freely by his blood. We praise Thee, O God, for so great salvation. May we, as a family, be all partakers of it; that, being justified by faith, we may have peace with Thee, through our Lord Jesus Christ.

We thank Thee, O Lord, for thy kind care of us through the past night. Help us now to enter upon the duties and conflicts of another week, in the strength derived from the religious influences of the Sabbath-day; and let not the world wear away the holy impressions which our hearts have received.

We beseech Thee, O Lord, hide not thy face from us this day. Keep us from evil, that we may not grieve Thee. May we not turn aside from the way in which Thou hast commanded us to walk, nor do evil in thy sight; but may we live this day according to thy will. Teach us to cast all our care upon Thee. Fortify our minds against all disappointments. Preserve us from despondency. Animate us to cheerfulness. May we be strong and of good courage, assured that in all right paths Thou wilt be with us. From all folly and falsehood, from all pride and meanness, from all error and accident, O Lord, deliver us this day. May we be deaf to all the voices of temptation, but gladly attentive to the faintest whispers of thy Holy Spirit. Guide us by thy counsel, and mercifully bring us to the close of the day in peace.

Bless all our dear family, and all our relatives, friends, and neighbours, with all things that are necessary and good for them this day. May grace, mercy, and peace rest upon them.

Prepare us for all thy will on earth; and when the days approach that we must die, may we, redeemed by the blood of Christ, and clothed in his righteousness, rise to glory, honour, and immortality. Hear us, O Lord, for Christ's sake. Amen.

READ IN HOLY SCRIPTURE 1 CORINTHIANS XV. 1—22.

ADORABLE and ever-blessed God, we, thine unworthy creatures, approach the footstool of the Divine grace, at the close of another day. Help us to come before Thee with becoming reverence and deep humility, conscious of thy greatness, and of our sinfulness. O Lord, the very heavens are not clean in thy sight, and Thou chargest thine angels with folly. What sinful creatures, then, must we be, who often transgress thy laws, forget thy presence, and are constantly guilty of unbelief! Looking back upon the day now past, what reason have we to abase ourselves in the dust, and to cry, "Unclean, unclean!"

Verily Thou art a God of long-suffering and of great kindness, in that Thou hast not dealt with us after our sins, nor rewarded us after our iniquities. Moreover, Thou hast not spared thine own dear Son, but didst freely give Him up for us all. O Lord, help us to be duly sensible of thy great kindness, in providing for us a way of escape from the wrath to come, and to be duly thankful for thy holy Word, which makes known to us the glad tidings of salvation, through faith in a crucified Redeemer. Help us to believe the record which Thou hast given us of thy Son; and in the prospect of the great and terrible day of the Lord, when all that are in their graves shall hear his voice, and shall come forth, give us grace so to live, that we may know that we are of God, and that we shall have part in the resurrection of the just. Enable us ever to keep in mind the Gospel of Christ, by which we are saved. Teach us constantly to rely on thy grace to help us in every time of need, and to rejoice that thy grace is sufficient for us. Help us in all our ways to acknowledge Thee, that Thou mayest direct our steps. Increase our faith. Wash us daily in the fountain opened for sin and uncleanness, and daily renew us, by thy Holy Spirit, in the spirit of our minds; and may we lie down in our beds each night at peace with Thee, through the blood of the cross. Take us, and all near and dear to us, under thine own Almighty wings, and give us comfortable and refreshing sleep, that we may be strengthened for the duties of another day.

Look with compassion on the afflicted and distressed. Give them patience under their sufferings, and a happy issue out of all their afflictions. Hasten the time when there will be no more night, when all sorrow and sighing shall flee away, and when the Lamb which is in the midst of the throne shall lead his people to fountains of living waters, and God shall wipe away all tears from their eyes.

All this we ask for Jesus' sake, to whom, with Thee and the Holy Ghost, be all honour and glory, world without end. Amen.

[Morning.]   TWENTY-NINTH WEEK.—TUESDAY.   [Evening.

READ IN HOLY SCRIPTURE DEUT. XXXII. 1—29. | READ IN HOLY SCRIPTURE ST. JOHN XXI.

ETERNAL God, whose glory filleth heaven and earth, adored be thy majesty, praised for ever and ever be thy name. Thou art our Rock and Refuge, our hope and our portion for ever. Clouds and darkness are round about thy throne, righteousness and judgment are the habitation of thy seat. Fill our hearts with a lowly reverence of thy holiness and majesty, and for thy dear Son's sake have respect unto the prayers and thanksgivings which now we present at thy footstool.

Thou hast renewed to us the mercies of the morning light, and from the experience of all thy goodness to us we gather hope of thy continued favour. Especially, O God, we recall thy gracious promises in Christ Jesus, and pray that Thou wouldst fulfil them to us, by pardoning our sins, and cleansing us from all the stains of guilt which defile us in thy sight. By thy Spirit assure our hearts of thy forgiveness and love, and enable us to rejoice in hope of thy glory.

Be with us, we beseech Thee, through all the day. Only as Thou keepest us shall we be safe. Strengthen us for duty. Show us in all things what is thy will, and enable us to fulfil it cheerfully and obediently. Subdue in us all pride and selfishness, and guide our feet in the footsteps of Him who was meek and lowly in heart. We pray that we may grow in grace, and in the knowledge of our Lord and Saviour Jesus Christ. Lord, give us more faith, a brighter hope, and a truer love. Unfold to us the unsearchable riches of Christ.

We pray that we may be preserved from everything which would displease Thee or grieve thy Spirit, or be inconsistent with our Christian profession. Suffer us not to fall into any snare of the enemy of our souls, and help us to avoid even the appearance of evil. We desire to do to all what is just and right, and that in all our intercourse with others we may speak and act with Christian kindness, courtesy, forbearance, and love. We feel, O God, that we are very ignorant and weak, and we cast ourselves on thy mercy. Watch over us and forsake us not. Let thy peace in all things rule our hearts.

Shed thy choicest blessings on all we love. [May the younger members of this household grow up in thy faith and fear; believing in Jesus, and copying his example.] Let thy blessing rest on our Sovereign and all in authority. Give thy Holy Spirit abundantly to all thy ministers, and let them see thy work prosper in their hands, at home and abroad. Cause all thy people to be more jealous of thy glory, and diligent in doing thy will. All these mercies we ask in the name of Jesus, thy dear Son, our Lord. Amen.

BLESSED be the God and Father of our Lord and Saviour Jesus Christ, who, according to his abundant mercy, hath begotten us again unto a lively hope by the resurrection of Jesus Christ from the dead. We bless Thee that, when our world was dead in trespasses and sins, Thou didst send forth thine only-begotten Son to live and die in our stead, so that He might deliver us, who were under the curse of the law. We would gratefully adore Thee that Jesus has fulfilled all righteousness.

We praise Thee for his perfect sacrifice for the sins of the whole world, and for his glorious triumph over all the powers of darkness. He hath led captivity captive, and hath obtained gifts for men. We rejoice in the thought that, after his resurrection, He still lingered for forty days in our world, showing Himself on many occasions to his disciples. We praise the love in which thy Son visited our earth, and hath now gone up on high to make intercession for us.

As we are now about to retire to rest, and as we remember that sleep is the image of death, so do we rejoice that the Captain of our salvation hath taken the sting from death, and robbed the grave of victory. May this our joy be deep and abiding, and arise from the witness of the Holy Ghost in our hearts that we are each of us born again, and have become new creatures in Christ Jesus. We beseech Thee, most merciful Father, that Thou wouldst deliver us from self-delusion. May we be indeed found in Jesus Christ.

Holy Saviour, we read with awe of the manner in which Thou didst search and test the love of Peter towards Thee. We feel that our love is weak and cold—is an utterly unworthy response to thy holy and mighty love to us. Help us, we entreat Thee, to love Thee; to love Thee more than we love all the world beside. We beseech Thee to increase our faith, to brighten our hope, and to fill our hearts more abundantly with thy Holy Spirit. Forgive the sins of this day. Accept our unfeigned thanks for all thy mercies, and now receive us into thy favour. May our names be enrolled in the Lamb's book of life.

Bless, we beseech Thee, thy catholic Church. Graciously hear the prayer of thy Son, our sole High Priest, that all thy believing people may be one, of one mind and one heart; one fold under one Shepherd. And grant, heavenly Father, that when we have done thy will on earth, we may also, like our Lord, ascend up to thy right hand, and enter into thy joy.

Hear our prayer, for the sake of Jesus Christ our Lord. Amen.

[199]

[Morning.] **TWENTY-NINTH WEEK.—WEDNESDAY.** [Evening.

READ IN HOLY SCRIPTURE DEUT. XXXII. 29–52.

O ETERNAL Lord God, who hast watched over and protected us during the past night, we desire to give Thee praise and glory for thy unceasing mercies, and to look to Thee, as the God of providence and of grace, for guidance and blessing throughout the coming day. We are ignorant, O Lord, and know not what a day may bring forth; we are weak, and cannot order our affairs aright; help us, then, to exercise continual dependence upon Thee. As the eyes of servants look unto the hand of their masters, so may our eyes and our hearts wait upon the Lord our God.

Pour down upon us, merciful Father, that heavenly wisdom which may lead us to consider our latter end, to remember that in the midst of life we are in death, and that we know not the day or the hour in which the Son of Man shall come. May we, then, live and walk this day in the light of eternity. We acknowledge that we have provoked Thee to anger with our vanities, seeking the things of this world instead of the things which are eternal, and desiring the favour of our fellowmen rather than thine. For this our folly and our sinfulness Thou mightest justly have abhorred us, and for our provocations Thou mightest have hidden thy face from us for ever; but Thou, O God, art a merciful God, long-suffering, and plenteous in goodness, and we are here living to praise Thee this day.

We pray Thee, Lord, that we may not presume upon thy mercy; yea, rather, let thy love in Christ Jesus constrain us to live no longer to ourselves, but unto Thee. Do Thou enable us to set our hearts towards all the words of instruction which are contained in the Holy Scriptures; may we, by the teaching of thy Spirit, understand that this is our very life, even to know Thee, the only true God, and Jesus Christ whom Thou hast sent. May we strive continually to put off the old man, and, being renewed in the spirit of our minds, to put on the new man, which is created in righteousness and true holiness. Assist us throughout this day to be watchful against sin, and ready to every good work, that we may glorify Thee by a holy walk and conversation. May we come out and be separate from an ungodly world; in our necessary contact with it, may we resist its temptations; in our business transactions, may we rise above its principles; in our family may there be a savour of spirituality; and in our intercourse with Thee, our God, may there be the loving heart, and close fellowship and communion. Thus, gracious God, do Thou guide us continually in the way of truth and holiness, for thy dear Son's sake, Jesus Christ our Lord. Amen.

READ IN HOLY SCRIPTURE PSALM XVI.

THE day is thine, O Lord, and the night also is thine. Thou hast held our souls in life through another day. We have been permitted to attend to the various duties of life. Preserved from evil and supplied by thy bounty, we have not lacked any good thing. Thou hast opened thine hand and satisfied us; and now, in unbroken peace and in the possession of numerous comforts, we are favoured with the precious privilege of gathering around our domestic altar. The lines are fallen to us in pleasant places, and we have a goodly heritage.

But while mercies and blessings belong unto Thee, O Lord, shame and confusion of face belong unto us. How much of imperfection and of sin attaches to us! We are conscious of many transgressions; and if our hearts condemn us, Thou art greater than our hearts, and knowest all things. God be merciful to us sinners. May the blood of Christ cleanse us from all iniquity, and the law of the Spirit of life in Christ Jesus make us free from the law of sin and death. May we afresh sincerely and solemnly say, "Thou art my Lord." May we do homage to no other God but Thee. May we suffer no power to usurp thy throne within us. Reign Thou over us supreme and alone.

Be Thou the portion of our inheritance and of our cup, and give us ever to set Thee before us, and act as with Thee at our right hand. May we not have the spirit of bondage again to fear, but the Spirit of adoption, whereby, with an assured hope, our heart may rejoice and our soul be glad, as we exclaim, "Abba, Father." Let us, with the faith of Jesus, believe that our flesh shall rest in hope, and that Thou wilt show us the path of life. Like Jesus, may we have the blessed assurance that in thy presence is fulness of joy, and at thy right hand there are pleasures for evermore. And thus, amidst all the temptations, toils, and sorrows of earth, may we aspire, with hope and confidence, after that better country which is the heavenly. Grant, O Lord, we beseech Thee, that these glorious views of immortality may be widely spread throughout the families of our own and other lands, until there shall be no longer occasion for any to say, Know the Lord, but all shall know Thee, from the least even to the greatest.

And now, O Father, we calmly and confidently commit ourselves to thy protection and blessing during another night. Suffer no evil to come near our persons or our dwelling. Let sleep refresh us and fit us for the duties of the morrow; and let all our days and nights on earth be passed in the fear and in the favour of God our Father, through Christ our Lord. Amen.

[MORNING.] TWENTY-NINTH WEEK.—THURSDAY. [EVENING.

READ IN HOLY SCRIPTURE JOSHUA I.

O GOD of Israel, grant us the light of thy Holy Spirit, that we may compare spiritual things with spiritual, and appropriate to ourselves the lessons of heavenly wisdom which appear in every portion of thy inspired Word. We rejoice with thankfulness that we are not under the law, but under grace. What the law could not do through the weakness of the flesh, thy Divine Son, our Redeemer, has fully accomplished. We bless Thee, we praise Thee, O God, for the great love with which Thou hast loved thy people, and for the fruits of that love which we have in the death and resurrection of Jesus, our Shepherd and our Head. Lead us nearer and nearer to Him, we beseech Thee. Place us more entirely under his care and guidance, and give us the spirit of loving obedience to his word and will.

How shall we sufficiently magnify Thee, our Father, that it hath pleased Thee to bring life and immortality to light by the Gospel? We contemplate with joy our heirship in Jesus, thy co-equal Son. We seek in faith the inheritance granted to Him, and to all thy children in Him, whom it hath pleased Thee to make heirs of God, and joint heirs with Christ. Oh, that we may delight to look out from the wilderness of the world, and view by this faith that better land of heavenly promise which Thou hast provided for the objects of thy fatherly care! Oh, that we may long and look for the appearance of Him who is coming again to lead his redeemed ones into the eternal enjoyment of the purchased possession! And while we wait for that glorious event, grant to us, our Father and our God, that we may feel we are not of this world, but that our citizenship is in heaven, from whence we are looking for Him in whose spotless righteousness we are to appear in thy presence, and to shine in thy kingdom. Having this blessed hope in Him, enable us to purify ourselves as He is pure.

We bless Thee for that record of thy wisdom and love, in which we are permitted to study thy Divine character, and to learn thy purposes in Christ. Make that sacred volume, we pray Thee, increasingly precious to our souls. Grant us thy Holy Spirit, without whose enlightening and sanctifying influences we can neither comprehend nor receive the precious truths which He has caused to be written for our instruction; and the more that blessed Book is scorned or traduced, the more fervently may we take it to our grateful and loving hearts, and the more valiantly strive for the life-giving doctrines which its pages contain. Graft it, we entreat Thee, inwardly in our hearts, that we may bring forth fruit thereof to the glory of thy name and the sanctification of our own souls, through Jesus Christ our Lord. Amen.

READ IN HOLY SCRIPTURE ACTS I.

WE give Thee thanks, O Lord, that Thou didst, in thine infinite compassion, look upon us in our low estate, and didst send thy well-beloved Son to deliver us from sin and condemnation. We bless Thee that Jesus was in this world as a man of sorrows, and suffered—the just for the unjust—to bring us to Thee; and having died for our offences, that he rose for our justification, and is even now at the right hand of the Majesty on high, to make intercession for us. By the eye of faith we would look up to Him as our advocate with Thee the Father. This is our encouragement in drawing near to Thee. We might well be afraid, in our sinfulness, to venture into thy sacred presence in our own name; but we come in the name of Him who is infinitely worthy; and our prayer is, "Behold, O God, our shield, and look upon the face of thine Anointed."

We thank Thee that our blessed Redeemer, before He ascended to his glory, gave his disciples the promise that he would send the Comforter, the Holy Spirit. And Thou, who hast in all ages been the Hearer and Answerer of prayer, didst fulfil thy word. Surely Thou art ready to fulfil thy promise to us. Help us, as the disciples of old, to abound in prayer and to wait upon Thee. Quicken us, and we will call upon thy name. We need thy Holy Spirit to help our infirmities, to give us the true Spirit of prayer, to enlighten us in the knowledge of thy Holy Word, to enable us to do thy will, to sanctify us, and to cheer us with the hope of glory. Thou hast promised thy Spirit to them that ask Thee. We pray that we may enjoy his life-giving influence, so that we may grow in grace and in the knowledge of Jesus Christ.

We beseech Thee to give more of the Spirit of prayer to the Church universal, and to pour out upon Zion the refreshing dews of thy heavenly grace. May thy people everywhere be revived; and in answer to the fervent prayer of thy children, do Thou give power from on high, that all the faithful may be more zealous, and that thy kingdom may advance throughout the world.

We commend unto Thee all our friends and relations. We pray Thee to encompass them with thy presence. Remember all the afflicted and distressed, comfort the mourners, bind up sorrowful and bleeding hearts, and pour the oil of holy joy into the wounded spirit.

And now, Lord, at the close of the day we acknowledge thy goodness in sparing us, and providing for all our wants. Thou who hast watched over us during all the days and nights of the past, do Thou protect us this night. We cast all our cares on Thee, and pray Thee to hear us, for Christ's sake. Amen.

[Morning.] **TWENTY-NINTH WEEK.—FRIDAY.** [Evening.

READ IN HOLY SCRIPTURE JOSHUA III.

READ IN HOLY SCRIPTURE ACTS II. 1–21.

O GRACIOUS and heavenly Father, who, though Thou dwellest on high, dost yet humble Thyself to behold the things that are in earth, we kneel in much humility at thy footstool, to thank Thee for the many mercies of the night, and to implore thy grace and protection for the day to which we have been spared. Accept us, we pray Thee, for Jesus' sake; and according to thy promise, send us not empty away. We are undeserving of thy goodness, and day by day adds to our many sins. Make us more thankful for what Thou hast done, and by thine indwelling Spirit so increase our love to Thee, that we may strive to spend this day as in thy sight, and in cheerful obedience to all thy will.

Graciously enlighten our minds, that we may more clearly understand thy Word. Thou, O God, who hast inspired holy men of old to write thy truth, alone canst enable us to believe what they have written, and to submit ourselves in all things to the teaching of thy Word. Remove, we beseech Thee, from us all ignorance and hardness of heart. Bestow upon us the spirit of meekness, and guide us into all truth. Let the way of salvation be so plain to us, that we may not err therein, nor be deceived by the temptations of Satan, or any false teaching of men. Be Thou, O Holy Ghost, our teacher. Take of the things of Christ and show them unto us, that we may grow in grace, and walking in his footsteps, live in all things to thy praise and glory.

Leave us not to ourselves, O God, this day. Our path is beset by many dangers and temptations, and our own sinful hearts are prone to wander to forbidden things. Even the duties of our calling may become a snare in the hands of our great enemy for the entanglement and ruin of our souls. Help, and defend, and keep us, for we are unable to keep ourselves. By thy Holy Spirit teach us what we ought to do, and strengthen us to do it. Suffer us not to shrink from any duty which Thou layest upon us, and especially preserve us from loving ourselves more than Thee, and from following our own will when it is contrary to thine. May the signs and tokens of thy presence with us be seen in our deeper love to Thee, our increasing hatred of sin, and our frequent triumphs over temptation. Grant us such an abundant experience of thy grace and love, that we may run in the way of thy commandments.

Do with those whom we would remember at thy throne. Let thy providence be about them, and thy love be shed abroad abundantly in all their hearts. We ask all for Jesus Christ's sake. Amen.

HOLY, holy, holy, Lord God of hosts; in old time Thou wast seen in Eden, in the bush that burned with fire, at the door of the Tabernacle, and within the Temple of Israel; but now Thou hast come down bodily to dwell amongst us. Fill—yea, as thou didst the place where the apostles came together—fill the earth with thy glory. Come, O Holy Ghost, and let thy power be known and seen in all the earth; cool the world's angry passions, quell all rage and enmity in loving peace. Still the rude sounds of war; hasten the time when Christ's kingdom shall be established in the earth, when men shall beat their swords into ploughshares, and nation shall not lift up sword against nation, neither shall they learn war any more.

Lord, touch the hearts of those who preach the Gospel; give them tongues of fire, with glowing words, to consume men's love of sin, and to inflame their souls with pure devotion. Send forth, O Holy Ghost, preachers in every land; that the nations may hear, in their own tongue, the Gospel of God, and be saved by Christ. If mockers scorn, let them be confounded. If unbelievers rise against Thee, abate their pride, and let unbelief be turned to faith. Make those who cavil at thy Word to stand in awe of it; and let the men who say there is no truth in it, be converted by its power.

We praise Thee, O God, for all the abundant blessings of this day. Add to them the gift of a thankful heart, and cause us to show forth thy praise, not only with our lips, but in our lives.

Blessed Spirit, enable us to realise thy presence more and more. If, during the day, we have forgotten Thee, done any sin, or left undone any act of righteousness, fill us with sorrow for these and all past offences. Wash us, O God, in the fountain once opened for sin, and for the sake of Jesus blot out all our offences. Help us, that we may speedily unlearn all evil, by knowing and doing all manner of good. Night is coming on; make it light with thy presence and favour. Death is drawing near; let us not be afraid, but may we find that death and the grave are, as Elijah's chariot and horses, carrying us to heaven. Go Thou with us in every duty and through every trial, that every dark day may be made bright with the gracious tokens of thy love. Keep us this night from all sin, and let us not fall into any snares of the evil one. Make thy strength perfect in our weakness, and leave us not, lest we fall.

We pray for our friends and relations. Enrich them with thy special blessing. Take them and us into thy keeping for the night, and let no harm befall us. We ask all for Jesus Christ's sake. Amen.

[Morning.] **TWENTY-NINTH WEEK.—SATURDAY.** [Evening.

READ IN HOLY SCRIPTURE JOSHUA IV.

READ IN HOLY SCRIPTURE ACTS II. 22—47.

O LORD, our gracious and merciful Father, with deep humility and sincere gratitude we desire to draw near to Thee in prayer this morning. Through the darkness of another night thine almighty arm has sustained us; and now we kneel at thy footstool, the monuments of thy forbearance and goodness.

We beseech Thee to stir up in our souls a more lively sense of our entire dependence upon Thee, and to a more obedient, grateful, and loving acknowledgment of thy merciful kindness. From Thee we have received all the blessings of our past lives. Thou art the author of all the mercies we at present enjoy. Thou art our only hope for all the future. As Thou didst lead thy people Israel in their journey through the wilderness, so hast Thou graciously led us in our earthly pilgrimage. We remember this morning thy special interpositions on our behalf. When in deep perplexity and distress, Thou hast relieved and comforted us; and when exposed to imminent danger, Thou hast delivered us, like Israel of old. We would call to mind the memorials of thy mercies, and mark the steps by which Thou hast thus far guided us. Still be our God and our guide, we beseech Thee, O Lord, even unto our life's end; and finally give us an abundant entrance into thine everlasting kingdom.

We ask special blessings both for ourselves and others this last day of the week. Help us so to order our temporal affairs, and discharge our duties, that we may not be unfitted for the high and holy exercises of the approaching Sabbath. Let thy good Spirit abide with all ministers of the Gospel, to aid them in the study of thy truth, that they may come forth to-morrow in the fulness of the blessing of the Gospel of Christ. To us, and to all thy people, let this day be a preparation day for the Sabbath.

We pray for all who are dear to us by the ties of nature and affection. Oh, let thy blessing rest upon them all. Have mercy, we beseech Thee, O Lord, upon our neighbours and acquaintances. Oh, let careless and impenitent sinners in this place be brought to Jesus Christ. May our influence, and the influence of other Christians around, lead them to Him, that they may obtain salvation and eternal life. In our midst, and throughout the whole earth, let thy kingdom come, and thy will be done even as it is done in heaven.

We supplicate before Thee, O Lord, the forgiveness of all our sins, the renewing and sanctifying influences of thy Holy Spirit, in the name and for the sake of thy beloved Son, Jesus Christ, to whom, with the Father and the Holy Ghost, be all honour and glory, world without end. Amen.

O GRACIOUS Lord God, who hast not dealt with us after our sins, nor rewarded us according to our iniquities, we bless Thee for the mercies of this day and of the week now past. Unceasing has been thy care, and infinite thy compassion. When we think of thy love, we are ashamed of the coldness of our hearts and the feebleness of our praise. Kindle within us, we beseech Thee, more fervent gratitude towards Thee, especially for the gift of thy dear Son, to redeem us, and of thy Holy Spirit, to convert and sanctify us. Show to us the exceeding greatness of thy mercy, by convincing us of our lost condition, and of our utter helplessness through sin. Glory be to thy name that, even when we were sinners and without strength, Christ died, the just for the unjust, the sinless for the sinful, that He might reconcile us to God. Lord, we pray that in all sincerity and truth we may grasp thy promises in Christ Jesus, and have peace through the blood of his cross. So by thy Holy Spirit work in us that, as Christ was raised from the dead by the glory of the Father, so we also may walk in newness of life. Fill us with all joy and peace in believing, and enable us to show forth the power of thy grace by a cheerful obedience to thy will, and a daily triumph over the power of sin and temptation.

Let thy watchful care be over us during the night. Grant that, through thy merciful protection, we and all whom we would remember at thy footstool may sleep in safety, and rise so refreshed as to enter with cheerfulness on the duties of the Lord's day.

We confess, O Lord, we have neglected our opportunities, and have not sought diligently the one thing needful. Let not our past sin cause Thee to withhold the continuance of spiritual privileges, or the tokens of thy presence in our use of them. [Give to the children of our family thy special grace. Convert them all from sin to holiness, and make them thine in Christ Jesus.]

We lift up our hearts on behalf of thy whole Church. Pour out thy Holy Spirit abundantly, as on the day of Pentecost. Cause thy ministers to preach as with tongues of fire the word of reconciliation, and bow many hearts day by day beneath the soul-subduing power of thy truth. Look in tender pity on the dark and desolate places of the earth. Lord, when shall thy light shine upon them, and thy Gospel be preached among all nations, and the whole earth be filled with thy glory? Hasten the time, we beseech Thee, when the glory of the Lord shall be revealed, and all flesh shall see it together.

We ask these and all other mercies in the name of thy dear Son, Jesus Christ. Amen.

[Morning.]   **THIRTIETH WEEK.—LORD'S DAY.**   [Evening.

READ IN HOLY SCRIPTURE JOSHUA VI.   READ IN HOLY SCRIPTURE ACTS III.

ALMIGHTY and most merciful Father, we thank Thee for thy constant care and kindness towards us. We praise Thee for our preservation during the past night, and that we behold another Sabbath day. We bless Thee for this day, as the memorial of our Lord Jesus Christ, the Captain of our salvation. We thank Thee that Thou didst send Him into the world, to seek and to save the lost. We adore Thee, O Son of God, that Thou didst bear our sins in thine own body on the tree; that Thou didst rise from the dead and ascend to heaven in our nature. We glorify thy name for the Gospel of thy love. O God, we beseech of Thee to grant that, by the power of thy Spirit, our hearts may be conquered for Christ. Give us faith in Jesus as our sacrifice, so that all our sins may be blotted out in his atoning blood. Enable us to trust in Him as our High Priest, through whom we present all our prayers and praises at thy throne. Give us grace to love Him with all our hearts, and serve Him with all our powers. May we be accepted in the Beloved, adopted into thy family, adorned with the beauty of thy holiness, and at last stand before Thee complete in Jesus. O righteous Father, we beseech Thee to have mercy upon all men. Let thy way be known upon earth, thy saving health among all nations. Stand by the ministers of Christ this day; accompany the preaching of thy Gospel with the power of thy Spirit; let it prove mighty to the pulling down of strongholds, and in bringing every thought into captivity to the obedience of Christ. Bless those who teach the young in Sabbath-schools or Ragged-schools; those who circulate the Scriptures, or religious tracts; those who visit the poor, the afflicted, the widows, and the fatherless. Smile upon all these labours, we beseech Thee, and crown them with success. Comfort those who mourn; and bind up the broken-hearted. May those who are longing for the sanctuary, but are detained at home, enjoy thy presence in their own dwellings. If we are permitted to go to thy house, help us to offer Thee spiritual worship, and to hear thy Word with meekness and love.

Grant us, O Lord, this day, some foretaste of the heavenly rest. Bless every member of our family, and all who are dear to us. May our relations and friends be our spiritual kindred in the bonds of everlasting love. If any of them know Thee not, awaken them this day to flee from the wrath to come, and to lay hold upon the hope set before them in the Gospel.

When our earthly Sabbaths are ended, then, Holy Father, admit us to the nobler worship of the heavenly temple, through Jesus Christ our Lord. Amen.

O ALMIGHTY and most merciful God, we magnify Thee for the mercies of another Sabbath-day. We thank Thee for the privileges we have enjoyed: for being permitted to go up to thy house, to join in the worship of thy people, and to mingle our voices with theirs in prayer and praise. We praise Thee too, O our Father, for the Gospel of thy grace. Blessed are they who know the joyful sound. Give us grace to love the tidings of peace, and to receive with meekness the engrafted Word, which is able to save the soul. May thy Gospel come to us not in word only, but in power, and, through the grace of the Spirit, be unto us the savour of life unto life. Help us to improve every means of grace which Thou hast in thy goodness bestowed upon us; and teach us to hallow our Sabbaths on earth, that they may be foretastes to us of an eternal Sabbath.

But while we thankfully acknowledge all thy goodness, we would humbly ask thy pardon for our sins. In many things we all offend, even on this thy holy day; we have grieved thy Spirit by wandering thoughts, by lifeless devotions, by a lack of fervour in our prayers, by a want of unction in our praises. Oh, forgive us, pardon our shortcomings, our failures, the feebleness of our faith, the coldness of our love, the languor of our hope. We would lay these and all our sins at the cross of Jesus. May we lie down this night washed, justified, and sanctified in the name of the Lord Jesus, and by the Spirit of our God.

Heavenly Father, we commend to thy tender care and keeping all whom we love, and all who seek an interest in our prayers. Make all grace abound towards them. May theirs be the love which passeth knowledge, the peace passing all understanding, the hope which maketh not ashamed, and the joy which is unspeakable and full of glory. Look graciously on all who are in affliction, and reveal Thyself to them as a God who comforteth those who are cast down; visit them in their distress, and heal their wounds. Give thy blessing, O God, to the Word that has been preached this day; sow the seed of eternal life in many hearts. May Christ, in the conversion of many sinners, see of the travail of his soul and be satisfied. Cause many of thine own people to go on their way rejoicing; arm them with renewed strength to run patiently the race that is set before them.

We commit ourselves, O God, and all that are near and dear to us, to thy care; guide, guard, and bless us, and receiving these our humble petitions, answer us not for our merit's sake, but for thy mercy, through Jesus Christ our Lord. Amen.

[Morning.]   **THIRTIETH WEEK.—MONDAY.**   [Evening.

READ IN HOLY SCRIPTURE JOSHUA VII.

O LORD, our heavenly Father, we thank Thee for the rest Thou hast graciously afforded us during the hours of darkness, and for the renewal of the morning light. We praise Thee for all the blessings which it brings, but chiefly for the refreshing of our souls with the saving light of thy Holy Word.

Oh, write upon our hearts and memories the Scripture we have just heard. May we hide it in our hearts, that we this day sin not against Thee. Teach us to look upon sin as the abominable thing which Thou hatest. May we fear to offend Thee, in thought or deed. May we tremble lest others offend, seeing that individually, and as members one of another, Thou dost call us to account. We acknowledge thy justice, and we humbly adore thy long forbearance in sparing us, though Thou dost set our sins in the light of thy countenance. As a people and as a Church, singularly favoured, yet in many ways abusing our high privileges, Thou mightest have given sentence against us. As a family, encompassed with mercies, yet far from being what we ought, Thou mightest have left us miserably to perish. As each one of us is prone to depart from Thee, and to covet this world's riches and honours, Thou mightest have brought us to a shameful end, as Thou didst Achan in the camp, leaving us the monuments of thy fierce anger. But, O thou Saviour of men, Thou hast given us abundant opportunity to repent; yea, Thou dost still plead with us, through the Son of thy love, to confess and to forsake our sin, that we may obtain mercy. We pray for grace to obey thy voice. May Jesus Christ and his great salvation be the object of our chief desire. May we give Him glory, by a full confession of our guilt; and, believing in the power of his blood, may we obtain of Thee, the God of all grace, perfect remission and forgiveness; that, being justified by faith, we may have peace with God, through Him who died for our sins, and rose again for our justification. And, O gracious Lord, do Thou seal us with that Holy Spirit of promise, and enable us henceforth to live unreservedly to thy glory.

We pray for all men. Bless our rulers. Give them wisdom from above; and in all times and circumstances enable them to look to Thee, and find guidance. Save our Sovereign, and all the Royal Family. Clothe thy ministers with righteousness, and make thy chosen people joyful. Visit with heavenly consolations the sick and the afflicted. And let thy choicest blessings, both for time and for eternity, rest upon us and upon all for whom we would pray; for the sake of our only Saviour, Jesus Christ; to whom be ascribed all honour and glory for ever. Amen.

READ IN HOLY SCRIPTURE ACTS IV. 1—31.

O LORD God of hosts, blessed is the man that trusteth in Thee. We trusted in Thee, and Thou hast delivered us; we called upon thy name, and Thou hast heard us in thy holy heaven. We call to remembrance the great things which Thou hast done for us, and for our fathers before us. Thou hast given to us, as well as to them, the light of revelation; and we read there of the trials and persecutions of thy Church; we read also of the strength and grace which Thou gavest to thy believing people to enable them to glorify Thee in the fires of affliction. Help us ever to remember that all that will live godly in Christ Jesus shall suffer persecution, and that thy people are called to be witnesses for Thee in the midst of a crooked and perverse generation.

At the close of another day we again acknowledge our sinfulness and unworthiness in thy sight. We have not this day adorned the Christian profession as we ought to have done; and we are conscious of much inconsistency in all our ways; yet Thou hast dealt mercifully with us; Thou hast not dealt with us after our sins, neither rewarded us after our iniquities. Oh, make us duly sensible of thy continual kindness, and that even trials and afflictions are intended for our good. Grant that our faith, though it be tried with fire, may be found unto praise, and honour, and glory, at the appearing of Jesus Christ. Convince us more and more that if Thou dost admit us to thy favour, we must ascribe this, not to our goodness, but solely to the merits of Jesus Christ. Conform us to his image, that like as He was raised from the dead by the glory of the Father, so we also may walk in newness of life. Forbid that any of us should be of the number of those who take counsel against thy holy child, Jesus; but rather let us esteem it a high honour to be counted worthy to suffer shame for his name, ever remembering that we must stand before his judgment seat, and be acknowledged or rejected by Him according as we have acknowledged or denied Him before the world. O Lord, give to each of us the grace which we severally require; and, if we have never prayed for grace before, or before believed on Jesus, help us to pray now, and to believe now, that we may lie down on our beds at peace with Thee, through the blood of the cross.

Bless all thy people, and strengthen them for the work which Thou hast given them to do. Bless our relations and friends, and may we rise from our knees convinced that Thou hearest the praises and supplications which are presented to Thee in the name of Jesus Christ; to whom, with Thyself and the Holy Ghost, be all honour and glory, world without end. Amen.

[MORNING.] **THIRTIETH WEEK.—TUESDAY.** [EVENING.

READ IN HOLY SCRIPTURE JOSHUA VIII. 1—22, 30—35.

READ IN HOLY SCRIPTURE ACTS IV. 32—V. 16.

O, ALMIGHTY God!—the God and Father of our Lord Jesus Christ; by Him we now venture to draw nigh to thy throne of grace. We would first praise and thank Thee for permitting us to see the light of another day, and to assemble before Thee for family worship. We thank Thee for all the temporal blessings we have received, and for thy forbearance and mercy and loving-kindness. We thank Thee for the means of grace and for the hope of glory;—for redemption through the blood of Christ;—and for the gift of the Holy Spirit; and we beseech Thee, make us duly sensible of all thy mercies; and enable us to show forth our gratitude, not merely in our lips but in our lives.

And now, Lord, we beseech Thee, speak peace to our souls. We have been reminded, by that portion of thy Word which we have just heard, of the blessings and the cursings contained in thy holy law: alas! we have justly deserved the curse; for we have in many things offended, and in all things we have come short. But we nevertheless can rejoice, that we have in Christ a Redeemer, who has endured the curse and its penalties for us;—who suffered, the just for the unjust: oh, enable us to look with steadfast faith upon that atoning blood, which taketh away the sin of the world; so that we may still have peace and joy in believing. Lord we praise Thee, that in Him we may look for the blessing instead of the curse, and rejoice in hope of the speedy manifestation of thy glory.

And help us, O Lord, in the meantime, to devote ourselves more entirely to thy service. Thou knowest the spiritual enemies with which we have to contend; and Thou knowest our weakness through the flesh,—the devices and desires of our corrupt hearts: help us therefore ever to remember the exhortation we have just heard,—"to fear not, neither to be dismayed." Help us to trust more entirely in Thee,—believing thy promises, and assured that Thou carest for us. And give us thy might in the inward man; that we may have the blessed experience, that greater is He that is in us, than he that is in the world. Make thy strength perfect in our weakness, and grant that we may bruise Satan under our feet shortly.

Finally we beseech Thee to bless, in like manner, all who are near and dear to us; and all for whom it is our privilege or duty to intercede. Convert those who know Thee not; strengthen the weak in faith; comfort the afflicted, the tempted, the distressed; raise up them that fall; and bring both them and us to thy everlasting kingdom and glory, through Jesus Christ our Lord. Amen.

THANKS be to Thee, O heavenly Father, that we have been brought to the close of another day in peace and safety. O Thou who makest the outgoings of the morning and evening to rejoice, grant that we may now conclude the day with Thee.

Blot out, we pray Thee, from thy book whatever Thou hast seen amiss in us this day, whether in the desires of our hearts, in the words of our mouths, in our tempers, or in our acts. Give us godly sorrow for every short-coming, and a steadfast resolution to amend and improve in time to come; and do Thou now sprinkle us with the blood of the Lamb, that we may rejoice in the sense of thy forgiveness.

We bless thy holy name for whatever good we have been enabled to do this day. Not unto us, O Lord, but unto thy name be the praise. We likewise thank Thee for whatever temptation we may have been enabled to overcome. Lord, still keep us, for we cannot keep ourselves. Oh, grant that we may be kept by the power of God, through faith, unto salvation; and that after all the trials and labours of life are ended, we may find ourselves numbered among thy chosen people.

Accept, we pray Thee, our intercessions for all mankind. Bless our dear friends and relatives, and make them partakers with us of thy blessing. Bless the universal Church of Christ, and grant that the multitude of them that believe may be of one heart and of one soul. May a spirit of liberality abound among them, and may they do good, and communicate to their poorer brethren. Give, we pray Thee, to all Christians holy consistency, that they may be just and honest, truthful and conscientious, and avoid all things contrary to their profession.

We beg to commend to Thee, O God, thine ancient people, the Jews. Take away the veil from their minds, that they may see Christ in the Old Testament, and that they may acknowledge Him to be the true Messiah.

Look with pity, we beseech Thee, on the dark places of the earth. Increase, O Lord, the labourers in thy vineyard, and do Thou dispose the hearts of those on whom Thou hast bestowed thy gifts, that they may seek a share in the ministry of Jesus, and strive to win souls to Him.

Do Thou sustain us and refresh us during the night, and grant that, if we are spared to see another day, we may consecrate it to Thee. But, O Lord, if Thou shouldest require our souls this night, oh, take us to Thyself, to dwell for ever with Thee in heaven, through Jesus Christ our Lord. Amen.

[MORNING.] THIRTIETH WEEK.—WEDNESDAY. [EVENING.

READ IN HOLY SCRIPTURE JOSHUA IX. 1—16.

GREAT and eternal God, who dwellest in glory and majesty, help us with reverence to approach unto Thee. Let our supplication arise from the sense of our necessities, and be the prayer which goeth not out of feigned lips. Thou hast permitted us as a family to gather once more before Thee, as we enter on another day. We thank Thee for the refreshment of sleep. We acknowledge the wisdom and the goodness with which Thou hast appointed alternate seasons of labour and of repose. We laid us down and slept; we awaked, for the Lord sustained us. We bless Thee that we are now strengthened for the work of this day. We give thanks for the support of our bodily and mental powers, for the bounties of thy providence, for the endearments of relationship and domestic affection, and for all the blessings which thy hand bestows. Blessed be the Lord, who daily loadeth us with his benefits.

We especially thank Thee for the light of thy Holy Word; and whilst we prize the fuller discoveries of thy will, and of thy great designs in the Gospel of thy Son, we bless Thee for these early records of thy dispensations in the past. May we be instructed by what we have now read. May we be as earnest in laying hold of eternal life as those of whom we have been hearing were in reference to their temporal safety. Give us all to embrace the opportunity which we now have of entering into a state of peace and harmony with Thee. Let it be our highest desire that we may possess thy favour, and share the blessed fellowship of thy people. Make us truthful and sincere in all our dealings with Thee, since, though creatures may deceive one another, Thou canst not be mocked, and knowest us altogether. Let our attention to religion be solemn reality. Help us all to embrace from the heart thy salvation, by putting away our sins, and by true faith in Jesus our Saviour. Thus may we enter into covenant with Thee, and become thine. Impress us, too, with the necessity of asking counsel of Thee in all things, since we are in ourselves so liable to error. May thy guidance be sought in every step; and do Thou save us from being deceived by false appearances and evil subtlety, and lead us in a right path.

Direct and help us in all the duties of this day. May all our works be begun, continued, and ended in Thee. Arm us against temptation. Keep us from all evil, whether in word or action. Save us from infirmities of temper. Cleanse the thoughts of our hearts by the inspiration of thy Holy Spirit. Prepare us for any trials which may befall us, and order all for our good. Hear thus our voice in the morning, and accept these our praises and prayers, for the sake of Christ our Saviour. Amen.

READ IN HOLY SCRIPTURE ACTS V. 17—42.

MERCIFUL God, and Heavenly Father, we thank Thee that we can draw near to Thee this night, in peace and safety, no man daring to make us afraid; that we can read together thy Holy Word, and worship Thee without let or hindrance. As our outward circumstances are favourable, so let our hearts be disposed to make good use of this sacred opportunity.

O God, our fathers have told us, and we have read in thy Holy Word, how persecutions and troubles have followed those who in old time testified for Thee, and who, by their faithful testimony, have secured for us the blessed freedom, and the knowledge of the truth as it is in Jesus, which we in these days enjoy. May we remember how dearly these privileges have been bought; may we value them more highly, and use them more thankfully. We praise Thee, O God, that thy truth hath triumphed, that neither kings nor nations have prevailed against it, and that all that resist it must fall before it and perish. We thank Thee that, notwithstanding all the craft of the wicked one, and the malice of ignorant men, thy Gospel is still extending its sway over the hearts of men, and the time fast approaching when the earth shall be filled with the knowledge of the Lord, as the waters cover the seas.

Oh, take out of the way everything that opposeth and exalteth itself against the Lord Jesus; bring back into the way of truth all who have erred or are deceived; shed forth upon all the Church thy Holy Spirit; remove the fears of the doubtful, and give faith and strength to the wavering.

We confess that when we ought to have obeyed Thee alone, the fear of man has often been a snare to us; and in seeking to please men we have forgotten our duty to Thee. Oh, pardon us for this; make us truly sorry for such folly and ingratitude, and make us henceforth bold and unflinching in doing what is pleasing to Thee, and in obeying God, rather than men. We pray for all who may be called to suffer for so doing, and to witness for Thee, either at home or abroad. Strengthen them according to their need; suffer not the enemy to obtain an advantage over them, but bring them out of the fiery trial, rejoicing that they are counted worthy to suffer shame for the name of Christ. O Thou almighty Lord and Saviour, give us grace to be faithful unto death; to suffer with Thee, Lord, for thy sake; to be ready not only to be bound, but to die for the Lord Jesus. Acknowledge us as thine; confess us before thy Father; and, though unworthy, vouchsafe to us, in accordance with thy gracious promise, the crown of life which fadeth not away. We ask all in the name of Jesus. Amen.

[Morning.]   THIRTIETH WEEK.—THURSDAY.   [Evening.]

READ IN HOLY SCRIPTURE JOSHUA X. 1–14.

O GOD of our life, we thank Thee that we have arisen this morning in health and peace. Our sleep has been sweet, and we have met together as a family in comfort and safety, because Thou, Lord, hast sustained us.

And now, O our God, hear us, as we ask for ourselves the help we need this day. We know not what may be required of us, or what may befall us. The way of man is not in himself: it is the Lord that directeth his steps. Guide us by thy counsel, strengthen us with thy grace, so that, whether in duty or in trial, we may do thy will, and glorify thy name. Especially, O heavenly Father, we implore help in our spiritual calling. We have duties to discharge, temptations to resist, and virtues to cultivate: to these we feel ourselves unequal, but Thou hast promised as our day our strength. Thou, O blessed Redeemer, hast said, "My grace is sufficient for Thee." Strengthen, O God, that which Thou hast wrought for us. May our souls be in health, and enjoy prosperity. Give us, we pray Thee, peace and joy through believing, that we may go on our way, whatever its obstructions or difficulties, rejoicing.

We earnestly pray for our beloved Sovereign and all the Royal Family. Endow them with heavenly grace, and prepare them for the crowns which never fade. Give wisdom to our senators, judges, and magistrates; may all our officers be peace, and our exactors righteousness. Make our country, we beseech Thee, a blessing to the world. Strengthen, we entreat Thee, all the ministers of religion, that they may be men of God, faithful, devout, and holy, and determined to know nothing among men but Christ Jesus and Him crucified. Make all the teachers of our youth to know their responsibilities, that the children may be so trained in thy way that they may never depart from it. May parents and children walk together in the paths of holiness, and finally dwell together in their Father's house in heaven.

We dare not leave thy throne of grace without entreating the forgiveness of all our sins. How numerous and aggravated have been our offences! but our hope is in that precious blood which cleanses from all sin. Thou art rich in mercy to all that call upon Thee; oh, hear and pardon us, for the sake of Jesus, who died for our offences, and rose again for our justification. With the consciousness of pardon we would rise from our knees, and go to the labours of the day. Oh, graciously accompany us; speak with us, that we may speak with Thee. Lift upon us the light of thy countenance, that we may praise and magnify thy name now and for evermore. Amen.

READ IN HOLY SCRIPTURE ACTS VI.

ALMIGHTY and most merciful Father, we draw near to Thee in the name Thou delightest to honour. We feel that we need an Advocate with Thee, for in everything we come short of thy glory. Our hearts are naturally full of sin; there is no health in us. But we look up to the atonement of thy dear Son, and his ceaseless intercession for us in thy presence. Bestow upon us a sweet sense of thy pardoning grace, and of our acceptance in thy sight. May we have the daily experience of thy forgiveness. Grant that every doubt and fear which disturbs us may be dispelled, and that we may rest in undoubting confidence on thine exceeding great and precious promises. Lord, if any of us have never yet desired that blessedness, awaken us now to seek for it.

We thank Thee for thy compassionate care of us through another day. To Thee we owe it that we have been preserved in health and strength, and that while others have been in trouble and sorrow, Thou hast given us refreshing rest. Supplied by thy bounteous hand, and covered by thy wings, may we learn to trust Thee more and more for what is seen and temporal, and to seek first the kingdom of God and his righteousness, the blessedness of Christ's friendship, conformity to his image, and fruitfulness in his service. Remember with thy favourable kindness our beloved kindred. Thou good Shepherd of the sheep, bring every one of them into thy fold, that they may feed in its green pastures, and drink at its still waters: then, as the flock is broken on earth, oh, re-unite it in the world above. We beseech Thee for thy universal Church. Do Thou increase the number of thy people, and clothe them with the beauty of holiness. Raise up many faithful pastors, who shall give themselves continually to prayer, and to the ministry of thy Word. Fill them with the Holy Ghost and with wisdom, and enable them to walk blamelessly before Thee. Defend those who are witnessing for Thee in high places, or in heathen lands. Inspire them with a courage which none can gainsay or resist. We magnify Thee for the example of thy saints in ages past, for the noble army of martyrs, for the glorious company of the prophets and apostles, for our own pious fathers and countrymen. Furnish thy truth with a succession of such standard-bearers, till Thou Thyself shalt return in glory, and every knee shall bow at thy footstool. Through the loneliness of the night be Thou our guardian; sleeping or waking, may our thoughts be with Thee. We make these our petitions for the sake of Jesus Christ our Lord and Saviour. Amen.

[Morning.] **THIRTIETH WEEK.—FRIDAY.** [Evening.

READ IN HOLY SCRIPTURE JOSHUA XXII. 11—29.

FATHER of mercies, we thank Thee that once more we are permitted to come to thy throne of grace, to render unto Thee the homage of our hearts, and to supplicate thy favour. In the morning will we direct our prayer unto Thee, for Thou art the fountain of all good, and the strength of our life.

Every day as it dawns upon us is a fresh proof of thy love; for thy mercies are new every morning, and Thou dost crown our lives with thy lovingkindness and tender mercy. Oh, that gratitude may be awakened in our hearts, with every acknowledgment of thy bounty. Thou who dost cause the darkness of the night to flee away, and the light to shine upon us, do Thou visit our souls with thy salvation, remove from our hearts the darkness of sin, and gladden us with the light of thy countenance. Help us this day to walk in the light, as Thou art in the light, and to have fellowship with Thee and thy Son Jesus Christ.

We thank Thee, O Lord, that we have liberty of access to thy mercy-seat at all times, and that, wherever we are, we may worship Thee; for our gracious Saviour has taught us that Thou art a Spirit, and they that worship Thee must worship Thee in spirit and in truth. Enable us by thy grace to use aright the high privilege Thou hast bestowed upon us, and to live in daily communion with Thee, the Father of our spirits. May we ever dwell in thy tabernacle, and enjoy the sweet tokens of thy presence. Conscious of our unworthiness, we would, whilst adoring Thee for thy mercy, confess unto Thee our numerous transgressions. Do Thou extend thy pardoning love to us, and forgive all our sins. Grant that the love of sin may be taken out of our hearts, and that we may turn from it as that which Thou dost hate. Teach us that our true happiness is not to be found in the way of transgression, but in doing thy righteous will. Implant within us a holy, reverential fear, and respect for thy Word, that we may be kept from the paths of the destroyer. Shed abroad thy love in our hearts, and draw out our affections to Thyself, as our supreme and everlasting portion. Strengthen us to resist temptation, and to overcome every evil desire of our corrupt natures; we would pray Thee to preserve us, and to hold up our goings in thy paths, that our footsteps slip not.

We bless Thee that Thou hast laid our help on One mighty to save, on One whose grace is sufficient for us day by day, whose blood cleanseth us from all sin, and whose power is able to keep us from falling. In his name we present our petitions; and to Him, and unto Thee, and to the Holy Spirit, we will give all the praise for ever. Amen.

READ IN HOLY SCRIPTURE ACTS VII. 1—29.

GRACIOUS and merciful Father and God, who hast magnified thy name in thy counsels of old; help us this night to look back with adoring gratitude on all the way by which Thou hast led and art still leading thy people, to the eternal enjoyment of the good things which Thou hast provided for them in Jesus Christ.

We are utterly worthless in thy sight. Even when we have been most enriched with the tokens of thy love, we have forgotten Thee, and have walked in the ways of our own heart. But Thou art Jehovah, Thou changest not; therefore we are not consumed. This is our only confidence, that Thou art gracious and merciful, slow to anger, and of great kindness. Grant that, being taught by the Holy Spirit our own deep guiltiness before Thee, and thy readiness to forgive and accept us, we may flee to the cross of Jesus as our only refuge from thy righteous condemnation.

We magnify the grace by which thy people have in every age been called, enlightened, and sustained. We adore the faithfulness with which they have been guided, corrected, and saved. O Lord, we feel that we have nothing to rest upon but thy grace and faithfulness. As believers in Jesus, the crucified and risen One, we know that we can claim a share in thy promises, and in thy fatherly love. O Lord, take away, we pray Thee, these evil hearts of ours, and give us clean hearts, that we may perfectly love Thee, and worthily magnify thy holy name. Amid all our trials and difficulties, do Thou guide and direct us. Hold up our goings in thy paths, that our footsteps slip not. Increase our faith in thy promises, and give us such experience of thy love, that we may find pleasure in a ready and constant obedience to thy commandments.

Take away, Lord, all bitterness, wrath, and malice out of our hearts. Give us the mind that was in Christ Jesus, that with lowliness and meekness we may esteem our brethren in Him better than ourselves; that we may love thy people everywhere, because they are thine, and recognise their claim to our sympathy and care; and that we may avoid all words and acts that gender strife, or that may wound the hearts of thy children.

We thank Thee, Lord, for the grace bestowed on thy people in every age; through which many have departed this life in hope of a glorious resurrection, through thy dear Son. Grant to us, we beseech Thee, the same grace, that while we live we may adorn the doctrine of God our Saviour in all things, and when we die we may die in the Lord. Make us to remember that the night is coming; and prepare us for an eternal day in heaven, for Jesus Christ's sake. Amen.

[Morning.]   THIRTIETH WEEK.—SATURDAY.   [Evening.

READ IN HOLY SCRIPTURE JOSHUA XXIII.

O THOU mighty and glorious God! hear us for Jesus Christ's sake. Preserve our land in peace; give the people prosperity, and raise men among us, wise, valiant, godly, as was Joshua. We have seen, O Lord, the many mighty works which Thou hast done for us, whereby we have been made a great nation; and we remember thy noble deeds in behalf of our forefathers, whom Thou didst deliver from the darkness and bondage of Popery. We have been delivered, O Lord, from the thrall of idolatry, from the deceitfulness of image-worship: may we evermore cleave unto Thee! Let the old be wise, the young be prudent, the rich liberal, the poor faithful. May Jesus Christ be the prince whom we serve, and heaven the home for which we long!

Pardon all our sins. Teach us rightly to use the world, to do good day by day, and be truly thankful. Whatever our lot, how many soever our trials, and great our dangers, may we remember that as Canaan was divided among Israel, so has our land been divided unto us, and the lot of every man fixed by the hand of God. Show unto the poor that they are poor because they would have been less happy, less useful, and more likely to die in sin, had they been born rich; and the rich have a wealthy place that they may do good, and help the poor man as they themselves would be helped of Christ. O God! bless them both; may the poor and the rich meet before Thee: the poor to be comforted, and the rich to be owned as good and faithful.

Have mercy upon the wicked of our land. Let them not perish by the darts of Satan, as did the Canaanites by the sword of Israel. Win them back, O God, unto Thyself; let them not be wicked any longer. O Holy Ghost, deliver the people, lest they die in their sin; give them repentance unto salvation, and translate them from the power of darkness into the kingdom of thy dear Son. Are we not all wicked? Great God, who can say, "I am righteous?" Are we not all passing away, going as all the earth goes? Oh, let thy mercy, which rests upon us and saves us; and thy Spirit which dwells in us and guides us; rest upon and save, dwell in and guide, all flesh: that Thou mayest be glorified.

We bless Thee for the good things of earth, and the promise of better things in heaven. May our every step this day bring us nearer to Jesus, in heart and life, that, through thy grace, we may strive in all things to have a conscience void of offence towards Thee and towards all men. May we never go back from Thee, but be daily growing in grace and in godliness. We offer all our petitions through Jesus Christ our Lord. Amen.

READ IN HOLY SCRIPTURE ACTS VII. 30—60.

HOLY and gracious God, in thy pity and love, let thy Holy Spirit teach and help us to pray. Bestow upon us true repentance and faith, and let us not depart from thy presence unforgiven and unblessed. Teach us, O Lord, to value our opportunities, and especially to number our days and apply our hearts unto wisdom. Thou hast added another week to our lives, and the account of it is now before Thee, with all our sins, and frailties, and neglects. Spare us, good Lord, spare us, whom Thou hast redeemed with thy precious blood, and let not thine anger turn against us. Oh, make us grateful for thy daily goodness, for the gifts of thy providence, the food and the raiment which Thou hast provided, and, above all, for the grace which keeps us from falling utterly from Thee, and being led captive of the devil at his will. So impress on our hearts a deep and abiding sense of all which Thou hast done for us, that we may see the wickedness of all those sins of which we are guilty, and be ashamed of them and forsake them. We long, O Lord, to be more perfectly consecrated to thy service, and to be more manifestly conformed in temper and character to the image of thy dear Son. Lord grant us this blessing for Christ's sake. May we believe in Him as a sacrifice for sin, and also endeavour daily to follow the blessed steps of his most holy life.

We implore thy blessing for all who are bound to us by ties of affection and friendship. Let thy good Spirit guide them and us in the way of peace and godliness. Fill all our hearts with more love to Thee, that thy service may be a delight and a joy to us. Be gracious and merciful to the young [and especially to those of this family]. Enable them as they grow in years to grow in grace and in the knowledge of our Lord and Saviour Jesus Christ. Bring them into thy fold, that the ranks of the Lord's people may be swelled continually by the accession of new disciples, who, like thy servant Stephen, may be full of faith, and not ashamed to confess Christ even to death. Give thy grace to all thy people, and grant that in all their trials, and in the persecutions that may come upon them for the truth's sake, they may exhibit the meekness and gentleness of Christ. Endue thy ministers with special help for the duties of thy holy day. Give them a message for all who shall come to thy house. Turn the feet of the Sabbath-breaker and of the ungodly from the paths of evil; bring them into the assemblies of thy people, and bow their hearts at the feet of Jesus.

Hear us, O Lord, for thy mercy is great, and help and answer us, for the sake of thy dear Son, Jesus Christ our Lord. Amen.

[210]

[MORNING.]   THIRTY-FIRST WEEK.—LORD'S DAY.   [EVENING.

READ IN HOLY SCRIPTURE JOSHUA XXIV.

O LORD God, enable us, we beseech Thee, to recall thy merciful dealings with us, from the beginning until now, and in thy presence, on this holy day, to lift up our hearts in praise and thanksgiving. We thank Thee for the blessings of thy daily providence, and the continuance of thy protecting care. Above all, we thank Thee that Thou didst not leave us to perish in our sins, but, in thy great compassion, hast redeemed us by the death of thy dear Son. We thank Thee for the message of reconciliation, and we pray, O God, that it may never be heard coldly or carelessly by any of us. Oh, that the rich mercies of thy redeeming love may call forth daily songs of praise, and every renewed experience of thy goodness quicken in us a more fervent desire to consecrate ourselves, body, soul, and spirit, to thy service. Enable us, in the spirit of sincere self-sacrifice, to devote ourselves to Thee, feeling that we have been redeemed, not with corruptible things, as silver and gold, but with the precious blood of Jesus Christ; and that it is our highest privilege, and should be our greatest joy, to do in all things thy will.

Mercifully bless us in all the engagements of this day. Enable us to sanctify it to Thee. Let it be to us a day of spiritual as well as bodily rest. As we assemble in the congregation, help us in all humbleness of mind to draw near to thy throne of grace. So convince us of sin, that our prayers may rise from hearts yearning for forgiveness. So reveal unto us our own deep need, that we may come to Thee hungering and thirsting after righteousness. May thy love encourage us, and the warnings of thy wrath kindle within us a holy fear. Open our hearts as the heart of Lydia, that we may receive with meekness the word which is able to save our souls.

We implore thy blessing on all who are united to us by ties of kindred or friendship. [Blessed Saviour, who didst suffer the little ones to be brought to Thee when upon earth, look tenderly and graciously on the children of our household, and win their hearts to thy service.] Let the tokens of thy presence be seen in all congregations who meet to-day in thy name. Clothe the lips of thy ministers with words of truth, and kindle their hearts with fervour, as they proclaim the unsearchable riches of Christ. Assist Sunday-school teachers. Cheer the hearts of all missionaries in their distant fields of labour, and so abundantly pour out thy Spirit on all flesh, that there may be a great increase of true believers, and that thy Name may be exalted. Answer us and bless us, and to Thee shall be all the glory. Amen.

READ IN HOLY SCRIPTURE ACTS VIII. 1—25.

HOLY and blessed Lord God, behold us in mercy as we draw near to the throne of thy heavenly grace, to offer up our evening prayer. Bestow upon us thy Holy Spirit, that He may show us our sinfulness, and reveal to us the riches of thy grace and the freeness of thy mercy in Christ Jesus.

We acknowledge with shame our deep sinfulness before Thee, O Lord. Enter not into judgment with us, O God, but grant unto us deep penitence and sincere repentance, that we may return to Thee with all our hearts, and evermore serve Thee with all our power.

We thank Thee that the Gospel which of old was preached in the cities and villages of Samaria has reached our ears, and that the Holy Ghost, who wrought effectually in the hearts of those who then believed, is here, able and willing to work in us, and to bring every thought into captivity to the obedience of Christ. O Holy Spirit, we beseech Thee to take possession of our hearts; to rule and govern our wills; to sanctify our thoughts, desires, and motives; and make us wholly and for ever the children of God. We pray that Thou wouldest strengthen our faith in thy Divine word, and help us constantly to realise its blessings. We pray that Thou wouldest assure us of our adoption into the family of God, and that Thou wouldest lead us, in all humility and loving confidence, to our heavenly Father; that in all our trials and sorrows, as well as all our prosperity and joy, we may have communion with Him, and with his Son Jesus Christ. Draw us, O Holy Spirit, nearer and nearer to our God, that we may have more frequent and fervent prayer, sweeter and holier fellowship with Him who is our life. Oh, that we may henceforth live in the Spirit, walk in the Spirit, and bring forth the fruits of the Spirit.

We offer to Thee, O heavenly Father, our humble and grateful acknowledgments for all the blessings of this Sabbath day; for rest from worldly care; for temporal mercies; but more especially for the spiritual favours Thou hast granted us. We bless Thee for thy Holy Word, the preaching of the Gospel, the privileges of prayer and praise, and for communion with thy people and Thyself. Let thy blessing follow all these engagements, and help us to bring forth fruits of holiness to thy praise and glory.

We humbly beseech Thee to crown with thy blessing the efforts of thy servants who to-day have sought to extend the knowledge of Jesus Christ. Answer Thou the prayer of thy universal Church, that thy kingdom may come, and thy will be done in earth as it is done in heaven. We ask it all in the name of Jesus Christ. Amen.

[MORNING.]   THIRTY-FIRST WEEK.—MONDAY.   [EVENING.

READ IN HOLY SCRIPTURE JUDGES II.

O ALMIGHTY God and heavenly Father, we thank Thee for the mercies of the past night, and the blessings of this returning day. We thank Thee for all the bounties of thy providence, and all the gifts of thy grace. Oh, make us more sensible of thy goodness, and enable us to show forth thy praise not only with our lips, but with our lives.

We confess that we are unworthy of the least of thy mercies. In thought, word, and deed, we have transgressed thy holy commandments, and grieved thy Holy Spirit. No language is too humble, no attitude too lowly, for us sinners. If Thou wert extreme to mark what we have done amiss, O Lord, we could not abide it. We plead before Thee the merits of Jesus; we ask thy pardon in his name, and for his sake. Cause us to know, in our own happy experience, that He is able to save to the uttermost all that come to Thee through Him. Enable us, through faith, to realise the blessedness of the man whose transgressions are forgiven, and whose sins are covered. Oh, hear us in heaven thy dwelling-place; and when Thou hearest, forgive. And not only blot out the sins of the past, but give us grace and strength against sin for the future. Help us, this and every day, to lay aside every weight, and the sin that doth most easily beset us. Give us power against all evil, and so conform us to the image of thy dear Son, that we may increase ever more and more in all the gifts and graces of the Holy Spirit.

We pray, not only for ourselves, but also for others. Bless all who are near and dear to us, and supply all their need. Guide them by thy counsel here, and afterwards receive them to glory.

Have compassion on all who are in sorrow, whether of mind, body, or estate; give them patience under all their trials, and a happy issue out of every affliction. May the light affliction, which is but for a moment, work for them a far more exceeding and eternal weight of glory.

We commend to thy love and tender mercy our gracious Sovereign and all the Royal Family. Spread around them the shield of thy protection, and cause them to live in thy faith and fear. May we be a people fearing Thee, and adorned with that righteousness which exalteth a nation.

Above all things, do Thou grant that this and every day which is added to our lives may be faithfully spent in thy service, and dedicated to thy glory. May we daily be more mindful of the things which belong unto our peace, and daily be more conformed to the likeness of thy dear Son.

Hear us, gracious God and Father, and do for us exceeding abundantly above all that we ask or think, through Jesus Christ our Lord. Amen.

READ IN HOLY SCRIPTURE ACTS VIII. 26—40.

O GOD, Father of all mercies, help us now to praise Thee, and to pour out our hearts in prayer before Thee. We thank Thee that Thou hast guarded us, guided us, and provided for us through another day. We are spared, preserved, and loaded with thy benefits, notwithstanding our transgressions against Thee. We adore Thee for the bounties of thy providence, and acknowledge that we are unworthy of the least of them.

But above all, we praise Thee for thine unspeakable gift. We bless Thee that Thou didst not spare thine own Son, but didst deliver Him up, the just for the unjust. We thank Thee that He was led as a lamb to the slaughter, that He poured out his soul unto death, and Thou didst lay upon Him the iniquity of us all. O Lamb of God, that takest away the sin of the world, have mercy upon us!

O God, we need the teaching of the Spirit; baptise us, we beseech Thee, with his renewing power. May the Comforter take of the things of Christ and show them to us. Enlighten us, O blessed Spirit, to behold the glory of God in the face of Jesus Christ. Make us thankful to receive instruction from any of thy servants who are enabled to expound the Word of life; but may we depend entirely on Thyself to convey the truth with power to our souls.

Deliver us, O God, from the fear of man, which bringeth a snare. Give us boldness to confess Christ before men, both with our lips and in our lives. May we honour all thine ordinances, and never be silent when we ought to speak for Thee.

O righteous Father, crown with success the efforts of thy people to publish the Gospel to all mankind. When thy ministers preach Jesus, may they never speak in vain; may their words, through thy grace, awaken dead souls to eternal life in Christ our Lord. We pray for the wealthy and powerful, that, like the Ethiopian treasurer, they may be humbled at the feet of Jesus. Teach them the vanity of earthly riches; incline them to spend and be spent for the glory of Christ and the good of men. Comfort those who are poor in this world; make them rich in faith, and heirs of thy kingdom.

Gracious God, smile upon us and all connected with us. May those at the head of this household be guided with wisdom from above in all their duties. Teach them to set a holy example to all who dwell under their roof. [Bless the children of this family; may they be born again of thy Spirit, and trained for glory.]

Grant, heavenly Father, that we may rest in peace this night; and on the morrow may we rise rejoicing in thy love, through Jesus Christ our Lord. Amen.

[212]

[Morning.]   THIRTY-FIRST WEEK.—TUESDAY.   [Evening.

READ IN HOLY SCRIPTURE JUDGES VI. 6—23.   READ IN HOLY SCRIPTURE ACTS IX. 1—22.

MOST merciful and gracious God, by whose kind providence we are permitted again to come to thy throne of grace, accept our sincere thanks that thy mercies are now to us every day, and that Thou dost bless the most unworthy when they seek Thee through thy dear Son. Kept safely through another night, and raised up again from our beds to discharge the duties of another day, we come to Thee now for those fresh supplies of grace, wisdom, and strength which we require for the right and conscientious discharge of our several duties.

Make us duly sensible of our insufficiency, that we may know that all our sufficiency is of Thee. Suffer us not to trust in our own strength of body or mind, but enable us to lean on thine almighty arm, stretched forth to support and direct us. We know, O Lord, by our own experience, as well as by the record concerning thine ancient people, that we are liable to forget thy presence, and to do evil; and that, by reason of our misdeeds, as well as to try our faith, Thou dost sometimes permit the enemy to prevail against us. We rejoice, however, to know that when thy people cry unto Thee, they are delivered. O Lord, we cry unto Thee now, and our prayer is, Hold Thou us up, and we shall be safe. Keep us this day without sin; and as Thou hast raised up a mighty Deliverer for us in the person of thy dear Son, enable us to fight manfully under Him, the Captain of our salvation, and to continue Christ's faithful soldiers and servants unto our lives' end. In thy providential dealings with us this day, show us some tokens for good, that we may be encouraged to trust in Thee. Touch our hearts by thy power, and kindle within us such a fire of Divine love, that we may be living sacrifices unto Thee, and may know that we are of God by the Spirit which Thou hast given us. Let the peace of God rule in our hearts, and whatsoever we do in word or deed, enable us to do all in the name of our Lord Jesus Christ, giving thanks unto God and the Father by Him.

If there be any amongst us not duly sensible of the value of true religion, give them grace to know that godliness is profitable for all things. Let thy Spirit bring home the truth to their hearts, and impart unto them the knowledge of salvation through Jesus Christ our Lord. Bless our relations and friends. Bless our Sovereign and all our rulers. Give them grace to execute justice and to maintain truth. Dispel all moral and spiritual darkness, and hasten the day when the Sun of righteousness will arise upon a benighted world, and give true light to every soul. All we ask is in Christ's name, and for his sake. Amen.

O LORD Jesus Christ, to whom all power is given in heaven and in earth, we desire to thank Thee for thy great glory. We praise Thee for thy loving-kindness towards thy redeemed Church, which Thou art exalted to reign over for ever.

Thou dost permit thy people to suffer persecution for the Word's sake, yet dost Thou never leave them. Should we be called to bear reproach and suffering for Thee, we pray Thee to make us faithful, and to overrule the trial for good. May we never be ashamed to own Thee, and never shrink from suffering in thy cause.

But what are we, that we should enjoy quietness and peace, none making us afraid? Surely this is a token of thy undeserved favour. Yet would we examine ourselves, whether we are not lukewarm and faithless in thy service, feeble-minded, and unable to resist unto blood, striving against sin; whether, therefore, Thou dost not the rather spare us because of our unworthiness to suffer shame for thy name. Lord, thy very goodness calls for deep searchings of heart. Help us to deal truly with ourselves, and to condemn and to correct whatever is amiss.

But Thou dost also magnify thy grace on thy bitterest foes. Thou didst in thine Apostle St. Paul show forth all long-suffering for a pattern to them that should after believe on Thee to life everlasting. We thank Thee for this wondrous record of thy love and power. Thou didst arrest him in his mad career, revealing Thyself as Him whom he persecuted, convincing him of his sin, and bringing him to repentance and newness of life. Exercise, O Lord, the same power now in the midst of thy enemies. Let the persecutor and injurious lowly submit themselves at thy feet. Let those who are afar off, whether Jews or Gentiles, be brought nigh. If any here present are not truly thine, save them from sin and unbelief.

And now, O Lord God of our salvation, accept, we humbly beseech Thee, our grateful tribute of praise for the mercies of the past day, for life and health preserved to us, and for the supply of our unnumbered wants. May we read thy goodness in all thy providential dealings, whether afflictive or comforting, and meekly submit ourselves to thy blessed will. Extend thy merciful protection over us this night. Refresh us with seasonable sleep, and fit us for the duties of the morrow. We commend ourselves, and all whom we would remember in prayer, to thy grace and ever-watchful providence: and we ask all these mercies in the name of our Lord and Saviour, Jesus Christ. Amen.

[213]

[MORNING.] THIRTY-FIRST WEEK.—WEDNESDAY. [EVENING.

READ IN HOLY SCRIPTURE JUDGES VI. 24—40.

READ IN HOLY SCRIPTURE ACTS IX. 23—43.

GLORY be to Thee, O God, because Thou hast protected us during the past night, and given us rest and sleep. As Thou hast renewed unto us the morning light, we pray Thee to renew our minds by thy Holy Spirit.

Follow with thy blessing, we pray Thee, the reading of thy Word. Grant that we may be nourished and grow thereby. Make us to take increasing delight in thy law, and to meditate in it day and night. Cause its sacred impressions to abide with us during the day, influencing our life, so that we may not be merely hearers but doers of thy word.

Fill our hearts, O Lord, with Christian love. Make us kind and gentle, and courteous and meek towards all men; and grant that we may adorn the Gospel by the sweetness of our tempers, and the amiability of our lives. Deliver us from all hardness of heart, and harshness, and suspicion, and uncharitableness, lest we should repel others from the religion which we profess.

Grant us likewise, O God, the gift of holiness. Help us to bear in mind that without holiness no man shall see the Lord. May we be ready to suffer for righteousness' sake, and count it an honour and a joy. Prevent us from ever sanctioning, or encouraging, or pleading for what is wrong or doubtful. May we never be partakers with the unfruitful works of darkness, but rather reprove them. And whilst we are striving to counteract the evil around us, and to influence others for good, grant that we may not ourselves be lukewarm or worldly, but that we may have the daily anointing of the Holy Ghost, and be continually living in a spiritual and heavenly frame of mind. When Thou pourest out thy blessings upon thy people, forget not us, O Lord; grant that we may not be dry while there is dew on all around.

Save us, blessed Lord, from self-deceit and from wrong views of thy character. Impress upon our minds that Thou, O God, seest us, and that there is not a word on our lips, nor a thought in our hearts, but Thou, O God, knowest it altogether. Make us sensible of our own mercies. Teach us the number of our gifts, and privileges, and advantages.

We humbly beseech Thee, let thy blessing accompany us during the day that is before us. O Lord, let us not forget Thee, and hide not Thou thy face from us. Help us to keep a conscience void of offence towards Thee, and towards all men. Enable us to walk circumspectly, not as fools, but as wise, redeeming the time; so that when we come together back to offer our evening sacrifice, our hearts may not reproach us with any wilful sins. Hear us, O God, in these our prayers, for the sake of Jesus Christ our Lord. Amen.

O THOU, who art glorious in holiness and fearful in praises,—before whom the angels veil their faces;—great need have we to blush before Thee. We were born in sin and conceived in iniquity, and have transgressed in thought, word, and deed against thy holy precepts. Every day's experience makes us sensible, that there is no health in us, and that how to perform that which is good we cannot find. But there is forgiveness with Thee; and Thou hast Thyself graciously taught us, that if we sin, we have an advocate with Thee, Jesus Christ the righteous, and that He is the propitiation for our sins. We therefore venture to appear before Thee: oh, help us to cleanse our defiled robes and to make them white in the blood of the Lamb; and again assure us of our perfect forgiveness through Him, who died for us and rose again.

And, O Lord, we beseech Thee, take not thy Holy Spirit from us; but vouchsafe to us richer communications of thy grace. Give us true repentance for the past;—that contrite heart and godly sorrow, which need not be repented of;—and for the time to come enable us, through the Spirit, more effectually to mortify the deeds of the body;—to grow in grace and in conformity to thy Divine nature;—and to go on from strength to strength until we finally appear before Thee in Zion.

And now Lord, we beseech Thee, give rest to thy Churches in these our days, as we have just heard with our ears Thou didst in the days of old. Let all, being rooted and grounded in Christ, the only foundation, be edified in Him. May all who call themselves Christians, be enabled to walk in the fear of the Lord, and in the comfort of the Holy Ghost. Make thy people everywhere full of good works and alms deeds, as Thou didst thy servant Tabitha; that others, beholding their light, may turn to the Lord, and that the number of the faithful may be greatly multiplied. Reveal Thyself to many, as Thou didst to thy servant Saul: speak to them in the way, O Lord, and turn them from darkness to light, and from the power of Satan unto God.

Send forth thy blessed Gospel into all lands. Speak Thou the promised word, and great shall be the number of them that publish it. Bless our beloved Sovereign with thy richest mercies. Bless all the Royal Family; especially him, who is likely hereafter to be ruler over us. Give to all our senators wisdom,—the spirit of counsel, and the spirit of the fear of the Lord. Give grace to all estates and conditions of men. And finally accept our humble thanks and praise for thy great mercies, thy long-suffering, and forbearance: all which we ask in the name and through the mediation of Jesus our Redeemer. Amen.

[Morning.]   THIRTY-FIRST WEEK.—THURSDAY.   [Evening.]

READ IN HOLY SCRIPTURE JUDGES VII.

O LORD of Hosts, who art worshipped by all the inhabitants of heaven, who go and come most willingly at thy holy command, and are delighted to obey the will of their King; we also would humbly present ourselves at thy footstool, and implore Thee to accept the cheerful homage of our hearts through Jesus Christ.

We confess unto Thee that the weakness of our nature and the naughtiness of our hearts has raised up against us many and powerful enemies; and we have one great and terrible adversary of our souls, to whose malice we are subject, and to whose fiery darts we are exposed. We acknowledge that we have become too much accustomed to the bondage and tyranny of sin, but we groan and sigh for deliverance from our spiritual enemies, and from the bonds of those sinful habits and ways by which we have so grievously been bound. O God, we have fallen by our iniquity, and in Thee alone is our help found. We look on the right hand, there is none to help but Thee; we look on the left hand, there is none other that fighteth for us but only Thou, O God.

When endeavouring to get the better of our sins, we have too often trusted in ourselves; we have thought vainly that we could successfully contend with them and overcome them, but they have been too many for us. We would henceforth put no trust in our own strength, but would go in the strength of the Lord God, even of Him who came to put away sin and overcome the wicked one. To this end do Thou give us faith in the Lord Jesus, that we may take Him as our leader; help us to believe in his severe conflict with sin and Satan, and in his triumphant victory; and whenever we contend with Satan, help us to remember we are fighting with one already overcome for us, and deprived of his deadly power by the victorious Son of God.

O Lord Jesus, we would renew this morning the consecration of ourselves, soul and body, to thy service, that we may follow and obey Thee as the Captain of our salvation. Make us humble yet faithful soldiers of the Cross. Clothe us with the whole armour of God, that we may be able to stand in the evil day. Cover us with the shield of faith; teach us how to use thy Holy Word, the sword of the Spirit; put upon us the helmet of salvation, and clothe us with righteousness and holiness of life; defend us against our unseen enemies; preserve us from the treachery of our sinful hearts; and lead us forth day by day conquering and to conquer, through the merits and grace of our Saviour, to whom we would ascribe, with the Father and the Holy Spirit, all might, glory, and dominion for ever. Amen.

READ IN HOLY SCRIPTURE ACTS X. 1–23.

O LORD, our heavenly Father, we come once more before Thee as the shades of evening are around us, to offer our united worship. Let our prayer be set forth before Thee as incense, and the lifting up of our hands as the evening sacrifice. Through this day Thy love has brought us. We sought thy guardianship in the morning, and now we say, "Hitherto the Lord hath helped us." We thank Thee for life and health, and active power, and for all the manifold mercies which strew our path. Above all, we adore Thee for the Lord Jesus Christ, who is our hope, and through whom we have confidence of access to Thee. For his sake we beseech Thee to forgive the shortcomings and sins of this day, and of our past lives. Pardon our coldness of heart, our languor in thy service, our defects of motive, our frequent failure to improve the opportunities of life. As he that is washed needeth yet to wash his feet, we would seek the pardon of our daily imperfections through our Saviour's all-cleansing blood.

Let a blessing rest on all in which we have been engaged to-day. Prosper, if it please Thee, our earthly employments, and continue to supply our temporal needs. May we ever be without excessive carefulness, and whilst in everything, by prayer and supplication with thanksgiving, we make known our requests unto Thee, let thy peace keep our hearts and minds through Christ Jesus. Bless any efforts in which we may have taken part for advancing the kingdom of thy Son. Prosper Thou our poor endeavours.

May we gather instruction from the events and experience of the day, and learn the lessons which thy providence affords. Teach us, too, from thy Word which we have now read. As we see how the knowledge and fear of Thee can sustain under all temptations, we ask Thee to uphold us by thy hand under all the dangers to which we are or may at any time be exposed. Thou dost guide those who wait habitually on Thee; we therefore pray Thee to lead us into the knowledge of truth and the way of duty, and to make us also useful to others.

We thank Thee that the Gentiles are now brought into thy Church, and that we partake of the privileges of thy people. May we stand by faith. We pray for the nations yet in heathen darkness. Let the dayspring from on high visit them, and guide their feet into the way of peace. Give abundant success to missionary labour, and send forth more labourers. Let the Spirit be poured out from on high, and the wilderness be a fruitful field, and the fruitful field be counted for a forest. Hear and accept us, through Christ our Saviour. Amen.

[Morning.]   THIRTY-FIRST WEEK.—FRIDAY.   [Evening.

READ IN HOLY SCRIPTURE 1 SAMUEL I. 9—28.   READ IN HOLY SCRIPTURE ACTS X. 24—48.

O THOU Father of mercies, it is meet and right, and our bounden duty, that we should bless Thee, for Thou hast kept us through the night watches, Thou hast renewed our health and strength; it is thy sun which now lights us, and thine air which we breathe. Nor are these thy best gifts to us. We sit under the vine and fig-tree of Christian privilege. We have thy Word to make us wise unto salvation, thy Spirit to sanctify us, thy beloved Son to redeem us. Surely the lines have fallen to us in pleasant places, and we have a goodly heritage.

Let a sense of thy exceeding kindness abide with us evermore, and be our peace, and be as the cords of love to bind us to thy service.

To that service we humbly desire to dedicate ourselves, in a sober, righteous, and godly life. Thy vows are upon us; confirm and aid us in the discharge of them. May we be faithful unto death in temptation; in tribulation, patient; in business, diligent; content with such things as we have, and ever mindful of that strict and solemn account which we must one day give before thy judgment-seat for the deeds done in the body. Lord, whilst Thou dost search and try us, do Thou apply the blood of sprinkling, and the washing of regeneration: then shall we be whiter than snow.

In reading of thy handmaiden, we have been reminded that Thou art the hearer of prayer, that no sigh nor tear escapes us but Thou writest it in thy book. Enable us to value our opportunities of seeking thy face. In the closet, and in the sanctuary, as we walk by the way, may we lift up our eyes to heaven, and pour out our petitions before Thee. Let no slothfulness or fear prevent us from knocking at that door from which none are sent empty away.

If Thou hadst not been merciful to us times without number, we had sunk in the waves of trouble, or yielded in the evil hour. Thine answers to our prayers have been precious to us. Draw thy people everywhere to commune with Thee. Bring them into thy banqueting-house, and let thy banner over them be love.

Preserve and bless our Sovereign. Be a mouth and wisdom to our magistrates and judges. Exalt this nation in righteousness. Let thy purposes of compassion to our lost world prosper in the hands of thy missionary servants; and hasten that happy period when Jew and Gentile, bond and free, shall unite in the same glad song which thy saints are singing before thy throne.

Lord, we commend ourselves to thy protection and governance, and taking thy yoke upon us, we once more go forth to our work until the evening.

All this we ask and offer in Jesus' name. Amen.

IMPRESS on all our hearts, we beseech Thee, O Spirit of the living God, the precious truths we have now read. We have heard the words of the living God; enable us to receive them with faith, and to obey them. We rejoice that Thou, O God, art no respecter of persons; for in every nation he that feareth Thee, and worketh righteousness, is accepted with Thee. Search out and bring to light thy hidden ones; reveal Thyself to them more fully; show unto them thy salvation, and bring them to confess Thee before the face of men. Thou, O God, hast granted unto Gentiles repentance unto life; may the Jews, thine ancient family, share also in the blessing. Take away the veil from their hearts; may they behold the beauty and glory of Jesus, the true Messiah, and acknowledge Him to be their Lord and Saviour. Pour out thy Spirit on all flesh. Let the people praise Thee, O God; let all the people praise Thee.

O our God and Father, who humblest Thyself to behold the things that are done on the earth, and dost specially reveal Thyself where two or three meet together in the name of thy dear Son, vouchsafe thy gracious presence to us now that we are assembled at thy footstool. We come to offer our evening sacrifice of prayer and praise. We would lift up holy hands without wrath and doubting; and would so live together as a family, that our prayers may not be hindered. Accept our thanksgivings for the favours so abundantly bestowed on us this day. Thou hast fed us and clothed us; Thou hast preserved our health, and protected us from danger. These blessings Thou hast of thine own free bounty bestowed; but we would acknowledge them also as given in answer to our morning prayer. We sought them at thy hand, and Thou hast mercifully granted them at our request. We would again approach Thee, and ask Thee, as we retire to rest, to grant us thy renewed providential care. During the defenceless hours of sleep, O God, be our Guardian and our Friend, and when morning dawns may we still find ourselves with Thee.

Forgive, we pray Thee, for the sake of Christ Jesus our Lord, all the sins of this day. Our personal offences and our family failings are many; but we entreat Thee to blot them all out of the book of thy remembrance. Cleanse our hearts and purify our thoughts. Shed thy Holy Spirit on us, that we may speak more freely and gratefully to Thee of all thy goodness and mercy to us; and when our days of meeting and of praise are closed on earth, may we rise to an eternal day in thy presence. These mercies and favours we ask for Christ the Redeemer's sake. Amen.

[Morning.] **THIRTY-FIRST WEEK.—SATURDAY.** [Evening.]

READ IN HOLY SCRIPTURE 1 SAMUEL II. 1–17.

O ALMIGHTY God, beside whom none other is holy, and who art the only rock of our salvation, we desire to thank Thee for thy many and great mercies. We thank Thee especially for keeping us and those near and dear to us safely during the night which is past, and for refreshing us for the discharge of the duties of another day. Thou alone, O Lord, killest and makest alive. Thou bringest down to the grave and bringest up. Thou makest poor and makest rich. Teach us, we pray Thee, during the day on which we are about to enter, to put our whole confidence in Thee alone. Dispose us humbly to accept, as that which in thine infinite wisdom Thou knowest to be best for us, whatever condition and circumstances of life Thou seest fit to appoint. Thou hast graciously promised to keep the feet of thy saints. Watch over us, we beseech Thee, at this present time, and protect us both in body and soul. Give us also, now that we are going forth to the active business of life, such an abundant measure of thy Holy Spirit as may enable us to discharge faithfully the duties assigned to us. Keep us also from being led away by wicked spirits or wicked men, or from being polluted by the pomps and vanities of the world.

We confess that our sins against Thee have been many and great. We have transgressed in thought, word, and deed. We have left undone those things which we ought to have done, and done those things which we ought not to have done. By Thee actions are weighed. But be not Thou extreme, O Lord, to mark what is amiss in us. Rather raise up, we pray Thee, us poor miserable sinners out of the dust. Lift up us wretched beggars from the dunghill; not for our own sake, O Lord, for we have no merits to plead, but for the merits of thy dear Son, our Lord and Saviour Jesus Christ. Do Thou vouchsafe to set us amongst princes, and make us inherit the throne of thy glory. By strength shall no man prevail; but the pillars of the earth are thine, and Thou hast set the world upon them. Give strength, therefore, unto us, who are wholly unable to help ourselves, and exalt the horn of thine Anointed.

And since, in order to godliness and prosperity, it is above all things necessary that thy Holy Word should be faithfully preached, and thy holy sacraments duly administered, we pray, Almighty God, that there may never be wanting amongst us a sufficiency of learned, devout, and faithful ministers. Save them, O Lord, from the sins which in the days of Eli made men abhor the offering of the Lord, and sanctify them, so that they may be a savour of life unto life. We ask all through Jesus Christ our Lord, to whom be everlasting praise. Amen.

READ IN HOLY SCRIPTURE ACTS XI.

O ALMIGHTY, eternal, and gracious Jehovah; the God of Abraham, the God of Isaac, and the God of Jacob; the God and Father of our Lord Jesus Christ: we thank Thee for the glorious Gospel which reveals to us a Saviour, and assures us of pardon, peace, and salvation in Him. The hearing ear and the seeing eye Thou hast made; the believing heart is thy gift; Thou preparest it to receive the incorruptible seed, even thy Word, which liveth and abideth for ever.

Thou hast purchased to Thyself an universal church by the precious blood of thy dear Son, the members of which are gathered from the east, and from the west, from the north, and from the south. The middle wall of partition between Jew and Gentile Thou hast broken down; both are now one in Christ Jesus; both reconciled unto Thee in one body by the cross. Peace is proclaimed by Jesus to them which were afar off as well as to them which were nigh, and all have access by one Spirit unto the Father. Called as Christians into the visible Church of Christ, we bear that Name which is above every name that is named, not only in this world, but in that which is to come. Suffer us not to rest content with mere outward profession, but give us grace to walk worthy of so high and holy a calling; unite us to Jesus by a living faith, and enable us to adorn the doctrine of God our Saviour in all things.

O Lord, our faith is weak; increase and strengthen it, we beseech Thee. Give us thy Holy Spirit to quicken our understandings, that we may understand the Scriptures; to open our eyes, that we may behold wondrous things out of the law; and to make the name of Jesus precious to us.

Bless the labours of thy ministers at home and abroad, and fill our hearts with joy and gladness when tidings of fresh spiritual conquests are brought home to us, through the agency of the ministering servants throughout the world.

We thank Thee for that providential care which has supplied our wants during this week, and surrounded us with many blessings. We commend to thy fatherly care all who are in sickness, distress, or trouble. Give them patience under their sufferings, and a happy issue out of their afflictions. Raise up friends to help the needy and necessitous, and sanctify all trials and afflictions to the soul's welfare.

And now that we are about to lie down to rest, grant us such refreshing sleep as may fit and prepare us for a right use of our Sabbath privileges; and with the morning light raise us up in safety, fit us for the duties of the day, and make it a day of blessing to us all, for Jesus Christ's sake. Amen.

[Morning.] **THIRTY-SECOND WEEK.—LORD'S DAY.** [Evening.

READ IN HOLY SCRIPTURE 1 SAMUEL II. 22-36.

READ IN HOLY SCRIPTURE ACTS XII.

O ETERNAL Jehovah, glorious in holiness, how shall sinners such as we are approach unto Thee? We here see, in the light of thy Word, that Thou art of purer eyes than to behold iniquity, and that Thou wilt by no means clear the guilty. And such, Lord, are we. We have sinned against the Lord: who shall entreat for us? We thank Thee that thy mercy has enabled us to say, "We have an Advocate with the Father, Jesus Christ the righteous, and He is the propitiation for our sins." We plead his merits; we trust in his intercession; we confess our sins; and we plead thy gracious promise that Thou wilt be faithful and just to forgive us our sins.

But, holy Father, never suffer us to think lightly of sin. Shall we continue in sin, because we are not under the law, but under grace? God forbid! May we ever regard it as the abominable thing that Thou hatest. And forasmuch as without Thee we cannot but fall, keep us ever by thy grace from all things hurtful, and lead us to love thy law, and to perfect holiness in thy fear.

Cause the ordinances of thy house this day, through the power and presence of thy Spirit, to assist and further our growth in grace. We thank Thee, Lord, on this thine own blessed day, not only for our creation, preservation, and all the blessings of this life, but especially for these means of grace, and for the hope of glory. When we go up to the tabernacle of the congregation to-day, may we remember that it is none other than the house of God. When approaching it, when present in it, and when returning from it, may we hate vain thoughts, and sanctify the Lord God in our hearts.

Lord, clothe thy priests with righteousness. May they be faithful to thy truth, and never suffer sin to go unrebuked, either in their flocks or their families. May they unsparingly expose the guilt of sin; but give them at the same time so largely of the spirit of Jesus that they may not break the bruised reed, or quench the smoking flax. Teach them to apply tenderly to convinced hearts the balm of Gilead, and lovingly to point them to the Physician there. In private and domestic life, may they rule their own houses well; and in all holy living may they be ensamples to their flocks. Bless in particular our minister, and may great grace be upon him in his holy work to-day.

And bless us, even us, O our Father. Bless old and young among us with all the grace we severally need. Be present this day in all the assemblies of thy people; and may the Lord add to the Church to-day such as shall be saved. And to Thee, by Christ Jesus, shall be all the glory, now and ever. Amen.

O LORD our God, we praise Thee for all that Thou didst accomplish for the salvation of men in the days of the apostles, and for the triumphs of the cross wheresoever uplifted. We adore Thee for the grace Thou didst confer on the first preachers of the truth, for the doors of usefulness Thou didst open for them, and for the proofs afforded, by the conversion of many, of the efficiency of the Gospel to meet every human want. We thank Thee that thy Word has lost nothing of its power, but is still the instrument of life and peace to all who believe it. We bless Thee for the multitudes by whom it is being diffused, for the thousands who are living in the purity and joy which it gives, and for the victories which it is accomplishing in many hearts and many lands. Hast Thou not promised that these victories shall extend? Fulfil, we beseech Thee, the Word on which Thou hast caused thy servants to hope. Send forth thy light and thy truth into every land. Give efficacy to the word of thy grace wheresoever proclaimed, and greatly increase the company of those who publish it. Let the darkness flee before its rising, the gods of the nations fall before its power, and the corruptions of men disappear before its influences. Glorify thy Son, that thy Son may also glorify Thee. Give Him the heathen for his inheritance, and the uttermost parts of the earth for his possession.

We bless Thee that the Gospel is known by us. Verily we are a people favoured of the Lord. Thou hast given to us thy Word, thy Son, thy Spirit, thine ordinances, and thy ministers. Oh, forbid that any of our privileges should ever testify against us. May we so use them as to secure by them every purpose for which they were given; growing in the knowledge of Christ, reaching the stature of perfect men in Him, and fulfilling the whole of our mission of life.

We thank Thee for another of the days of the Son of man, for the words of mercy and instruction to which we have listened, and for the hallowed and happy influences of thy house. May we remember the truths we have heard, follow the directions to which we have hearkened, and carry with us the influences and spirit of the Sabbath into the associations and engagements of life. Oh, suffer not any of the impressions which have this day been made by thy truth to pass away. Quicken, by thy Spirit, all the seed that has been sown, and magnify thy Word in the conversion of many souls.

Hear us in these our prayers, pardon our sins, and take us as a family into thy keeping for the night. We ask all in the name of thy dear Son, Jesus Christ. Amen.

[Morning.] **THIRTY-SECOND WEEK.—MONDAY.** [Evening.

READ IN HOLY SCRIPTURE 1 SAMUEL III.

READ IN HOLY SCRIPTURE ACTS XIII. 1—15.

O LORD, who art the light and life of thy people, grant us thy peace whilst we now approach thy mercy-seat, in the name of Jesus Christ thy Son. Reconciled to Thee through Him, may we have boldness of access to thy presence; and for his sake be gracious towards us, we beseech Thee.

We praise Thee for the mercies of another night; that Thou hast watched over us when we were helpless, refreshed us with sleep, and raised us up in safety. How many during the past night have tossed restlessly to and fro upon beds of weariness and pain! How many have closed their eyes for ever upon this world, and have entered upon their eternal destiny. The dead cannot praise Thee; but the living, the living, they shall praise Thee, as we do this day.

Enable us, O Lord, to devote ourselves to thy service. We thank Thee that Thou art ever calling us, as Thou didst Samuel of old. Speak to us, gracious Lord, nor suffer us to turn a deaf ear to thy voice. We know not what is before us this day; but we humbly ask that we may spend it in thy fear. Be near to us, as our Helper and our Guide. Suffer no evil to befall, no temptation to assail, no sin to beguile, no spiritual adversary to gain the advantage over us. May we keep very close to Thee, conscious that we can be happy only as Thou shalt smile, and safe only as Thou shalt afford us thy protection.

Should we meet with unexpected trials, give to us a spirit of holy resignation to thy will. If sorrowful tidings are brought to us, may we be still, and know that Thou art God, tracing our sorrows to thine appointment, and believing in the infinite wisdom and loving-kindness that order all the events of life. May it be enough for us to know that it is the Lord. Let this rebuke every suspicion, remove every fear, silence every complaint. Take from us, in mercy take from us, our self-will, and help us, not from coercion, but from choice, to submit ourselves to Thee.

Enable us so to live that we may escape those chastisements with which Thou dost punish thy people's sins. [May we rule our households in thy fear, and train our children for Thee.] Mercifully grant us the strength that we need for the faithful discharge of duty, and for the meek endurance of trial. We mourn because of our self-confidence, our vain glory, and our pride. Oh, teach us that our sufficiency is in Thee. Make us so conscious of our weakness, that we may lean this day upon thine arm, and glorify Thee. Pour out thy grace on all our relations. May they be found in Christ at the great day. Hear us for Jesus Christ's sake. Amen.

O MERCIFUL and gracious God, to thy name be the praise for the many blessings which we have enjoyed this day. Oh, awaken in us lively gratitude for all thy goodness, and especially for not having spared thy dear Son, on whom Thou hast laid the sins of us all. Give us faith to believe the word which Thou hast spoken concerning Him, and grant that, believing in Him, we may have life everlasting. We have sinned against Thee, and are liable to condemnation; but we pray that for his sake all our sins may be put away, and our souls be washed in his precious blood. Deepen in us a godly sorrow for sin, and help us to hate and forsake it. O Lord, by thy Holy Spirit transform and renew our hearts into the likeness of thy dear Son, that we may be to the praise of thy glory, and be as living epistles of Christ, known and read of all men. Fill us with all joy and peace in believing, and enable us to abound in hope, through the power of the Holy Ghost. Constrain us by the love of Christ to live not for ourselves, but for Him who died for us, and rose again, that we may in all things prefer what is pleasing and acceptable to Thee.

We confide ourselves, and all that concerns us, to thy gracious care. Our circumstances, our trials and temptations, are all known to Thee. We beseech Thee, O God, to guide and overrule them all for our good. Suffer us never to distrust thy love, or to forget that not even a sparrow can fall to the ground without thy knowledge. Weak and ignorant as we are, we look up to Thee for wisdom and guidance; and pray that we may be enabled to cling to thy promises, and rest daily on thy Word. Take us into thy keeping for the night. Cause thy richest blessings to descend on all who are dear to us, and make them partakers with us of the everlasting inheritance which Christ is gone to prepare for his people. [We implore specially thy mercy on behalf of the younger members of our family. From their early childhood draw them to Thyself, bring their wills into conformity with thine own, and consecrate them to thy service by the indwelling of thy Spirit in their hearts.]

Crown with success whatever has been done this day for the enlargement of the Redeemer's kingdom. Increase the zeal of thy people, and grant that all who profess and call themselves Christians may be led into the way of truth, and adorn the doctrine of God their Saviour in all things. Speed onward the progress of thy truth, and hasten the time when the whole earth shall be full of thy glory. We ask all for the sake of Jesus Christ our Lord, to whom with Thee and the Holy Ghost be all glory for evermore. Amen.

[219]

[Morning.] **THIRTY-SECOND WEEK.—TUESDAY.** [Evening.

READ IN HOLY SCRIPTURE 1 SAMUEL IV.

O LORD, our God, vouchsafe to receive us, thy servants, who come before Thee, not trusting in any righteousness of our own, but in thy great and manifold mercy. We approach thy throne in deep humility, knowing the greatness of thy power and majesty. All the hosts of heaven bow before Thee in fear and reverence. We are a fallen and sinful race, unworthy of thy favour and regard; and yet Thou art graciously pleased to behold the inhabitants of earth with thy loving-kindness.

From Thee, O God, cometh all our strength and wisdom, and every victory we obtain over the enemies of our souls is the effect of thy grace in our hearts. Be Thou mercifully with us this day. Guide us continually in the way of life, and cheer our hearts with the joys of thy salvation. We desire to walk in the path of duty, to resist temptation, to serve and please Thee in all our doings, and to glorify thy name. May thy grace be sufficient for us, and may we know the perfectness of thine almighty strength.

Pardon, O gracious God, all our past sins, and let not our transgressions be remembered against us. We rejoice to know that, if any man sin, we have an Advocate with Thee: that we have a merciful and compassionate High Priest, to whose sympathy and intercession we may look for the acceptance of our prayers. Make us to be more constant in the use of our religious privileges; and may we indeed find grace to help in all time of need.

Deliver us especially, O Lord, from all dependence on ourselves, or upon our own wisdom. While we desire thy promises, may we love thy commands, and may thy way be made plain before our face. Give us the comfort of thy presence and favour: since, if Thou art in the midst of us, we shall not be moved; if Thou art for us, none can be against us.

And while we trust in Thee alone for spiritual mercies and temporal happiness, we beseech Thee to grant that thy blessing may continue with us, even to the end. May thy glory never depart from our families or our churches. Day by day, and year by year, we need thy protecting and preserving care. Let all before Thee, in their several stations, devote their hearts and lives to Thee and to thy service. [May the young experience thy guidance, and the elder among us testify to thy continual support.] Thus, as life advances, may we grow in grace and knowledge, and be changed ever more and more into the likeness and image of thy dear Son, until at length we see Thee as Thou art, in thine everlasting kingdom, through the same Jesus Christ, our blessed Mediator and Redeemer. Amen.

READ IN HOLY SCRIPTURE ACTS XIII. 16—52.

EVER gracious Father, we come at the close of this day to bow ourselves before the throne of thy grace. We have many mercies to thank Thee for, and we have had fresh proof of thy loving-kindness. Now let our prayer, offered through the merits of our Redeemer, be set forth before Thee as the incense, and the lifting up of our hands be as the evening sacrifice. It is only in his blessed name, and relying on his merits, that we dare thus approach Thee, for our sins of omission and of commission are more than we can number. Thou hast chosen us and exalted us to high Christian privileges, but for how many years hast Thou suffered our manners, and borne with our waywardness, and our frequent instances of rebellion. When we have looked to Thee, Thou hast helped us, and made our way plain before us, and afterwards we have forgotten Thee again and again. Were it not that through Jesus Christ is preached unto us the forgiveness of sins, we should be in despair; but, glory be to thy holy name, by Him all that believe are justified from all things from which they could not be justified by the deeds of the law. For his sake, receive us graciously, and love us freely.

Let us not be of the number of those who hear or read the Word of God, and yet know not Christ. We rejoice that the promise which was made unto the fathers God hath fulfilled the same unto us, their spiritual children, in that he hath raised up Jesus again. Let not these great blessings turn to our condemnation, through our misuse or neglect of them, lest that come upon us which is spoken of in the prophets, "Behold, ye despisers, and wonder, and perish." Gracious Lord, by thy Spirit enable us to read, mark, learn, and inwardly digest the sacred truths of thy Holy Word, which alone can make us wise unto salvation, through faith which is in Christ Jesus our Lord.

And let the solemn consideration that these things were first preached to the Jews, and then offered to us Gentiles, make us humble, and stir us up to increased watchfulness, lest we, like them, put away the Word of God from us, and so judge ourselves unworthy of everlasting life. Look again upon thine ancient people: make them to behold with the eye of faith Him whom they pierced, and mourn. Hasten the time when they shall cease to set themselves against the Lord, and against his anointed.

[We pray for our dear children; help us to train them up for Thee, and to set them a right example.] Bless all our relatives, and help the sick and needy. Give us now refreshing sleep, and answer all our petitions, for thy dear Son's sake. Amen.

[MORNING.] THIRTY-SECOND WEEK.—WEDNESDAY. [EVENING.

READ IN HOLY SCRIPTURE 1 SAMUEL VI.

O LORD God, the High and Holy One, who dwellest in heaven, and yet stoopest in mercy to regard the supplications of thy believing people, hear us and have mercy upon us. Turn not thy face away because of our many sins and our great unworthiness, but fulfil to us thy promises, and be very gracious unto us. Cleanse us from all sin in the fountain once opened. Lamb of God, that takest away the sins of the world, grant us thy peace.

With deep humility and reverence, O God, we crave thy Divine help and strength for the day to which Thou hast brought us. Leave us not to ourselves, or our own wisdom, for it is but foolishness. Guide and direct us in all our words and works, and enable us in everything to consider what will please Thee. We are set in the midst of many and great dangers, through the weakness of our own hearts, and the temptations of the world and the devil, and by reason of the frailty of our nature, we cannot always stand upright. Grant us thy protection, and uphold us by thy power, that we may be kept from all evil, and fall this day into no kind of sin. Give us such a constant sense of thy love to us, that we may love Thee, and cheerfully obey thy commandments.

Graciously overrule and direct all things for our good. In the midst of prosperity and peace, we would never forget whence these blessings come. In the experience of trial or disappointment we desire to bow submissively to thy will. We commend both ourselves and all whom we love to thy merciful care during this day. [Look in special tenderness on the young members of our family. Preserve them from sin, and fill their hearts with love to Thee and thy dear Son. Incline them in all things to do thy will; may they find thy ways to be ways of pleasantness and peace.]

We thank Thee for the renewed mercies of the morning. Enable us to trace thy hand in all our blessings, and especially to remember with daily gratitude all that Thou hast done for us in and through thy dear Son. We would shun the sin of unthankfulness, and ascribe to Thee all praise and glory for thy goodness and love.

Regard with thy favour our Sovereign, and all in authority. Let Divine wisdom preside in their councils, and a gracious Providence overrule all their plans and purposes for thy glory and the increase of true godliness in the land. Attend with thy blessing the labours of all faithful pastors, and teachers, and missionaries. Bring many this day to the cross of Jesus. Make thy people zealous of good works, and glorify Thyself in the purity and obedience of thy Church. We ask it all for Jesus Christ's sake. Amen.

READ IN HOLY SCRIPTURE ACTS XIV.

ALMIGHTY and most merciful God, by whose kind and gracious care we have been safely brought to the close of another day, help us to approach thy footstool with humble, grateful, and loving hearts. We praise Thee that thy tender mercies are over all thy works, and that thy loving-kindness is especially shown to them that fear Thee, and delight in thy commandments. We bless Thee that all the day long Thou hast been our Guide and Friend, keeping us in the way we should go, prospering our labours, and filling our mouths with food and gladness.

How wonderful and mysterious, O our Father in heaven, are the dispensations of thine hand to thy most faithful servants and thy dearest children! We trace in thy Holy Word the progress of thy servants by whom the Gospel was first proclaimed to men. We see them rejected by the heathen, hated by their own brethren, and persecuted even unto death; but we see them endued with the grace of patient perseverance and continuance in well-doing. We praise Thee, O Lord, who didst fill them with thy Spirit, and crown their labours with such great success. Let their example animate us, who are so languid in zeal, that we also may not grow weary in well-doing. Especially give us the same spirit of courage and holy fidelity to Thee, that we may never fear to testify for Christ, and make known to our fellow-men the riches of thy grace.

O Lord, we acknowledge with shame our want of love for thy service, and the numerous sins that mark our progress every day. But we bless Thee that the blood of Jesus Christ, thy Son, cleanseth us from all sin; and we once more repair to that fountain which Thou hast opened for sin and uncleanness. Let us have the sweet assurance that our sin is covered, and that our transgressions are blotted out, so that there may be peace in our consciences as we lie down to rest.

We pray Thee to let thy favour rest upon all our beloved friends. Enfold them in thy kind embrace. If they are in trouble, do Thou comfort them; and in all their necessities do Thou draw them unto Thyself, that they may find strength in the Strength of Israel. Bless our country, and give us peace. Let our gracious Sovereign be guarded by thy watchful care. Give wisdom and grace to all our rulers; and let this land, so long and so signally favoured by thy goodness, be evermore a sanctuary for liberty and pure religion, and a source of spiritual light to the whole world. Thus we commit ourselves into thy gracious hands, through Jesus Christ our Lord, to whom, with Thee, O Father, and Thee, O Holy Ghost, our triune God, be equal honour and endless praise. Amen.

[Morning.]   THIRTY-SECOND WEEK.—THURSDAY.   [Evening.

READ IN HOLY SCRIPTURE 1 SAMUEL VII. 1–15.

READ IN HOLY SCRIPTURE ACTS XV. 1–21.

O LORD, our God, we are now in thy presence! Solemnise our minds, we pray Thee, and aid us by thy Holy Spirit to draw near to Thee through that blessed Redeemer who is the Way, the Truth, and the Life.

We humbly confess that, like thine ancient people, we have sinned against the Lord. If we have not fallen into gross idolatry, we have in heart often backslidden from Thee, and provoked Thee to withdraw from us thy presence and favour. We deeply need thy pardoning mercy; we plead the merits of the great Sacrifice; we trust in the Lamb of God, that taketh away the sins of the world, and who ever liveth to make intercession for them who come unto Thee by Him. But we would not rest satisfied with the forgiveness of our past sins. We would return unto the Lord with all our hearts, and serve Him only. Help us to resist the powerful temptations of Satan. By faith may we overcome the world, and still more fervently we ask Thee to strengthen us to resist and subdue the pride, selfishness, and sensuality of our fallen nature. May we walk in the Spirit, that we fulfil not the lusts of the flesh.

We praise Thee for thine abounding mercies to us in past years. Thou hast delivered our soul from death, our eyes from tears, and our feet from falling, and we would gratefully exclaim, "Hitherto the Lord hath helped us." Another night bears witness to thy watchful love and care. We have laid us down to sleep; we have awaked, because Thou hast sustained us. We are here, the living, to praise Thee. Bless, we beseech Thee, each member of this family with all temporal and spiritual good. May we dwell together in unity, peace, and the fear of the Lord. May our intercourse be sanctified by thy grace and presence. Increase the number of those who call upon thy name, who acknowledge the Lord to be their God; and hasten the time when in every family there shall be an altar erected to thy praise.

Bless those who occupy important positions among thy people. May they be men who have understanding of the times, and who know what Israel ought to do. Make them mighty alike in counsel and in prayer.

And now, O Lord, we pray Thee to be with us this day. Amid the busiest scenes of life may the thought of thy presence rest upon our mind. May we set the Lord always before us. Make us upright, truthful, and honourable in all our transactions, and let us seek to have a conscience void of offence towards God and towards man. Grant that in nothing we may dishonour thy holy name.

These mercies we entreat in the name of our Lord and Saviour Jesus Christ. Amen.

FATHER of mercies, we adore Thee as the fountain and giver of every good and perfect gift. Help us this evening to surround thy throne with devout thankfulness for all the mercies that have attended our path this day. We confess our utter unworthiness of the least of thy mercies, for we have all sinned, and come short of thy glory. How, then, shall we bless Thee for the grace that willeth not the death of a sinner, but preferreth that he should turn from his wickedness and live? Turn us, O God of our salvation, and we shall be saved, through the grace of our Lord Jesus Christ.

We thank Thee, O God, for the grace shown to thine ancient people the Jews, for the Gospel preached before unto Abraham; but we bless Thee much more for the Gospel which is now the glad tidings of great joy to all people. We thank Thee for the removal of every hindrance to the unity of mankind through a crucified Saviour. We adore Thee that Thou hast visited us who were once afar off, to make of us a people to glorify thy name. Help us to appreciate as we ought to do the infinite freeness of thy salvation. May we never rest our hope on ceremonial observances, from whose yoke Thou hast graciously released us, nor let our piety become formal and lifeless.

We adore the grace which has entrusted us with this glorious Gospel for diffusion in all the world. Make us faithful, we beseech Thee, to our great commission. Give us the most Christ-like compassion for perishing souls. May we join with angels in rejoicing over sinners that repent and turn to God. Hasten the time when the heathen world shall have heard the Gospel and believe. Bless the churches of Christ in heathen lands, with all their native teachers, evangelists, and pastors. May every minister and missionary of the cross be filled with the Holy Ghost and with power. Keep them from all error. Make us all ready to contend earnestly for the faith once delivered to the saints. Give us grace to see Christ in all the Scriptures, and therefore to cling to thy Word with ever-growing zeal. Help us to abstain from all appearance of evil. Having the Gospel, may we live according to the Gospel, purifying our hearts by faith in Christ, who is the Way, the Truth, and the Life.

Heavenly Father, we commend each other, and all we love, with all who love us, to thy watchful care this night. May our sleep prepare us for the duties of the morrow, if thy mercy spare us to another day. In many things we have all offended against Thee this day. Blot out our iniquity, for it is great, and grant us thy peace. Hear and answer us, we beseech Thee, for Christ's sake. Amen.

[Morning.]   THIRTY-SECOND WEEK.—FRIDAY.   [Evening.]

READ IN HOLY SCRIPTURE 1 SAMUEL VIII.

O LORD God omnipotent, who art the King of all the earth, from whom proceed all mercies, temporal as well as spiritual, we present ourselves before Thee, to acknowledge all thy goodness towards us. We bless Thee that Thou hast spared us to the beginning of another day, and that Thou art pouring afresh all thy benefits upon us, providing for all the wants of our body, and supplying spiritual good for our souls. Truly, thy mercies are new every morning, and great is thy faithfulness.

But, while we acknowledge thy gracious dealings with us, we feel that we are utterly unworthy of the least of all thy mercies. Our transgressions are many and great. We entreat Thee to forgive and blot out by the blood of thy dear Son all that we have done amiss, the sins of our heart and of our life; and enable us by thy grace to resist every temptation to evil, and to walk in thy ways.

In entering upon our daily duties, and in coming in contact, as we must, with the world, we dare not lean on our own wisdom, or on our own strength. Be near, O Lord, to guide and uphold us; and constrain us, under a deep sense of thy presence, to be bold for what is right, and faithful in contending against all evil. Make us watchful and circumspect in all our conduct, that we may give no occasion to the enemies of thy truth to blaspheme. Write the precepts of thy Word in our heart, that we may not sin against Thee. Amid all our engagements, may it ever be our chief aim to grow in grace, and in the knowledge of our Lord and Saviour Jesus Christ.

We entreat thy favour, gracious Lord, on all dear to us. May every member of our family be drawn by the power of thy Holy Spirit unto Christ, and made a partaker of his salvation. Bestow thy mercy also on all who are connected with us, whether as friends and neighbours, as fellow-worshippers, or fellow-labourers in thy cause. Pour upon them the riches of thy grace continually.

Deal mercifully with our country. Continue all thy mercies to us, and fill our hearts with thankfulness for them. Abundantly bless our Sovereign. Be thou always her guide and strength, her consolation, and her peace. Look graciously upon all the Royal Family. Endue them with thy Holy Spirit, enrich them with thy heavenly grace, prosper them with all happiness, and bring them, through thy mercy, unto thine everlasting kingdom. Mercifully cause thy Holy Word to have free course and be glorified. Give abundant success to all preachers and teachers, and daily bring many souls into the fold of thy Church.

We present all our supplications and prayers in the name of thy dear Son Jesus Christ. Amen.

READ IN HOLY SCRIPTURE ACTS XV. 22—41.

ALMIGHTY God, who from day to day revealest unto us thy goodness and mercy, and enrichest us with the bounties of thy providence and the blessings of thy grace, incline thine ear to our prayer, and accept, we beseech Thee, our united tribute of thanksgiving and praise. We desire to worship Thee in spirit and in truth. Oh, awaken in us heartfelt gratitude and love, and kindle our affections as with heavenly fire, that with all fervour of spirit we may delight to speak thy praise, and to tell what the Lord hath done for us.

We thank Thee that Thou hast kept us safely amidst the dangers of the day now past. We feel that in many things we have fallen short of what it was our duty to do, and thereby have displeased Thee, and brought on our souls the guilt of sin. How coldly have we served Thee; with what slow and sluggish hearts have we fulfilled thy will; how frequently have we forgotten thy presence, and preferred our own way to thy way, and followed the promptings of our own hearts instead of thy gracious Spirit's teaching and guidance. Forgive us, we pray Thee, all our offences and disobedience. It is our comfort to know that Jesus died for us, and that his blood cleanseth from all sin. Cleanse us, and blot from the book of thy remembrance all our transgressions. Open our eyes to understand the great mystery of godliness, and teach us by thine own Spirit the things which belong to our peace. We pray that we may have faith to grasp thy promises, and diligently to fulfil thy commandments. Show us, O God, the evil of the sin which is in us, that we may hate and forsake it. Lord Jesus, come and dwell in our hearts by faith, and so reveal unto us thy love, which passeth knowledge, that we may be filled with the fulness of God. Preserve us from the sin of putting anything in the place of Christ. We desire to use all thy ordinances as means of grace to our souls, but, O God, forbid it that we should rest on anything for peace and salvation but the finished work of thy dear Son.

Take us under thy merciful and Almighty protection. Keep us during the hours of darkness, and let thy presence be with us as our security and our peace. We cast all our care upon Thee, for Thou carest for us. We ask thy favour, not for ourselves alone, but for all who are dear to us. Thou knowest their wants and temptations. Bless them according to their need and the greatness of thy love, and overrule all things for their good. Especially cause them to increase in the knowledge and love of thy dear Son our Lord.

The Lord be with us and bless us; the Lord lift up the light of his countenance upon us, and be gracious unto us; the Lord give us peace, now and ever, for his mercies' sake. Amen.

[Morning.] **THIRTY-SECOND WEEK.—SATURDAY.** [Evening.]

READ IN HOLY SCRIPTURE 1 SAMUEL IX. 15–27.

READ IN HOLY SCRIPTURE ACTS XVI. 1–18.

LORD God, Father of mercies, Giver of every good gift, bow down thine ear, and hear us. We desire to begin the day with Thee, and, in the remembrance of another night's protecting care, to lift up our hearts to Thee in praise and thanksgiving. O God, we are indeed unworthy of thy goodness, for we have sinned against Thee, and been ungrateful for thy mercy, and disobedient to thy commands. But we are emboldened by thy Word to come at all times to the throne of grace, and to ask mercy of Thee, and grace to help in time of need.

O God, give us now, we beseech Thee, these blessings. We ask them in Christ's name, pleading his merits, and resting on the assurance of his perpetual intercession. If Thou forgive, who can condemn? Gracious Father, in mercy grant us every good and perfect gift; and, above all, let the light of thy love continually shine upon our hearts, that we may cheerfully follow wherever Thou leadest, and be willing to bear whatever cross Thou layest upon us. Oh, keep us steadfast in the presence of temptation, and ready in all things to deny ourselves, and to follow Christ. O gracious Spirit, abide with us, and instruct us in the fuller knowledge of Divine things. Increase our faith, and cause us to grow in grace, and in godliness, and to reflect in all our life the holy example of Jesus. Fill our hearts with love to God, and work in us the blessed experience which witnesses to our adoption, and is the earnest of coming glory.

Be with us, O God, in all that we do this day. Prosper us in all our plans, and purposes, and undertakings; and enable us to feel that Thou, God, seest us. Especially grant that amidst the engagements of time, we may be mindful of the nearness of eternity, and of the coming of the Lord Jesus Christ. In the world, preserve us from a worldly spirit, and teach us in our place and station to walk circumspectly. Set a watch over our lips, that we offend not in word. By thy Divine providence supply our temporal wants, giving us this day our daily bread. Impart to us a spirit of contentedness, that we may be thankful for present blessings, and leave the future in thy hand.

Be gracious and merciful to our land. Guide the counsels of all in authority. Teach them what is right in thy sight, and give them courage to do it. Be with all thy ministers, at home and abroad, and make them wise to win souls. Establish and strengthen all thy people in their most holy faith, and make them zealous in every good word and work. For all who are dear to us we implore thy grace. Watch over them, and enrich them with the tokens of thy love. Hear us, and accept us, for the sake of Jesus Christ our Lord. Amen.

O LORD God, assist us to render unto Thee our evening sacrifice of thanksgiving and praise. Help us to call to mind the mercies, not only of the past day, but of the past week. We cannot reckon them in order unto Thee; if we were to declare and speak of them, they are more than can be numbered. We bless Thee for holding us back from danger, and for leading us in a safe path. We bless Thee for the continued supply of our manifold needs, and for the power of enjoying thy gifts. We bless Thee for extending thy longsuffering toward us, though, by our many failures in duty and repeated transgressions of thy law, we have sorely tried thy patience. For these and all thy mercies, deign, O most gracious Lord, to accept our ascriptions of grateful praise.

Let thy mercy lighten upon us, O Lord, as our hope is in Thee. We confess before Thee that during the past week, yea, during the past day, we have often had evil thoughts in our hearts, and in many instances have committed acts of sin. O Thou who searchest the heart and observest the life, if we are not conscious of our sinfulness, do Thou graciously convince us of it; and let us not retire to rest without the assurance of thy free forgiveness. For the sake of the great Sacrifice that was offered on Calvary, O Lord, forgive.

Be pleased to bless to us, sacred Spirit, our reading of the Scriptures. Open our hearts, that we may attend to its blessed truths, and be the faithful followers of Jesus. [May the younger members of this household become like Timothy in their early knowledge of the Holy Scriptures, and in their youthful devotion to Christ and his service. To this end, sanctify the instructions communicated to them, and the influences that are brought to bear upon them, both by parents and other teachers. O Lord, open our children's hearts to thy truth, while they are yet children.]

O Lord, shelter us all to-night beneath thine almighty wing. Bless us with sleep, and restore us in the morning to a peaceful and happy consciousness. Let the Sabbath-day be ushered in with Thee, so shall it be to us a day of rest and devotion—a time of refreshing from the presence of the Lord.

We commend unto Thee thy servants who show unto men the way of salvation. Assist them in their preparation of mind and heart for the exercise of their ministry on the morrow. We beseech Thee to make the preaching of the Gospel a means of spiritual life to all who hear it; and let the kingdom of Christ be established through the world. Hear us, O Lord God, according to thy great compassion, and abundantly answer and bless us, for our Saviour's sake. Amen.

[Morning.]   THIRTY-THIRD WEEK.—LORD'S DAY.   [Evening.]

READ IN HOLY SCRIPTURE 1 SAMUEL X. 1–9, 18–27.   READ IN HOLY SCRIPTURE ACTS XVI. 19–40.

ALMIGHTY God, our gracious Father, we thank Thee for the ordinance of the Sabbath; and on this thine own appointed day of rest, we would bow the knee before Thee, and thank Thee for our creation, preservation, and all the blessings of this life. As a Sabbath, this day should remind us of creation, and draw our affections to Thee as the Creator. Thou, Almighty Father, wast pleased to rest from all thy work which Thou hadst created and made, and didst sanctify a day of rest for thy people to observe throughout all generations. On this day, too, we are reminded of the work of redemption. On the first day of the week the blessed Jesus arose from the grave, and showed redemption to be complete. We would adore, and bless, and glorify Thee for the gift of a Saviour, and for all the means of grace and hopes of glory we enjoy in Him. Sanctify our hearts this day. Prepare us for the duties of the sanctuary, and bless the religious exercises in which we shall be engaged. Make these our earthly Sabbaths foretastes of that heavenly Sabbath which is the promised portion of the people of God.

Bless the labours of thy ministering servants; anoint them with the oil of grace; make them burning and shining lights; grant that the word spoken may have much success. Thou, O Lord, wilt have mercy upon whom Thou wilt have mercy. Thine own are known to Thee, but in calling them out from the world Thou art pleased to use human agency. Bless the agency Thou hast appointed. The instruments are feeble, but the power is of Thee. They are a sweet savour of Christ in them that are saved, and in them that perish. Give unction from above, that they may be a band of men whose hearts Thou hast touched; and give fruit to their labours, that they to whom they minister may not rest in outward change of manners, but may have a real inward change of heart, wrought by the power of the Holy Ghost.

We would intercede for the ungodly, who know Thee not, and have no regard for thy name, thy day, or thy service; for the Sabbath-breakers, profane swearers, drunkards, and all who live after the flesh. Send forth thy light and thy truth; convince, convert, and save them; remove the darkness which surrounds them; show them the love and the power of Jesus, and bow them down at the foot of the cross.

We praise Thee for thy grace which has called us to thy service; and for any good thing that is in us, not unto us, O Lord, not unto us, but unto thy name be the praise and the glory. Hear us, answer us, and bless us, we pray Thee, for the sake of thy dear Son Jesus Christ, our adorable Redeemer and Saviour. Amen.

ALMIGHTY God, who hast mercifully set apart one day out of seven to be kept holy to Thyself, we desire to thank Thee for this thy great lovingkindness to the children of men. We might have been, as in heathen lands, the victims of incessant toil and labour. But Thou, in thy mercy, hast proclaimed a day of rest. Grant us thy servants grace, while we thank Thee heartily for the relief which Thou hast thus mercifully given to our weary bodies, so faithfully to use thy holy Sabbaths as that they may minister abundantly to the wellbeing of our immortal souls.

Preserve us especially, we pray Thee, O Lord, from being either afraid or ashamed of serving Thee on this holy day. Grant that neither the seductions of pleasure nor the ridicule of the profane may avail to tempt us to join in polluting thy Sabbaths, or keep us away from the courts of thy house. Give us rather, we pray, the same bold spirit which Thou gavest in olden time to thy faithful servants, Paul and Silas. Grant that, like them, we may have grace and strength to bear cheerfully whatever the wicked world may lay upon us, rather than forsake thy service, or cease to promote thy honour and glory.

Thou hast graciously promised to hear the prayers of any two or three who are gathered together in thy name. The walls of the dungeon are no hindrance to Thee, and Thou dost listen to the voice of the poorest prisoner. Grant, then, O Lord, that the preaching of the Gospel by thy ministers this day may have been as a great earthquake in the hearts of the hearers. Grant that the doors of the prison in which Satan has shut them may have been opened, and the bonds of sin may have been loosed. Grant that the light of thy Holy Spirit may have shined into very many dark hearts. Grant that many may have been roused to ask what they must do to be saved, and by thy merciful leading, may find the true answer through faith in the Lord Jesus Christ.

And now, O Lord, we heartily pray Thee, wash away, in the most precious blood of thy dear Son, the stains of our many and great sins. Baptize us, also, with thy Holy Spirit. Grant that we may be Christians, not only in word and profession, but in deed and in truth. Change our hearts, as in olden time Thou didst change the heart of the jailer at Philippi; and grant that as in him, so in us, the change may be manifested in a loving conduct towards all them with whom we have to do. Bless all whom we love, and grant that we and they may rest to-night free from harm beneath thy protecting and over-ruling care. We offer up this our Sabbath evening prayer, through Jesus Christ, thy Son, our Lord. Amen.

[225]

No. 29.

[Morning.] **THIRTY-THIRD WEEK.—MONDAY.** [Evening.

READ IN HOLY SCRIPTURE 1 SAMUEL XI.

READ IN HOLY SCRIPTURE ACTS XVII.

ALMIGHTY and eternal God, our ever-living and ever-loving Father, receive the thanksgivings we now offer for the sleep of the past night, the light of another morning, and the privileges and mercies to which we have risen. We bless Thee that our rest has not been broken by the cry of alarm, the sound of war, or the approach of death. Thou hast done great things for us, whereof we are glad. Bless the Lord, oh, our souls, and all that is within us, bless his holy name.

We now pray Thee to prepare us for the duties of another day. Strengthen us for the work we have to perform. Give us grace to act conscientiously with regard to all trusts, faithfully in all engagements, forbearingly towards others, and watchfully in all things. May there be nothing in the spirit we cherish, the friends we make, and the pursuits we follow, inconsistent with Christian character and the lessons of thy Word. May the life that we lead be one of faith in our Lord Jesus Christ, of submission to the Divine will, and of fruitfulness in purity and goodness.

We bless Thee for the assurance that all things work together for good to them that love Thee. Oh, let the assurance be realised in us. Loving Thee with the affection of children, the fortitude of saints, and the joy of servants, may all our associations on earth tend to prepare us for the fellowships of eternity, the activities of daily life for the engagements of heaven, and the sufferings of this present time for the glory to be revealed.

All within us which is wrong, we pray Thee to rectify. Suffer us not to go forth into the occupations of the day with guilt on the conscience, under any subjection to evil, or with any misgivings of mind as to our acceptance in Christ. May we know in whom we have believed, that Thou hast forgiven all our sins, and that Jesus Christ has been made to us wisdom, and righteousness, and sanctification, and redemption. And knowing this to be our condition, may we walk accordingly, perfecting holiness in the fear of the Lord, and letting our light so shine before men, that, seeing our good works, they may glorify our Father who is in heaven. But so to act we need Divine help; work in us, then, all the good pleasure of thy will, strengthen us with might by thy Spirit in the inner man, and keep us in close and constant nearness to thyself.

We put ourselves into thy hands. May the day be one of safety to us, not of danger; of good, not of evil; of mindfulness of God, not of forgetfulness of Him. These blessings, with the pardon of all our sins, we ask in the name and for the sake of our Lord Jesus Christ. Amen.

HEAVENLY Father, we thank Thee that Thou hast made Thyself known in thy Gospel, and that thy only begotten Son hath revealed Thee unto us. In Him we know Thee as our Creator, Preserver, and Benefactor. We are thine offspring, and in Thee we live, and move, and have our being; and for life and breath, and all things received this day, we are indebted to Thee. But above all, we know Thee as our Redeemer. Thy holy Word has taught us that Thou hast given thy dear Son to die for our sins, and to rise again for our justification. We know Thee also as our Sanctifier. Thou hast given us thy Holy Spirit to convert and renew our hearts. Oh, may the blood of Jesus be applied to our consciences to take away our guilt, especially the guilt that we may have contracted this day. And may the Holy Spirit be granted unto us in greater measure, that we may walk more worthily as thy children in days to come.

Lord, have mercy, we pray Thee, on those to whom Thou art still an unknown God. Specially have mercy upon thine ancient people Israel, that they may see that this Jesus whom thy Gospel preaches unto them is indeed the Christ. Oh, take the veil from their hearts, that they may look on Him whom they pierced, and believe.

Have mercy on all idolaters who know Thee not. Oh, spread thy Gospel to the ends of the earth, so that all may know Thee, from the least unto the greatest.

And if any amongst ourselves, living in the midst of Gospel light, are still ignorant of Thee, open their eyes, that they may indeed know Thee as the only true God, and Jesus Christ whom Thou hast sent, for this knowledge is life eternal.

To us who do know Thee, give a desire to know Thee better. And, in order to this, give us the noble spirit of the Bereans, to search the Scriptures daily. May we bring everything to the touchstone of thy holy Word. And may thy Spirit enable us readily to receive what thy Word teaches, and faithfully to avoid what is contrary thereto.

May we ever have one King, Jesus. O Lord Jesus! defend us this night, and protect thy needy and imperilled people everywhere. Especially defend all thy missionaries and evangelists; and, oh, wherever they preach thy Gospel, do Thou induce many to believe unto life eternal. Make thy Church to be a praise in the earth, fruitful in all good works, and zealous for thy glory.

Take us, and all our friends and relatives, into thy protection for the night; and give us rest of body and peace of conscience. We ask it all for thy dear Son's sake. Amen.

[MORNING.]   THIRTY-THIRD WEEK.—TUESDAY.   [EVENING.

READ IN HOLY SCRIPTURE 1 SAMUEL XII.

BLESSED Lord, who hast caused all Holy Scripture to be written for our learning, bring home to our hearts, we beseech Thee, by thy Holy Spirit, that portion of thy sacred Word which we have now just read.

We know, O Lord, that those bright examples of godliness which that Word contains were not set before us merely to excite our admiration, but that we should copy and imitate them. One of these we behold in thy faithful servant Samuel. In him Thou hast taught us to see the course of the man of God made perfect unto all good works. In him we behold an illustration of the rejoicing in the testimony of a good conscience, that in simplicity and godly sincerity, not with fleshly wisdom, but by the grace of God, he had his conversation in the world. Oh, that we, like him, may be able to appeal to men for the integrity of our conduct, and that we may receive the like testimony which he received.

Thou hast given us all our respective parts to perform; we have all our trusts to fulfil; we have all our spheres to occupy, be they ever so contracted; we have all our accounts to render up. Oh, that we may do so, not with grief, but with joy. Thou, O Lord, hast called us, and separated us from an ungodly world, to be a peculiar people, zealous of good works; to be lights and examples in the midst of a crooked and perverse generation. And such, O Lord, we shall be, if we answer the purpose and end of our vocation. Oh, enable us by thy grace to do so. Thus may we adorn the doctrine of God, our Saviour, in all things.

And while we are zealous to maintain good works, and to walk worthy of the Lord unto all pleasing, we would put no trust in anything that we do. While we labour to abound in the fruits of righteousness, we would desire to be found in Christ, not having our own righteousness, which is of the law, but that which is through the faith of Christ. Lord, we would ever remember that by the grace of God we are what we are; that salvation is all of grace. To Thee we would ascribe all the glory of our salvation; and our only hope is that the same grace which commenced the good work will carry it on until the day of Jesus Christ. O Lord, depending on that grace, we trust that we shall be enabled to maintain our steadfastness unto the end; and that, amidst the trials, and dangers, and temptations of this life, we shall go on, from faith to faith, from strength to strength, until, at length, we appear before our God in Zion. Grant this, O heavenly Father, for the sake of thy dear Son Jesus Christ. Amen.

READ IN HOLY SCRIPTURE 1 THESSALONIANS I.

O GOD, our Father, and the Father of our Lord Jesus Christ, we would again make known our requests unto Thee by prayer and supplication, with thanksgiving. May we be accepted through Him, in whom Thou art always well pleased, even thy Son Jesus, who delivered us from the wrath to come, and who ever liveth to make intercession for us. We praise Thee for the gift of a Saviour; for the atonement which he has made for our sins; for the manifestation of thy power in raising Him from the dead; and for the assurance that he will come again from heaven, to the eternal glorification of them that believe, and look for his appearing. May grace and peace, and all spiritual blessings, descend upon us from God the Father, and the Lord Jesus Christ.

We would offer our thanksgivings for the mercies of another day. O Lord, we are unworthy of the least of thy favours; but we pray Thee to continue them to us. Protect and guard us this night from evil. Cleanse us from all the sins and pollutions of the past day; and give us increasing power against temptation, that we may not hereafter offend against Thee. Keep us steadfast in the narrow way that leadeth to eternal life.

We praise Thee, O Lord, for the blessed Gospel of thy grace. May it come to each of us, not in word only, but in power, and in the Holy Ghost, and in much assurance. Fill us with faith, hope, and love. And, if we are truly born again from above, may we remember what manner of persons we ought to be in all holy conversation and godliness. May all around take knowledge of our work of faith, and labour of love, and patience of hope in our Lord Jesus Christ; so that we may be ensamples to all them that believe.

We would plead with Thee, O heavenly Father, on behalf of others. We pray for the world. Oh, may the word of the Lord sound out from this and every other Christian nation, unto them that are in the darkness of ignorance and superstition, causing them to turn to God from idols, to serve the living and true God. Let the labourers in the Gospel field be multiplied; and may thy Spirit render their work effectual. Wherever thy true religion is professed, may it be honoured and adorned by holy living. Grant thy richest blessings to our dear relatives and friends. Sanctify their hearts, and bring them, through Christ, to glory. We would give Thee thanks, also, for those who have gone before to that rest which remaineth for the people of God. Prepare us, by thy grace, to follow them; and, when our earthly course is ended, may we partake of the same blessed immortality, and dwell in thy presence for evermore. We ask all through Jesus Christ, our Saviour. Amen.

[Morning.] **THIRTY-THIRD WEEK.—WEDNESDAY.** [Evening.]

READ IN HOLY SCRIPTURE 1 SAMUEL XIII. 1—14.

READ IN HOLY SCRIPTURE 1 THESSALONIANS II.

ALMIGHTY God, our heavenly Father, we adore Thee as the Author of all the mercies which we daily and hourly receive. Under the shadow of thy wings we have rested through the night. We laid ourselves down to sleep, and have awaked, because Thou didst sustain us, and we would together as a family this morning unite in offering praise, adoration, and thanksgiving to thy great name.

Assist us this day, we beseech Thee, in all the duties which it brings. Without thy help we can do nothing; but if we acknowledge Thee in all our ways, we know that Thou wilt direct our path. Let us not shrink from duty because it seems hard, but resolve in the strength of the Lord to take up our cross daily, and to follow Christ. As we are enlisted under Christ's banner, make us valiant and good soldiers, giving no quarter to our spiritual enemies; but, O God, make us watchful unto prayer. Arm us for every attack. When the enemy shall come in like a flood, do Thou, O Spirit of the Lord, lift up a standard against him.

And should help seem long in coming, may we, nevertheless, possess our souls in patience, and tarry the Lord's leisure. Thy time must be the best time. Let us not do foolishly, nor depart from keeping the commandments of the Lord our God which He has commanded us. It may be that our extremity is thy opportunity; therefore may we wait patiently for the Lord. And do Thou incline thine ear unto us, and hear our cry, so that our minds be not overcharged with the cares of this life. Let not our enemy triumph over us. May the Philistine be driven from our hearts. Be pleased, O Lord, to deliver us. O Lord, make haste to help us.

And in all our varied relations this day, whether ruling or ruled, as masters or servants, grant us grace to act a consistent part. May each of us have a single eye to thy glory; may we strive to be men after God's own heart, hating all iniquity, and seeking to bring forth the peaceable fruits of righteousness, which are by Jesus Christ, to the praise and glory of God. Enable us so to act and speak in all things as to please Thee, and to show the power of thy grace in our hearts.

Bless all thy ministering servants, and make them wise to win souls, and faithful in rebuking sin. God be gracious to our beloved Sovereign and her royal offspring; and increase among all ranks and orders that righteousness which exalteth a nation: so shall our people be thy people: so shall our kingdom be established, and the Lord shall be our God.

Hear us, Father of mercies, and send us an answer of peace, for Jesus Christ's sake. Amen.

GRACIOUS God and Father, who art glorious in thy greatness and majesty, behold in mercy our family now gathered at thy footstool for supplication and thanksgiving. Adored be thy goodness for permitting us to draw near to Thee, and for assuring us of thy favour and love in Christ Jesus. We are sinful and unworthy, and have offended Thee times without number, by doing what we ought not to have done, and leaving undone what we ought to have done. But to Thee belong mercies and forgivenesses. Hear us, then, good Lord, and, in thy gracious compassion, put away our sins, and let them not hinder the coming down of thy blessing in answer to these our evening prayers.

We praise Thee for all thy goodness to us during the past day. The gifts of thy providence have been renewed in such measure as Thou seest fit. Life has been spared, and fresh opportunities have been afforded us for doing thy work and will in the world. We have again access to thy throne, and can again plead thy promises and the finished work of thy dear Son. To thy name be all the praise. Add to all thy mercies the blessing of a thankful heart, and kindle within us such a deep sense of thy goodness and mercy as will constrain us to consecrate ourselves afresh to thy service, and make us ashamed of our own self-pleasing and unreadiness of spirit. Work in us, we beseech Thee, that thorough change of heart which we are all unable to work in ourselves. Though we be tied and bound with the chain of our sins, yet, in the pitifulness of thy great mercy, loose us. Draw us, by thy Spirit and by thy Word, from every evil way, and let not sin or Satan have dominion over us. So will we praise and bless thy name for ever and ever.

Impress the lessons of thy Holy Word upon our hearts. Give us the willing ear, that we may receive it as the Word of the living God, which is able to save our souls, and which worketh effectually in them that believe. May it be in us as the incorruptible seed, which shall take root in the good ground of prepared hearts, and bring forth the fruits of a holy and religious life, to thy glory. Preserve us from ignorance, hardness of heart, and contempt of thy Word; and let not Satan, or the world, or our own weak and wayward wills, cause us to fall from Thee. Especially, O God, regard with pity and tender compassion those of us who may have hitherto received thy message of mercy in vain. Oh, let not one of ourselves, or of all who are dear to us, make shipwreck of our souls, and fail of eternal life. We commend ourselves and them to thy Divine protection. Hear us, for Christ's sake. Amen.

[MORNING.] THIRTY-THIRD WEEK.—THURSDAY. [EVENING.

READ IN HOLY SCRIPTURE 1 SAMUEL XV. 10—31. | READ IN HOLY SCRIPTURE 1 THESSALONIANS III.

O LORD God, who art a God of holiness, we bow before Thee with humility, reverence, and godly fear; for thou hatest iniquity and sin, and we are vile before Thee, and have been sinners from the beginning. We bless Thee that Thou art merciful and long-suffering even with us sinners, for the sake of Jesus Christ, our Advocate and Redeemer. We adore Thee for the hope that we are accepted in thy beloved Son, that our sins are blotted out, and shall be brought into remembrance against us no more for ever. We accept it as a new proof of thy love that we are permitted once more to see the cheerful light of day, and we desire, with the assistance of thy Holy Spirit, to consecrate it wholly to thy service and praise. Many days have we passed in sin, but this day we would devote to Thee, our Lord and our God.

Let us not deceive ourselves, O Lord; but do Thou graciously teach us the plague of our own hearts. Preserve us this day from turning aside to folly, and from any wilful indulgence of the lusts of the flesh. Help us to crucify the flesh with its affections and lusts, and enable us to walk not after the flesh, but after the Spirit, that we may keep a conscience void of offence, and enjoy this day, and evermore, the blessedness of thine approving smile. Strengthen us, that we may boldly resist the devil, until he flee from us. We thank Thee for the assurance that He who is for us is greater than all they that are against us. Keep this in our remembrance, we beseech Thee, all the day long; let it be our stay and comfort when the enemy shall arise against us, so that we may not provoke Thee to righteous anger by yielding to the enticements of the world, the flesh, or the devil.

We praise Thee, merciful God, for thy preserving grace until this day, and we would confidently commit our way to Thee, believing that Thou ever goest before us, and wilt constantly direct our steps. [Regard those of us who are young with peculiar tenderness and favour; teach them to be watchful and humble, and to keep their eyes from beholding vanity. Help the elder to set a worthy example to the younger, and to show forth the praises of Jesus by a holy walk and conversation.]

We pray, O Lord, for the prosperity of thy Church universally, and the sanctification in heart and life of all thy people. Fill thy ministering servants with Divine wisdom, and enable them to unfold to a perishing world the unsearchable riches of Christ. So let thy kingdom come, and thy will be done on earth as it is in heaven. O Lord, accept our morning sacrifice, and hear the voice of our supplication, through Jesus Christ our Saviour. Amen.

O LORD, our Father and our God, we kneel at thy footstool at the close of another day. The day is thine, the night also is thine, and alike by day and by night we are with Thee.

We adore Thee for thy providential care. From our earliest infancy to the present moment Thou hast watched over and blessed us; and whilst caring for others, Thou hast not forgotten us, though we have been so unmindful of thy goodness.

We thank Thee for thy Holy Word. May its promises comfort us in every season of sorrow; may its precepts teach us the nature of that obedience which Thou dost require. Help us to derive profit and encouragement from that portion of thy Word which we have read to-night. It has taught us not to be moved by the afflictions of life, and we humbly pray that we may so regard them as the discipline of thine hand, that we may never lose our confidence in Thee; and grant, O Lord, that however numerous or powerful our temptations may be, the tempter may never triumph. Bring us off more than conquerors through Him that loved us; and though in ourselves we are weak, let us find our strength in Thee.

We pray that we may live more holy and useful lives, that we may be known by our faith and charity, and that Thou wilt enable us to increase and abound in love one towards another. Save us from an unforgiving and an uncharitable spirit. From pride and passion, from malice and revenge, O Lord, deliver us. Holy Spirit, who alone canst sanctify our fallen nature, come and make our hearts thy temple. Dwell within us, to cleanse our thoughts, to purify our motives, to restrain our evil dispositions and desires. Conform us more and more to the likeness of our blessed Lord. Take from us the image of the earthy, and put upon us the image of the heavenly.

And now we invoke thy blessing before retiring to rest to-night. Abide with us, O Saviour, for the day is far spent. O Lamb of God, who takest away the sins of the world, take away our sins. May the atoning blood which Thou hast shed for sinners cleanse our souls. We gather around thy cross, and bring to Thee the burden of our guilt. Lord, remember us! Son of David, have pity upon us! Resting in thy love, and sheltered by thy power, may we lie down and sleep in peace, and in the morning rise strengthened and refreshed for the duties of another day.

We know not how near we are to our final rest. Grant, we beseech Thee, that when we close our eyes in death, we may awake in thy likeness, and be for ever satisfied. And to Thee, O Father, Son, and Spirit, we ascribe eternal praises. Amen.

[MORNING.] **THIRTY-THIRD WEEK.—FRIDAY.** [EVENING.]

READ IN HOLY SCRIPTURE 1 SAMUEL XVI.

ALMIGHTY and Omniscient God, Thou only searchest and knowest the hearts of men. Aid us, we entreat Thee, by thy good Spirit, to worship Thee this morning, and at all times, in spirit and in truth. May the words of our lips answer to the thoughts and desires of our hearts. We confess with shame our proneness to substitute form for spirit in thy worship, and to be often carried away with appearances merely, in the preferences we give to our fellow-men. Help us, O Lord, to discern between the evil and the good, in ourselves and others.

Help us, O Lord, to remember that every natural and spiritual endowment is from Thee; that all the success of our secular and spiritual enterprises is from Thee. Incline us, in humble gratitude, to lay all we are and all that we have at thy feet. In our very heart teach us to say, "Not I, but the grace of God that was with me." Help us always to abase ourselves, that Thou mayest exalt us. May we bear our abasements with meekness, and the exaltations of others without envy. Keep us when in low degree from repining, and when in high degree from pride. Choose Thou our lot, and teach us, in whatever state we are, to be content.

Almighty God, impress upon our minds, we beseech Thee, that as Thou art holy, so is thy service holy. Humble us in the dust as we see Thee putting down one and setting up another. Suffer us not to provoke Thee, by our obstinacy and presumption, to cast us away from thy presence, nor to take thy Holy Spirit from us, lest evil spirits enter and possess our hearts, and our last state be worse than the first. Oh, quicken us, that we may feel the least departure from Thee. May we dread nothing so much as the loss of thy favour. If we fall into sin, oh, suffer us not to cloak our offences, nor have recourse to false methods of restoration and peace. Preserve us from associates who will flatter and palliate rather than reprove and heal our backslidings. Almighty Saviour, destroy within us the works of the devil. Let us not be of those who draw back unto perdition, but of those who believe unto the saving of the soul. Daily increase our sense of thine infinite excellence. May our souls know Thee, indeed, as the chief among ten thousand, and the altogether lovely. Impress thy beauty upon us, that we may show forth thy praise.

Kind Guardian of our sleeping and waking hours, we give Thee heartiest thanks for refreshing sleep, and for the rich mercies of this morning. Be with us amid the duties of the day. Keep us this day without sin. We ask all for Christ's sake. Amen.

READ IN HOLY SCRIPTURE 1 THESSALONIANS IV.

ACCEPT, we pray Thee, O Lord God, our offering of praise at the close of this day. We thank Thee for countless and undeserved mercies; for food and raiment, and a home to dwell in; for turning away many evils, known and unknown; for guarding us in the midst of dangers that might have imperilled body and soul. We thank Thee for thy Holy Word, and the revelation of thy surpassing love in Jesus Christ, and the promise of the Holy Spirit. We thank Thee that, through the death of thy dear Son, Thou hast provided reconciliation for sinners, and opened the kingdom of heaven to all believers. We thank Thee that Thou hast shown us how we ought to walk, and to please God, and that in all our temptations, and perplexities, and weakness, we may come to Thee for strength, and guidance, and protection. Great, indeed, is thy love to us; it passeth knowledge. We deserve thy wrath, but Thou thinkest upon mercy. Enable us to receive thy gifts with thankfulness, and to grow in all wisdom and goodness.

We pray, O God, for a deeper sense of our own guiltiness before Thee. Oh, that Thou wouldest melt and break our hearts to a true repentance and contrition. Teach us, by thy Holy Spirit, the exceeding sinfulness of sin; show to us how it grieves Thee, and dishonours thy name; stir up in our hearts a holy indignation against it, that we may allow it no resting-place within us, but strive against it in thy strength, and come off more than conquerors, through Him who loved us, and died and rose again, that we, being dead to sin, may walk in newness of life. We desire, O God, that thy will should be more fully accomplished in us, even our sanctification, remembering that blessed are the pure in heart, for they shall see God. We desire and pray that the same mind may be in us which was in Christ Jesus, and that in all things we may speak and act as true disciples of our holy Lord and Master. Clothe us with humility, and give us a spirit of meekness. Fill our hearts with brotherly love, that we may bear and forbear, returning good for evil, and doing unto all around us as we would that they should do unto us. O God, so carry on and perfect thy work of grace in us, that when the Lord cometh we may be found of Him in peace, and enter in with Him into his glory.

We implore thy blessing on all who are dear to us. Take them and us under thy gracious protection and fatherly care for the night. In thy goodness and love, guard us against all evil. Give us rest of body, and peace of mind; and do for us more than we can ask or think, according to thy gracious promise in Christ Jesus, our Lord. Amen.

[Morning.] **THIRTY-THIRD WEEK.—SATURDAY.** [Evening.]

READ IN HOLY SCRIPTURE 1 SAMUEL XVII. 1—31.

READ IN HOLY SCRIPTURE 1 THESSALONIANS V.

GRACIOUS God, bring our hearts, by thy Holy Spirit, into a humble and reverent frame as we kneel at thy footstool. Make us sensible of thy presence, as the presence of the High and Holy One, in whose sight we are but as sinful dust and ashes. Increase our faith in thy promises. Give us a child-like spirit; and of thy great goodness do for us above all we can ask or think, for Jesus Christ's sake. We have sinned in thy sight, and are unworthy, through our deep sinfulness, of thy favour. But accomplish in us the work of thy grace, and cleanse, and renew, and sanctify us.

We praise Thee, O Lord, for the guardianship and care by which Thou hast preserved us during the night. We praise Thee for family mercies renewed to us this morning; for the message of thy Holy Word, and the gracious promise of help and strength for the day's engagements and duties. Let no evil spirit of unthankfulness cause us to forget thy goodness and forbearance towards us. In everything we desire to give thanks for what Thou hast bestowed and for what Thou hast withheld. Kindle within us a more earnest gratitude, that we may show forth thy praise and our own deep sense of thy mercy.

Leave us not this day to our own wisdom, which is but folly, or our own strength, which is but weakness; In all our ways we desire to acknowledge Thee, and pray that Thou wouldest direct our paths. Especially, O Lord, help us in the great conflict with sin and Satan. O Thou who, by the hand of the stripling David, didst destroy the enemy of thy people, mightily work in us, and help us to slay the sins which have so often risen up and gained the mastery over us. Glorify thy name, and give us the victory. We pray that in all we do this day we may act and speak as becometh the Gospel of Christ, and bring neither dishonour nor reproach on thy holy name.

Graciously bestow thy blessing [on the younger members of our family, and] on all who are dear to us. Bless, guide, and govern thy whole Church, and grant that all who profess and call themselves Christians may be led into the way of truth, and hold the faith in unity of spirit, in the bond of peace, and in righteousness of life. Give much success to the labours of all ministers, missionaries, and to every effort which is made in thy name for the enlargement of the Redeemer's kingdom, and the subversion of Satan's power. Lord, make bare thine arm in the midst of the nations, and let it be seen that Thou art God, and Thou alone. Grant us these our prayers, which we offer in the name of thy dear Son, to whom be honour and glory for ever and ever. Amen.

O LORD, who in thy Word hast taught us that thy dear Son, Jesus Christ, whom Thou hast exalted unto thy kingdom in heaven, will come again to be the Judge of the quick and the dead, and hast forewarned us that the day of the Lord so cometh as a thief in the night, make us ready, we beseech Thee, for the hour of his appearing.

We desire to live as those who have obtained salvation through faith in his blood. We would that we might be sanctified wholly, and that our whole spirit, soul, and body might be preserved blameless unto the coming of our Lord Jesus Christ. But, alas! we come far short of all that we desire. Each day, as we review it, presents its catalogue of sins and shortcomings, of evil thoughts and feelings, of evil acts and words, of duties neglected and love grown cold. The day we are now bringing to a close might witness, as other days, against us. O God of mercy and of peace, do Thou freely and fully pardon us! Through the precious blood of thy dear Son, cleanse us from all unrighteousness, and enable us, by simple faith in Him, who is the Lord our Righteousness, to realise true peace. And oh, that Thou wouldest give us more grace, that we might live before Thee as becometh saints. We are continually harassed and hindered, in running the race set before us, by the many and powerful enemies of our souls. Clothe us with the whole armour of God, that we may be defended against every assault, and may be strong to overcome every adversary. Make us bold and faithful in thy service, never shrinking from what we know to be right, whatever the doing it may cost us. Give us wisdom to prove all things, and strength of mind and purpose to hold fast that which is good. Make us ever watchful, lest by sinful compliances we grieve and quench thy Holy Spirit. Endue us with the spirit of prayer, that we may continually come to Thee, in simple dependence, for all the grace we need. And as we receive at thine hands the many gifts we so earnestly seek, fill our hearts with gratitude and praise.

And now, O Lord, we commit ourselves, our household and family, and all whom we love, to thy care and keeping during the night. Preserve us from all danger, refresh us with sleep, and enable us to rise on the morrow renewed in strength for all our duties. And day by day endue us with more of energy and of love, with more of holiness and heavenly-mindedness, that we may live as those who are looking for and hasting unto the coming of the Lord Jesus.

Hear us, O our gracious Father and Almighty God, and grant all that Thou knowest we need, for the sake of Jesus Christ, our only Mediator and Advocate. Amen.

[Morning.] **THIRTY-FOURTH WEEK.—LORD'S DAY.** [Evening.

READ IN HOLY SCRIPTURE 1 SAMUEL XVII. 32—58.

READ IN HOLY SCRIPTURE ACTS XVIII. 1—17.

LORD of the Sabbath, we thank Thee that Thou hast safely brought us to the beginning of this day. We bless Thee for appointing and preserving to us the holy Sabbath, and for thy good providence which enables us to keep it. Help us to consecrate its hours to Thee; and whether we be in thy house, or in our own dwellings, may we feel that Thou art near, and be filled with light and gladness.

In waiting upon Thee to-day, may we renew our strength of soul. In ourselves we are unable to contend with the powers of evil that assault us. Whenever we have gone to the conflict alone, we have failed. Hence we have to acknowledge before Thee that we have been overcome by temptation, and that many sins mar our character. If Thou, Lord, shouldest mark iniquity, we could not stand. But there is forgiveness with Thee. Pleading the merits of our Lord Jesus Christ, we are emboldened to ask Thee to remember our sins and iniquities no more; and oh, may the sense of thy forgiving love awaken in us a holy fear of transgressing against Thee.

We adore Thee, O Lord, for every instance of thy gracious help and deliverance which we can call to mind. May the remembrance of past mercies strengthen us for new duties and for new conflicts. We are sure that in dealing with our spiritual adversaries the weakest shall be as David, if Thou wilt give wisdom and might. Nerve us, blessed Lord, with holy courage to fight the good fight of faith. Strengthen us with all might by thy Spirit in the inner man, that we may be more than conquerors.

We glorify Thee, O Lord, on account of thy servants, who, like mighty men of valour, have gained signal victories over the powers of evil which have beset thy Church. We bless Thee, too, that Thou hast often made the weak mighty in pulling down the strongholds of error and wickedness. Awake, O arm of the Lord; awake, as in the ancient times. May thy ministers be men full of faith and of the Holy Ghost. Go forth with them in their warfare with all wickedness, and let the conversion of sinners and the increasing holiness of thy people testify to the success of their enterprise. Let new victories be won for Christ to-day. Make all ministers and missionaries, and Sunday-school teachers and tract distributors, to feel that God is working with them.

[Make this Sabbath a happy day to the children of the household. May the sacred stories of the Bible, such as we have now read, make a way for the entrance of thy truth to their young minds.]

Listen to our Sabbath morning petitions, and mercifully give us an answer of peace, for our Lord Jesus Christ's sake. Amen.

ALMIGHTY and ever-blessed God, we would now as a family approach thy throne, and offer our evening sacrifice of prayer and praise through Jesus Christ.

We bless Thee for the sacred privileges of another Sabbath, for the opportunity of uniting in worship with the thousands of thy children who have this day been instructed in thy truth, comforted by thy Spirit, and cheered on their way heavenward. Many a heart has, we trust, been relieved of its sorrows, and braced for the renewed struggle of life. Many have had sweet fellowship with the Father and the Son, and have been enabled joyfully to anticipate the rest that remaineth for the people of God. Help us all, that we may know the day of our merciful visitation, and that we may carry the spirit of the Sabbath into the duties of the week. Have mercy on those who oppose themselves, and reject the gracious counsel of God. Show them that they fight against their own interest, and wrong their own souls. Pity those lands where persecution, tyranny, and superstition prevail. Turn the heart of the persecutor, and make him a pattern of thy long-suffering, and a promoter of the faith which he has laboured to destroy. Eternal thanks be to thy name, O Lord, that thy Gospel has been sent to the Gentiles. We pray for the time when the Jews shall acknowledge their Messiah, and be brought in with the fulness of the Gentiles. Our hearts' desire and prayer for Israel is, that they may be saved.

Lord, follow with thy blessing the faithful labours of thy servants this day. Ever animate them in their work by the assurance that sustained the Apostles themselves: "Be not afraid, for I am with Thee." Help them to set forth Christ as the one Mediator between God and man, the only way of safety and peace, and may they be enabled, by their faithfulness and consistency, to commend themselves to every man's conscience, as in the sight of God. We would remember those who have been detained from thy sanctuary this day by affliction. Thou art able, O Lord, to make up to all such the loss of outward ordinances. Speak grace and comfort to the souls of thy suffering people. Make their bed in their sickness. Sanctify to them their trials, and in thine own time give them a happy issue out of all their afflictions.

And now, O Lord, take charge of us this night. Give rest to our wearied bodies, and strengthen us to serve Thee with renewed vigour on the coming day. Into thy hands we commit ourselves and all our interests for time and eternity. Be Thou the everlasting home and resting-place of our souls, through Jesus Christ our Lord, to whom be all praise, now and for ever. Amen.

[Morning.] **THIRTY-FOURTH WEEK.—MONDAY.** [Evening.

READ IN HOLY SCRIPTURE 1 SAMUEL XVIII. 1—16.

O LORD our God, we bless Thee for thy great goodness in bringing us to the light of another day. Grant us the help of thy grace, that we may glorify Thee with our bodies and our spirits, which are thine. Help us to serve Thee better than we have done, for in many things we have offended and fallen short of our duty; and it is of thy mercy only that we are still able to approach Thee, and in the name of Jesus to ask pardon for the past and help for the time to come.

Morning after morning have we come before Thee, confessing our unworthiness, and lamenting our offences; morning after morning we have asked for thy grace to keep us from evil; and yet how little have we profited by all thy loving-kindness! In thought, and word, and deed, we have sinned against Thee. Leave us not to ourselves, for without Thee we can do nothing; but wash us in the blood of Jesus, and let the knowledge of thy great love be ever with us, that loving Thee because Thou hast loved us, we may be strong to resist temptation, and may delight to keep thy commandments.

We go forth to our daily business. O Lord, Thou knowest how frail we are, and how the power of the world and sin press against us to lead us to evil. Thou knowest the special need of each of us; strengthen us by thy grace, that we may be ready to do the thing that is right.

O Lord Jesus, who wast tempted like as we are, we believe that as our Great High Priest Thou art ever ready to hear and to bless; be Thou our guide this day. Save us from the fear of man; may we not be ashamed of following Thee. Teach us thy love, that with all humbleness towards God, and all gentleness towards man, we may seek the way of righteousness. Save us from all pride, vain-glory, and self-sufficiency. If it please Thee to give us any success or prosperity, enable us to remember that all we have is thine, that our ability to plan and to act comes from Thee. Grant that we may bear disappointment with cheerfulness and patience, so that if it please Thee to send us any loss or trial, we may yet be able to see our neighbour's prosperity without murmuring or fretfulness, and may go on trusting in the Lord with good courage. May no provocation lead us to sin with our lips or in the thoughts of our heart, but as thy true disciples may we abound in brotherly love towards all men. Be Thou our guide. Give us light to follow Thee.

Bless, O God, thy people everywhere; supply their wants, sustain their weakness, comfort them in sorrow, and increase their faith. Have mercy on sinners, lead them into the way of peace. Hear us, for Christ's sake. Amen.

READ IN HOLY SCRIPTURE 2 THESSALONIANS I.

O THOU God and Father of our Lord Jesus Christ, who hast appointed a day in which Thou shalt judge the world in righteousness, we pray to be made ready by thy grace for the great day of Christ's appearing. May we know Him now joyfully as our Saviour and Advocate, and be enabled to look forward without fear to the hour when we must stand at his bar. Then may we hear Him say to us, "Come, ye blessed of my Father." We know that we cannot be justified before Thee by our own works. If Thou, O Lord, shouldest mark iniquity, O Lord, who could stand? But we plead thy mercy, and trust in the refuge of our Redeemer's love and righteousness.

O God, moved by thought of the terrors of the Lord, when He shall come revealed in flaming fire, we would heartily plead to-night on behalf of infidels and heretics, and careless and wicked persons, who obey not Thee. Oh, that they were wise, that they understood these things, and would consider their latter end! Revive thy Church in these realms, that her influence for the salvation of the multitudes around may go forth with a new power. Awake them that sleep, call to the dead to arise, and cause men to know the merciful day of their visitation. Stretch thy hand forth to the dying this night, and where the death-bed is yet uncheered by the hopes of the Gospel, oh, show the greatness of thy power and of thy grace, and at the very last hour pluck brands from the burning. Glory be to thy name for all the saved who are walking in the light of life, their faith growing, their love abounding, their actions glorifying the name of the Lord Jesus Christ. Multiply Thou their number, and add yet to their graces continually. Mercy and peace be to all such as love the Lord Jesus in sincerity.

We look back with gratitude on the way in which Thou hast preserved and led us this day. We pray Thee to forgive all the ills we have this day done. We would retire to rest under the covert of thy wings. When Thou sealest our eyes in sleep, let it be the sleep of thy beloved. Shouldst Thou hold them waking, let our thoughts be with Thee. When the morning returns, may we find ourselves called to raise a new song of thankfulness for safety, and peace, and health. Or should the eyes of any of us, closing in sleep, open no more on earth, may they behold the glories of the better country. We desire to associate the thought of death with the memory of thy promise, O gracious Saviour, and with untroubled hearts to wait for thy coming, according to thy Word, to receive us to be with Thyself, that we may be where Thou art for ever. To Thee, with the Father and the Holy Spirit, be all the glory. Amen.

[MORNING.] **THIRTY-FOURTH WEEK.—TUESDAY.** [EVENING.

READ IN HOLY SCRIPTURE 1 SAMUEL XX. 1–23, 35–42.

READ IN HOLY SCRIPTURE 2 THESSALONIANS II.

ALMIGHTY God, we pray Thee to bless to us the reading of thy Holy Word. May the portion we have just heard be impressed upon our minds and hearts. Help us rightly to form and profitably to use our earthly friendships. If we are called, like thy servant David, to pass through heavy and sore trial, may Christian friends be raised up to counsel and comfort us. But we especially pray for the presence and help of our loving Saviour, who is a Friend that sticketh closer than a brother; and who has graciously said that the very hairs of our head are all numbered.

We thank Thee for the doctrine of Divine providence, and for the inspired assurance that all our concerns, whether personal or domestic, are under thine eye and control. At this family altar we gratefully acknowledge the mercies of another night. We laid us down and slept; we awaked; for the Lord sustained us. Our temporal wants are again supplied, and we are permitted to enter upon the duties of a new day. We beseech Thee to preserve us from the destruction that wasteth at noon, as well as from the pestilence that walketh in darkness. Help us to fulfil our worldly engagements in a Christian spirit. While we are not slothful in business, may we be fervent in spirit, serving the Lord. If trials lie before us, make us willing to suffer; and whether we are called to labour or to endure affliction, may the promise be fulfilled, "My grace is sufficient for thee; my strength is made perfect in weakness." Give us power this day to maintain a living, personal union with Christ. May He be made unto us wisdom, and righteousness, and sanctification, and redemption. Help us to feel our dependence on the Holy Spirit for religious light and influence. May He supply to us holy thoughts and resolutions; and by his help may we rest with calmness and confidence on the atonement of the cross. In moments of perplexity may He guide us. When the enemy shall come in like a flood, may He lift up a standard against him. If the sun of prosperity shine upon us, may He chasten our joys; and if the clouds of adversity gather, may He inspire us with resignation and hope.

Hear our prayers for all who are dear to us. Let our households live before Thee. May the children of thy people be brought to a knowledge of the truth. Give to them an early connection with thy Church. Preserve them from the follies of the world. Guide them through life with thy counsel, and afterward receive them to glory.

Bless all Christian churches with peace and prosperity. We ask all for Jesus Christ's sake. Amen.

OUR Father who art in heaven, we desire to bow ourselves before Thee, and to acknowledge thy greatness and glory, and thy right to do with us and with all thy creatures according to thy holy will. We bless Thee for the revelation of mercy made known to us, and for the Lord Jesus Christ, thine unspeakable gift to a fallen and sinful world, and we pray that he may dwell in our hearts the hope of glory. We thank Thee for what thine inspired prophets have told us respecting his cause of righteousness and truth, and rejoice that, notwithstanding many apostacies and evils, it shall finally triumph gloriously. We praise Thee that the mystery of iniquity shall not always pervert the truth as it is in Jesus; and oh, may we be among those who receive this truth in love, and grow up unto Him in all things, who is the Head of the Church, and to whom Thou hast given the pre-eminence. Keep us graciously from every delusion and error; number us with thy children whom Thou hast from the beginning chosen to salvation, through sanctification of the Spirit and belief of the truth; and may we feel in our blessed experience that Thou hast effectually called us by the Gospel to the obtaining of the glory of our Lord Jesus Christ. Give us good hope through grace, even that hope that maketh not ashamed, and which is one of the fruits of thy Holy Spirit. May we know that we are Christ's, and have the witness in our hearts that we are born of God; and as our days pass on, do Thou make us meet for the inheritance of the saints in light, so that the full blessedness of thy children may be ours at the coming of our Lord Jesus Christ, and our gathering together unto Him.

We thank Thee, most merciful God, for thy kind dealings with us this day; for the bread which has sustained us, for the measure of health we have enjoyed, for the continuance of reason, for domestic comforts, and for every other blessing, whether for the body or the soul. Pardon, we beseech Thee, the sins and errors of this day. Oh, forgive, for the blessed Saviour's sake, all our shortcomings in thought, and word, and action; and let us lie down on our beds with our consciences at peace, through the sprinkling of the blood of atonement. Favour us with a peaceful night and refreshing sleep; let no evil come near our dwelling or persons, but be Thou our shield, our guardian, and our God. We rejoice that the darkness and the light are both alike to Thee; therefore will we lie down in peace and sleep, for Thou, Lord, only makest us to dwell safely. And now, O God of our salvation, accept our thanksgiving, and hear and answer our humble prayer, for the sake of our only Lord and Saviour Jesus Christ. Amen.

[MORNING.] **THIRTY-FOURTH WEEK.—WEDNESDAY.** [EVENING.

READ IN HOLY SCRIPTURE PSALM XXXI.

BOW down thine ear unto us, O Lord, for we put our trust in Thee. In Thee, the Rock of Ages, we place all our confidence, and rest assured that we shall never be ashamed. We rejoice that our times are in thy hand. Thy wisdom appoints, and thy gracious providence accomplishes, all that concerns us. In all the mercies of life we desire to see thy smile; and when the shadow of earthly sorrow crosses our path, we would remember that it is the shadow of thy mighty hand at work for our highest good. Let thy great goodness fill our hearts with thankfulness, and our lips with praise. May the past deliverances Thou hast wrought on our behalf never be forgotten, but always strengthen our belief that thine unfailing mercy will pardon our sins, subdue our corruptions, and supply all our need.

Make thy face to shine upon thy servants this morning, that all day long we may walk in thy favour. We desire to perform all the duties of life in thy strength, and so to do common things that they may glorify Thee. Preserve us, we beseech Thee, O Lord, from our spiritual foes, and direct our feeble steps, that the snares of Satan may not prevail against us. Let our judgment of all things be formed by the light of thy sacred word, and suffer not the conflicting opinions of men to estrange our hearts from Thee. Should the strife of tongues disturb us, enable us with patience to endure, and by meekness to commend to others the Gospel we profess, and the God we serve.

Most merciful Father, accept our thanksgivings for the blessings bestowed upon us during the night, and for the daily bread with which Thou hast supplied our table. Shield us now from the dangers of the day, and richly satisfy our souls with the bread of life. Go before us in all our ways, and bring us in peace and comfort, at the close of the day, to our family altar. Let thine undeserved love to us fill us with compassion and tenderness to all our suffering fellow-creatures; and, for thy sake, may we in all things do unto others as we would that they should do to us. Hear our supplications for all men. May those who are near and dear to us be one with us in thy service on earth, and in thy glory in heaven. Abundantly bless our beloved Sovereign and all the Royal family. Enrich our native land with all seasonable gifts of thy good providence, and with the abundant light of thy Gospel truth. Be with our countrymen in distant colonies and foreign lands, and hasten the glorious time when the whole earth shall know Thee, the only true God, and Jesus Christ, whom Thou hast sent. Grant this, we beseech Thee, for his sake. Amen.

READ IN HOLY SCRIPTURE 2 THESSALONIANS III.

O HOLY and Eternal God, help us, in this our evening praise and prayer, to worship Thee in spirit and in truth. The name of Jesus is our plea, and his intercessions on high the source of all our confidence. We trust in Him, and recall with thankfulness the gracious promise that whatsoever we shall ask in his name, believing, we shall receive. We believe; O Lord, help our unbelief.

Glory be to thy name for the multiplied blessings of this day. With what gracious care hast Thou watched over and preserved us! With what unwearied love hast Thou borne with our infirmities and sins! How hast Thou withheld the punishment we have deserved, and bestowed mercy instead of judgment! Oh, fill us with thankfulness and praise, and grant us grace with renewed purpose of heart to cleave unto Thee in all things. Especially we implore thy forgiveness for this day's many sins. Suffer not our guilt to remain upon us, but cleanse us in the fountain once opened for uncleanness. O God, grant us thy peace, and enable us to lie down on our beds this night in the blessed experience of thy forgiveness.

Gracious Father, in thy truth and faithfulness strengthen our hearts, and keep us from all evil. Enable us to do in all things what Thou hast commanded; and to live in the constant assurance of thy love, and the blessed hope of the Lord's coming. By thy Spirit awaken in us a sincere love to Thee, that we may be ready to every good word and work, and never grow weary in well-doing. Preserve us, we pray Thee, from the sin of idleness. Help us to look upon our time, and talents, and opportunities as a stewardship from Thee. Oh, that we may use them all in thy service, and for the good of others. Show us, O Lord, by the leadings of thy providence, and by the teaching of thy Holy Spirit, what we ought to do, and give us the will and the strength to do it, that we may be living epistles of Christ.

Look in mercy upon thy Church, and preserve it from false teachers, who would turn thy children from the way of truth into the paths of error. Guide thy ministers to a deeper knowledge and experience of thy truth, and make them instruments of great and lasting blessing to their people. Have compassion on all men, and raise up labourers for Thee, who shall go into thy vineyard and gather in a rich harvest of souls for Christ.

We crave thy blessing for all who are dear to us [and especially for the children of our family]. Take us and them under thy gracious care; and so refresh us with needful rest, that when the morning dawns upon us, we may enter with renewed diligence on the work of another day. Hear us, we pray Thee, for Christ's sake. Amen.

[Morning.]   THIRTY-FOURTH WEEK.—THURSDAY.   [Evening.

READ IN HOLY SCRIPTURE 1 SAMUEL XXII.

O GOD, the Lord, the holy and heavenly Father, be merciful unto us, and bless us, and cause thy face to shine upon us. In the shining of thy face we feel our life and comfort ever lie. If Thou art angry all our strength is gone, and we walk in weary dread of perishing under thy frown. Only in thy favour do we live, and only in thy mercy can we rejoice. Oh, satisfy us early with thy mercy, that we may rejoice, and be glad all the day.

We bless Thee for thy Son, whom Thou hast anointed, and sent to save us. He is our refuge from guilt and our rest in trouble, and we come unto Him, seeking salvation in Him. As they of old, the distressed of Judah, came unto David, unto the hold, seeking for refuge in the son of Jesse, so do we, in our heavier distress, come unto Jesus, unto the cleft of the Rock, seeking salvation in the Son of the living God. Oh, that we may be received of Him, and admitted into the number of his disciples, and find the salvation we need in Him! Grant, also, O Lord, that we may be united to his person, and made partakers of his overflowing grace. As the branch is united to the vine, so may we be united to Jesus, and receive of his fulness, and grace for grace.

Regard, O Lord, the state of this household, and look Thou to our peace and safety. We are subject to many evils; we are pursued by many foes; we know not what a day or an hour may bring upon us; but be Thou our shield and sure defence, and we shall not be greatly moved. What time we are afraid, we will trust in God; as our fathers trusted, so will we, and we shall not be confounded. Thou hast been our help, therefore in the shadow of thy wings will we confide. In quietness and confidence shall be our strength. When we are troubled, let us not be distressed; when we are perplexed, let us not be in despair; if we should be persecuted, let us not be forsaken; or if we should be cast down, let us not be destroyed. In Thee may we find our peace in trouble, our comfort in sorrow, our strength in weakness, and our deliverance in every time of danger. While Thou, Lord, art for us, who can be against us?

We beseech thy providential care throughout this day. Guide us with thine eye, and enable us in all our ways to acknowledge Thee. Help us to carry about with us a praying heart, and to be diligent in business, fervent in spirit, serving the Lord. Grant us grace to acquiesce in all thy dispensations; and may we in all things be able to say sincerely, "Thy will be done." Hear us in these things, O Lord, for Jesus Christ's sake, to whom with Thee and the Holy Ghost be all honour and praise for evermore. Amen.

READ IN HOLY SCRIPTURE ACTS XVIII. 18–28.

O GOD, the Father of all mercies, and the God of all consolation, look upon us with the favour Thou bearest towards thy people, and visit us with thy salvation. Thy good providence has kept us in being and in blessings during the day past, and we now come before Thee, in the name of thy dear Son, to obtain thy blessing. We would humbly and heartily confess our sins unto Thee; we acknowledge that this day, and during all the days of our life, we have not served Thee as we ought; and if we have not fallen into open sin, it is owing to thy restraining grace, and not to our own merit.

We pray Thee, pardon our sins, and grant to us peace and joy in believing in Jesus. Shed abroad in our hearts the Holy Ghost, to renew us in righteousness, and to strengthen us against our besetting sins. Teach us to recognise thy providence ordering all events, so that not a sparrow falls to the ground without thy knowledge. Help us in all our worldly business to remember that our life is but a vapour, appearing for a little time, and then vanishing away.

Preserve us, O Lord, from a vain and contentious spirit; may we seek first the kingdom of God and its righteousness, and, in diligent attention to our duty, feel sure that all necessary things will be added unto us. We praise Thee for our temporal blessings, for health and happiness, food and raiment, the use of our reason, and all those family comforts by which we are surrounded. Let thy goodness lead us to repentance, and produce a hearty devotion to thy service. Remember this night the needy and the afflicted: supply their wants; sustain them in their trials; and make all things to work together for their good.

Bless our country with peace and prosperity. Grant to those who rule in the state the spirit of godly grace and wisdom, and may true religion and virtue prosper in our land to all generations. Remove, O Thou Prince of Peace, all the causes of strife and war, and grant to all nations unity, peace, and concord. Grant success to every effort that is made to teach the young their duty to God and man, and prosper the preaching of thy Gospel to every creature. Be present with all Christian missionaries in foreign lands; cause the heathen to be turned from idols to serve the living and true God, and to wait for his Son from heaven; and the Jews to look on Him whom they pierced, and mourn. And now, Lord, we commit ourselves to Thee, our Creator, Preserver, and Redeemer. Keep us this night in safety of body and in peace of mind, and strengthen us for the duties of each returning day, through our Lord Jesus Christ. Amen.

[Morning.]   THIRTY-FOURTH WEEK.—FRIDAY.   [Evening.]

READ IN HOLY SCRIPTURE 1 SAMUEL XXIV.

OUR Father who art in heaven, to whose grace we look for the pardon of all our sins, teach us, we pray Thee, by thy Holy Spirit, to offer in sincerity the petition taught us by our blessed Lord, and to say, " Forgive us our debts, as we forgive our debtors." Thou didst enable thy servant David to withhold his hand from hurting his cruel persecutors, when placed within his power; and surely it becomes us, with the yet brighter example before us of Him who, being reviled, reviled not again, and who in suffering, threatened not, to refrain from recompensing evil for evil. Oh, grant us the spirit of charity and love, that we may forbear with one another, and forgive one another, even as Thou, for Christ's sake, dost forgive us. If in the course of the day on which we have now entered we meet with those who injuriously asperse us or rail at us, may we be enabled to answer in the meekness of wisdom, and to approve ourselves followers of the patient and gentle Sufferer, who endured the contradiction of sinners against Himself, and prayed for them that nailed Him to the cross. And may we ever be kept from all that tends to hurt or wrong another. Let us do good, and not evil, all the days of our life.

We pray Thee, O Lord, to succour with thy grace such as are persecuted for righteousness' sake. Deliver them, if it please Thee, turning the hearts of their persecutors to justice and truth; and while their trials last, may He who walked with the Hebrew youths in the furnace of Babylon manifest his presence to their hearts, and stay them up with his all-sufficient grace. Remember in thy mercy all who are enslaved and oppressed. Break, we pray Thee, every yoke. Oh, in thy mercy, break all over the world the yokes of ignorance and sin, and destroy the dominion of the wicked one. We thank Thee for the civil and religious freedom we enjoy. Oh, that all the subjects of our Sovereign (whom do Thou bless) were also freed by the truth, and found walking in the glorious liberty of the children of God!

We now commend all the members of this household to thy safe keeping for the day. As we go to our various tasks and duties, may we remember that we are under thine eye, and always strive to please Thee. Keep us in our going out and our coming in. Preserve our souls from sin. Lead us not into temptation, but deliver us from evil. Prosper, if it please Thee, our work this day; and with our daily bread, give us a Father's blessing. We praise Thee for the rest and refreshment of the bygone night, and for all the mercies with which this morning Thou hast surrounded us. And to thy holy name we ascribe honour and glory, for ever and ever, through Jesus Christ our Saviour. Amen.

READ IN HOLY SCRIPTURE ACTS XIX. 1—20.

AT the close of the day, we would again seek thy presence, O Lord God. May thy Word just read be felt by us in all its fulness. Help each one of us to examine ourselves, whether we are in the faith. Let not our profession be only a bending of the knee, whilst our heart is not humbled. Let not our prayer come only from the lip, whilst our heart is far away from Thee. Heavenly Father, forgive all our lukewarmness. Give us a heart to pray more—to ask oftener for thy Holy Ghost, to seek a deeper interest in dying to sin and living unto Thee, so that by our lives we may show that we are under the power of the Holy Ghost.

We commenced this day with reading thy Word, and asking help that we might live up to the privileges promised in that Word. Now we come to grieve over another day's shortcomings and weaknesses. Whilst the spirit is willing, oh, how weak we often find the flesh to be! We would not hide one sin; help us, O God, by thy Spirit, to confess every sin. As Thou dost deepen the sense of sin within us, so let thy Word mightily grow in our minds, and be enjoyed in our lives, through the forgiveness which is in Christ Jesus our Lord.

When we testify to others about the happiness of true godliness, oh, may we do it with our lives as well as by our words!

Keep us from the influence of false doctrine, and make those who preach thy Word themselves to enjoy the forgiveness of sins.

We pray for every member of our family. May thy Word grow mightily amongst them. We pray for our friends and neighbours: may thy Word grow mightily amongst them also. We pray for our enemies, O Lord God: may thy Word grow mightily amongst them.

Help each of us to take away the stumbling-block out of our brother's way, whatever seems to stop the spreading of the Word. To this end, bless, O Lord, all Sabbath-schools, all faithful preachers of the Word, all missionary and other societies, which seek to place the sinner under the powers of the Gospel, or which seek to remove the vice and iniquity which so mightily prevent the Word having free course.

As we pray for success on these undertakings, so lead each one of us to do our part in helping on thy blessed work. As we can each be useful in our day and generation, may we so live that no one shall hereafter charge us with not helping them to receive the Gospel.

We commend each other into thy gracious care for the night. Graciously watch over us, and defend us from all evil. Hear us, and have mercy upon us, for Jesus Christ's sake. Amen.

[Morning.] **THIRTY-FOURTH WEEK.—SATURDAY.** [Evening.

READ IN HOLY SCRIPTURE PSALMS CXLI., CXLII.　　READ IN HOLY SCRIPTURE 1 CORINTHIANS I.

O LORD God, who in all ages hast been a refuge for thy people, we rejoice to know that Thou art the unchangeable God whose compassions fail not. We thank Thee that in thy Word Thou hast recorded for our encouragement the experience of thy saints, and thereby hast revealed to us thy goodness and mercy. Oh, enable us to walk in their footsteps, and to lean upon Thee in all our weakness and temptation with child-like trust, and to feel that Thou art indeed the God of our salvation, a very present help in every time of need. Thou hast helped us hitherto, and we bless thy holy name. We remember thy goodness and love, and desire to cast all our care upon Thee, for Thou carest for us. May the mercies of the night now past, and those now renewed to us, stir us up to thankfulness and praise, and especially constrain us this day cheerfully and obediently to do thy will. Suffer us not to wander from Thee, but keep us ever near Thyself. Draw our hearts away from all evil, and let not sin have dominion over us. We would keep our hearts with all diligence, and set a watch over our lips, that we offend not in word.

Gracious Father, give us a clearer knowledge of heavenly things, and especially make us acquainted with Thyself and thy dear Son Jesus Christ. Work in us, we beseech Thee, a true repentance for all those sins which we from time to time have most grievously committed by thought, word, and deed against thy Divine Majesty, provoking most justly thy wrath and indignation against us. Increase our faith and multiply upon us thy mercy, that Thou being our ruler and guide, we may so pass through things temporal, that we finally lose not the things eternal.

We seek thy blessing on all the duties and engagements of this day. Only as Thou shalt defend and protect us shall we escape the snares of sin and the shafts of the great enemy. Almighty God, we commit ourselves to thy care, and earnestly pray that Thou wilt not leave us nor forsake us. Take charge of all our circumstances, whether at home or in the world. If Thou sendest trial or disappointment, may we profit by it: if peace and prosperity is given, may we see thy hand in it and be thankful.

Help every effort which shall be made this day for bringing souls to Christ. Fill the hearts of thy believing people with a fervent zeal for thy glory, and with an earnest desire to bring the sinful and guilty into the fold of Jesus. Send forth daily fresh labourers into thy vineyard, and grant much success to all thy ministers. Give thy choicest blessing to all whom we love, and answer all our prayers for ourselves and others, for Jesus Christ's sake. Amen.

O LORD, our heavenly Father, at the close of another week we would offer to Thee our sacrifice of prayer and thanksgiving. We bless thy name for the mercies that have followed us all our life long unto this day. Above all, we thank Thee that Thou hast called us to be saints, and hast translated us out of the kingdom of darkness into the kingdom of thy dear Son. Oh, help us to walk worthy of our high calling, in all lowliness and meekness, forbearing one another, and forgiving one another, even as Christ forgave us. O Lord, have mercy upon us. Pardon our offences; cleanse the thoughts of our hearts by the inspiration of thy Holy Spirit, that we may be full of love to Thee, and to thy people, and to all mankind. May all old things die in us, and all things belonging to the Spirit live and grow in us. May we be blameless and harmless, children of God without rebuke in the midst of a crooked and perverse generation.

We are now on the eve of another holy day. Prepare our hearts for entering on its sacred duties. Help us to lay aside all thoughts of our worldly business or amusement, and to spend the day, if we are spared to enter on it, in earnest endeavours for our own spiritual improvement, and for that of others. Keep us from all anxious thoughts about the things of this life. May we be careful for nothing, but in everything, by prayer and supplication, make our requests known unto Thee.

Help us to use the world as not abusing it, knowing that the fashion thereof passeth away.

We would again implore thy Fatherly blessing on all who are near and dear to us. Give them, if it be thy holy will, all the blessings of this life; but, above all, give them thy Holy Spirit, and defend them with thy heavenly grace, that they may be Thine now, and Thine for ever.

We pray Thee, O Lord, to bless our native land, and all ranks of men among us. Make our officers peace, and our exactors righteousness. Bless and keep the magistrates, and give them grace to execute justice, and to maintain truth. Give to all nations unity, peace, and concord. Give and preserve to our use the kindly fruits of the earth, so as in due time we may enjoy them. Have mercy upon all men. Succour, help, and comfort all that are in danger, necessity, and tribulation, giving them patience under their sufferings, and a happy issue out of all their afflictions.

Hear, O Lord, we beseech Thee, those our petitions; and those things which for our unworthiness we dare not, and for our ignorance we cannot ask, vouchsafe to give us for the worthiness of thy Son, Jesus Christ our Lord. Amen.

[MORNING.] THIRTY-FIFTH WEEK.—LORD'S DAY. [EVENING.

READ IN HOLY SCRIPTURE 1 SAMUEL XXVI.   READ IN HOLY SCRIPTURE 1 CORINTHIANS II.

ALMIGHTY God! who hast, in all ages, ordered the course of this world according to thine unerring wisdom and righteousness, we beseech Thee so to assist us in reading the record of thy dispensations, that we may learn to delight in the ways of thy providence, and to yield ourselves more humbly and readily to thy will.

Teach us, O Lord, to meditate profitably on the wonders of thy power and wisdom as they are unfolded in thy Word. We remember how Thou didst watch over thy servant David in the wilderness, not leaving him, though poor and persecuted, without faithful followers. By granting him the help of thy Holy Spirit, Thou didst make him valiant, wise, and loyal; and when he had suffered much, and encountered the cruel hatred of many enemies, didst give him the victory, and seat him on his throne in peace and glory.

And thus it was that Thou didst foreshow how thy dear Son Jesus should endure many afflictions, and, having been made perfect by suffering, should be crowned with glory everlasting. In Him is our hope. In Him thy people are a chosen generation, a royal priesthood, a nation of kings. Grant us, therefore, O Lord, both the will and the strength to follow Him whithersoever it may be his good pleasure to call us. Let us never be unfaithful to Him, nor ashamed to confess that we serve and adore a crucified Saviour. Suffer us not to shrink from bearing the burdens or exercising the patience and humility which may show that we are his.

Mercifully be with us in all the sacred duties and engagements of this day. Help us in all our infirmities, that we may worship Thee in spirit and in truth, and receive with meekness the lessons of thy Word. Give us, we beseech Thee, the hearing ear and the understanding heart, and grant that every Lord's Day may find us holier and wiser, increasing in spiritual strength, and having a deeper experience of thy saving power and love. Mightily, O God, work in the hearts of men. By thy Spirit awaken the careless, and arouse the slumbering. Convince sinners of their sins; humble them in godly sorrow; melt their hearts by thy love; and show them the grace and sufficiency of Jesus Christ. Inspire thy ministers with a holy boldness, and cause thy Word from their lips to be a means of blessing and comfort to many. Guide those who are in error into the way of truth. Assist all Sunday-school teachers in their labours. Be with all missionaries and churches in other lands, and make them lights to reflect thy glory.

Lord, have mercy and help us, according to thy great love in Jesus Christ our Lord. Amen.

O GOD our Father, at the close of the Sabbath we gratefully acknowledge thy goodness in sending to us the ministry of thy Word. We thank Thee that thy servants preach unto us Jesus Christ, and Him crucified. Grant, we beseech Thee, that these precious truths may come in demonstration of the Spirit and of power. Under their influence may we grow up into Christ, be made wise unto salvation, and fruitful in every good work. And if to-night our minds are darkened, so that we discover not the beauties of Jesus and the greatness of his salvation, O Eternal Spirit, who searchest all things, yea, the deep things of God, reveal them unto us. Make us to know the things that are fully given to us of God. In the Lord Jesus may we have righteousness and strength. Through Him give us to enjoy a happy sense of sins forgiven, the entire renewal of the heart, and a lively hope of everlasting glory. And may we know nothing among men, as the ground of our hope, as the source of our blessing, save Jesus Christ, and Him crucified.

We praise and glorify Thee for all the privileges of this day. Blessed be the Lord for these days of rest! We would examine ourselves to-night, in thy presence, as to the spirit we have cultivated, and the improvement we have made. O God, Thou knowest whether or not we have called the Sabbath a delight, the holy of the Lord, honourable. Thine omniscient eye has seen much sin in our services — we have in many respects been doing our own ways, or finding our own pleasure, or speaking our own words: Lord, we humbly confess the sin, and pray for pardon. Even before we retire to rest, be merciful unto us, and bless us with full and free forgiveness; and help us to carry through the week the hallowing influences of thy grace. May thy Word dwell richly in our hearts in all wisdom. In all the circumstances of life may we do justly, love mercy, and walk humbly with our God. And if we should never see another earthly Sabbath, oh, may we be fitted for an eternal Sabbath at thy right hand.

We pray for all congregations that have been assembled in thy name. Send upon them showers of blessing. And may all Christian efforts be rendered effectual to the pulling down of the strongholds of sin.

We commit ourselves, our relatives, and friends, to thine especial care. O Thou that keepest Israel, defend us from all harm. Evermore give us thy grace; and when we have served Thee and our generations according to thy will, may we have an entrance ministered unto us abundantly into thine everlasting kingdom, through Jesus Christ our Lord. Amen.

[Morning.] **THIRTY-FIFTH WEEK.—MONDAY.** [Evening.

READ IN HOLY SCRIPTURE 1 SAMUEL XXVIII.

HOLY, holy, holy, Lord God of Hosts: heaven and earth are full of thy glory. Glory be to Thee, O Lord, most high. We praise and thank Thee for thy protecting care over us during the past night, and for the light of another day. But more especially do we praise Thee for that revelation which Thou hast given us to be a light to our feet, and a lamp for our paths. Oh, let thy Word find a fruitful place in our hearts, and make it to be continually profitable to us for doctrine, for reproof, for correction, for instruction in righteousness. Therein are set forth for our profit the lives of men of old time: give us grace to follow the examples of the good, and to take warning by those whose ways bear testimony that they departed from Thee, and provoked thy righteous indignation. O Lord, leave us not to ourselves, nor to the power of the great enemy of our souls; and make us to know not only that it is by grace we are saved, but that it is by grace we also stand; else we, like others, may commit the very sins which we once abhorred, and run the risk of being left to the counsels of our own hearts, and of the spirit that worketh in the children of disobedience. Forbid that we should seek for the living amongst the dead; and, while we duly prize the advice of the holy and the good, let us look only to Thee for wisdom and infallible truth; and, coming to thy lively oracles, may we always find in them a word in season. Let us not be wise in our own eyes, or prudent in our own sight; and do Thou give us not only contrite hearts, but also humble spirits, meekly to receive the engrafted Word, which is able to save our souls. Daily and hourly beset with spiritual enemies, help us to fight against them in thy strength, and in the persuasion that as our day, so shall our strength be. Bring constantly to our remembrance that Scripture which saith, " Cursed be the man which trusteth in man, and maketh flesh his arm, and whose heart departeth from that Lord ; " " Blessed is the man that trusteth in the Lord, and whose hope the Lord is."

We bless Thee that Thou hast reconciled the world unto Thyself through thy dear Son, and that through Him we can ask all the blessings which we require. Be with us throughout this day. Suffer us not to fall into sin, or to run into any kind of danger; but let all our doings be ordered by thy governance, to do always that which is righteous in thy sight. Bless our relatives, our acquaintances, and our neighbours. Bless our country, and the rulers thereof. Guide them in their councils and overrule their plans for good. Let thy blessing rest on all, O Lord, and thy Word be glorified. We ask all through Jesus Christ our Lord. Amen.

READ IN HOLY SCRIPTURE 1 CORINTHIANS III.

MERCIFUL Lord! the God and Father of our Lord Jesus Christ, we praise Thee for the great goodness vouchsafed us this day. Thy love has spared us. Thy bounty has satisfied our wants. Thy watchful care has preserved our going out and coming in. Well may our hearts rejoice to feel that it is in Thee we live, and move, and have our being; that Thou, Lord, dost compass us with thy favour as with a shield.

But, Lord, we are often so engrossed and overwhelmed with the cares and struggles of this life that we forget how our Father knoweth what things we have need of; and in our weakness, resting upon an arm of flesh, we neglect Thee, our God, days without number. Oh, quicken us by thy Holy Spirit!—draw us, and we will run after Thee. Help us to rest in thy faithful love.

O Lord, Thou knowest us altogether. How solemn is this thought when we look forward to the great day of account! Then shall every man's work be declared of what sort it is. Give us grace so to live that we may look up in that day, with holy confidence. Let us not deceive ourselves with a name to live while we are dead in trespasses and sins. Let us not be content with a form of godliness. Give us the indwelling, humbling, renewing grace of thy Holy Spirit. Alas, Lord! how little we know ourselves! How often the pride and selfishness of the carnal heart intrudes into our holy things! Oh, for the outpouring of the Holy Spirit, that his grace in us may be exceeding abundant in faith and love towards Jesus Christ; that we may grow up into Him our head, in whom we have redemption through his blood.

Adorable Redeemer, head over all things to thy Church, look upon thy people. Glorify thy grace in the growing consistency of those who are called by that name. Stir up the love and zeal of thy people for the spread of the Gospel. Have compassion on the multitudes who are in darkness and unbelief—some in our own families, many round about us. O Lord, let not our inconsistencies be stumbling-blocks to any of them. Rather, through thy grace, may our light so shine, that they may glorify our God and Saviour in seeking and embracing the great salvation.

Gracious Father, we ask thy blessing upon the sick and afflicted, the destitute and the tried. Visit them especially with thy salvation. Uphold them by thy good Spirit. Comfort, strengthen, and in thine own time relieve them.

And now we yield ourselves to Thee. Watch over us and all whom we would specially remember at thy footstool this night. Keep us, bless us, give us refreshing sleep, O our God, through Jesus Christ our adorable Redeemer. Amen.

[MORNING.]   THIRTY-FIFTH WEEK.—TUESDAY.   [EVENING.

READ IN HOLY SCRIPTURE 1 SAMUEL XXXI.

O LORD, the Almighty Creator of all things in heaven and earth, whose ever-present providence supplies the wants of all which thy hand hath made, Thou art our God, and we will exalt Thee; Thou art our God, and we will praise thy name. Wonderful art Thou in thy dealings unto the children of men. Thou hatest nothing that Thou hast made, and even when we were yet sinners, Thou didst look down in tender compassion, and, through thy dear Son, redeem and save us. Adored be thy glorious name for thy saving grace. Lord, cause the remembrance of this thy great mercy, and the daily experience we have of thy goodness and care, to quicken our souls with grateful affection towards Thee. Oh, prevent us by thy grace from adding to all our many sins the grievous sin of unthankfulness! Take away the blindness of our hearts, and unfold to us all the riches of thy grace, that we may know the love of Christ, which passeth knowledge, and be filled with all the fulness of God.

Gracious Father, be with us, we beseech Thee, this day, and guide our wayward hearts in the paths of righteousness and truth. Cause the warnings of thy Word to awaken in us a holy fear, lest we, too, should fall from our steadfastness, and incur thy righteous displeasure. In thy favour alone is life and peace. If Thou cast us off, we perish. Help us, then, to walk circumspectly, not as fools, but as wise, that we grieve not thy Spirit, and quench his light within us. In faith we desire to live, seeing Thee, who art invisible, ever about our path, a very present help in the hour of need. Looking up to Jesus, our all-prevailing Mediator and Intercessor, enable us to lay aside every weight, and the sin which easily besets us, and to run with patience the race which is set before us. Guard us, we pray Thee, against the assaults of the great enemy, the temptations of the world, and the deceitfulness of our own hearts. Let not sin bring us under its power to-day, but give us strength to resist and overcome.

We earnestly implore thy grace and blessing on behalf of all who are dear to us. Merciful God and Father, teach them by thy Spirit, and by thy Word, and by the lessons of thy providence. Let not one of them be deaf to thy voice, or receive thy grace in vain. We pray that they may all find Christ, and be found of Him; and that under the protection of thy providence, and the guidance of thy Spirit, they and we may tread the narrow way of life in faith and love, ever pressing onward towards the end. Speed this day the work of thy Gospel, and make it the power of God to the salvation and comfort of many hearts. We ask all in the name of Jesus Christ our Lord. Amen.

READ IN HOLY SCRIPTURE 1 CORINTHIANS IV.

O GOD, our Father, whose merciful providence has kept us through this day, now that its work is done, and we are brought again together to read thy Word and worship Thee, enable us to render hearty thanks for all thy great goodness towards us. In Thee we live, and move, and have our being; from Thee has come every blessing which has been ours this day. Whatever success has attended us, whatever power we have had to resist sin, or to live as followers of Jesus, has been thy gift, and for these do we render thanks; but most of all for thy revealed Word, for the gift of thy Son, and for the knowledge of thy free forgiveness and ready help to all who seek Thee in simple trust on Him.

It is in the strength of that knowledge and of this truth that we are bold to come unto Thee; for when we remember our shortcomings and errors, the wanderings of our hearts this day, our shrinking from honest service before Thee, and our actual transgressions of thy law, we are convinced of our unworthiness to claim any good at thy hands. But we come to Thee, as to our Father in Christ Jesus, knowing that in Him Thou art willing to hear, and to bless; and we ask Thee, for his sake, to pardon all our sins, all wherein we have this day offended, all in which we have done evil, or neglected to do good. Help us to search our hearts, and to try ourselves by the standard of thy Word. Save us from carelessness, from the folly which shuns self-examination, or strives to make little of sin, and give us courage and faithfulness to bring ourselves to the light, that, learning our own weakness, we may the more earnestly seek thy grace and promised help.

We are thy stewards, O God. Time, talent, strength, opportunity to do good, and power of example are given by Thee, that we may in them glorify Thee. O Thou who searchest the heart, forgive us all the error of the past, and quicken us by thy Spirit, that we may be found faithful in the time to come. Help us to care more and to do more for the spread of thy Gospel. May the Spirit of our Master stir our hearts with earnest desire for the salvation of sinners. Prosper all efforts to make known the name and love of Jesus. Wherever the good seed is sown, in church or school, abroad or at home, may thy blessing give the increase. Have mercy on our country; may thy Word have free course and be glorified among us. Have pity on all who are in trouble, and sanctify to them their trials. And now, O Father, we commit to Thee ourselves and all our friends and neighbours; keep us during the night, and raise us up to live to thy glory for Jesus' sake. Amen.

[Morning.] **THIRTY-FIFTH WEEK.—WEDNESDAY.** [Evening.

READ IN HOLY SCRIPTURE 2 SAMUEL I.

READ IN HOLY SCRIPTURE 1 CORINTHIANS V.

GRACIOUS God, to whom we come this morning in the name of our Lord and Saviour Jesus Christ, mercifully hear our prayer and accept our thanksgiving. Thou hast been pleased to preserve us in safety through the darkness of the night, and hast gathered us together now at the throne of thy heavenly grace : and not unto us, but to thy name be the glory, for we have not merited these favours at thy holy hand. Grant us grateful hearts, O Lord; especially make us thankful for thy Holy Word ; may it be a light to our foot and a lamp to our path, to show us the way in which we ought to walk, until we see Thee in the blessed world above, where Christ sitteth at the right hand of God.

Bless to our edification the Scripture we have just read, and hasten the time when nation shall not lift up sword against nation, neither shall they learn war any more. Let mourning and weeping, lamentation and woe, come to an end under the reign of the ever blessed Prince of Peace. Give the King thy judgments, O God, and thy righteousness unto the King's Son. Let Him have dominion from sea to sea, and from the river unto the ends of the earth. We adore Thee for the promise that his name shall endure for ever, that men shall be blessed in Him, and that all nations shall call Him blessed. Help us to love Him whose love to us is wonderful, and to rejoice that He dieth no more, but ever liveth to make intercession for us. Search us and try us by thy Holy Spirit, O God, and root up from our hearts every plant which Thou hast not planted; strengthen faith, and love, and every grace within us, that we may bring forth fruit to thy glory by Jesus Christ ; and purify us to Thyself, that we may show forth thy praise. May we be jealous of thine honour, over remembering that we are not our own, but bought with a price, even the precious blood of Christ, who gave Himself for us, that he might bring us to God.

Mercifully keep us in the narrow way this day. If tempted, let us not yield to temptation. If troubled, do Thou strengthen and uphold us. In thy mercy forgive all our many sins against Thee. And let us receive every gift of providence which Thou mayest give us this day as a fresh proof of thy fatherly kindness in Christ Jesus. Give us this day our daily bread ; enable us to hold fast the Word of truth among all with whom Thou mayest bring us in contact ; prosper the work of our hands upon us ; give peace in our hearts and peace in our dwelling; make all things work together for our good; according to thy gracious promise, to those who love Thee; and do all this for the sake of our ever blessed Lord and Saviour Jesus Christ, to whom be glory and praise for ever and ever. Amen.

MOST gracious God, we bless Thee for the assurance of thy Word that Christ our Passover is sacrificed for us. May we constantly feel that we have an interest in the atonement for sin which he has offered, and which Thou hast accepted. Vouchsafe to us all the benefits of his passion, and fill us with peace and joy by believing in Him. Oh, show unto us that the evils of our nature can only be overcome by the power of Christ. Help us to purge out the old leaven of corruption, and do Thou make us new creatures in Christ Jesus. Give us grace to put off concerning the former conversation the old man, which is corrupt according to the deceitful lusts, and be renewed in the spirit of our minds ; and to put on the new man, which after God is created in righteousness and true holiness. May we ever remember that the grace of God that bringeth salvation hath appeared to all men, teaching us that, denying ungodliness and worldly lusts, we should live soberly, righteously, and godly, in this present world.

Through our Saviour's atoning merit we have been preserved during another day. Make us deeply penitent in the review of its sins and neglected opportunities. Forgive the evil thoughts and conversations in which we have indulged. Blot out from thy book and memory our forgetfulness of Thee. Graciously accept our desires and efforts to promote thy glory, and mercifully fulfil thy promise that those who sow in tears shall reap in joy.

Bestow thy blessing upon all for whom we should pray. May the Holy Spirit be largely given to the churches. Unite the hearts of all Christians, and make them zealous for the spread of the Gospel. Bless all missionary enterprises with great success. Be gracious to all godly ministers, and render their word effectual to salvation.

Look upon the land of our birth, and make us a holy people. Be merciful to all classes of our population. Bless our soldiers and seamen. Establish among us the gift of peace, and establish unity and concord on the earth. Comfort the poor and the afflicted in their sorrow. Cause the widows to trust in Thee ; and be Thou a Father to the fatherless.

And now, O God of mercy, make us thankful for so large an exemption from the trials which many suffer, and for so large a possession of the comforts which many do not enjoy. Watch over our persons and dwelling during this night. Renew our physical and mental strength for future duty, and bring us and ours to the house not made with hands, eternal in the heavens, through Jesus Christ our Lord, to whom, with Thee and the Holy Spirit, be everlasting praise. Amen.

[Morning.] THIRTY-FIFTH WEEK.—THURSDAY. [Evening.

READ IN HOLY SCRIPTURE 2 SAMUEL VI.

O ETERNAL God, heaven and earth are full of thy glory. Holy and reverend is thy name, and we are unworthy to take it on our lips, or to come into thy presence. Thou art, indeed, gracious and merciful, and thy tender pity to us is shown by daily mercies, and above all in the gift of Jesus Christ to be the Redeemer of the world. We adore Thee for thy goodness, and we pray that an abiding sense of it may ever be in our hearts. We thank Thee also for thy preserving care during the past night. Thy hand has been over us while we slept. To Thee be all the praise for the health and strength which Thou hast bestowed, and for the blessings which have been renewed to us this morning. O God, dwell in us by thy Holy Spirit, and enable us to consecrate life and all its powers to thy service. Deepen in our hearts the conviction that we are not our own, but thine; that we are bought with a price, even with the precious blood of Jesus. In the remembrance of this, we pray that our wills may be conformed to thine, and that in the station of life in which Thou hast placed us we may truly and godly serve Thee.

We confess our sinfulness before Thee. Alike by things done and things left undone, we transgress thy commandments. Merciful Father, for thy name's sake pardon our iniquity, for it is great; and grant us the assurance of forgiveness. Cause us to hate sin as Thou hatest it, and enable us to watch against it with a holy jealousy. Guard and keep us this day from its power and dominion, that we may not wilfully offend Thee, or do wrong in thought, word, or deed to our fellow-creatures. Awaken in us a love for what is just and truthful, and grant that in all our intercourse with others to-day, at home and abroad, we may not bring reproach on thy name by inconsistency, but adorn the Gospel of Christ in all things. Preserve us from the fear of the world. Inspire us with the courage which springs from the fear and love of Thee. Make us zealous for thy honour, and ready cheerfully to confess Thee at all times, careless of the smile or the frown of men. Gladden our hearts by the assurance of thy love and of thy protection, that we may cheerfully show forth thy praise.

We commend all whom we love to thy gracious care. Convert such of them as are unconverted, and reveal unto them thy power and grace in Christ Jesus. Draw the hearts of the young to Thee in their youth, and make the hoary head a crown of righteousness. Make the name of Jesus a praise in the earth, and hasten the coming in of thy kingdom.

Have mercy upon us, and bless us in all things, for thy dear Son's sake. Amen.

READ IN HOLY SCRIPTURE 1 CORINTHIANS VI.

O MIGHTY God, Thou art of purer eyes than to behold evil, and canst not look on iniquity. We confess that we have fallen by sin, and our bodies and spirits, which were formed to be the temples of thy praise, have been all defiled. We adore the exceeding riches of thy grace, by which Thou hast redeemed us from the power of darkness, and we most earnestly pray that we may now appear before Thee, washed, and sanctified, and justified, in the name of the Lord Jesus, and by the Spirit of our God. Bought with the precious blood of Christ, make us daily and hourly to feel that we are not our own, that we are not the world's, but thine, and thine alone, for time and for eternity. May our lives testify that we are Christ's, that we have received his Spirit, and walk in his steps. Give unto us, O Lord, the gentleness of Jesus, that we may overcome evil with good, and thus be preserved from all strife and envying. Teach us to take wrong rather than do it, and always to prefer affliction to sin. Give unto us, O Lord, the purity of Jesus, that our minds and bodies may not fall under the power of intemperance or uncleanness. Preserve us from impure thoughts and unholy practices. When we are tempted, supply us with strength to resist, and grace to overcome.

We mourn that while we thus bow down before Thee, multitudes of our fellow-creatures are dishonouring Thee, and provoking thine indignation by abominable vices. Lord, have mercy upon them, and recover them from their evil doings. We confess that it is only by Thee that we are kept from running in the ways of death. Keep us by thy mighty power, even unto the end.

We beseech Thee, O our God, to cleanse our country from those dreadful crimes which dishonour thy name. Bless every effort that is made to raise the fallen, to restore the wandering, and to preserve the weak. Bless our young men and maidens, and turn their feet from the paths of the destroyer. Let our sons be as plants grown up in their youth, and our daughters as the polished corners of the temple. Forgive us, O Lord, wherein we have this day, in thought, word, or deed, sinned against Thee, and ever grant us grace to glorify Thee in our body and our spirit, which are thine. Protect us while we sleep, restore our exhausted strength, and let us rise on the morrow to serve Thee in newness of life. Look down, O Lord, upon all the afflicted, and hear their cry. Be with the watchers of the night; and whether they pace our streets, or sail on the ocean, or guard the sick, give them pleasant thoughts of Thee and of thy protecting care. We ask all in Jesus' name. Amen.

[Morning.] **THIRTY-FIFTH WEEK.—FRIDAY.** [Evening.

READ IN HOLY SCRIPTURE PSALM XXIV.

ALMIGHTY God, Lord of heaven and earth, we approach Thee, in the name of our Advocate, Jesus Christ, the Righteous One, and for his sake we beseech Thee to grant that the words of our mouth and the meditation of our heart may be acceptable in thy sight.

We confess, O Lord, our sins against Thee; we acknowledge ourselves unworthy the least of thy mercies, and plead for pardon, and the continuance of our blessings, temporal and spiritual, only for the merit of our Redeemer.

The earth, O Lord, is full of thy goodness, and thy mercy is over all thy works. Supply our temporal wants as seemeth good in thy sight, teaching us, in having food and raiment, therewith to be content. Above all, make us to hunger and thirst after righteousness, and satisfy our souls with the bread of life. Enable us in all our actions this day to maintain pure hands, and in all our thoughts a pure heart. Give us an abiding sense of thy presence and nearness to us; may we do all as in thy sight, and with a single eye to thy glory.

Strengthen us against the vanities of the world, the deceitfulness of our own heart, and the devices and assaults of Satan. Increase our love to the Scriptures, and help us to study them more prayerfully and diligently. In time of danger and difficulty, let thy Word be a light unto our feet, and a lantern to our path, and in times of sorrow the joy of our heart. Bless each member of our family, both present and absent. Thou knowest, O Lord, the circumstances of each one, for unto Thee all hearts are open, all desires known, and no secrets are hid. Adapt thy blessings to their several wants, granting to us and them, in this world, a saving knowledge of thy truth, and in the world to come life everlasting.

We desire, also, to offer up prayers and giving of thanks for all men; for our Sovereign, and all that are in authority, that we may lead a quiet and peaceable life, in all godliness and honesty. Comfort, O Lord, those in trouble, support the feebleminded, supply the wants of the poor, and have mercy upon all men.

Bless the whole Church of God with the spirit of grace, unity, and concord. Prosper the preaching of the Gospel in all lands, and prepare us to share in the Redeemer's glory and kingdom. Make us to watch and wait for Christ's appearing, that when He shall come and knock, He may find us ready. Be at our right hand, O Lord, to-day, and suffer us not to be drawn aside from the path of duty. Pardon our ignorances and shortcomings, and deal with us according to thine own riches in glory. Hear us, O God, Thou King of Glory, for the sake of Jesus Christ our Lord. Amen.

READ IN HOLY SCRIPTURE 1 CORINTHIANS X.

O GOD, the Lord, the Holy One of Israel, Thou art glorious in holiness, and Thou art glorious also in love. Blessed be Thou, O Lord, for the boundless mercy which from day to day Thou showest us in the Gospel of thy Son. Oh, that thy goodness to us may teach us to love Thee with all the heart.

Thou knowest them that trust in Thee. Thy people are thy peculiar care upon earth. The pillar of thy presence is with them that fear Thee, and Thou givest them manna from heaven, and water out of the Rock. Bless us with this guidance, then we shall never wander; and with this provision; then we shall never faint. May we never forget what thou canst do for us, but remember it, and confide in it with thankfulness. May we never cease to fear lest, a promise being left us of entering into rest, any of us should seem to come short of it; and may this godly fear make us depart from all waywardness and unbelief, and cleave to Thee with full purpose of heart.

Help us, O God, to live agreeably to our profession. Help us to walk worthy of the vocation wherewith we are called. Help us to shun all alliance with the world, and to stand fast in the communion of saints. Enable us to show our Christian principle in all things, and, when the good of others calls for self-denial on our part, may we deny ourselves cheerfully for others' sakes. As we have received Christ Jesus the Lord, so may we walk in Him, rooted and built up in Him, and established in the faith, as we have been taught, abounding therein with thanksgiving.

O Lord, we come unto Thee: we look unto Thee for help and succour. Be Thou a Father to us: make us thy children, and nurture and train us up in righteousness. Be Thou a Shepherd over us: make us the sheep in thy fold, and lead us to the green pastures and still waters of thy gracious promises. Be Thou our Deliverer, our Saviour, our Redeemer; redeem us from all iniquity, and purify us unto Thyself a peculiar people, zealous of good works.

Increase our faith and confirm our hope in Thee evermore. Clothe us with that charity that never faileth, and work in us that poverty of spirit unto which thou hast promised the vision of Thyself; as we hope for mercy, enable us also to show mercy and be kind.

And now, O Lord, receive us graciously, and watch over us throughout the night, as Thou hast throughout the day. Grant that we may sleep in peace, and rise with renewed strength to the activities of to-morrow. This and every other petition we present for Jesus Christ's sake. Amen.

[MORNING.] **THIRTY-FIFTH WEEK.—SATURDAY.** [EVENING.]

READ IN HOLY SCRIPTURE 2 SAMUEL VII.

LOOK down, O Lord God, from thy holy place, and open thine ear to our prayer. Help us, O God of our salvation, and let the light of thy countenance shine upon us. Thou hast indeed been gracious unto us. We desire to acknowledge thy hand and to trace thy love in all that befalls us day by day, and in the Divine protection which guards us from evil night by night. What are we, and what is our house, that Thou hast so graciously dealt with us? Enable us ever to be thankful for all things—for a quiet and peaceful home, for religious privilege and opportunity, for thy Holy Word, and the unsearchable riches of Christ Jesus. By the experience of thy goodness, kindle in our hearts a fervent zeal for thy glory, that we may honour Thee by our obedience to thy will, and the consecration to Thee of all which Thou hast given us.

As Thou hast preserved us through the night, we pray that thy blessing may be upon us during the day. We are set in the midst of many and great dangers, and by reason of the frailty of our nature we are continually liable to fall. In Thee alone is our help and strength; only as Thou keepest us shall we be safe, either from the temptations of the world and the devil, or from the sinfulness of our own hearts. Merciful Father, be Thou near us all the day. Leave us not to ourselves, but by thy Spirit teach and guide us. Whatever our hands find to do, we would do it with our might, and be diligent in every good word and work. In the calling and occupation of life to which thy providence hath appointed us, may we have peace and strength to serve Thee. Preserve us from everything that is inconsistent with a Christian profession; and when we are tempted to wander from the path of holiness, let thy restraining and preserving grace keep us in safety, and cause us to maintain our steadfastness. Oh, that by thy help we may strive in all things to have a conscience void of offence towards God and man, and in the full assurance of thy forgiveness may boldly and faithfully set our faces against whatever would dishonour Thee, or hinder thy Gospel in the world around us.

Be merciful, O God, to this fallen world. Oh, snatch many souls this day like brands from the burning. Send home thy Word with power to the hearts of those who shall hear it. Glorify thy dear Son by drawing the sinful and guilty in increasing numbers to his cross. We commend to Thee our friends and relatives. Do for them according to thy great mercy, and grant them thy Holy Spirit, to enlighten and sanctify them, and prepare them for thy kingdom. For thy dear Son's sake hear us, and to Thee shall be honour and praise for evermore. Amen.

READ IN HOLY SCRIPTURE 1 CORINTHIANS XI. 17—34.

O GOD of truth and mercy, who art the same yesterday, to-day, and for ever, and whose unfailing compassions abound to the guilty and the unworthy, inspire our hearts with a simple and trusting faith. Draw us by thy Spirit, and give us real communion with Thee in this our evening worship. Preserve us from wandering and sinful thoughts, and cause the remembrance of thy great majesty and glory to make us reverent and humble in thy presence. It is in the name of thy dear Son that we approach Thee. Only through the precious merits of his blood do we hope for acceptance; and through his perpetual intercessions we look for an answer to our prayers.

O Lord, convince us deeply of our sin. Enable us to search our own hearts, and in thy light to see the guiltiness, and impurity, and worldliness which are in us. So by thy Spirit teach us our own coldness of affection towards Thee, and the imperfection of our obedience, that we may be ashamed and blush for our many transgressions. We feel, O God, that we do not know all the evil of sin, and how it grieves thy Spirit and puts our Saviour, who died for us, to shame. Lord Jesus, wash us in thy blood, and make us by thy power and grace free from the bondage of sin and Satan.

We praise Thee for countless mercies. Thou art indeed most merciful to us, and we pray for grace and strength of purpose, that we may show our thankfulness in deeds as well as in words. Add to the blessings of the week now past the blessing of thy favour and protection through this night. In the silence and darkness of the night, let thine unslumbering care be round about us. Prepare us for the thankful enjoyment of the rest and the spiritual privileges of the Lord's day. We desire, O Lord, that all our spiritual engagements may be carried on with a believing heart. Give us courage to examine ourselves whether our repentance and faith be indeed sincere and truthful, and our waiting upon Thee be really with a desire for spiritual blessing. Teach us that Thou art an holy God, and that Thou requirest truth in the inward parts.

Prepare thy ministers and all who shall be engaged in teaching the young or the afflicted for their special work. Pour out thy Spirit abundantly upon them, and make them a blessing in the earth. We pray for all who are engaged as evangelists in heathen lands or among thine ancient people. Oh, let the time to favour Zion come. Gather in thine elect from the nations of the earth, and hasten the day when the glory of the Lord shall be revealed, and all flesh shall see it together. Hear us, O God and Father, for Jesus Christ's sake. Amen.

[MORNING.] **THIRTY-SIXTH WEEK.—LORD'S DAY.** [EVENING.

READ IN HOLY SCRIPTURE 2 SAMUEL XII. 1—23.   READ IN HOLY SCRIPTURE 1 CORINTHIANS XII.

O LORD, our heavenly Father, who hast caused all Holy Scriptures to be written for our learning, impress on our minds what we have now read. May we learn, from the grievous fall of thy servant David, ever to remember our own weakness, and to watch and pray, that we enter not into temptation. We thank Thee if Thou hast kept us from sins which would have ruined our peace, and brought dishonour on our Christian profession. But, when we review our past lives, we feel how often and how grievously we have offended against thy holy laws. We have done those things that we ought not to have done, and we have left undone those things that we ought to have done. Sin has mingled with our best actions, and we are altogether as an unclean thing. Have mercy upon us, O God, according to thy loving-kindness; according to the multitude of thy tender mercies, blot out all our iniquities. Wash us in that blood which cleanseth from all sin. Create in us clean hearts, O God, and renew a right spirit within us. Strengthen us with all might by the power of thy Holy Spirit, that we may be able to resist all the wiles of the devil, all the temptations of this wicked world, and all the evil desires of our own corrupt hearts.

We thank Thee for the spiritual privileges of this holy day. Enable us to spend it in thy faith and fear. We desire to feel thy presence in the house of prayer, and to find it the very gate of heaven. Pour out thy Spirit on our own hearts and on the hearts of all who worship with us. Shed thy richest blessings on thy Church, and increase the faith and zeal of thy people. Grant that the name of thy dear Son may be exalted, and that this day He may see abundantly of the travail of his soul. Strengthen the hands of thy ministers, and make them a blessing to all who hear thy Word at their lips. Lord, we pray for the day when thy purposes of mercy shall be fulfilled, and the whole earth be filled with thy glory.

We thank Thee for thy great goodness to us throughout all our past lives. Thou hast given us food and raiment, and unnumbered mercies, temporal and spiritual, of the least of which we are unworthy. Oh, give us grateful hearts, that we may show forth thy praise, not with our lips only, but in our lives, even by giving up ourselves to thy service.

We pray not for ourselves alone, but for all who are near and dear to us. May all whom we love be loved of Thee; may they be bound with us in the Lamb's bundle of life, and be heirs with us of the heavenly inheritance.

All these blessings we ask in the name and for the sake of our Lord Jesus Christ. Amen.

HELP us, O Lord, in approaching thy mercy-seat, to come with lively faith in the intercession of Jesus, our exalted Redeemer. Whilst we confess our unworthiness to come into thy presence, and deplore our sinfulness, enable us to look to Him who died for our sins, and rose again for our justification.

We bless Thee that our adorable Lord, after He had made atonement for our sins, ascended to thy right hand; that He is there a Prince and a Saviour, to give repentance and remission of sins, to receive gifts for men, even for the rebellious; and we praise Thee that Thou hast given unto us pastors and teachers, for the perfecting of the saints, for the work of the ministry, for the edifying of the body of Christ. We adore Thee for the bounty with which Thou hast scattered spiritual blessings on the children of men, and that the same Spirit through whose power marvellous works were wrought in the early Church is given to enlighten and to sanctify our hearts, and to lead us into the truth of thy Word. May we ever be under the influence of thy Holy Spirit, so that we may not only confess with the lip, but with the heart, that "Jesus is the Lord;" and may our lives testify that we have been with Him, and learnt of Him.

As members of the body of Christ, help us to promote the well-being of our brethren; and, however humble our place in thy Church, may we be filled with the spirit of Jesus, our Head, so that we may have sympathy with those who are called to suffer. Preserve us from living to ourselves, and as we have opportunity, help us to do good unto all men, especially unto those who are of the household of faith. May thy Church be more united in spirit, and more manifestly one before men.

We have to thank Thee for the mercies and privileges of another Christian Sabbath. May this day not close without thy blessing on its engagements. Grant that the truths of thy Word to which we have listened may have an abiding place in all our hearts; enable us to carry into all the pursuits of this week the sacred influences of thy house; and as Sabbaths come to us and pass away, may we be gaining fitness for the eternal Sabbath of heaven, the rest which remains for the people of God.

We implore thy blessing to rest upon our friends and relatives. Fill them with thy grace, and bring them with us into thy glory. Gracious God and Father, we are unworthy in thy sight, but do Thou have mercy upon us and hear us, according to thy blessed promises in Jesus Christ our Lord. Amen.

[Morning.] THIRTY-SIXTH WEEK.—MONDAY. [Evening.

READ IN HOLY SCRIPTURE 2 SAMUEL XV. 13–37.

O GOD, who art the Great and the Holy God, we bow down to worship Thee; and we pray that Thou wouldst write upon our minds the teachings of thy Word. We rejoice to learn how thine ancient servants, under the pressure of their sorrows, drew near to Thee. They knew that thine eyes were over the righteous, and thine ears open to their prayers; and when they poured out their hearts before Thee, they found that Thou, Lord, wast a shield for them, their glory, and the lifter up of their heads. Help us, like them, in all times of our trouble, to trust in the Lord with all our hearts, and lean not unto our own understanding. Thou hast taught us to expect great tribulation in our pathway to the kingdom; for many are the afflictions of the righteous. But salvation belongeth unto the Lord: thy blessing is upon thy people. We therefore cry unto Thee, O Lord; do Thou hear us out of thy holy hill. May all our doings be in humble imitation of the meek and lowly Jesus, who when He was reviled reviled not again; when He suffered He threatened not, but committed Himself to Him that judgeth righteously.

Another Sabbath has gone, for ever gone; and we are about to engage in the concerns of life. Be pleased to give us right motives in every act that we perform this day, and may we always be governed by the blessed principle of love to God. We would not be slothful in business; but oh, for fervour of spirit in the service of the Lord! Let not the good seed of the Word, which on the past Sabbath was sown in our hearts, be choked by the cares of the world, the deceitfulness of riches, or the pleasures of this life. And amidst the varying circumstances of the world, may our hearts find refuge and hope in an ever present Saviour.

We pray not for ourselves only, but for all that are associated with us by family ties. May all that we love be loved by Jesus! Guide them all by thy counsel. As a family may we pass safely and happily through the scenes of the present life, till all are brought in triumph to eternal life.

And now, O Thou holy God, we make humble confession to Thee of our unnumbered sins. Thou hast seen all the actions of our lives, all the principles and feelings of our hearts, all the tempers that we have displayed, and all our omissions of duty. We deserve thy wrath, but spare us, good Lord. Be merciful to us through the death and intercession of our blessed Saviour, and through this day give us the testimony of an approving conscience, and the smile of an approving God.

We ask these and all other mercies through Jesus Christ our Lord. Amen.

READ IN HOLY SCRIPTURE 1 CORINTHIANS XIII.

WE thank Thee, O heavenly Father, with reverent joy and hope, for all the blessings assured us by the Gospel; but especially do we desire to glorify Thee as revealed to us in thy dear Son. Humbly, O Lord, we pray for the forgiveness of all our sins, and to be made partakers of the inheritance of thy children. Humbly do we seek to enjoy such fellowship with Jesus, that as, by the indwelling of his Spirit, the life of our souls is renewed day by day, so we may experience more and more the influence of divine charity, inclining us to do all things acceptable in thy sight.

We confess that we are often tempted to resist and set aside thy holy teachings. We come to Thee with offerings, of great price in our reckoning, but rejected by Thee because not the offerings of love. So help and enlighten us, O Lord, that we may no longer offend Thee by thus substituting an earthly oblation for the spiritual sacrifice of ourselves. But enable us so to employ all that we are and have to thy honour, and the benefit of our neighbour, that whatever we do or offer may tend to the accomplishing of the designs of thy mercy.

We know, O God, how impossible it is, by any thought or virtue of our own, to subdue the evil which is in us. But nothing is impossible with Thee. Thou canst give us the victory over all our sins and infirmities. Let, then, the power of thy Word so prevail in us, that all covetous desires, all reserves and exceptions to the forgiveness of injuries, all envy and boastfulness, with every other indulgence of a base selfishness, may cease in us through the power of divine charity.

Thus let thy grace work in us, O Lord, for the sake of Jesus; then will that mind be in us which was in Him. Then, too, may we look to become wise as well as holy; and we shall no longer think or understand as children only, but as those who are growing up to the measure of Christ's stature. We acknowledge that, as yet, the eyes of our understanding are very weak and dim. The promised land of peace and joy is seen but through a glass darkly. We discern not yet the rays of thy glory in the face of Jesus Christ. To the pure in heart only is granted this heavenly vision. Therefore we beseech Thee, O most gracious and compassionate Father, make us pure, and fill us with that love toward Thee wherewith Thou hast loved us.

Take us beneath thy care and protection during the night. Accept our united thanksgivings for the blessings of this day, and grant that we may live in the constant sense of thy providential guidance. Hear us, we beseech Thee, for Jesus Christ's sake. Amen.

[Morning.] THIRTY-SIXTH WEEK—TUESDAY. [Evening.

READ IN HOLY SCRIPTURE PSALMS III. & IV.

O OUR God, through thy great goodness we have laid us down in peace and slept, and Thou, Lord, hast made us to dwell in safety. We beseech Thee, have mercy upon us, and hear our prayer. In ourselves weak and helpless, guilty and unworthy, we flee unto Thee, for thy mercies are great. We indeed are the people of thy hand and the sheep of thy pasture. Alas! we have erred and strayed from thy ways like lost sheep. We have followed too much the devices and desires of our own heart. We have done what we ought not to have done, and have not done what we ought to have done, and there is no health in us. But thine it is always to have mercy and to forgive. We have destroyed ourselves, but in Thee is our help found. Blessed be thy holy name, salvation belongeth unto the Lord. Lord, lift Thou up the light of thy countenance, and by thy Holy Spirit enable us to see the light of the knowledge of the glory of God in the face of Jesus Christ. Lord, increase our faith. Give us such a deep sense of our sinfulness, and such a comforting sense of thy great love in the redemption of the world by our Lord Jesus Christ, that we may rejoice in his great salvation. So gracious Lord, this day and every day, may the life we now live in the flesh be by the faith of the Son of God; that as He died and rose again for us, so may we die unto sin and live unto righteousness; that, in our daily business and callings, we may serve the Lord Christ; and whatsoever we do, in word or deed, do all in the name of the Lord Jesus, giving thanks to our God and Father by Him.

So may our eye be single to thy glory as we go forth to our work and to our labour until the evening. Lord, keep us back from all self-seeking or self-pleasing. May the power of Christ strengthen us in every duty. May the love of Christ be a watch upon our lips, that we sin not with our tongue. May the meekness and gentleness of Christ mould our spirits and tempers into his own blessed image. So may all our habits and intercourse with each other as a family, and with those we meet in our daily employments, be as it becometh the Gospel of Christ.

We have, indeed, no power of ourselves to help ourselves. Arise, O Lord; save us, O our God. Subdue our sins, heal our infirmities, and lead us in the paths of righteousness for thy name's sake.

Blessed Lord, we commit ourselves, body, soul, and spirit, to thy gracious care. Keep us, if it be thy will, in health and strength. Give us this day our daily bread. Prosper the work of our hands upon us. In Thee would we put our trust. Lord, hear our prayer, and do Thou for us and all who are dear to us according to thy mercy, for the sake of thy dear Son Jesus Christ our Saviour. Amen.

READ IN HOLY SCRIPTURE 1 CORINTHIANS XIV.

MOST merciful Father, the Father of our Lord Jesus Christ, we again prostrate ourselves before Thee, and cry, "Unclean, unclean." Every day testifies that we are a people of unclean lips, and dwell amongst a people of unclean lips; for daily we transgress thy laws, and come short of thy glory.

But Thou hast mercifully opened a fountain for sin and for uncleanness, in which we may wash and be clean. The blood of Jesus Christ cleanseth us from all sin, and through Him we have access by one Spirit unto Thee as our reconciled Father. Help us to exercise a lively faith in Jesus Christ, and to come as dear children to the throne of grace, persuaded that Thou wilt accept us and bless us, and supply all our need according to thy riches in glory by Christ Jesus.

We are this night one stage nearer to the end of our mortal life; oh, give us grace to consider our latter end, and to apply our hearts unto wisdom. May we know that Jesus Christ is made unto us wisdom, and righteousness, and sanctification, and redemption. Pour into our hearts that most excellent gift of charity, and constrain us by the Holy Ghost to love Thee who first loved us, and sent thy Son to be the propitiation for our sins. We would earnestly desire of Thee the best spiritual gifts; and we ask, also, that Thou wouldst give us grace to edify others. Help us to grow in grace and in the knowledge of the Lord and Saviour Jesus Christ; and, advancing in the Divine life, may we learn in malice to be children, but in understanding to be men.

Look down upon the whole Church, and give grace to all its members, that they may keep the unity of the Spirit in the bond of peace, and do all things decently and in order. Forbid that the tongues of thy ministering servants should give any uncertain sound; and do Thou enable them faithfully to preach thy Word, not shunning to declare the whole counsel of God. Look in mercy on all who are ignorant of Thee, and also on all thy suffering children. Enlighten the eyes of those who are sitting in darkness and the shadow of death, and sanctify all afflictions and trials to those who are bowed down under them. Bless all our relations, our friends, and our neighbours with the choicest of thy blessings. Bless our Sovereign and our country, and have mercy upon all men. Hasten the day, we pray Thee, when thy purposes of mercy and grace in Christ Jesus shall be fulfilled, and the earth be full of thy glory. Take us again under thy protecting care this night, and do for us and all for whom we pray more abundantly than we can ask or think, for the sake of thy dear Son Jesus Christ our Lord. Amen.

[Morning.] **THIRTY-SIXTH WEEK.—WEDNESDAY.** [Evening.

READ IN HOLY SCRIPTURE 2 SAM. XVIII. 1—17, 31—33.   READ IN HOLY SCRIPTURE 1 CORINTHIANS XV. 1—28.

O LORD, our heavenly Father, by whose undeserved mercy it is that we are preserved to the beginning of another day, we desire humbly and reverently to lift up the voice of praise and thanksgiving to Thee, the Author of every good and every perfect gift.

We are unworthy to approach Thee. We are in ourselves poor, and miserable, and blind, and naked; but we bless thy holy name that Thou hast provided for us unsearchable riches in Christ Jesus: Thou hast promised that all who love Thee shall behold thy face in righteousness, and shall be clothed with immortality. Fill, we beseech Thee, our hearts with a due sense of all these thy priceless blessings, and grant us this day and evermore to live as those who recognise Thee as their Father and their God.

Make us, we pray Thee, docile and obedient, contented in that position in which Thou hast placed us, and earnestly desirous of accomplishing thy will therein. Keep us from rebellion against thy sovereignty; apply to our hearts the warnings of thy holy Word, so that we may understand and feel that "rebellion is as the sin of witchcraft, and stubbornness is as idolatry." Enable us, by thy Holy Spirit, to love Thee as our Father, and truthfully to obey Thee in all things as our King.

We implore Thee to bless and sanctify all whom Thou hast placed in any offices of command, whether in thy Church or elsewhere. Especially we pray for our Sovereign, that she may be guided by thy wisdom and comforted by thy love. Strengthen her hands for the prosperity of thy people, and grant that in her time we may enjoy the blessing of peace. We commend to thy fatherly protection all those who are bound to us by the ties of kindred or affection: make us one family in love; teach us to bear one another's burdens, and so fulfill the law of love.

In all the engagements of this day, impress, O Lord, on our hearts the sense of thy presence, so that whatever we do we may do as unto the Lord and not unto man. Keep us from sin, as that which is hateful to Thee and harmful to ourselves. Alarm the impenitent by the terrors of thy wrath; comfort the afflicted by the consolations of thy name; guide the perplexed by the heavenly monitions of thy wisdom; and draw the wavering to Thee by the cords of thy everlasting love.

Finally we thank Thee for the mercies of the past night, and for all thy loving-kindness, beseeching Thee that, as hitherto Thou hast helped us, so goodness and mercy may follow us all the days of our lives.

Grant us, O Lord, these blessings, for the sake of Jesus Christ our Lord. Amen.

O GRACIOUS God and Father, we bless Thee for the Word of Truth, which is a lamp unto our feet and a light unto our path. Thou hast spoken unto us by thy servants and by thy Son, and thy Word is true from everlasting. Heaven and earth shall pass away, but thy Word shall not pass away. Thou hast fulfilled the things which were written in the Law of Moses, and in the Prophets, and in the Psalms, concerning Christ. We thank Thee that He died for our sins according to the Scriptures, and that He was buried, and that He rose again the third day, according to the Scriptures.

Grant to us, we earnestly pray, the Holy Spirit, that we may be in deed and in truth brought into the family of Christ thy dear Son; that as we have inherited sin and sorrow and death from the first Adam, we may obtain righteousness and heaven and eternal life from the second Adam, who is the Lord from heaven.

O our Father, we trust that we are now able to say, "I know whom I have believed." Keep us humble in this confidence, and help us to say more heartily every day, "By the grace of God, I am what I am." May the words of Christ become daily more precious to us: "I am the Resurrection and the Life: he that believeth in me, though he were dead, yet shall he live." Lord, we believe; help Thou our unbelief.

We earnestly pray that we may grow exceedingly in faith and hope and love; make us steadfast in the faith of the crucified and risen Saviour, so that our path on earth may be as the shining light, and that at length through the grave and gate of death, we too may pass to a joyful resurrection. Prepare us by thy grace for that glorious day when He shall appear the second time without sin unto salvation—all things under his foot, the last enemy destroyed, and the kingdom which has been gained by the might of the Son, delivered up to the glory of the Father. Fill our hearts with a grateful sense of thy goodness, adorn our walk with the beauty of holiness, and crown our life with the gift of thy peace. Teach us to love all those who love the Lord Christ, and fill us with such pity for the world that lieth in sin, that we may labour and pray that all may know and serve Him as the King of kings and the Prince of Peace.

Take us, and all that are dear to us, under thy protection this night; keep us in peace during the hours of darkness, and give us such refreshing sleep as shall fit us to engage with renewed strength in the duties of the ensuing day. We ask all these blessings in the name of thy dear Son our Saviour. Amen.

[Morning.] **THIRTY-SIXTH WEEK.—THURSDAY.** [Evening.

READ IN HOLY SCRIPTURE 2 SAMUEL XIX. 1–15, 39–43.

READ IN HOLY SCRIPTURE 1 CORINTHIANS XV. 35–58.

O LORD, open Thou our understanding, that we may understand the Scriptures; enable us to profit by that portion of thy holy Word which we have now been reading. We have seen, O Lord, the terrible consequences of Absalom's sin to himself, his father, and the whole land: and have we not this morning cause to mourn over our offences also? Truly, we have rebelled against thine anointed King, and said, We will not have this Man to reign over us. All we like sheep have gone astray, we have turned every one to his own way. Justly, then, might we have been cut off and left to perish for ever. But Thou didst pity thy erring ones, and such was thy love to a guilty world that Thou didst give thine only-begotten Son, that whosoever believeth in Him might not perish, but have everlasting life. Enable such of us as are thine to walk worthy of our high and holy calling. May we be blameless and harmless, as thy sons, without rebuke in this crooked and perverse generation. And if there should be one before Thee dead in trespasses and sins, may thy Holy Spirit bid the sleeper awake, this dead one arise. Oh, that all such may be led by Him to Jesus, the Shepherd and Bishop of their souls.

We acknowledge thy goodness to us during the past night. We laid us down and slept in peace, for Thou alone, O Lord, sustained us. What shall we render unto Thee for all Thy benefits bestowed upon us? O Lord, open Thou our lips, and our mouth shall show forth thy praise.

We know not what trials may be before us this day, but in all our ways we acknowledge Thee, knowing that Thou wilt direct our paths. Go with us then, to our various duties; and whatsoever our hands find to do, may we do it with all our might. Supply the wants of others, and give us grateful hearts for the many comforts we possess. Bless all who are near and dear to us [especially our beloved children; may they all be taught of Thee, and may their peace be great]. Grant that our relations may be thy relations, and our friends thy friends.

Help us to seek the salvation of the poor, wandering sinner this day. May our conscience not have power this evening to say—"Why spake ye not a word of bringing the King back?"

Oh that there may be amongst thy people a holy jealousy for thine honour. Awake, awake, put on strength, O arm of the Lord; bow the hearts of thy people as the heart of one man to this glorious work.

And now, Lord, what wait we for? truly our hope is even in Thee. Hear us in these our prayers, through Jesus Christ our Lord. Amen.

O GOD, our Father, who hast made all things, and hatest nothing that Thou hast made, hear us, we pray Thee, in thy great mercy, and answer and help us. Unwearied is thy forbearance towards us, and unceasing are the gifts of thy bounty. Teach us to be thankful. Show us how much we owe to Thee, and how great are the riches of thy loving-kindness and the tenderness of thy deep compassion. What can we render unto Thee, O Lord, for all thy mercy? We bless Thee, O Lord, with all our hearts; we praise thy holy name.

Forgive, we pray Thee, all our sins. We look in faith unto Jesus, who loved us and gave himself for us. For his sake blot from the book of thy remembrance all our transgressions, and give us peace. Renew our hearts by thy Holy Spirit, that we may put off every sinful habit, and be confirmed in spirit and in life to the Lord Jesus Christ. Oh give us grace to search out whatever in us is displeasing to Thee, and to resolve, thy grace helping us, that we will die unto sin and live unto God. Cause the fruits of the Spirit to abound in us, that we may adorn the doctrine of God our Saviour in all things, and be as living epistles of Christ, known and read of all men.

We praise Thee, O God, that Thou hast so clearly revealed to us the doctrine of the future resurrection of the dead. Enable us to realise the solemn lessons of the great day in which all that are in the grave shall hear the voice of the Son of God, and shall come forth, some to the resurrection of life and some to the resurrection of condemnation. Lord God, by thy Spirit awaken in us a spirit of holy and constant diligence, that we may make our calling and election sure, and be found of Christ in peace. Prevent us from slumbering in unconcern. Show us our true state before Thee, and draw us by thy grace nearer to Jesus and nearer to Thyself, that we may now gain the victory over sin, and in the great day be made partakers of his triumph over death and the grave. Give us, we pray Thee, such a fervent hope of a resurrection unto life, that we may be steadfast and earnest in every good word and work. When we are growing weary in well-doing, and complaining of the greatness of our trials and the grievousness of our temptations, let thy Spirit remind us of the promise that our labour shall not be in vain in the Lord.

Spread the shield of thy guardianship over our family and all those we love. Mercifully grant us all rest of body and peace of mind, and fit us for the duties of another day. We pray to be heard and answered for the alone sake of thy dear Son Jesus Christ our Lord. Amen.

[Morning.] **THIRTY-SIXTH WEEK.—FRIDAY.** [Evening.]

READ IN HOLY SCRIPTURE 2 SAMUEL XXII. 1—30.

O LORD God of Hosts, who art the aid of all that need, look down, we beseech Thee, upon us whilst as a family we kneel before Thee. Help us by the gift of thy Holy Spirit to worship Thee with holy worship. Strengthen us to meet every trial that may await us this day, and deliver us from every temptation.

We do not presume to come before Thee, O merciful God, trusting in our own merits or righteousness; our trust is only in the perfect righteousness and all-sufficient merits of thy dear Son Jesus Christ, our Lord. Whatever may have been the purity of our hearts, the cleanness of our hands, or the uprightness of our walk as before our fellow-sinners upon earth, before Thee, O Lord, we are constrained to bow our faces to the dust, and to lay our hands upon our mouths, and cry out, "Unclean! unclean!" If in any way we have differed from others around us, it is thy grace alone that hath made us to differ. By nature we were all dead in trespasses and sins, and, if so be we are now alive from the dead, Thou only hast quickened us. O gracious Father, let not one of us remain unquickened. Reveal to us more clearly each day the mystery of the cross of Christ. Bow thy heavens, and come down, and take possession of us, and make us wholly Thine, and kindle such a fire of love in our hearts as may consume all our carnal affections, and purge away all our dross.

And whilst we pray unto Thee, O Lord, we would not forget to praise Thee, who alone art worthy to be praised. It is to Thee we owe our life and breath and all things. Thy grace alone hath spared us hitherto; thy merciful providence hath carried us through temptations, guided us in our difficulties, guarded us in danger, saved us from violence, comforted us in affliction, given us strength in our weakness, and been our lamp in the darkness. For these and countless other mercies we laud and magnify thy holy name.

And now, Lord, we would intercede for all near and dear to us. Bless them all with all spiritual blessings in Christ Jesus, and make us and them mutually blessings to each other. Bless also our neighbours and acquaintances, our spiritual teachers and pastors, our country, and especially our Sovereign and all the Royal Family. Make this nation to be a nation fearing Thee and working righteousness, that thy name may be known upon earth, thy saving health upon all people.

Hear us, O Lord, we beseech Thee, in these our humble petitions, and accept our grateful praises, in the name and for the sake of Jesus Christ, our only Mediator and Advocate, to whom be glory for ever and ever. Amen.

READ IN HOLY SCRIPTURE ACTS XIX. 21—41.

O GRACIOUS God, we bless thy name that thy mercy endureth for ever. Spared by thy loving-kindness through another day, we draw near to thy throne of grace with hearts filled with adoring gratitude. Accept, we beseech Thee, our tribute of praise and thanksgiving. May thine undeserved mercy to us, sinful creatures, lead to more entire devotedness of heart and life. Bless that portion of thy Word we have just read. Oh, may very many not only see the power of Christ in us, but also, being reconciled in Christ Jesus, feel that power in themselves, in their translation from darkness to light, and from the hard service of Satan to the loving service of God. Make us to pity the poor benighted heathen, who, like the Ephesians, are worshipping idols. Bless all societies formed for sending the Gospel of the grace of God to them. Bless all who are labouring in distant lands, and striving to bring poor, perishing sinners to a saving knowledge of the true God. Truly, the harvest is great, but the labourers are few! Lord of the harvest, send forth labourers into thy harvest. Hasten the time when we shall not have to say, each to the other, "Know the Lord," for all shall know Him, from the least to the greatest. Grant, when that day dawns, that all of us who are now worshipping Thee may be amongst those who shall see the Lord in his glory, and for ever be with Him.

Deepen the work of grace in those of us in whom Thou hast begun it, and commence it in the souls of any of us who are still unconverted. Bring us more and more under the powerful influence of thy Word; that being begotten again unto a lively hope by the resurrection of Jesus Christ from the dead, we may daily grow in grace. Make us, therefore, more earnest students of the Bible, and grant that our increased knowledge of Jesus as our wisdom, righteousness, sanctification, and redemption, may make us to give more diligence to add to our faith virtue, and to virtue knowledge, and to knowledge temperance, and to temperance brotherly kindness, and to brotherly kindness charity; for if these things be in us and abound, we shall neither be barren nor unfruitful in the knowledge of our Lord Jesus Christ.

Now, Lord, we commit ourselves to thy care and keeping this night. Should we be spared through the night, may Jesus be first in our thoughts when we wake in the morning. Oh, grant that our bodies and minds, refreshed by sleep, may be fitted and prepared by prayer and meditation for thy service during the day.

Pardon all our sins during the past day. Accept our prayers and thanksgivings for the sake of Jesus Christ our Lord and Saviour. Amen.

[Morning.] **THIRTY-SIXTH WEEK.—SATURDAY.** [Evening.]

READ IN HOLY SCRIPTURE 2 SAM. XXII. 31—XXIII. 5. | READ IN HOLY SCRIPTURE 2 CORINTHIANS I.

ALMIGHTY God, our Heavenly Father, who of thine infinite love and goodness towards us hast given thy dearly beloved Son Jesus Christ to be our Redeemer to ransom us from death, and our Advocate and Intercessor to plead for us on high, hear us for his sake, and enable us in faith and love to present our morning prayer and praise. For the great benefits which in thy mercy and tender pity Thou hast bestowed upon us, we bless thy name, and especially for the revelation of Thyself which Thou hast given us in thy Word. Increase our knowledge of Thee; enable us to know Thee as God the Father who created us, as God the Son who redeemed us, as God the Holy Ghost who sanctifieth us. Oh that we may acquaint ourselves with Thee as the Author and Giver of salvation, and have peace. Through the teaching of thy Spirit cause us to increase and go forward in the knowledge and faith of Thee and of thy dear Son, that we may love Thee more and serve Thee better, and have the witness of thy Spirit within us that we are thine.

But, O God, we greatly need thy strength to sustain us. Thou knowest our weakness, and the many and powerful temptations which beset us, and draw our hearts from Thee, and our feet from thy ways. Leave us not, we beseech Thee, this day. Suffer us not to fall into the snares which our great enemy or the world may spread for us. We trust in thy Word, we lean on thy strength, we would take refuge beneath thy protection. Be Thou our shield and defence, and we will not fear. Especially we beseech Thee to awaken in us a holy watchfulness against the peculiar temptations which arise in our daily calling. Oh, let us not, through fears of others, hide our religion, or be ashamed of doing what is right. Give us a sound judgment of all things, grace to know what we ought to do, and a holy boldness to do it. In the presence of temptation shed on our hearts such a sense of the love of Christ to us, that we may be constrained to forsake evil and to follow Him fully in all things. Impress thy gracious promises on our hearts, and enable us to see our own interest in the covenant of grace and in the work of thy dear Son.

We ask, O God, thy grace and forgiveness, not only for ourselves, but also for all our relations and friends. Bestow on them all thy richest blessings. May we and they be all thy children in the faith of Jesus Christ, and be so endued with thy grace from day to day as to rejoice in hope of thy glory. Look down upon us mercifully from heaven and bless us. Hear us in these our prayers and thanksgivings, and withhold not the answer of peace, for Jesus Christ's sake. Amen.

MOST exalted Lord, Father of all mercies and God of all comfort, we magnify thy holy name. Thou art worthy of our highest praise. Every good and every perfect gift cometh from Thee. All our temporal and spiritual deliverances, and the consolations which have abounded to us by Christ, are from Thee. We trust not, therefore, in ourselves, but in thy great name, for Thou wilt hear and deliver those that hope in Thee.

When we review the week about to close, we are astonished at thy long-suffering and forbearance towards us. We have broken thy most holy law, and committed many offences against thy Divine majesty. We would sincerely repent and earnestly beseech Thee to pardon us for the time we have spent unprofitably, for our careless words, the wrongs we have done, the duties we have neglected, and the unholy tempers we have manifested. Remember not these our offences, neither take thou vengeance of them, but spare and pardon all thy people whom Thou hast redeemed.

That we may henceforth more truly serve Thee, pour out upon us an abundant measure of heavenly wisdom and strength. Confirm us in thy faith and love. Anoint us with the Holy Ghost, and seal us thine. Give the earnest of the Spirit in our hearts, the assurance that Thou art our Father, reconciled through thy Son, and that our ways please Thee.

Thou, O Lord, knowest the state of all in thy presence, and the trials and afflictions they have to endure. May the number and nature of these never lead us to despair of serving Thee, or prove a hindrance in leading a godly life. Make Thou us stedfast in thy service, and enable us to experience that if we are partakers of the sufferings of the Gospel, we shall be also of its consolations.

And now, O Lord, before we retire to rest this night, prepare us for the coming of thy holy day; enable us to fix our minds on things above; fortify them with thy grace, that we may not seek our own pleasure, nor turn our feet from thy holy house. Let the coming Sabbath, if we are spared to see it, be a delight to our souls. Vouchsafe also thy special blessing to all thy true and faithful servants, at home and abroad, that they may fully set forth grace and peace through our Lord Jesus Christ. Strengthen and enable them to comfort all thy servants that are in any trouble, by the comfort wherewith they are comforted of God.

Bless with thine especial favour and protection every member of this family; number them among thy saints, and grant that, when we shall awake from the sleep of death, it may be to spend in the courts of thine house above, a Sabbath of eternal praise, through Christ our Lord. Amen.

[Morning.] THIRTY-SEVENTH WEEK.—LORD'S DAY. [Evening.]

READ IN HOLY SCRIPTURE 1 CHRONICLES XXI. | READ IN HOLY SCRIPTURE 2 CORINTHIANS II.

O GOD, the Father of our Lord Jesus Christ, who didst not suffer thine Holy One to see corruption, but didst declare Him to be thy Son with power, by the resurrection from the dead; we give Thee thanks, that He was delivered for our offences, and raised again for our justification; that He is the propitiation for our sins; and that, being justified by his blood, we are saved from wrath through Him, and made heirs of the kingdom which Thou hast promised to them that love Him. Our Father in heaven, we acknowledge with godly sorrow that we have sinned greatly and have done wickedly in thy sight; but we beseech Thee to do away the iniquity of thy servants, and enter not into judgment with us; for if Thou, Lord, shouldest mark iniquity, who shall stand? With Thee there is mercy that Thou mayest be feared; and with Thee there is plenteous redemption. Let us fall into thy hand, for very great are thy mercies; so will we sing and give thanks unto Thee all the days of our life; and our mouth shall praise Thee with joyful lips.

O God, to whom belong mercies, spare Thou them that confess their faults; and let thy mercy lighten upon us, as we hope in Thee. So will we compass thine altar, that we may publish with the voice of thanksgiving, and tell of all thy wondrous works. Make us to love the habitation of thy house, and the place where thine honour dwelleth. Let it please Thee so to enrich our hearts this day with thy grace, that we may come into thy courts in the multitude of thy mercy; and in thy fear may we worship towards thy holy temple. Make thy face to shine upon thy servants; and save us for thy name's sake. Abundantly satisfy us with the fulness of thy house, and make us drink of the river of thy pleasure; for with Thee is the fountain of life, and in thy light we shall see light. Open Thou our eyes, that we may behold wondrous things out of thy law; and let the Spirit of truth lead us into all truth, that so we may grow in grace, and in the knowledge of our Lord and Saviour Jesus Christ, and be made meet for the inheritance of the saints in light.

Arise, O Lord, into thy rest; Thou and the ark of thy strength. Let thy priests be clothed with righteousness, and let thy saints sing for joy. Feed thine inheritance; and lift them up for ever. Send thy people help out of the sanctuary; and strengthen them out of Zion. Gather together thine elect, and let the kingdoms of this world become the kingdoms of our Lord and of his Christ.

Answer us, O God, and accept this our morning worship, which we present in the name of thy adorable Son, Jesus Christ our Saviour. Amen.

IT is a good thing to give thanks unto Thee, O Lord, and to show forth thy praise, O Thou most High; to show forth thy loving-kindness in the morning, and thy faithfulness every night. We are permitted by thy great goodness to see the close of another day of sacred rest. We have worshipped in thy holy temple with the congregation of thy people. We have listened to the words spoken by thy servants; we have joined in the prayers and thanksgivings of thy Church. The good seed has been sown, and we now pray, most merciful Father, that Thou wouldest cause to fall upon our hearts the dew of thy grace, that we may know Thee more, love Thee more, and serve Thee more faithfully.

Thou, O Lord, not only lovest the gates of Zion, but the dwelling-places of thy people. We are now as a family permitted to unite in prayer in our own habitation. May thy richest blessing, O our heavenly Father, rest upon us, and thy watchful care be over us for evermore. How full of counsel and encouragement is that lesson of thy holy Word which we have just read! We adore the longsuffering and tender mercy of our God. Thou art ready to forgive; Thou art ever near to heal the broken in heart, and to bind up their wounds. Thou hast revealed the fulness of thy truth and love in Jesus Christ, in whom we have redemption through his blood, even the forgiveness of sins, according to the riches of thy grace. May the Spirit reveal to our hearts his tender compassion towards sinners. Are we, our Father, forgiven and saved? O help us to remember the mercy showed to us, and which we daily need. Teach us, we most humbly pray Thee, to cherish towards all men thine own spirit. While we abhor evil, may we seek to restore and save the evil doer. Help us to go about this Christ-like work in the spirit of our Divine Saviour, who did not break the bruised reed nor quench the smoking flax.

Have pity, O heavenly Father, on every backslider who has been overborne by temptation, who has suffered himself to be led captive by the enemy of souls. Let the rebukes of conscience, the action of thy Holy Spirit, and the chastisement of thy Providence, awaken him to a sense of his danger and misery.

Keep Thou us, O Shepherd of Israel, through the silence and dangers of this night. With divine repose in our souls may we close our eyes in sleep, anticipating the everlasting rest of thy children. Be with us through the dangers and trials of the coming week. Keep us by thy grace from evil, and strengthen us to follow that which is good. Pardon us and accept us, through Jesus Christ our Saviour. Amen.

[253]

[Morning.] **THIRTY-SEVENTH WEEK.—MONDAY.** [Evening.

READ IN HOLY SCRIPTURE 1 CHRONICLES XXVIII.

READ IN HOLY SCRIPTURE 2 CORINTHIANS III.

ALMIGHTY God, the fountain of all good gifts, who knowest our necessities before we ask, and our ignorance in asking, we beseech Thee have mercy upon us, compassionate our infirmities, and, for the sake of thy dear Son, give us those things which for our unworthiness we dare not, and for our blindness we cannot ask. We have laid us down in peace, and taken our rest, and are now raised up again, because Thou, Lord, hast made us dwell in safety. Blessed be thy name for this and for all the tokens of thy grace, especially for the gift of thy dear Son. Suffer us never, we beseech Thee, to think lightly of thy redeeming love, or to forget at how great cost and from what eternal misery Thou hast redeemed us. Oh, that the love of Christ may constrain us, as those who have been bought with a price, to live not for ourselves but for Thee. We have gone astray like a sheep that is lost; graciously keep us in thy fold, and preserve us from wandering from Thee. Give us a continual sense of thy forgiving love, that we may live every day as in the light of thy countenance, and under the constant guidance of thy Holy Spirit.

Holy Father, we commit ourselves to thy merciful care and protection for the day on which we have entered. Thou knowest how we are often sorely hindered in our Christian race, and how often when we would do good, evil is present with us. O Lord, whither can we look for help but to Thee, who hast loved us with an everlasting love, and desirest not that even the least and lowliest of thy people should perish? All strength and wisdom are thine. Be Thou our defender, and spread around us the shield of thy protection. We look up to Thee, O Father, and pray Thee to keep us this day from falling. By thy grace we would guard our lips, and keep our very thoughts, lest we sin against Thee. Through thy help we would subdue the inclinations which would prompt us to what is wrong. O Lord, make us thine entirely; consecrate us as the temples of the Holy Ghost, and make us as vessels of honour to thy glory.

Glorify thy name in the daily triumphs of thy Gospel. Increase the zeal of thine own people for the enlargement of the Redeemer's kingdom. Open the eyes of many blind sinners this day, to see in Jesus their Saviour and their God. Comfort the sorrowing, and instruct them through the season of trial in the things of God. Graciously regard all whom we love, and suffer them not to neglect the great salvation. For them, and for ourselves, and for thy whole Church, we implore every blessing. Grant it, O Lord, for thy dear Son's sake. Amen.

O LORD our God, we kneel before Thee at the close of another day, to offer our evening worship. Thou hast again surrounded us with manifold mercies, not one of which we have merited. Praise the Lord, our souls, and all that is within us, bless his holy name.

We thank Thee for all the glory connected with the Gospel dispensation, that things but dimly disclosed to holy men of God in ancient times, are revealed to us in all their grandeur. We implore thy help that we may live in a manner worthy of the name we bear and the hopes we entertain. Enable us to stand before an ungodly world as the epistles of Christ, known and read of all men.

But what thanks can we render Thee for all the promises of thy Word? By the teaching of the Spirit may we be made like Christ, and after the darkness and desolation of the grave may we be for ever satisfied with thy likeness. Perfect that which concerneth thy servants; keep us from falling, and present us faultless in the presence of thy glory with exceeding joy.

We entreat Thee to fulfil thy gracious promises respecting the enlargement of thy Church. May the Spirit of glory and of God rest upon it, that the Gentiles may come to its light, and kings to the brightness of its rising. Take away the veil which yet rests upon the hearts of thine ancient people, and bring them into the fold of thy Church.

Take care of us during the darkness of the night. Give us refreshing sleep; invigorate our wearied powers; and fit us for the discharge of duty on the morrow. May we lie down every night beneath the wings, and wake every morning with the remembrance, of thy presence and protection.

We ask thy blessing upon our dear relatives and friends. Give them the mercies we have sought for ourselves. If in the feebleness and decay of age, grant them the special consolations they may require. May the little ones growing up into life be preserved from danger, be made partakers of thy grace, and be fitted by thy Holy Spirit for honour and usefulness.

Almighty God, in thy great mercy pardon our manifold sins. We are painfully conscious of waywardness, and folly, and frequent transgression. For Christ's sake forgive us; for Christ's sake sanctify us; and accept us in the Beloved. We close this day, as we hope to close life itself, resting upon the sacrifice of the cross.

Almighty God, the God of all the families of the earth, accept this our evening devotion, and be our friend and helper, our God and our guide, even unto death, for the sake of Jesus Christ our blessed Lord and Saviour. Amen.

[MORNING.] **THIRTY-SEVENTH WEEK—TUESDAY.** [EVENING.

READ IN HOLY SCRIPTURE 1 CHRONICLES XXIX.

FATHER in heaven, we meet once more round our family altar, to thank Thee for the care bestowed on us during the past night, for refreshing sleep, and for renewed health and strength. We thank Thee for the returning light of day, and ask Thee in like manner to shed forth upon us the light of thy Holy Spirit, to illumine our path, and teach us to do such things as shall please Thee.

Do Thou keep us from sin this day; help us to tread the narrow path that leads through this world to a better and a brighter. Suffer us not to be exposed to temptation; or if we are tempted, make a way for us to escape. Keep us very near to Jesus; may we never be permitted to wander far from Him.

We desire, O our Father, to consecrate our service this day to Thee: enable us by thy grace to serve Thee in our varied pursuits. Whether engaged in our domestic and household duties, or in our more public engagements, may we do everything in the name of the Lord Jesus, and with a single eye to his glory. Lord, make us willing in the day of thy power. May we ever remember that we are not our own, but bought with a price; that all things come of Thee, and that all that we can give is thine own. Blessed Saviour, give us willing hearts; make us fellow-labourers with Thee, in the great work that Thou art doing in these latter days. Thou art building up thy spiritual temple, and adding to thy Church daily such as shall be saved. The work is great and glorious. Yet, Lord, Thou art pleased to use very feeble instruments to build up the temple of the Lord. Wilt Thou use us, though we be but hewers of wood, or drawers of water? Yet use us, Lord, and Thou shalt have all the glory. Make us earnest to work for Thee while it is day, for the night cometh, when no man can work.

And now, Lord, to these our petitions would we add our praises; we would address Thee in the words that have been put into our mouths this day: "Blessed be Thou, Lord God, for ever and ever. Thine, O Lord, is the greatness, and the power, and the glory, and the victory, and the majesty: for all that is in the heaven and in the earth is thine; thine is the kingdom, O Lord, and Thou art exalted as head above all. Both riches and honour come of Thee, and Thou reignest over all; and in thine hand is power and might; and in thine hand it is to make great, and to give strength unto all. Now therefore, our God, we thank Thee, and praise thy glorious name."

Wilt Thou accept these our praises, and answer these our prayers, for the sake of thy Son, our Saviour Jesus Christ? Amen.

READ IN HOLY SCRIPTURE 2 CORINTHIANS IV.

IT is good for us to draw near to God. As for us, we will call upon God, and the Lord shall save us. Evening and morning will we pray and cry aloud, and God shall hear our voice. Thou makest the outgoings of the morning and evening to rejoice.

Our gracious God and Father, Thou crownest our days with thy goodness. Thou hast crowned this day with thy goodness; and whilst the mercies of the day are still all fresh in our memories, we come to thy footstool to thank and bless Thee for them all. We bless Thee for the strength of the day, for the food of the day, for the employments of the day, and for the enjoyments of the day. We bless Thee that a Father's love has watched us, that a Father's power has kept us, and that a Father's bounty has fed us. And we pray Thee that a Father's care may be over us through the night, and that a Father's hand may smooth our pillows and guard our slumbers.

We ask thy forgiveness for all the sins of the day, for all our angry tempers, for all our hasty words, for all our sinful thoughts. May they be covered over, all of them, by the precious blood of Christ. We pray Thee to make us feel more the exceeding sinfulness of sin. We pray to be taught more the exceeding fulness of thy pardoning mercy in Jesus Christ. We pray that we may know more of the glorious Gospel of Christ, and that more of its life and peace may be received into our hearts.

We pray that we may be more patient under all the afflictions of life. We confess with shame that we are often so little patient under our afflictions. Alas! that they do not seem to us light afflictions, but very heavy. Help us to look away from our own afflictions to the afflictions of Christ. Help us to look more often and more seriously on that face so marred more than any man's, and that form more than the sons of men. Oh, that we may remember that He was wounded for our transgressions, and bruised for our iniquities, that the chastisement of our peace was upon Him, and that by his stripes we are healed!

We praise Thee that there is no sorrow with God. We bless Thee that in thy presence is fulness of joy, and that at thy right hand are pleasures for evermore. We praise Thee that, when we have done with sin, we shall have done with sorrow. And we pray that we may think more of sin, and less of sorrow; and that our sorrows may make Christ more than ever dear to us. We pray that we may live in his love, and die in his love. We ask, O our Father, this great blessing and all other mercies which Thou seest we have need of, through Jesus Christ our Saviour. Amen.

[Morning.] **THIRTY-SEVENTH WEEK.—WEDNESDAY.** [Evening.

READ IN HOLY SCRIPTURE 2 CHRONICLES I.

O LORD our God, and our fathers' God, our voice shalt Thou hear in the morning, for thine ear is ever attent to the cry of those who call upon Thee. The heaven of heavens cannot contain Thee, but Thou hast promised to dwell with him that is of a contrite heart and who trembleth at thy word. Behold us met in the name of thy dear Son Jesus Christ, and look with favour upon us, as thine adopted children.

We praise Thee for that fatherly love which promises to supply our wants and satisfy our desires out of the fulness of thy blessing; and we thank Thee for thine assurances so free and full, that every one who asketh receiveth, and he that seeketh findeth, and to him that knocketh the door is opened; and it is in confidence that Thou art still the same, still faithful to thy word, that we come to Thee at this time for pardon, and peace, and grace to help in our time of need.

We know not what we should pray for as we ought; we know not our own real wants, nor the value of things which we should ask for; and we therefore seek thy guiding Spirit, to teach us now and at all times how to pray. May He bring our will into conformity to thy will; may He set our desires upon those things which Thou approvest and wilt be willing to grant.

We ask, as thy servant Solomon, for a wise and understanding heart, to do our duty in that position in life in which Thou hast been pleased to place us. We know not what is best for us; we would not fix our lot, nor appoint our station in life; but we ask for thy special grace, so to conduct us, that we may fulfil the object of our being, and set forth thy glory.

We always need wisdom, and too often do we lean to our own understanding; we ask for that knowledge which will enable us to guide our affairs with discretion, and to avoid the manifold evils to which we are exposed.

At all times of perplexity and doubt, show us our path, and keep us in the right way; and if we have strayed, bring us back to the Shepherd and Bishop of our souls.

O God of holiness, make us holy in all manner of conversation; and teach us to follow the instruction of our blessed Saviour. May we be transformed into his likeness, that men may take knowledge of us that we have been with Jesus, and glorify Him in us, his humble followers.

We thank Thee for having placed all the treasures of wisdom and knowledge in Jesus Christ, with whom Thou wilt freely give us all things. Unworthy of the least of thy mercies, we pray Thee still to continue them to us this day and ever, for the sake of our blessed Saviour. Amen.

READ IN HOLY SCRIPTURE 2 CORINTHIANS V.

HOLY, holy, holy, Lord God Almighty, who art to be worshipped in spirit and in truth, fill all our minds, we beseech Thee, with reverence and love. At the close of this day we come again to Thee, for Thou alone art worthy of our devoted service and of our constant praise. We remember with gratitude thy manifold goodness in answer to the prayers of the morning. Thou hast not forsaken us. Thou hast been at hand to teach, to encourage, and to strengthen us; Thou hast wisely and tenderly disciplined us for our good; Thou hast cheered us in trial, and preserved us in danger; Thou hast crowned us with thy lovingkindness, and we are glad. Yet, notwithstanding all thy claims upon us, and thy favour towards us, we have sinned against Thee this day. Our hearts condemn us for the unkind and unwise words we have spoken, for the worldly and selfish thoughts we have cherished, for the corrupt motives we have indulged, for the unchristian acts we have committed. It is thy love we have slighted, and thine authority we have set at nought. Enter not into judgment with us, O Lord! Again exercise towards us, through the sacrifice of our Redeemer, Jesus, thy pardoning grace. Say to each of us, "Peace, be of good cheer; thy sins, which are many, are all forgiven." We praise Thee for the work of reconciliation through the Lord Jesus Christ, so that we may be made the righteousness of God in Him. We praise Thee for the word of reconciliation with which Thou hast favoured us. Fix its truths in all our hearts. Let there be no coldness and distance between Thee and our souls. Constrain us, by thy love towards us, to love Thee supremely, and to love each other wisely. In anticipation of the final judgment, help us effectually to watch and pray against all sin. Teach us so to live, in trustful dependence upon the Saviour, that the day of judgment may be the day of our complete redemption. Lord, increase our faith. Give us to feel the presence of the Comforter, the Holy Ghost, as the earnest of our heavenly home. When the earthly house of our tabernacle is taken down, graciously receive us to dwell for ever with Thee. Suffer not one of our family to be shut out of heaven.

Give to us refreshing sleep, and prepare us for the morrow. Bless with thy love all our kindred and friends. Make thy Church increasingly prosperous. Help all missionaries, and pastors, and teachers in the ministry of reconciliation. Destroy all idolatry, and Mahometanism, and Judaism, and corrupt Christianity, and bring the world, in penitence and faith, to the feet of Jesus the Reconciler. We ask all blessings in his name and for thy glory, now and ever. Amen,

[Morning.]   THIRTY-SEVENTH WEEK.—THURSDAY.   [Evening.

READ IN HOLY SCRIPTURE 2 CHRONICLES V.—VI. 11.   READ IN HOLY SCRIPTURE 2 CORINTHIANS VI.

ALMIGHTY and infinitely holy God, in whose sight the heavens are unclean, and who chargest thine angels with folly, but who graciously condescendest to dwell with the humble and the contrite, help us to draw near to Thee this morning with unfeigned humility and contrition of heart. Give to us, for Christ's sake, thy Holy Spirit; help us to realise, in our approach to the throne of grace, that we are the temples of the Holy Ghost. May He now help our infirmities. May He make intercession for us, heavenly Father, according to thy will; teaching us how to pray, and what to pray for. As Thou didst of old fill thine house with thy presence, so give us to know that Thou art present with us, thy children, at all times, according to the promise of thy covenant; but especially when we draw near to Thee in our private chamber, at the family altar, and in the public sanctuary, that our prayers may always be the petitions of those who, having received the Spirit of adoption, cry, "Abba, Father." May thy glory be our one object. We would not, O Lord, trust in our own strength, but in thine. We would make no resolutions leaning on our own power to carry them out. We have often done so, but have ever found our own strength to be perfect weakness. Pardon us, gracious Father, in all our shortcomings, and in all that we have done wrong in times past. Oh, may all our failures, by which thy name has been dishonoured, lead us to closer communion and fellowship with Jesus Christ by the Holy Spirit. May we, through Him, the source of all grace, wisdom, and strength, be found always walking before our God, doing according to his commands, observing his statutes and judgments. Give to us clear views of Gospel truth. Help us to read thy Word in a teachable spirit. May we hide it in our hearts, that we may not sin against Thee. In the temptations of Satan, the world, and the flesh, help us rightly to use the sword of the Spirit. Enable us, in the strength of the Captain of our salvation, to overcome our spiritual foes to the glory of thy name. When our souls cleave to the dust, quicken us by thy word. When we are cast down by the workings of inward corruption, encourage us by thy precious promises. Help us to realise that all who believe have redemption in Jesus; that he has put away their sins by the sacrifice of Himself; that to them there is no condemnation. May our names be written in the Lamb's book of life; and may we be included in the promise, "I give unto my sheep eternal life, and they shall never perish, neither shall any one pluck them out of my hand." Grant it, O Lord, for Christ's sake. Amen.

AGAIN, O Lord, gracious and merciful, do we come before Thee, to render unto Thee our evening offering of grateful adoration. How great has been the sum of thy mercies to us-ward this day! From how many dangers hast Thou preserved us! from what sins have we not been kept by thy restraining grace! Impress upon us, we beseech Thee, the magnitude of these blessings, and day by day bring our hearts more into harmony with thy Spirit. We thank Thee for the ministry of thy Word; that Thou hast not allowed our teachers to be removed into a corner, but that our eyes see them, and our souls acknowledge them, as bearing unto us the glad tidings of salvation, the ever-blessed and glorious Gospel. Enable us to be fellow-labourers with them, holding up their hands by our prayers and sympathy, and recognising that all thy people are privileged to be kings and priests to God and to the Lamb for ever. As such, do Thou, O King of kings, bless and strengthen us. Fight with the sword of thy Spirit on our behalf, so that we may overcome the evil that is in the world through sin, utterly defeat and destroy the enemy that is within us, and offer our hearts unto Thee as temples wherein no idol shall remain, but where Jesus, and Jesus only, shall be worshipped and glorified. Join us all into one body; make manifest unto us our oneness in Christ, that as soldiers in his great army, we may recognise our dependence one on another, and of all on Him, the Captain of our salvation. Subdue in us, O Lord, all self-righteousness, and preserve us from all unholy associations. And now that we are about to rest from the labours of the day, we beseech Thee, who hast been our guide during its busy season, to be our guardian during the silent watches. Lighten with thy sanctifying influence the hours of darkness, keep us from all which might disturb our rest, and purify our souls from all evil thoughts, so that, shouldest Thou call us, we may be found ready. We would lie down in peace with all men, praying Thee to pour out thy Spirit upon them in these our later days. Make up the number of thy saints, O Lord, we beseech Thee, and hasten thy kingdom. We acknowledge our unworthiness, and bewail our continual transgression. Forgive, O Lord, graciously forgive the sins of thy servants. Oh, our God, grant us that repentance which is not to be repented of, and purify the tears of our contrition by the blood of a crucified Saviour. We commend ourselves unto Thee, in the all-prevailing name of Jesus Christ our Saviour. Amen.

[MORNING.] THIRTY-SEVENTH WEEK.—FRIDAY. [EVENING.

READ IN HOLY SCRIPTURE 2 CHRONICLES VI. 12—42.

O LORD, the God of Israel, and of all that trust in Thee, look down upon us. There is no God like unto Thee in heaven or in the earth; yet Thou keepest covenant and showest mercy unto thy faithful servants. It is to Thee that we direct our prayer this morning. Have respect unto us, and hearken to our supplication. Hear from heaven, thy dwelling-place; and when Thou hearest, forgive.

We praise Thee, O God, for permitting and encouraging us to draw near to Thee, and to make our requests known. Now that we kneel at thy footstool, show thy mercy, and pardon our sins. Enable us to enjoy a sense of thy presence. Set a watch, O Lord, before us, that we offend not in thought, word, or deed; and give us grace that we may walk according to thy will. We are weak and compassed with infirmity, but we look to Jesus for strength, and to thy Holy Spirit for guidance in all our engagements this day. Help us, we beseech Thee, to discharge the duties of our several stations with diligence and good will; and whatsoever we may be called to do or suffer, may we so act as becometh those who serve the Lord Christ. Grant, Lord, that we may not offend against Thee, the supreme Governor of all things, whose power no creature can resist. It belongeth to Thee to punish sinners, and to be merciful to them that truly repent. Be pleased, therefore, to judge and defend thy servants. May no weapon formed against them prosper, but in great mercy deliver and protect them.

May it please Thee to look favourably upon us as a nation. Accept our thanksgivings for the many and great deliverances which Thou hast wonderfully wrought for us. Graciously continue to bestow upon us thy loving-kindness and favour. Save us from all dangers. Visit us not in thy displeasure for our sins, nor for those of our forefathers; but be merciful, and preserve us from all evil.

Hear us in our supplications on behalf of our Sovereign, and every member of the Royal family. Keep them in thy faith and fear, and help them to seek thy honour and glory. Bless all that are in authority in our land. Guide all judges and magistrates. Give them grace to execute justice and maintain truth, so that we may lead a quiet and peaceable life in all godliness and honesty.

We commit ourselves to thy protection this day. Preserve us from every false and evil way. Guide us by thy counsel, and when we have done and suffered thy righteous will on earth, receive us to Thyself, through our Lord and Saviour Jesus Christ, to whom with Thee and the Holy Spirit, the Triune God, be all adoration and praise. Amen.

READ IN HOLY SCRIPTURE 2 CORINTHIANS VII.

O LORD, our heavenly Father, bow down thine ear to us, and graciously accept, for Christ's sake, this our evening sacrifice of prayer and praise. Thou art a Spirit; help us to worship Thee in spirit and in truth. We confess before Thee the sins and failings of this day, rejoicing to know that Thou canst be faithful and just, and yet forgive us our sins. Teach us to cleanse ourselves from all filthiness of the flesh and spirit, perfecting holiness in the fear of God. Oh, that we may not feel the sorrow of the world, which worketh death, but that which worketh repentance to salvation, not to be repented of.

How shall we thank Thee for the exceeding great and precious promises which we have in thy Son: for the forgiveness of our sins, the acceptance of our persons, the gift of thy Holy Spirit, everlasting life begun, and eternal glory awaiting us? Enable us, we beseech Thee, to consecrate to Thee all that we are and all that we have: the faculties of our mind, the members of our body, our time, our influence over others, to be all used for thy glory, and resolutely employed in obedience to thy commands, so long as Thou continuest us in life. And this we do, not to obtain thy favour, but because for the sake of Jesus Thou hast vouchsafed it unto us. This day may be our last; it may be that our work is done, our conflicts passed. Grant that we may know that, through thy dear Son, there is laid up for us a crown of glory, which Thou hast promised to all that love Thee.

Protect our beloved home this night. May no evil befall us, but refresh our weary frames with sweet and pleasant rest. Especially would we commend to thy care the sons and daughters of affliction. O God, pity those who are homeless and friendless, having no place to lay their head. Look upon our Sovereign and our country. Bless all ministers of thy everlasting Gospel. Remember all missionaries, give increased power to their words, and may the truth preached by their lips be the incorruptible seed springing unto everlasting life in very many souls. We thank Thee for thy care over us as a kingdom. May we increasingly learn that righteousness alone exalteth a nation, and that sin is the reproach of any people. Enable us to love our enemies, to bless them that curse us, to do good to them that hate us, and to pray for them that despitefully use us and persecute us. Thus may we pass through things temporal, so that finally we lose not those that are eternal. Grant this, O Lord, for the sake of Jesus Christ, to whom, with Thee and the Holy Ghost, be all honour and glory, world without end. Amen.

[Morning.] **THIRTY-SEVENTH WEEK.—SATURDAY.** [Evening.]

READ IN HOLY SCRIPTURE 2 CHRONICLES VII.

READ IN HOLY SCRIPTURE 2 CORINTHIANS VIII.

O FATHER, we bless Thee that Thou hast not spared Thine own Son, but delivered Him up for us all. We thank Thee that by the one offering of the body of Jesus, once for all, Thou hast destroyed death, spoiled Satan, brought in everlasting righteousness, and opened the gate of heaven to all that believe. Eternal thanks be unto Thee for the one Mediator between God and man, the great High Priest over the house of God, by whom we have access at all times and in every place to Thee.

We are ashamed when we think of our sinfulness. Be merciful to us, cleanse our souls, and visit us with thy salvation; so shall we see the good of thy chosen, rejoice in the gladness of thy nation, and glory with thine inheritance.

And as Thou hast done great things for us, whereof we are glad, we ask Thee still to do great things for us, for thy name's sake and for thy glory. We are no more our own, for Thou hast bought us with the precious blood of Jesus; help us to glorify Thee in our bodies and in our spirits, which are thine. We desire to dedicate ourselves, our souls and bodies, unto Thee. Preserve us from the guilt and danger of keeping back anything from Thee. We would offer ourselves to Thee as a living sacrifice, holy, acceptable through Christ, and rejoice in this as a reasonable and a happy service. Send, we pray Thee, thy promised Spirit into our hearts, and make us living stones in his Church. May we become the temples of the Holy Ghost, the habitation of God through the Spirit. May Christ be formed in us the hope of glory. May old things pass away, and all things become new.

Give us every day an increasing hatred of sin, in all its forms, and under all its disguises. Cleanse us from secret faults. Keep us back from presumptuous sins. Subdue every fleshly lust. Restrain every unsanctified temper. Change evil habits into good. May we watch over our own souls, be instant and constant in prayer, and careful readers of thy Word. Bring every thought into captivity unto the obedience which is in Christ, and may all who see us take knowledge of us that we have been with Jesus. Bless all dear to us, and make them thine. Bless our enemies, if we have any, and turn their hearts. Add to thy Church daily such as shall be saved. Undo the heavy burden, and let the oppressed go free. Break every yoke. Bring in the latter day glory. Thy kingdom come. Then shall the earth bring forth her increase, and God, even our own God, shall give us his blessing. O Lord, we beseech Thee to hear us, and answer us for thy dear Son's sake. Amen.

O GRACIOUS God, who art ever the merciful hearer of prayer, incline thine ear unto us whilst we kneel before Thee, in the name of Jesus Christ, thy dear Son.

We bless Thee, O Lord, for thy fatherly care over us since the last Sabbath-day, and that Thou hast brought us to the close of another week in peace and safety. We bless Thee for the enjoyment of such a measure of health and strength as Thou, in thy good providence, hast seen fit to bestow upon us. We bless Thee for food and raiment, for preservation from danger, for deliverance from evil, for strength to resist the world, the flesh, and the devil; for all the countless privileges which are ours, as a Christian family in a Christian land; and for the disposition Thou hast given us to serve and worship Thee. Above all we bless Thee for the gift of thy dear Son Jesus Christ, to be unto us both a sacrifice for sin and also an example of godly life. We are verily less than the least of all thy servants, and utterly unworthy, O Lord, to receive any blessing from Thee. Until Thou didst visit us with thy salvation, and awaken and quicken us by thy grace, if so be we have tasted that Thou art gracious, we lived wholly to ourselves and this present evil world. And even since Thou hast called us, how often have we sinned against Thee by word, and thought, and deed; yea, even this very day we have grieved thy Holy Spirit, doing many things that we ought not to have done, and leaving undone many things that we ought to have done.

Yet, O gracious Father, we come to Thee with full confidence, having access through the blood of Jesus. For his sake we pray Thee to have mercy upon us, and to give us grace to walk more closely with Thee for the rest of our lives.

And, O blessed Jesus, who art our God and Saviour, fulfil thy gracious promise unto us, and pour down upon us thy Holy Spirit, to guide us into all truth. Make us to know more of thy grace and love, so that we may abound in every Christian grace, and may have a readiness to will, and a forwardness to perform every good work, giving ourselves to Thee, who for our sakes didst become poor, that we through thy poverty might be rich.

We commit ourselves, most merciful God, to thy care and keeping this night. Let thy good Spirit watch over us and all near and dear to us. Give us refreshing rest and sleep, and so prepare our hearts for the service of the sanctuary, that thy holy day may be unto us a foretaste of the rest that remaineth for thy people. Hear us, and grant us an answer of peace, for Jesus Christ's sake. Amen.

[Morning.]   THIRTY-EIGHTH WEEK.—LORD'S DAY.   [Evening.

READ IN HOLY SCRIPTURE 2 CHRON. VIII. 12.–IX. 12.

READ IN HOLY SCRIPTURE 2 CORINTHIANS IX.

O MOST Holy and Almighty God, who dwellest on high, but yet humblest thyself to behold the things that are in heaven and earth, have regard, we humbly beseech Thee, to our prayers, and let our praises rise before Thee as the incense of grateful hearts, and be acceptable through the intercession of thy dear Son. Let not our sins hide thy face from us on this thy day, but enable us to enter on the spiritual duties of the day with fervent hearts.

Glory be to thy name for the mercies of the past night. Mercifully continue thy protection and care through the day, preserving us from all evil, temporal and spiritual, and sustaining us in health and safety to its close. We look up to Thee in all our necessities, and rely on thy grace for the supply of all our wants. Be not far from us, but according to thy goodness and mercy help us and bless us. Especially do we seek the presence of thy Holy Spirit, without whose grace we shall be able neither to receive the truth we hear, nor to pray to Thee in sincerity and truth. Oh, grant that He may dwell in us, convincing us deeply of our sin, and melting our hearts with true repentance, as we kneel at thy footstool, taking of the things of Christ and showing them unto us, increasing our faith, and kindling within us a more fervent consecration to thy service. Prepare our hearts to receive the message of thy Word. Let it not be that she who came from the uttermost parts of the earth to hear the wisdom of Solomon should rise up in the judgment against us, for neglecting the precious Gospel of thy Son, our Saviour. Fill us with love to Him, and by thy Spirit stir up in us an intense desire to know Him more intimately, in the glory of his person, and the riches of his grace.

Bless to us all the ordinances of this Lord's day. Be present in all congregations which shall call upon thy name. Send forth thy Spirit in his might and power, and make the truth which shall be proclaimed effectual to the conversion and quickening of many souls. Thy Word is a hammer; so apply it that hard hearts may be broken, and stubborn hearts be subdued. It is fire; oh, grant that it may consume and burn up the sins that hinder the work of grace among thy people. It is a sword; oh, that it may pierce the souls of the self-righteous, and convince them of their sinfulness and their need of a Saviour. Strengthen and encourage all thy faithful ministers. Such as are in error do Thou guide to the knowledge of thy truth, and make them wise to win souls. Graciously attend with thy blessing all the labours of those who teach the young. Let man be everywhere humbled, and thy dear Son be exalted. We ask all in his name, and for his sake. Amen.

O GOD, to Thee be all the glory and the praise for the many mercies with which Thou hast visited us this day. Receive us graciously, and deal with us not according to our sins, but according to thy tenderness and pity, for Jesus Christ's sake. All our trust is in Thee. We are thine, body, soul, and spirit. Our health and strength are thy gifts. Our privileges come from thy goodness to us, and it is entirely through thy love to our souls that we have had another Sabbath on earth, and the renewed opportunities of worshipping Thee in the congregation, and hearing the appointed ministrations of thy Word. O God, accept our praise for all thy loving-kindness. Having not spared thy dear Son, Thou hast with Him given us all other needful blessings. Suffer us not to think coldly of what Thou hast done for us, and art doing for us every day. Again and again, O God, we would raise the song of praise before Thee.

Heavenly Father, bless to us all the holy engagements of this day. May we reap such spiritual benefit as shall convince us, by our own experience, that a day in thy courts is better than a thousand spent with the world in pleasure or in sin. Forgive, we pray Thee, all that has been amiss in our services; the coldness of our praise, the wanderings of our hearts, the feebleness of our faith, the insincerity of our repentance, and our inattention to thy Word. Gracious Saviour, who knowest our infirmities, suffer not these things to hinder our spiritual profit. We pray that we may be preserved from the sin of receiving the grace of God in vain. Cleanse and blot out all our sins in thy precious blood, and grant that they may be remembered no more. Our only plea is thy sacrifice, and our only hope is in thy Divine intercession on high. Magnify thy name in our salvation. Dwell Thou in our hearts, and cause us to know thy love, and to be filled with all the fulness of God.

Mercifully attend with thy blessing all the ministrations of thy holy Word throughout the world. We trust that Thou hast indeed broken down, by thy grace, the strongholds of sin and Satan in many hearts this day, and that angels are rejoicing over repenting sinners drawn to Christ. O Almighty Saviour, let it be seen that Thou hast been present, according to thy promise, wherever two or three have been gathered in thy name, by the hearts that have been subdued, the sorrows that have been cheered, and the spiritual wounds that have been healed.

Take us under thy care for the night. Bless us and all we love with the constant experience of thy goodness, and in all things help us and save us, for the sake of the Lord Jesus Christ, our only Redeemer and Saviour. Amen.

[Morning.] **THIRTY-EIGHTH WEEK.—MONDAY.** [Evening.

READ IN HOLY SCRIPTURE 1 KINGS XII.

READ IN HOLY SCRIPTURE 2 CORINTHIANS X.

MOST merciful Father, we, thy weak and sinful children, desire to approach unto Thee in prayer and worship. Let our prayer come before Thee as incense, and the lifting up of our hands as the morning sacrifice of old.

We give thanks at the remembrance of thy holiness and love, which are revealed in thy well-beloved Son, our Saviour. Enrich us, we beseech Thee, in Him with all heavenly blessings. We give thanks and rejoice that we live in a land where the true light shineth. We rejoice that while to others there are lords many, and gods many, to us there is but one God the Father, of whom are all things, and we of Him; and one Lord Jesus Christ, by whom are all things, and we by Him.

Let our hearts rise in thankfulness unto Thee on the morning of this new day, for the new mercies by which we are surrounded. We acknowledge, O Lord, thy gracious care over us through the silence and darkness of another night. We pray for a blessing to rest on that portion of Holy Scripture which we have read. We desire to thank Thee for the great national privileges which we enjoy. We pray that the shield of thy protection may evermore surround our country; that Thou wouldest preserve us from internal discord and from foreign wars, and cause that righteousness to abound amongst us which is the strength and glory of any nation.

We pray, as we are taught, for all that are in authority over us; that we may lead a quiet and peaceable life, in all godliness and honesty, for this is good and acceptable in the sight of God our Saviour. Bless our gracious Sovereign, and all our rulers, and magistrates, and judges. Give all needful wisdom to those who guide the affairs of this great empire. May the spirit of peace, and a high sense of right, distinguish our legislations, and grant thy special guidance in all times of perplexity and trial.

Pity Thou, O God, the enslaved and oppressed everywhere, and set them free. Let tyranny and oppression cease, and kings be raised up who shall be the true shepherds of their people.

And now, our heavenly Father, we commend ourselves to Thee, and the word of thy grace. We are weak, but our strength is in Thee. We are ignorant, but thy Spirit can teach and guide us. Keep us in thy fear and love this day, and help us to live as thy children and to adorn the doctrine of thy Gospel in all things. May thy peace rest on our house, and thy blessing prosper us in our daily work. Mercifully accept us and our prayers through thy Son, our blessed Lord and Saviour. Amen.

O LORD our God, all whose paths are mercy and truth unto such as keep thy covenant and thy testimonies, we beseech thee to enable us to love Thee. Remember not against us former iniquities, and let thy tender mercies speedily prevent us. Help us, O God of our salvation, for the glory of thy name. Deliver us, and purge away our sins; so we, thy servants, will give thanks unto Thee for ever.

O God, who hast redeemed us with the precious blood of thy Son, and hast called us to glory and to virtue, grant us grace that we may walk worthy of the Lord unto all well-pleasing; that we may approve things that are excellent; that we may be sincere and without offence till the day of Christ, being filled with the fruits of righteousness, which are by Jesus Christ, unto thy glory and praise. Make us harmless and sincere, the children of God, without rebuke, in the midst of a crooked and perverse generation, among whom may we shine as lights in the world, holding forth the Word of life, that whereas they speak evil of us, they may by our good works glorify Thee, our Father in heaven. We bless Thee that though we walk in the flesh, we do not war after the flesh; for the weapons of our warfare are not carnal, but mighty, through Thee, to the pulling down of strongholds, casting down imaginations, and every high thing that exalteth itself against the knowledge of God, and bringing into captivity every thought to the obedience of Christ.

Be pleased, O God, who givest grace to the humble, to clothe us with humility, and to sanctify our hearts by thy good Spirit, that we may ever esteem thy servants in the ministry very highly in love for their work's sake; and as we have received freely the blessings of redeeming grace, freely may we give. Our hearts' desire and prayer for all men is, that they may be saved. Make bare thine arm, O Lord, and subdue all nations to Thyself.

O God, our Father, accept our humble and hearty thanksgiving for the blessings of this day. Be pleased still to remember us, and those who are dear unto us, with thy favour. Let it please Thee to keep us through the watches of the night, giving sleep to our eyes and slumber to our eye-lids, and suffering no evil to befall us; that when we awake, we may still be with Thee. Let thy blessing be on all those who love our Lord and Saviour Jesus Christ; and let every tongue confess that he is Lord, to the glory of Thee, the Father.

O Lord, hear, for Jesus Christ's sake; and to Thee, Father, Son, and Holy Ghost, one God, shall be given glory and dominion for ever. Amen.

[Morning.] **THIRTY-EIGHTH WEEK.—TUESDAY.** [Evening.

READ IN HOLY SCRIPTURE 1 KINGS XIII.

READ IN HOLY SCRIPTURE GALATIANS III.

ALMIGHTY God, help us to approach Thee with that profound reverence with which we ought at all times to draw near, remembering that Thou art in heaven, and we upon the earth. Behold us, a part of thy great family, bowing before Thee, and offering our lowly worship. We confess our sins, we acknowledge our dependence upon Thee, and humbly bless Thee for continued life and continued mercies. We desire to go forth to our allotted duties this day, strong in the grace of the Lord Jesus.

We thank Thee for all thy good and great gifts: for the works of thy hands, the arrangements of thy providence, and for thy wonderful testimonies; for the privileges of the Church, the joys of a holy life, and for hopes which are full of immortality; for the substantial comforts of our home, the interchange of affectionate thought and feeling, and for the numberless mercies of our daily life, we offer our lowly lacknowledgments. Thou hast dealt well with thy servants, O Lord. Help us so to study thy holy Word, that we may discover its hidden meaning, and know the deep things of God. Give us grace to obey all thy holy commandments, to form habits of holiness, to follow every conviction of duty, and save us from those miseries and punishments which, sooner or later, overtake the transgressor.

We cannot tell what a day may bring forth, but we know that the eye of the Lord rests upon the righteous, and that his ear is open to their cry. And though we know not whether unexpected mercies or unexpected sorrows await us this day, we rejoice to know that all things work together for good to them that love God, and that all the events of our life are parts of a merciful discipline, by which Thou wouldest train and prepare us for heaven. Help us, therefore, diligently to perform our duties, calmly to wait thy will, and to stay our minds upon Thee, that we may have peace. Let thy blessing rest upon all our engagements. Prosper the work of our hands. Preserve us not only from sin, but from error and indiscretion. Help us, in the different relationships of life, to manifest the dignity, and purity, and attractiveness of the Christian character.

We thank Thee for the many assurances in thy written Word that the altars of heathen gods shall be overthrown. We devoutly thank Thee for the extension of thy kingdom, and entreat Thee speedily to accomplish the number of thine elect.

O Thou who dost ever hear the prayers of all who address Thee in the name of Jesus Christ, hear these our prayers, and accept this act of household worship, for the sake of Jesus Christ our Saviour. Amen.

MOST gracious God, the Father of our Lord Jesus Christ, look down upon us, we pray Thee, from thy holy place, and let thine ear be open to the prayers and praises which we now offer before Thee. We thank Thee for thy preserving mercy and sustaining care through this day. How kindly hast Thou provided for us! How tenderly hast Thou dealt with us! With what compassionate forbearance hast Thou borne with our self-love and self-will! And now, O Lord, Thou waitest to be gracious, and to accept and answer the prayers we offer up for the forgiveness of our many sins, and for the renewal to us of thy many mercies. Praised be thy name, O God. Honour, and glory, and thanksgiving be unto Thee for all that Thou hast done, for the riches of thy redeeming grace, and for all the gifts of thy providence. We confess we are unworthy even to gather up the crumbs of mercy which fall from thy table. We have strayed often from thy ways, and this day have done many things displeasing to Thee. Enter not into judgment with us, O God, for in thy sight shall no man living be justified. Hide thy face from our sins, and blot out all our iniquities. O Lamb of God, that takest away the sins of the world, have mercy upon us. Thou that sittest at the right hand of God the Father, a Prince and a Saviour, awaken in us a true repentance, and bestow the unspeakable blessing of a full forgiveness.

Heavenly Father, renew in us, we pray Thee, whatever has been decayed this day by the fraud and malice of the devil, or through our own sinful departure from Thee. Strengthen us by thy blessed Spirit, carry on in us the work of salvation, and cause us to grow every day in all spiritual knowledge and experience. Especially, O God, awaken in our hearts a deep and constant hatred of sin, that we may shrink from the unclean thing which Thou abhorrest. Awaken in us the sincere love of what is holy and truthful, and so fulfil in us the work of the Spirit, that the fruits of the Spirit may abound in us, and love, joy, peace, goodness, faith, meekness, and temperance be seen in our life and conduct, to the praise of thy name. Mercifully grant, O God, that none of us may receive thy grace in vain. Arouse the careless among us. Deepen the impressions of the anxious. Decide the hearts of the wavering. Oh, that when Christ shall come in the power and glory of his second advent, we, and all whom we love, may be found of Him in peace, cleansed, accepted, and sanctified.

Take us into thy care for the night. Bestow upon us needful rest, and, if it please Thee, raise us in the morning to the duties of another day. We ask all for Christ's sake. Amen.

[Morning.] **THIRTY-EIGHTH WEEK.—WEDNESDAY.** [Evening.

READ IN HOLY SCRIPTURE 1 KINGS XIV.

OUR Father who art in heaven, Almighty and All-merciful God, we thank Thee for thy kind care of us during the darkness. We bless Thee that Thou hast given thine angels charge over us, and that no evil hath befallen us, neither hath any plague come nigh our dwelling. We praise Thee that we have laid ourselves down and slept, and that we have awaked, because the Lord hath sustained us. Truly the light is sweet, and a pleasant thing it is for the eyes to behold the sun. We bless Thee for the sweeter light, and for the brighter sun, which in Christ Jesus Thou hast made to shine on us; and we pray that in his light we may see light. We pray that we may see more of the darkness and sinfulness of our own evil nature. They that are whole need not a physician, but they that are sick. O Holy Spirit of God, acquaint us with the sickness of our souls. May we know how deeply sinful we are. May we so feel our sins, and so mourn under them, as to be led in humble faith to seek for pardon and salvation in Jesus Christ. We bless Thee that Thou art the Lord that healeth us. We praise Thee that Thou forgivest all our iniquities, and healest all our diseases. We thank Thee that we have no need to send, as Jeroboam did, to any human prophet, when anxiously concerned about the health of those we love. We adore thy gracious name that, all poor and sinful as we are, we may bring our unworthy petitions and lay them with our own hands at the feet of our most loving and pitiful Saviour. We thank Thee that we know that He is touched with the feeling of our infirmities, and that in his blessed name we may come boldly to the throne of grace, sure of obtaining mercy, and of finding grace to help in time of need.

We pray that we may trust Jesus more, and love Him better. We pray that we may each one of us know this precious Saviour to be our Saviour and our Friend, the Friend who loveth at all times, and sticketh closer than a brother. We pray, O Thou all-blessed Saviour, that we may not be over-troubled with any of the cares, or sicknesses, or sufferings which Thou mayest appoint for us to bear on earth. Oh, teach us each day afresh to cast our burden upon the Lord, and to trust Thee in all things.

Help us in all the duties, and joys, and sorrows of this day. May we keep close to Christ, and do thou, O Christ, keep close to us, and cause all grace, throughout this day, to abound toward us all in all things. O our Father, forsake us not; fail not to bless us, through Jesus Christ our Saviour, to whom with Thee and the Holy Spirit be everlasting praise. Amen.

READ IN HOLY SCRIPTURE 2 CORINTHIANS XII.

LORD God Almighty, our heavenly Father in Christ Jesus, we thy children kneel before thy mercy-seat another evening. We thank Thee for the care and protection granted to us during the past day. Teach each believing heart before Thee to feel that we are in the very presence of our God; that Thou art within these walls. Teach us that our fellowship is with the Father, and with his Son Jesus Christ. Teach us by thy Holy Spirit, this evening, that we may be enabled to see what is our relation to Jesus thy Son. Teach us to look within the veil, and above this world of sin, and to know something of that new and better life which is beyond. Holy Spirit, take of the things of Jesus, and show them unto us. Teach us that in Him, our risen Head, we may draw near to the very presence-chamber of the King of kings.

But, Lord, while we thus wait upon Thee, and would fain linger in sight of thy glory, we forget not that the thorn in the flesh is given us. The old nature is still ours, and though crucified, it is always striving to regain the mastery; it is very strong to buffet us. We are still in this body of sin, still wearing our pilgrim garb, still treading an enemy's land. Keep us low in the dust of self-abasement; empty us of ourselves. We are nothing. We have nothing to bring to Thee but our sins. Our only plea is that we are sinners, and that in stead of sinners Jesus died. We are so weak and feeble as to be utterly unable to save ourselves. Teach us to listen to those loving words which Jesus says to us to-night, "My grace is sufficient for thee." May we be content with whatever Thou dost appoint for us, whether it be joy or sorrow, whether it be poverty or riches; and glory in our infirmities, that the power of Christ may rest upon us. Oh, that we may know more of the power of Christ in our daily conflict with sin and Satan. Saviour, do Thou never leave us, or we fall. Keep us ever looking to Thee, and to Thee only.

Heavenly Father, we pray for others, for friends and relatives, and those endeared to each of us by ties of earthly relationship. Do Thou bless them in Jesus. And if there be any of them, or any of those who are now kneeling before Thee, who do not know Jesus as their Saviour, teach them their danger; show them their need of a Saviour; show them that the great debt of sin has been paid; teach them to trust their never-dying souls to the blood shed upon Calvary, and Thou shalt have all the glory now and throughout eternity.

Hear us, O Lord God, in these and all our unworthy prayers, for the sake of thy Son, our Saviour Jesus Christ. Amen.

[Morning.]   THIRTY-EIGHTH WEEK.—THURSDAY.   [Evening.

READ IN HOLY SCRIPTURE 1 KINGS XVII.

RIGHTEOUS and merciful Father, help us to come acceptably to Thee, who art ready to manifest thy love to all who seek it, through the mediation of Jesus Christ our Lord. In his name, and in his only, we plead with Thee now. Graciously regard, and aid, and bless us all. We thank Thee for sleep and rest; for the powers we now enjoy, and for fresh opportunities of using them in thy service. We thank Thee for our daily bread. Suffer not the commonness of thy blessings to make us insensible to their value and to thy goodness. Teach us to see thy hand in the ordinary supply of our wants, as plainly and gratefully as Elijah did in the miracles wrought for his support. We thank Thee for thy Word, to guide us on our pilgrimage to heaven; for Jesus Christ, the Bread of life, to nourish and strengthen us; and for the Holy Spirit, to enlighten, to purify, and to gladden our souls. Guard us, O Lord, from repeating this day sins we have confessed and deplored in past times. Let not Satan prevail against us. Help us in everything to think more of pleasing Thee than of pleasing ourselves. Make it our delight to know Thee, to love Thee, to extol Thee. Through the merits of thy Son, our Redeemer, mercifully accept, and sanctify, and encourage us amidst all the dangers and trials, the duties and joys of the day before us. Keep us from Ahab's spirit of worldliness, and unbelief, and pride. Gracious Father, save us from all formalism in religion; from all vain confidence; from every impure, selfish, and unchristian thought. If sharp discipline be awaiting us, enable us to receive it with meekness and submission. Should death be near us, or any one of our kindred, prepare our minds for thy will. Draw us nearer to Christ and to each other. Increase continually our fellowship with the Saviour, so that death, whenever it comes, may be gain. Has any one of us arisen without a due sense of obligation to Thee? be pleased to awaken that sense now. Is any heart trembling in anticipation of trial and toil? inspire such with Christian courage and hope. Be to us, merciful God, all that we need, from the beginning of the day unto the end of it. [Give to the children thy Holy Spirit. Teach them to follow Jesus in everything. Help them to love and to trust Thee with all their hearts.] Remember for good all who are suffering from want, from sickness, from bereavement. Bind up the broken-hearted, and heal their wounds. Make all happy in doing good to each other and in glorifying thy holy name. Let this our morning sacrifice be as incense before Thee, O God, and do for us exceeding abundantly above all we ask or think, through Jesus Christ our Lord. Amen.

READ IN HOLY SCRIPTURE 2 CORINTHIANS XIII.

ALMIGHTY and ever-present God, who searchest out all our ways, and to whom all hearts are open, help us to remember that Thou, with whom we have to do, seekest truth in the inward parts, and that Thou hatest all falsehood and lying.

We acknowledge that we do not know ourselves as we ought; we are blind to our own faults, sharp-sighted at the failings of others, and too ready to justify and excuse our conduct. Make us to deal more honestly by ourselves; place us before the glass of thy holy Word, that we may see what manner of persons we are. Teach us to examine into our state before Thee; to know how we stand in thy sight, as believers or unbelievers, as accepted in Christ or still afar off, without Christ, and therefore without hope. We mourn that there is so little of Christ in us; that we are so unlike to Him, and so unworthy in many respects of the name we bear. May a solemn sense of our obligations lead us to greater effort to be conformed to his image, and to be made new creatures in Him, without deception.

Blessed Jesus, we would look upon Thee with the eye of faith, contemplating thy perfect example, watching thy footsteps, and steadily following thy guidance. Correct us where we are wrong. May we suffer no sin to pass unrepented of, nor rest with any unforgiven. When we see others sin, may we be kept from following a multitude to do evil; and if this day we have done anything simply because we have seen others do it, may we be in future watchful against so great a danger. Grant us thy Holy Spirit, to assist us in examining ourselves; and when overwhelmed with a sense of our sinfulness, direct our eyes to the Lamb of God, who taketh away the sin of the world. Thus pardoned and at peace with all, we would retire to rest this night, looking for the mercy of our Lord Jesus unto eternal life.

We cannot close the day without thanking Thee for its manifold blessings, and for all the good things Thou hast caused to fall to our lot. We would call upon our souls and all within us to bless and praise thy holy name. Grant that the remembrance of thy blessings, which we share with so many, may lead us to love our fellow-men, as partakers of the benefit, as fellow-heirs and recipients of grace, as those for whom Jesus shed his most precious blood, redeemed from sin and reserved for glory. And now, O blessed, glorious, and undivided Trinity, Three and One, we reverence Thee as God, humbling ourselves before the mystery of thy nature, but looking to the effectual power of thine operations, and praying that the grace of the Lord Jesus, the love of God, and the communion of the Holy Ghost, may be with us all evermore. Amen.

[Morning.] **THIRTY-EIGHTH WEEK.—FRIDAY.** [Evening.

READ IN HOLY SCRIPTURE 1 KINGS XVIII. 1–20.

ALMIGHTY and ever-living God, the gracious Giver of all blessings, accept our thanks for the mercies of the night, through which Thou hast safely preserved us. By thy Holy Spirit make us more deeply sensible of thy loving-kindness, and stir up our hearts to praise, not only for the daily bounties of thy providence, but also for the unsearchable riches of Christ. Lord God, who is like unto Thee, pardoning iniquity, transgression, and sin; long-suffering, and of great kindness, causing thy sun to shine on the evil and the good, and sending rain on the just and on the unjust?

We desire, O God, to enter on this day's duties with thy favour and protection. Our pathway in the world is beset by many and constant temptations; the great enemy of souls is ever on the watch for our souls, and we are weak, ignorant, and sinful, unable to do anything that is good without Thee. Give us now, we pray Thee, forgiveness and peace, that we may go forth with the assurance that Thou art our God, and that in all our ways Thou art at hand to help and defend us. Suffer us not to turn aside from the straight path of thy commandments into ways of our own choosing, or to forget in all our engagements that Thou, God, seest us. Keep us upright, sincere, and truthful in everything, anxious to do what is just and pure in the sight of God and man, and thus to adorn the doctrine of God our Saviour in all things. We feel how unworthy is all our obedience; but, O God, accept it for thy dear Son's sake, and give us so largely of thy heavenly grace that it may be more cheerful and self-denying, and spring from hearts full of love to Thee. Especially give us a tender conscience, that we may not harden our hearts against thy Word, or be insensible to the teachings of thy Spirit. Fulfil in us all thy work, and make us monuments of mercy and grace for ever and ever.

Look in thy tender compassion on all who are dear to us, and guide them, by thy grace, in the narrow way of eternal life, and give them the blessed experience of thy great salvation. [Convert the hearts of the children of our household to Jesus Christ. Teach them, O Lord, the things of God, that even from tender years they may grow in grace and in the knowledge of their Lord and Saviour. Spread around them the shield of thy Divine guardianship, and suffer not the influence of an evil world to keep them away from Thee.] Let thy blessing rest on the whole Church of Christ. Prosper all its labours for thy glory, and make it an honour and a praise in the earth.

These and all other mercies we implore at thy hand, in the name of our adorable Redeemer, Jesus Christ. Amen.

READ IN HOLY SCRIPTURE ACTS XX. 1–12.

HEAVENLY Father, we kneel before thy mercy-seat this evening, praising Thee for our creation, preservation, and for all the blessings of this life, but above all for the means of grace, and for the hope of glory. Enable us, O Lord, to see the depth of thy love towards us, in sending thy dear Son to atone for our sins, and to give us access to thy throne of grace.

But we are sorely beset and hindered in running the race set before us. It is not indeed with us as it was with thy servant St. Paul, that the preaching of thy Word excites an uproar amongst the people, and endangers life; but still thy people have trials and temptations, and spiritual enemies lay wait for their souls. We are dwelling in tabernacles of flesh, and too often do our souls partake of the drowsiness and sleep that creeps over our mortal frames when wearied with worldly labours; but we pray that we may be kept from the sleep of death, to which the frailty of human nature ever leads the soul.

Let thy good Spirit, O God, breathe upon us the breath of life, and let thy right hand be stretched out to defend us from all our enemies. May we and all whom we love rejoice together in Christ Jesus. Prepare us, O Lord, day by day, for eternity. Send down answers to our prayers. Let the labours of thy ministering servants be blessed to our souls; let the various means of grace be valued by us. Give us increasing love for thy holy Word, and a sincere and earnest faith in thy promises. Deepen in us godly sorrow for sin, and unfold more clearly to us the riches of thy love in Christ Jesus.

Forbid that anything should stand between us and our high Christian duties and privileges, and suffer not coldness and apathy to seize our souls, because persecution for Christ's sake does not now drive thy servants to upper chambers and secret places that they may worship their Lord; but rather may gratitude for our favoured lot make us more earnest, more loving, more active, more self-denying in carrying on the work for which thy servants of old suffered, even unto death, willingly accepting martyrdom if Jesus might be honoured through them. May we enjoy constant communion with Thee. Come, O Thou Holy Spirit of Jesus, and reign in our hearts, and suffer no other lord to have dominion there.

Come and put within us real and living faith, that we may experience the love of Christ, and become the honoured instruments of making known to others thy salvation.

Hear us, O God, our Father, for Jesus Christ's sake, to whom be everlasting praise and glory. Amen.

[Morning.] **THIRTY-EIGHTH WEEK.—SATURDAY.** [Evening.

READ IN HOLY SCRIPTURE 1 KINGS XVIII. 21—40.

READ IN HOLY SCRIPTURE GALATIANS I.

O LORD God of Abraham, of Isaac, and of Jacob, let it be known to us this day that Thou art the Hearer and Answerer of prayer. We acknowledge Thee to be the Lord, and desire to humble ourselves before Thee, and invoke thy favour and blessing. We adore Thee for thy mercy in permitting us to begin another day in peace and safety. The repose enjoyed by us during the night has been vouchsafed by Thee. Our preservation is due to thy watchful care. We would renew our covenant with Thee this morning, and dedicate to Thee afresh all the powers of our mind and body. We thank Thee for that portion of thy Word on which we have been meditating. May thy good Spirit impress its teaching on our hearts. We confess with shame that our conduct has often been such as to make men doubt the sincerity of our profession. We have been backward in the confession of our faith. We have been slow to defend the honour of our Master in the presence of unbelievers. We have sought the approval of the world rather than that of our God, and have often followed its maxims and neglected the holy precepts of the Book of life. Oh! remove from us all traces of indecision of character. If any now before Thee have been seeking to unite the service of the world and that of God, oh, give them grace to relinquish so vain and profitless a pursuit. Unite their scattered affections, and let the love of Christ, who shed his blood for sinners, bring them to repentance. [We pray especially for the children of this household, that they may early choose that good part which shall never be taken away from them.]

And now, Lord, what wait we for? Truly our hope is in Thee. Let the sacred fire of the Holy Ghost purify our hearts, and inflame our zeal. Help us to go forth to the duties of the day in the strength of our Redeemer. May our services be accepted, and our sins and shortcomings forgiven, through his gracious intercession.

Bless this day all the ministers of the everlasting Gospel. Assist them in their preparation for their solemn office. Give us all grace to lay aside worldly cares at the close of this day, and set our house in order for the duties of the blessed Sabbath. May many souls be added to the Church on the morrow, as living stones in the temple of grace. Hear us, O God, hear us, that our nation may know that Thou art God. We wait for the fulfilment of thy promise. Send down showers of blessings on our land, and the whole world. Wilt thou not revive us again, that thy people may rejoice in Thee? We ask all in the name of Jesus Christ, to whom with Thee, O Father, and Thee, O blessed Spirit, be everlasting glory. Amen.

O THOU gracious and ever blessed Lord God Almighty, Thou who art the God and Father of our Lord Jesus Christ, through whom alone we dare to approach Thee, and whose name alone we mention in thy presence, look down upon us in Him, O Lord, and for his sake receive us graciously and love us freely.

We humbly thank Thee for the mercies of the past day; for having preserved us amid many perils, and for having provided for us, out of the riches of thy grace, things needful both for our souls and for our bodies. We acknowledge with shame and confusion of face that we are unprofitable servants—that we have not rendered unto Thee according to that we have received. Whilst Thou hast been showering down blessings upon us, we have been turning away from Thee. We have gone after other gods, and we have served them. Pardon our iniquity, O Lord, for it is great. Wash us in that fountain which Thou hast opened for sin and uncleanness. Pour down upon us thy holy, regenerating, and sanctifying Spirit. Make us new creatures. Create in us a clean heart, O God, and renew a right spirit within us.

We remember, O Lord, that another of thy precious Sabbaths is near at hand. We desire at this time to plead for those who on the morrow shall plead for Thee. Grant them to speak only in full accordance with thy Word. Let their preaching be with all clearness and distinctness of doctrine. Let no error be intermingled therewith. Work mightily through them to the turning of many from darkness to light, and from the power of Satan unto Thee; and grant that the whole body of thy Church may be comforted, refreshed, and edified.

And, gracious Father, we desire now to commit ourselves to thy care. Watch over us and keep us through the night unto which Thou hast brought us; strengthen us to rise on the morrow so refreshed in mind and body as to be prepared to join in the services of thy sanctuary, and worship Thee with great delight. Let thy blessing rest upon all the means of grace which Thou hast appointed for us. Grant us to pray in faith, to sing thy praises with the understanding, and to give attentive heed to the preaching of thy Word. Reveal unto us more and more of thy dear Son. Grant us to seek justification, not by the works of the law, but by the righteousness of Christ. And lest we should frustrate the grace of God and make Christ in any way to have died in vain, oh, grant that henceforward, being crucified with Christ, we may live the life we now live in the flesh by the faith of Him who loved us and gave Himself for us. Amen.

[Morning.] **THIRTY-NINTH WEEK.—LORD'S DAY.** [Evening.

READ IN HOLY SCRIPTURE 1 KINGS XIX.

TO Thee, O God, all hearts are open. Thou knowest how often we have gone astray from Thee by the failing of our faith in the hour of temptation and trial, and have forgotten thy sure words of comfort, "I will never leave thee nor forsake thee." Thou knowest the weakness of our mortal nature. Oh, grant us such strength and protection as shall carry us through all temptations, and shall keep us steadfast in thy faith and fear. Help us ever to look unto Jesus, the Author and Finisher of our faith, who fainted not under sorrow and suffering, but endured the cross, despising the shame.

We also pray Thee, O Lord, that when we read the records of thy mercy to thy people of old, our faith may be strengthened in that never-failing providence which ordereth all things both in heaven and earth. Thou didst feed thy people with manna in the wilderness, and didst refresh thy servant Elijah with food from heaven, teaching us thereby that, like as a father pitieth his children, so the Lord pitieth them that fear Him. Thou hast said that not a sparrow falleth to the ground without Thee, and Thou hast taught us to ask Thee for our daily bread: O God, we thank Thee for these thy mercies, and we would seek to keep far from us all anxious thoughts of the morrow, knowing that Thou art faithful who hast promised.

Let the wondrous food wherewith Thou didst strengthen thy servant Elijah remind us of that true bread of life with which Thou dost vouchsafe to feed us in the wilderness of this world, even Jesus Christ, thine unspeakable gift, who is the bread of God, coming down from heaven, and giving life unto the world. Lord, evermore give us this bread. Give us a living faith in Him, that we may rest our hopes on Him alone for pardon, peace, and eternal life. And we thank Thee, O God, for that Thou hast given thy Son, our Saviour, Jesus Christ, not only to die for us, but also to be our exalted High Priest, who ever liveth to make intercession for us. Oh, help us to value more and more the ordinances of thy house. May they be to us means of grace. Hear our prayers, and accept our praises. Guide us by thy Spirit into all truth, that we may grow in grace, and in the knowledge of our Lord and Saviour, Jesus Christ.

And grant, O Lord, that when life's journey is ended, we may sit down at the marriage supper of the Lamb, when He who is in the midst of the throne shall feed us, and shall lead us unto living fountains of waters, and God shall wipe away all tears from our eyes. Hear us, for the sake of Jesus Christ, our Lord. Amen.

READ IN HOLY SCRIPTURE GALATIANS II.

O ETERNAL God, our Father in heaven, hallowed and adored be thy name. All glory and honour be to Thee for the great mercies with which Thou hast crowned our life this holy day. For all our temporal blessings, food to eat, raiment to put on, and the mercies of health and strength Thou hast given us, we thank Thee. For the privileges of the house of prayer, for the ministrations of thy Gospel, whereby are made known to us anew thy matchless grace and love in Christ Jesus, we thank Thee. Gracious Father, bestow, with all thy blessings, the new heart and the right spirit, that we may be truly grateful to Thee for all that Thou hast done, and be anxious to show our thankfulness, not only with our lips, but in a life of dedication to thy service.

But, O God, with our thanksgivings we are constrained to mingle sorrowful confessions of sin and earnest supplications for pardon. Thou hast been near, but how little have we been conscious of thy presence! with how much irreverence has our worship been marred and defiled! How have our thoughts wandered from Thee! how careless have we been in listening to thy holy Word! Lord, we are ashamed of our poor and worthless services. But for thy tenderness and compassion, and the prevailing efficacy of Christ's intercession, we dare not hope for acceptance. Have mercy upon us, O God, and blot out all our sins, for thy name's sake, for they are great. Quicken our hearts, and arouse our languid affections, that we may worship and serve Thee better in future, and come to thy ordinances with that hungering and thirsting of soul to which Thou hast promised thy blessing.

Merciful Father, cause thy Word, which we have heard, to be treasured up and remembered by us all, even when the day of rest is gone. Let not Satan snatch it away or the cares and pleasures of life choke it. We desire to be growing in grace and the knowledge of our Lord and Saviour Jesus Christ, who loved us and gave Himself for us. Let the warnings of thy ministers be fastened on our consciences, and the promises of thy Word encourage us to diligence in every duty. Increase our weak faith, and nourish in us all thy work of grace. Preserve us and all thy people from false doctrine, and especially make clear to us the way of salvation through faith in Jesus Christ. Bless all the ministrations of thy servants this day, and make thy Gospel to triumph in the conversion both of Jews and Gentiles.

Take us now into thy gracious keeping. Bless us and all for whom we would pray, according to thy mercy and our need, for Jesus Christ's sake, to whom, with Thee and the Holy Spirit, be everlasting praise. Amen.

[267]

[Morning.] **THIRTY-NINTH WEEK.—MONDAY.** [Evening.]

READ IN HOLY SCRIPTURE 1 KINGS XXI.

O GOD, we thank Thee for again permitting us to draw near to Thee. We bless thy name for the mercies of the past night. We praise Thee for the sacred privileges of the Sabbath, which we have been permitted to enjoy. May the influence of its holy engagements abide with us all the week. Help us to remember the sacred lessons we have learned, and to exhibit to the world that we have indeed been with Jesus.

Again we enter upon the world's duties, and go forth to life's trials and temptations. Go Thou with us, blessed God, and we shall not fall. Abide Thou near us, and we shall be safe from evil, and strong for labour. Make us more than conquerors in every temptation. We know not what may lie before us. Let the thought that Thou knowest all, and canst prepare us for all, take away all fear. May we be careful for nothing, but in everything, by prayer and supplication with thanksgiving, make known our requests unto Thee. Make us, above all things, earnest about our souls, seeking first thy kingdom and thy righteousness, and all else shall be added unto us.

We thank Thee for the lessons Thou hast taught us this morning in thy Word. Keep us from all the iniquities that polluted king Ahab. Let us not be tempted to think that such sins could never overtake us. Without thy grace there is no depth of iniquity to which we might not fall.

Keep us very humble. Make us over watchful. Let him that thinketh he standeth, take heed lest he fall. Put far from us all covetous desires. May we be content with such things as we have. Help us to overcome all evil desires in their beginnings, and to close our eyes against everything that would lead us astray. Preserve us from the evil influences of bad companionship. Keep us from making those who know Thee not our friends. Help us to guard against entering into close relationship with any who are not thy children. May we give no heed to the dearest friend we have if his influence be for evil. May we lead many along the narrow way of life, but never draw any from duty and holiness.

Imprint deeply upon our minds the solemn thought that every sin we ever commit will assuredly find us out, and that no wicked word or deed shall be hidden from thy sight. O Lord, as we call to mind the many and grievous sins that we have committed, help us to cry to Thee earnestly for pardon, through Jesus Christ. We have greatly sinned against Thee. Our iniquities cry to Thee for vengeance. We have deserved thy wrath. Good Lord, deliver us.

O God, pardon—sanctify—bless us, for Jesus Christ's sake. Amen.

READ IN HOLY SCRIPTURE GALATIANS III.

ALMIGHTY and most merciful Father, another day has been numbered with eternity since we last met before Thee, and we have new mercies to praise Thee for, and new sins for which to seek thy forgiveness. Lord, teach us to pray. Mercifully bow down thine ear and hear us, and give us an answer of peace.

Blessed art Thou, O God, far above all our praises. All the hosts of heaven, ten thousand times ten thousand, and thousands of thousands, sing thy praises, and rest not day and night, saying, "Holy, holy, holy, Lord God of hosts; heaven and earth are full of thy glory." We would join their glorious company above, and desire with them to say, "Worthy is the Lamb that was slain to receive power, and riches, and wisdom, and strength, and honour, and glory, and blessing." With every creature in heaven, and on earth, and under the earth, we would join in praising Thee. But chiefly would we praise Thee for that wonderful manifestation of thy love towards a ruined world, in that Thou gavest thine only-begotten Son to die that we might live. In the greatness of that gift enable us to see at once the greatness of thy love, and the greatness of sin; that nothing could vindicate thy broken law, and satisfy thy offended justice, but the doings and sufferings of thy dear Son; that nothing could save us from the withering curse but our blessed Saviour standing in our stead, and being made a curse for us. Oh, help us, as we gaze upon the cross and its woe, to see sin as Thou seest it, as that which stained thy glory, crucified the Son of God, and as that abominable thing which Thou hatest. Lord, we would hate sin, even as Thou hatest it; we would look upon Him whom we have pierced, and mourn. Our sins are many, and they are great; for thy name's sake pardon our iniquity; look upon us for Jesus' sake. We have no other name to plead, but we know that his name is all-prevailing with Thee. Our only plea, then, to-night, is the atoning sacrifice of thy dear Son. Wash us in the fountain of his blood, and accept us in the Beloved.

Thou knowest the dangers in our paths; pour out upon us more and more of the Holy Ghost, to keep us and to guide us. Hedge up our way, if necessary, with thorns, so that we may never turn aside out of the right path. Guard us against all declension in heart or in practice. Conform us more and more to the image of Christ, and help us so to live to Christ, that others may be won to Jesus by our life. Lord, make us holy, as Thou art holy.

And now take us, and all dear to us, under thy keeping this night, and bless us, O our Father, for Jesus Christ's sake. Amen.

[Morning.] THIRTY-NINTH WEEK.—TUESDAY. [Evening.

READ IN HOLY SCRIPTURE 1 KINGS XXII. 1—38.

WE praise Thee, O Lord, for thy goodness in permitting us to see the light of another day. Refreshed by sleep, we now go forth to the duties Thou hast given us to fulfil; and wherever thy providence may lead us, there grant that thy grace may prove sufficient for us. Enable us to learn from thy holy Word the lessons Thou hast designed it to teach us. May the light of thy truth irradiate our minds, and cheer and gladden our hearts.

If this day we should be placed in circumstances of perplexity, circumstances in which we know not where to walk, or how to act, oh, let us not lean on our own understanding. Do Thou direct our steps; and, as we seek thy guidance, may we hear a voice behind us, saying, "This is the way, walk ye in it." In all times of weakness, be Thou our strength; in the hour of sorrow, be Thou our joy; and in every season of difficulty and doubt, be Thou, O Lord, alone our wisdom and our guide.

Grant thy blessing on thy ministering servants. May they all be messengers of the Lord of hosts! Cause them faithfully to declare thy truth, whether men will hear or whether they will forbear; and let neither the flattery of a smiling world nor the opposition of a frowning world move them from the path of duty.

O Lord, Thou art God alone. Thou sittest on thy throne, and all the hosts of heaven surround Thee. Thou orderest all things according to the counsel of thine own righteous will. The bow may be drawn at a venture, but the arrow is directed by Thee. Enable us to feel that nothing is beneath thy notice, nothing beyond thy control. Give us grace to see thy hand in the events of our daily life; and whether those events be prosperous or adverse, whether they be agreeable to our natural preferences or opposed to them, grant that we may look beyond and above the instruments, and see Thee, our Father, in all.

Vouchsafe, O Lord, to keep us this day without sin. Give us a holy dread of tampering or trifling with it. May we not nourish in our hearts anything displeasing to Thee. In the fall of Ahab may we see how certainly sin is followed by punishment, and how impossible it is for man's efforts to avert the punishment Thou hast righteously denounced.

Lord, we are sinners: we all deserve thy wrath. But, oh! we praise Thee that the punishment we have deserved has been borne for us by our sinless Substitute, Jesus Christ the righteous, perfect God and perfect man, our ever-blessed and adorable Redeemer. For his sake, hear and help and save us, and to Him, with Thee, O Father, and Thee, O Holy Ghost, one God, we will ascribe everlasting praise. Amen.

READ IN HOLY SCRIPTURE GALATIANS IV.

O THOU eternal, omniscient, and omnipresent Jehovah, our most gracious Father in Christ Jesus. We bow ourselves before thy Divine Majesty, and entreat Thee, for the sake of thy dear Son, to hear, to answer, and to bless us. We confess our sins unto Thee; our many sins, in thought, word, and deed; and we pray Thee to pardon and deliver us for Christ's sake.

We praise Thee that Thou didst, in the fulness of time, send forth thy Son, made of a woman, made under the law, to redeem them that were under the law, that we might receive the adoption of sons. And, O our Father, if thou hast made us thy children by adoption and grace, we beseech Thee to send forth the Spirit of thy Son into our hearts, enabling us, in all sincerity and truth, to cry unto Thee, Abba, Father. We rejoice that Thou dost not look upon us, who believe in Jesus, merely as servants, but as sons and daughters of Thee, the Lord Almighty; and if we are children, then we are heirs of God, and joint-heirs with Christ. We bless Thee for the privilege Thou hast conferred upon us, in having admitted any of us unworthy creatures into the family and household of Thee, our God. We pray that we may be preserved from all evil, from formality or hypocrisy in thy service. If thy truth hath made us free, then are we free indeed; we would not turn again to weak and beggarly elements, but having been justified by faith, we would enjoy peace with Thee, through Jesus Christ our Lord. If we are called to suffer persecution for Christ's sake, seeing that he who is born after the flesh will persecute him who is born after the Spirit, then let us ever remember thy words, O Lord Jesus, "In the world ye shall have tribulation; but be of good cheer, I have overcome the world."

We pray unto Thee on behalf of our friends and relatives: bless them with all spiritual blessings in Christ Jesus. Take them and us into thy care this night, and protect us from all evil. Look with thy favour upon our Sovereign; may she always seek first thy kingdom and thy righteousness. Give her councillors wisdom, that they may so guide the affairs of this nation, that thy name may be glorified in all they do. May thy Word have free course, and be glorified amongst us. Let all thy ministering servants be clothed with righteousness. Enable them rightly to divide thy Word, and grant that thy Word preached may be instrumental both in the conversion of sinners and in the edifying of thy saints. Grant this, and every other needful blessing, we humbly beseech Thee, for Jesus Christ's sake, our most blessed Lord and Saviour, to whom, with Thee and the Eternal Spirit, be everlasting praise. Amen.

[Morning.] THIRTY-NINTH WEEK.—WEDNESDAY. [Evening.

READ IN HOLY SCRIPTURE 2 CHRONICLES XX. 1—20.

READ IN HOLY SCRIPTURE GALATIANS V.

O LORD our God, we desire to be filled with holy confidence and reliance upon thine aid. For our sins and iniquities, and for the trial of our faith, are we made to feel the malice of many foes. But may we learn through each affliction to trust Thee more implicitly, and to call upon Thee unceasingly. Are not the wicked thy sword, O Lord, and they who trust in Thee the sheep of thy pastures? But chiefly when the sons of wickedness arise up against us, and our souls are sore tried with many fears, may we remember thy wonders of old. Are not the children of faith counted for thy people, and the seed of Abraham thy servant dear in thy sight? Thou dost permit us to rejoice in the promises, and to experience the exceeding joy which arises to them who are clothed in the justifying righteousness of Jesus. Thou hast given to us the promise of an inheritance among the saints in light. Thou hast shown to us that the path of faith is the path of safety, and that they who know Thee now by faith shall attain one day to the fruition of thy glorious Godhead.

Graciously pour into our hearts, in fuller measure, the spirit of grace and of supplication. Teach us not to fear though the earth be removed, and though the mountains be carried into the midst of the sea. But rather may we expect perpetually to be cheered and sustained by thy gracious interposition, and made to delight more and more in the safety which Thou dost accord to them who love Thee.

Send, we pray Thee, thy Holy Spirit upon thy people. Enlighten the minds of those whom Thou dost set in authority, and enable them to perceive and know what they ought to do. Give a word of wisdom to all thy watchmen, and teach them to lift up the voice and to cry, and to instruct and teach thy people. Above all would we pray for the monarch whom Thou hast set over us. Oh, may her heart be fixed, and not fear for evil tidings. May she be cheered and comforted by the words of them whom Thou hast charged to speak in thy name, and may she reverently hear and obey when thou dost deign to teach.

Thus, O Lord, shall thy people fear no evil tidings. The hearts of all that trust Thee shall be established, and have great peace. The word of God shall grow and prosper through the fidelity of them that serve Thee, and Thou shalt get Thee honour, O Lord, through thy mercy and goodness unto thy chosen.

And now we pray that Thou wilt keep us this day, and every day, and make all thy dispensations of thy providence to work in us according to the good pleasure of thy will, through Jesus Christ our Lord. Amen.

AGAIN, O Lord, hast Thou, by thy good providence, brought us to the close of a day in which grace, mercy, and peace have been multiplied unto us. May we be enabled, by thy Holy Spirit's aid, to look backward, and say, "Hitherto hath the Lord helped us with his providence and his grace," supplying all our temporal and our spiritual necessities. May we look forward with quietness and confidence to all that may befall us and ours in time to come. And yet, O Lord, the very thought and mention of so marvellous a proof of thine unmerited goodness in giving a promise of grace and glory, fills us with shame, and brings us into the dust, while we lay our hands upon our mouths and say, "Behold we are vile; what shall we say unto Thee? Enter not into judgment with thy servants, O Lord; spare us from those evils which we most righteously have deserved."

The day is past, and in the book of thy remembrance innumerable sins and ignorances must be recorded. We pray Thee, blot them out with Christ's most precious blood; deal not with us after our sins; pardon our iniquity, for it is great. The night has now arrived, and in closing it with Thee, we have not forgotten to read thy holy Word. Have any fallen from grace? do Thou restore them, and though making them to feel how evil and bitter thing it is to depart from Thee, yet take away all their iniquity, receive them graciously, love them freely. Have any of us begun to run well but are hindered? remove every obstacle out of the way; renew them with fresh strength, so to run that they may obtain the prize set before them. Are any in danger of misusing Christian liberty? Give them a right judgment, a sound faith, and establish them in thy truth.

Grant that all of us may be endued with, and be taught and led by the Holy Spirit. May the works of the flesh be mortified, subdued, and overcome. May the fruits of the Spirit—love, joy, peace—be especially apparent amongst us, as individuals and as a family. May we all live in the Spirit, walk in the Spirit, and finally, by thy mercy, reach thy glory.

To our confessions and petitions we add our praises and thanksgivings for mercies countless as the sands, for creation, preservation, and all the blessings of this life; and with an earnest, hearty prayer for thy blessing on all we love, and for whom in duty we are bound to pray, and a petition for thy watchful eye to be on us through the night, we lay ourselves down in peace, and take our rest, for it is Thou only that maketh us to dwell in safety. We ask all for Jesus Christ's sake. Amen.

[Morning.] **THIRTY-NINTH WEEK.—THURSDAY.** [Evening.

READ IN HOLY SCRIPTURE 2 KINGS II.

MERCIFUL and gracious God, let thy favour rest upon us in this our morning worship, and give us, we beseech Thee, the spirit of fervent prayer and praise. Increase our faith in thy promises, and whenever we approach thy footstool grant that it may be with a deep sense of our own sinfulness and a full assurance of thy grace and love in Jesus Christ, our Lord.

Again Thou hast preserved us while we slept, and hast raised us up in such health and strength as Thou seest good for us. Praised be thy name for temporal mercies, but above all for the spiritual blessings which Thou hast provided for us and promised to us in the Gospel of thy Son. Warm our cold and languid hearts by the constant experience of thy grace, and the more we receive at thy hands the more may our thankfulness abound, and the heartier be our devotion to thy service.

Work in us, we pray Thee, a godly sorrow for sin, and a saving faith in our Lord Jesus Christ. Cleanse us in his precious blood from every guilty stain; clothe us with his righteousness; sanctify us by the Holy Ghost; and increase in us that holiness without which none can see the Lord. Oh, enable us to enter on this day's duties with the consciousness of thy favour and grace; then shall we have courage in thy strength to do such things as please Thee. Leave us not to the frailty of our own hearts and the power of temptation, but be Thou with us, to deliver us from all dangers, and to uphold us in all temptations. Let thy blessed Spirit guide us in all our perplexities, and teach us thy holy will. Let neither the comforts of home nor the cares of the world steal our hearts from Thee. In the midst of the concerns of time, we desire to live in the remembrance of eternity, and to labour diligently in the station to which Thou hast called us, as those who serve the Lord Christ. Come, O Holy Ghost, and enlighten our dark understandings, that we may know the love of Christ in all its constraining power, and be filled with the fulness of God.

Heavenly Father, we pray for all whom we love. Let thy blessing be upon them, and thy protection be over them this day. Guard them from all evil, and guide their steps in the ways of thy commandments. [Regard with thy special favour the children of our family. Suffer them not to grow up without the teaching of thy Holy Spirit. Show them their sin, and reveal to their hearts the tenderness and love of Jesus.] Prosper thy Word in all the world this day, and make it effectual to the salvation of the unsaved and the comfort of the sorrowing. Hear us and bless us, O God, for Jesus' sake. Amen.

READ IN HOLY SCRIPTURE GALATIANS VI.

ALMIGHTY God and, most merciful Father, we come before Thee again this evening to acknowledge with thankfulness thy continued daily mercies to us in Christ Jesus. Raise our hearts to Thee in true love: for we would be followers of Thee, as dear children.

Give us grace to live in the spirit of meekness, gentleness, and Christian forbearance towards all men. Teach us to bear one another's burdens, and to bear with one another's infirmities. As disciples of Christ, enable us to fulfil the law of Christ, which is the law of love. May that mind be in us which was in Him; so shall we do nothing through strife or vain-glory, but in lowliness of mind shall we learn, by thy grace, to esteem others better than ourselves.

Teach us to know and to feel the burden and the guilt of sin. Make us to know our infirmities and our besetting sin. O heavenly Father, show us to ourselves, that we may know what we are in thy sight; thus lead us to lay our burden of sin on Jesus Christ.

O Lord, Thou showest unto us, in thy Word, that whatsoever a man soweth, that shall he also reap. Help us to search our heart and our ways, that we may know what we are sowing in preparation for the day of judgment. Oh, mercifully grant that in that day none of us shall be heard to say, "The harvest is past, and I am not saved!" O our God and Father, give to us that inward and spiritual grace by which we may be new creatures in Christ Jesus, born again of the Holy Spirit; and so, being led by Him in our daily life here, may reap life everlasting.

Bless us, as a family, according to our special need. Make us each to know that we are in the place which Thou hast appointed for us, and that Thou art leading us by the right way. Enable us faithfully to discharge the duties that lie before us every day; so that, whether we rule or serve, we may rule or serve according to the light of thy Word and the power of thy grace. So shall peace and mercy be our portion, and the grace of our Lord and Saviour Jesus Christ be upon us, as our strength and sure defence.

Bless all our relations, friends, and neighbours, especially the sick and afflicted; bless our enemies, if we have any, and turn their hearts. Greatly bless the ministers of thy Word; own, honour, accept their work, and make them successful winners of souls to Christ for salvation.

And now, O Lord, take us unto thy fatherly care and protection. May we sleep in peace, in the assured hope of the forgiveness of all our sins through Jesus Christ, our Mediator and Redeemer. Amen.

[Morning.] **THIRTY-NINTH WEEK.—FRIDAY.** [Evening.

READ IN HOLY SCRIPTURE 2 KINGS IV. 1—37.

ALMIGHTY, ever-living God, the God and Father of our Lord Jesus Christ, we come once more into thy presence, to offer up the tribute of our morning sacrifice of praise and thanksgiving. We adore and bless thy holy name for all that thou art in Thyself, and for all that Thou hast done for us, thy sinful creatures. Blessing, and honour, and glory, and power be unto Thee, that sittest upon the throne, and to the Lamb, for ever and ever. Hearken, O gracious God, unto the cry of thy servants, who now draw nigh unto Thee, to seek thy blessing and guidance during this day.

We pray Thee to watch over, preserve, and bless us; keep us from evil; guide us in all our ways; and grant that all we do this day may be to the glory of thy holy name. But we come to Thee more especially to pray for spiritual blessings, which Thou art ever ready to vouchsafe to thy waiting people.

We implore Thee to increase our faith. Give us a real, living faith in the Lord Jesus Christ. Enable us so to lay hold on Him, that we may be able to appropriate to our souls everlasting benefit, the rich blessings of his blood, and righteousness, and merits. May we be washed in the fountain of his blood, clothed in the robe of his righteousness, and thus, when called to stand before Thee in judgment, may we be justified from all things from which we could not be justified by the law.

Grant, we beseech Thee, that our love to Thee may increase day by day. May our faith work by love, and bring forth much fruit, to the praise and glory of thy great name. Thou hast commanded us to love Thee with all the heart, and soul, and mind, and strength; enable us so to do. May our life be hid with Christ in Thee, and may all our energies and powers of body, soul, and spirit, be laid as a willing and glad offering on the altar of thy love. But, Lord, Thou knowest how depraved our hearts are, how utterly unable we are in ourselves either to love or serve Thee; we therefore implore Thee to give unto us the Holy Ghost, the Comforter, whose gracious office it is to convert, renew, and sanctify the heart of sinful man.

Anoint us this day with the blessed unction of thine own Holy Spirit, and as Thou didst in days of old, by the agency of thy servant the prophet, fill the empty vessels with oil, so be pleased to fill our hearts, which are truly empty of all goodness in themselves, with the sanctifying and strengthening influences of the Holy Ghost. Hear us, most gracious and merciful Father, in these our imperfect supplications and prayers, and answer us according to the fulness of thy great mercy in thy dear Son, Jesus Christ, our Lord. Amen.

READ IN HOLY SCRIPTURE ROMANS I. 1—19.

ALMIGHTY Father, we come this night to thy throne, beseeching Thee to give us boldness and access with confidence by faith in Jesus Christ. We thank Thee, O our God, for the invitation to come to Thee, that we may obtain mercy, and find grace to help us. We thank Thee for thy Gospel concerning Jesus Christ, thy Son, our Lord. Oh, help us to live day by day as those who have been begotten again to a lively hope by the resurrection of Christ from the dead, and as those who are each day advancing nearer to the inheritance that is undefiled, and that fadeth not away. Give us not only to rejoice in the glorious Gospel of the blessed God, but earnestly to seek that others may have their eyes opened to see its glory, and their hearts transformed so as to experience its happiness. Oh, may each of us in this household be, according to our opportunities and duties, separated, as thy servants, unto the Gospel, embracing it by our faith, adorning it by our life, and commending it by simplicity and sincerity in our conversation in the world.

Most gracious God, keep us from being ashamed of the Gospel of Christ. Oh, help us to bear in mind that it is a message for all the world, and that it is the power of God unto salvation to every man who believeth. Give us so to experience its influence upon our own hearts, as to know that its power is thine, unto the salvation of our own souls; and thus, instead of being ashamed of our religion, may we have given to us the spirit of power, and of love, and of a sound mind. O God of all grace, we need not only thy revelation, but also grace to use it aright.

Oh, send forth the Spirit of thy Son into our hearts, that thy Word may come to us, not in word only, but in power, and in the Holy Ghost, and with much assurance. Teach us, by thy Spirit, that thy Word is truth. Sanctify us by thy truth. Give us to feel that it is a sacred trust committed to us for our salvation, and that we are debtors to Jews and Gentiles, so far as in us lies to make it known for their salvation.

Bless all, we pray Thee, who serve Thee in the Gospel of thy Son, giving them, in all their sacred occupations, love, and fidelity, and success. Oh, send forth thy light and thy truth among Jews and Gentiles over all the world. And now, good Lord, we commit ourselves, our souls and bodies, our lives and all our interests, to Thee, for this night, and for all time, and all eternity. Bestow upon those we love the same blessings, both for body and soul, which we ask for ourselves. Accept, we beseech Thee, our persons and our prayers, for the sake of Jesus Christ our Strength and our Redeemer. Amen.

[Morning.] **THIRTY-NINTH WEEK.—SATURDAY.** [Evening.]

READ IN HOLY SCRIPTURE 2 KINGS V.

O ALMIGHTY God, who hast begotten us again unto a lively hope by the resurrection of Jesus Christ from the dead—in whose name we may draw near thy mercy-seat, and boldly ask for a portion in thy great and precious promises, listen to this our morning prayer. We need not go and wash in the waters of Jordan seven times, for there is a fountain opened for sin and uncleanness, which can wash away all sin, and make the sinner pure and clean. Give each of us now before thee strong faith in Christ's atoning blood, and, like him of whom we have now read, whose flesh became clean and pure, like that of a little child, may our souls lose all their defilement, and be made perfectly whole, and become like little children.

We earnestly pray for the gift of thy Holy Spirit, that we may be cleansed by the blood of Christ, and renewed into his image. Wean our affections from the world, and help us to follow our Lord in his walk of holiness, of humility, of patience, of sympathy, of love, and of goodness, and to keep his footprints ever in sight, while, with self-denying zeal for thy glory, and the extension of thy Church on earth, we carry on the work which He began when here, and left for his Church to complete. May this now day given to us be one spent in our Master's work, both in ruling our own spirits and in humble efforts to serve Thee amongst men. Give us grace to go forth this day in the spirit of the Syrian girl; doing our part, however small, to give comfort to the afflicted, and to point the way to the great Physician. Bless all who are engaged in the work of evangelising the world of darkness around us, and in building up saints in their most holy faith. Let not thy professing people bring discredit on their Lord's name, by their worldliness and apathy; nor let them resemble Gehazi, who stood before his master desirous of being thought faithful, while in his right hand he grasped a lie. Let the name of Jesus be hallowed in all hearts, and then will hypocrisy and deceit make way for righteousness, sincerity, and truth, and the cleansing power of the blood of Christ will be made manifest, and there shall be much joy in heaven.

O God, let the Spirit of Jesus come down and rest upon our own country in particular, that the light of truth may dispel all the darkness of error, of heresy, of false teaching, and of worldliness, and that the atoning blood of Jesus may be honoured amongst us and by all nations under heaven, and the reign of sin be cut short, through a general outpouring of the Holy Ghost. Hear us, O God, for thy dear Son's sake, to whom, with Thee and the Holy Ghost, be all praise for ever and ever. Amen.

READ IN HOLY SCRIPTURE ROMANS II.

O HEAVENLY Father, who in thy tender love didst reconcile the world unto Thyself by Jesus Christ, and through Him hast regard unto the prayers and praises of all who come nigh to Thee, enable us to lift up our hearts to Thee as thy children, and in all thankfulness and adoring love to worship at thy footstool. We confess we are unworthy to look upon thy face, or to open our lips in thy presence. With lowly reverence we offer our evening worship, trusting to thy great mercy in Christ Jesus.

As we look back through the day, we feel that all its events and circumstances have been in thy hand, and ordered by thy providence. Its mercies have been of thy giving. That we have reached its close in safety is the result of thy watchful care. And now that we can plead at thy footstool, and in the full assurance of thy grace implore forgiveness for all our sins, and peace through the blood of Jesus, this also is of Thee. All praise be to Thee, O our God, for these many and great tokens of thy love. We lament over our many sins against Thee, and take shame to ourselves that we serve Thee so feebly, and feel so little thy love prompting us in daily duty. Have mercy upon us, O God, for these and all our other sins, and blot them out for ever from thy remembrance. Do Thou convince us deeply of our sin. Preserve us from that deadness of heart which despises the riches of thy goodness, and forbearance, and long-suffering. As every day passes, we desire to have a deeper sense of thy mercy, and to be led by it to see more clearly what cause we have for shame and repentance before Thee. Awaken in us a salutary fear of thy judgments, and a vivid sense of the responsibility which the possession of Christian privileges entails upon us. Thou hast favoured us beyond others. We pray that we may be guided by thy Spirit in the profitable use of thy mercies, lest the very heathen should rise against us in judgment. Impress deeply on our hearts the importance of being sincere in our religious profession, that we may not serve Thee with our lips while our hearts are far from Thee. Oh, may our religion be a religion of the heart, in the spirit and not in the letter, whose praise is not of men but of God.

Take us, and all whom we love, into thy Divine keeping for the night. May we rest in safety and rise refreshed and thankful for the blessings of another Lord's day. Lord, by thy Spirit so stir up our hearts, that we may long after Thee in thy ordinances as the hart for the water-brook, and know thy grace and glory in the sanctuary. Hear us and help us in all we need, for the sake of Jesus Christ our Lord. Amen.

[Morning.] **FORTIETH WEEK.—LORD'S DAY.** [Evening.

READ IN HOLY SCRIPTURE 2 KINGS VI. 1–23.

READ IN HOLY SCRIPTURE ROMANS III.

HOLY, holy, holy, Lord God Almighty, Thou who art the first and the last, the greatest and the best of beings, we would enter into thy presence with grateful hearts, and bless and praise thy holy name for the return of the morning light. Verily, thy mercies are new every morning, and great is thy faithfulness.

It is of thy mercy that we have been preserved through another night; that we have been raised up to behold the light of another day; that we are permitted once more to know the sweet enjoyment of another of thy holy Sabbaths. We would this day enter into thy gates with thanksgiving, and go into thy courts with praise. Enable us to realise thy presence in the midst of us, and to feel that Thou art with us of a truth. Help us to worship Thee acceptably and in godly fear. Keep us from the sin of those who draw near unto Thee with their lips while their heart is far from Thee. Let our prayers and praises ascend up as incense before Thee, through our Lord Jesus Christ.

We thank thee, O Lord, that our lot is fallen unto us in pleasant places; that we have a goodly heritage; that we live in a land where thy Word is faithfully preached, and thy Gospel fearlessly proclaimed. Be with all those who shall this day stand up in thy name, to speak unto us of the things which belong unto our peace. Having themselves tasted that the Lord is precious, enable them to declare fully and plainly to all who wait upon their ministry the riches of thy grace. Give them to lay the axe to the root of all that is contrary to Thee. Let them strike home by the power of thy Spirit, that they who are proud in heart may fall low in the dust before Thee. Grant that through their instrumentality many souls may this day be converted unto Thee, and a cry be heard going up to Thee from thy people on every side, saying, "This place is too strait for us to dwell in."

Many and great are the adversaries opposed to us; but we rejoice to know, O Lord, that, if our enemies are mighty, Thou art all-mighty; that, if they are many, we can yet say, "More are they that be with us, than they that be with them." Arise, O God, and disappoint the wicked one. Let them be ashamed and confounded that seek after our soul to destroy it. Let them be turned back and put to shame that desire our hurt. Uphold us by thy right hand, and give us to be more than conquerors at the last.

Hear, O Lord, the prayers of thy servants, and give ear unto these our supplications. O Lord, hearken, and do the things that we have asked, for thy dear Son's sake, Jesus Christ, our only Saviour and Redeemer, to whom, with Thee and the Holy Ghost, be eternal praises. Amen.

MERCIFUL God, we bless and praise thy holy name for the rest and privileges of this sacred day. It has been good for us to draw near to thy throne of grace, and unite with thy people in the worship of thy name. We glorify Thee for such a provision for our spiritual wants and weakness. Oh, may we prize this holy day more and more. May our prayers and thanksgivings be more fervent, and may each returning Sabbath find us more fitted to enjoy the eternal Sabbath in thy heavenly kingdom. Bless the labours of thy ministers. We confess the iniquities of our holy things. O Lord Jesus, intercede for us, as Thou hast promised. Wash us from all our sins in thy precious blood. Clothe us with thy righteousness, and enable us to lean upon thine Almighty arm in all time of our tribulation and weakness.

We pray especially that the words we have heard outwardly with our ears this day may be so engrafted inwardly in our hearts as to bring forth in us the fruits of good living throughout the week on which we have entered. Let the remembrance of this holy day quiet us amidst life's distractions, and assist us to maintain a constant fear and love for thy most holy name. We would close the Sabbath services by commending one another to thy care. May every member of this family be a member of the household of faith.

When we read thy Word together, day by day, may we profit from its instructions, and grow in grace continually. Give unto us all the Spirit of truth, to guide our study of the Word of life. Show unto us our unworthiness and helplessness. May we be deeply convinced of our inability to help ourselves without thy mighty succour, and may we lay aside all self-righteousness and confidence in human effort. Our best doings are nothing worth; our prayers and our tears of repentance need to be washed in the blood of Jesus, our Redeemer. Thy Word declares that we are altogether become unprofitable, and that there is none righteous, no, not one. As unprofitable servants, we entreat Thee to be merciful unto us.

We thank Thee for the hope of the blessed Gospel, and for the gift of Jesus to be a propitiation for our sins. Give us faith in his atoning sacrifice, and may we ever enjoy peace with God through the offering of his dear Son. We would pray also for our beloved friends and relatives. Number them among thy saints in glory everlasting. Comfort those who are in sorrow, and help them to flee to Jesus as the only refuge of the troubled soul. We ask all through Jesus Christ, our Lord. Amen.

[Morning.] **FORTIETH WEEK.—MONDAY.** [Evening.

READ IN HOLY SCRIPTURE 2 KINGS VII.

O LORD God, heavenly Father, accept the offering which we now present unto Thee at the beginning of another day. We thank Thee, O Lord, for the blessings of the past Sabbath day, both temporal and spiritual; for bodily rest; for grace to serve Thee with a quiet mind; for an open Bible and a preached Gospel; and for the strengthening and refreshing of our souls in thy sanctuary.

Grant, Lord, that a sweet savour of the day may remain with us throughout the week; that we may abide under the shadow of the Almighty, mindful of thy presence in our commonest occupations; and that we may do all things as unto the Lord, and not unto men, looking ever unto Jesus as both the Author and Finisher of our faith.

But whilst we thus praise Thee, O our God, for mercies past, and pray unto Thee for grace to live to thy glory, we acknowledge our own utter unworthiness and corruption. We have provoked Thee to anger by the multitude of our transgressions, and it is only of thy mercy that we have not been cast off for ever and consumed. We are still prone daily to wander from thy ways, and we have no power to keep ourselves from evil, or to help ourselves in the path of righteousness; but, blessed be thy holy name, Thou hast laid help for us upon One that is mighty, even upon Jesus Christ our Lord. He is able to save to the uttermost all who come unto Thee through Him. Grant unto each one of us, O heavenly Father, that we being engrafted into Christ Jesus by a living faith, and being made temples of God by the indwelling of the Holy Ghost, may seek and keep all thy commandments, and may walk steadfastly in thy precepts, serving Thee with a perfect heart and a willing mind, and yielding our whole selves and all our substance unto Thee as dedicated things, as holy vessels of the sanctuary meet for thy use.

And now we would intercede with Thee, O merciful God, for all whom we love upon earth, that they may be one with us in Christ Jesus; for our neighbours and acquaintances, that those amongst them who know the Lord may have peace and joy in believing, and that those who are afar off may be brought nigh by the blood of Christ. We pray also for our country, that it may be more and more influenced by the truth as it is in Jesus; and for our Sovereign and all in authority, that they may ever have before their eyes the fear of the Lord, which is the beginning of wisdom, and may thus govern the nation with a view to thy glory.

We ask all in the name and for the sake of Jesus Christ, our only Mediator and Advocate. Amen.

READ IN HOLY SCRIPTURE ROMANS IV.

O ALMIGHTY Father, who hast exalted thy Son, our Lord Jesus Christ, to be a Prince and a Saviour, for to give repentance and remission of sins, grant unto each one now kneeling before Thee the blessedness of him whose iniquities are forgiven, and whose sins are covered.

O Lord, if we say that we have no sin, we deceive ourselves, and the truth is not in us; but we confess, O God, that we have erred and gone astray from Thee, and from the ways of thy commandments. We have not loved Thee as we ought, and we have lived too much to ourselves, instead of seeking thy will and thy glory. But Thou hast comforted our hearts by the blessed assurance that the blood of Jesus Christ cleanseth from all sin, and by the promise that whosoever believeth on Him shall not perish, but have everlasting life. O God, give unto us the obedience of faith, that we may receive these thy promises, and believe in them to the saving of our souls. Thou knowest our unbelief and hardness of heart; oh, give unto us true faith, even the faith of thy servant Abraham, that, like him, we may not stagger at the promises of God through unbelief, but be strong in faith, giving glory to God, being fully persuaded that what He hath promised He is able to perform. And grant, O Lord, that, having these promises, we may cleanse ourselves from all filthiness of the flesh and of the spirit. May we, by thy grace helping us, depart from all iniquity, and be a peculiar people unto Thee, zealous of good works. Suffer us not to sin against Thee by receiving thy grace in vain, but grant that, being justified by faith and having peace with Thee through Jesus Christ, we may show that faith by all good works.

Finally, we beseech Thee, O heavenly Father, to enable us to look unto Christ crucified for support and comfort under pain and sickness, loss and bereavement. May we have the same mind that was in Christ, being patient under tribulation, and submitting ourselves to thy holy will. Give us an increasing sense of the realities of eternity, that we may lightly esteem the sufferings of this present time, and reckon them not worthy to be compared with the glory that shall be revealed.

And we bless thy holy name for thy promise that death shall be swallowed up in victory. Thou hast raised up thy Son Jesus from the dead, and hast promised that because He lives, we shall live also. Let us take these gracious words to our great and endless comfort, that so, when we lie down to die, we may rest in peace, and sleep in Him who is alone our hope and trust, even Jesus Christ, thy dear Son, our ever-living Lord and Saviour. Amen.

[Morning.] **FORTIETH WEEK—TUESDAY.** [Evening.

READ IN HOLY SCRIPTURE 2 KINGS IX.

O LORD God Almighty, whose eyes run to and fro in the earth, to show Thyself strong in behalf of those that fear Thee, look down from heaven thy dwelling-place upon us thy unworthy creatures, approaching Thee in his name whom Thou hearest always. O most gracious God, we are sinners before Thee, sinners in thought, in word, and in deed; and we know, were it not for thy mercy, sin must be our ruin. Like the publican of old, we dare not lift up our eyes unto heaven, but humbly from our hearts would cry, God be merciful to us sinners. And, oh, blessed be thy holy name, thy mercy is great, for where sin hath abounded, grace hath much more abounded; there is forgiveness with Thee, that Thou mayest be feared; Thou hast not spared thine own Son, but freely delivered Him up for us all. He hath suffered, the just for the unjust, that, reconciled to Thee by his death, we might be saved by his life. Forgive us, O good Lord, forgive us all our sin, for Jesus' sake; wash us in his precious blood, clothe us in his spotless righteousness, receive us graciously, and love us freely. Pour out upon us thy life-giving Spirit; anoint us with the Holy Ghost. May He dwell in our hearts as the Spirit of wisdom to enlighten us, as the Spirit of grace to quicken us, as the Spirit of supplication inciting us to prayer, as the Spirit of truth to guide us into all truth, and as the Spirit of holiness to sanctify us, and make us meet for the inheritance of the saints in light.

Grant to each of us, merciful Lord, and to all near and dear to us, thy peace, that peace which passeth all understanding. Help us to understand the source and nature of true peace, and let us never rest until we can feel the truth of the Apostle's words, "Being justified by faith, we have peace with God, through our Lord Jesus Christ."

Give us earnest zeal for the cause of Christ; zeal according to knowledge, zeal tempered with prudence and with love; and while we seek to call others to that Saviour whom to know is life and peace, may we strive to follow Him more closely, and to serve Him more fully. O Lord, grant us more and more of thy quickening grace, so that we may never have to complain, "Other vineyards have I kept, but mine own vineyard have I not kept."

With these our prayers accept our praises for mercies countless as the sands; mercies in providence, mercies in grace. Lord God, when we think of them, we can only exclaim, "Thy mercies are new every morning; surely, goodness and mercy have followed me all the days of my life." Hear us, O Lord; and, as Thou hearest, forgive, for Jesus Christ's sake. Amen.

READ IN HOLY SCRIPTURE ROMANS V.

BLESSED God, accept our praises this night for the many new proofs of thy love vouchsafed to us throughout the day. We thank Thee for thy protecting care. We magnify thy name for thy tender and unspeakable love. As we meditate upon all that Thou hast graciously done for us, may our cold hearts be warmed into glowing love towards Thee. No friendship is so faithful as thine; no tenderness so loving as thine; no long-suffering and forbearance so great as thine. Thou so loved us as to give thy dear Son for us. Thou hast so loved us as to redeem our souls at the price of his most precious blood. When we were yet without strength, in due time Christ died for us. Even for our dearest friend, which of us would be content to die? But Thou didst commend thine unutterable love to us in that, while we were yet sinners, Christ died for us. When we were yet enemies, we were reconciled to Thee by the death of thy Son. Thy wrath lay on us on account of our sin; but Thou hast given everlasting life to all who truly believe on Jesus. Help us to believe! Give us saving faith! Melt our hearts with his tenderness! May his unexampled love constrain us to give the rest of our days to Him. O God, take away all that keeps us from Him: crucify every desire that holds us back. Help us to cut off the right hand, and pluck out the right eye, rather than be lost. Let the sweet thought, that the blood of Christ cleanses from all sin, encourage us to come to Him for full pardon for the past. We pray that his all-constraining grace may lead us to full consecration to Him for the future, that we may feel that we are not our own but his, and glorify Him henceforward in our bodies and in our souls, which are his. Being justified by faith in Him, give us peace. Help us to rejoice in the blessed hope of being partakers of thy glory. In the world we shall have tribulation, but in Jesus Thou wilt vouchsafe peace.

O God, sanctify all thy providential dealings with us. Make them blessed messengers of mercy: the means of drawing us more closely to Thee, and of purifying us for Thyself. May tribulation work patience in us; and patience experience; and experience hope; and hope make us not ashamed; because thy love is shed abroad in our hearts by the Holy Ghost, which is given us.

And now, O God, we again retire to rest. Watch Thou over us. Dwell Thou within us, even in our slumbers. May we awake with new love to Thee. We pray that by thy grace tomorrow, if we live, may be holier than any day we have ever known. Hear us and bless us, for Jesus Christ's sake. Amen.

[Morning.]   FORTIETH WEEK.—WEDNESDAY.   [Evening.]

READ IN HOLY SCRIPTURE 2 CHRONICLES XXIV. 1—22.

READ IN HOLY SCRIPTURE ROMANS VI.

ALMIGHTY and everlasting God, our heavenly Father, we are permitted, through thy tender mercy, to meet together at the beginning of another day to present our prayers and supplications at the throne of grace. For Jesus Christ's sake we beseech Thee to look upon us with thy favour, and to bless us with all spiritual blessings in Him. We are not worthy of the least of thy mercies through our manifold trangressions. We have erred and strayed from thy ways like lost sheep, but, O Thou good Shepherd, who didst come into this world of sin and sorrow to seek and to save that which was lost, we entreat Thee to compassionate our infirmities, and to pardon all our sins. Strengthen us with might in the inner man, that we may love Thee more and serve Thee better than we have ever yet done. Suffer us not to be conformed to this world, but may we be daily transformed by the renewing of our minds, and thus may we prove more and more what is that good, and acceptable, and perfect will of thine. O Holy and Eternal Spirit, do Thou increasingly enlighten our minds. Be Thou our teacher, that we may learn more of the great truths contained in thy holy Word.

O Thou King of kings, and Lord of lords, the only ruler of princes, we pray to Thee on behalf of our Sovereign and all in authority. May they seek to promote thy glory, and to advance thy cause in all they do. We know that all hearts are in thy hands; do Thou so dispose and turn them as it seemeth best to thy godly wisdom. May the rich in the world be rich in good works, ready to distribute, willing to communicate, and not trust in uncertain riches, but in Thee, the living and the true God. May multitudes among all classes be constrained by the love of Christ, and give to Thee of their substance who giveth us richly all things to enjoy. Thou hast taught us that righteousness exalteth a nation, but that sin is a reproach to any people. Let the evil example of those wicked persons recorded in thy Word be a warning to all who are in authority, that they may not follow a multitude to do evil; but grant that the pious efforts of thy servants, who did good in Israel toward God and toward their own house, may stimulate them to follow in their steps. Restrain the young who shall be the future rulers of our country from all evil counsels, and thus bringing reproach on thy name, injury to their own souls, and wrath upon the people of this land, and so direct them that they may seek first the guidance and the teaching of thy blessed Spirit, and then the counsel of thy faithful servants.

We ask these and every mercy in and through Jesus Christ. Amen.

O OUR Father, grant to us, thy children, the spirit of prayer. Enable us, through Christ, by one Spirit, to have access to Thee.

With our whole hearts we desire to praise Thee for the grace Thou hast manifested towards us. By grace we are saved; by grace we live; by grace we stand. From the first moment when, with penitent heart and weeping eyes, we saw Thee as Thou art, our Father and our God, through all the changes and trials of our earthly pilgrimage, up to the present hour, we have been debtors to thy free and sovereign grace.

O our Father, teach us to live righteously, soberly, and godly in this wicked world. Forbid, O Lord, that we should ever continue in sin that grace may abound. May we live as those who are dead with Christ, dead to the condemnation and guilt of sin, but dead also to the power and dominion of sin. May we live as those that are alive from the dead, raised up with Christ to newness of life. May we know the power of Jesus and his resurrection. May the life that we live be a life of faith in the Son of God, as we know and experience the precious truth that He loved us, and gave Himself for us. May we grow day by day in spirituality, in heavenliness of mind, in crucifixion of self, in conformity to Christ.

O Lord, we confess it with shame, we too were once the servants of sin. Once we yielded our members, even as others, servants to uncleanness, to iniquity unto iniquity. And the fruit that we reaped in that service was disappointment, and bitterness, and sorrow; and the end to which it led was everlasting death. But, blessed be thy name, Thou hast redeemed us. Oh, how shall our stammering lips praise Thee enough for the grace that rescued us from a slavery so base, and a doom so dread! May we ever obey from the heart that form of doctrine which was delivered us. Now Thou hast bought us for Thyself; now we are no longer our own. All that we are, and all that we have, is thine. Oh, teach us not only to realise our unspeakable dignity, but to manifest our great responsibility. Now let us yield ourselves as instruments of righteousness unto Thee. Now, in every thought, and word, and work, in all our intercourse with the world, in every station and relationship of life, enable us to bear fruit more and more unto holiness, as we realise more and more the blessed end that is before us, everlasting life.

Pardon all that Thou hast seen amiss in us this day. Be with us this night. And if spared to see another day, may our desire be to glorify Thee afresh in our bodies and in our spirits, which are thine. We ask all for Christ's sake. Amen.

[Morning.] **FORTIETH WEEK.—THURSDAY.** [Evening.]

READ IN HOLY SCRIPTURE 2 KINGS XIII.

O LORD God, who hast given us thy holy Word to be the comfort of our hearts, and the guide of our lives, grant that we may, by thy Holy Spirit's aid, enjoy its consolations, and in all our thoughts, words, and works be ruled by its guidance. We have just read of one who did evil in the sight of the Lord, for he followed the sins of Jeroboam, who made Israel to sin. Preserve us this day and ever from that to which we are all exposed, following a multitude to do evil, lest thine anger should be kindled against us as it was against Israel. We are this day, in our various duties and callings, of necessity exposed to temptations. Keep us from them, deliver us out of them. Guide us, by thy counsel, through this life, till we attain thy glory in the life which is to come; and teach us to be very watchful over ourselves, that it never be said of us we have caused others to sin. We would humbly confess before Thee our manifold sins, negligences, and ignorances, and pray Thee, for Christ's sake, to forgive us all that is past. Blot out our sins in his cleansing blood, we would earnestly pray. Supply all our need according to thy riches in glory by Christ Jesus, and ever incline our hearts to love and serve Thee, that grace, mercy, and peace may be multiplied unto us. We heartily thank Thee for thy protecting care over us, thy watchful providence, in ordering and arranging all things for us so well, so wisely, and so lovingly; and above all, for the redemption of our souls, and the forgiveness of sin, to each and all who believe in Jesus. That we may be more humble, more prayerful, more grateful, give unto us more of the light, life, power, and unction of thy Holy Spirit; more love for thy Word, more and more earnest longing and looking for thy kingdom and glory. [Teach our children dutiful obedience to their parents in all things, for this is well pleasing to Thee, O Lord.]

As Thou hast taught us to make prayers and supplications for all men, we pray for our nation. Bless the whole race of mankind with all things needful for life and godliness. Vouchsafe thy blessing to this nation, and grant that peace and happiness, truth and justice, religion and piety, may be established amongst us. Bless the Royal Family with all temporal and spiritual blessings. Take under thy special protection all those who are travelling by land or by water. Accept, O Father of mercy, our humble and hearty thanks for all thy mercies towards us, more especially, and above all, for thy great love in giving thine only Son for our redemption. Hear, we pray Thee, our imperfect supplications, and give us an answer of peace, for the sake of Christ Jesus, our most blessed Lord and Saviour. Amen.

READ IN HOLY SCRIPTURE ROMANS VII.

O GRACIOUS and merciful Father, enable us to approach Thee, under a deep sense of unworthiness, through Jesus Christ our Lord. We bless Thee that Thou hast taught us somewhat of the excellence of thy commandments. And yet, O Lord, we confess that this thy law condemns us, and reveals to us perpetually our sinfulness in thy sight. But we love it nevertheless, and adore thy holiness therein. To Thee alone we give all the praise. But how severe in the souls of thy servants are the contentions and sorrows to which they are subjected. When we would do good, evil is present with us. Not only is it present in our memory, but present within us. We feel its influence and its power. Blessed be thy name, O Lord, for those amongst us who are truly thy servants, and give our hearts to Thee. May we freely dedicate body, soul, and spirit to thy service. May we render to Thee a perfect obedience, and devote every thought, and effort, and purpose to thy work, and the promotion of thy glory. But the force of temptation from without, and of evil from within, constrains us to exclaim, under a deep conviction of weakness, "O wretched man, who shall deliver me from the body of this death?" But, gracious Lord Jesus, Thou hast redeemed, and Thou wilt not withhold thy Spirit. Thy presence and thy grace are pledges of our final victory. Our souls Thou hast bought unto Thyself with thy precious blood. Our bodies Thou hast redeemed from the power of the grave, so that they shall not remain in eternal corruption. Thou hast ascended up on high, and hast led captivity captive; and we pray that we may one day dwell in that place whither Thou hast already gone before. Teach us, then, O blessed Jesus, to occupy until Thou come. Enable us to grow in our love of thy holy law. Write it perpetually upon our hearts. Nay more, may we advance in holiness, and daily glorify Thee; and may the blood of the Saviour Jesus, applied perpetually to our spirit, cleanse us from all iniquity. Thus, O Lord, may we be a peculiar people, zealous of good works, and shining as lights in the world, living to thy glory, and when we die, dying in thy peace, O blessed and eternal God, through Jesus Christ our Lord.

In his name we bless Thee for all the mercies of the day now past, and implore Thee to take us under thy protection for the night to which Thou hast brought us. O God, visit with thy richest blessings all who are dear to us. Oh, make them thine more and more, and keep them thine for ever, that they may live to thy praise here, and with us share thy glory hereafter. We ask all for Christ's sake. Amen.

[Morning.] **FORTIETH WEEK.—FRIDAY.** [Evening.

READ IN HOLY SCRIPTURE 2 CHRONICLES XXVI.

READ IN HOLY SCRIPTURE ROMANS VIII. 1—18.

HEAVENLY Father, spared by thy mercy in Christ Jesus, we meet together again this morning in peace and with thankfulness, to hear thy holy Word, to tell Thee all our wants, and to ask for grace and strength to walk according to thy will. Make us, we beseech Thee, very attentive to thy voice speaking to us. Write thy Word on our hearts by the power of God the Holy Spirit.

We would begin the day with Thee; for blessed is that family that knows the joyful sound of thy voice; they shall walk, O Lord, in the light of thy countenance.

We humbly confess unto Thee, heavenly Father, that we are sinful, and have of ourselves no desire for that which is holy and pleasing unto Thee; we are weak, and have no power to do what is good. Oh, leave us not to ourselves, but enable us to think and to do always that which is righteous in thy sight.

We would remember that as long as we seek Thee, Thou wilt make us to prosper; Thou wilt help us against the enemies of our soul, the world without, and our deceitful hearts within; Thou wilt marvellously help us, and we shall be strong. Whilst we thank Thee for this assured hope of spiritual strength, we pray Thee to make and to keep us humble, lest our heart be lifted up to our destruction. We would remember the solemn word of warning, "Let him that thinketh he standeth, take heed lest he fall." Hold Thou up our goings, O Lord, in thy ways, that our footsteps slip not.

Make us each to know and to do our duty in that station of life in which Thou hast placed us, with diligence and faithfulness, and to abide therein with contentment; let there be in us no feeling of discontent with what thy goodness gives us, or thy loving care denies.

Keep us, heavenly Father, from the power of evil example, and unholy agreement with anything that is sinful. Give us grace, not only to avoid all evil, but all appearance of evil, that we may glorify Thee in all that we do.

O Lord, we have nothing to boast of in ourselves; we have much to be ashamed of, to repent of, and to forsake. We know that the wages of sin is death, but thy free gift is eternal life through Jesus Christ our Lord: his blood cleanseth from all sin; his righteousness is unto and upon all those who believe. We would make glad mention of all this before Thee, O our God and Father, as the only ground of our hope in the great day of his appearing.

And now we commit to thy loving care ourselves, and all who are dear to us. Bless and accept us, for Jesus Christ's sake, our only Mediator and Redeemer. Amen.

O BLESSED Lord, drawing near to thy mercy-seat as a family, we desire to render unto Thee our humble thanks for all thy tender mercies vouchsafed to us this day. Thy loving-kindness hath encompassed us round about; and under the shadow of thy wings we have dwelt in safety. To Thee we owe every good that we possess; by Thee we have been made strong to labour; Thou hast been our rest when weary, our help in seasons of difficulty, and our strength in weakness. Thou canst sanctify our joys, alleviate our sorrows, keep us in peace, and give us a sure prospect of everlasting life through Jesus Christ our Lord. For all thy countless mercies we adore and magnify thy holy name.

But, O Lord God, when we turn our thoughts to ourselves, we are covered with shame and confusion of face. Though Thou hast been so mindful of us, we have been unmindful of Thee. How many have been our failings and shortcomings, our transgressions and sins. Hear us in thy mercy, O Lord, and have pity upon us; pardon all our iniquities for Jesus Christ's sake, and blot out all our guilty stains. Take away all the enmity of our carnal nature, and impart to us the spiritual mind which is life and peace. Subdue and mortify in us all sin, and give us the witness of the Spirit that we are thy children, heirs of God, and joint-heirs with Christ.

And now, heavenly Father, we beseech Thee to be near to us during the silent hours of the night. Mercifully defend us from all harm. Let the everlasting arms of thy love be underneath us. Be Thou our Keeper, Guardian, and Defender whilst we sleep, and may our repose be refreshing to our bodies and invigorating to our minds. If it should please Thee to spare us till the morrow, prepare us for its duties; or if it should be thy will to summon us to thy judgment seat, may we be found in Christ Jesus without spot and blameless.

We would finally commend to Thee, O gracious God, all who are near and dear to us on earth, the absent members of this household, our friends in Christ Jesus, and all for whose temporal and spiritual health we desire to pray. Bless thy whole Church. Send thy holy Word throughout the world, and let it have free course everywhere. Give thy Holy Spirit abundantly to all thy faithful servants; and hasten the time when the number of Thine elect shall be completed, and when there shall be one fold and one Shepherd. Until then, keep us steadfast in the faith, diligent in labour, and fervent in prayer, waiting for the coming of our Lord and Saviour Jesus Christ. Accept, we beseech Thee, O Lord, these our supplications, for the sake of Jesus Christ our Lord. Amen.

[Morning.]   FORTIETH WEEK.—SATURDAY.   [Evening.]

READ IN HOLY SCRIPTURE 2 KINGS XVII. 6—41.   READ IN HOLY SCRIPTURE ROMANS VIII. 19—39.

MOST merciful Father, we come with thanksgiving to thy throne for thy unwearied and unmerited goodness. How precious are thy thoughts to usward! they are more in number than the sand. When we awake we are still with Thee. Verily, O Lord our God, Thou hast been patient and long-suffering to us; Thou hast been gracious, full of compassion, and slow to anger.

Oh, teach us, we beseech Thee, to observe thy providence, not only in thy dealings with man in the days of old, but in thy wonderful works unto ourselves. Thou art the same yesterday, to-day, and for ever; and as Thou didst carry captive and punish Israel for their rebellion, so Thou dost still reveal thy wrath from heaven against all ungodliness and unrighteousness of men. O righteous Father, help us to remember that Thou dost search our hearts; that Thou settest our secret sins in the light of thy countenance; that Thou seest all our worldliness, all our idolatry of heart, all our preference of the creature, and all our forgetfulness of Thee. Have mercy upon us, we beseech Thee, leading us to consider that in the present, as in the past, Thou dost exercise righteousness, and judgment, and loving-kindness in the earth.

Most gracious God, we come anew this morning, through our Lord Jesus Christ, to find refuge and shelter in thy mercy. We can find no safety, or peace, or strength, in ourselves or in our services. We would seek all in Jesus Christ our Lord. We would come anew, therefore, to the blood of sprinkling, to the fountain opened for sin and for uncleanness, and would seek there cleansing and strength. Keep us this day mindful of thy presence. Incline our hearts, as thy servants, to do all in the name of the Lord Jesus. Help us to carry our religion into all our occupations, doing what we ought to do with all our might, and with a view to thy glory, so that our employments may be a part of our religion, that our work may be a service done heartily, as to Thee the Lord, and that our servitude to Thee may be enjoyed by us as a blessed liberty.

All our dear friends we commend this day to Thee and to the Word of thy grace, which is able to build them up and give them an inheritance among all the saints. Our Father, who art in heaven, keep them; guide and guard them; deliver them from all evil; and lead them by thy good Spirit to the land of uprightness. We pray for thy universal Church, for its purity, for its unity, for its extension through all the world. Let the people praise Thee, O Lord, let all the people praise Thee; and let the whole earth be filled with thy glory, for the sake of Jesus Christ our Saviour. Amen.

GRACIOUS and merciful Father, we present ourselves before thy throne of grace, at the close of another day and of another week, to bless and praise thy holy name for the continuance of all thy goodness and mercy towards us. We thank Thee for having watched over and preserved us from evil. We bless Thee for our health, our friends, our food and raiment, and the many mercies which Thou hast so long vouchsafed unto us; but especially do we bless Thee for spiritual mercies, for the gift of thy dear Son, for the means of grace, and for the hope of glory.

But, Lord, we desire to humble ourselves before Thee for our many sins. In looking back upon the past week, alas! in how many ways have we transgressed thy holy laws by thought, word, and deed! Blot out our transgressions, and purge away our iniquities, that we may be whiter than snow. Create in us a clean heart, O God, and renew a right spirit within us. Make us to hate sin, and to fight against it with steadfast perseverance.

And now, O gracious God, in the prospect of another sacred day of rest, may our hearts be calmed from worldly turmoil, and our souls be prepared for the duties and privileges of thy blessed Sabbath. We desire to be in the Spirit on the Lord's day, and to find Christ very near to us. May nothing be permitted to separate us from the love of Christ; draw out our hearts towards Him with tender affection. We pray for a blessing on all thy ministering servants. May they preach the Word with all fidelity, speaking the truth in love, and holding forth the Word of life. May sinners be awakened and converted, and the souls of believers be edified and strengthened. Oh, hasten thy kingdom and the coming of thy dear Son in glory. Look down with compassion on the heathen nations who are sitting in darkness and the shadow of death. Raise up and send forth to the harvest many more labourers to preach the unsearchable riches of Christ. Bless thy servants already in the field, enduring the heat and burthen of the day. Strengthen their hands, prosper their labours, and give them many souls for their hire, that they may rejoice in the day of Christ that they have not run in vain, neither laboured in vain. Bless all missionary societies at home; give wisdom to their counsels, and provide them with men and means to circulate more widely the Gospel of the grace of God to the ends of the earth. We now commend ourselves, and all that are near and dear to us, to thy care and protection this night; give us rest and sleep, and raise us up again, in health and safety, for the sacred duties of thine own day. We ask all in the name of Jesus Christ our Lord. Amen.

[Morning.] **FORTY-FIRST WEEK.—LORD'S DAY.** [Evening.

READ IN HOLY SCRIPTURE 2 KINGS XVIII.

READ IN HOLY SCRIPTURE ROMANS IX.

EVER blessed and glorious Jehovah, trusting in the merits and intercession of thy dear Son, we bow ourselves this morning before the throne of thy majesty. Thy goodness hath spared us through the past night, while its darkness and repose have ministered to our necessities and recruited our wearied frames. We have been mercifully kept from sickness and from accident of every kind: for these great benefits we offer to Thee the sacrifice of praise. Especially do we thank Thee for the return of another Sabbath morning. Grant that we may value the Sabbath for its blessed rest, and for its many precious privileges. Help us to do that which is right in thy sight this day, not forsaking the assembling of ourselves together in thy sanctuary. Enable us to offer to Thee a pure and spiritual service. If in any degree we are in danger of worshipping the creature more than the Creator; if anything interposes between our souls and thy majesty, to which our corrupt hearts are inclined to burn incense and offer worship, oh, disclose it to us, and give us grace wholly to remove it, and to put it away from us. Oh, that we may cleave unto the Lord, and not depart from following Thee, but ever keep thy commandments. Then wilt Thou give us power over every foe, and none shall harm us if we are followers of that which is good.

Have mercy upon them who neither value thy great salvation nor love thy people. Graciously convert them, and bring them to repentance and the knowledge of thy truth. Cause many this day to feel their sins, and to look unto Christ for peace. Let not the great enemy triumph this day. O Thou that art stronger than he, snatch perishing souls from his grasp, and glorify thy grace in their salvation.

Bless the ministrations of thy servants, the pastors of thy flock. Make them faithful in declaring thy message, and zealous to win souls to Christ. Help them rightly to divide the word of truth, and thus to give each his portion of spiritual food in due season. May we strive to profit by their godly admonitions, and let thy Holy Spirit carry the arrow of conviction to many dead souls this day, so that not a few may be added to thy Church who shall be eternally saved.

Bless our beloved Sovereign and all the Royal Family. Make them solicitous for the spread of true religion throughout the land. Bless all orders and ranks among us, and may this prove a Sabbath of holy rest, of hallowed communion, and of spiritual joy to all.

Hear us, heavenly Father, for thy dear Son's sake, Jesus Christ our Lord. Amen.

ETERNAL Father, with filial reverence we desire, at the close of this sacred day, to bow down before Thee, and once more call upon thy holy name. There is no unrighteousness with Thee. We thank Thee for the glad tidings of great joy that have been proclaimed afresh to us. Blessed be thy name for the hallowed privileges of public praise, and prayer, and meditation on thy holy truth. In the spiritual rest of this day may our strength be renewed, so that we may go forth on the morrow the better furnished for every good word and work.

Merciful God, save us from boasting in our privileges. Keep us from the vain and sinful thought that by the mercies of this day we have established our own righteousness. Suffer us not to attribute thy great favours to us to our own worthiness, and grant us the spirit of tender compassion towards those whose advantages are less than ours. Soften our hearts with the gentleness and the overflowing sympathy of thy dear Son, and hear our prayer that all thy rebellious children, whether Jew or Gentile, may be saved.

Graciously follow with thy blessing the preaching of thy Word. Encourage by thy promises all who have sincerely ministered in thy name. If their hearts are now drooping at the remembrance of their own feebleness, cheer them, O Thou Son of God, by making thy strength perfect in their weakness. Keep them from looking merely at the outward signs of success, and help them to leave their labours in thy hands. Deepen every impression that has been made upon the hearts of those who have listened to thy Word. Give contrition to the impenitent. Destroy the confidence of such as are trusting in themselves. Confirm the faith of every believer in the Lord Jesus. Heal the backsliding; subdue the proud; reclaim the wandering; and deliver from the thraldom of Satan all who are being led captive by him at his will. Strengthen those whom Thou hast called out of darkness into light to walk worthy of their high vocation. Let thy Church fulfil aright its mission, that in every place where it may be said "Ye are not my people," there they may be called the children of the living God.

And now, O loving Father, forgive all that has been sinful in us. Pardon our coldness of heart, our carelessness and inattention in thy house. Apply to us that blood which cleanseth from all sin, and so in thy great mercy fit us for the rest which remaineth for the people of God. Watch over us, we beseech Thee, during the night; let our sleeping and our waking thoughts be with Thee, and thine shall be the glory, through our Lord Jesus Christ. Amen.

[MORNING.]   FORTY-FIRST WEEK.—MONDAY.   [EVENING.

READ IN HOLY SCRIPTURE 2 KINGS XIX.   READ IN HOLY SCRIPTURE ROMANS X.

O MOST mighty God, the Sovereign of thy people, and the triumphant Defender of all the rights and privileges of thy spiritual Israel, we humbly worship at the feet of thy Divine majesty. Unto Thee, O Lord most high, do we give our most hearty thanks for the shadow of thine all-surrounding care which has so safely protected us from the perils of another night. Thou hast mercifully kept us, and caused us to see the light of this day. With joy, O Lord, do we magnify thy name; for Thou hast been to us a strong Rock, and a Tower of defence.

Continue, O God, to be mindful of us, for many also are the perils of the day. In the mystery of thine infinite wisdom, in the greatness of thine unspeakable mercy, we are placed in a world full of temptations, and we ourselves are frail and feeble, with no power of ourselves to help ourselves. Lord, do Thou help us, and in all our necessities stretch forth the right hand of thy power to defend and deliver us. Especially preserve us from the sinfulness and deceitfulness of our own hearts. Suffer us not to wander from Thee. Guide us, we beseech Thee, to a clearer knowledge of thy truth. May our hearts be cheered by thy promises, and our lives this and every day be controlled by thy precepts. Give us thy Holy Spirit: oh, that He may abide with us for ever, establishing us in the faith, and kindling in us a more earnest love for Thee, and a heartier zeal in thy service.

Thou, O Lord God of Israel, which dwellest between the cherubim, art the God, even Thou alone, of all the kingdoms of the earth; Thou hast made heaven and earth. O Lord, we hope in Thee. Hitherto Thou hast helped and defended us, and graciously delivered all them that have trusted in Thee. Take us and all whom we love under thy gracious care this day. Overrule all outward trials for good, and forsake us not in the time of adversity. Suffer us not to fall into sin, but deliver us out of all our trouble.

And inasmuch as our sins have merited thy displeasure, and we righteously deserve punishment and correction, oh, save us, pardon us, and evermore help us to walk before Thee in holiness and newness of life. We would fall into thine hands, O Lord; for Thou knowest our frame, and rememberest that we are dust.

With us, O God, succour all them that are in trouble, and enable them to come to Thee for help and deliverance. Thine, O Lord, is the victory. Ever bestow it upon thy militant Church, that unto Thee we may evermore give the praise and the glory. Accept and answer us in these our prayers, for Jesus Christ's sake. Amen.

FATHER of mercies and God of all comfort, how can we sufficiently praise Thee for thy great love in Christ Jesus, and for the gracious promise that whosoever shall call upon Thee shall be saved! We thank Thee for thus encouraging us to cast all our care upon Thee, and to lay at thy footstool our sins and shortcomings. Have mercy upon us for thy mercies' sake. Especially we beseech Thee to give us a clear understanding of the way of salvation, that we may see how Christ was made sin for us, though He knew no sin, that we may be made the righteousness of God in Him. We have no goodness of our own to plead before Thee; all our hope is in thy dear Son, on whom Thou didst lay the iniquities of us all. Lord, increase our faith, that we may believe in Christ with the heart, and not be ashamed to confess Him with the lips. While others are tossed about by various winds of doctrine, may we be rooted, grounded, and settled in the faith of Jesus. Suffer not our faith to be of a dead and unpractical character. May it be seen in the fruits of righteousness, which are by Jesus Christ to the praise and glory of God.

We have been preserved by thy goodness, O Lord, through another day. We have gone in and out in peace and comfort; and while many have been either incapacitated for duty by affliction, or smitten down by death, we come together to our domestic altar to bless Thee, O God, who hast aided us in duty and preserved us from danger. How many mercies have we received from thy hand! How rich and varied have been the benedictions of thy love! Now that we are all here present before thy throne, we offer Thee the service of gratitude and praise. But in many things we have all offended. We need forgiveness. We intreat the application of the blood of atonement. Now let us close the day, and lie down with a consciousness of thy favour, which is life. Unite us to each other and to Thee in bonds of loving devotedness; and when at length we shall be separated by death, may we be re-united in a brighter and a better world. Pity the families suffering from sickness and calamity. Let the light of thy smile cheer them. What multitudes of families know Thee not! O Lord, enlighten them. Look especially on thine ancient people. Our heart's desire and prayer for Israel is that they may be saved. Take away the blindness from their hearts, and turn them in repentance unto Jesus their King. Send forth the light of thy truth through the world, and make it the power of God, day by day, to the salvation of many believing souls. Grant us, O God, thy fatherly protection during the night, accept our evening sacrifice, and answer our prayers, for Jesus Christ's sake. Amen.

[Morning.] **FORTY-FIRST WEEK—TUESDAY.** [Evening.

READ IN HOLY SCRIPTURE ISAIAH XXXVIII.

O THOU who art the Lord God of the holy prophets, Thou before whom our fathers did walk, we come into thy presence with thanksgiving, and bring to Thee an offering of praise. Thou hast spared our lives through another night, and we continue in the land of the living, the monuments of thy goodness and mercy. We will bless the Lord at all times; his praise shall continually be in our mouth. O God, we know not what this day may bring forth. Thou mayest soon say to one or other amongst us, "Set thine house in order, for thou shalt die, and not live." We pray Thee, help us, that we may be found prepared for all thy will; whilst we live, may we live unto the Lord; and when we die, may we die unto the Lord. But if it be thy will, O God, to lengthen our lives upon the earth, we beseech Thee to lead us not into temptation, and to deliver us from evil. As our day is, so let our strength be. Help us to glorify Thee with our bodies and spirits, which are thine. We look up to Thee, O our Father, for all the help we shall need for the duties of this day. Help us to do all in the name of the Lord Jesus. Assist us to remember that Thou, God, seest us. Thou desirest truth in the inward parts: may we keep consciences void of offence toward God and man.

We pray Thee to have compassion on all who are our kinsmen according to the flesh. Make all the members of our household fellow-citizens with the saints, and fellow-heirs with us of the grace of everlasting life. May all our friends, however distant from us in this earthly abode, be united with us for ever in our Father's house above. O Lord, we intercede with Thee for our native country, that it may enjoy peace and prosperity; for our Monarch, that the throne may long be established in righteousness; and for all our rulers and governors, that we may live quiet and peaceable lives under their laws, in all godliness and honesty. Hear us, we entreat Thee, for all who are in affliction or poverty. Grant to them that contentment which, with the fear of the Lord, is great gain. Do Thou, O God, provide of thy goodness for the poor, and bind up the broken in heart. Let thy kingdom come, O God, and let thy will be done on earth, as it is done in heaven. May the true light of the Gospel shine into all lands. Grant that Jesus Christ, having been lifted up upon the cross, may draw all men unto Him; that in all things, throughout the whole earth, He may have the pre-eminence. Grant this, O merciful Father, for his name's sake; and unto Him, to Thyself, and to the holy Ghost, ever one God, be ascribed all the glory and the majesty, world without end. Amen.

READ IN HOLY SCRIPTURE ROMANS XI.

O MOST gracious God and Father, ere we retire to rest, we kneel once more before thy footstool, to ask of Thee the blessing of pardon and peace. We come to Thee, O Lord, for Thou only canst bless us—Thou only canst save us. Oh, hear us now, we humbly beseech Thee, for Jesus Christ our Saviour's sake. We are not worthy, O Lord, to offer unto Thee any petition. We have broken thy covenant, transgressed thy law, and daily provoked Thee by our sins. If Thou wert to deal with us as we deserve, we should soon be cut off in thy just and righteous indignation. But, blessed be thy name, Thou art a merciful God. Thy ways are not as our ways. Thou wilt have mercy on whom Thou wilt have mercy. Oh, have mercy upon us. Cast us not away. Leave us not to the blindness and ignorance of our natural hearts, but engraft us into Christ. Unite us to Him, that partaking of the root and fatness of the Divine olive tree, we may evermore bear much fruit to the glory of thy grace.

And save us, we entreat Thee, from vain and foolish presumption. Give us not over to an evil heart of unbelief. May we call to mind thy dealings of old with thine ancient people Israel; and may the remembrance warn us not to be highminded, but to fear. Lord, increase our faith. Enable us so to believe in the Lord Jesus Christ that our souls may be saved in the great day of his appearing. Oh, fill us over with a godly fear, lest, a promise being left us of entering into his rest, any of us should seem to come short of it.

We pray for others, O Lord, as well as for ourselves. Look down, we beseech Thee, upon thy whole Church. May every member of it be more and more filled with thy grace and heavenly benediction. Extend the knowledge of thy name throughout all lands. Gather in the dispersed of Israel. May they look up in faith to Him whom they have pierced, and own Him as their promised Messiah. Remember, O Lord, thy covenant with Abraham, Isaac, and Jacob, and speedily accomplish the number of thine elect. Oh, hasten the time when, according to thine own gracious promise, the kingdoms of this world shall become the kingdom of our Lord and of his Christ, and when the earth shall be filled with the knowledge of the glory of the Lord, as the waters cover the seas. Once more we commend ourselves to thy gracious care. Be with us this night, and with all who are near and dear to us. May we lie down in peace, sleep in safety, and if it be thy will, rise up in the morning with renewed health and strength to run the way of thy commandments. We ask this and every blessing in the name of Jesus Christ our Lord. Amen.

[Morning.] **FORTY-FIRST WEEK.—WEDNESDAY.** [Evening.]

READ IN HOLY SCRIPTURE 2 CHRONICLES XXXII. 22—33.

READ IN HOLY SCRIPTURE ROMANS XII.

MOST merciful God, our heavenly Father, we thank Thee that Thou hast permitted us to lie down in peace and awake in safety; that Thou hast watched over us and preserved us from all dangers. Now that a new day is added to our lives, we ask Thee that through all its hours we may be kept and guided by thine Almighty hand, and enabled to walk as thy children.

Accept our grateful thanks for the many mercies with which thy love has surrounded us this morning. May all thy gifts lead us nearer to Thee, and all be held as talents to be used for Thee. But whatever may be the earthly blessings Thou art pleased to give us, help us to lay up our treasure in heaven, where neither moth nor rust corrupt, nor thieves break through and steal. Suffer no outward prosperity to draw our hearts away from this enduring treasure. May they ever be fixed where true joys are to be found. Especially we ask Thee never to leave us to ourselves. Whatever trials or temptations Thou mayest see to be right and good for us, deliver us out of every temptation, strengthen us to endure every trial: and, O Lord, we do earnestly ask Thee to be with us in every time of need. We know ourselves to be weaker than a bruised reed, to need help every moment, and therefore again we pray Thee, leave us not, neither forsake us, O God of our salvation.

We thank Thee for the portion of health and strength we enjoy this morning. Whenever it shall be thy will that sickness should visit us, help us to receive the sickness, as we do the health, as from Thee, and may each state be to thy glory; each promote that conformity of our spirits to the likeness of Christ which is our chief desire. O Lord, in all things bend our wills to thine. May it be no mere form of words, but the expression of our inward souls, when we say "Thy will be done."

Not only in our hearts and by us may thy will be done, but throughout the world: may all nations and all people be made subject to Thee. We remember now before Thee the many thousands of China, of India, and of other lands, who have never heard thy name, upon whom the light of the Gospel has not yet shined. Lord, have mercy upon them. Arouse those who know Thee and Jesus Christ whom Thou hast sent, to put forth more strenuous efforts to send the Gospel more abundantly to the heathen. May we all pray more for this, seeing Thou hast said that for all these things Thou wilt be inquired of by thy people. O Lord, help us then to continue in prayer until Thou shalt make Jerusalem a praise in the earth. All these things we ask for Jesus Christ's sake. Amen.

ETERNAL and ever blessed God, in whom we live, and move, and have our being, we feel that thy goodness to us this day has laid us under fresh obligations to love and serve Thee. We are unworthy of thy notice, for we are but dust and ashes in thy sight. We have not walked before Thee this day as humbly and as obediently as we ought to have done. Thoughts have arisen in our minds, and feelings in our hearts, and words may, in an unguarded moment, have escaped our lips that have displeased Thee. We confess this with shame and sorrow, and pray that, ere we retire to rest, we may be forgiven, and that our consciences, through the blood of sprinkling, may be cleansed and made peaceful.

By the aid of thy Holy Spirit we would turn away from all iniquity, and strive with more earnestness to please Thee, by constantly looking unto Jesus, and by walking in the way of thy commandments.

We bless Thee for that instructive portion of Holy Scripture we have just read, and we beseech Thee to incline our hearts to keep those thy statutes. The presentation of our bodies to Thee, a living sacrifice, holy and acceptable, is our reasonable service. May we not be conformed to the world, and may we daily be renewed in the spirit of our minds, and put on the new man, which after God is created in righteousness and true holiness. As members of the same family, as parts of the great brotherhood of mankind, and as heirs of the grace of life, may we discharge all our respective duties, whether parents or children, masters or servants, in thy fear. While attending to things temporal, may we not neglect things eternal; and may the piety of our hearts appear in our lives. Deliver and preserve us from pride, covetousness, slothfulness, and selfishness, evils to which our fallen nature is so prone. With the sick and the mourning help us to sympathise, and with kind words and generous actions may we remind them of Him who went about doing good, and convince them that godliness is profitable unto all things, having promise of the life that now is, and of that which is to come. May we rather suffer wrong than needlessly provoke the ill-doer, and by gentleness and forbearance disarm the unkindness and malice of all who would injure us. Lord, soften their hearts, and help us to forgive them, as we hope to be forgiven by Thee.

And now, gracious God, we commend ourselves, one another, relatives and friends, and all for whom we should pray, to thy loving care for the night. Hear and answer us, for the Lord Jesus Christ's sake; to whom, with Thee and the Holy Spirit, be everlasting praise. Amen.

[Morning.]   FORTY-FIRST WEEK.—THURSDAY.   [Evening.]

READ IN HOLY SCRIPTURE 2 CHRONICLES XXXIII.

O LORD God Almighty, look down upon us assembled before Thee this morning, and for Jesus' sake pardon our manifold and grievous transgressions. Let not this prayer come only from our lips, but may it be the earnest supplication of our hearts. Mercifully grant, O holy Father, that we may see, by the light afforded by thy Holy Spirit, how utterly lost and corrupted we are by nature; how far we wander from Thee, even after we have heard thy loving voice inviting us to return unto Thee; how apt we continually are to yield either to the assaults or to the allurements of the enemy of our souls; and how unspeakably imperfect are our best efforts in thy service. Grant, O Lord, that we may see and feel all this, and may come again and again to the fountain opened for all sin and for all uncleanness, even the precious blood of Jesus Christ thy Son, which is able to wash away all sin.

We bless Thee, O Lord, that Thou dost invite us to return unto Thee, though we have gone astray from Thee. We bless Thee that Thou dost invite even the chief of sinners. We bless Thee that Thou hast left upon record, in thy holy Word, the cases of many who, from being rebels against Thee, became faithful servants; from being blasphemers, became saints. May these examples encourage us unto repentance. May they encourage others to turn unto Thee. May they render the ministers of thy holy Word more zealous in seeking to win souls unto Thee; may they render them more earnest in their expostulations with poor sinners madly hastening to destruction, but whom Thou art ready even now to receive; to whom Thou art crying even now, "Why will ye die?"

We would beseech Thee, O heavenly Father, to direct us in all the business and employments of this day. May we endeavour in all things to serve Thee, in all things to glorify Thee. Permit us not, O Lord, to set up any idol in our heart. Let not self, let not pleasure, let not eagerness after the things of this world occupy thy place. Our hearts should be as a temple prepared for Thee. Set up thy throne there, O God, and reign there evermore.

We would pray for those dear to us. Bless them, O gracious Father, with every blessing. Enrich them with all spiritual mercies. If any are in trouble, sanctify the afflicting dispensation unto them. May we not only be enabled to receive thy loving correction with meekness and patience when it pleases Thee to afflict us, but may it be so sanctified unto us, that it may prove to us a priceless blessing. These mercies we humbly ask for Jesus' sake. Amen.

READ IN HOLY SCRIPTURE ROMANS XIII.

O THOU, in whom we live, and move, and have our being, we unite together at thy footstool to offer our evening tribute of praise and prayer. Give us, we beseech Thee, the help of thy Holy Spirit. May He make intercession within us, while Jesus, the one Mediator, makes intercession for us before thy throne.

We have much to thank Thee for. Our debt of gratitude is always increasing. This day has given us fresh proofs of thy goodness. O Thou bountiful Giver of all good, we acknowledge thy hand in the common mercies of our every-day life, and we praise Thee for thy constant care, and providence, and love.

Let the lawful occupations of this day be followed with thy blessing. Let thy mercy cover our transgressions, and let the blood of Jesus Christ thy Son cleanse us from all sin. Being cleansed from the guilt of sin, may we be released from its power. Let us not nourish in our hearts anything that is opposed to thy holy will. O Thou great Deliverer, let not sin any longer have dominion over us, but do Thou help us to put on the Lord Jesus Christ and make not provision for the flesh to fulfil the lusts thereof.

We pray Thee to enable us to profit by the lessons of instruction we have now read from thy holy Word. As subjects, may we be obedient to those whom Thou hast appointed to rule over us. Do Thou rule over them, and ever incline their hearts to rule in thy fear, so that they may be a terror only to those who do evil, and a praise to them that do well.

Help us to fulfil the duties we owe to our fellow-citizens. May we cultivate that love which is the fulfilling of the law. May we willingly do whatever may contribute to our neighbour's welfare, and carefully avoid whatever would injure him. Save us, by the power of thy Spirit working in us, from a selfish regard to our own interests, and a forgetfulness of the rights and claims of others.

Help us, O our Father, to walk as the children of light. May the light of Divine truth illumine our understandings. May the light of thy love shine upon our hearts. May the light of advancing holiness shine in our whole character. Enable us by Divine grace to let our light so shine before others that they seeing our good works, may glorify Thee, our Father in heaven. So do Thou help us, to spend the remaining days of our life, that when we come to the end of them, we may receive an entrance abundantly into thy kingdom, through the infinite merits of thy dear Son; to whom, with Thee and the Holy Spirit, be everlasting praises. Amen.

[Morning.] **FORTY-FIRST WEEK.—FRIDAY.** [Evening.

READ IN HOLY SCRIPTURE 2 CHRONICLES XXXIV.

ALMIGHTY and merciful God, who art always more ready to hear than we are to pray, enlarge our hearts in prayer this morning, that we may so ask as to receive, and so seek as to find. Our plea in praise and prayer is the name of Jesus, that name which is above every name, and prevaileth with Thee. Oh, enable us by thy grace to plead it at all times with an earnest faith. May it inspire us with confidence before Thee, and drive away all doubt and fear.

Gracious God, we recall with thankful hearts the mercies of the night: how Thou hast watched over us and kept us, how Thou hast blessed us with such rest as was good for us, and how Thou permittest us again to meet around thy footstool. Thou never weariest of blessing us; may we never weary of praising Thee, or of meditating on thy goodness. We desire to have such an abiding sense of thy grace and love as shall constrain us to live not for ourselves, but for Thee. We pray that when our hearts grow cold in thy service, Thou wouldst kindle them anew by a fresh manifestation of thy goodness. O Lord, preserve us from the grievous sin of ingratitude. As we daily enjoy thy mercies, open our eyes to see the hand which bestows them, and fill us with the spirit of praise.

We implore thy forgiveness for every sin of which Thou knowest. We also implore Thee to give us that tenderness of heart which would cause us to fear above all things grieving thy Spirit, or displeasing Thee. Thou, O God, knowest our feebleness, and how easily we are drawn aside from the ways of godliness and obedience. Keep us, we beseech Thee, this day from all sin, and of thy great mercy strengthen us to resist all temptation. We pray that we may be preserved from the sin of idolatry, from provoking thy anger by putting anything in the place of Thee, or preferring anything to thy favour. Spread around us the shield of thy protection, and defend us against all dangers. Give us thy Holy Spirit abundantly, that in all our conduct the fruits of the Spirit may be manifest, and our life be framed after the example of thy dear Son. O God, we want to feel more and more that we are thy children, and that Thou art training us day by day for a place in thy kingdom.

Let thy favour rest on all whom we love, and for whom we pray. Pour out thy gracious Spirit on the hearts of thy people, and make them zealous for thy glory. Bless thy Word wherever it is preached and made known, and glorify thy grace in the conversion day by day of many hearts to Christ. Give to all in authority wisdom and guidance, and overrule all that they do for the increase of true religion. We ask these mercies in the name of Jesus Christ our Lord. Amen.

READ IN HOLY SCRIPTURE ROMANS XIV.

OUR Father and our God, brought safely through the day, we praise Thee for all its blessings, and desire now at its close to commend ourselves to thy fatherly protection. The darkness and the light are both alike to Thee. As Thou hast been with us in the light, so be with us and watch over us during all the hours of darkness.

Whatever Thou hast seen amiss in us during the day that is now gone, do Thou graciously forgive. In many things we all offend. If Thou, Lord, shouldst mark iniquity, O Lord, who should stand? We cast ourselves upon thy forgiving mercy this night. Thou hast said that if we confess our sins, Thou art faithful and just to forgive us our sins, and to cleanse us from all unrighteousness. Confessing our sins before Thee at this time, we trust thy promise both for pardon and for purity.

Give us increasing carefulness, we pray Thee, in the conduct of our daily life. Beset with evils on the right hand and on the left, prone to evil by the motions of sin that are within us, may we seek to cleanse our way by taking heed thereto according to thy Word. Give our consciences increased tenderness, teach us to give attention to their admonitions, and enable us to purify our souls by obeying the truth.

Enable us to live in anticipation of that time when we shall all stand before the judgment-seat of Christ, and when every one of us shall give account of himself to God. Above all, by thy Spirit, convince us of the sin of unbelief.

Increase our faith, and help us to look unto Jesus, the Author and Finisher of faith. Reveal thy Son in us, O God, as the Way, and the Truth, and the Life, and as the hope of glory. And as He lives for us, so may we live to Him; and as He died for us, so, when we die, may we die to Him. Whether we live, may we live unto the Lord, or whether we die, may we die unto the Lord.

Bending together at our domestic altar, may we also here remember what is promised and provided for us as a family in Christ. In Him may our family be blessed. Believing in Him, may we be saved and our house. In all our exercises of devotion, give us true spirituality and deep sincerity. May we seek after a kingdom of God which is not meat and drink, but righteousness, peace, and joy in the Holy Ghost. In all our convictions, give us conscientiousness. May every one of us be fully persuaded in his own mind. In all our dealings with our brethren, teach us charity. May we at all times follow after things which make for peace, and things wherewith one may edify another. May we never cause our brother, by our example, to think lightly of sin, or to turn aside from Thee. We ask all for Christ our Saviour's sake. Amen.

[Morning.] **FORTY-FIRST WEEK.—SATURDAY.** [Evening.

READ IN HOLY SCRIPTURE 2 CHRONICLES XXXVI.

O LORD God Almighty, terrible art Thou in thy majesty, and resistless in thy power. None can successfully oppose Thee, or say unto Thee, "What doest Thou?" Thou doest according to thy will in the armies of heaven and amongst the inhabitants of the earth. Thou art a jealous God, and wilt not give thy glory unto another. Thine eyes behold, and thine eyelids try the children of men. Thou takest knowledge of the works and the character of all men, high and low, rich and poor. Thou visitest the sins of the fathers upon the children, from one generation to another; but righteous art Thou in all thy ways, and holy in all thy works. Sin is the abominable thing which thy soul hateth, and Thou wilt not permit it to pass unpunished. Whatsoever a man soweth, that shall he also reap. Impress our hearts very deeply with that terrible visitation of thy righteous judgment of which we have now been reading. May we flee from sin as from the face of a serpent, conscious that whatever may be the rank or circumstances of men, their sin will find them out. But there is mercy with Thee, that Thou mayest be feared, and plenteous redemption, that Thou mayest be sought unto. Through Jesus Christ thy Son, Thou wilt forgive, accept, and save all that repent and believe. We come now to the altar of God, to God our exceeding joy. The past night of safety and rest has laid us under fresh obligations to Thee, and this new day calls us to seek fresh supplies of grace and blessing.

As members of a family, may we be anxious, by thy grace, efficiently to discharge all our duties as unto the Lord, and not unto men, and to perform the work of each day in the day. We know not what of danger or difficulty, of sorrow or of joy, lies before us: help us to feel that we are in thy hand, and Thou wilt make all things to work together for good to them that love Thee. Give us a watchful, prayerful spirit, and help us to derive instruction and holiness from all the scenes through which we pass, and the circumstances in which we may be placed. Let us dwell together as a family in unity. May all our relatives be sons and daughters of the Lord God Almighty. Hasten the time when all the families of our land and of the world shall fear God and work righteousness.

We commend ourselves, individually and collectively, to thy paternal care during this day. Anoint us with the Holy Ghost, and pour upon us blessings temporal and blessings spiritual, according to our necessities. Bless us, O our God, and make us blessings, and thine shall be the praise for evermore, through Jesus Christ our Lord. Amen.

READ IN HOLY SCRIPTURE ROMANS XV.

MOST blessed God, the God of the spirits of all flesh, we prostrate ourselves again before thy throne of grace, and approach thy mercy-seat in the name of thy dear Son. Thou hast spared us through another week, and blessed us during this period of our existence in various ways. Indeed, we acknowledge that every moment of our lives testifies to mercies spiritual and temporal continually vouchsafed to us, and testifies likewise to our unworthiness of the least of thy mercies. Thou hast made us partakers of the spiritual things of thine ancient people Israel. Thou hast called us to the light and knowledge of thy glorious Gospel, that we might have joy and peace in believing in Jesus, and that we might abound in hope by the power of the Holy Ghost. Thou hast given us a holy standard of conduct in the example of thy dear Son; and Thou hast ordained ministers, whose duty it is to watch for our souls. Oh, make us to be duly sensible of these thy great mercies, and of our shortcomings in reference to them; and send down the Holy Ghost to quicken us, that we may become more and more dead to the world, and more and more alive to our spiritual interests; so that, at the close of each successive week of our lives, we may have some humble but distinct assurance that we have made some progress on our heavenward way, and that we are hastening towards that eternal Sabbath—the rest which remaineth for the people of God. Give us stronger faith in the all-sufficiency of the sacrifice of Jesus to atone for all our transgressions, and enable us so to appropriate that blessed sacrifice each of us to himself and herself, that being justified by faith we may have peace with Thee; and, in order that we may know that we are of God, make us to be conformed to the image of Him who pleased not Himself, who went about doing good, and who said, "It is more blessed to give than to receive." Help us to deny ourselves for thy sake, and for the relief of the afflicted and distressed; and if we cannot at all times assist them by contributions of our worldly goods, give us grace to do so by our prayers, seeing that Thou dost condescend to hear us on the behalf of others as well as on our own.

We would pray earnestly for all who minister in holy things. Enable them to come before the people, on the forthcoming Sabbath-day, in the fulness of the blessing of the Gospel of Christ. Take us again, we beseech Thee, under thy gracious protection this night. Bless all for whom it is our duty to pray, and grant us an answer of peace. We ask all for Jesus Christ's sake, to whom, with Thee and the Holy Ghost, be everlasting praises. Amen.

[Morning.] FORTY-SECOND WEEK.—LORD'S DAY. [Evening.

READ IN HOLY SCRIPTURE DANIEL I.

ALMIGHTY and eternal God, impress on our minds a deep sense of our utter unworthiness. Help us to come to Thee through Christ thy Son, who is the Way, the Truth, and the Life, and humbly relying for acceptance in thy sight, most holy God, on his atoning sacrifice and death, and in his intercession in heaven for all that come to Thee by Him.

Mercifully accept our thanks for thy great goodness in giving us rest during the night that is gone, and for all other gifts of thy gracious providence. But on this day especially we would rejoice and be exceeding glad. Go with us into thine house of prayer. Help us to sing thy praise with the heart as well as the voice. Fill us with the spirit of true devotion. May we hear the Word which shall be spoken to us with faith, and receive it meekly as the engrafted Word of life. May we be fed and grow thereby.

Bless, we beseech Thee, O Lord, all the assemblies of thy saints throughout the whole earth. Give a great success to the preachers of thy Gospel, and comfort and stablish their converts. O Lord God, make bare thine arm among the nations, and shortly accomplish the number of thine elect. May we never forget the Scripture which has now been read in our hearing. We commend all who may be suffering for righteousness' sake to thy sustaining power and grace. We know not what may happen to ourselves, but we pray that in all things, in all temptations, and in all places we may manifest the prudence, wisdom, courage, integrity, and the fear and love of Thee, for which thy servant Daniel and his followers were distinguished, that we, like them, may also triumph.

Most merciful God, grant, we beseech Thee, that this day may be to us a foretaste of heaven. May thy house be the gate thereof to our souls; and may we, by waiting upon Thee, be so strengthened as to be able to bear every trial, and discharge every duty which may await us during the week. Command thy blessing to rest on our gracious Sovereign and the Royal Family, and on our rulers and governors, judges and magistrates, that they may be a terror to evil-doers, and a praise to them that do well. Be pleased in thy great mercy to hear these prayers. Forgive whatever Thou seest to be amiss in them. Grant what Thou knowest we need, for we ask all in the name of Christ Jesus, in whose most precious blood we pray that our sins may be washed away, and in whose righteousness we hope to stand justified before thy judgment-seat. To Him with Thyself and the Holy Ghost, the ever-living God, be all honour and glory, for ever and ever. Amen.

READ IN HOLY SCRIPTURE ROMANS XVI.

ALMIGHTY and immortal God, we magnify thy glorious name for thy great goodness in the Sabbath mercies and privileges vouchsafed to us this day. We bless Thee for our creation, preservation, and all the blessings of this life, but above all for thine inestimable love in the redemption of the world by our Lord Jesus Christ, for the means of grace, and for the hope of glory.

Thankful for the opportunities of communion with Thee which we have enjoyed on this thy holy day, we would earnestly supplicate once more thy blessing on its closing hours.

We bow before thee as the members of a Christian family, and we pray that our household may be distinguished as a household of faith—a household whose purpose it is to serve the Lord. United in the bonds of natural affection, unite us more closely still in the bonds of spiritual union to Christ, so that each may be doubly beloved in the Lord. Thus united in heart, and in the faith and hope of the Gospel, make us, we beseech Thee, increasingly anxious to adorn the doctrine of God our Saviour in all things, emulating the example of the early believers, who laboured much in the Lord. And to this end multiply upon us thy manifold gifts of grace: supply all our spiritual need: stablish, strengthen, settle us; for without Thee we can do nothing.

Bless, we pray Thee, to our profit, and to the profit of the universal Church, the reading and the preaching of thy holy Word in all the churches of the saints. By thy Spirit, the only infallible teacher, guide thy people into all truth, and accompany the Word of thy grace with demonstration and with power to the hearts and consciences of all who are living in and loving the darkness of error and sin. May the blind eyes be opened, and the deaf ears be unstopped. Pour out thy Spirit upon all flesh, and grant that the ends of the earth may speedily see the salvation of our God.

And now, O merciful Father, taught to believe that Thou art more ready to hear than we are to pray, and wont to give more than we desire or deserve, and deeply feeling that we have cause for shame in the remembrance of the poverty of desire and the unworthiness of spirit which have characterised our approaches this day to thy throne of grace, we would close it with the final and large petition for ourselves and for others, that Thou wouldst pour down upon us the abundance of thy mercy, forgiving us those sins whereof our conscience is afraid, and giving us those good things which we are not worthy to ask, but through the merits and mediation of Jesus Christ, thy Son, our Lord. Amen.

Morning.]   FORTY-SECOND WEEK.—MONDAY.   [Evening.

READ IN HOLY SCRIPTURE DANIEL III.

ALMIGHTY God, Thou art the King, eternal, immortal, invisible, the only wise God, and unto Thee, and Thee alone, will we ascribe honour and glory, for ever and ever.

We beseech Thee, this morning, to accept our thanks for thy great goodness to us. We praise Thee for having taught us to love and trust Thee alone. Teach us, we pray Thee, yet more and more by the Holy Spirit to believe in Thee, that we may never be brought to confusion. Conform us, in thought, and word, and deed, to the image of thine honourable, true, and only Son. Help us to live the life of faith in Thee which He lived. Make it our meat to do thy will, and thus, though the outward man perish, let the inward man be renewed day by day.

Pity, O righteous Father, our weakness, we entreat Thee; pardon our worldliness. We confess with shame that we have too often trembled at the fear of man, or sought anxiously the praise of man. But grant that the bright example of faith in Thee which thy Word has brought before us this morning, may help to nourish our souls in all holy boldness in our obedience to thy laws. Let no fiery furnace of earthly wrath over daunt our courage. Let no persecution or distress tempt us to deny Thee. In every hour of danger help us to witness for Thee, and to realise thy presence and protection. O Thou who once didst endure for us the contradiction of sinners against Thyself, be our strength, our comfort, our joy. Help us not to be careful to answer our adversaries when they threaten us for thy sake. Thou art able to deliver us, for all power in heaven and on earth is thine.

Vouchsafe, O Lord, to keep us this day without sin. Make us sincere and conscientious in all we do or say. May all that we do be done as unto the Lord, and not unto men. Suffer us not to be afraid openly and honestly to serve Thee; and by our well-doing may we have grace to put to silence the ignorance of foolish men, who desire to set up their own gods of this world in opposition to Thee.

O Lord, hear our prayer for those who know Thee not. Send forth to them thy light and thy truth. Turn their hearts from all pride and self-worship, and lead them to submit as thy children to Thee. Bless all kings and rulers, all magistrates and judges. Help them to walk humbly in thy fear, and to govern in uprightness of heart. Preserve to us our freedom of worship, and grant the same blessing to all the nations of the earth. Holy Father, keep us now and ever in thy name, through Jesus Christ, our Lord and Saviour, to whom, with Thee and the ever blessed Spirit, be everlasting praise. Amen.

READ IN HOLY SCRIPTURE ACTS XX. 13–38.

GRACIOUS and merciful Lord God, who art the supreme Disposer of all things in heaven and earth, and in whose hands are the issues of life and death, pour upon us the spirit of grace and of supplication, while we draw nigh to thy mercy-seat this evening. We confess that we have sinned against Thee in thought, word, and deed, and that we are unworthy of the least of thy mercies. Yet hast Thou spared us, and loved us, and given thy dear Son to die for us. Oh, let thy goodness lead us to repentance, and thy longsuffering prove our salvation.

We acknowledge that thy way is in the sea, and thy footsteps are not known. That we, who are sinful dust and ashes, should be privileged to listen to the joyful sound, and hear thy Gospel proclaimed, is wonderful! Oh, that we may value it more than we have ever done; and let it prove a savour of life unto life to us. Mercifully enrich our souls with the blessed experience of thy grace and love in Christ Jesus. Bestow the peace which passeth all understanding, and grant that we may know the love of Christ, and be filled with all the fulness of God. Sanctify our sinful hearts, and make us anxious in all things to be conformed to thy will. Strengthen our weak resolutions, and preserve us from the sin of grieving thy Holy Spirit by our negligence and coldness of heart in thy service.

Grant that we may be more earnest in prayer for all thy ministering servants who are set over us in the Lord. Make them faithful to their high commission, serving the Lord with all humility of mind, keeping back nothing that is profitable unto their flocks, and solemnly adjuring all to repentance towards God, and faith towards our Lord Jesus Christ. If Thou art pleased to permit days of persecution to try thy Church, be with those thy servants who will be found in the forefront of the battle. When difficulties beset their path, and the Holy Ghost witnesseth that bonds and afflictions await them, may none of these things move them, neither may they count their lives dear unto themselves; so that they may finish their course with joy, and the ministry which they have received of the Lord Jesus, to testify the Gospel of the grace of God. Like the holy Apostle, may they be pure from the blood of all men, and not shun to declare unto their hearers all the counsel of God; so that, taking heed to themselves and to all the flock over which the Holy Ghost has made them overseers, they may feed the Church of God, which He hath purchased with his own blood.

Bless our relatives [our dear children], our Sovereign, our country. Protect us this night, and keep us faithful unto death, for Jesus Christ's sake. Amen.

[Morning.]   FORTY-SECOND WEEK.—TUESDAY.   [Evening.

READ IN HOLY SCRIPTURE DANIEL V.

O THOU most holy, most merciful, and loving Father, with deep humility and sincere gratitude we approach thy footstool, to offer to Thee our morning worship. Graciously incline thine ear to our prayer, and by thy good Spirit help our weakness, and grant us the happiness of those who know that they are accepted of Thee.

We unitedly offer our devout thanksgiving for thy sustaining and protecting mercies through the darkness and helplessness of the night. How kind hast Thou been to us in preserving our health, in restoring our strength, and refreshing our spirits with rest and sleep! Thy bountiful hand has furnished all the mercies which we now enjoy, and which contribute to our comfort and happiness. We feel thy goodness, O Father; we acknowledge thy love; and we pray that our minds and hearts may be so influenced by thy favours, that we may lovingly and heartily use them all for the promotion of thy glory, and for the best interests of our fellow-men.

Be pleased, merciful Lord, to write upon our hearts the lessons of thy most holy Word. By the terrible evils which Thou didst send in ancient times on those who despised thy Word, may we be led to consider the exceeding sinfulness of sin, and how fearful a thing it is to fall into the hands of the living God. Of thine infinite mercy, O God, deliver us from the sin of pride and unbelief. Whatever else Thou deniest us, give us a contrite and humble spirit, that trembleth at thy word. We confess our many shortcomings. Enter not into judgment with us, for in thy sight shall no man living be justified; but in thy mercy forgive and bless us.

We humbly supplicate thy blessing for all the members of our family, and for all our relations and friends. May it please Thee to bestow upon us all thy Holy Spirit, that we may evermore walk in thy ways, and do all things for thy glory.

As we go forth to the duties of this day, we pray that thy presence may go with us. Guide us in every step we take. Guard us from the snares and temptations by which Satan may seek our spiritual injury. Let every trial find us strong in the Lord, and every earthly joy be heightened by the joy of our God.

Receive our prayers, O merciful Father, on behalf of thy people throughout the world, that it may please Thee to clothe them with salvation as a garment; and help them so to exalt our Redeemer and Lord, that the world may be drawn unto Him, until thy kingdom shall come, and thy will be done on earth even as it is in heaven. We ask all in the name of thy dear Son, Jesus Christ our Lord. Amen.

READ IN HOLY SCRIPTURE ACTS XXI. 1—10.

TO Thee, O gracious God, we lift up our hearts to praise and pray. Help us to cast off the burden of earthly care and thought, and to worship Thee in spirit and in truth.

We thank Thee that Thou hast this day delivered us from evil, and saved us from many sins and from much sorrow. Through the blood of the Lamb we have overcome, and this evening can sing aloud of thy delivering mercy. Deign to receive the song of our joyful praise, and help us to bless thy holy name. We praise Thee, O Lord, because Thou hast exempted us from many trials which fell upon thy Church in ancient times. The lines have fallen to us in pleasant places, and we have a goodly heritage. Suffer us never to forget the Giver of all our mercies. May we never wax wanton and abuse thy bounteous grace, but unto Thee may we constantly offer the sacrifice of a grateful and holy heart.

Forgive, O Lord, our sins, for they are many, and especially our contempt of thy Word and our neglect of the ministry of reconciliation. Most justly mightest Thou have taken away our pastors and teachers from the midst of us, for we have often been heedless of their warnings, and unmindful of their instructions and reproofs. Blot our sins from the book of thy remembrance, and still send to us the messengers of peace. In the greatness of thy mercy, O thou great Head of the Church, multiply the number of thy faithful ministers who shall be ready to live and to die for the name of the Lord Jesus. Oh, grant, heavenly Father, that we may not receive thy message in vain. We believe: do Thou help our unbelief. Teach our ignorance. Soften and melt our hearts, that we may know and love thy truth, and find it the power of God to our salvation.

Succour, O God, and defend all thy servants who, in sickly climes and barbarous lands, are swiftly exhausting health, and strength, and life in endeavouring to bring the heathen into thy fold. Oh, sustain their faith; preserve their piety; uphold their lives; and if they should early fall before the power of disease or persecution, oh, give them the victory, and an abundant entrance into eternal life.

To ministers of thy Gospel in all lands give thy prospering blessing, and let the abundance of the seas and the forces of the Gentiles be converted unto Thee. May the mountain of the Lord's house soon be established upon the top of the mountains, and all nations flow unto it. We ask all in the name and through the all-prevailing intercession of our adorable Redeemer, Jesus Christ. For his sake hear, and help, and bless us this night. Amen.

[Morning.] **FORTY-SECOND WEEK.—WEDNESDAY.** [Evening.

READ IN HOLY SCRIPTURE DANIEL VI.

O THOU God and Father of our Lord Jesus Christ, the Author of our being and the Preserver of our lives, look down upon us, we beseech Thee, in thy compassion and love, as we once more kneel before thy throne of grace to offer our united tribute of prayer and praise. By thy good providence Thou hast brought us in safety to the beginning of another day: defend us in the same with thy mighty power, and grant that this day we may fall into no sin, neither run into any kind of danger, but that all our doings may be ordered by thy governance to do always that which is righteous in thy sight, through Jesus Christ our Lord.

We live in an ensnaring world. Oh, make us wise as serpents, and harmless as doves. Be Thou evermore our Ruler and Guide. Hold up our goings in thy paths, that our footsteps slip not. Keep us as the apple of the eye; hide us under the shadow of thy wings. Help us at all times to walk before Thee with holy vigilance and godly circumspection. Knowing how frail we are, and how prone to sin, remembering how crafty is the enemy of our souls, and how many are the dangers to which we are exposed, may we always so continually set Thee before us, that, trusting to thy power, confiding in thy love, and daily seeking the promised help of the Holy Spirit, we may evermore be safe under thy protection.

We thank Thee, O Lord, for the encouragement Thou hast so abundantly given us in thy holy Word to put our whole trust and confidence in thy power and love. Impress upon our hearts, we beseech Thee, the lessons of life we may learn from the instructive history we have now been reading. Like thy servant Daniel of old, may we walk in wisdom toward them that are without. By our upright, consistent, and Christian conduct, may we, as he was, be living epistles known and read of all men. Like him, may we obey God rather than men, and be ready to suffer the loss of all things rather than deny the God of our salvation. Amidst all the trials, and difficulties, and uncertainties of life, may we see and feel, as Daniel did, that the path of duty is the only path of safety, and may we so act that thy name may be glorified in us. But, above all, endue us, O Lord, with a spirit of fervent, persevering prayer. In everything, by prayer and supplication, may our requests be made known unto Thee, and do Thou in mercy give us an answer of peace.

Accept our thanks, O Lord, for thy preserving care of us during the past night. Keep us this day in thy faith and fear, and if spared to the close of it in safety, may we lie down at night at peace with Thee, through Jesus Christ our Lord. Amen.

READ IN HOLY SCRIPTURE ACTS XXI. 20—40.

ALMIGHTY and everlasting God, we thine unworthy servants acknowledge before Thee, with shame and confusion of face, that the heart of man is deceitful above all things, and desperately wicked. It is not subject to the law of God, neither indeed can be. They that walk only after the flesh cannot please Thee. From the beginning of thy Gospel, the children of darkness have persecuted the children of light. The servant has been treated like the Master, and the disciple like his Lord. But we thank Thee, and praise Thee, that thy Word has nevertheless prospered, and been magnified. Holy men of God, apostles and martyrs, have resisted even unto blood, striving against sin, not counting their lives dear unto them, for thy name's sake. We bless Thee that Thou hast still in the world a faithful Church, against which the gates of hell cannot prevail; and we call upon Thee to give more and more of thy Holy Spirit to us, and to all thy servants, that we may hold fast the truth as it is in Jesus, and contend earnestly for the faith once delivered unto the saints. Let no man take our crown. Let us not be ashamed of the Gospel of Christ, never be afraid to take up the cross, and follow Him who redeemed us with his most precious blood, that, when He shall come a second time, we may be counted worthy to stand before Him good and faithful servants, to enter into the joy of our Lord. We thank Thee, O Lord, for another day's benefits and loving-kindnesses. Day unto day uttereth speech, night unto night showeth knowledge. Thy mercies are new every morning, and repeated every evening. But, whilst Thou hast been loading us with favours, we have been forgetting Thee, and breaking thy commandments. Yet Thou, O Lord, have mercy upon us, have mercy upon us. Spare Thou them, O God, which confess their faults, and cleanse us this night with the blood which cleanseth from all sin. We pray Thee, moreover, to grant us thy watchful care and providence throughout this night. Let not the darkness make us afraid: to Thee the night shineth as the day; the darkness and the light are both alike to God. Restore in sleep the strength of mind and body exhausted through the daytime; let no evil thoughts disturb us, whether waking or sleeping; but under the shadow of thy love may we dwell safely.

For all our dear relatives and acquaintances, far away or nearer home, we entreat thy mercy. The Lord lift up the light of his countenance upon them, and be gracious unto them. O Lord, hear us; hear us in heaven, thy dwelling-place; and when Thou hearest, pity and forgive, for Jesus Christ's sake. Amen.

[Morning.] **FORTY-SECOND WEEK.—THURSDAY.** [Evening.

READ IN HOLY SCRIPTURE DANIEL IX.

ALMIGHTY God, behold us, we beseech Thee, with favour, as we kneel at thy footstool this morning; and permit us, through the Lord Jesus Christ, our only Mediator, to call upon thy name.

Accept our thanksgiving for nightly rest, and for the morning mercies spread out so plentifully before us. The light of this new day we hail as thy gift; and we desire to humble ourselves in thy sight on account of our manifold sins, and to take refuge from thy righteous displeasure at the cross of Jesus, where, if we seek Thee, we are assured Thou wilt be found of us. We desire, O Lord, to be more deeply impressed with a sense of our guilt and pollution; we ask that the blood of Christ, which cleanseth from all sin, may be more precious to us; and that we may more earnestly thirst for that holiness without which no man shall see the Lord. Our iniquities, like the wind, have taken us away; but as Thou art plenteous in mercy and ready to forgive, we are not without hope that Thou wilt receive us graciously and love us freely. And we beseech Thee to subdue within us all that is contrary to thy holy will and injurious to our best interests; and to bring us, through faith in the Divine Redeemer, into peace with Thee, and into the liberty wherewith Christ makes his people free.

Thou most high God, may we be as mindful of thine honour, and as faithful to truth and conscience, as Daniel was, of whose confessions and supplications we have been reading, and whose contrition and devout earnestness we desire to imitate. We praise Thee for enabling him to hold fast his integrity, and to be faithful to Thee and to thy cause. May the spirit that actuated him influence us, so that there may be no fault found in us, except it be found against us concerning the law of our God.

We deplore our personal and our family transgressions, the sins of our rulers, and of the people at large; for, alas! we and they, too, have rebelled against Thee. And is there not, O Lord, amongst those who bear the Christian name, much evil—evil that grieves thy good Spirit? Oh, enter not, Thou righteous Lord, into judgment with us, but pardon and save us for the glory of thy name.

O Lord, go forth with us as our Guide, Teacher, and Guard to the duties of this day. Help us to resist every temptation to evil speaking and evil doing. Assisted by thy grace, may we order all our affairs in the house and in business with discretion; and by our faith in Christ Jesus, and our practical love to his name, give evidence of being thy children.

Hear us, gracious Father, for the sake of Jesus Christ our Lord. Amen.

READ IN HOLY SCRIPTURE ACTS XXII.

HEAVENLY Father, we come to Thee at the close of another day to confess our sins, to thank Thee for thy great mercies, and to ask thy protection during the night that is before us. Pardon all our transgressions, we beseech Thee, and make us know the blessedness of those whose sins are forgiven and whose iniquities are covered. We acknowledge that we are all the children of wrath even as others; but we pray that each one of us, through the great love wherewith Thou hast loved us, even when we were dead in trespasses and sins, may be quickened together with Christ. We thank Thee for the grace and mercy shown to thy servant Paul, that in him first Jesus Christ might show forth all long-suffering for a pattern to them who should hereafter believe on Him to life everlasting. May he be a pattern to us; may we all know for ourselves what it is to be changed, as he was, from death unto life, to be made new creatures in Christ, to be born again, being assured by the existence within us of a Divine life and of a growing desire to be like Jesus, that we have really been translated from the kingdom of Satan to the kingdom of thy dear Son. In the manifestation of that life, may we follow thine Apostle Paul as he followed Christ; follow him in devotedness to thy service, in willingness to count all things but loss for the excellency of the knowledge of Jesus Christ our Lord, and in a determination to glory only in the cross of Christ.

Not for ourselves alone, O Lord, do we ask this, but for all our relations and friends, for all our countrymen, and for the whole world, so that the time may come when all men shall become the children of God by faith in Christ Jesus, and the whole earth be filled with the glory of the Lord even as the waters cover the sea.

We confidingly look for thy protection and care during this night. Through the day thy love has spared us, and still we ask Thee to continue thy lovingkindness to us, so that while we sleep no harm may happen to us, but that we may be refreshed and strengthened by rest for the duties of another day.

Blessed be thy holy name for all the mercies we have received, not only through the past day, but through all our lives. For sins forgiven, for health preserved, for loving friends, for a happy home, for the supply of all our bodily wants, for the Word of God, and for the hope of glory, we heartily thank Thee. We are unable to mention with our lips a hundredth part of thy mercies, but with our hearts we would thank Thee for them all.

We offer all our prayers and our praises through our beloved Saviour Jesus Christ. Amen.

[Morning.]　　　　　FORTY-SECOND WEEK.—FRIDAY.　　　　　[Evening.

READ IN HOLY SCRIPTURE NEHEMIAH I.

O LORD God of heaven and of earth, we adore Thee as the high and holy God. Who would not fear Thee, O Lord, and magnify thy name for ever and ever? May our fear ever be the fear of reverence and love; the fear of children, and not of servants or slaves. While we reverence thy greatness and thy terribleness, may we, at the same time, be able to rejoice in thy love, and to hope in thy mercy.

We thank Thee that thy love and mercy have been made known to us in the person and through the work of thy Son and our Saviour Jesus Christ. For Him, as for thine unspeakable gift, we praise Thee; and through his merits and intercession we draw near to Thee now, and offer our morning worship. Hear Him, O our Father, on our behalf; and hear us through Him, and let our words and thoughts, our praises and prayers, be acceptable in thy sight.

We praise Thee, O Thou Ruler of nations, for the privileges by which our lot has been marked. We thank Thee that we are not in captivity, mourning over the desolations of our native land; that our homes have not been invaded, our liberties crushed, or our temples closed. Make us grateful, we beseech Thee, for our security and peace. Help us to acknowledge Thee as the Author of our national mercies, and to do all we can to contribute to our national piety.

Like thy servant Nehemiah, may we mourn over our national sins, and our personal departures from Thee. We and our fathers' house have sinned. Our princes, our priests, and our people have sinned. Oh, deal not with us as we have deserved. Spare Thou them that confess their faults. Hear our intercessions for those who confess them not. In thy great mercy awaken piety in those who love Thee, and give repentance to those who love Thee not. Let the wickedness of the wicked come to an end; let the careless be brought to reflection; let the indifferent become serious; let the worldly become spiritual. And do Thou, O God of our salvation, so prosper every effort to evangelise and save our fellow-citizens, that soon the whole land may become like the garden of the Lord.

Vouchsafe to us, O Lord, thy gracious help for every duty of this day. Be Thou at our right hand, that we be not moved. Oh, keep us this day from temptation and sin. If placed in any difficulty, do Thou direct and guide us. If overtaken with any sorrow, O Thou great Comforter, help us to bear it. Let thine arm be our strength and stay. Let thy grace sanctify us, and fit us for thy service in this world, and for thy glory in the next. O Lord, hear and answer our prayers, for Jesus Christ's sake. Amen.

READ IN HOLY SCRIPTURE ACTS XXIII.

O HOLY and glorious Lord God, Father, Redeemer, Sanctifier, once more Thou dost permit us to offer up unto Thee praises, and thanksgivings, and supplications. Fill our hearts with lively gratitude unto Thee, we entreat Thee, for thy unspeakable mercies to us. Thou hast spared us. Thou hast blessed us. Thou hast kept us in comfort and in peace. Thou hast permitted us now to listen once more to thy holy Word, and to hear of thy dealings with thy faithful servant of old; and Thou dost grant us the inestimable privilege of lifting up our voice and hearts unto Thee, assured that Thou wilt hear us, and wilt, if we pray in faith, grant us our petitions.

Make us to understand, O Lord, how vast are these benefits. While so many of our fellow-creatures are living in darkness, never having heard of thy glorious Gospel, we have the full beams of the Sun of Righteousness streaming upon us. While multitudes more, though they have heard of Thee, are not permitted to read in thy holy Word, we enjoy that priceless blessing. We have thy Word in our house, and may at all times read and ponder it, none daring to make us afraid. While many who live in this privileged land, and who likewise have thy holy Word, study it not, and live without Thee in the world, we have been brought, by thy great mercy, to read therein, and to assemble together to offer up our prayers to Thee. For these great and inestimable privileges, O God, we would praise and thank Thee. But oh, let us not rest in them. Let not a false security take possession of our souls. Deeply impress upon us the necessity that we should live according to our privileges. Make us to remember ever that Thou Thyself hast said, "To whomsoever much is given, of him shall be much required." Oh, may we seek a closer walk with Thee, a more tender conscience, a more heavenly frame of mind, a more entire devotedness to Thee.

Forgive, O merciful God, all our sins, iniquities, and shortcomings this day. Make us to hate and abhor sin, and to fight more vigorously and more successfully against it day by day. Protect us, preserve us in body and soul, while we lie down to rest this night; and if Thou sparest us to the morrow, may we commence the day with a determination to be more faithful in thy service.

Finally, we pray, O Lord, that Thou wouldst hasten the glad time when thy Church shall cover the whole world; when the knowledge of thy truth shall fill the earth as the waters cover the sea. Hear us, gracious Father, and according to thy great mercy answer us and help us, and to thy name shall be all the praise. We ask all in Jesus' name. Amen.

[Morning.] **FORTY-SECOND WEEK.—SATURDAY.** [Evening.

READ IN HOLY SCRIPTURE NEHEMIAH II.

ALMIGHTY God, our heavenly Father, we bless Thee that Thou hast once more permitted us to see the light of day. And now that another day has dawned upon us, help us not only to begin it, but also to spend it, in thy love and fear. Make us conscious that thy presence is evermore about us. In our going out and coming in, in our downsitting and uprising, may we know that Thou, God, seest us. May the thought of Thee be pleasant to us, cheering and sustaining us in all our difficulties, stimulating and helpful in all our undertakings.

And while we seek thy favour as our shield, may we also gratefully endeavour to promote thy glory in the earth. May our whole lives be conformed to thy will, and may our characters reflect thine image. Whatsoever we do, in word or deed, may we do all in the name of the Lord Jesus; even when we eat or drink, may we concern ourselves about thy glory. Oftentimes restrained from speech by circumstances, may we ourselves become epistles of Christ, known and read of all men.

Teach us contentment with our earthly lot. Thou art the Judge: Thou puttest down one, and settest up another. Let it satisfy us to know, whatever may be the portion of our inheritance, that it is appointed unto us of Thee; and let us, by an equal fidelity to the talents entrusted to our care, seek to obtain at last an equal commendation to that which others may receive who have discharged a weightier trust.

We thank Thee that the morrow is the Sabbath. May we find rest unto our souls. Wearied with the labour of the week, and oppressed with all the cares of life, may the house of God be to us the gate of heaven. There are some sorrows which we cannot tell our fellow-men: incline us to bring all our burdens to thy sanctuary, and there roll them on the Lord. And may the zeal of thine house consume us. Not merely when we worship in the holy place, but at all times, may we be pervaded with the spirit of the sanctuary. In the midst of worldly duties, may the interests of the kingdom of heaven be continually upon our hearts.

Let thy kingdom come, and let thy will be done on earth even as it is in heaven. May thy kingdom come in all our hearts. May it enter, and include with it every member of this family. May the kingdoms of this world become the kingdoms of our Lord and of his Christ. In all these things may the God of heaven prosper us; and may we at last have our portion, our right, and our memorial in the heavenly Jerusalem. And all we ask is for the sake of Jesus Christ our blessed Lord and Saviour. Amen.

READ IN HOLY SCRIPTURE ACTS XXIV.

O LORD, our heavenly Father, in the name of thy Son Jesus Christ, our Lord, we now draw near to the footstool of thy mercy-seat to acknowledge thy goodness and love, to render to Thee the worship of our hearts, and to seek for the blessings we need both for our bodies and our souls.

By the riches of thy goodness, forbearance, and love, we have been spared and are brought in safety to the close of another week. Every morning and evening have brought some new token of thy care, and every day a fresh proof of thy long-suffering mercy. Our food and raiment, our health and homes, our friends and comforts, have all come from Thee, our God. To Thee we are indebted for every blessing we receive, for every breath we draw. We acknowledge our entire and constant dependence upon Thee, and our obligation to render to Thee the highest and best services of our hearts and lives.

But we confess, and we deplore before Thee, that we have frequently transgressed thy commandments. We have been unmindful of thy mercies, and ungrateful for thy love. We are ashamed, O Lord, when we think of our unkindness and ingratitude to Thee, our Father in heaven, and our entire unworthiness of thy favourable regard. Pardon us, good Lord, we humbly beseech Thee, these our numerous and oft-repeated sins. Oh, forgive us for the sake of thy beloved Son, Jesus Christ. We plead before Thee his obedience and death as the ground of our hope of forgiveness and acceptance. And, O Lord, bestow upon us thy Holy Spirit, that He may show us our sin, and check us when we begin to wander from Thee.

Especially we pray that we may be preserved from the sin of procrastination. When Thou speakest, may we cheerfully listen; when Thou commandest, may we instantly obey; when thy judgments threaten us, may we humble ourselves in true contrition before Thee. In all our words and works make it our earnest desire to live soberly, godly, and righteously, in this present world. Holy Spirit, take Thou entire possession of our spirits. Make our hearts thy dwelling-place, and bring Thou all our faculties and capacities into entire subjection to the will of God; and by thy grace fit us to dwell in holiness and happiness in his kingdom and glory for ever.

We commit ourselves and each other to thy watchful and loving care through this night, and we pray that when we rise we may be in the Spirit of the Lord, and be prepared to use and to improve all the blessed privileges of thy sacred day, for Jesus Christ's sake. Amen.

[Morning.] **FORTY-THIRD WEEK.—LORD'S DAY.** [Evening.]

READ IN HOLY SCRIPTURE NEHEMIAH IV.

O LORD Jesus Christ, who hast ascended on high, who hast led captivity captive, and received gifts for men, yea, for the rebellious also, we beseech Thee to help us to realise what Thou hast said, that "where two or three are gathered together in my name, there am I in the midst of them," and give us faith to expect blessings at thine hands. On the first day of the week Thou didst rise from the dead to carry on thy work; and on this morning we have been raised from our beds to glorify the God of our salvation, and to seek for special blessings on our souls.

But, O Lord, we are continually exposed to spiritual foes, who try to mar thy work, and to hinder our spiritual progress; and without Thee we can do nothing. Oh, send us help from the sanctuary, strengthen us out of Zion: strengthen us with might by thy Holy Spirit in the inner man, and enable us to fight the good fight of faith, and to lay hold on eternal life. Keep us this day from walking in our own ways, and finding our own pleasure, and speaking our own words. Our souls cleave to the dust; but do Thou quicken us, and fight for us, and in us. So shall we come off more than conquerors over our spiritual enemies; our adversaries shall acknowledge thy power, and we shall be encouraged in the good hope, that in due time, through faith in Thee, we shall be inhabitants of that glorious city whose builder and maker is God. Help us this day to watch and pray that we enter not into temptation; and enable us to resist the devil, that he may flee from us.

O Lord, Thou hast commanded thy Gospel to be preached to every creature under heaven, and by the foolishness of preaching Thou dost save them that believe; but there are many adversaries. Do Thou be pleased to enable thy servants to overcome every obstacle to the preaching of thy Word, and help them forward in the work of building up thy people in their most holy faith, and in converting sinners from the error of their ways. Enable them with the sword of the Spirit to contend earnestly for the faith once delivered unto the saints, and to be very valiant for the truth as it is in Jesus. Let the Gospel trumpet be so faithfully blown this day, that thy people may prepare themselves for any spiritual conflict, and may know that it is through much tribulation we shall enter the kingdom of God. Comfort all that mourn in Zion. Assist thy people who may this day be engaged in spreading thy truth, and hasten the day when every knee shall bow to Thee, and every tongue shall confess that Thou art Lord, to the glory of God the Father, to whom with Thyself and the Holy Ghost be ascribed all honour and glory, world without end. Amen.

READ IN HOLY SCRIPTURE ACTS XXV.

GRACIOUS Lord God, we praise Thee for the many blessings of this Sabbath day. For preserving care and sustaining grace, for the renewed opportunity of serving Thee in the congregation of thy saints, and for the precious ministrations of thy holy Word, we thank Thee. So teach us our sinfulness and convince us of our sin, that the message of thy Gospel may be to us, indeed, glad tidings of great joy, and that we may find comfort and peace in thy promises of deliverance and acceptance. O Lord, we earnestly pray for thy Holy Spirit so to work in us a believing and an obedient spirit, that we may not receive the grace of God in vain, nor turn away from thy truth. We desire to be thine; take our hearts and cleanse them from every stain of guilt in the fountain once opened, and sanctify us by a holy consecration to thy service for ever and ever. Teach us what we owe to Thee for the gift of thy dear Son. Oh, that we may comprehend with all saints the love of Christ to us which passeth knowledge, and be filled with the fulness of God. Great and constant is our need; but in Him Thou hast provided for all our wants. Give us grace to open our mouth wide that Thou mayest fill it; and that we may be for ever the monuments of thy mercy, saved, sanctified, and glorified with Thee for ever.

Bless to our souls all the ordinances of thy house, and let not the sinfulness of our services cause Thee to withhold from us thy blessing. Fix in our hearts the lessons of thy Word which have been brought before us, and so water the seed sown that it may bring forth fruit many fold to thy praise. Preserve us from the sin of unbelief and negligence. Show us in all things what Thou wouldst have us to do, and enable us to do it as in thy sight and for Thee. Have compassion on our weakness and ignorance. Pity our sinful state. Draw us, O God, by thy Spirit, and we will run in the way of thy commandments.

We pray, O God, on behalf of all who have to-day heard thy Word. Make it effectual to their salvation, and to the increase of the Redeemer's kingdom. May thy people be stimulated by the example of the saints to be bold for Thee, and manfully to confess Christ's name and bear his cross. Watch over us and all who are dear to us this night. May the hours of darkness be hours of rest and peace, and the savour of the Sabbath abide with us even on the morrow. May all our days be spent in thy fear, in the love of our Saviour, and in the love of each other. Assist us, watch over us, and bless us, even to the end, so that when life here is terminated, we may enjoy eternal life with Thee in heaven. We ask all in the name of Jesus Christ. Amen.

[Morning.] **FORTY-THIRD WEEK.—MONDAY.** [Evening.]

READ IN HOLY SCRIPTURE NEHEMIAH V.

O LORD our God, Thou art worthy to be praised. There is no end of thy greatness, and there is no limit to thy goodness. Again Thou hast granted us life and favour, and at our family altar we behold Thee, the present God, waiting to be gracious in the supply of our spiritual and temporal necessities for another day.

Replenish us, we beseech Thee, with thy Holy Spirit. Quicken us according to thy Word, that this day we may run in the way of thy commandments, and please Thee, both in will and deed. Resuming the duties, taking part once more in the trials of the week, and remembering our past experience, we feel how weak and feeble we are in ourselves. We would maintain the temper and conversation which become the Gospel of Christ; we would walk in wisdom toward them that are without; we would preserve a conscience void of offence toward God and toward man: but who is sufficient for these things? Left to ourselves, the first temptation will turn us aside, the smallest sorrow will overpower us. We pray Thee, for Christ's sake, to endue us with power from on high. Make us sensitive to the approach of evil. Set a watch at the door of our lips, and cleanse the thoughts of our hearts. Enable us to retain the Sabbath spirit whilst we discharge the week-day duty. Like thy servant Nehemiah, who in the time of trial, and difficulty, and temptation, and evil example, was able to say, "So did not I, because of the fear of God," give us grace to set Thee always before us; and though others give place to the devil and fall into his snares, enable us to retain our Christian integrity and uprightness. We put no confidence in the flesh; we know that we can do no good thing without Thee; but we know also that we can do all things through Christ strengthening us; and we pray that his strength may be perfected in our weakness. By a fresh act of faith we would this morning look unto Jesus as our all in all, who of God is made unto us wisdom, and righteousness, and sanctification, and redemption.

We supplicate for our beloved relatives thy choicest gifts. Let none be strangers to thy Gospel. Cause the light of thy countenance to rest upon them, and enrich them with spiritual blessedness. Regard with thy favour our country and our Sovereign. Bestow upon our rulers grace, wisdom, and understanding. Revive and extend all Churches in all lands which hold the truth as it is in Jesus. Send forth labourers into the harvest of the heathen world, and kindle afresh in the hearts of thy people the flame of missionary devotion, liberality, and zeal. Hear us, pardon us, and sanctify us, for our Redeemer's sake. Amen.

READ IN HOLY SCRIPTURE ACTS XXVI.

THOU ever blessed God, who art the King eternal, immortal, and invisible, the only wise God our Saviour, we would reverently come into thy presence, and devoutly take thy holy name on our lips.

We heartily thank Thee that the throne of grace is always open to us, and that we can worship Thee in any place and at any time. We believe that thou art, and that Thou art the rewarder of them that diligently seek Thee.

Thou hast mercifully conducted us to the close of another day. We devoutly thank Thee, O God, for continuing to us the health and strength needed to enable us to attend to the duties of the station in which Thou hast placed us. We desire to conduct our affairs with integrity and justice. Suffer us not to yield to the influence of worldly maxims and polity, nor to an inordinate desire for wealth. In all our transactions may we ever remember the words of thy Son, our Lord and Saviour, "Whatsoever ye would that men should do unto you, do ye even so to them."

And now, Almighty God, assure us, ere we retire to rest, of the forgiveness of all our sins. May we be truly penitent on account of them, and seek for pardon through faith in the atoning sacrifice of Christ thy Son. We lament our imperfect service, and the presence of sin in all our thoughts and actions. But purify and accept our service, we beseech Thee. We long to be filled with the Holy Ghost, that every day we may grow in grace, and in meetness for thy kingdom in glory. Search us, O God, and try our hearts, and see if there be any evil way in us, and lead us in the way everlasting.

We would remember all those who are in trial and adversity. Shelter the defenceless; feed the hungry; comfort the mourner; raise up the fallen; strengthen the weak; restore the backslider; humble the proud; give wisdom to the foolish; repentance and faith to the hardened and careless. Pity the widow and the fatherless. Defend all who may be in peril, whether on the land or on the sea. Be nigh to those who are sick, and sanctify their afflictions to their souls' good; and put thine everlasting arms beneath the dying, that when heart and flesh fail, God may be the strength of their heart and their portion for ever. And do Thou, most gracious God, mercifully forgive all our sins, graciously guide us through the journey of life by thy counsel, and afterward receive us to glory. These great and undeserved mercies we humbly and earnestly ask Thee to bestow upon us for the alone sake of our Lord and Saviour Jesus Christ, to whom be everlasting praise. Amen.

[Morning.]   FORTY-THIRD WEEK.—TUESDAY.   [Evening.

READ IN HOLY SCRIPTURE NEHEMIAH VI.   READ IN HOLY SCRIPTURE ACTS XXVII. 1–26.

INFINITE and eternal God, who dwellest on high, and yet dost graciously stoop down to minister to the necessities of the meanest and lowliest of men, we adore Thee in the glory of thy majesty, thy power, and unfailing compassions. Before the mountains were brought forth, or ever Thou hadst formed the earth and the world, even from everlasting to everlasting, Thou art God. Bow our hearts, we beseech Thee, at thy footstool with lowly reverence and awe, and at the same time give us an encouraging sense of thy tenderness and grace. We acknowledge with thankfulness and praise thy daily goodness to us in temporal and spiritual things. Cause us to hear thy voice and to see thy hand in all the mercies which crown our life, that they may be memorials of thy love to us, and the means of kindling our love to Thee.

The returning day has brought with it fresh necessities: Lord, we implore Thee to supply them according to the riches of thy grace in Jesus Christ. Especially grant us anew thy forgiveness for whatever sin Thou hast seen in us. We confess our guiltiness before Thee: our very nature is sinful in thy sight, and all our best services are marred by unholiness and shortcoming. O Lord, work in us to will and to do of thy good pleasure. Take away all our guilt, and change, renew, and sanctify us. Fulfil to us the purposes of thy love, and set the seal of thy Spirit upon us, that we may be more than ever thine, by a thorough consecration to thy service.

Leave us not to ourselves or to the devices of our own hearts this day. We desire to go forth to its duties and engagements under the protection of thy gracious providence, and with the guidance of thy Holy Spirit. We have no power of ourselves to resist temptation; be Thou our strength in every hour of trial. Prompt us by thy grace to what is pure, and upright, and holy, and suffer us not to stray into paths of sin and worldliness. We commend ourselves to thy grace. Give us, we beseech Thee, a tender conscience, which will shrink from displeasing Thee; a simple faith, which can trust in Thee; and an obedient heart, which will follow Thee.

We pray for thy Church. O God, thwart and disappoint the designs of all who oppose thy truth and would hinder its progress in the world. Make all thy people zealous for thy glory, and willing to do what in them lies, for the building up of thy spiritual temple.

We pray for all who are dear to us. Let none of us, young or old, depart from thy presence unblessed, but cause thy favour to rest upon us now and all the day, for Jesus Christ's sake, to whom be honour and praise for ever. Amen.

O ALMIGHTY God, our heavenly Father, we desire to approach to Thee this night with the sacrifice of thanksgiving; to praise Thee for the mercies of the past day; and to implore thy blessing before we lie down to rest.

Thou hast kept us this day from many dangers, seen and unseen; Thou hast preserved us in our going out and our coming in; Thou hast crowned us with mercies and loving-kindness. For these things, most gracious Father, we thank and bless Thee; but, most of all, for thine inestimable love in the redemption of the world by our Lord Jesus Christ, for the means of grace, and for the hope of glory.

But, Lord, notwithstanding all thy goodness, we have this day sinned against Thee in thought, and word, and deed; and if Thou shouldest mark iniquities, who shall stand? But there is forgiveness with Thee; and now, O Lord, we pray for pardon through the blood of Jesus. Wash our souls from the stain of every sin. Create in us clean hearts, O Lord, and renew right spirits within us. Convince us more and more of the exceeding sinfulness of sin and of its hatefulness in thy sight, that so we may be more constantly on the watch against it. Help us to resist the devil: may we never give way to evil thoughts, or idle words, or an unforgiving spirit. Sanctify us by the indwelling of thy Holy Spirit. May He in all things direct and rule our hearts; and oh, grant us greater likeness to our Divine Master. May that mind be in us which was also in Him. We are thine, O Lord: may we serve thee with all our hearts; may the love of Christ constrain us to yield up ourselves, body, soul, and spirit, to thy service, that henceforth we may live entirely to Thee. Teach us to be instant in doing thy work. Whatsoever our hand findeth to do, may we do it with all our might. We know not what a day may bring forth! May we, then, live as those who feel that their time is short, and that they must soon render an account to Thee. Prepare us, O Lord, for that solemn time. Let each day, as it comes to its close, find us more prepared for heaven. Grant that we may be daily growing in grace and in the knowledge of our Lord and Saviour Jesus Christ. May we count all things but loss for the excellency of that knowledge. May we be ever pressing towards the mark for the prize of our high calling of God in Christ Jesus. Keep our eyes ever fixed upon Jesus; and in all times of danger and of difficulty may we feel his presence with us.

And now, gracious God, we commit ourselves to Thee for the night. Mercifully accept, pardon, and bless us, for Jesus Christ's sake. Amen.

[Morning.]   FORTY-THIRD WEEK.—WEDNESDAY.   [Evening.

READ IN HOLY SCRIPTURE NEHEMIAH VIII.   READ IN HOLY SCRIPTURE ACTS XXVII. 27—44.

ALMIGHTY God, we adore Thee for thy protecting care during the past night. Thou hast renewed our lives and our health this morning, and we call upon our souls, and all that is within us, to bless thy holy name. For all thy gifts we thank Thee, but especially for the great love wherewith Thou hast loved us in the gift of thy Son for our salvation. We rejoice that in Jesus Thou hast provided a Saviour able to save to the uttermost all that come unto Thee by Him. Lord, we come to Thee now in Jesus' name, and for his sake alone ask the forgiveness of all our sins, negligences, and ignorances. We confess with shame how unmindful we have often been of all our obligations unto Thee, and our duty towards Thee. Our own hearts condemn us, and Thou art greater than our hearts, and knowest all things. Enter not into judgment with thy servants, O Lord; but for the sake of Him who died, the Just for the unjust, receive us graciously and love us freely.

Vouchsafe to us, O Lord, the teaching of thy Holy Spirit, that we may rightly understand the things belonging to our peace, and learn to give all diligence to make our calling and election sure. When we hear or read thy holy Word, may it come in power and demonstration of thy Spirit to our hearts, and build us up in the faith and love of thy holy name. Assist us, O Lord, against all the temptations that surround us, that we be not entangled by the pursuits of the present world, and enable us to set our affections on the things which are above. May Christ and his great salvation be daily more precious in our eyes, and his love constrain us to a ready obedience to all thy commandments. May we have the witness of thy Spirit with our spirits that we are thy children, that the joy of the Lord may be our strength.

Make us, we pray Thee, anxious to do good to others, by active efforts on their behalf, as well as by the blamelessness of our walk and conversation. May those around us see in us that thy ways are ways of pleasantness and paths of peace, and be constrained to say, "We will go with you, for God is with you of a truth." Bless the whole world with the knowledge of the Gospel of Jesus. Send out thy light and thy truth to the dark places of the earth, that many may come from the east and west and north and south, to sit down in the kingdom of God. Have mercy upon Zion, and turn again the captivity of Israel.

Let thy hand be upon us for good throughout this day, and spare us to end it with fresh praises. All these mercies we ask for ourselves and others, in the all-prevailing name of Jesus our Lord and Saviour, to whom be all praise and glory for ever and ever. Amen.

ALMIGHTY God, our heavenly Father, whom truly to know is eternal life, and who hast graciously revealed Thyself to us in thy holy Word, grant us, we beseech Thee, so to know thy dear Son Jesus Christ as the Way, the Truth, and the Life, that we may evermore rejoice in the comforts of thy holy Gospel. We bless Thee for the zeal and boldness of thy servants in former days, who counted not their lives dear unto them, that they might make known the unsearchable riches of Christ. Oh, grant that we may prize thy Gospel, and experience its power, as they did; so that, like them, we may be filled with zeal for thy glory, and for the salvation of men.

We live, O Lord, in the midst of troubles and dangers. We adore Thee for the sure refuge we have in Christ. Grant that in Him we may be secure from every trouble, and safe against all dangers. Deliver us from the snares of ungodly men. Preserve us from the allurements of the world. Enable us to triumph, by thy Spirit, over the sinful affections that dwell in our own deceitful hearts. Suffer us not to make shipwreck of faith or of a good conscience. May we hold fast the profession of our faith without wavering, and preserve always a conscience void of offence towards God and towards man. Have mercy upon the many thousands around us who are living in sin and ignorance of Thee. Show them their danger ere it be too late, and teach them the value of the safety that is in Christ. Bless the labours of all faithful ministers of thy Gospel. Give them boldness to make known thy truth, and grant that thy Word, spoken by them, may never be spoken in vain.

And now, O Lord, we beseech Thee to pardon the sins which we have committed against Thee this day. As every day thy mercies are renewed, so every day do we sin against Thee by ingratitude and sloth. We thank Thee for the finished work and perfect righteousness of our Lord Jesus Christ. Heavy-laden, with a sense of sin, we desire to look to Him anew this night, in the assurance which Thou hast given us that his blood cleanseth from all sin. Strengthen, we beseech Thee, our resolutions of amended life, and nourish in us all holy desires. Our time here is but short. May we have grace to work while it is day, remembering that the night cometh, in which no man can work. We commend to thy mercy all the afflicted, the destitute, and the suffering. Have mercy upon them, O Lord. May the trials of thy people issue in their increased holiness, and the sufferings of those who know Thee not be overruled by thy grace to their salvation. We ask all in the name of our Lord Jesus Christ. Amen.

[MORNING.] **FORTY-THIRD WEEK.—THURSDAY.** [EVENING.]

READ IN HOLY SCRIPTURE NEHEMIAH IX.

O OUR God, the great, the mighty, and the terrible God, who keepest covenant and mercy, blessed be thy glorious name, which is exalted above all blessing and praise. Assembled here as one family, we desire, O Lord, to confess, in deep humility, our sins and our iniquities committed against Thee.

Thy mercies and loving-kindnesses have been renewed to us as of old. Thy providential care has protected us by day and by night. Thou hast given us bread for our hunger and water for our thirst. Thou hast preserved our health, and Thou hast defended our property and home from invasion and loss. Thou hast moreover spoken to us from heaven in thy holy Word, giving us therein thy true laws, good statutes, and right judgments. Thou hast not spared thy Son, thine only Son, but hast freely given Him up for us all, and Thou hast put thy Holy Spirit within us. What shall we render unto Thee for these, and all other thy manifold mercies, vouchsafed to us? Oh, help us, gracious Lord, to praise Thee with our lips, and to magnify Thee in our lives. For we have not always been mindful of thy wonders, which Thou hast done amongst us. We have oftentimes dealt very proudly, as though our own power or might could have gotten us these good things, and we have forgotten to be thankful. Yea, we have even rebelled against our gracious God, and done dishonour to the precious Saviour who has purchased and redeemed us. We have grieved thy Spirit. But, blessed Lord, Thou art a God ready to pardon, gracious and merciful, slow to anger, and of great kindness. Oh, forsake us not, though we have forsaken Thee. Let thy good Spirit still instruct us, let not thy pillar of cloud depart from us by day nor thy pillar of fire by night; lead us in the way wherein we should go, and forgiving, through the merits of thy dear Son, our past transgressions, keep us henceforth, by thy Spirit, stedfast in thy fear. Let each one of us be specially the object of thy sustaining grace to-day, and may our every thought, our every word, our every work, be holiness unto the Lord. Help us by each act at home, and by each deed abroad, to prove that this household is a family that fears the Lord, and that every member of it is a child of thine.

We desire thy blessing, Lord, in all our occupations, and in all our trials we implore thy strength. Help us to bring into subjection every temper, passion, and desire. Send to us and ours every blessing, temporal and spiritual, which Thou seest good for us, and hear us, Lord, in these our prayers, for the sake of Jesus Christ, thy dear Son, our Lord. Amen.

READ IN HOLY SCRIPTURE ACTS XXVIII.

O LORD, our God in Christ, help us to worship Thee at this time in spirit and in truth. Accept our thanks for all thy mercies to us during the day. Thou hast preserved us in life, health, and grace; Thou hast been with us in our going out and coming in; Thou hast continued to us the precious blessing of reason; and for all these things we ascribe the glory and the praise to Thee. Our fathers trusted in Thee, and they were not put to shame; they trusted in Thee, and Thou didst deliver them from many a peril, and didst put the glad song of deliverance and thanksgiving in their lips.

We bless Thee for the history of thy dealings with thine honoured Apostle, as he went from place to place, teaching the idolatrous Gentiles the great truths of salvation. Blessed be thy name, the Gospel which he taught is still the power of God unto salvation to every one that believeth. We praise Thee for all that it has done in our fallen and sinful world, under the mighty influence of thy Holy Spirit. Nations that sat in darkness have seen a great light, and to them who sat in the region and shadow of death, light has sprung up. Multitudes who were far off have been made nigh, and many who wandered in darkness, and barbarism, and guilt, are now at the feet of Jesus, clothed, and in their right mind. For all these evidences of the truth of our holy faith we praise Thee, O Lord, and pray that the day may soon come when the prejudices of the Jew, and the idolatry and pride of the Gentile, shall give way before the truth as it is in Jesus; when all nations shall be blessed in Him, and call Him blessed; and when the light of the knowledge of the glory of the Lord shall cover the earth, as the waters cover the sea.

We entreat Thee, O Lord, to keep us from indifference, and from the sin and danger of unbelief. Preserve us from the guilt of hearing and not understanding, of seeing and yet not perceiving the Word of the living God. Give us hearts to feel, and minds to perceive the things that belong to our peace. May we accept Christ as made of God unto us wisdom, and righteousness, and sanctification, and redemption. Graciously make our consciences tender, and our hearts thankful, that we may hate and flee from everything that offends Thee, and run in the path of obedience, perfecting holiness in the fear of God. We pray that our lives may show that we are reconciled to Thee by Him whom Thou didst freely give to redeem us, and that it is our joy to seek the promotion of his glory. May we love Him who first loved us, and may we be kept in safety this night, for his sake. Amen.

[Morning.]   FORTY-THIRD WEEK.—FRIDAY.   [Evening.]

READ IN HOLY SCRIPTURE NEHEMIAH XIII.   READ IN HOLY SCRIPTURE PHILEMON.

ETERNAL and ever-blessed Jehovah, we desire reverently to acknowledge Thee to be the Lord, the Lord God, merciful and gracious, long-suffering and abundant in goodness and truth, keeping mercy for thousands, forgiving iniquity, transgression, and sin. Graciously look down from heaven, thy dwelling-place, upon us thine unprofitable servants, and, according to the multitude of thy tender mercies, blot out our transgressions. Oh, do Thou wash us thoroughly from our iniquity, and cleanse our hearts from sin. Strengthen us, that we may perfectly love Thee and worthily magnify thy holy name.

We praise Thee, O Lord, for making known to us, through the Scriptures, the knowledge of thy will. Grant that we may never neglect these lessons of thy grace; establish us in all thy ways, and make us complete in thy blessed will.

When we compare our lives with thy most holy law, we are constrained to confess that we are vile. Our iniquities have been many and great: they have increased over our head; and our trespass is grown up unto heaven. Be merciful unto us, we beseech Thee; visit us not as our offences deserve, but spare us, good Lord; spare them whom Thou hast redeemed through thy Son.

We bless thy holy name for all thy servants departed this life in thy faith and fear, and pray that we may not only desire to die their death, and to be partakers with them of thy heavenly kingdom, but that Thou wouldst give us grace to follow their good example. Make us partakers of the favour which Thou didst bear unto them. May no wicked design or weapon formed against us prosper, but keep us in peace and safety.

Hear our prayers also on behalf of our country. Thou hast wondrously favoured and highly exalted us as a nation, yet we have not served Thee as we ought. Thy law is broken, thy Sabbaths are profaned, the ordinances of thy house are neglected, and the institutions of our holy religion despised. We beseech Thee, O Father of mercy, to turn from us all the evils which we most righteously deserve, and grant that we may evermore serve Thee in holiness and pureness of living, to the honour and glory of thy name. Hasten the time when all the people shall praise Thee. Do Thou be pleased to qualify us for thy service by giving us wisdom and strength, whereby we may be instruments in thy hands of reproving the ungodly and turning many to righteousness.

We commit ourselves to thy keeping this day. Watch over our paths, and finally bring us all ours into thy kingdom in glory, for the sake and through the merits of our Lord and Saviour Jesus Christ. Amen.

O FATHER of mercies, graciously regard us in this our evening worship. Our only plea in approaching thy footstool is the name of thy dear Son: for his sake bow down thine ear and hear, and according to thy goodness bless us with all things which are needful for life and for godliness. Thou hast mercifully preserved us amid the dangers of the day, and hast supplied our many wants. Make us more deeply sensible of thy goodness to us, and more constantly anxious to show our thankfulness by an habitual consecration to thy service. We confess that in many things this day we have displeased Thee. Thou knowest how much and how often we have preferred our own will to thine, and walked in the ways of the world instead of in the footsteps of our Lord and Saviour. O God, reckon not against us these our sins, but have mercy upon us. Graciously forgive and enable us to lie down to rest in the assurance of being at peace with Thee. If Thou seest us careless and unconcerned beneath the burden of sin, arouse us by thy grace, and leave us not to perish. Quicken our hearts, and shed upon them the light of thy truth, that we may understand all the greatness of our need and the riches of thy grace in Christ. Lead us in the right way, and grant that at the close of every day we may be holier, and wiser, and better, increasing in the knowledge of God and in the faith of Jesus Christ. Make thy grace effectual to the entire sanctification of our hearts, and let it be seen in our love to Thee and to thy people, that we have indeed passed from death to life. Living or dying, we pray that we may be thine. Take away the love of self and of sin. In every spiritual perplexity do Thou guide us, and from all dangers do Thou preserve us. Deliver us from a spirit of formalism, and enable us in all things to seek thy glory and the spiritual welfare of those around.

Watch over us through the night, and turn away all evil from our dwelling. Look, in thy mercy, on all our dear relations and friends [and bring the children of our family early, by thy grace, into the fold of the good Shepherd]. Both for them and for ourselves, and for the whole Church, we implore every good gift, beseeching Thee to complete in us all the work of thy grace, and to prepare us for a place in thy kingdom of glory.

Graciously have regard to the state of thy Church. Heal its divisions and enlarge its borders. Mightily work by thy truth in the hearts of men, and make thy ministers zealous to prepare the way of the Lord, and to make ready, even in the desert, a highway for our God. Grant us these our petitions, and bless us abundantly, for Jesus Christ's sake. Amen.

[Morning.]   FORTY-THIRD WEEK.—SATURDAY.   [Evening.

READ IN HOLY SCRIPTURE JOB I.

ALMIGHTY God, we desire to come before Thee in the name and through the intercession of thy dear Son, humbled under a sense of our own unworthiness, and yet filled with holy confidence in the merits of Him who ever liveth to make intercession for us.

We praise Thee, O Lord, for the mercies of the past night, and we now implore thy blessing and thy presence with us in all the duties that lie before us this day. Grant, we pray Thee, that we may in all our ways acknowledge Thee, and do Thou graciously direct our paths. Order our goings in thy ways, that our footsteps slip not. Keep us mindful, good Lord, of the dangers to which we are ever exposed in our intercourse with the world, even in the pursuit of our lawful callings; and give us grace that, conscious of our own weakness, we may never presume to depend upon ourselves, but may look up unto Thee for wisdom to direct us, and for thy Holy Spirit's gracious teaching and influence to lead and guide, to uphold and keep us in all our ways. Grant that, setting the Lord always before us, and remembering that Thou, God, seest us, we may have grace so to pass through things temporal as not to forget or finally lose the things that are eternal. And, forasmuch as we know not what trials may befall us, or with what afflictions it may please Thee in thy providence to visit us, grant that we may ever have our hearts and hopes there surely fixed, where alone true joys are to be found. Teach us patiently to endure, and in all our troubles enable us to submit ourselves to thy hand, knowing that Thou dost not willingly afflict the children of men, but chastenest thy people for their profit, that they may be partakers of thine holiness.

We have read of the patience of Job, and have seen the end of the Lord in all his dispensations; how that the Lord is very pitiful and of tender mercy. Give us grace to take thy servant, of whom we have now been reading, for an example of suffering affliction and of patience; and with him may we learn, in all sincerity, to say, under every trial, "Shall we receive good at the hand of God, and shall we not receive evil?" "The Lord gave, and the Lord hath taken away; blessed be the name of the Lord." Above all, may we be enabled, in this and in all things, to follow the example of our blessed Saviour Jesus Christ, and, rejoicing in the assurance that in Him we have an High Priest who is able to succour them that are tempted, may we each be taught from our hearts to say, "Not my will, O Lord, but thine be done."

Hear us, we beseech Thee, O merciful Father, and give us an answer of peace and a blessing, for thy dear Son's sake. Amen.

READ IN HOLY SCRIPTURE COLOSSIANS I.

O THOU who art the God and Father of our Lord Jesus Christ, and in Him our God and Father, behold us thy servants, who desire, at the close of another day, to approach Thee with our supplications. Hearken unto the voice of our cry, our King and our God, for unto Thee will we pray. We adore Thee as the Lord of heaven and earth, and as the giver of all our mercies, and our guardian from those evils which our sins deserve. We confess that we have too often done that which we ought not to have done, and have left undone those things which we ought to have done; and that there is within us a tendency to forget thy presence, and to depart from thy faith and fear. We therefore draw near to Thee, to implore not only forgiveness for the past, but great strength for the future, that we may be filled with the knowledge of thy will, and live as becomes those who are the disciples of Christ. Grant that we may be fruitful in every good work, increasing in the knowledge of God, and ever abounding in thanksgiving to Him who hath called us from the power of darkness into the kingdom of Christ. Grant that we may no longer be tied and bound with the chain of our sins, but that Christ may dwell in us, the hope of glory. May we abound in the graces of faith and Christian charity, and may our hope be fixed not on the uncertain and transitory things of this life, but where true joys are to be found. May we receive the Gospel as the word of truth, and may we adorn the principles we profess by a consistent and holy life. Bestow upon us, through the Spirit, the graces of humility, of faith, of prayer, of love, of watchfulness, and of obedience, that we may walk worthy of the Lord unto all pleasing, and pass our life here in the enjoyment of grace, mercy, and peace from Thee, O heavenly Father, and from our Lord and Saviour Jesus Christ, in whose hallowed name we plead for ourselves, our kindred, and for all with whom we are concerned.

We beseech Thee to take us and them under thy gracious protection this night. Protect us, we pray Thee, during the hours of darkness; bestow upon us refreshing rest, and grant that we may wake on the morrow fitted for the duties of another day. Preserve within us a grateful recollection of thy mercies. Thy goodness and long suffering towards us demand our morning and our evening praise. To Thee therefore, O Thou Keeper of Israel, who never slumberest or sleepest, let all love and gratitude be rendered by the members of this household, and by all the faithful brethren of Christ throughout the world, this night, henceforth, and for evermore. Amen.

[MORNING.] **FORTY-FOURTH WEEK.—LORD'S DAY.** [EVENING.

READ IN HOLY SCRIPTURE JOB II.

MOST bountiful and ever-blessed God, our heavenly Father, we adore Thee for all the wonders of thy providence and the blessings of thy grace. Thou hast once more kindly preserved us during the hours of the darkness; and from thy hand proceed all the comforts and enjoyments we possess. Add, Lord, to thy other gifts a heart to love and serve Thee all our days.

We praise Thee, O God, for this sacred day; and we earnestly pray Thee to make this Sabbath a time of refreshing to us from thy presence. Give us holy affections and heavenly desires, and make us sincere and upright in thy ways. Let thy Word dwell in us richly, that our knowledge of Thee may increase, and we may be enabled to avoid the snares of Satan, which continually beset us. When we shall go to present ourselves before the Lord, let no vain, wandering thoughts molest our worship; may all the cares of life be put far from us, that nothing may prevent our profiting by the ordinances of thy house.

Number us amongst those who fear God and eschew evil. In the severest temptations enable us to hold fast our integrity. Strengthen us, O Lord, to resist sin in every form; and as we know not what Thou hast appointed for us, prepare us alike to serve Thee with active diligence or to suffer for Thee with perfect patience, as it seemeth good in thy sight. When Thou art pleased to afflict us, let us neither utter a presumptuous word nor cherish a rebellious thought. Only let all things draw us nearer to Thyself in child-like confidence, cheerful submission, and complete approval of thy ways. Make all seeming evil good to us, and permit not our unruly hearts to pervert thy goodness to that which is evil.

We supplicate thy richest blessing on behalf of all thy faithful worshippers this day. Vouchsafe the aid of thy good Spirit to all preachers of the Gospel, and grant that wonders of grace may be wrought in the name of the Lord Jesus. Mercifully behold in love all who, by sickness or other lawful impediment, may be deprived of the privilege of entering into thy courts; comfort them with thy good Word, and give unto them the oil of joy for mourning and the garments of praise for the spirit of heaviness. Crown with thine effectual blessing all Sabbath-school instructions and every endeavour to promote thy glory in the world.

We beseech Thee, for the sake of thy dear Son Jesus Christ, to pardon all our sins; through the merits of his intercession accept and answer our petitions; and to the Father, the Son, and the Holy Ghost be everlasting praises. Amen.

READ IN HOLY SCRIPTURE COLOSSIANS II.

O LORD Jesus, the Lord of the Sabbath, let our prayers this day be set forth before Thee as the incense, and let the lifting up of our hands be as the evening sacrifice. We are not worthy to offer unto Thee any sacrifice, nor to gather up the crumbs that fall from thy table; but, we beseech Thee, our great High Priest and Intercessor, to accept our sacrifice of praise and thanksgiving. O Lord God, Lamb of God, Thou that takest away the sins of the world, have mercy upon us! And because, O Lord, thy mercies are great, we beseech Thee to enable us by thy grace to present our bodies living sacrifices, holy and acceptable unto God, which is our reasonable service.

O Lord, our heavenly Father, who didst so love the world as to give thine only begotten Son that we might not perish, but have everlasting life, give us grace to receive and to praise Thee for thine unspeakable gift. Help us and all ours so to receive Christ Jesus the Lord as to walk in Him; may we be rooted and built up in Him, and established in the faith, as we have been taught, abounding therein with thanksgiving. Let no man spoil us through philosophy and vain deceit, after the tradition of men, or after the rudiments of the world; but may we, O Lord, be buried with Christ in baptism, and raised with Him through the faith of the operation of God, who raised Him from the dead, and exalted Him to be the Head over all things for his Church.

And O Thou blessed Spirit, whose office it is to take of the things of Christ and show them to us, open our eyes to behold wondrous things; and grant that whatsoever in thy holy Word we shall profitably learn, we may in very deed fulfil the same. Follow with thy blessing all that has been spoken in the name of Jesus this day throughout our land and throughout our world. May thy Word never be spoken in vain, but make it a word of life, a word of comfort, and a word of power; and may all who have spoken it be themselves partakers of thy grace.

Take away our guilt, O Lord, and pardon the iniquity of our holy things. Pour down upon our Sovereign, our rulers, and our people, the riches of thy grace. And especially upon ourselves and upon all dear to us, bestow thy fatherly blessing. May we all, young and old, be risen with Christ, and seek those things which are above, where Christ sitteth at the right hand of God; and when Christ, who is our Life, shall appear, may we also appear with Him in glory.

O Lord, forgive us; O Lord, answer us; O Lord, hearken and do, for the sake of our Lord and Saviour Jesus Christ. Amen.

[Morning.]   FORTY-FOURTH WEEK.—MONDAY.   [Evening.

READ IN HOLY SCRIPTURE JOB XLII.

O LORD God of hosts, look on us in mercy as we kneel before Thee, and as Thou hast brought us in peace and safety to the beginning of this week, so guide and guard us to the close of it. Let our walk be such as becometh the Gospel of our salvation. Keep us from all evil, that we may serve Thee with a quiet mind, for Jesus Christ's sake.

Make us, O Lord, to see ourselves as Thou seest us. We daily confess our sins and acknowledge our unworthiness; give us grace to feel more deeply the sins which we confess, and the unworthiness which we acknowledge. Send thy Holy Spirit to take of the things of Christ, and to show them unto us. Teach us to see in the death of Christ thy holiness, thy justice, and thy hatred of sin, that we may understand the utter depravity of our nature, which demanded so great a sacrifice; that we may abhor ourselves in dust and ashes; that we may pour contempt on all our pride, and may cast off our own righteousness as nothing but filthy rags in thy sight.

Enable us at the same time to see in the sacrifice of the cross that mercy and truth are met together, that righteousness and peace have kissed each other, so that we may know the love of God, which passeth knowledge, and may be ever encouraged to come to Thee with all boldness, having access through the blood of Jesus.

O Thou great and glorious Jehovah, all things are possible with Thee. Thou art able to do for us exceeding abundantly above all that we can ask or think. O God the Father, grant us, according to the riches of thy glory, to be strengthened with might by thy Spirit in the inner man. O God the Son, dwell in our hearts, and fill us with Thyself, that, like Thyself, we may be full of grace and truth. O God the Holy Ghost, sanctify us wholly, that our walk may testify to all around that Jesus Christ is made unto us wisdom, righteousness, sanctification, and redemption, and that we are complete in Him.

These are the blessings for which we ask, O our God. We ask Thee not to deal with us after our follies and our sins. We ask Thee for pardon and peace. We ask for acceptance in the Beloved. We ask for all spiritual blessings in heavenly places in Christ Jesus. We plead also for our relatives, our friends, and our acquaintance; accept them and bless them together with us, that we may together serve Thee here, and together enter into thy glory. Bless our country and our Sovereign, and grant that the Gospel may have free course and be everywhere glorified.

We ask all in the name and for the sake of Jesus Christ our Lord. Amen.

READ IN HOLY SCRIPTURE COLOSSIANS III.

MOST gracious God, the Father of our Lord Jesus Christ, look down upon us, we pray Thee, from thy holy place, and let thine ear be open to our prayers and thanksgivings. We pray for thy grace, that our worship may be sincere and truthful, the offering of hearts touched with a deep sense of thy goodness, and of our own constant need. We thank Thee for thy preserving mercy and sustaining care through the day. How kindly hast Thou provided for us! How tenderly hast Thou dealt with us! With what compassionate forbearance hast Thou borne with our self-love and self-will! And now, O Lord, Thou waitest to be gracious. Accept and answer, we implore Thee, the prayers we offer up for the forgiveness of our many sins, and the renewal to us of thy mercies. We confess ourselves unworthy even to gather up the crumbs of mercy which fall from thy table. We have strayed often from thy ways, and this day have done many things displeasing to Thee. Enter not into judgment with us, O God; for in thy sight shall no man living be justified. Hide thy face from our sins, and blot out all our iniquities. O Lamb of God, who hast taken away the sins of the world, have mercy upon us. Thou that sittest at the right hand of God the Father, a Prince and a Saviour, awaken in us a true repentance, and bestow the unspeakable blessing of a full forgiveness. Show us the evil of sin. Convince us of our own unrighteousness, and clothe us with thine own righteousness, that we may be without spot and blemish in the great day.

Heavenly Father, who hast so abundantly provided for us in the Gospel of thy dear Son, make us anxious to obtain and to enjoy the great blessings which are promised to thy believing people. By thy Holy Spirit raise our affections to things above, where Christ sitteth at the right hand of God. Oh, cause us to be partakers of his death and resurrection, and grant us grace so to live by faith in Him, that when He appeareth we may also appear with Him in glory. Oh, that we may be enabled to deny ourselves, and to forsake all those things which displease Thee! So fulfil in us the work of the Spirit, that we may show in all our conduct before Thee and before all men that we are indeed thy children, and that the word of Christ and the Spirit of Christ dwell in us day by day. We pray for Divine help, that in all we do we may have an eye to thine honour and the glory of our Lord Jesus Christ.

Take us and our dear relations into thy care for the night. Give us needful rest, and, if it please Thee, raise us in the morning to the faithful discharge of another day's duties. We ask all for Jesus Christ's sake. Amen.

[303]

[Morning.] **FORTY-FOURTH WEEK—TUESDAY.** [Evening.

READ IN HOLY SCRIPTURE JONAH I.

O GOD, our Father in Jesus Christ, we praise Thee that Thou hast preserved us through another night, and permitted us again to worship at thy throne of grace. Thou invitest us with humble boldness to bring our wants to Thee. Earnestly, then, would we beg of Thee to give us understanding to know, and a heart and will to choose thy ways. Lord, we confess with shame that we have often rebelled against Thee, and have followed too much the devices and desires of our own hearts. Again would we plead this morning the blood of our great Sin-offering. Again would we seek the intercession before Thee of our great High Priest. By thy cross and passion, by thy glorious resurrection and ascension, Lord Jesus, save and deliver us.

Give us grace to follow thy bright example, O Thou whose meat it was to do the will of Him who sent Thee, and to finish his work. Take away the proud self-will, the slothful self-indulgence, so natural to our carnal minds; and may the constant inquiry of each of us be, not what we like best to do, but what Thou wilt have us to do. Oh, dispose of us as Thou wilt; and, as we are permitted to lay upon Thee the heavy burden of our sin and care, may we gladly take upon us the light burden of thy commandments, and thus find rest for our souls.

Father of mankind, look in thy mercy on the great cities and towns, yea, and on the little villages also, of our favoured land. Alas! notwithstanding that Bibles and means of grace are to be found everywhere, what numbers are there who are living in rebellion against Thee! Thou seest the open and grievous sins that prevail among the ungodly, and the lukewarmness and worldly conformity which is manifest among thy professing Church. Oh, send forth bold and faithful preachers of thy Word, to warn sinners of thy terrible wrath revealed from heaven against all ungodliness and unrighteousness of men; and, as the preacher's voice reaches their ears, may the Spirit's power touch their hearts, and lead them to repent, and turn to God, and do works meet for repentance. Hear us also in behalf of all who are sitting in spiritual darkness and in the shadow of death. Look on the waste places of heathenism. Oh, remember thy promise that in thy dear Son all the families of the earth should be blessed. Look upon the covenant, for the dark places of the earth are full of the habitations of cruelty. Oh, send forth labourers into thy harvest, and make the Gentiles obedient by the power of the Spirit of God. Let all flesh see thy salvation, and the whole earth be filled with thy glory. We ask all through Jesus Christ our Lord. Amen.

READ IN HOLY SCRIPTURE COLOSSIANS IV.

ALMIGHTY and everlasting God, assist us, we beseech Thee, to approach thy throne with deep reverence for thy majesty and thankfulness for thy loving-kindness towards us. We feel that we are utterly unworthy to come into thy presence. We have sinned against Thee times without number. But we venture to come in the name of Jesus Christ thy Son. We implore the aid of thy promised Spirit. Oh, look not upon our unworthiness apart from Christ. Pardon our sins for his sake. Give unto us the sense of pardon through Him. Help us to believe that in Him we are thy forgiven children.

May thy Word, read to us this night, prove a light to our feet and a lamp to our paths. Enable us to act towards all men with kindness and justice, even as we would they should act towards us. Give us the spirit of prayer. Humbly, earnestly, believingly, and frequently, incline us to pray unto Thee. Help us to watch as well as pray, that the tempter may never find us unprepared to resist his open assaults and baffle his malignant wiles. On all the pastors of thy flock, especially upon him who is set over us in the Lord, we implore thy heavenly blessing. In the study, and in the pulpit, and in their pastoral visits, be Thou with them. May they speak the mystery of Christ with fulness and power. Give us grace to profit from their ministrations. Whatever we learn from them, out of thy holy Word, may we indeed fulfil the same. Help us to bridle our tongue, to avoid in our conversation all that may displease Thee, and to use for thy glory and the good of men the gift of speech with which Thou hast endowed us. We know, O Eternal God, that our life is short and that it is fast hastening away. Every hour brings us nearer to the judgment-day. Oh, teach us so to redeem our time, and to number our days, that we may apply our hearts unto wisdom. Finally, may we learn from thy holy Word just read that as thy servants of old entertained a kindly feeling towards each other, so should we also love as brethren. Bound together by the strong and holy bands of family affection, let no family divisions trouble us. And while contending earnestly for the faith once delivered to the saints, may we love all those, whatever their name amongst men, who are united with us in the body of thy Son.

We commend ourselves to thy safe keeping during the hours of this night. Underneath the shadow of thy wings may we sleep in peace. From all evils do Thou in mercy deliver us; and when we lie down to sleep the sleep of death, may it be to awake in thy presence, where there is fulness of joy, and to glorify Thee, world without end, through Jesus Christ our Lord. Amen.

[Morning.] **FORTY-FOURTH WEEK.—WEDNESDAY.** [Evening.]

READ IN HOLY SCRIPTURE JONAH II., III.

ALMIGHTY and most merciful God, again we bow the knee before Thee. Give us boldness, and access with confidence, by the faith of Jesus. Thy compassions fail not; they are new every morning. We desire to thank Thee for the mercies of the past night, for refreshing sleep, for renewed health, and for the many blessings that Thou bestowest upon us. And now, O God, with the returning light we would dedicate ourselves afresh to Thee. Let thy blessing this day go before and follow us. Grant that we may fall into no sin, neither run into any kind of danger. Hold up our goings in thy paths, that our footsteps slip not. Grant us this day the help of thy Holy Spirit, that we may not only think those things that be good, but also have grace and power faithfully to do the same.

We confess before Thee, O Lord, our sinfulness in the days that are past. We have wandered far from Thee. We have too often neglected thy laws and broken thy commandments, and have provoked most justly thy wrath and indignation against us. Oh, deliver us from the burden of past sins. As far as the east is from the west, so far do Thou remove our iniquities from us. Reveal to us more and more the preciousness of the Lord Jesus and the cleansing efficacy of his blood. And grant, Lord, that the remembrance of thy past goodness may make us more zealous in doing thy work. How often hast Thou delivered us when we were in trouble! How often hast Thou heard us, when out of the depths we have cried unto Thee? May we be diligent in extending the knowledge of the Saviour and of his great salvation. Bless, O Lord, abundantly all those who are truly labouring for Thee; all who in this or in other lands are seeking to spread abroad the knowledge of thy truth. Increase their numbers a hundredfold. Pour upon thy Church a greater spirit of self-denial, and grant that still larger efforts may be made to extend its bounds. May thy Word everywhere have free course and be glorified. Cause multitudes from amongst the heathen to be turned from darkness to light. Take away blindness from the Jews. Let them receive Thee, O Jesus, as their Messiah, and help to proclaim thy saving name amongst the Gentiles. Give to us all, we pray Thee, more zeal, more love, more devotedness, a single eye to thy glory, and a greater desire for the promotion of thy kingdom.

We ask thy blessing, O Lord, upon our families. Bring into thy fold any who are wandering in ignorance of Thee. Hear these our unworthy prayers for Jesus Christ's sake, to whom be all praise and glory for ever and ever. Amen.

READ IN HOLY SCRIPTURE EPHESIANS I.

O GOD, our Father, great and wonderful are thy mercies to us in Christ Jesus; how can we worthily praise Thee? Feeble are all our efforts to comprehend the exceeding length and breadth of thy redeeming and saving love; O Lord, kindle in our hearts a deeper sense of what we owe to Thee. Reveal to us more clearly the riches of thy grace, and enable us to receive the Gospel of our salvation in the simplicity of a child-like faith. Enlighten the eyes of our understanding, and let us ever experience the greatness of thy power. Raise our thoughts to Jesus in his glory, and give us exalted views of his majesty and grace. We pray for the Spirit of Truth, that He may guide us into all truth, that He may take of the things of Christ and show them unto us.

Enable us to read the message of thy love in all our life. We thank Thee for all that Thou hast given us during this day. We confess, O Lord, that we have not deserved thy goodness. We have done what we ought not to have done, and have not done what we ought. Merciful Father, forgive us these our sins, and let them not be remembered against us. We pray for increased faith in thy promises, and for the blessed assurance of our adoption into the family of God. Grant us these blessings, and day by day conform us more entirely to the image and likeness of thy dear Son.

Gracious Saviour, to whom all power is given in heaven and earth, who art exalted far above all principalities and powers, and art made the Head over all things to thy Church, we adore Thee for thy great love to us, and we pray Thee to enrich us continually with the gifts of thy grace. Abide with us this night, and shed upon us the blessed tokens of thy presence. Cause our hearts to burn within us as we recall what Thou hast done for our salvation. O Lord, forbid it that we should be cold and lukewarm in thy service, or count as an unholy thing the blood of thy cross. Stir up, we pray Thee, our sluggish affections, and kindle them into a fervour of zeal for thy glory. Make us thine and keep us thine for ever.

Spread round us through the hours of darkness the shield of thy protection. May we, and all whom we love, enjoy this night every blessing which is good for us. O Lord, grace, and strength, and wisdom are thine. Bestow them, not according to our imperfect and sinful petitions, but according to thy knowledge of our need and the riches of thy goodness in Jesus Christ. To Him with Thee, O Father, and Thee, O Holy Ghost, one Triune Jehovah, be honour, praise, and glory for ever. Amen.

[Morning.] **FORTY-FOURTH WEEK.—THURSDAY.** [Evening.

READ IN HOLY SCRIPTURE JONAH IV.

WE praise Thee, O our God, for the blessed truth, that Thou art a God gracious and merciful, slow to anger, and of great kindness, repenting Thee of the evil! We thank Thee that this is so clearly revealed in thy holy Word. May thy precious promises vouchsafed to the truly penitent, and the many instances of thy forgiving mercy in past times, ever encourage us to come to Thee for pardon and peace. Lord, we acknowledge our sins before Thee, and would humble ourselves under thy mighty hand. But, O Lord, be not extreme to mark what we have done amiss. Spare us, though we have deserved thy wrath. There is in us no worthiness; but we bless Thee that we can plead the worthiness of thy dear Son. In his name we come before Thee, pleading the merits of his most precious blood. Renew to us, we beseech Thee, this morning the assurance of thy forgiving love. Stir us up to a hearty repentance for all our sins. Quicken and increase our faith. Pour down upon us thy Holy Spirit, and enable us, by his mighty power, to turn from every evil way, and to serve Thee in holiness all the days of our life.

Help us, O Lord, to be watchful against the infirmities of our evil nature. Preserve us from pride, and anger, and impatience of spirit. In our daily cares and trials help us, we beseech Thee, to look to Thee for grace to enable us to control our wayward and evil inclinations. May we be kind and tender-hearted, forbearing one another in love; and grant that, looking to the merits of thy dear Son as our only plea before Thee, we may likewise look to Him as our example, and endeavour to follow in the blessed footsteps of his most holy life. Be with us, we pray Thee, throughout this day. We thank Thee for peace, rest, and safety during the past night. We thank Thee for the many blessings by which we are surrounded. Lord, continue thy goodness to us, we beseech Thee. Supply us with all things needful for the body, and feed our souls with the bread of life. Give us strength for our various duties, wisdom in our perplexities, and victory over every temptation. Sanctify to us all the dealings of thy providence. Help us so to love and serve Thee here, that an abundant entrance into thy heavenly kingdom may be ministered to us hereafter.

Mercifully regard with thy favour all who are dear to us, and give them thy richest blessings. Lord, hear us, and let our cry come before Thee; and do for us exceeding abundantly above all that we can ask or think, for the sake of thy dear Son, Jesus Christ our Lord, to whom be honour and glory for ever. Amen.

READ IN HOLY SCRIPTURE EPHESIANS II.

O ALMIGHTY God, at the close of another day we assemble before Thee, to praise Thee for the continuance of thy loving-kindness towards us. Thou art never weary of doing us good, though we are often weary of doing Thee service. We would therefore now humble ourselves before Thee, encouraged by the promise of thy Word, that if we confess and forsake our sins we shall find mercy. Speak peace unto us through the Son of thy love, who gave Himself a sacrifice for our sins, that He might open the kingdom of heaven to all believers.

We are ashamed for our past unprofitableness before Thee. Our privileges are many and great. Give us, Lord, a deeper sense of the great love wherewith Thou hast loved us. Let thy goodness so pass before us that adoring wonder may fill our hearts, and our lives continually speak thy praise. May Christ, who is our peace, dwell richly in our hearts by faith. May we be rooted and built up in Him, and strengthened daily with all might, by thy Spirit in our souls, that we may resist all temptation, and overcome those sins which most easily beset us.

Teach us, by the things which are passing around us, that here we have no continuing city. Save us from the snare of seeking our portion in this world, lest we be poor through eternity. May the one thing needful in our estimation be, to know our adoption into thy family, and to have the light of thy countenance shining upon us. In the sweet assurance of thy love, may we be enabled to take up our cross daily, to endure hardship, and to fight the good fight of faith, looking for the blessed hope, even the glorious appearing of our great God and Saviour, Jesus Christ.

Look in mercy, Lord, upon all for whom it is our duty to pray. Be especially gracious to our relations and friends. Let none of them remain strangers to the power of true religion. May they all know Thee, and Jesus Christ whom Thou hast sent, and walk together with us as heirs of the grace of life.

Look in mercy upon the sick and afflicted. Support them under their trials, and sanctify their sorrows to the good of their souls. Help them to see thy fatherly hand in all that befalls them, and submissively to say, "It is the Lord; let Him do what seemeth Him good."

To thy heavenly care we commend ourselves this night. Save us from all evil. Let our last thoughts be of Thee, and when we awake may the desire of our souls be again towards Thee. Hear us, O Thou God of love, for the sake of Him in whom Thou art ever well pleased, even Jesus, our only Lord and Saviour. Amen.

[Morning.] **FORTY-FOURTH WEEK.—FRIDAY.** [Evening.

READ IN HOLY SCRIPTURE JOEL I.

READ IN HOLY SCRIPTURE EPHESIANS III.

ALMIGHTY and most merciful God, who hast most graciously watched over us through the silence of another night, and hast allowed us to see the light of this day, we thank Thee for these fresh tokens of thy love, and adore Thee as the giver of every good and perfect gift. We confess ourselves unworthy of the least of thy mercies. Hadst Thou dealt with us after our sins, and rewarded us according to our iniquities, we had not been here before Thee this morning at the throne of thy heavenly grace. But Thou hast had mercy upon us, for thy great name's sake, Thou hast given us the Gospel of thy dear Son, and Thou hast said that whosoever believeth in Him shall be saved. Lord, increase our faith; help us humbly and steadily to rely upon Him who poured out his soul unto death, that we might live and not die. Make us to grow in grace and in Christian knowledge, and may our conduct and conversation prove that we are indeed alive unto God through Jesus Christ.

As we are reminded by the Scripture we have read of our entire dependence upon Thee for temporal blessings, may we have grateful hearts for thy manifold mercies. The corn, the wine, and the oil, and all the fruits of the field, are thine. Thou canst send plenty, or visit a nation with the calamity of famine. In thy hand it is to enrich or make poor, to build up or to pull down. May old and young, rich and poor, rulers and people, in our highly favoured nation, remember that there is no happiness and no prosperity without thy Divine blessing.

Lord, teach us all to turn to Thee with full purpose of heart, to mourn over our sins, to confess and forsake them, and to acknowledge Thee in all our ways. Let us not abuse thy providential gifts, but may we be sober, temperate, and thankful, using the world as not abusing it, and ever remembering that we are stewards of the manifold gifts of God. Whether we eat or drink, or whatsoever we do, may we do all to thy glory. We are not our own, but bought with a price, even with the precious blood of Christ, as of a lamb slain from the foundation of the world: do Thou, therefore, give us much grace, that we may live not unto ourselves, but unto Him who died for us and rose again; living or dying, may we be for ever his. Be pleased, O Lord, to give us this day our daily bread, and health to enjoy it. Keep us from all evil, and graciously grant us wisdom rightly to discharge the duties of our station, whilst we look to Thee for guidance in all things. We rejoice that thy grace is sufficient for us, and that thy strength is made perfect in weakness. May we ever find it so, for Christ's sake. Amen.

WE bow our knees unto Thee, O God, the Father of our Lord Jesus Christ, of whom the whole family in heaven and earth is named, that Thou wouldest grant us, according to the riches of thy glory, to be strengthened with might by thy Spirit in the inner man. Help us, Lord, with boldness and in the confidence of faith in Christ to come and enjoy freedom of access to Thee. To us, who are the least of all saints, is this grace given, that we may approach and supplicate our God. Oh, for thy Spirit's help, that we may avail ourselves to the full of this precious privilege tonight!

Lord, forgive us all those evil things we have done, and said, and thought to-day. They crowd upon our memory now, and they have not been hidden from Thee. We have dishonoured Thee before men; our own souls have been injured through sin, and we have caused mischief to the souls of others by our unfaithfulness to Thee. How much good we might have done which we have left undone! O Lord, here, in thy presence at our family altar, we would abase ourselves and repent us truly of our unprofitable day so much misspent. Let us not lie down with guilt upon our consciences. Lord, forgive us; and, for Jesus' sake, speak to us of pardon and of peace by thy Holy Spirit.

Thou hast not wearied of doing us good, and we have to add another day of ceaseless mercy to the record of the years of loving-kindness Thou hast afforded to us. Our cup of blessing runneth over. Take, Lord, our hearts, and make them wholly thine: it is all that we can give Thee in return for all Thou hast bestowed on us.

Preserve us, gracious Lord, from every danger and from every harm to-night. Keep far from this our home all evils, and let us all in undisturbed repose enjoy the sleep we need.

Above all earthly blessings we implore thy Holy Spirit, and seek for more of sweet communion with Thee in our souls. May Christ dwell in our hearts by faith. May we be rooted and grounded in love, and be enabled to comprehend with all saints what is the breadth, and length, and depth, and height; and to know the love of Christ, which passeth knowledge, that we may be filled with all the fulness of God.

Nor would we ask these blessings for ourselves alone. Lord, we have others, whom we love, that are not here with us to-night. If disease, or want, or threatening dangers press upon them, Lord, disperse these evils, and be present with them to bless them and to do them good. Above all, make and keep them thine for ever. We ask all through Jesus Christ our Lord. Amen.

[Morning.] **FORTY-FOURTH WEEK.—SATURDAY.** [Evening.

READ IN HOLY SCRIPTURE JOEL III.

READ IN HOLY SCRIPTURE EPHESIANS IV. 1—16.

ALMIGHTY God, the Fountain of all good gifts, who knowest our necessities before we ask, and our ignorance in asking, have mercy upon us, compassionate our infirmities, and for the sake of thy dear Son give us those things which for our unworthiness we dare not, and for our blindness we cannot ask. Thy mercies are new to us every morning, and we would blend praise with prayer, and with thanksgiving for past goodness would make known our requests unto Thee. We have laid us down in peace and taken our rest, and are now raised up again, because Thou, Lord, hast made us dwell in safety. Blessed be thy name for this and for all the tokens of thy grace, especially for the gift of thy dear Son. Suffer us never, we pray Thee, to think lightly of thy redeeming love, nor to forget at how great cost Thou hast redeemed us. We have gone astray like a sheep that is lost; graciously keep us in thy fold, and preserve us from wandering from Thee. Give us a continual sense of thy forgiving love, that we may be cleansed from all our sins, and live every day as in the light of thy countenance, and under the constant guidance of thy Holy Spirit.

Holy Father, we commit ourselves to thy merciful care and protection for the day on which we have entered. Thou knowest how we are often sorely hindered in our Christian race, and that when we would do good evil is present with us. With hearts so prone to the love of sin, and self, and the world, and a great enemy ever on the watch to lure us from Thee, whither, Lord, can we look for help but to Thee, who hast loved us with an everlasting love, and desirest not that even the least and the lowliest of thy people should perish? All strength and wisdom are thine. Be Thou our Defender, and spread around us the shield of thy protection. We look up to Thee, O Father, and pray Thee to keep us this day from falling. By thy grace we would guard our lips, and keep our very thoughts, lest they sin against Thee. Through thy help we would subdue the inclinations which would prompt us to what is wrong. O Lord, make us thine entirely, consecrate us as the temples of the Holy Ghost, and keep us thine for ever.

Glorify thy name in the daily triumphs of thy Gospel. Increase the zeal of thine own people for the enlargement of the Redeemer's kingdom. Open the eyes of many blind sinners this day to see in Jesus their Saviour and their God. Comfort the sorrowing, and instruct them through the season of trial in the things of God. Graciously regard all whom we love, and suffer them not to neglect the great salvation. For them, and for ourselves, and for thy whole Church, we implore every blessing, for thy dear Son's sake. Amen.

O THOU Fountain of light and life, we seek thine assistance, that we may rightly offer our evening sacrifice of prayer and praise. Send thy Holy Spirit to help us in our devotions, and guide us to the understanding of thy Word.

Glory be to Thee, O Lord our God. We owe it to thy mercy that our lives have been spared through another week, and that we are now in the enjoyment of so many mercies. Create within us a thankful remembrance of thy preserving care. Above all, help us to praise Thee for thy great love in the redemption of our souls by our Lord Jesus Christ. We come as weak and unprofitable servants, humbling ourselves before Thee, and confessing that we have sinned and are guilty in thy sight. Our only hope is in Thee, the Lord our righteousness. Cast us not away from thy presence, restore unto us the joy of thy salvation, and take not thy Holy Spirit from us. Sanctify our souls. Thou hast purchased them to Thyself; grant, therefore, that we may live to Thee, and walk worthy of our vocation, with all lowliness, meekness, and longsuffering, forbearing one another in love.

Lord, we entreat Thee to hear our prayers on behalf of thy Church. Cleanse and defend it, and because it cannot continue in safety without thy succour, preserve it continually. Grant that it may be so governed, that all who profess themselves Christians may be true members of the one body, and partakers of the Holy Ghost. Enable them to hold the faith in the unity of the Spirit, in the bond of peace, and in righteousness of life.

We praise Thee, O God, for the ample provision Thou hast made for thy Church in the ascension of thy Son. Thou hast exalted Him that He might fill all things, and give gifts to men. Pour down upon all thy people a large measure of those gifts necessary for the perfecting of the saints, the work of the ministry, and the edifying of the body of Christ. Bring all thy disciples to the perfect knowledge of the truth, that they may attain to the measure of the stature of the fulness of Christ. Preserve them from instability of mind and from unbelief, from false doctrine, and every form of evil and deceit. Enrich them with thy grace, that they may speak the truth in love, and grow up into Christ in all things. Increase the number of faithful ministers, and give great success to the preaching of the Gospel.

We now commend ourselves to thy protection. Bless every member of our family. May we be affectionately united together, constantly seeking thy honour, and the edification of each other in truth and love. Bestow these and all other needful blessings, for Jesus Christ's sake. Amen.

[MORNING.]   FORTY-FIFTH WEEK.—LORD'S DAY.   [EVENING.

READ IN HOLY SCRIPTURE AMOS IV.

ALMIGHTY God, the Creator of the heavens and the earth, in mercy behold us, who now desire to appear before thy sacred majesty, and to offer unto Thee the sacrifice of prayer and praise. What are we, that we should venture to bend our knees before Thee? We are but sinful dust and ashes; and if Thou shouldest enter into judgment with us, we could not stand in thy presence. We humbly confess our unworthiness; we acknowledge the proneness there is within us perpetually to depart from the obedience which is due to the Lord our God; and that we have no strength of our own to resist that which is evil, or to do that which Thou dost command. We therefore bow ourselves before Thee this day, not trusting in our own goodness, but pleading the merit of our Advocate, Jesus Christ the righteous. For his sake we implore Thee to regard our prayers, to absolve us from all our unworthiness, and to bestow upon us that grace by which we may be enabled to fulfil the duties of the state of life in which Thou hast in thy providence placed us. Whether it be our lot to command, or our duty to obey, may we alike remember that we are the servants of the living God, and that we have a Master in the heavens.

Be with us this day in thy house of prayer, and in all our going out and our coming in; fit us for the faithful discharge of all that we owe to Thee, to our kindred, our neighbours, and ourselves; preserve us from whatever is unwise in word, or unholy in thought or deed. Prosper, we pray Thee, during the ensuing week our lawful undertakings; and while we are seeking those things which are needful for this life, suffer us not to forget the things that pertain to the life hereafter. Bless us this day in all our religious duties, and endow all who minister in holy things with love and power, and a sound mind. Teach them by thy Spirit, that they may teach others. Grant that the word they shall preach may through thy grace be the power of God to the salvation, the comfort, and the edification of many souls.

Daily enable us to keep in mind the truth which we have now heard, that Thou wilt come to be our Judge. Enable us, O Lord our God, so to live that we may meet Thee at thy coming with holy joy, knowing that our redemption from sin and conflict then draweth nigh. Graciously supply the necessities, spiritual and temporal, of all who are dear to us, and cause them to grow in grace, and in the knowledge of our Lord and Saviour. These mercies, for ourselves and for others, we ask in the name of our adorable Lord and Master, Jesus Christ, in whom we trust, and to whom, with Thee, O Father, and Thee, O Eternal Spirit, be ascribed everlasting praise. Amen.

READ IN HOLY SCRIPTURE EPHESIANS IV. 17—32.

O LORD, our heavenly Father, who art the Author and Giver of all good things, we beseech Thee to look upon us this evening with thy favour, and grant us thy blessing.

We are now, through thy gracious providence, brought to the close of another Sabbath; and we desire to bless thy holy name for the mercies and privileges which we have this day enjoyed. Let the prayers which we have offered up in thine house find acceptance with Thee, and bring down an abundant blessing upon us. May the praises which we have rendered to thy Divine Majesty be likewise graciously accepted of Thee; and grant, we beseech Thee, Almighty God, that the words which we have heard this day may be so inwardly grafted in our hearts, that they may bring forth in us a lively faith in the Son of thy love, and the fruits of righteousness, which are by Jesus Christ, to the praise of thy holy name.

Forgive, we pray Thee, all that has been amiss in our services; and accept ourselves and our worship, for the sake of our blessed Lord and Saviour. Give us to know the truth as it is in Jesus; and grant that the fruits of thine Holy Spirit may abound in us; that we may put off concerning the former conversation the old man, and be renewed in the spirit of our minds, that we may put on the new man, which after God is created in righteousness and true holiness. Deliver us, O Lord, from the sin of grieving the Holy Spirit of God; and give us grace that we may be enabled to put away from us all bitterness, and wrath, and anger, and clamour, and evil speaking, with all malice, that we may be kind one to another, tender-hearted, forgiving one another, even as God for Christ's sake hath forgiven us. May we be found followers of God as dear children, glorifying thy name, and adorning the doctrine of God our Saviour in all things.

Unto thy gracious care and fatherly protection we commend ourselves this night; beseeching Thee to watch over us for good, and to preserve us from all evil. And if we are spared to see the light of another day, and to enter again upon our respective duties in life, may we show in our whole walk and conduct that we have not only heard of Christ, but have indeed learned of him, and have been taught by his Holy Spirit. Grant that our profiting may so appear that all men may take knowledge of us that we have been with Jesus; and have imbibed of his spirit—the spirit of holiness and love. Regard with thy gracious favour all who are dear to us, and enrich them with all spiritual blessings in Christ Jesus. Hear us, we beseech Thee, gracious God, in these our supplications and prayers, for Jesus Christ's sake. Amen.

[Morning.]   FORTY-FIFTH WEEK.—MONDAY.   [Evening.

READ IN HOLY SCRIPTURE AMOS V.

O LORD God, we come to Thee this morning, not because we are righteous, but because our transgressions are manifold, and our sins are great. We have sinned against Thee, yet Thou, even Thou, hast said, "Seek the Lord, and ye shall live." Yea, Thou, even Thou, blessed Lord, hast said, "Look unto me, and be ye saved;" "Come unto me, all ye that are weary and heavy laden, and I will give you rest."

And now, Lord Jesus, to whom shall we go but unto Thee? for Thou only hast the words of everlasting life. Thou, Lord, wast lifted up to draw all men unto Thee; draw us, and we will run after Thee. Thou didst bid Peter to come to Thee on the raging waters; bid us come. Let no waves of passion hinder us; let no storms of this world's opposition scare us; let no gusts of temptation turn us aside; let no winds of false doctrine draw us away from Thee. Lord, let thy good Spirit lead us, and bid us come.

We come just as we are: receive us, we beseech Thee, and give us the comfort of thy Spirit. We come for wisdom to direct; we come for grace to strengthen; we come for peace to quiet and to pacify our hearts and minds; we come for a blessing on the ordinances of thine house during the Sabbath that is past. Let the seed sown in our hearts bring forth fruit to life eternal. May we grow by it, and live according to thy Word; doers of thy Word, and not hearers only. Let not Satan snatch the Word out of our hearts, and let neither the cares nor the lusts of this world choke it and make it unfruitful. Let our lives abroad and our tempers at home show that we serve Thee and love Thee. Make the week begun a week of blessing to us and to all whom we love. Preserve us outwardly in the body, and inwardly in the soul, defending us from all dangers, and so ministering to our weakness that we may live to thy praise.

Bless, O Lord, our Sovereign, our princes, our people. Defend the nation from the devices of all our enemies, spiritual and temporal, and especially from the craft and malice of those who hate and oppose thy blessed Word. Keep us as a nation in the simplicity of thy Gospel, and let judgment run amongst us as waters, and righteousness as a mighty stream.

Hear us, O Lord, for thy mercies are great; and make haste to help us and to bless us. Let thy presence go with us, and abide with us. Dwell in our hearts, dwell in our homes, and dwell amongst us as a people; and hasten the day when Thou, Lord, shalt dwell with men, and thy people, whom Thou hast redeemed, shall dwell with Thee for ever in thy glory. We ask it for Christ's sake. Amen.

READ IN HOLY SCRIPTURE EPHESIANS V.

IN the name of our Lord Jesus Christ, we draw near to Thee, O our God, humbly beseeching that the exhortations we have now read from thy holy Word may be written upon our hearts, and bring forth fruit in our lives. Constrained by the love of Him who gave Himself an offering and a sacrifice to God for us, we desire to be followers of Thee as dear children, even as children of the light. We therefore pray that our whole body, and soul, and spirit, may be so sanctified by thy Spirit that we may live in all goodness, and righteousness, and truth, being preserved from the works of darkness, and made meet for an inheritance in the kingdom of Christ and of God.

We are reminded by the approach of another night that our time is short; and we have seen enough in another day of the sins and sorrows of our fellow-men to make us feel that the days are evil. Preserve us, good Lord, we beseech Thee, in thy fear, and promote in us thy praise. Make thy will the rule of our conduct; thy glory the supreme object of our desire; and let the sweet sense of thy approval comfort our hearts. O God, give us grace to adorn the doctrine of Christ in all the relations of life. May He be our constant example who was holy, harmless, undefiled, and separate from sinners. We desire to partake of his spirit, that pure and fervent love to one another may abound in us. Let no unkindness, no unfaithfulness disturb our peace, but make our dwelling the abode of joys which the world can neither give nor take away. Humbly we confess at thy footstool that in many things we all offend; forgive all the wrong we have done to Thee or to each other, and cleanse us by the blood of Jesus and the washing of his Word, that no iniquity may defile or dwell in us. Accept our heartfelt thanks for all the mercies we have enjoyed this day: prosper the work of our hands, and now surround us with thy gracious protection, that we may sleep in safety and without fear of evil. We supplicate thy blessing, as Thou seest they need, for all our relations, friends, and neighbours. [And we specially pray that our children may be blessed with health and strength, and that, by true religion, they may be preserved from the evil that is in the world through sin. Enable us, O God, by prayer, by example, and by faithful counsel, to lead them in the way they should go, and bring them with us, when this mortal life shall end, to thine own everlasting habitation.] Bless, O God, our country and our Monarch, and pour down thy grace upon all sorts and conditions of men. Preserve us in peace; prosper our commerce; suppress sin, and let truth and righteousness fill all the earth, through Jesus Christ. Amen.

[Morning.] FORTY-FIFTH WEEK.—TUESDAY. [Evening.

READ IN HOLY SCRIPTURE AMOS VIII.

O ALMIGHTY God, heaven is thy throne and the earth thy footstool; yet, in thy tender compassion, Thou stoopest down to the lowliest and meanest of men, caring for us day by day, protecting us night by night, and supplying all our wants. All praise be to Thee for thy great goodness. Help us ever to recall with thankfulness the undeserved mercies with which Thou crownest our life, and in a spirit of praise to live for Thee. To Thee we lift our hearts in the prospect of another day's duties and engagements. To Thee we come for grace and strength, for pardon and peace. For thy dear Son's sake have mercy upon us, and bless us. We pray that we may be daily cleansed from all sin in the blood of Jesus, and that by thy Holy Spirit we may be consecrated, body, soul, and spirit, to thy service. Go with us, we beseech Thee, to all the duties of our several callings this day. Oh, preserve us from falling before the power of any temptations. Make us strong to resist sin, and so fill us with love to Thee, and an earnest desire to obey thy will in all things, that we may not feel thy commandments to be grievous. Keep us humble before Thee, and conscious of our own utter weakness, that we may not be lifted up with pride and self-conceit, and so fall into sin. Remind us of thy presence, and so quicken our faith that we may look to Thee and lean upon Thee for wisdom and strength. In our intercourse with others may we be watchful over our words and works, lest we give the enemy occasion to blaspheme, or put a stumbling-block in the way of thy children, and cause them to fall. In tenderness of conscience and with a spiritual mind we desire to walk before Thee. We are frail and ignorant; but, O Lord, Thou canst supply all our need. Grant us every good thing, for Jesus Christ's sake.

Graciously have pity on a lost and sinful world. Let the dark places of the earth be enlightened with the light of thy truth. Feed famishing souls with the bread of life. Kindle the zeal and love of thy Church, that it may be more diligent in scattering abroad the knowledge of Christ and Him crucified. And oh, bless all the ministrations of thy Gospel, that souls may daily be added to the Church, and that Jesus may see of the travail of his soul. Oh, that we and all we love may be saved and sanctified through Him, and be numbered among thy saints in glory everlasting.

Look on our country. Give wisdom to our rulers, and control all that they do to the increase of godliness and the welfare of thy Church. Merciful Father, hear us in these our prayers, and answer us, for Christ's sake, Amen.

READ IN HOLY SCRIPTURE EPHESIANS VI.

O MOST merciful God, the God of all the families of the earth, but very especially the God and Father of all them that believe, we pray Thee give unto us the Spirit of adoption, that we may together adore Thee as our Father.

And whilst with one heart and one mind we thus call upon Thee as members of thy redeemed family in heaven, make us as an earthly family to recognise our relative duties one towards another and towards all men. Let none seek their own things, but let each desire to promote the happiness of others, for Jesus Christ's sake. Thus would we walk together in love, O gracious Father; thus would we glorify Thee with our bodies and our spirits, which are thine. But when we would do good, evil is present with us, and we are beset and hindered in running the race Thou hast set before us. Within, the evil heart of pride, and selfishness, and unbelief, is ever striving for the mastery over us. Without, we have to contend with the world that lieth in wickedness, and with the wicked one, who, as the god of this world and the prince of the power of the air, is ever seeking to destroy us. And who and what are we, O Lord God, that we should be able to withstand these mighty foes? We are indeed utterly unable of ourselves to help ourselves, unable to mortify sin, to overcome the world, or to stand against the wiles of the devil. But Thou Thyself hast laid help for us upon One that is mighty. Thou hast provided for us armour of proof, even the whole armour of God. Gird us with this, O Lord God of Hosts. Enable us to wield with power the sword of the Spirit, which is thy Word. Make us ever watchful unto prayer with all perseverance. Thus shall thy strength be made perfect in our weakness; thus shall we stand in the evil day, and at the last shall stand before thy throne without being ashamed, in all things more than conquerors, through Him who loved us.

We bless Thee, we praise Thee, we worship Thee, we glorify Thee, O Lord God, heavenly Father, for giving unto us, guilty and unworthy sinners, the light of the knowledge of thy glory in the face of Jesus Christ. We desire to yield our bodies, souls, and spirits unto Thee, as those who are in very deed alive from the dead, that we may be ensamples to each other, to all who are near and dear to us; to our friends, our neighbours, and to all with whom we have any dealings; ensamples of truth, and sincerity, and uprightness; of temperance, sobriety, and moderation; of gentleness, meekness, and charity, and of all godliness of living, to the praise of the glory of thy grace. Gracious God and Father, we ask it all through Jesus Christ our Lord, Amen.

[Morning.] **FORTY-FIFTH WEEK.—WEDNESDAY.** [Evening.

READ IN HOLY SCRIPTURE AMOS IX.

O THOU great and glorious Jehovah, humbly and reverently would we worship Thee. Deeply would we feel and sincerely acknowledge our own nothingness and thine infinite greatness. We are weak; Thou art almighty. We are sinful; Thou art holy. We are the creatures of a day; Thou art eternal. We are but as dust and ashes; Thou dwellest in light inaccessible, the Maker, and Preserver, and Ruler of the great universe. Yet we entreat Thee to accept our adoration, for the sake of our Mediator and Advocate, Jesus Christ.

Fearful art Thou in thy judgments, O Lord God. None can resist thy power, or flee from thy presence. Oh, help us to worship Thee aright. May we tremble at the thought of offending Thee. Bitterly may we regret, and earnestly strive against, all that can displease Thee. Forgive the sins of our past lives. Blot them out of the book of thy remembrance. Bring them no more against us for ever. Give us the blessedness of the man to whom Thou dost not impute sin. Wash us in the blood that cleanseth from all guilt. Let thy Holy Spirit work within us, to will and to do of thy good pleasure. Make us, by his influences, to hate that which Thou hatest, to love that which Thou dost love, to practise that which Thou wilt bless. So we, being thy people, and the sheep of thy pasture, shall be saved from sin and death, and give Thee praise for ever and ever.

O God, bring thine ancient people into the fold of the Saviour. Forgive their unbelief and disobedience. Teach them to see in Jesus their Saviour and their God. Give renewed energy and wisdom to those who labour for their conversion, and in thine own good time prosper the efforts made with an abundant blessing.

Fulfil, we entreat Thee, thy promises to thy Church. Heal all her divisions. Take away her corruptions. Kindle into a flame the lukewarm zeal of all her members. Let all pastors, teachers, and missionaries receive a large outpouring of thy Holy Spirit. Lord of the harvest, send forth more labourers into thy harvest, and so hasten the coming of thy kingdom, that thy ways may be known upon earth, thy saving health amongst all nations.

Accept our thanksgiving for thy preserving care during the past night, and for all the blessings we now have, and hope still to enjoy. Preserve us, we beseech Thee, throughout this day. If it be thy will, let health, peace, and prosperity attend us. Above all, order our thoughts, and words, and deeds aright, that our lives may correspond with our prayers, and be an acceptable sacrifice unto Thee; and to thy name shall be all the praise, through Jesus Christ our Lord. Amen.

READ IN HOLY SCRIPTURE PHILIPPIANS I.

O GRACIOUS God and Father, we are met together at the close of another day to acknowledge thy great mercies. We praise Thee for innumerable blessings pertaining to the present life; but above all, we thank Thee for the unspeakably precious gifts of thy dear Son and thy Holy Spirit; for thy holy Word, and for an open door of access unto Thee. Lord, we are sinful creatures. We humbly confess that in us, that is, in our flesh, there dwelleth no good thing. If there has been begun in any of our souls a good work, it is thy sovereign and undeserved grace that has wrought it. Oh, that there may not be a member of this family, nor an inmate of this house, destitute of that new birth of thy Spirit, without which none can enter into the kingdom of God. May we all be of one mind in the Lord, united to each other by our common union to Christ; so that, though we must expect separation on earth, we may spend an eternity together in glory.

And if Thou hast begun a good work in us, we pray that Thou wouldest strengthen and perfect it. May our love abound more and more in knowledge and in all judgment; that we may approve things that are excellent; that we may be sincere, and without offence till the day of Christ, being filled with the fruits of righteousness which are by Him, to the glory and praise of God. Grant that to us to live may be Christ, and while it is our joy to do his work here below, may it be our earnest desire to depart and to be with Christ, which is far better.

O God, look down in compassion upon thy whole Church. Pity those who, though they are called Christians, are in reality the enemies of Christ. Bring conviction of sin to their hearts, and may they know Jesus as their Saviour, who alone can deliver them from its punishment and its power. Oh, that all the ministers of thy Word may be men of much prayer, and be wise to win souls for Christ. Grant that all their flocks may manifest a conversation becoming the Gospel. Grant that, as faithful pastors are called to their rest, their places may be abundantly supplied by men determined, like Paul, to know nothing save Jesus Christ and Him crucified. For this end, bless our schools, colleges, and universities with a plenteous outpouring of thy Spirit. Overrule, for the furtherance of thy Gospel, all the efforts of its opposers. When the enemy cometh in like a flood, may the Spirit of the Lord lift up a standard against Him.

And now, O Father, we commit ourselves to thy care. Thou that never slumberest nor sleepest, watch over us. Be our God for ever and ever, through Jesus Christ our Lord. Amen.

[312]

[Morning.] **FORTY-FIFTH WEEK.—THURSDAY.** [Evening

READ IN HOLY SCRIPTURE MICAH IV.

READ IN HOLY SCRIPTURE PHILIPPIANS II.

MOST gracious and merciful Lord God, we yield Thee hearty thanks that, with the renewal of the face of the earth by the morning light, Thou hast renewed to us thy loving-kindnesses, which have been ever of old. It is of thy goodness alone that we again kneel before the face of thy glory, waiting for the riches of thy grace. Oh, Thou Fountain of light, let the Sun of righteousness shine in our souls. Suffer not the god of this world, or an evil heart of unbelief, to blind our minds. Remove from us the doubts and confusions of a troubled soul, and cause the light of thy countenance to shine upon us.

We thank Thee for thy promises, by thy servant Micah, of light, life, peace, and joy to be given under the dispensation of thy Spirit; may we now richly enjoy all those blessings. Hasten, we beseech Thee, the day of the establishment of the Redeemer's kingdom over the earth. Thou hast given unto thy Church the earnest of the Spirit, and hast shown thy faithfulness in the conversions of Pentecost, in reviving from time to time thy work in the world, and in blessing the missions of thy Church to the heathen. Oh, increase and strengthen those missions. Give wisdom to those who conduct them, and convert, through them, many souls. Grant that thy law, which went forth out of Zion at Pentecost, may soon become the rule of faith and obedience to all nations.

Restore peace through the world. Scatter the nations that delight in war. O Thou Prince of Peace, who hast reconciled us when we were enemies to thy Father, do Thou, in fulfilment of thy great work, speak peace to us, and command that it reign universally. May we, and all who name thy precious name, feel the security of walking in that name, none making us afraid. Thou art our stronghold: the tower of thy flock. May our cry be ever unto Thee. Forbid it, O our Saviour, that we should, under any dispensations of thy providence, murmur or fear, as though our King, the Wonderful Counsellor, were perished. May we feel thy presence calming our souls, thy great might succouring us, thy love gladdening us.

We implore thy mercy, O Lord, to forgive our sins. We pray for the experience of all joy and peace in believing. Give us the sweet assurance of reconciled love. Work in us a growing desire for conformity to thy will, and to the blessed image of Jesus. May He be formed within us the hope of glory. Enable us to follow his steps. Give us strength to walk in love, as He hath loved us. Cause us daily to live as in thy sight and to thy praise. Make us holy in all manner of conversation, as Thou art holy, and hear these our prayers, for the sake of Jesus Christ our Saviour. Amen.

GREAT and gracious God, assist us in our devotions. Give us the spirit and power of prayer. We confess that we are sinful, unworthy, weak, and dependent. We cannot pray as we ought, or as we would. Send us help, receive us graciously, bless us abundantly, and pardon us freely, through Jesus Christ our Lord.

O heavenly Father, give to us the ornament of a meek and quiet spirit. Enable us to walk in lowliness of mind, in love, and with one accord. Let the same mind be in us which was in Christ Jesus, who, being in the form of God, thought it not robbery to be equal with God, but took upon Himself the form of a servant, and was made in the likeness of men.

Keep us from strife and vain-glory, from murmurings, disputings, and discontent, that we may be blameless and harmless, the sons of God, without rebuke, in the midst of a crooked and perverse nation. Enable us to be an example of godliness at all times, and useful to all men; to hold forth the Word of life faithfully and constantly, the testimony of God's marvellous grace and mercy, in Jesus Christ our Lord.

O Lord, our God, confirm our hope, and enable us to grow in grace and in the knowledge of our Lord Jesus Christ. Give strength to our faith, firmness to our resolutions, earnestness to our prayers, fervour to our praise, spirituality to our worship, and zeal in every good word and work. Pour thy Holy Spirit upon us, to renew our corrupt hearts, to enlighten our dark understandings, to subdue our stubborn wills, and to purify our depraved affections. Make us all more attentive to our duties: public, social, domestic, and private. Reveal to us more fully the preciousness of Christ, that we may know Him in all the glory of his Godhead, and in all the perfection of his manhood; in his justifying righteousness, in his all-sufficient sacrifice, in his all-prevailing intercession in heaven, and in his willingness and power to save to the uttermost all who come unto God by Him. Bless all the members of our family [our dear children and servants] with every blessing in Christ Jesus. Enable us to bear patiently all those domestic trials and grievances which Thou seest good to permit, and to meet them not in our own strength, but in that strength which is made perfect in our weakness.

We thank Thee, O Lord, for all thy goodness to us, for life and preservation, health and strength, friends and benefactors, the redemption of the world by Christ Jesus, the means of grace, and the hope of glory.

Bless and protect us during the night. We ask all through Jesus Christ our Lord. Amen.

[Morning.] **FORTY-FIFTH WEEK.—FRIDAY.** [Evening.

READ IN HOLY SCRIPTURE MICAH VI.

O GOD, we come into thy presence and bow ourselves before Thee, trusting for acceptance, not to anything in us, but entirely to the righteousness and sacrifice of our great Redeemer. We thank Thee that Thou hast brought us out of darkness into light, and hast redeemed us from the degrading service of Satan and of sin; and we entreat Thee that Thou wilt grant us thy Holy Spirit to enlighten and sanctify our minds, and to strengthen us with might in the inner man, working in us to will and to do of thy good pleasure, and enabling us at all times to do justly, to love mercy, and to walk humbly with our God. We are poor and weak in ourselves, and ever liable to fall; but do Thou make us watchful against every temptation, and give us grace and strength to help us in every time of need. We would remember with grateful hearts all thy past providential kindness towards us; and feeling confident that Thou wilt never leave us nor forsake us, we would cast all our care upon Thee, who carest for us; and we humbly entreat of Thee to grant that we may at all times walk worthy of the vocation wherewith we are called, in all lowliness and humility, keeping ourselves unspotted from the world, and so passing through things temporal, that finally we lose not the things that are eternal.

We thank Thee that Thou hast mercifully preserved us to another day. Grant that this day we may fall into no sin, but that all our thoughts, words, and actions may be regulated by thy Spirit, and in accordance with thy Gospel, so that, whether we eat or drink, or whatsoever we do, we may seek to glorify Thee, our God, with our bodies and our spirits, which are thine.

We would pray for others as well as for ourselves. Bless with all suitable grace and mercy all who are connected with us by the ties of relationship or of friendship. Instruct the ignorant, strengthen the weak, relieve the distressed. Lead all whom Thou hast visited with affliction to hear the rod, and who hath appointed it, and mercifully grant that they may find all things working together for their good. Graciously overrule all the concerns of this present earthly scene for the everlasting welfare of thy Church and people, and hasten the time when all the kingdoms of the world shall acknowledge Christ our Redeemer as King of kings and Lord of lords.

And now, O God, we beseech Thee to pardon all our sins, to wash us in the blood of the Lamb, to grant us more of that peace which passeth all understanding, to guide, direct, and sanctify us by thy Holy Spirit. In mercy hear and answer these our prayers, which we offer up in the name of thy well-beloved Son, our Saviour. Amen.

READ IN HOLY SCRIPTURE PHILIPPIANS III.

ASSIST us mercifully, O Lord, in these our supplications and prayers, with thy Holy Spirit, and graciously grant that, through thy help, we may faithfully and devoutly ask what is according to thy will, through Jesus Christ our Lord, and may obtain those things which Thou seest that we need, for his sake.

In coming before Thee, O Lord, to present this our evening sacrifice of prayer and praise, we humbly confess our misdeeds, and seek forgiveness for all our sins of thought, word, and deed, beseeching Thee to pardon them for thy dear Son's sake. Teach us, O Lord, ever to remember that we are poor, sinful creatures, depending entirely upon thy grace and mercy revealed to us in the Gospel. We desire to renounce all confidence in ourselves, and all trust in anything which we have ever done or can do. We would be found in Christ, pardoned on account of his sacrifice on the cross, and accounted righteous on account of his obedience to the law, through faith in Him. Grant that, knowing Him and the power of his resurrection, we may live as those whose citizenship is in heaven.

We beseech Thee, also, O Lord, to remove from us, and all thy people, all love of contention and vain-glory. Reveal thy truth more and more to us all by thy Holy Spirit. We beseech Thee, also, O Lord, to preserve us from worldly cares, and undue anxiety about earthly things. Grant that, seeking first thy kingdom and righteousness, all other things may be added unto us. We beseech Thee, also, to grant thy blessing upon all our lawful plans and undertakings, and to give us that measure of worldly success which may be well for us; and do Thou be pleased so to order and direct all the events of our future lives that they may promote our eternal welfare, and that all things may work together for our good.

We also intercede with Thee, O Lord, on behalf of all whom we should remember at the throne of grace. We beseech Thee to give to our dear relatives and friends the same blessings which we have asked for ourselves. We also beg thy blessing upon our Sovereign, the Royal Family, the ministers of state, and all who are in authority, that they may seek thy glory and the good of those who are placed under them.

And now, O Lord, we thank Thee for thy care and goodness during the present day, and we commend ourselves to thy gracious care during the night, beseeching Thee to refresh us with comfortable rest and sleep, to preserve us from all dangers, and to bring us safely to the beginning of another day, through Jesus Christ our Lord, to whom be glory, praise, and adoration, for ever and ever. Amen.

[Morning.] **FORTY-FIFTH WEEK.—SATURDAY.** [Evening.

READ IN HOLY SCRIPTURE HOSEA VI.

ENABLE us, O our Father, in drawing near to Thee, to come with true hearts, in the full assurance of faith. Grant that our worship may be the service of the heart, and that we may now realise the truth that Thou art the hearer and answerer of prayer.

We bless Thee that Thou wilt not disregard the cry of our helplessness, nor turn away from the prayer of thy humble and contrite people. We are conscious that Thou mightest justly spurn us from thy presence, and leave us to our misery and shame. But thy ways are infinitely above our ways; Thou delightest in mercy, and though Thou art a holy God, and canst not look on sin, yet, for the sake of Jesus, our Substitute and Intercessor, Thou wilt graciously pass by our transgressions. We praise Thee that Thou art a God of love, and that Thou hast given us the fullest assurances of thy good will towards us, and the clearest proofs of thy compassionate regard, in the gift of thy dear Son. Oh, let not any of us stand afar off from Thee, when Thou art willing that we should come nigh to Thee through Jesus Christ. May none of us cherish slavish fear or sinful distrust in our hearts, for like as a father pitieth his children, so Thou dost pity them that fear Thee. We confess with shame, O God, that our goodness has too often been as a morning cloud, and as the early dew it has passed away. Good impressions have been transitory, convictions of duty have been resisted, resolutions which we formed have been broken, our desires and affections have not gone out to Thee with ardour and with constancy. We pray Thee to convince us of our weakness, to show us our unworthiness, that we may be humbled; and to lead us by faith to take hold of thy strength, so that we may persevere in thy ways, and endure unto the end. Revive our souls by the presence of thy Holy Spirit; refresh us with the dew of thy heavenly grace, as the parched earth is refreshed by the rain, and make us to bring forth fruit to thy praise.

We desire, O Lord, to live continually in the enjoyment of thy favour. Withdraw not thy presence from us. Unitedly we would say, "Come, and let us return unto the Lord." We wish to live evermore in thy sight, and to feel that we are encircled with thy love, and that we walk in the light of thy countenance. May we thus advance in the way of holiness, and follow on to know the Lord.

We beseech of Thee to forgive all our sins, to accept our thanks for the mercies of this morning, to be with us throughout this day, and to enable us to bear about with us the thought of thy presence, for the Redeemer's sake. Amen.

READ IN HOLY SCRIPTURE PHILIPPIANS IV.

O THOU gracious God, who hearest prayer, teach us to pray. Pour down upon us the spirit of grace and supplication, and grant that, being reconciled to Thee through the blood and righteousness of Jesus, thy dear Son, we may worship Thee in full assurance of faith. Awaken in us spiritual desires, that our souls may thirst for God, and look up to thy throne in the sure hope and expectation of thy blessing. Great are thy lovingkindnesses and tender mercies to us. We thank Thee for them all, for the bounties of thy providence, and for all thy gifts of grace. Oh, that our experience of thy mercy and goodness may be in us a spring of joy and peace, and make us ever glad in the remembrance of what Thou hast done for us. Then shall we indeed be zealous for thy glory, and diligent in thy service.

Especially, O Lord, enable us now to enjoy the blessed sense of thy forgiveness for this day's sins. We confess them before Thee : sins of thought, and word, and act; things said and done which have grieved thy Spirit, and been contrary to thy commandments. Have mercy, O God, and let us not lie down to-night with the burden of unforgiven sin on the conscience. Spare us, good Lord! spare thy servants whom Thou hast redeemed with thy most precious blood. We are very weak and sinful, and when we would do good, evil is present with us; and we are unfaithful to Thee, and stray from thy holy ways. Yet, O Lord, do us good, and supply all our need, according to thy riches in glory by Jesus Christ. Establish us more surely in the faith, and make us stronger to resist temptation. We cast all our care upon Thee, and in the name of thy dear Son pray Thee to help us, that we may abound in the work of the Lord, and be ready to receive Him at his coming.

Graciously bless us as a family with all spiritual and temporal mercies. Enable us by love to serve one another. Comfort and relieve all those who are afflicted in mind, body, or estate. Let thy presence be with them, and thy Spirit teach them in their affliction the things of Christ. We pray for the unconverted, whether in our own household or in the world around us. O Lord, pity the miserable slaves of sin, and worldliness, and superstition; break their bands, and stir up in them the desire for that liberty with which Christ makes his people free. Make them to feel their ruin and danger, and to flee to Christ for deliverance and salvation.

Finally, we pray Thee to prepare us for the coming Sabbath. May thy ministers be blessed in all their labours for thy glory. Lord God, hear us. We ask all in the name of thy dear Son, and our Saviour. Amen.

[Morning.] **FORTY-SIXTH WEEK.—LORD'S DAY.** [Evening.

READ IN HOLY SCRIPTURE HOSEA XIII.

O ETERNAL and ever-blessed Lord God, who, in the midst of wrath, thinkest upon mercy, and beside whom there is no Saviour, verily we have destroyed ourselves through sin; yet in Thee, and in Thee only, is our help. We magnify thy holy name for the unspeakable gift of thy dear Son, and for that wonderful manifestation of thy righteousness whereby Thou declarest Thyself to be just, and still the justifier of them that believe in Him. O Lord Jesus Christ, Lamb of God, Son of the Father, who, through the sacrifice of Thyself once freely offered, hast abolished death, and brought life and immortality to light through the Gospel, look down upon us, we humbly beseech Thee, on this the morning of thine own holy day, and enable us to approach Thee with the worship of sincerity and truth. O Lord, we humble ourselves before Thee as miserable sinners, and trust in Thee alone for pardon and acceptance. We confess not only our utter unworthiness and sin, but also our great weakness and helplessness. We desire ever to feel and to acknowledge that we are not sufficient of ourselves even to think anything as of ourselves, but that the very preparations of the heart, and all our sufficiency, must be of Thee. Oh, graft in our hearts the love of thy name. Increase in us true religion. Vouchsafe unto us the aid of thy Holy Spirit, that we may cheerfully perform the duties and enjoy the precious privileges of this day of rest. Oh, that it may bring grace and refreshment to all our souls; a happy earnest and foretaste of that unchangeable and glorious rest that remaineth for thy people in heaven.

Go with us, we earnestly entreat Thee, to thy house of prayer this day. Pour forth in our waiting hearts the spirit of adoption, and be Thou present in the midst of the assemblies of thy saints, wheresoever two or three are gathered in thy name. Give grace to all thy ministers, that they may rightly divide the Word of truth, and be faithful stewards and dispensers of thy mysteries. Bless those especially who have gone forth into distant lands, to proclaim amongst the heathen the unsearchable riches of Christ. Carry home, we pray Thee, thy Word with power this day to all who shall hear or read it, and unto thy Church multitudes of such as shall be saved.

We would ask for a peculiar blessing upon all our own dear friends, relations, and neighbours. Strengthen them every one to enter by the strait gate, and to walk perseveringly in the narrow way which leadeth to eternal life. May they and we be all thine, in the day when Thou makest up thy jewels. O Lord, hear us, pardon and bless us, and give us more than we know how to ask or think, for Jesus Christ's sake. Amen.

READ IN HOLY SCRIPTURE HEBREWS I.

HOLY, holy, holy, Lord God of hosts, we implore Thee to help us by thy Spirit, as we draw near to Thee in the name of thy Son, that we may worship Thee acceptably, with reverence and godly fear. We plead the merits and intercession of Him who died for us. For his sake bow down thine ear and hear us.

We earnestly thank Thee, O Lord, for all the blessings of the day of rest now coming to its close. We thank Thee for all the privileges we have enjoyed in the communion of thy saints, for the means of grace of which we have been partakers, and for the Word of life which we have heard this day. Grant, gracious Lord, that we may not receive thy grace in vain. May we be deeply impressed with reverence for thy holy Word. May we receive its heavenly truth in our minds and hearts, and find it to be to us the seed of eternal life.

Hear us also, we beseech Thee, while we pray that thy blessing may descend in rich abundance on all the congregations of thy people throughout the world. May the Word which has been taught and preached prevail to the conversion of the ungodly, and to the edification of thy people in their holy faith. May the time soon come when thy Word shall be known in all lands, thy saving health amongst all nations. Send forth the messengers of salvation to every land. Prepare the way for the entering in of the Gospel. Guide and protect thy servants. Send forth thy ministering spirits who serve Thee in heaven, to succour and defend all who are exposed to sorrow and peril in doing thy work. Be Thou the stay and comfort of those who are suffering here on earth for the testimony of thy truth, that, in communion with Thee, they may find strength equal to their need, and in all things prove more than conquerors, through Him that loved them.

And now, Lord, we earnestly commend ourselves, and all whom we should remember, to thy divine protection during the hours of night. We would lie down at peace with Thee, through the atonement and intercession of thy beloved Son. Keep us from all evil in body and soul, and refresh and strengthen us for the cheerful discharge of every duty. Look in mercy on those around on whom the shades of night are closing in sorrow or in pain. May they remember Thee on their beds, and meditate on Thee in the night watches, and find comfort and relief to their souls.

Hear us for the sake of our Divine Redeemer, to whom, with Thee, O Father, and the Holy Spirit, we would ascribe all honour and glory, adoration and praise, world without end. Amen.

[Morning.] **FORTY-SIXTH WEEK.—MONDAY.** [Evening.

READ IN HOLY SCRIPTURE NAHUM I.

O ALMIGHTY Lord and everlasting God, who knowest them that trust in Thee, dispose our hearts again to call upon thy name.

The holy Sabbath is past, and we enter upon our daily course of life. Oh, grant that the cares of the world may not choke the Word we have lately heard, nor its pleasures render it unfruitful. Once again has thy goodness preserved us when we have provoked Thee by our sins, and the greatness of thy power hast Thou restrained by the abundance of thy mercy. Forgive us all our offences, but most of all our past neglects of thy grace, and our want of ready obedience to the calls of thy Gospel. May thy goodness lead us to repentance, and may we show forth thy praise this day both with our lips and in our lives. Break the power of our besetting sins; unloose our tongues, and make all our members instruments of righteousness unto holiness. Lord, strengthen our faith, that we may believe thy promises, and trust Thee for our daily bread. Oh, shed abroad thy love in our hearts, that we may be filled with it, and that all we do, or think, or say may be done in charity.

Preserve this household and family; may it never with truth be said of us, or of any belonging to us, that we have been deaf to thy call, and received thy grace in vain. Make us to abhor that which is evil, and to cleave to that which is good. Guard us against temptation, and prepare us for whatever dangers may be this day before us. Be Thou, O good Lord, a stronghold in the day of our trouble, and may thy fear be our refuge. Should wicked counsellors arise and imagine evil against Thee, and teachers of falsehood try to seduce thy people, let thy good Spirit resist them: but when thy messengers of mercy bring good tidings and publish peace, may they be regarded with favour; may the people follow in multitudes to hear and keep the solemn feasts; and may they daily perform their vows.

Look in mercy, O Lord, upon the dark places of the earth: bless, protect, and prosper thy missionary servants who labour in heathen lands. Give unto them the faith that can remove mountains of difficulty, and charity that never faileth. Wherever Thou hast given dominion to our country, there may Christian truth be spread, and happy fruits of righteousness abound.

In every land let slavery come to an end. Let the fetter be everywhere loosed, and minds that have been in bondage to ignorance and error be set free. O Thou King of kings, bless our Sovereign and all in authority under her; may they rule in thy fear, and ever enjoy thy favour. Hear and answer us, for Jesus Christ's sake. Amen.

READ IN HOLY SCRIPTURE HEBREWS II.

O LORD God, humble us in the dust when we take thy holy name on our lips. Work in us a godly sorrow for sin, leading to a true repentance, and faith in Jesus Christ, the Lamb of God, who taketh away the sin of the world. O God, fill our hearts with gratitude and our lips with praise, when we contemplate the exceeding riches of thy grace towards us, in providing for us a Saviour, who is Christ the Lord. Truly, Thou hast laid help for us on One who is mighty to save.

Oh, help us by the teachings of thy Holy Spirit to receive aright the great salvation which has been wrought out for us by thy dear Son. May this love of thine, which is manifested in the Lord Jesus Christ, constrain us to hate our sins, and to love Him who thus suffered even unto death, that we who deserved to die might have eternal life. O blessed Jesus, who art partaker of our flesh and blood, and who dost condescend to call us brethren, make us deeply sensible of our unspeakable obligations to thy redeeming love; and give us grace day by day to trust in thy blood-shedding for the pardon of all sin, and in thy perfect righteousness as the only ground of our acceptance in the sight of God.

O blessed Jesus, help us to meditate much and often on the depths of thy humiliation, to which Thou didst so willingly stoop, to accomplish the work of mercy which brought Thee to this earth. Help us to rejoice in thy exaltation to the right hand of the Majesty in the highest heavens, where Thou ever carriest on the work of intercession in behalf of thy people. And enable us, amidst present imperfections and tribulations, to enjoy that peace with God which was thy parting gift to thy sorrowing disciples.

O God the Father, Son, and Holy Ghost, we bless thy thrice holy name that Thou hast watched over our goings out and our comings in this day. We give Thee humble and hearty thanks for the varied blessings bestowed upon us, for we acknowledge Thee as the Author of them all. O God, forgive our want of gratitude, our want of service: forgive wherein we have failed in duty to Thee, or to our fellow-creatures, or to one another as members of the same family; forgive wherein we have sinned in thought, in word, or in deed. Oh, forgive us freely, forgive us fully, and wash us in that fountain which Thou Thyself hast opened for sin and for uncleanness; and thus may we lie down in our beds at peace with God, with ourselves, and with all men. O God, the hearer of prayer, we pray Thee to hear and answer us, and to bless us more than we can ask or think, for Jesus Christ's sake. Amen.

[Morning.]   FORTY-SIXTH WEEK.—TUESDAY.   [Evening.

READ IN HOLY SCRIPTURE ISAIAH I.

O LORD God Almighty, before whom the seraphim stand with veiled faces, and cry, "Holy, holy, holy is the Lord of hosts," and before whom thy saints in glory stand and exclaim, "Who shall not fear Thee? for Thou art holy," how shall we come into thy presence, who are sinful dust and ashes? We confess that we are a people laden with iniquity, a seed of evil-doers; yea, and too often we have been the corrupters of others, and tempted them to sin. We have often forsaken Thee, and provoked Thee to anger by our sinful tempers, and foolish and wicked words; by our hatred, and malice, and bitterness; by our want of faith, and hope, and love. We are altogether vile in heart, and lips, and life; and if Thou hadst visited us with thy heavy judgments, as Thou didst the Jews of old, and hadst scattered us through the nations, and taken away our Church, and our Bible, and our ministers, and our Sabbaths, Thou wouldest have been justified in thy dealings with us; but we bless and praise thy name that Thou hast not so dealt with us. Thou hast still continued to us our undeserved blessings. Thou hast given to us many temporal mercies: food, and raiment, and health, and strength, so that we can do our daily work; and Thou hast given us our Bible to read at home, and the ordinances of the Sabbath; and Thou offerest to us pardon of our sins, and justification before Thee, and sanctification through thy dear Son, Christ Jesus, and by his Holy Spirit. O Lord most holy, we beseech Thee, for Jesus' sake, take all the members of this household, and wash them clean in the fountain Thou hast opened for sin and uncleanness; and grant that, though our sins are now as glaring as scarlet, they may be removed, and we may become white as snow: though they are deep and doubly dyed like crimson, we may become as the pure wool. Take all our sins, as Thou hast promised, and cast them into the depths of the sea, that they may be seen and remembered no more for ever. Grant that we may each come out of that fountain like Naaman out of the Jordan, with our flesh made as the flesh of a little child, without any spot, or blemish, or any such thing.

And, O Lord, as Thou knowest we shall never forsake sin or practise holiness, unless Thou give us thy Holy Spirit and a new heart, we beseech Thee to create a new heart in each of us, and send us thy Holy Spirit, that He may make us new creatures, and incline us this day to love thy Word and thy commandments, and to practise them.

Bless, gracious Father, each member of this family. Make us to love one another, and help each other this day on our heavenly way. Grant us these our prayers, for Christ's sake. Amen.

READ IN HOLY SCRIPTURE HEBREWS III.

O LORD Christ, blessed art Thou, O Thou King of glory. We rejoice in thy mercy, O Lord, and especially in the glorious fact that Thou, our risen Saviour, art Head of thine elect Church, which Thou hast knit together in one holy communion and fellowship.

Enable us to hold fast the confidence and rejoicing of our hope in Thee unto the end. Remember us in our low estate, now that Thou art in thy kingdom. Save us from hardness of heart, and contempt of thy Word, and every form of unbelief.

From the deceitfulness of sin and every root of bitterness, good Lord, deliver us. Help us, O God, and daily strengthen our hearts to be steadfast unto the end, that when Christ, who is our life, shall appear, we also may appear with Him in glory. Oh, come down, Thou Spirit of God, and make clean our hearts within us. Establish and increase in us whatsoever of faith and love Thou hast wrought in us. Heal our distempers, help our infirmities, succour our weaknesses, and in thy great goodness supply all our wants.

Blessed be thy name, O God, for the promise of eternal rest and peace. Through the grace and merits of thy dear Son, we pray Thee that we may not come short of it through unbelief and sin. Make us watchful against all that would hinder us in the heavenly race, and as Thou knowest how many temptations beset us, we pray that Thou wouldest defend and keep us in the midst of all dangers. Keep our hearts tender, and so make known to us the preciousness of thy love in Christ, and the faithfulness of thy promises, that we may follow the Lord fully, and not turn back from Thee to our ways.

Spread around us to-night the shield of thy care. Give rest and peace to us and to all whom we would remember at thy throne of grace. Compassionate the sick, the sorrowful, and the dying. Extend the borders of thy Church in every land, and hasten the time when Christ's name shall be a theme of praise on every tongue, and every knee shall bow at his footstool. Let thy Spirit guide the counsels of our rulers and all in authority. Make them good men and godly, that they may fear Thee, love thy Sabbaths, and honour thy name.

And now, O God, we beseech Thee mercifully to incline thine ears to us that have made our prayers and supplications to Thee. Grant that those things which we have faithfully asked according to thy will may effectually be obtained, to the relief of our necessity, and to the setting forth of thy glory, through Jesus Christ our Lord. Amen.

[Morning.] FORTY-SIXTH WEEK.—WEDNESDAY. [Evening.

READ IN HOLY SCRIPTURE ISAIAH II.

O MERCIFUL and ever-living God, praised be thy name for renewed mercies. With unfeigned humility we cast ourselves at thy footstool. We are utterly unworthy to look up to Thee, for sin is in our hearts, and pollutes all our services. Yet, gracious Father, turn not thy face away from us, nor withhold thy blessing. For the sake of Jesus, thy dear Son, and in fulfilment of thy promises, answer us and help us. Many and constant are our wants, and Thou alone art all-sufficient. Convince us of our need, and give us the faith which will venture all on Thee, and not doubt of thy grace and blessing.

We look for thy presence to be with us, and for thy mercy to be around us all the day. Leave us not, O God, nor forsake us, for by Thee alone can we be kept safely amidst the dangers of an evil world and the temptations of life. Oh, reveal unto us the exceeding greatness of thy love, and the tenderness of thy compassions, that we may love Thee, and trust in Thee, and come in all our necessities to Thee for help and for blessing. Especially do Thou, O Holy Ghost, come and abide with us, and show us of the things of Christ, that our hearts may go forth to Him in simple faith, and that we may be daily cleansed in his blood, and evermore live for Him. Lord God, we pray that this day we may be enabled to do such things as please Thee. Give us a tender conscience, that will shrink from sin, and that watchfulness of spirit which will guard against temptation, and make us shun even the appearance of evil. Oh, enable us to live as in the light of thy countenance, and in all the duties of our daily life to experience the blessedness of thy presence. We desire, O our Father, to be in all things thine, and that thy shield may be ever around us, and thy love be ever abiding upon us.

And not only for ourselves, but for others do we implore thy blessing; for all who are dear to us, that they may be dear to Thee in Christ Jesus; for all thy believing people, that they may be richly endued with the gifts of thy Spirit, and magnify thy name in the world; for all who are living in darkness and death, that they may be quickened from their death in trespasses and sins, and live unto Thee; for all in station and authority, that they may use their talents wisely and well, for the glory and the welfare of Christ's kingdom. Lord, pour out thy grace on the hearts of Jews and Gentiles, that they may every day be inquiring the way to Zion. Exalt and magnify the name of thy dear Son in the world, and fulfil speedily thy promise that idolatry and sin shall be cast out, and wars cease, and the Lord alone be glorified. We ask all through Jesus Christ our Lord. Amen.

READ IN HOLY SCRIPTURE HEBREWS IV.

GRACIOUS God, we approach thy heavenly footstool in the name of our great High Priest, who is passed into the heavens, and who is there, we trust, making intercession for us. What thanks do we owe to Thee, for thy unspeakable love in sending thy Son to die for our sins, and to rise again for our justification! We thank Thee that He ever liveth to sympathise with us in all our sufferings and temptations, for He is now touched with the feeling of our infirmities, as He was in the days of his humiliation. Forgive, O heavenly Father, our forgetfulness of this blessed truth, that Jesus our Saviour, though far removed out of our sight, is our compassionate High Priest, Himself afflicted in all our afflictions, and ever ready to succour and defend us. May we for the future cherish the remembrance of this fact, and seeing more and more our own weakness, and daily need of forgiveness, may we come boldly unto the throne of grace, that we may obtain mercy, and find grace to help in every time of need.

Lord, increase our faith, deliver us from the sin of unbelief, that we may not dishonour thy Son, grieve thy Holy Spirit, and finally exclude ourselves from that rest which remaineth to the people of God. We trust that Thou hast made us thy children by adoption and grace, that we have passed from death unto life; but may we bear in mind that if any man have not the Spirit of Christ, he is none of his. We are weak in ourselves; strengthen us to fight the good fight of faith, defend us with thy heavenly grace, that we may continue thine for ever, and daily increase in thy Holy Spirit more and more.

Bless those who minister among us in holy things; may their words, spoken in thy name from time to time, sink deep into our hearts and the hearts of all committed to their charge; may their own souls be refreshed and comforted by the dew of thy heavenly grace, and may they be shining lights in this dark world. Give great success to all efforts which are made to make known thy living truth among all nations. Bless all our relations and friends, hear our prayers on their behalf. Bring back to thy fold those who are wandering from Thee. Defend us through the silent hours of the night, refresh us with sweet sleep, pardon all our sins, and in thy great mercy grant that, as we grow in years, we may grow in grace, and be so sanctified by the Spirit, as to be prepared for a place in thy kingdom. We pray also for all who are near and dear to us. Let thy blessing rest upon them now and ever. Hear us for the sake of Jesus Christ, thy Son, our Lord. Amen.

[MORNING.] **FORTY-SIXTH WEEK.—THURSDAY.** [EVENING.

READ IN HOLY SCRIPTURE ISAIAH VII. 1—16.

ALMIGHTY and most merciful Father, through whose watchful care we have laid us down and slept, make us thankful for these thy daily mercies, and keep us humble. May thy goodness lead us to repentance, and make us ashamed of our unbelief, and unthankfulness, and sin. Lord God, we acknowledge we are not our own, and we now dedicate ourselves afresh to thy service. Sprinkle us with the blood of Jesus, sanctify us by the Holy Ghost, and make our hearts the temples of God, that we may live to Thee, and glorify Thee in our bodies and our spirits, which are thine. Preserve us this day, we beseech Thee, from the evil which is in the world. Suffer us not to yield to temptation, or to be guilty of sin. In the station to which Thou hast called us we pray for grace to honour Thee, and to be as the living epistles of Christ, known and read of all men.

O God, how can we sufficiently praise Thee for thy great love in sending thy dear Son to redeem and to save us? Draw, we pray Thee, our hearts to Jesus. Reveal unto us more clearly his Divine glory, the freeness and sufficiency of his sacrifice as the atonement for sin. Increase our faith in Him, that we may love Him more and serve Him better.

We commend all who are dear to us to thy fatherly care and love. Cause all who are unconverted to feel their need of Jesus, and to seek in Him for the blessings of salvation. O Thou Lord of the harvest, send forth labourers into the harvest. Remember for good all faithful missionaries and ministers. Bless them in their own souls, and make them a blessing to others. Increase abundantly the number of thy believing people, and deliver us as a Church from the lukewarmness which dishonours Thee and grieves thy Spirit. Make the formal sincere, the proud humble, the careless anxious, the indolent diligent, and the unholy holy, that every member of thy Church may truly and godly serve Thee.

Look, O God, in mercy on our land. Forgive our national sins, and turn aside the judgments we deserve. Root up the covetousness and love of this world which choke the good seed and make it unfruitful. Check the progress of infidelity, and let it be seen that thy Word is indeed the truth, and the power of God unto the salvation of all who believe. Gracious God, in thy tenderness and compassion, hear us in these our prayers and thanksgivings. Guilty and sinful as we are, yet we hope that Thou wilt hear and bless us, and enrich us with the fulness of thy heavenly grace; for we offer all our worship in the glorious and saving name of thy dear Son, Jesus Christ, our Lord. Amen.

READ IN HOLY SCRIPTURE HEBREWS V.

ALMIGHTY and most merciful God, who desirest not the death of a sinner, but that all should turn unto Thee and live, we desire to approach Thee with a deep sense of our unworthiness, confessing that we have sinned against Thee. We have done things which we ought not to have done, and have left undone those things which we ought to have done. O Lord God, our heavenly Father, do Thou have mercy upon us, and forgive us all these our sins and offences. Humbled under a sense of our guiltiness, we bless thy holy name for all thy goodness towards us. Thou hast mercifully cared for our temporal wants, and hast protected and preserved us amid the dangers and temptations of the past day. For this great mercy we thank Thee. But we especially praise Thee for the precious gift of thy dear Son, that Thou hast sent Him into the world to partake of our nature, sharing all its sorrows, and weaknesses, and trials. We thank Thee that He lived and died for us, and for our salvation; and we adore Thee for the assurance that He ever liveth as our all-prevailing Intercessor, to plead at the throne of grace on behalf of all who desire to approach Thee through Him, as the Way, the Truth, and the Life. Look with compassion upon us, and strengthen us by thy grace, that we may rightly value the great blessings which Thou hast provided for us in the Gospel of thy dear Son. Lead us into the way of life, that we may no longer wander as sheep going astray, but follow the example of our Divine Guide, and henceforth walk in the way of righteousness, and learn obedience to Thee, the Lord our God. To this end, we beseech Thee, sanctify to us all the passing events of life, that they may draw us nearer to thy blessed self; and grant that we may, through the sacred influence of the eternal Spirit, experience the comfort of thy Word. May the Gospel be the guide of our lives; may it animate us in the hour of affliction, and its sacred truths be our consolation in times of peril. Enable us to grow in grace, and increase in all godliness, until our souls are filled with a sense of the Divine goodness, leading us with grateful hearts to present unto Thee the sacrifice of unceasing praise.

Take us, O our God, into thy Divine care this night. Feeble and helpless in ourselves, we cast ourselves entirely on thy mercy and strength. Accept, we beseech Thee, through our High Priest, Jesus Christ, thy Son, our thanksgivings for ourselves, and regard with compassion our supplications for others. Pardon all our sins, strengthen our good desires, increase our faith, and keep us unto salvation, to thy glory, through Jesus Christ our Lord. Amen.

[Morning.] **FORTY-SIXTH WEEK.—FRIDAY.** [Evening.

READ IN HOLY SCRIPTURE ISAIAH XI., XII.

O LORD our God, bless and sanctify us through this portion of thy Word. Thy Word is truth. Let the same good Spirit which rested on Christ, the Root and Offspring of David, the Rod out of the stem of Jesse, rest upon us; plant in us a holy, filial, and reverential fear, and enable us to worship Thee in spirit and in truth.

Bless thy Church, revive thy work amongst us, that Christ may be exalted, sinners converted, and the earth filled with the knowledge of the Lord, as the waters cover the sea. Curb and subdue the unruly passions of sinful men; hasten the time when righteousness and truth, peace and harmony, shall reign throughout the wide world; when the wolf shall dwell with the lamb, and the leopard shall lie down with the kid.

O Lord, we thank Thee that Thou hast caused the light of revealed truth to penetrate the darkness of the Gentile world. We thank Thee also, O Lord, for the hope Thou hast given of the restoration and conversion of thy ancient people, the Jews. May the natural branches soon be grafted in, and both Jew and Gentile be made one in Christ Jesus.

We desire to thank Thee, O Lord, for all thy mercies to us as a family, for thy tender care and protection during the helplessness of sleep, for sweet rest and calm repose, and for all thy numerous and great mercies, temporal and spiritual. Enable us this day to show our gratitude by word and deed, and to manifest the strength of our convictions and the depth of our love, by the extent of our exertions and the consistency of our lives.

Safely keep us this day, both outwardly as to our bodies, and inwardly as to our souls. Suffer us not to run into any kind of danger, sin, or temptation. Go with us where we go, and dwell with us where we dwell. Enable us to put our whole trust and confidence in Christ. Make us strong in his strength, wise in his wisdom, holy in his holiness, and righteous in his righteousness. Be Thou, O God, our rock of defence, our shield and buckler, that we may be able to quench all the fiery darts of the wicked one, and be more than conquerors through Christ, who loved us and died for us.

Grant us the help of thy Holy Spirit, O our Father, to renew, to enlighten, to guide, to cheer, to seal, and to comfort us. Wash us in that fountain opened for sin and uncleanness. [Bless our dear children, and make them holy, good, and happy.] We commend to thy favour those who are dear to us. All their wants are known to Thee. Mercifully supply them out of thy fulness, for Jesus Christ's sake. Amen.

READ IN HOLY SCRIPTURE HEBREWS VI.

HEAVENLY Father, give unto us thy servants grace to enter now into thy presence, pleading the merits and trusting in the intercession of Christ. Oh, let our prayer be set forth in thy sight as the incense, and let the lifting up of our hands be an evening sacrifice.

Lord, we thank Thee that Thou hast called us to the knowledge of thy grace, and faith in Thee. We praise Thee for the principles of the doctrine of Christ which Thou hast revealed. Enable us to cleave unto thy Word, rooted and grounded in the faith. We pray, moreover, that through the teaching of thy Spirit we may advance in all wisdom and spiritual understanding. Give us spiritual experience, by which we may comprehend, with all saints, what is the breadth, and length, and depth, and height of the Redeemer's love. Oh, save us from blindness and from all backsliding in the inner life. Grant that thy warnings against apostacy may be thine own means of keeping us steadfast in the truth. Leave us not, O our God, to the wickedness and waywardness of our own hearts. Maintain within us the full assurance of hope unto the end. So strengthen in us the assurance of hope, that we may believe all thine exceeding great and precious promises. Give us an appropriating faith. Oh, that we may walk with Thee, blessed with the inward sealing of thy Spirit. As Thou hast begotten us to a lively hope of entering into thy joy, quicken, we pray Thee, that hope until we experience a blessed foretaste of heaven. Grant that it may be as an anchor of the soul, entering into that within the veil. May Jesus be its supreme object. Enable us, O Lord, to live on the fulness which is in Him, in sanctifying belief of the truth that He ever liveth to make intercession for us.

We bless Thee, O our adorable Forerunner, that Thou hast already taken possession in our name, and for us, of our glorious inheritance. Thou hast ascended up on high, to prepare a place for thy people in the mansions of thy Father's house. Oh, prepare us by thy Holy Spirit for the place.

Our Father, daily increase in us, of thy goodness, the plenteous gifts of thy Spirit. Enable us to be pure, even as Christ was pure. Lead us to pant after increasing holiness. Cause us to be partakers in thine own way of thine own holiness. Take us this night under thy protection, O Thou keeper of Israel. Give us refreshing rest and sleep. May our last thoughts to-night and the waking thoughts of the morning be of Thee. Hear us, O Lord, according to the multitude of thy tender mercies, for his sake who loved us and gave Himself for us, thy Son, Jesus Christ, our Saviour and Mediator. Amen.

[Morning.] FORTY-SIXTH WEEK.—SATURDAY. [Evening.

READ IN HOLY SCRIPTURE ISAIAH XXV.

ALMIGHTY God, our heavenly Father, we thank Thee for all thy mercies, and seek the continuance of thy favour and blessing. We praise Thee for all thy loving-kindness to us in the time past of our lives. Day by day thy goodness and mercy have followed us. The comforts of our earthly condition, and the privileges of our spiritual life, have come to us from Thee, the Author and Giver of every good and perfect gift. Thou hast guided our steps and strengthened our hearts, and drawn us to Thyself by the invitations of thy Word, and the influence of thy Spirit, and the dispensations of thy providence towards us; and we desire with unfeigned hearts to thank Thee for all these instances of thy care and love. Especially do we praise and magnify thy holy name for the gift of thy dear Son, in whom all thy other gifts are made to be sources of blessing to our souls.

We beseech Thee to pardon all our past sins, negligences, and ignorances; to deliver us from the fears of a guilty conscience, by the assurance of thy forgiving grace in Christ Jesus. Do Thou increase our knowledge and our love of Thee, and enable us to live and walk as thy pardoned and reconciled children here on earth, and so to be prepared in heart and mind for thy perfect service in the world to come. May we be so blessed of Thee ourselves as to prove a daily blessing unto others.

We thank Thee, O Lord, for all that we have heard of thy wonderful works to thy people in our fathers' days and in the old time before them. Make known amongst all nations thy faithfulness and truth. Oh, that the power of evil may be broken, and the dominion of Satan put down in every land, that there may be found the fruits of righteousness and truth, of peace and charity, to the honour of thy great name, and to the comfort and salvation of immortal souls.

For the sake of all, we pray Thee to help thy ministering servants this day in preparing for their work to-morrow. May all who shall go forth to teach and preach thy truth be enlightened and strengthened of Thee, so that their work may prosper, and be found hereafter to praise, and honour, and glory, at the appearing of Jesus Christ. And now, O Lord, we earnestly commend ourselves, and all whom we love, to thy Divine protection and guidance throughout this day. We would go forth to our appointed work in the experience of thy favourable presence with us. Enable us to be diligent in business, fervent in spirit, serving the Lord; and when all our earthly work is done, may we be found ready for an eternal Sabbath, through Christ our Lord. Amen.

READ IN HOLY SCRIPTURE HEBREWS VII.

O GOD, our heavenly Father, who art the Father of mercies and the God of all consolation, we, thy unworthy servants, desire to approach thy throne of grace, deeply sensible of our great sinfulness, and expecting only to be heard for the sake of Him whom Thou hast exalted to thy right hand as a Prince and a Saviour, to give repentance and remission of sins, and who is able to save to the uttermost all that come unto Thee through Him.

We have sinned grievously in thought, word, and deed; we have done much which we ought not to have done, and have neglected much which we ought to have done; but Thou art a God who pardoneth iniquity, and Thou hast sent thy Son to fulfil the law, and to die as a sacrifice upon the cross for our redemption; thus to prove that Thou art a God who delightest in mercy. For his sake we entreat of Thee to grant us a full and free forgiveness, and to enable us to rejoice in a knowledge of our acceptance through his finished work. And do Thou send down upon us thine Holy Spirit, to teach us more about the things of Christ, and to lead us into all truth. May He strengthen us with might in the inner man, and shed abroad the love of Christ in our hearts, so as to kindle in us a holy flame of love towards Him, which will constrain us to live, not to ourselves, but to Him who shed his precious blood for our redemption. And do Thou enlighten our understandings, that we may understand the Scriptures. May they dwell in us richly in all wisdom. May we ever be instructed by thy precepts, and encouraged by thy promises, so as to run with patience the race that is set before us, and at length to obtain an immortal crown.

And now, O God, we ask that Thou wilt prepare us for the sacred engagements of the coming Sabbath. May we enjoy a double measure of thy presence with us on thine own day. May we find it profitable and delightful to wait upon Thee in the ordinances of thy temple. Enable us to worship Thee, who art a Spirit, in spirit and in truth. Give grace to all thy servants, that they may open their mouths boldly to preach the unsearchable riches of Christ. May many sinners be led to acknowledge Jesus as their Saviour; may thine own people be edified and comforted by the ministrations of thine house of prayer; and may our thanksgivings for all the mercies of providence and of grace ascend as a holy sacrifice to thy throne, which shall be accepted, as we trust these our humble petitions are, through Jesus, our great High Priest, who ever liveth to make intercession for us. Amen.

[MORNING.] **FORTY-SEVENTH WEEK.—LORD'S DAY.** [EVENING.]

READ IN HOLY SCRIPTURE ISAIAH XXVI.

O LORD our God, in kneeling before Thee this morning, to seek Thee early, and to ask thy blessing upon another Sabbath-day, we thank Thee for thy watchful providence during the past night, and for thy merciful protection throughout the same. Grant that we may all be in the Spirit on this thy holy day, and feel the Sabbath to be a delight and honourable. Grant that we may derive profit and benefit from all the public services of the sanctuary. Enable us also to worship Thee in private, in sincerity and in truth, devoutly to read and meditate upon thy holy Word, and so to apply its precepts to ourselves as to correct whatever may be amiss in our hearts and lives.

Pour out thy Spirit, O Lord, upon all the churches of thy saints; that, as in the days of old, walking in the fear of the Lord and in the comfort of the Holy Ghost, they may be multiplied and established in the faith. We beseech Thee also, O Lord, to send thy Holy Spirit down upon all Christian ministers, especially those in this place and neighbourhood, that they may be stirred up to watch for souls, and to diligently and faithfully preach thy holy Word; and do Thou give an abundant blessing upon their labours in every place.

We beseech Thee also to bless all Sunday-school teachers and Scripture-readers, and all others who in any place may be striving to make known the way of salvation unto others.

We also beseech Thee to bless us in our going out and coming in, from this day forth and for evermore, and to enable us to set Thee always before us. We beseech Thee also to vouchsafe thy blessing upon all our lawful plans and undertakings during the remainder of the present week and always, and to grant that whatever we do, we may do all to the glory of God. Enable us to trust in the Lord Jehovah for ever, in whom is everlasting strength; and grant that we may each and all experience that they shall be kept in perfect peace whose minds are stayed on Thee. And do Thou, O Lord, so work in us, that we may serve Thee truly, and, renouncing all worldly idols, may serve Thee alone, and make mention of thy name.

We thank Thee for all the many and great religious privileges and advantages which Thou hast vouchsafed unto us in our highly favoured land, beseeching Thee to grant that we may never grow careless or lukewarm, or provoke Thee to withdraw these blessings from us. Grant that we, and all about us, may duly profit by them. Accept and answer us. We ask all through Jesus Christ our Lord. Amen.

READ IN HOLY SCRIPTURE HEBREWS VIII.

O GOD of our salvation, let our prayer come up before Thee, and do Thou incline thine ear, and hear and answer us. Look on the face of thy beloved Son, whom Thou hast exalted to thy right hand in glory, who hath entered into the holy place for us, our great High Priest and everliving Mediator, and for his sake do us good, and bestow upon us thy blessing.

All our ways and works have been this day before Thee. Whether we have honoured thy holy day, or done our own will, thine eye hath been upon us. Thou wast with us in the sanctuary, and didst read the secret thoughts of our hearts as we knelt at thy footstool, or lifted up our voice in praise: Thou hast been with us at home, and wherever else we have gone this day. Oh, could we but see ourselves as Thou seest us, and know all the sinfulness that has defiled us and our services this day, we should be ashamed to appear in thy presence, O Thou holy and heart-searching God. Have mercy upon us, we beseech Thee; subdue our hearts by the knowledge and remembrance of our multiplied sins, and by the experience of thy grace and love. We deserve not thy favour, yet, O God, be gracious unto us; pardon, accept, and bless us. We long to be holier and better; to have our hearts filled with a sense of thy love; and to be growing in grace and in godliness. We mourn, heavenly Father, that we are so tied and bound with the chains of sin, and the power of the world, and the love of self. Deliver us, for thy mercy's sake, and suffer us not to fall under the dominion of evil. Take away all our hardness of heart, and guide us in the paths of peace.

Hear us, we beseech Thee, while we plead for the outpouring of thy grace on all men. Have pity upon those for whom Christ died, but who are yet in the gall of bitterness and the bond of iniquity. Snatch from the burning the souls that are ready to perish; and grant that even now thy Word this day declared may be rankling as a sharp arrow of the Spirit in many a heart, making it to feel its misery and its sin, and to long for the balm which only gives health. Let the sorrowful be comforted and the weak be strengthened by the ordinances of this thy day. Uphold the hands of thy ministers, and attend with thy blessing the labours of all who have been engaged in feeding Christ's lambs.

All praise be to thy name, O our God, for all thy goodness. In the remembrance of it, we look up with hope and confidence to thy protection and blessing this night, praying that Thou wouldest keep us safely in the hours of darkness, and fit us, both in body and soul, for the duties of the coming week. Hear us for Christ's sake. Amen.

[Morning.] FORTY-SEVENTH WEEK.—MONDAY. [Evening.]

READ IN HOLY SCRIPTURE ISAIAH XXXII.

UNTO Thee, O Lord God, we look at the beginning of this day, and at thy Divine hand we implore all favour and blessing. All thy works praise Thee, and we ourselves are the monuments of thy grace and forbearance. Behold us, O our Father, and fulfil to us thy promises. Thou art faithful and true, keeping mercy for them that fear Thee. For the sake of Jesus Christ, do Thou hear, and help, and bless us. Thy providence has watched over us in the night. For rest and sleep we are indebted to thy mercy, and also for the renewed opportunity of spreading our wants this morning at thy footstool. We adore thy glorious name for all this goodness. Oh, that our thankfulness were proportioned to thy mercy, and that our hearts were more deeply sensible of thine exceeding great love and tender compassions. We confess with shame, O God, the coldness of our hearts. Cleanse us in the fountain once opened, and grant us thy peace.

In the prospect of the day's duties and temptations we cast our care upon Thee, and implore thy protection, and presence, and blessing. Grant that thy truth preached to us yesterday may have an abiding influence on our hearts and our lives. Let it not be choked, O God, by the cares and pleasures of life, and so be unfruitful. Suffer us not to forget eternity, amid the occupations and pursuits of time. Wean us from the love of earthly things, and remind us continually that this world is not our rest. We pray that thy blessings may not turn our hearts from Thee, or make us forgetful of thy will concerning us. Oh, teach us to trace back every good gift to Thee, and to see thy hand in all the circumstances of life, whether of prosperity or of trial. Above all, we desire to have our hearts enlarged with the love of Christ, and to feel evermore that Thou art leading us by thy Spirit into the deeper experiences of thy truth and faithfulness. Make us thine. Set the seal of thy love upon us, and guard, and guide, and defend us as thy children, until we reach the land of rest and peace. Have compassion on our ignorance. Bear with our want of faith. Pity our weakness, and do for us abundantly above all we can ask or think, for thy name's sake, in Jesus Christ our Lord.

Mercifully, O Lord, enrich with thy choicest blessings all whom we love. Convert the unconverted, awaken the careless and the backsliding, and give us all increasing knowledge of Christ, in the glory of his power and the greatness of his salvation. [Turn the hearts of the children before Thee to Christ, and cause them, even from their early years, to submit to the guidance and teaching of thy Spirit.] We ask it all through Jesus Christ our Lord. Amen.

READ IN HOLY SCRIPTURE HEBREWS IX.

O LORD God, who art of purer eyes than to behold evil, and canst not look on iniquity, how shall we venture to approach thy footstool, to lift up our eyes to Thee, and to make application for thy forgiveness? Verily, in many things we offend all; and if Thou wert to deal with us according to our deserts, we should be outcasts for ever from thy presence, and from the enjoyment of the glory of thy power. How unmindful have we been of Thee this day: how little have we watched over our thoughts, and words, and ways: how much have we done that we ought not to have done, and how much of our known duty have we neglected or done amiss! O gracious God, well might we despair, when we look back upon the course of one single day, and remember what Thou art, and what we are!

But, blessed be thy holy name, Thou hast, in thine infinite loving-kindness, provided a way of access for sinners to Thyself. Thou hast given thine own dear Son to be the great High Priest and Mediator of the new covenant; that by the one offering of Himself, once offered, He might make propitiation for our sins, and open the kingdom of heaven to all believers. O Lord, we plead the merits of that precious blood, which taketh away the sin of the world. We trust in the sufficiency of that perfect righteousness, even the righteousness of the Lord Jesus Christ, which is unto all and upon all them that believe. May we go to rest this night with a sweet sense of sin forgiven for his sake, and in the full confidence of faith, that, if we wake no more in this world, we shall wake with Him, and be with Him for ever, where He is. Oh, that we, and all who are near and dear to us after the flesh, may be looking for and hasting unto that glorious day, when He shall appear the second time, without sin, unto salvation; and may we so love and follow Him now, that we may rejoice and reign with Him in glory. Save us all, O Lord, we beseech Thee, from the sin of presuming on thy goodness; and grant that the Holy Spirit may shed abroad thy love in our hearts, so as constantly to constrain us not to live unto ourselves, but unto Him who died for us and rose again. Refresh, we pray Thee, our wearied bodies with comfortable rest, and strengthen us for the duties of to-morrow; and vouchsafe to others also, and especially to those who desire our prayers, the same blessings, both for soul and body, which we ask for ourselves. Cause the light of thy Gospel still to spread; and may those who know the name of Jesus rejoice evermore in its heavenly comfort. All which we ask for his sake who liveth and reigneth with Thee and the Holy Ghost, one God, world without end. Amen.

[Morning.] **FORTY-SEVENTH WEEK—TUESDAY.** [Evening.]

READ IN HOLY SCRIPTURE ISAIAH XXXV.

O LORD GOD, who art from everlasting to everlasting, and by whom, and for whom, and through whom are all things; pour upon us thy Holy Spirit at this time, that we may realise thy glorious perfections, and humble ourselves at thy footstool under a sense of our great unworthiness and manifold necessities. Help us, O God, to approach Thee, trusting alone to the merits and mediation of thy dear Son, our Saviour Jesus Christ; and for his sake freely pardon the multitude of our transgressions, and extend to us thy loving favour.

We offer our praise and thanksgiving for thy merciful goodness in still sparing us. And now, whilst prostrate in thy presence, our Creator and Preserver, we commit ourselves, and all those who are dear to us, to thy heavenly care and keeping for the day on which we have entered. We know not what is before us, but to Thee are all things known. And we earnestly pray Thee so to guide our steps and to uphold our goings, that we may walk in the way of thy commandments, and turn not aside into the paths of sin and folly. Without Thee we can do nothing that is good. We therefore beseech Thee to support us under every trial, to furnish us for every duty, to strengthen us in the faith of Jesus Christ, that we may successfully resist all the assaults of the devil, and show ourselves fruitful in every good word and work.

Grant us grace ever to make thy blessed Word our companion and our counsellor. May its promises of help in every time of need comfort our hearts. May we live by faith and not by sense. Enable us to rely so confidently on thy faithfulness, that we may be cheered with the bright hope of better times, when the curse denounced on the very ground because of man's disobedience shall be taken away; when the wilderness shall be fruitful with the blessing of the Spirit, and the desert rejoice and blossom as the rose. O God, we praise Thee for the promises of present salvation. We praise Thee for the prospects of coming glory. We praise Thee for the redemption of sinful men, which Jesus Christ, thine incarnate Son, has died to accomplish. And we pray that we ourselves may have a place among those blessed persons who are waiting with patience, and rejoicing in hope, for the glorious day of his appearing, when all the ransomed of the Lord shall obtain joy and gladness, and when sorrow and sighing shall for ever flee away.

These and all other necessary blessings we ask and expect for the sake of Jesus, whom Thou hearest always, and to whom, with the Father and the Holy Ghost, we ascribe the kingdom, the power, and the glory, for ever and ever. Amen.

READ IN HOLY SCRIPTURE HEBREWS X. 1–18.

O GOD of glory and of grace, we humbly draw near to Thee; be ready, we beseech Thee, to receive our prayers through the mediation and sacrifice of Jesus Christ, thy Son, our Lord. We thank Thee that we are not under the law, but under grace. Our transgressions are many in number; every day increases the long catalogue, and leaves us without excuse; for we cannot plead ignorance, nor say that thy service is hard. It is to the hardness of our hearts we trace the cause of our many and oft-repeated sins: for these thy law justly condemns us; but Thou hast laid our judgment upon thine own beloved Son, and we are spared for his sake. We lay hold of the covenant, which promises that our sin and iniquities Thou wilt remember no more; in this we rest for pardon and for holiness. Oh, may we never abuse thy great mercy, nor allow ourselves in sin that grace may abound. O Lord, sanctify us wholly; make us perfect and complete in Christ Jesus. Forgive us all our sins, and more particularly those of the day past. Grant us thy Holy Spirit and true repentance; and since Thou hast made so great a sacrifice for our sins, may we offer and present unto Thee ourselves, our souls and bodies, to be a living sacrifice unto Thee daily.

Praised be thy name, O Lord, for the knowledge of thy truth, and that we can read and hear it, none making us afraid. May all who profess and call themselves Christians hold the faith in unity of spirit, in the bond of peace, and in righteousness of life. May all ministers of religion be examples to those they teach; may they who administer justice be themselves just, and know how to temper justice with mercy. May this whole nation be exalted in righteousness, fear thy name, and love to obey thy commandments. O Thou God of peace, we pray that wars may cease unto the ends of the earth. May brother not lift up sword against brother, nor nation against nation; but peace be within all our borders. Where persecution rages may thy dominion be extended, O Prince of Peace. Let the idols be utterly abolished, and all the horrid rites of idolatrous worship come to an end. Bless every member of this household; may love and concord ever here prevail. May the younger submit themselves unto the elder, and all be happy in the service of Christ. If any be visited with affliction, may we know how to bear it, and how to improve the day of adversity. Be present, merciful Father, with all the sick and suffering; make Thou all their bed in their sickness; and let the weak and weary find this night a resting-place for their sorrows on the bosom of thy love. We ask all through Jesus Christ our Lord. Amen.

[325]

[MORNING.] FORTY-SEVENTH WEEK.—WEDNESDAY. [EVENING.

READ IN HOLY SCRIPTURE ISAIAH XL.

BLESSED be Thou, O God, the Father of mercies, and of all comfort. We are unworthy of one gracious look from Thee. Deal not with us, Lord, after our sins; neither reward us according to our iniquities. Pity us, we pray Thee. Speak comfortably to our souls. Declare to us thy salvation, and let our souls be satisfied with thy mercy, O Lord, so shall our mouths be filled with thy praise and with thine honour all the day long. Reveal thy glory, O God. Oh, let all flesh see thy mercy and thy power. Take out of the way every stumbling-block. Make a glorious path for thy Truth in the world, and cause all thy ministering servants so to proclaim the Gospel of thy grace, that multitudes may see the good of thy chosen, and glory with thine inheritance. O Thou good Shepherd, feed thy flock, and defend it from all attacks of the wicked one. Gently deal with the weak and the weary. Raise up the fallen, and carry the lambs in thy bosom. For Thou, O Jesus Christ, art almighty in power and omniscient in wisdom. All the multitudes of the nations are but as a drop of the bucket. Thou only art the Lord. Thou only, O Christ, with the Holy Ghost, art most high in the glory of God the Father. Thou alone art strong to save and mighty to deliver. Oh, do Thou increase our strength, and when we faint and are weary give us power. Hast Thou not promised, O God, that they that wait upon Thee shall be strengthened? Fulfil in us this day thy gracious word, and uphold our goings in thy paths, that our footsteps slip not. We long and pray that the work of thy grace may be fulfilled and perfected in us, that our faith may be increased, that the lukewarmness of our hearts may be changed into the earnestness of a sincere love for Thee, and that the power of Christ may transform us more and more into his own blessed image. Oh, prepare us for the coming of the Lord in his glory and majesty, and grant that, through thy grace and mercy now vouchsafed to us, when He cometh we may be found of Him in peace, without spot and blameless, cleansed from all sin, and sanctified in body, soul, and spirit.

Watch over us all this day, and bless the work of our hands. Let thy favour rest on our land, and thy wisdom be the guide of all in authority. Cause to abound among us the righteousness which exalteth a nation, and let thy fear rule in the homes and hearts of the people. Gracious God, in thy tenderness and mercy hear Thou our prayers, and accept our thanksgivings for all thy goodness and love. We offer all in the name of thy beloved Son, to whom be everlasting praise and glory. Amen.

READ IN HOLY SCRIPTURE HEBREWS X. 19—39.

O LORD, who dwellest in light, to which no man can approach; whom no man hath seen nor can see; though we are altogether unworthy and full of sin, yet we would come boldly to thy throne, because Thou hast invited us, and because Thou waitest to be gracious, and hast assured us that our dear Redeemer, thine own Son, ever lives to make intercession with Thee on our behalf. Hear us, gracious God, the Father of our Lord Jesus Christ, and, for the Lord Jesus Christ's sake, give each of us before Thee, and every one in this house, thy blessing this evening.

We have not boldly confessed Thee this day before men, as we should have done. We have not provoked one another to love and to good works, as we might have done. We have not endured hardness as good soldiers of Jesus Christ, as it was our duty to do. We have not had that strength of faith by which we might have been willing to suffer the loss of all things rather than deny Thee; and we have not been patient under affliction and provocation, as became Christ's people. But, O heavenly Father, for thy dear Son's sake, forgive us all our offences against Thee. Thou hast assured us there is plenteous redemption, and we beseech Thee to grant that we may be among thy redeemed ones, who are cleansed from all sin, and redeemed from all iniquity. Grant that we may each have thy Holy Spirit working in us a hatred of sin and a love of holiness, and that we may henceforth strive to please Thee in all things.

We desire to praise Thee, O heavenly Father, for thy many mercies vouchsafed to us this day. Thou hast watched over us in our going out and in our coming in, and hast been round about us, to protect us from all evil. Oh, grant that our hearts may be filled with love toward Thee for thy daily mercies to us, and that our faith in Thee may so increase that we may carry every care to Thee, and cast it down before Thee, assured that Thou carest for us, and wilt count no concern of ours too small for thy regard. To thy gracious care and keeping we would now commend every one of this family, and pray Thee to give to us that sleep which Thou hast promised to thy beloved, that we may rise refreshed in body and mind, and fitted for the duties of the morrow. Bless our relations, and acquaintances, and friends; bless our neighbourhood, and grant that the people may be a God-fearing, and a Sabbath-loving, and a church-going people. Bless all the ministers of thy Word in all lands: those who labour at home and those who toil among Jews and Gentiles; and grant that soon the Gospel may spread over the whole earth, for Jesus' sake, our only Lord and Saviour. Amen.

[323]

[Morning.] FORTY-SEVENTH WEEK.—THURSDAY. [Evening.

READ IN HOLY SCRIPTURE ISAIAH XLI.

O HEAVENLY Father, we seek thy face, and draw near unto Thee, through Jesus Christ, thy dear Son. Thou art the first and the last, without beginning and without end. Thou art a great and holy God, yet dost Thou graciously condescend to listen to the prayers of thy most unworthy, sinful children.

We thank Thee, O our God, for all the mercies of the past night, and that Thou hast brought us to the beginning of another day in health and strength, to fulfil the duties which lie before us.

Praise be to Thee that Thou hast cast our lot in a land where the true Gospel shines, and where we have heard of Jesus, and his great salvation, from our earliest childhood. We thank Thee that we are permitted to look unto Thee as a reconciled Father in Christ Jesus, and that in all our troubles, anxieties, and dangers, we may be greatly comforted and sustained by the assurance that Thou knowest all our circumstances, and dost still hold us up, as Thou didst thy people of old, by thy right hand, and dost speak unto us sweet words of comfort, saying, "Fear not, I will help Thee, saith Jehovah, and thy Redeemer, the Holy One of Israel." But, O gracious God, what unworthy returns do we make for all thy goodness towards us! How unmindful have we been of thy love, thy kindness, thy glory! Truly, we are unprofitable servants! Forgive, for Jesus Christ's sake, our past ingratitude, and our guilty neglect of Thee, who hast never been unmindful of us. Wash away all our sins in the blood of Jesus, and blot them out of the book of thy remembrance.

May we go forth to the duties of the day in the happy assurance that that blessedness is ours which belongs to those whose transgression is forgiven, and whose sin is covered. May we prove our gratitude to Thee for so great a blessing, by giving up ourselves more unreservedly to thy service, and by walking before Thee in holiness and righteousness this and all our days. [Let our children grow up before Thee, and early give themselves to thy service. Make them truly thine, and sanctify them in body, soul, and spirit.] Bless all efforts for the spread of thy Gospel, both among Jews and Gentiles, in our own and in far distant lands. Revive thy work in the Churches at home, and send forth labourers into the missionary fields abroad, and grant them a glorious harvest. Regard with favour our land; give grace and wisdom to all in authority, and make them instruments for the fulfilment of thy gracious purpose in the world. Be Thou with us, and all dear to us, this day, and keep us near to Thyself. We ask every mercy for the sake of Jesus, thy Son, our Redeemer. Amen.

READ IN HOLY SCRIPTURE HEBREWS XI. 1–22.

ALMIGHTY God, the Preserver of our life, the Giver of all grace, oh, reveal unto us the greatness of thy glory and the plenteousness of thy mercy. We bend the knee at thy footstool, and pray that our hearts may be touched by living fire from thine altar, and our prayer and praise be accepted through the merits and intercession of Jesus our Lord. Oh, give us faith to grasp firmly thy promises, and day by day to bring near to us the things that are unseen and eternal. Thou permittest us to enter in within the veil, whither Jesus has entered for us. Bless us, O God, with a clear perception of divine things, that we may seek earnestly for the full enjoyment of all which Thou hast provided for us, and live in the constant experience of thy saving grace and mercy.

Forgive us the many sins of which we have been guilty this day. If we say that we have no sin, we deceive ourselves, and the truth is not in us. Lord God, preserve us from this self-deceit; convince us of sin; make us to feel all its grievousness, and to know that by things done and things left undone we are constantly disobeying Thee and transgressing thy commandments. Graciously bestow the assurance of thy favour. Mercifully accept us, and let not our offences be remembered before Thee. Come, O Holy Ghost, and abide in us; take away the love of sin, and kindle in us a fervent desire to be more conformed to the likeness of Jesus.

We pray, O God, that Thou wouldest increase our faith in thy Word, and make us bold to do and patient to suffer thy will, in the assurance that heaven and earth shall pass away before thy Word can fail. By the example of thy servants in old time, stir up our hearts to diligence, that we be not slothful, but followers of them who through faith and patience inherit the promises. Oh that, like them, we may seek earnestly a better country, even a heavenly, and rest under thy protection, and with thy blessing press on in the narrow way, overcoming the world and its temptations, and glorifying thy name by our holy consistency.

We implore thy blessing for the night on ourselves and all those we love. Let grace, mercy, and peace be on us all, from God our Father and the Lord Jesus Christ. Shed on thy Church, O Lord, the abundance of all good gifts, and so water the seed of thy Word which has been sowed this day, that it may bring forth much fruit to thy praise. Accept our grateful and hearty thanksgivings for this day's mercies; and grant that we may read in them the tokens of thy love, and be encouraged to trust Thee and to love Thee even more and more. Holy Father, hear and help us, for thy dear Son's sake. Amen.

[Morning.] **FORTY-SEVENTH WEEK.—FRIDAY.** [Evening.

READ IN HOLY SCRIPTURE ISAIAH XLIII.

O THOU who fillest the heavens with the glory of thy presence, and yet condescendest to regard the supplications of the children of men, receive, we beseech Thee, the prayers and the praises which we now present unto Thee, through Jesus Christ our Lord. Blessed be thy name, O our Father, for the mercies of the past night. We acknowledge our unworthiness, and while confessing our sinfulness, we look up to Thee for thy pardoning mercy and thy sanctifying grace. Thou art our God, and we will praise Thee. Enrich us with thy blessing, and guide our steps into the way of peace. We beseech Thee in thy mercy to hide thy face from our sins, and to blot out all our iniquities. Animate us, we implore Thee, by thy good Spirit, that we may not be led astray by an undue regard to things temporal. Enable us, by thy grace, to remember the lessons which we have now been taught in thy holy Word, and to feel that it is thy favour that imparts comfort and protection, and that as thy redeemed people we are called to thy service. Number us, we beseech Thee, among thy saints, that we may know, by joyful experience, that they who have the Lord for their God need fear no evil.

We pray Thee, that as Thou didst of old guide, protect, and nourish thine ancient people Israel, so Thou wilt guide, protect, and nourish us. If Thou art pleased to appoint trials for our lot, overrule them for thy glory and for our good, that we may learn to value aright the comforts of thy promises and the blessings of thy providence. May grace, mercy, and peace be with us. Thou hast assured us of thy pardoning mercy and of thy watchful care; graciously touch our hearts, that we may be impressed with a sense of thy goodness, and by a life of faith adorn our Christian profession. Give us faith daily to live near to Thee, and power to dedicate ourselves to thy service.

May thy blessing rest upon all who are now present before Thee. Cause the young to grow in grace as they grow in years. Convert the ungodly among us, and make thy Gospel the power of God unto their salvation. Be with us wherever our duty calls us this day; prosper the work of our hands, and crown our efforts with success. Keep us in thy faith and fear; preserve us from sin. Set a watch over the door of our lips, that we offend not in word, nor bring dishonour on thy holy Gospel. Sanctify our hearts, and grant that peace and good-will may dwell within our walls, and that by a life of watchfulness, prayer, and grateful obedience, we may shew forth thy praise. These blessings we ask for ourselves, and for all for whom it is our duty to pray, in the name and for the merit of Jesus Christ our Lord. Amen.

READ IN HOLY SCRIPTURE HEBREWS XI. 23—40.

O THOU who hast been the strength and support of thy saints in all ages, we rejoice that Thou art from everlasting to everlasting. Help us to believe that Thou art the same yesterday, to-day, and for ever, that thy compassions fail not, and that what Thou hast been to thy people in ancient times Thou wilt be to us who now call upon thy name. We thank Thee that, for our instruction and encouragement, Thou hast recorded in thy Word the faith of thy servants in bygone ages; as we read of their firm trust in Thyself, and their unshaken confidence in the truth of thy promises, we pray that we may take them as our example, and be found followers of all those who, through faith and patience, are now inheriting the promises. We give Thee thanks, O God, for the fuller revelation of thy purposes of grace and mercy we possess, and that we see what prophets and righteous men of old were not permitted to see. Grant that, as Thou hast increased our privileges, our faith, and love, and hope may be increased. May we have that faith which will help us to endure as seeing Thee who art invisible, the faith that will bring near to us the unseen glories of the heavenly country, and that will purify our hearts, and enable us to overcome the world, with its allurements, its temptations, and its trials. If Thou shouldest see fit to permit our faith to be tried by opposition, affliction, and reproach, for the sake of Christ, may we be able to stand steadfast, and at last to be more than conquerors through Him that loved us. May nothing move us away from Thyself, but grant us so abundantly thy grace, that even adverse influences around us may drive us nearer to thy side. Amidst the trials and difficulties that beset our path, help us to keep in view the end of our faith, the salvation of our souls, and constantly to have respect unto the recompence of the reward. Let the hope of heaven, the rest, and peace, and joy that are there, cheer us during all our pilgrimage here below, and at last may we be brought into thy presence, where there is fulness of joy, and to thy right hand, where there are pleasures for evermore.

And now, O Father, we thank Thee that through another day Thou hast spared us, and supplied all our wants, and with quiet and trustful hearts would we commit ourselves to thy care through the night. Hear us on behalf of all our dear friends. The blessings we have sought for ourselves we would desire Thee to bestow on them. Let thine eye be upon them, and whatever their circumstances, do Thou suit thy mercy to them.

Hear these our humble prayers, we beseech Thee. We offer them all through Jesus Christ our Lord. Amen.

[Morning.] **FORTY-SEVENTH WEEK.—SATURDAY.** [Evening.

READ IN HOLY SCRIPTURE ISAIAH XLV.

READ IN HOLY SCRIPTURE HEBREWS XII.

O LORD, Thou art great, and greatly to be exalted, and thy glory shall endure for ever. Thou art the Lord, and there is none else; there is no God beside Thee. There is no might nor power that exalts itself against Thee, but Thou wilt bring it down. Thou canst raise up deliverance for thy people in their hour of deepest sorrow, and canst save them out of the hand of their enemies by thy outstretched arm, when they feel that they can do nothing for themselves. Thou hast made the earth and created man upon it, and Thou canst turn the hearts of kings and make them do thy pleasure. But we adore Thee for a greater than Cyrus, and for a more glorious deliverance than that of Jacob from his captivity. In thy pity and compassion Thou hast had mercy upon us, and sent thine only begotten Son into the world, that we may live through Him. Thou hast laid help upon One that is mighty, and hast said, Deliver from going down to the pit, for I have found a ransom. Give us grace to believe in and to trust and adore this great Redeemer. May He have our hearts entirely, and may we feel it our chief joy to follow where He leads. They that trust in Him shall not be ashamed or confounded world without end, but they shall be saved with an everlasting salvation.

Grant us this salvation, O Lord our God. May the love of Christ constrain us, so that we shall find his yoke easy, his burden light, and his service perfect freedom. Adored be thy name for the invitation to look and be saved. By thy grace enable us to say, In the Lord alone have we righteousness and strength, and in him may we be justified from all things from which we cannot be justified by the law. Alas! O God, we have broken thy holy law, and cannot be delivered from the curse by any act of our own; but we praise thy most gracious name that Jesus died in our stead, and was made a curse for us, that we might be made the righteousness of God in Him. We bless Thee that this Gospel message is so plain and clear, and so exactly suited to our fallen and sinful condition. May we feel its effects in daily increasing spiritual strength, and in ever-growing conformity to the Lord our Righteousness.

We thank Thee for the peaceful rest of the past night, and for a new day with its new mercies. Give us this day our daily bread, and grace to walk as those who have been redeemed, not with silver or gold, but with the precious blood of Christ. Keep our bodies from danger, and our souls from sin; and enable us, whatever temptations may beset us, to be more than conquerors through Him that loved us and gave Himself for us; and all we ask is for his sake. Amen.

MERCIFUL Father in Christ Jesus, who dost regard with favour them that are of a meek and contrite spirit, accept thy unworthy servants who, at the close of another week, meet before thy throne for prayer and praise. Taught by thy Holy Spirit, we would remember how short our time is, and as each stage of life is passed, solemnly ask how we are prepared to meet our God. Gracious God, we seek the pardon of our sins through the blood of the cross. Lord Jesus, remove every weight from our souls that keeps us back from Thee; sin unforgiven, sin practised, harassing cares, and sorrows; and let us run patiently the race set before us, looking unto Thee. Oh, help us to realise our immortality and responsibility; to remember that the soul never dies, and that for the deeds done here we must render an account to Thee. Make us consult thy honour more than the world's favour, fearing eternal exclusion from thy love more than temporary affliction. Give us all, day by day, the grace of patience; possessing the great light of the Gospel, may none of us fail of the grace of God, but persevere faithfully to the end. Thanks to thy name for that Gospel of Jesus, and for the mercy which extends to us the day of grace. Awake, O arm of the Lord! convince the careless and impenitent of the guilt of rejecting Jesus, of refusing Him who speaketh in grace and truth. Enable us who now worship Thee to know by experience the nature of true faith, to adorn the doctrine of God our Saviour in all things, and to attain the blessed assurance of having received a kingdom that cannot be moved.

Bless the present and absent members of this family; all relations, friends, and neighbours; and dispose their hearts to the attainment of everlasting salvation. For the whole household of faith, singly and collectively; for our fellow-citizens, fellow-countrymen, and fellow-creatures, we implore thy grace, to edify, comfort, alarm, or convert them, according to their several needs. Give thy Spirit to our Sovereign and the Royal Family. May they diligently fulfil the duties of their exalted station as in thy sight, remembering their own subjection, in all things, to a King in heaven. Preside over our national councils; may they be pervaded by Christian integrity and truth; and remove far from all who take part in them any contempt for thy holy Word. We thankfully acknowledge our countless blessings, while deploring our unworthiness as a people. Quicken us, O Lord, in our love to Thee and to each other. Now grant unto our bodies the rest they need, and to our souls peace in Jesus; and raise us up in health to worship Thee acceptably on the Lord's day, through Christ our Saviour. Amen.

[Morning.] **FORTY-EIGHTH WEEK.—LORD'S DAY.** [Evening.

READ IN HOLY SCRIPTURE ISAIAH XLVIII.

O LORD, Thou art the First and the Last; help us this morning with reverence and godly fear to approach thy footstool. We thank Thee for thy watchful guardian care. We have been protected and preserved by thine overruling providence. Teach us always to look up to Thee as the Author of our existence, and the Source and Giver of every good, and to trace thy love in every blessing. We beseech Thee now to give us thy Holy Spirit. We would go forth to the duties of the day in thy strength. Keep us by thy grace, for we are not able to keep ourselves. Be Thou our Sun and Shield, and grant us constantly to live under the beams of thy grace, beneath the protection of thy power. Thou art the Redeemer and the Holy One of Israel, lead us by the way that we should go, and prosper us in all we do. Thou hast graciously declared unto us thy Word and will; cause us attentively to hearken to thy commandments, and dutifully to obey thy precepts, that so our peace may be as a river, and our righteousness as the waves of the sea. Thine ancient people thirsted not when Thou didst lead them through the desert land; for then Thou didst cause waters to flow out of the rock. Oh, satisfy us early with thy mercy. Feed us with the bread of heaven, and from the streams of that Rock, which is Christ, give us now to drink, that our souls may be refreshed, and that we may go on our way rejoicing.

Thou hast said that Thou wilt not give thy glory to another. We desire to render unto Thee the glory due unto thy name. We would worship the Lord our God, and Him only would we serve. We are not our own. We are bought with a price, even the precious blood of Christ. Give us thy Holy Spirit, that we may glorify Thee with our bodies and spirits, which are thine; adorn the doctrine of God our Saviour in all things, and serve our generation according to thy will.

As a family may we live before Thee; having the light of thy love on our home, and every member of our household a member of the household of faith, and the family of God. Hear our prayers for all who love our Lord Jesus Christ in sincerity and truth. Make thy presence felt in all congregations gathered this day in thy name. Strengthen the hands of thy faithful pastors. Guide all who are in error to the knowledge of thy truth. Let the power and love of Christ be realised in many hearts, and the steps of wanderers be turned to the fold of the Good Shepherd. Send forth thy Gospel into all lands. Cause the wickedness of the wicked to come to an end; and pity and convert them. Lord answer and accept, sanctify and save us, for the Redeemer's sake. Amen.

READ IN HOLY SCRIPTURE HEBREWS XIII.

O LORD, we thank Thee for having permitted us to go up to thy sanctuary to-day, that we might offer spiritual sacrifices, and think of thy loving-kindness in the midst of thy temple. Impress upon our minds, we beseech Thee, the doctrines and precepts of thy Gospel. May we always be found looking unto Christ, and, trusting in the shadow of his wings, may we be delivered from the guilt and power of our sins. Clothe us with his righteousness, and fill us with his Spirit.

We also thank Thee, Lord of the Sabbath, for thy day of rest, and for bestowing upon us in connection with it such priceless privileges. We adore thy wisdom and love embodied in the ministry of reconciliation. May we ever obey those that have the rule over us, knowing that they watch for our souls. Give us, we beseech Thee, grace to receive with meekness and faith thy holy Word. Enable us at all times to find unfailing consolation in thine exceeding great and precious promises, and to feel that Thou wilt never leave nor forsake us, so that we may boldly say "The Lord is my helper; I will not fear what man can do unto me." Cause our Christian life to be characterised by a holy courage. Firmly rooted and grounded in the faith, may we ever be ready to suffer for the sake of Christ, and to bear his reproach. May we hold the world with a light hand, and, while we remain in it, show by our conversation that we are not of it. Make us perfect, through the blood of the everlasting covenant, in every good work, that we may do that which is well pleasing in thy sight.

Thou, O Lord, art the God of all the families of Israel. Be our God, we entreat Thee. Let our home be sanctified by thy presence. [Let our sons be as plants grown up in their youth, and our daughters as corner-stones of thy temple.] May our friends and all connected with us be numbered amongst thine elect people. During this night grant us thy protecting care. We would not forget that here we have no continuing city. Soon our last Sabbath evening on earth will come. Enable us to keep the eternal Sabbath before our eyes, so that when we have done thy will here below, we may enter upon that rest which Thou hast prepared for thy people. We would unite with our own petitions the intercessions presented by thy Church to-day in behalf of all ranks and conditions of men; especially do we remember before Thee all that are in bonds and that suffer adversity. May the works of darkness come to an end, and all the nations find rest in Jesus. The Lord bless us and keep us. The Lord lift up the light of his countenance upon us. The Lord give us grace and peace, now and ever. Amen.

[330]

[Morning.] **FORTY-EIGHTH WEEK.—MONDAY.** [Evening.

READ IN HOLY SCRIPTURE ISAIAH L.

O GOD, the Father of our Lord Jesus Christ, and our Father, as Thou renewest thy mercies to us every day, so waken our ear morning by morning to the voice of thy lovingkindness, and stir us up to call upon thy name.

With shame we confess before Thee that, although from our birth under the strongest obligation to obey Thee as our Creator and Preserver, we have yet sinned against Thee by our disobedience, and brought ourselves into bondage by our iniquities. Hadst Thou recompensed us as we deserve, we must have lain down in despair; but thy hand was not shortened that it could not redeem, nor thy power unequal to deliver us.

We praise Thee for the gift of thy dear Son, who knowing how to speak a word in season to him that is weary, has invited the heavy laden to come unto Him, that they may find rest unto their souls. Blessed be thy name, that under the painful sense of our many transgressions, while Satan accuses and condemns us, He is near that justifieth us. Suffer us no more to rebel against Thee, nor to turn away from thy commandments. For his sake, who gave his back to the smiters, and his cheeks to them that plucked off the hair, forgive us our past transgressions, and enable us henceforth to set our face like a flint to go and sin no more. Help us, O our God, and then we shall not be ashamed; but shall delight ourselves in thy commandments, and ever find them ways of pleasantness and paths of peace.

To these our humble prayers and thanksgivings, we venture to add our intercession for all men; for our Sovereign and the Royal Family, for the Parliament of the nation, and for all that are in authority; that all orders and ranks of men may unite in seeking the glory of their God. We especially pray for the Church of Christ, and for all who, though fearing the Lord, yet walk in darkness and have no light; enable them to trust in the Lord, and to stay themselves upon their God. Remembering the anguish of mind and body through which the Captain of our salvation passed to glory, may they find comfort in following his steps. We pray for the world, that those who are seeking happiness in temporal things, or who are relying for salvation on their own wisdom, strength, or righteousness, may by thy Holy Spirit be taught their folly. Pour down on all who are dear to us thy richest blessings. Give them all the constant experience of thy love, and guide them in the ways of godliness and peace. Graciously hear us in all that we ask, according to thy will, for the sake of thy well-beloved Son, our adorable Redeemer, to whom with Thee and thy Holy Spirit be everlasting praise. Amen.

READ IN HOLY SCRIPTURE JAMES I.

ALMIGHTY and Eternal God, who art unchangeably the same, our Creator, our Preserver, and the Author and Giver of all our mercies; awaken in us, as we kneel before Thee, a spirit of reverent humility and thankful praise. Of thine own, O Lord, alone can we give Thee. The heart to praise, and the desire to pray, come only from Thee. Faith, and wisdom, and strength are thine. Gracious Father, bestow these gifts on us, then shall we worship Thee with the spirit and with the understanding, and our mouth will be filled with thy praise.

Great has been thy goodness and forbearance towards us this day. We have often sinned against Thee by saying things we ought not to have said, and by doing things we ought not to have done. We have forgotten that thine eye was upon us, and that we should have done thy will, not our own; and yet Thou art long-suffering and patient, and still waitest to be gracious to us. Blessed be thy name, that we have gone in and out in peace and safety throughout the day, that our wants have been supplied, and that now, in the name of thy dear Son, we can come to thy footstool and obtain forgiveness and acceptance. O God, enable us to rejoice in thy gifts, to see in them all thy hand and thy love. We pray that we may lie down to rest forgiven, accepted, and blessed by Thee. We pray that every day we may be made more deeply sensible of thy mercy, and more anxious in all things to do thy will. Holy Father, write thy law on our hearts, and by thy Spirit stir us up to a daily, and diligent, and loving obedience. Lord Jesus, come and dwell in us, and enable us to feel thy presence, and to experience the greatness and excellence of thy love. Then shall we be thine indeed, and live unto Thee, and follow thy footsteps. Fulfil thy promise, O God, and give us the Spirit to guide us into all truth, and to teach us the things of God. Especially suffer us not to be forgetful hearers of thy Word, unmindful of its warnings, or coldly indifferent to its promises, as those whose religion is vain. Kindle in our hearts a deep hatred of sin, as displeasing and dishonouring to Thee. In the midst of all our temptations and trials, be Thou with us, O Jesus, who thyself hast suffered being tempted. By the mercies and afflictions of life train us for heaven, and in thine unchanging love perfect in us thy work.

We seek for ourselves, and all who are dear to us, thy Divine protection, O Lord, for this night. Let thy sheltering wing guard us from evil, and thy power raise us again in life and strength for duty and service. We ask it all in the adorable name of Jesus, thy dear Son; for his sake, heavenly Father, help, answer, and bless us. Amen.

[Morning.] FORTY-EIGHTH WEEK—TUESDAY. [Evening.

READ IN HOLY SCRIPTURE ISAIAH LII.

GREAT and glorious God, spared by thy mercy, we would begin another day by worshipping Thee. Meet and right it is that we should do so. Help us always to esteem it not only our duty, but our highest privilege, to draw near to Thee in prayer and praise.

Blessed, for ever blessed be thy name, that we have heard the glad tidings of thy Gospel; that peace with God, salvation from sin, and eternal life and glory, have been published in our ears, through Jesus Christ, whom Thou hast sent to be the Saviour of the world. Through Him, and Him alone, we dare to approach Thee. Through Him we call Thee our Father, and look to Thee for every blessing, both those pertaining to the present life and those of the life to come.

While we slept, Thou, who never slumberest nor sleepest, hast been our protector. But, Lord, we need thy care as much when we are awake as when we are asleep; for we have no wisdom or strength to take care of ourselves. Keep us, then, oh, keep us this day from all adversities that might happen to our bodies, and from all evil thoughts that might assault and hurt our souls. Bestow upon us thy Holy Spirit. Enable us to remember that we are not our own, but thine. Shed abroad thy love in our hearts. Put into our minds good desires. Enable us to live in the world as those who are not of it, as those who are the servants of another King, the citizens of another kingdom. And oh, give us courage, not only to confess Christ with our lips, but to adorn his Gospel by our lives. Help us to do our duty in the stations to which Thou hast called us. May we touch no unclean thing. May the words of our mouths and the meditation of our hearts be always acceptable in thy sight, O Lord, our strength and our Redeemer.

Oh, our Father, Thou hast taught us to be careful for nothing, but in everything by prayer and supplication with thanksgiving to make our requests known unto Thee. We commit, therefore, to Thee all our temporal wants. Provide for us. Feed us with food convenient for us. Be with us in our daily business as Thou wast with Joseph of old, and make all that we do to prosper.

And, Lord, we pray that Thou wouldest accomplish thy promises concerning the future blessedness of our sin-stricken world. May he who died in suffering and shame on Calvary, be exalted and extolled, and be very high. May the Jews repent and be converted to Him; and may the Gentile nations bow at his footstool, and many be saved through his atoning blood. Oh, that those times of refreshing may speedily come! We ask all through Jesus Christ. Amen.

READ IN HOLY SCRIPTURE JAMES II.

ALMIGHTY God, with whom is no respect of persons, help us to approach Thee acceptably, and teach us how to pray. May thy gracious Spirit help our infirmities. Sensible of our unfitness for thy presence, we feel the precious value of Immanuel's intercession, in whose name we offer our prayer.

Thy goodness has accompanied us through this day. Life, health, and blessing have thy hands dispensed to us. Thou hast kept us in safety; Thou hast not suffered disease to invade our dwelling, nor accident to befall us. What shall we render to Thee, giver of all good, for thine abounding mercy! Make us grateful, and may our lives and our lips show forth thy praise.

Humbly do we confess our unworthiness. Our sins are many, and we acknowledge them with shame before Thee. It is of the Lord's mercy we are not consumed. Thou hast compassion upon us. Work in us, we beseech Thee, a true sense of sin, that we may be contrite and humble before Thee; that we may receive the forgiveness of sins, according to thy word; that we may once more prove the pacifying, cleansing virtue of that blood which taketh away sin. Speak thy peace to our souls, ere we enter upon the silent hours of the night.

Grant thy favour according to our respective wants, which are known to Thee. Make us aware of these wants, and bring us to thine inexhaustible fulness to supply them. Enlighten our darkness, and make us wise in the understanding of thy Word. Take from us all pride, and give us humility of heart. Shed abroad thy love in our hearts, and enrich us with the treasures of thy grace. Out of thy riches in glory by Christ Jesus supply all our need.

Oh, send out thy light and truth to all mankind. Give efficacy to thy Gospel, and let it soon be possessed by all people. Smile upon the labours of thy servants, at home and abroad. Give to thy Son the heathen for his inheritance, that the desert may be glad, and the wilderness rejoice and blossom as the rose. Thus let thy kingdom come; wars cease to the end of the earth; oppression, slavery, and sin be brought to an effectual end.

God be merciful to us, and bless us, and cause thy face to shine upon us, that thy way may be known upon earth, thy saving health among all nations. Let the people praise Thee, O God; let all the people praise Thee.

To thy gracious care we commit ourselves this night. Give refreshing rest and renewed vigour of body and soul. All these mercies we ask in the name of Jesus Christ. Amen.

[Morning.] **FORTY-EIGHTH WEEK.—WEDNESDAY.** [Evening.]

READ IN HOLY SCRIPTURE ISAIAH LIII.

LORD, we pray Thee to open our understandings, that we may understand the Scripture which we have been reading. Let thy Spirit, who in thy servants the prophets testified beforehand the sufferings of Christ, and the glory that should follow, ever guide us. Lord, we tremble for ourselves when we see the blindness of the people to whom were committed thy oracles, but who did not perceive that the Spirit bore witness to Jesus as their Messiah. We believe in thy Word. O Lord God, help our unbelief, and increase our faith in thy dear Son as the Redeemer of mankind. Reveal thy truth to our souls, and make it effectual to our salvation. May He who was once despised and rejected of men be in our eyes the chief among ten thousand, and altogether lovely. What sufficient thanks and adoration can we offer unto Thee, that thy Son our Lord became obedient unto death for us men, and for our salvation that he was smitten of Thee, and afflicted. Though we cannot resemble Him in his innocency, may we imitate his meekness; and, under all circumstances of provocation, follow his steps. If we are ever reviled, suffer us not to revile again; if called to suffer, preserve us from threatening, and enable us to commit ourselves to Him who judgeth righteously. Set a watch at all times over our lips, that we offend not in word. And whilst in Him, bearing our sins in his own body on the tree, we see a sacrifice for our guilt, and an example of patience, let us learn also to become dead unto sins, continually mortifying all our evil and corrupt affections. Convince us of our individual wanderings from the fold of Christ. O God, we have indeed sinned and come short of thy glory. Blessed be thy name, that Thou hast laid on Christ the iniquities of us all. Through his blood, shed for us, we implore thy pardon and peace.

We adore thy goodness, O Lord, for having shielded us from harm during the hours of darkness, and renewed to us this morning the blessings of thy providence and grace. Add to all thy mercies, we pray Thee, the gift of a thankful heart, and give us so to feel the love of Christ in our hearts, that we may cheerfully consecrate our life to thy service.

Go with us, merciful Father, to all the duties of this day. Let neither sin nor Satan obtain the victory over us. Show us, under all circumstances, what we ought to do, and give us grace and strength faithfully to do it. Gracious Spirit, dwell Thou in our hearts, and work in us all the will of God. Adorable Redeemer, in thy name we offer these our prayers and praises; answer us for thy truth's sake. Amen.

READ IN HOLY SCRIPTURE JAMES III.

SET a watch, O Lord, before our mouth; keep the door of our lips; let us not be hasty to utter anything before God; for Thou art in heaven, and we upon the earth; therefore should our words be few. Grant unto us to have our hearts and our lips prepared, now, and at all times when we draw near to Thee. Gracious God, never permit our lips to utter in thy presence that which our hearts do not feel, for Thou searchest the hearts and triest the reins of the children of men. We acknowledge that thy holy Word convinces us of having sinned with our mouths. We are a people of unclean lips, and we fervently pray for thy pardoning mercy to be extended to every one of the countless sins we have spoken, or thought, or done; and we beseech of Thee to give us that wisdom that is from above to teach and to keep us, so that the fruits of righteousness may abound in our lips and our lives. May our mouths be sealed against all that is false, impure, unkind, idle, or vain; may they be opened in behalf of thy truth. Lord, help us to speak for the helpless and the oppressed. We also entreat Thee to preserve us from hasty words to our fellow-creatures. Make us like unto Him who, when he was reviled, reviled not again; who, when he suffered, threatened not; who did no sin, neither was guile found in his mouth. Thus may we be peacemakers, and by words of kindness refresh and comfort all around.

O God of mercy pardon all the profanity of the sons of men, and give to the people a pure language, that they may all call upon the name of the Lord, to serve him with one consent. Bless us as a family, that envy, and strife, and confusion, and every evil work, may be kept far from us. And now that another night has set in, great God, we ask thy protecting care to be over our dwelling, and our persons, and all that appertains to us.

We rejoice to know that while we slumber thy praises will be sung in other portions of our world; and we pray that we may serve Thee eternally in that world in which there shall be no night. O Lord, preserve those who are this night journeying by land or by water, and let thy gracious presence be enjoyed by the afflicted. Grant strength unto those who watch beside the suffering, and may those who die awake to endless day with Thee. Shouldst Thou spare us to rise again on the morrow, enable us to serve Thee more diligently and devotedly than in the day which is past, and in every thing to seek the honour of thy name. Grant unto us now to enjoy the assurance of thy pardoning love, and to rest in thy favour through the abounding merit of thy dear Son, Jesus Christ, for whom we bless Thee. To Father, Son, and Holy Spirit be glory for ever. Amen.

MORNING. FORTY-EIGHTH WEEK.—THURSDAY. [EVENING.

READ IN HOLY SCRIPTURE ISAIAH LIV.

O LORD our Redeemer, the Holy One of Israel, we desire to approach unto Thee this morning, and to worship Thee, the only living and true God. Thou art the God of the whole earth. We unite with all the families that call upon thy name to render to Thee the tribute of our praise for thy goodness and thy love, and to seek from Thee in prayer the blessings we need at thy hand. Listen, we beseech Thee, O Lord, to our humble cry, and grant us thy fatherly blessing.

We thank Thee, most merciful Father, that we have not been called to sleep the sleep of death, but that whilst many of our fellow-sinners have been called to exchange the darkness of night for the blackness of darkness and despair, we appear at thy footstool the monuments of thy sparing mercy. For life and health, and all things we enjoy, we give Thee our most humble and hearty thanks. We call upon our souls, and all that is within us, to bless and to praise thy holy name. Thou hast redeemed our life from destruction; Thou crownest us with loving kindness and tender mercies. We humbly beseech Thee to impress upon our hearts the consideration of our entire dependence upon Thee, and make us feel the deep and solemn obligation we are under to worship and to serve Thee with all the faculties and capacities of our being.

We come to Thee for the blessings which we need this day. We beseech Thee to keep us by thine almighty power in all the temptations which may assail us in the discharge of our lawful duties. Help us to honour Thee even in our trials and afflictions. We ask Thee to give us the wisdom we need to walk in the path of virtue and holiness. We implore thy grace to enable us to honour the Lord with our substance, and to exemplify that spirit of benevolence and self-sacrifice which ever distinguished our divine Redeemer when he was upon earth. May we be enabled this day to commend the religion of Jesus Christ to some who have hitherto rejected it, and by our holy walk and conversation may we draw souls to the Saviour. Impress upon our minds, O Lord, the lessons of thy holy Word we have now read. Assure our hearts that, if we are thy children by faith in Jesus Christ, we have an all-sufficient friend in Thyself, one from whom no powers of earth or hell can ever separate us.

Bestow thy blessing, we beseech Thee, upon all who are dear to us. Make them the objects of thy special care, and the subjects of thy saving grace, and grant that we may all be found at thy right hand, and with all thy redeemed children may we attain unto eternal glory, through Jesus Christ our Lord. Amen.

READ IN HOLY SCRIPTURE JAMES IV.

MOST gracious Saviour, Thou alone canst enable us to walk according to the precepts of thy blessed Gospel. It is only through divine strength imparted to us that we can do what we know to be right. Grant, heavenly Father, for Jesus Christ's sake, that we may be anxious in all our thoughts, words, and actions, to be guided by the Holy Spirit, and by the doctrines and precepts of thy Word. May it ever be our desire to follow after peace, to avoid all that pertains to envy and strife, to flee from all sinful and hurtful lusts, to be content with the things that we have, and to cast our care upon God, who careth for us. May the Spirit which is of God triumph in us over the spirit which is of the world, and may we regard the friendship of Jesus as of greater value than all that the world can afford.

We beseech Thee to help us to walk humbly in thy presence and before our fellow-men. Suffer us not at any time to give way to evil influence; grant that we may resist temptation; that we may be strong in the day of trial, and ever manfully strive to keep ourselves unspotted from the world. Amidst the various duties of life help us ever to remember Thee. Let not health, prosperity, or riches lead us to trust in an arm of flesh. And if surrounded by adversity, sickness, and sorrow, may our faith still be strong in Thee, who art able to deliver us through our Lord Jesus Christ. May we guard our thoughts as in thy sight. Help us to set a watch over our lips, that no evil word may escape. Let no provocation stir us up to wrath. May we be gentle and kind to all men, and when our patience is sorely tried, bring to our remembrance the example of Him who, when he was reviled, reviled not again. From all rash and uncharitable judgments deliver us. Enable us in all things, as far as in us lies, to practise the charity that thinketh no evil. By thy grace helping us, may we ever cultivate a meek and quiet spirit; and if wronged at any time by our neighbour, may we commit ourselves to Him that judgeth righteously. In all our daily engagements give us heavenly wisdom to direct us, and in all our plans prosper us by thy blessing. May we do the duties of life as they daily arise in our path, ever remembering that only the present time is ours.

And now we thank Thee for all the mercies of this day. We confess before Thee our sins; we ask thy mercy and implore thy pardon. We commend each other to thy gracious protection this night. May we abide in safety under thy loving care. What we seek for ourselves we ask for the whole family of God. In mercy hear us, and answer us for Jesus' sake. Amen.

[Morning.] **FORTY-EIGHTH WEEK.—FRIDAY.** [Evening.

READ IN HOLY SCRIPTURE ISAIAH LV.

O ALMIGHTY and ever-blessed God, we beseech Thee, in the name of our Lord Jesus Christ, by thy Holy Spirit to help us now to worship Thee acceptably with reverence and godly fear. We desire to return unto Thee our hearty thanks for thy watchful care over us during the past night, beseeching Thee to take us all into thy care and keeping during the present day, and to preserve us from all evil. Grant also that, wherever we are, and whatever we do, we may endeavour to glorify Thee, and may always remember that thine eye is ever upon us, and may never undertake anything upon which we dare not ask thy blessing. Teach us to hunger and thirst after righteousness, and may we eat of the bread of life, and drink of those living waters which thy Son Jesus Christ, our Lord, has promised to give to all who come unto Him.

And if, O Lord, any of those who are now before Thee be as yet strangers to those sure mercies of the everlasting covenant promised in thy only-begotten Son, Christ our Lord, grant that they may at once forsake their evil ways and unrighteous thoughts, and turn unto Him in hearty repentance and true faith, that they may receive the fulfilment of thy promise to have mercy upon them, and to abundantly pardon them. Grant also that we may all be so led and guided by thy Holy Spirit, that thy Word may dwell in us richly in all wisdom, and that we may be enabled so to speak and act, that by our means the truths of thy Word may be conveyed to others also, and may accomplish thy purpose in the salvation of sinners, and in the edification of thy saints. Grant also that we ourselves may be living epistles of Christ, written by thy Holy Spirit, and known and read of all men as exemplifying the doctrines of thy grace; that if any whom we meet obey not the written Word, they may, without the Word, be won by our holy conversation, and that Thou in all things mayest be glorified through Jesus Christ.

We beseech Thee also to grant thy blessing upon all our temporal affairs, and give us an abiding faith in thy gracious promise that, if we seek first the kingdom of God and thy righteousness, all worldly necessaries may be added unto us.

And while we pray for new mercies, we desire also to heartily thank Thee for all the various blessings which in thy merciful providence Thou hast bestowed upon us. We adore thy grace which has so constantly provided for all our need. By thy Holy Spirit enable us to prove our thankfulness by our lives, through Jesus Christ our Lord, who liveth and reigneth with Thee and the Holy Ghost in the glory of the Triune Godhead everlastingly. Amen.

READ IN HOLY SCRIPTURE JAMES V.

UNTO Thee do we lift our eyes, O our God. In the multitude of thy tender mercies, regard us for the sake of Jesus Christ our Saviour. For his sake enter not into judgment with us for the sins of another day. In how many ways have we offended Thee in thought, word, and deed! In how many ways have we come short of thy holy commandments! We do confess our sins, and are sorry for our misdeeds; blot them out, we beseech Thee, from the book of thy remembrance. Oh, wash us, and we shall be clean; purge us, and we shall be whiter than snow. Thou hast declared, by the mouth of thine apostle, that Thou art very pitiful, and of tender mercy. Oh, extend that pity to us who now kneel before Thee; enable us to know by happy experience that tender mercy which has borne with us so long, and yet bears with us, though we deserve judgment. Enable us now, by the teaching of the Holy Spirit, to offer up that effectual, fervent prayer which with Thee, the God of mercy, through thy dear Son, availeth much, and which will bring down upon us showers of heavenly blessings. And above all, O Lord, give us that patient waiting for thy second coming, which will stablish our hearts in thy fear and love. Let us remember that the day of the Lord cometh as a thief in the night, and when men shall slumber, then the sign of the Son of man shall be seen in the heavens, and the kingdom of God shall come. May we be found then amongst the sheep of his pasture at his right hand, washed in his own precious blood, and clothed with his perfect righteousness, that we may stand complete in him.

O Lord, we praise and magnify thy holy name for all the blessings of another day. Surely goodness and mercy have followed us; we have been preserved from many dangers, seen and unseen, we have been sustained by thy fatherly hand, and we desire to give Thee all the glory. Take us now under thy heavenly keeping during the defenceless hours of the night; oh, may we lie down at peace with Thee. Give us refreshing rest, and grant that if spared to see the light of another day, we may begin it in thy fear and love, and spend it to thy glory; that thus we may strive each day we live on earth to live more as thy people; more as those whom thy mercy hath spared, and thy love hath redeemed.

Hear us, gracious God, in these our humble supplications; accept our heartfelt praises, and do for us more and better than we can ask or think, for the alone sake of Him who is worthy to receive the adoration of heaven and earth, even Jesus Christ thy dear Son our Lord. For his sake answer and bless us. Amen.

[Morning.] **FORTY-EIGHTH WEEK.—SATURDAY.** [Evening.

READ IN HOLY SCRIPTURE ISAIAH LIX.

READ IN HOLY SCRIPTURE 1 PETER I. 1–12.

MOST holy and most merciful Lord, we would humbly acknowledge our sins before Thee. We have done the things which we ought not to have done, and we have left undone the things we ought to have done; we have erred and strayed from thy ways, and there is no health in us. But our sins are not greater than Thou canst forgive. Lord, extend to us thy pardoning mercy, and as redeemed by the blood of Christ may we walk in newness of life. May the vastness of thy love, the efficacy of Christ's atonement, the renewing power of the Holy Ghost, be known by and illustrated in us. May we be the subjects of a personal conviction of sin, and of the repentance that leads into the way of peace, and into the light of our Father's countenance.

We have come, through thy mercy, to the beginning of another day. We thank Thee for strength to do its work, and for power of thought to comprehend and meet its responsibilities. May the day be spent under the influence of a holy, childlike fear of God. Let heavenly wisdom guide us. Suffer us not to fall before temptation. If unexpected or sudden trouble come to-day, may it be met with the calmness that springs from trust in God. In all our joys and pleasures may the giver be devoutly and thankfully recognised. Let no rash, unkind, or idle words proceed from our lips. Keep, we pray Thee, our consciences sensitive, our thoughts and emotions pure, our aims unselfish. May all our dealings with our fellow-men be marked by truth and uprightness, and the value of our time be deeply appreciated through each passing hour. May the close of the day find us, not merely nearer to our graves, but matured in character, strengthened in faith, grown in likeness to God, and preparedness for eternity.

Surround with thy Divine protection all whom we love. Their wants and temptations are known to Thee. Do Thou for them, O God, above all that we can ask or think, and especially train and guide them in the way of eternal life. [Give thy Holy Spirit, we pray Thee, to the children before Thee, and cause them earnestly to seek the one thing needful.]

May the Redeemer's kingdom be extended and strengthened to-day. May those who are looking forward to the work of spiritual teaching on the approaching Lord's Day be divinely directed, and enabled to meditate on thy Word with clearness of thought, and with warmth and delight of heart. Hear, O Lord, the cry of the sorrowing. Protect the defenceless. Strengthen the tempted. Vindicate those that are wronged. Let thy way be known upon earth, thy saving health among all nations, through Jesus Christ our Lord. Amen.

BLESSED be thy name, O God; to Thee, O God the Father, to thee, O God the Son, to Thee, O God the Holy Ghost, we present our sacrifice of praise and adoration. Eternal thanks be to Thee, O redeeming God, for thy love to lost and ruined men, that Thou hast prepared for them who believe in Jesus a place among the children of God, and reserved an inheritance that fadeth not away.

We bless Thee that we can look forward with confidence to that blissful inheritance which our blessed Redeemer has gone to prepare for us. May we be accounted worthy for his sake to be owned as sons of God and joint-heirs with Christ. Blessed Saviour, who hast purchased this inheritance for thy true disciples, fit and prepare us for it, and fill our hearts with such faith in Thee, and such love towards Thee, that we may never be ashamed of Thee; but that when tried we may come forth as gold.

Thou hast brought us safely to the close of another week; a step further on our pilgrimage, and nearer to the end of our days. If we have been kept from any sin, it is due to thy grace; if we have done anything to thy glory, it is due to thy assistance, but if we have sinned and walked carelessly, it has been our own fault, and we would confess it as such.

Thou hast given us to know things which others sought to know in vain; to us it is granted to enjoy those mercies for which holier and better men sighed, but died without partaking of them; Oh, how little return have we made to Thee. We have been unprofitable indeed, and not availed ourselves of our great advantages as we might have done. Open our eyes to their value ere they be removed, and given to those who shall bring forth more fruit. To this end help us to use the coming Sabbath aright. May we lay aside the cares and thoughts, and plans of the six days, to rest and attend especially to the interests of our souls. Send us the Holy Spirit to open our understandings, to bring home the Word of truth to our consciences, and to sanctify us through the means of grace.

When we attend the house of God, may the same Holy Spirit who inspired the Scriptures engrave their teachings on our hearts, and draw our minds to the contemplation of those glorious truths, so clearly revealed to us, into which even the angels desire to look. Thus may we grow in grace and knowledge, delighting ourselves in the Lord; having our fruit unto holiness, and becoming daily more meet for the inheritance of the saints in light, through the merits and mediation of Jesus Christ our adorable Lord and Saviour. Amen.

[Morning.] **FORTY-NINTH WEEK.—LORD'S DAY.** [Evening.

READ IN HOLY SCRIPTURE ISAIAH LXIII.

WITH deep humility and reverence, O God, we gather around thy footstool. Thou art high and holy, the King of kings, and Lord of lords. Power and wisdom, grace and truth, are thine. Adored be thy name, O heavenly Father, that Thou hast opened a way of access to thy throne, and that, through Jesus Christ, Thou wilt be gracious unto us, and hear our prayer. Have mercy upon us, and in fulfilment of thy Divine promises give us an answer of peace, and supply all our need, for Christ's sake. Frail and feeble in ourselves, we lean on thy strength. Ignorant and foolish, we implore Thee to give us wisdom, that under thy Divine teaching we may grow in grace, and be instructed in that knowledge which maketh wise unto salvation. Sinful and unworthy, we beseech thy gracious forgiveness. Give us the assurance of thy pardon, and grant us thy peace. We are thine; oh, save us. Dwell Thou in our hearts, and stir us up with a holy jealousy to cast down everything which exalts itself against Thee.

We praise Thee for thy lovingkindnesses, and for all the goodness which Thou hast bestowed upon us in thy great mercy. We thank Thee for the daily gifts of thy bounty; and, above all, for sending thy dear Son to seek and to save the lost. Unfold to us more clearly all the riches of his grace, that the assurance of his sympathy may encourage and comfort us in every trial, and the remembrance of his love and pity deepen our faith and awaken our love.

Preserve us this day from sin. We pray that through thy help we may realise thy presence with us in the house of prayer, and be comforted. In mercy take away from us all worldliness of thought, and raise our hearts to thy footstool, that we may worship Thee in spirit and in truth. Impress thy word on our hearts, and suffer us not to grieve thy Spirit by our rebellion against thy will, or to err from thy ways. Oh, that we may all be thy children indeed, loving thy will and cheerfully following in our Lord's footsteps.

Strengthen the hands of thy ministers by the assurance of thy presence, and kindle in the hearts of all who shall this day be gathered in thy name, a zeal for thy glory. Make thy word mighty to the conversion of many from sin to holiness, from Satan and the world to Christ. Lord, we long and pray for the coming of thy kingdom, when Jesus shall be exalted, and every knee bow at his footstool, and every tongue confess that He is Lord. Pour out the Holy Spirit abundantly on thy Church; and grant that we, and all whom we love, may be so taught and led by Him as that none of us may be found wanting in the day of Christ. Answer and bless us for his sake. Amen.

READ IN HOLY SCRIPTURE 1 PETER I. 13—25.

O GOD and Father of our Lord and Saviour Jesus Christ, and our God and Father in Him, we would unite together at the close of this blessed Sabbath, to render Thee thanks for the renewed opportunity we have this day had of reading, and hearing, and thinking about our Saviour and his redeeming love. Bless to our souls thy Word, read or heard. Let it not rise up in judgment against us. May it not add to our condemnation that we have been born in a land so highly privileged as to have the light of the glorious Gospel shining in it brightly; but may we have grace to improve our privileges, to gird up the loins of our mind, as travellers to a better country; to be sober, and hope to the end for the grace that is to be brought unto us at the revelation of Jesus Christ. O Lord, make us indeed obedient children, new creatures, sheep of the Redeemer's fold, followers of Him, and heirs of eternal life.

Help us, O God, to pass the time of our sojourning on the earth in faith and in the fear of God, remembering that here we have no continuing city, and that we profess to look for one to come. May thy Gospel preached this day be to us, and to all who heard it with holy reverence, the savour of life into life; and may many who have hitherto been careless about thy glory and their own salvation be arrested by its mighty power, through the operation of the Holy Spirit, and be convinced, and converted, and made new creatures in Christ Jesus. We bless Thee that the Gospel is the power of God unto salvation to every one that believeth, and that fresh proofs of its blessed effects upon the hearts and lives of men are continually appearing for the honour of our ever blessed Saviour. Glory be to thy name, O Lord, for the great truth just read, that we are not redeemed with corruptible things, as silver and gold, but with the precious blood of Christ, as of a lamb without blemish and without spot. Let us ever remember this, and let it have its due influence upon our minds, leading us continually to strive after a more perfect conformity to Christ, and righteousness, and true holiness. Thou hast said, Be ye holy, for I am holy. May thy good Spirit lead us more and more into the truth, sanctifying our hearts by faith, and taking of the things of Jesus and shewing them unto us. Pardon our sins and shortcomings during this day, even the iniquities of our most holy things. May the truths we have heard influence our hearts and lives through the week, and be fruitful in all godliness and obedience. And now, O Guardian of thy children, keep us through the coming night, for Christ's sake. Amen.

[337]

[MORNING.] FORTY-NINTH WEEK.—MONDAY. [EVENING.

READ IN HOLY SCRIPTURE ISAIAH LXIV.

ALMIGHTY and Everlasting Father, for thy lovingkindness and tender care during the night, and for the renewed bounties of thy providence, we adore thy glorious name. Day by day we lift our hearts to Thee in praise. Make us ever more and more deeply sensible of thy goodness, and stir us up by thy grace to live to thy praise. It is with shame and confusion of face, O Lord, that we confess our transgressions against thy holy law. We have wandered and strayed from thy holy ways like lost sheep; not only have we wilfully disobeyed thy holy commands, but we have not given Thee the chief place in our affections, nor even retained Thee in our thoughts. We have sinned. We are all as an unclean thing; sin mingles with and defiles our best services, our purest actions. We all do fade as a leaf, and our iniquities like the wind have taken us away. Yet would we take hold of thy strength, that we may be at peace with Thee. Though we are thus weak and sinful, Thou wilt not despise our cry. Thou didst show mercy to our fathers when they sought Thee. As Thou wast merciful unto them, be Thou also gracious unto us, and save us. Lift us, we pray Thee, from the dust; fill our hearts with thoughts of peace. May we enjoy the assurance of acceptance in the Beloved. Cause thy Holy Spirit ever to dwell in us richly, subduing our stubborn will, enlightening our darkened understanding, purifying our thoughts and affections, and bringing our whole nature into the obedience of Christ.

Enable us as a family ever to experience, as we have done through the past night, thy lovingkindness and tender mercy. May our beloved children live before Thee. May our relatives and friends obtain like precious faith with us, and rejoice in the possession of the peace that passeth understanding. Cause the truth to which we listened in thy house on the past day to bring forth fruit in our hearts during the week. Help us to be diligent in business, fervent in spirit, serving the Lord. May we ever be in thy hand as clay in the hands of the potter, and do Thou mould us according to thine own will, so that we may become vessels meet for thy use. Let the knowledge of thy holy name be extended on every side. There are but few that call upon thy name, or that stir up themselves to take hold upon Thee. Revive thy work, O Lord, in the midst of us. Oh, that Thou wouldest rend the heavens and come down, and, by the manifestations of power and grace, bring all mankind to thy feet. We ask all these things for the sake of Christ our Lord, who is worthy with Thyself, O Father, and the Eternal Spirit, to receive honour, and glory, and blessing, throughout all ages, world without end. Amen.

READ IN HOLY SCRIPTURE 1 PETER II.

O GOD, Thou hast laid in Zion a chief cornerstone, elect and precious, and he that believeth on Him shall not be confounded. May we, as we come to the family altar this evening, be a spiritual house, a holy priesthood, offering up spiritual sacrifices acceptable to Thee by Jesus Christ. We thank Thee for the mercies and blessings that have encompassed our path during the day. Thou hast not suffered us to want any good thing. O Lord, we will praise Thee; for Thou makest the outgoings of the morning and evening to rejoice. We pray Thee to forgive whatsoever sin we have committed to-day. We are conscious of many errors, infirmities, and backslidings. We have been as sheep going astray; but we would return to the Bishop and Shepherd of our souls. The Lord Jesus bore our sins in his own body on the tree; may we receive healing by his stripes, and, dying unto sin, live unto righteousness.

Help us, we beseech Thee, to show forth the praises of Him who hath called us out of darkness into his marvellous light. May we abstain from fleshly lusts, which war against the soul; be very careful to maintain good works; and under any wrong which we may at any time suffer, continue in well-doing, and commit ourselves to Him who judgeth righteously, following the example of Christ who suffered for us, and who has left us an example that we should follow in his steps. We thank Thee for the example of Christ. May we imbibe his Spirit, have the same mind dwelling in us that dwelleth also in Him, and be in the world even as He was. May we grow up into his likeness, and beholding in his human life the Divine pattern of what manner of persons we ought to be in all holy conversation and godliness, be changed into his image from glory to glory, as by the Spirit of the Lord.

We commend ourselves to thy care for the night. May the angels of the Lord encamp around our dwelling, and may we rest in peace beneath thy sheltering wing.

Command thy blessing upon thy universal Church. Enlarge the borders of thy kingdom. Let those who have not obtained mercy, now obtain mercy. Let those who are not thy people, soon become thy people. Bring in the Jew with the fulness of the Gentiles. Give to thy Son the heathen for his inheritance, and the uttermost parts of the earth for his possession. And let thy name be hallowed, and thy will be done on earth, even as it is in heaven. Mercifully hear us; graciously answer us, and do exceeding abundantly for us above all we ask or think, through Jesus Christ our Lord and Saviour. Amen.

[MORNING.] **FORTY-NINTH WEEK.—TUESDAY.** [EVENING.

READ IN HOLY SCRIPTURE ISAIAH LXVI.

O LORD God, have mercy upon us and hear us; receive our praises and answer our prayers. Born in sin, and guilty every day of many transgressions against Thee, we deserve not thy favour. But we are emboldened by thy gracious promises to spread our wants before Thee. Give us true contrition and sorrow of heart for our sins; fulfil thy word, and come and dwell in us, and make us the temples of God. Cleanse us from all defilement, and let the assurance of thy grace bring peace to our consciences.

We praise Thee, Holy Father, for thy countless mercies, for thy watchful care during the night, for the gifts of thy providence this morning, and, above all, for the opportunity of again kneeling at thy footstool, and, in the name of Jesus, seeking mercy and grace to help in time of need. Thou never weariest of doing us good; we pray that we may never weary of loving and serving Thee. Enlarge our hearts with a true knowledge of thine unspeakable love. Enable us to see it in all the circumstances and events of our life, and through thy grace make it the means of kindling in us a fervent love towards Thee, that it may be our highest joy to do thy will. O Lord, quicken these cold, dull hearts of ours, and inflame them with zeal for thy glory. Reveal to us so manifestly thy tenderness and grace in Christ Jesus that we may feel ashamed of our past sins, and strive more diligently to walk in the footsteps of thy dear Son.

In humble dependence on thy grace and protection, we enter on the duties of the day to which Thou hast spared us. We are weak and ignorant; O God, leave us not to ourselves; suffer us not to be led astray into the paths of evil, or to become the prey of the destroyer. While engaged in the world, preserve us from a worldly spirit. Amid the engagements of this life we pray that we may never be suffered to forget the life to come, or to bring dishonour on the name of Jesus by our inconsistency and unbelief. So mould our tempers and dispositions by the Holy Ghost, that the mind which was in Christ may be in us, and that, thinking much of his cross and passion, we may deny ourselves, for his sake, and set our affections on things above.

We would seek a blessing from thy hand for all who are dear to us. Let thy Providence watch over them, and thy Spirit train them for glory. Stretch out thy hand, O God, over the great family of man, and cause Jews and Gentiles to submit themselves to the truth. Hasten the fulfilment of thy promise that all men shall worship before Thee, and that Jesus shall see of the travail of his soul and be satisfied. Gracious Father, grant us thy mercies, for Jesus Christ's sake. Amen.

READ IN HOLY SCRIPTURE 1 PETER III.

HEAVENLY Father, we approach the mercyseat this evening, conscious of our own unworthiness, yet encouraged by the knowledge that Jesus is gone into heaven, and is now on thy right hand. We humbly confess that in many things we offend against Thee. Our own hearts condemn us; but Thou art greater than our hearts, and knowest all things. We grieve to think we should so often have broken that law which is holy, and just, and good. For his sake, who suffered for sins, and died, the just for the unjust, that he might bring us to God, we humbly entreat thy forgiveness of all our offences and shortcomings this day.

Give us, we beseech Thee, the aid of thy Holy Spirit, that we may be followers of that which is good, and may maintain a conscience void of offence towards men. But that we may also have a good conscience towards our God, let our hearts be cleansed with the blood of sprinkling. When called to suffer, with all thy children, grant that it may never be for evil doing; that the world may have no evil thing to say of us with truth. May we sanctify Thee, O Lord God, in our hearts; that living in thy fear, we may not be afraid of the terror of any that might harm us.

To these requests we would add our thanksgiving that Thou hast called us to inherit a blessing; and we praise thy name on behalf of all those who, with us, are partakers of the grace of life. Grant that they may have a good reason for the hope that is in them, and, day by day, show the power of thy grace in their hearts and lives. Make them all to be of one mind, and teach them to love as brethren. Permit us also to intercede for the many who are called Christians, but obey not the word, that they may be led to repentance by the longsuffering of our God, which still waits to be gracious. If we have any enemies who speak against us, or do us evil, O Lord, forgive them, and change their hearts; but suffer us not at any time to render evil for evil, or railing for railing, but contrariwise blessing, that we may be the followers of the meek and lowly Saviour.

And now, Father of mercies, gratefully acknowledging the many favours of another day, we commit ourselves to thy keeping, whose eyes are over thy people, and whose ears are open to their prayers. Mercifully regard with thy favour all our dear relatives and friends, and let this our evening sacrifice be acceptable in thy sight. We offer it through our great High Priest: and to the triune Jehovah, Father, Son, and Holy Spirit, be ascribed salvation, and glory, and praise, and thanksgiving, for ever and ever. Amen.

[MORNING.] **FORTY-NINTH WEEK.—WEDNESDAY.** [EVENING.

READ IN HOLY SCRIPTURE ZEPHANIAH III.

O GOD, who is a God like unto Thee, that pardoneth iniquity? We would begin this day feeling how much we owe to thy pardoning mercy, which blots out all our transgressions; and to thy forbearance and pity which has blessed us hitherto. May we learn from thy dealings of old, the holiness and the love of our God and Father; and trace in them the light of grace, which for thy children, is never quenched.

Fill us with a true hatred of sin, and in the cross of our Lord Jesus Christ, who gave himself for our sins, may we read the fearful character of that one thing which Thou dost abhor. Deepen in our hearts a spirit of true repentance, and by the power of thy Holy Spirit train us up in the knowledge of thy will, and in the fear of thy name.

O God, we beseech Thee, fulfil thy gracious promise towards this fallen world. Awaken the hearts of the unconverted in this and in all lands, that they may call upon thy name and through thy dear Son obtain pardon and peace. Make us to rejoice with all the heart, in a sweet sense of thy love in Jesus Christ. Let each of us who are now worshipping Thee go forth in the strength of the Lord, and overcome all the temptations of the world, the flesh, and the devil.

Help us in our duties this day; that we may do them in thy fear, and for thy glory. Succour us when tempted; that we may not forget Thee. Keep us from all evil, in the heart, in the thoughts, in the words of our lips, and in the actions of our life. May we find thy grace sufficient for us; and find thy strength made perfect in our weakness. From self-righteousness keep us free; and let us walk humbly before the Lord.

Sanctify to us events in thy providence. Thou rulest over all, a King for evermore. May prosperity make us thankful; and adversity lead us to discern the good which is working together in all things for thy children. Of thy great mercy give to us family blessings according to our need. May parents and children be under thy guiding care in all things; and be sheltered by thine unfailing love.

Bless with thy special favour our gracious Sovereign, and all the Royal Family. Guide and overrule the counsels of all in authority, to the happiness of our people, and the welfare of the world. May ours be the righteousness which exalteth a nation, and ours the blessedness of that people whose God is the Lord.

The sacrifice of thanksgiving for thy mercies, so rich, so constant, so satisfying, we would humbly lay at thy footstool; craving pardon, and acceptance, and thy guardian care this day, through Jesus Christ our Redeemer; to whom be all praise now and ever. Amen.

READ IN HOLY SCRIPTURE 1 PETER IV.

ONCE more, heavenly Father, we draw near to thy throne of grace with our prayers and our praises. To Thee we owe all our blessings. For life and health, food and raiment, protection from bodily dangers, and preservation from the assaults of Satan, we praise thy holy name. We are not worthy of the least of all the mercies and of all the truth which Thou hast showed unto thy servants.

Lord, we profess to be followers of thy dear Son, who gave himself to be unto us both a sacrifice for sin, and also an ensample of godly life. Forgive, we pray Thee, the many and grievous failures of our obedience during the day that is past; and may the recollection of the dying love of Jesus animate us for the time to come to live a life of holiness. Give us thy gracious Spirit to conform us to thy will. May the time past of our lives indeed suffice us to have wasted in sin and folly; and may we live the rest of our time in the flesh not to the lusts of men, but to the will of God, making it our constant aim to be unto Thee a peculiar people, zealous of good works.

Help us now at the end of another day to remember that the end of all things is at hand, and to prepare for the solemn account that we must give to Him who shall judge the quick and the dead at his appearing. Oh that the Judge may then be our Friend! Jesus, Thou advocate for sinners, plead our cause! May we be found in Thee, not having our own righteousness, but thine, the righteousness that is of God by faith. May we lie down to rest this night with the sweet hope that in Thee we are safe for time and for eternity!

And grant, O Lord, that when we shall enter upon the cares and business of another day, we may do so, not in a worldly and thoughtless, but in a prayerful, sober, watchful spirit; remembering that this is not our rest, and waiting for the coming of our Lord Jesus Christ. Seeing that the difficulties in the way of our salvation are such that even the righteous scarcely are saved, may we be thoroughly in earnest to secure eternal life. May all under this roof be of one mind in seeking the Lord.

[May we who are parents especially receive grace to train up our children for Thee, and may the dear children fear the Lord from their youth, and so escape the corruptions that are in the world.]

Lord, bless our neighbours. Make the poor rich in faith. Comfort the sorrowful. Turn the wicked to repentance. May our minister be wise to win souls. May the Queen and all in authority under her be guided by wisdom from Thee. Hasten the conversion of Jews and Gentiles, and the coming of our Lord Jesus Christ. We ask all in his name. Amen.

[Morning.]   FORTY-NINTH WEEK.—THURSDAY.   [Evening.

READ IN HOLY SCRIPTURE HABAKKUK III.

O THOU, who art glorious in holiness, fearful in praises, doing wonders, we approach Thee with reverence and godly fear. Thy glory covereth the heavens, and the earth is full of thy praise. We bless Thee that Thou hast not spoken to us only in thy majesty and thy power, but in the still, small voice of thy mercy and thy love. Thou art terrible out of thy holy places to them that provoke thine anger; but Thou art the strength and the joy of all who trust in Thee.

Give unto us, we beseech Thee, O Lord, that strong faith which will trust Thee at all times. We confess that we are prone to confide in thy mercies rather than in Thyself. Blessed be thy holy name for all our comforts: but, oh, be Thou our Comforter, then, though our labour fail, and all the pleasant things of life be withheld from us, we shall joy in Thee, the God of our salvation. We implore thy mercy on our world. Gracious and merciful God, who art slow to anger and of great kindness, make known thy saving health among all nations. We thank Thee for the knowledge of salvation through our Lord Jesus Christ; and we pray that all men may be brought to love and serve Him.

And now that another day calls us to our duties, O God, be Thou our strength. By Thee only can we resist sin, and so perform all our labour that thy sacred name may be glorified in us and by us. We bless thy faithful care and loving-kindness for the safety and the sleep we have enjoyed throughout the night. We thank Thee for the morning meal provided for our bodies, and for the spiritual food which thy Word has furnished to our souls. Let thy holy Word make music in our hearts all day, to soothe the toil of our hands, and may the glory of our Father in heaven cheer and encourage us with noble thoughts. We pray that we may faithfully discharge all our duties to our fellowmen, owing no man anything, but to love one another. Be Thou, O God the Spirit, our helper in every difficulty, our guide in perplexity, our present help in the time of trouble, and our God to all eternity. Bless with all needful good our friends and relations. Make the neighbourhood in which we dwell peaceful and happy. Deliver us from all public sins that would provoke thine indignation, and put it into the hearts of all our countrymen to seek to please Thee. O God, bless our Sovereign, and all who rule over us; our soldiers and sailors; our employers and employed. Watch over the aged and the young, and bless us, even us, O our Father, as Thou seest that we need; for we present these our supplications in the name and for the sake of our Lord Jesus Christ, to whom, with Thee and the Holy Spirit, be glory for ever. Amen.

READ IN HOLY SCRIPTURE 1 PETER V.

ALMIGHTY God, we beseech Thee graciously to behold this portion of thy family and of thy flock which Thou hast bought with thine own blood. Hear our prayers, and graciously help us. We pray that we may be at all times fed with food convenient for us, by those to whom Thou hast committed the oversight of thy Church. Preserve its ministers from low and ambitious motives, that so, having proved themselves faithful and true pastors, they may receive from the Chief Shepherd, at his appearing, a crown of glory that fadeth not away. To all thy people and sheep of thy pasture, give thy heavenly grace, that with meek hearts and due reverence the younger members of the body of Christ may submit themselves to the instruction and guidance of the older; and all, of whatever degree, be animated by the spirit of mutual subjection, forbearing one another in love. May all be clothed with the beautiful garment of humility, and enable us each one to cast our burden upon Thee, who carest for us. Let us not sleep as do others, but be watchful and obedient in all things.

We praise thy great mercy, O God, that we have been kept in safety this day. How many evils have befallen others from which we have been graciously preserved! How many have been called away from life, and opportunity, and privilege, while we are spared! Accept, O God, our thanksgivings for all thy goodness to us, and make us thankful. Especially forgive us all our sins and transgressions against Thee. We are guilty in thy sight, and confess with shame our misdoings. Have mercy upon us, and wash us in the fountain opened for sin and uncleanness. Fill us with all joy and peace in believing, and give us a good hope of eternal life.

Hear us, we beseech Thee, on behalf of all who are bound to us by the ties of kindred or friendship. Their wants are all known to Thee. Grant to them, O Lord, all gifts of grace and peace. Comfort them if sorrowing, and enrich them with the blessed tokens of thy presence. We pray for the unconverted among us. Almighty Spirit, subdue, change, and quicken their hearts. Convince them of sin, and then show them the power and sufficiency of Christ to save. [Draw the hearts of the children of our family to Thyself. Fill them with love to Jesus, and cause them from childhood to walk obediently in his footsteps.] Bless whatever has been done this day for bringing sinners to Christ, and for the increase of thy kingdom.

Guard us through the night by thy Divine care, and cause us to rest in peace and safety. We ask all for Jesus Christ's sake. Amen.

[Morning.]　　　FORTY-NINTH WEEK.—FRIDAY.　　　[Evening.

READ IN HOLY SCRIPTURE JEREMIAH I.

GOD of all power and might, who art the Author and Giver of all good things, we come before Thee to seek thy gracious favour. Give us, we beseech Thee, thy Holy Spirit to help our infirmities, for we know not what to pray for as we ought. Unworthy as we are in ourselves, we come to Thee with full confidence, in the name and through the blood of Jesus. He is thy well-beloved Son, in whom Thou art well pleased. He is worthy to receive all things for us. Accept us, good Lord, for the sake of his righteousness. Make us all thy sons and daughters in Him, and out of his fulness supply all our necessities.

Thou, Lord Jesus, art our Creator; by thine own power Thou didst form us, and for Thyself. Thou also art our Redeemer, and didst purchase us unto Thyself by thine own most precious blood. Thine, therefore, we are, and not our own, and Thee we ought to serve. Give us grace to serve Thee as we ought. Sanctify us wholly unto Thyself, as a peculiar people, zealous of good works. Mercifully assist us to show forth thy praise, not only with our lips, but in our lives. Take possession of all our hearts. Make us to be followers of God as dear children, and to walk in love one towards another, and towards all men, as Thou also lovedst us and didst give Thyself for us.

Bless each one of us in our several duties. Let all our work, of whatever kind, be begun, continued, and ended in Thee. Let the comfort and happiness of all around us be as dear to us as our own. Let all our intercourse with others be such as becomes the Gospel of Christ, so that all who know us may know us as thy people.

Bless thy Church, O gracious Father, in every land. Knit all thy people together as one in Christ Jesus, so that thy truth may be known upon earth, thy saving health among all nations. Let the glorious Gospel of the blessed God have free course and be glorified everywhere. Make thy ministering servants to be as defenced cities, and as iron pillars, and brazen walls, against every form of error, and ungodliness, and sin. Be Thou ever near to them. Uphold and strengthen them, so that none may prevail against them, and that they may be mighty through God to the pulling down of strongholds.

We would more especially intercede for thine ancient people Israel. Visit them, O Lord, with thy salvation in all lands. Remove thy judgment from the midst of them. Restore them again to thy favour, that they may yet be for a praise and a blessing throughout the earth, and that through them all nations may flow unto Thee.

We ask all in the name of Jesus Christ, our blessed Lord and Saviour. Amen.

READ IN HOLY SCRIPTURE 2 PETER I.

O GOD, the Father of our Lord Jesus Christ, we bless Thee that in thy Son, our Saviour and Redeemer, Thou hast given us all things that pertain unto life and godliness. We come to Thee this evening to supplicate the gift of thy Holy Spirit, that He may write upon each of our hearts thy gracious words contained in our evening lesson. Oh that He may come and make each of us a partaker of the Divine nature, that we may escape the corruption that is in the world through sin. Oh that He would enable us to make our calling and election sure. O Lord, how absolutely we need thy Spirit for this great and important work. Without Him we can do nothing. Come, Holy Spirit, and enlighten all our minds. Lead us each to the Lamb of God that taketh away the sin of the world, and help us to follow in his footsteps, until we safely arrive with Him in glory above.

Hear, we beseech Thee, most merciful Father, the supplications which we this evening make before Thee for our beloved relations and friends. Oh that in thine infinite mercy Thou wouldst interpose on behalf of those who are living in sin, and are exposed to the danger of the second death. Pity them, O Lord, in thy great love, and turn their feet into the way of peace and life. Sanctify, gracious Saviour, all those who are thy children. May they daily enjoy the tokens of thy presence and love, and be ever more and more prepared for the kingdom of heaven.

Have mercy, O Lord, we beseech Thee, upon a lost world. We know that Thou hast so loved the world as to give thine only-begotten Son for its salvation. Yet, O God, how many still lie under the power of darkness, without hope, because without Thee! Interpose, O Almighty God, and deliver the world from his power. Inspire all thy servants with the spirit of Jesus Christ, that in his strength they may go forth and bring the nations unto Thyself. Hasten the coming of Messiah's kingdom, that all men may be blessed in Him, that He may reign over a redeemed and regenerated world.

We now commit ourselves and each other unto thy care. We would lay ourselves down in peace, and sleep, knowing that Thou, Lord, only makest us to dwell in safety. If it be thy will, strengthen our bodies and invigorate our minds with rest and sleep, that we may be fitted for the duties of life. Enable us to live as in the prospect of the Lord's coming; and grant that when He cometh we may be found of Him in peace, without spot, and blameless, cleansed, accepted, sanctified. Hear us and answer us, Holy Father, for Jesus Christ's sake. Amen.

[Morning.] **FORTY-NINTH WEEK.—SATURDAY.** [Evening.

READ IN HOLY SCRIPTURE JEREMIAH VIII.

O LORD our God, who dwellest in the heavens, and yet hast respect unto all who draw near unto Thee in the name of thy dear Son Jesus Christ, we come unto thy throne of mercy this morning for fresh blessings and mercies, as well as renewed pardon. We know, O our God, that we are sinners in thy sight, and that the very angels are not pure before Thee. Oh, look upon us, then, in love this day, and blot out our iniquities; wash us afresh in the fountain of redeeming blood, and fill us with thy Holy Spirit, that we may think, speak, and do only such things as are well-pleasing in thy sight and tend to the glory of thy great name.

O Lord, enable us to take warning from the portion of thy Word which we have now been reading. Enable us to see and understand that the troubles and calamities of thy people of old were thy just judgments upon them for their sins and stubbornness of heart, because they had slidden back by a perpetual backsliding, and had held fast deceit, and refused to return. O Lord, turn Thou us, and we shall be turned unto Thee. Draw us by thy Holy Spirit, that we may run after Thee. Oh, make our hearts willing to hearken unto Thee now, in the time of our visitation, that we may follow Thee all the days of our life.

O God, who hast given us such holy privileges in the land of our birth; who hast left us thy blessed Word of truth to be a light to our feet and a lamp to our path; who hast sent the ministers of thy Gospel to proclaim salvation through a crucified and risen Saviour to every one that believeth in Him; who hast appointed thy holy Sabbaths to be a sign between Thee and man— O Lord, let not these things turn to our greater condemnation. Let it not be said of us that we have rejected the Word of the Lord, and there is no wisdom in us; that we have neglected thy mercies and thy warnings, and have not listened to the voice of the charmer, charm he never so wisely. The harvest is passing, the summer is ending; O Lord, let us ask our own hearts, as in thy sight, "Are we saved? Have we found the balm in Gilead for our own disease? Have we sought for the good Physician? Has He healed our souls? Are we thine by and through Him who came to open the kingdom of heaven to all believers?"

O God, take us under thy care and keeping this day. Watch over us for good, and over all of whom we should make mention in our prayers. May we acknowledge Thee in all we do, and so strive to let our light shine before men, that they, seeing our good works, may glorify thy holy name, through Jesus Christ our Lord. Amen.

READ IN HOLY SCRIPTURE 2 PETER II.

O GOD, by whose almighty power we have been preserved this day, we desire now to thank Thee for all thy blessings, beseeching Thee to forgive, for thy dear Son's sake, whatever we have thought, said, or done amiss this day. We beseech Thee also of thy great mercy to watch over, protect, and defend us during this night. Preserve us from all danger, and raise us up in peace and safety to see the light of another Lord's day. Prepare our minds, O Lord, by thy Holy Spirit, for all the employments of the morrow, and grant that we may derive spiritual profit and benefit from all its sacred services, and may grow in grace and in the knowledge of our Lord and Saviour Jesus Christ. We beseech Thee to enlighten all ministers of thy Church with true knowledge and understanding of thy Word, and to grant that both by their preaching they may set it forth, and in their lives may exhibit it according to their teaching.

We also beseech Thee, O Lord, to bring into the way of truth all who are in error, that they may be led to teach the truth faithfully, according to thy Word. Have mercy also upon all men, and grant that they may be brought to the saving knowledge of thy truth, and be saved through Christ for ever. Give thy abundant blessing upon all efforts which are being made for gathering in Christ's people out of the world, and stir up all thy people diligently and constantly to pray for the coming in of thy kingdom. Grant also that we and all thy people may labour, and strive, and pray to be instrumental in turning from their evil ways all those whom we know to be living in sin and error, that they may obtain salvation through our Lord and Saviour Jesus Christ.

We also beseech Thee, O Lord, to bring into a right mind, so that they may duly regard thy holy day, all who now encourage the use of thy Sabbaths as days of pleasure or worldly profit; that they may cease to hold out any inducements or temptations to others to neglect their religious privileges and duties for amusement or earthly gain; and do Thou dispose them and all orders of society to a better observance of thy Sabbaths as days of holy rest for all classes of the community. Grant also that we ourselves may steadfastly persevere unto the end in well-doing, to thy honour and glory.

We implore thy choicest blessings for all who are dear to us. Look upon them in thy great mercy, and according to their need do thou graciously help them. We ask all for them and for ourselves through our Saviour Jesus Christ, who liveth and reigneth with Thee and the Holy Ghost, ever one God, world without end. Amen.

[Morning.] **FIFTIETH WEEK.—LORD'S DAY.** [Evening.

READ IN HOLY SCRIPTURE JEREMIAH XVII.

O LORD, the hope of thy people, the confidence of all who put their trust in Thee, draw near unto us on this the morning of thy holy day, for we come to Thee in the name of Jesus, whom Thou hearest always.

As we approach Thee, we would not regard iniquity in our hearts, we would cherish no secret sin, nor allow iniquity to cleave unto us. Search and try our ways, and see if there be any way of wickedness in us. Cleanse us from our secret faults, and keep us from presumptuous sins.

We acknowledge that we have been ever too ready to make self our aim; in heart to depart from Thee, and to look for help from ourselves; but henceforth we would more entirely own our dependence on Thee. Heal us, O Lord, and we shall be healed; save us, and we shall be saved; and to Thee will we ascribe all the praise.

We rejoice in the return of the day when it is said unto us, "Let us go up into the house of the Lord." And we thank Thee that the Word of the Lord is so freely and fully distributed in these our days. May we receive it with meekness, and may it be the means of our salvation, leading us to faith in the Lord Jesus Christ, and to a cheerful obedience to thy holy commandments.

Grant thy special presence to all assemblies in the houses of God in our land. Assist with thy Holy Spirit the preachers of thy truth. Bind all Christians together in the bonds of true fellowship; and wherever the good seed of the Word is sown, prepare men's hearts to receive it, and to bring forth fruit with patience. Bless all seminaries of sound learning and religious education, that there never may be wanting a supply of persons duly qualified to serve Thee in all important positions both in the Church and in the State. Grant long life and prosperity to our beloved Sovereign and the Royal Family, and that, this life ended, they may receive a crown of glory which fadeth not away.

We pray for our relations, friends, neighbours, and all our fellow countrymen. Bring them all to the knowledge of thy name, and to faith in the only Redeemer.

Show to those who are in error the light of thy truth, that they may return into the way of righteousness. Have mercy upon those all who are disposed to neglect or profane thy holy day; show them their sin, give them a better mind, teach them that Thou hast said, "Them that honour me I will honour, and those that despise me shall be lightly esteemed." And grant to us all that, by keeping diligently thy Sabbaths here, we may be the better prepared for the eternal rest of thy heavenly kingdom hereafter, through Jesus Christ our Lord. Amen.

READ IN HOLY SCRIPTURE 2 PETER III.

WE thank Thee, O God, that we are spared to the close of another day, and that we may come in praise and prayer to Thee, with whom one day is as a thousand years, and a thousand years as one day.

Impart unto us and preserve within us a simple and immovable faith in thy holy Word. May we follow it with humble, diligent, trustful obedience. If there be men around us professedly or practically disbelieving and despising thy Word, guard us, we beseech Thee, from falling into the same spirit; cause our faith and love to be thereby deepened, since Thou hast foretold that the unbeliever and the scoffer shall arise. Through all that is dark and perplexing to our minds in the condition and ways of the world, may we be assured that our unseen Father is working out his own ends. Let no seeming delay in the fulfilment of thy promises cause us to mistrust Thee. Let no tarrying of the punishment of sin make us careless. Grant that the longsuffering of God may work a deep repentance in the hearts of sinners.

We earnestly ask to be rightly impressed with the solemn truth of the coming day of the Lord: for its suddenness may we be prepared. Oh that our sins may be pardoned and washed away in the blood of the Lamb, that we may be able to pass its scrutiny, to be calm in its terrors, and to rejoice in its decisions. Let thy blessed Spirit quicken the hope of glory in our hearts, and help us to become the manner of persons we ought to be in all holy conversation and godliness.

Give unto us this night, O most merciful Father, the blessings that are specially suited to the close of a Christian Sabbath-day. Deepen every holy impression that has been produced in us. Give us thy strength to carry out every holy resolution we have formed. May it be with more spirituality of mind that we return, if spared to see another morning, to our daily work and cares.

Water, we beseech Thee, in the heart of every hearer of the Gospel to-day, the seed of truth that has been sown. May the awakened sinner find no escape from his convictions and fears but in his Saviour. May every Christian who has been raised to nearer fellowship with God this day be kept from sinking back into worldliness again. May a heavenly peace and comfort, springing from the words of truth they have heard, now fill the hearts of sufferers and mourners. May those who have faithfully preached, or taught, or visited, or conversed in the service of the Gospel, rest in the blessed confidence that they have been labouring for God, and sowing imperishable seed. Hear, answer, and help us for the sake of Jesus Christ our Lord. Amen.

[MORNING.] FIFTIETH WEEK.—MONDAY. [EVENING.

READ IN HOLY SCRIPTURE JEREMIAH XXIII. 1–32.   READ IN HOLY SCRIPTURE 1 JOHN I.

BLESSED and praised be thy name, O Thou Shepherd of Israel! Thou neither slumberest nor sleepest, but in tender compassion to our helpless condition, dost keep watch and ward over thy people. We thank Thee that Thou hast permitted us again to assemble around the family altar to offer up our praises and thanksgivings, and to implore thy blessing.

Thou hast taught us that the welfare of the soul is of all things the most needful; do Thou in mercy so influence our minds, that, amidst the anxieties of this world, we forget not the things of the world to come. For our soul's welfare, we beseech Thee continue to us the blessing of wise and faithful pastors, men after thine own heart, who shall feed thy flock, and shall neither scatter nor destroy the sheep of thy pasture; but, above all, give us grace to seek the aid of thy Holy Spirit to guide us into all truth. Grant that our desires may be ever unto Thee, and not unto ourselves; to do thy will, and not our own. Enable us to love and serve Thee, and to delight in the way of thy commands. Hasten, we beseech Thee, the time when the knowledge of the Lord shall cover the earth as the waters cover the sea; and when judgment and justice shall dwell in the land; when Judah shall be saved, and Israel shall dwell safely. Dispose us, we beseech Thee, to prize aright the counsels of thy Word, and cause us so to take heed unto our ways that no unchristian actions may be seen in our lives, nor unholy speech be heard proceeding from our lips.

Unworthy as we are, set us not in a slippery path, and bring not evil upon us; but bless to our good the means of grace, and incline those who minister in holy things to seek that wisdom which is from on high, that they may not cause thy people to err, as did the teachers of old time. Preserve us, we beseech Thee, from all participation in the sinful ways of worldly men. Let us not strengthen the hands of evil doers, but rather seek to turn them from their evil ways; and to this end, give us grace to remember the assurance of thy Word, that a day will come when Thou wilt enter into judgment, and none shall be able to hide himself from thy sight. Prepare us for that day that we may give up our account with joy.

O Thou who fillest the heavens and the earth with thy presence, accompany thy Word with power, and grant that it may be like fire to consume the dross, and like a hammer to break the stony heart, so that sinners may be converted unto Thee and live; and grant that we may live this day as thy believing, loving, and obedient people, for Jesus Christ's sake, to whom with Thee and the Holy Ghost be everlasting praise. Amen.

ALMIGHTY God, our heavenly Father, help us, thine unworthy servants, to make our common supplications unto Thee. May our prayer be heard and answered through the merits of our gracious Saviour.

We rejoice, heavenly Father, in the assurance given us in thy Holy Word that if we confess our sins, Thou art faithful and just to forgive us our sins, and to cleanse us from all unrighteousness. May the blessedness of perfect pardon be the possession of each soul now before Thee. Blessed Redeemer, may we, who have never seen Thee with our mortal eyes, behold Thee by faith, and become thy true disciples, thy loving and obedient followers.

We have reason to bless Thee, O our Father, not only for the glorious hope of everlasting life through Jesus Christ, but also for the constant care and watchful providence which have this day been our guard from many evils. Thou hast mercifully supplied our wants. Thou hast enabled us to discharge our daily duties. The health that we possess, our reason, and all our faculties of mind and body, come from Thee. It is of the Lord's mercies that we are not consumed. Great is thy faithfulness. Oh, make us thankful for what we enjoy, patient and resigned under all that we suffer; and thus may we prove ourselves to be the children of our Father in heaven.

Have pity upon those who call not upon thy name. The dark places of the earth are full of the habitations of cruelty. Let iniquity no longer abound. Let thy Gospel be everywhere received, and the Saviour's love be felt in the heart, uniting men in a holy brotherhood. Prosper the labours of faithful preachers of the cross.

Grant, Lord, that it may be our chief concern, as a family, to glorify Thee. May we delight to do thy will. Make us useful and happy in our various stations of life, and enable us at last to obtain a place amongst thy redeemed people.

And now be pleased, gracious Father, to receive us this night into thy keeping. Suffer no evil to befall us. Be with our relations, and friends, and neighbours. Visit them with thy salvation. Convince of sin all such as have erred. Bring back the wanderer to the fold of the good Shepherd. Have mercy upon the young in years. Let them not depart from Thee. Establish and confirm the weak-hearted. Succour the tempted. Relieve the distressed. Comfort all that mourn. Guide such as are in perplexity and difficulty into the right way. Console the aged, and let their latter days be bright with the promise of the heavenly inheritance. And all this we beg for Jesus Christ's sake. Amen.

[Morning.] FIFTIETH WEEK.—TUESDAY. [Evening.

READ IN HOLY SCRIPTURE JEREMIAH XXXVI.

READ IN HOLY SCRIPTURE 1 JOHN II.

BLESSED Lord, who hast caused all holy Scriptures to be written for our learning, we pray Thee to make us to receive all thy Word as the Word of God. Endue us with heavenly wisdom. May that same Spirit who inspired holy men of old, now abide in our hearts, to enable us to understand the Bible and to show us the things of Christ; that so, by comfort and patience of thy holy Word, we may eschew all evil, and over hold fast the blessed hope of everlasting life, which Thou hast given us in thy Son Jesus Christ.

Great is the anger and the wrath which Thou hast pronounced against impenitent sinners. Yet, O Lord, Thou art a gracious God, full of tender pity and compassion. Thou dost threaten, in order that men may return from their evil ways, and that Thou mayest forgive their iniquity and their sin. Thou willest not the death of a sinner. Oh that men would see the goodness of the Lord! We pray Thee to put forth thy great power, and come among us. Melt the hard hearts of those who sin against their own souls, and draw them to Jesus. O Lord, pardon their unbelief, and give them grace to receive with meekness the engrafted Word which is able to save their souls.

Most gracious God, help us to contend earnestly for the faith once delivered to the saints. Enable us to speak the truth in love, and to commend the truth by our Christian behaviour. Help us to be living epistles, known and read of all men, that the gainsayers may be rebuked when they perceive the grace of God in us. Father of mercies, we confess with deep sorrow how little our lives adorn the Gospel of Christ. Sanctify us by the Word of truth. Make us more meek, more gentle, more patient, more full of loving-kindness and charity. May the fruits of faith abound in us, that so the Gospel of our blessed Saviour may be glorified in us, and sinners may be converted unto Thee.

O Lord our God, be with us this day in our going out and coming in. Prosper upon us the work of our hands. Help us to be diligent in business, fervent in spirit, serving the Lord.

Bless every member of our families. Preserve their bodies in health. Bless their souls. Convert, by thy grace, those who know Thee not. [Especially we entreat Thee to look with tender care upon the little children in our family.] Bless all thy people with increasing faith and love. Brighten their hope; and when all the days of life are past, and their appointed work is done, may they rest in Jesus.

We heartily thank Thee, O Lord, for all thy mercies, and beseech Thee to receive our prayers for Christ's sake. Amen.

O THOU that hearest prayer, Thou hast assured us that if we ask we shall receive, and that if we seek we shall find, listen to our supplications, and send us not empty away, but fill us with peace and joy in believing.

We bless thy holy name that we can make mention of One whom Thou hearest always. We have an Advocate with the Father, Jesus Christ the Righteous, who is the propitiation for our sins, and not for ours only, but also for the sins of the whole world. We beseech Thee to pardon and accept us, for Jesus Christ's sake, granting us in this world the blessings of thy salvation, and in the world to come life everlasting.

All things around us are changing; but thou art the same, and thy years have no end. Enable us evermore to rest our weary hearts upon the promise of thy Son: "Lo, I am with you always, even unto the end of the world."

Help us to be forbearing and forgiving, that loving our brother we may abide in the light. Keep us from wrath, envy, malice, and uncharitableness. Make us like unto Him who, when He was reviled, reviled not again; who, when He was persecuted, threatened not. May the same mind be in us which was in Christ Jesus our Lord.

We bless Thee for all the bounties of another day; and now that the evening time has come, help us to remember the evening of life, and prepare us all to meet our God.

Sanctify unto us all the events, the sorrows and joys, the trials and crosses, of this day. Incline us to honour the Lord with our substance, and with the first-fruits of all our gains.

Teach us to die indeed unto the world, that we may live unto our God. Help us to crucify the flesh with its affections and lusts; to set our affections on things above, and not on things of the earth; and when the place which knows us now shall know us no more for ever, then, absent from the body, may we be present with the Lord.

Send down, we beseech Thee, upon our hearts the dew of thy Holy Spirit, and enrich us with thy heavenly grace. Bless all who are near and dear to us everywhere. Comfort them in all their sorrows. Cheer them by the light of thy blessed presence, and may we meet at last where there will be no more separation, and no more death, but where we shall be together with the Lord.

Pardon all our faults, and follies, and sins. Wash us in the blood of the Lamb, and enable us to rejoice in God, by whom we have received reconciliation and peace. Now unto Him who loved us, and washed us in his own blood, be praise and glory for ever and ever. Amen.

[Morning.] **FIFTIETH WEEK.—WEDNESDAY.** [Evening.

READ IN HOLY SCRIPTURE LAMENTATIONS III. 22—41.

LET us lift up our hearts unto God in the heavens, assured that He is ever good to them that wait for Him.

We approach Thee, heavenly Father, as the Sovereign Disposer of all events; out of whose mouth proceedeth whatsoever evil and good befalls thy creatures, so that none saith, and it cometh to pass, when the Lord commandeth it not. Accept our grateful thanks for thy numberless bounties. It is of thy goodness that we are not consumed, because thy compassions fail not. Thy mercies are new every morning, and to thy hand we trace all the temporal and spiritual blessings by which we, this day, find ourselves surrounded. Continue them to us, we beseech Thee, for Christ's sake, in wise and gracious abundance. Suffer us not to misuse any of them to our own injury; but in the midst of our comforts may we frequently search and try our ways and turn afresh to the Lord. We are assured that Thou dost not afflict willingly, nor needlessly grieve the children of men. Whensoever, therefore, it shall seem good to Thee to cause us grief, teach us to bear the yoke with silent and confiding submission. May we prove how good it is both to hope and quietly wait for thy salvation. Let our sorrows deepen our humility; may we put our mouth in the very dust, feeling how far our chastisements fall short of our deserts. Above all things, dispose our souls to claim and enjoy the Lord as our portion. Help us to do so this day, and on all our days; and when heart and flesh fail, be Thou the strength of our hearts and our portion for ever!

We would not limit our supplications to the little circle now kneeling at thy footstool. Bestow all blessings, O Lord, upon our relatives, friends, and neighbours, especially upon such as are peculiarly dear to us. Shower down upon them thy choicest gifts, and from thy dealings, whether indulgent or severe, enable them to derive the highest good. Let thy favour rest upon our native land. Let thy Holy Spirit work through thy Word, and gather many souls into the kingdom of thy Son. We confess that unless thy compassions had exceeded our provocations, we had long ago been rejected, and discarded like thine ancient people Israel. We would plead for that once favoured family. Thou hast promised that Thou wilt not cast them off for ever. Hasten the time when all Israel shall be saved, and when their recovery shall be as life from the dead to our fallen race; and the kingdoms of this world shall become the kingdoms of our God and his Christ.

We ask these things for ourselves and others, in the name of the same Jesus Christ our Lord. Amen.

READ IN HOLY SCRIPTURE 1 JOHN III.

WE approach thy mercy seat, O Lord, through the mediation of thy well-beloved Son; rejoicing that there is forgiveness with Thee and plenteous redemption, and that those who come to Thee Thou wilt in no wise cast out. Have mercy upon us, O, Lord, according to thy loving-kindness, and according to the multitude of thy tender mercies blot out all our transgressions. For we acknowledge our sins unto Thee. In many things we all offend and come short of thy glory. We have gone astray like lost sheep. We have done the things which we ought not to have done, and have left undone the things we ought to have done; and there is no health in us. Through Jesus Christ, who was delivered for our offences, we beseech Thee, O Lord, to pardon the iniquity of thy servants. May our transgressions be blotted out as a thick cloud, and as a cloud our sins. Cause thy face to shine upon us, be gracious to us, and give us peace.

Oh, how great is thy goodness which Thou hast laid up for them that fear Thee! Thou hast given them the unsearchable riches of Christ; called them to thy kingdom and glory; bestowed upon them the adoption of children; sent forth the Spirit of thy Son into their hearts, whereby they cry Abba Father; given them eternal life; and prepared for them a place at thy right hand. Lord, what is man that Thou art mindful of him, and the Son of man that Thou visitest him? We are not worthy of the least of all thy mercies, and Thou hast blessed us with all spiritual blessings in heavenly places in Christ.

Oh, let not thy grace be in vain. May we taste that Thou art gracious, and all be partakers of thy great salvation. Shed abroad thy love in our hearts. Deliver us from the dominion of sin, and destroy within us all the works of the devil. Strengthen us to live by faith and not by sight; and may it be manifest to all that we are thine, by the Spirit that is within us.

May the mind that was in Christ Jesus be also in us, and may we be filled with the Holy Ghost, so that we may bring forth the fruits of good living, and be to the praise and glory of thy grace, wherein Thou hast made us accepted in the Beloved.

Grant that all men may hear of the great love wherewith Thou hast loved us, that they may believe and be saved. Let all the ends of the earth see the salvation of our God.

And now, O Father, cover us with thy feathers; let no evil come nigh our dwelling; preserve us to thy everlasting kingdom, where there is no more night. We ask all through Jesus Christ, our only Lord and Saviour. Amen.

[Morning.] **FIFTIETH WEEK.—THURSDAY.** [Evening.]

READ IN HOLY SCRIPTURE EZEKIEL XIV.

O GRACIOUS and merciful God, who hast granted to us the light of another day, we will direct our prayer unto Thee, and look up. Be with us always, and especially at the hour of prayer. Sanctify us to be thy priests to serve Thee, and grant that the holy thoughts and desires of our morning prayers may not pass away like the morning cloud, but may abide with us, so that we may wait on Thee in spirit all the day long.

We humbly own thy great goodness in delivering us and our land from all forms of outward and visible idolatry. But we confess with conscious shame our continual proneness to inward idolatry. Thou mightest justly set thy face against us, because we have set up our idols in our hearts. We are verily guilty, O Lord, before Thee. Pardon us, we pray Thee, for thy dear Son's sake, and help us by thy grace to give our hearts unreservedly to Thee. Deliver us from the sin of loving and serving the creature more than Thee, our Creator. Save us from selfishness and self-pleasing; from trusting in an arm of flesh; from excessive devotion to business; and from all undue anxiety about earthly things. Sanctify our wills. Cleanse our affections. Purify our imagination, and cast out everything that defileth. Occupy our whole souls with thy presence; set up thy throne in our hearts, and rule there supreme, so that we may be thy people, and Thou mayest be our God.

All-seeing God, if we regard iniquity in our hearts, Thou wilt not be inquired of by us. Suffer, then, no iniquity to get the dominion over us, but grant to us an entire sincerity of heart before Thee, that our prayer may be the prayer of the upright.

Keep this family, all its members present or absent, safe under thy protection, and far from every evil way; and grant that we may walk this day and evermore in thy faith and fear.

In mercy preserve our country from all those sins which bring down thy judgments upon a guilty people; and if Thou shouldest visit us for public chastisement and correction, be gracious still to preserve amongst us a large remnant of thine own people, who shall pour out before Thee the effectual, fervent prayer of the righteous. And do Thou teach them so to plead with Thee, after the manner of Moses, and Job, and Daniel, that the great Intercessor in thy temple above may receive their prayers into the golden censer, and present them with acceptance before thy throne.

Be as the dew unto Israel. Extend thy compassions as far as the wants and miseries of this fallen world, and bring the heathen into thine inheritance. We ask all for the sake of Jesus. Amen.

READ IN HOLY SCRIPTURE 1 JOHN IV.

O MERCIFUL Father, we kneel before Thee this evening as thine own children. Do Thou grant unto us the teaching of thine own Spirit, that we may believe the love wherewith Thou hast loved us, in sending thine only begotten Son into the world, that we might live through Him. Help us to examine our own hearts: whether this thy gracious will is being accomplished in us; whether we are living through Him, and are therefore no more of the world, and speaking of the world. May thy love constrain us to love Thee, and daily to confess Thee in our words and actions. Forgive us, for our Saviour Jesus Christ's sake, the many occasions on which we have failed thus to confess Thee to-day. We are ashamed that we have so little shown our grateful sense of thy love to us, by self-denying love to others. We too much please ourselves, rather than others for their souls' good. Oh, give unto us more of this blessed gift of love; of love to Thee, and of love to man for thy sake.

Grant unto us also, by the same Spirit, to have a right judgment in all things. Help us to try all doctrines brought before us by that Word which He inspired, and thus to overcome all those temptations to wander to the right hand and to the left, which are continually presented to us in the world.

Vouchsafe unto us so firm a faith in thy love through Christ, that we may render unto Thee not the trembling service of slaves, but the willing, thankful, loving service of children. May we ever ask, What shall I render unto the Lord for all his benefits toward me? How shall I show my love to Him who first loved me? Do Thou, in answer to this desire, open before us doors of Christian usefulness, and bestow on us the honour and the privilege of being fellow-labourers with Thee. May we, like Philip of old, tell others of that Saviour whom we have found, and invite them to taste and see how gracious He is. Oh, grant that if Thou dost permit us to go forth to our daily work to-morrow, it may be with the prayerful determination that, as we have opportunity, and according to our ability, we will speak of the Saviour to those with whom we may have to do.

And now, O heavenly Father, we commend ourselves to thy care for this night. Watch over all our dear relations and friends. Bless them both in body and soul. Have pity upon any amongst them who are living at a distance from Thee, and do Thou bring them nigh by the blood of Christ. Extend the preaching of thy Gospel throughout the world, and gather sinners unto thy dear Son. We offer all our prayers in his name, who loved us, and gave himself for us, Jesus Christ our Saviour. Amen.

[Morning.] **FIFTIETH WEEK.—FRIDAY.** [Evening.]

READ IN HOLY SCRIPTURE EZEKIEL XVIII. 20—32.

O LORD God, the holy, just, and true, we bless thy name for the glad tidings of thy mercy, for the assurance that Thou wouldest not the death of a sinner, but rather that he should turn unto Thee and live. Accept us, O Lord, guilty, and unworthy though we are ever to come unto Thee, for the sake of Jesus, thy dear Son; and now, in this our morning worship, lift up the light of thy countenance upon us and be gracious unto us.

We praise Thee, O God, for the mercies of the night. Oh, how great is thy goodness to us! how ceaseless thy love! how unwearied thy patience! how multiplied are thy bounties! how wonderful and passing knowledge the riches of thy grace! Forgive, O Lord, the coldness and deadness of our hearts under the experience of all this thy love. We are ashamed that we feel it so little, and so feebly show our thankfulness. Take our hearts, holy Father, and mould them anew by thy Spirit, that we may love Thee more and serve Thee better than we have ever done.

In the prospect of the day's duties, we look up to Thee for strength and wisdom. Create in us a desire to do thy will in all things, and to seek such things as please Thee. We pray that the station of life in which Thou hast placed us may be as a training school for heaven, and that in all our intercourse with others it may be seen that we are the disciples of Him who was meek and lowly in heart. Be Thou, O Lord, with us; and enable us, wherever we are, to feel that Thou art near, our Father, our Friend, our Guide, even unto death. Our hearts are frail, our faith is feeble, our steadfastness uncertain. Do thou mercifully quicken and establish us in thy ways, that our footsteps slip not. Kindle within us a fervent love for all that is holy and good, that we may have the spiritual mind which is life and peace. Stir up our souls to a holy jealousy against sin, and such a zeal for thine honour as will make us cast away all our transgressions, as those who are alive from the dead, through Jesus Christ our Lord.

We pray for all who are dear to us. [We entreat thy special favour for the children of this family. Make them thy children in Christ Jesus, and give them the Holy Ghost, even from earliest years, consecrating them and enduing them with a spirit of love to Thee, obedience to their parents, and a desire to please Thee.] Look in mercy on the ungodly, and on all who are living for things temporal, and forgetting the things eternal. Melt their hearts by thy grace, and turn their feet unto the ways of godliness and peace.

We pray for every blessing in the name of Jesus Christ our Lord. Amen.

READ IN HOLY SCRIPTURE 1 JOHN V.

O HOLY and eternal Lord God, we kneel before Thee this evening as guilty sinners. We have all of us transgressed against Thee. During this very day, now closing over us, we have all sinned against Thee. Even if Thou hast graciously preserved us from open and evident transgression of thy commandments, yet how far, how very far! have we been from that entire devotedness to thy service, and that entire conformity to thy will, which Thou dost justly claim at our hands. We cannot present unto Thee a single action which shall stand the just severity of thy judgment. This is true, O Lord, of the best of us. Perhaps there are some of us who have to confess that in everything we have said or done since the morning we followed our own desires entirely, and have not sought to please Thee. Verily, and in any case, we are a company of sinners.

And as we confess this, O Lord, with our lips, so we beseech Thee to work in us, that we may feel it in our hearts. Make us to know our transgressions and our sins. Make us to see in how many things we have all gone astray like lost sheep. And cause us also, we beseech Thee, to be sensible of the exceeding sinfulness of all sin, and to see how evil a thing it is even to desire what thy sovereign wisdom has seen fit to forbid; or, as we all of us so often do, even to forget Thee in our hearts. Impress upon us by thy Holy Spirit, as Thou only canst do, these great truths. Impress upon us also our own weakness and inability to resist, so that we may see that our only safety is in Thee. Enable us finally to tread Satan under our feet, and keep us ever by thy grace from falling back from Thee, for Thou art all our strength, even Thou alone. O Lord God, we freely acknowledge that if we are saved at all from this great world that lieth in wickedness, it has not been of ourselves. It has been by the power of thy regenerating Spirit, and for the sake of thy Son. And in so far, therefore, as this is true of any of us, we would lift up our hearts to Thee now in the spirit of devout thanksgiving.

We thank Thee also for the many encouragements held out to us all. What golden sentences we have just read! This is the record that God hath given to us eternal life, and this life is in his Son. If we ask anything according to his will, he heareth us. Oh, that these heavenly promises may follow us to-night when we separate, and give earnestness, and life, and success to our private prayers before Thee.

We ask this, and all that Thou seest good for ourselves and for those who are dear to us, for our Saviour's sake. Amen.

[349]

[Morning.] **FIFTIETH WEEK.—SATURDAY.** [Evening.

READ IN HOLY SCRIPTURE EZEKIEL XX. 33—49.

READ IN HOLY SCRIPTURE 2 & 3 JOHN.

O LORD of hosts, the God of Israel, that dwellest between the cherubim, Thou art the God, even Thou alone, of all the kingdoms of the earth. Thou art a God that doest wonders; Thou hast declared thy strength among the people; Thou hast with thine arm redeemed thy people, the sons of Jacob and Joseph. We thank Thee for the glorious things Thou hast spoken of Zion. Hasten, we beseech Thee, the time when Thou wilt bring thine ancient people again to thine holy mountain, and be sanctified in them before the heathen. Guide them under thy rod, O Shepherd of Israel, into the bond of the covenant. Soon may they look on Him whom they have pierced and mourn, and serve Thee with acceptance on the mountain of the height of Israel. Soon may Jew and Gentile be one fold, under the one good Shepherd.

Awake, awake, put on strength, O arm of the Lord. O Shepherd of Israel, shine forth. Speed the triumphs of the Gospel. Bless all preachers this day in their preparatory studies. On the coming Sabbath, may they be as flames of fire; as polished shafts in thy hand, may they reach the hearts of many. Gird thy sword upon thy thigh, O most mighty. May thine arrows be sharp in the hearts of thine enemies. May these enemies everywhere become thy friends, and all the ends of the earth see the salvation of our God.

Give us grace, O Lord, to take warning from thine ancient people, and to take encouragement from the riches of thy forbearance and mercy. We are as prone as they were to forget thy works and thy wonders in providence and grace. Help us to set our hope in God, and not to forget his commandments. If Thou shouldest see fit to try us as silver is tried, and lay affliction upon our loins, give us strength to bear it, and grace to improve it, so that the result may be found, through the blessing of thy Holy Spirit, the Sanctifier and the Comforter, unto praise, and honour, and glory, at the appearing of the Lord Jesus.

O Thou Keeper of Israel, who dost neither slumber nor sleep, we thank Thee for the refreshing rest and providential protection thou hast vouchsafed to us during the past night. Bless us as a family, and as a family circle, present and absent, in soul, body, and spirit. We would lay our living powers anew, as a free-will offering, on thine altar, and serve Thee this day with our bodies and with our spirits, which are thine. Mercifully forgive us all our sins for Christ's sake, and give us peace and joy in believing. Fit us for this day's duties; support us under its trials; arm us against its temptations; and the glory shall be thine, through the blessed Redeemer. Amen.

BLESSED Lord, who hast graciously made known to us, through thy Word, the truth as it is in Jesus, grant that this saving truth may dwell in us, and be with us for ever. May we abide in it and walk in it. Enable us to give a cordial acceptance to the faithful saying, that Christ Jesus came into the world to save sinners. And may we be so rooted and grounded in this faith as to be proof against the many deceivers who are entered into the world. If any come unto us and bring not this saving doctrine, may we give him no welcome and no hearing, but shun him as a deceiver and an antichrist. May we seek rather to be fellow-helpers to the truth, and be always ready, by our prayers and contributions, to strengthen the hands of those who carry it abroad. Oh, that we may fervently fulfil that law of Christ which teaches his believing people to love one another; and may every other commandment He has given us to keep be written in our hearts. Let us not be of the number of those who love the pre-eminence, but of those rather who are clothed with humility, and in honour prefer others above themselves. Give us grace to shun that which is evil and to follow that which is good, so as to have a good report of all men and of the truth itself. Help us to do faithfully whatsoever we do, to the glory of thy great name, and ever fill us with the gifts of thy Spirit in all wisdom and understanding.

Bless, O Lord, our dear relatives and friends. May they in all things prosper and be in health; but especially may their souls prosper. Oh that, like thine apostle, we may have no greater joy than to hear that our dear friends walk in truth. Alas! that there are so many in our land who abide not in the doctrine of Christ, but speak perverse things to draw away disciples after them. Oh, bring into the way of truth all such as have thus erred, and may believers be daily added to the Lord, multitudes both of men and women.

Have mercy, Lord, we beseech Thee, on the perishing heathen nations; bless the work of those societies who send to them the Gospel; and multiply a thousandfold the number of those to whom there is this grace given to preach among the Gentiles the unsearchable riches of Christ. Accept, gracious Lord, our thanksgivings for all the mercies of the week; prepare us for the holy duties of to-morrow; and grant that we may give a joyful hearing to the glad tidings of salvation. Prepare the hearts of all who shall hear the Gospel preached or be taught it in schools, and grant that it may be the spiritual birthday of many, for Christ's sake, in whose name we ask protection for the night and all other mercies. Amen.

[Morning.] **FIFTY-FIRST WEEK.—LORD'S DAY.** [Evening.]

READ IN HOLY SCRIPTURE EZEKIEL XXXIII.

READ IN HOLY SCRIPTURE JUDE.

O GOD, Thou that art the God and Father of our Lord Jesus Christ, the Father of mercies, the God of all grace, bow down now the ears of thy love to us, who now draw near unto Thee in prayer and praise. We bless Thee for all thine overflowing goodness to us, especially for the gift of thy beloved Son, to be unto us wisdom, righteousness, sanctification, and redemption; and for the outpouring of thy Holy Spirit, to soften our hard hearts, to convince us of our manifold need, to show to us our ruined state, by nature and by sin, to bring us to the saving knowledge of thine eternal love, and to faith in all the work of our redeeming Jesus. We bless Thee, too, for all the means of grace.

We humbly confess unto Thee our grievous neglect and misuse, in times past, of our religious privileges. While we cry unto Thee for the pardon of all past sins, through the blood of the Lamb, especially do we pray Thee to blot out the iniquity of our Sabbath days. We bewail that we have often come before Thee, as thy people come, and seemingly tendered the worship of our lips, while our hearts have been straying far away. We bewail that we have often heard the preacher's testimony of thy saving grace, unmelted and unmoved. May it be so with us no more. Suffer no further neglect of this holy day to testify against us.

Be with us, we pray Thee, when we enter thy house. Sanctify us wholly. May we confess our sins as they who feel the burden to be grievous. Enable us to pray as they who wrestle with their God for life. May we praise as they who feel how tenderly Thou hast dealt with them. Enable us to adore as they who know the preciousness of grace, and are rejoicing in hope of the glories of heaven. Cause thy Word to come to us this day with power. May we learn more of Christ than we have ever learned before. Cause our love to be kindled into brighter flame. May we be led to more entire surrender of ourselves, body, soul, and spirit, to thy holy service. Especially do we pray Thee to bless the labours of thy faithful ministers. Give them wisdom, zeal, tenderness, and affection; firm determination to warn the sinner, and boldness to proclaim the unsearchable riches of Christ. To all the congregations of true worshippers, give thy heavenly grace. Add to thy Church many that shall be saved. Grant that the wicked may forsake their ways, and the unrighteous their thoughts, and that there may be joy among the angels in heaven over many a repenting sinner. Have mercy on those who are accustomed to profane thy holy day, and give them repentance unto salvation. Hear us and bless us for Jesus Christ's sake. Amen.

ALMIGHTY God, we desire at the close of another Sabbath day, to present ourselves together before Thee in the name of thy Son Jesus Christ. We were born in sin, and, if Thou hadst left us to ourselves, we should still have been enemies unto Thee by wicked works; but Thou hast received and sanctified them that believe, and called them unto thine eternal glory by Christ Jesus. We adore Thee, O God, for thine inestimable love in thine only begotten Son. We thank Thee also for the various means of grace which Thou hast provided for us; the Scriptures which Thou hast caused to be written for our learning; and the Sabbath, whereon Thou hast commanded us to rest from work, that we may keep it holy. Grant that in the contemplation of thy manifold mercies we may know and believe the love that Thou hast to us; and while we trust in thy promises, make us diligently to keep thy commandments.

We beseech Thee, O God, to bless unto us the services of the Sabbath, and make them conducive to our growth in grace, and in the knowledge of our Lord Jesus Christ. Grant the petitions which we have this day offered up unto Thee. Pardon whatever of sin Thou hast seen in us. Forgive us if, through the infirmity of the flesh, or want of watchfulness over our thoughts, we have taken thy name in vain; and may each succeeding Sabbath find us strengthened, more and more, with might by thy Spirit, and pressing towards the mark for the prize of the high calling in Christ Jesus. Thou hast warned us that, as the Israelites, who believed not, after they had been brought out of Egypt, died in the wilderness, and never entered the promised land; so we, if we fall after the same example of unbelief, shall be shut out from the the heavenly Canaan, and perish for ever. May we, therefore, while we think we stand, take heed lest we fall. Protect us, we pray Thee, from the wiles of the devil, whereby he would corrupt our minds from the simplicity that is in Christ. Enable us to resist the allurements of those who, walking after their own ungodly lusts, would entangle us again in the pollutions of the world. Grant that our confidence in thy Word may never be shaken by the vain reasoning of men, who, thinking themselves wise, have become fools; but give us grace that, building ourselves up in our most holy faith, and praying always in the Holy Ghost, we may keep ourselves in thy love, looking for the mercies of our Lord Jesus Christ unto eternal life. O God, our strength is in Thee, who alone art able to keep us from falling, and to present us, with all thine elect people, before the presence of thy glory, in the kingdom of thy dear Son, to whom, be praise and dominion, now and for ever. Amen.

[351]

[MORNING.] **FIFTY-FIRST WEEK.—MONDAY.** [EVENING.

READ IN HOLY SCRIPTURE EZEK. XXXIV. 11—31.

O ALMIGHTY God, who art the Shepherd of Israel, regard with thy favour the members of thy flock throughout the world. Feed them, we beseech Thee, with food convenient for them, leading them day by day to the pastures which Thou hast thyself provided, and causing them to lie down by the waters of quietness.

We adore Thee for the goodness and wisdom which have prepared for us the great things of thy law. We bless Thee for the revelation of thy will, and for the hope of eternal life which Thou hast given us through Christ our Lord. Send, we pray Thee, thy Holy Spirit, and direct us into the right understanding and love of thy truth, that we may reverently obey the same. Cause thy blessing to rest upon the ministry of thy faithful servants, that they may see the fruit of their labour in bringing many souls to Christ. Raise up thy great power, and come among us, and succour us by sending forth pastors who shall feed thy flock with knowledge, and with a true heart. Look upon all our universities and seminaries of sound religious learning, and grant that the tutors and students may all be taught by Thee, that so there may never be wanting a supply of godly and learned men for the ministry of thy word, and for the edification of thy Church. Remember thine ancient people Israel, that they may no longer be as sheep not having a shepherd, but may be brought into the fold of Christ, and be one flock, under one Shepherd.

Bless those who are labouring as missionaries to the Jews and to the heathen, that they may be enabled to bring many souls out of darkness and misery into the light and peace of the Gospel. Be with thy ministering servants in our colonies, that they may maintain thy truth and forward the salvation of those committed to their care. Look upon our beloved country. Bless our gracious Sovereign, and all in authority. Give peace in our time, O Lord, and grant that we may be godly and quietly governed. We have sinned against thy Divine Majesty in thought, word, and deed, and if Thou wert extreme to mark what we have done amiss we could not stand before Thee. Our mercies and our privileges have been without number, and we have not rendered unto Thee according to thy goodness. Hear, we pray Thee, our confession, and when Thou hearest, forgive. Look upon the face of thine Anointed, and accept us in him thy well beloved Son. Make us a blessing in all places. Prepare us for the duties of this day. Keep us continually in the love and service of Thee, and bring us finally into the presence of our Redeemer with exceeding joy. We ask these mercies for his great name's sake. Amen.

READ IN HOLY SCRIPTURE REVELATION I.

O LORD Jesus Christ, how utterly unworthy are we to approach thy footstool or to look on the glory of thy countenance. Thine eyes are as a flame of fire, searching us through, and bringing to light all the hidden sin and impurity of our fallen and guilty natures. We confess our unholiness of heart and will, and our many and often-repeated offences against Thee and against our Father who is in heaven. Convince us of our sin, and by thy Spirit work in us a true repentance. Have mercy upon us, O Thou loving Saviour, deliver us from sin and condemnation, which we deserve, and give us peace.

Impress our hearts with a deep sense of thy majesty. Open our understandings, and reveal Thyself unto us as Thou dost not to the world. Take away the darkness of sin and infirmity, and give us the anointing of the Holy One, and show us as we can bear it the greatness of thy power and glory as the Redeemer of our fallen world. We pray that the Holy Ghost may take of these things and show them unto us, and that while we are humbled in the dust in the presence of so great Majesty we may be encouraged by the assurance that Thou art indeed mighty to save, and strong to deliver.

How can we praise Thee enough, O Lord Jesus, for all the love wherewith Thou hast loved us, and for all the sacrifice and self-denial, and shame, and suffering which Thou didst endure for us even to death! Do Thou by thy Spirit kindle in us a flame of loftier devotion, and purer love. Revive and increase thy work in us, that these cold hearts of ours may be fervent, and that the worldliness which clings to us may be more and more consumed by thy constraining love. Lead us on to higher degrees of holiness, and grace, and knowledge, and cause the fruit of our union with Thee to be seen in our homes and in the world, and in the readiness with which we deny ourselves to please Thee. We look onward to the day when Thou shalt come with clouds, and every eye shall see Thee, and all kindreds of the earth shall wail because of Thee. Quicken in us, day by day, an earnest anxiety to be ready for thy coming, that it may be to us a joy and not a dread. Awaken in thy Church a longing for the day when sin and Satan shall be cast out. Stir up thy ministers and people to greater watchfulness and prayer. Bless all the trials and tribulations of thy people to the correction of sin and the increase of godliness.

Humbly commending to thy gracious care ourselves and all who are dear to us, we ascribe unto Thee, O Divine Saviour, with the Father and the Spirit, everlasting praise and glory. Amen.

[Morning.] FIFTY-FIRST WEEK.—TUESDAY. [Evening.

READ IN HOLY SCRIPTURE HAGGAI 1—11. 9.

ALMIGHTY and merciful God, we praise Thee for thy care over us during another night, and for the light and blessings of this morning. We thank Thee that Thou hast granted us refreshing sleep, and permitted us, as a family, to bow at thy footstool, and to present to Thee our praises. We praise Thee, O God, not only for the bounties of thy providence, but for the blessings of thy grace, for thy Son who died to redeem us, and for thy Spirit, whom Thou hast promised to renew our depraved natures. Let thy blessing be upon us through the whole of this day. Give to us a constant sense of thy presence. Incline us to hate all that is displeasing in thy sight. Inspire our hearts with thy love, that with alacrity and delight we may obey thy precepts. If Thou art pleased to favour us with prosperity, help us to remember its perils while we fulfil its responsibilities. Let all our enjoyments be received as from a Father's hand, and be sweetened by a Father's love. If Thou seest fit to visit us with affliction, disappointment, or sorrow, enable us to bow with submission to thy will, and confide in thy wisdom, faithfulness, and love. In every season of perplexity do Thou guide us, and in every hour of temptation and weakness succour us by thy strength.

We thank Thee, O Lord, for thy holy Word, and we pray Thee to bless to us that portion of it which we have now read. Preserve us from that spirit of procrastination in spiritual things into which thine ancient people fell in the building of the temple. Let those who are undecided in religion remember that now is the accepted time, and that now is the day of salvation; and let thy servants, in seeking the salvation of souls and the extension of the Redeemer's kingdom, labour with promptitude and diligence. Preserve us from the spirit of selfishness and sloth. Never may we seek our own honour and ease, while we are indifferent to thy cause; and forbid that, as a chastisement for our sins, we should be visited with famine and temporal privation.

We bless Thee, O God, that the Desire of all nations has come, and that thy people are erecting a spiritual temple to his praise. We pray that we may all be living stones in this edifice, and that we may contribute our parts to aid the progress of its erection. Let thy blessing be with us throughout this day. We are weak, do Thou strengthen us with all spiritual grace and power. We are ignorant, mercifully teach us, and guide our feet in the way of godliness and peace. Let all the members of this family, and all for whom we ought to pray, receive from Thee all needful favours. And finally bring us all to thy heavenly kingdom, through Jesus Christ our Saviour. Amen.

READ IN HOLY SCRIPTURE REVELATION II. 1—11.

O THOU, who art the watchful Guardian of thy people, and the Head of thy Church, as in days of old, we know that Thou art ever present to mark our deeds and to receive our prayers. Incline our hearts to receive with an obedient spirit the things which Thou hast spoken. Give us grace to labour in thy service, and to walk patiently in the path of duty. Enable us to manifest to those around us purity of doctrine in our creed, and the power of godliness in our lives. Grant us wisdom to shun the doors of evil, and to depart from those who delight in error. Bestow upon us, at all times, the ability to test the truth, that we may not be led astray by false teachers, and that the light of thy Gospel may not be removed from us. Cause it to be our desire, like the members of the Ephesian Church, to show forth our works and labours, our patience and our zeal, from no spirit of self-righteousness or vain-glory, as seeking the praise of men, but as seeking to commend ourselves to God, through Jesus Christ our Lord. Grant that by a diligent use of the privileges we enjoy, we may become rich in faith and in good works, rejoicing in hope, and comforted with the assurance of grace to help us in every time of need. Cause the instruction which Thou hast given to us in thy revealed will to guide us in safety, to support us under conflict, and to comfort us in the hour of sorrow; for thy commandment is a lamp, and thy law is light, and the reproofs of instruction are the way of life. Enable us, throughout our lives, to remember that Thou art ever beholding alike the evil and the good, and that Thou hast commanded us to have no fellowship with the unfaithful works of darkness, but rather to reprove them. Teach us that watchfulness, obedience, and purity of life and conversation become thy servants; for we confess, from the infirmity of our nature, and from the sinfulness that dwells within us, we have too often wandered from thy ways, and done that which is evil in thy sight. We pray Thee, absolve us from our transgressions, and by thy mercy enable us to retrace our steps, to repent of our misdoings, and to delight in the works of godliness; and as without thy aid we can do no good thing, teach us to hate that which Thou hatest, and love that which Thou lovest. Let thy Spirit witness with our spirits that we are the servants of Christ and the children of God; and when, in thy wisdom, Thou dost call us hence, grant that we, and all that are dear to us, may be numbered among that glorious assembly of the first-born, who shall not be hurt by the second death, but shall obtain the tree of life which is in the paradise of God. Grant it, Lord, for the Redeemer's sake. Amen.

[353]

[Morning.] **FIFTY-FIRST WEEK.—WEDNESDAY.** [Evening.

READ IN HOLY SCRIPTURE ZECHARIAH III.—IV. 7.

READ IN HOLY SCRIPTURE REVELATION II. 12—29.

WHO shall not fear Thee, O Lord, and glorify thy name, for Thou only art holy? Thou chargest thine angels with folly, and the heavens are not clean in thy sight. Yet so great is thy condescension, that Thou regardest the prayer of the humble. Oh, that we may deeply feel our unworthiness, whilst we ascribe unto Thee all blessing and praise.

We thank Thee O Lord, our heavenly Father, that Thou hast in thy great mercy made known thy willingness to receive all such as repent of their sins, and believe in the atoning sacrifice of thy dear Son. There is forgiveness with Thee, that Thou mayest be feared. We have an Advocate with Thee, the Father, even Jesus Christ, the righteous. For his sake, may we be justified, adopted into thy family, and made heirs of eternal salvation. Take away our filthy garments from us, and clothe us with the spotless robe of the Redeemer's merits. Enable us to live a holy life. May we feel persuaded of the existence of that better country to which we are fast hastening, and be prepared to enter, with the Captain of our salvation, into the promised inheritance.

Our Father which art in heaven, we have this morning renewed reason for dedicating ourselves afresh to thy service. We have laid down, and slept, and awaked, because Thou hast sustained us. We will remember thy loving-kindness in the morning. Keep us, we pray Thee, this day without sin. Lead us not into temptation. May holy thoughts possess our souls. Let nothing enter into them which defileth, or worketh abomination, or maketh a lie. Give us this day our daily bread. May thy blessing rest upon all our honest endeavours and lawful undertakings. We commend to thy fatherly benediction our relatives and friends, our neighbours and acquaintances. Let thy fear be ever before them. Bring back those who may have departed from Thee. Strengthen the good purposes of those who are weak and tempted. Heal the broken-hearted. May the fatherless find mercy in Thee, and the friendless learn to stay themselves upon their God.

Finally, we would entreat Thee, heavenly Father, to have compassion upon all men. Hear Thou the cry of the sorrowful. Pity the captive. Restore the sick. Remove violence from the earth. May all people learn righteousness. Let thy will be done, O Lord, and thy kingdom come on earth as it is in heaven.

Hear Thou in heaven thy dwelling place, and when Thou hearest, forgive, answer, and bless us for the sake of Jesus Christ, our blessed Lord and Saviour, to whom with Thee and the Holy Ghost be all honour and praise. Amen.

O LORD, the Creator of heaven and earth, from everlasting to everlasting Thou art God. We praise Thee, we glorify Thee, we give thanks to Thee for thy great glory, O heavenly King, God the Father Almighty. Heaven and earth are full of the majesty of thy glory. By the power of thy Spirit, and the sense of thy greatness, bow our hearts in reverence at thy footstool. Suffer us not to think lightly of thy glorious perfections, nor to lose sight of thy holiness, which hates sin, and of thy truth, which has pledged Thee to punish it.

O Lord, convince us of sin. Make us to feel ashamed of our many transgressions against Thee, and with all earnestness of faith to seek forgiveness and cleansing through the blood of Jesus. Urge us onward, by thy Spirit and thy Word, in the narrow way. Thou knowest how we are sore let and hindered in running the race that is before us. Only in thy strength, and under thy guidance, can we hope to overcome and to subdue the power of the world, the flesh, and the devil. Help us, O Lord our God, help us for thy name's sake, and make thy grace to abound towards us more and more. Increase in us all holy and heavenly gifts, that we may not dishonour our Christian calling, and bring reproach on thy holy name. Make us thine, and keep us thine for ever and ever, that we may continue Christ's faithful disciples and servants even to our lives' end.

Thy past mercies, and thy gracious promises in the Gospel, embolden us, O Lord God, to seek from Thee such grace and blessing as Thou seest needful for us. We cannot live without Thee by day; we cannot rest without Thee in peace by night. Stretch over us thy hand, and defend us from all evil. Regard every member of this family, and all whom we love. Descend upon them in all the power of the Spirit, and make their hearts burn within them at the assurance of thy help and blessing.

We beseech Thee, O Lord God, to grant thy blessing to everything which has been done this day for thy glory, and for the ingathering to thy fold the souls that have wandered away from Thee, and hardened themselves against the truth in Jesus. We pray for the spread of thy Gospel. Oh, let the true light shine wherever men are sitting in darkness and the shadow of death. Remove the veil from the eyes of the Jews, and take away the evil heart of unbelief. Let the Gentiles be turned away from idols to serve Thee, the living God. Make bare thy arm in the midst of the nations, and let it be seen, even to the ends of the earth, that Thou art God and God alone. Merciful Father, hear and help us, for thy dear Son's sake. Amen.

MORNING.] FIFTY-FIRST WEEK.—THURSDAY. [EVENING.

READ IN HOLY SCRIPTURE ZECHARIAH XIII.

ALMIGHTY God, our heavenly Father, who rulest and reignest over all, we bless Thee for life, and breath, and all things. We come into thy presence with deep humility, for we have sinned against heaven and before Thee. We adore and magnify thy holy name that Thou didst not spare thine only begotten Son, but didst deliver Him up for us all; and we come now to that fountain once opened for sin and uncleanness, of which we have now been reading in thy most holy Word. Assist us, O God, we beseech Thee, to draw near with faith to the throne of the heavenly grace, that we may obtain mercy, and find grace to help us in all the duties and difficulties of daily life. Keep our hearts right with Thee, and help us to run with patience the race that is set before us, looking unto Jesus, the Author and Finisher of our faith.

Do Thou, O Lord, quicken our zeal, increase our faith, and inflame our love, that forgetting the things which are behind, we may press forward to those which are before. Let thy Holy Spirit expel all evil from our hearts, and fill us with peace, and love, and joy. Give us, we beseech Thee, the confidence of children, that we may realise our adoption into thy family, and be enabled to call Thee by the endearing name of Father; and thus, O God, cause us to realise that all things are working together for our good. Keep us from murmuring and repining, and help us to remember thine own blessed words: " In the world ye shall have tribulation: but be of good cheer; I have overcome the world."

We bless Thee for all the common mercies of daily life, for friends and food, for reason and for raiment; but, above all, for Him whom, not having seen, we love, who died for our sins, and who now intercedes as our High Priest before the throne.

Look down with compassion, we beseech Thee, on all mankind. Let thy truth be known upon earth, thy saving health among all nations. Bless all missionaries of the cross of Christ in all parts of the heathen world, and crown their labours with success.

We commend to Thee the sick, the suffering, and the dying, beseeching Thee to remember the outcast, to be the Father of the fatherless, and the Husband of the widow. Comfort all who are afflicted, with the precious promises of thy holy Word, and help them to cast their burthens upon the Lord, that He may sustain them.

Forgive, we earnestly beseech Thee, all our sins; cleanse us in the blood, and cover us with the righteousness of our Redeemer, and prepare us to be with Him in glory. We ask all these mercies in the name of Jesus Christ, our ever-living Lord and Saviour. Amen.

READ IN HOLY SCRIPTURE REVELATION III.

ALMIGHTY God, by whose providence we are brought to the evening of another day, enable us to close it as becomes thy faithful soldiers. Thou hast called us to maintain a life-long conflict in the prospect of an unfading crown. If thine all-seeing eye detects among us any who have only a name to live while we are dead, vouchsafe to quicken those lifeless souls, that Christ may give them light. Awaken any of us that are relapsing into carelessness and unfaithfulness, and strengthen within us the things that remain that are ready to die. If any of us have offended Thee by lukewarmness, if any of us are incurring thy rebuke and chastisement, graciously forgive us for Christ's sake. Accompany the reproof by the influence of thy Holy Spirit, that we may be zealous and repent, and be warmed with gratitude. Thus be pleased to meet our several necessities. Cause us to lie down this night accepted in the Beloved, and may we sleep in peace under the guardianship of a heavenly Father. If we are spared to see the light of the morrow, awaken us to renewed fidelity in our holy warfare. Preserve us from every delusion. Never may we deem ourselves rich and in need of nothing; but, sensible of our own dependence, and of thy bounty, may we buy of Thee gold tried in the fire, that we may be rich, and white raiment that we may be clothed. Thus prepared, may we be followers of them whom of old Thou didst commend. Let the presence of the ungodly only serve to increase our watchfulness. Let the remembrance that Thou knowest our ways confirm and encourage us to keep the word of thy patience without denying thy name; and, O Lord, do Thou vouchsafe to keep us from the hour of temptation, or bring us safely through it.

Thus may we prove more than conquerors, and gain the promised reward. We know not, O blessed Saviour, its greatness and its value. We understand not, as yet, how inestimable is the privilege of those whom Thou shalt confess before thy Father's face, and whom Thou shalt make everlasting pillars in his temple. But grant, O Lord, that this blessedness may be ours. Enable us, therefore, so to pass through things which are temporal, that we may finally lose not those benefits eternal.

Furthermore, revive thy languid churches, Lord. May they remember their responsibilities, and how they have received and known thy truth. Preserve them (especially preserve that church to which we belong) from the unfaithfulness of Sardis, and from Laodicean lukewarmness. Keep all thy people in faithfulness, duty, and love, and make the world to know that Thou hast loved them, O holy and gracious Jesus. Amen.

[355]

[MORNING.] **FIFTY-FIRST WEEK.—FRIDAY.** [EVENING.

READ IN HOLY SCRIPTURE ZECHARIAH XIV.

O LORD of Hosts, and God of all the families of the earth, we desire to draw near thy holy presence to worship thy great and glorious name. We praise Thee, O God; we acknowledge Thee to be the Lord. Thou art God in the heaven above, and in the earth beneath, and all things come of Thee. In thy hands our breath is, and thine are all our ways. We have laid us down and slept, and awaked, because Thou, Lord, makest us to dwell in safety. To Thee we owe our preservation and defence from all the perils and dangers of the night; the refreshing of our bodies and the renewal of our powers through thy gracious gift of sleep. Thou art the Father of all our mercies. Thou art the Father of lights, and from Thee cometh down every good and every perfect gift. Bless the Lord, O our souls, and all that is within us, bless his holy name. Bless the Lord, O our souls, and forget not all his benefits.

To Thee, O Lord, we would again direct our prayer, and to Thee we would once more look up. Let thy mercy be upon us according as we hope in Thee. Vouchsafe, O Lord, to keep us this day without sin, and grant that we may yield ourselves unto Thee as those that are alive from the dead, and help us through thy Holy Spirit to walk before Thee in newness of life. Create within us a clean heart, and renew a right spirit within us. Put thy laws into our hearts and write them in our minds, that we may not sin against Thee. Wash us in the blood of Christ, and purge our consciences from dead works to serve the living God. Cleanse the thoughts of our hearts by the inspiration of thy Holy Spirit, and make us vessels unto honour meet for the Master's use. Assist us to glorify Thee in our body and spirit; and whatever we do, whether we eat or drink, may we do all to the glory of God. Grant that we may be made perfect in every good work to do thy will, and work in us that which is well pleasing in thy sight.

We beseech Thee, O Lord, to grant unto us those things which are requisite and necessary as well for the body as the soul. We cast our cares upon Thee, for Thou carest for us, and Thou numberest the hairs of our head. Watch over and preserve our life and health. Give us neither poverty nor riches; feed us with food convenient for us. Lead us in the way we should go; guide us with thy counsel, and after we have fulfilled thy will on earth, receive us into glory, granting unto us an abundant entrance into the everlasting kingdom of our Lord and Saviour Jesus Christ, to whom, with the Father, and the Holy Ghost, we ascribe all honour and glory, world without end. Amen.

READ IN HOLY SCRIPTURE REVELATION IV.

O LORD Almighty, the Father of men and angels, Thou sittest upon the throne of thy glory, and orderest all things after the counsel of thy will. We are sinful and unclean; but blessed be thy name that, in the light of the Sun of Righteousness, we behold the rainbow round about the throne; the sign of wrath appeased, and of justice and mercy reconciled. We come before Thee in the name of Jesus, hear us for his sake, and help us.

The angels, with many eyes and many wings, stand before thy throne, and rest not day and night, saying, Holy, holy, holy, Lord God Almighty! And with them the spirits of the just made perfect and the whole company of the Church on earth, whose names are written in heaven as priests and kings, worship and serve Thee. To this company of holy angels and redeemed men, we, unworthy as we are, humbly desire to join ourselves, that we may give our heart and voice to sing thy praise.

We adore Thee for all that Thou art in thyself, thou glorious King, and for all that Thou art to us, thou gracious Saviour. We adore Thee for thy infinite power, majesty, and glory; for thy infinite justice, holiness, and truth; for thy infinite mercy and love. We bless Thee for the manifestation of thy goodness to us sinners. We praise Thee for all temporal mercies, for food and raiment, for health and strength, and for all the blessings which flow around our homes, and pour their comforts into our bosoms; but above all thy gifts to us, we praise Thee for the gift of thy dear Son, and the promise of thy Holy Spirit. Thy love to us is wonderful. We thank and praise Thee that thy Son has died and is alive again for us; that Thou makest his flesh to be meat indeed, and his blood to be drink indeed to our souls, and that by Him Thou takest away the sting of death and the victory of the grave, and fillest our hearts with hopes full of immortality.

When we think of all thy greatness and glory, of all thy grace and mercy, we are lost in wonder, love, and praise. With angels, and archangels, and all the company of heaven, we laud and magnify thy glorious name, evermore praising Thee and saying, Holy, holy, holy, Lord God of Hosts! heaven and earth are full of thy glory. Glory be to Thee, O Lord most high.

Gracious Father, forgive us all the sins of this day, and grant us such a deep sense of their sinfulness that we may hate them as Thou hatest them. Bestow on us the peace that passeth understanding. Spread around us, and all whom we love, the shield of thy loving care, and preserve us now and ever, for Christ's sake. Amen.

[Morning.] **FIFTY-FIRST WEEK.—SATURDAY.** [Evening.

READ IN HOLY SCRIPTURE PROVERBS IV.

O THOU only wise God, we come unto Thee in the name of thy beloved Son, in dependence on the assurance of thy Word, that Thou givest to all men liberally and upbraidest not. May thy Holy Spirit convince us more and more of our natural ignorance, and of our need of that wisdom which is from above. Grant that Jesus himself may be made unto us wisdom, as well as righteousness, and sanctification, and redemption. May we be made wise unto salvation, through faith which is in Him.

Let none of us think highly of ourselves, because of any wisdom which we may possess; for if any man think that he knoweth anything, he knoweth nothing yet, as he ought to know. Sanctify to thine own service and glory whatever of earthly knowledge Thou hast permitted us to acquire. May we, as faithful stewards of thy manifold gifts, employ them all for Thee, remembering thy command, "Occupy till I come." Oh, make us wise for eternity, wise to consider our latter end, wise unto that which is good and simple concerning evil.

May we never, by willingly entering into the path of the wicked, provoke Thee to leave us to ourselves. Oh, turn away our eyes, lest they behold vanity. Strengthen us, by thy Spirit, to avoid those persons and places which may tempt us to sin. May we think no trouble too great, no sacrifice too costly, for this holy end. May we ponder the path of our feet, and let our eyes look right on. Hedge up our way that we may not walk in our own paths. May we ever hear thy voice saying unto us, "This is the way, walk ye in it," when we turn to the right hand, or when we turn to the left.

Thou didst command thy people of old to make preparation beforehand for the rest of thy holy Sabbath. Incline our hearts, we beseech Thee, to set all things in order this day for the quiet and devout observance of the morrow. Be with all thy ministers in their reading and meditation, that they may be able to bring forth out of their treasure things new and old. May they bear the names of their people on their hearts before thy mercy seat, and rightly divide the Word of Truth, giving to each his portion in due season. And oh, pour out abundantly of thy Spirit upon thy whole Church. Awaken both ministers and people to a deeper sense of their heavenly calling. May there be more fruit-bearing branches, glorifying Thee by bringing forth much fruit. Oh, hear the united prayers of thy believing people, and send down the Holy Ghost to quicken thy Church, that it may serve Thee singly and devotedly. We ask all for Christ's sake. Amen.

READ IN HOLY SCRIPTURE REVELATION V.

HEAVENLY Father, we thank Thee that we have been brought in safety to the close of this week. Thy goodness and mercy have followed us all the days of our life, and we lift our hearts to Thee in praise and adoration. Unable to count up the multitude of thy mercies, we pray that we may not be ungrateful. Do Thou graciously hear our prayer, and open our eyes to see all the greatness of thy love in the bounties of thy providence and the gifts of thy Gospel, that we may be constrained to render to Thee the tribute of a life consecrated to thy service. We beseech Thee also to give us an increasing knowledge of Thyself, O God. Unfold to us, by thy Spirit and through the teaching of thy Word, the greatness and glory of thy Divine perfections, and enable us to see how they all meet in the person of thy dear Son, our Incarnate Lord. Reveal Thyself unto us as the God of grace, more ready to hear us than we are to pray to Thee; able and willing to forgive us all sin, and to help us in every time of need. Blot from thy book the sins of this day. Remember not against us what we have said, or thought, or done, which is displeasing to Thee. O Lord, give us peace of conscience in the remembrance of our transgressions, and seal to our hearts the promise of thy gracious pardon.

O Thou exalted Redeemer, mighty to save, our atonement for sin, the conqueror of Satan, and our deliverer from death and hell, we would mingle our praise and adoration with the songs of the blessed who surround thy throne. With angels and archangels, and all the company of heaven, we laud and magnify thy holy name. Thou that art exalted to the right hand of the Father, have mercy upon us, and accept our praise. Thou art the king of glory, O Christ; Thou art the everlasting Son of the Father. All praise be to thy name. O Lord Jesus, make our hearts to overflow with love to Thee. Chide and correct the coldness of our love, and the indolence of our service, and the feebleness of our devotion. Draw us, and we will run after Thee. Reveal the power of thy Spirit within us, and make us partakers of thine abounding grace here, and of thine everlasting glory hereafter. Show us clearly thy footsteps, and strengthen us with a holy courage and an undaunted faith to follow Thee, bearing the cross which Thou layest upon us, and zealous to set forth thy praise.

Lord God, who never slumberest, guard and defend us to-night from evil. Shed on us, and all whom we love, the peace that passeth understanding, and fit us for the spiritual engagements of the morrow. We beseech Thee to hear, and answer, and bless us in these our prayers, which we offer through Jesus Christ our Lord. Amen.

[Morning.] **FIFTY-SECOND WEEK.—LORD'S DAY.** [Evening.

READ IN HOLY SCRIPTURE PROVERBS VIII.

READ IN HOLY SCRIPTURE REVELATION VII. 9—17.

O ALMIGHTY and All-seeing God, we call upon Thee out of a world of uncertainty and darkness. When the morning light ariseth, it doth not show us what the day will bring forth. When we avail ourselves to the utmost of the natural faculties Thou hast given us, many solemn and eternal realities are still concealed from our eyes; our minds have been blinded by sin. We are but poor, weak, and ignorant creatures, unable of ourselves to know or to think that which is good. We therefore humbly and earnestly seek from Thee this morning, O Thou great Fountain of all true knowledge and Father of lights, the gift of wisdom. Thou hast given us the light of the day. Give us also, we beseech Thee, the light of thy grace. Thou hast given us the light of thy holy Word. Give us power to discern and understand it. Open Thou our eyes to behold the wondrous things of thy law.

We would encourage ourselves in asking these blessings by the words which we have just heard. May they teach us that if our ignorance is great, so is thy willingness to remove it. Doth not wisdom cry, and understanding put forth her voice; and that to assure us of this truth? Oh, cause us, we beseech Thee, thus to hear and believe; and make us, thy servants, to be amongst those who, loving heavenly wisdom, are beloved in return.

We desire to thank Thee, also, if, in any measure, Thou hast already enlightened our dark minds. Especially we thank Thee that all the wisdom which we require for our duties and our hopes, is treasured up for our enrichment in thy crucified Son. May He be made unto us wisdom, and righteousness, and sanctification, and redemption. And may the atoning work of that blessed One who was possessed by Thee in the beginning of thy way, be at once the power and wisdom of God in our experience and our minds.

We ask further for that practical wisdom which shall make us hate evil and fear Thee. May we have that great evidence of knowing and loving truth, a hearty willingness to obey.

These are the petitions, O Lord, which we offer to Thee on this the morning of thy day. May we go in the spirit of them to thy house. May we follow up these our family prayers by joining there in supplication with the congregation of thy people. And may the lessons we learn in thy sanctuary perfect our trust in that Fatherly wisdom which is always good to Israel, even to those of clean heart. Our daily necessities are many, but Thou art all-sufficient. Hear us and answer us, we humbly beseech Thee, for our Redeemer's sake. Amen.

EVER blessed Jehovah, with angels and the redeemed we would devoutly exclaim, "Salvation to our God which sitteth upon the throne, and unto the Lamb. Blessing, and glory, and wisdom, and thanksgiving, and honour, and power, and might be unto our God for ever and ever." We thank Thee, O Lord, for here uplifting the veil, and vouchsafing to us a glimpse of the celestial Holy of Holies. With thy entranced servant, we can, in our measure, as through a glass darkly, behold this white-robed throng, and rejoice to find it made up of victorious saints from all nations, and kindreds, and peoples, and tongues. We thank Thee that Jesus stands related to our whole race as their Redeemer; that he gave Himself a ransom for all. May the joyful sound given forth this day prove, through faith, the power of God to the salvation of sinners and the increased sanctification of saints. Bless, in particular, our own church and pastor; and may the work of God increasingly prosper in our hearts and hands.

We bless thy name, most merciful Father, for our Sabbaths, for our sanctuaries, for all our religious privileges, and especially for the promise of the Divine Spirit. Pardon all the sins of our holy things—all the strange fire we have this day allowed to blend with the incense of our devotion. May the Word we have read or heard profit us, being mixed with faith, and watered by thy Spirit. May every good impression received this day, either in God's house or our own, be deepened, prolonged, and matured, to our increased holiness and comfort, and to thy glory. Help us more and more to receive thy truth in the faith and love of it, and may it abound in all manner of fruits in our lives. Be with us, and all near and dear to us, during this week, if it be thy will to spare us. Fit us for its duties. Fortify us for its trials. May Sabbath and sanctuary impressions follow us into week-day avocations; may every day be to us a Sabbath, and every place holy ground.

O God of peace and of all consolation, give us grace to put on the whole armour of God, to fight the good fight of faith, to overcome by the blood of the Lamb, to follow Him faithfully whithersoever He goeth, to walk in the Spirit, to glorify our Heavenly Father, and in all duty, and under all trial, to be faithful unto death; that we, too, may emerge at last victorious out of great tribulation, having washed our robes and made them white in the blood of the Lamb, and serve Thee day and night in thy heavenly temple. We commend ourselves, and all whom we love, to thy gracious care, and we ask every mercy for Jesus' sake, who, with Thee, O Father, and Thee, O Holy Ghost, reignest one God, world without end. Amen.

[Morning.] **FIFTY-SECOND WEEK.—MONDAY.** [Evening.]

READ IN HOLY SCRIPTURE PROVERBS X.

O LORD, who hast said that they who worship Thee must worship Thee in spirit and in truth, may we thus come to Thee this morning. Enable us with our spirits within us to seek Thee early. Oh, grant us to-day that blessing of thine which maketh rich without sorrow. May we be rich in faith, rich in grace, rich in the unsearchable riches of Christ. May all the good things He has purchased by his death, be given to us richly to enjoy.

We thank Thee for thy Word, which is a lamp to our feet, and a light unto our paths. May the lessons contained in it be written in our hearts. Give us grace to be diligent, not only in our earthly but our heavenly calling; gathering, during the summer of our opportunities, the blessings of thy free salvation, laying up knowledge, keeping instruction, and fulfilling that labour of the righteous which tendeth to life. As in the multitude of words there wanteth not sin, enable us to take heed to our ways that we sin not with our tongue, and to keep our mouth with a bridle. Preserve us from lying lips, from slanderous lips, from prating lips; and may our tongues be as choice silver, speaking what is good to the use of edifying, and what may minister grace to the hearers. Thus may our mouth be as a well of life. Oh, cleanse our heart from evil passions, and, instead of that hatred which stirreth up strife, fill us with that love that covereth, as far as may be, a neighbour's sins. Put into our hearts such good desires as we may believe, according to thy promise, Thou wilt grant, and fill us with that hope which shall be gladness in the latter end. May we be built on the everlasting foundation which Thou hast laid for us in Christ, so that our expectation shall not perish.

And what we thus ask for ourselves we would ask also for others. Grant to our dear relatives and friends that they also may build upon the Rock of Ages, and put on that righteousness which delivereth from death. Be favourable to our land. Bless our Sovereign, and all the Royal Family, with the healthful spirit of thy grace. May our rulers rule in thy fear, and be the counsellors of peace. May our ministers be clothed with righteousness, and may their lips feed many. Bless all the efforts which are making in these times to convert sinners from the error of their ways, and to save souls from death by guiding them to Jesus. May infidelity be put to shame, the days of antichrist be shortened, peace be given to the earth, and the kingdoms of this world soon become the kingdom of our Lord and of his Christ.

Accept, O Lord, our grateful praises for all thy goodness to us, and hear us for the sake of Jesus Christ our Lord. Amen.

READ IN HOLY SCRIPTURE REVELATION XIV.

O GOD, the Author and Preserver of our frame, and the Fountain of all our enjoyments, we approach thy mercy-seat at the close of another day to give thanks for all thy mercies, and to commend ourselves to thy protection and care. We are conscious how far short we have come this day of what we ought to have been, that many duties have been neglected, that many sins have been committed against Thee. We come again to the blood of sprinkling for pardon and for purification, and beseech Thee to seal upon our consciences a sense of thy forgiving love, and to impart to us that peace which the world can neither give nor take away.

We bless Thee that we have been permitted to read of the redeemed assembly before the throne, and we pray that thy grace may enable us, like them, boldly to avow a Saviour's name; that it may preserve us from the defilements of the world, and help us to follow the Lamb in whatever path he may lead us. We bless Thee for the saving virtue of the blood of Christ, and that what it has done for those who have gone before us, it can do for us also. Oh, that we may have redemption through his blood, even the forgiveness of sins. Deliver us from the love and power of sin, no less than from its guilt and condemnation; and though conscious now of numberless faults, may we be presented at last without fault, before the throne of God.

We praise Thee, O Father, that already so vast an assembly has been gathered to the heavenly Zion, and are singing the new song to the Redeemer in the heavenly temple. Let us learn on earth the song of heaven, and possess a foretaste of the joys of eternity. Give success, O Lord, to all the heralds of salvation; let the everlasting Gospel be speedily published to all the inhabitants of the earth; and may this our globe become one great temple in which Thou wilt delight to dwell, and in which man will delight to worship. Let the people praise Thee, O God; let all the people praise Thee. We pray for the destruction of antichrist, and for the coming of thy kingdom in power and great glory. Help us all to live to the Lord, that we may at last die to the Lord; to work for Christ here, that we may rest with Christ hereafter. Prepare us all for the great harvest, the end of the world. Let us all remember that we are ripening either for heaven or for hell. Oh, gather not our souls with sinners; but bind us up in the bundle of life, and number us among thy redeemed in glory everlasting. And now, O God, be with us all this night, and bestow upon us the fulness of thy grace and blessing, for our Redeemer's sake. Amen.

[Morning.] **FIFTY-SECOND WEEK.—TUESDAY.** [Evening.

READ IN HOLY SCRIPTURE PROVERBS XIII. | READ IN HOLY SCRIPTURE REVELATION XV.—XVI. 7.

ADORED be thy great name, O our God, that we, so sinful and unworthy, are still the objects of thy merciful care and tender compassion. Accept, we beseech Thee, our united praise for the rest of the night, for life, and strength, and spiritual blessing. Enable us, in sincerity and truth, to worship Thee. We trust in the merits and mediation of Jesus Christ, our exalted Mediator and Saviour. For his sake, and in fulfilment of thy faithful promise, let us not leave thy footstool unforgiven or unblessed. We pray that it may please Thee to give us true repentance for all our ignorance, indolence, and disobedience, and so to put away our sins from before thy face, that they may not be remembered against us in the day of Christ's appearing. In the name of Jesus, grant us peace.

Incline our hearts, O God, this day to love thy precepts. Take away all hardness of heart, and unbelief, and disobedience, and by thy gracious Spirit enable us to tread the narrow way of life as the followers of a holy Master. We pray that our service may be a cheerful service, and that our obedience may spring from a fervent love and a sincere desire to please Thee, our God, in all things. But show us our weakness, and our daily need of grace and wisdom from above. Without thy strength to meet them, the temptations which beset us from the world, the devil, and our own fallen hearts and stubborn wills, will work our ruin. Merciful Father, help us, guide us, and uphold us. Suffer us not to be discouraged in our Christian course by the hardness of the way, nor to murmur, though the lot which Thou dost appoint for us be one of trial. Hold us by thy hand, richly bless us with the tokens of thy favour, and abundantly fulfil thy promise, that as our day is so our strength shall be.

Gracious God, all things are in thy hand, and Thou reignest on high as King for evermore. Thou feedest the fowls of the air, and clothest the grass of the field. Not even a sparrow falleth to the ground without thy knowledge, and the very hairs of our head are all numbered. We cast all our daily care upon Thee. We commit our life, our circumstances, our trials, our dangers, our fears, our perplexities, our wants to Thee. Our hope is in thy truth and love, and we know Thou carest for us. Defend and keep us this day, prosper us in all that we do, keep us from sin, and shed in our hearts the assurance of thy grace and love.

Bless all whom we love; supply their daily need, and make all things work together for their good. Those, and all other mercies which Thou seest good for them or ourselves, we ask in the name of Jesus Christ our Saviour. Amen.

O LORD of Hosts, the mighty God, to whom vengeance belongeth, we stand in awe, and tremble before the majesty of thy righteous indignation. Fill us, O Lord, with a holy courage, that we may be witnesses of thy truth without fear of man; knowing in whom we have believed, and that He is able to keep us from falling, and to preserve us unto his glorious kingdom.

Gracious Lord, fill our hearts with an earnest desire for the salvation of our perishing fellow-sinners. We plead thy blessed promise, to give the heathen to thy Son, and the utmost parts of the earth for his possession. Fulfil thy gracious Word, O Lord. Cause the nations to fear thy name, and bless thine inheritance. Be with the missionaries who preach the glad tidings of redeeming love. Grant unto those that hear them a listening ear and a believing heart; and oh, may the day quickly come, when the whole earth shall be filled with the knowledge of the glory of the Lord.

Heavenly Father, Thou hast led us through another day with loving care. We bless Thee for a happy home, for health and safety. We bless Thee for the grace which has prospered our work in our hand. If we have fulfilled our appointed labour, if we have had any success, if we have been saved in temptation, if we have been able to confess Jesus before men, if we have ministered comfort to any sorrowing heart, if we have experienced any joy and peace, to Thee be all the praise. Yet, O God, too often we have sinned and done amiss. God has not been in all our thoughts; we have rebelled against thy providence; we have spoken unadvisedly with our lips; we have been forgetful to watch and pray. Many temptations have prevailed against us. We are ashamed when we think of resolutions broken, and work left undone. O God, the Father of our Lord Jesus Christ, our only hope is in thy grace. Spare us, good Lord. Spare thy people, whom Thou hast redeemed with thy precious blood, and be not angry with us for ever.

We commend ourselves and the absent members of our families to thy mercy. In the silent hours of night, when we cannot take care of ourselves, be Thou our defence and shield. If it be thy will that we should live to see the light of the morning, may we awake strengthened by thy Holy Spirit to serve Thee more perfectly, or else receive us into those heavenly habitations which Thou hast prepared for them that love Thee.

Hear us, O Lord, in these our prayers this night, for the sake of our Saviour, Jesus Christ, to whom with the Father and the Holy Spirit, be all honour and glory, world without end. Amen.

[Morning.] **FIFTY-SECOND WEEK.—WEDNESDAY.** [Evening.

READ IN HOLY SCRIPTURE PSALM XXXII.

ALMIGHTY and everlasting Father, who dost give thy Holy Spirit to convict of sin, help us, we beseech Thee, by his influences, after the manner of thy servant David of old, to acknowledge our sins, to confess our transgressions, and to seek the blessedness of the man whose transgressions are forgiven, whose sin is covered. Sinful in nature, we have been sinful in practice. How many words have we spoken, how many thoughts and feelings have we indulged, of which Thou canst not approve! How seldom have we worshipped Thee in spirit and in truth! How many opportunities of seeking thy favour and doing thy will have we neglected! Thou art our Master; but we have been unprofitable servants. Thou art our King; we have been rebellious subjects. Thou art our Father; we are ungrateful and disobedient children. Notwithstanding all thy loving-kindness towards us, we have deserved thy wrath and curse. Oh, hadst Thou been extreme to mark our sins, we should long ago miserably have perished. But Thou art a God merciful and gracious. Thou hast provided pardon for us in Jesus Christ. Thou hast exalted Him to give repentance and remission of sins. We implore the grace of repentance. Teach us to grieve over our misdeeds. Save us from the power as well as the guilt of sin. Save us from sinning. Let the life we live in the flesh be a life of faith in the Son of God. That we may be justified, and have peace with Thee, withhold not from us, we beseech Thee, a justifying faith. May we believe with the heart unto righteousness. Lord, increase our faith. Thus may we have the blessedness of the man unto whom Thou dost not impute sin, and in whose spirit there is no guile.

Bless, O God, all our relatives, neighbours, and friends. If any are impenitent and unbelieving, give unto them opportunities and incentives to repent, believe, and obey. Estranged from Thee by sin, may they be brought nigh to Thee by the blood of the cross. Give them a new heart and a right spirit, that they may live and not die. Thou who willest not the death of him that dieth, have mercy upon them, we beseech Thee. Stir up thy faithful people to labour more earnestly and pray more fervently for the salvation of men. Bless all the efforts that are made in all branches of thy true Church for the furtherance of this glorious object. Let ministers at home and missionaries abroad be successful in preaching Christ and Him crucified. May it be the holy ambition of all thy people to turn many to righteousness, that, obeying thy command, they may enjoy thy promise, and shine as the stars for ever and ever. Grant this, O merciful Father, for Jesus Christ's sake. Amen.

READ IN HOLY SCRIPTURE REVELATION XIX.

O LORD, the great and glorious God, we render to Thee our most humble and hearty thanks for the unspeakable gift of thy Son, through whom Thou canst forgive the transgressor and show mercy to thousands. In Him Thou canst be just, and yet the justifier of the ungodly. Help us, we beseech Thee, that we neglect not so great salvation; coming to Thee through the sacrifice of the Redeemer, may we lay hold of thy strength, and be at peace with Thee.

This night, O God, we have new cause to be thankful, and we offer Thee our evening sacrifice of praise. Throughout this day, when we have hungered, Thou hast fed us; when we have thirsted, Thou hast given us drink. Thy hands have provided raiment convenient for us. Thou hast crowned our life with loving-kindnesses and tender mercies. Thou hast kept our souls from death, our eyes from tears, and our feet from falling. Bless the Lord, O our souls, and all that is within us, bless his holy name.

But to us, O our heavenly Father, belong shame and confusion of face. We have offended against thy holy laws. We have gone astray like lost sheep. Pardon our iniquity, for it is great. Look upon thy Son, and forgive all our transgressions. Behold, O God our Shield, and look upon the face of thine anointed. May we be cleansed in the blood of thy dear Son our Saviour, and go and sin no more.

And now, O God, we beseech Thee for another night's rest. We have not yet come to the world where thy servants serve Thee day and night. We cannot, for we are feeble and frail, worship Thee without weariness. The spirit may be willing, but the flesh is weak. Now, therefore, O Lord, cover us this night with the shadow of thy wing. Peace be to this house. Let no harm come nigh our dwelling. Save us from the pestilence that walketh in darkness. Give to thy beloved sleep.

We pray Thee to look in great mercy upon all our friends and kinsfolk. Let great grace be upon them all. Seek and save those among them who know Thee not. Increase in others, who belong to Thee, every good gift. May our different paths in the journey of life all end at length in our Father's house within the veil.

Hear us for our country, for our monarch, and the Royal Family; for the Sovereign's counsellors, for the senate of the land, and for all judges and magistrates. Hear us for the poor, the sick, the dying; and grant that many sorrowing hearts may this night rejoice in Thee. We ask all these blessings in the Saviour's name, and ascribe to Father, Son, and Holy Ghost the kingdom, the power, and the glory for ever and ever. Amen.

[Morning.]   FIFTY-SECOND WEEK.—THURSDAY.   [Evening.]

READ IN HOLY SCRIPTURE PSALM XXXIII.

WE would begin this day, O Lord, heavenly Father, with the sacrifices of praise and thanksgiving. All thy works are done in truth, and the earth is full of thy goodness. Grant, we beseech Thee, to each of us such a knowledge of the greatest of all thy blessings, the blessings of the Gospel of Christ, that our hearts may ever be tuned to thy praise. We adore Thee for the finished work of our redemption in Christ Jesus. Oh, how great is thy loving-kindness to the sons of men! Thou pardonest sin, and openest the kingdom of heaven to all believers. Lord, may we by thy grace be enabled to believe in thy dear Son with all our hearts. Convince each of us more deeply of our lost and ruined condition by nature, and enable us by faith to cast our sins on Jesus. May the blessedness of those whose God is the Lord be ours, that our mouth may be filled with laughter and our tongue with joy; and that we may walk worthy of our high calling as thy children in Christ Jesus, fill our hearts, we pray Thee, with a holy fear of thy great name. Impress upon us the solemn truth that thine eye is in every place, beholding the evil and the good, and by the power of thy Spirit help us to walk before Thee in holiness and true righteousness.

Keep us mindful, O Lord, of our weakness and frailty. May we never so presume on our own strength as to run into temptation, or fall from our dependence on thy grace. Give us an increasing love for thy holy Word. May we make it a light for our feet and a lamp for our path. May we esteem it more than our necessary food, and may thy testimonies be the very joy of our hearts. Be with us this day in our several employments. Help us to engage in every duty in dependence on thy grace, and with a humble desire, whether we eat or drink, or whatsoever we do, to do all to thy glory. Thou hast promised, O Lord, to preserve the souls of thy people who wait on Thee. Fulfil to us, we beseech Thee, that promise. Be Thou our help and shield, a very present help in every time of trouble. Sanctify to us our crosses as well as our comforts; and grant that, being kept steadfast in thy faith and fear, we may so pass through the waves of this troublesome world as finally to come to the land of everlasting life.

Bless, we pray Thee, the efforts of thy servants to proclaim thy truth among all nations. Hasten the time when all men shall have heard the Gospel of thy salvation, and when all the inhabitants of the world shall stand in awe of Thee. Bring in thy kingdom of righteousness and peace. Hear these our prayers, O Lord, and accept the praises and thanksgivings which we offer unto Thee, through Jesus Christ our Lord. Amen.

READ IN HOLY SCRIPTURE REVELATION XX.

HOLY, holy, holy, Lord God Almighty, the Creator of angels and of men, just, O Lord, are all thy ways. We pray Thee to lay the restraint of thy great might upon the powers of darkness. Grant unto us a daily victory over all their temptations and over the corruptions of our own hearts, through Him who has redeemed us with his precious blood.

Animate us with the same spirit that filled the holy martyrs, who in former days witnessed for Jesus and for the Word of God. May we be valiant for the truth, displaying its inward power by a life according to the powers of godliness, and confessing it openly in our daily conduct. In thine infinite mercy forgive us those things wherein we have failed in faithfulness to Thee and thy Word. May the blood of Jesus Christ thy Son cleanse us from all sin. May we be found in Him at his coming.

Day by day we draw nearer to that great white throne from which shall be made the final manifestation of thy holiness, authority, and justice. Suffer us not to forget that we must all stand at thy judgment-seat to give account of the things done in the body. Blot out all our sins from thy book of remembrance, and grant that our names may be found written in the book of life.

We implore Thee to bless our [children,] relations, and friends, with thy salvation, that when Christ shall come in the glory of the Father we may be re-united with them in that world of everlasting life and glory which shall then be opened to thy redeemed, and where there shall be no more death.

Thou hast shown us that earth and heaven shall flee away before the throne of the Judge, and that our present state is but temporary and corruptible. Suffer us not to bind our hearts to those things which must soon be no more. May our affections be fixed on those objects which are beyond the reach of change, and on Him who shall then come in his glory, that when He shall appear we may have confidence, and not be ashamed before Him at his coming.

Hasten, O Lord, the fulfilment of thy purposes. May the long conflict between good and evil be speedily decided. Crown thine own cause with victory. Let superstition and all delusion and unrighteousness pass away and cease for ever, and let thy kingdom come.

We commit ourselves to thy grace, in his name for the day of whose coming we would look with holy fear and joy. The Lord grant unto us that we may find mercy of the Lord at that day. Accept us now and at the last, for Jesus Christ's sake. Amen.

[MORNING.] **FIFTY-SECOND WEEK.—FRIDAY.** [EVENING.

READ IN HOLY SCRIPTURE PSALM XXXIV.

O LORD, in whom we live, and move, and have our being, Thou art great, and greatly to be praised. We adore Thee for thy glorious perfections; Thou art infinite in holiness, justice, power, wisdom, goodness, and love. But more especially would we magnify Thee for the riches of thy grace as displayed in thy dealings with us. We deserve to be shut out of thy presence for ever; but in thy wonderful love to us, Thou hast provided a way, in the death of thy dear Son, whereby we may be brought back to Thee. And through that new and living way Thou permittest us, though we are sinful and mean, to come before Thee with unhesitating confidence, and to ask Thee for everything we need, not only for the life to come, but for the present life; to disburden ourselves from every care by laying it upon Thee. Oh, how many of thy believing people have looked to Thee in their times of darkness, and been lightened, and enabled to triumph in thy truth and mercy. We, too, O Lord, would look up to Thee. We, too, would taste and see that Thou art good. Known unto Thee are the peculiar wants, and fears, and dangers of each of us here present. Let none of us rise from our knees this morning without the blessing which we need. Make us all partakers of the Holy Ghost. Give to each pardon of sin, peace of conscience, a broken and contrite heart, a spirit of submission to thy will, and of assured trust in thy love. And may we feel that it is an unspeakable honour and blessing to be the servants of such a Master; yea, the children of such a Father.

Oh, help us to live this day as becomes thy children. Give us that fear of the Lord which is the beginning of wisdom, and may it influence us in all our ways. Enable us to keep our tongues from evil, and our lips from speaking guile. May we do what is good in thy sight, and what will do good to our fellow-creatures. Cause us to live in peace, provoking no quarrels, and promoting love and goodwill among all around. Thus may our light so shine before men, to the glory of Thee, our Father in heaven.

Hear us while we pray for others as well as for ourselves. May those who are in affliction find it good for them to be afflicted. Let the poor and distressed learn to call upon Thee, and find by experience that they that seek the Lord shall not want any good thing. Cause the wicked to repent and turn to Thee ere it is too late, lest they perish in their sins. Raise up faithful ministers throughout the land, and give them great success in their blessed work; and send forth thy glorious Gospel to all nations, for the sake of Jesus Christ, our Mediator and Redeemer. Amen.

READ IN HOLY SCRIPTURE REVELATION XXI.

O GOD, the King of heaven, supreme, unchangeable, and holy, look down with pity upon us, the creatures of thine almighty hand. Consider the sinful character of the world in which we live, the way in which our souls are deluded by sin, and the calamities under which our bodies suffer. Look upon us from thy dwelling-place on high. Blessed for ever be thy name that we may look forward to a better state than this. We thank Thee, too, for the glimpses of those coming glories, which break upon us in thy last revelation of things to come. We are lost in its wonders, but our minds are exalted in the thought of them. We rise above the world and its narrow confines. We praise Thee that Jesus has his place in the vision of that heavenly city; that thy dear Son, our Redeemer, fills it with the lustre of his light. We rejoice to know that in that heavenly state He whom we love is one with Thee, whom we adore. We thank Thee for the gift of Him to mortal man, to reveal unto us thy glory and all the exceeding tenderness of thy great compassion. We hope to bless and praise Thee to all eternity for what we have seen in Him, what we have learned by Him, and what He has been to us. We should not have known Thee but by Him. We could not have loved Thee; we could not have come to Thee. The glories of thy infinite holiness would have made us recoil in alarm; but Thou didst send Him to bear the penalty of our sins, and to reconcile us unto Thee by the sacrifice of his cross. By the teaching of thy Spirit enable us to understand the happy destinies in store for us, the dignity to which we shall be raised as sons of God and joint-heirs with Jesus. We shall drink of the water of life. We shall bathe in unsullied light. We shall bask in the light of thy countenance, in that city where nothing that defileth can enter, no temptation shall approach us, nor the fear of sin distract our peace. Amid the sounds of heavenly harmonies, the sights of all beauty and glory, the apprehension of all knowledge, the attainment of all grace, what bliss will be ours! Endless ages will bring us nearer to Thee continually; and yet thy fulness will ever pass knowledge. O glorious God, our Father; O most gracious, most tender Son, our Saviour; most mighty Spirit, our Sanctifier, all praise from multitudes of the human race be ever thine! Let the angels echo man's rejoicing song; let all creatures magnify Thee; let the whole universe celebrate thy glory. And, oh, grant that, with thy redeemed and sanctified people, we and all who are dear to us may be found at the last without fault, because cleansed in Christ's blood, and made holy by thy indwelling Spirit. Hear and help us, for Christ's sake. Amen.

[Morning.] **FIFTY-SECOND WEEK.—SATURDAY.** [Evening.]

READ IN HOLY SCRIPTURE PSALM XLII.

READ IN HOLY SCRIPTURE REVELATION XXII.

GIVE us thy blessing, gracious Father, in again approaching thy mercy-seat. Raise up our souls to newness of life, as Thou dost day by day raise our bodies refreshed and strengthened by rest and repose. It is of thy goodness that we still live, and move, and have our being. It is of thy mercies that we are not consumed. Thou hast commanded thy loving-kindness to visit us in the day-time, and thy faithfulness all the night through. O God, Thou art our rock, Thou art our defence and our salvation. As the hart panteth after the water-brooks, so pant our souls after Thee, O God. Without thy presence we are miserable and lost. If Thou forsake us we are undone.

O God of our salvation, abide with us all this day. Remove the load of sin from our oppressed consciences. Raise our downcast souls. Speak peace to our troubled spirits. Tune our hearts to praise and gladness, and make thy goodness all our song in the days of our pilgrimage. May all our troubles seem light to us if Thou art near. Life's sorrows will be no sorrows to us if Jesus sweetly whisper amid them all, "Peace, be still; it is I, be not afraid." When thy billows go over us, may thine arms be underneath us. Comfort us in all our trials with the assurance that Thou wilt not leave us nor forsake us. May our oppressed souls look on to the day when we shall yet praise Thee for thy tender love. Thou art the health of our countenance, and our God. Let not our souls be disquieted within us, but give us glad hope in Thee. There remaineth a rest for the people of God; may the ever-present remembrance of that rest be a stronghold in the day of trouble. Make all trials to work for our eternal good. Draw us nearer to Thyself day by day. Make us more and more like our precious Saviour. May his spirit be ours, and our walk be like unto his most holy walk. May our sufferings be thine own appointed means of sanctification. We pray that we may come out of sorrow as gold purified in the fire, and have cause to thank Thee for ever that Thou hast so graciously dealt with us.

Again the week draws to a close. May this last day be spent only in thy service. Help us to redeem the time, because the days are evil. May we be strengthened and guided rightly to complete the week's labours. Prepare us for the coming Sabbath-day. Let the thought of it stimulate us to greater zeal in the discharge of all life's duties. Remind us, O God, by thy Spirit that we must work the works of our heavenly Master while it is day, because the night cometh when no man can work. Grant this for our dear Redeemer's sake. Amen.

SPARED by thy mercy to the end of another week, we come before Thee, most merciful Father, offering Thee our thanksgivings not only for the blessings of the past week, but also for the mercies of our whole lives. From the hour of our birth up to the present moment Thou, with tender care, hast watched over us. Surely goodness and mercy have followed us all our days. Oh, that all this care and love had met with due gratitude from us, and that our lives had been as much devoted to thy service as they have been blessed with thy bounties! Alas! we can only say, "We are a foolish people and unwise;" for we have sinned against Thee, we have walked in our own ways, and followed the devices and desires of our own hearts. Cleanse us, we pray Thee, from all our sins, in the precious blood of Jesus Christ.

We believe, according to thy Word, that if we confess our sins, Thou art faithful and just to forgive us our sins, and to cleanse us from all unrighteousness. O Lord, help us every day to strive more earnestly against all forms of sin. Cause us to grow in grace, and to be entirely conformed to the image of thy dear Son. Make us all citizens of that blessed city which Thou hast revealed to us in the portion of thy Word we have just been reading. May we drink of the water of life, and be among that blessed number who live where there shall be no more curse, where thy servants see thy face, and where they need no candle, neither light of the sun; for the Lord God giveth them light, and they shall reign for ever and ever. We pray Thee to prepare all ministers for their expected services on the morrow. Speak by them, and let the word they preach be with the demonstration of the Spirit and with power. Bless all who shall endeavour to spread the knowledge of the Saviour, whether in Christian congregations, in Sunday-schools, in the homes of the people, or in the lanes and alloys of cities and country places; and while the Spirit and the Bride say "Come," may all that hear say "Come," and multitudes come and drink of the water of life freely.

And now, O merciful and gracious Father, before this week close, bless to us all the circumstances in which we have been placed, all the work which we have done aright, all our reading and conversation. Cause all things to work together for our good. Accept our work as service to Thyself, and bless it to our true spiritual improvement. Keep us in safety this night; give us quiet and refreshing sleep, and prepare us for the privileges and enjoyments of the coming Sabbath. Hear our prayers, for the sake of Jesus Christ, our adorable Redeemer. Amen.

[MORNING.] **FIFTY-THIRD WEEK.—LORD'S DAY.** [EVENING.

READ IN HOLY SCRIPTURE PSALM LXXXIV.

O LORD of hosts, who art adored by those who dwell in thy house above: they worship Thee in the vision of thine eternal majesty; they see thy face. They are blessed, for they continually praise Thee.

We rejoice, O Lord, in the return of the day of rest. Thou art the giver of our earthly Sabbaths. We thank Thee for the rest they bring from our daily toils and cares, and for the solace and refreshment of spirit they afford under the trials and burdens of this mortal life. Help us this day to rejoice in Thee, our peace and strength. May we feel that Thou, Lord, art very near to us as the God of our salvation. Cause us to meditate with joy on thy great love to us in Christ Jesus. May our minds be enlightened by thy Word; our affections be raised by thy Spirit above every transient and fading object; our desire, love, confidence, and hope be drawn towards Thee, and more surely fixed on heavenly things. Correct our worldly inclinations; bring our wayward will into conformity with thy holy will, and free us from every hindrance to fellowship with Thee, and with the Church above. Give fervour and strength to our best desires, that our words may be the true expression of our emotions as we say, "Our heart and our flesh cry out for the living God."

Thou art the Lord of all the assemblies of the saints, whether in heavenly places or in thy earthly courts. Lead us to thine house with praise and holy gladness of heart. Give us the spirit of grace and of supplication. Remove far from us whatever would hinder or restrain our prayers. May we receive with meekness the Divine lessons thy servants shall teach us from thy Word. Thou who art eternal truth, lead us, through the ministry which Thou hast appointed, unto Thyself.

Prosper the word of thy servants to the conversion of sinners, and the progress of thy people in all godliness. Bless it especially unto ourselves [and to our dear children. Fulfil, in their salvation, the word of thy covenant, "I will be a God unto thy seed"], that we may rejoice in thy great salvation.

Thus, Lord, give us communion with thy saints. With them, may we this day draw near to Thee, the Father, through the full atonement and rich merits of thy beloved Son; and so, in fellowship with thy redeemed, advance from strength to strength, till we join the triumphant hosts of those to whom Thou didst give thy grace here, and hast given thy glory for ever. Thus may we know, both here and hereafter, the blessedness of the man whose trust is in Thee. Hear us, O Lord of hosts, for Jesus Christ's sake, to whom be everlasting praise. Amen.

READ IN HOLY SCRIPTURE PSALM XIX.

O THOU God of nature and of grace, in lowly reverence we bow before Thee, and offer our evening prayer. We thank Thee that when we call Thou wilt hear, and when we ask Thou wilt give.

Grant us, we beseech Thee, a near approach to thy throne at this time. Give us correct views of Thyself. Give us an interest in the pleadings of our great Advocate. Give us the promised aid of the Holy Spirit. Then the words of our mouth and the meditation of our hearts will be acceptable in thy sight, O Lord, our strength and our Redeemer.

For all the light Thou hast given us we devoutly thank Thee. While the heavens declare thy glory, do Thou help us to listen to their voice; and while the firmament showeth thy handy work, do Thou help us to learn the lessons it teacheth respecting Thee. In all thy works may we trace thy hand, and through all thy ways may we understand the loving-kindness of our God. Mercifully teach us by the purer light of thy holy Word. Let thy perfect law convert the unconverted. Let thy testimony make wise the simple. Let thy statutes rejoice our hearts. Let thy commandments enlighten our eyes.

Write upon our memories and our hearts, O Lord, we beseech Thee, the truths that have been brought under our notice this day. Let the prayers we have offered in thy house be graciously answered, and let our praises be accepted through the intercession of our adorable High Priest.

Oh, let the services of this day strengthen us for the duties of all the days of the week. Under their influence, may we be the better prepared for the trials and temptations of life. Oh, our Father, help us to resist every evil; help us to cleave to that which is good; and if permitted on the morrow to mingle again in the busy pursuits of this life, may we go and bring forth fruit unto God.

We ask Thee of thy great mercy, O Lord, to forgive the sins and imperfections of this day. Remember not against us the wanderings of our thoughts nor the coldness of our affections. We come even with our holy things to the cross, and pray that they may be sprinkled with the precious blood. O Lord, have mercy upon us, and permit us to go to rest to-night at peace with Thee, through our Lord and Saviour Jesus Christ.

Let thy best blessing rest on all faithful ministers of the Gospel, and on all congregations of Christian worshippers. May the labours of this day promote the cause of true piety in this land, and may that cause prosper throughout the world.

Hear, sanctify, and save us, for Jesus Christ's sake. Amen.

[Morning.] **LAST DAY BUT ONE OF LEAP YEAR.** [Evening.

READ IN HOLY SCRIPTURE PSALM CII.

O LORD, we thank Thee that Thou dost cheer us with hope whenever we call upon Thee. Our sins have deserved continual wrath, and yet Thou surroundest us with continual blessing. O Lord, we come unto Thee now, and ask thy blessing, O gracious Father, through thy beloved Son Jesus Christ. Oh, teach us to know Thee in Him as our forgiving God.

We have so often sinned and so grievously against Thee, that we could not dare to come into thy presence had not Christ loved us and died for us. In Him we know there is hope. Thou lovest to bless them that come in his name, and through Him we come, and we lay hold on the hope set before us. Thou, too, O our God and Father, art most ready to receive us, and most willing to pardon us. Else why didst Thou send Him to die for us? Thy great love sent Him to us, and his great love made Him willing to come, and glad to suffer for us. We yield Thee, O God, Father, Son, and Spirit, equal praise.

And when we think of thy mercy, we have hope. We have strong confidence that Thou wilt abide with them that seek Thee, and wilt never leave them till Thou hast brought them to thy heavenly glory. Dangers encompass us around. Temptations assail us, and Satan is ever scheming against us with all the craft of the fallen son of the morning. Give us grace to stand against all his wiles, that we may be more than conquerors through Him that loved us. But we are weak, and our resolutions often fail us, and there are rebel lusts within that spring up to lead us captive. Help us to resist them, and to tread them under foot, dying unto sin as Jesus died, and rising again into new life in holiness, as He rose again from the grave. May we be crucified with Christ, and live the life we now live in the flesh by the faith of the Son of God, who loved us and gave Himself for us. As He died for sin, so may we die to sin; and as He rose again, so may we rise unto all holy practices, all lively emotions, and all heavenly desires. May we be found walking with Christ here, that we may rest in Him after Death, having lived to his glory above all things, and finally glorified Him by dying in Him. We pray for daily help and grace from above, that if we live we may live unto the Lord; and if we die, we may die to be yet more the Lord's. Be with us during the day to which Thou hast brought us. Help us in all our work, our trials, and our temptations, and mercifully answer our prayers. Thou, Lord, knowest best what we need, whether for the body or the soul. We cast all our care upon Thee; do Thou for us above all we ask or think, for the sake of thy dear Son, Jesus Christ. Amen.

READ IN HOLY SCRIPTURE PSALM XCVII.

GREAT and glorious Jehovah! clouds and darkness are around Thee; righteousness and judgment are the habitation of thy seat! Thou art to thine enemies a consuming fire. Yet we thank Thee that Thou hast revealed Thyself as a God in whom we may rejoice. Thyself a Spirit, and the Father of spirits, we thank Thee that though we have lost thine image by sin, Thou dost restore it by grace. Thyself eternal, Thou hast brought life and immortality to light by the Gospel. Almighty, all-present, and unchangeable, we rejoice in thy power to guard, in thy presence to sustain, and in the constancy of thine enduring love towards us. Just art Thou, O Lord God; and we thank Thee that Thou canst be just and the justifier of them that believe in Thee. Holy and righteous art Thou, but Thou canst impute to us the righteousness, and transform us into the likeness of thy Son. Trusting in his merits and intercession, we can come to Thee as reconciled children to a Father.

Exposed as we are to many temptations, and subject to many trials and infirmities, over endue us with thy Holy Spirit, we beseech Thee, that we may always delight in the contemplation of thy character and doings. When we have any doubts about the revelations Thou hast made, when we are cast down by the chastisements we have to endure, when we grieve over the varied frailties of our nature, do Thou in thy mercy scatter our doubts, and take away our fears, and enable us to believe that Thou art making all things to work for our good.

And if, O God, we are deceiving ourselves in respect to our relationship with Thee in Christ, do Thou, in thy love and pity, undeceive us. Help us to examine ourselves, to prove our own selves. Shine into our hearts, and discover to us our true state. We ardently desire and fervently pray that we may be thine. Body, soul, and spirit, property and life, we would consecrate to Thee. Accept us; pardon, sanctify, and glorify us; and we shall be amongst those who shall be to the praise and glory of thy grace for ever and ever.

Extend thy kingdom in the hearts of all people. Confound them that delight in graven images. On the dark places of the earth let the Sun of Righteousness arise. To this end, endue thy Church with more of apostolic zeal and success, that the song of heaven may soon become the song of earth, "Hallelujah, the Lord God Omnipotent reigneth."

As time is lengthened and years are increased, may we be more fitted for thy presence, where there is fulness of joy, and for thy right hand, where are pleasures for evermore. We ask all for Christ's sake. Amen.

[Morning.]   NEW YEAR'S DAY.   [Evening.]

READ IN HOLY SCRIPTURE PSALM CXLV.

O LORD our heavenly Father, from everlasting to everlasting Thou art God. A thousand years in thy sight are but as yesterday when it is passed, and as a watch in the night. But man is vanity; his days are as a shadow; as a flower of the field so he flourisheth. And yet, O Lord God, Thou hast kept our souls in life; and because thy compassions fail not, we all are here waiting upon Thee on this first morning of another year. Oh, give us grace to glorify Thee. Fill our hearts with thankfulness, and our mouths and our lives with praise. May we never be weary of giving Thee thanks, for Thou art good, and doest good, and thy tender mercies are over all thy works. Bless the Lord, O our soul, and all that is within us bless his holy name, who forgiveth all our iniquities, who healeth all our diseases, who redeemeth our life from destruction, and crowneth us with loving-kindness and tender mercies.

And now, O Lord our Saviour, be nigh unto us who call upon Thee, and fulfil all our desire. We wait upon Thee, and upon Thee only do we depend for all temporal good and spiritual blessing. Do thou graciously open thy hand day by day, and satisfy us whilst we sojourn here with those things that Thou knowest we need. Uphold us, that we fall not. If bowed down under trial or sorrow, lift us up. Increase in us true religion, and nourish us with all goodness. Under the teaching of the Holy Ghost, may we grow daily in the knowledge of Thyself and of Jesus Christ thy Son. May we enjoy continually the peaceful sense of pardoning mercy through his atoning blood and righteousness. May He be unto us wisdom, and righteousness, and sanctification, and redemption; and may the life we live in the flesh be by the faith of Him who loved us and gave Himself for us. May the Lord the Spirit dwell in us and walk in us. May He guide us by his counsel, and may fruit unto holiness abound in our lives. Strengthen us with strength by the same Spirit in our souls; and oh, hold Thou up our goings, that our footsteps slip not. Sanctify to us all thy providences, and let health and sickness, prosperity and adversity, alike work together for our good.

Finally, O God, hear our intercessions. May grace, mercy, and peace be multiplied to all thy people. Bless with all blessing those who are near and dear to any of us. Add to thy Church daily such as shall be saved; and so, completing the number of thine elect, come, Lord Jesus, to be glorified in thy saints, and admired in all them that believe. May we be numbered with thy saints, and be with Thee where Thou art, beholding thy glory. So will we always praise thy name, and be giving Thee thanks for ever and ever. Amen.

READ IN HOLY SCRIPTURE 1 PETER I. 13–25.

O HOLY and most merciful God, in whose sight the very heavens are unclean, give us, we beseech Thee, a lively sense of the infinite holiness of thy nature. We are prone, O Lord, to think that Thou art such a one as ourselves. Remove, we pray Thee, the dulness of our blinded sight, and give us right impressions of the glory of thy great name. We bless Thee for that perfect justification in thy sight which is unto all and upon all that believe in the Lord Jesus Christ. We bless Thee for our adoption in Christ Jesus as thy children. Grant, O Lord, that, rejoicing in the grace that has adopted us to be thy children, we may be enabled to follow Thee as dear children, and as He which hath called us is holy, to be ourselves holy in all manner of conversation. Help us, Lord, to gird up the loins of our mind; to be sober, and hope to the end for the grace that is to be brought unto us at the revelation of Jesus Christ. Help us to remember that we have not been redeemed with corruptible things, but with the precious blood of Christ; and as bought with such a price, may we seek to glorify Thee in our bodies and spirits, which are thine.

Strengthen us by thy Spirit to be watchful against our spiritual enemies, and especially those that lie concealed in our own deceitful hearts. Give us a holy fear of offending against Thee. Cleanse us, O Lord, from our secret sins. Let the bright beams of thy truth rise in our souls and purify them. Subdue our self-will, and give us grace to be obedient unto Thee in will and deed. Give us a spirit of pure and fervent love. May all anger, clamour, and bitterness be put away from us, and love, joy, peace, long-suffering, and gentleness abound in us. We are entering on a new year, through thy mercy. Strengthen us, we pray Thee, for the duties and trials that may be before us. So order and dispose the events that shall befall us that they may conduce to our advancement in true religion and goodness. Help us to keep ever present in our minds the solemn truth that the time is short. Bless each member of this family. May none of us neglect the great salvation. May we abound in love one towards another, and endeavour to help each other in our Christian course.

Have mercy, we pray Thee, on the sick and destitute around us. Look also in compassion on the many thousands around us who are walking in the ways of sin, and give them grace to repent and turn to Thee. Let this year see a great increase to thy Church.

Hear us, O Lord, for thy mercy is great, and do for us exceeding abundantly above all that we can ask or think, for the sake of thy Son, our Lord Jesus Christ. Amen.

[Morning.] **LAST DAY OF THE YEAR.** [Evening.

READ IN HOLY SCRIPTURE 2 CORINTHIANS V. 1—9.

O GOD, who art the giver of every good and perfect gift, we desire to render our heartfelt thanksgivings unto Thee for having filled our hearts with joy and gladness, in bringing us to the last morning of another year, and for all the unnumbered mercies we have received from thy fatherly hand. Thy mercies have indeed been renewed every morning and repeated every evening; oh, how great is the sum of them! The terror by night, and the arrow that flieth by day, have not hurt us. Thousands have fallen at our side, and ten thousand at our right hand, but Thou hast preserved us alive. Spiritual blessings, great in number and infinite in value, have been vouchsafed to us. What shall we render unto Thee, O God, for all thy goodness towards us? We would call on all that is within us to bless and praise thy holy name. Oh, enable us to render unto Thee the homage of a grateful heart, and the praise of a holy life.

One year after another of our existence on earth is passing away. Soon, O God, the time Thou hast allotted for us will have gone for ever. Every passing year reminds us that we are drawing nearer to the close of our days. May we live in the constant apprehension of this our end. Help us to set our affections on things above; to live above the world, and in hope of thy glory. Give us a larger measure of thy Holy Spirit. Within us may we have a stronger witness, and in our outer life an ever-growing evidence, that we are thy children. Thus seal us with the Holy Spirit of promise, the earnest of our inheritance—making us always confident that when our earthly house of this tabernacle shall be taken down, we shall have a mansion in our Father's house above; a building not made with hands, eternal in the heavens, where we shall glorify Thee for ever.

Pour out thy blessed Spirit on all ranks and degrees of men, and turn the hearts of the disobedient into the ways of truth and godliness. Graciously protect and defend thy Church against all the powers of darkness, and the devices and desires of wicked men. Largely increase the number of thy believing people, and stir up the hearts of all who know Thee by faith to be diligent in every good word and work. Cheer the hearts of the sorrowing, and minister to them abundantly of thy grace and strength. We pray for all ministers and missionaries at home and abroad. Lord God, encourage them under their disappointment and trials, and strengthen their hands in thy work. Glorify thy Gospel in the conversion of souls, and make all things ready for the coming in of thy kingdom. Hear us, we beseech Thee, and have mercy upon us for Jesus Christ's sake. Amen.

READ IN HOLY SCRIPTURE PSALM CXI.

MOST merciful and gracious Father, through thy good hand upon us, we are brought in safety to the close of another year, and we bless Thee because thy goodness and truth have followed us daily. From Thee have come all our supplies. Thou hast caused us to lie down night by night, and Thou hast protected us; we have gone in and out daily, because Thou hast kept us. Thou hast made our bed in sickness, and hast raised us up again when we have been brought low. Thou hast refreshed us when weary, and hast comforted us with thy comforts. Thou hast endued our souls with much strength, and hast upheld us, saying to our souls, "Fear not, I am thy salvation." Thou hast blessed us with the means of grace, hast sent redemption unto thy people, and commanded thy covenant for ever. Thou hast made known to us thy Son crucified for our sins, and raised again for our justification; and Thou hast given thy good Spirit to teach and to sanctify the hearts of thy faithful people, and to witness to them that they are the children of God. O Lord, Thou hast done all this for us, and delighted over us to do us good; notwithstanding all our sins, our negligences, and our backslidings. O God, we acknowledge that we have not rendered unto Thee according to all that Thou hast done for us. We cast ourselves anew on the atonement of Jesus, our divine Redeemer. We pray Thee for his sake forgive us all that is past. Renew to us now this evening the sense of thy free pardon for his merit's sake, and so give us peace. Yea, so fill us with thy grace and heavenly benediction, that we may rejoice and be glad in Thee all the days of our life.

And now, Lord, may we be all taught so to number our days as to apply our hearts more simply, sincerely, and wholly, to heavenly wisdom. Thou, and Thou only, knowest when they shall be cut off. Only give us grace that we may always stand ready and prepared for the coming of Jesus, and may be found of Him in peace. Finally, we pray Thee to bless our Sovereign, and to look in mercy on our country. Pardon our national sins, and the sins of thy people. Oh, let not our abuse of the Christian privileges which Thou hast bestowed bring down thy judgments on the land. But turn us, O Lord, that we may be turned. Continue to us, we beseech Thee, our national and Christian blessings, and make thy people zealous for thy glory. Hear us, O Lord, and stir up thy strength and come among us, and with great might succour us. May the power of the Spirit accompany the preaching of the Gospel everywhere, and hasten the time when all shall know Thee, from the least to the greatest, through Jesus Christ our Lord. Amen.

PRAYERS AND THANKSGIVINGS

FOR

SPECIAL OCCASIONS.

	PAGE
LAST DAY BUT ONE OF LEAP YEAR	366
NEW YEAR'S DAY	367
LAST DAY OF THE YEAR	368
CHRISTMAS DAY	371
GOOD FRIDAY	371
EASTER DAY	372
ASCENSION DAY	372
WHIT SUNDAY	373
TRINITY SUNDAY	373
BIRTH OF A CHILD	374
BAPTISM OF A CHILD	374
BIRTHDAY IN THE FAMILY	375
MARRIAGE IN THE FAMILY	375
SICKNESS OF A MEMBER OF THE FAMILY	376
RECOVERY OF A MEMBER OF THE FAMILY	376
DEATH OF A MEMBER OF THE FAMILY	377
DEATH OF A PARENT	377
FUNERAL OF A MEMBER OF THE FAMILY	378
DURING DOMESTIC TRIALS	378
A MEMBER OF THE FAMILY ENTERING A NEW SPHERE	379
ENTERING UPON A NEW ABODE	379
DEPARTURE OF A MEMBER OF THE FAMILY ON A JOURNEY	380
SAFE ARRIVAL OF A MEMBER OF THE FAMILY FROM A JOURNEY	380
DURING THE ILLNESS OF A MINISTER	381
DEATH OF A MINISTER	381
COMMENCEMENT OF A NEW MINISTER'S LABOURS	382
DURING PREVALENT SICKNESS	382
A LOCAL MISSIONARY MEETING	383
ON BOARD SHIP	383
FOR FRIENDS AT SEA	384
FOR FRIENDS IN DISTANT LANDS	384
IN A TIME OF NATIONAL PERPLEXITY	385
THANKSGIVING FOR NATIONAL BLESSINGS	385
IN TIME OF WAR	386
THANKSGIVING FOR PEACE	386
DEATH OF THE SOVEREIGN	387
ACCESSION OF A SOVEREIGN	387
FOR RAIN	388
FOR FAIR WEATHER	388
FOR A FRUITFUL HARVEST	389
THANKSGIVING AFTER HARVEST	389

No. 47.

PRAYERS FOR SPECIAL OCCASIONS.

CHRISTMAS DAY.

READ IN HOLY SCRIPTURE JOHN I. 1—14, OR HEBREWS II. 14—18.

ALMIGHTY and gracious God, we especially adore Thee on this day. When we were fallen through sin, Thou didst have compassion upon us. When we had no power of our own to deliver ourselves from death, Thou didst undertake our cause, and in thy great love didst give thy dear Son to be our Redeemer and Saviour. Wonderful, indeed, is thy goodness! Help us evermore to be thankful. Suffer us not to look coldly and indifferently on the mystery of mercy which this day recalls. Give us grace to read in it a love which passes knowledge, and by thy Holy Spirit unfold to us all its meaning and purpose for ourselves. Blessed are the eyes which see the things that we see, and hear the things that we hear. We thank Thee, O God, we praise thy name for thy unspeakable gift, and pray that we may more and more experience in our own souls the blessed fruits of thy grace and mercy.

O Lord Jesus Christ, who didst make Thyself of no reputation, but wast made flesh, and dwelt among us, sharing our weakness, and bearing the burden of our sorrows, bone of our bone, and flesh of our flesh—one with us in all things, sin only excepted, we adore Thee as God over all, blessed for ever. From everlasting to everlasting Thou art God. We humbly accept the mysteries of thy incarnation, O Lord God. Thou art our Immanuel, God with us. All praise and glory be thine, that Thou didst stoop so low to redeem and to save us. Oh, suffer us not to neglect thy great salvation, nor to live unmindful of thy tenderness, and sympathy, and power. Give us faith in Thee, and so lead us by thy Spirit in the ways of truth and holiness, that we may have the witness of the Spirit that we are indeed the children of God, and have received the adoption of sons.

O God, Father, Son, and Holy Ghost, accept our adoration and praise, hear us in these our prayers, and when thou hearest forgive, for thy great name's sake. Amen.

GOOD FRIDAY.

READ IN HOLY SCRIPTURE JOHN III. 14—18.

O THOU God of our redemption, we come before Thee this day more especially to adore Thee for the gift of thy dear Son, who died the just for the unjust, that He might bring us to God.

It becomes us to humble ourselves in the very dust before Thee, when we reflect that so great was our guilt, that no less sacrifice than that of the Incarnate God would suffice to atone for it. Blessed Jesus, it was our sins that caused thy agonies! Oh, how great was thy love, even to us whose very nature is enmity to Thee! Oh, crown thy work by giving us thy Holy Spirit to take away our hard hearts, and to give us hearts to feel our own guilt and thy love, to lead us to look unto Him whom we have pierced, and to mourn for Him. Give us, O Lord, by the renewing influence of the Holy Spirit, that godly sorrow which worketh repentance unto salvation not to be repented of. Oh, that we may see that Jesus is our peace, that we have redemption through his blood, even the remission of our sins. And, oh, that we may no longer stand in doubt whether we love Christ or not; but may each be able to say from the depth of our hearts, "Lord, Thou knowest all things; Thou knowest that I love Thee."

Grant that the cross of Christ may kill our pride. May the same mind be in us which was in Him, who came down from the throne of glory to take the form of a servant, and die the death of a malefactor. Let nothing ever be done by us through strife or vain-glory, but may we be clothed with humility. We pray that the cross of Christ may kill our worldliness. By it may the world be crucified to us, and we to the world.

And, oh, that the cross may triumph throughout the earth! May Jesus see of the travail of his soul and be satisfied. May He who was lifted up upon the cross draw all men unto Him. Gracious God, pour out thy Spirit on the hearts of men, that they may believe and be saved. To Him be glory, in earth and in heaven, for ever and ever. Amen.

PRAYERS FOR SPECIAL OCCASIONS.

EASTER DAY.

READ IN HOLY SCRIPTURE MARK XVI. 1—16.

WITH grateful joy, O Lord, we hail this blessed day. We thank Thee with our whole hearts that He who died for our sins has risen again for our justification. We bless Thee that Jesus Christ our Lord, who was made of the seed of David according to the flesh, has been declared to be the Son of God with power by the resurrection of the dead. We adore Thee that Jesus, thy beloved Son, is not sleeping in the tomb, but is risen as He said, and that He has thus become the first-fruits of them that sleep in death. Strengthen our faith in the assurance that as in Adam all die, even so in Christ shall all be made alive. We pray Thee most earnestly, O heavenly Father, to bring all our hearts more and more under the power of the revelation, that the hour is coming in which all that are in their graves shall hear the voice of the Son of God and come forth; they that have done good unto the resurrection of life, and they that have done evil unto the resurrection of damnation. Awaken in each one of us a living faith in Jesus Christ, that we may in that hour hear joyfully the voice that will break the sleep of death.

Grant us the help of thy grace, that we may all now so die unto sin, so live unto God, and so set our affections on things above, as that when Christ, who is our life, shall appear, we also may appear with Him in glory. Strengthen us, by the teaching of thy Holy Spirit, for every trial. Help us to resist all sin, and lead us to purify ourselves, even as Christ is pure. Especially do we ask to be delivered from the miserable bondage of the fear of death. When Thou shalt be pleased to call us, may we be enabled by thy grace to say, "O death, where is thy sting? O grave, where is thy victory? Thanks be to God, which giveth us the victory through Jesus Christ our Lord." These, our praises and prayers, we offer in the name of Him who, though he was dead, still lives to make intercession for us. For his sake hear us, O Lord God, and help and bless us. Amen.

ASCENSION DAY.

READ IN HOLY SCRIPTURE EPHESIANS I. 15—23.

O ALMIGHTY and ever-living God, Thou art the author of life and the only source of all true happiness. We bless Thee for the incarnation, death, and resurrection of thy beloved Son, Jesus Christ, that through Him this world, sunk in sin and exposed to everlasting destruction, might be restored to thy favour and the possession of eternal life. We thank Thee that when He had conquered death, and him that had the power of death, He ascended up on high, and is now seated on thy right hand, far above all principality, and power, and might, and dominion, and every name that is named, not only in this world, but also in that which is to come. We adore Thee that in Jesus Christ we have a great High Priest, who, though He is passed into the heavens, is still touched with the feeling of our infirmities, and that He ever lives to make intercession for us before thy throne.

We beseech Thee, O God, to assist us by that mighty power which wrought in Him when Thou didst raise Him from the dead, that we may be quickened together with Christ unto newness of life, and sit together with Him in heavenly places. May we henceforth have our affections raised above the things of this world, and fixed on those things which are above, where Christ sitteth at the right hand of God.

Whilst we are here upon earth, may the remembrance of our risen and exalted Saviour stimulate to all holy obedience and love. May we have our treasure and our conversation in heaven, amidst all the sorrows and trials of this mortal life. Give us grace to live as the children of God and as heirs of eternal glory. We pray that when the Lord Jesus Christ himself shall come again, with all his holy angels, to judge the world, we may meet Him with joy, and receive his commendation, "Well done, good and faithful servant; enter thou into the joy of thy Lord." These, and all needful things, we ask, O God, in the name of our adorable Saviour, Jesus Christ. Amen.

PRAYERS FOR SPECIAL OCCASIONS.

WHIT SUNDAY.

READ IN HOLY SCRIPTURE ST. JOHN XVI. 7—14.

O THOU who art great and greatly to be feared, we come with reverence and godly fear to thy footstool, and call upon thy most holy name. We adore Thee as God almighty, infinite, and glorious. We acknowledge that we cannot by searching find Thee out, we cannot find Thee out unto perfection. And yet we praise Thee, that Thou hast not left us altogether in the dark respecting thy nature and perfections. We worship Thee as Father, Son, and Holy Spirit; and, at the same time, as the one only true God, the one God of our creation, and the one God of our salvation.

Holy and blessed Father, we thank Thee for the gift of thy Son, and not less for the gift of thy Spirit. Holy and blessed Son of God, we thank Thee for thy sufferings and death, through which the Spirit has been given to us. Holy and blessed Spirit, we thank Thee that Thou didst come, and that Thou dwellest in the midst of us. Oh, take up thine abode in our hearts, and make us the temples of the Holy Ghost.

We beseech Thee, O Lord, that our minds may be enlightened by the Spirit's teaching, and that our nature may be renewed by the Spirit's power. If any in our circle have not been convinced of sin, oh, may the Spirit convince them of sin, of righteousness, and of judgment to come. If any have been convinced, may the Spirit take of the things of Christ, and show them the all-sufficiency of his grace and the preciousness of His death. By the Spirit's abundant consolations may the sorrowing be comforted, may the dead be quickened, may the wavering be established, may the wandering be converted, and may all be sanctified. And oh, do Thou, in thine infinite mercy, help us so to live as that we may never grieve the Spirit, or cause Him to depart from us.

Hear these our prayers, O God, and grant us all mercies, through the merits of our Saviour, to whom, with Thee, O Father, and the Eternal Spirit, be everlasting praises. Amen.

TRINITY SUNDAY.

READ IN HOLY SCRIPTURE ISAIAH VI. 1—7.

GREAT God, give us, we beseech Thee, grace to receive, to believe, and, before men, to confess whatsoever Thou hast revealed concerning Thyself in thy holy Word. Let our reason, conscience, and will be guided by Thee. Grant to us a child-like spirit, that, without presumptuous questionings or doubts, we may hold the "mystery of the faith in a pure conscience."

Holy Father, who dwellest in light inaccessible; whom no man hath seen or can see, we praise and magnify thy holy name. The heavens and the earth declare thy glory. By Thee have we been created; in Thee we live, and move, and have our being. And though we have fallen from Thee, yet hast Thou provided for our redemption and salvation in the gift of thy blessed Son. May we love and serve Thee for thy marvellous love towards us. May we fear thy justice, and adore thy greatness.

Blessed Jesus, who art the only-begotten Son of the Father, who hast become man, and suffered, and died, and art risen again, for us men and our salvation; who now dost intercede for us in heaven, and bless us with thy presence on earth : do Thou accept our prayer. Let thy sacrifice be our hope, thy life our example, thy promises our consolation; and when Thou shalt come to judge the world, may we be presented by Thee without spot to God.

O Thou most Holy Spirit, the Lord and Giver of life, raise us, we beseech Thee, from the death of sin to the life of righteousness. Sanctify us by thy grace, and bless all our labours for the advancement of truth and righteousness.

O Thou Divine and Holy Trinity, three persons in one God, we adore Thee, we magnify Thee! While all holy beings worship Thee, let our voices blend with theirs, and at length may it be ours to unite with cherubim and seraphim in saying, Holy, holy, holy, Lord God of hosts, world without end. Lord hear and answer, for thy great name's sake. Amen.

PRAYERS FOR SPECIAL OCCASIONS.

BIRTH OF A CHILD.

READ IN HOLY SCRIPTURE PSALM CXXVII.

GRACIOUS and merciful God, thy wise and gracious providence has been, in all ages, the refuge and the rejoicing of those that know thy name. Thy mercy endureth for ever. We approach Thee at this time with peculiar joy, because Thou hast done great things for us, of which we are glad. We bless Thee, O Lord, for thy lovingkindness in the gift of the precious babe Thou hast intrusted to our charge; and we render unto Thee our heartfelt praises for the life which Thou hast preserved, as well as for that which Thou hast bestowed, and we pray that both may be dedicated to thy service for ever and ever.

O Thou Saviour God, who didst Thyself become an infant of days, by that great mystery of godliness, thy manifestation in our flesh, we invoke thy blessing upon this beloved infant. Let *him* continually enjoy thy favour; make *him* the object of thy constant protection; grant unto *him* health of body and vigour of mind. We seek not for this child the great things of this world, but we do supplicate the blessings of the covenant which is ordered in all things and sure. Number *him* among thy faithful followers in this world, and make *him*, with them and with ourselves, a partaker of the glory of the world to come.

We beseech Thee, O Lord, to grant unto all whom Thou hast honoured to be parents, grace to train their children in thy fear; that by example, by instruction, and by constant prayer, they may secure the blessing Thou hast promised to those who train their children in the nurture and admonition of the Lord. Suffer not our sins to bring distress or trouble upon the children now born into the world, but grant that, cleansed by the precious blood of Jesus, parents and child may in heaven rejoice before Thee with exceeding joy. Graciously behold the other children of thy household, and shed on their hearts thy heavenly grace. We ask all through thy dear Son, Jesus Christ our Saviour, to whom, with Thee and the Holy Spirit, shall be praise and glory for ever. Amen.

BAPTISM OF A CHILD.

READ IN HOLY SCRIPTURE JOHN III. 1—13.

O GOD of our fathers, whose loving sympathy is ever manifested towards them that call upon thy name, behold us as, in obedience to thy command, we have dedicated our young child to thy service.

We confess, with deep humiliation, the mournful truth that all men are by nature born in sin, and the children of wrath. We are corrupt before Thee, and there is none that doeth good, no, not one. We know that Thou hast provided for us a Saviour, able to save to the uttermost all that come to God by Him, and that through his merits and mediation Thou wilt give the Holy Spirit to them that ask for it. Only to as many as receive Christ dost Thou give authority to become thy sons, even to them who are born, not of blood, nor of the will of the flesh, nor of the will of man, but of God. May that Divine birth early take place in the child for whom we pray, and to this end pour out thy Spirit upon our seed, and thy blessing upon our offspring.

Enable *his* parents to watch over *him*, and bring *him* up in the nurture and admonition of the Lord. Ever may we feel our solemn responsibility, and be faithful to our trust, and by wise instruction and holy example attract *him* to the service of *his* Lord. Spare this child, and grant that as *he* grows in years *he* may grow in favour with God and man. Fill *him* with the Holy Ghost, that *he* may be a vessel fit for the Master's use. May *he* reverence thy Word and ordinances, and over all temptations be more than conqueror, through Him that loved *him*. Strengthen *him*, we beseech Thee, O God, day by day, and ever increase in *him* the manifold gifts of thy grace. Defend *him* continually from all evil, and grant that *he* may be thine, and continue thine for ever and ever. If life be prolonged, may *he* prove a joy to our hearts. If Thou art pleased to remove *him* in the freshness of childhood, may we be submissive to thy will, rejoicing in the assurance that of such is the kingdom of heaven. Hear us for Christ's sake. Amen.

PRAYERS FOR SPECIAL OCCASIONS.

BIRTHDAY IN THE FAMILY.

READ IN HOLY SCRIPTURE PSALM CIII.

O LORD God Almighty, thou art from everlasting to everlasting, God over all, blessed for evermore. With Thee is no variableness or the shadow of turning. Thou art the same yesterday, to-day, and for ever. We are creatures of a day, and soon the place which knows us now will know us no more. Thou hast divided our life into days, and months, and years, that we may be often reminded of the rapid flight of time, and of the nearer approach of eternity.

To one of our number, O Lord, this day brings lessons of solemn interest. Another year has fled, never more to return. As we look back, O God, we remember with unfeigned thankfulness thy great kindness, thy continued and unmerited favours. Every day has brought some new token of thy love; every moment has been laden with blessing. We bless and praise thy holy name for thy goodness and love.

Whatever Thou hast seen wrong in us during the past year, we humbly beseech Thee, in infinite mercy, to forgive. We all have reason to deplore our numerous follies and transgressions against thy most righteous law. For the sake of thy beloved Son, Jesus Christ, blot out all our sins, assure us of thy pardoning grace, and day by day grant us thy peace.

O most gracious Father, we unitedly and earnestly supplicate a special blessing upon *him* who this day enters upon a new period of time. Be pleased, we humbly beseech Thee, to grant a birthday gift from Thyself. We ask the blessing of thy favour, the gift of the Holy Ghost. As this year passes away, may it be the happiest, the holiest, and best which our dear relative has yet spent upon earth. If consistent with thy Divine will, spare to us in health and prosperity the life so dear to us; but should this year bring a season of trial, then grant to us, O merciful Lord God, that thine all-sustaining grace may be equal to our need, for the sake of thy beloved Son Jesus Christ, our Lord. Amen.

MARRIAGE IN THE FAMILY.

READ IN HOLY SCRIPTURE JOHN II. 1—11.

O GOD, who hast promised to be the God of all the families of Israel, and whose blessed Son, while here on earth, did once manifest his glory at the marriage feast in Cana of Galilee, and did there increase the provision made for those who were present with Him, to their great joy and comfort; we beseech Thee to be at this time also present with those thy servants in whose welfare we feel a more especial interest, and who this day intend to enter upon the holy state of matrimony. Fulfil the humble and earnest hope that thy protecting hand shall ever bless and defend those who shall be joined together this day in thy house with prayer and supplication. Pour down upon them the abundance of thy blessing. Hear and answer the petitions which shall be offered for them in the house of prayer. Give them grace so to take heed to the instruction contained in thy holy Word, that thy law may teach them, and thy Gospel comfort them, and that under the guidance of thy Holy Spirit they may steadfastly walk in the narrow road which conducts to everlasting life; and grant that in all places, circumstances, and relations they may live to thy glory, and walk as in thy presence. And do Thou sanctify to them the new and lasting relation into which they are about to enter, that their hearts may be knit together in holy and perpetual love. May no previous ties of kindred or of affection be broken, or even weakened, by the separation which is caused; but may others be formed thereby.

Finally, we beseech Thee, make us all to be accepted in Him who is the Head of his body, the Church. Cleanse us this day, and every day, in his precious blood. Enrich us with thy heavenly grace; renew us constantly by thine indwelling Spirit; make us holy as Thou art holy; and grant that we may be presented without spot before Thee, and be partakers of the marriage supper of the Lamb, through Him who liveth and reigneth with Thee and the Holy Ghost, one God, for ever and ever. Amen.

PRAYERS FOR SPECIAL OCCASIONS.

SICKNESS OF A MEMBER OF THE FAMILY.

READ IN HOLY SCRIPTURE PSALM XXXVIII. 1—15.

O THOU God of all compassion, who art a very present help in trouble, we come unto Thee in this season of anxiety. In Thee, O Lord, do we hope: Thou wilt hear, O Lord our God. We meet together, therefore, to plead with Thee on behalf of that beloved member of our family who is visited with illness. We know that sickness came into the world through sin. Our many and grievous sins have justly deserved that we should be visited with sickness and death. But, Lord, thine only Son came to take our sins upon Him; and in bearing them, Himself took our infirmities, and bare our sicknesses. For his sake forgive our sins, and comfort us by healing our dear relative.

Blessed Jesus, we remember what Thou didst for those who brought to Thee the sick of the palsy; how Thou saidst, "Son, thy sins be forgiven Thee," and didst then command him to arise and walk. Oh, do the same, we humbly pray Thee, for us. Give to thy sick servant the blessed assurance of thy pardoning love; and give *him* likewise renewed health, that *he* may live to Thee, and be an instrument of thy glory, by serving Thee faithfully, and doing good in *his* generation.

But, O Lord, we desire from the heart to say, "Thy will be done." We know that it is appointed unto all men once to die. But Jesus has taken away the sting of death, and made it to his people the pathway to immortality. Oh, if it be thy will to call our beloved one hence, prepare *him* for the momentous change. Renew *him* by thy Spirit. May *he* be found in Christ, not having his own righteousness, but that which is by the faith of Jesus Christ. In Him may *he* triumph over death, and be received into thine everlasting kingdom.

And, oh, teach us all so to number our days that applying our hearts to wisdom, we may sit loose to this fleeting world, and esteem Jesus as the pearl of great price. Cause us daily to set our affections on things above, that we may die unto sin and live unto God. Hear us, we pray Thee, and answer us, for Jesus Christ's sake. Amen.

RECOVERY OF A MEMBER OF THE FAMILY.

READ IN HOLY SCRIPTURE PSALM XXX.

MOST merciful and gracious Lord God, Thou liftest up all those that be bowed down. Verily God hath heard us, and hath not turned away our prayer, nor his mercy from us.

We bring to Thee now, in great humility, our most hearty thanks for thy deliverance wrought in this household. Thou didst smite, but Thou hast healed. Thou didst lay low, but Thou hast brought back our beloved friend from the gates of the grave. Because Thou hast been mindful of us, therefore in the shadow of thy wing will we rejoice. O Lord, we beseech Thee, sanctify to all this family the affliction that is passing away. Let not our hearts grow cold towards Thee, in forgetfulness of thy great mercy. May thy servant who is spared to us remember the way through which Thou hast led *him*, and live henceforth a life of thankfulness and holiness unto the Lord. Help all of us, we pray Thee, to join in this renewed sacrifice of praise; and may we, too, be prepared, at thy bidding, to part with health and strength, and suffer all thy will. Whether we live, may we live unto the Lord; and whether we die, may we die unto the Lord; whether we live or die, may we be the Lord's.

And grant, O our Father, we earnestly pray, that when our pilgrimage on earth is finished, as it soon will be, there may remain to all who dwell in this house the building of God, the house not made with hands, eternal in the heavens; where the inhabitants shall no more say, "I am sick;" where there shall be no more pain; and where this corruptible shall put on incorruption, and this mortal shall put on immortality. May thy mercies lead us to repentance, and thy love in Christ Jesus constrain us to live for thy praise.

O Lord our God, we will give thanks unto Thee for ever for thy loving goodness and for thy truth and faithfulness.

Glory be unto the Father, unto the Son, and unto the Holy Ghost; as it was in the beginning, is now, and ever shall be, world without end. Amen.

PRAYERS FOR SPECIAL OCCASIONS.

DEATH OF A MEMBER OF THE FAMILY.

READ IN HOLY SCRIPTURE PSALM XXXIX.

O LORD, the Sovereign Ruler and Disposer of all things, without whom not even a sparrow falleth to the ground, happy are we that we may draw nigh Thee in the hour of overwhelming trouble; that sorrowing, we may look up to Thee as our loving, wise, and gracious Father, and even in the presence of death trust Thee, lean on Thee, and draw from Thee the grace that upholds, comforts, and blesses.

Draw near, O our God. Let the cry of our sorrow come before Thee. We acknowledge thy right over us, and ask of Thee a holy, child-like submission. Teach us the lessons Thou desirest us to learn. Let us not remain unmoved in the presence of so great an affliction, neither let us sinfully murmur. Sanctify this our loss to the good of our souls, and humble us with fresh views of our sinfulness, the wrongs we have done to Thee, to each other, and to our departed relative.

Teach us to know our end, and the measure of our days what it is, that we may know how frail we are. May we live as those who must soon die, valuing each moment as an opportunity of serving Thee, of blessing others, and of growing in the grace and knowledge of our Lord. Grant us a holy diligence in well-doing, a conscientious discharge of duty, a single eye to thy glory, and a more intense longing for the coming of the great day of Jesus Christ.

We thank Thee, our Father, for the joyful hope of the resurrection-day. And now what wait we for? Our hope is in Thee, and our eyes are towards Thee. Help us so to live that to die may be gain. Work in us all that is well-pleasing in thine eyes. Change us into the image of Christ, from glory to glory, so that when the Master calleth we may be found in Jesus, and be for ever with the Lord.

Glorify thy great name, and save us; sanctify us with thy Holy Spirit, and enrich us with thy heavenly grace, for thy dear Son's sake, our Saviour Jesus Christ. Amen.

DEATH OF A PARENT.

READ IN HOLY SCRIPTURE GENESIS L. 1-14.

OUR Father, who art in heaven, the ever-living and unchanging God, hear us. We bow before Thee, oppressed by the mournful visitation of death. Meekly and submissively would we kiss the rod that has smitten us; and, though it be with trembling lips, exclaim, "Even so, Father; for so it seemeth good in thy sight."

Help us with filial tenderness to remember *him* who has gone from us, and cherish with profound veneration the memory of departed goodness, of loving watchfulness, and parental care. May we be followers of them who through faith and patience inherit the promises.

We bless Thee, amid all our sorrows, for the bright light which the Gospel sheds over the grave; for the assurance that though in Adam all die, in Christ shall all be made alive. While pursuing our course without the smile and counsel we have been wont to enjoy, may we be comforted by the thought that when father and mother forsake us, the Lord will take us up; that like as a father pitieth his children, so the Lord pitieth them that fear Him. Blessed be thy name for all the cheering promises given us in thy Word, designed to soothe our aching hearts. May we, with an unwavering faith in the Divine goodness, rise from the dust, into which this bereavement has cast us, and go forth to the duties of life with more firm dependence on thy grace. Hold Thou us up, and we shall be safe. Guide us by thy counsel, and afterwards receive us unto glory. Enable us to prepare for our own departure, by daily exercising fresh confidence in Christ our Redeemer, by the cultivation of a spirit of love and obedience to Thee, and by aiming at perfect holiness in the fear of God; and at last, through the intercession of our glorious High Priest, may we receive an abundant entrance into the kingdom of our Lord and Saviour. Hear this our prayer, and do for us abundantly, above all we ask or think, for his sake. To whom, with Thee and the Holy Spirit, be glory for ever and ever. Amen.

PRAYERS FOR SPECIAL OCCASIONS.

FUNERAL OF A MEMBER OF THE FAMILY.

READ IN HOLY SCRIPTURE 1 THESS. IV. 13—18.

LORD, have mercy upon us; Christ, have mercy upon us. O God, in thy hands are the keys of death and the world to come. Thou openest, and no man can shut; Thou shuttest, and no man can open. Even now, O our Father, we will pray that as our day our strength may be. Lord, we believe; help Thou our unbelief.

The Lord gave, and the Lord hath taken away; blessed be the name of the Lord. We have been to the grave, to weep there. We have buried our dead out of our sight. It is the Lord; let Him do what seemeth Him good.

Blessed Saviour, we thank Thee that Thou canst be touched this day with the feeling of our infirmities. Thou too hast been at the mouth of the sepulchre. Jesus wept. Give to our sorrowing hearts, we implore Thee, grace to believe thy words, "I am the Resurrection and the Life." Our *brother* shall rise again. Thy grave, moreover, we will recollect. Thou Thyself hast suffered the last agony, and Thou hast risen from the dead. It is not, therefore, thought a thing incredible with us that God should raise the dead; for now is Christ risen from the dead, and become the first-fruits of them that slept.

Meanwhile, O blessed Saviour, comfort our hearts, and fill up in this house the void thy providence has made. Let us not be filled with overmuch sorrow. May we look beyond the grave to the everlasting world, and set our affections ever on the inheritance incorruptible, undefiled, eternal in the heavens.

Prepare us, O Lord, for our own departure. For us the windows must be darkened. We too shall be carried to the burial. Grant, we humbly pray, that our friends may bury us when we depart in sure and certain hope of the resurrection to eternal life. And may we all meet together again in the world where they die no more, where the tears shall be wiped away for ever from our eyes, and the day of our mourning shall be ended, for Jesus Christ's sake. Amen.

DURING DOMESTIC TRIALS.

READ IN HOLY SCRIPTURE HEBREWS XII. 1—13. OR PSALM LVII.

O GOD, Thou art our refuge in all times of distress. Thou hast said, "Call upon me in the day of trouble, and I will answer Thee." We know that Thou art true, and that thy promise cannot fail. In this, the time of our sorrow and distress, we come to Thee. Thou knowest the peculiar trial which now afflicts us. In thy great love and pity, behold us as we approach thy footstool for help. O Lord, our spirits are bowed down with grief. We are utterly helpless, and all human aid fails us. Extend to us, we beseech Thee, thine almighty arm, and grant us thy supporting and delivering grace.

We know, O Lord, that every affliction we bear is sent in mercy, and is designed for our good. We would not murmur or repine at thy dealings with us. We confess that our severest trials are far lighter than we deserve. Thou hast not dealt with us after our sins, nor rewarded us according to our iniquities. Oh, that we may receive the lessons which Thou art now teaching us. Forbid that we should lose the benefit of this trial. Though we at present feel it grievous to bear, may it produce in us the peaceable fruits of righteousness, to thy praise and glory.

If consistent with thy holy will, we pray that this end may soon be answered, and then we humbly beseech Thee to remove the trial from us. Whilst it lasts, do Thou, O merciful Father, help us to bear it with patience and resignation to thy will. In all our trials assist us, that we may be continually looking to Jesus, who, for the joy that was set before Him, endured the cross, despising the shame. Strengthen us with the spirit of grace and of glory, that whilst we suffer with Him here, we may be sustained by the abundant consolations of his love; and when our trials are ended, and the time for our departure has arrived, may we be received into his kingdom, to reign together with Him in glory everlasting. We ask this in Jesus' name. Amen.

PRAYERS FOR SPECIAL OCCASIONS.

A MEMBER OF THE FAMILY ENTERING A NEW SPHERE.

READ IN HOLY SCRIPTURE PSALM I.

MOST gracious God and Father in Christ Jesus, we give Thee thanks and praise that we are commanded to acknowledge Thee in all our ways, and that Thou hast promised to direct our steps. We know that there cannot be prosperity in the affairs of this life except Thou give the blessing; but Thou hast promised thy blessing to them that seek first the kingdom of God and his righteousness, and Thou hast told us that godliness is profitable for all things, having promise of the life that now is, and also of that which is to come. And now, believing these gracious words, and trusting that thy hand is in the movement which one of our number is making, we earnestly commit *him*, and all that concerns *his* well-being, to thy Divine care. Grant that it may be found that this matter is of Thee, of thy gracious ordering, and therefore for the good of all concerned. Let integrity and truth preserve *him*; give *him* wisdom, that *he* may order *his* affairs with discretion, and let the pure principles of the Gospel regulate *his* intercourse with the world. Bestow as much prosperity as Thou seest best for *his* highest interests. Fulfil in *his* case the promise made to the man that walketh not in the counsel of the ungodly, nor standeth in the way of sinners, nor sitteth in the seat of the scornful; but whose delight is in the law of the Lord; that *he* may be as a tree planted by rivers of water, that bringeth forth *his* fruit in due season. If it be thy pleasure to bless *him*, and to prosper the work of *his* hands, give *him* grace always to remember *his* obligations to Thee, and to act as a steward of thy manifold gifts. And, above all, may we ever keep in mind the solemnity of the great day when we shall stand before the judgment-seat of Him who knows even our inmost thoughts, and, through thine infinite mercy in Christ Jesus, stand accepted before Thee then, and be for ever gathered together with the congregation of the righteous. Hear our prayers, for the sake of Jesus Christ our Lord. Amen.

ENTERING UPON A NEW ABODE.

READ IN HOLY SCRIPTURE HEBREWS XI. 8—16.

O LORD our heavenly Father, who, in the arrangements of thy providence, hast appointed us another habitation on which we have entered this day, we bless Thee that though we have not now the visible sign of thy leading us with which Israel in the wilderness was favoured, even the pillar of cloud and of fire, at whose removal they moved forward, and at whose tarrying they rested, yet we have sure and certain guidance in thy holy Word, and in thy ever-encompassing providence. It is joy to us, O Lord, to feel that all our movements on earth may be entirely guided and sanctioned by Thee, and that if we seek Thee Thou wilt go with us wherever we go, and dwell with us where we dwell.

O Lord, as Thou hast been with us in our old house, so be with us in the new. Let our present abode be only the shadow and earnest of that blessed home from which there shall be no removal; and if any of our number should be called away from this house by death, oh, grant that it may be only to enter that better home in glory. Help us to dwell here as Abraham in the land of promise, looking for the city that hath foundations, whose builder and maker is God, and confessing that we are strangers and pilgrims on the earth. Cause our chief aim here to be to glorify Thee, and help us all, in our different relationships and spheres of duty, to seek to let our light so shine before men that they may glorify Thee, our Father, in heaven. Assist us to live as a Christian household, knit together in love; to be kind one to another, tender-hearted and forgiving; seeking not our own good exclusively, but each seeking the welfare of the whole family. Pour down in rich abundance thy blessing upon this household, and hereafter gather us all safely into the heavenly kingdom, where all the family of God shall dwell with Thee for ever. Every blessing we need to render this new dwelling the abode of peace, and joy, and righteousness, and love, we seek in the name of Jesus Christ our Lord. Amen.

PRAYERS FOR SPECIAL OCCASIONS.

DEPARTURE OF A MEMBER OF THE FAMILY ON A JOURNEY.

READ IN HOLY SCRIPTURE PSALM CXXI.

O GOD, most holy and blessed, we desire to lift up our hearts to Thee as our glorious Creator, in whom we live, and move, and have our being. We know not what a day may bring forth, and cannot go out or come in without thy gracious help. We would acknowledge Thee in all our ways, and lift up our eyes to the hills whence our help cometh. Be pleased, for Christ our Saviour's sake, to show thy salvation to every member of this family. May we all know Thee as our Father, and walk before Thee as obedient children, called out of the world, and set apart to thy service and glory. Especially would we commend to thy care and protection that member of our family who is about to leave us for a time. Grant thy merciful protection and presence to *him*, O Lord, during the journey upon which *he* is about to enter. Let no evil befall our dear one. May *he* be preserved in peace of mind, and in health and safety of body, and feel that Thou art with *him* continually. We praise Thee for the promises of the psalm we have read, and for the assurance that the Lord is the keeper of his people, and their shade upon their right hand. We thank Thee for the privilege of prayer, and that we can pray for one another, though separated; for Thou art in every place, and hearest the prayers of thy people when they make intercession for their brethren in the name of the Lord. And grant, O God, that we may all be preserved safely through the whole journey of life; that we may be enabled to set the Lord always before us; that we may walk in the narrow path that leads to everlasting life; and that, finally, when with us all the changes of time are over, we may meet in heaven, a redeemed family, to be employed for ever in the noble service of the upper sanctuary, where we shall see the Lord, and our joy shall be full. All this we humbly but earnestly ask in the name of our Lord and Saviour Jesus Christ. Amen.

SAFE ARRIVAL OF A MEMBER OF THE FAMILY FROM A JOURNEY.

READ IN HOLY SCRIPTURE PSALM CXLV.

GRACIOUS and compassionate Lord God, whose tender mercies are over all thy works, we render praise and thanks to Thee for thy special goodness in bringing thy servant in safety to the end of *his* journey. We commended *him* to thy care, and Thou hast graciously heard our petitions, and brought *him* to the haven where *he* would be. What shall we render to Thee for these and thy many other mercies, for thy watchful care, for thy sustaining grace, and for help in every time of trouble? How many are thy thoughts which are to usward! how many evils dost Thou keep far from us! and from how many snares dost Thou preserve our feet, that they slip not! The eyes of all wait upon Thee. Thou openest thine hand, and satisfiest the desire of every living thing. We have ever found Thee to be ready to hear, and nigh unto us when we have called upon Thee in truth.

Let a sense of thy continued mercies, and of this fresh instance of thy goodness, lead us more devotedly to give ourselves to thy service, and to desire to please Thee in all our ways, that wherever our lot may be cast, in our own native land or far away from our home, we may do thy will in that position of life to which Thou hast been pleased to call us.

As we accomplish our earthly journeys, may we remember that we are but pilgrims and strangers here; that this is not our rest, and that the world can give us no real satisfaction, but that we must seek it in heaven, where Christ is, at thy right hand. Help us to hasten on to that blessed state, setting our affections upon things above, abstaining from fleshly lusts that war against the soul, and earnestly desiring, after this long and wearisome journey of life, to enter upon the everlasting enjoyment of that rest which remaineth for the people of God, to which may God, of his mercy, bring us, for the sake of Jesus Christ, our blessed Lord and Saviour. Amen.

PRAYERS FOR SPECIAL OCCASIONS.

DURING THE ILLNESS OF A MINISTER.

READ IN HOLY SCRIPTURE JOHN XI. 1—16.

O GOD, in whose hand our breath is, and whose are all our ways, we bow ourselves before Thee, in humble supplication on behalf of our beloved and valued pastor, now prevented from ministering to us.

We are encouraged to come to Thee in this matter, after the example of our sympathising Saviour, who mourned over the sickness, and wept over the grave of his friend; so now may we learn to weep with them that weep, and to suffer with them, as being members one of another, bearing one another's burdens, and so fulfilling the law of Christ.

Now that Thou hast afflicted him, cause our pastor to feel all the power of those blessed truths he has testified to others. May the comfort with which he has comforted others return into his own bosom an hundredfold. May he be perfectly assured of thy good-will towards him, that Thou wilt perfect that which concerns him, and not forsake the work of thine own hands. Enable him to commit the care of his flock and family into the hands of the good Shepherd, and to feel that Thou wilt provide for the sheep of thy pasture.

If it be thy will, restore him speedily to health and strength, that with renewed vigour, and in the enjoyment of re-established health, he may continue his important and arduous task, and again refresh our souls with the saving truths of the everlasting Gospel.

If this should not be in accordance with thy will, yet vouchsafe thy suffering servant a special sense of thy presence, increase of faith in that Saviour whom he has preached to others, and greater meetness for the inheritance of the saints. Comfort his heart by the assurance of thy love; and give him a reasonable hope that many to whom he has ministered here will be his joy and crown of rejoicing in the day of the Lord, when thy Church shall be complete and the number of thy elect gathered in. We beseech Thee to hear and help and bless us, for Jesus Christ's sake. Amen.

DEATH OF A MINISTER.

READ IN HOLY SCRIPTURE HEBREWS XIII. 7—17.

O THOU who art the same yesterday, and to-day, and for ever, Thou alone art our undying Friend; grant that in thy unchangeable perfections we may ever find sufficient consolation from the sorrows of this changing world. In this season of suffering we desire to bow to thy sovereign will; we rejoice that all thy ways are right, and thy dominion is an everlasting dominion over all creatures and all events. Clouds and darkness are round about Thee, but justice and judgment are the habitation of thy throne. O our God, bless unto us and to all our fellow-worshippers that stroke of thy providence which has removed one of our best earthly friends, thy servant, who taught us in thy truth, and led us in thy ways. While we mournfully exclaim, "The prophets, where are they? and the fathers, do they live for ever?" do Thou, O Lord, graciously comfort our hearts, and preserve us from undue sorrow.

Be pleased, great God, to sanctify to us, and to our neighbourhood, this bereavement. We confess that we have not profited as we might have done by the labours of thy faithful servant, and we pray that even now he, being dead, may speak to us in our frequent recollection of his words. We bless Thee, O Lord, for thy servant's fidelity, for his consistent life, and for every instance in which he has been the means of turning men from sin unto God. We rejoice in the firm belief that he is honoured with thine own approval, and has received a large reward. We commend to thy loving care all his afflicted relatives, beseeching Thee to provide for all their necessities, and to comfort them in this season of grief. Graciously send unto us, O God, a pastor after thine own heart, and permit us not, by indifference to thy holy Word, to call down the chastisement of our sins and the loss of our spiritual privileges. Hear us, good Lord, and according to thine exceeding great and precious promises, give us an answer of peace, for Jesus Christ's sake, to whom with Thee and the Holy Ghost be all honour and glory. Amen.

PRAYERS FOR SPECIAL OCCASIONS.

COMMENCEMENT OF A NEW MINISTER'S LABOURS.

READ IN HOLY SCRIPTURE 1 COR. III. 1—15.

O ALMIGHTY God, who in thy good providence hast sent forth many ministers in thy Church, and who hast in all ages used them as instruments in thy hand for leading men to the saving knowledge of thy truth; we beseech Thee to look down in mercy upon all thy ministers in all parts of the world (and especially in this place and neighbourhood), and to fill them with thy grace and heavenly blessing. Grant that they may never attempt to lay any other foundation than that of Jesus Christ; and that they may so teach and preach Jesus Christ and him crucified, both in public and private, and set him forth as lifted up for the salvation of mankind, that all classes of men may be drawn unto him as their Redeemer and their Saviour.

The things which we thus ask, O Lord, for all the churches of the saints, and for the ministers thereof, we do more especially ask at this time for this place, and for the ministers thereof; beseeching Thee to grant a special blessing to him who is newly called to labour therein for Thee, and also to the people committed to his charge, that they may duly profit by the ministry of the Gospel. Grant that thy Word spoken by thy ministers in this place may never be spoken in vain; and that the work of God may so prosper in these parts that all may be constrained to say, "What hath God wrought!" Enable us, and all the people, to fulfil all the duties of those who are taught in the Word; but grant that we may never so put our trust in man as to forget that Thou alone workest in us to will and to do of thy good pleasure. May we therefore work out our own salvation with fear and trembling, looking to Thee alone.

These and all other blessings, for us, and thy whole Church, and the people of this place, and all that are dear unto us, which Thou seest that we need, we ask in the name of our Lord and Saviour Jesus Christ. Amen.

DURING PREVALENT SICKNESS.

READ IN HOLY SCRIPTURE PSALM XCI.

O THOU Almighty and gracious God, our only Helper and most sure Refuge, turn Thou unto us, and help us who are in so great and pressing need. Thou knowest our sad estate, and what danger we are in. Disease, sickness, death are on every side, and Thou art chastening us, and filling our eyes with tears and our hearts with anguish. Oh, our God, wilt Thou not pity, help, and save us, who humbly and with sorrow of heart do cast ourselves at thy feet? Deal not with us as we have deserved, neither remember against us our iniquities. For who are we, that the Lord should contend with us? and how can we, who are but dust and ashes, stand before Thee?

We do confess our sins this day, the sins of our past lives, and are ashamed and confounded because of our transgressions against Thee. Humble us beneath thy mighty hand. Cleanse Thou us from secret faults. Wash us, and make us white in the blood of the Lamb, and restore unto us the joy of thy salvation.

Thou art good, and just, and righteous in all thy dealings; but, oh, our God, who hast promised thy protection and blessing to thy people, remember us as a family for good. Keep from our home, if it seem good in thine eyes, the sickness that alarms us. Let no evil happen to us and ours. Lord, we trust in Thee, we rely upon thy gracious promises, we call to mind all thy love to us, and the great gift of thy dear Son which Thou hast bestowed upon us, and that Word of thine in which Thou hast caused thy servant to hope: "Call upon me in the day of trouble, and I will answer thee." But shouldst Thou will otherwise, thy will be done. Teach us a cheerful submission, an unfaltering confidence in Thee, a trustful reliance on our gracious Saviour, a meetness for thy kingdom, and an abundant entrance therein, through Jesus Christ our Lord, who ever liveth at thy right hand in glory, our all-prevailing Mediator and Saviour, so that at last we may enter upon the blessings prepared for us for His sake. Amen.

PRAYERS FOR SPECIAL OCCASIONS.

A LOCAL MISSIONARY MEETING.

READ IN HOLY SCRIPTURE ISAIAH LV.

O GOD, who hast given thine only-begotten Son to die for sinners, and willest not that any should perish, but that all should come to the knowledge of the truth, be present at our assembling together to-day for the spread of thy glorious Gospel among the heathen. Thou hast commanded us to send the message of salvation to every creature, and hast given us the cheering promise that the heathen wilderness shall yet blossom abundantly, and rejoice with joy and gladness. Do Thou graciously fulfil thy promise, and enable us more earnestly to obey thy blessed command. Bless the society on whose behalf we have met. May its means of spreading thy truth be greatly increased. May its promoters be more numerous. Increase their zeal and liberality. Bless those who guide its counsels. Strengthen those engaged in its glorious work. Especially look with favour upon its missionaries. May they ever be men of God, full of faith, and power, and the Holy Ghost. Comfort them in their distant and lonely homes. Be Thou their stay and support, and great consolation. More than make up to them all that they have forsaken in their own land. Gather thousands and tens of thousands of perishing souls into thy fold by their means; and may thy will be done, and thy kingdom come over all the world.

Bless our efforts in this place in the great work of sending the Gospel to the heathen. Make us all more self-denying and prayerful. Increase our interest in the blessed work, and multiply our labours. Above all, make us individually partakers of the inestimable benefit of Christ's salvation. Let us not perish ourselves while we are sending the good news of pardon to others. Give us thy Holy Spirit that we may know Thee and love Thee in our own souls, anxious to adorn the Gospel of God our Saviour, and make known thy love to the whole earth.

Graciously hear us and answer us, according to thy abundant mercy, for the sake of Jesus Christ our Lord. Amen.

ON BOARD SHIP.

READ IN HOLY SCRIPTURE PSALM CVII. 21—31.

O THOU who makest the outgoings of the morning and evening to praise Thee, accept the tribute of our hearty, though most unworthy thanksgiving. Thy providence has led us to journey over the sea, and thy hand has kept us in safety. We are passing through dangers unknown, above us, below us, and around us; but beneath thy wings we are secure from all things that can hurt us. O Lord, great is thy goodness; thy thoughts to us-ward are more in number than the sand upon the sea-shore.

Abide with us, we beseech Thee, O Lord. Let thy protecting love continue to preserve us and those who are our companions in the ship. Say to the storms, "Peace, be still," and bid the winds prosper our course towards the haven where we would be. O Lord God of hosts, who is a strong Lord like unto Thee? or to thy faithfulness round about Thee? Thou rulest the raging of the sea: when the waves thereof arise, Thou stillest them.

Protect, we entreat Thee, O God of grace, our souls as well as our bodies, and comfort us with thy peace, that passeth understanding. Keep us day by day, that we may not sin against Thee in thought, or word, or work. Fill us with a deep sense of thy majesty and power, who madest the sea and all that is therein. Let thy believing people in this ship adorn their profession in all things, and boldly witness for Thee before all men. And for them who know Thee not, we beseech Thee to teach them by thy Spirit; that seeing the works of the Lord, and thy wonders in the deep, they may feel their dependence on thy strength, and their need of thy forgiveness. Give them repentance unto salvation, and stablish them with thy free Spirit. Oh, make them thine, and keep them thine for ever and ever.

Hear us, O God, and answer these our imperfect petitions, which we offer up relying upon the merits and prevailing intercession of Jesus Christ, thy Son, our Lord; to whom be glory for ever and ever. Amen.

PRAYERS FOR SPECIAL OCCASIONS.

FOR FRIENDS AT SEA.

READ IN HOLY SCRIPTURE ISAIAH XLIII. 1—11.

ALMIGHTY Lord God, graciously hear us and help us, for thy great name's sake. Thou hast created heaven and earth, the sea, and all things that are therein. The winds and waves are thy servants, and fulfil in all things thy will. Thou sittest above the water-floods, a King for evermore. We cast our care upon Thee, for Thou carest for us, and supplicate all grace and blessing for our friends now exposed to the perils of the deep. Merciful Father, look down upon them and watch over them. Fulfil thy gracious promise; while they pass through the waters, be Thou with them, and let not the flood overtake them. Stretch around them the everlasting arms, and bring them in safety to the haven where they would be. By day and by night, in calms and tempests, wherever they are, do Thou shield and protect them. When danger threatens them, do Thou interpose for their preservation, and in the hour of trial, do Thou, O Jesus, help and deliver. And while Thou dost mercifully preserve and protect them from temporal evils, oh, make them thine by the converting and renewing power of thy Holy Spirit. If they are unconverted, do Thou convert them. Carry on in them the purposes of thy love, and seal them unto the day of redemption, that we and they may be one in Christ Jesus, and look forward with a common hope to the rest which remaineth for the people of God.

And not only for our own friends, but for all who go down to the sea in ships, we implore thy grace and protection. Mercifully look upon them, O God, and by thy Spirit stir up their hearts to spiritual anxiety. Impress them by the visible displays of thy power, and teach them thy greatness and glory. Cause thy goodness to lead them to repentance, and the constant nearness of danger to prompt them to earnestness in the great work of their souls' salvation.

We ask these mercies, O our God, all for Jesus Christ's sake, our only Saviour and Redeemer. Amen.

FOR FRIENDS IN DISTANT LANDS.

READ IN HOLY SCRIPTURE PSALM VIII.

WE adore Thee, Lord God Almighty, that Thou art, at all times and in all places, the hearer and the answerer of prayer; and we now come to Thee, beseeching that thy gracious regard may be especially displayed towards our beloved relatives and friends in distant lands. We rejoice to feel that, although far removed from us, they are near to Thee, for Thou art not far from any one of us. Behold now, O God, those over whom our hearts yearn; and though the seas divide us as to the body, let thy grace unite us in spirit at thy footstool. The Lord watch between us while we are absent one from the other.

We know not what may be the circumstances in which our beloved friends are now placed; but this is our comfort: thine eye, O God, is upon them, and thine ear is open to their cry. Bless them, O Lord, with the consciousness of thy presence, with the mercies of thy providence, and with the rich fulness of thy sanctified Word. In worship and in work, in labour and in rest, in rising up and in sitting down, in going out and in coming home, by night and by day, in solitude and in society, enrich them with the enjoyment of thy love. Enable them ever to continue instant in prayer, and may the God of their fathers attend to their petitions, and in each new scene give them new impressions of his favour. Grant unto them, O Lord, the public means of grace, the faithful ministry of thy truth, and the sweet enjoyments of the Sabbath; bless them with friends who fear thy name, and preserve them from the error of the wicked: suffer not the sun to smite them by day, nor the moon by night; the Lord preserve them from all evil. Father of mercies, grant that, when the wanderings of our earthly pilgrimage shall cease, we and those we love may meet in thy heavenly mansions, to go out no more for ever.

We ask these blessings, and whatever else Thou seest good, O gracious God and merciful Father, in the name of our Lord and Saviour Jesus Christ. Amen.

PRAYERS FOR SPECIAL OCCASIONS.

IN A TIME OF NATIONAL PERPLEXITY.

READ IN HOLY SCRIPTURE PSALM XLVI.

ALMIGHTY God, enthroned in the highest heavens, who art governor among the nations of the earth, give ear to the cry of thy people who, in their trouble, visit Thee, and pour out their prayer while thy chastening is upon them. We acknowledge our manifold offences against thy law and thy love. We have sinned, and come short of thy glory. O Lord, righteousness belongeth unto Thee; but unto us confusion of face, as at this day. Now, therefore, O our God, hear the prayer of thy servants, and cause thy face to shine upon us. O Lord, forgive; O Lord, hearken and do; defer not for thine own sake, O our God, for we are called by thy name.

Amid all our national perplexities, do Thou appear on our behalf. When men's hearts are failing them for fear, be Thou our refuge and strength: a very present help in trouble. Give wisdom to those who are at the head of public affairs: wisdom that is profitable to direct. May all be sensible that apart from thy guidance it is not safe to act. May the fear of thy holy name ever direct all their deliberations and doings. Control all the complicated movements of men and nations, and overrule their passions and prejudices, that thy name may be glorified. Make the wrath of men praise Thee. If calamities shall visit us as a people, may we bow submissively beneath thy stroke, and acknowledge that Thou art justified when Thou speakest, and clear when Thou judgest. Yet, Lord, in the midst of wrath remember mercy.

May the dawn of a bright and happy day soon again be seen breaking on the darkness of our perplexity, and the heart of this nation be filled with thanksgiving, because Thou, Lord, hast helped us and comforted us. May the influence of thy Gospel be more widely and deeply felt among all classes. Send forth more labourers into thy spiritual harvest. Let the people praise Thee, O God; let all the people praise Thee. Hear our prayer, for Jesus Christ's sake. Amen.

THANKSGIVING FOR NATIONAL BLESSINGS.

READ IN HOLY SCRIPTURE PSALM CXV.

O THOU God of grace, who art the bounteous givor of every mercy that gladdens, comforts, and blesses, to Thee do we turn with gratitude in our hearts, and praises on our tongue, for all thy undeserved goodness. We would speak good of Thee who art doing us good, and tell how Thou hast always been mindful of us, and that not one thing has failed of all the Lord our God has promised.

While we praise Thee for all thy mercies vouchsafed to us, especially would we now declare thy gracious dealings with us as a people. For Thou hast made us a land great, and granted us a name and influence mighty among the nations of the earth. To a great pinnacle of wealth and glory hast Thou raised us, not for our righteousness' sake, but because Thou hast a love to us. Oh, that we may use all our power, and riches, and influence to glorify Thee, advance thy cause, and make known the great and saving name of the Lord Jesus.

But how can we sufficiently acknowledge our spiritual mercies? Once we were far off like other Gentiles; but now, brought nigh by the blood of Jesus, we can serve Thee without fear, in righteousness and holiness, all the days of our life. We have an open Bible. Thy houses of prayer cover our land, and thy truth is our inheritance and our children's. Thou hast poured out upon us the refreshing dews of thy Spirit. What have we that we have not received? and it is Thou alone that hast distinguished us in privileges and mercies above others. Make us to walk worthy of thy great goodness and our high privileges. Teach us as a people to fear sin, to walk closely with Thee, to obey Thee because we love Thee, and day by day to show forth the praises of Him who hath called us to his kingdom and glory.

Lord, may our life be one song of praise and holy gratitude for all thy goodness and mercy towards us, through Jesus Christ our Lord. Amen.

PRAYERS FOR SPECIAL OCCASIONS.

IN TIME OF WAR.

READ IN HOLY SCRIPTURE PSALM LXXVI.

ALMIGHTY and most gracious God, who hast all power in heaven and upon the earth, and who knowest all that takes place in all worlds, we come to Thee. Accept us at this time, O Lord, for the sake of thy dear Son, who was delivered for our offences and raised again for our justification. We desire to adore Thee for him, who is our peace, and to pray that his peaceable kingdom of righteousness and truth may soon be set up over the whole earth, when the sins and woes of war shall be known no more, and when men shall beat their swords into ploughshares and their spears into pruning-hooks. We mourn over the wickedness of our fallen nature, O Lord, so fearfully seen in the day of battle. Oh, that these horrors may soon come to an end for ever. Have mercy, O Lord, upon the wounded and the dying, and upon those who may yet perish by the sword; and, if it please Thee, put an end to the slaughter which is now making many hearts desolate, and causing the bitter cry of the widow and the orphan to ascend to Thee. Thou hast the hearts of kings in thy hand, and canst turn them in favour of peace. To Thee we therefore look, O Lord. Be Thou pleased to stay the progress of this destruction, to make the wrath of man to praise Thee, and to restrain the remainder thereof. Let men learn righteousness when thy judgments are abroad in the earth, and do Thou graciously bring good out of the great evil of war. May nations learn that they are mutually dependent, that Thou hast made them of one blood, that they are all entirely in thy hand, and that they ought to seek each other's welfare. We feel, O God, that there is no security for a nation or an individual but in thy protection. Only as Thou blessest us shall we be blessed, and only as Thou carest for us, can all things work for good. Keep Thou us, and we shall be safe; and preserve us to thy heavenly kingdom and glory, for the sake of our Lord and Saviour Jesus Christ; to whom, with Thyself and the Holy Ghost, be everlasting praises. Amen.

THANKSGIVING FOR PEACE.

READ IN HOLY SCRIPTURE PSALM CXXIV.

O LORD God, who rulest over all from the beginning, we acknowledge, with deep humiliation before Thee, the power of thy Almighty hand in sending thy recent scourge of war upon this our nation, and we return Thee our humble and hearty thanks for the great things which Thou hast done for us in the restoration of peace and tranquillity, whereof we are now glad.

We acknowledge before Thee, O Lord, that it was not by our own power or might that we have obtained this blessing. Our help standeth in the name of the Lord, who hath made heaven and earth. Grant that, by the manifestation of thy judgments being seen on the earth, the inhabitants of the world may learn righteousness, and thy name may be honoured among all nations. We beseech Thee also to grant that all the changes in the kingdoms of this world may tend to hasten the setting up of thy heavenly kingdom.

We pray Thee to dispose the hearts of all men so to value and to desire the blessings of peace, that they may be more and more desirous to avoid all provocation to enter upon war. Look down likewise, O Lord, in mercy upon all those who have suffered in any way from the calamities of the recent war, and grant that their sufferings and their sorrows may so work together for their eternal good, that though they now sow in tears, yet they may hereafter reap in joy, and rejoice for ever in thy eternal kingdom.

Finally, we beseech Thee to hasten the reign of the Prince of peace, when men shall beat their swords into ploughshares and their spears into pruning-hooks; when nation shall not any longer lift up sword against nation, neither shall they learn war any more. Lord make bare thine arm in the midst of us, and let it be seen that Thou art overruling all things for the coming in of thy glorious kingdom. Prepare us, O Lord, for that happy time, by a believing reception of the Gospel of peace, and preserve us now and for ever, for Jesus Christ's sake. Amen.

PRAYERS FOR SPECIAL OCCASIONS.

DEATH OF THE SOVEREIGN.

READ IN HOLY SCRIPTURE ECCLESIASTES XII.

O GOD, who art the God of the spirits of all flesh, look mercifully upon thy servants, and accept us for thy Son's sake. Thou hast taken away the head, whom Thou hadst set to rule over us. O Lord, righteousness belongeth unto Thee, and to us shame and confusion of face, as at this day. But Thou art a merciful God, full of compassion, long-suffering, and of great mercy. Spare us, good Lord; spare thy people.

Pour down, we beseech Thee, at this time the special grace of thy good Spirit upon all the people of this land, and upon all who are put in authority over us. Teach us to remember that the powers that be are ordained of Thee. Enable us to be subject unto them for conscience' sake, and to render unto all their due: tribute to whom tribute, custom to whom custom, fear to whom fear, honour to whom honour.

Enable us to recognise thy hand, O Lord God, in all things. Teach us to lay to heart that it is appointed unto all men once to die, and after death the judgment. Let the mourners, as they go about the streets, learn righteousness. Grant that we, being reconciled by the blood of the covenant, and sanctified by thy Spirit, may so live by the faith of the Son of God, that when our time of departure comes, we may render up our account with joy.

Finally, we beseech Thee to comfort them that mourn, and to bind up the broken heart. Be Thyself the refuge and strength of the sorrowful. And since by Thee kings rule and princes execute judgment, we beseech Thee to bestow upon the future ruler of this land thy heavenly benediction. Overrule all things for thine own glory and our salvation. Hasten to accomplish the number of thine elect, and bring in thy kingdom. Evermore hear, in heaven thy dwelling-place, look down in mercy upon us, and bless us, and grant us all things needful for our souls and bodies, through Jesus Christ, our adorable Redeemer and Lord. Amen.

ACCESSION OF A SOVEREIGN.

READ IN HOLY SCRIPTURE PSALM XX.

ALMIGHTY and everlasting God, Thou hast taught us in thy holy Word that the hearts of kings are in thy rule and governance. Pour down thy blessing, O Lord, upon thy servant whom Thou hast chosen to rule over this land. Endow *him* with every gift Thou seest necessary for *him*. Bestow upon *him* the spirit of wisdom and counsel, and a right judgment in all things, that *he* may devise such things as shall please Thee. Replenish *him* with the grace of thy Holy Spirit, that *he* may alway incline to thy will, and walk in thy way. Give *him* faith in Thee, zeal for thy truth, love for thy name, and reverence for thy majesty, that *he* may reign in thy faith, and fear, and love, as remembering the solemn account *he* must one day give. Bless *him* now with the knowledge of thy truth, and in the world to come with life everlasting.

Give peace in our time, O Lord, we beseech Thee. Direct the counsels of all who are in authority over us in righteousness and equity. Divert the malice and frustrate the designs of those who would do us harm. Defend our Sovereign and this nation from all assaults of our enemies, that we, surely trusting in thy defence, may not fear the power of any adversaries, and may serve Thee in quietness and peace all the days of our life.

Send thy Spirit into all our hearts, O Lord, and prosper the ministry of thy Word amongst us. Prosper every good work that is done for Thee, and make it effectual for the glory of thy name and the salvation of souls. And so extend the influences of thy truth in every home throughout our land, that peace and happiness, truth and justice, religion and piety, may be established among us for all generations.

We are unworthy, O Lord, of the least of all these thy mercies; yet we beseech Thee, who art ever more ready to hear than we to pray, to bestow them upon us, and give unto us of thy abundant goodness more than we can desire or deserve, through Jesus Christ, thy Son, our Lord. Amen.

PRAYERS FOR SPECIAL OCCASIONS.

FOR RAIN.

READ IN HOLY SCRIPTURE 1 KINGS VIII. 35.

ALMIGHTY God, who art the ruler of all things, and who doeth what pleaseth Thee in the heaven above and in the earth beneath, we approach Thee with deep humility, through the merits of thy Son. Thou hast bidden thy people to come boldly unto the throne of thy grace, through that great High Priest who is passed into the heavens; and we come to Thee pleading thy promise. Hast Thou not said, that whatsoever we ask believing, we shall receive? Lord, we believe; help Thou our unbelief; and at this time do for us exceeding abundantly above all that we can ask or think.

Thou hast laid thine afflicting hand upon thy servants, O Lord, and hast commanded the clouds that they give no rain. The heaven is shut up; the skies are as brass over our head, and the earth as iron beneath our feet. The fields yield no meat, and the flock is cut off from the fold. We call upon Thee for mercy. Thou makest a fruitful land barren for the wickedness of them that dwell therein; and again, Thou turnest the wilderness into a standing water, and dry ground into watersprings. We confess that we have grievously sinned against Thee, and have justly provoked thy wrath and indignation against us. But stay thine avenging hand, we beseech Thee, O Lord, and have pity upon us. Cover the heaven with clouds, and prepare rain for the earth. Send us the early and the latter rain, and so preserve for us the kindly fruits of the earth, that in due time we may enjoy them. For thy Son's sake, spare us, O Lord, who confess our sins unto Thee. Hear us, for thy mercy is great; and in the multitude of thy mercies look upon us. We humble ourselves beneath thy mighty hands, O Thou most Holy. Above all, sanctify our national trouble to the removal of our national sins. Grant us, we beseech Thee, the supply of our need, and all things that Thou seest necessary, both for our souls and for our bodies, for the sake of thy dear Son, Jesus Christ, our Lord. Amen.

FOR FAIR WEATHER.

READ IN HOLY SCRIPTURE GENESIS IX. 8—17.

ALMIGHTY God, our heavenly Father, who makest the sun to rise on the evil and on the good, let it please Thee of thy great mercy to forgive the iniquity of thy people, and be favourable to this our land. Remember, O God, thy covenant, that while the earth remaineth, seed-time and harvest, and cold and heat, and summer and winter, and day and night, shall not cease. And so increase our faith that we may trust in Thee, who givest us all things richly to enjoy, and whose tender mercies are over all thy works.

O God, who bindest up the waters in the thick cloud, and the cloud is not rent under them, be pleased to stay the clouds of heaven, that it may not rain, and grant such weather as that the ground may give its increase; that our fields may yield the precious fruits brought forth by the sun; and that our barns being filled with plenty, we may eat and bless Thee, the Lord, in whom we live, and move, and have our being; and whose hand is ever open to supply the wants of every living thing.

We praise Thee, O God; we acknowledge Thee to be the Lord, in whose hand are all things, and who workest all things after the counsel of thine own will. Let it please Thee of thine infinite goodness so to fill our hearts with thy grace, that we may take no thought for the morrow; but having food and raiment, may we therewith be content. Mercifully remove our unbelief, and disappoint our fears, that we, confiding in the promises of thy Word and the bountifulness of thy providence, may pass our days in peace and quietness, knowing that we have our treasure in heaven, and an inheritance that fadeth not away.

We humbly confess, O God, that we are not worthy of the least of all the mercies and of all the truth which Thou hast showed unto thy servants; but we plead the merits of thy Son, Jesus Christ, our Saviour. Hear us at this time, and bless us, O our God and Father, for His sake. Amen.

PRAYERS FOR SPECIAL OCCASIONS.

FOR A FRUITFUL HARVEST.

READ IN HOLY SCRIPTURE PSALM CVII. 31—43.

O GOD, our heavenly Father, who hast never left Thyself without witness, in that Thou hast done good in giving us rain from heaven and fruitful seasons, filling our hearts with food and gladness, let it please Thee to look upon us in our necessities, and grant that the earth, which drinketh in the rain which cometh upon it, may bring forth all that is meet for the use of man, that the voice of rejoicing may be heard in the tabernacles of the righteous.

O God, the Father of lights, from whom cometh down every good gift, we thy servants beseech Thee to hear the prayers of thy people, and to crown the year with thy goodness. By thy blessing upon the land, let our valleys be covered over with corn, wherewith the mower may fill his hand, and he that bindeth up the sheaves his bosom. Grant that our fields may be reaped in safety; and so fill our hearts with thy grace, that while we eat our bread in plenty, we may also labour for that meat which endureth unto everlasting life.

O God, in whom are all our springs, we acknowledge our dependence on Thee for life and all its comforts. Thou hast borne us even from the womb, and during all the dangers and temptations of our lives Thou hast never ceased to watch over us and bless us. Thou hast of thine infinite goodness supplied all our need, and not one good thing has failed of all which Thou hast promised. Thy loving-kindness Thou hast never taken from us, nor suffered thy faithfulness to fail.

Let it please Thee, holy Father, to continue thy goodness and mercy unto us, that our land may still yield her increase, and that we, thy servants, living here as strangers and pilgrims, may worthily magnify thy holy name, and finally come to thine heavenly inheritance. May the sure hope of thy kingdom quicken us to greater diligence in thy service. And this we humbly beg, O Lord our God, in the name and through the merits of our Saviour Jesus Christ. Amen.

THANKSGIVING AFTER HARVEST.

READ IN HOLY SCRIPTURE PSALM LXV.

EVER-BLESSED God, who keepest covenant with thy people, and showest mercy unto all men, we offer our grateful adorations to Thee for the bountiful harvest with which Thou hast crowned the labours of the husbandman, and hast provided for us our daily bread. Thou hast fulfilled thine ancient promise, that seed-time and harvest should not fail. Thou hast graciously given fertility to the soil, hast made it soft with showers, and blessed the springing thereof. Thy paths drop fatness. Oh, that men would praise the Lord for his goodness, and for his wonderful works to the children of men.

May it ever be our delight, as it is our duty, to trace thy hand in the blessings that meet us in our daily path. Continue thy favours, although we are undeserving of them, and deepen in our hearts a sense of our obligation to Thee. May our lives, so wonderfully preserved and so richly endowed by thy bounty, be daily consecrated to thy service and glory.

Help us, O Lord, with devout thankfulness of heart, to recognise the rich provision made for our spiritual necessities. Thou hast dealt bountifully with us. Thou hast given us the inestimable gift of the holy Scriptures. May our souls be sustained and invigorated by the blessed truths and promises of the Gospel, and be fruitful in all godliness.

May every nation under heaven soon be favoured with the same privileges that we enjoy, and yield to Thee its increase. Send forth thy light and thy truth, that they may bring men unto thy holy hill and to thy tabernacles. Lord of the harvest, send forth labourers into thy harvest; and grant, for Christ's sake, that when thy angels, the reapers, shall come, at the end of the world, we and those we love may be gathered into the heavenly garner.

We humbly implore these mercies, and all the fulness of thy grace and peace in the name of Jesus Christ our Lord. Amen.

www.ingramcontent.com/pod-product-compliance
Lightning Source LLC
Chambersburg PA
CBHW051248300426
44114CB00011B/944